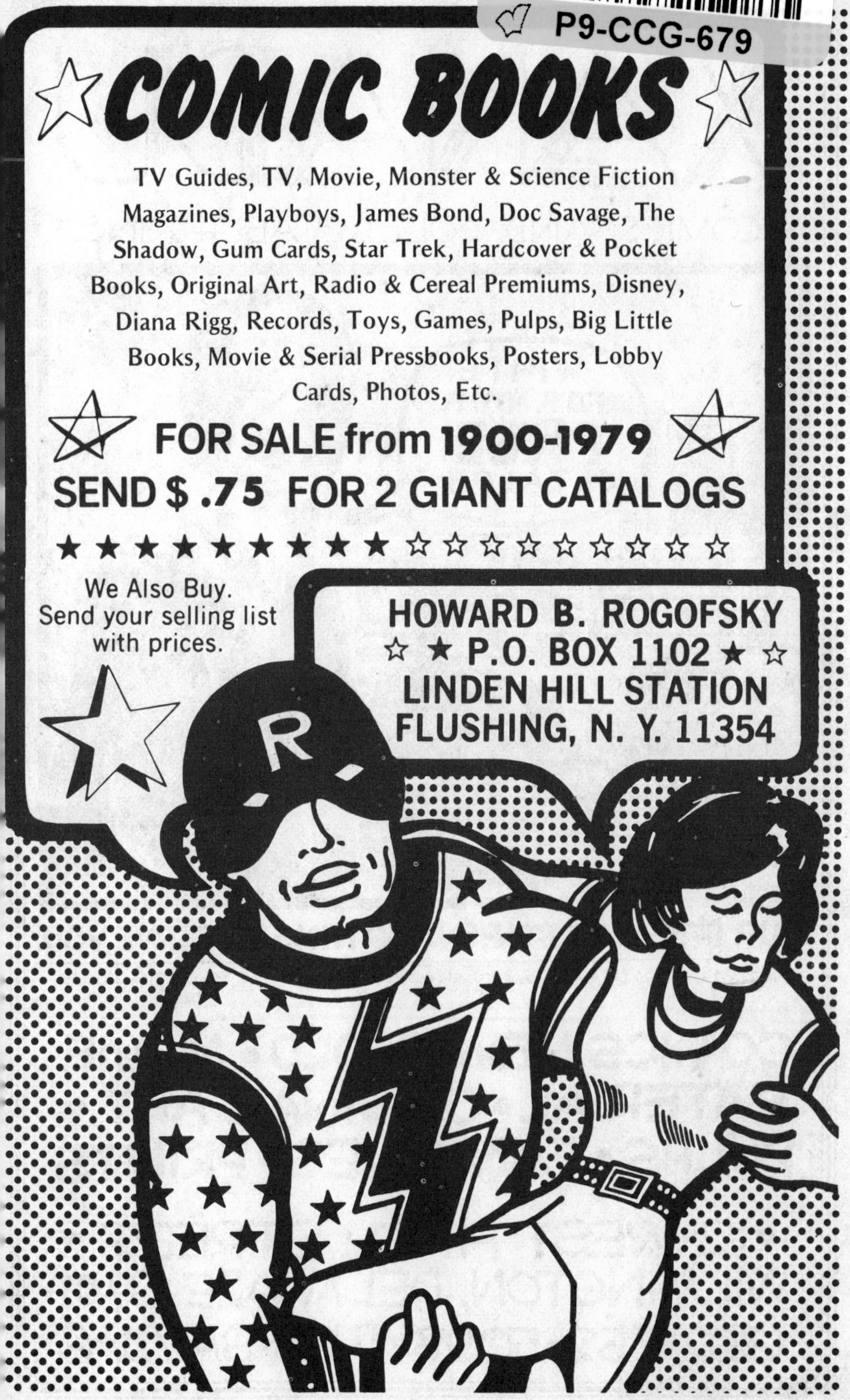

William M. Gaines produced a line of comic magazines which influenced and set the trend for the whole comic book industry. These books, known as EC's, represent some of the best illustrated and written comics ever produced. This edition pays tribute to Bill and the whole EC Gang who made it all possible.

ACKNOWLEDGEMENTS

Larry Bigman (Frazetta-Williamson data); Glenn Bray (Kurtzman data); Gary Carter (D. C. data); J. B. Clifford Jr. (E. C. data); Gary Coddington (Superman data); Wilt Conine (Fawcett data); Dr. S. M. Davidson (Cupples & Leon data); Al Dellinges (Kubert data); Kim Weston (Disney and Barks data); Kevin Hancer (Tarzan data); Charles Heffelfinger and Jim Ivey (March of Comics listing); Grant Irwin (Quality data); Fred Nardelli (Frazetta data); Mike Nolan (MLJ, Timely, Nedor data); George Olshevsky (Timely data); Richard Kravitz (Kelly data); Frank Scigliano (Little Lulu data); Gene Seger (Buck Rogers data); Rick Sloane (Archie data); David R. Smith, Archivist, Walt Disney Productions (Disney data); Don and Maggie Thompson (Four Color listing); Mike Tiefenbacher, Jerry Sinkovec, and Richard Yudkin (Atlas and National data); Tom Bocci (Classic Comics data); Raymond True (Classic Comics data); Greg Robertson (National data); Jim Vadeboncoeur Jr. (Williamson and Atlas data); Andrew Zerbe and Gary Behymer (M. E. data).

My appreciation must also be extended to Dan Hering, Bruce Hamilton, James Ward, and Jim Friedman who loaned material for photographing and especially to Hugh O'Kennon who again spent a weekend helping me photograph his stock. Special acknowledgement is also given to Everett Raymond Kinstler, Ron Russell, Scott Pell Joseph Vucenic, Larry Wingate, W. T. Michaelson, Bruce Hamilton, Robert Selvig, and Dave Noah for submitting an unusual amount of corrective data; to Dr. Richard Olson for rewriting grading definitions; to Charles Heffelfinger for rewriting "Understanding the Classics;" to Robert Selvig, Hugh O'Kennon, Jay Maybruck, John Snyder, Bill Cole, Rick Sloane (pricing); to Tom Inge for his "Chronology of the American Comic Book;" to E. B. Boatner for her exclusive article on E.C., and especially to Bill Gaines for his encouraging support; to Wally Wood for his outstanding cover; to Marie Severin for coloring the cover; to Carl Macek for his article on "Seduction of the Innocent;" to Al Williamson for his inspiring full color page; to Harvey Kurtzman, John Severin, and Wally Wood for their art contributions for the article; to Mike Gold (DC Comics) for data; to Jerry DeFuccio for his counsel and help; to Bill Spicer and Zetta DeVoe (Western Publishing Co.) for their contribution of data, and especially to Bill for his front cover EC logo design and lettering as well as his kind permission to reprint portions of his and Jerry Bails' America's Four Color Pastime; to Robert Crestohl for his statistical compilation; and to Walter Presswood and Dave Noah for their help in editing this volume.

I will always be indebted to Jerry Bails, Landon Chesney, and Larry Bigman whose advice and concern have helped in making The Price Guide a reality; to my wife, Martha, for her encouragement and help in putting this reference work together; and to everyone who placed ads in this edition.

Acknowledgement is also due to the following people who have so generously contributed much needed data for this edition:

Peter Adamakos
Perry Adams
Gary Arbuckle
Darrow Autry
John M. Baker
Steve Barrington
Robert T. Beck
Tommy Billhartz
Sandy Blatt
Glenn Bray
Christopher Brown
Dr. Bruce C. Brumfield
Roger A. Budnick
Capitol City Comics
Peter Cocking
Chuck Combs
J. Keith Contarino
Kyle Corbin
Robert A. Dane
Howard Leroy Davis
Joe Desris
Zetta DeVoe
Paul DiLella
Andy Dunn
Rod Dyke
Greg Eide
Cliff Erickson
John Evans
Ron Evry
Bill Ewing
Sam Falin
Mark Feldman
Jim Friedman
Mike Friedrich
Richard Gagnon
John Garbarino
Fred Garcia
Thomas Garcia, Jr.
David E. Gifford
Paul Gilbert
Richard H. Gilliam
Max Gottfried
Jim Gray
Jerry Gruschke
Lowell Guddall
Scott Guenther
Micky Guiley
Richard Gummer
Elias Hafich
Terry Harms
Aubrey Harness
Dave Harper
Jon Hart
Charles Heffelfinger
Steven Hill
Kendall Hopkins
D. W. Howard
Paul Howley

John A. Hultgren
Jim Hyland
John S. Iavarone
Jackson E. Jeffrey
Willford King
Mark A. Kingdon
Mike Kirby
Mark Kirkpatrick
Leonard Knappenberger
Jim Kovacs
Harry Kremer
Kent Krumvieda
Stuart Labovitz
Jeff Langstaff
John Lebar
Mervin Lee
Philip M. Levine
Dan Levitt
Rodney J. Lockwood
Tom Long
Rick Lowell
John Lykins
Carl Macek
Greg Z. Manos
Ruben V. Marcelo
Bill Massie
Tom Mattevi
Raymond May
Jay Maybruck
Herbert F. McCaulla
Paul A. McKlveen
Mitchell Mehdy
Chris Melancon
Jeff Mendel
W. T. (Butch) Michaelson
Stan Molson
Dick Mosso
Gerald Mowery
James Moyer
Richard Nanson
Richard O'Brien
Bill Olver
Peter Ommundsen
Buddy Paige
Pierre R. Paradis
Jeff L. Patton
Scott Pell
Dennis Petilli
Adam R. Philips
Don Pierce
Albert E. Poling
John H. Preble
Ron Puckett
Don L. Puff
Walker Reddick III
Chuck Redding
Bob Reed

Richard A. Register
Philip Ressegiue
Rob Ripin
Lee Roberts
James R. Rogers, D.D.S.
Peter Roman
Steve Roselius
Gary Rowell
Ron Russell
Louis B. Sager
Michael Sager
Ken Sanders
Joe Sarno
William K. Schoch
Steven M. Scholz
Horst Schroder
Herb Scott
Randy Scott
Jack Seabrook
Shep Sheppard
Keith Sillman
Jim Silva
Roderick H. Silva
R. H. J. Silva, Jr.
Calvin Slobodian
Sparkle City Comics
Nick & Lee Spassky
Ed Spiegil
William Steinfelt
Dan Stevenson
Mike S. Stoeckig
Jeff Stone
Ray Storeh
Klaus Strzyz
Matt Sturm
Craig Van Grasstek
Hal Verb
Roland C. Verville
Joseph A. Vucenic
Jim Walsh
Bill Ward
H. W. Ward
Jim Ward
David Weaver
Jack Weaver
Bob Weintz
Stephen Weisenbach
Frank Wilcox
Rev Winfree
Larry Wingate
Bill Wong
Chris Wrenn
David Yaruss
Chuck Yeaman
Ronald J. Young
Richard Yudkin
Tex Ziadie

The
Comic Book
PRICE GUIDE
1979-1980

BOOKS FROM 1900—PRESENT INCLUDED

CATALOGUE & EVALUATION GUIDE—ILLUSTRATED

By

ROBERT M. OVERSTREET

SPECIAL CONTRIBUTORS TO THIS EDITION

E. B. Boatner
and Carl Macek

SPECIAL ADVISORS TO THIS EDITION

●*Larry Bigman* ●*L. C. Chesney* ● *Bruce Hamilton*
●*Steve Geppi* ● *Hugh O'Kennon* ●*Robert Selvig* ●*David Noah*

PREFACE

Comic book values listed in this reference work were recorded from convention sales, dealers' lists, adzines, and by special contact with dealers and collectors from coast to coast. Prices paid for rare comics vary considerably from one locale to another. We have attempted to list a realistic average between the lowest and highest range observed. The reader should keep in mind that the prices listed only reflect the market just prior to publication. Any new trends that have developed since the preparation of this book would not be shown.

The values listed are reports, not estimates. Each new edition of the guide is actually an average report of sales that occurred during the year; not an estimate of what we feel the books will be bringing next year. Even though many prices listed will remain current throughout the year, the wise user of this book would keep abreast of current market trends to get the fullest potential out of his invested dollar.

Everyone connected with the publication of this book advocates the collecting of comic books for fun and pleasure, as well as for nostalgia, art, and cultural values. Second to this is investment, which, if wisely-placed in the best quality books (condition and contents considered), will yield dividends over the long term.

Some comic book titles listed are incomplete, especially in regard to first and last issues, but this will be remedied in future editions as the information becomes available. All titles are listed as if they were one word, ignoring spaces, hyphens and apostrophes. Page counts listed will always include covers.

The Guide will be listing only American comic books. Canadian, English and other foreign comics will not be listed due to space limitation (See Canadian Comics). Some variations of the regular comic book format will be listed. These basically include those pre-1933 comic strip reprint books with varying size--usually with cardboard covers, but sometimes with hardback. As forerunners of the modern comic book format, they deserve to be listed despite their obvious differences in presentation. Other books that will be listed are giveaway comics--but only those that contain known characters or work by known artists.

Many books of the late 1940s had pages cut out of them before distribution to help the paper drives. In recent years many of the Gold Key, Marvel & DC books are also published by Whitman and are generally considered to be worth less than the originals.

By the same token, books in the rare class are seldom offered for sale. This makes it difficult to arrive at a realistic market value. Arbitrary values are placed on these, although even this varies considerably. Among the issues in this category are: Action No. 1, Marvel Comics No. 1, Batman No. 1, Jumbo No. 1, More Fun Nos. 52, 53, Captain America No. 1, Walt Disney Nos. 1,2, Four Color No. 4, Silver Streak No. 6, Wow No. 1, Black and White Nos. 16, 20, Shock Illustrated No. 3, Superman No. 1, Motion Picture Funnies Weekly No. 1, Detective Nos. 27, 28, Whiz No. 2(No. 1), and the no-number Feature Books.

This book is the most comprehensive listing of comic books ever attempted. Comic book titles, dates of first and last issues, publishing companies, origin and special issues are listed when known. Many of the better artists are pointed out also. When more than one artist worked on a story, their names are separated by a (/). The first name did the pencil drawings and the second did the inks. When two or more artists work on a story, only the most prominent will be noted. There has been some confusion in past editions as to which artist to list and which to leave out. We wish all good artists could be listed, but due to space limitation, only the very best can. The following list of artists are considered to be either the best in the comic field or are historically significant and should be pointed out. Artists designated with an (*) indicate that only their most noted work will be listed. The rest will eventually have all their work shown as the information becomes available. This list could change from year to year as new artists come into prominence. It should also be noted that there are several artists who are as prolific as they are talented and whose works cannot be listed simply because of space limitations. Among these are John Severin and Russ Heath.

Adams, Neal	Feldstein, Al	Nostrand, Howard
*Baker, Matt	Fine, Lou	Orlando, Joe
Barks, Carl	Foster, Harold	Raboy, Mac
Beck, C.C.	Fox, Matt	Raymond, Alex
Brunner, Frank	Frazetta, Frank	Siegel & Shuster
*Buscema, John	Gottfredson, Floyd	Simon & Kirby (S&K)
*Check, Sid	Ingels, Graham	Smith, Barry
Cole, Jack	Johnson, Walter	Stanley, John
Cole, L.B.	Jones, Jeff	Starlin, Jim
Craig, Johnny	Kamen, Jack	Steranko, Jim
Crandall, Reed	Kelly, Walt	Torres, Angelo
Davis, Jack	Kirby, Jack	Toth, Alex
Disbrow, Jayson	Krenkel, Roy	Ward, Bill
*Ditko, Steve	Krigstein, Bernie	Williamson, Al
Eisner, Will	*Kubert, Joe	Wolverton, Basil
*Elder, Bill	Kurtzman, Harvey	Wood, Wallace
Evans, George	Manning, Russ	Wrightson, Bernie
Everett, Bill	*Meskin, Mort	

The following abbreviations are used with the cover reproductions throughout the book for copyright credit purposes. The companies they represent are listed here:

(ACE) Ace Periodicals	(KING) King Features Syndicate
(ACG) American Comics Group	(LEV) Lev Gleason Publications
(AJAX) Ajax-Farrell	(MCG) Marvel Comics Group
(AP) Archie Publications	(ME) Magazine Enterprises
(ATLAS) Atlas Comics (see below)	(MLJ) MLJ Magazines
(AVON) Avon Periodicals	(NOVP) Novelty Press
(BP) Better Publications	(PG) Premier Group
(C & L) Cupples & Leon	(PINE) Pines
(CC) Charlton Comics	(PMI) Parents' Magazine Institute
(CEN) Centaur Publications	(PRIZE) Prize Publications
(CCG) Columbia Comics Group	(QUA) Quality Comics Group
(CG) Catechetical Guild	(REAL) Realistic Comics
(CHES) Harry 'A' Chesler	(RH) Rural Home
(DC) DC Comics, Inc.	(S & S) Street and Smith Publishers
(DELL) Dell Publishing Co.	(SKY) Skywald Publications
(DMP) David McKay Publishing	(STAR) Star Publications
(DS) D. S. Publishing Co.	(STD) Standard Comics
(EAS) Eastern Color Printing Co.	(STJ) St. John Publishing Co.
(EC) E. C. Comics	(SUPR) Superior Comics
(ENWIL) Enwil Associates	(TC) Tower Comics
(EP) Elliott Publications	(TM) Trojan Magazines
(ERB) Edgar Rice Burroughs	(TOBY) Toby Press
(FAW) Fawcett Publications	(UFS) United Features Syndicate
(FF) Famous Funnies	(VITL) Vital Publications
(FH) Fiction House Magazines	(WDP) Walt Disney Publications
(FOX) Fox Features Syndicate	(WEST) Western Publishing Co.
(GIL) Gilberton	(WHIT) Whitman Publishing Co.
(GK) Gold Key	(WHW) William H. Wise
(GP) Great Publications	(WMG) William M. Gaines (E. C.)
(HARV) Harvey Publications	(WP) Warren Publishing Co.
(HILL) Hillman Periodicals	(YM) Youthful Magazines
(HOKE) Holyoke Publishing Co.	(Z-D) Ziff-Davis Publishing Co.

ATLAS COMICS. The following list of publishers all printed ATLAS comics and are coded throughout the book. The ATLAS GLOBE insignia first appeared in November 1951 and lasted until September 1957 after which Marvel took over.

ATLAS Publisher's Abbreviation Codes:

ACI: Animirth Comics, Inc.	CPC: Chipiden Publishing Corp.
AMI: Atlas Magazines, Inc.	CnPC: Cornell Publishing Corp.
ANC: Atlas News Co., Inc.	CPI: Crime Publications, Inc.
BPC: Bard Publishing Corp.	CmPI: Comedy Publications, Inc.
BFP: Broadcast Features Pubs.	CPS: Canam Publishing Sales Corp.
CSI: Classics Syndicate	CmPS: Complete Photo Story
CCC: Comic Combine Corp.	SSI: Classics Syndicate, Inc.
CDS: Current Detective Stories	EPI: Emgee Publications, Inc.
CFI: Crime Files, Inc.	FPI: Foto Parade, Inc.
	GPI: Gem Publishing, Inc.

TERMINOLOGY. The following terms are used occasionally in this edition and are explained here: "B & W"—Black and White art; "Bondage cover"—usually denotes a female in bondage; "cameo"—when a character appears briefly in one or two panels; "debut, first app., intro"—mean the same thing, i. e., the first time that a character appears anywhere; "flashback"—when a previous story is being recalled; "G. A."—Golden Age (1930s - 1950s); "origin"—when the story of the character's creation is given; "extremely rare"—1 to 5 copies known to exist; "very rare"— 5 to 50 copies; "rare"— 50 to 100 copies; "scarce"—100 to 1,000 copies (the quantities given will change as new information is compiled; "S & K"—Simon & Kirby (artists); "X-over"—when one character crosses over into another's strip.

A SPECIAL PLEA. Please notify us of any omissions, corrections, or deletions of data in this volume so that we may include it in the next edition.

IMPORTANT. This book is not a "for sale" list of comic books. The publisher of this reference work is a collector, and has no comic books for sale. Therefore, the prices are for your information only.

DEALERS' POSITION. Prices listed herein are an indication of what collectors (not dealers) would probably pay. For one reason or another, these collectors might want certain books badly, or else need specific issues to complete their runs. Dealers are not in a position to pay the full prices listed, but work on a percentage depending largely on the amount of investment required and the quality of material offered. Usually they will pay from 20 to 70 per cent of the list price depending on how long it will take them to sell the collection after making the investment; the higher the demand and better the condition, the more the percentage. Most dealers are faced with expenses such as advertising, travel, telephone and mailing plus convention costs: entrance, table fee, hotel, etc. These costs all go in before the books are sold. The high demand books usually sell right away but there are many other titles that are difficult to sell due to low demand. Sometimes a dealer will have cost tied up in this type of material for several years before finally moving it. Remember, his position is that of handling, demand and overhead. Most dealers are victims of these economics. Good Luck and Happy Hunting.

Robert M. Overstreet

Advertise in the Guide

s book reaches more serious comic collectors than any other publication and has proven
results due to its world-wide circulation and use. Your ad will pull all year long until the
edition comes out.

play Ad space is sold in full, half, fourth, and eighth page sizes. Ad rates are set in the early
prior to each edition's release. Write at that time for rates (between Oct.—Dec.).

PRINTED SIZES AND RATES

FULL PAGE—8" long x 5" wide. HALF PAGE—4" long x 5" wide.
FOURTH PAGE—4" long x 2½" wide. EIGHTH PAGE—2" long x 2½" wide.
CLASSIFIED ADS will be retyped and reduced about one-half. No
artwork permitted. Rate is based on your 4" typed line. DISPLAY
CLASSIFIED ADS: The use of borders or bold face type or cuts or other
decorations change your classified ad to display—rates same as regular
display.

NOTE: Submit your ad on white paper in a proportionate version
of the actual printed size. All full —Quarter page advertisers will
receive a complimentary copy of the Guide. The NEW Guide will
be professionally done throughout...so to reflect a consistently high
quality from cover to cover, we must ask that all ads be neatly and
professionally done. Full payment must be sent with all ads. All
but classified ads will be run as is.

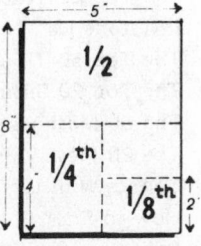

Ad deadline next edition—Jan. 15

BOB OVERSTREET
780 Hunt Cliff Dr. N.W.
Cleveland, Tennessee 37311

The PRICE GUIDE has become the STANDARD REFERENCE WORK in the field and is
distributed to thousands of comic collectors throughout the world. Don't miss this opportunity
to advertise in the Guide.

NOTICE: All advertisements are accepted and placed in the Price Guide in good faith. However,
we cannot be held responsible for any losses incurred in your dealings with the advertisers.
If, after receiving legitimate complaints, and there is sufficient evidence to warrant such action,
these advertisers will be dropped from future editions.

SPECIAL NOTICE

If copyrighted characters are planned for your ad, the following must be done: Send a copy of
your ad layout (including characters) to the company(s) or copyright owner(s) involved request-
ing permission for their use. A copy of this permission must be sent to us with your ad. DC
Comics and Marvel Comics have indicated that you will have no problem getting permission,
so if you must use their characters...write for the permission. For DC, write: Public Relations,
DC Comics, Inc., 75 Rockefeller Plaza, N. Y., N. Y. 10019. For Marvel, write: Marvel Comics,
c/o Sol Brodsky, 575 Madison Ave., N. Y., N. Y. 10022. Other companies such as Disney could
be more of a problem. At any rate, we cannot accept any ads with copyrighted characters
without a copy of the permission.

TABLE OF CONTENTS

GRADING COMIC BOOKS

Before a comic book's true value can be assessed, its condition or state of preservation must be determined. In most comic books, especially in the rarer issues, the better the condition, the more desirable the book. The scarcer first and/or origin issues in PRISTINE MINT condition will bring several times the price of the same book in POOR condition. The grading of a comic book is done by simply looking at the book and describing its condition, which may range from absolutely perfect newsstand condition (PRISTINE MINT) to extremely worn, dirty, and torn (POOR). Numerous variables influence the evaluation of a comic's condition and **all** must be considered in the final evaluation. More important characteristics include tears, missing pieces, wrinkles, stains, yellowing, brittleness, tape repairs, water marks, spine roll, writing, and cover lustre. The significance of each of these will be described more fully in the grading scale definitions. As grading is the most subjective aspect of determining a comic's value, it is very important that the grader must be careful and not allow wishful thinking to influence what the eyes see. It is also very important to realize that older comics in above MINT condition are extremely scarce and are rarely advertised for sale; most of the nicer comics advertised range from NEAR MINT to MINT. To the novice, grading will appear difficult at first, but as experience is gained, accuracy will improve. Whenever in doubt, consult with a reputable dealer or experienced collector in your area. The following grading guide is given to aid the hobbyist:

GRADING DEFINITIONS

The hardest part of evaluating a comic is being honest and objective with yourself, and knowing what characteristics to look for in making your decision. The following characteristics should be checked in evaluating books, especially those in higher grades: degree of cover lustre, degree of color fading, staples, staple areas, spine condition, top and bottom of spine, edges of cover, centering, brittleness, browning/yellowing, flatness, tightness, interior damage, tape, tears, folds, water marks, color flaking, and general cleanliness. After examining these characteristics a comic may be assigned to one of the following grades:

PRISTINE MINT (PM): File copies; perfect; absolutely perfect in every way, regardless of age. The cover has full lustre, is crisp, and shows no imperfections of any sort. The cover and all pages are white, the spine is tight, flat, and clean; not even the slightest blemish can be detected around staples, along spine, at corners or edges. Arrival dates pencilled on the cover are not acceptable. As comics must be truly perfect to be graded PM, they are obviously extremely scarce even on the newsstand. Books in this grade bring 10 to 20 per cent more.

MINT (M): Almost perfect, as above but with slight loss of lustre, or a slight off-centered cover, or a minor printing error. Could have pencilled arrival dates, slight color fading, and near white to white cover and pages. No physical defects are acceptable of any sort; e.g., a tiny color flake missing from spine or side of cover would make an otherwise MINT comic grade NEAR MINT.

NEAR MINT (NM): Almost perfect; tight spine, flat and clean; just enough minor defects of wear noticeable with close inspection to keep it out of the MINT category; i. e, a small flake of color missing at a staple, corner or edge or slight discoloration on inside cover or pages; near perfect cover gloss retained.

VERY FINE (VF): Slight wear beginning to show; possibly a small wrinkle or crease at staples or where cover has been opened a few times; still clean and flat with most of cover gloss retained.

FINE (FN): Tight cover with some wear, but still relatively flat, clean and shiny with no subscription crease, writing on cover, yellowed margins or tape repairs. Stress lines around staples and along spine beginning to show; minor color flaking possible at spine, staples, edges or corners.

VERY GOOD (vg): Obviously a read copy with original printing lustre and gloss almost gone; some discoloration, but not soiled; some signs of wear and minor markings, but none that deface the cover; usually needs slight repair around staples and along spine which could be rolled; cover could have a minor tear or crease where a corner was folded under or a loose centerfold; no chunks missing, tape or brown pages.

GOOD (g): An average used copy complete with both covers and no panels missing; slightly soiled or marked with possible creases, minor tears or splits, rolled spine and small color flaking, but perfectly sound and legible. A well-read copy, but perfectly acceptable with no chunks missing, tape or brown pages.

FAIR (f): Very heavily read and soiled, but complete with possibly a small chunk out of cover; tears needing repairs and multiple folds and wrinkles likely; damaged by the elements, but completely sound and legible.

POOR (p): Damaged; heavily weathered; soiled; or otherwise unsuited for collection purposes.

COVERLESS (c): Coverless comics turn up frequently and bring 20 to 50 per cent of the good price depending on condition and demand.

IMPORTANT: Books with defects such as pages or panels missing, coupons cut, torn or taped covers and pages, brown or brittle pages, restapled, taped spines, pages or covers, water-marked, printing defects, rusted staples, stained, holed, or other imperfections that distract from the original beauty, are worth less than if free of these defects. Coverless comics in nice condition will bring about one-fifth to one-half Good price (retail) depending on the title, and more on the key books.

Many of the early reprint comics were printed in hardback with dust jackets. Books with dust jackets are worth more. The value can increase from 20 to 50 per cent depending on the rarity of book. Usually, the earlier the book, the greater the percentage. The condition of the dust jacket should be graded independently of the book itself.

CAUTION: Tape should not be used under any circumstances for comic repair. Most tapes contain harmful chemicals that will eventually destroy the paper which they touch. Today, many collectors find it objectionable and resist collecting books repaired in this way, as it destroys the natural beauty of the comic. Comic repair should be left to those who know how.

STORAGE AND DEACIDIFICATION OF COMIC BOOKS
by Bill Sarill

The enemies of comic books are heat, light, mold, moisture, air pollution and acidity. Books should be stored upright (not flat) in a dark unheated or air-conditioned room, with an ideal relative humidity (RH) of 50%. Higher RH will promote mold growth and rusted staples, whereas at lower RH paper will tend to lose its flexibility. Serious collectors should invest in a sling psychrometer, an inexpensive device for measuring RH which is available through laboratory suppliers. RH itself can be controlled by use of household humidifiers and dehumidifiers. Sunlight and ultraviolet light (from fluorescent fixtures) are harmful to paper; incandescent lamps should be used when illumination is needed, the books stored in darkness at all other times.

Tests by the Barrow Research Laboratory show that the lifetime of book paper is multiplied by a factor of 4.5 with every drop in temperature of 27 degrees Fahrenheit. Conversely, higher temperatures lead to a rapid aging of paper with subsequent browning and embrittlement. Air conditioning at the lowest comfortable temperature is therefore recommended. Air filters and purifiers should also be used to reduce dust and pollutants.

Collectors often seal their books in polyethylene bags. Although inexpensive, such bags offer only limited protection. Polyethylene film is relatively permeable to moisture; in addition it may contain volatile plasticizers which penetrate and discolor books in as little as one year. Vinyl and vinyl-related products (such as Saran Wrap) are even more destructive to paper, and should never be used for wrapping books. The preferred material is Mylar type S, a clear polyester film which is the least permeable and most inert of all the plastics. Mylar envelopes for book storage can be made from sheet Mylar sealed with 3M double coated tape No. 415. (This tape has been tested and found safe for archival use.)

Books, whether bagged or not, should never be stored in ordinary cardboard boxes. Most cardboard is dangerously acidic and this acid can penetrate through polyethylene bags. File boxes (sold by stationers and some dealers) are not suitable for permanent storage unless constructed of acid-free board.

It is our conviction that binding books is not a suitable method of preservation. Binding of itself will not protect books from environmental deterioration, and the mutilation caused by sewing and trimming is of course irreversible. For those who desire the appearance of a library of bound volumes, an alternative is to have a competent bookbinder construct cases of acid-free millboard in which comic books may be stored. These cases can be made to resemble books, and their cost is generally no more than the cost of binding.

Acidity remains the chief culprit in the aging of paper. In addition to acid migration from cardboard, sources of acidity include air pollution, alum-rosin size, residual bleaches from the papermaking process, and lignin, a complex organic acid found in most pulpwood papers. As described in the 1977 edition of The Guide, acidity may be neutralized by a variety of processes of which the least expensive is vapor phase deacidivication (VPD). The use of cyclohexylamine carbonate in the form of VPD paper continues to remain the most popular VPD method. In this process sheets of VPD paper are interleaved among pages of a stack of books, and the books sealed within an airtight bag for one week; at the end of this time, the sheets may be discarded and the treatment is complete. NOTE: It has reached our attention that some collectors have been leaving

VPD sheets within books for as long as six months. VPD paper should NEVER be kept within books for extended periods, as the sheets may eventually fuse to the comic book pages.

One difficulty in deacidifying comic books has been the presence of lignin, which tends to evolve gradually in comic book paper and which necessitates continuing deacidification of books at intervals of 10 to 15 years.

THE 1978 MARKET REPORT

Like 1977, the winter of 1978 went down in the records as one of the coldest. But the freezing weather did not "freeze" the comic book market. From the beginning, the market was active with collectors' interest expanding more and more into new areas. The so-called GOOD GIRL art books such as PHANTOM LADY, MEET CORLISS ARCHER, VENUS, SLAVE GIRL, RULAH, BRENDA STARR, CLAIRE VOYANT, MISS FURY, SUNNY, NAMORA, SEVEN SEAS, TORCHY, UNDERCOVER GIRL, LADY LUCK & BLUE BEETLE took off. Even the later issues of many of the Fiction House titles that contain Matt Baker and Kamen art such as JUMBO, WINGS, and RANGERS are now selling well. With the success of "Star Wars" and "Close Encounters," science fiction books are becoming more and more in focus: Fiction House's PLANET, Avon's CAPTAIN SCIENCE, ROCKET TO THE MOON, SPACE DETECTIVE, ROBOT MEN OF THE LOST PLANET, STRANGE WORLDS, OUT OF THIS WORLD, EC's WEIRD SCIENCE AND WEIRD FANTASY, Aragon's WEIRD TALES FROM THE FUTURE with Wolverton art and DC's STRANGE ADVENTURES are representative.

All EC titles as well as Avon's, i. e. MASK OF FU MANCHU, EERIE, MOLLY O'DAY, KING SOLOMON'S MINES, AN EARTH MAN ON VENUS, and THE HOODED MENACE, to name a few, continue to be in very high demand. Due to the higher prices of Silver-Age books, a trend back to collecting Golden Age was noticed, even though many of the rare Silver-Age titles in nice condition again set record prices such as FANTASTIC FOUR No. 1, SHOWCASE No. 4, DETECTIVE No. 225, ADVENTURE No. 247, HULK No. 1, FLASH No. 105, BRAVE & THE VOLD No. 28, AMAZING FANTASY No. 15 and TALES TO ASTONISH No. 27, among others.

Another area that is becoming highly collected are the books either mentioned or illustrated in *The Seduction of the Innocent*, such as PHANTOM LADY No. 17, SUPERMAN No. 55, HOWDY DOODY No. 6, TOM MIX No. 9, and REFORM SCHOOL GIRL as examples. A prototype of REFORM SCHOOL GIRL—INTIMATE CONFESSIONS No. 1—has become a very hot seller. Many new "Seduction" comics have been identified and are listed in this edition. The most classic find in this category is a drug book called TRAPPED (See listings).

For the past several years the market has been focusing on the books from the late 1940's to early 1950's. Much new information has been uncovered out of this period including many interesting new titles such as: BOLD STORIES, CANDID TALES, THE CENTURION OF ANCIENT ROME, DOC CARTER VD COMICS, FOR GIRLS ONLY, 40 BIG PAGES OF COMICS, IT RHYMES WITH LUST, and TARZAN OF THE APES TO COLOR. Other titles that are really coming on strong are: RICHIE RICH, DENNIS THE MENACE, ARCHIE books, ABBOTT & COSTELLO, GREEN GIANT, ELSIE THE COW, SUPERBOY, REAL SCREEN, THE THREE STOOGES, CLASSIC Comics, Movie Comics, Early Love comics and many early 1950's DC titles.

Some of the Horror-Mystery titles outside of E. C. like TERRORS OF THE JUNGLE & VOODOO (Baker, Kamen art), WEIRD MYSTERIES, WEIRD CHILLS, MR. MYSTERY, MARVEL TALES and MYSTIC (Wolverton art), WEIRD HORRORS, WITCHCRAFT, SON OF SINBAD (Kubert art), BLUE BOLT WEIRD (L. B. Cole, Wolverton art), EERIE, A STAR PRESENTATION (Wood art), THE THING (Ditko art), and STRANGE WORLD OF YOUR DREAMS (Simon and Kirby art) are but a few examples of books collectors are seeking.

Many of the early '50s crime comics have good potential for investment as a great number were used in *The Seduction of the Innocent* (TRUE CRIME, CRIME REPORTER, WANTED, MURDER INC., and CRIME DETECTIVE) or contain art by artists such as Matt Baker (AUTHENTIC POLICE CASES). Many contain drug stories such as CRIME MYSTERIES (Marijuana) and bring higher prices.

Love comics are becoming more and more collected these days. The most classic example of this genre is FORBIDDEN LOVE No. 1 which is commanding very high prices. All the St. John Love comics with Matt Baker and Kubert art, i.e. PICTORIAL ROMANCES, HOLLYWOOD CONFESSIONS, TEEN-AGE ROMANCES, --TEMPTATIONS, & DIARY SECRETS are in high demand. The Avon and Realistic books, i. e. INTIMATE CONFESSIONS, REALISTIC ROMANCES, ROMANTIC LOVE and FRONTIER ROMANCES with their seductive covers and beautiful Kinstler art are setting record prices in the market. The Quality Books with Bill Ward, Crandall, Everett, and Krigstein art are much sought after. Examples are BROADWAY ROMANCES, CAMPUS LOVES, LOVE CONFESSIONS, LOVE LETTERS, FLAMING LOVE, and UNTAMED LOVE. Wally Wood art is in very high demand and his love comic work is no exception: LOVE STORIES, MY CONFESSIONS, MY EXPERIENCE, CONFESSIONS OF ROMANCE, and POPULAR TEEN-AGERS. Star Publications put out a much-collected series of love books such as FILM STARS ROMANCES, FLAMING WESTERN ROMANCES and TARGET WESTERN ROMANCES, all with L. B. Cole covers. Even the Simon and Kirby books such as YOUNG LOVE and YOUNG ROMANCE are becoming more popular. We predict that many of the choice love comics as outlined above will continue to be good investments in the years ahead.

Books featuring unusual themes are in high demand. Some examples are: Catechetical Guild's BLOOD IS THE HARVEST and IF THE DEVIL WOULD TALK, Harvey's TEEN-AGE DOPE SLAVES, Hillman's MONSTER CRIME, the giveaways IS THIS TOMORROW, LUCKY FIGHTS IT THROUGH by Kurtzman, REDDY KILOWATT, TRAPPED, and books with covers showing extreme sex, violence or torture. Other sought-after books in this category are ALL-NEGRO, NEGRO HEROES and NEGRO ROMANCE. In 1953 and 1954 many publishers produced comics in 3-D. The 3-D craze (both movies and comics) went out as fast as it came in. These books have good investment potential and the demand for them is increasing.

During the 1940's many covers were drawn with an INFINITY theme and collectors are beginning to pick up on this. An infinity cover shows a scene that repeats itself to infinity. These covers will be listed in future editions as they are discovered.

Last year *The Price Guide* acquired a near complete set of SPIRIT

SECTIONS which is completely documented for the first time in this edition. At last, all special issues, etc. are now known (See Listings).

The top collected artists in 1978 were: Wolverton, Matt Baker, Krigstein, Bill Ward, Ditko, Toth, Kurtzman, Wood, Frazetta, Williamson, Neal Adams and Wrightson. The work of Jayson Disbrow and the psychedelic covers of L. B. Cole are bringing higher prices now and show indications of being good investment material for the future.

No news of the sale of Barks paintings in 1978, although some were offered with prices ranging between $6,000 and $12,000. Carl is currently doing a series of water colors, "Famous Ducks in Hisotry," while his wife, Gare', keeps turning out her beautiful landscapes. His Duck books went up an average of 105 per cent last year which is the biggest "Thank You" his many fans could give him.

Everett Raymond Kinstler continues to do portraits of congressmen and some movie stars, such as John Wayne. His early '50s covers and stories continue to climb in demand.

Original Schomburg paintings featuring the Timely characters were auctioned off and sold in 1978 bringing prices upwards to $2,400. We have been informed that only a total of ten paintings will be done.

After almost 30 years, Bill Gaines has finally decided to sell the EC original art. The plan is to sell the art after Russ Cochran publishes it in his EC book series. It will go to the highest bidder with the first batch to be released winter 1978-79.

1978 was a lean year for collections turning up which is probably one of the reasons for the increased demand for Golden Age books. Some dealers went out of business while many others started. The Guide's circulation went up 33 per cent in 1978 and probably received more publicity through magazines and newspapers than in any other year. We were even contacted by a foreign printer that wants to reprint the Guide in a foreign language.

The Poughkeepsie books mentioned in the No. 8 Guide continued to come out in small dribbles during the year. The availability of mint Dell runs is mind boggling to those of us who have spent years systematically putting our collections together. Nonetheless, they are coming out in a limited supply and no one knows when it will end. The opinion is that only a few more copies of each title will be released in the future. Surely not enough to over-supply the market, but just enough to feed the market, keeping the demand high.

In June, 1978, DC cancelled many of their current titles. The finished art for the next issue of those titles was published in two volumes CANCELLED COMIC CALVACADE. Only 35 copies were printed and distributed.

Comic characters continued to be in the limelight with the TV shows, the Superman movie and the new Conan newspaper strip.

As we traveled around the country this year we were diverted from our usual itinerary and visited Project Starlight International in Austin, Texas. This is a privately funded organization that investigates UFO phenomena. They have an ad in this edition promoting a book "Socorro Saucer" which documents a 1964 UFO landing in Socorro, New Mexico. The book is fascinating as was our visit with them.

We visited Camelot in Houston and spent hours pawing through 3,000 love comics as well as many other varieties, collecting material for the Guide. Many changes in the market have occurred this year. In some areas, prices varied tremendously making it harder for us to arrive at realistic averages. Avon's and Fox books fit into this category. However, we feel confident that the prices settled on are realistic and reflect the market more accurately from coast to coast.

WHY PEOPLE COLLECT COMICS

Collecting is one of the most universal avocations of man. There is no end to the list of things people collect. Every artifact of man and nature—from matchbook covers to great works of art—is, at one time or another, the object of some collector's frantic search. To the non-collector this mania must seem incomprehensible; but to the collector himself, it is a fascinating and continuously rewarding pastime.

Many people would be surprised to learn that along with coins, stamps, and books, one of the most prized collectors' items throughout the world is panel art—i. e., comic magazines, newspaper comic strips, and related material. People of all ages, from all walks of life collect "comics." Scientists, engineers, teachers, actors, artists, writers, businessmen, laborers, students, and people from every possible background spend many delightful hours with this hobby.

People collect panel art for a variety of reasons. Some collectors are amateur comic artists and writers, or even professionals in the field, who collect outstanding examples of cartoons and strips as inspiration for their own work. Others collect and study the comics as examples of popular art, interesting in their own right, or because they reflect the culture of the period in which they are produced. However, the vast majority of panelologists (i. e., comic collectors) want only to enhance their own enjoyment of this popular medium or recapture "the sense of wonder" that the comics provided in their youth. In addition to true collectors, there are also those who speculate in comics—i. e., merely buy comics to resell at a profit. There is a little bit of the speculator in all collectors.

SCARCITY OF COMIC BOOKS

Most all comic books prior to 1942 are very hard to find and rarely turn up. The paper drives of World War II and beyond consumed untold millions of comic books, not to mention the hundreds of thousands sent overseas to the armed services. This, associated with the American tradition of burning what few comics and magazines were left, has produced today an extremely rare collector's item—the comic book.

Because of the publicity given comic collecting by the news media, plus the ever-growing ranks of serious collectors, unknown numbers of people were influenced to save their comics. Comic books of the 1960s-70s were searched out and bought up in the thousands by (l) dealers, to supply the growing numbers of comic collectors, and (2) others speculating that they, like the golden age books, would someday become valuable. Due to this, books from 1964 to present are for the most part in plentiful supply, while books prior to this time are scarce and their rarity increases with age. Sometimes local distributing problems can produce temporary scarcity in certain issues, but usually this is only a localized condition.

Most collectors pay the highest prices for first issues, origin issues, or books with special covers, stories, and artists. This "higher demand" produces a scarcity on these particular books, forcing the price up. Unless collecting habits change dramatically in the near future, this trend should continue.

TOP HUNDRED TITLES

The following statistical table, compiled by Robert Crestohl, lists the top (most valuable) 100 titles in mint condition. The place in rank is given for each title by year, with its corresponding value. These tables can be very useful in forecasting trends in the market place. For instance, the investor might want to know which title is yielding the best dividend from one year to the next, or you might just be interested in seeing how the popularity of titles change from year to year.

During the past year Action Comics continued to gain on Marvel Mystery ending with a 23 per cent increase. Big gains have also been noted by the following titles: Archie (up 47%); Donald Duck (up 105%); Fantastic Four (up 47%); Flash Comics (up 38%); Phantom Lady (up 65%); Peter Wheat (up 73%); Superboy (up 51%); and World's Finest (up 36%). Donald Duck jumped from ninth to fourth place while several other titles came into the top hundred for the first time: Two-Fisted Tales, Phantom Lady, Archie, Fight, Peter Wheat and Strange Tales.

As the tables indicate, Silver Age titles are still on the go and continue to be a good investment.

TOP HUNDRED TITLES 1977-78 WITH TOTAL VALUE OF MINT RUN
(Figures Listed Denote Rank and Total Value of Mint Run for Each Year)

TITLE	1978 RANK	& VALUE	1977 RANK	& VALUE
MARVEL MYSTERY COMICS	1	$26236	1	$21130
ACTION COMICS	2	24598	2	19972
DETECTIVE COMICS	3	18633	3	15682
DONALD DUCK	4	16175	9	7892
WHIZ COMICS	5	15970	4	12874
MORE FUN COMICS	6	14811	5	12183
WALT DISNEY'S COMICS & STORIES	7	13874	6	11327
ADVENTURE COMICS	8	10769	7	9527
CAPTAIN AMERICA	9	10733	8	8974
SUPERMAN	10	10265	10	7788
FLASH COMICS	11	7360	14	5320
BATMAN	12	7069	12	5765
ALL STAR COMICS	13	7010	11	5934
CAPT. MARVEL ADVENTURES	14	6305	13	5552
MASTER COMICS	15	6286	15	5272
MOTION PICTURE FUNNIES WEEKLY	16	6000	18	4500
ALL AMERICAN COMICS	17	5512	16	4748
MICKEY MOUSE MAGAZINE	18	5255	22	3452
POLICE COMICS	19	5194	19	4278
FAMOUS FUNNIES	20	4975	17	4732
HUMAN TORCH	21	4735	21	3767
WORLD'S FAIR & FINEST	22	4698	23	3448
DICK TRACY	23	4683	20	3966
JUMBO COMICS	24	4030	26	3255
WOW COMICS	25	4007	33	2581
SUBMARINER	26	3885	25	3266
PEP COMICS	27	3754	27	3197
SILVER STREAK COMICS	28	3650	29	2855
STAR SPANGLED COMICS	29	3526	28	2974
KING COMICS	30	3439	24	3304
PLANET COMICS	31	3407	30	2806
DAREDEVIL	32	3257	31	2702
HIT COMICS	33	3195	37	2459
SENSATION COMICS	34	3178	34	2572
NATIONAL COMICS	35	3156	32	2628
MYSTIC COMICS	36	3060	42	2360
DARING MYSTERY COMICS	37	3000	41	2385
SMASH COMICS	38	2989	36	2462
CRACK COMICS	39	2900	40	2392
WONDER WOMAN	40	2894	46	2208
CLASSIC COMICS	41	2879	35	2489
USA COMICS	42	2850	44	2265
MILITARY COMICS	43	2810	38	2432
ALL WINNERS COMICS	44	2760	39	2395
FEATURE COMICS	45	2697	45	2224
TIP TOP COMICS	46	2581	50	2072
POPULAR COMICS	47	2460	43	2289
LOONEY TUNES	48	2435	49	2076
OUR GANG	49	2288	53	1931
MICKEY MOUSE	50	2274	57	1713
JUNGLE COMICS	51	2239	51	1985
SUPER COMICS	52	2198	48	2169
TARGET COMICS	53	2196	56	1735

TITLE	1978 RANK & VALUE		1977 RANK & VALUE	
CAPTAIN MARVEL JR.	54	2154	52	1976
FANTASTIC FOUR	55	2145	64	1462
SHADOW COMICS	56	2058	60	1638
LITTLE LULU	57	1993	58	1664
ACE COMICS	58	1955	54	1910
SHOWCASE	59	1942	83	1188
BLACKHAWK	60	1930	61	1601
TARZAN	61	1926	65	1448
TOP NOTCH COMICS	62	1864	59	1642
SUPERBOY	63	1854	78	1222
THE FUNNIES	64	1839	55	1839
ANIMAL COMICS	65	1810	62	1525
RED RAVEN COMICS	66	1800	80	1200
ZIP COMICS	67	1772	63	1514
PLASTIC MAN	68	1763	70	1380
AIRFIGHTERS & AIRBOY	69	1693	66	1436
WEIRD FANTASY	70	1615	71	1323
EXCITING COMICS	71	1592	72	1311
WINGS COMICS	72	1588	73	1293
WEIRD SCIENCE	73	1583	74	1290
NEW FUNNIES	74	1580	69	1385
YOUNG ALLIES	75	1575	75	1288
AMAZING SPIDERMAN	76	1563	85	1177
RED RYDER COMICS	77	1536	84	1183
BLUE BOLT COMICS	78	1489	67	1430
BOY COMICS	79	1488	68	1402
SPARKLER COMICS	80	1480	77	1272
JOURNEY INTO MYSTERY & THOR	81	1474	100	1055
HAUNT OF FEAR	82	1465	90	1139
VAULT OF HORROR	83	1440	87	1167
COMIC CAVALCADE	84	1439	76	1276
PETER WHEAT	85	1425	----	822
MAD COMICS & MAGAZINE	86	1390	86	1175
TWO FISTED TALES	87	1388	----	1050
UNCLE SCROOGE	88	1386	89	1144
COMICS ON PARADE	89	1347	81	1191
MYSTERY MEN	90	1344	79	1203
ALL FLASH COMICS	91	1330	88	1149
THRILLING COMICS	92	1316	94	1101
STARTLING COMICS	93	1271	----	995
WONDERWORLD	94	1240	97	1078
PHANTOM LADY	95	1231	----	745
ARCHIE	96	1228	----	817
SPEED COMICS	97	1215	91	1108
FIGHT COMICS	98	1206	----	939
BLUE RIBBON COMICS	99	1201	82	1189
STRANGE TALES	100	1186	----	1004

TOP TWENTY TITLES (Silver Age)
1978

N. B. To qualify for the SILVER AGE TOP TWENTY TITLES, the title must have begun no earlier than 1955. In the case of Tales of Suspense, Tales To Astonish, Journey into Mystery and Strange Tales, since the superheroes are the main concern, these sets are computed from where superheroes first appear.

TITLE	1978 RANK & VALUE	
FANTASTIC FOUR	1	$ 2145
SHOWCASE	2	1942
AMAZING SPIDERMAN	3	1563
FLASH	4	1448
THE BRAVE AND THE BOLD	5	1062
TALES TO ASTONISH & THE HULK	6	1033
JOURNEY INTO MYSTERY & THOR	7	837
JIMMY OLSEN	8	795
LOIS LANE	9	658
THE AVENGERS	10	579
GREEN LANTERN	11	553
CHALLENGERS OF THE UNKNOWN	12	546
TALES OF SUSPENSE & CAPT. AMERICA	13	541
JUSTICE LEAGUE	14	488
STRANGE TALES & DR. STRANGE	15	351
RICHIE RICH	16	321
MY GREATEST ADV. & DOOM PATROL	17	315
X-MEN	18	308
CONAN	19	295
DAREDEVIL	20	264

INVESTOR'S DATA

The following tables denote the rate of appreciation of the top 50 Golden Age titles and the top 20 Silver Age titles over the past eight years (1971-78) since the first Price Guide was published. The retail value for a complete mint run of each title in 1978 is compared to its corresponding value in 1971. By dividing the 1978 value by the 1971 value, it is easy to calculate the exact rate of appreciation of each title in terms of percentage points.

For example: a complete mint run of ACTION COMICS retailed at $24,598 in 1978 and $2,354 in 1971. From these figures it is calculated that every $100 investment in this title in 1971 would be worth exactly $1,044.94 in 1978. Whether the run be in mint, fine or good condition, this figure would remain relatively constant.

The following table is meant as a guide to the investor and it is hoped that it might aid him in his decision in what titles to invest. However, it should be pointed out that trends may change at any time and that some titles can develop into real comers from a presently dormant state. In the long run, however, if the investor sticks to the titles that are appreciating steadily every year, he can't go very far wrong.

It is interesting to note that even the titles that are appreciating the slowest are still increasing much faster than economic inflationary values during the same period.

TOP 50 TITLES — RATE OF INCREASE OVER 1971 VALUES

TITLE	1978 RANK & VALUE		1971 RANK & VALUE		1978 VALUE FOR EACH $100 IN 1971
MARVEL MYSTERY COMICS	1	$26236	4	$2584	$1018.81
ACTION COMICS	2	24598	6	2354	1044.94
DETECTIVE COMICS	3	18633	3	2747	678.30
DONALD DUCK	4	16175	49	604	2677.98
WHIZ COMICS	5	15970	13	1357	1176.86
MORE FUN COMICS	6	14811	2	2816	525.96
WALT DISNEY'S C & S	7	13874	11	1487	933.02
ADVENTURE COMICS	8	10769	1	3066	351.24
CAPTAIN AMERICA	9	10733	17	1303	823.71
SUPERMAN	10	10265	12	1460	703.08
FLASH COMICS	11	7360	14	1344	547.62
BATMAN	12	7069	19	1246	567.34
ALL STAR COMICS	13	7010	9	1657	423.05
CAPT. MARVEL ADVENTURES	14	6305	26	1009	624.88
MASTER COMICS	15	6286	25	1021	615.67
MOTION PICTURE FUNNIES WEEKLY	16	6000	----	N/A	N/A
ALL AMERICAN COMICS	17	5512	23	1189	463.58
MICKEY MOUSE MAGAZINE	18	5255	18	1252	419.73
POLICE COMICS	19	5194	27	903	575.19
FAMOUS FUNNIES	20	4975	7	2343	212.33
HUMAN TORCH	21	4735	42	632	749.21
WORLD'S FAIR & FINEST	22	4698	30	841	558.62
DICK TRACY	23	4683	24	1116	419.62
JUMBO COMICS	24	4030	16	1320	305.30
WOW COMICS	25	4007	53	574	698.08
SUBMARINER	26	3885	50	601	646.42
PEP COMICS	27	3754	28	880	426.59
SILVER STREAK COMICS	28	3650	82	394	926.40
STAR SPANGLED COMICS	29	3526	32	830	424.82
KING COMICS	30	3439	5	2490	138.11
PLANET COMICS	31	3407	48	613	555.79
DAREDEVIL	32	3257	41	639	509.70
HIT COMICS	33	3195	64	523	610.90
SENSATION COMICS	34	3178	38	681	466.67
NATIONAL COMICS	35	3156	39	676	466.86
MYSTIC COMICS	36	3060	95	340	900.00
DARING MYSTERY COMICS	37	3000	----	220	1363.64
SMASH COMICS	38	2989	31	833	358.82
CRACK COMICS	39	2900	48	613	473.08
WONDER WOMAN	40	2894	62	537	538.92
CLASSIC COMICS	41	2879	----	N/A	N/A
USA COMICS	42	2850	87	365	780.82
MILITARY COMICS	43	2810	65	520	540.38
ALL WINNERS COMICS	44	2760	57	545	506.42
FEATURE & FEATURE FUNNIES	45	2697	20	1214	222.16
TIP TOP COMICS	46	2581	8	2088	123.61
POPULAR COMICS	47	2460	10	1598	153.94
LOONEY TUNES	48	2435	54	558	436.38
OUR GANG	49	2288	----	338	676.92
MICKEY MOUSE	50	2274	----	266	854.89

TITLE	1978 RANK & VALUE		1971 RANK & VALUE		1978 VALUE FOR EACH $100 IN 1971
FANTASTIC FOUR	1	$2145	2	$254	$ 844.49
SHOWCASE	2	1942	1	280	693.57
AMAZING SPIDERMAN	3	1563	6	155	1008.39
THE FLASH	4	1448	7	142	1019.72
THE BRAVE AND THE BOLD	5	1062	3	184	577.17
TALES TO ASTONISH & THE HULK	6	1033	5	163	633.74
JOURNEY INTO MYSTERY & THOR	7	837	10	123	680.49
JIMMY OLSEN	8	795	4	170	467.65
LOIS LANE	9	658	11	108	609.26
THE AVENGERS	10	579	----	61	949.18
GREEN LANTERN	11	553	14	96	576.04
CHALLENGERS OF THE UNKNOWN	12	546	8	140	390.00
TALES OF SUSPENSE & CAPT. AMER.	13	541	15	83	651.81
JUSTICE LEAGUE	14	488	13	99	492.93
STRANGE TALES & DR. STRANGE	15	351	12	100	351.00
RICHIE RICH	16	321	----	N/A	N/A
MY GREATEST ADVENTURE	17	315	9	138	228.26
X-MEN	18	308	----	41	751.22
CONAN	19	295	----	N/A	N/A
DAREDEVIL	20	264	----	51	517.65

The following table shows the rate of increase of the 50 most valuable single books and the 20 most valuable Silver Age books over the past two years. Comparisons would be the same as the previous table of the Top 50 titles. Ranking in most cases is relative since so many books fall under the same value. These books are listed alphabetically.

50 MOST VALUABLE BOOKS

ISSUE	1978 RANK & VALUE		1977 VALUE
MARVEL COMICS No. 1	1	$10000	$ 7500
ACTION COMICS No. 1	2	7500	5250
MOTION PICTURE FUNNIES WEEKLY No. 1	3	6000	4500
WHIZ COMICS No. 1	4	5000	3750
DETECTIVE COMICS No. 27	5	4200	3600
SUPERMAN No. 1	6	3000	2400
WALT DISNEY'S COMICS & STORIES No. 1	7	2500	1800
WOW COMICS No. 1	8	2400	1200
MORE FUN COMICS No. 52	9	2250	1500
CAPTAIN AMERICA No. 1	10	2250	1800
BATMAN No. 1	11	2200	1800
CAPT. MARVEL ADVENTURES No. 1	12	2000	1500
MARVEL MYSTERY COMICS No. 2	13	1800	1350
MARVEL MYSTERY COMICS No. 5	14	1800	1500
ACTION COMICS No. 2	15	1800	1500
RED RAVEN No. 1	16	1800	1200
DONALD DUCK TELLS ABOUT THE KITES S.C.E.	17	1800	1500
MORE FUN COMICS No. 53	18	1500	900
WHIZ COMICS No. 2	19	1500	1125
DONALD DUCK Four Color No. 9	20	1500	1200
DONALD DUCK Black & White No. 20	21	1500	900
DONALD DUCK March of Comics No. 4	22	1500	1350
ACTION COMICS No. 3	23	1350	1200
ACTION COMICS No. 5	24	1350	1200
DETECTIVE COMICS No. 28	25	1350	1200
DONALD DUCK TELLS ABOUT THE KITES P.G.&E.	26	1350	1200
MICKEY MOUSE Four Color No. 16	27	1300	975
MARVEL MYSTERY COMICS No. 3	28	1200	1050
DONALD DUCK Four Color No. 4	29	1200	1200
DONALD DUCK Black & White No. 16	30	1200	900
DONALD DUCK Four Color No. 29	31	1125	900
DONALD DUCK March of Comics No. 20	32	1050	900
WALT DISNEY'S COMICS & STORIES No. 2	33	1000	900
HUMAN TORCH No. 1	34	975	855
MARVEL MYSTERY COMICS No. 4	35	900	750
MARVEL MYSTERY COMICS No. 9	36	900	675
CAPTAIN AMERICA No. 2	37	900	750
ACTION COMICS No. 4	38	900	750
ALL AMERICAN COMICS No. 16	39	900	750
BOY EXPLORERS No. 2	40	900	900
DARING MYSTERY COMICS No. 1	41	900	750
DETECTIVE COMICS No. 33	42	900	750
SILVER STREAK COMICS No. 6	43	900	750
SUPERMAN No. 2	44	900	750
WHIZ COMICS No. 3	45	900	750
SPECIAL EDITION No. 1	46	825	750
USA COMICS No. 1	47	750	600
SUBMARINER No. 1	48	750	600
MARVEL MYSTERY COMICS No. 8	49	750	675
MYSTIC COMICS No. 1	50	750	600

ISSUE	1978 RANK & VALUE		1977 VALUE
FANTASTIC FOUR No. 1	1	$600	$360
SHOWCASE No. 4	2	450	180
AMAZING FANTASY No. 15	3	360	255
AMAZING SPIDERMAN No. 1	4	300	255
HULK No. 1	5	240	120
JOURNEY INTO MYSTERY No. 83	6	255	120
FANTASTIC FOUR No. 2	7	210	135
FANTASTIC FOUR No. 3	8	150	90
FLASH No. 105	9	150	105
SHOWCASE No. 8	10	150	75
THE AVENGERS No. 1	11	120	60
JIMMY OLSEN No. 1	12	120	75
BRAVE AND THE BOLD No. 1	13	120	105
TALES TO ASTONISH No. 27	14	120	90
SHOWCASE No. 1	15	120	105
SHOWCASE No. 14	16	120	60
TALES OF SUSPENSE No. 39	17	105	60
FANTASTIC FOUR No. 4	18	105	75
AMAZING SPIDERMAN No. 2	19	90	75
HULK No. 2	20	90	60

COMICS WITH LITTLE IF ANY VALUE

There exists in the comic book market, as in all other collector's markets, items, usually of recent origin, that have relatively little if any value. Why even mention it? We wouldn't, except for one thing—this is where you could probably take your worst beating, investment-wise. Since these books are listed by dealers in such profusion, at prices which will vary up to 500 per cent from one dealer's price list to another, determining a realistic "market" value is almost impossible. And since the same books are listed repeatedly, list after list, month after month, it is difficult to determine whether or not these books are selling. In some cases, it is doubtful that they are even being collected. Most dealers must get a minimum price for their books; otherwise, it would not be profitable to handle. This will sometimes force a value on an otherwise valueless item. On the other hand, you might buy a vastly over-priced golden-age comic and still expect to recover your loss after a reasonable passage of time. This, unfortunately, is not true of so many titles that we are put in a rather awkward position of listing.

THE PRICE GUIDE'S POSITION: We don't want to leave a title out just because it is presently valueless. And at the same time, we don't want to presume to "establish" what is collectible and what isn't. The passage of time and a change in collectors' interests can make almost any comic potentially valuable. Some books, by virtue of their age, will someday obtain a value as a cultural or historical curiosity. Therefore, we feel that all books, regardless of the demand for them, should be listed.

Since speculation in the comic book market began around 1964, most all titles since that time have been saved and are in plentiful supply. These books have been included for your information and can be found listed throughout The Guide with arbitrary values assigned (under 50 cents). The collector would be well advised to compare prices between several dealers' lists before ordering this type of material.

HOW TO START COLLECTING

Most collectors of comic books begin by buying new issues in mint condition directly off the newsstand. (Subscription copies are, as a rule, folded and, hence, unsuited for collecting purposes.) Each week new comics appear on the stands that are destined to become true collectors items. The trick is to locate a store that carries a complete line of comics. In several localities this may be difficult. Most panelologists frequent several magazine stands in order not to miss something they want. Even then, it pays to keep in close contact with collectors in other areas. Sooner or later, nearly every collector has to rely upon a friend in Fandom to obtain for him an item that is unavailable locally.

Once you have located a good source of new comics, find out on what days the books are delivered. Plan to drop by regularly as soon after the comics are checked in as possible. This way you may avoid missing an issue, and you will also stand a better chance of getting mint copies. You will find that comics rapidly become damaged on the stands, especially when they are displayed in certain kinds of racks.

Before you buy any comic to add to your collection, you should carefully inspect its condition. Unlike stamps and coins, defective comics are generally not highly prized. The cover should be properly cut and printed. Remember that every blemish or sign of wear depreciates the beauty and value of your comics.

The serious panelologist usually purchases extra copies of popular titles. He may trade these multiples for items unavailable locally (for example, foreign comics), or he may store the multiples for resale at some future date. Such speculation is, of course, a gamble, but unless collecting trends change radically in the future, the value of certain comics in mint condition should appreciate greatly, as new generations of readers become interested in collecting.

COLLECTING BACK ISSUES

In addition to current issues, most panelologists want to locate back issues. Some energetic collectors have had great success in running down large hoards of rare comics in their home towns. Occasionally, rare items can be located through agencies that collect old papers and magazines, such as the Salvation Army. The lucky collector can often buy these items for much less than their current market value. Placing advertisements in trade journals, newspapers, etc., can also produce good results. However, don't be discouraged if you are neither energetic nor lucky. Most panelologists build their collections slowly but systematically by placing mail orders with dealers and other collectors.

Comics of early vintage are extremely expensive if they are purchased through a regular dealer or collector, and unless you have unlimited funds to invest in your hobby, you will find it necessary to restrict your collecting in certain ways. Every enthusiast defines his collection in a different manner. Some collect only runs of certain titles. Others collect only selected issues, which carry special stories or work by a favorite artist. Many collect only incomplete runs of their favorite titles, concentrating on certain periods. However you define your collection, you should be careful to set your goals well within your means.

HOW TO SELL YOUR COMICS

If you have a collection of comics for sale, large or small, the following steps should be taken. (I) Make a detailed list of the books for sale, being careful to grade them accurately, showing any noticeable defects; i. e., torn or missing pages, centerfolds, etc. (2) Decide whether to sell wholesale to a dealer all in one lump or to go through the long laborious process of advertising and selling piece by piece to collectors. Both have their advantages and disadvantages.

In selling to dealers, you will get the best price by letting everything go at once—the good with the bad—all for one price. Simply select names either from ads in this book or from some of the adzines mentioned below. Send them your list and ask for bids. The bids received will vary depending on rarity and condition of the books you have. The rarer and better the condition, the higher the bids will be.

On the other hand, you could become a dealer and sell the books yourself. Order a copy of one or more of the adzines. Take note how most dealers lay out their ads. Type up your ad copy, carefully pricing each book (using the Guide as a reference). Send finished ad copy with payment to adzine editor to be run. You will find that certain books will sell at once while others will not sell at all. The ad will probably have to be retyped, remaining books repriced, and run again. Price books according to how fast you want them to move. If you try to get top dollar, expect a much longer period of time. Otherwise, the better deal you give the collector, the faster they will move. Remember, in being your own dealer, you will have overhead expenses in postage, mailing supplies and advertising cost. Some books might even be returned for refund due to misgrading, etc.

In selling all at once to a dealer, you get instant cash, immediate profit, and eliminate the long process of running several ads to dispose of the books; but if you have patience, and a small amount of business sense, you could realize more profit selling them directly to collectors yourself.

WHERE TO BUY AND SELL

Throughout this book you will find the advertisements of many reputable dealers who sell back-issue comics magazines. If you are an inexperienced collector, be sure to compare prices before you buy. Never send large sums of money through the mail. Send money orders or checks for your personal protection. Beware of bargains, as the items advertised sometimes do not exist, but are only a fraud to get your money.

The Price Guide is indebted to everyone who placed ads in this volume, whose support has helped in curbing printing costs. Your mentioning this book when dealing with the advertisers would be greatly appreciated.

Attend a comic convention this year. There you will find an abundance of comic material for sale, as well as a chance to meet others who share your interest. Check the following publications for announcements of cons to be held in your area:

THE BUYERS GUIDE
DYNAPUBS, 15800 Rt. 84 North
East Moline, Ill. 61244

COLLECTOR'S DREAM MAGAZINE
P.O. Box 127, Station T.
Toronto, Ont. M6B 3Z9 Canada

MEET THE DEALERS
Box 711
Lindenhurst, NY 11757

THE COMICS JOURNAL
P.O. Box 292
Riverdale, Md. 10840

THE RBCC
1014 Salzedo, Apt. 10
Coral Gables, Fla. 33134

The Price Guide highly recommends the above adzines, which are full of ads buying and selling comics, pulps, radio tapes, premiums, toys and other related items. You can also place ads to buy or sell your comics in the above publications.

COMIC BOOK MAIL ORDER SERVICES

The following offer a mail order service on new comic books. Write for rates and details:

BILL COLE, P.O. Box 60, Wollaston, Mass. 02170 (Disney Comics)

DELTA - T COMICS, 11407 55 Avenue, Edmonton, Alberta, Canada T6H 0X3

THE FANTASY MAIL CO., P. O. Box 7476, Rochester, N. Y. 14615

FOUR COLOR DREAMS COMIC SERVICE, 9 St. Catherine Drive, St. Peters, Mo. 63376

SEA GATE DIST., INC., P. O. Box 177, Coney Island Station, Brooklyn, N. Y. 11224

STYX COMIC SERVICE, P. O. Box 3791, Winnipeg, Manitoba, Canada R2W 3R6

HOW TO SELECT FANZINES

In the early 1960s, only a few comic fanzines were being published. A fan could easily afford to subscribe to them all. Today, the situation has radically changed, and it has become something of a problem to decide which fanzines to order.

Fanzines are not all of equal quality or general interest. Even different issues of the same fanzine may vary signficantly. To locate issues that will be of interest to you, learn to look for the names of outstanding amateur artists, writers, and editors, and consult fanzine review columns. Although you may not always agree with the judgements of the reviewers you will find these reviews to be a valuable source of information about the content and quality of the current fanzines.

When ordering a fanzine, remember that print runs are small and the issue you may want may be out of print (OP). Ordinarily in this case, you will receive the next issue. Because of irregular publishing schedules that nearly all fanzines must, of necessity, observe, allow up to 90 days or more for your copy to reach you. It is common courtesy when addressing an inquiry to an ama-publisher to enclose a self-addressed, stamped envelope.

FAN PUBLICATIONS OF INTEREST

THE ARTISTS INDEX—OVR Comics, 1114 Devons Rd., London, England.

BATMANIA—Richard H. Morrissey, 55 Claudette Circle, Framingham, Mass. 01701—for Batman fans.

CAPTAIN GEORGE'S WHIZZBANG—"Captain George" Henderson, 594 Markham St., Toronto, Ontario, Canada.

CARTOON—The Cartoon Museum—Jim Ivey, 561 Obispo Ave., Orlando, Fla. 32807.

CHRONICLE—George Breo., 5600 Milwaukee Ave., Chicago, Ill. 60646.

CLASSICS COLLECTORS CLUB NEWSLETTER—Raymond True, 1930 W. Warwick Lane, Roselle, Ill. 60172.
THE CLASSICS READER—W. J. Briggs, P.O. Box 1191, Station 'Q' Toronto, Ontario, Canada M4T 2P4.

COLLECTORS WORLD—Tom Crawford, 35 Fort Hill Ave., Canandaigua, NY 14424. Contains ads & articles about comic collecting.

COMIC DETECTIVE—Bart Bush, 713 Sugar Maple, Ponco City, Okla. 74601.

COMIC FAN VENTURE—632 Gibbon St., Williams Lake, B. C., Canada.

COMIC MEDIA—Richard Burton, 22 Woodhaw, Egham, Surrey TW20, 9AP, England.

THE COMIC PRESS—Russell Condello, 34 Burt Street, Rochester, New York 14609, Articles about Silver Age Comics, 90 cents.

THE COMIC READER—Street Enterprises, P.O. Box 255, Menomonee Falls, Wisc. 53051. (Gives advance information on all new comics being published).

THE COMICS NEWS FANZINE—BEM, 3 Marlow Court, Britannia Square, Worcester WR1.3DP, England.

COMIX WORLD—Clay Geerdes, 915 Indian Rock Road, Berkeley, Calif. 94707 -zine on underground comics.

THE COMPLETE EC LIBRARY—Russ Cochran, P.O. Box 437, West Plains, Mo. 65775. A must for all EC collectors. The first four volume set reprints Weird Science Nos. 1-22. Reprinting of the complete EC line is planned. Write for details.

CRAWFORD'S ENCYCLOPEDIA OF COMIC BOOKS (Hardcover format, 448 pages, color illustrated) Comicade Ent./Jonathan David Publishers, 1978. Book contains comprehensive history of the comic book industry, $19.95.

DENIS GIFFORD'S BRITISH COMIC CATALOGUE—1874-1974; $30, 224 p., clothbound with 1700 titles listed. Write: ISBS Inc., 10300 S.W. Allen Blvd. Beaverton, Oregon 97005.

THE DUCKBURG TIMES—Paul Anderson III, 1407 Spring Creek Dr., Laramie, WY 82070—A bi-monthly fanzine for Barks & Disney fans.

ERBANIA—D. Peter Ogden, 8001 Fernview Lane, Tampa, Fla. 33615—ERB Zine.
ERB-dom—Camille Cazedussus Jr., Rt. 2, Box 119, Clinton, La. 70722.

FAN INFORMER—Arvell M. Jones, 5729 Cadillac, Detroit, Mich. 48213.

FANDOM MEDIA—Paul Hugli, 9440 Nichols, Bellflower, Calif. 90706.

FANDOM FUNNIES—Jay Zilber, 81 Webster Park, Columbus, Ohio 43214 (Fandom Humor Magazine) $1.00

FANTASY TRADER—Mike Cruden, 35, Sandringham Rd., Gee Cross, Hyde, Cheshire, England.

FANTASY UNLIMITED—Alan Austin, 47 Hesperus Crescent, Millwall, London, E14 9A8, England.

GLX SPTZL GLAAH!—Ken Gale, 220 E. 85th Street, No. 5-R, New York, N.Y. 10028 (for Sheldon Mayer collectors and fans) 50 cents.

GRAPHIC STORY MAGAZINE—Bill Spicer, 329 North Ave. 66, Los Angeles, Cal. 90042.

GRAPHIC STORY QUARTERLY & WONDERWORLD—Richard Kyle, P.O. Box 16168, Long Beach, Calif. 90806.

THE HEROINES SHOWCASE—The Comics Heroines Fan Club—Steven R. Johnson, P.O. Box 1329, Campbell, Calif. 85008.

INFINITY—Gary Berman, 19750 F. Peck Ave., Flushing, N.Y. 11365.

INVESTORS NEWSLETTER—Sparkle City Comics, P.O. Box 24238, Dayton, Ohio 45424. A guide to comic investing.

LOLLAPALOOSA—(Published annually; focuses on comic art.) Mitch O'Connell, 266 Spruce, Boulder, Colo. 80302.

MEDIASCENE—Supergraphics, Box 445, Wyomissing, Pa. 19610 (Subscriptions: 6/$4. Articles on current comics media).

THE MENOMONEE FALLS GAZETTE—A weekly newspaper featuring the best daily adventure strips. Write: P.O. Box 255, Menomonee Falls, Wisc. 53051.

NIMBUS—Frank Lovece, editor—Write Sam de la Rosa, 328 Canavan, San Antonio, Texas 78221.

OLDE TIME COMICS—64 page tabloid reprinting early newspaper strips. Published quarterly by Tower Press, Inc., Folly Mill Road, Seabrook, N.H. 03874.

PHANTACEA—Jim McPherson, 1749 Collingwood St., Vancouver, Canada V6R 3K2.

PHANTASMAGORIA— Kenneth Smith, Box 20020-A, L. S. U. Station, Baton Rouge, La. 70803. Articles on fine art & science fiction.

SCIENCE FICTION REVIEW—Richard E. Geis, P.O. Box 11408, Portland, Oregon 97211.

STRIP SCENE—Carl Horak, Remuda Publ., 6312 Crowchild Trail S.W., Calgary, Alberta, Canada T3E SR5 — For strip collectors (403) 242-8532.

SQUA TRONT—John Benson, editor. For back and recent issues write: Jerry Weist c/o The Million Year Picnic, 36 Boylston St., Cambridge, Mass. 02138.

SUPERZINE!—Chris Lareau, 2018 Commonwealth Ave., Brighton, Mass. 02135. Contains ads and articles.

TREK—The Phantom Empire, 5600 N. Freeway No. 341, Houston, Texas 77022—A full tabloid zine for Star Trek fans.

TETRAGRAMMATION FRAGMENTS—Jay Zilber, 81 Webster Park, Columbus, Ohio 43214. (Monthly newsletter of United Fanzine Organization) 50 cents.

COMIC BOOK CLUBS
NEW YORK—Little Lulu Fan Club, Norman F. Hale, 110 Bank St. Apt. 2H, New York, N.Y. 10014.

Note: Anyone wanting their clubs listed in next year's guide, please send information.

COLLECTING STRIPS

Collecting newspaper comic strips is somewhat different than collecting magazines, although it can be equally satisfying.

Obviously, most strip collectors begin by clipping strips from their local paper, but many soon branch out to strips carried in out-of-town papers. Naturally this can become more expensive and it is often frustrating, because it is easy to miss editions of out-of-town papers. Consequently, most strip collectors work out trade agreements with collectors in other cities in order to get an uninterrupted supply of the strips they want. This usually necessitates saving local strips to be used for trade purposes only.

Back issues of strips dating back several decades are also available from time to time from dealers. The prices per panel vary greatly depending on the age, condition, and demand for the strip. When the original strips are unavailable, it is sometimes possible to get photostatic copies from collectors, libraries, or newspaper morgues.

COLLECTING FOREIGN COMICS

One extremely interesting source of comics of early vintage—one which does not necessarily have to be expensive—is the foreign market. Many American strips, from both papers and magazines, are reprinted abroad (both in English and in other languages) months and even years after they appear in the states. By working out trade agreements with foreign collectors, one can obtain, for practically the cover price, substantial runs of a number of newspaper strips and reprints of American comics books dating back five, ten, or occasionally even twenty or more years. These reprints are often in black and white, and sometimes the reproduction is poor, but this is not always the case. In any event, this is a source of material that every serious collector should look into.

Once the collector discovers comics published in foreign lands, he often becomes fascinated with the original strips produced in these countries. Many are excellent, and have a broader range of appeal than those of American comic books. They are published in magazines of every conceivable size and description. Any comics collection is enhanced by the addition of foreign comics. It is possible to build substantial collections of these magazines through the generous assistance of fans in countries like Australia, England, South Africa, Ireland, Scotland and Canada. Look for their ads in the adzines listed under "Where to Buy and Sell" or check with dealers, some of which stock foreign comics.

CANADIAN REPRINTS
EC's: by J. B. Clifford

Several EC titles were published in Canada by Superior Comics from 1949 to at least 1953. Canadian editions of the following EC titles are known: (Pre-Trend) Saddle Romances, Moon Girl, A Moon A Girl. . .Romance, Modern Love, Saddle Justice; (New-Trend) Crypt of Terror-Tales From the Crypt, Haunt of Fear, Vault of Horror, Weird Science, Weird Fantasy, Two-Fisted Tales, Frontline Combat, and Mad. Crime SuspenStories was also published in Canada under the title Weird SuspenStories (Nos. 1-3 known). No reprints of Shock SuspenStories by Superior are known, nor have any "New Direction" reprints ever been reported. No reprints later than January 1954 are known. Canadian reprints sometimes exchanged cover and contents with adjacent numbers (e. g. a Frontline Combat 12 with a FC No. 11 cover). They are distinguished both in cover and contents. As the interior pages are always reprinted poorly, these comics are of less value (about ½) than the U. S. Editions; also, they were printed later than the U. S. editions from asbestos plates made from the original plates. On some reprints, the Superior seal replaces the EC seal. Superior publishers took over Dymamic in 1947.

Dells: by Ronald J. Ard

Canadian editions of Dell comics, and presumably other lines, began in March-April, 1948 and lasted until February-March, 1951. They were a response to the great Canadian dollar crisis of 1947. Intensive development of the post-war Canadian economy was financed almost entirely by American capital. This massive import of money reached such a level that Canada was in danger of having a grossly disproportionate balance of payments which could drive it into technical bankruptcy in the midst of the biggest boom in its history. The Canadian government responded by banning a long list of imports. Almost 500 separate items were involved. Alas, the consumers of approximately 499 of them were politically more formidable than the consumers of comic books.

Dell responded by publishing its titles in Canada, through an arrangement with Wilson Publishing Company of Toronto. This concern has not existed for a number of years and it is reasonable to assume that its sole business was the production and distribution of Dell titles in Canada. There is no doubt that they had a captive market. If you check the publication data on the U. S. editions of the period you will see the sentence "Not for sale in Canada." Canada was thus the only area of the Free World in those days technically beyond the reach of the American comic book industry.

We do not know whether French editions existed of the Dell titles put out by Wilson. The English editions were available nationwide. They were priced at 10 cents and were all 36 pages in length, at a time when their American parents were 52 pages. The covers were made of coarser paper, similar to that used in the Dell Four Color series in 1946 and 1947 and were abandoned as the more glossy cover paper became more economical. There was also a time lag of from six to eight weeks between, say, the date an American comic appeared on a Seattle comics rack and the date that the Canadian edition appeared on its Vancouver counterpart.

Many Dell covers had seasonal themes and by the time the Canadian edition came out (two months later) the season was over. Wilson solved this problem by switching covers around so that the appropriate season would be reflected when the books hit the stands. Most Dell titles were published in Canada during this period including the popular Atom Bomb giveaway, Walt Disney Comics and Stories and the Donald Duck and Mickey Mouse Four Color one-shots. The quality of the Duck one-shots is equal to that of their American counterparts and generally bring about 30% less.

By 1951 the Korean War had so stimulated Canadian exports that the restrictions on comic book importation, which in any case were an offense against free trade principle, could be lifted without danger of economic collapse. Since this time Dell, as well as other companies, have been shipping direct into Canada.

COLLECTING ORIGINAL ART

In addition to magazines and strips, some enthusiasts also collect the original art for the comics. These black and white, inked drawings are usually done on illustration paper at about 30 per cent up (i. e., 30 per cent larger than the original printed panels). Because original art is a one-of-a-kind article, it is highly prized and often difficult to obtain.

Interest in original comic art has increased tremendously in the past several years. Many companies now return the originals to the artists who have in turn offered them for sale, usually at cons but sometimes through agents and dealers. As the collection grows, extra or less pleasing items are often used as swapping material with other collectors. Cartoons have now become generally accepted as an art form by academics; museums are purchasing comic art for their permanent collections. As with any other area of collecting, rarity and demand governs value. Although the masters' works bring fine art prices, most art is available at moderate prices. Comic strips are the most popular facet with collectors, followed by comic book art. Once scarce, current and older comic book art has surfaced within the last few years. In 1974 several original painted covers of vintage comic books and coloring books turned up from Dell, Gold Key, Whitman, and Classic Comics. Gag, sports, political, and other type cartoons are sought by relatively few.

The following are sources for original art:

Tony Dispoto
Comic Art Showcase
P. O. Box 425
Lodi, N. J. 07644

Russ Cochran
P.O. Box 437
West Plains, Mo. 65775

THE HISTORY OF COMICS FANDOM

At this time it is possible to discern two distinct and largely unrelated movements in the history of Comics Fandom. The first of these movements began about 1953 as a response to the then-popular, trend-setting EC line of comics. The first true comics fanzines of this movement were short-lived. Bhob Stewart's EC FAN BULLETIN was a hectographed newsletter that ran two issues about six months apart; and Jimmy Taurasi's FANTASY COMICS, a newsletter devoted to all science-fiction comics of the period, was a monthly that ran for about six months. These were followed by other newsletters, such as Mike May's EC FAN JOURNAL, and George Jennings' EC WORLD PRESS. EC fanzines of a wider and more critical scope appeared somewhat later. Two of the finest were POTRZEBIE, the product of a number of fans, and Ron Parker's HOOHAH. Gauging from the response that POTRZEBIE received from a plug in an EC letter column, Ted White estimated the average age of EC fans to lie in the range of 9 to 13, while many EC fans were in their mid-teens. This fact was taken as discouraging to many of the faneds, who had hoped to reach an older audience. Consequently, many of them gave up their efforts in behalf of Comics Fandom, especially with the demise of the EC groups, and turned their attention to science-fiction fandom with its longer tradition and older membership. While the flourish of fan activity in response to the EC comics was certainly noteworthy, it is fair to say that it never developed into a full-fledged, independent, and self-sustaining movement.

The second comics fan movement began in 1960. It was largely a response to (though it later became a stimulus for) the Second Heroic Age of Comics. Most fan historians date the Second Heroic Age from the appearance of the new FLASH comics magazine (numbered 105 and dated February 1959). The letter departments of Julius Schwartz (editor at National Periodicals), and later those of Stan Lee (Marvel Group) and Bill Harris (Gold Key) were most influential in bringing comics readers into

Fandom. Beyond question, it was the reappearance of the costumed hero that sparked the comics fan movement of the sixties. Sparks were lit among some science-fiction fans first, when experienced fan writers, who were part of an established tradition, produced the first in a series of articles on the comics of the forties—ALL IN COLOR FQR A DIME. The series was introduced in XERO No. 1 (September 1960), a general fanzine for science-fiction fandom edited and published by Dick Lupoff.

Meanwhile, outside science-fiction fandom, Jerry Bails and Roy Thomas, two strictly comics fans of long-standing, conceived the first true comics fanzine in response to the Second Heroic Age. The fanzine, ALTER EGO, appeared in March 1961. The first several issues were widely circulated among comics fans, and were to influence profoundly the comics fan movement to follow. Unlike the earlier EC fan movement, this new movement attracted many fans in their twenties and thirties. A number of these older fans had been active collectors for years but had been largely unknown to each other. Joined by scores of new, younger fans, this group formed the nucleus of a new movement that is still growing and shows every indication of being self-sustaining. Although it has borrowed a few of the more appropriate terms coined by science-fiction fans, Comics Fandom of the Sixties was an independent if fledging movement, without, in most cases, the advantages and disadvantages of a longer tradition. What Comics Fandom did derive from science-fiction fandom it does so thanks largely to the fanzines produced by so-called double fans. The most notable of this type is COMIC ART, edited and published by Don and Maggie Thompson.

Listed below are some of the major events in the Comics Fan Movement of the early 1960s.

1960
Sept. XERO No. 1 (Dick Lupoff) with "AICFAD" on First Heroic Age.

1961
Feb. locs in BRAVE & BOLD No. 35 initiate wide-scale fan contacts.
Mar. ALTER EGO No. 1 (Jerry Bails and Roy Thomas).
Apr. COMIC ART No. 1 (Don Thompson).
Sept. THE COMICOLLECTOR No. 1 (Jerry Bails).
Oct. ON THE DRAWING BOARD (J. Bails); later THE COMIC READER.
Dec. THE ROCKET'S BLAST No. 1 (G. B. Love).

1962
June First ALLEY AWARDS POLL.
July KOMIX ILLUSTRATED No. 1 (Bill White).
Sept. THE KOMIX NO. 1 (John Wright, South Africa)
        MASQUERADER No. 1 (Mike Vosburg).
        SUPER HERO No. 1 (Mike Tuohey).
Dec. THE COMIC WORLD No. 1 (Robert Jennings).

1963
Apr. FIGHTING HERO COMICS NO. 1 (G. B. Love).
June STAR-STUDDED COMICS NO. 1 (The Texas Trio).
Aug. DATELINE: COMICDOM NO. 1 (Ronn Foss).
Oct. Ratification of the ACADEMY CHARTER.

1964
Feb. FANTASY ILLUSTRATED NO. 1 (Bill Spicer).
Mar. ALLEY TALLY, first weekend fan party.
Apr. WHO'S WHO IN COMICS FANDOM (L. Lattanzi).
May First Detroit fan-meet.
        First Chicago fan-meet.
        Fanclave at the home of Russ Manning.
June SLAM-BANG NO. 1 (Rick Weingroff).
July BATMANIA NO. 1 (Bill White).
Oct. VOICE OF COMICDOM NO. 2 (first issue) (Golden Gate Publishers).
        CAPA-alpha No. 1 (first comics-oriented APA).
        FORUM NO. 1 (Paul Gambaccini).
        reprints of first BUCK ROGERS strips (Edwin Aprill).
Dec. DOWN UNDER NO. 1 (John Ryan, Australia).

1965

Mar., Apr. Widespread publicity about Comicdom in magazines and newspapers throughout the world.

July THE GUIDEBOOK OF COMICS FANDOM (Bill Spicer).

COMIC BOOK CONVENTIONS

As is the case with most other aspects of comic collecting, comic book conventions, or cons as they are referred to, were originally conceived as the comic-book counterpart to science-fiction fandom conventions. There were many attempts to form successful national cons prior to the time of the first one that materialized, but they were all stillborn. It is interesting that after only three relatively organized years of existence, the first comic con was held. Of course, its magnitude was nowhere near as large as most established cons held today.

What is a comic con? As might be expected, there are comic books to be found at these gatherings. Dealers, collectors, fans, whatever they call themselves can be found trading, selling, and buying the adventures of their favorite characters for hours on end. Additionally if at all possible, cons have guests of honor, usually professionals in the field of comic art, either writers, artists, or editors. The New York cons virtually ooze pros out of every nook and cranny, because most of them do live in New York. The committees put together panels for the con attendees where the assembled pros talk about certain areas of comics, most of the time fielding questions from the assembled audience. At cons one can usually find displays of various and sundry things, usually original art. There might be radio listening rooms; there is most certainly a daily showing of different movies, usually science-fiction or horror type. Of course there is always the chance to get together with friends at cons and just talk about comics; one also has a good opportunity to make new friends who have similar interests and with whom one can correspond after the con.

It is difficult to describe accurately what goes on at a con. The best way to find out is to go to one or more if you can.

WHERE TO GO TO SEE WHAT YOU WANT TO SEE

If you are seriously into the many varied aspects of comic fandom, then the opportunity to attend a comic convention will be difficult to pass up. Any of the large cons has its own distinguishing features which guarantee its enjoyability. As is obvious, though, each con is different; each has activities that may not appeal to everyone. Therefore, if you can only afford to visit one convention, your choice is important in relation to your interests. This section is to guide one's decision as to which convention should be attended.

If you want to see professionals, there is no question that any of the New York cons are best, as well as the San Diego convention. Of course, because of the dearth of pros in the other areas of the country, the other cons sometimes get guests to attend who are not usually seen at cons. So don't discount the other cons outside New York and San Diego. For example, Orlando Con '75 specialized in the many fine artists and writers in the comic strip field.

If it's comics and more comics that you want, once again the New York cons would probably be best because of the heavy dealer attendance. Of course, the increasing scarcity and prices of the older comics makes it difficult to find and to buy them at almost any con. So the solution to this is to go to all the cons. Actually, though, the New York cons (those being the N. Y. Comic Art Convention and Creation) are best, with the other national cons trailing not too very far behind. Many people, though, dislike the New York cons due to their immensity and impersonality. For these persons, the other national cons are the only ones worth attending. The decision is yours.

If you are looking for cinematic thrills, conventions all have varied film

The WIZARD KING is Wallace Wood's finest (and final) contribution to comic art. Volume I is finished and will be going to press shortly. Volume II is currently in production, and will be published in the near future. There will be four volumes in all. He has been working on it for ten years (and thinking about it for possibly forty). He started it in WITZEND #4, made a couple of false starts for other publishers, and finally began to work on it in earnest in 1974. He finished it in 1977, and decided to publish it himself. To do this he needs to raise some capital.

You can help, by joining F.O.O. (The Friends of Odkin) and by buying some of his other publications: SALLY FORTH, CANNON and HEROES, INC.

$5.00 membership fee. For this you'll receive:
1. A membership card, good until Jan. 1, 1980
2. 25% off on all books published by Wood
3. Four issues of THE WOODWORK GAZETTE, the club's official newsletter (easily worth the price of membership alone).

OR - Send $3.00 more and receive a copy of the current issue of one of his publications at the member discount.

OR - Send $15.00 and get the whole works, which includes SALLY FORTH #3, and #4, CANNON #1 and HEROES INC. #2.

DEALERS ... A flat rate of 50% off on all orders of 30 copies or more. SALLY or CANNON cover price is $4.00, HEROES INC. #2 is $2.00.

FORTHCOMING from WOODWORK PRESS ... Immediate plans are for 3 more issues of CANNON, 4 WIZARD KING books in hard cover, a SALLY FORTH hard cover book, THE BEST OF WITZEND, WARP, and WOODWORK, which may take several volumes and several years to complete.

So SUPPORT FREE ENTERPRISE! Be a Patron of the Arts! This stuff will only gain in value as time goes by, so it's a good investment ... WITZEND #1 sold for a dollar ten years ago and now it's $25 IF you can find a copy of it. And if you care at all about ever seeing another Wallace Wood comic job, now is the time to do something about it.

WALLACE WOOD
BOX 3733
AMITY STATION
NEW HAVEN, CT. 06525

EC

EXCELLENCE IN COMICS

In the early 1950's a small comic book publisher known as EC began producing a new line of comics. The stories and illustrations were of such high quality that they launched a new era in comic publishing. The caliber of art produced is evidenced by this beautifully rendered page by Al Williamson, one of EC's leading science fiction artists.

The EC story can best be told by showing a good assortment of their cover illustrations, which break down into three major divisions: Pretrend, 1945-1950; New Trend, 1950-1955; and New Direction, 1955-1956.

The PRETRENDS.....

Blackstone No. 1, 1947. © 1979 by William M. Gaines

Crime Patrol No. 15, 1949. © 1979 by William M. Gaines. First appearance The Crypt Keeper

Gunfighter No. 8, 1949. © 1979 by William M. Gaines. Graham Ingels cover art

Modern Love No. 7, 1950. © 1979 by William M. Gaines. Feldstein cover art

Moon Girl No. 2, 1948. © 1979 by William M. Gaines. Johnny Craig cover art

Saddle Justice No. 7, 1949. © 1979 by William M. Gaines. Graham Ingels cover art

The PRETRENDS, cont'd. . . .

Crime Patrol No. 7, 1948.
© 1979 by William M. Gaines.
Johnny Craig cover art

Land Of The lost No. 2, 1946.
© 1979 by William M. Gaines

A Moon, A Girl...Romance No. 9,
1949. © 1979 by William M.
Gaines. Feldstein cover art

Picture Stories From American
History No. 1, 1945. © 1979
by William M. Gaines

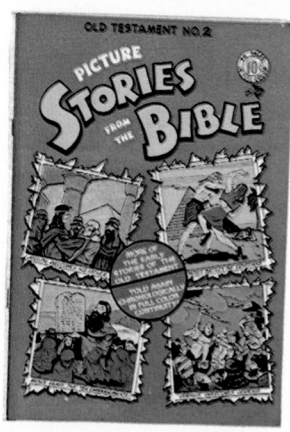

Picture Stories From The Bible
No. 2, 1943. © 1979 by
William M. Gaines

Reddy Kilowatt No. 2, 1947.
© 1979 by William M. Gaines

Saddle Romances No. 10, 1950.
© 1979 by William M. Gaines.
Feldstein cover

Tiny Tot Comics No. 8, 1947.
© 1979 by William M. Gaines

War Against Crime No. 10, 1949.
© 1979 by William M. Gaines.
First app. the Vault Keeper

Weird Fantasy No. 13/1, 1950.
© 1979 by William M. Gaines.
Feldstein cover art

Weird Fantasy No. 14/2, 1950.
© 1979 by William M. Gaines.
Feldstein cover art

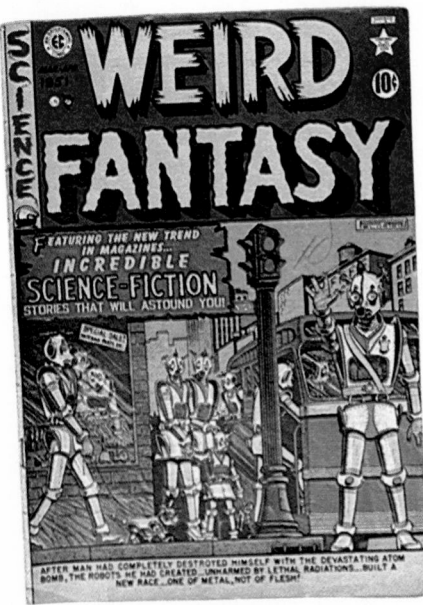

Weird Fantasy No. 6, 1951.
© 1979 by William M. Gaines.
Feldstein cover art

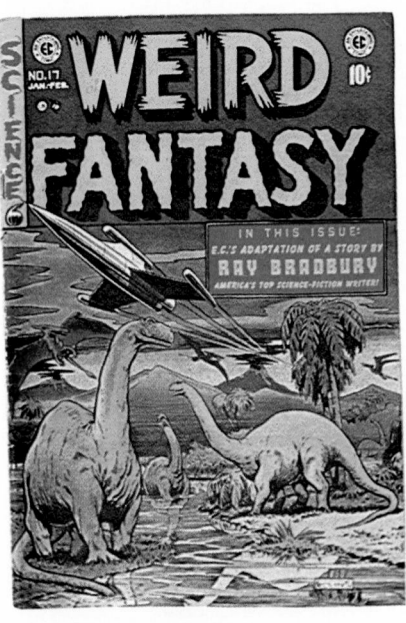

Weird Fantasy No. 17, 1952.
© 1979 by William M. Gaines.
Feldstein cover art

Weird Fantasy No. 7, 1951.
© 1979 by William M. Gaines.
Feldstein cover art

Weird Fantasy No. 10, 1951.
© 1979 by William M. Gaines.
Feldstein cover art

Weird Fantasy No. 15, 1952.
© 1979 by William M. Gaines.
Feldstein cover art

Weird Science No. 14/3, 1950.
© 1979 by William M. Gaines.
Feldstein cover art

Weird Science No. 15/4, 1950.
© 1979 by William M. Gaines.
Feldstein cover art

Weird Science No. 9, 1951.
© 1979 by William M. Gaines.
Wood cover art

Weird Science No. 18, 1952.
© 1979 by William M. Gaines.
Wood cover art

Weird Science-Fantasy No. 29,
1955. © 1979 by William M.
Gaines. Frazetta cover art

Weird Science-Fantasy Annual,
1952. © 1979 by William M.
Gaines. Feldstein cover art

Weird Science No. 12/1, 1950.
© 1979 by William M. Gaines.
Feldstein cover art

Weird Science No. 12, 1951.
© 1979 by William M. Gaines.
Wallace Wood cover art

Weird Science No. 16, 1952.
© 1979 by William M. Gaines.
Wallace Wood cover art

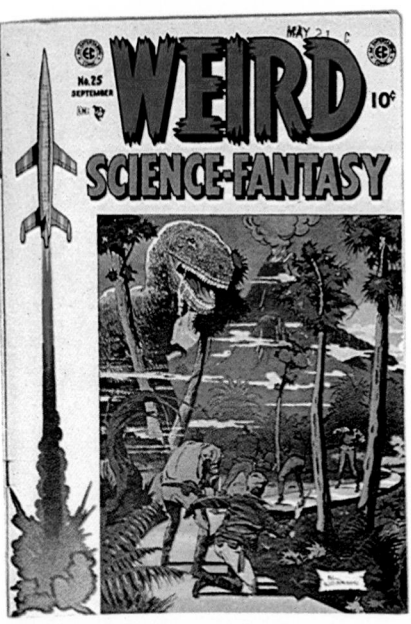

Weird Science-Fantasy No. 25, 1954.
© 1979 by William M. Gaines. Al
Williamson cover art

The Crypt Of Terror No. 18, 1950. © 1979 by William M. Gaines. Johnny Craig cover

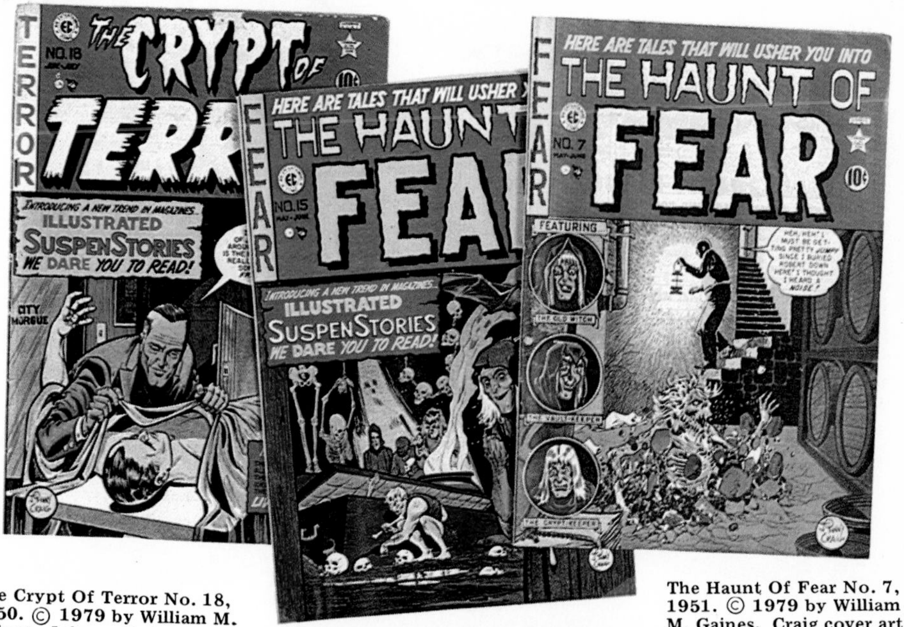

The Haunt Of Fear No. 15/1, 1950. © 1979 by William M. Gaines. Johnny Craig cover art

The Haunt Of Fear No. 7, 1951. © 1979 by William M. Gaines. Craig cover art

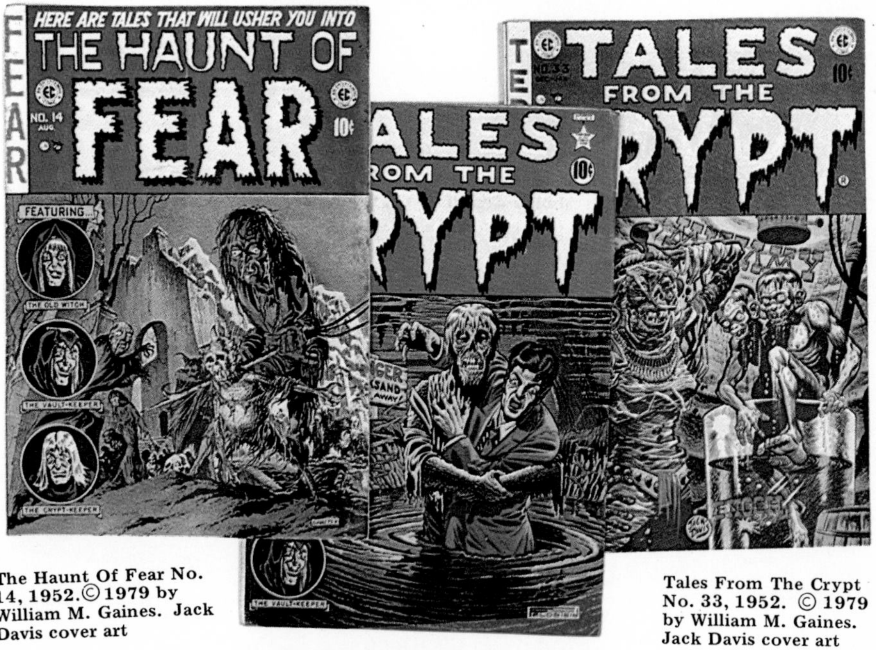

The Haunt Of Fear No. 14, 1952. © 1979 by William M. Gaines. Jack Davis cover art

Tales From The Crypt No. 24, 1951. © 1979 by William M. Gaines. Feldstein cover art

Tales From The Crypt No. 33, 1952. © 1979 by William M. Gaines. Jack Davis cover art

Tales From The Crypt
No. 39, 1953. ©1979
by William M. Gaines.
Jack Davis cover art

The Vault of Horror No.
15, 1950. ©1979 by
William M. Gaines.
Johnny Craig cover art

The Vault Of Horror No. 18,
1951. © 1979 by William M.
Gaines. Johnny Craig cover

The Vault Of
Horror No.
12, 1950.
© 1979 WMG
Johnny Craig
Cover art

The Vault Of Horror No. 39,
1954. ©1979 by William M.
Gaines. Craig cover art

NEW TREND - Horror Specials. . . .

Three Dimensional EC Classics
No. 1, 1954. ©1979 by William
M. Gaines. Kurtzman cover art

Three Dimensional Tales From
The Crypt Of Terror, 1954. ©
1979 by William M. GAines

Tales Of Terror Annual, 1952.
©1979 by William M. Gaines.
Feldstein cover art

NEW TREND - Crime and Shock. . . .

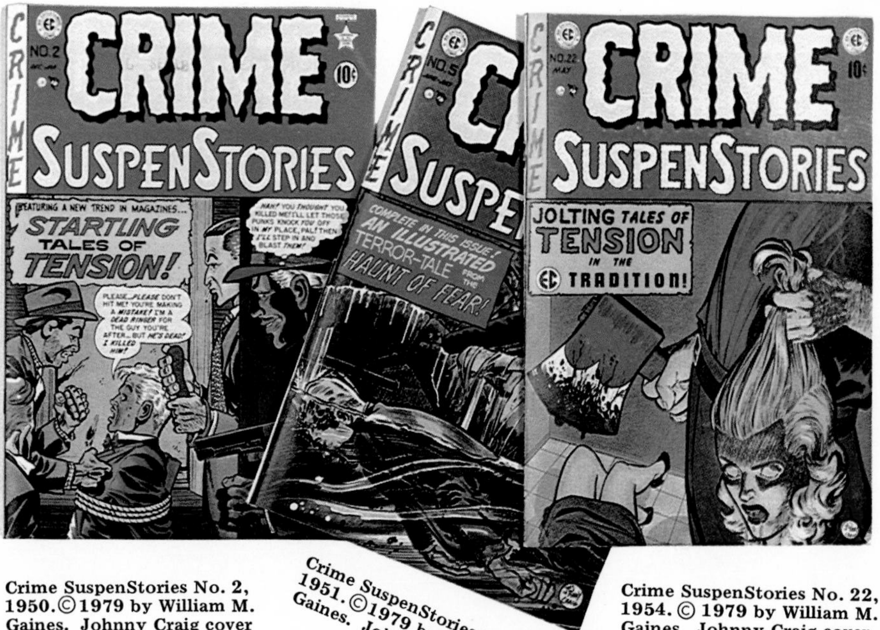

Crime SuspenStories No. 2,
1950.©1979 by William M.
Gaines. Johnny Craig cover

Crime SuspenStories No. 5,
1951.©1979 by William M.
Gaines. Johnny Craig cover

Crime SuspenStories No. 22,
1954. © 1979 by William M.
Gaines. Johnny Craig cover

Crime SuspenStories No. 7, 1951.
© 1979 by William M. Gaines.
Johnny Craig cover art

Shock SuspenStories No. 1, 1952.
© 1979 by William M. Gaines.
Feldstein cover art

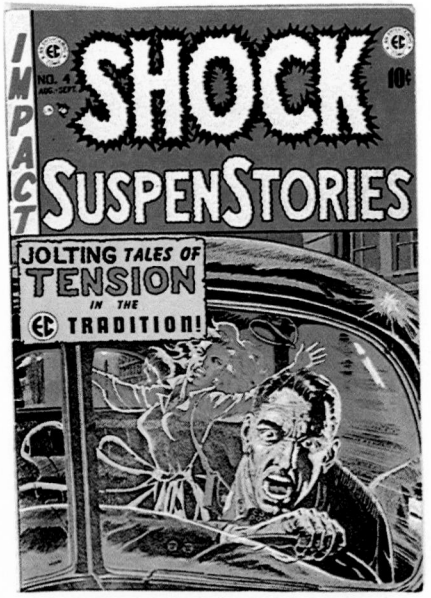

Shock SuspenStories No. 4, 1952.
© 1979 by William M. Gaines.
Wallace Wood cover art

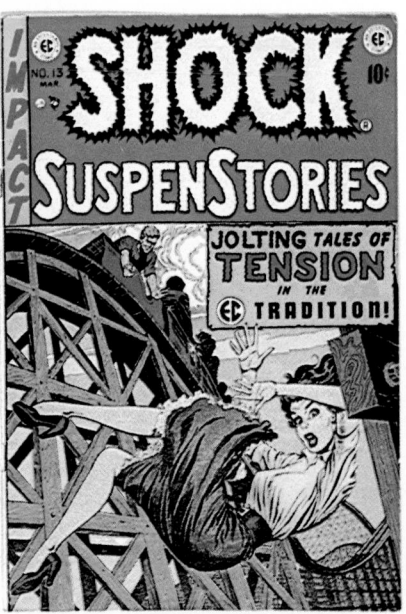

Shock SuspenStories No. 13, 1953.
© 1979 by William M. Gaines.
Kamen cover art. Frazetta story

NEW TREND - War, Humor. . . .

Frontline Combat No. 3, 1951.
©1979 by William M. Gaines.
Kurtzman cover art

Frontline Combat No. 9, 1952.
©1979 by William M. Gaines.
Kurtzman cover art

Frontline Combat No. 12, 1953.
©1979 by William M. Gaines.
Jack Davis cover art

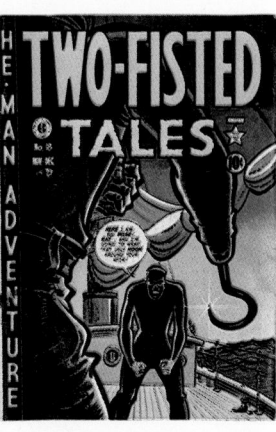

Two-Fisted Tales No. 18, 1950.
©1979 by William M. Gaines.
Kurtzman cover art

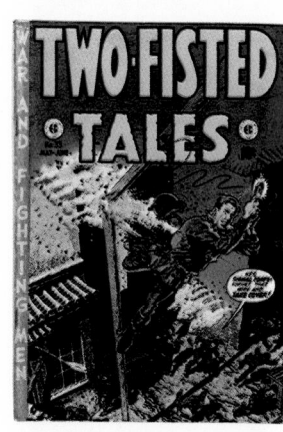

Two-Fisted Tales No. 33, 1953.
©1979 by William M. Gaines.
Wallace Wood cover art

Two-Fisted Annual, 1953
©1979 by William M. Gaines.
Jack Davis cover art

Mad No. 2, 1952.©1979 by
E.C. Publications, Inc.   Jack
Davis cover art

Mad No. 5, 1953. © 1979 by
E.C. Publications, Inc. Bill
Elder cover art

Panic No. 1, 1953. © 1979 by
William M. Gaines. Feldstein
cover art

Aces High No. 3, 1955.
©1979 by William M. Gaines.
George Evans cover art

Extra! No. 4, 1955.©1979
by William M. Gaines. Johnny
Craig cover art

Impact No. 1, 1955.©1979 by
William M. Gaines. Jack Davis
cover art

Impact No. 3, 1955.©1979 by
William M. Gaines. Jack Davis
cover art

Incredible Science-Fiction No.
32, 1955.©1979 by William M.
Gaines. Jack Davis cover art

MD No. 3, 1955.©1979 by
William M. Gaines. Johnny
Craig cover art

Piracy No. 1, 1954.©1979 by
William M. Gaines. Wallace
Wood cover art

Psychoanalysis No. 3, 1955.
© 1979 by William M. Gaines.
Jack Kamen cover art

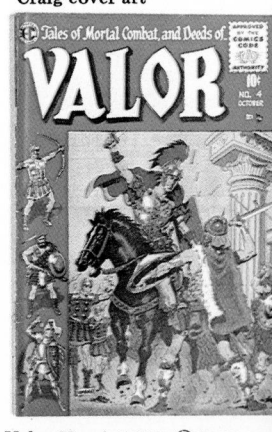

Valor No. 4, 1955.©1979 by
William M. Gaines. Wallace
Wood cover art

MARVEL COMICS GROUP™
INVITES YOU...

TO THE WONDERS OF THE
MARVEL UNIVERSE

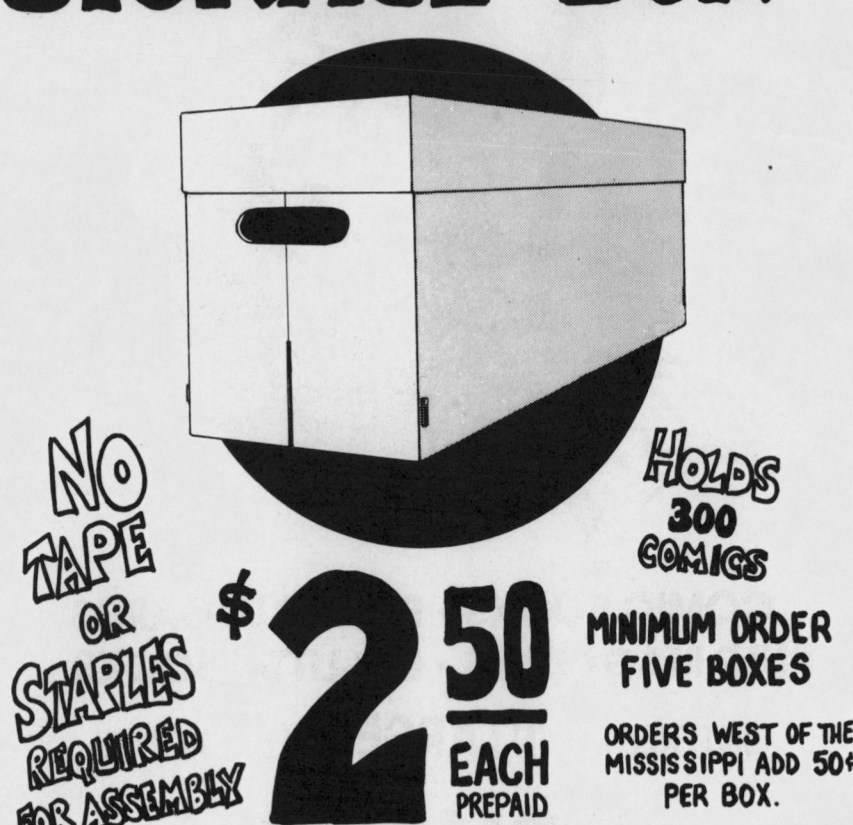

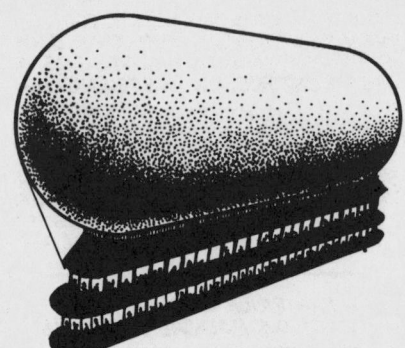

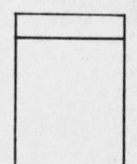
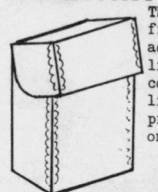

BASIL WOLVERTON 8-6-56

VERY UNORIGINAL ORIGINAL
OF *SPACEHAWK* ESPECIALLY FOR
JERRY DE FUCCIO

RICK ELFMAN
REEVEN ELFMAN

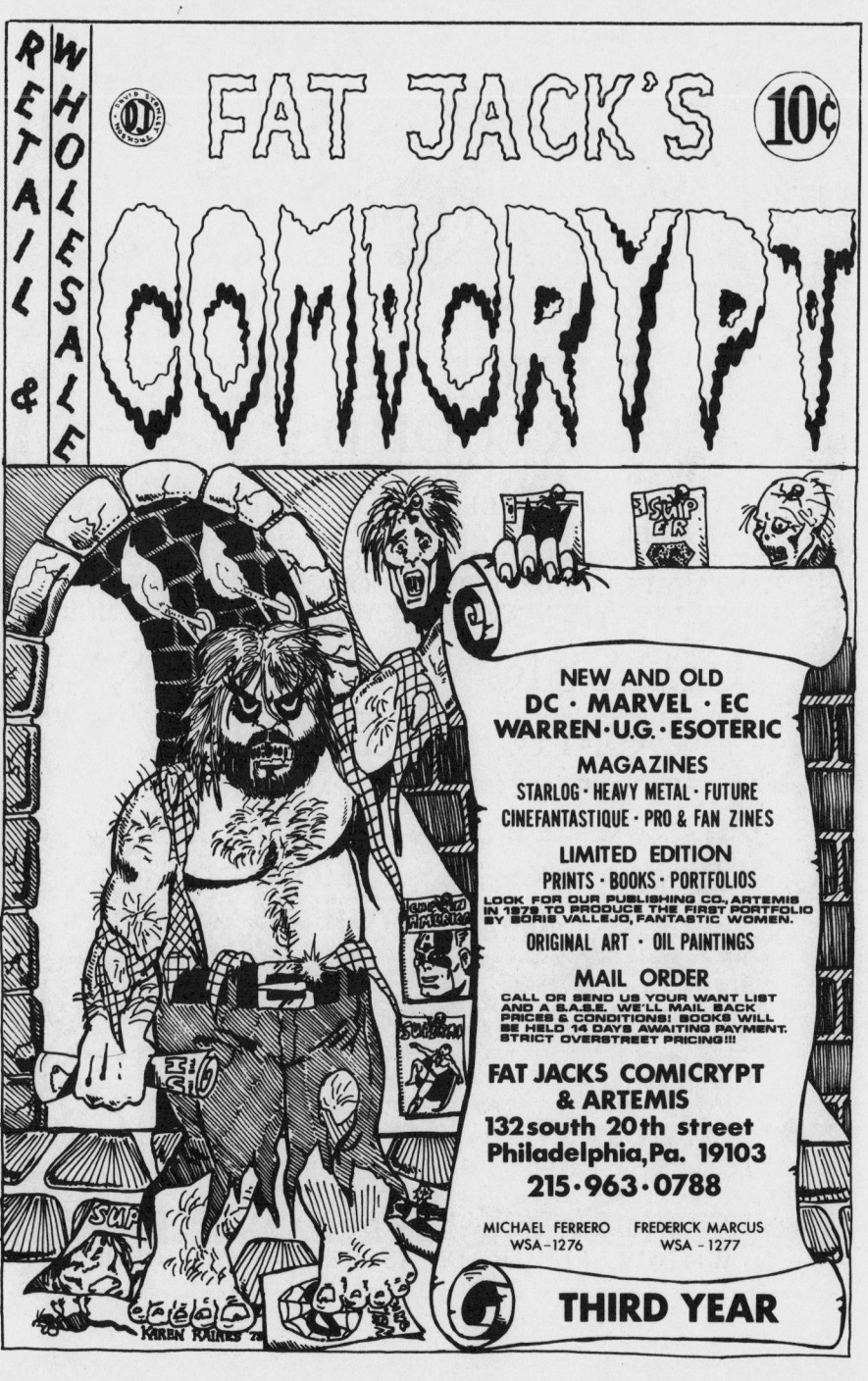

BOB SMART, 8 SEFTON AVENUE,CONGLETON,

Phone: 026-02-3417   CHESHIRE,CW12 3DB,ENGLAND.

As one of Englands largest dealers in American and
British Comics, I'm always interested in making new
contacts abroad, with a view to buying, selling, or
trading comics and related items.

BUYING BUYING BUYING

If you have a current sales list, please send it to the
above. I'm always interested in buying Marvels, D.C.,
Gold Key, Dell, EC, Warren, Golden age and many more.

SELLING OR TRADE

I can supply most of the British Comics (old and new)
in large quantities, E.G., EAGLE COMICS featuring the
famous Dan Dare strip with art by Frank Hampson and
Frank Bellamy. T.V.21 COMICS with Thunderbirds, Fire-
ball XLS, Zero X and Dr.Who strips, featuring Art by
Frank Ballamy also.
Other titles available are MICKEY MOUSE WEEKLYS (1930)
RUPERT THE BEAR, AVENGERS (T.V.SERIES), JOE 90, JAMES
BOND (OO7), MARVELMAN, TARZAN (1950) SMALL FORMAT
PICTURE LIBRARY COMICS (COWBOY DETECTIVE, THRILLER),
CAPTAIN BRITAIN (as listed in Overstreet), BRITISH
MARVEL WEEKLYS (these are reprints of American Marvels)
titles supplied on request. HARDBACK ANNUALS of MARVEL
and D.C., CHARACTERS, plus many other publications, too
numerous to list here. If not familiar with British
Comics, I would be prepared to send sample copies on
request. _ _ _ _ _ _ _ _ _ _ _

Are there collectors who wouldn't mind having there
Marvel back issues with the price on the front cover in
pence instead of cents. If there is, I'd like to hear
from you. They are priced on average at 50% of Overstreet
e.g. HOWARD THE DUCK No1 at $6.For bulk orders, I will do
certain titles at less than 50% Overstreet.

Earlier Marvels from 1960 onwards with an English price
instead of cents, can also be supplied at between 50% and
75% of Overstreet, comics that fit the above description
include Spiderman, Fantastic Four, Avengers, X Men (All
from issue No1 onwards) also Journey into Mystery No83
onwards, plus most of the other sort after earlier Marvels.
PLEASE NOTE: the only difference between the English and
American copies is the price on the cover, they were distributed in England the same time as they were in America,
and except for the difference in cover price, are identical
in every way to the American issues,.
ALL LETTERS WILL BE ANSWERED.

WHY YOU SHOULD OWN A COMIC BOOK!

Norman Mingo

VIC GHIDALIA – ANTHOLOGIST

LITTLE MONSTERS
BEWARE THE BEASTS
HORROR HUNTERS
THE VENUS FACTOR
THE DEVIL'S GENERATION
MORE LITTLE MONSTERS
BEWARE MORE BEASTS
ANDROIDS, TIME MACHINES AND BLUE GIRAFFES
GOOSEFLESH!
SATAN'S PETS
NIGHTMARE GARDEN
WIZARDS AND WARLOCKS
THE ODDBALLS
THE YOUNG DEMONS
EIGHT STRANGE TALES
FEAST OF FEAR
THE MUMMY WALKS AMONG US
DRACULA'S GUEST AND OTHER STORIES

MOST COMIC COLLECTORS
HAVE OLD RECORDS, TOO!

MUSIC WORLD
Dept. 630
400 S. Cortez St.
Prescott, Az 86301

SUBSCRIPTION RATES:

Single Copies: 75 cents
Introductory Subscriptions:
12 Issues: $6.00 domestic
12 Issues: $7.50 foreign
24 Issues: $10.00 domestic
24 Issues: $12.50 foreign
48 Issues: $17.00 domestic
48 Issues: $25.00 foreign

For FIRST CLASS or for
AIR MAIL rates: Inquire.

The team of Osborne and Hamilton have done it again! We've been struck with amazement over the years that whenever we visit a comic collector, he invariably has some old records he's amazed to find are worth money. In four years the team —incorporated as Jellyroll Productions— has produced six price guides on record collecting, with the seventh, eighth and ninth in the works. We've advertised them all, so far, to comic collectors, because we've found enough of a common link between these fields to warrant telling one about developments in the other.

If you walked around any city block in your neighborhood, how many people do you think you'd find with some old records? We've done it! You'd be amazed. More people do than don't. Music is, after all, the common language.

Since people don't throw away records (unfortunately, as they have often done with comic books) there are a lot more of them around. But then, too, there are so many people who *like* records, no wonder record collecting is one of the fastest growing hobbies in the world!

The need for a biweekly tabloid newspaper for collectors to get together, to advertise what they want to buy, sell or trade with each other was apparent. So *Music World* was born. It comes off the press like clockwork, every other Monday, and is in the mail to 5000+ collectors and others who are interested by Wednesday. Single copies cost 75 cents, but a 12 issue introductory subscription for $6.00 drops the per copy price down to only 50 cents. If you just want a peek, though, we'll be happy to send you a complimentary copy for only 25 cents (in coin or stamps) to cover postage and handling.

Records go out of print quickly. For that reason a record only a year old is sometimes worth good money to a collector who missed it or only became recently interested. If you want to find out what *your* old 45's or albums (or the old 78's in your grandmother's garage) are worth, pick up a copy of one of the Official Price Guides for Record Collecting at your book store, or drop a line to Jellyroll Productions, Box 3017, Scottsdale, AZ 85257 and we'll send you information on what's currently available to order directly from us.

After you've found out what they're worth, do you want to sell them to a collector who may be interested? You can run an ad for as little as $2.00 in *Music World* and start getting response in just two weeks!

What about your favorite albums that you *don't* want to sell, but which you've practically worn out from replaying so much? Through *Music World* you can find people who specialize in digging up exactly what you'd like to replace in your own record library, but can't find yourself.

If you've read this far, you're interested enough to gamble a quarter! Send *Music World* 25 cents in coin or stamps right now, while you're thinking about it! You'll be glad you did!

GET A FREE SAMPLE COPY FOR
25 CENTS IN COINS OR STAMPS
TO COVER POSTAGE & HANDLING

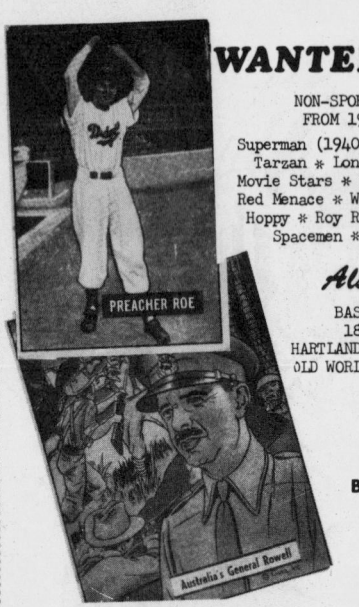

HUGH O'KENNON

2204 HAVILAND DRIVE
RICHMOND, VA. 23229

Tel. (804) 270-2465

Buying - Selling - Collector's Comic Books

I Offer The Following To ALL Customers:

- ACCURATE GRADING

- SATISFACTION GUARANTEED

- PROMPT DEPENDABLE SERVICE

- REASONABLE PRICING

- EXPERIENCE

Selling - A list of all Comics for sale is available. Please forward 50 cents for a copy (refundable with first order).

Buying - Write for MY offer before you sell your comic books.

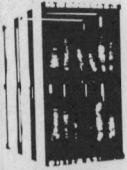

NOSTALGIA PRESS
PUBLICATIONS

Flash Gordon No. 1—The Planet Mongo (Color, Hard, 164 pgs.) $14.95
Flash Gordon No. 2—The Water World (Color, Hard, 164 pgs.) $14.95
Flash Gordon No. 3—In Arboria, Ice (Color, Paper, 112 pgs.) $9.95

Flash Gordon No. 4-Versus Frozen Terrors (Color, Paper, 92 pgs.) $9.95
Flash Gordon No. 5-Joins the Power Men (Color, Paper, 100 pgs.) $9.95

Incredible Upside-Downs by Verbeek (Color, Hard, 32pgs.) $7.95
Little Nemo 1905-1910 (Hard, 256 pgs., 120 in color (Slight Damage)
                  Reg. $25 $16.95
Little Nemo in Slumberland (B&W, Paper, 32 pgs.) $2.50

Mandrake the Magician (B&W, Paper, 96 pgs.) $5.95
Nostalgia Comics Nos. 1-6 (B&W, Paper, 80 pgs.) . . . . each $5.95
Phantom (B&W, Paper, 82 pgs.) $6.95

Popeye the Sailor (B&W, Paper, 128 pgs.) $7.95
Prince Valiant No. 1-King Arthur's Court (Color, Hard, 164 pgs.) $14.95
P.V. No. 2-Companions in Adventure (Color, Hard, 164 pgs.) $14.95

P. V. No. 3-Queen of the Misty Isles (Color, Hard, 144 pgs.) $14.95
P. V. No. 4-Adventure in Two Worlds (Color, Hard, 144 pgs.) $14.95
Prince Valiant Story Library—Text With B&W Illustrations:
   No. 1-Prince Valiant (B&W, Hard, 128 pgs.) $7.95
   No. 2-Atilla the Hun (B&W, Hard, 128 pgs.) $7.95
   No. 3-The Inland Sea (B&W, Hard, 128 pgs.)d$7.95
   No. 6-The New World (B&W, Hard, 128 pgs.) $7.95
   No. 7-Three Challenges (B&W, Hard, 96 pgs.) $7.95

Scorchy Smith No. 1-Soldier of Fortune (B&W, Paper, 92 pgs.) $6.95
Scorchy Smith No. 2-Partners in Danger (B&W, Paper, 92 pgs.) $6.95
Secret Agent X-9 by Alex Raymond and Dashiel Hammett (B&W, Paper, 176 pgs.)
                    8.95

Terry and The Pirates Adventure Library:
   No. 1-China Journey (B&W, Paper, 108 pgs.) $6.95
   No. 3-Meet Burma (B&W, Paper, 96 pgs.) $6.95
   No. 4-Dragon Lady (B&W, Paper, 96 pgs.) $6.95

American Card Catalog-1960 edition-Listings and Values of Paper Collectibles
            (B&W, Paper, 212 pgs)$6.95
Burdick's Pioneer Postcards-Ill.-History of Early Postcards (B&W, Paper, 200 pgs.)
                    $12.95
Charlie Chaplin-The Picture History of His Fabulous Career (B&W, Paper, 64 pgs)
                    $3.95
Fleischer Story-An Illustrated History of the Popeye, Betty Boop, and Superman
Animation Studio (B&W, Hard, 186 pgs.) $12.50
Franklin Booth-A Collection of This Master's Art
From the 1920's (B&W, Paper, 72 pgs.) . . . . .Reg. $9, Now $2.95
Great Old Bubble Gum Cards-A Punch Out Book of Reproductions
from the 1900's to the 1940's (Color, Paper, 20 pgs.) $6.95

Please add 75 cents handling
charge on each order and 75 cents
postage for each book ordered.
Thank you. NYC & NY State
Residents, Add tax.

NOSTALGIA INC.
Box 293C
Franklin Square,
New York 11010

lineups. The Texas and Oklahoma cons have the con circuit cornered in the genres of serials and B-westerns. As would be expected, though, most conventions concentrate on science fiction and horror movies, with minimal straying from this format. Again, if the movie schedule is your deciding factor, take a look at the convention advertisements in the various adzines. The committees usually have firmed up the lineups early enough for a potential attendee to decide whether he wishes to make the trip.

The addresses below are those currently available for conventions upcoming in 1978-79. Unfortunately, addresses for certain major conventions are unavailable as this list is being compiled. Once again, the best way to keep abreast of conventions is through the various adzines. Please remember when writing for convention information to include a self-addressed, stamped envelope for reply. Most conventions are non-profit, so they appreciate the help. Here is the list:

COMIC BOOK CONVENTIONS FOR 1979

THE ALL-AMERICAN COMIC-CON— c/o Old Weird Herald's, 6804 N.E. Broadway, Portland, Oregon 97213 Phone (503) 254-4942. May 5 & 6, 1979

ATLANTA COMICS & FANTASY FAIR '79—Marilyn White, 784 Ponce de Leon Terrace, Atlanta, Ga. 30306. Aug. 10-12, 1979

BAYCON 5— Salvador Dichiera, P.O. Box 3931, San Francisco, Ca. 94119

CHICAGO COMICON—Larry Charet, 1219-A West Devon Ave., Chicago, Ill. 60660—July 20-22, 1979.

CHICAGO-MONTHLY MINI CON—Write Yesteryears, 508 Clyde Ave., Suite No. 27, Calumet City, Ill. 60409.

COLLECTORS' MEET (Burlington, Mass.)—R. C. Gesner, 8 Belmont St., Lowell, Mass. 01851. April 8 & Nov. 18, 1979.

CREATION CON—Box 6547, Flushing, N. Y. 11365.

DELAWARE VALLEY COMICART CONSORTIUM—Box 62, Maple Shade, N.J. 08052. Attn: Frederick Marcus. Nov. 17,18,19, 1979.

HOLLYWOOD COMIC BOOK & SCIENCE FICTION CONVENTION—Bruce Schwartz, 921 N. Gardner, Apt. 9, L.A., Calif. 90046.

HOUSTON CON '79—P.O. Box 12613, Houston, Tx. 77087.

ITHACON IV, Ithaca, N. Y.—Bill Turner, 1043 Auburn Rd., Groton, N. Y. 13073. April 21-22, 1979.

MINNEAPOLIS COMIC CONVENTION—Box 3221 Traffic Station, Minneapolis, Minn. 55403.

NEW YORK COMIC ART CONVENTION '79—Phil Seuling, P.O. Box 177, Coney Island Station, Brooklyn, N. Y. 11224.

NEWCON '79—Don Phelps, P.O. Box 85, Cohasset, Mass. 02025.

SAN DIEGO COMIC-CON—Box 17066, San Diego, Calif. 92117.

A Chronology of the Development of
THE AMERICAN COMIC BOOK

By
M. Thomas Inge*

Precursors: The facsimile newspaper strip reprint collections constitute the earliest "comic books." The first of these was a collection of Richard Outcault's **Yellow Kid** from the Hearst **New York American** in March 1897. Commerical and promotional reprint collections, usually in cardboard covers, appeared through the 1920s and featured such newspaper strips as **Mutt and Jeff, Foxy Grandpa, Buster Brown,** and **Barney Google.** During 1922 a reprint magazine, **Comic Monthly,** appeared with each issue devoted to a separate strip, and in 1929 George Delacorte published 13 issues of **The Funnies** in tabloid format with original comic pages in color, becoming the first four-color comic newsstand publication.

1933: The Ledger syndicate published a small broadside of their Sunday comics on 7" by 9" plates. Employees of Eastern Color Printing Company in New York, sales manager Harry I. Wildenberg and salesman Max C. Gaines, saw it and figured that two such plates would fit a tabloid page, which would produce a book about 7½" x 10" when folded. Thus 10,000 copies of **Funnies on Parade**, containing 32 pages of Sunday newspaper reprints, was published for Proctor and Gamble to be given away as premiums. Some of the strips included were: **Joe Palooka, Mutt and Jeff, Hairbreadth Harry,** and **Reg'lar Fellas.** M. C. Gaines was very impressed with this book and convinced Eastern Color that he could sell a lot of them to such big advertisers as Milk-O-Malt, Wheatena, Kinney Shoe Stores, and others to be used as premiums and radio give-aways. So, Eastern Color printed **Famous Funnies: A Carnival of Comics** , and then **Century of Comics** , both as before, containing Sunday newspaper reprints. Mr. Gaines sold these books in quantities of 100,000 to 250,000.

1934: The give-away comics were so successful that Mr. Gaines believed that youngsters would buy comic books for ten cents like the "Big Little Books" coming out at that time. So, early in 1934, Eastern Color ran off 35,000 copies of **Famous Funnies, Series 1,** 64 pages of reprints for Dell Publishing Company to be sold for ten cents in chain stores. Selling out promptly on the stands, Eastern Color, in May 1934, issued **Famous Funnies** No. 1 (dated July 1934) which became, with issue No. 2 in July, the first monthly comic magazine. The title continued for over 20 years through 218 issues, reaching a circulation peak of nearly one million copies. At the same time, Mr. Gaines went to the sponsors of Percy Crosby's **Skippy** , who was on the radio, and convinced them to put out a Skippy book, advertise it on the air, and give away a free copy to anyone who bought a tube of Phillip's toothpaste. Thus 500,000 copies of

----

With the invaluable assistance of Bill Blackbeard and helpful suggestions and comments by William M. Gaines, Bob Overstreet, Hames Ware, Don and Maggie Thompson, Jerry Bails, and Ron Goulart, to all of whom the compiler is grateful.

Skippy's Own Book of Comics was run off and distributed through drug stores everywhere. This was the first four-color comic book of reprints devoted to a single character.

1935: Major Malcolm Wheeler-Nicholson's National Periodical Publications issued in February a tabloid-sized comic publication called **New Fun,** which became **More Fun** after the first issue and converted to the normal comic-book size after issue six. **More Fun** was the first comic book of a standard size to publish original material and continued publication until 1949. **Mickey Mouse Magazine** began in the summer, to become **Walt Disney's Comics and Stories** in 1940, and combined original material with reprinted newspaper strips in most issues.

1936: In the wake of the success of **Famous Funnies**, other publishers, in conjunction with the major newspaper strip syndicates, inaugurated more reprint comic books: **Popular Comics** (News-Tribune, February), **Tip Top Comics** (United Features, April), **King Comics** (King Features, April), and **The Funnies** (new series, NEA, October). Four issues of **Wow Comics**, from David McKay and Henle Publications, appeared, edited by S. M. Iger and including early art by Will Eisner, Bob Kane, and Lou Fine.

1937: The first non-reprint comic book devoted to a single theme (although single-theme pulp magazines had included comic strips earlier) was **Detective Comics**, an offshoot of **More Fun**, which began in March to continue to the present. The book's initials, "D.C.," have long served to refer to National Periodical Publications, which was purchased from Major Nicholson by Harry Donenfeld late this year.

1938: "D.C." copped a lion's share of the comic book market with the publication of **Action Comics** No. 1 in June which contained the first appearance of Superman by writer Jerry Siegel and artist Joe Shuster, a discovery of Max C. Gaines. The "man of steel" inaugurated the "Golden Era" in comic book history. Fiction House, a pulp publisher, entered the comic book field in September with **Jumbo Comics**, featuring Sheena, Queen of the Jungle, and appearing in over-sized format for the first eight issues.

1939: The continued success of "D.C." was assured in May with the publication of **Detective Comics** No. 27 containing the first episode of Batman by artist Bob Kane and writer Bill Finger. **Superman Comics** appeared in the summer. Also, during the summer, a black and white premium comic titled **Motion Picture Funnies Weekly** was published to be given away at motion picture theatres. The plan was to issue it weekly and to have continued stories so that the kids would come back week after week not to miss an episode. Four issues were planned but only one came out. This book contains the first appearance and origin of the Sub-Mariner by Bill Everett (8 pages) which was later reprinted in **Marvel Comics**. In November, the first issue of **Marvel Comics** came out, featuring the Human Torch by Carl Burgos and the Sub-Mariner reprint with color added.

1940: The April issue of **Detective Comics** No. 38 introduced Robin the Boy Wonder as a sidekick to Batman, thus establishing the "Dynamic Duo" and a major precedent for later costume heroes who would also have boy companions. **Batman Comics** began in the spring. Over 60 different comic book titles were being issued, including **Whiz Comics** begun in February by Fawcett Publications. A creation of writer Bill Parker and artist C. C. Beck, **Whiz's** Captain Marvel was the only superhero ever to surpass Superman in comic book sales. Drawing on their own popular pulp magazine heroes, Street and Smith Publications introduced **Shadow Comics** in March and **Doc Savage Comics** in May. A second trend was established with the summer appearance of the first issue of **All-Star Comics**, which brought several superheroes together in one story and in its third issue that winter would announce the establishment of the Justice Society of America.

1941: Wonder Woman was introduced in the spring issue of **All-Star Comics** No. 8, the creation of psychologist William Moulton Marston and artist Harry Peter. **Captain Marvel Adventures** began this year. By the end of 1941, over 160 titles were being published, including **Captain America** by Jack Kirby and Joe Simon, **Police Comics** with Jack Cole's Plastic Man and later Will Eisner's Spirit, **Military Comics** with Blackhawk by Eisner and Charles Cuidera, **Daredevil Comics** with the original character by Charles Biro, **Air Fighters** with Airboy also by Biro, and **Looney Tunes & Merrie Melodies** with Porky Pig, Bugs Bunny, and Elmer Fudd, reportedly created by Bob Clampett for the Leon Schlesinger Productions animated films and drawn for the comics by Chase Craig. Also, Albert Kanter's Gilberton Company initiated the **Classics Illustrated** series with **The Three Musketeers**.

1942: **Crime Does Not Pay** by editor Charles Biro and publisher Lev Gleason, devoted to factual accounts of criminals' lives, began a different trend in realistic crime stories. **Wonder Woman** appeared in the summer. John Goldwater's character Archie, drawn by Bob Montana, first published in **Pep Comics**, was given his own magazine **Archie Comics**, which has remained popular over 35 years. The first issue of **Animal Comics** contained Walt Kelly's "Albert Takes the Cake," featuring the new character of Pogo. In mid-1942, the undated Dell Four Color title, No. 9, **Donald Duck Finds Pirate Gold**, appeared with art by Carl Barks and Jack Hannah. Barks, also featured in **Walt Disney's Comics and Stories**, remained the most popular delineator of Donald Duck and later introduced his greatest creation, Uncle Scrooge, in **Christmas on Bear Mountain** (Dell Four Color No. 178).

1945: The first issue of **Real Screen Comics** introduced the Fox and the Crow by James F. Davis, and John Stanley began drawing the **Little Lulu** comic book based on a popular feature in the **Saturday Evening Post** by Marjorie Henderson Buell from 1935 to 1944.

1950: The son of Max C. Gaines, William M. Gaines, who earlier had inherited his father's firm Educational Comics (later Entertaining Comics), began publication of a series of well-written and masterfully drawn titles which would establish a "New Trend" in comics magazines: **Crypt of Terror** (later **Tales from the Crypt**, April), **The Vault of Horror** (April), **The Haunt of Fear** (May), **Weird Science** (May), **Weird Fantasy** (May), **Crime SuspenStories** (October), and **Two-Fisted Tales** (November), the latter stunningly edited by Harvey Kurtzman.

1952: In October "E.C." published the first number of **Mad** under Kurtzman's creative editorship.

1953: All Fawcett titles featuring Captain Marvel were ceased after many years of litigation in the courts during which National Periodical Publications claimed that the super-hero was an infringement on the copyrighted Superman.

1954: The appearance of Fredric Wertham's book **Seduction of the Innocent** in the spring was the culmination of a continuing war against comic books fought by those who believed they corrupted youth and debased culture. The U. S. Senate Subcommittee on Juvenile Delinquency investigated comic books and in response the major publishers banded together in October to create the Comics Code Authority and adopted, in their own words, "the most stringent code in existence for any communications media."

1955: In an effort to avoid the Code, "E. C." launched a "New Direction" series of titles, such as **Impact, Valor, Aces High, Extra, M.D.,** and **Psychoanalysis**, none of which lasted beyond the year. **Mad** was changed into a larger magazine format with issue No. 24 in July to escape the Comics Code entirely.

1956: Beginning with the Flash in **Showcase** No. 4, Julius Schwartz began a popular revival of "D.C." superheroes which would lead to the "Silver Age" in comic book history.

1960: After several efforts at new satire magazines (**Trump** and **Humbug**), Harvey Kurtzman, no longer with Gaines, issued in August the first number of another abortive effort, **Help!** , where the early work of underground cartoonists Jay Lynch, Skip Williamson, Gilbert Shelton, and Robert Crumb appeared.

1961: Stan Lee edited in November the first **Fantastic Four**, featuring Mr. Fantastic, the Human Torch, the Thing, and the Invisible Girl, and inaugurated an enormously popular line of titles from Marvel Comics featuring a more contemporary style of superhero.

1962: Lee introduced **The Amazing Spider-Man** in August, with art by Steve Ditko, **The Hulk** in May and **Thor** in August, the last two produced by Dick Ayers and Jack Kirby.

1965: James Warren issued **Creepy**, a larger black and white comic book, outside Comics Code's control, which emulated the "E.C." horror comic line. Warren's **Eerie** began in September and **Vampirella** in September 1969.

1967: Robert Crumb's **Zap** No. 1 appeared, the first popular underground comic book.

1970: Editor Roy Thomas at Marvel begins **Conan the Barbarian** based on fiction by Robert E. Howard with art by Barry Smith.

1972: **The Swamp Thing** by Berni Wrightson begins in November from "D.C."

1973: In February, "D.C." revived the original Captain Marvel with new art by C. C. Beck and reprints in the first issue of **Shazam** and in October **The Shadow** with scripts by Denny O'Neil and art by Mike Kaluta.

1974: "D.C." began publication in the spring of a series of over-sized facsimile reprints of the most valued comic books of the past under the general title of "Famous First Editions," beginning with a reprint of **Action** No. 1 and including afterwards **Detective Comics** No. 27, **Sensation Comics** No. 1, **Whiz Comics** No. 2, **Batman** No. 1, **Wonder Woman** No. 1, **All-Star Comics** No. 3, and **Flash Comics** No. 1.

1975: In the first collaborative effort between the two major comic book publishers of the previous decade, Marvel and "D.C." produced together an over-sized comic-book version of **MGM's Marvelous Wizard of Oz** in the fall, and then the following year in an unprecedented cross-over produced **Superman vs. the Amazing Spider-Man**, written by Gerry Conway, drawn by Ross Andru, and inked by Dick Giordano.

1976: Frank Brunner's Howard the Duck, who had appeared earlier in Marvel's **Fear** and **Man-Thing**, was given his own book in January, which because of distribution problems became an over-night collector's item. After decades of litigation, Jerry Siegel and Joe Shuster were given financial recompense and recognition by National Periodical Publications for their creation of Superman, after several friends of the team made a public issue of the case.

1977: Stan Lee's **Spider-Man** was given a second birth, fifteen years after his first, through a highly successful newspaper comic strip, which began syndication on January 3 with art by John Romita. This invasion of the comic strip by comic book characters continued with the appearance on June 6 of Marvel's **Howard the Duck**, with story by Steve Gerber and visuals by Gene Colan. In an unusually successful collaborative effort, Marvel began publication of the comic book adaption of the George Lucas film **Star Wars**, with script by Roy Thomas and art by Howard Chaykin, at least three months before the film was released nationally on May 25. The demand was so great that all six issues of **Star Wars** were reprinted at least seven times, and the installments were reprinted in two volumes of an over-sized Marvel Special Edition and a single paperback volume for the book trade.

1978: In an effort to halt declining sales, Warner Communications drastically cut back on the number of "D. C." titles and overhauled its distribution process in June. The interest of the visual media in comic book characters reached a new high with the Hulk, Spider-Man, and Doctor Strange, the subjects of television shows; with various projects begun to produce film versions of Flash Gordon, Dick Tracy, Popeye, Conan, the Phantom, and Buck Rogers; and with the movement reaching an outlandish peak of publicity with the release of 'Superman' in December. Two significant applications of the comic book format to traditional fiction appeared this year: **A Contract with God and Other Tenement Stories** by Will Eisner and **The Silver Surfer** by Stan Lee and Jack Kirby.

For Those Who Know How To Look

by
Carl Macek

The most influential arguments set forth in favor of comic book self-censorship were delivered in Dr. Frederic Wertham's *Seduction of the Innocent* (New York, 1954). The publication of this book capped seven years of intense public criticism by Wertham against "crime" comics and their effect on the children who read them. Throughout the three hundred and ninety-seven pages of text (which included a sixteen-page photo layout), Wertham tried to show how comic books were a major cause of juvenile delinquency and psychological trauma. A noted child psychologist, Wertham interviewed numerous children and their parents in and around the Lafargue Clinic in Harlem as source material for his book, articles and various lectures. His attack was not solely based on story content and the graphic depiction of violence found in comics but he also attempted to show how advertisements for bad skin and hygenic products could be seen as key factors in creating a society of warped children. He was convinced that the comic medium was extremely harmful to normal childhood development.

His arguments were heard in an atmosphere of paranoia and fear created, in part, by the Cold War and the Black-list, witch-hunting days of McCarthyism. The Ameri-can public was ready for Wertham's indoctrination. His arguments fell on ears eager to hear that the blame for juvenile delinquency lay else-where, that the responsibility for maintaining a high level of civil normalcy was not the responsibility of institutions like the family, education or government. Rather Wertham was confinced that the burden of guilt in regard to juvenile delinquency rested squarely on the shoulders of the comic book publishers and the artists and writers who worked for them. This approach to substitute responsibility was not unique to comic books. Motion pictures and paperback books underwent a similar intense scrutiny during this same period (movies for a more political reason), culminating in various black-lists and self-enforced codes.

It is not germane to the discussion of Wertham's book and its ultimate effect on comics to determine whether he was right or wrong in his diagnosis of the influence which comics have on young minds. What is important is that his book was published. The damage had been done. The response to Wertham's zealousness in proving his ideas can be seen in a code created in 1954 by comic book publishers which forbids certain actions, situations and even specific words from appearing in comics which were to bear their seal. That code is still in effect today.

In order to put the question of comic book self-censorship into proper perspective, it is necessary to look back to the roots of Wertham's public attack upon comics and trace the development of his ideas as well as the public's acceptance of them.

Prior to 1947 the hotttest bit of news concerning comics in major American periodicals either dealt with the huge amounts of money made by selling cartoons to newspaper syndicates or *Li'l Abner*'s latest dilemma. For all practical purposes comic strips seemed to garner most of the attention. During the spring of that year, however, a group of distinguished panelists writing in the *Saturday Review of Literature* (John Mason Brown, Al Capp, et al.) began discussing, pro and con, the effect of comics on those who read them. This brief series of charges and counter-charges inspired Dr. Frederic Wertham to write a key article which he felt would once and for all expose the true "criminal" nature of comics.

It was in the May 29 issue of the *Saturday Review of Literature* that Wertham's thoughts first found a mass audience. In his essay Wertham cited various comics (specifically TRUE CRIME No. 2, JO-JO No. 15, *Great Expectations* and *The Mysteries of Paris*) in both text and through illustrations which he felt proved his point that comics were a harmful influence on children. The response to his article was intense and immediate.

Hundreds of letters flooded the executive offices of the *Saturday Review*. Many of them eventually were printed in subsequent issues of

Drug story from Truce Crime No. 2. Classic example that Wertham attacked. © 1979 by Mag. Village

the weekly magazine. One of the most lucid letters came from a teenage comic book collector who eloquently presented his case in favor of comic books. The controversy that followed triggered Wertham to devote a large portion of the next seven years of his career to discovering the cause of juvenile delinquency. One of his main targets was the comic book. There was a consistency to his methodology. By using what has been called a hypodermic approach to problem-solving, Wertham saw practically every comic as a "crime" comic. He made little distinction between Jungle, Western, Crime, Horror or Super-hero titles. If the comic dealt with the concept of good vs. evil, chances were that Wertham considered it a crime comic. He saw that many comics contained ultra-violent scenes and was convinced that this form of conditioning and de-sensitizing was a major cause of juvenile delinquency. He tried to bend every fact and every case study he could find to support his theory. Any child who put a bath towel around his neck and thought he could fly was a potential tool for Wertham to use against the producers of comics. Throughout his attack upon comics however, Wertham maintained that he was not in favor of censorship. He merely wanted to prevent the perverted minds of those who created this fodder of near-pornographic material (to paraphrase Wertham) from continuing their "seduction of the innocent."

"Headlight Comics," from Blue Beetle No. 54. Ill. in S.O.T.I. © **1979 Fox**

His book singled out nearly one hundred and sixty different comics as specific examples of his charges. The most flamboyant of these examples appear in the photo section in the middle of his book. Using thirty-six panel blow-ups or cover reproductions Wertham was able to coin such popular phrases as "injury-to-the-eye-motif," "headlight comics" and "there are pic-

tures within pictures for children who know how to look." He talked about bondage, homosexuality, sado-masochism and the associations of sex and violence. He missed no opportunity to point out gross brutality and underlying racial hatred. The pictures shown in this book were meant to represent an unhealthy cross section of comics read by children every day. Of the comics used by Wertham the easiest to identify are those which reproduce covers to specific issues. These are CRIME SUSPENSE No. 20, CRIME DETECTIVE No. 9, PHANTOM LADY No. 17, and REFORM SCHOOL GIRL. The identity of the rest of these illustrations is less clear. It falls into the domain of the comic book scholar to determine title and issue number.

There are several reasons why it is significant to identify these comics. The most obvious is to determine exactly how Wertham's interpretation of various scenes and panels (often taken out of context) relate to his overall criticism and central theme of innocence seduced. By cutting out individual panels and arranging them out of context (or even detailing a specific panel in which Wertham saw, concealed in the shadows, a woman's pubic area), this child psychologist was himself conditioning a specific response out of parents and other adults who took the time to read his book. A more extreme reason for discovering the exact comics used by Wertham in *The Seduction of the Innocent* is the desire to see exactly which comics Wertham was exposed to while he was conducting his research. Were there consistencies in the titles, publishers, artists, genres, scenes portrayed on the covers? What was it that caused

THE FOLLOWING ILLUSTRATIONS APPEAR IN
<u>SEDUCTION</u> OF <u>THE INNOCENT</u>

From All Top No. 14. ©1979 Fox

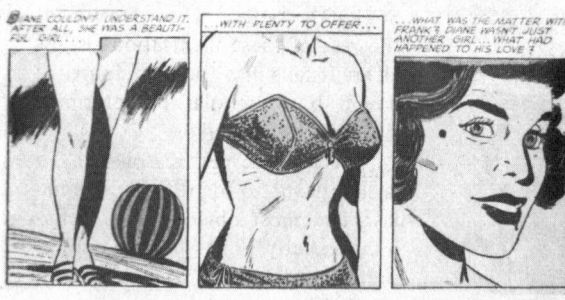

**ABOVE: From Weird Mysteries
NO. 7.** ©1979 by Gillmore

**RIGHT: From Crime Smashers
No. 1.** ©1979 by D.S.

**BELOW: From Weird Mysteries
No. 7.** ©1979 by Gillmore

Wertham to choose those specific comics?

Through extensive research a majority of these Seduction illustrations have been decoded. In the process it should be noted that they do represent a solid cross-section of many of the primary publishing houses—Fiction House, Avon, E. C., Fox, Atlas, Harvey, Hillman and D. C. (a notable exception was Dell). The comics found at this time which contain panels reproduced in Wertham's book are as follows: HAUNT OF FEAR No. 19, TRUE CRIME VOL. 1 No. 2 (two illustrations), WOMEN OUTLAWS No. 1, FRONTIER ROMANCES No. 1, WEIRD MYSTERIES No. 7 (two illustrations), FIRST LOVE No. 35, ALL-FAMOUS CRIME No. 9, JUNGLE No. 98, CRIME SMASHER No. 1, BLUE BEETLE No. 54, STRANGE ADVENTURES No. 39, DYNAMIC No. 17, RED SEAL No. 16, ALL-TOP No. 14, LAW-BREAKERS ALWAYS LOSE No. 7, EXPOSED Vol. 1 No. 6 and WEIRD SCIENCE No. 19. There are still several illustrations which have eluded most collectors of the seduction material. Several books which have been cited as having a reference in the *Seduction of the Innocent* are, I feel, hasty judgments or apparently incorrect. The most blatant is OUTLAWS No. 1. Although containing scenes of incredible violence this comic does not appear to have been mentioned or illustrated in Wertham's book. This is not to saw that it shouldn't have been, possibly leading to an entire classification of books that Wertham overlooked.

Getting deeper into the structure of *The Seduction of the Innocent* a pattern emerges in regard to Wertham's use of specific reference

in the text portion of the book. A careful reading of passages in which a particular comic is singled out as a prime example of deviancy shows that Wertham is extemely careful not to expose the exact title or issue number. TEGRA No. 1 is mentioned on page 31 when Wertham, talking about S&M in comics, discusses an unnamed example of sexual extravagance: "They contain such details as one girl squirting fiery 'radium dust' on the protruding breasts of another girl

From Outlaws No. 1. © 1979 by D.S.

('I think I've found your Achilles' heel chum!')." MY LIFE No. 4 is cited on page 39 by Wertham with, "Another confession comic book is the reincaranation of a previous teen-age book with an innocuous title. That one was despite its title, one of the most sexy, specializing in highly accentuated and protruding breasts in practically every illustration. Adolescent boys call these 'headlight comics'. . .The confession comic into which this one turned has a totally different style, the new-love comics formula. One story, 'I Was a Spoiled Brat,' begins with a big picture of an attractive girl looking at herself in the mirror and baring herself considerably. . . ." HOWDY DOODY No. 6 is mentioned on page 309 as follows: "Take one that looks even more harmless, HOWDY DOODY. . .The book depicts colored natives as stereotyped caricatures, violent, cowardly, cannibalistic, and so superstitious that they get scared by seltzer tablets and popping corn and lie down in abject surrender on their faces before two little white boys " TOM MIX No. 9 is given an incredible treatment by Wertham on page 323. Even the esoteric drug giveaway TRAPPED is discussed by Wertham as a valuable comic on page 350. The list could go on, citing Wertham's text and the comics the information was derived from. It would serve no real purpose except to show how much of what Wertham interpreted from these various comics was a product

of his active imagination, the interpretation of a scholarly scientist driven by an unnaturally overzealous desire to end juvenile delinquency. At this time over one-third of the references are documented.

One unusual aspect to the books used by Wertham in *The Seduction of the Innocent* is the fact that a number of them were reprinted prior to the publication of his book. The scene of torture with the "red hot poker" from DYNAMIC No. 17 was reprinted in CRIME REPORTER No. 2. The "lovers-lane" panel from an L. B. Cole drawn story entitled "Crimson Trail of the Lipstick Slayer' from ALL-FAMOUS CRIME No. 9 was reprinted in LAW/CRIME No. 3. (Interestingly enough if one looks at the panel in Wertham's book it looks as though the couple was shot in their heads, whereas in actuality the circular marks in the middle of their foreheads is the tell-tale lipstick mark of the sadistic killer.) GIANT COMICS No. 4 reprints the "we'll drain this dame dry" story

ABOVE: "Lovers Lane," from All-Famous Crime No. 9. ©1979 by Star

LEFT: "Red Hot Poker," from Dynamic No. 17. © 1979 by Ches

from RED SEAL No. 16. In these particular cases it is difficult to know with much certainty which comic Wertham actually used when conducting his "investigation." That problem does not arise in the case of FUGITIVES FROM JUSTICE No. 3–a mistakenly identified Seduction book. This most unusual Seduction *reprint* is from a Walter Johnson story where one of his classic pin-up type drawings was illustrated as the "invitation to learning" panel in Wertham's book. The original drawing shows a girl lounging on a bed in a sheer negligee. It was reprinted in FUGITIVES FROM JUSTICE No. 3 with the woman wearing a bright red dress. This is one example in which the comic had been censored and lost the initial sexiness of the original drawing but still contained the innuendo suggested by Wertham.

All of this leads to one question. Was Wertham's attack of comic book publishing effective? That particular answer is neither complex or difficult to determine. Where the

difficulty begins is in interpreting the answer.

A Senate sub-committee headed by Senator Estes Kefauver investigated juvenile delinquency in the early 1950's. Wertham was called as a key witness (along with Bill "E. C." Gaines and others). The inconclusive findings of this public hearing served as a springboard for Wertham and the success of his book. People needed an answer to the problem of juvenile delinquency. Many sought to find it in the pages of *Seduction of the Innocent*. Once this occurred and the Comics Code Authority was established, the rest was downhill. Comics were censored. At times this censorship took place for no apparent reason. E. C. Comics initiated their policy of "New Direction" titles which ultimately proved to be the death blow for what was one of the most ambitious ventures in comic book publishing. Many secondary titles ceased publication. Others were consolidated into other formats. Migration of comic book writers and artists to other less controversial media was widespread. The entire period was one of radical change.

The scatterbrained approach to this problem of indiscriminate censorship can nowhere better be illustrated than in two particularly undistinguished Harvey romance comics: TEEN-AGE BRIDES No. 5 (pre-code) and TRUE BRIDE-TO-BE ROMANCE No. 20 (a code issue). These two comics contain the same stories and art and are exact in every way except that in the newer code issue a new cover has been added and certain images where minor evidence of cleavage, cheescake and behavior of a "sexual" nature has been eliminated. A story drawn by Bob Powell shows the fanatical desire on the part of the censor to blacken out anything too explicit in comic books. In the bottom left-hand panel of the noncode issue a husband is kissing his wife on the neck while whispering, "I love you, baby!"—in the code issue his head is taken completely out of the frame and yet the word balloon remains. The question is, "Where is the husband?" For those who know how to look the answer is obvious.

It has been twenty-five years since Wertham's book exposed the "true" nature of comics. The effect is still present today when parents who grew up in the Fifties still refuse to buy comics for their children because they are considered bad influences. The effect is still present today when comic books are considered "junk" literature. It is a classic case of misguided motives. Wertham was partially right. There were extremes of violence in comics, but they were not the main cause of juvenile delinquency. Comics were censored in 1954 and children still smoked dope, cut up their friends in street fights, broke windows, stole whatever they could get away with. The diagnosis was wrong. Rather than cleaning up the elements of an environment that reflected a society and culture that was itself desensitized by the violence of two major wars, Wertham should have concentrated on creating a sociological climate in which healthy material could appear. Once the fear of potential harm is eliminated it is not difficult to see that comics, along with most mass entertainment during the late 1940's and early 1950's, got one of the worst deals in contemporary social freedom.

LEFT: From Teen-Age Brides No. 5(pre-code). RIGHT: From True Bride-To-Be Romances No. 20(post-code). © 1979 by Harv

The DC
Super Heroes Poster Book

Together in one giant poster book—the DC Super Heroes and their
archenemies, the DC Super Villains. Featured in full-color are such
greats as Superman, Batman, Wonder Woman, the whole Shazam
family, Green Arrow, the Joker, Luther, Penguin, and many more.
**By far and away this is the biggest and brightest collection of
comic art ever published!** A Harmony Book / 48 pages/$6.95

24 FULL-COLOR, PULL-OUT, 11¼ x 15¼ POSTERS

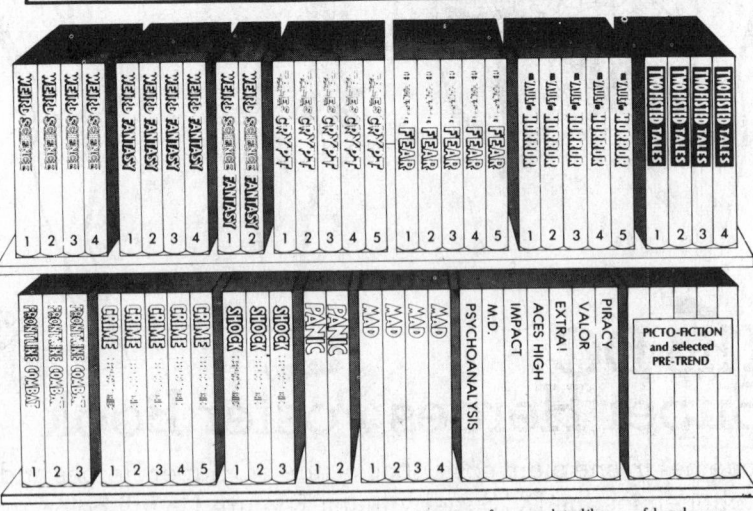

wood.

Good Lord! choke... gasp... It's EC!

By E. B. BOATNER*

From The Vault Of Horror No. 28, "We Ain't Got No Body!," by Ingels.©1979 by William M. Gaines.

"It was a weird tableau ... the five of them! The two feet hopped along! Behind them! ... a hand dragged itself! The other hand lay, palm upward, upon the back of the moving hand! The directing hand rested in the upper hand's palm!" *(The Vault of Horror 28).*

A weird tableau for the uninitiate perhaps, but for five years between 1950 and 1955 this econoline of walking corpses was standard fare for readers of Entertaining Comics horror titles, and was typical of the startling ingenuity and inventiveness of their science fiction, suspense, war, and humor books.

With my special thanks to Bill Gaines, Al Feldstein, Harvey Kurtzman and Jerry De Fuccio for their time, help and patience.

In 1950 EC released seven titles in what it called a New Trend of comic books, including horror books, *The Crypt of Terror, The Vault of Horror, The Haunt of Fear,* science fiction comics, *Weird Science* and *Weird Fantasy;* crime with a twist ending, *Crime Suspen-Stories;* and an adventure-war book, *Two-Fisted Tales.*

Reader response to these books was immediate and enthusiastic. Here were books with a fresh approach — high quality scripts featuring plots with an O. Henry ending rather than the standard linear development, unusual and varied illustration by artists who were encouraged to develop their own idiosyncratic styles, and an editorial sense of humor that drew the reader directly into the EC ambiance.

The New Trend was the Golden Age of EC, and like all such halcyon times was preceded by a Bronze Age, and followed all too soon by a declining Silver Age. In EC terminology, these periods would be the Pre-Trend years of 1947-1950, and the New Direction and Picto-Fiction period of 1955-56. But back to the beginning.

EC as Entertaining Comics was launched in 1947 by twenty-five-year-old William Maxwell Gaines who book over his father's company when M. C. Gaines was killed in a motor boat accident. Before that time, as "Educational Comics," EC had consisted of a line of juvenile books: *Picture Stories From the Bible, Animal Fables, Dandy Comics, Fat and Slat, Tiny Tot Comics* and the like.

Just as Bill Gaines was picking up the reins at EC, a young artist named Al Feldstein was growing restless with the erratic pay at Fox Studios and came to EC thinking he

might get in on the ground floor of the new enterprise. Feldstein was slated to do a teen-age book in the *Archie* format which never made it to the drawing board, but he did meet Gaines which sparked a rare and happy chemistry that is still working today.

They immediately dropped the "Freddy Firefly Versus Atomic Bug!" type stories *(Animal Fables No. 7)* to develop their line of crime, western and romance books, including Maxwell Gaines' *War Against Crime, International Comics, Moon Girl and the Prince,* and Sol Cohen's *Gunfighter and Saddle Justice* and their own *Crime Patrol, Modern Love* and *Saddle* Romances. Many of the first Pre-Trend books soon underwent a series of byzantine title changes to satisfy second class postage regulations.

From Gunfighter No. 10, by Ingels.
© 1979 by William M. Gaines.

Gaines and Feldstein's first Pre-Trend efforts were fairly standard shoot 'em ups and love books with dialogue ranging from the quaint, "ZaZa LaFleur was raised in cow country," *(Gunfighter No. 10)* to the obscure, "Get down off them horses yuh coyotes, before I salivate yuh!" (GF No. 5). Figuring that if romance sells and oaters sell, then love on horseback should be twice as good. *Saddle Justice* was turned into *Saddle Romances*. There was even an editor-to-cowpoke advice column entitled "Chat With Chuck" similar to the "Advice From Amy" and "Advice From Adrienne" pages in *A Moon, A Girl . . . Romance* and *Modern Love*.

They hadn't yet hit their stride; not even the titles were all their own yet. "Like *Gunfighter*," recalls Gaines. "These were mostly Sol Cohen's things. He started a book called *Gunfighter* because Gregory Peck had just come out in the movie and it was a big success. And that was about the extent of his editorial thinking." Of his own early editorship he says, "Oh, it was fun. I never took it seriously. I was down there because my mother thought the business should be continued."

The New Trend style began to emerge through the last issues of the Pre-Trend books. Early horror and science fiction appeared in *Crime Patrol* No. 15, *War Against Crime* No. 10, and *Moon Girl* No. 5, while *Modern Love* No. 8 featured a comic industry satire titled "The Love Story to End All Love Stories." There was no attempt to test-market the proposed New Trend, says Gaines, and with the long lead time on the books there would not have been time to assess reader response. "We put out these stories and we enjoyed them so much that we decided to change the books." The three GhouLunatics, the Old Witch, Crypt Keeper and Vault Keeper, were spawned in the Pre-Trend stories, and they quickly set up crypt-keeping in their New Trend baliwicks, hosting *The Haunt of Fear*, *Tales From the Crypt*, and *The Vault of Horror*, respectively.

Gaines and Feldstein wanted to be trend setters, rather than followers, and between April and October 1950 they introduced the seven previously mentioned titles that formed the nucleus of their heralded New Trend. They came as a revelation to the jaded comic book reader. Here were unpredictable stories; stories that did not condescend, and which brought a refreshing, if macabre, sense of humor to the fledgling horror field. Their science fiction stories had substance and were not simply "Saddles in the Sky" with rockets. If the "SF was far beyond the competition," EC war stories were like nothing that had ever appeared in the heavily nationalistic books of the 40s, and the suspense books undercut everything Superman had taught about justice prevailing.

A certain synergy was generated by the Gaines-Feldstein collaboration, the transformation of their plots through the artist's rendering, and the personal interaction between the EC reader and editors via the letter pages. The small staff and Feldstein's insistence on giving the

From Saddle Justice No. 5, by Craig.
© 1979 by William M. Gaines.

artists high visibility (Johnny Craig was featured as early as 1949 at the end of "Colorado Rose" in SJ No. 5) contirbuted to the personal family feeling of the books. Gaines and Feldstein made personal appearances as characters from time to time, poking fun at themselves and their creations. They are killed off at the end of "A Love Story to End All Love Stories" leaving office boy Paul Kast shouting, "I, the office boy of T. Tot Publications, am the only one left! So if you like this type of story, and want to see more like it in future issues ... which I will publish ... Write ME!"

The bulk of the horror, crime, suspense, and science fiction books were written and edited by Al Feldstein, who turned out four stories a week for nearly five years. Johnny Craig edited and wrote lead stories for *The Vault of Horror* and Harvey Kurtzman edited and wrote most of the *Two-Fisted Tales* (later taken over by John Severin), *Frontline Combat,* and *MAD* comics. Towards the end of the New Trend, Carl Wessler and Jack Oleck wrote for the horror books, submitting scripts which would be rewritten by Feldstein. Writers Robert Bernstein and Irving Wirstein also contributed to later books, mainly in the New Direction series.

Recalling their writing sessions, Feldstein says, "Bill and I would get together early in the morning and plot out something. First of all we would figure out who we were writing for, because each guy had his own style. So if we were doing an Ingles piece we would figure out something with walking corpses, and if we were doing a Jack Kamen, we would figure on something with a love triangle, something sexy, or little kids.

"We'd try to get it pretty well plotted by lunch time, then go out and have a big lunch at Patrissy's and get bloated with Italian food,

and then I'd go into my office and write. I'd lay the story out and write it at the same time so that it was written right on the boards that the artists were eventually going to draw on, the actual illustration boards. They were then given out to our letterer, who would letter what I wrote, and then the artist would draw. If I didn't write too much they'd have some space to draw, and if I did, they had nothing and no place to draw."

The Leroy lettering was a distinctive feature of the EC books and gave a precision and literary quality to the already lengthy and complicated texts. EC books were written to be read, not skimmed. The lettering was done by Jim Wroten and his wife Skippy, and by Gaines' cousin Buddy Rogin. "Wroten's kind of stuff matched my personality, which is precise and exact," says Gaines. "And I could give him corrections over the phone — you can't do that with a hand letterer." However, Harvey Kurtzman detested the rigidity of this template lettering, and after his first few stories always used Ben Oda to hand-letter his own books and his work in Feldstein's books.

After the illustration boards were returned by the artists, they were colored by Marie Severin — sister of John — who managed to color *all* of the hundreds of EC stories as well as many of the covers. Some of the artists did color their own covers.

Feldstein always left the artist free to work within the framework of his text. "I didn't believe in sketching out my conception of what the particular panel would look like," he says "because I thought that inhibited each individual artist's style. That's like asking an artist to sign his name on my handwriting. The only thing that I asked was that they show me pencils to make sure that they had the elements for carrying the story forward.

"Every guy did his own concepts, and unless it jarred me as an editor and as author of the material, I wouldn't have any objection to it. I would just make sure that the elements that were necessary to tell the story were there."

The sources of most EC plots came from Gaines' own reading in science fiction pulps and from hundreds of "springboards" that he kept on 3x5 cards, one idea to a card. "I would read a story," he explains, "and I would get two or three springboards out of it. We would just take the basic premise, like making a woman out of a package of dehydrated powder in a bathtub, and fashion our own story.

"We'd gotten beyond the point of stealing the plot, we were stealing the springboard. And then one springboard would lead to another. Sometimes we would get many original thoughts from reading a story. I found reading stories was my best way to come up with original ideas. By and large, most of our ideas were original, but it all came out of reading."

An entire article could be done on the origins of EC plots, and one can ferret out numerous authors' contributions in addition to the recognized adaptations of Eando (Earl and Otto) Binder and Ray Bradbury. Roald Dahl's "The Sound Machine" for "The Sounds From Another World" (WS No. 14)

From Weird Science No. 14/3, by Kurtzman. © 1979 by William M. Gaines.

From Crime SuspenStories No. 5, "The Sewer!," by Craig.
© 1979 by William M. Gaines.

From VOH No. 17, "Terror On The Moors!," by Craig. © 1979 by William M. Gaines.

and Henry Hasse's "He Who Shrank" for "Lost in the Microcosm" (WS No. 12) are only two.

Unfortunately for EC historians, that goldmine of 3x5 cards was destroyed. "We had a burglar down on Lafayette Street who would come in and steal our subscription money every so often," explains Gaines. "Finally, because we got a safe and didn't leave money around, he got furious and burned a lot of things from my desk. One of the things he burned was my whole file of plots — hundreds and hundreds and hundreds of springboards."

Complementing the consistently high quality of the scripts was the superior art of the EC illustrators. While over 30 artists worked on the New Trend books, there is a nucleus of regulars who did most of the stories, and who can be easily recognized by their style.

Already mentioned is Johnny Craig who was drawing Pre-Trend crime, western, and romance, by 1948. All the *Crime Patrol's* featured Craig's stunning cover art which was dominated by heavy areas of black pierced with slashes of light — spotlights, headlights, interrogation lights, and bullet streaks. Craig delineates his characters with a fine clean line, never cluttering a panel even when there are numerous figures. ("Johnny Craig drew the only clean sewers I've ever seen," Wally Wood recalls.) Craig's killers frequently featured dapper young men, stylish ladies, or distinguished white-mustached older gentlemen who all broke out in discreet beads of sweat in moments of stress or impending death.

Most easily identifiable in the horror line is the reclusive Graham Ingles — known as Ghastly — who drew even normal people in a way that made people want to wash their hands after finishing a story. Ingles specialized in walking corpses and in people deformed in body and spirit who oozed and dripped across his pages. He did many covers for *The Haunt of Fear,* and Nos. 14 and 17, the first one a procession of things with pitchforks; the second a collection of rotting heads, show the distinctive Ghastly touch.

Ingles had been an editor at Standard Comics before coming to EC. Oddly enough, he started in the love and western books where his nascent talent for the loathsome is noticeable only fleetingly in a character's skewed smile or a drunkenly tilted lamppost. "Graham was someone we pulled out of love and western," says Gaines, "and I wasn't at all sure that he could do horror. Looking back on it, it's absurd! You typecast artists just like you do actors and actresses, and I just couldn't believe that Graham was a horror artist."

Al Feldstein drew covers and stories for many of the Pre- and New Trend books in a rather heavy, deceptively simple line technique with rounded corners that gave an almost Bahaus effect. His science fiction is reminiscent of a restrained Basil Wolverton, as Wolverton drew in "The Brain Bats of Venus" *(Mister Mystery No. 7, 1952),* although he was unaware of Wolverton's work at the time.

Feldstein's ghouls and corpses were tattered but not unwholesome, and his aliens had a functional appearance. A Feldstein rotting corpse wouldn't track up the kitchen floor, while the average Ingles human would have left a trail

From HOF No. 13, "For The Love Of Death!," by Ingels. © 1979 by William M. Gaines.

Classic Early Feldstein horror story from The Vault Of Horror No. 12. © 1979 by William M. Gaines.

Old Witch by Ingels from The Haunt Of Fear No. 10. © 1979 by William M. Gaines.

THE BRAIN-BATS of VENUS

THERE ARE SOME PLANETS ON WHICH MAN SHOULD NEVER SET FOOT! TWO EARTHMEN FOUND THAT OUT --- TOO LATE!

EC CONFIDENTIAL!

HORNS WERE BLOWING. COWBELLS WERE RINGING. CHIMES WERE SOUNDING OUT THE FATEFUL HOUR OF MID-NIGHT. *THIS WAS NEW YEAR'S EVE, 1963.* THIS WAS *JAM-PACKED TIMES SQUARE. THIS WAS THE SCENE OF DEATH.* HIGH OVERHEAD, IN THE WINTRY STARLESS SKY, AN ARMY BOMBER BOUND FOR MITCHEL FIELD, LONG ISLAND, SUDDENLY NOSED DOWN AND STREAKED EARTHWARD...STREAKED UNCONTROLLABLY TOWARD THE FESTIVE CROWD...*STREAKED TOWARD THE SCENE OF DEATH.* ITS ROAR WAS GREATER THAN THE CROWD ROAR. ITS WHINING SCREAMING DIVE WAS SHRILLER THAN THE HORNS. THE HORNS STOPPED BLOWING. THE BELLS STOPPED RINGING. THE CROWD FELL INTO A FROZEN TERRORIZED SILENCE. THE BOMBER'S LIGHTS EXPLODED FROM THE DARKNESS BETWEEN THE TOWERING BUILDINGS. THE SILVERY SHAPE HURTLED AT THE CROWD, AND NOW, THE SCREAMING DIVE WAS GREATER THAN THE PLANE ROAR, SHRILLER THAN ITS DIVE. AND NOW THE SCREAMING CROWD WAS AWARE...

ABOVE: From Mister Mystery No. 7, by Wolverton. © 1979 by Aragon Magazines.

LEFT: From Weird Science No. 21, by Wood. © 1979 by William M. Gaines.

From cover of Weird Science No. 6, by Feldstein. © 1979 by William M. Gaines.

of slime. The *Weird Science* No. 6 cover is representative of his science fiction work, while the corpse on the cover of *Tales From the Crypt* No. 23 is making a tidy, albeit rotted, exit from its casket. "I'm a well-organized person," comments Feldstein, "so I guess I have well-organized aliens. I was taught in the High School of Music and Art that form follows function."

Wally Wood arrived at EC out of Eisner through Pre-Trend with Harry Harrison, where they did westerns and romances. An incredibly speedy draftsman, Wood could turn out a story a week drawn with minute detail. The splash panel for "EC Confidential" (WS No. 21), for example, shows an Army bomber plunging into a vast New Year's crowd in Times Square. Not only are the hundreds of figures each drawn in, but they all have faces.

Wood doted on elaborate scenes, crowded with muscular males and scantily-clad females, little creatures peeping from crannies, or-

From cover of Tales From The Crypt No. 23, by Feldstein. © 1979 by William M. Gaines.

ganic statuary and animated bric-a-brac. His multi-tentacled aliens had a texture midway between that of Feldstein and Ingles, giving an impression of slipperiness rather than sliminess. Both Feldstein and Wood enjoyed drawing lush women, but Wood's had deeper cleavage and fewer clothes. The prolific Wood drew extensively for the science fiction and war books — where he excelled in space hardware and war paraphenalia — as well as for the horror, suspense and humor.

Rebel Jack Davis added his unique densely-inked artwork to the EC books in 1950. His loose redneck characters gave both a dimension of reality to the war books, and the right touch of distance and lunacy to even the grimmest horror tales. Of his brief foray into science fiction Gaines says, "Davis can do many things. On the other hand, he can't do science fiction very well. I think we gave him a cover once (three — ISF No. 30-32), but Jack doesn't have it like some of the other guys did for science fiction. But he sure had it for everything else."

"Davis came up to New York from Atlanta and he was looking for work," remembers Feldstein. "Finally he got to our place, which was a small place, so he must have tried somewhere else and didn't get anywhere. We gave him his first work, and I let him go in his own way without inhibiting him or telling him he couldn't put in the scratchy little lines or the oversized feet or anything like that. Davis has a kind of earthy style, and he's very good for war stuff.

Jack Kamen slipped easily from romance books into EC's horror, science fiction and suspense tales, using essentially his romance characters — handsome men, voluptuous girls, and wide-eyed children. Kamen did for eyelashes what Craig did for sweat beads on nervous killers. Kamen's forte was the triangle story and the innocent — or not so innocent — child menaced by an evil adult.

While a Craig triangle tale usual-

From Crime SuspenStories No. 6, "Out Of My Mind!," by Kamen. © 1979 by William M. Gaines.

From The Haunt Of Fear No. 7, by Kamen. © 1979 by William M. Gaines

From Weird Fantasy No. 17, "Ahead Of The Game!," by Elder.
© 1979 by William M. Gaines.

From Tales From The Crypt No. 38, "Last Laugh," by Elder.
© 1979 by William M. Gaines.

ly involved a walking corpse, Kamen opted for nice wholesome family types doing each other in. The editors played up his strengths and weaknesses in "Kamen's Kalamity" (TftC No. 31) having mild-mannered Jack turn into a killer werewolf in an attempt to put more horror in his horror stories.

Will Elder's fine lunatic imagination came into its own with his work in *MAD,* where his ability to imitate any style of art proved an invaluable skill for parodying ads, other comic strips, movies, etc. He embellished backgrounds with his own zany free-association graffiti, perhaps the most arcane of which was a poster in "Mickey Rodent" (*MAD* No. 19) reading "Attention bloodhounds — become a Donner!"

Elder worked originally as inker for John Severin's pencils. The two did many fine war stories for Kurtz-

man's books, and Elder made a few sallies alone into the horror and science fiction fields. The lurking satire in Elder's pen was subtly at variance with the general tenor of the science fiction books, however, and "Ahead of the Game" (WF No. 17), in which a demented professor wires up living heads into a computer, is too close to parody. In the same way, even though the horror books were done tongue-in-cheek, "Strop! You're Killing Me!" and "Last Laugh" (TftC 37 and 38), were, in Elder's hands, more a parody of an EC horror story. But he was perfectly suited for *MAD* and *Panic.*

Elder's high school chum Harvey Kurtzman, so the story goes, came to EC in 1949 looking for work in an Educational vein, unaware that Entertaining had taken over. Gaines recalls looking at Kurtzman's portfolio. "Al and I sat there and giggled and laughed all afternoon and then said, 'We're not really Educational Comics, that's a hold-over from years ago. We're putting out horror and science fiction and so on. But would you like to do some of that?'

"So Harvey said yes — reluct-antly, but he had to eat — and he did horror and science fiction for us. Then he came to us with the concept of an adventure book. I had no feeling at all for adventure — I didn't know what he was talking about. If you want to see a dreadful example of adventure, Al and I did one story for the first *Two-Fisted Tales*, and I don't think you'll have any trouble picking out which one it is. . . . So I started him on *Two-Fisted Tales*. It wasn't do-ing well but it wasn't doing badly. And then the war came, and he switched it to war and added *Front-line Combat.*"

Harvey drew with thick sloopy buush lines which looked effortless but which, on the contrary, were worked and reworked by the me-ticulous Kurtzman. He was never comfortable with EC crime or hor-ror — "They fell into an attitude or a system or style where it became very Freudian, very ghoulish," he says now, but he was justifiably proud of his 13 science fiction stories which included " . . . Greg-ory Had a Model T" (WS No. 7) and "Mysterious Ray From Anoth-er Dimension!" (WF No. 16). Kurtzman drew covers and stories for his war books and covers for the *MAD* comics although he un-fortunately did not draw any new *MAD* stories.

Al Williamson began to draw for

From Weird Fantasy No. 6, by Kurtzman. ©1979 by William M. Gaines.

A-54

EC in 1952 at the age of 21. Influenced by the more realistic and physical style of Alex Raymond, he beautifully illustrated prehistoric tales with amply fleshed warriors and muscular young women. He was frequently helped out on deadline by, and shared credits with, close friend Frank Frazetta, which relationship Williamson now describes as "doing a lot of stuff together, but we were not a team." Frazetta did one story alone, "Squeeze Play" (SSS No. 13) and a cover for WSF No. 29. This cover was originally done for *Famous Funnies* who rejected it as being too violent—It was redone for Ec.

Innovative Bernie Krigstein came late to EC in 1953, but his versatility of style and techniques made the reader vividly aware of his presence in the New Trend and New Direction books. Unlike Jack Kamen, Krigstein was able to adapt his style to the type of story he was illustrating, from the crude, heavily lined "Pipe Dream" (VOH No. 36),

From Shock SuspenStories No. 13, "Squeeze Play," by Frazetta. © 1979 by William M. Gaines.

to the delicate and airy adaptation of Bradbury's "The Flying Machine" (WSF No. 23) to the stylized Hirschfield cartoon style of

From Weird Science Fantasy No. 23, by Krigstein.© 1979 by William M. Gaines.

"From Eternity Back to Here" (*MAD* No. 12).

Krigstein chafed at the limitations of the 6 to 8 page format and often reworked the text and subdivided panels to gain more space. The most famous of these stories is "Master Race" from the New Direction's *Impact* No. 1, which Feldstein assigned as a six-page story, and which Krigstein expanded to eight. His cinematic technique is evident on the opening page, where the repeated overlay of a figure in the final frame, for example, perfectly conveys the movement of the subway train within a single panel.

Other excellent artists who contributed to the New Trend, New Direction and Pictofiction books included George Evans, Reed Crandall, Joe Orlando, Angelo Torres, Roy Krenkel, Joe Kubert and Alexander Toth.

The fresh Gaines/Feldstein scripts and the innovative talent of these artists gave EC an impressive lineup of books with solid content and eyecatching format. EC never had the print run of Gleason and Biro's books — *Crime Does Not Pay* might sell as many as 4,000,000 copies per issue, while EC sold somewhere in the neighborhood of 1,500,000 copies monthly for the entire group, or 400,000 as a top figure for the best horror comic sale per issue — but they had a devoted following of fans who read and corresponded faithfully.

Despite distribution problems, it was an exciting time for EC's young staff. "The New Trend days were happy days from the creative point of view," agrees Gaines. "In those days I had nothing to do with the business and to speak of, so I was all involved in the editorial end, creating story lines, and creating magazines and titles. I guess there were the usual aggravations, but somehow I remember them all as very pleasant days."

It was as happy a time for Al Feldstein. "Generally, I loved doing the stuff, and it was great fun. I was a very fortunate person, and have been most of my life, in being able to earn a living at something I enjoy doing. And also, of course, it's very exciting to be able to do things that haven't been done before so that you're free within your art — from my own personal stiff-simple style, to Graham Ingles' drippy-gooky and Jack Davis' hairy-scratchy, and Jack Kamen's sweetsy-cutsie — we all had our own statements to make and we were encouraged.

We were fortunate in having a publisher like Bill Gaines who permitted us to be that way."

Feldstein not only managed to turn out four stories a week, but he was able to keep clear editorial distinctions between the EC genres, giving the horror, science fiction, and suspense their own special flavors. Horror tales were done tongue-in-cheek, usually with an awful Old Testament eye-for-an-eye retribution awaiting the villain. For example, a charlatan who offers quick weight loss to his victims and peddles them encapsulated tape worms, is finally trapped in a vault and devoured by a giant worm that has battened on one of the deceased weight watchers. ("Dying to Lose Weight" VOH No. 18).

The horror reader could safely anticipate such deliciously just punishments, but as the stories grew more realistic in the crime and shock books, justice became increasingly elusive, and the reader's sense of assurance increasingly shaky. Feldstein showed that a

HERE IS AN ELECTRIFYING STORY WITH SOLID IMPACT IN ITS STARTLING CONCLUSION!

THE PATRIOTS!

A SHOCK SuspenStory

From Shock SuspenStories No. 2, by Davis. © 1979 by William M. Gaines

Korean veterans' homecoming parade ("The Patriots" SSS No. 2) could be as lethal as the giant worm and far more likely to happen.

Feldstein played the science fiction straight, using humor on occasion as an integral part of the story, but not to lampoon the science fiction genre per se, unless the parody revolved around the EC editors, as in "EC Confidential" (WS No. 21). A number of the stories were "message" plots, used to make a statement about man's inhumanity to man; "The Loathsome" (WS No. 20), man's in-humanity to other creatures; "The Probers" (WS No. 8), and man's inhumanity to aliens; "The Teacher From Mars" (WSF No. 24), an Eando Binder adaptation.

After the first cluster of new books appeared in 1950, the New Trend was filled out with *Frontline Combat* (1951), *MAD* (1952), *Shock SuspenStories* (1952), and latecomers *Panic* (1954) and *Piracy* (1954). Title changes made *Tales From the Crypt* out of *The Crypt of Terror,* and the two science fiction books were merged, first into *Weird Science-Fantasy* and

From Weird Science No. 8, "The Probers," by Wood. ©1979 by William M. Gaines.

A-57

**From The Haunt Of Fear No. 17/3, "Horror Beneath The Streets!,"
by Feldstein. ©1979 by William M. Gaines.**

then retitled *Incredible Science Fiction.*

The five crime and horror books were EC's bread and butter, and the horror books in particular drew readers with Gaines and Feldstein's Planter's Punch of bad puns, outrageous jokes and grisly grue all offered through the miasmic hospitality of the three GhouLunatics.

The reason that Gaines and Feldstein were forced to collaborate with the unwholesome three was explained in "Horror Beneath the Streets" (HOF No. 17) where the terrified editors are pursued through the sewers of New York and forced to sign binding contracts with the Old Witch, the Crypt Keeper and the Vault Keeper. One of the three introduced each story, trading insults with the others and inviting correspondence to their letter columns.

"Al and I had a strange rapport in those days," says Gaines, "where he could start something and I'd finish it, or vice versa, or he'd say three words and I'd say three words — we literally were writing together. And when we did the GhouLunatics, it was almost like you hear these mythological things where the ventriloquist's dummy takes over. Because we'd write a letter, and Goddamn if one of the GhouLunatics wouldn't answer that letter, and it didn't matter whether I said it, or Al said it, or we both said it — it wasn't us! It was one of those devilish creatures!"

Within this framework, the atmosphere of the horror books can be conveyed in just a few of the egregious story titles: "Ooze in the Cellar?" (HOF No. 11); "Horror We? How's Bayou?" (HOF No. 17); "Ants in Her Trance!" (TftC No. 28); "Tain't the Meat, It's the Humanity!" (TftC No. 32); and

"Fare Tonight, Followed by Increasing Clottyness. . ." (TftC No. 36).

Points of view varied, and stories were narrated variously by a trunk which traps a killer and squeezes him out of its keyhole like toothpaste ("Tight Grip!" TftC No. 38); a swamp shack forced to house a loathsome ghoul ("Swamped" HOF No. 27); and a lonesome grave, yearning for a corpse of its own to cuddle ("The Craving Grave!" TftC No. 39).

EC horror opened new vistas of death from sources previously unimagined by the reader. Victims were serial-sectioned by giant machines, eaten by ghouls, devoured by rats — from inside and out, pecked by pigeons, stuffed down disposals, skewered on swords, buried alive, dismembered and used as baseball equipment, hung as living clappers in huge bells, made into sausages and soap, dissolved, southern fried, hacked up by maniacs in Santa Claus suits, and offed in unusually high percentages by their wives or husbands.

Discussing these spouse-cide tales which were also a staple of the crime and shock books, Gaines says only, "Well you have to realize that most of the EC springboards were mine, and the direction that the springboards took was the result of my neuroses. And I've probably said more than I should say at this point! For whatever reason, I got enjoyment out of those. That's why I thought them up, much the way that Thurber did. Thurber's stuff was full of the same nuttiness. I won't say that my problems were exactly Thurber's problems but we both showed them through our work."

From Tales From The Crypt No. 38, "Tight Grip!," by Davis.
© 1979 by William M. Gaines.

From The Haunt Of Fear No. 27, "Swamped," by Crandall.
© 1979 by William M. Gaines.

A popular horror feature was the "Grim Fairy Tale," the first of which was illustrated by Ingles and the remaining 13 by Kamen, The humor that Feldstein would later turn into *Panic* could be seen in "Snow White and the Seven Dwarfs" (HOF No. 22) in which a compulsive neat Snow White drives the dwarfs to homicide and ends, ' So the seven little dwarfs stormed back into their spotless little house and proceeded to turn it into a miserable hovel again. . ."

"It was the biggest shock to me," Feldstein says, "when guys like Wertham and this whole catastrophe exploded on us, talking about how these comics were affecting our children and causing juvenile delinquency. I couldn't believe it. I don't believe that children are that vulnerable and that gullible that they're going to accept this as reality. Except ill children, of course, and for this country to guide its way by the standards of ill people is a frightening thing."

It did become apparent, however, that a certain overkill marred some of the scripts. One of the most widely-quoted examples was "Foul Play!" (HOF No. 19) illustrated by Jack Davis at his grisliest. In revenge for a teammate murdered by an opponent's poisoned spikes, the Bayville baseball team dismembers the killer and sets up a midnight memorial game.

"See the long strings of pulpy intestines that mark the base lines," intones the narrator. "See the two lungs and the liver that indicate the bases ... the heart that is home plate. See Doc White bend and whisk the heart with the mangy scalp, yelling, 'Play ball. . .' See the batter come to the plate swinging the legs, the arms, then throwing all but one away and standing in the

From The Haunt Of Fear No. 19, "Foul Play!," by Davis. Used In Seduction Of The Innocent. © 1979 by William M. Gaines.

From Shock SuspenStories No. 11, "In Gratitude...," by Wood. © 1979 by William M. Gaines.

box waiting for the pitcher to hurl the head to him. See the catcher with the torso strapped on as a chest protector, the infielders with their hand-mitts, the stomach rosin bag, and all the other pieces of equipment that once was Central City's star pitcher, Herbie Satten. . . ."

"One of the traps that Bill and I fell into," admits Feldstein, "was that we were beginning to formularize our material. A problem like that always happens when you're constantly pushing the stuff out. There were mistakes, no question about it. In retrospect, I'm sorry that there were some things that we did — we just got a little wild. When you're trying to outdo yourself week after week, issue after issue, sometimes you overstep the bounds and we were beginning to stretch our taste standards a bit in order to get all the stories written. That was wrong, because we got into areas that were really kind of tacky, like that baseball game

thing."

"None of them ever bothered me in terms of being too horrible." he adds. The only thing that bothered me was bad taste. After all, why should a well written, well conceived horror story bother you? To me that's not bad taste; it may curdle your blood, but that's exactly what we were trying to do. That means you should be proud that you were successful."

While the GhouLunatics and their off-the-shroud humor put the reader at one remove from the mayhem in the stories, a number of EC's most vivid stories found in the Suspense books dealt with serious issues of racial hatred, religious intolerance, and sexual abuse; themes seldom touched in *any* media in the early 50s.

A young soldier returns from Korea ("In Gratitude . . ." SSS No. 11). He has lost an arm in a grenade exploison in which a friend died to save him. Since the friend had no family, the young soldier has brought the body back to his hometown for burial. But when he asks to visit the grave before the welcoming ceremonies, his parents confess that the friend is buried "over in Greendale."

"We couldn't go through with it, Joey!" cries his mother, and his father adds, "The whole town was on our necks, our friends ... the family ... I had my business to consider, son. We couldn't do it."

Standing alone that afternoon on the bunting-draped high school stage Joey faces his friends and family. "I gave my right hand defending freedom and equality and I was *proud* of it ... I *was* proud, that is until today. I had a buddy in Korea. We ate together ... slept together ... laughed together ... cried together. We fought for democracy together ... he gave his life for that cause ... and he saved mine in doing it. He threw himself on a live grenade ... and got blown up ... to save me. But when his body was sent back here, it wasn't good enough to be buried in Fairlawn Cemetery. It wasn't good enough because its skin wasn't the right color. ... Well that grenade that tore that skin to pieces didn't know its color ... didn't care if it was white or black. What did he die for? You say you're proud of me. Well, I'm not proud of you. I'm ashamed of you ... and for you!"

Not only is the message powerful, but it sustains the reader's

From Shock SuspenStories No. 5, "Hate," by Wood.
© 1979 by William M. Gaines.

From Shock SuspenStories No. 8, "The Assault," by Wood. © 1979 by William M. Gaines.

interest through 13 panels focused on a single character delivering a monologue. Wood varies distance and point of view in his illustrations, changing the focus like a movie camera, always keeping an American flag in the panel as an ironic counterpoint to Joey's bitter words.

"Hate"(SSS No. 5) also drawn by Wood, is a brutal story of religious prejudice in which a neighborhood gang tries to force a Jewish family to move out. Wood-illustrated stories "The Assault" (SSS No. 8) and "A Kind of Justice" (SSS No. 16) painted opposite sides of the same sexual coin, and drew reams of mail, both pro and con, from readers.

Such stories jolted the reader's complacency and his assurance that in real life justice would prevail. The horror stories, and many of the lurid crime tales were too farfetched to befall the average reader, but these plots struck close to home, and were definitely unnerving. "That's a different kind of bother," says Feldstein. "That's a bother in terms of feeling badly for some innocent person, and I can understand that. We tried a lot of things that were unorthodox for their day, like having innocent people die and criminals get away with their crimes."

Horror and crime were their bread and butter, but the editors always maintained that "We at EC are proudest of our Science-Fiction." EC SF *was* good. Parsecs ahead of any competition, the EC stories were lovingly scripted by Feldstein and brilliantly rendered by the sceince fiction artists. They have held their own against the science fiction book market over the last 25 years, and are just as readable now as the day they appeared on the stands.

For the most part following the EC formula of psychological surprise and unexpected denouement, they were on a consistently higher level than Buck Rogers' ray gun and rocket thrillers. Feldstein preferred to explore more subtle questions — how would man act in the void of outer space? What treatment would man receive at the hands — or tentacles — of aliens?

The "As ye vivisect so shall ye be vivisected" theme was repeated in stories like "The Probers" (WS No. 8) where a space scientist who has been experimenting on small lab animals ends up on the other end of an alien's scalpel. Other turnaround stories, "A Gobl Is a Knog's Best Friend" (WS No. 12 Wood) and "Bum Steer" (WS No. 15 Orlando), offered the unpleasant possibilities of powerful aliens turning humans into pets — or pate'.

The chances for snafus and misunderstandings even among friendly or neutral races were legion. In "Chewed Out" (WS No. 12 Orlando) aliens being talked down by a ham radio operator do land in the midst of a jubilant crowd — but are so tiny that ship and crew are lost in a vat of sauerkraut on a hot dog stand, and, adding injury to insult, are served up and eaten by an oblivious general.

Unfortunate earthmen managed to land on a giant gaming table, risking annihilation in a cosmic crap game ("The Die Is Cast!" WF No. 12 Wood), touched down with a bang on a child's balloon at an alien carnival ("Snap Ending!" WS No. 18) and ended ingloriously as vermin in the salad of a fastidious six-legged diner ("Revulsion!" WF No. 15 Orlando).

From Weird Science No. 18, "Snap Ending," by Williamson. © 1979 by William M. Gaines.

From Weird Science No. 6, "Sinking Of The Titanic!," by Wood. © 1979 by William M. Gaines.

From Weird Science No. 15, "Bum Steer!," by Orlando. © 1979 by William M. Gaines.

From Weird Science No. 12, "Chewed Out," by Orlando. © 1979 by William M. Gaines.

THE UTTERLY FANTASTIC EVENTS LEADING UP TO THE

DESTRUCTION OF THE EARTH!

From Weird Science No. 14/3, by Feldstein.
© 1979 by William M. Gaines.

Feldstein tackled the paradox of time travel in such fine stories as "Why Papa Left Home" (WS No. 11 Orlando) in which the protagonist discovers that he is his own father who deserted his mother 22 years ago, and "Sinking of the Titanic!" (WS No. 6 Wood) in which attempts to return to save passngers on that fatal night causes the original collision.

Feldstein himself illustrated a set of five "holocaust" or "end of the world" stories in 1950. In "Destruction of the Earth" (WS No. 14), the entire world is sucked into the sun's inferno. Its absence is explained to a class of wide-eyed students by their instructor who recalls "I and other elders here on Mars remember it well . . . glowing brightly in our southern skies!"

Desperately searching for a plot gimmick for *Weird Science* No. 11, editors Gaines and Feldstein dream up a weapon already under secret production by the U.S. Government ("Cosmic Ray Bomb Explosion" WF No. 14). Whisked to the Pentagon, Al and Bill are cleared by a loyalty test, but it is too late.. . . . Scientists deep in the Kremlin have already studied their copies of WS No. 11. As Al and Bill stroll by the Capitol dome, the Russian bomb falls.

Basil Wolverton did an annihilation story for *Marvel Tales* No. 102 a year later, and a glance at "The End of the World" in this issue will show the similarity of his art and Feldstein's.

Future technologies and human-alien liasons inspired baroque sex plots that went far beyond the triangle-adultery-murder themes of the crime and horror books. A jealous father who slips his daughter's fiance an overdose of sex hormones ("Transformation Completed" WS No. 10 Wood) is chagrined when the wedding goes on as scheduled — after she also takes a few injections. Her daughter, he conceded, "made a very handsome groom . . . and Lee, a lovely bride."

"Arnold, Baby! I wish you'd hurry up and change . . . so that things can be normal," pleads the newly-bearded bride whose horrified groom has just discovered that Gastropodians change sex for the second half of their lives.("There'll Be Some Changes Made!" WS No. 14 Wood). The disgusted bride in "Right on the Button" (WS No. 19 Elder) takes matters into her own hands, killing her husband on their wedding night when she discovers the loathsome alien has a navel. EC sex isn't much fun in the crime/horror present, and promises to be even more appalling in the SF future, when lovely women will turn out to be butterfly creatures who deposit their eggs to feed and grow in their human lovers. . . ("The Maidens Cried" WS No. 10 Wood).

In 1952 Feldstein began a series of adaptations of Ray Bradbury's science fiction stories which evoked a heavy reader response ranging from "I thought a comic version would dim the Bradbury brilliance, but it comes across like an arc lamp" to "very interesting . . . but a bit over my head" (WS No. 19). One surprised reader was Bradbury, who had been unaware of his part in the springboard system.

In a 1977 letter Bradbury says "There's not much to say. EC stole from me. I caught them at it. They admitted the crime. They then proceeded to adapt 30 or more of my stories and did some fine work at it, which pleased me. Gaines has a nice sense of humor about the whole

From Weird Science No. 10, "The Maidens Cried," by Wood. © 1979 by William M. Gaines.

From Weird Fantasy No. 13, 1952, "Home To Stay," by Wood. © 1979 by William M. Gaines.

plagiarism bit. Ask him to show you a copy of my Christian letter, where I pointed out their crime, nicely, and asked for a small check which they immediately sent."

Bradbury's Christian letter of April 19, 1952 read, "Dear Sir: Just a note to remind you of an oversight. You have not as yet sent on the check for $50.00 to cover the use of secondary rights on my two stories, "The Rocket Man" and "Kaleidoscope" which appeared in your *Weird Fantasy* May-June '52 No. 13, with the cover-all title of "Home to Stay." I feel that this was probably overlooked in the general confusion of office-work, and look forward to your payment in the near future. My very best wishes to you."

Bradbury-EC relations remained cordial, and Bradbury was paid $25 each for adaptations of such superb pieces as "I, Rocket" (WS No. 20 Williamson), "King of the Grey Spaces!" (WF No. 19 Severin & Elder), "The Million Year Picnic"

(WF No. 21 Severin & Elder), "Mars Is Heaven!" (WS No. 18 Wood), "There Will Come Soft Rains . . ." (WF No. 17 Wood), and "The Long Years!" (WS No. 17 Wood) in addition to horror classics "The Small Assassin!" (SSS No. 7 Evans), "The Screaming Woman!" (CSS No. 15 Kamen), and "The October Game" (SSS No. 9 Kamen) for the other books.

Bradbury also wrote several letters to the Cosmic Correspondence pages, one of them to praise "Judgment Day!" (WF No. 18 Orlando-reprinted in ISF No. 33) one of the most famous EC science fiction stories that Bradbury felt "should be required reading for every man, woman, and child in the United States." "I realize you have been battling, in the sea of comics, to try to do better things," he wrote. "You've done a splendid thing here, and deserves the highest commendation."

The story begins as the space--suited Earthman Tarlton arrives to inspect Cybrinia, planet of mechanical life, to see if the inhabitants are ready to receive the wonders and greatness of Earth. An orange robot steps forward to guide Tarlton around the spacious streets and gleaming plant where orange citizens are made and educated.

But what of the *blue* robots, asks Tarlton. Reluctantly, the orange guide leads him aboard a mobile-bus — where the blue citizens sit in the back — and takes him to Blue Town and the shabby plant where blue robots are constructed and educated on inferior machines. Tarlton points out that only the blue sheathing differentiates the two groups. "Would you deny that the differences between you and the blue robots are taught . . . in your educator?"

The orange guide replies unhappily, "You are lecturing me as though all this were my fault, Tarlton! This existed before I was made! What can I do about it? I'm only one robot." "I'm sorry, my friend!" answers Tarlton. "Yes. I

know you are only one robot. That is why I am afraid that Cybrinia is not ready to join the Galactic Republic." But he leaves the orange robot with words of comfort. "For awhile on Earth, it looked like there was no hope! But when mankind on Earth learned to live together, real progress first began, the universe was suddenly ours."

The great ship rockets up into the void, "and inside the ship, the man removed his space helmet and shook his head, and the instrument lights made the beads of perspiration on his dark skin twinkle like distant stars. . ."

While thousands were moved by "Judgment Day," comics Code watchdogs in 1954 attempted to keep Gaines from reprinting it in *Incredible Science Fiction* No. 33 "on the basis that the perspiration on the black's face in the last panel was offensive." (The slot was open because the Association had already rejected Angelo Torres' "An Eye for an Eye" — later printed in Gelman's *Horror Comics of the*

From Weird Fantasy No. 18, "Judgement Day!," by Orlando.
© 1979 by William M. Gaines.

1950s.) Gaines recalls that he threatened, "'I'm going to sue you if you don't let it through,' and they said, 'All right.' They let it through and that was the end of my association with *the Association.*"

While Feldstein was busy with the science fiction, crime and horror books, Harvey Kurtzman was offering a serious look at war in *Two-Fisted Tales and Frontline Combat.* His books were the antithesis of the "Captain Kill Crushes the Yellow Peril" fare of the '40s. Kurtzman looked at war from Caesar's legions to the Korean conflict, examining the men who run the wars, the dog soldiers who fight them, and the hapless civilians over whose homelands and homes the wars are fought.

The first issues of *Two-Fisted Tales* were straight adventure books with standard spy tales like "Hong Kong Intrigue" (TFT No. 18) which was burdened with descriptions like "evil-slanting eyes" and "obscenely fat Oriental" (and was probably the Gaines-Feldstein effort), but with the advent of the Korean War, the book went entirely to war stories, adding *Frontline Combat* in 1951.

"I think that my constant preoccupation was to put down some form of truth," Kurtzman explains. "At that time there were war stories in comic books, and they were just the worst kind of crap that you can imagine. Bad in the sense that they glamorized war. They idealized, glamorized, and made a joke of this horrible business of war."

"In any case, I was depressed by the lack of accuracy in war fiction, and I was determined to make war fiction reflect reality. That's been my underlying platform in a sense; I am constantly intrigued by areas where I sense that great lie fantasies are being built out of proportion. So the direction that my war stories took was not satirical at all, but I was traveling a different route to arrive at the same place — a criticism of popular war attitudes in fiction and print."

Kurtzman's war is not glamorous. Qualities of bravery, cowardice, cruelty, compassion are individual — not racial or national — characteristics. And brave or cowardly, the individual's fate depends on chance; a stray bullet, a moment's hesitation, and one man's life is cut short, another's spared. Kurtzman presented the enemy as human, and his even-handed treatment of all participants gave his stories an unusual and disturbing angle, and prevented the reader from making easy judgments.

From Frontline Combat No. 4, "Combat Medic!," by Davis. © 1979 by William M. Gaines.

Kurtzman researched his stories meticulously, even to the point of using authentic Korean phrases in "Combat Medic!" (FC No. 4 Davis). He and legman Jerry DeFuccio (who also wrote EC fillers) spent countless hours aloft in experimental aircraft, below decks in submarines, and immersed in the American History room at the Fifth Avenue Library. "Kurtzman wanted you to really absorb all the atmosphere through your pores," DeFuccio says. "He hated anything

From Two-Fisted Tales No. 35, by Davis.
© 1979 by William M. Gaines.

that was watered down. If you drew a weapon, it wouldn't be from another drawing or plate, it had to be from some kind of a scale model that had every bolt and rivet."

Kurtzman's accuracy paid off, both in historical ambiance and emotional impact. The reader might delude himself that the events in "Hate" or "A Kind of Justice" never happen, but he couldn't deny Kurtzman's historicity. Stonewall Jackson *was* accidentally killed by the very men who loved him, whether it happened like "Stonewall Jackson!" (FC No. 5) or "Chancellorsville!" (TF No. 35), and the 442nd Combat Team of Japanese Americans were fighting against the Germans in 1944 (FC No. 5).

Kurtzman experimented with several special issues, FC No. 7 and No. 12 on Iwo Jima and the Air Force; TFT No. 26 on "The Changjin Reservoir." He had hoped to cover the entire Civil War in

seven books, but only three of these were completed, FC No. 9, and TFT Nos. 31 and 35. All were exhaustively researched and executed with the legwork of Jerry DeFuccio, the aid of the American History room's Mr. Vigilante, and the advice of historian Fletcher Pratt.

Whether it was his quest for perfection or his tendency to worry, Kurtzman exercised greater control over the finished product and took longer to complete his books than did Feldstein. "He was looking for perfection in a ten cent comic book, which is very nice, but it wasn't economically feasible," comments Gaines.

Kurtzman's tight control was not always well-received by the artist. "Sometimes my roughs inspired the artist, sometimes they made the artist angry because they boxed him in," he says. For a highly creative artist to take one of my roughs and work from it took a certain amount of discipline, because creativity does not like limitations and my roughs would limit things constantly.

The irony of Kurtzman's war plots was turned to satire and parody in *MAD,* that breath of fresh humor in the comic desert. For the first time the comic book reader saw his everyday surroundings — including comic books — lampooned by a writer who included him in the joke. The first issue satirized the very stories that EC was publishing, and went on in later issues to tackle movies, advertising, television, the classics, super markets and the McCarthy hearings which Kurtzman courageously took on in "What's My Shine!"

"The stuff I liked to do generally was provocative," he says. "I don't consider myself a good humorist, but what I did, that I think I identify with my stuff — and I can point it out in the old *MAD*s — was that I did thought-provoking humor."

What, for example, Kurtzman asked, would happen if comic strip violence was carried over into real life? His answer was "Bringing Back Father" (No. 17) in which Elder and Krigstein did simultaneous parodies of George McManus' "Bringing Up Father." Elder, the perfect mimic, copied the original strip on one page, while on the facing page Krigstein realistically rendered the bloody homelife of characters who actually threw crockery and punches indiscriminately. The contrast is convincingly horrific, and as gruesome as the average EC tale of domesticity in the shock stories.

Davis, Elder, and Wood were the principal *MAD* artists —22 (1955) was, in fact, an Elder tour-de-force: "Special Art Issue: The Bill Elder Story," taking the artist from "Childhood" to "Senility" with a Kurtzman cover and the rest drawn entirely by Elder.

MAD parodied movie and comic book favorites in such classics as Wood's "Superduperman!" (No. 4), "Black and Blue Hawks!" (No. 5),

From Mad No. 5, by Wood. © 1979 by E.C. Publications. Inc.

"Flesh Garden!" (No. 11), "Prince Violent!" (No. 13), "Gopo Gossum!" (No. 23); Davis' "Lone Stranger!" (No. 3), "Mark Trade!" (No. 12), " 'Hah! Noon!' " (No. 9), Elder's "Dragged Net!" (No. 3), "Ping Pong!" (No. 6), "Woman Wonder! (No. 10), "Starchie" (No. 12); and Severin's "Melvin of the Apes!" (No. 6).

These stories alone would make MAD a memorable creation, but Kurtzman went further in the manipulation of his material with cover designs that mimicked the "Racing Form" or a school composition book, and experimentation with unusual visuals in the stories themselves. Jack Davis, for example, illustrated "Captain TVideo" (No. 15) entirely in black and white TV frames overlaid with black interference lines, while "3-Dimensions" (No. 12) brought the wonders of that fad to the 2-dimensional page.

"When I look around me I seem to find that there's much in this little world of ours that looks silly," comments Kurtzman. "The way people carry on. And that's where my material came from. I made fun of what the material was. Of its silliness. Of, in certain cases, its lack of truthfulness, its contradictions. Satire is the kind of thing where you really come to bear on the immediate things that are happening in the world."

MAD lasted 23 issues as a comic book before increasing censorship pressures on the whole EC line and Kurtzman-Gaines conflicts determined that it be changed to the black and white magazine format that is still going strong today in its 206th issue. MAD spawned a number of imitators, the best of which was EC's own Panic which appeared on the stands in late 1953 and was edited by the prolific Al Feldstein along with his six other magazines.

Feldstein used other writers on Panic, among them Jack Mendelson together with the familiar artists Davis, Elder, Feldstein, Kamen, Orlando, Wolverton (who appeared in MAD Nos. 10, 11, and 17), and Wood. Panic had the distinction of being banned in Boston — indeed, throughout the entire Commonwealth — because of Bill Elder's lunatic rendering of "The Night Before Christmas" in issue No. 1 which featured a "Just Divorced" sign on the back of Santa's sleigh.

In the February 14, 1954 issue of the Hartford Courant, the first of a four-part feature by Irving M. Kravsow appeared under the banner headline "Depravity for Children — 10 Cents a Copy!" Mr. Kravsow went on to describe the offending Panic No. 1 as "having a reprint of the lovely Christmas poem "The Night Before Christmas" illustrated by gross and obscene drawings that defy descriptions." (Mr. Kravsow's decriptive faculties would have been permanently impaired had the illustrator been S. Clay Wilson rather than Will Elder.)

The spirit of McCarthy was abroad in the land, and comic books were fair game for the censorious. "It was really a frightening time," says Feldstein. "It was the time of the red herring, and parents were looking for someone who could do their job. There were also, I think, a lot of ulterior motives in terms of opening the door to censorship."

Censorship was nothing new to comics, having been on the horizon since the mid- to late 40's, and EC was involved in all with three regulartory periods. Covers of the early EC books carry a small star labeled

"Conforms to the Comics Code" under the logo "Authorized A.C.M.P." This Association of Comics Magazine Publishers was headed by one Henry Schultz, attorney and sole employee, whose job consisted of reading books and suggesting changes. When he suggested too many changes and sales went down, that was the end of A C.M.P.

A second period of censorship, according to Gaines, was during a time of difficulty with wholesalers when his distributor, the head of Leader News, insisted that his son, another attorney named Stanley Estrow, have the power to order changes. Craig's VOH No. 32 cover and story "Out of His Head!" must have been censored during this period, after Schultz and before the Code. An advance ad for this book ran uncensored in TftC No. 37 and showed a corpse with a meat cleaver wedged in its skull about to confront its killer. By the time No. 32 had been published the cleaver had been opaqued, leaving the corpse with an ambiguous nimbus about its head throughout the story.

The third and final period of censorship for EC came with the introduction of the Comics Code Authority in September 1954, the year that earlier saw the publication of Dr. Fredric Wertham's *Seduction of the Innocent* and the Hearings Before the Subcommittee to Investigate Juvenile Delinquency. Gaines testified voluntarily at these hearings, and said in part, "I was the first publisher in these United States to publish horror comics. I am responsible, I started them. Some may not like them. That is a matter of personal taste. It would be just as difficult to explain the

harmless thrill of a horror story to a Dr. Wertham as it would be to explain the sublimity of love to a frigid old maid. My father was proud of the comics he published, and I am proud of the comics I publish. We use the best writers, the best artists; we spare nothing to make each magazine, each story, each page, a work of art."

Later he asked, "What are we

The Vault Of Horror No. 32; Craig cover. © 1979 by William M. Gaines.

afraid of? Are we afraid of our own children? Do we forget that they are citizens too, and entitled to the essential freedom too? Or do we think our children so evil, so vicious, so simple-minded, that it takes a comic magazine story of murder to set them to murder, of robbery to set them to robbery?"

In the end, the Senate hearings did not produce the Code; the industry itself set up the Comics Code Authority under former New York City Magistrate Charles F. Murphy, and allowed cooperative publishers to stamp their books

"Approved by the Comics Code Authority." Says Feldstein, "I've always maintained that the comic book industry castrated itself. The industry ran scared, and the whole thing was terrible."

The Code, which prohibited the very words "horror" and "terror," together with Gaines' existing financial and distribution problems, dealt a body blow to the New Trend books. The final issues of the horror comics in 1954 printed "IN MEMORIAM" which read in part, "As a result of the hysterical, injudicious, and unfounded charges leveled at crime and horror comics, many retailers and wholesalers throughout the country have been intimidated into refusing to handle this type of magazine. We are forced to capitulate. We give up. We've had it!"

"But enough mush!" the editors continue. "This is not only an obituary notice; it is also a birth announcement!" EC rebounded from the depths of 1954 with its New Directions books for 1955: *Aces High, Extra!, Impact, M.D., Psychoanalysis* and *Valor.* They still had *MAD, Panic, Incredible Science Fiction* and — retitled from *Weird Science-Fantasy* for its final four issues — and the swashbuckling *Piracy,* which had been introduced late in 1954 and was not, strictly speaking a New Directions book.

Feldstein edited all the new books except *Extra!* which was handled by Johnny Craig. Although the new books drew upon the same artists and added the writing skills of Carl Wessler and Jack Oleck, the New Directions died within the year. There was talent, but it was fettered by the code restrictions, and the cream of the readership, Gaines feels, had been turned away from comics by the sensationalism of the censors. The first issue of each title was published without the code seal but wholesale resistance forced Gaines to capitulate. Under the seal the books still did poorly, perhaps because of continued difficulties with wholesalers perhaps because the old spirit was gone.

Krigstein's "Master Race" in *Impact* 1 was certainly equal to the best of the New Trend, but more typical of the new scripts was "Spads Were Trump" (AH No. 5) also drawn by Krigstein, WWI tale in which an American ace named Muller was forced to shoot down a German ace who, improbably, is his

From Impact No. 1, "Master Race," by Krigstein.
© 1979 by William M. Gaines.

brother. The plotting is slack, the characters one-dimensional, and there is no explanation, either psychological or logistical, for the national allegiance of either brother.

In a last-ditch attempt to avoid the Code restrictions, Gaines launched the short-lived Adult Picto-Fiction books *Crime Illustrated, Confessions Illustrated, Shock Illustrated,* and *Terror Illustrated.* The four were published in *MAD*-sized magazine format, sold for a quarter, and contained black and white pictures with a block of text rather than balloon dialogue. Freed of the Code, the Picto-fiction dealt even more explicitly with themes of infidelity, sexual aberration, and abnormal psychology. Stories like "Sin Doll" (SI No. 3 Kamen), "I Sold My Baby" (CoI No. 2 Kamen) and "The Lipstick Killer" (SI No. 2 Crandall) were not bad reading, and the quality of illustration was high, but the format was static, and the content perhaps too unusual for public taste.

In any case the financial bottom had dropped out of EC. *Confessions, Crime* and *Terror* lasted only 2 issues, and 250,000 copies of *Shock* No. 3 were destroyed because there was no money to bind them. Perhaps a scant hundred were saved and hand-bound. There were bleak days at EC before the infant *MAD* magazine took hold and rose phoenix-like from the comic ahses. Kurtzman edited the first five magazine issues (No. 24-No. 28) and then following his departure after financial disagreements with Gaines Feldstein took over and continues as *MAD* editor today.

The question inevitably arises what might have been the fate of the New Trend books if the Code

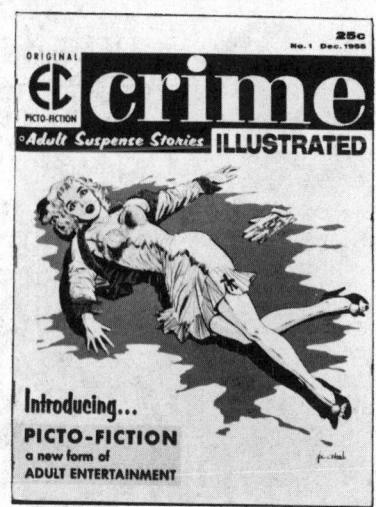

Crime Illustrated No. 1. © 1979 by William M. Gaines.

had not killed them? "The horror books never did badly," notes Gaines ' Right up to the end the horror books made money." There were plans even to the end to add a fourth horror book – *The Crypt of Terror* was to be resurrected – and ads for it had already appeared in *The Vault of Horror* No. 40. There were sales problems with the science fiction, but neither Gaines nor Feldstein had any intention of abandoning them.

"That was our trick," confides Gaines. "We published everything we wanted to publish with the horror profits, which were considerable right up to the end." Adds Feldstein, 'We were always going to keep the science fiction going, just for our own ego. I loved writing them, and editing them, and I loved doing the covers. We weren't going to let them go even though they weren't doing too well. The horror certainly made it up."

As for the future, Feldstein speculates that EC might have gone on to develop even better material. "I

THE VAULT OF HORROR!

HER! HER! HOW Y'ALL, LI'L OL' HARPIES AND HOBGOBLINS? PARDON MAH SOUTHERN-TYPE DROOL, CHILLUN, BUT IF YOU'LL JUST HUSTLE INTO THE VAULT OF HORROR SO'S I CAN CLOSE THE CREAKY DOOR AND KEEP OUT THAT FILTHY FRESH AIR, YOUR VAULT-KEEPER WILL LEAD YOU ON A TOUR THROUGH SOME STINKING, MIASMIC SWAMPS...THAT IS, IF IT'S ALL RIGHT BAYOU? YOU REMEMBER DRUSILLA, DON'T YOU? SHE'S MY ONLY COMPANION HERE IN THE VAULT, OTHER THAN THE RATS! TOGETHER WE DUG UP THIS SORROWFUL SELECTION OF SWAMPLAND SPOONING CONCERNING A LONELY LAD AND HIS LACHRYMOSE (LACHRYMOSE? WHAT DAT??) LOVE FOR A LASS. I CALL IT...

DEADLY BELOVED!

From The Vault Of Horror No. 39, Craig art. © 1979 by
William M. Gaines. Right up to the end there were plans
for a fourth horror book. Even the Vault Keeper got his
own assistant, DRUSILLA (Above), who unfortunately
was buried along with the rest of the line.

think there could have been an improvement — I think we would have perfected our art as we went along. The material was good and we were developing good writers. The whole area was wide open. In those days Bill always had a certain ambition to make money, but he also wanted to enjoy what he was doing."

Enjoyment was the word during those five years — and integrity, imagination, innovation, and talent. The EC days are gone, but time, ironically, has brought respectability. In a typical EC-style ending,

in 25 years *MAD* has gone from outlaw to institution, transforming Gaines from dealer in depravity to kindly humor publisher. But scratch the surface, and EC addicts are still acrawl. Fanzine *Squa Tront* is still in print as of this writing, EC artists are in demand at cons, collectors are buying EC books at premium prices, while the beautiful Cochran reprints should assure that they will be both available and affordable for future generations. Ec lives. Spa Fon!

—————————

Abbott & Costello #10, ©STJ   Ace Comics #21, © DMP   Action Comics #1, © DC

The correct title listing for each comic book can be determined by consulting the indicia (publication data) on the beginning interior pages of the comic. The official title is determined by those words of the title in capital letters only, and not by what is on the cover.

Titles are listed in this book as if they were one word, ignoring spaces, hyphens, and apostrophes, to make finding titles easier.

A-1 (See A-One)

ABBIE AN' SLATS (--With Becky #1-4) (See Fight for Love, Treasury of Comics, & United
1940 - 1948 (Reprints)   Comics)
United Features Syndicate

	Good	Fine	Mint
Single Series #25,28('40)	9.00	18.00	27.00
#1(1947)	4.00	8.00	12.00
2-4: #3 reprints from Sparkler #68-72			
	2.50	5.00	7.50

ABBOTT AND COSTELLO (--Comics)
1948 - 56 (Mort Drucker art in most issues)
St. John Publishing Co.

#1	5.00	10.00	15.00
2-9(#8-8/49)	3.00	6.00	9.00
10-Son of Sinbad story by Kubert (not a reprint of S.O.S. #1).(8/50)			
	4.00	8.00	12.00
11-20	1.75	3.50	5.25
21-30	1.40	2.80	4.20
31-40	1.00	2.00	3.00
3-D #1 (11/53)	5.00	10.00	15.00

ABBOTT AND COSTELLO (TV)
Feb, 1968 - #22, Aug, 1971 (Hanna-Barbera)
Charlton Comics

#1	.40	.80	1.20
2-10	.25	.50	.75
11-22		.25	.50

ABC (See America's Best TV Comics)

ABRAHAM LINCOLN LIFE STORY
1958   (25¢)
Dell Publishing Co.

#1	2.50	5.00	7.50

ABSENT-MINDED PROFESSOR, THE (See 4-Color Comics #1199)

ACE COMICS
April, 1937 - #151, Oct-Nov, 1949
David McKay Publications

#1-Jungle Jim by Alex Raymond, Krazy Kat			
begin	60.00	120.00	180.00
2	25.00	50.00	75.00

	Good	Fine	Mint
3-5	17.50	35.00	52.50
6-10	12.00	24.00	36.00
11-The Phantom begins	12.00	24.00	36.00
12-25	9.00	18.00	27.00
26-Origin Prince Valiant	35.00	70.00	105.00
27-30	7.00	14.00	21.00
31-34: #37-Krazy Kat ends	6.00	12.00	18.00
41-50	5.00	10.00	15.00
51-60	4.00	8.00	12.00
61-90	3.25	6.50	9.75
91-100	2.50	5.00	7.50
101-127	2.00	4.00	6.00
128-Brick Bradford begins	2.00	4.00	6.00
129-133	1.75	3.50	5.25
134-Last Prince Valiant	1.75	3.50	5.25
135-The Lone Ranger begins	1.75	3.50	5.25
136-151	1.75	3.50	5.25

ACE KELLY (See Tops Comics)

ACES HIGH
Mar-Apr, 1955 - #5, Nov-Dec, 1955
E.C. Comics

#1-Not approved by code	10.00	20.00	30.00
2-5	6.00	12.00	18.00

NOTE: *All have stories by Davis, Evans, Krigstein, & Wood; Evans covers #1-5.*

ACTION ADVENTURE (War)
June, 1955 - #4, Oct, 1955
Gillmore Magazines

V1#2-4	.60	1.20	1.80

ACTION COMICS
June, 1938 - Present
National Per. Publ./Detective Comics/DC

#1-Origin & 1st app. Superman by Siegel & Shuster, Marco Polo, Tex Thompson, Pep Morgan, Chuck Dawson & Scoop Scanlon; intro. Zatara; reprinted in Famous 1st Edition. Superman story is missing 4 pgs. which was included when reprinted in Superman #1.   2100.00 5250.00 8400.00
(Prices vary widely on this book)
#1(1976)Paper cover, 16pgs. in color; reprints complete Superman story from #1('38) (Giveaway)(NOTE: *A large number turned up in N.Y. in 1978 causing a set-back in price*)

2	.20	.40	.60
2		600.00	1200.00	1800.00
3 (Scarce)	450.00	900.00	1350.00
4	300.00	600.00	900.00
5 (Rare)	450.00	900.00	1350.00
6-1st app. Jimmy Olsen (called office boy)			

1

	Good	Fine	Mint
	250.00	500.00	750.00
7,10-Superman covers	250.00	500.00	750.00
8,9	225.00	450.00	675.00

11,12,14:#14-Clip Carson begins, ends #41
110.00 220.00 330.00
13-Superman cover; last Scoop Scanlon
150.00 300.00 450.00
15-Superman cover 125.00 250.00 375.00
16 80.00 160.00 240.00
17-Superman cover; last Marco Polo
80.00 160.00 240.00
18-Origin 3 Aces 60.00 120.00 180.00
19,20-Superman covers 70.00 140.00 210.00
21,22,24,25 40.00 80.00 120.00
23-1st app. Luthor & Black Pirate by Moldoff
50.00 100.00 150.00
26-30 27.50 55.00 82.50
31,32 22.00 44.00 66.00
33-Origin Mr. America 25.00 50.00 75.00
34-40: #37-Origin Congo Bill. #40-Last Black
Pirate 22.00 44.00 66.00
41 22.00 44.00 66.00
42-Origin Vigilante; Bob Daley becomes Fatman; Black Pirate ends 25.00 50.00 75.00
43-50: Intro. Stuff #45 17.50 35.00 52.50
51 15.00 30.00 45.00
52-Fatman & Mr. America become the Ameri-
commandos; origin Vigilante retold
17.50 35.00 52.50
53-60: #56-Last Fatman. #58-Kubert Vigilante
begins, ends #70 15.00 30.00 45.00
61-70: #63-Last 3 Aces 12.00 24.00 36.00
71-80: #74-Last Mr. America. #80-2nd app.
Mr. Mxyztplk 9.00 18.00 27.00
81-90 8.00 16.00 24.00
91-100 7.00 14.00 21.00
101-120 6.50 13.00 19.50
121-140: #127-Vigilante by Kubert; Tommy
Tomorrow begins. #135,136,138-Zatara by
Kubert 6.00 12.00 18.00
141-160 5.00 10.00 15.00
161-180 4.00 8.00 12.00
181-200: #191-Intro. Janu in Congo Bill.
#198-Last Vigilante 3.50 7.00 10.50
201-220 3.00 6.00 9.00
221-240: #224-1st Golden Gorilla story
2.50 5.00 7.50
241-251: #242-Origin & 1st app. Brainiac(7/58)
#248-Congo Bill becomes Congorilla. #251-
Last Tommy Tomorrow 2.00 4.00 6.00
252-Origin & 1st app. Supergirl and Metallo
17.50 35.00 52.50
253,255-260 1.75 3.50 5.25
254-2nd app. Bizarro, 1st Bizarro World story
2.50 5.00 7.50
261-270: #261-Last Congorilla; origin Streaky

	Good	Fine	Mint
the Super Cat	1.50	3.00	4.50

271-290: #276-1st app. Brainiac 5, Phantom
Girl & Triplicate Girl. #280-Congorilla
app. 1.20 2.40 3.60
291-300: #292-1st Superhorse. #293-Origin
Comet 1.00 2.00 3.00
301-320 .75 1.50 2.25
321-340: #334-Giant G-20 (Origin Supergirl).
#340-Origin, 1st app. Parasite
.60 1.20 1.80
(80 pg. Giant G-20) 1.00 2.00 3.00
341-360: #341-Triplicate Girl becomes Duo Dam-
sel. #347-Giant Supergirl G-33. #360-Giant
Supergirl G-45 .50 1.00 1.50
(80 pg. Giant G-33, G-45) .75 1.50 2.25
361-380: #373-Giant Supergirl G-57. #376-Last
Supergirl in Action. #377-Legion begins
.40 .80 1.20
(80 pg. Giant G-57) .65 1.35 2.00
381-402: #392-Last Legion in Action. Saturn
Girl gets new costume. #393-402-All Superman issues .30 .60 .90
403-420: #403-1st 52pg. ish; last #413. #411-
Origin Eclipso(reprt.). #413-Last 25¢ ish;
Metamorpho begins; ends #418. #419-Intro.
Human Target .25 .50 .75
421-424: #422 & 423-Origin Human Target; Green
Arrow app. #421,424 .20 .40 .60
425-Adams art; Atom begins .80 1.60 2.40
426-436,438-442,444-448,450 .20 .40 .60
437,443-100pg. Giants .60 1.20 1.80
449-68pg. ish .40 .80 1.20
451-460: #458-Last Green Arrow
.20 .40 .60
461-490: #467-Last Atom .25 .50
491 .20 .40
U.S. Navy Giveaway #1 (1944)-Regular comic
format 25.00 50.00 75.00
--Special Edition #2(1944)-U.S. Navy Giveaway (68 pgs.) Regular comic format
25.00 50.00 75.00

NOTE: *Supergirl's origin in #262,280,285,291,
305,309. Adams covers-#356,358,359,361-64,
366,367,370-74,377-79 (inks), 398-400,402,
404-06,419,466,468,473,485. Infantino cov-
ers-#396,397; stories-#419,437. Bob Kane's
Clip Carson-#14-41. Meskin art-#42-121
(most). Toth stories-#406,407,413.*

ACTION MINIATURE
1946
National Periodical Publications

No#-Vigilante story based on movie serial
7.00 14.00 21.00

Action Comics #17, © DC

Action Comics #28, © DC

Action Comics #86, © DC

Adventure Comics #34, © DC

Adventure Comics #47, © DC

Adventure Comics #56, © DC

ACTUAL CONFESSIONS (Formerly Love Adventures)
#13, October, 1952
Atlas Comics (MPI)

	Good	Fine	Mint
#13	.75	1.50	2.25

ACTUAL ROMANCES
Oct, 1949 - #2, 1949 (52 pgs.)
Marvel Comics (IPS)

	Good	Fine	Mint
#1	1.50	3.00	4.50
2	.80	1.60	2.40

ADAM AND EVE
1975
Spire Christian Comics (Fleming H. Revell Co.)

By Al Hartley	.25	.50	.75

ADAM-12 (TV)
Dec, 1973 - #10, Feb, 1976
Gold Key

#1	.25	.50	.75
2-10	.15	.30	.45

ADDAMS FAMILY (TV)
Oct, 1974 - #3, Apr, 1975 (Hanna-Barbera)
Gold Key

#1-3	.25	.50	.75

ADLAI STEVENSON
Dec, 1966
Dell Publishing Co.

#12-007-612-Life story	2.00	4.00	6.00

ADULT TALES OF TERROR ILL. (See Terror Ill.)

ADVENTURE BOUND (See 4-Color Comics #239)

ADVENTURE COMICS (Formerly New Adventure)
#31, Oct, 1938 - Present
National Periodical Publ./DC Comics

#31	17.50	35.00	52.50

32-39: #32-Anchors Aweigh (ends #52), Barry
O'Neil (ends #60, not in #33), Captain
Desmo (ends #47), Dale Daring (ends #57),
Federal Men (ends #70), The Golden Dragon
(ends #36), Rusty & His Pals (ends #52)
by Bob Kane, Todd Hunter (ends #38) and
Tom Brent (ends #39) begin; #39-Jack Wood
begins, ends #42. 14.00 28.00 42.00
40-Intro. & 1st app. The Sandman. Socko
Strong begins, ends #54
                    140.00 280.00 420.00

	Good	Fine	Mint
41	40.00	80.00	120.00

42-47: #47-Steve Conrad Adventurer begins,
  ends #76   30.00 60.00 90.00
48-Origin & 1st app. The Hourman by Bernard
  Baily   125.00 250.00 375.00
49,50   30.00 60.00 90.00
51-60: #53-Intro. Jimmy "Minuteman" Martin
  & the Minutemen of America in Hourman;
  ends #78. #58-Paul Kirk Manhunter begins,
  ends #72   27.50 55.00 82.50
61-Intro. & 1st app. Starman by Jack Burnley
                    100.00 200.00 300.00
62-65   30.00 60.00 90.00
66-Origin Shining Knight 40.00 80.00 120.00
67,68   30.00 60.00 90.00
69-Intro. Sandy the Golden Boy (Sandman's
  sidekick); Sandman dons new costume
                    32.00 64.00 96.00
70-Last Federal Men 27.50 55.00 82.50
71-Jimmy Martin becomes costume aide to the
  Hourman   27.50 55.00 82.50
72-1st Simon & Kirby Sandman
                    90.00 180.00 270.00
73-Origin Manhunter by Simon & Kirby; begin
  new series   110.00 220.00 330.00
74-Thorndyke replaces Jimmy, Hourman's
  assistant   40.00 80.00 120.00
75,76   40.00 80.00 120.00
77-Origin Genius Jones; Mist story
                    40.00 80.00 120.00
78-80-Last Simon & Kirby Manhunter & Burnley
  Starman   40.00 80.00 120.00
81-90: #83-Last Hourman. #84-Mike Gibbs begins, ends #102   25.00 50.00 75.00
91,92-Last Manhunter & Simon & Kirby Sandman
                    22.00 44.00 66.00
93-102-Last Starman, Sandman, & Genius Jones.
  Most-S&K covers   12.00 24.00 36.00
103-Aquaman, Green Arrow, Johnny Quick, Superboy begin   20.00 40.00 60.00
104-110   15.00 30.00 45.00
111-120   10.00 20.00 30.00
121-130   7.00 14.00 21.00
131-140: #132-Shining Knight 1st return to
  King Arthur time; origin aide Sir Butch
                     5.00 10.00 15.00
141-149   4.00   8.00 12.00
150,151,153,155,157,159,161,163-All have 6pg.
  Shining Knight stories by Frank Frazetta.
  #159-Origin Johnny Quick
                    15.00 30.00 45.00
152,154,156,158,160,162,164-166-Last Shining
  Knight   4.00   8.00 12.00
167-200   3.50   7.00 10.50
201-220   3.00   6.00   9.00
221-246,248-250: #207-Last Johnny Quick (not
  in #205). #210-1st Krypto app.
                     2.50   5.00   7.50

(Adventure Comics cont'd)

	Good	Fine	Mint
247-(Scarce)-1st Legion of Super Heroes app.			
	35.00	70.00	105.00
251-255: All Kirby Green Arrow. #255-Intro. Red Kryptonite in Superboy			
	2.50	5.00	7.50
256-Origin Green Arrow by Kirby			
	3.50	7.00	10.50
257-259	1.75	3.50	5.25
260-Origin Aquaman	2.50	5.00	7.50
261-270: #262-Origin Speedy in Green Arrow. #269-Intro. Aqualad; last Green Arrow (not in #206). #270-Congorilla begins, ends #281,283.			
	1.50	3.00	4.50
271-280: #275-Origin Superman-Batman team. #279-Intro. White Kryptonite in Superboy			
	1.25	2.50	3.75
281-290: #281-Last Congorilla. #282-Intro. Star Boy of Legion. #283-Intro. The Phantom Zone. #284-Last Aquaman in Adv. #285-1st Bizarro World story (ends #299) in Adv.-see Action #260. #288,289-Intro. Devin, the Knave from Krypton.			
	1.00	2.00	3.00
291-299: #294-1st Legion of Super Pets. #299-Last Bizarro World story.80	.80	1.60	2.40
300-Legion series begins	4.00	8.00	12.00
301-310: #304-Death of Lightning Lad in Legion. #307-Intro. Element Lad in Legion. #308-Intro. Lightning Lass of Legion			
	1.00	2.00	3.00
311-320: #312-Lightning Lad back in Legion. #315-Last new Superboy story. #317-Intro. Dream Girl in Legion; Lightning Lass becomes Light Lass; Hall of Fame series begins			
	.90	1.80	2.70
321-330: #327-Intro. Lone Wolf in Legion			
	.80	1.60	2.40
331-350: #345-Last Hall of Fame; returns in #356,371. #346-1st app. Karate Kid, Princess Projectra, Ferro Lad, & Nemesis			
	.75	1.50	2.25
351-380: #353-Death of Ferro Lad in Legion. #380-Last Legion in Adv.	.60	1.20	1.80
381-400: #381-Supergirl begins. #390-Giant Supergirl G-69. #399-Unpubbed G.A. Black Canary story	.40	.80	1.20
(80 pg. Giant G-69)	.75	1.50	2.25
401-410: #403-Giant Legion ish G-81; #409-52pg. ish begins; ends #420			
	.35	.70	1.05
(68pg. Giant G-81)	.60	1.20	1.80
411-416: #412-Animal Man origin reprt/Str. Adv. #180. #413-Hawkman by Kubert; G.A. Robotman reprt/Det. #178. #416-100pg. Giant Supergirl DC-10 feat. Black Canary, Wonder Woman, Phantom Lady (Police), Girl			

	Good	Fine	Mint
of 1000 Gimmicks	.25	.50	.75
(Giant DC-10)	.50	1.00	1.50
417-Morrow Vigilante; Frazetta Shining Knight reprt/Adv. #161	.40	.80	1.20
418-Black Canary by Toth; unpubbed G.A. Dr. Mid-Nite story	.25	.50	.75
419-Black Canary by Toth & Zatanna story			
	.25	.50	.75
420-430: #424-Last Supergirl in Adv. #425-New look, content change to adventure; Toth art, origin Capt. Fear. #428-Black Orchid begins, ends #430; Dr. 13 app.			
	.20	.40	.60
431-Spectre revived, ends #440; Toth art			
	.20	.40	.60
432-440: #435-Aquaman begins. #438-Unpubbed 7 Soldiers of Victory begins, ends #443			
	.20	.40	.60
441-458: #446-The Creeper begins. #452-Aquaman ends. #453-Superboy begins			
	.15	.30	.45
459-462 ($1.00 size)	.50	1.00	1.50

NOTE: _Legion app.-#287,282,290,293. Vigilante app.-#420,426,427. Adams covers-#365-69, 371-73,375-79,381-83. Guardineer cover-#45. Infantino art-#399,411,416. Kaluta cover-#425. Kirby art-#250-256. Kubert art-#413. Meskin story-#81. Morrow stories-#413-18,422. Newton stories-#459,460. Nino art-#432,433. Orlando pencils-#457,458. Simon/Kirby covers-#72-102. Staton stories-#456-60; cover-#458. Toth story-#425._

ADVENTURE COMICS
No date (Early 1940's) Paper cover, 32 pgs.
IGA

	Good	Fine	Mint
Two different issues; Super-Mystery reprints from 1941	12.00	24.00	36.00

ADVENTURE INTO FEAR
1951
Superior Publ. Ltd.

	Good	Fine	Mint
#1	2.00	4.00	6.00

ADVENTURE INTO MYSTERY
May, 1956 - #8, July, 1957
Atlas Comics (OPI #1-7/BFP #8)

	Good	Fine	Mint
#1-Everett cover	2.00	4.00	6.00
2,3,6,8	1.00	2.00	3.00
4-Williamson story, 4pgs.	3.00	6.00	9.00
5-Everett cover/story + Orlando story			
	1.25	2.50	3.75
7-Torres story	1.50	3.00	4.50

Adventure Comics #81, © DC

Adventure Comics #172, © DC

Adventure Into Mystery #1, © MCG

4

Adventures Into Darkness #7, © BP   Adventures Into Terror #43, © MCG   Adventures Into The Unknown #3, © ACG

ADVENTURE IS MY CAREER
1945   (36 pgs.)
U.S. Coast Guard Academy/Street & Smith

	Good	Fine	Mint
No #-Simon art	4.00	8.00	12.00

ADVENTURES FOR BOYS
Dec, 1954
Bailey Enterprises

Comics, text, & photos	1.50	3.00	4.50

ADVENTURES IN DISNEYLAND   (Giveaway)
1955, 12 pgs.   (Dist. by Richfield Oil)
Walt Disney Productions

	3.00	6.00	9.00

ADVENTURES IN PARADISE   (See 4-Color #1301)

ADVENTURES IN ROMANCE
Nov, 1949   (Slightly large size)
St. John Publishing Co.

#1-Two Leonard Starr stories; Frank Bolle, Warren King art	4.00	8.00	12.00

ADVENTURES IN SCIENCE   (See Classics Special)

ADVENTURES IN 3-D.
Nov, 1953 - #2, Jan, 1954
Harvey Publications

#1-Nostrand + Powell art, #2-Powell art	5.00	10.00	15.00

ADVENTURES INTO DARKNESS
#5, 1952 - #14, 1954
Better-Standard Publications/Visual Editions

#5-7	1.40	2.80	4.20
8-Toth art	2.00	4.00	6.00
9-14	1.25	2.50	3.75

ADVENTURES INTO TERROR   (Formerly Joker)
#43, Nov, 1950 - #31, May, 1954
Marvel/Atlas Comics (CDS/ACI)

#43, 44	2.50	5.00	7.50
#3-5	1.75	3.50	5.25
6,8	1.50	3.00	4.50
7-Wolverton art, 6pgs.	10.00	20.00	30.00
9,10,12-Krigstein stys.	2.00	4.00	6.00
11,13-20	1.00	2.00	3.00
21-31	.80	1.60	2.40

NOTE: _Colan_ art-#5,25. _Everett_ cover-#13,21,
25. _G. Kane_ story-#7. _Don Rico_ art-#4,5. Wolverton _cover panel-#5. Wolvertonesque art by
Matt Fox-#25._

ADVENTURES INTO THE UNKNOWN
Fall, 1948 - #174, Aug, 1967 (#1-33, 52pgs.)
American Comics Group
   (1st continuous series horror comic)

	Good	Fine	Mint
#1-Wood story, 51+ pgs.	15.00	30.00	45.00
2,4,5	5.00	10.00	15.00
3-Feldstein story, 9pgs.	8.00	16.00	24.00
6-10	2.50	5.00	7.50
11-20	2.00	4.00	6.00
21-26,28-30	1.50	3.00	4.50
27-Williamson/Krenkle story, 8pgs.	9.00	18.00	27.00
31-50	1.25	2.50	3.75
51-59 (3-D effect)	1.50	3.00	4.50
60,61-Last pre-code ish	.80	1.60	2.40
62-90	.60	1.20	1.80
91,95,96(#95 on inside),107,116-All contain Williamson stories	2.25	4.50	6.75
92-94,97-106,108-115,117-127	.40	.80	1.20
128-Williamson story reprinted from Forbidden Worlds #63	1.00	2.00	3.00
129-150	.35	.70	1.05
151-153: #153-Magic Agent app.	.25	.50	.75
154-Nemesis series begins (origin), ends #170	.40	.80	1.20
155-167,169-174: #157-Magic Agent app.	.25	.50	.75
168-Ditko story	.50	1.00	1.50

NOTE: _"Spirit of Frankenstein" series in #5,
6, 8-10,12,16. Buscema story-#100,106,109,
110,158. Craig story-#11,160._

ADVENTURES INTO WEIRD WORLDS
Jan, 1951 - #30, June, 1954
Marvel/Atlas Comics(ACI)

#1-Heath story	3.00	6.00	9.00
2	2.00	4.00	6.00
3-9	1.25	2.50	3.75
10-Krigstein story	2.00	4.00	6.00
11-30	1.00	2.00	3.00

NOTE: _Everett story-#10; covers-#6,8,10,12,
13,18-20,22,24. Robinson story-#13._

ADVENTURES IN WONDERLAND
Apr, 1955 - #5, Feb, 1956 (Jr. Readers Guild)
Lev Gleason Publications

#1-Maurer art	1.75	3.50	5.25
2-4	1.20	2.40	3.60
5-X-Mas issue	1.50	3.00	4.50

5

ADVENTURES OF ALAN LADD, THE
Oct-Nov, 1949 - #9, Feb-Mar, 1951
National Periodical Publications

	Good	Fine	Mint
#1	5.00	10.00	15.00
2-9	3.00	6.00	9.00

NOTE: *Toth art in some issues.*

ADVENTURES OF ALICE (Also see Alice in Wonderland & -- at Monkey Island)
1945
Pentagon Publishing Co./Civil Service

#1	3.00	6.00	9.00
2-Through the Magic Looking Glass			
	2.50	5.00	7.50

ADVENTURES OF BOB HOPE, THE
Feb-Mar, 1950 - #109, Feb-Mar, 1968
National Periodical Publications

#1	6.00	12.00	18.00
2	3.00	6.00	9.00
3-10	2.00	4.00	6.00
11-20	1.50	3.00	4.50
21-50	1.00	2.00	3.00
51-93,95-105: #103-Infantino art			
	.60	1.20	1.80
94-Aquaman cameo	.70	1.40	2.10
106-109-Adams cvrs/stories	1.50	3.00	4.50

ADVENTURES OF DEAN MARTIN & JERRY LEWIS, THE
(Jerry Lewis #41 on)
July-Aug, 1952 - #40, Oct, 1957
National Periodical Publications

#1	6.00	12.00	18.00
2	3.00	6.00	9.00
3-10	2.00	4.00	6.00
11-20	1.50	3.00	4.50
21-30	1.00	2.00	3.00
31-40	.80	1.60	2.40

ADVENTURES OF G.I. JOE
1969   (3½"x7")
Giveaways

#1-Danger of the Depths. 2-Flying Space Adventure. 3-Secret Mission to Spy Island. 4-White Tiger Hunt. 5-Fantastic Free Fall. 6-Eight Ropes of Danger. 7-Capture of the Pygmy Gorilla. 8-Hidden Missle Discovery. 9-Space Walk Mystery. 10-Fight for Survival. 11-The Sharks' Surprise. 12-Secret of the Mummy's Tomb. each.... .20   .40   .60

ADVENTURES OF HOMER COBB, THE
Sept, 1947

Say/Bart Prod. (Canadian)

	Good	Fine	Mint
#1-Feldstein art	10.00	20.00	30.00

ADVENTURES OF HOMER GHOST
June, 1957 - #2, August, 1957
Atlas Comics

V1#1, V1#2	.40	.80	1.20

ADVENTURES OF JERRY LEWIS, THE (Dean Martin & Jerry Lewis #1-40)(See Super DC Giant)
#41, Nov, 1957 - #124, May-June, 1971
National Periodical Publications

#41-60	.70	1.40	2.10
61-80	.50	1.00	1.50
81-91,93-96,98-100	.40	.80	1.20
92-Superman cameo	.50	1.00	1.50
97-Batman/Robin x-over	.50	1.00	1.50
101-104-Adams cvrs/stys.	1.50	3.00	4.50
105-Superman x-over	.50	1.00	1.50
106-111,113-116	.40	.80	1.20
112-Flash x-over	.50	1.00	1.50
117-Wonder Woman x-over	.50	1.00	1.50
118-124	.30	.60	.90

ADVENTURES OF MANUEL PACIFICO, TUNA FISHERMAN, THE
1951 (Giveaway) (16pgs. in color)
Breast O' Chicken Giveaway (Frieda-Bart Hind)

#1-4	2.50	5.00	7.50

ADVENTURES OF MIGHTY MOUSE (Mighty Mouse Adventures #1)
#2, Jan, 1952 - #16, Jan, 1955
St. John Publishing Co.

#2-5	2.00	4.00	6.00
6-16	1.50	3.00	4.50

ADVENTURES OF MIGHTY MOUSE (2nd Series)
(Two #144's; formerly Paul Terry's Comics; #128-137 have no #'s)(Becomes Mighty Mouse #161 on)
#126, Aug, 1955 - #160, Oct, 1963
St. John/Pines/Dell/Gold Key

#126(8/55), 127(10/55)-St. John			
	1.00	2.00	3.00
No#(128, 4/56)-#144(8/59)Pines			
	1.00	2.00	3.00
#144(10-12/59)-#155(7-9/62)Dell			
	.80	1.60	2.40
#156(10/62)-#160(10/63)Gold Key			
	.80	1.60	2.40

NOTE: *Early issues titled "Paul Terry's Adventures of --".*

Adventures Into Weird Worlds #24. ☺ MCG   Adventures Of Bob Hope #109. ☺ DC   Adventures Of Mighty Mouse #146. ☺ Terry Toons

Advs. Of Ozzie & Harriet #4, © DC   Advs. Of The Big Boy #1, © MCG   Advs. Of The Jaguar #12, © AP

ADVENTURES OF MR. FROG & MISS MOUSE (See
Dell Jr. Treasury #4)

ADVENTURES OF OZZIE AND HARRIET, THE
Oct-Nov, 1949 - #5, June-July, 1950 (Radio)
National Periodical Publications

	Good	Fine	Mint
#1	3.00	6.00	9.00
2-5	2.00	4.00	6.00

ADVENTURES OF PATORUZU
Aug, 1946 - Winter, 1946
Green Publishing Co.

No #'s-Contains Animal Crackers reprints
                        1.00   2.00   3.00

ADVENTURES OF PINKY LEE, THE (TV)
July, 1955 - #5, Nov, 1955
Atlas Comics

#1	2.50	5.00	7.50
2-5	1.75	3.50	5.25

ADVENTURES OF QUAKE & QUISP, THE
(See Quaker Oats "Plenty of Glutton")

ADVENTURES OF REX THE WONDER DOG, THE
Jan-Feb, 1952 - #46, Nov-Dec, 1959
National Periodical Publications

#1(Scarce)-Toth art	10.00	20.00	30.00
2,3-Toth art	5.00	10.00	15.00
4,5	2.50	5.00	7.50
6-10	2.00	4.00	6.00
11-20	1.50	3.00	4.50
21-46	1.00	2.00	3.00

NOTE: *Infantino, Gil Kane art in most issues.*

ADVENTURES OF ROBIN HOOD, THE (Formerly
Robin Hood)
#8, Nov, 1957 (Based on Richard Green TV Show)
Magazine Enterprises (Sussex Publ. Co.)

#8	1.25	2.50	3.75

ADVENTURES OF ROBIN HOOD, THE
March, 1974 - #7, Jan, 1975 (Disney Cartoon)
Gold Key

#1(90291-403)-Partial reprints of $1.50 ed-			
itions	.30	.60	.90
2-7	.20	.40	.60

ADVENTURES OF THE BIG BOY (Eastern & Western
editions of early issues)
1956 - Present (Giveaway)
Timely Comics/Webs Adv. Corp./Illus. Features

	Good	Fine	Mint
#1-Everett art	50.00	100.00	150.00
2-5,7,8-Everett art	8.00	16.00	24.00
6,9-50	1.20	2.40	3.60
51-100	.50	1.00	1.50
101-150	.25	.50	.75
151-240	.15	.30	.45
#1-12('77-'78)		.15	.25
Summer, '59 ish, lg.size	2.00	4.00	6.00

ADVENTURES OF THE DETECTIVE
No date(1930's) 36pgs.;9½x12" B&W(soft cover)
Humor Publ. Co.

Not reprints; Ace King by Martin Nodle
                        6.00 12.00 18.00

ADVENTURES OF THE DOVER BOYS
Sept, 1950
Archie Comics (Close-up)

#1	2.00	4.00	6.00

ADVENTURES OF THE JAGUAR, THE
Sept, 1961 - #15, 1963
Archie Publications (Radio Comics)

#1-Origin Jaguar	2.50	5.00	7.50
2,3	1.40	2.80	4.20
4,5-Catgirl app.	1.00	2.00	3.00
6-10: #6-Catgirl app.	.70	1.40	2.10
11-15: #13,14-Catgirl, Black Hood app. in			
both	.60	1.20	1.80

ADVENTURES OF TINKER BELL (See 4-Color #982)

ADVENTURES OF TOM SAWYER (See Dell Jr.
Treasury #10)

ADVENTURES OF YOUNG DR. MASTERS, THE
Aug, 1964 - #2, Nov, 1964
Archie Comics (Radio Comics)

#1,2	.80	1.60	2.40

ADVENTURES ON THE PLANET OF THE APES
Oct, 1975 - #11, Dec, 1976
Marvel Comics Group

#1-Reprints from Planet of the Apes in color;			
Starlin cover	.50	1.00	1.50
2-5	.25	.50	.75
6-11	.15	.30	.45

NOTE: *Alcala reprints-#10,11. Starlin
cover-#6.*

AFRICA
1955
Magazine Enterprises

(Africa cont'd)

	Good	Fine	Mint
#1(A-1 #137)-Cave Girl & Thun'da; Powell cover + 4 stories	5.00	10.00	15.00

AFRICAN LION (See 4-Color #665)

AFTER DARK
May, 1955 - #8, Sept, 1955
Sterling Comics

	Good	Fine	Mint
#6-8-Sekowsky art in all	1.20	2.40	3.60

AGGIE MACK
Jan, 1948 - #8, Aug, 1949
Superior Comics Ltd.

	Good	Fine	Mint
#1-Feldstein "Johnny Prep"	7.00	14.00	21.00
2,3-Kamen covers	4.00	8.00	12.00
4-Feldstein "Johnny Prep"; Kamen cover	5.00	10.00	15.00
5-8-Kamen cvrs/stys.	3.50	7.00	10.50

AGGIE MACK (See 4-Color Comics #1335)

AIN'T IT A GRAND & GLORIOUS FEELING?
1922 (28pgs.)(Full color; 9x9½";stiff card-
Whitman Publishing Co.   board cvr)

	Good	Fine	Mint
Sunday strip reprints; Briggs art	12.00	24.00	36.00

AIR ACE (Bill Barnes #1-12)
V2#1, Jan, 1944 - V5#8, Feb-Mar, 1947
Street & Smith Publications

	Good	Fine	Mint
V2#1-12	2.00	4.00	6.00
V3#1-8	1.50	3.00	4.50
V4#1-8	1.20	2.40	3.60
V5#1-8: #8-Powell art	1.00	2.00	3.00

AIRBOY COMICS (Airfighters #1-22)
V2#11, Dec, 1945 - V10#4, May, 1953(No V3#3)
Hillman Periodicals

	Good	Fine	Mint
V2#11,12-Valkyrie in #12	6.00	12.00	18.00
V3#1,2(no #3)	4.00	8.00	12.00
4-The Heap app. in Skywolf	3.00	6.00	9.00
5-8: Valkyrie in #6	3.00	6.00	9.00
9-Origin The Heap	3.00	6.00	9.00
10,11	3.00	6.00	9.00
12-Skywolf & Airboy x-over; Valkyrie app.	5.00	10.00	15.00
V4#1-Iron Lady app.	3.00	6.00	9.00
2-Rackman begins	2.00	4.00	6.00
3,10,12	2.00	4.00	6.00

	Good	Fine	Mint
4-Simon & Kirby cover	3.00	6.00	9.00
5-9,11-S&K stories	4.00	8.00	12.00
V5#1-9: #4-Infantino Heap	2.00	4.00	6.00
10-Origin The Heap	2.00	4.00	6.00
11,12	2.00	4.00	6.00
V6#1-5,7	2.00	4.00	6.00
6,8-Origin The Heap	2.00	4.00	6.00
9-12	2.00	4.00	6.00
V7#1-7,9,11,12	2.00	4.00	6.00
8,10-Origin The Heap	2.00	4.00	6.00
V8#1-12	1.50	3.00	4.50
V9#1-12: #2-Valkyrie app.	1.50	3.00	4.50
V10#1-4	1.50	3.00	4.50

NOTE: *Krigstein story-V5#12(pencils),V8#4.*
McWilliams art-V3#7. Powell story-V8#1,6.
Starr story-V5#1.

AIR FIGHTERS COMICS (Airboy #23, V2#11 on)
Nov, 1941 - V2#10, Fall, 1945
Hillman Periodicals

	Good	Fine	Mint
V1#1-Black Commander only app.	50.00	100.00	150.00
2-Origin Airboy & Iron Ace; Black Angel, Flying Dutchman & Skywolf begin; 1st Valkyrie app.; Fuji art	80.00	160.00	240.00
3-Origin The Heap & Skywolf	35.00	70.00	105.00
4	25.00	50.00	75.00
5,6	20.00	40.00	60.00
7-12	15.00	30.00	45.00
V2#1-9: #2-Intro. Valkyrie. #7-Valkyrie app.	12.00	24.00	36.00
10-Origin The Heap & Skywolf	12.00	24.00	36.00

AIR FORCES (See American Air Forces)

AIR WAR STORIES
Sept-Nov, 1964 - #8, Aug, 1966
Dell Publishing Co.

	Good	Fine	Mint
#1-Glanzman cvr/art begins	.50	1.00	1.50
2-8	.30	.60	.90

ALADDIN (See Dell Jr. Treasury #2)

ALAN LADD (See Adventures of --)

ALARMING ADVENTURES
Oct, 1962 - #3, Feb, 1963
Harvey Publications

	Good	Fine	Mint
#1-Williamson + Crandall art	2.00	4.00	6.00
2,3- " " "	1.75	3.50	5.25

Aggie Mack #6, © SUPR

Air Ace #12, © S&S

Airboy Comics V2#11, © HILL

8

Air Fighters Comics #3, © HILL   Album Of Crime No.#, © Fox   Al Capp's Dogpatch #2, © UFS

ALARMING TALES
Sept, 1957 - #6, July, 1958
Harvey Publications (Western Tales)

	Good	Fine	Mint
#1(1st Series)-Kirby cover & 4 stories			
	3.00	6.00	9.00
2-Four Kirby stories	2.50	5.00	7.50
3,4-Kirby stories	1.75	3.50	5.25
5-Kirby/Williamson story	1.50	3.00	4.50
6-Williamson/Torres sty.	1.50	3.00	4.50

ALBERT THE ALLIGATOR & POGO POSSUM
(See 4-Color Comics #105, 148)

ALBUM OF CRIME
1959   (132 pgs.)
Fox Features Syndicate

No#-See Fox Giants. Contents can vary and
    determines price.

ALBUM OF LOVE
1949   (132 pgs.)
Hero Books (Fox)

No#-See Fox Giants. Contents can vary and
    determine price.

AL CAPP'S DOGPATCH (Also see Mammy Yokum)
#71, June, 1949 - #4, Dec, 1949
Toby Press

#71(#1)-Reprints from Tip Top #112-114			
	2.00	4.00	6.00
#2-4: #4-Reprints from Little Abner #73			
	1.75	3.50	5.25

AL CAPP'S SHMOO (See Oxydol-Dreft)
July, 1949 - 1950   (None by Al Capp)
Toby Press/Harvey Publications

#1	5.00	10.00	15.00
2-5	3.00	6.00	9.00

AL CAPP'S WOLF GAL
1952
Harvey Publications/Toby Press, #2

#1,2-Edited reprint from Li'l Abner #63,64			
	5.00	10.00	15.00

ALEXANDER THE GREAT (See 4-Color #688)

ALGIE
Dec, 1953 - #3, 1954
Timor Publ. Co.

#1	.60	1.20	1.80

	Good	Fine	Mint
2,3	.40	.80	1.20
Super Reprint #15	.30	.60	.90

ALICE (New Advs. in Wonderland)
1952
Ziff-Davis Publ. Co.

#2-Davy Berg art	1.50	3.00	4.50
3-9	1.20	2.40	3.60
10,11-Davy Berg art	1.20	2.40	3.60

ALICE AT MONKEY ISLAND (See The Advs. of Alice)
#3, 1946
Pentagon Publ. Co. (Civil Service)

#3	2.50	5.00	7.50

ALICE IN WONDERLAND (See Advs. of Alice,
4-Color #331,341, Dell Jr. Treasury #1, Movie
Comics, Single Series #24, Walt Disney Showcase #22, & World's Greatest Stories)

ALICE IN WONDERLAND
1965
Western Printing Company

--Meets Santa Claus('50's), no date, 16 pgs.			
	2.00	4.00	6.00
Rexall Giveaway(1965, 16pgs., 5x7¼") Western Printing(TV-Hanna-Barbera)			
	1.50	3.00	4.50
Wonder Bakery Giveaway(16pgs. color, no #, no date)(Continental Baking Co.)			
	1.50	3.00	4.50

ALIENS, THE
Dec, 1967; 1972
Gold Key

#1-Reprints from Magnus #1,3,4,6-10, all by Russ Manning	.65	1.35	2.00
#1-2nd printing ('72)	.35	.70	1.05

ALL-AMERICAN COMICS (-- Western #103-126,
-- Men of War #127 on)
April, 1939 - #102, Oct, 1948
National Periodical Publ./All-American

#1-Hop Harrigan, Scribbly, Toonerville Folks, Ben Webster, Spot Savage, Mutt & Jeff, Red White & Blue, Adv. in the Unknown, Tippie, Reg'lar Fellars, Skippy, Bobby Thatcher, Mystery Men of Mars, Daiseybelle, & Wiley of West Point begin			
	70.00	140.00	210.00
2-Ripley's Believe It or Not begins, ends #24	40.00	80.00	120.00

(All-American Comics cont'd)

	Good	Fine	Mint
3-5: #5-The American Way begins, ends #10			
	22.00	44.00	66.00
6,7: #6-Last Spot Savage. #7-Last Bobby Thatcher			
	17.50	35.00	52.50
8-The Ultra Man begins	27.50	55.00	82.50
9,10	22.00	44.00	66.00
11-15: #12-Last Toonerville Folks. #13-Popsicle Pete begins, ends #26,28. #15-Last Tippie & Reg'lar Fellars			
	16.00	32.00	48.00
16-Origin & 1st app. Green Lantern (Rare)			
	350.00	700.00	1050.00

(Prices vary widely on this book)

	Good	Fine	Mint
17-(Scarce)	80.00	160.00	240.00
18	60.00	120.00	180.00
19-Origin & 1st app. The Atom; Last Ultra Man			
	80.00	160.00	240.00
20-Atom dons costume; Hunkle becomes the Red Tornado; Rescue on Mars begins, ends #25			
	50.00	100.00	150.00
21-23: #21-Last Wiley of West Point & Skippy. #23-Last Daiseybelle; 3 Idiots begin, end #82			
	40.00	80.00	120.00
24-Sisty & Dinky become the Cyclone Kids; Ben Webster ends	40.00	80.00	120.00
25-Origin & 1st app. Dr. Mid-Nite; Hop Harrigan becomes Guardian Angel; last Adventure in the Unknown	60.00	120.00	180.00
26-Origin & 1st app. Sargon, the Sorcerer			
	40.00	80.00	120.00
27-Intro. Doiby Dickles, Green Lantern's sidekick	40.00	80.00	120.00
28-(#28 on cvr, #27 on inside) Hop Harrigan gives up costumed identity)			
	25.00	50.00	75.00
29,30	25.00	50.00	75.00
31-40: #35-Doiby learns Green Lantern's I.D.			
	18.00	36.00	54.00
41-50: #50-Sargon ends	14.00	28.00	42.00
51-60	12.00	24.00	36.00
61-Origin Solomon Grundy	25.00	50.00	75.00
62-70: #70-Kubert Sargon	10.00	20.00	30.00
71-Last Red White & Blue	9.00	18.00	27.00
72-Black Pirate begins (not in #74-82); last Atom	9.00	18.00	27.00
73-80: #73-Winky, Blinky & Noddy begins, ends #82	9.00	18.00	27.00
81-88,90: #90-Origin Icicle			
	8.00	16.00	24.00
89-Origin Harlequin	10.00	20.00	30.00
91-99-Last Hop Harrigan	8.00	16.00	24.00
100-1st app. Johnny Thunder by Alex Toth			
	14.00	28.00	42.00
101-Last Mutt & Jeff	10.00	20.00	30.00
102-Last Green Lantern, Black Pirate & Dr. Mid-Nite	10.00	20.00	30.00

NOTE: *No Atom in #47,62-69. Moldoff covers-#16-23. Toth stories-#88,92,96,98-102; covers-#92,96-102.*

ALL-AMERICAN MEN OF WAR (Previously All-American Western)
#127, Aug-Sept, 1952 - #117, Sept-Oct, 1966
National Periodical Publications

	Good	Fine	Mint
#127,128 (1952)	6.00	12.00	18.00
#2(12-1/'52-53)-#5	3.00	6.00	9.00
6-20	2.50	5.00	7.50
21-28	1.75	3.50	5.25
29,30,32-Wood stories	3.50	7.00	10.50
31,33-50	1.40	2.80	4.20
51-70: #67-1st Gunner & Sarge by Andru			
	1.00	2.00	3.00
71-80	.80	1.60	2.40
81-100: #82-Johnny Cloud begins, ends #111, 114,115	.50	1.00	1.50
101-117: #112-Balloon Buster series begins, ends #113. #115-Johnny Cloud app.			
	.35	.70	1.05

NOTE: *Drucker story-#65,74. Infantino story-#8. Krigstein story-#128('52),2,3,5. Kubert story-#36,38,41,43,47,49,50,52,53,55,56,60, 63,65,69,71-73,103; cover-#41. Tank Killer in #69,71,76 by Kubert.*

ALL-AMERICAN SPORTS
October, 1967
Charlton Comics

#1	.20	.40	.60

ALL-AMERICAN WESTERN (Previously All-American Comics; Becomes All-American Men of War)
Nov, 1948 - #126, June-July, 1952
National Periodical Publications

	Good	Fine	Mint
#103-110-Johnny Thunder continues by Toth			
	4.50	9.00	13.50
111-126-All Toth art	3.00	6.00	9.00

NOTE: *Kubert art-#103-105,107,111,112(1 pg.), 113-115,121. Kurtzman 1 pg.-#112(Pot-Shot Pete).*

ALL COMICS
1945
Chicago Nite Life News

#1	2.50	5.00	7.50

ALLEY OOP (See 4-Color #3 & Super Book #9)

ALLEY OOP
1947 - #18, Aug, 1949
Standard Comics

All-American Comics #7. © DC

All-American Comics #49. © DC

All-American Western #106. © DC

Alley Oop #17, © STD

All Famous Crime #4, © STAR

All-Flash #15, © DC

(Alley Oop cont'd)	Good	Fine	Mint
#1	7.00	14.00	21.00
2-5	5.00	10.00	15.00
6-18	4.00	8.00	12.00

ALLEY OOP
1955 - #3, 1956 (Newspaper reprints)
Argo Publ.

#1	4.00	8.00	12.00
2,3	3.00	6.00	9.00

ALLEY OOP
1963; 1965
Dell Publishing Co.

#1,2('63)	1.75	3.50	5.25
#1,2('65)	1.25	2.50	3.75

ALL-FAMOUS CRIME
1949 - #10, Nov, 1951
Star Publications

#1	2.50	5.00	7.50
2-8,10	1.25	2.50	3.75
9-Used in Seduction of the Innocent, illo- "The wish to hurt or kill couples in lovers' lanes is not uncommon perversion;" L. B. Cole cover & story reprint/Law-Crime #3	6.00	12.00	18.00

NOTE: *All have L. B. Cole covers.*

ALL FAMOUS CRIME STORIES
1949   (132 pgs.)
Fox Features Syndicate

No#-See Fox Giants. Contents can vary and determines price.

ALL-FAMOUS POLICE CASES
Oct, 1951 - #16, Sept, 1954
Star Publications

#1	1.50	3.00	4.50
2-6	1.15	2.30	3.45
7-Kubert art	2.00	4.00	6.00
8-16	1.00	2.00	3.00

NOTE: *All have L. B. Cole covers.*

ALL-FLASH
Summer, 1941 - #32, Dec-Jan, 1947-48
National Periodical Publ./All-American

#1-Origin The Flash retold by E. E. Hibbard			
	90.00	180.00	270.00
2	40.00	80.00	120.00
3,4	30.00	60.00	90.00
5-Winky, Blinky & Noddy begins, ends #32			

	Good	Fine	Mint
	25.00	50.00	75.00
6-10	20.00	40.00	60.00
11-13: #12-Origin The Thinker. #13-The King app.	15.00	30.00	45.00
14-Green Lantern cameo	17.50	35.00	52.50
15-20: #18-Mutt & Jeff begins, ends #22	11.00	22.00	33.00
21-31	9.00	18.00	27.00
32-Origin The Fiddler	10.00	20.00	30.00

NOTE: *Book length stories #2-13,15,16.*

ALL FOR LOVE
Apr-May, 1957 - V3#2, Jun-July, 1959
Prize Publications

V1#1	.80	1.60	2.40
2-6	.40	.80	1.20
V2#1-5	.30	.60	.90
V3#1,2: #2-Powell art	.25	.50	.75

ALL FUNNY COMICS
Winter, 1943-44 - #23, May-June, 1948
National Periodical Publications (Detective)

#1-Genius Jones begins	3.50	7.00	10.50
2	2.00	4.00	6.00
3-12,15,16-Last Genius Jones			
	1.50	3.00	4.50
13,14,17-23	1.20	2.40	3.60

ALL GOOD (-- Comics)
1944 (132 pgs.); Spring, 1946 (36 pgs.)
R. W. Boigt Publ.(1944)/Fox Features Synd.

#1(1944)-The Bouncer, Purple Tigress, Puppeteer, & The Green Mask	5.00	10.00	15.00
1946-Joy Family, Dick Transom, Rick Evans, One Round Hogan	4.00	8.00	12.00

ALL GOOD
1949   (260 pgs.) (50¢)
St. John Publishing Co.

(8 funny animal comics bound together)
	4.00	8.00	12.00

ALL GREAT
1944; 1945 (132 pgs.); 1946 (36 pgs.)
Fox Features Syndicate

1944-Capt. Jack Terry, Rick Evans, Jaguar Man	6.00	12.00	18.00
1945-Green Mask, Bouncer, Puppeteer, Rick Evans, Rocket Kelly	6.00	12.00	18.00
#1(1946)-Crazy Horse, Bertie Benson, Gussie the Cub	2.00	4.00	6.00

ALL GREAT (Dagar, Desert Hawk #14 on)
#14, Oct, 1947 - #13, Dec, 1947
Fox Features Syndicate

	Good	Fine	Mint
#14-Brenda Starr reprts.	10.00	20.00	30.00
13-Origin Dagar, Desert Hawk; Brenda Starr (all reprts.); Kamen cover	12.00	24.00	36.00

ALL-GREAT CONFESSIONS
1949   (132 pgs.)
Fox Features Syndicate

No#-See Fox Giants. Contents vary and
determines price.

ALL GREAT CRIME STORIES
1949   (132 pgs.)
Fox Features Syndicate

No#-See Fox Giants. Contents vary and
determines price.

ALL GREAT JUNGLE ADVENTURES
1949   (132 pgs.)
Fox Features Syndicate

No#-See Fox Giants. Contents vary and
determines price.

ALL HERO COMICS
March, 1943   (100 pgs.) (Cardboard cover)
Fawcett Publications

	Good	Fine	Mint
#1-Captain Marvel Jr., Capt. Midnight, Golden Arrow, Ibis the Invincible, Spy Smasher, & Lance O'Casey	40.00	100.00	160.00

ALL HUMOR COMICS
Spring, 1946 - #17, December, 1949
Quality Comics Group

	Good	Fine	Mint
#1	2.00	4.00	6.00
2-9	1.20	2.40	3.60
10-17	1.00	2.00	3.00

ALL LOVE (-- Romances #26)(Formerly Ernie)
#26, May, 1949 - 32, May, 1950
Ace Periodicals (Current Books)

	Good	Fine	Mint
#26(#1)-Ernie app.	1.00	2.00	3.00
27-L.B. Cole story	1.25	2.50	3.75
28-32	.80	1.60	2.40

ALL-NEGRO COMICS
June, 1947   (15¢)
All-Negro Comics

	Good	Fine	Mint
#1 (Rare)	80.00	160.00	240.00

ALL-NEW COLLECTORS' EDITION (Formerly Limited
Collectors' Edition)
January, 1978 - Present
DC Comics, Inc.

#C-53-Rudolph the Red-Nosed Reindeer	.50	1.00	1.50
C-54-Superman Vs. Wonder Woman	.80	1.60	2.40
C-55-Superboy & the Legion of Super-Heroes	.80	1.60	2.40
C-56-Superman Vs. Muhamad Ali-Story & wrap-around cover by Adams	1.00	2.00	3.00
C-58-Superman Vs. Shazam!	.50	1.00	1.50
C-60-Rudolph's Summer Fun(8/78)	.50	1.00	1.50

ALL-NEW COMICS (-- Short Stories #1-3)
Jan, 1943 - #14, Nov, 1946; #15, Mar-Apr, 1947
Harvey Publications

#1-Steve Case, Crime Rover, Johnny Rebel, Kayo Kane, The Echo, Night Hawk, Ray O'Light, Detective Shane begin; Red Blazer on cover only	27.50	55.00	82.50
2-Origin Scarlet Phantom	16.00	32.00	48.00
3	12.00	24.00	36.00
4,5	10.00	20.00	30.00
6-The Boy Heroes & Red Blazer (text story) begin; Black Cat app.; Intro Sparky in Red Blazer	10.00	20.00	30.00
7-Kubert & Powell art; Black Cat & Zebra app.	12.00	24.00	36.00
8-Shock Gibson app.; Kubert & Powell art	12.00	24.00	36.00
9-Black Cat app.; Kubert art	12.00	24.00	36.00
10-The Zebra app.; Kubert art (3 stories)	12.00	24.00	36.00
11-Girl Commandos app.	9.00	18.00	27.00
12-Kubert art	9.00	18.00	27.00
13-Stuntman by Simon & Kirby; Green Hornet, Joe Palooka, Flying Fool app.	12.00	24.00	36.00
14-The Green Hornet & The Man in Black Called Fate by Powell, Joe Palooka app.	8.00	16.00	24.00
15-(Extremely Rare)-Small size (5½x8½"-Black & White, 32pgs.) Distributed to mail subscribers only. Black Cat and Joe Palooka app.			

15-(Extremely Rare)... (Sold in San Francisco
in 1976 for $500.00)
*(Also see Boy Explorers #2, Flash Gordon #5,
and Stuntman #3.)*

All Love =27. © ACE

All-Negro Comics #1. © All-Negro Comics

All-New Comics #5. © HARV

All-Select Comics #3, © MCG

All Star Comics #5, © DC

All Star Comics #17, © DC

ALL PICTURE ADVENTURES
Oct, 1952 - #2, Nov, 1952 (100pg. Giants)
St. John Publishing Co.

	Good	Fine	Mint
#1-War comics	3.50	7.00	10.50
2-Horror-crime comics	4.00	8.00	12.00

NOTE: *Above books contain three St. John
comics rebound; variations possible.* <u>Baker</u>
art known in both.

ALL PICTURE ALL TRUE LOVE STORY
October, 1952 (100 pgs.)
St. John Publishing Co.

#1-Canteen Kate by Matt Baker			
	7.00	14.00	21.00

ALL-PICTURE COMEDY CARNIVAL
October, 1952 (100 pgs.)
St. John Publishing Co.

#1-(4 rebound comics)-Contents can vary;
Baker art   7.00   14.00   21.00

ALL REAL CONFESSION MAGAZINE
#3, Mar, 1949 - #4, Apr, 1949 (132 pgs.)
Hero Books (Fox)

#3,4-See Fox Giants. Contents can vary and
determines price.

ALL ROMANCES (Mr. Risk #7 on)
Aug, 1949 - #6, June, 1950
A. A. Wyn (Ace Periodicals)

#1	1.20	2.40	3.60
2-6	.80	1.60	2.40

ALL-SELECT COMICS (Blonde Phantom #12 on)
Fall, 1943 - #11, Fall, 1946
Timely Comics (Daring Comics)

#1-Capt. America, Human Torch, Sub-Mariner be-
  gin; Black Widow app.120.00 240.00 360.00
2-Red Skull app.   50.00 100.00 150.00
3-The Whizzer begins 35.00 70.00 105.00
4,5-Last Sub-Mariner 24.00 48.00 72.00
6-The Destroyer app. 20.00 40.00 60.00
7-9: #8-No Whizzer   20.00 40.00 60.00
10-The Destroyer & Sub-Mariner app.; last
  Capt. America & Human Torch issue
                      16.00 32.00 48.00
11-1st app. Blonde Phantom; Miss America app.
                      24.00 48.00 72.00

ALL SPORTS COMICS
Oct-Nov, 1948 - #4, Apr-May, 1949 (52 pgs.)
Hillman Periodicals

	Good	Fine	Mint
#1	1.25	2.50	3.75
2-Krigstein pencils	1.50	3.00	4.50
3,4	.80	1.60	2.40

ALL STAR COMICS (-- Western #58 on)
Summer, 1940 - #57, Feb-Mar, 1951; #58, Jan-
Feb, 1976 - #74, Sept-Oct, 1978
National Per. Publ./All-American/DC Comics

#1-The Flash(#1 by Harry Lampert), Hawkman
  (by Shelly), Hourman, The Sandman, The
  Spectre, Biff Bronson, Red White & Blue
  begin; Ultra Man's only app.
                     225.00 450.00 675.00
2-Green Lantern, Johnny Thunder begin
                     120.00 240.00 360.00
3-Origin Justice Society of America; Dr.
  Fate & The Atom begin, Red Tornado cameo;
  last Red White & Blue; reprinted in <u>Fam-
  ous First Edition</u> 275.00 550.00 825.00
4   100.00 200.00 300.00
5-Intro. & 1st app. Shiera Sanders as
  Hawkgirl   90.00 180.00 270.00
6-Johnny Thunder joins JSA
                     70.00 140.00 210.00
7-Batman, Superman, Flash cameo; last Hourman; Doiby Dickles app.
                     70.00 140.00 210.00
8-Origin & 1st app. Wonder Woman; Dr. Fate
  dons new helmet; Dr. Mid-Nite & Starman
  begin; Shiera app.; Hop Harrigan JSA
  guest   120.00 240.00 360.00
9-Shiera app.   65.00 130.00 195.00
10-Flash, Green Lantern cameo, Sandman new
  costume   65.00 130.00 195.00
11-Wonder Woman begins; Spectre cameo;
  Shiera app.   60.00 120.00 180.00
12-Wonder Woman becomes Secretary of JSA
                     55.00 110.00 165.00
13-15: Sandman w/Sandy in #14&15; #15-Origin
  Brain Wave; Shiera app.
                     50.00 100.00 150.00
16-19: #16(?)-Last Hop Harrigan. #19-Sandman
  w/Sandy   45.00 90.00 135.00
20-Dr. Fate & Sandman cameo
                     45.00 90.00 135.00
21-Spectre & Atom cameo; Dr. Fate by Kubert;
  Dr. Fate, Sandman end 35.00 70.00 105.00
22,23: #23-Origin Psycho Pirate; last Spectre & Starman   35.00 70.00 105.00
24-Flash & Green Lantern cameo; Mr. Terrific
  only app.; Wildcat, JSA guest; Kubert
  Hawkman begins   35.00 70.00 105.00
25-27: #25-The Flash & Green Lantern start
  again. #27-Wildcat, JSA guest
                     30.00 60.00 90.00
28-30   27.50 55.00 82.50

13

(All Star Comics cont'd)　　Good　Fine　Mint
31,32　　　　　　　　25.00　50.00　75.00
33-Solomon Grundy, Hawkman, Doiby Dickles
　app.　　　　　　45.00　90.00 135.00
34,35-Johnny Thunder cameo in both
　　　　　　　　25.00　50.00　75.00
36-Batman & Superman JSA guests
　　　　　　　　45.00　90.00 135.00
37-Johnny Thunder cameo; origin Injustice
　Society; last Kubert Hawkman
　　　　　　　　25.00　50.00　75.00
38-Black Canary begins; JSA Death issue
　　　　　　　　30.00　60.00　90.00
39,40: #39-Last Johnny Thunder
　　　　　　　　22.50　45.00　67.50
41-Black Canary joins JSA; Injustice Society
　app.　　　　　　20.00　40.00　60.00
42-Atom & the Hawkman don new costume
　　　　　　　　20.00　40.00　60.00
43-49　　　　　　20.00　40.00　60.00
50-Frazetta art, 3 pgs.　25.00　50.00　75.00
51-56　　　　　　20.00　40.00　60.00
57-Kubert story, 6 pgs. (Scarce)
　　　　　　　　25.00　50.00　75.00
58('76)-Flash, Hawkman, Dr. Mid-Nite, Wild-
　cat, Dr. Fate, Green Lantern, Star Spang-
　led Kid, Robin & Power Girl app.
　　　　　　　　.50　1.00　1.50
59-74　　　　　　.20　.40　.60
NOTE: *No Atom-#27,36; no Dr. Fate-#9,13; no
Flash-#8,9,11-23; no Green Lantern-#9; no
Johnny Thunder-#5,36; no Wonder Woman-#9,10,
23. Burnley Starman-#8-13. Kubert Hawkman-
#24-30,33-37. Moldoff Hawkman-#3-23. Simon &
Kirby Sandman-#14-17,19. Staton stories-inks
#66-74; covers-#71-74. Wood story-#58-65;
covers-#63,64.*

ALL STAR WESTERN　(All Star #1-57)
Apr-May, 1951 - #120, Aug-Sept, 1961
National Periodical Publications

#58-Trigger Twins begin, end #116
　　　　　　　　5.00　10.00　15.00
59-66　　　　　　2.50　5.00　7.50
67-Johnny Thunder begins; Gil Kane art
　　　　　　　　3.50　7.00　10.50
68-80　　　　　　2.00　4.00　6.00
81-98　　　　　　1.50　3.00　4.50
99-Frazetta reprinted from Jimmy Wakely #4
　　　　　　　　4.00　8.00　12.00
100-107,109-116,118-120　1.50　3.00　4.50
108-Origin Johnny Thunder 2.00　4.00　6.00
117-Origin Super Chief　2.00　4.00　6.00
Note: *Infantino art in most issues. Madame
app.-#117-119.*

ALL STAR WESTERN (Weird Western Tales #12 on)

Aug-Sept, 1970 - #11, Apr-May, 1972
National Periodical Publications
　　　　　　　　Good　Fine　Mint
#1-Reprints; Infantino art .40　.80　1.20
　2-Outlaw begins; El Diablo by Morrow be-
　gins　　　　　　.30　.60　.90
　3-8: #3-Origin El Diablo. #5-Last Outlaw
　ish. #6-Billy the Kid begins, ends #8
　　　　　　　　.30　.60　.90
　9-3pg. Frazetta reprint .50　1.00　1.50
10-Jonah Hex begins, #11 .20　.40　.60
NOTE: *Adams covers-#1-5; #7-11, 52 pgs.;
Morrow stories-#2-4,10,11.*

ALL SURPRISE
Fall, 1943 - #12, Winter, 1946-47
Timely/Marvel(CPC)

#1-Super Rabbit & Gandy & Sourpuss
　　　　　　　　1.50　3.00　4.50
2-10,12　　　　　1.20　2.40　3.60
11-Kurtzman "Pigtales" story
　　　　　　　　4.00　8.00　12.00

ALL TEEN　(Formerly All Winners; Teen #21 on)
#20, January, 1947
Marvel Comics (WFP)

#20　　　　　　　1.50　3.00　4.50

ALL-TIME ROMANCE
1955
Ajax/Farrell Publications

#22　　　　　　　.80　1.60　2.40

ALL TIME SPORTS COMICS
Oct-Nov, 1948 - #7, Oct-Nov, 1949
Hillman Periodicals

#1　　　　　　　1.20　2.40　3.60
2-7　　　　　　　.80　1.60　2.40

ALL TOP
1944　(132 pgs.)
William H. Wise Co.

Capt. V, Merciless the Sorceress, Red Robbins, One Round Hogan, Mike the M.P., Snooky,
Pussy Katnip app.　4.00　8.00　12.00

ALL TOP COMICS　(My Experience #19 on)
1945 - #18, Mar, 1949; 1957 - 1959
Fox Features Synd./Green Publ./Norlen Mag.

#1-Cosmo Cat & Flash Rabbit begin
　　　　　　　　2.00　4.00　6.00
2-7　　　　　　　1.40　2.80　4.20

All Star Comics #55. ⓒ DC

All Star Western #63. ⓒ DC

All Top Comics #9, ⓒ FOX

All-True Crime #27, © MCG   All True Romance #20, © Four Star   All Winners Comics #18, © MCG

(All Top Comics cont'd)   Good   Fine   Mint
8-Blue Beetle, Phantom Lady, & Rulah, Jungle Goddess begin (11/47); Kamen cover
                        40.00   80.00 120.00
9-Kamen cover   30.00   60.00   90.00
10-Kamen bondage cover 30.00   60.00   90.00
11-13   25.00   50.00   75.00
14-No Blue Beetle; used in Seduction of the
Innocent, illo-"Corpses of colored people
strung up by their wrists"
                        30.00   60.00   90.00
15-17: #15-No Blue Beetle
                        22.50   45.00   67.50
18-Dagar, Jo-Jo, Rulah app. only; No Phantom
Lady, Blue Beetle 15.00 30.00 45.00
#6(1957-Green Publ.)-Patoruzu the Indian;
Cosmo Cat on cover only .75   1.50   2.25
#6(1958-Literary Ent.)-Muggy Doo; Cosmo Cat
on cover only   .75   1.50   2.25
#6(1959-Norlen)-Atomic Mouse; Cosmo Cat on
cover only   .75   1.50   2.25
#6(1959)-Little Eva   .75   1.50   2.25
#6(Cornell)-Supermouse on cover
                        .75   1.50   2.25
#6(Cornell)   .75   1.50   2.25
NOTE: *Jo-Jo by Kamen-#12,18.*

ALL TRUE ALL PICTURE POLICE CASES
Oct, 1952 - #2, Nov, 1952   (100 pgs.)
St. John Publishing Co.

#1-Three rebound St. John crime comics
                        7.00   14.00   21.00
2-Three comics rebound 5.00   10.00   15.00
NOTE: *Contents may vary.*

ALL-TRUE CRIME (-- Cases #1,26-35; Formerly
Official True Crime Cases)
#26, Feb, 1948 - #52, Sept, 1952
Marvel/Atlas Comics(LMC/OCI #27/CFI #28,29)

#1 (100 pgs.)   4.00   8.00   12.00
26(#1)   2.00   4.00   6.00
27(4/48)   1.20   2.40   3.60
28-41,43-48,50-52   1.00   2.00   3.00
42,49-Krigstein art   2.00   4.00   6.00
NOTE: *Robinson art-#47.*

ALL-TRUE DETECTIVE CASES (Kit Carson #5 on)
Feb-Mar, 1954 - #4, Aug-Sept, 1954
Avon Periodicals

#1   3.50   7.00   10.50
2-Wood art, 8 pgs.   5.00   10.00   15.00
3   2.50   5.00   7.50
4-Wood(?), Kamen stories 5.00 10.00   15.00
No# (100 pgs.)-7 pg. Kubert story, Kinstler
back cover   5.00   10.00   15.00

ALL TRUE ROMANCE (-- Illustrated #3)
Mar, 1951 - #34, Mar, 1958; #4, Nov, 1957
Artful Publ. #1-3/Harwell(Comic Media)/Ajax-
Farrell(Excellent Publ.)/Four Star Comic Corp.
                        Good   Fine   Mint
#1(3/51)   3.50   7.00   10.50
2,3(12/51)-#5   2.00   4.00   6.00
6-Wood art, 9pgs. (exceptional)
                        5.00   10.00   15.00
7-10   1.75   3.50   5.25
11-20   1.25   2.50   3.75
21-34   .80   1.60   2.40
#4(Farrell, 1957)   .45   .90   1.35

ALL WESTERN WINNERS (Formerly All Winners;
becomes Western Winners with #5)
#2, Winter, 1948-49 - #4, April, 1949
Marvel Comics(CDS)

#2-Origin Black Rider, Kid Colt & Two-Gun
Kid   6.00   12.00   18.00
3,4   4.00   8.00   12.00

ALL WINNERS COMICS (All Teen #20; Official
True Crime Cases #22 on; #1 advertised as
All Aces)
Summer, 1941 - #19, Summer, 1946; #21, Win-
ter, 1946-47 (no #20) (#21 continued from
Yound Allies #20)
Timely/Marvel Comics (USA, Young Allies, Inc.)

#1-The Angel & Black Marvel only app.; Capt.
America by Simon & Kirby, Human Torch &
Sub-Mariner begin 225.00 450.00 675.00
2-The Destroyer & The Whizzer begin; Simon
& Kirby Capt.America 100.00 200.00 300.00
3   70.00 140.00 210.00
4,5   60.00 120.00 180.00
6-The Black Avenger only app.; no Whizzer
story   50.00 100.00 150.00
7-10   40.00   80.00 120.00
11-18: #12-Last Destroyer; no Whizzer story;
no Human Torch #14-16 30.00   60.00   90.00
19,21-All Winners Squad, Miss America only
app.   40.00   80.00 120.00
NOTE: *Everett Sub-Mariner-#1,3,4; Burgos
Torch-#1,3,4.*

        (2nd Series-Aug, 1948)
(Becomes All Western Winners with #2)

#1-The Blonde Phantom, Capt. America, Human
Torch, & Sub-Mariner app.
                        35.00   70.00 105.00

ALL YOUR COMICS
1944 (132 pgs.); 1946 (36 pgs.)
Fox Features Syndicate (R. W. Boight)

(All Your Comics cont'd)   Good   Fine   Mint
#1-(1944)-The Puppeteer, Red Robbins, &
    Merciless app.   5.00   10.00 15.00
#1-(1946)-Red Robbins, Merciless the Sorcer-
    er app.   4.00   8.00 12.00

ALMANAC OF CRIME
1948   (148 pgs.)
Fox Features Syndicate

No#-Contain 4½ rebound Fox titles. See Fox
    Giants. Contents can vary and determines
    price.

ALONG THE FIRING LINE WITH ROGER BEAN
1916   (Hardcover, B&W)(6x17")(66 pgs.)
Chas. B. Jackson

#3-by Chic Jackson(1915 daily strips)
                             7.00   14.00 21.00

AL OF FBI   (See Little Al of the FBI)

ALPHONSE & GASTON & LEON
1903 (15x10" Sunday strip reprints in color)
Hearst's New York American & Journal

by Fred Opper   20.00 50.00 80.00

ALVIN (TV) (See 4-Color Comics #1042)
Oct-Dec, 1962 - #28, Oct, 1973
Dell Publishing Co.

#12-021-212   .40   .80   1.20
2-28   .25   .50   .75
Alvin For President(10/64) .20 .40   .60
-- & His Pals in Merry Christmas With Clyde
   Crashcup & Leonardo #1(02-120-402)12-2/64,
   reprinted in 1966   .40   .80   1.20

AMAZING ADULT FANTASY (Amazing Adventures
#1-6; Amazing Fantasy #15)
#7, Dec, 1961 - #14, July, 1962
Marvel Comics Group (AMI)

#7   3.50   7.00 10.50
8-14: All Ditko stories 3.00   6.00   9.00

AMAZING ADVENTURE FUNNIES (Fantoman #2 on)
June, 1940 - #2, Sept, 1940
Centaur Publications

#1-The Fantom of the Fair by Gustavson, The
   Arrow, Skyrocket Steele From the Year X
   by Everett - All reprints from Amazing
   Mystery Funnies & Funny Pages; Burgos art
                        40.00 80.00 120.00

                             Good   Fine   Mint
2-Reprints. This issue came out after
Fantoman #2   25.00 50.00 75.00

AMAZING ADVENTURES
1950 - #6, Fall, 1952
Ziff-Davis Publ. Co.

1950 (no month given) (8½x11")(8 pgs.) Has
   the front & back cover + Schomburg story
   used in Amazing Advs. #1 (possibly a pre-
   publication proof)
           Estimated value 45.00
#1-Wood, Schomburg, Anderson, Whitney
   stories   10.00 20.00 30.00
2-5-Anderson art   4.00   8.00 12.00
6-Krigstein story   5.00 10.00 15.00

AMAZING ADVENTURES (Amaz. Adult Fantasy #7)
June, 1961 - #6, Nov, 1961
Marvel Comics Group (AMI)

#1-Origin Dr. Droom by Kirby; Ditko & Kirby
   art in all; Kirby covers #1-6
                         9.00 18.00 27.00
2   5.00 10.00 15.00
3-6: Last Dr. Droom   3.00   6.00   9.00

AMAZING ADVENTURES
Aug, 1970 - #39, Nov, 1976
Marvel Comics Group

#1-Inhumans by Kirby & Black Widow begin
                         1.00   2.00   3.00
2-Last Kirby Inhumans   .75   1.50   2.25
3,4   .60   1.20   1.80
5-8-Adams art; #8-Last Black Widow
                         1.00   2.00   3.00
9,10: #10-Last Inhumans(origin reprint by
   Kirby)   .50   1.00   1.50
11-Beast begins, ends #17 .30   .60   .90
12-14   .30   .60   .90
15-17-Starlin covers. #17-2pg. Starlin pencils   .40   .80   1.20
18-War of the Worlds begins; 1st app. Kill-
   raven; Adams art   1.20   2.40   3.60
19-26   .30   .60   .90
27-Starlin cover   .35   .70   1.05
28-39: #34-Death of Hawk .25   .50   .75
NOTE: Adams covers-#6-8, pencils part-#18.
Chaykin story-#19. Everett inks-#3-5,9. Ploog
inks-#12. Craig Russell art-#27-39.

AMAZING ADVENTURES OF CAPTAIN CARVEL AND
HIS CARVEL CRUSADERS, THE (See Carvel Comics)

AMAZING CHAN & THE CHAN CLAN, THE (TV)
May, 1973 - #4, Feb, 1974 (Hanna-Barbera)

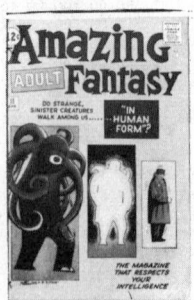

Amazing Adult Fantasy #11, © MCG

Amazing Adventure Funnies #2, © CEN

Amazing Adventures #5, © Z-D

Amazing-Man Comics =11, © CEN   Amazing Mysteries #32, © MCG   Amazing Mystery Funnies V3#1, © CEN

(Amazing Chan & the Chan Clan cont'd)
Gold Key

	Good	Fine	Mint
#1-4	.15	.30	.45

AMAZING COMICS   (Complete #2)
Fall, 1944
Timely Comics

#1-The Destroyer, The Whizzer, The Young
  Allies, Sergeant Dix 45.00 90.00 135.00

AMAZING DETECTIVE CASES (Formerly Suspense #2?)
#3, Nov, 1950 - #14, Sept, 1952
Marvel/Atlas Comics(CCC)

#3	1.25	2.50	3.75
4-6	1.00	2.00	3.00
7-10,11,14	.85	1.70	2.55
12-Krigstein art	2.00	4.00	6.00
13-Everett story, 4 pgs.	1.20	2.40	3.60

AMAZING FANTASY   (-- Adult Fantasy #7-14;
Amazing Adventures #1-6)
#15, Aug, 1962
Marvel Comics Group(AMI)

#15-Origin & 1st app. of Spider-Man by Ditko;
  Kirby/Ditko cover   150.00 300.00 450.00

AMAZING GHOST STORIES (Formerly Nightmare)
#14, Oct, 1954 - #16, Feb, 1955
St. John Publishing Co.

#14-Kinstler art	2.00	4.00	6.00
15-Reprints Weird Thrillers #5			
	1.20	2.40	3.60
16-Kubert reprints of Weird Thrillers #4;			
Matt Baker cover	1.75	3.50	5.25

AMAZING-MAN COMICS
#5, Sept, 1939 - #27, Feb, 1942
Centaur Publications

#5(#1)-Origin A-Man the Amazing Man by Bill
  Everett; The Cat-Man by Tarpe Mills (also
  #8), Mighty Man, Minimidget & sidekick
  Ritty, & The Iron Skull begin
                    65.00 130.00 195.00
6-Origin The Amazing Man retold; The Shark
  begins   35.00 70.00 105.00
7-Magician From Mars begins
                    25.00 50.00 75.00
8-11: #11-Zardi, the Eternal Man begins;
  Amazing Man dons costume; last Everett
  issue   17.50 35.00 52.50
12,13   14.00 28.00 42.00
14-Dr. Hypno begins 12.00 24.00 36.00

	Good	Fine	Mint
15-20	12.00	24.00	36.00
21-TNT Todd app.	9.00	18.00	27.00

22-Dash Darnell, the Human Meteor & The Voice
  app.   9.00 18.00 27.00
23-Intro. Tommy the Amazing Kid; The Marksman only app.   9.00 18.00 27.00
24,27   9.00 18.00 27.00
25,26-Meteor Martin by Wolverton in both
                   25.00 50.00 75.00

AMAZING MYSTERIES (Formerly Sub-Mariner #31?)
#32, May, 1949 - #35, Jan, 1950
Marvel Comics (CCC)

#32-The Witness app.	3.50	7.00	10.50
33-35	1.50	3.00	4.50

AMAZING MYSTERY FUNNIES
Aug, 1938 - V3#8, Sept, 1940 (#24)
Centaur Publications

V1#1-Everett cover; Dick Kent Adv. story;
  Skyrocket Steele in the Year X on cover
  only   60.00 120.00 180.00
2-Everett & Eisner art
                   30.00 60.00 90.00
3-Everett & Eisner art; Everett cover
                   20.00 40.00 60.00
3(#4, 12/38)-No# on cover, #3 on inside
                   15.00 30.00 45.00
V2#1-3: #1-Everett art 12.00 24.00 36.00
4-Dan Hastings begins; ends #5
                   12.00 24.00 36.00
5,6   12.00 24.00 36.00
7-Intro. The Fantom of the Fair; Everett,
  Gustavson, Burgos art 35.00 70.00 105.00
8-Origin & 1st app. Speed Centaur
                   20.00 40.00 60.00
9-11   12.00 24.00 36.00
12-Wolverton art   20.00 40.00 60.00
V3#1(#17)-Intro. Bullet (1/40)
                   12.00 24.00 36.00
18,20   10.00 20.00 30.00
19,21-24-All have Space Patrol by
Wolverton   25.00 50.00 75.00

AMAZING SAINTS
1974   (39¢)
Logos International

True story of Phil Saint .15   .30   .45

AMAZING SPIDER-MAN, THE (See Amazing Fantasy, Aurora, Book & Record--, Giant Comics
to Color, Marvel Treasury Ed., Spectacular
--, & Spidey Super Stories)

AMAZING SPIDER-MAN, THE
March, 1963 - Present
Marvel Comics Group

	Good	Fine	Mint
#1-Retells origin by Steve Ditko; F.F. x-over; Kirby cover	135.00	270.00	405.00

1-Reprint from the Golden Record Comic set

	Good	Fine	Mint
	1.50	3.00	4.50
with record....	2.00	4.00	6.00
2-1st app. The Vulture	40.00	80.00	120.00

3-Human Torch cameo; intro. & 1st app.

Doc Octopus	25.00	50.00	75.00
4	20.00	40.00	60.00
5,6: #5-Dr. Doom app.	15.00	30.00	45.00
7-10: #8-Fant.-4 app. #9-1st app. Electro (origin)& The Sandman	11.00	22.00	33.00

11-15: #14-Intro. Green Goblin; Hulk x-over

	7.00	14.00	21.00
16-20: #18-Fant.-4 app.	4.50	9.00	13.50
21-30: #28-Origin & 1st app. Molten Man	2.50	5.00	7.50
31-38-Last Ditko ish.	2.00	4.00	6.00
39,40	1.50	3.00	4.50
41-60	1.20	2.40	3.60
61-80	.90	1.80	2.70
81-89	.75	1.50	2.25
90-Death of Capt. Stacy	1.00	2.00	3.00
91-93,95,99	.60	1.20	1.80
94-Origin retold	.80	1.60	2.40

96-98-Drug books not approved by CCA

	1.50	3.00	4.50
100	1.20	2.40	3.60
101-Intro. Morbius	.90	1.80	2.70
102-Origin Morbius (52pgs.)	.90	1.80	2.70
103-112	.70	1.40	2.10
113,114-Starlin in part	.75	1.50	2.25
115-120	.60	1.20	1.80

121-Death of Gwen Stacy (reprinted in Marvel

Tales #98)	3.00	6.00	9.00
122-Death of Green Goblin	3.00	6.00	9.00

123-140: #124-Intro. Man Wolf, origin-#125.
#129-1st app. The Punisher

	.40	.80	1.20
141-150	.30	.60	.90
151-170	.25	.50	.75
171-Nova x-over	.30	.60	.90

172-181: #181-Origin retold; gives life history
of Spider-Man

	.20	.40	.60

182-190: #190-1st app. Hans The Herder

	.15	.30	.45
Annual #1(1964)	7.00	14.00	21.00
Annual #2	4.00	8.00	12.00
Special #3,4	2.00	4.00	6.00
Special #5-8(12/71)	1.20	2.40	3.60
King Size #9 ('73)	.80	1.60	2.40

Annual #10(6/76)-1st app. Human Fly

	.60	1.20	1.80
Annual #11(9/77),#12(8/78)	.30	.60	.90

	Good	Fine	Mint
Giant-Size #1(7/74)-Dracula app.	.80	1.60	2.40
Giant-Size #2	.60	1.20	1.80

Giant-Size #3-6(9/75): #4-The Punisher app.

	.50	1.00	1.50

Giveaway-Esquire & Eye Magazines(2/69)-Miniature)-Still attached 2.50 5.00 7.50
-- vs. the Prodigy Giveaway, 16pgs. in color
('76)-5x6½"-Sex education; (1 million
printed) Can be ordered from Planned Parenthood, M-76 Publ., 810 Seventh Ave.,
N. Y., N. Y. 10019 at 35c each

	.15	.30	.45

NOTE: _Ditko art-#1-38, Annuals #1,2. Kirby
story-#8._

AMAZING WILLIE MAYS, THE
No Date (Aug, 1954?)
Famous Funnies Publ.

No# (Scarce)	4.00	8.00	12.00

AMBUSH (See 4-Color Comics #314)

AMERICA IN ACTION
1942; 1945 (36 pgs.)
Dell(Imp. Publ. Co.)/Mayflower House Publ.

1942-Dell-(68pgs.)	3.00	6.00	9.00

#1(1945)-Has 3 adaptations from American history; Kiefer, Schrotter & Webb art

	3.00	6.00	9.00

AMERICAN COMICS
1940's
Theatre Giveaways (Liberty Theatre, Grand
Rapids, Mich. known)

Many possible combinations. "Golden Age"
superhero comics with new cover added and
given away at theatres. Following known:
Superman #59, Capt. Marvel #20, Capt. Marvel
Jr. #5, Action #33, Whiz #39. Value would
vary with book and should be 50-70% of the
original.

AMERICAN AIR FORCES (See A-1 Comics)
1944 - 1945; 1951 - 1954
William H. Wise(Flying Cadet Publ. Co./Hasan
(#1))/Life's Romances/Magazine Ent. #5 on

#1-Article by Zack Mosley, creator of Smilin'
Jack   3.50 7.00 10.50
2-4   2.00 4.00 6.00
NOTE: _All part comic, part magazine. Art by
Whitney, Chas. Quinlan, H.C. Kiefer, and Tony
Dipreta._

Amazing Spider-Man #1. © MCG

Amazing Spider-Man #10. © MCG

Amazing Spider-Man #22. © MCG

American Air Forces #2. © WHW   America's Best Comics #23. © BP   America's Greatest Comics #8. © FAW

(American Air Forces cont'd)

	Good	Fine	Mint
#5(A-1#45),6(A-1#54),7(A-1#58),8(A-1#65), 9(A-1#67),10(A-1#74),11(A-1#79),12(A-1#91)	1.75	3.50	5.25

NOTE: *Powell art-#5-12.*

AMERICAN GRAPHICS
#1, 1954; #2, 1957   (25¢)
Henry Stewart

1-The Maid of the Mist, The Last of the
   Eries (Indian Legends of Niagara)(Sold
   at Niagara Falls)   2.50   5.00   7.50
2-Victory at Niagara & Laura Secord (Heroine
   of the War of 1812)   2.00   4.00   6.00

AMERICAN INDIAN, THE (See Picture Progress)

AMERICAN LIBRARY
1944   (68 pgs.)   (15¢)
David McKay Publications

#3-6: #4-Case of the Crooked Candle-Perry
   Mason   4.00   8.00   12.00

AMERICA'S BEST COMICS
Feb, 1942 - #31, July, 1949
Nedor/Better/Standard Publications

#1-The Woman in Red, Black Terror, Captain
   Future, Doc Strange, The Liberator, & Don
   Davis, Secret Ace begin
                   40.00 80.00 120.00
2-Origin The American Eagle; The Woman in
   Red ends   20.00 40.00 60.00
3-Pyroman begins   15.00 30.00 45.00
4   13.50 26.75 40.00
5-Last Captain Future-not in #4; Lone Eagle
   app.   12.00 24.00 36.00
6,7-American Crusader app. in #6
                   10.00 20.00 30.00
8-Last Liberator   8.00 16.00 24.00
9-The Fighting Yank begins; The Ghost app.
                    8.00 16.00 24.00
10-13,15-20   6.00 12.00 18.00
14-Last American Eagle 6.00 12.00 18.00
21,24   5.00 10.00 15.00
22-Capt. Future app.   5.00 10.00 15.00
23-Miss Masque begins; last Doc Strange
                    8.00 16.00 24.00
25-Last Fighting Yank; Sea Eagle app.
                    6.00 12.00 18.00
26-The Phantom Detective & The Silver Knight
   app.   6.00 12.00 18.00
27,28-Commando Cubs app.; Doc Strange in #27
                    6.00 12.00 18.00
29-Last Pyroman   6.00 12.00 18.00

	Good	Fine	Mint
30,31	6.00	12.00	18.00

NOTE: *American Eagle not in #3,8,9,13.
Fighting Yank not in #10,12,14. Liberator
not in #2,6,7. Pyroman not in #9,11,14-16,
23,25-27. Schomburg (Xela) covers-#23-31.*

AMERICA'S BEST TV COMICS
1967   (Produced by Marvel Comics)
American Broadcasting Company

#1-Spider-Man, Fantastic Four, Casper, King
   Kong, George of the Jungle, Journey to
   the Center of the Earth app. (Promotes
   new TV cartoon show)   1.20   2.40   3.60

AMERICA'S BIGGEST COMICS BOOK
1944   (196 pgs.)   (One Shot)
Better Publications

#1-The Grim Reaper, The Silver Knight, Zudo,
   the Jungle Boy, Commando Cubs, Thunder-
   hoof app.   7.00 14.00 21.00

AMERICA'S FUNNIEST COMICS
1941   (80 pgs.)   (15¢)
William H. Wise

No#(#1), 2   2.00   4.00   6.00

AMERICA'S GREATEST COMICS
1941 - #8, Summer, 1943 (100pgs.)(Soft card-
Fawcett Publications   board covers)

#1-Bulletman, Spy Smasher, Capt.Marvel, Min-
   ute Man & Mr. Scarlet begin
                   75.00 187.50 300.00
2   35.00 87.50 140.00
3   22.50 56.25 90.00
4-Commando Yank begins; Golden Arrow & Ibis
   the Invincible & Spy Smasher cameo in
   Captain Marvel   20.00 50.00 80.00
5   20.00 50.00 80.00
6   12.50 31.25 50.00
7-Balbo the Boy Magician app.; Captain
   Marvel, Bulletman cameo in Mr. Scarlet
                   12.50 31.25 50.00
8-Capt. Marvel Jr. & Golden Arrow app.; Spy
   Smasher x-over in Capt. Midnight; no Minute Man or Commando Yank
                   12.50 31.25 50.00

AMERICA'S SWEETHEART SUNNY (See Sunny)

ANARCHO DICTATOR OF DEATH (See Comics Novel)

ANCHORS ANDREWS (The Saltwater Daffy)
1/53 - #4, 7/53 (Anchors the Saltwater -- #4)

(Anchors Andrews cont'd)
St. John Publishing Co.

	Good	Fine	Mint
#1-Canteen Kate by Matt Baker, 9 pgs.	4.00	8.00	12.00
2-4	1.00	2.00	3.00

ANDY & WOODY (See March of Comics #40,55,76)

ANDY BURNETT (See 4-Color Comics #865)

ANDY COMICS
June, 1948
Current Publications

#20-Archie-type comic	.80	1.60	2.40

ANDY DEVINE WESTERN
Dec, 1950 - 1952
Fawcett Publications

#1	6.00	12.00	18.00
2-10	3.00	6.00	9.00
11-21	2.00	4.00	6.00

ANDY GRIFFITH (See 4-Color #1252,1341)

ANDY HARDY COMICS (See Movie Comics #3, Fic-
1952 - #6, 9-11/54   tion House)
Dell Publishing Co.

4-Color #389	1.20	2.40	3.60
4-Color #447,480,515	1.00	2.00	3.00
#5,6	.80	1.60	2.40
-- & the New Automatic Gas Clothes Dryer('52, 16pgs.,5x7¼")-Bendix Giveaway			
	1.50	3.00	4.50

ANDY PANDA
1943 - Nov-Jan, 1962   (Walter Lantz)
Dell Publishing Co.

4-Color #25('43)	25.00	50.00	75.00
4-Color #54('44)	15.00	30.00	45.00
4-Color #85('45)	8.00	16.00	24.00
4-Color #130('46),154,198	4.00	8.00	12.00
4-Color #216,240,258,280,297			
	2.50	5.00	7.50
4-Color #326,345,358	1.40	2.80	4.20
4-Color #383,409	1.20	2.40	3.60
#16-30	.80	1.60	2.40
31-56	.60	1.20	1.80

(See March of Comics #5,22,79 & Super Book
#4,15,27.)

ANDY PANDA
Aug, 1973 - #23, Jan, 1978   (Walter Lantz)
Gold Key

	Good	Fine	Mint
#1-Reprints	.25	.50	.75
2-10-All reprints	.15	.30	.45
11-23-All new stories		.15	.30

ANGEL
Aug, 1954 - #16, Nov-Jan, 1958-59
Dell Publishing Co.

4-Color #576(8/54)	.70	1.40	2.10
#2(5-7/55) - #16	.45	.90	1.35

ANGEL AND THE APE (Meet Angel #7)
11-12/68 - #6, 9-10/69   (See Showcase #77)
National Periodical Publications

#1-Not Wood art	.40	.80	1.20
2-6-Wood art in all	.50	1.00	1.50

ANGELIC ANGELINA
1909   (11½x17"; 30pgs.; 2 colors)
Cupples & Leon Company

By Munson Paddock	10.00	20.00	30.00

ANIMAL ADVENTURES
Dec, 1953 - #3, 1954
Accepted Publications

#1-3	.65	1.35	2.00

ANIMAL ANTICS (Movie Town -- #20 on)
Mar-Apr, 1946 - #19, Mar-Apr, 1949
National Periodical Publications

#1-Raccoon Kids begin	3.00	6.00	9.00
2-10	1.50	3.00	4.50
11-19: #14-Post art	1.20	2.40	3.60

ANIMAL COMICS
1942 - #30, Dec-Jan, 1947-48
Dell Publishing Co.

#1-1st Pogo app. by Walt Kelly (Dan Noonan art in most issues)	175.00	350.00	525.00
2-Uncle Wiggily begins	70.00	140.00	210.00
3,5	50.00	100.00	150.00
4,6,7-No Pogo	25.00	50.00	75.00
8-10	27.50	55.00	82.50
11-15	20.00	40.00	60.00
16-20	12.00	24.00	36.00
21-30: #25-30-"Jigger" by John Stanley			
	9.00	18.00	27.00

NOTE: #18-30-*Dan Noonan* art. *Gollub* art in
most later issues.

ANIMAL CRACKERS (Also see Advs. of Patoruzu)
1946 - #31, July, 1950; 1959

Andy Panda Four Color #297, © Walter Lantz

Animal Comics #12, © Dell

Animal Comics #6, © Dell

Animated Movie-Tunes #2, © MCG   Annie Oakley #18, © Dell   A-1 Comics No#, © ME

(Animal Crackers cont'd)
Green Publ. Co./Norlen/Fox Feat.(Hero Books)

	Good	Fine	Mint
#1-Super Cat begins	1.20	2.40	3.60
2-31	.50	1.00	1.50
#31(Fox)-Formerly My Love Secret			
	.75	1.50	2.25
9(1959-Norlen)	.40	.80	1.20
No#, no date, no publ.	.40	.80	1.20

ANIMAL FABLES
July-Aug, 1946 - #7, Nov-Dec, 1947
E.C. Comics

#1	15.00	30.00	45.00
2-6	10.00	20.00	30.00
7-Origin Moon Girl	25.00	50.00	75.00

ANIMAL FAIR (Fawcett's --)
March, 1946 - #11, Feb, 1947
Fawcett Publications

#1	2.50	5.00	7.50
2-6	1.20	2.40	3.60
7-11	1.00	2.00	3.00

ANIMAL FUN
1953
Premier Magazines

#1-(3-D)	5.00	10.00	15.00

ANIMAL WORLD, THE (See 4-Color Comics #713)

ANIMATED COMICS
No date given (Summer, 1947?)
E.C. Comics

#1 (Rare)	50.00	100.00	150.00

ANIMATED FUNNY COMIC TUNES (See Funny Tunes)

ANIMATED MOVIE-TUNES (Also see Movie Tunes)
Fall, 1945
Margood Publishing Co. (Timely)

#1-Super Rabbit	1.20	2.40	3.60

ANNETTE (See 4-Color Comics #905)

ANNETTE'S LIFE STORY (See 4-Color #1100)

ANNIE OAKLEY
Spr, 1948 - #4, 11/48; #5, 6/55 - #11, 6/56
Marvel/Atlas Comics(MPI #1-4/CDS #5 on)

#1 (1st Series)(1948)	6.00	12.00	18.00
2-Kurtzman art	5.00	10.00	15.00

	Good	Fine	Mint
3,4	4.00	8.00	12.00
5 (2nd Series)(1955)	2.50	5.00	7.50
6-8: #8-Woodbridge art	2.00	4.00	6.00
9-Williamson story, 4pgs.	3.00	6.00	9.00
10,11	1.50	3.00	4.50

ANNIE OAKLEY AND TAGG
1953 - 1965
Dell Publishing Co./Gold Key

4-Color #438	2.00	4.00	6.00
4-Color #481,575	1.75	3.50	5.25
#4(7-9/55)-#10	1.25	2.50	3.75
11-18(1-3/59)	1.00	2.00	3.00
#1(7/65-G.K.)	.50	1.00	1.50

ANOTHER WORLD (See Strange Stories From --)

ANTHRO (See Showcase)
July-Aug, 1968 - #6, July-Aug, 1969
National Periodical Publications

#1-Howie Post art in all	.50	1.00	1.50
2-6: #6-Wood inks	.30	.60	.90

ANTONY & CLEOPATRA (See Ideal, A Classical Comic)

A-1 COMICS (A-1 appears on covers #1-18 only)
See individual title listings. 1st two issues not numbered.
1944 - #139, Sept-Oct, 1955
Life's Romances Publ.-#1/Compix/Magazine Ent.

No#-Kerry Drake, Johnny Devildog, Rocky, Streamer Kelly	6.00	12.00	18.00
#1-Dotty Dripple(1 pg.), Mr. Ex, Bush Berry, Rocky, Lew Loyal(20pgs.)			
	1.50	3.00	4.50
2-8,10-Texas Slim & Dirty Dalton, The Corsair, Teddy Rich, Dotty Dripple, Inca Dinca, Tommy Tinker, Little Mexico & Tugboat Tim, The Masquerader & others			
	1.40	2.80	4.20
9-Texas Slim (all)	1.50	3.00	4.50
11,12-Teena	1.25	2.50	3.75
13-Guns of Fact & Fiction (1948). Ingels & J. Craig art	4.00	8.00	12.00
14-Tim Holt Western Adventures #1 (1948)			
	15.00	30.00	45.00
15-Teena	1.25	2.50	3.75
16-Vacation Comics	1.00	2.00	3.00
17-Tim Holt #2	8.00	16.00	24.00
18-Jimmy Durante. Last issue to carry A-1 on cover	5.00	10.00	15.00
19-Tim Holt #3	7.00	14.00	21.00
20-Jimmy Durante	4.00	8.00	12.00

	Good	Fine	Mint
21-Joan of Arc(1949)-Ogden Whitney art			
	3.50	7.00	10.50
22-Dick Powell(1949)	1.50	3.00	4.50
23-Cowboys 'N' Indians #6	1.20	2.40	3.60
24-Trail Colt #1-Frazetta, reprinted in Manhunt #13. Ingels cvr.	12.00	24.00	36.00
25-Fibber McGee & Molly(1949)			
	1.50	3.00	4.50
26-Trail Colt #2-Ingels cover			
	9.00	18.00	27.00
27-Ghost Rider #1(1950)-Origin Ghost Rider			
	20.00	40.00	60.00
28-Christmas-(Koko & Kola #6)(5/47)			
	1.20	2.40	3.60
29-Ghost Rider #2-Frazetta cover (1950)			
	18.00	36.00	54.00
30-Jet #1-Powell art	6.00	12.00	18.00
31-Ghost Rider #3-Frazetta cover & origin (1951)	18.00	36.00	54.00
32-Jet Powers #2	4.00	8.00	12.00
33-Muggsy Mouse #1('51)	.60	1.20	1.80
34-Ghost Rider #4-Frazetta cover (1951)			
	18.00	36.00	54.00
35-Jet Powers #3-Williamson & Evans story			
	10.00	20.00	30.00
36-Muggsy Mouse #2	.60	1.20	1.80
37-Ghost Rider #5-Frazetta cover (1951)			
	18.00	36.00	54.00
38-Jet Powers #4-Wiliamson & Wood story			
	12.00	24.00	36.00
39-Muggsy Mouse #3	.60	1.20	1.80
40-Dogface Dooley #1('51)	1.25	2.50	3.75
41-Cowboys 'N' Indians #7	1.20	2.40	3.60
42-Best of the West #1	7.00	14.00	21.00
43-Dogface Dooley #2	1.25	2.50	3.75
44-Ghost Rider #6	6.00	12.00	18.00
45-American Air Forces #5	1.75	3.50	5.25
46-Best of the West #2	3.50	7.00	10.50
47-Thun'da, King of the Congo #1-Frazetta cover & stories('52)	150.00	300.00	450.00
48-Cowboys 'N' Indians #8	1.20	2.40	3.60
49-Dogface Dooley #3	1.25	2.50	3.75
50-Danger Is Their Business #11 (1952)			
	2.50	5.00	7.50
51-Ghost Rider #7 ('52)	6.00	12.00	18.00
52-Best of the West #3	3.50	7.00	10.50
53-Dogface Dooley #4	1.25	2.50	3.75
54-American Air Forces #6(8/52)			
	1.75	3.50	5.25
55-U.S. Marines #5-Powell art			
	1.75	3.50	5.25
56-Thun'da #2	10.00	20.00	30.00
57-Ghost Rider #8	5.00	10.00	15.00
58-American Air Forces #7	1.75	3.50	5.25
59-Best of the West #4	3.50	7.00	10.50
60-The U.S. Marines #6	1.75	3.50	5.25
61-Space Ace #5(1953)-Guardineer art			

	Good	Fine	Mint
	5.00	10.00	15.00
62-Starr Flagg, Undercover Girl #5			
	12.00	24.00	36.00
63-Manhunt #13-Frazetta reprinted from A-1 #24	10.00	20.00	30.00
64-Dogface Dooley #5	1.25	2.50	3.75
65-American Air Forces #8	1.75	3.50	5.25
66-Best of the West #5	3.50	7.00	10.50
67-American Air Forces #9	1.75	3.50	5.25
68-U.S. Marines #7	1.75	3.50	5.25
69-Ghost Rider #9(10/52)	5.00	10.00	15.00
70-Best of the West #6	2.50	5.00	7.50
71-Ghost Rider #10(12/52)	5.00	10.00	15.00
72-U.S. Marines #8	1.75	3.50	5.25
73-Thun'da #3	9.00	18.00	27.00
74-American Air Forces #10			
	1.75	3.50	5.25
75-Ghost Rider #11(3/52)	4.50	9.00	13.50
76-Best of the West #7	2.50	5.00	7.50
77-Manhunt #14 (classic cover)			
	6.00	12.00	18.00
78-Thun'da #4	9.00	18.00	27.00
79-American Air Forces #11			
	1.75	3.50	5.25
80-Ghost Rider #12(6/52)	4.50	9.00	13.50
81-Best of the West #8	2.50	5.00	7.50
82-Cave Girl #11(1953)-Powell art (Origin)			
	15.00	30.00	45.00
83-Thun'da #5	8.00	16.00	24.00
84-Ghost Rider #13(8/53)	4.50	9.00	13.50
85-Best of the West #9	2.50	5.00	7.50
86-Thun'da #6	8.00	16.00	24.00
87-Best of the West #10	2.50	5.00	7.50
88-Bobby Benson's B-Bar-B Riders #20			
	2.25	4.50	6.75
89-Home Run #3-all Powell art			
	1.20	2.40	3.60
90-Red Hawk #11(1953)-Powell art			
	2.50	5.00	7.50
91-American Air Forces #12			
	1.75	3.50	5.25
92-Dream Book of Romance #5			
	1.50	3.00	4.50
93-Great Western #8('54)-Origin The Ghost Rider	4.00	8.00	12.00
94-White Indian #11-Frazetta reprints			
	25.00	50.00	75.00
95-Muggsy Mouse #4	.60	1.20	1.80
96-Cave Girl #12, with Thun'da; Powell art			
	10.00	20.00	30.00
97-Best of the West #11	2.50	5.00	7.50
98-Undercover Girl #6	9.00	18.00	27.00
99-Muggsy Mouse #5	.60	1.20	1.80
100-Badmen of the West #1-Meskin art(?)			
	6.00	12.00	18.00
101-Dream Book of Romance #6			
	1.50	3.00	4.50

A-1 Comics #8, © ME

A-1 Comics #18, © ME

A-1 Comics #32, © ME

A-1 Comics #52, © ME   Apache #1, © FH   Aquaman #23, © DC

(A-1 Comics cont'd)	Good	Fine	Mint
102-White Indian #12?-Frazetta reprints			
	25.00	50.00	75.00
103-Best of the West #12	2.50	5.00	7.50
104-White Indian #13-Frazetta (1954)			
	25.00	50.00	75.00
105-Great Western #9-Ghost Rider app.; Powell art, 6pgs.; Bolle cvr.	2.00	4.00	6.00
106-Dream Book of Love #1-Powell & Bolle art			
	2.00	4.00	6.00
107-Hot Dog #1	.80	1.60	2.40
108-Red Fox #15 (1954)	3.50	7.00	10.50
109-Dream Book of Romance #7 (7-8/54)			
	1.50	3.00	4.50
110-Dream Book of Romance #8			
	1.50	3.00	4.50
111-I'm A Cop #1('54)	2.00	4.00	6.00
112-Ghost Rider #14('54)	4.50	9.00	13.50
113-Great Western #10	2.00	4.00	6.00
114-Dream Book of Love #2-Guardineer, Bolle art	1.50	3.00	4.50
115-Hot Dog #3	.80	1.60	2.40
116-Cave Girl #13	10.00	20.00	30.00
117-White Indian #14	6.00	12.00	18.00
118-Undercover Girl #7	9.00	18.00	27.00
119-Straight Arrow's Fury #1			
	3.00	6.00	9.00
120-Badmen of the West #2	3.00	6.00	9.00
121-Mysteries of Scotland Yard #1; reprints from Manhunt	3.00	6.00	9.00
122-Black Phantom #1(11/54)	8.00	16.00	24.00
123-Dream Book of Love #3(10-11/54)			
	1.50	3.00	4.50
124-Dream Book of Romance #8(10-11/54)			
	1.50	3.00	4.50
125-Cave Girl #14	10.00	20.00	30.00
126-I'm A Cop #2-Powell art	1.50	3.00	4.50
127-Great Western #11('54)	2.00	4.00	6.00
128-I'm A Cop #3-Powell art	1.50	3.00	4.50
129-The Avenger #1('55)	8.00	16.00	24.00
130-Strongman #1	6.00	12.00	18.00
131-The Avenger #2('55)	4.00	8.00	12.00
132-Strongman #2	4.00	8.00	12.00
133-The Avenger #3	4.00	8.00	12.00
134-Strongman #3	4.00	8.00	12.00
135-White Indian #15	6.00	12.00	18.00
136-Hot Dog #4	.80	1.60	2.40
137-Africa #1	5.00	10.00	15.00
138-The Avenger #4	4.00	8.00	12.00
139-Strongman #4-Powell art			
	4.00	8.00	12.00

APACHE
1951
Fiction House Magazines

#1	2.50	5.00	7.50
I.W. Reprint #1	.80	1.60	2.40

APACHE KID (Formerly Reno Browne; Western Gunfighters #20 on)(Also see Two-Gun Western)
#53, 12/50 - #10, 1/52; #11, 12/54 - #19,4/56
Marvel/Atlas Comics(MPC #53-10/CPS #11 on)

	Good	Fine	Mint
#53(#1)	2.50	5.00	7.50
2-5	1.50	3.00	4.50
6-10 (1951-52)	1.35	2.75	4.00
11-19 (1954-56)	1.00	2.00	3.00

APACHE MASSACRE (See Chief Victorio's --)

APACHE TRAIL
Sept, 1957 - #4, June, 1958
Steinway/America's Best

#1	1.00	2.00	3.00
2-4	.50	1.00	1.50

APPROVED COMICS
March, 1954 (All painted covers)(no cover price)
St. John Publishing Co.

#1-Contains The Hawk #5	1.00	2.00	3.00
2-Contains Invisible Boy	1.00	2.00	3.00
3(4/54)-Contains Wild Boy of the Congo #11 ('51)	1.00	2.00	3.00
7-Contains The Hawk #6	1.00	2.00	3.00
12-Contains North West Mounties(8/54)			
	1.00	2.00	3.00

AQUAMAN (See Showcase, Brave & the Bold, Super DC Giant, Adventure, DC Super-Stars #7, Detective, and World's Finest)

AQUAMAN
Jan-Feb, 1962 - #56, Mar-Apr, 1971;
#57, Aug-Sept, 1977 - #63, Aug-Sept, 1978
National Periodical Publications/DC Comics

#1-Intro. Quisp	5.00	10.00	15.00
2,3	2.50	5.00	7.50
4-10	1.20	2.40	3.60
11-20: #11-Intro. Mera. #18-Aquaman weds Mera	.80	1.60	2.40
21-30: #23-Birth of Aquababy. #29-Intro. Ocean Master, Aquaman's step-brother	.60	1.20	1.80
31,32,34-40	.50	1.00	1.50
33-Intro. Aqua-Girl	.50	1.00	1.50
41-47,49	.40	.80	1.20
48-Origin reprinted	.50	1.00	1.50
50-52-Adams Deadman	2.00	4.00	6.00
53-56('71)	.30	.60	.90
57('77),59,60-63	.20	.40	.60
58-Origin retold	.20	.40	.60

NOTE: *Aparo* story-#40,52-59. *Newton* story-#60-63.

AQUANAUTS (See 4-Color Comics #1197)

ARCHIE AND ME
Oct, 1964 - Present
Archie Publications

	Good	Fine	Mint
#1	2.50	5.00	7.50
2-5	1.50	3.00	4.50
6-10	1.00	2.00	3.00
11-30	.50	1.00	1.50
31-42	.30	.60	.90
43-63-(All Giants)	.25	.50	.75
64-103-(Reg. Size)	.15	.30	.45

ARCHIE...ARCHIE ANDREWS, WHERE ARE YOU?
Feb, 1977 - Present (Digest size, 160 pgs.)
Archie Publications

	Good	Fine	Mint
#1	.40	.80	1.20
2-7	.30	.60	.90
8-Reprints origin The Fly by Simon & Kirby			
	.40	.80	1.20

ARCHIE AS PUREHEART THE POWERFUL
Sept, 1966 - #6, Nov, 1967
Archie Publications (Radio Comics)

	Good	Fine	Mint
#1	1.20	2.40	3.60
2-6	.70	1.40	2.10

NOTE: *Evilheart cameos in all. Title: -- As
Capt. Pureheart the Powerful-#4,6; -- As Capt.
Pureheart-#5.*

ARCHIE AT RIVERDALE HIGH
Aug, 1972 - Present
Archie Publications

	Good	Fine	Mint
#1	.80	1.60	2.40
2-10	.50	1.00	1.50
11-30	.25	.50	.75
31-56		.20	.40

ARCHIE COMICS (See Pep & Oxydol-Dreft)
Winter, 1942-43 - Present
MLJ Magazines/Archie Publications #20 on

	Good	Fine	Mint
#1-Intro. Veronica	70.00	140.00	210.00
2	30.00	60.00	90.00
3-5	15.00	30.00	45.00
6-10	12.00	24.00	36.00
11-20	7.00	14.00	21.00
21-30	4.00	8.00	12.00
31-40	3.00	6.00	9.00
41-50	2.50	5.00	7.50
51-70: #69-Katy Keene sty.	2.00	4.00	6.00
71-100	1.50	3.00	4.50
101-130	.90	1.80	2.70
131-190	.50	1.00	1.50

	Good	Fine	Mint
191-220	.35	.70	1.05
221-240	.20	.40	.60
241-273	.15	.30	.45
Annual #1('49)(Scarce)	15.00	30.00	45.00
Annual #2('51)	6.00	12.00	18.00
Annual #3-6(1952-55)	4.00	8.00	12.00
Annual #7-15(1956-65)	2.00	4.00	6.00
Annual #16-26(1966-75)	1.00	2.00	3.00
Annual #27	.30	.60	.90
Annual Digest #27('75)-#32('78): #29-196pgs., rest are 160 pgs.	.60	1.20	1.80

--All-Star Specials(Wint.'75)-$1.25; 6 re-
 maindered Archie comics rebound in each;
 titles: "The World of Giant Comics",
 "Giant Grab Bag of Comics","Triple Giant
 Comics", & "Giant Spec. Comics".

	1.00	2.00	3.00

Mini-Comics (1970-Fairmont Potato Chips
 Giveaway-Miniature)(8 issues-No#'s, 8pgs.
 each)   .60   1.20   1.80

ARCHIE SHOE-STORE GIVEAWAY
1944-45; 12-15 pgs. of games, puzzles, stories like Superman-Tim books. No #'s - came
out monthly.
Archie Publications

	7.00	14.00	21.00

ARCHIE COMICS DIGEST
Aug, 1973 - Present (Small size, 160 pgs.)
Archie Publications

	Good	Fine	Mint
#1	.70	1.40	2.10
2-10	.40	.80	1.20
11-31	.25	.50	.75
32-The Fly reprint by S&K	.30	.60	.90

ARCHIE GIANT SERIES MAGAZINE (--'s Christmas
Stocking #1-6)(No #36-135, No #252-451)
1959 - Present
Archie Publications

#7-Katy Keene Holiday Fun 5.00 10.00 15.00
 8-Betty & Veronica Summer Fun ('60)
 9-The World of Jughead(12/60)
10-Archie's Christmas Stocking(1/61)
11-Betty & Veronica Spectacular(6/61)
12-Katy Keene Holiday Fun(9/61)
13-Betty & Veronica Summer Fun(10/61)
14-The World of Jughead(12/61)
          each.... 2.50   5.00   7.50
15-Archie's Christmas Stocking(1/62)
16-Betty & Veronica Spectacular(6/62)
17-Archie's Jokes(9/62)
18-Betty & Veronica Summer Fun(10/62)
19-The World of Jughead(12/62)

Archie & Me =5. ⊙ AP

Archie Comics =1. ⊙ AP

Archie Comics =62. ⊙ AP

(Archie Giant Series Mag. cont'd)

	Good	Fine	Mint
20-Archie's Christmas Stocking(1/63)			
each....	2.00	4.00	6.00

21-Betty & Veronica Spectacular(6/63)
22-Archie's Jokes(9/63)
23-Betty & Veronica Summer Fun(10/63)
24-The World of Jughead(12/63)
25-Archie's Christmas Stocking(1/64)
26-Betty & Veronica Spectacular(6/64)
27-Archie's Jokes(8/64)
28-Betty & Veronica Summer Fun(9/64)
29-Around the World With Archie(10/64)
30-The World of Jughead(12/64)
31-Archie's Christmas Stocking(1/65)
32-Betty & Veronica Spectacular(6/65)
33-Archie's Jokes
34-Betty & Veronica Summer Fun(9/65)
35-Around the World With Archie(10/65)

| each.... | 1.50 | 3.00 | 4.50 |

136-The World of Jughead(12/65)
137-Archie's Christmas Stocking(1/66)
138-Betty & Veronica Spectacular(6/66)
139-Archie's Jokes(6/66)
140-Betty & Veronica Summer Fun(8/66)
141-Around the World With Archie(9/66)

| each.... | 1.00 | 2.00 | 3.00 |

142-Archie's Super-Hero Special - Origin Capt.
   Pureheart, Capt. Hero, & Evilheart

| | 1.50 | 3.00 | 4.50 |

143-The World of Jughead(12/66)
144-Archie's Christmas Stocking(1/67)
145-Betty & Veronica Spectacular(6/67)
146-Archie's Jokes(6/67)
147-Betty & Veronica Summer Fun(8/67)
148-World of Archie(9/67)
149-World of Jughead(10/67)
150-Archie's Christmas Stocking(1/68)
151-World of Archie(2/68)
152-World of Jughead(2/68)
153-Betty & Veronica Spectacular(6/68)
154-Archie Jokes(6/68)
155-Betty & Veronica Summer Fun(8/68)
156-World of Archie(10/68)
157-World of Jughead(12/68)
158-Archie's Christmas Stocking(1/69)
159-Betty & Veronica Christmas Spect.(1/69)
160-World of Archie(2/69)

| each.... | .80 | 1.60 | 2.40 |

161-World of Jughead(2/69)
162-Betty & Veronica Spectacular(6/69)
163-Archie's Jokes(8/69)
164-Betty & Veronica Summer Fun(9/69)
165-World of Archie(9/69)
166-World of Jughead(9/69)
167-Archie's Christmas Stocking(1/70)
168-Betty & Veronica Christmas Spect.(1/70)
169-Archie's Christmas Love-In(1/70)
170-Jughead's Eat-Out Comic Book Mag.(12/69)
171-World of Archie(2/70)
172-World of Jughead(2/70)
173-Betty & Veronica Spectacular(6/70)
174-Archie's Jokes(8/70)
175-Betty & Veronica Summer Fun(9/70)
176-Li'l Jinx Giant Laugh-Out(8/70)
177-World of Archie(9/70)
178-World of Jughead(9/70)
179-Archie's Christmas Stocking(1/71)
180-Betty & Veronica Christmas Spect.(1/71)
181-Archie's Christmas Love-In(1/71)
182-World of Archie(2/71)
183-World of Jughead(2/71)
184-Betty & Veronica Spectacular(6/71)
185-Li'l Jinx Giant Laugh-Out(6/71)
186-Archie's Jokes(8/71)
187-Betty & Veronica Summer Fun(9/71)

	Good	Fine	Mint

188-World of Archie(9/71)
189-World of Jughead(9/71)
190-Archie's Christmas Stocking(12/71)
191-Betty & Veronica Christmas Spect.(2/72)
192-Archie's Christmas Love-In(1/72)
193-World of Archie(3/72)
194-World of Jughead(4/72)
195-Li'l Jinx Christmas Bag(1/72)
196-Sabrina's Christmas Magic(1/72)
197-Betty & Veronica Spectacular(6/72)
198-Archie's Jokes(8/72)
199-Betty & Veronica Summer Fun
200-World of Archie(10/72)

| each.... | .50 | 1.00 | 1.50 |

201-Betty & Veronica Spectacular(10/72)
202-World of Jughead(11/72)
203-Archie's Christmas Stocking(12/72)
204-Betty & Veronica Christmas Spect.(2/73)
205-Archie's Christmas Love-In(1/73)
206-Li'l Jinx Christmas Bag(12/72)
207-Sabrina's Christmas Magic(12/72)
208-World of Archie(3/73)
209-World of Jughead(4/73)
210-Betty & Veronica Spectacular(6/73)
211-Archie's Jokes(8/73)
212-Betty & Veronica Summer Fun(9/73)
213-World of Archie(10/73)
214-Betty & Veronica Spectacular
215-World of Jughead
216-Archie's Christmas Stocking(12/73)
217-Betty & Veronica Christmas Spect.(2/74)
218-Archie's Christmas Love-In(1/74)
219-Li'l Jinx Christmas Bag(12/73)
220-Sabrina's Christmas Magic(12/73)
221-Betty & Veronica Spectacular(Advertised
   as World of Archie)(6/74)
222-Archie's Jokes(Advertised as World of
   Jughead)(8/74)
223-Li'l Jinx(8/74)
224-Betty & Veronica Summer Fun(9/74)
225-World of Archie(9/74)
226-Betty & Veronica Spectacular(10/74)
227-World of Jughead(10/74)
228-Archie's Christmas Stocking(12/74)
229-Betty & Veronica Christmas Spect.(12/74)
230-Archie's Christmas Love-In(11/74)
231-Sabrina's Christmas Magic(1/75)
232-World of Archie(3/75)
233-World of Jughead(4/75)
234-Betty & Veronica Spectacular(6/75)
235-Archie's Jokes(8/75)
236-Betty & Veronica Summer Fun(9/75)
237-World of Jughead(9/75)
238-Betty & Veronica Spectacular(10/75)
239-World of Jughead(10/75)
240-Archie's Christmas Stocking(12/75)
241-Betty & Veronica Christmas Spect.(12/75)
242-Archie's Christmas Love-In(1/76)
243-Sabrina's Christmas Magic(1/76)
244-World of Archie(3/76)
245-World of Jughead(4/76)
246-Betty & Veronica Spectacular(6/76)
247-Archie's Jokes(8/76)
248-Betty & Veronica Summer Fun(9/76)
249-World of Archie(9/76)
250-Betty & Veronica Spectacular(10/76)
251-World of Jughead(10/76)

| each.... | .20 | .40 | .60 |

452-Archie's Christmas Stocking(12/76)
453-Betty & Veronica Christmas Spect.(12/76)
454-Archie's Christmas Love-In(1/77)
455-Sabrina's Christmas Magic(1/77)
456-World of Archie(3/77)
457-World of Jughead(4/77)
458-Betty & Veronica Spectacular(6/77)

Archie's Girls, Betty & Veronica #5. © AP   Archie's Joke Book #19. © AP   Archie's Madhouse #22. © AP

(Archie Giant Series Mag. cont'd)

	Good	Fine	Mint
459-Archie's Jokes(8/77)-Shows 8/76 in error			
460-Betty & Veronica Summer Fun(9/77)			
461-World of Archie(9/77)			
462-Betty & Veronica Spectacular(10/77)			
463-World of Jughead(10/77)			
464-Archie's Christmas Stocking(12/77)			
465-Betty & Veronica Christmas Spect.(12/77)			
466-Archie's Christmas Love-In(1/78)			
467-Sabrina's Christmas Magic(1/78)			
468-World of Archie(2/78)			
469-World of Jughead(2/78)			
470-Betty & Veronica Spectacular(6/78)			
471-Archie's Jokes(8/78)			
each....	.20	.40	.60

ARCHIE'S CHRISTMAS LOVE-IN (See Archie Giant
Series Mag. #169,181,192,205,218,230,242,454,
466)

ARCHIE'S CHRISTMAS STOCKING (Archie Giant Ser-
1954 - #7, 1959 (Annual)(25¢) ies Mag. #7 on)
Archie Publications

#1	7.00	14.00	21.00
2-4	4.00	8.00	12.00
5-7	3.00	6.00	9.00

(See Archie Giant Ser. Mag. #10,15,20,25,31,
137,144,150,158,167,179,190,203,216,228,240,
452,464)

ARCHIE'S CLEAN SLATE
1973   (35¢)
Spire Christian Comics (Fleming H. Revell Co.)

#1	.25	.50	.75

ARCHIE'S GIRLS, BETTY AND VERONICA
1950 - Present
Archie Publications

#1	16.00	32.00	48.00
2	10.00	20.00	30.00
3-5	7.00	14.00	21.00
6-10	5.00	10.00	15.00
11-20: #14-Katy Keene app.	3.00	6.00	9.00
21-30	2.50	5.00	7.50
31-60	1.50	3.00	4.50
61-100	1.00	2.00	3.00
101-140: #118-Origin Superteen. #119-Last			
Superteen story	.50	1.00	1.50
141-180	.30	.60	.90
181-220	.20	.40	.60
221-275	.15	.30	.45
Annual #1(1953)	7.00	14.00	21.00
Annual #2-5(1958)	3.00	6.00	9.00
Annual #6-8(1960)	2.50	5.00	7.50

ARCHIE'S JOKE BOOK MAGAZINE (See Joke Book--)
1953 - #3, Summer, 1954; #15, 1954 - Present
Archie Publications

	Good	Fine	Mint
1953-One Shot (Rare)	10.00	20.00	30.00
#1	6.00	12.00	18.00
2,3 (No #4-14)	4.00	8.00	12.00
15-30: #16,17-Katy Keene app. (#15 formerly			
Archie's Rival Reggie)	2.00	4.00	6.00
31-40,42,43	1.50	3.00	4.50
41-1st comic work by Neal Adams('59), 1 pg.			
	4.00	8.00	12.00
44-48-Adams art in all, 1-2 pgs.			
	2.50	5.00	7.50
49-60	.80	1.60	2.40
61-100	.50	1.00	1.50
101-140	.30	.60	.90
141-200	.20	.40	.60
201-250		.20	.40
Drug Store Giveaway(#39 with new cover)			
	1.35	2.75	4.00

ARCHIE'S JOKES (See Archie Giant Series Mag.
#17,22,27,33,139,146,154,163,174,186,198,
211,222,235,247,459,471)

ARCHIE'S LOVE SCENE
1973   (35¢)
Spire Christian Comics(Fleming H. Revell Co.)

#1	.40	.80	1.20

ARCHIE'S MADHOUSE (Madhouse Ma-ad #67 on)
Sept, 1959 - #66, Feb, 1969
Archie Publications

#1	6.00	12.00	18.00
2	3.50	7.00	10.50
3-5	2.50	5.00	7.50
6-10	2.00	4.00	6.00
11-16	1.00	2.00	3.00
17-21,23-40	.50	1.00	1.50
22-1st app. Sabrina, the Teen-age Witch(9/62)			
	1.00	2.00	3.00
41,42,44-66	.50	1.00	1.50
43-Mighty Crusaders cameo	.50	1.00	1.50
Annual #1(1962-63)	1.50	3.00	4.50
Annual #2-6('64-69)(Becomes Madhouse Ma-ad			
Annual #7 on)	.40	.80	1.20

NOTE: Cover title #61-65 is "Madhouse" and
#66 is "Madhouse Ma-ad Jokes."

ARCHIE'S MECHANICS
Sept, 1954 - 1955
Archie Publications

#1(15¢)-52pgs. (Rare)	10.00	20.00	30.00
2,3(10¢) (Scarce)	7.00	14.00	21.00

26

ARCHIE'S ONE WAY (Religious)
1972 (39¢) (36pgs.)
Spire Christian Comics(Fleming H. Revell Co.)

	Good	Fine	Mint
#1	.25	.50	.75

ARCHIE'S PAL, JUGHEAD (Jughead #127 on)
1949 - #126, Nov, 1965
Archie Publications

#1	20.00	40.00	60.00
2	10.00	20.00	30.00
3,4	8.00	16.00	24.00
5-Intro. Moose & Midge	9.00	18.00	27.00
6-10	5.00	10.00	15.00
11-20	3.00	6.00	9.00
21-40	2.50	5.00	7.50
41-60	2.00	4.00	6.00
61-80	1.50	3.00	4.50
81-100	1.00	2.00	3.00
101-126	.60	1.20	1.80
Annual #1(1953)	6.00	12.00	18.00
Annual #2-5(1954-56)	3.00	6.00	9.00
Annual #6-8(1957-60)	2.00	4.00	6.00

ARCHIE'S PALS 'N' GALS
1951 - #6, 1957-58; #7, 1958 - Present
Archie Publications

#1(116 pgs.)	8.00	16.00	24.00
2(Annual)(1957)	5.00	10.00	15.00
3-7(Annual, '57-58)	3.00	6.00	9.00
8(1958)-#10	2.00	4.00	6.00
11-20	1.50	3.00	4.50
21-40	1.00	2.00	3.00
41-60	.50	1.00	1.50
61-90	.30	.60	.90
91-125	.15	.30	.45

ARCHIE'S PARABLES
1973 (36 pgs.)
Spire Christian Comics(Fleming H. Revell Co.)

By Al Hartley	.40	.80	1.20

ARCHIE'S RIVAL REGGIE (See Reggie)

ARCHIE'S RIVAL REGGIE (Archie's Joke Book Mag.
1950 - #14, Aug, 1954   & Reggie #15 on)
Archie Publications

#1	12.00	24.00	36.00
2	6.00	12.00	18.00
3-5	4.00	8.00	12.00
6-14	2.50	5.00	7.50

ARCHIE'S SOMETHING ELSE
1975 (36 pgs.) (39¢)

Spire Christian Comics(Fleming H. Revell Co.)

	Good	Fine	Mint
No#	.25	.50	.75

ARCHIE'S SONSHINE
1973 (36 pgs.) (39¢)
Spire Christian Comics(Fleming H. Revell Co.)

No#	.25	.50	.75

ARCHIE'S SUPER HERO SPECIAL (See Archie
Giant Series Mag. #142)

ARCHIE'S TV LAUGH-OUT
1969 - Present
Archie Publications

#1	.80	1.60	2.40
2-10	.40	.80	1.20
11-20	.20	.40	.60
21-60		.20	.40

ARCHIE'S WORLD
1973 (39¢)
Spire Christian Comics(Fleming H. Revell Co.)

	.25	.50	.75

ARCHIE WHERE ARE YOU DIGEST
1977
Archie Publications

#3(8/77), #4(11/77)	.25	.50	.75

ARISTOCATS (See Movie Comics & Walt Disney
Showcase #16)

ARISTOKITTENS, THE (--Meet Jiminy Cricket #1)
Oct, 1971 - #9, 10/75 (#6-52pgs.) (Disney)
Gold Key

#1	.20	.40	.60
2-9	.15	.30	.45

ARIZONA KID, THE
March, 1951 - #6, Jan, 1952
Marvel/Atlas Comics(CSI)

#1	3.00	6.00	9.00
2-4	1.75	3.35	5.00
5,6	1.35	2.75	4.00

ARMY AND NAVY (Supersnipe #6 on)
May, 1942 - #5, Sept, 1942
Street & Smith Publications

#1-Cap Fury & Nick Carter			
	12.00	24.00	36.00

Archie's Mechanics #2, © AP

Archie's Pals 'N' Gals #1, © AP

Archie's Pal Jughead #23, © AP

The Arrow #2, © CEN   Astonishing #5, © MCG   Astonishing #14, © MCG

(Army and Navy cont'd)	Good	Fine	Mint
2- " " " "	5.00	10.00	15.00
3,4	4.00	8.00	12.00
5-Supersnipe app.; see Shadow V2#3 for 1st app.	8.00	16.00	24.00

ARMY AT WAR (Also see Our Army at War, Can-
celled Comic Cavalcade)
Oct-Nov, 1978
DC Comics

#1		.20	.40	.60

ARMY ATTACK (Formerly U.S. Air Force #1-37)
July, 1965 - #47, Feb, 1967
Charlton Comics

V1#1	.25	.50	.75
2-5	.20	.40	.60
V2#38(7/65)-#47	.15	.30	.45

NOTE: *Glanzman art-#1-3. Montes/Bache art-#44.*

ARMY WAR HEROES
Dec, 1963 - #38, June, 1970
Charlton Comics

#1	.50	1.00	1.50
2-20	.25	.50	.75
21-38: #23-Origin & 1st app. Iron Corporal series by Glanzman. #24-Intro. Archer & Corp. Jack series	.20	.40	.60

NOTE: *Montes/Bache art-#1,16,17,21,23-25,27-30.*

AROUND THE BLOCK WITH DUNC & LOO (See Dunc
and Loo)

AROUND THE WORLD IN 80 DAYS (See 4-Color
Comics #784 & A Golden Picture Classic)

AROUND THE WORLD UNDER THE SEA (See Movie
Classics)

AROUND THE WORLD WITH ARCHIE (See Archie
Giant Series Mag. #29,35,141)

AROUND THE WORLD WITH HUCKLEBERRY & HIS
FRIENDS (See Dell Giant #44)

ARRGH! (Satire)
Dec, 1974 - #5, Sept, 1975
Marvel Comics Group

#1-Everett reprint	.30	.60	.90
2-5	.20	.40	.60

NOTE: *Alcala art in #2; cover-#3. Everett re-
print-#2.*

ARROW, THE

Oct, 1940 - #3, Oct, 1941
Centaur Publications

	Good	Fine	Mint
#1-The Arrow begins	30.00	60.00	90.00
2	16.00	32.00	48.00
3-Origin Dash Darwell, the Human Meteor; origin The Rainbow	16.00	32.00	48.00

NOTE: *Gustavson art-#1,2.*

ARROWHEAD
April, 1954 - #4, Nov, 1954
Atlas Comics (CPS)

#1-Sinnott art in all	2.00	4.00	6.00
2-4	1.20	2.40	3.60

ASTONISHING (Marvel Boy #1,2)
#3, April, 1951 - #63, Aug, 1957
Marvel/Atlas Comics(20CC)

#3-Marvel Boy cont'd.	9.00	18.00	27.00
4-6-Last Marvel Boy; #4-Stan Lee app.	7.00	14.00	21.00
7-10	1.75	3.50	5.25
11,12,15,17,18,20	1.40	2.80	4.20
13,14,16,19-Krigstein stories	2.00	4.00	6.00
21-24	1.20	2.40	3.60
25-Crandall story	1.75	3.50	5.25
26-36-Last pre-code ish (1/54)	1.00	2.00	3.00
37-44,46,48-53,56,58,59	.80	1.60	2.40
45,47-Krigstein stories	1.75	3.50	5.25
54-Torres art	1.25	2.50	3.75
55-Crandall & Torres art	1.75	3.50	5.25
57-Williamson/Krenkel story, 4 pgs.	2.50	5.00	7.50
60-Williamson/Mayo story, 4 pgs.	2.50	5.00	7.50
61,63	.80	1.60	2.40
62-Torres + Powell story	1.20	2.40	3.60

NOTE: *Berg story-#53,56. Gene Colan story-
#29. Ditko story-#50,53. Drucker story-#41.
Everett story-#3-6,12,37,47,48,58; covers-
#4,5,15,18,29,47,51,53,55,57,59-62. Kirby
story-#56. Morrow story-#52,61. Orlando sto-
ry-#47,58. J. Romita story-#7,43. Woodbridge
story-#62,63. Canadian reprints exist.*

ASTONISHING TALES (See Ka-Zar)
Aug, 1970 - #36, July, 1976
Marvel Comics Group

#1-Ka-Zar by Kirby(pencils)& Dr. Doom by Wood begin	1.00	2.00	3.00
2-Kirby & Wood art	.70	1.40	2.10
3-6: Smith art; Wood art-#3,4; Everett inks-#6	.90	1.80	2.70

(Astonishing Tales cont'd)

	Good	Fine	Mint
7-9: #8-Last Dr. Doom	.50	1.00	1.50
10-(52pgs.)Smith/Buscema art			
	.80	1.60	2.40
11,14-20: #11-Origin Ka-Zar; #20-Last Ka-Zar			
	.35	.70	1.05
12-Man Thing by Adams	1.00	2.00	3.00
13-Man Thing app.	.40	.80	1.20
21-24: #21-It! the Living Colossus begins, ends #24	.25	.50	.75
25-Deathlok the Demolisher begins			
	.60	1.20	1.80
26-30: #29-Guardians of the Galaxy app.			
	.25	.50	.75
31-Wrightson cover inks	.25	.50	.75
32-36	.20	.40	.60

NOTE: *Buscema art-#9,10.*

ASTRO BOY (TV)(Also see March of Comics#285)
August, 1965
Gold Key

#1(10151-508)	.60	1.20	1.80

ASTRO COMICS
1969 - 1978   (Giveaway)
American Airlines (Harvey)

No#-Has Harvey's Casper, Spooky, Hot Stuff, Stumbo the Giant, Little Audrey, Little Lotta, & Richie Rich reprints
.65   1.35   2.00

ATLANTIS, THE LOST CONTINENT (See 4-Color Comics #1188)

ATLAS (See First Issue Special)

ATOM, THE (See Action, All-American, Brave & the Bold, Detective, Showcase, & World's Finest)

ATOM, THE (-- & the Hawkman #39 on)
Jun-Jul, 1962 - #38, Aug-Sept, 1968
National Periodical Publications

#1	6.00	12.00	18.00
2	3.00	6.00	9.00
3-1st Time Pool story; origin Chronos	2.50	5.00	7.50
4,5: #4-Snapper Carr x-over	2.00	4.00	6.00
6-10: #7-Hawkman x-over. #8-Justice League	1.50	3.00	4.50
11-20: #18-Zatanna x-over	1.00	2.00	3.00
21-30: #29-Golden Age Atom x-over	.60	1.20	1.80
31-38: #31-Hawkman x-over. #36-G.A. Atom x-			

	Good	Fine	Mint
over #37-Intro. Major Mynah; Hawkman cameo	.50	1.00	1.50

NOTE: *Anderson art-#39,43,44; inks-#1-11,13, 40,41; cover inks-#1-25,31-35,37. Gil Kane art-#1-37; covers-#1-37. Pool stories also in #6,9,12,17,21,27,35.*

ATOM AGE (See Classics Special)

ATOM-AGE COMBAT
June, 1952 - #5, April, 1953
St. John Publishing Co.

#1	3.00	6.00	9.00
2-5: #3-Mayo art, 6pgs.	2.50	5.00	7.50
1(2/58-St. John)	2.00	4.00	6.00

ATOM-AGE COMBAT
Nov, 1958 - #3, March, 1959
Fago Magazines

#1	2.00	4.00	6.00
2,3	1.50	3.00	4.50

ATOMAN
Feb, 1946 - #2, April, 1946
Spark Publications

#1-Origin Atoman; Jerry Robinson & Mort Meskin art; Kidcrusaders, Wild Bill Hickok, Marvin the Great app.	10.00	20.00	30.00
2	6.00	12.00	18.00

ATOM AND THE HAWKMAN, THE (Formerly The Atom)
#39, 10-11/68 - #45, 10-11/69
National Periodical Publications

#39,42-45	.40	.80	1.20
40,41-Hawkman by Kubert; covers-#39-45			
	.50	1.00	1.50

ATOM ANT (TV)
January, 1966   (Hanna-Barbera)
Gold Key

#1(10170-601)	.25	.50	.75

ATOMIC ATTACK
1952 - #8, Oct, 1953
Youthful Magazines

#1 (Exist?)	3.00	6.00	9.00
2-8	2.00	4.00	6.00

ATOMIC BOMB
1942
Jay Burtis Publications

The Atom #7, © DC   Atom-Age Combat #2, © STJ   Atoman #2, © Spark Publ.

Atomic Mouse #16, © CC   Atomic Spy Cases #1, © AVON   Attack On Planet Mars No#, © AVON

	Good	Fine	Mint
(Atomic Bomb cont'd)			
#1-Airmale & Stampy	3.50	7.00	10.50

ATOMIC BUNNY
1958 - #19, Dec, 1959
Charlton Comics

#12-19	.40	.80	1.20

ATOMIC COMICS
1946   (Reprints)
Daniels Publications (Canadian)

#1-Rocketman, Yankee Boy, Master Key			
	3.00	6.00	9.00
2-4	2.00	4.00	6.00

ATOMIC COMICS
Jan, 1946 - #4, July-Aug, 1946
Green Publishing Co.

#1-Radio Squad by Siegel & Shuster; Barry			
O'Neal app.	3.50	7.00	10.50
2-Inspector Dayton; Kid Kane by Matt Baker;			
Lucky Wings, Congo King, Prop Powers			
(only app.) begin	6.00	12.00	18.00
3,4: #3-Zero Ghost Detective app.			
	3.00	6.00	9.00

ATOMIC MOUSE   (See Blue Bird)
March, 1953 - #54, June, 1963
Capitol Stories/Charlton Comics

#1-Origin	2.00	4.00	6.00
2-10	.80	1.60	2.40
11-25,27-54	.50	1.00	1.50
26-(68 pgs.)	1.00	2.00	3.00

ATOMIC RABBIT
August, 1955 - #11, March, 1958
Charlton Comics

#1-Origin; Al Fago art	2.00	4.00	6.00
2-10-Fago art in most	.80	1.60	2.40
11-(68 pgs.)	1.00	2.00	3.00

ATOMIC SPY CASES
Mar-Apr, 1950
Avon Periodicals

#1	7.00	14.00	21.00

ATOMIC THUNDERBOLT, THE
Feb, 1946 - #2, April, 1946
Regor Company

#1-Intro. Atomic Thunderbolt & Mr. Murdo,			
2	5.00	10.00	15.00

ATOMIC WAR!
Nov, 1952 - #4, 1953
Ace Periodicals (Junior Books)

	Good	Fine	Mint
#1	5.00	10.00	15.00
2-4	3.50	7.00	10.50

ATOM THE CAT
Aug, 1955 - #16, May, 1959
Charlton Comics

#1	.60	1.20	1.80
2-10,12-16	.40	.80	1.20
11-(64 pgs.)	.50	1.00	1.50

ATTACK
May, 1952 - #60, Nov, 1959
Youthful Mag./Trojan/Charlton #54 on

#1	1.50	3.00	4.50
2-10	1.00	2.00	3.00
11-20	.80	1.60	2.40
21-40	.60	1.20	1.80
41-53,55-60	.25	.50	.75
54-(100 pgs.)	.40	.80	1.20

ATTACK! (Attack at Sea V4#5)(Also see
Special War Series #2)
1962 - #4, Oct, 1967; 9/71 - #15, 3/75
Charlton Comics

No#(#1)-('62) Special Edition			
	.50	1.00	1.50
2('63), 3(Fall, '64)	.25	.50	.75
V4#2(10/65),3(10/66),4(10/67)			
	.20	.40	.60
#1(9/71)	.25	.50	.75
2-15(3/75): #4-American Eagle app.			
	.20	.40	.60

ATTACK!
1975   (39¢)   (36 pgs.)
Spire Christian Comics(Fleming H. Revell Co.)

No#	.25	.50	.75

ATTACK AT SEA   (Formerly Attack!, '67)
October, 1968
Charlton Comics

V4#5	.20	.40	.60

ATTACK ON PLANET MARS
1951
Avon Periodicals

No#-Infantino, Kubert & Wood art; adaptation			
of Tarrano the Conqueror by Ray Cummings			
	25.00	50.00	75.00

AUDREY & MELVIN (Formerly Little --?)
#62, September, 1974
Harvey Publications

	Good	Fine	Mint
#62	.15	.30	.45

AUGIE DOGGIE (TV) (See Whitman Comic Books)
Oct, 1963   (Hanna-Barbera)
Gold Key

	Good	Fine	Mint
#1	.25	.50	.75

AURORA COMIC SCENES INSTRUCTION BOOKLET
1974   (Slick paper, 8pgs.)(6-1/4"x9-3/4")
(Included with superhero model kits)
Aurora Plastics Co. (in full color)

#181-140-Tarzan; Adams art
                1.00   2.00   3.00
#182-140-Spider-Man; #183-140-Tonto(Gil Kane
   art); #184-140-Hulk; #185-140-Superman;
#186-140-Superboy; #187-140-Batman; #188-140-
   The Lone Ranger(1974); #192-140-Captain
   America(1975); #193-140-Robin
         each....   .40   .80   1.20

AUTHENTIC POLICE CASES
Feb, 1948 - #37, Jan, 1955
St. John Publishing Co.

#1-Hale the Magician by Tuska begins
                3.00   6.00   9.00
2-Lady Satan app.   2.50   5.00   7.50
3-Veiled Avenger app.   2.50   5.00   7.50
4,5,7: #5-Late '30's Jack Cole reprint. #7-
   Masked Black Jack app. 1.50   3.00   4.50
6-Matt Baker cover; Walter Johnson story.
   Used in Seduction of the Innocent; illo-
   "An invitation to Learning"-reprinted in
   Fugitives From Justice #3
                6.00   12.00   18.00
8,10-14: Vic Flint in all. Matt Baker art
   begins #8   3.00   6.00   9.00
9-Drug story (reprinted in #34); no Vic
   Flint   4.00   8.00   12.00
15-Drug story; Vic Flint app.
                3.50   7.00   10.50
16-24   1.75   3.50   5.25
25-28 (All 100 pgs.)   4.00   8.00   12.00
29-33,35,37   1.25   2.50   3.75
34-Drug cover/story (reprinted from #9)
                2.50   5.00   7.50
36-Vic Flint strip reprts.1.40   2.80   4.20
NOTE: *Matt Baker covers-#8-10,12,13,19.*

AVENGER, THE (See A-1 Comics)
1955 - #4, Aug-Sept, 1955
Magazine Enterprises

	Good	Fine	Mint
#1(A-1#129)-Origin	8.00	16.00	24.00
2(A-1#131),3(A-1#133),4(A-1#138)			
	4.00	8.00	12.00

IW Reprint #9('64)-Reprints #1(new cover)
   ('60-61)   1.35   2.75   4.00
NOTE: *Powell stories-#2-5; covers-#1-4.*

AVENGERS, THE
Sept, 1963 - Present
Marvel Comics Group

#1-Origin The Avengers (Thor, Iron Man, Hulk,
   Ant-Man, Wasp)   50.00 100.00 150.00
2   25.00   50.00   75.00
3   15.00   30.00   45.00
4-Revival of Captain America who joins the
   Avengers   15.00   30.00   45.00
4-Reprint from the Golden Record Comic set
                1.00   2.00   3.00
         With Record.... 1.50   3.00   4.50
5   7.00   14.00   21.00
6-10: #9-Intro. Wonder Man-joins Avengers &
   dies in same story   5.00   10.00   15.00
11-19: #15-Death of Zemo. #16-New Avengers
   line-up(Hawkeye, Quicksilver, Scarlet
   Witch join; Thor, Iron Man, Giant-Man &
   Wasp leave). #19-Intro. Swordsman; origin
   Hawkeye   2.50   5.00   7.50
20-22: Wood inks   1.75   3.50   5.25
23-30: #28-Giant-Man becomes Goliath
                1.25   2.50   3.75
31-40   1.00   2.00   3.00
41-50: #48-Origin new Black Knight
                .80   1.60   2.40
51-56,59,60: #59-Intro. Yellowjacket. #60-
   Wasp & Yellowjacket wed .70   1.40   2.10
57-Intro. The Vision   1.50   3.00   4.50
58-Origin The Vision   1.50   3.00   4.50
61-65,68-70: #63-Goliath becomes Yellowjacket;
   Hawkeye becomes the new Goliath
                .60   1.20   1.80
66,67-Smith stys/cvr #66 1.50   3.00   4.50
71-80: #80-Intro. Red Wolf .60   1.20   1.80
81-92: #83-Intro. The Liberators (Wasp, Val-
   kyrie, Scarlet Witch, Medusa & the Black
   Widow). #87-Origin the Black Panther. #92-
   Adams cover   .60   1.20   1.80
93-(52pgs.)-Adams cvr/sty.4.00   8.00   12.00
94-96-Adams cover/stories 2.00   4.00   6.00
97-G.A. Capt. America, Sub-Mariner, Human
   Torch, Patriot, Vision, Blazing Skull,
   Fin, Angel, & New Capt. Marvel x-over
                .60   1.20   1.80
98-Goliath becomes Hawkeye; Smith cover/stor-
   ies w/Buscema   1.50   3.00   4.50
99-Smith art/cover   1.50   3.00   4.50
100-Smith art/covers; featuring everyone who

Authentic Police Cases #4, © STJ

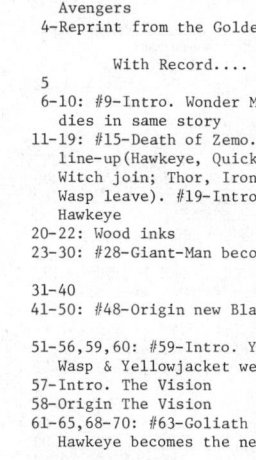

The Avengers #7, © MCG

The Avengers #34, © MCG

The Avengers #100, © MCG   Babe #11, © PRIZE   Baby Huey #1, © HARV

	Good	Fine	Mint
(The Avengers cont'd)			
was an Avenger minus Wonderman			
	2.00	4.00	6.00
101-106,108-110	.50	1.00	1.50
107-Starlin story	.70	1.40	2.10
111-119: #114-1st app. Mantis			
	.40	.80	1.20
120-Starlin cover pencils	.50	1.00	1.50
121-130: #123-Origin Mantis	.35	.70	1.05
131-140: #134,135-True origin The Vision.			
#135-Starlin cover	.30	.60	.90
141-149: #144-Origin & 1st app. Hellcat			
	.25	.50	.75
150-Kirby art; reprints	.25	.50	.75
151-170: #151-Wonderman returns with new			
costume	.20	.40	.60
171-180	.15	.30	.45
Annual #7(11/77)-Starlin cover/story			
	.60	1.20	1.80
Annual #8(10/78)	.25	.50	.75
Special #1(9/67)	2.25	4.50	6.75
" #2(9/68)	1.20	2.40	3.60
" #3(9/69)	1.00	2.00	3.00
" #4(1/71),#5(1/72)	.80	1.60	2.40
" #6(11/76)	.60	1.20	1.80
Giant Size #1(8/74)	.80	1.60	2.40
" " #2(11/74),#3(2/75)			
	.50	1.00	1.50
" " #4(6/75),#5(12/75)			
	.50	1.00	1.50

NOTE: *John Buscema stories-#41(1st at Marvel)-65,68-77,79-85,87-91,97,98,152,153; covers-#41-66,68-91,97,98,178. Kane/Everett cover-#97. Kirby stories-#1-8,16; covers-#1-30,148, 151-158; layouts-#14,15.*

AVENGERS, THE (TV)
11/68 ("John Steed & Emma Peel" cover title)
Gold Key

#1	1.20	2.40	3.60

NOTE: *The Avengers is official title on inside.*

AVIATION ADVENTURES & MODEL BUILDING
12/46 - #17, 2/47 (True Aviation Adv.--#15)
Parents' Magazine Institute

#16,17-Half comics and half pictures			
	1.00	2.00	3.00

AVIATION CADETS
1943
Street & Smith Publications

	2.00	4.00	6.00

AWFUL OSCAR (Formerly Oscar)
#12, Aug, 1949 - #13, Oct, 1949
Marvel Comics Group

	Good	Fine	Mint
#12,13	1.00	2.00	3.00

BABE (--, Darling of the Hills, later issues)
6-7/48 - 1950 (Also see Big Shot, Sparky Watts)
Prize/Headline/Feature

#1-Boody Rogers art	5.00	10.00	15.00
2-11-All by Boody Rogers	3.00	6.00	9.00

BABE AMAZON OF OZARKS
#5, 1948
Standard Comics

#5	2.50	5.00	7.50

BABE RUTH SPORTS COMICS
April, 1949 - #11, Feb, 1951
Harvey Publications

#1-Powell art	2.00	4.00	6.00
2-11: #8-Powell art	1.00	2.00	3.00

BABES IN TOYLAND (See 4-Color #1282 and
Golden Pix Story Book ST-3)

BABY HUEY AND PAPA (See Paramount Animated--)
May, 1962 - #33, Jan, 1968
Harvey Publications

#1	2.00	4.00	6.00
2-10	.80	1.60	2.40
11-20	.35	.70	1.05
21-33		.25	.50

BABY HUEY IN DUCKLAND
Nov, 1962 - #14, Sept, 1966 (25¢ Giant)
Harvey Publications

#1	1.50	3.00	4.50
2-5	.60	1.20	1.80
6-14	.30	.60	.90

BABY HUEY, THE BABY GIANT (Also see Casper,
Harvey Hits #22, & Paramount Animated Comics)
Sept, 1956 - #97, Oct, 1971; #98, Oct, 1972
Harvey Publications

#1	10.00	20.00	30.00
2	5.00	10.00	15.00
3-5	2.00	4.00	6.00
6-10	1.00	2.00	3.00
11-30	.60	1.20	1.80
31-60	.30	.60	.90
61-98	.15	.30	.45

BABY SNOOTS (Also see March of Comics #359,
Aug, 1970 - #22, Nov, 1975   371,396,401)
Gold Key

(Baby Snoots cont'd)	Good	Fine	Mint
#1	.25	.50	.75

2-22: #22-Titled Snoots, the Forgetful Ele-
fink   .15   .30

BACHELOR FATHER (TV)
1962
Dell Publishing Co.

4-Color #1332(#1)	.70	1.40	2.10
#2-Written by Stanley	.80	1.60	2.40

BACHELOR'S DIARY
1949
Avon Periodicals

#1-King Features panel cartoons & text re-
prints   4.00   8.00 12.00

BADGE OF JUSTICE
#22, 1/55 - #23, 3/53; 4/55 - #4, 10/55
Charlton Comics

#22(1/55),#23(3/55),#1	.80	1.60	2.40
2-4	.60	1.20	1.80

BADMEN OF THE WEST
1951   (Giant - 132 pgs.)
Avon Periodicals

#1-Contains rebound copies of Jesse James,
King of the Bad Men of Deadwood, Badmen
of Tombstone; other combinations possible
Issues with Kubert stories......
7.00 14.00 21.00

BADMEN OF THE WEST! (See A-1 Comics)
1953 - #3, 1954
Magazine Enterprises

#1(A-1#100)-Meskin art?	6.00	12.00	18.00
2(A-1#120), 3	3.00	6.00	9.00

BADMEN OF TOMBSTONE
1950
Avon Periodicals

No#	3.00	6.00	9.00

BAFFLING MYSTERIES (Formerly Indian Braves
#1-4; Heroes of the Wild Frontier #26-28)
#5, Nov, 1951 - #26(10/55),29,30, 1955
Periodical House (Ace Magazines)

#5	2.00	4.00	6.00

6,7,9,10: #10-E.C. Crypt Keeper copy on
cover   1.75   3.50   5.25
8-Harrison/Wood story?   4.00   8.00 12.00

	Good	Fine	Mint
11-20	1.50	3.00	4.50
21-26,29,30	1.25	2.50	3.75

NOTE: *Cameron stories-#16,20.*

BALBO (See Mighty Midget Comics)

BALOO & LITTLE BRITCHES
April, 1968   (Walt Disney)
Gold Key

#1-From the Jungle Book	.50	1.00	1.50

BALTIMORE COLTS
1950
American Visuals Corp.

	2.50	5.00	7.50

BAMBI (See 4-Color #12,30,186, Movie Comics,
Movie Classics, and Walt Disney Showcase #31)

BAMBI (Disney)
1941, 1942
K. K. Publications (Giveaway)

1941-Horlick's Malted Milk & various toy
stores-text & pictures; most copies mailed
out with store stickers on cover
15.00 30.00 45.00
1942-Same as 4-Color #12, but no price
(Scarce)(Same as '41 ish?)
30.00 60.00 90.00

BAMM BAMM & PEBBLES FLINTSTONE
Oct, 1964   (Hanna-Barbera)
Gold Key

#1	.25	.50	.75

BANANA OIL
1924   (52 pgs.) (Black & White)
MS Publ. Co.

Milt Gross art; not reprints
8.00 16.00 24.00

BANANA SPLITS, THE (TV) (See March of Comics
2/69 - #8, 10/71   (Hanna-Barbera)   #364)
Gold Key

#1	.20	.40	.60
2-8	.15	.30	.45

BAND WAGON (See Hanna-Barbera --)

BANG-UP COMICS
Dec, 1941 - #3, June, 1942
Progressive Publications

Badmen Of Tombstone #1. © AVON

Baffling Mysteries #8. © ACE

Bang-Up Comics #1. © Progressive Publ.

33

The Barker #5, © QUA   Barney Google Four Color #19, © News Synd.   Barry M. Goldwater, © DELL

(Bang-Up Comics cont'd)   Good   Fine   Mint
#1-Cosmo Mann & Lady Fairplay begin; Buzz
   Balmer by Rick Yager in all
                       25.00 50.00 75.00
2,3   15.00 30.00 45.00

BANNER COMICS (Captain Courageous #6)
#3, May, 1941 - #5, Jan, 1942
Ace Magazines

#3-Captain Courageous & Lone Warrior & Side-
   kick Dicky begin   30.00 60.00 90.00
4,5   25.00 50.00 75.00

BARBARIANS, THE
June, 1975
Atlas Comics/Seaboard Periodicals

#1-Origin, only app. Andrax; Iron Jaw app.
                         .50   1.00   1.50

BARBIE & KEN
May-July, 1962 - #5, Nov-Jan, 1963-64
Dell Publishing Co.

#01-053-207(#1)   1.00   2.00   3.00
2-5   .50   1.00   1.50

BARKER, THE
Autumn, 1946 - 1949
Quality Comics Group/Comic Magazine

#1   2.50   5.00   7.50
2   1.50   3.00   4.50
3-10   1.25   2.50   3.75
11-14   .80   1.60   2.40
15-Jack Cole pencils   1.20   2.40   3.60
NOTE: *Jack Cole art in some issues.*

BARNEY AND BETTY RUBBLE (Flintstones' Neighbors)
Jan, 1973 - #23, Dec, 1976 (Hanna-Barbera)
Charlton Comics

#1   .30   .60   .90
2-23   .15   .30   .45

BARNEY BAXTER
1938 - 1956
David McKay/Dell Publishing Co.

Feature Book #15(McKay-'38)
                       12.00 24.00 36.00
4-Color #20('42)   12.00 24.00 36.00
#4,5   8.00 16.00 24.00
1,2(1956-Argo)   2.00   4.00   6.00

BARNEY GOOGLE (See Comic Monthly)
1923 - 1928(Daily strip reprints;B&W)(52pgs.)
Cupples & Leon Co.

                       Good   Fine   Mint
#1-By Billy DeBeck   15.00 30.00 45.00
2-6   10.00 20.00 30.00
NOTE: *Started in 1918 as newspaper strip;
Spark Plug began 1922, 1923.*

BARNEY GOOGLE & SNUFFY SMITH
1942 - April, 1964
Dell Publishing Co./Gold Key

4-Color #19('42)   17.50 35.00 52.50
4-Color #40('43)   7.00 14.00 21.00
Large Feature Comic #11(1943)
                       10.00 25.00 40.00
#1(1950-Dell)   3.00   6.00   9.00
2,3   2.00   4.00   6.00
#1(10113-404)Gold Key, 4/64
                        1.20   2.40   3.60

BARNEY GOOGLE & SNUFFY SMITH
May, 1951 - #4, Feb, 1952 (Reprints)
Toby Press

#1   3.00   6.00   9.00
2,3   2.00   4.00   6.00
4-Kurtzman story "Pot Shot Pete", 5pgs.;
  reprints/John Wayne #5 2.50   5.00   7.50

BARNEY GOOGLE AND SNUFFY SMITH
March, 1970 - #6, Jan, 1971
Charlton Comics

#1   .50   1.00   1.50
2-6   .25   .50   .75

BARNYARD
1944 - 1950; 1957
Nedor/Polo Mag./Standard(Animated Cartoons)

#1   2.00   4.00   6.00
2-12,16   .80   1.60   2.40
13-15,17,20,21,23,27-All contain Frazetta
   text illos   2.50   5.00   7.50
18,19,22,24,25-All contain Frazetta stories
   & text illos   6.00 12.00 18.00
26,28-31   .60   1.20   1.80
10(1957)   .30   .60   .90

BARRY M. GOLDWATER
March, 1965 (Complete Life Story)
Dell Publishing Co.

#12-055-503   2.00   4.00   6.00

BASEBALL AS THE STARS PLAY IT
1954 (3½x4")(8 diff.)(16pgs. in color)
Wilson Certified Franks giveaway

(Baseball As the Stars Play It cont'd)

	Good	Fine	Mint

#1-Pointers on Pitching. 2-Batting & Field-
ing Secrets. 3-Playing the Infield. 4-How to
Catch. 5-Circus Cut-Out & Fun Book. 6-Western
Cut-Out & Fun Book. 7-Dress-Up & Fun Book
8-Travel Cut-Out & Fun Book

each....	.50	1.00	1.50

BASEBALL COMICS
Spring, 1949
Will Eisner Productions

#1-Will Eisner cvr/stys.	12.00	24.00	36.00

BASEBALL HEROES
1952   (One Shot)
Fawcett Publications

No#	3.00	6.00	9.00

BASEBALL THRILLS
1951 - #10, Summer, 1952
Ziff-Davis Publ. Co.

#1	1.20	2.40	3.60
2-10	.60	1.20	1.80

BASIL (-- the Royal Cat)
Jan, 1953 - #4, Sept, 1953
St. John Publishing Co.

#1	.60	1.20	1.80
2-4	.40	.80	1.20

BAT LASH (See Showcase #76)
Oct-Nov, 1968 - #7, Oct-Nov, 1969
National Periodical Publications

#1	.60	1.20	1.80
2-7	.40	.80	1.20

BATMAN (See Aurora, Book & Record Set, Detec-
tive, 80-Pg. Giants, Giant Comics to Color,
Limited Coll. Ed., 100-Pg. Super Spec., 3-D
Batman, & World's Finest)

BATMAN
Spring, 1940 - Present
National Per. Publ./Detective Comics/DC Comics

#1-Origin The Batman retold by Bob Kane; see
Detective #33 for 1st origin; 1st app.
Joker & Catwoman; has Batman story without Robin originally planned for Detective #38; reprinted in Famous 1st Editions

	600.00	1500.00	2400.00

(Prices vary widely on this book)

	Good	Fine	Mint
2	225.00	450.00	675.00

3-1st Catwoman in costume

	125.00	250.00	375.00
4	100.00	200.00	300.00
5	70.00	140.00	210.00
6-10: #8-Infinity cover	50.00	100.00	150.00

11-15: #13-Jerry Siegel, creator of Superman
appears in a Batman story

	35.00	70.00	105.00
16-Intro. Alfred	40.00	80.00	120.00
17-20	20.00	40.00	60.00

21-30: #24-Last app. of Tweedledum & Tweed-
ledee. #25-Only Joker-Penguin team-up

	17.50	35.00	52.50

31-40: #32-Origin Robin retold

	12.00	24.00	36.00
41-46	9.00	18.00	27.00

47-Origin The Batman retold

	22.00	44.00	66.00

48-50: #49-1st Vicki Vale. #50-Two-Face app.

	8.00	16.00	24.00

51-60: #57-Centerfold is a 1950 calendar

	7.00	14.00	21.00
61-70: #68-Two-Face app.	6.00	12.00	18.00
71-80	4.50	9.00	13.50
81-90: #81-Two-Face app.	4.00	8.00	12.00
91-100	3.50	7.00	10.50
101-110	3.00	6.00	9.00
111-120	2.50	5.00	7.50
121-130: #127-Superman app.	2.00	4.00	6.00

131-140: #131-Intro. 2nd Batman & Robin series. #139-Intro. old Bat-Girl

	1.50	3.00	4.50
141-150	1.20	2.40	3.60

151-170: #164-New look & Mystery Analysts

series begins	.90	1.80	2.70
171-180: #176-Giant G-17	.70	1.40	2.10
(80 pg. Giant G-17)	1.00	2.00	3.00

181-190: #181-Contains poster of Batman &
Robin. #182-Giant G-24. #185-Giant G-27.

#187-Giant G-30	.50	1.00	1.50
(80 pg. Giant G-24,27,30)	.80	1.60	2.40

191-200: #193-Giant G-37. #197-New Bat-Girl
app. #198-Giant G-43, reprints origin.
#200-Retells origin of Batman & Robin

	.50	1.00	1.50
(80 pg. Giant G-37,43)	.60	1.20	1.80

201-210: #203-Giant G-49. #208-Giant G-55-New
art by Gil Kane

	.35	.70	1.05
(80 pg. Giant G-49,55)	.50	1.00	1.50

211-218: #213-Giant G-61-origin Alfred; new
origin of Robin. #214-Alfred given a last
name-"Pennyworth". #218-Giant G-67

	.25	.50	.75
(80 pg. Giant G-61,67)	.50	1.00	1.50

Baseball Heroes No#. © FAW

Batman #1. © DC

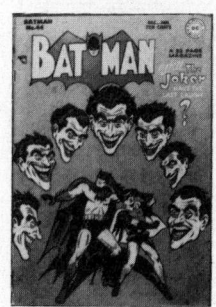

Batman #44. © DC

Batman #59, © DC

Battle #5, © MCG

Battle Action #3, © MCG

(Batman cont'd)	Good	Fine	Mint
219-Adams story	1.75	3.50	5.25
220	.25	.50	.75
221,223-231: #223-Giant G-73. #228-Giant G-79			
	.25	.50	.75
(80 pg. Giant G-73,79)	.50	1.00	1.50
222-Beatles take-off	1.00	2.00	3.00
232,234,237: Adams stories. #234-52pg. ish begin, end #242	1.50	3.00	4.50
233,235,236,238-242: #233-Giant G-85. #238-DC-8 100pg. Super Spec.; unpubbed G.A. Atom, Sargon, Plastic Man stories; Doom Patrol origin reprint; Adams cover			
	.25	.50	.75
(80 pg. Giant G-85)	.50	1.00	1.50
(100 pg. DC-8)	.80	1.60	2.40
243-245-Adams stories	1.25	2.50	3.75
246-250	.25	.50	.75
251-Adams story; Joker app.	1.25	2.50	3.75
252,253: #253-Shadow app.	.25	.50	.75
254-100pg. editions begin	.50	1.00	1.50
255-Adams story	1.25	2.50	3.75
256-261-Last 100pg. issue	.50	1.00	1.50
262-68pgs.	.25	.50	.75
263-280	.20	.40	.60
281-299	.15	.30	.45
300(52pgs.)-308	.15	.30	.45
Annual #1(8-10/61)Curt Swan cover			
	5.00	10.00	15.00
Annual #2	3.00	6.00	9.00
" #3(Summer, '62)	2.50	5.00	7.50
" #4-7(7/64)	1.75	3.50	5.25
Pizza Hut giveaway(12/77)-exact reprints of #122 & #123	.25	.50	.75
Prell Shampoo giveaway('66)-16pgs."The Joker's Practical Jokes"(6-7/8"x3-3/8")			
	1.00	2.00	3.00

NOTE: _Adams_ covers-#200,203,210,217,219,220-222,224-27,229,230,232,234,236-41,243-45,251,255. _Burnley_ stories-#10,12-18,20,25,27;
cover-#28. _Infantino_ stories-#234,235,255;
covers-#164-75,177-81,183,184,188-92,194-99.
Kaluta covers-#242,248,253. _Bob Kane_ stories-#1,2; covers-#1-5,7. _Newton_ story-#305.
Robinson/Roussos stories-#13,15-17,20,22,24,25,27,28,31,33,37. _Robinson_ stories-#12,14,18; covers-#6,8-10,12-15,18,21,26,27,30,37,39.
Simonson pencils-#300. _Wrightson_ inks-#265.

BATMAN (Kellogg's Poptarts comics)
1966 (set of 6) (16 pgs.)
National Periodical Publications

"The Man in the Iron Mask", "The Penguin's Fowl Play", "The Joker's Happy Victims", "The Catwoman's Catnapping Caper", "The Mad Hatter's Hat Crimes", "The Case of Batman II"

each....	1.00	2.00	3.00

NOTE: _Infantino_ art on Catwoman and Joker issues.

BATMAN FAMILY, THE
9-10/75 - #20, 10-11/78   (68pgs.-#1-4)
(Combined with Detective Comics with #481)
National Periodical Publications/DC Comics

	Good	Fine	Mint
#1-Origin Bat Girl-Robin team-up(The Dynamic Duo); reprints + one new story begins; Adams reprint.	.50	1.00	1.50
2-5	.30	.60	.90
6-12,14-16	.25	.50	.75
13-Newton story	.25	.50	.75
17-($1.00 size)-Kaluta cvr.	.40	.80	1.20
18-Starlin cvr, Staton art	.40	.80	1.20
19,20: Staton stories; #19-Kaluta cover. #20-Starlin wraparound cover			
	.40	.80	1.20
Power Record giveaway(12¼x12¼")Gorilla City, 16pgs. ($1.00 size)	.40	.80	1.20

BATMAN MINIATURE   (See Batman Kellogg's)

BATMAN RECORD COMIC
1966   (One Shot)
National Periodical Publications

#1	1.00	2.00	3.00

BATMAN SPECTACULAR   (See DC Special Ser.#15)

BAT MASTERSON   (TV)
8-10/59; 12-1/59-60 - #9, 11-1/61-62
Dell Publishing Co.

4-Color #1013 (8-10/59)	.80	1.60	2.40
#2-9	.50	1.00	1.50

BATS   (See Tales Calculated to Drive You —-)

BATTLE
March, 1951 - #70, June, 1960
Marvel/Atlas Comics(FPI #1-62/Male #63 on)

#1	2.00	4.00	6.00
2-10: #4-1st Buck Pvt. O'Tool			
	1.00	2.00	3.00
11-20	.80	1.60	2.40
21,23-Krigstein story	1.75	3.50	5.25
22,24-36,38-40	.60	1.20	1.80
37-Kubert story	1.50	3.00	4.50
41-Kubert/Moskowitz story	1.50	3.00	4.50
42-48	.60	1.20	1.80
49-Davis story	2.00	4.00	6.00
50-54,56-58	.50	1.00	1.50
55-Williamson story, 5pgs.	2.50	5.00	7.50
59-Torres story	1.20	2.40	3.60

(Battle cont'd)	Good	Fine	Mint
60-62: Combat Kelly app.-#60,62; Combat Casey			
app.-#61	.50	1.00	1.50
63-65: #63-Ditko story. #64,65-Kirby stories			
	1.50	3.00	4.50
66-Kirby, Davis stories	1.75	3.50	5.25
67-Williamson/Crandall story, 4 pgs. + Kirby			
story + Davis	2.50	5.00	7.50
68-Williamson w/Kirby pencils, 4 pgs. +			
Kirby/Ditko story	2.50	5.00	7.50
69-Kirby story	1.00	2.00	3.00
70-Kirby/Ditko story	1.00	2.00	3.00

NOTE: *Berg* stories-#8,60,62. *Everett* story-#36,50,70; cover-#56,57. *Kirby* cover-#64-69. *Orlando* story-#47. *Powell* story-#53,55. *Robinson* story-#9,39. *Severin* art-#28,32,34. *Woodbridge* story-#52,55.

BATTLE ACTION
Feb, 1952 - #12, 5/53; #13, 10/54 - #31, 8/57
Atlas Comics(NPI)

	Good	Fine	Mint
#1	1.50	3.00	4.50
2-7,9,10: #6-Robinson cover/story			
	1.00	2.00	3.00
8-Krigstein story	1.75	3.50	5.25
11-26,28,29,31	.70	1.40	2.10
27,30-Torres stories	1.20	2.40	3.60

NOTE: *Battle Brady* app. #5,6,10-12. *Woodbridge* stories-#28,30.

BATTLE ATTACK
Oct, 1952 - #8, Dec, 1955
Stanmor Publications

	Good	Fine	Mint
#1	1.20	2.40	3.60
2-8	.60	1.20	1.80

BATTLE BRADY (Men in Action #1-9)
#10, Jan, 1953 - #14, June, 1953
Atlas Comics (IPC)

	Good	Fine	Mint
#10-14	.80	1.60	2.40

BATTLE CLASSICS (See Cancelled Comic Caval-
Sept-Oct, 1978 (44 pgs.)   cade)
DC Comics

	Good	Fine	Mint
#1-Kubert reprint, new Kubert cover			
	.20	.40	.60

BATTLE CRY
1952 - #20, Sept, 1955
Stanmor Publications

	Good	Fine	Mint
#1	1.20	2.40	3.60
2-10: #8-1st Pvt. Ike app.(also in #10-12,17)			
	.70	1.40	2.10

	Good	Fine	Mint
11-20	.50	1.00	1.50

BATTLEFIELD (War Adventures on the --)
April, 1952 - #11, May, 1953
Atlas Comics (ACI)

	Good	Fine	Mint
#1	1.20	2.40	3.60
2-5	1.00	2.00	3.00
6-11	.60	1.20	1.80

BATTLEFIELD ACTION
#16, Dec, 1957 - #62, Feb-Mar, 1966
Charlton Comics

	Good	Fine	Mint
#16	.30	.60	.90
17,18,20-30	.25	.50	.75
19-Check story	.60	1.20	1.80
31-62	.15	.30	.45

NOTE: *Montes/Bache* art-#43,55,62.

BATTLE FIRE
April, 1955 - #7, 1955
Aragon Magazine/Stanmor Publications

	Good	Fine	Mint
#1	1.00	2.00	3.00
2-7	.60	1.20	1.80

BATTLEFRONT
June, 1952 - #48, Aug, 1957
Atlas Comics (FPI)

	Good	Fine	Mint
#1	1.50	3.00	4.50
2,5	1.00	2.00	3.00
3,4-Robinson book-length story in each			
	1.20	2.40	3.60
6-10: Combat Kelly in all	.80	1.60	2.40
11-21,23-30: Battle Brady in #14,16			
	.60	1.20	1.80
22-Kubert story	1.50	3.00	4.50
31-39	.50	1.00	1.50
40,42-Williamson story	2.50	5.00	7.50
41,44-47	.50	1.00	1.50
43-Check story	.60	1.20	1.80
48-Crandall art	.90	1.80	2.70

NOTE: *Drucker* story-#28. *Everett* story-#44. *Morrow* story-#41. *Orlando* story-#47. *Powell* story-#21,25,47. *Robinson* story-#1,2,4,5; cover-#4. *Woodbridge* story-#45,46.

BATTLEFRONT
#5, 1952
Standard Comics

	Good	Fine	Mint
#5-Toth art	1.75	3.50	5.25

BATTLE GROUND
Sept, 1954 - #20, 1957

Battle Attack #4, © Stanmor Publ.

Battle Fire #4, © Stanmor Publ.

Battlefront #1, © MCG

37

Battle Report #1, © AJAX

Battle Squadron #1, © Stanmor

Bee 29, The Bombardier #1, © Neal Publ.

(Battle Ground cont'd)
Atlas Comics (OMC)

	Good	Fine	Mint
#1	1.50	3.00	4.50
2-8,10	.70	1.40	2.10
9-Krigstein story	1.50	3.00	4.50
11,13,18-Williamson story in each(4pgs. #11)			
	2.50	5.00	7.50
12,15-17,19,20	.60	1.20	1.80
14-Kirby story	1.00	2.00	3.00

NOTE: *Drucker story-#7,12,13. Orlando story-#17. Severin story-#19.*

BATTLE HEROES
Sept, 1966 - #2, Nov, 1966   (25¢)
Stanley Publications

#1,2	.30	.60	.90

BATTLE OF THE BULGE (See Movie Classics)

BATTLE REPORT
Aug, 1952 - #6, June, 1953
Ajax/Farrell Publications

#1	1.00	2.00	3.00
2-6	.50	1.00	1.50

BATTLE SQUADRON
April, 1955 - #5, Dec, 1955
Stanmore Publications

#1	1.00	2.00	3.00
2-5	.50	1.00	1.50

BATTLE STORIES
1952 - #11, 1953
Fawcett Publications

#1-Evans story	1.75	3.50	5.25
2-11	1.00	2.00	3.00

BATTLE STORIES
1963 - 1964
Super Comics

Reprints #10-12,15-18; Jet Powers in #15 by Powell	.40	.80	1.20

BEACH BLANKET BINGO (See Movie Classics)

BEAGLE BOYS, THE (Walt Disney)
Nov, 1964 - Present
Gold Key

#1	.70	1.40	2.10
2-5	.40	.80	1.20
6-10	.35	.70	1.05

	Good	Fine	Mint
11-20	.25	.50	.75
21-47	.15	.30	.45

BEANBAGS
Winter, 1951 - #2, Spring, 1952
Ziff-Davis Publ. Co. (Approved Comics)

#1,2	1.20	2.40	3.60

BEANIE THE MEANIE
1958 - #3, May, 1959
Fago Publications

#1-3	.35	.70	1.05

BEANY AND CECIL (TV) (Bob Clampett's --)
Jan, 1952 - 1955; 7-9/62 - #5, 7-9/63
Dell Publishing Co.

4-Color #368	2.00	4.00	6.00
4-Color #414,448,477,530,570,635			
	1.20	2.40	3.60
#01-057-209	1.00	2.00	3.00
2-5	.80	1.60	2.40

BEAR COUNTRY (Disney) (See 4-Color #758)

BEATLES, THE (See Strange Tales #130, My
Little Margie #54, Jimmy Olsen #79, Summer
Love)

BEATLES, LIFE STORY, THE
Sept-Nov, 1964   (35¢)
Dell Publishing Co.

#1-Stories with color photo pin-ups			
	9.00	18.00	27.00

BEATLES YELLOW SUBMARINE (See Movie Comics
under Yellow --)

BEAVER VALLEY (See 4-Color Comics #625)

BEDKNOBS & BROOMSTICKS (See Walt Disney
Showcase #6)

BEE 29, THE BOMBARDIER
February, 1945
Neal Publications

#1-(Funny Animal)	1.35	2.75	4.00

BEEP BEEP, THE ROAD RUNNER (TV)
July, 1958 - #14, 8-10/62; 10/66 - Present
Dell Publishing Co./Gold Key

4-Color #918,1008,1046	1.00	2.00	3.00

(Beep Beep, the Road Runner cont'd)

	Good	Fine	Mint
#4-14(Dell)	.50	1.00	1.50
#1	.70	1.40	2.10
2-5	.50	1.00	1.50
6-18	.30	.60	.90
19-with pull-out poster	.30	.60	.90
20-40	.25	.50	.75
41-75(Gold Key)	.20	.40	.60
Florida Power & Light Giveaway ('67)	.25	.50	.75

(See March of Comics #351,353,375,387,397)

<u>BEETLE BAILEY</u> (Also see Comics Reading Libr.)
#469, 5/53 - #38, 5-7/62; #39, 11/62 - #53,
5/66; #54, 8/66 - #66, 1968; #67, 2/69 -
#119, 11/76; #120, 4/78 - Present
Dell Publishing Co./Gold Key #39-53/King #54-
66/Charlton #67-119/Gold Key #120 on

4-Color #469,521,552,622	1.00	2.00	3.00
#5-10	.50	1.00	1.50
11-50	.35	.70	1.05
51-124	.15	.30	.45
Bold Detergent Giveaway(1969)-same as regular ish (#67) minus price	.25	.50	.75
Cerebral Palsy Assn. Giveaway V2#71(1969)- V2#73(1/70)	.25	.50	.75
Giant Comic Album(1972, 59¢, 11x14")Color cover, B&W interior, modern promotions (reprints)	.25	.50	.75

<u>BEHIND PRISON BARS</u>
1952
Realistic Comics (Avon)

#1-Kinstler cover	5.00	10.00	15.00

<u>BEHOLD THE HANDMAID</u>
1954   (Religious giveaway)
George Pflaum

	2.50	5.00	7.50

<u>BELIEVE IT OR NOT</u> (See Ripley's --)

<u>BEN AND ME</u> (See 4-Color Comics #539)

<u>BEN BOWIE & HIS MOUNTAIN MEN</u>
1952 - #19, May-July, 1959
Dell Publishing Co.

4-Color #443	1.50	3.00	4.50
4-Color #513,557,599,626,657			
	1.25	2.50	3.75
#7-10	1.00	2.00	3.00
11-Intro. & origin Yellow Hair			
	.80	1.60	2.40

	Good	Fine	Mint
12-19	.60	1.20	1.80

<u>BEN CASEY</u> (TV)
June-July, 1962 - #10, June-Aug, 1965
Dell Publishing Co.

#12-063-207	1.00	2.00	3.00
#2(10/62)-#10	.50	1.00	1.50

<u>BEN CASEY FILM STORY</u>
November, 1962
Gold Key

#30009-211-All photos	2.00	4.00	6.00

<u>BENEATH THE PLANET OF THE APES</u> (See Movie
Comics)

<u>BEN FRANKLIN KITE FUN BOOK</u>
1975, 1977   (16 pgs.) (5-1/8"x6-5/8")
Southern Calif. Edison Co./PG&E ('77)

	.30	.60	.90

<u>BEN HUR</u> (See 4-Color Comics #1052)

<u>BEN ISRAEL</u>
1974   (39¢)
Logos International

	.30	.60	.90

<u>BEOWULF</u>
Apr-May, 1975 - #6, Feb-Mar, 1976
National Periodical Publications

#1	.50	1.00	1.50
2-6	.30	.60	.90

<u>BERRYS, THE</u>
May, 1956
Argo Publ.

#1-Reprints daily & Sunday strips & daily Animal Antics by Ed Nofziger.			
	1.00	2.00	3.00

<u>BEST COMICS</u>
Nov, 1939 - 1940
Better Publications

#1-Red Mask begins	13.50	26.75	40.00
2-4	8.00	16.00	24.00

<u>BEST FROM BOY'S LIFE, THE</u>
Oct, 1957 - #5, Oct, 1958   (35¢)
Gilberton Company

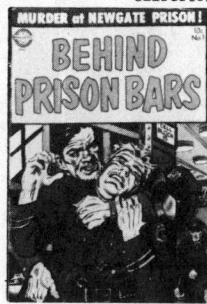

Beetle Bailey #5, © KING   Behind Prison Bars #1, © AVON   Best Comics #4, © BP

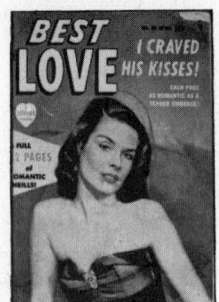

Best Love #36, © MCG

The Best Of D.T.M. #1, © FAW

Best Romance #5, © STD

(Best From Boy's Life cont'd)

	Good	Fine	Mint
#1-Space Conquerors & Kam of the Ancient			
Ones app.; also #3	1.00	2.00	3.00
2-5	.70	1.40	2.10

BEST LOVE (Formerly Sub-Mariner)
#33, Aug, 1949 - #36, April, 1950
Marvel Comics (MPI)

#33,34	.80	1.60	2.40
'35,36-Everett stories	2.00	4.00	6.00

BEST OF BUGS BUNNY, THE
Oct, 1966 - #2, 1968
Gold Key

#1,2	.60	1.20	1.80

BEST OF DENNIS THE MENACE, THE
Summer, 1959 - #5, Spring, 1961 (100 pgs.)
Hallden/Fawcett Publications

#1	1.75	3.50	5.25
2-5	1.50	3.00	4.50

BEST OF DONALD DUCK, THE
Nov, 1965 (36 pgs.)
Gold Key

#1-Reprints 4-Color #223 by Carl Barks			
	7.00	14.00	21.00

BEST OF DONALD DUCK & UNCLE SCROOGE, THE
Nov, 1964 - #2, Sept, 1967 (25¢)
Gold Key

#1(#30022-411)('64)-Reprints 4-Color #189 &			
408 by Carl Barks	12.00	24.00	36.00
2(#30022-709)('67)-Reprints 4-Color #256 &			
"7 Cities of Cibola" by Barks			
	9.00	18.00	27.00

BEST OF MARMADUKE, THE
1960 (A Dog)
Charlton Comics

#1-Brad Anderson's strip reprints			
	.50	1.00	1.50

BEST OF THE WEST (See A-1 Comics)
1951 - #12, April-June, 1954
Magazine Enterprises

#1(A-1#42)-Ghost Rider, Durango Kid, Straight			
Arrow, Tim Holt begin	7.00	14.00	21.00
2(A-1#46),3(A-1#52),4(A-1#59),5(A-1#66)			
	3.50	7.00	10.50

	Good	Fine	Mint
6(A-1#70),7(A-1#76),8(A-1#81),9(A-1#85),			
10(A-1#87),11(A-1#97),12(A-1#103)			
	2.50	5.00	7.50

BEST OF UNCLE SCROOGE & DONALD DUCK, THE
November, 1966 (25¢)
Gold Key

#1(#30030-611)-Reprints part 4-Color #159 &			
456 & Uncle Scrooge #6 by Carl Barks			
	9.00	18.00	27.00

BEST OF WALT DISNEY COMICS, THE
1974 (In Color)(Walt Disney)($1.50)(52 pgs.)
8½x11" cardboard covers; 32,000 printed of ea.
Western Publishing Co.

#96170-Reprints 1st two stories less 1 pg. ea.			
from 4-Color #62	1.20	2.40	3.60
96171-Reprints Mickey Mouse and the Bat			
Bandit of Inferno Gulch from 1934 (strips)			
by Gottfredson	1.20	2.40	3.60
96172-Reprints Uncle Scrooge #386 & 2 other			
stories	1.20	2.40	3.60
96173-Reprints "Ghost of the Grotto" (from			
4-Color #159) & "Christmas on Bear Mtn."			
(from 4-Color #178)	1.20	2.40	3.60

BEST ROMANCE
#5, Feb-Mar, 1952 - #6, May, 1952
Standard Comics (Visual Editions)

#5-Toth art	2.00	4.00	6.00
6	.80	1.60	2.40

BEST SELLER COMICS (See Tailspin Tommy)

BEST WESTERN (Formerly Terry Toons?)(Western
Outlaws & Sheriffs #60 on)
#58, 6/49 - #59, 8/49
Marvel Comics (IPC)

#58,59-Black Rider	2.00	4.00	6.00

BETTY AND HER STEADY (Going Steady With Betty
#2, Mar-Apr, 1950   #1)
Avon Periodicals

#2	2.00	4.00	6.00

BETTY AND ME
Aug, 1965 - Present (Giants #36 on)
Archie Publications

#1	2.00	4.00	6.00
2-5: #3-Origin Superteen; in new costume			
#4-7; dons new helmet #5, ends #8			
	1.00	2.00	3.00

(Betty and Me cont'd)	Good	Fine	Mint
6-10	.60	1.20	1.80
11-35	.50	1.00	1.50
36-55(52pgs.)	.25	.50	.75
56-95		.20	.40

BETTY & VERONICA (See Archie's Girls --)

BETTY & VERONICA CHRISTMAS SPECTACULAR (See
Archie Giant Series Mag. #159,168,180,191,
204,217,229,241,453,465)

BETTY & VERONICA SPECTACULAR (See Archie
Giant Series Mag. #11,16,21,26,32,138,145,153,
162,173,184,197,201,210,214,221,226,234,238,
246,250,458,462,470)

BETTY & VERONICA SUMMER FUN (See Archie
Giant Series Mag. #8,13,18,23,28,34,140,147,
155,164,175,187,199,212,224,236,248,460)

BEVERLY HILLBILLIES (TV)
Apr-Jun, 1963 - #21, Oct, 1971
Dell Publishing Co.

#1	.60	1.20	1.80
2-10	.35	.70	1.05
11-21	.20	.40	.60

BEWARE (Formerly Fantastic; Chilling Tales
#10, 6/52 - #12, 10/52   #13 on)
Youthful Magazines

#10-Pit & the Pendulum adaptation; Wildey art			
	1.75	3.50	5.25
11,12	1.20	2.40	3.60

BEWARE
Jan, 1953 - #15, May, 1955
Trojan Magazines/Merit Publ.

#13(#1)	1.50	3.00	4.50
14-16(#2-4)	1.20	2.40	3.60
5-7,11	1.00	2.00	3.00
8,9-Check art	1.50	3.00	4.50
10-Frazetta/Check cover; Disbrow art			
	15.00	30.00	45.00
12-Harrison story	2.00	4.00	6.00
13,15	1.00	2.00	3.00
14-Krenkel/Harrison cvr.	2.00	4.00	6.00

BEWARE! (Tomb of Darkness #9 on)
March, 1973 - #8, May, 1974
Marvel Comics Group

#1	.20	.40	.60
2-6,8	.15	.30	.45
7-Torres reprt./Mystical Tales #7			

	Good	Fine	Mint
	.20	.40	.60

BEWARE TERROR TALES
May, 1952 - 1953
Fawcett Publications

#1-Powell art	1.75	3.50	5.25
2-11: #8-Powell art	1.20	2.40	3.60

BEWARE THE CREEPER (See 1st Issue Special &
5-6/68 - #6, 3-4/69   Showcase)
National Periodical Publications

#1-Ditko art	1.00	2.00	3.00
2-6-Ditko art	.70	1.40	2.10

BEWITCHED (TV)
April-June, 1965 - #14, Oct, 1969
Dell Publishing Co.

#1	.30	.60	.90
2-14	.20	.40	.60

BEYOND, THE
Nov, 1950 - #33, 1955
Ace Magazines

#1	2.00	4.00	6.00
2-Matt Baker story(pencils)			
	2.00	4.00	6.00
3-5,7-9	1.00	2.00	3.00
6-Baker story	2.50	5.00	7.50
10-Harrison/Wood? story	3.00	6.00	9.00
11-20	.90	1.80	2.70
21-33	.80	1.60	2.40

NOTE: *Cameron story-#20-22,24-26,30. #1 was
to appear as Challenge of the Unknown #7.*

BEYOND THE GRAVE
July, 1975 - #6, June, 1976
Charlton Comics

#1	.20	.40	.60
2-6	.15	.30	.45

NOTE: *Ditko stories-#1-3,5; covers-#2,3.*

BIBLE TALES FOR YOUNG FOLK
Aug, 1953 - #5, Mar, 1954
Atlas Comics (OMC)

#1	3.00	6.00	9.00
2-Everett, Krigstein sty.	2.00	4.00	6.00
3-5	1.50	3.00	4.50

BIG ALL-AMERICAN COMIC BOOK, THE
1944   (One Shot)   (132 pgs.)
All-American/National Periodical Publ.

Beware #12, © YM

Beware Terror Tales #7, © FAW

The Beyond #10, © ACE

Big Book Of Fun Comics #1, © DC   Big Book Romances #1, © FAW   Big Shot Comics #3, © CCG

	Good	Fine	Mint
(Big All-Amer. -- cont'd)			

#1-Wonder Woman, Green Lantern, Flash, The
Atom, Wildcat, Scribbly, The Whip, Ghost
Patrol, Hawkman by Kubert (1st on Hawkman),
Hop Harrigan, Johnny Thunder, Little Boy
Blue, Mr. Terrific, Mutt & Jeff app.; Sar-
gon on cover only   120.00 240.00 360.00

BIG BOOK OF FUN COMICS
Spring, 1936   (52 pgs.)
National Periodical Publications

#1 (Rare) - Large size; reprints New Fun
#1-5(1st DC Annual)   75.00 150.00 225.00

BIG BOOK ROMANCES
February, 1950   (148 pgs.)
Fawcett Publications

#1-Contains remaindered Fawcett romance com-
ics - several combinations possible
3.00   6.00   9.00

BIG BOY   (See Adventures of the --)

BIG CHIEF WAHOO
1942
Eastern Color Print./George Dougherty

#1-Newspaper reprints	7.00	14.00	21.00
2-Steve Roper app.	4.00	8.00	12.00
3-5	3.00	6.00	9.00
6-10	2.00	4.00	6.00
11-23	1.50	3.00	4.50

NOTE: *Kerry Drake in some issues.*

BIG CIRCUS, THE   (See 4-Color #1036)

BIG COUNTRY, THE   (See 4-Color #946)

BIG DADDY ROTH
Oct-Nov, 1964 - #4, Apr-May, 1965 (Mag. 35¢)
Millar Publications

| #1-Toth art | 3.00 | 6.00 | 9.00 |
| 2-4-Toth art | 1.75 | 3.50 | 5.25 |

BIG HERO ADVENTURES   (See Jigsaw)

BIG JIM'S P.A.C.K.
No date   (16 pgs.)
Mattel, Inc. (Marvel Comics)

Giveaway with Big Jim doll   .15   .30

BIG JOHN AND SPARKIE
1952   (Formerly Sparkie, Radio Pixie)
Ziff-Davis Publ. Co.

	Good	Fine	Mint
#4	2.00	4.00	6.00

BIG LAND, THE   (See 4-Color #812)

BIG RED   (See Movie Comics)

BIG SHOT COMICS
May, 1940 - #104, Aug, 1947
Columbia Comics Group

#1-Intro. Skyman; The Face (Tony Trent), The
Cloak (Spy Master), Marvelo, Monarch of
Magicians, Joe Palooka begin
50.00 100.00 150.00
2-Origin Skyman	25.00	50.00	75.00
3-The Cloak called Spy Chief			
	17.50	35.00	52.50
4,5	12.00	24.00	36.00
6-10	8.00	16.00	24.00
11-13	7.00	14.00	21.00
14-Origin Sparky Watts	8.00	16.00	24.00
15-Origin The Cloak	9.00	18.00	27.00
16-20	7.00	14.00	21.00
21-30: #29-Intro. Capt. Yank. #30-Bo (a dog)			
newspaper strip reprints by Frank Beck			
begins, ends #104	5.00	10.00	15.00
31-40: #32-Vic Jordan newspaper strip reprints			
begin, end #50	4.00	8.00	12.00
41-50: #42-No Skyman. #50-Origin The Face			
retold	3.00	6.00	9.00
51-60	2.00	4.00	6.00
61-70: #63 on- Tony Trent, the Face			
	1.50	3.00	4.50
71-80: #73-The Face cameo. #74,80-The Face			
app. in Tony Trent. #78-Last Charlie Chan			
strip reprints	1.25	2.50	3.75
81-90: #85-Tony Trent marries Babs Walsh			
	1.25	2.50	3.75
91-104	1.00	2.00	3.00

(Skyman in Outer Space #70-94)
NOTE: *Mart Bailey art on "The Face"-#1-104.
Sparky Watts by Boody Rogers-#14-42,77-104,
(by others #43-76). Others than Tony Trent
wear "The Face" mask in #46-63,93. Skyman by
Ogden Whitney-#1,2,4,12-37,49,70-101. Skyman
covers-#1,6,10,11,14,16,20,27,89,95,100.*

BIG TEX
June, 1953
Toby Press

| #1 | 1.20 | 2.40 | 3.60 |

BIG-3
Fall, 1940 - #7, January, 1942
Fox Features Syndicate

(Big-3 cont'd)

	Good	Fine	Mint
#1-Blue Beetle, The Flame, & Samson begin	40.00	80.00	120.00
2	20.00	40.00	60.00
3-5	12.00	24.00	36.00
6-Last Samson	10.00	20.00	30.00
7-V-Man app.	10.00	20.00	30.00

BIG THRILL BOOKLET (See Tom Mix & Chewing Gum)
1934 (3x2½")(8pgs., cover & centerfold in color)(24 books in set)(4 sets)
Goudey Chewing Gum (Giveaway)

Buck Jones #1-6	3.00	6.00	9.00
Buck Rogers #1-6	6.00	12.00	18.00
Dick Tracy #1-6	5.00	10.00	15.00
Tailspin Tommy #1-6	3.00	6.00	9.00

NOTE: *Prices are per book. There are 24 different books under each title or 96 in all.*

BIG TOP COMICS, THE
1951 (No month)
Toby Press

#1,2	1.00	2.00	3.00

BIG TOWN (Radio/TV)
Jan, 1951 - #50, Mar-Apr, 1958
National Periodical Publications

#1	4.00	8.00	12.00
2	2.00	4.00	6.00
3-10	1.50	3.00	4.50
11-50	.80	1.60	2.40

BIG VALLEY, THE (TV)
June, 1966 - #6, Oct, 1969
Dell Publishing Co.

#1-6	.30	.60	.90

BILL BARNES COMICS (Air Ace V2#1 on)
Oct, 1940 - #12, 1942
Street & Smith Publications

#1	12.00	24.00	36.00
2-Barnes as The Phantom Flyer app.	7.00	14.00	21.00
3-5	5.00	10.00	15.00
6-12	3.00	6.00	9.00

BILL BATTLE, THE ONE MAN ARMY
Oct, 1952 - 1953
Fawcett Publications

#1	1.20	2.40	3.60
2-6	.80	1.60	2.40

BILL BOYD WESTERN
Jan, 1950 - #23, June, 1952
Fawcett Publications

	Good	Fine	Mint
#1	6.00	12.00	18.00
2-10	3.00	6.00	9.00
11-23	2.00	4.00	6.00

BILL BUMLIN (See Treasury of Comics #3)

BILL STERN'S SPORTS BOOK
Spring-Summer, 1951 - V2#2, Winter, 1952
Ziff-Davis Publ. Co.

V1#10(1951)	.80	1.60	2.40
V2#2(1952)-Krigstein art	1.75	3.50	5.25

BILLY AND BUGGY BEAR
1958; 1964
I.W. Enterprises/Super

I.W. Reprint #1(Early Timely Funny Animal), 7(1958)	.40	.80	1.20
Super Reprint #10(1964)	.40	.80	1.20

BILLY BUCKSKIN WESTERN (Two-Gun Western #4)
Nov, 1955 - #3, March, 1956
Atlas Comics (IMC #1/MgPC #2,3)

#1-Mort Drucker art	2.00	4.00	6.00
2- " " "	1.00	2.00	3.00
3-Williamson story + Drucker art	2.50	5.00	7.50

BILLY BUNNY (Black Cobra #6 on)
Feb-Mar, 1954 - #5, Oct-Nov, 1954
Excellent Publications

#1-5	.40	.80	1.20

BILLY BUNNY'S CHRISTMAS FROLICS
1952 (100 pgs.)
Farrell Publications

#1	1.20	2.40	3.60

BILLY MAKE BELIEVE (See Single Series #14)

BILLY THE KID
#7, 1957 - #121, 12/76; #122, 9/77 - #123, 10/77; #124, 2/78 - Present
Charlton Publ. Co.

#7-14,17-19: #11-68pgs.	.65	1.35	2.00
15-Origin	1.00	2.00	3.00
16-Two pgs. Williamson	1.50	3.00	4.50
20-22-Three Severin stys.	1.20	2.40	3.60
23-40	.40	.80	1.20

Big 3 #1, © FOX

Bill Barnes Comics #4, © S&S

Bill Boyd Western #4, © FAW

Billy West #6, © STD   Black & White #13, © N.Y. News Synd.   Black & White #23, © N.Y. News Synd.

	Good	Fine	Mint
(Billy the Kid cont'd)			
41-60	.25	.50	.75
61-80: #66-Bounty Hunter series begins. Not			
in #79,82,84-86	.20	.40	.60
81-121: #87-Last Bounty Hunter. #11-Origin			
& 1st app. The Ghost Train; Sutton art.			
#117-Gunsmith & Co., The Cheyenne Kid app.,			
122,123('77)	.20	.40	
124(2/78)-127: All Severin	.20	.40	
Modern Comics #109(1977 reprint)	.15	.30	

BILLY THE KID ADVENTURE MAGAZINE
Oct, 1950 - #30, 1955
Toby Press

#1-Williamson/Frazetta, 2 pgs.			
	7.00	14.00	21.00
2,4-8,10	1.50	3.00	4.50
3-Williamson/Frazetta "The Claws of Death",			
4pgs.+Williamson sty.	10.00	20.00	30.00
9-Kurtzman Pot-Shot Pete	4.00	8.00	12.00
11,12,15-20	1.20	2.40	3.60
13-Kurtzman reprint/John Wayne #12 (Genius)			
	1.75	3.50	5.25
14-Williamson/Frazetta; reprint of #1, 2pgs.			
	3.00	6.00	9.00
21,23-30	1.00	2.00	3.00
22-One pg. Williamson/Frazetta reprint/#1			
	1.50	3.00	4.50

BILLY THE KID AND OSCAR
Winter, 1945 - #3, Summer, 1946 (Funny Animal)
Fawcett Publications

#1	1.00	2.00	3.00
2,3	.60	1.20	1.80

BILLY WEST (Bill West #9,10)
1949 - #10, April, 1951
Standard Comics (Visual Editions)

#1	2.00	4.00	6.00
2-10: #7,8-Schomburg cvr.	1.20	2.40	3.60

NOTE: *Celardo* art-#1-5,9; cover-#2,3.
Moreira story-#3.

BING CROSBY (See Feature Films)

BINGO (-- Comics) (H. C. Blackerby)
1945 (Reprints National material)
Howard Publ.

#1-L. B. Cole opium cover	4.00	8.00	12.00

BINGO, THE MONKEY DOODLE BOY
Aug, 1951; Oct, 1953
St. John Publishing Co.

	Good	Fine	Mint
#1(8/51)-by Eric Peters	1.75	3.50	5.25
1(10/53)	1.20	2.40	3.60

BINKY (Formerly Leave It To --)
#72, 4-5/70 - #81, 10-11/71; #82, Sum/77 -
National Per. Publ./DC Comics   Present

#72-81	.15	.30	.45
82('77)		.15	.30

BINKY'S BUDDIES
Jan-Feb, 1969 - #12, Nov-Dec, 1970
National Periodical Publications

#1	.20	.40	.60
2-12		.15	.30

BIONIC WOMAN, THE (TV)
October, 1977 - #5, June, 1978
Charlton Publications

#1-5	.15	.30	.45

BLACK AND WHITE (Large Feature Comics #25 on)
1939 - 1941 (All strip reprints)
Dell Publishing Co.

#1-Dick Tracy Meets the Blank			
	70.00	175.00	280.00
2-Terry & the Pirates	40.00	100.00	160.00
3-Heigh-Ho Silver! The Lone Ranger (text &			
ill)(76 pgs.)	24.00	60.00	96.00
4-Dick Tracy Gets His Man			
	35.00	87.50	140.00
5-Tarzan by Harold Foster (origin); reprints			
1st dailies from '29-100.00	250.00	400.00	
6-Terry & the Pirates & The Dragon Lady; re-			
prints dailies from 1936			
	30.00	75.00	120.00
7-(Scarce)-52pgs.; The Lone Ranger-Hi-Yo			
Silver the L.R. to the Rescue			
	35.00	87.50	140.00
8-Dick Tracy Racket Buster			
	35.00	87.50	140.00
9-King of the Royal Mtd.	15.00	37.50	60.00
10-(Scarce)-Gangbusters (# appears on inside			
front cover)	20.00	50.00	80.00
11-Dick Tracy Foils the Mad Doc Hump			
	35.00	87.50	140.00
12-Smilin' Jack	15.00	37.50	60.00
13-Dick Tracy & Scotty	35.00	87.50	140.00
14-Smilin' Jack	15.00	37.50	60.00
15-Dick Tracy & the Kidnapped Princess			
	35.00	87.50	140.00
16-Donald Duck-1st app. Daisy Duck on back			
cover(6/41-Disney) 350.00	875.00	1400.00	

(Prices vary widely on this book)

(Black and White cont'd)

	Good	Fine	Mint
17-Gangbusters(1941)	12.00	30.00	48.00
18-Phantasmo	15.00	37.50	60.00
19-Dumbo Comic Paint Book (Disney); partial reprint 4-Color #17	70.00	175.00	280.00
20-Donald Duck Comic Paint Book (Rarer than #16) (Disney)	400.00	1000.00	1600.00

(Prices vary widely on this book)

	Good	Fine	Mint
21-Private Buck	5.00	12.50	20.00
22-Nuts & Jolts	6.00	15.00	24.00
23-The Nebbs	6.00	15.00	24.00
24-Popeye (Thimble Threatre) 1/2 by Segar	25.00	60.00	100.00

NOTE: *The Black & White Feature Books are oversized 8½"x11-3/8" comics with color covers and black and white interiors. The first nine (9) issues all have rough, heavy stock covers and, except for #7, all have 76 pages, including covers. #7 and #10-24 all have 52 pages. Beginning with #10 the covers are slick and thin and, because of their size, are difficult to handle without damaging. For this reason, they are seldom found in fine to mint condition. The paper stock, unlike Wow #1 and Capt.Marvel #1, is itself not unstable...just thin.*

BLACKBEARD'S GHOST (See Movie Comics)

BLACK BEAUTY (See 4-Color #440)

BLACK CAT COMICS (-- Western #16-19; -- Mystery #29 on)
June-July, 1946 - #28, April, 1951
Harvey Publications (Home Comics)

	Good	Fine	Mint
#1-Kubert art	25.00	50.00	75.00
2-Kubert art	15.00	30.00	45.00
3	10.00	20.00	30.00
4-The Red Demons begin (The Demon #4 & 5)			
5,6-The Scarlet Arrow app.; S&K art in both; Powell story #6	11.00	22.00	33.00
7-Vagabond Prince by S&K + 1 more story	12.00	24.00	36.00
8-S&K art	10.00	20.00	30.00
9-Origin Stuntman by S&K (reprint/Stuntman #1); Kerry Drake begins, ends #12	17.50	35.00	52.50
10-20: #13-Kerry Drake app. #15,17-Mary Worth app. + Invisible Scarlett O'Neil-#15	6.00	12.00	18.00
21-28	5.00	10.00	15.00

BLACK CAT MYSTERY (Formerly Black Cat; -- Western Mystery #54; --Western #55,56; --Mystery #57; --Mystic #58-62; Black Cat #63-65)
#29, June, 1951 - #65, April, 1963

Harvey Publications

	Good	Fine	Mint
#29-Black Cat bondage cover; Black Cat stories	5.00	10.00	15.00
30-Black Cat on cvr only	3.00	6.00	9.00
31-35,37,38,40	2.50	5.00	7.50
36,39-Used in Seduction of the Innocent: #36-Pgs. 270,271; #39-Pgs. 386,387,388.	6.00	12.00	18.00
41-43,50	2.25	4.50	6.75
44,46-49,51-Nostrand art in all	3.00	6.00	9.00
45-Classic "Colorama" by Powell; Nostrand art	5.00	10.00	15.00
52,53	2.25	4.50	6.75
54-Two Black Cat stories	4.00	8.00	12.00
55,56, Black Cat app.	3.00	6.00	9.00
57-Kirby cover	2.50	5.00	7.50
58-60-Four Kirby stys.	4.00	8.00	12.00
61-Nostrand story & classic "Colorama" reprinted from #45	3.00	6.00	9.00
62-E.C. story swipe	1.75	3.50	5.25
63-65-All Giants(25¢)-Black Cat app.	2.50	5.00	7.50

NOTE: *Check story-#50. Kirby cover-#57. Meskin story-#51. Nostrand art-#44-49,61. Powell story-#32-35,40,41,43-52,57. Bondage covers-#32,34,43.*

BLACK COBRA (Formerly Billy Bunny)
#1, 10-11/54; #6(#2), 12-1/54-55; #3,2-3/55
Ajax/Farrell Publications

	Good	Fine	Mint
#1	3.50	7.00	10.50
6(#2)-Formerly B.Bunny	2.50	5.00	7.50
3	2.50	5.00	7.50

BLACK DIAMOND WESTERN (Desperado #1-8)
#9, 1949 - #60, 1956
Lev Gleason Publications

	Good	Fine	Mint
#9-Origin; Wolverton art	5.00	10.00	15.00
10-15	1.75	3.50	5.25
16-28-Wolverton's Bing Bang Buster	3.00	6.00	9.00
29,30,32-60	.80	1.60	2.40
31-One pg. Frazetta	1.35	2.75	4.00

BLACK FURY (Wild West #58)(See Blue Bird)
May, 1955 - #57, 3-4/66 (Horse stories)
Charlton Comics Group

	Good	Fine	Mint
#1	.80	1.60	2.40
2-15	.50	1.00	1.50
16-18-Ditko art	1.20	2.40	3.60
19-57	.25	.50	.75

Black Cat Comics #14, © HARV

Black Cat Comics #45, © HARV

Black Diamond Western #17, © LEV

Blackhawk #57, © DC

Blackhawk #102, © DC

Black Knight #5, © MCG

BLACK GOLIATH
Feb, 1976 - #5, Nov, 1976
Marvel Comics Group

	Good	Fine	Mint
#1	.40	.80	1.20
2-5	.25	.50	.75

BLACKHAWK (Formerly Uncle Sam #1-8)
#9, Winter, 1944 - #243, Oct-Nov, 1968;
#244, 1-2/76 - #250, 11-12/76
Comic Magazines(Quality)#9-107; National Per.
Publ., #108(1/57) on

#9(1944)	60.00	120.00	180.00
10(1946)	30.00	60.00	90.00
11-15	20.00	40.00	60.00
16-20	14.00	28.00	42.00
21-30	10.00	20.00	30.00
31-40	7.00	14.00	21.00
41-60: #50-1st Killer Shark; origin in text			
	5.00	10.00	15.00
61-80: #70-Return of Killer Shark. #71-Ori-			
gin retold. #75-Intro. Blackie the Hawk			
	4.00	8.00	12.00
81-107: #93-Origin in text	3.00	6.00	9.00
108-Re-intro. Blackie, the Hawk, their mascot;			
not in #115	4.00	8.00	12.00
109-117	2.00	4.00	6.00
118-Frazetta reprint/Jimmy Wakely #4, 3pgs.			
	7.00	14.00	21.00
119-130	1.50	3.00	4.50
131-142,144-160: #133-Intro. Lady Blackhawk			
	.90	1.80	2.70
143-Kurtzman reprt/Jimmy Wakely #4			
	1.00	2.00	3.00
161-163,165-190	.60	1.20	1.80
164-Origin retold	1.00	2.00	3.00
191-197,199-202,204-210: Combat Diary series			
begins. #197-New look for Blackhawks			
	.50	1.00	1.50
198-Origin retold	.60	1.20	1.80
203-Origin Chop Chop	.60	1.20	1.80
211-243(1968): #228-Batman, Green Lantern,			
Superman, The Flash cameos. #230-Black-			
hawks become superheroes. #242-Return to			
old costumes	.35	.70	1.05
244,245('76)-Kubert covers; Evans story in ea.			
	.25	.50	.75
246-250: #250-Check dies; Evans stories in all			
	.25	.50	.75

NOTE: *Crandall stories-#10,11,16,18-20,22-26,
30-33,39-44,46-50,52-58,60,63,64,66,67; cov-
ers-#18-20,22. Kubert cover-#245. Ward stor-
ies-#16-27(Chop Chop, 8pgs. ea.); pencilled
stories-#17-63(approx.).*

BLACKHAWK INDIAN TOMAHAWK WAR, THE
1951
Avon Periodicals

	Good	Fine	Mint
No#-Kinstler cover; Kit West story			
	3.00	6.00	9.00

BLACK HOOD COMICS (Formerly Hangman #2-8;
Laugh Comics #20 on)
#9, Winter, 1944 - #19, Summer, 1946
MLJ Magazines

#9-The Hangman & The Boy Buddies cont'd.			
	12.00	24.00	36.00
10-The Hangman & Dusty, the Boy Detective			
app.	7.00	14.00	21.00
11-Dusty app.; no Hangman	5.00	10.00	15.00
12-18	5.00	10.00	15.00
19-I.D. exposed	6.00	12.00	18.00

BLACK JACK (Rocky Lane's --)
#20, Nov, 1957 - #30, Nov, 1959
Charlton Comics

#20-22,25,27,29,30	.70	1.40	2.10
23-Williamson art	2.00	4.00	6.00
24,26,28-Ditko art	1.00	2.00	3.00

BLACK KNIGHT, THE
1952 - 1953
Toby Press

#1(1952)	4.00	8.00	12.00
1(5/53)(Toby)	2.50	5.00	7.50
Super Reprint #11(1963)	1.00	2.00	3.00

BLACK KNIGHT, THE
May, 1955 - #5, April, 1956
Atlas Comics (MgPC)

#1	10.00	20.00	30.00
2-5	7.00	14.00	21.00

BLACK LIGHTNING (See Cancelled Comic Caval-
April, 1977 - #11, 9-10/78   cade)
National Periodical Publ./DC Comics

#1	.30	.60	.90
2-11	.20	.40	.60

BLACK MAGIC (--Magazine)(Becomes Cool Cat)
10-11/50 - V7#3, 7-8/60; V7#4,9-10/60 - V8#5,
11-12/61
Crestwood Publ. to V4#5/Headline to V7#2/
Crestwood (Prize)

V1#1-S&K story, 10pgs.; 2 Meskin stories			
	9.00	18.00	27.00
2-S&K cvr./sty.,17pgs.	6.00	12.00	18.00
3(2-3/51)-S&K story	5.00	10.00	15.00
4-S&K cvr./sty.,9pgs.	5.00	10.00	15.00
5-S&K story	4.00	8.00	12.00

(Black Magic cont'd)	Good	Fine	Mint
6-S&K cvr/sty, 3pgs.	4.00	8.00	12.00
V2#1(10-11/51),4,5,7,(6/52,#13 on cover)- S&K art	3.00	6.00	9.00
2,3,6,10,11-S&K covers only	1.75	3.50	5.25
8,9,12-S&K art	3.00	6.00	9.00
V3#1-6(5/53)-S&K cvrs/stories in all(#19-24)	2.25	4.50	6.75
V4#1(6-7/53)-#5(3-4/54)-S&K covers/stories in all(#25-30)	2.00	4.00	6.00
V5#1-3(no#4-6)-S&K covers/stories(#31-33)	2.00	4.00	6.00
V6#1(9-10/57)-#6(7-8/58)	1.50	3.00	4.50
V7#1(9-10/58),#2(11-12/58),#3(7-8/60)	1.00	2.00	3.00
#4(9-10/60),#5(11-12/60)-Torres art in all	1.50	3.00	4.50
6(1-2/61)	.80	1.60	2.40
V8#1(3-4/61)	.80	1.60	2.40
2(5-6/61)-E.C. story swipe, Ditko art	1.20	2.40	3.60
3(7-8/61)-#5	.80	1.60	2.40

NOTE: *Ditko art-#27-29. Meskin art-#6. S&K*
means Simon & Kirby.

BLACK MAGIC
Oct-Nov, 1973 - #9, Apr-May, 1975
National Periodical Publications

#1-S&K reprints	.25	.50	.75
2-9-S&K reprints	.15	.30	.45

BLACKMAIL TERROR (See Dick Tracy)

BLACKOUTS (See Broadway Hollywood --)

BLACK PANTHER, THE
January, 1977 - Present
Marvel Comics Group

#1-Kirby cover/art	.30	.60	.90
2- " " "	.20	.40	.60
3-12-" " "	.15	.30	.45

BLACK PHANTOM (See Wisco)
Nov, 1954 - #2, 1955
Magazine Enterprises

#1(A-1#122)	8.00	16.00	24.00
2 (Rare)	10.00	20.00	30.00

BLACK RIDER (Formerly Western Winners; Western Tales of Black Rider #28-31; Gunsmoke Western #32 on)
#8, 3/50 - #18, 1/52; #19, 11/53 - #27, 1/55
Marvel/Atlas Comics(CDS #8-17/CPS #19 on)

	Good	Fine	Mint
#8(#1)	5.00	10.00	15.00
9	3.00	6.00	9.00
10-Origin Black Rider	3.50	7.00	10.50
11-20	2.50	5.00	7.50
21-27: #21,23-Two-Gun Kid story. #24-Arrow- head story. #26,27-Kid Colt Outlaw story	1.75	3.50	5.25

BLACK RIDER RIDES AGAIN!
Sept, 1957
Atlas Comics (CPS)

#1-Three Kirby stories + Powell; Severin cover	3.50	7.00	10.50

BLACKSTONE (See Wisco Giveaways & Super Magician Comics)

BLACKSTONE, MASTER MAGICIAN COMICS
Mar-Apr, 1946 - #3, Jul-Aug, 1946
Vital Publications/Street & Smith Publ.

#1	3.50	7.00	10.50
2,3	2.50	5.00	7.50

BLACKSTONE, THE MAGICIAN
#2, May, 1948 - #4, Sept, 1948 (No #1)
Marvel Comics (CnPC)

#2-4-The Blonde Phantom in all (--Detective on cover only #3,4)	10.00	20.00	30.00

BLACKSTONE, THE MAGICIAN DETECTIVE FIGHTS CRIME
Fall, 1947
E.C. Comics

#1	15.00	30.00	45.00

BLACK SWAN COMICS
1945
MLJ Magazines

#1-The Black Hood reprints from Black Hood #14	4.00	8.00	12.00

BLACK TARANTULA (See Feature Presentations#5)

BLACK TERROR (See Exciting & America's Best)
1942 - #27, June, 1949
Better Publications/Standard

#1-Black Terror, Crime Crusader begin	35.00	70.00	105.00
2	20.00	40.00	60.00
3	15.00	30.00	45.00
4,5	10.00	20.00	30.00
6-10: The Ghost app. #7	8.00	16.00	24.00

Black Magic #6, © PRIZE

Blackstone The Magician #2, © MCG

The Black Terror #20, © STD

Blazing Combat #1, © WP   Blazing Comics #2, © RH   Blazing West #20, © ACG

(Black Terror cont'd)	Good	Fine	Mint
11-19	6.00	12.00	18.00
20-The Scarab app.	6.00	12.00	18.00
21-Miss Masque app.	5.00	10.00	15.00
22-Partial Frazetta art on one Black Terror			
story	7.00	14.00	21.00
23-Robinson/Meskin art	5.00	10.00	15.00
24-½pg. Frazetta art + Meskin art			
	5.00	10.00	15.00
25-27-Robinson/Meskin art	5.00	10.00	15.00

NOTE: *Most issues have* Schomburg (Xela) *covers. Bondage cover-#17.*

BLAKE HARPER (See City Surgeon --)

BLAST (Satire Magazine)
Feb, 1971 - #2, May, 1971
G & D Publications

#1-Wrightson & Kaluta art	1.20	2.40	3.60
2-Kaluta art	.80	1.60	2.40

BLAST-OFF (Three Rocketeers)
October, 1965
Harvey Publications (Fun Day Funnies)

#1-Two Kirby/Williamson stories; Crandall/ Williamson, Williamson/Crandall, & Williamson/Torres/Krenkel story			
	2.50	5.00	7.50

BLAZE CARSON (Rex Hart #6 on) (See Wisco)
Sept, 1948 - #5, June, 1949
Marvel Comics (USA)

#1	3.00	6.00	9.00
2-5	2.00	4.00	6.00

BLAZE THE WONDER COLLIE (My Love #1?)
#2, Oct, 1949 - #3, Feb, 1950
Marvel Comics

#2(#1),3	1.20	2.40	3.60

BLAZING BATTLE TALES
July, 1975
Seaboard Periodicals (Atlas)

#1-Intro. Sgt. Hawk & the Sky Demon; McWilliams art; Thorne cover	.20	.40	.60

BLAZING COMBAT (Magazine) (35¢)
Oct, 1965 - #4, July, 1966 (B&W)
Warren Publishing Co.

#1-Frazetta cover	8.00	16.00	24.00
2-4-All Frazetta covers; #4-Frazetta ½ pg.			
	4.00	8.00	12.00

NOTE: *Above has art by* Crandall, Evans, Morrow, Orlando, Severin, Torres, Toth, Williamson, *and* Wood.

BLAZING COMICS
June, 1944 - #6(V2#3), April, 1945
Enwil Associates/Rural Home

	Good	Fine	Mint
#1-The Green Turtle, Red Hawk, Black Buccaneer begin; origin Jun-Gal			
	4.00	8.00	12.00
2-4	2.50	5.00	7.50
5-Black Buccaneer cover; Cloak & Dagger on inside	2.50	5.00	7.50
6(V2#3-inside)-Indian/Jap cover; Will Rogers on inside	2.50	5.00	7.50

BLAZING SIXGUNS
December, 1952
Avon Periodicals

#1-Kinstler cover/story	4.00	8.00	12.00

BLAZING SIXGUNS
1964
I.W./Super Comics

I.W. Reprint #1,8,9-Kinstler cover #8			
	.65	1.35	2.00
Super Reprint #10,11,13-16(Buffalo Bill, Swift Deer),17(1964)	.50	1.00	1.50
#12-Reprints Bullseye #3; S&K art			
	2.50	5.00	7.50
18-Powell's Straight Arrow			
	1.00	2.00	3.00

BLAZING SIX-GUNS
Feb, 1971 - #2, April, 1971 (52 pgs.)
Skywald Comics

#1-The Red Mask, Sundance Kid begin, Avon's Geronimo reprint by Kinstler			
	.30	.60	.90
2-Wild Bill Hickok, J. James, Kit Carson reprints	.20	.40	.60

BLAZING WEST (Hooded Horseman #23 on)
Fall, 1948 - #22, Mar-Apr, 1952
American Comics Group(B&I Publ./Michel Publ.)

#1-Origin & 1st app. Injun Jones, Tenderfoot & Buffalo Belle; Texas Tim & Ranger begins, ends #13	3.50	7.00	10.50
2,3,5	2.00	4.00	6.00
4-Origin & 1st app. Little Lobo; Starr art			
	2.00	4.00	6.00
6-10	1.75	3.50	5.25
11-13	1.50	3.00	4.50

(Blazing West cont'd) Good Fine Mint
14-Origin & 1st app. The Hooded Horseman;
   Whitney cover   1.75 3.50 5.25
15-22   1.20 2.40 3.60

BLAZING WESTERN
Jan, 1954 - #5, Sept, 1954
Timor Publications

#1-Text story by Bruce Hamilton
                              1.20 2.40 3.60
2-5   .75 1.50 2.25

BLITZKRIEG!
Jan-Feb, 1976 - #5, Sept-Oct, 1976
National Periodical Publications

#1-Kubert cover   .25   .50   .75
2-5   .15   .30   .45

BLONDE PHANTOM (Formerly All-Select #1-11;
Lovers #23 on)(Also see Marvel Mystery &
#12, Wint/46-47 - #22, 3/49   Blackstone)
Marvel Comics (MPC)

#12-Miss America begins, ends #14
                             25.00 50.00 75.00
13-Sub-Mariner begins   17.50 35.00 52.50
14,15   15.00 30.00 45.00
16-Captain America with Bucky app.; Kurtzman's "Hey Look"   15.00 30.00 45.00
17-22   12.00 24.00 36.00

BLONDIE (See Eat Right to Work -- & Comics
Reading Libraries)
1942 - 1946
David McKay Publications

Feature Book #12 (Rare) 40.00 80.00 120.00
Feature Book #27-29,31,34(1940)
                          6.00 12.00 18.00
Feature Book #36,38,40,42,43,45,47
                          4.00   8.00 12.00

BLONDIE & DAGWOOD FAMILY
10/63 - #4, 12/65   (68 pgs.)
Harvey Publications (King Features Synd.)

#1   .75 1.50 2.25
2-4   .50 1.00 1.50

BLONDIE COMICS (-- Monthly #16-141)
Spring, 1947 - #163, 11/65; #164, 8/66 -
#175, 12/67; #177, 2/69 - #222, 11/76
David McKay #1-15/Harvey #16-163/King #164-
175/Charlton #177 on

#1   4.00   8.00 12.00

                       Good   Fine   Mint
2-5   2.50   5.00   7.50
6-10   1.75   3.50   5.25
11-20   1.20   2.40   3.60
21-30   .80   1.60   2.40
31-50   .60   1.20   1.80
51-80   .50   1.00   1.50
81-100   .35   .70   1.05
101-130   .30   .60   .90
131-139   .25   .50   .75
140-(80 pgs.)   .50   1.00   1.50
141-166(#148,155,157-159,161-163 are 68pgs.)
                        .40   .80   1.20
167-One pg. Williamson ad .20   .40   .60
168-175,177-222   .20   .40   —
Blondie, Dagwood & Daisy #1(100pgs., 1953)
                       2.00   4.00   6.00
1950 Giveaway   1.50   3.00   4.50
1962,1964 Giveaway   .60   1.20   1.80
N.Y. State Dept. of Mental Hygiene Giveaway-
   ('56,'61) Reg. size (diff. issues) 16pgs.
No#   1.00   2.00   3.00

BLOOD IS THE HARVEST
1950   (32 pgs.) (Soft cover)
Catechetical Guild

(Very Rare) Anti-communism
                    400.00 800.00 1200.00

BLUE BEETLE, THE (Also see Mystery Men &
Weekly Comic Mag.)
Winter, 1939-40 - #60, Aug, 1950
Fox Publ., #1-11, #31-60; Holyoke #12-30

#1-Reprints from Mystery Men #1-5; Blue
   Beetle origin; Yarko the Great reprints
   from Wonderworld #2-5 all by Eisner; Master Magician app.; (Blue Beetle in 4 diff.
   costumes)   55.00 110.00 165.00
2   27.50 55.00 82.50
3   17.50 35.00 52.50
4,5: #4-Two Powell stys.14.00 28.00 42.00
6-Dynamite Thor begins 10.00 20.00 30.00
7,8-Dynamo app. in both. #8-Last Thor
                       10.00 20.00 30.00
9,10-The Blackbird & The Gorilla app. in
   both   8.00 16.00 24.00
11-The Gladiator app.   8.00 16.00 24.00
12-The Black Fury app. 8.00 16.00 24.00
13-V-Man begins, ends #18; Kubert art
                        8.00 16.00 24.00
14,15-Costumed aide, Sparky called Spunky
   #15-19   8.00 16.00 24.00
16-20: #19-Kubert art   7.00 14.00 21.00
21-26: #24-Intro. & only app. The Halo
                        6.00 12.00 18.00
27-Tamra, Jungle Princess app.

Blonde Phantom #16, © MCG

Blondie Comics #5, © KING

Blood Is The Harvest, © CG

Blue Beetle #47, © FOX

Blue Beetle #50, © FOX

Blue Bolt V7#12, © NOVP

(Blue Beetle cont'd)	Good	Fine	Mint
	5.00	10.00	15.00
28-30	4.00	8.00	12.00
31-40: "The Threat from Saturn" serial in			
#34-37	3.50	7.00	10.50
41-45	2.50	5.00	7.50
46-The Puppeteer app.	2.50	5.00	7.50
47-Kamen/Baker covers/stories begin; The			
Puppeteer app.	12.00	24.00	36.00
48-50	10.00	20.00	30.00
51,53	10.00	20.00	30.00
52-Kamen bondage cover	9.00	18.00	27.00
54-Used in <u>Seduction of the Innocent</u>. Illo-			
"Children call these 'headlights' comics"			
	15.00	30.00	45.00
55,57-Last Kamen issue	9.00	18.00	27.00
56-Used in <u>Seduction of the Innocent</u>,			
page 145	12.00	24.00	36.00
58-60-No Kamen art	2.50	5.00	7.50

NOTE: <u>*Kamen*</u> *stories-#47-51,53,55-57; covers-
#47,49-52.*

BLUE BEETLE (Formerly The Thing; becomes
Mr. Muscles #22 on) (See Space Adventures)
#18, Feb, 1955 - #21, Aug, 1955
Charlton Comics

#18,19,21-Pre-1942 reprts.	2.50	5.00	7.50
20-Joan Mason by Kamen	3.00	6.00	9.00

BLUE BEETLE (Unusual Tales #1-49; becomes
Ghostly Tales #55 on)
V2#1, 6/64 - V2#5, 3-4/65; V3#50, 7/65 -
V3#54, 2-3/66; #1, 6/67 - #5, 11/68
Charlton Comics

V2#1-Origin Dan Garrett-Blue Beetle			
	1.00	2.00	3.00
2-5, V3#50-54	.70	1.40	2.10
#1(1967)-Question series begins by Ditko			
	1.20	2.40	3.60
2-Origin Ted Kord-Blue Beetle; Dan Garrett			
x-over	.90	1.80	2.70
3-5(#1-5-Ditko art)	.60	1.20	1.80
#1,3(Modern Comics-1977) Reprints .15			.30

BLUEBIRD
1977   (50¢)
Power Comics

#1,2	.20	.40	.60

BLUE BIRD COMICS
Late 1940's - 1964   (Giveaway)
Various Shoe Stores/Charlton Comics

No#(1947-50)(36pgs.)-Several issues; Human
Torch, Sub-Mariner app. in some

	Good	Fine	Mint
	5.00	10.00	15.00
1959-Wild Bill Hickok #1	.65	1.35	2.00
1959-(6 titles)(All #2) Black Fury #1,4,			
Freddy #4, Timmy the Timid Ghost #4, Mask-			
ed Raider #4, Li'l Genius, Wild Bill Hick-			
ok (Charlton)	.65	1.35	2.00
1960-(6 titles)(All #4) Black Fury #8,9,			
Masked Raider, Freddy #8,9, Timmy the			
Timid Ghost #9, Li'l Genius #9 (Charlton)			
	.40	.80	1.20
1961,1962(All #10's) Atomic Mouse #16, Black			
Fury #12, Freddy, Li'l Genius, Masked			
Raider, Six Gun Heroes, Timmy the Ghost,			
Wild Bill Hickok, Wyatt Earp #3,12,16-18			
(Charlton)	.30	.60	.90
1963-Texas Rangers #17 (Charlton)			
	.25	.50	.75
1964-Mysteries of Unexplored Worlds #18, War			
Heroes #18 (Charlton)	.20	.40	.60
1965-War Heroes #18	.15	.30	.45

NOTE: *More than one issue of each character
could have been published each year. Numbering is sporatic.*

BLUE BIRD CHILDREN'S MAGAZINE, THE
1957   (16 pgs.)(Soft cover)(Reg. size)
Graphic Information Service

V1#2-6: Pat, Pete & Blue Bird app.			
	.60	1.20	1.80

BLUE BOLT
June, 1940 - #100 (V10#2), Sept-Oct, 1949
Novelty Press/Premium Group of Comics

V1#1-Origin Blue Bolt by Joe Simon, Sub-Zero,			
White Rider & Super Horse, Dick Cole, Won-			
der Boy & Sgt. Spook 75.00	150.00	225.00	
2-S&K story(1st S&K teamup)			
	55.00	110.00	165.00
3-S&K cover/story	40.00	80.00	120.00
4,5-S&K story in each; #4-Bill Everett			
cover; #5-Everett art begins on Sub-			
Zero	35.00	70.00	105.00
6,8-10-S&K story	25.00	50.00	75.00
7-S&K cover/story	30.00	60.00	90.00
11,12	10.00	20.00	30.00
V2#1-Origin Dick Cole & The Twister			
	4.00	8.00	12.00
2-Origin The Twister retold			
	4.00	8.00	12.00
3-5-Intro. Freezum #5	3.50	7.00	10.50
6-Origin Sgt. Spook retold			
	3.00	6.00	9.00
7-12: #7-Lois Blake becomes Blue Bolt's			
costume aide	2.50	5.00	7.50
V3#1-3	2.50	5.00	7.50

```
(Blue Bolt cont'd)               Good    Fine    Mint
    4-Blue Bolt abandons costume,
    5-12                         2.00    4.00    6.00
V4#1-12                          1.50    3.00    4.50
V5#1-8                           1.00    2.00    3.00
V6#1-10, V7#1-12                 1.00    2.00    3.00
V8#1-12, V9#1-9, V10#1,2          .80    1.60    2.40
```

BLUE BOLT (--Weird Tales of Terror #111,112;
--Weird Tales #113-119; becomes Ghostly Weird
Stories #120 on; cont. of Novelty Blue Bolt)
#102, Nov-Dec, 1949 - #119, May-June, 1953
Star Publications

```
#102-104-The Chameleon app.; last Target-
    #104                         3.00    6.00    9.00
 105-Origin Blue Bolt(from #1) retold by
    Simon; Chameleon & Target app.
                                 5.00   10.00   15.00
 106-Blue Bolt by S&K begins; Spacehawk re-
    prints from Target by Wolverton begins,
    ends #110; Sub-Zero begins
                                 7.00   14.00   21.00
 107-110: #108-Last S&K Blue Bolt reprint
                                 6.00   12.00   18.00
 111-Reprints Red Rocket, Blue Bolt & The
    Mask                         3.00    6.00    9.00
 112-Last Blue Bolt & Torpedo Man app.
                                 3.00    6.00    9.00
 113-Wolverton's Spacehawk reprint/Target
    V3#7                         6.00   12.00   18.00
 114,116,119: #116,119-Jungle Jo app.
                                 3.00    6.00    9.00
 115-Sgt. Spook app.            3.00    6.00    9.00
 117-Reprints Jo-Jo & Blue Bolt
                                 3.00    6.00    9.00
 118-"White Spirit" by Orlando?
                                 4.00    8.00   12.00
```
NOTE: *L. B. Cole covers-#102 on. Disbrow
stories-#112,114,115(2 stories ea.),#116-118
(1 story).*

BLUE CIRCLE COMICS
June, 1944 - #6, May, 1945
Enwil Associates/Rural Home

```
#1-The Blue Circle begins; origin Steel
    Fist                         3.00    6.00    9.00
2-6                              2.00    4.00    6.00
```

BLUE PHANTOM, THE
June-Aug, 1962
Dell Publishing Co.

```
#1(#01-066-208)-by Fred Fredericks
                                 1.00    2.00    3.00
```

BLUE RIBBON COMICS (-- Mystery Comics #9-18)

Nov, 1939 - #22, March, 1942
MLJ Magazines

```
                              Good    Fine    Mint
#1-Dan Hastings, Ricky the Amazing Boy, Rang-
    A-Tang the Wonder Dog begin; Little Nemo
    app. (not by W. McCay); Jack Cole art
                            35.00   70.00  105.00
 2-Bob Phantom, Silver Fox (both in #3), Rang-
    A-Tang Club & Cpl. Collins begin; Jack
    Cole art                 17.50   35.00   52.50
 3                           10.00   20.00   30.00
 4-Doc Strong, The Green Falcon, & Hercules
    begin; origin & 1st app. The Fox & Ty-Gor,
    Son of the Tiger         15.00   30.00   45.00
 5-8: #8-Last Hercules       10.00   20.00   30.00
 9-Origin & 1st app. Mr. Justice
                             45.00   90.00  135.00
10-12: #12-Last Doc Strong
                             27.50   55.00   82.50
13-Inferno, the Flame Breather begins, ends
    #19                      27.50   55.00   82.50
14,15,17,18: #15-Last Green Falcon
                             22.00   44.00   66.00
16-Origin & 1st app. Captain Flag
                             40.00   80.00  120.00
19-22: #20-Last Ty-Gor; #22-Origin Mr. Just-
    ice retold               15.00   30.00   45.00
```

BLUE RIBBON COMICS (Teen-Age Diary Secrets
#6)(See Heckle & Jeckle)
Feb, 1949 - #6, Aug, 1949
Blue Ribbon (St. John)

```
#1,3-Heckle & Jeckle         1.00    2.00    3.00
 2(4/49)-Diary Secrets; Matt Baker cover only
                             2.00    4.00    6.00
 4(6/49)-Teen-Age Diary Secrets; Matt Baker
    cover, 2 stories         4.00    8.00   12.00
 5(8/49)-Teen-Age Diary Secrets; photo cover;
    two Baker stories        4.00    8.00   12.00
 6-Dinky Duck(8/49)           .65    1.35    2.00
```

BLUE STREAK (See Holyoke One-Shot #8)

BLYTHE (See 4-Color #1072)

B-MAN (See Double-Dare Adventures)

BO (Also see Big Shot #32)
June, 1955 - #2, Aug, 1955
Charlton Comics Group

```
#1,2-(a dog) Newspaper reprints by Frank
    Beck                     1.00    2.00    3.00
```

BOATNIKS, THE (See Walt Disney Showcase #1)

Blue Bolt #105. © STAR

Blue Bolt Weird #112. © STAR

Blue Ribbon Comics #7. © MLJ

51

Bobby Benson's--#11, © ME   Bob Steele Western #5, © FAW   Bonanza #9, © GK

BOBBY BENSON'S B-BAR-B RIDERS (See Model Fun)
May-June, 1950 - #21, 1953
Magazine Enterprises

	Good	Fine	Mint
#1-Powell art	6.00	12.00	18.00
2	3.50	7.00	10.50
3-5: #4-Lemonade Kid cvr.	3.00	6.00	9.00
6-8,10	2.50	5.00	7.50
9,11,13-Frazetta covers; Ghost Rider in			
#13-15	10.00	20.00	30.00
12,14-20(A-1#88)	2.25	4.50	6.75
21-Frazetta cover	12.00	24.00	36.00
--in the Tunnel of Gold(5¼x8";84pgs.)-Radio			
giveaway by Hecker-H.O. Company(H.O. Oats)			
contains only 12 color pgs. of comics,			
rest in novel form	3.00	6.00	9.00

NOTE: *Powell* art *in #1-13; covers-#1-8,10,12.*

BOBBY COMICS
May, 1946
Universal Phoenix Features

#1-by S. M. Iger	1.50	3.00	4.50

BOBBY SHELBY COMICS
1949
Shelby Cycle Co.

	1.20	2.40	3.60

BOBBY SHERMAN (TV)
Feb, 1972 - #7, Oct, 1972
Charlton Comics

#1-7-Based on TV show "Getting Together"			
	.25	.50	.75

BOBBY THATCHER & TREASURE CAVE
1932   (86 pgs.) (B&W; hardcover; 7x9")
Altemus Co.

Reprints; art by Storm	6.00	12.00	18.00

BOB COLT WESTERN
Nov, 1950 - #9, March, 1952
Fawcett Publications

#1	5.00	10.00	15.00
2-9	2.50	5.00	7.50

BOB HOPE (See Adventures of --)

BOBMAN & TEDDY (See The Great Society)
1966
Parallax Publications

Bob & Ted Kennedy - Political satire			
	1.50	3.00	4.50

BOB SCULLY, TWO-FISTED HICK DETECTIVE
No date (1930's)   36 pgs.; 9½x12"; B&W;
Humor Publ. Co.   paper cover

	Good	Fine	Mint
By Howard Dell-not reprts.	4.00	8.00	12.00

BOB SON OF BATTLE (See 4-Color #729)

BOB STEELE WESTERN
Dec, 1950 - #10, June, 1952
Fawcett Publications

#1	5.00	10.00	15.00
2-10	2.50	5.00	7.50

BOB SWIFT (Boy Sportsman)
May, 1951 - #5, Jan, 1952
Fawcett Publications

#1	1.50	3.00	4.50
2-5	.75	1.50	2.25

BOLD STORIES
May, 1950 - July, 1950 (Digest size)(144pgs.)
Kirby Publishing Co.   (Full Color)

May issue (Very Rare) - Contains "The Cobra's			
Kiss"by Graham Ingels	20.00	40.00	60.00
July issue (Very Rare) - Contains "The Ogre			
of Paris" by Wally Wood			
	25.00	50.00	75.00

BOMBARDIER (See Bee 29, the Bombardier)

BOMBA, THE JUNGLE BOY
Sept-Oct, 1967 - #7, Sept-Oct, 1968
National Periodical Publications

#1	.40	.80	1.20
2-7	.25	.50	.75

BOMBER COMICS
March, 1944 - #4, Winter, 1944-45
Melverne Herald/Elliot Publ./Farrell/
Sunrise Times

#1-Origin Wonder Boy; Kismet, Man of Fate			
begins	5.00	10.00	15.00
2-4	3.00	6.00	9.00

BONANZA (TV)
June-Aug, 1960 - #37, Aug, 1970
Dell/Gold Key

4-Color #1110,1221,1283, also #01070-207,			
01070-210	1.00	2.00	3.00
#1(12/62-G.K.)	.75	1.50	2.25
2-10	.50	1.00	1.50
11-37	.30	.60	.90

BONGO (See Story Hour Series)

BONGO & LUMPJAW (See 4-Color #706,886, and Walt Disney Showcase #3)

BON VOYAGE (See Movie Classics)

BOOK AND RECORD SET
1975 (16 pgs.) (7¼x10") ($1.49)
A Power Records Production

	Good	Fine	Mint
PR-10-Spider-Man, PR-11-The Hulk, PR-12-Capt. America, PR-13-Fantastic Four, PR-14-Frankenstein, PR-15-Dracula, PR-16-The Man-Thing, PR-17-Curse of the Werewolf (Adams cover reprint/Marvel Spotlight #2), PR-18-Planet of the Apes, PR-19-Escape From the Planet of the Apes, PR-20-Beneath the Planet of the Apes, PR-21-Battle for the Planet of the Apes, PR-24-Spider-Man, PR-25-Star Trek (Adams cover), PR-26-Star Trek, PR-27-Batman (Adams cover/story), PR-28-Superman, PR-29-Space: 1999, PR-30-Batman (Adams art), PR-31-Conan the Barbarian (Adams cover), PR-32-Space: 1999			
each..(w/45rpm record)	.60	1.20	1.80

BOOK OF ALL COMICS
1945 (196 pgs.)
William H. Wise

	Good	Fine	Mint
Green Mask, Puppeteer	5.00	10.00	15.00

BOOK OF COMICS, THE
1944 (132 pgs.)
William H. Wise

	Good	Fine	Mint
#1-Captain V app.	4.00	8.00	12.00

BOOK OF LOVE
1950 (132 pgs.)
Fox Features Syndicate

No#-See Fox Giants. Contents can vary and determines price.

BOOTS AND HER BUDDIES
#5, 1948 - #9, 1949; Dec, 1955 - #3, 1956
Standard Comics/Visual/Argo

#5-8	2.50	5.00	7.50
9-(Scarce)-Frazetta art, 2 pgs.	8.00	16.00	24.00
1-3(Argo-1955-56)Reprts.	1.50	3.00	4.50

BOOTS & SADDLES (See 4-Color #919,1029,1116)

BORDER PATROL
May-June, 1951 - #3, Sept-Oct, 1951

P. L. Publishing Co.

	Good	Fine	Mint
#1	1.50	3.00	4.50
2,3	1.00	2.00	3.00

BORIS KARLOFF TALES OF MYSTERY (--Thriller #1,2)
#3, April, 1963 - Present
Gold Key

#3-8,10	.60	1.20	1.80
9-Wood story	1.35	2.75	4.00
11-Williamson story, Orlando story, 8pgs.	1.50	3.00	4.50
12-Torres, McWilliams + 2 Orlando stories	1.00	2.00	3.00
13,14,16-20	.40	.80	1.20
15-Crandall art	.80	1.60	2.40
21-Jones art	.90	1.80	2.70
22-40	.30	.60	.90
41-54	.25	.50	.75
55(10/63),55(11/63)	.20	.40	.60
56-60	.20	.40	.60
61-73,75-88 (#80-86, 52pgs).	.15	.30	.45
74-Origin & 1st app. Taurus.	.20	.40	.60
Story Digest #1(7/70-G.K.)-All text	.30	.60	.90

(See Mystery Comics Digest #2,5,8,11,14,17, 20,23,26)
NOTE: Bolle stories-#51-54,56,58,59. McWilliams stories-#12,14,18,19. Orlando stories-#11-15,21.

BORIS KARLOFF THRILLER (TV) (Becomes Boris Karloff Tales of Mystery #3)
Oct, 1962 - #2, Jan, 1963 (80 pgs.)
Gold Key

#1	1.20	2.40	3.60
2	.80	1.60	2.40

BOUNCER, THE (Formerly Green Mask?)
1944 - #14, Jan, 1945
Fox Features Syndicate

No#(1944)-Same as #14	3.50	7.00	10.50
#11(#1)(9/44)-Origin	3.00	6.00	9.00
12-14	2.50	5.00	7.50

BOUNTY GUNS (See 4-Color Comics #739)

BOY AND THE PIRATES, THE (See 4-Color #1117)

BOY COMICS (Captain Battle #1&2; Boy Illustories #43-108)(Stories by Charles Biro)
#3, April, 1942 - #119, March, 1956
Lev Gleason Publications

#3(#1)-Origin Crimebuster, Bombshell & Young

Boris Karloff #7. © GK

The Bouncer #14. © FOX

Boy Comics #7. © LEV

53

Boy Comics #12, © LEV

Boy Commandos #5, © DC

Boy Detective #1, © AVON

(Boy Comics cont'd)   Good Fine Mint
Robin Hood; Yankee Longago, Case 1001-1008,
Swoop Storm, Boy Movies, & Yankee Lon begin; intro. Iron Jaw 70.00 140.00 210.00
4   35.00 70.00 105.00
5   30.00 60.00 90.00
6-Origin Iron Jaw; Little Dynamite begins,
ends #39   35.00 70.00 105.00
7-10: #7-Bombshell ends. #10-Case 1001-1008
ends   22.50 45.00 67.50
11-14   12.00 24.00 36.00
15-Death of Iron Jaw 15.00 30.00 45.00
16-20   10.00 20.00 30.00
21-29: #28-Yankee Lon ends
               5.00 10.00 15.00
30-Origin Crimebuster retold
               7.00 14.00 21.00
31-40: #32-Swoop Storm, Young Robin Hood ends
               3.00   6.00   9.00
41-50   2.50   5.00   7.50
51-59: #57-Dilly Duncan begins, ends #71
               1.50   3.00   4.50
60-Iron Jaw returns 2.00   4.00   6.00
61-Origin Crimebuster & Iron Jaw retold
               2.50   5.00   7.50
62-Death of Iron Jaw explained
               1.50   3.00   4.50
63-72   1.35   2.65   4.00
73-Frazetta 1-pg. ad 1.75   3.35   5.00
74-80: #80-1st app. Rocky X of the Rocketeers; becomes "Rocky X" #101; Iron Jaw-
Sniffer & the Deadly Dozen begins, ends
#118   1.00   2.00   3.00
81-88   1.00   2.00   3.00
89-92-The Claw serial app. in all
               1.40   2.80   4.20
93-Claw cameo   1.00   2.00   3.00
94-97,99,100   1.25   2.50   3.75
98-Rocky X by Sid Check 2.50 5.00   7.50
101-107,109-111,119: #111-Crimebuster becomes
Chuck Chandler. #119-Last Crimebuster
               1.00   2.00   3.00
108,112-118-Kubert stories 1.75 3.50   5.25
   (See Giant Boy Book of Comics)
NOTE: *Boy Movies in #3-5,40,41. Iron Jaw*
app.-#3,4,6,8,10,11,13-15; returns-#60,61,62,
68,69,72-79,81-118. Fuje art-#55, 18pgs.

BOY COMMANDOS (See Detective Comics)
Winter, 1942-43 - #36, Nov-Dec, 1949
National Periodical Publications

#1-Origin Liberty Belle; The Sandman & The
Newsboy Legion x-over in Boy Commandos;
S&K art, 48pgs.
          80.00 160.00 240.00
2-Last Liberty Belle; S&K art, 46pgs.
          40.00 80.00 120.00

               Good Fine Mint
3-S&K art, 45 pgs.   25.00 50.00 75.00
4-S&K art   17.50 35.00 52.50
5   12.00 24.00 36.00
6-10: #6-S&K art   10.00 20.00 30.00
11-Infinity cover   7.00 14.00 21.00
12,15-S&K art   8.00 16.00 24.00
13,14,16-20   6.00 12.00 18.00
21,22,24-28,30   3.00   6.00   9.00
23-S&K art, 2 stories 6.00 12.00 18.00
29,31-S&K story   5.00 10.00 15.00
32-36   3.00   6.00   9.00
NOTE: *Most issues signed by Simon & Kirby*
are not by them. S&K covers-#1-9.

BOY COMMANDOS
Sept-Oct, 1973 - #2, Nov-Dec, 1973
National Periodical Publications

#1,2-S&K reprints   .30   .60   .90

BOY DETECTIVE
May-June, 1951 - #4, May, 1952
Avon Periodicals

#1   4.00   8.00 12.00
2,3   3.00   6.00   9.00
4-Wood story   4.00   8.00 12.00

BOY EXPLORERS COMICS
1946 - #2, Sept-Oct, 1946
Harvey Publications

#1-Kirby story, 12pgs. + S&K cover
          30.00 60.00 90.00
2-(Extremely Rare)-Small size (5½x8½"-B&W,
32pgs.) Distributed to mail subscribers
only. S&K art
  (Sold in Minneapolis, 1978 for $1000.00)
  (Another copy with no subscription address label sold in 1978 for $2000.00)
(Also see All New #15, Flash Gordon #5, and
Stuntman #3).

BOY ILLUSTORIES (See Boy Comics)

BOY LOVES GIRL (Boy Meets Girl #1-25)
#26, Aug, 1952 - #57, June, 1956
Lev Gleason Publications

#26(#1)   1.00   2.00   3.00
27,29-42   .80   1.60   2.40
28-Drug story   2.50   5.00   7.50
43-Toth story   2.00   4.00   6.00
44-57   .50   1.00   1.50

BOY MEETS GIRL (Boy Loves Girl #26 on)
Feb, 1950 - #25, July, 1952
Lev Gleason Publications

(Boy Meets Girl cont'd)	Good	Fine	Mint
#1-Guardineer art	1.20	2.40	3.60
2-10	.80	1.60	2.40
11-25	.50	1.00	1.50

BOYS' AND GIRLS' MARCH OF COMICS (See March of Comics)

BOYS' RANCH (Also see Witches' Western Tales)
10/50 - #6, 8/51 (#1-3, 52pgs.; #46, 36pgs.)
Harvey Publications

	Good	Fine	Mint
#1-Three S&K stories	25.00	50.00	75.00
2-Three S&K stories	15.00	30.00	45.00
3-Two S&K stories + Meskin story	10.00	20.00	30.00
4-S&K art(5pg.)/cover	7.00	14.00	21.00
5,6-S&K splashes & centerspread only; Meskin art	6.00	12.00	18.00
Shoe Store Giveaway #5,6 (Identical to regular issues except S&K centerfold replaced with ad)	5.00	10.00	15.00

NOTE: *Simon & Kirby covers-#1-6.*

BOZO THE CLOWN (TV)
July, 1950 - #4, Oct-Dec, 1963
Dell Publishing Co.

4-Color #285	1.75	3.50	5.25
#2(7-9/51)-#7(10-12/52)	.80	1.60	2.40
4-Color #464,508,551,594	.80	1.60	2.40
#1-4(1963)	.40	.80	1.20

BRADY BUNCH, THE (TV)
Feb, 1970 - #2, May, 1970
Dell Publishing Co.

#1,2	.20	.40	.60
Kite Fun Book (PG&E, 1976)	.20	.40	.60

BRAIN, THE
Sept, 1956 - 1958
Sussex Publ. Co./Magazine Enterprises

#1	1.00	2.00	3.00
2,3	.65	1.35	2.00
4-7	.35	.70	1.05
IW Reprints #1,3,4,8,9,10('63),14	.35	.70	1.05
IW Reprints #2-Reprints Sussex #2 with new cover added	.35	.70	1.05
Super Reprint #17,18(no date)	.35	.70	1.05

BRAIN BOY
April-June, 1962 - #6, Sept-Nov, 1963
Dell Publishing Co.

	Good	Fine	Mint
4-Color#1330-Gil Kane art	1.00	2.00	3.00
#2-6(7-9/62 - 9-11/63)	.60	1.20	1.80

BRAND ECHH (See Not Brand Echh)

BRAND OF EMPIRE (See 4-Color Comics #771)

BRAVADOS, THE (See Wild Western Action)
August, 1971 (52 pgs.) (One Shot)
Skywald Publ. Corp.

#1-Red Mask, The Durango Kid, Billy Nevada reprints	.25	.50	.75

BRAVE AND THE BOLD, THE (See Super DC Giant)
Aug-Sept, 1955 - Present
National Periodical Publications/DC Comics

#1-Kubert Viking Prince, Silent Knight, Golden Gladiator begin	50.00	100.00	150.00
2	30.00	60.00	90.00
3,4	20.00	40.00	60.00
5-Robin Hood begins	15.00	30.00	45.00
6-10: #6-Kubert Robin Hood, G. Gladiator last app., Silent Knight; no V. Prince	12.00	24.00	36.00
11-22: #22-Last Silent Knight	10.00	20.00	30.00
23-Kubert Viking Prince origin	12.00	24.00	36.00
24-Last Kubert Viking Prince	12.00	24.00	36.00
25-27-Suicide Squad	2.00	4.00	6.00
28-Justic League intro.; origin Snapper Carr	25.00	50.00	75.00
29-30-Justice League	10.00	20.00	30.00
31-33-Cave Carson	2.00	4.00	6.00
34-Origin Hawkman & Byth by Kubert	6.00	12.00	18.00
35,36-Kubert Hawkman; origin Shadow Thief #36	4.00	8.00	12.00
37-39-Suicide Squad	1.50	3.00	4.50
40,41-Cave Carson Inside Earth; #40 has Kubert art	2.00	4.00	6.00
42,44-Kubert Hawkman	2.50	5.00	7.50
43-Origin Hawkman by Kubert	3.00	6.00	9.00
45-49-Infantino Strange Sports Stories	1.00	2.00	3.00
50-Green Arrow & Jonn' Jonzz'	1.00	2.00	3.00
51-Aquaman & Hawkman	1.00	2.00	3.00
52-Kubert Sgt. Rock, Haunted Tank, Johnny Cloud, & Mlle. Marie	1.50	3.00	4.50
53-Toth Atom & Flash	1.50	3.00	4.50
54-Kid Flash, Robin & Aqualad	1.00	2.00	3.00

Boys' Ranch #6, © HARV

Brave & The Bold #5, © DC

Brave & The Bold #20, © DC

Brave & The Bold #28, © DC

Brave & The Bold #31, © DC

Brave & The Bold #36, © DC

	Good	Fine	Mint
(Brave and the Bold cont'd)			
55-Metal Men & The Atom	.75	1.50	2.25
56-Flash & Jonn' Jonzz'	.75	1.50	2.25
57-Origin Metamorpho	.75	1.50	2.25
58-Metamorpho	.75	1.50	2.25
59-Batman & Gr. Lantern	.75	1.50	2.25
60-Teen Titans	.75	1.50	2.25
61,62-Starman & Black Canary by Anderson			
	.90	1.80	2.70
63-Supergirl & W. Woman	.75	1.50	2.25
64-Batman & Eclipso	.75	1.50	2.25
65-Flash & Doom Patrol	.75	1.50	2.25
66-Metamorpho & Metal Men	.75	1.50	2.25
67-Infantino Batman & The Flash			
	.75	1.50	2.25
68-Batman & Metamorpho	.75	1.50	2.25
69-Batman & Gr. Lantern	.75	1.50	2.25
70-Batman & Hawkman	.75	1.50	2.25
71-Batman & Gr. Arrow	.75	1.50	2.25
72-Infantino Flash & Spectre			
	1.00	2.00	3.00
73-Aquaman-Atom	.60	1.20	1.80
74-Batman-Metal Men	.60	1.20	1.80
75-Batman-The Spectre	.60	1.20	1.80
76-Batman-Plastic Man	.60	1.20	1.80
77-Batman-Atom	.60	1.20	1.80
78-Batman-W. Woman-Batgirl	.60	1.20	1.80
79-Batman-Deadman by Adams	2.00	4.00	6.00
80-Batman-Creeper; Adams art			
	1.75	3.50	5.25
81-Batman-Flash;Adams art	1.75	3.50	5.25
82-Batman-Aquaman; Adams art			
	1.75	3.50	5.25
83-Batman-Teen Titans; Adams art			
	1.75	3.50	5.25
84-Batman-Sgt Rock; Adams	1.75	3.50	5.25
85-Batman-Green Arrow; New costume for Green			
Arrow by Adams	1.75	3.50	5.25
86-Batman-Deadman; Adams	1.75	3.50	5.25
87-Batman-Wonder Woman	.60	1.20	1.80
88-Batman-Wildcat	.60	1.20	1.80
89-Batman-Phantom Stranger	.60	1.20	1.80
90-Batman-Adam Strange	.60	1.20	1.80
91-Batman-Black Canary	.60	1.20	1.80
92-Batman-Intro. The Bat Squad			
	.50	1.00	1.50
93-Batman-House of Mystery; Adams art			
	1.50	3.00	4.50
94-Batman-Teen Titans	.50	1.00	1.50
95-Batman-Plastic Man	.50	1.00	1.50
96-Batman-Sgt. Rock	.50	1.00	1.50
97-Batman-Wildcat; 52pgs. begin, end #102;			
1st Deadman reprt/Strange Adv. #205			
	.60	1.20	1.80
98-Batman-Phantom Stranger	.50	1.00	1.50
99-Batman-Flash; Adams cover; Kubert Viking			
Prince	.50	1.00	1.50
100-Batman-Green Lantern-Green Arrow-Black			

	Good	Fine	Mint
Canary-Robin; Adams art	1.20	2.40	3.60
101-Batman-Metamorpho; Kubert Viking Prince			
	.40	.80	1.20
102-Batman-Teen Titans; Adams pencils			
	.60	1.20	1.80
103-Batman-Metal Men	.40	.80	1.20
104-Batman-Aparo Deadman	.40	.80	1.20
105-Batman-Wonder Woman	.40	.80	1.20
106-Batman-Green Arrow	.40	.80	1.20
107-Batman-Black Canary	.40	.80	1.20
108-Batman-Sgt. Rock	.40	.80	1.20
109-Batman-Demon	.40	.80	1.20
110-Batman-Wildcat	.40	.80	1.20
111-Batman-The Joker	.30	.60	.90
112-Batman-Mr. Miracle; 100pg. issues begin,			
end #117	.30	.60	.90
113-Batman-Metal Men; Kubert; Hawkman ori-			
gin reprint from #34; origin Multi-Man/			
Challengers/Unknown#14	.30	.60	.90
114-Batman-Aquaman	.30	.60	.90
115-Batman-Atom; Kubert origin Viking Prince/			
#23	.30	.60	.90
116-Batman-Spectre	.30	.60	.90
117-Batman-Sgt. Rock; last 100pg. issue			
	.25	.50	.75
118-Batman-Wildcat-Joker	.25	.50	.75
119-Batman-ManBat	.25	.50	.75
120-Batman-Kamandi-68pgs.	.25	.50	.75
121-Batman-Metal Men	.25	.50	.75
122-Batman-Swamp Thing	.25	.50	.75
123-Batman-Plastic Man-Metamorpho			
	.25	.50	.75
124-Batman-Sgt. Rock	.25	.50	.75
125-Batman-Flash	.25	.50	.75
126-Batman-Aquaman	.20	.40	.60
127-Batman-Wildcat	.20	.40	.60
128-Mr. Miracle	.20	.40	.60
129-Batman-Green Arrow-The Atom, Part 1 (Also			
Two-Face & The Joker)	.20	.40	.60
130-Batman-Green Arrow-The Atom, Part 2 (Also			
Two-Face & The Joker)	.20	.40	.60
131-Batman-Wonder Woman	.20	.40	.60
132-Batman-Kung-Fu Fighter	.20	.40	.60
133-Batman-Deadman	.20	.40	.60
134-Batman-Green Lantern	.20	.40	.60
135-Batman-Metal Men	.20	.40	.60
136-Batman-Metal Men-Green Arrow			
	.20	.40	.60
137-Batman-The Demon	.20	.40	.60
138-Batman-Mr. Miracle	.20	.40	.60
139-Batman-Hawkman	.20	.40	.60
140-Batman-Wonder Woman(60¢)	.20	.40	.60
141-Batman-Black Canary(vs. The Joker)			
	.30	.60	.90
142-Batman-Aquaman	.30	.60	.90
143-Batman-Creeper-Human Target			
	.20	.40	.60

NOTE: #14, 8/55 does exist; #13,15 in question.

(Brave and the Bold cont'd)

	Good	Fine	Mint
144-Batman-Green Arrow-Human Target			
	.20	.40	.60
145-Batman-Phantom Stranger	.20	.40	.60
146-Batman-Unknown Soldier	.20	.40	.60
147-Batman-Supergirl	.20	.40	.60
148-Batman-Plastic Man; Staton art			
	.20	.40	.60
149-Batman-Teen Titans	.20	.40	.60

NOTE: *Adams* stories-#79-86,93,100,102; covers-#75,76,79-86,88-90,93,95,99. *Infantino* stories-#97,98; covers-#45-49,67,69,70,72; w/*Anderson*-#96. *Kubert &/or Heath* art-#1-24. *Kubert* covers-#22-24,34-36,40,42-44,52. *Giant issue*-#112.

BRAVE AND THE BOLD SPECIAL, THE (See DC Special Series #8)

BRAVE EAGLE (See 4-Color #705,770,816,879, 929)

BRAVE ONE, THE (See 4-Color Comics #773)

BREEZE LAWSON, SKY SHERIFF
Summer, 1948   (Also see Exposed)
D. S. Publishing Co.

#1-Edmond Good art	3.00	6.00	9.00

BRENDA LEE STORY, THE
Sept, 1962
Dell Publishing Co.

#01-078-209	1.25	2.50	3.75

BRENDA STARR (Also see All Great)
#13, 9/47; #14, 3/48; V2#3, 6/48 - V2#12,12/49
Four Star Comic Corp./Superior Comics Ltd.

V1#13-By Dale Messick	8.00	16.00	24.00
14-Kamen bondage cvr.	10.00	20.00	30.00
V2#3,5-Kamen covers	7.00	14.00	21.00
4-Used in Seduction of the Innocent, pg.			
21; Kamen bondage cover			
	12.00	24.00	36.00
6-10-Kamen covers	6.00	12.00	18.00
11,12 (Scarce) Kamen covers			
	8.00	16.00	24.00

NOTE: *Newspaper reprints + original material through #6. All original #7 on.*

BRENDA STARR (-- Reporter)
#13?, 1955 - #15, 10/55?
Charlton Comics

#13?-#15?-Newspaper reprints			
	2.50	5.00	7.50

BRENDA STARR REPORTER
October, 1963
Dell Publishing Co.

	Good	Fine	Mint
#1	1.50	3.00	4.50

BRER RABBIT (See 4-Color #129,208,693 and Walt Disney Showcase #28)

BRER RABBIT IN "A KITE TAIL"
1956   (14 pgs.) (Walt Disney) (Premium)
Pacific Gas & Electric Co.

(Rare)	12.00	24.00	36.00

BRER RABBIT IN "ICE CREAM FOR THE PARTY"
1955   (14 pgs.) (Walt Disney) (Premium)
American Dairy Assn.

(Rare)	5.00	10.00	15.00

BRICK BRADFORD
1948 - 1949   (Ritt & Grey reprints)
King Features Syndicate/Standard

#5-8	5.00	10.00	15.00

BRIDE'S DIARY
#4, May, 1955 - #9, May, 1956
Ajax/Farrell Publ.

#4-9	.80	1.60	2.40

BRIDES IN LOVE (Summer Love #46 on)
Aug, 1956 - #45, Jan, 1965
Charlton Comics

#1	.60	1.20	1.80
2-10	.30	.60	.90
11-45	.15	.30	.45

BRIDES ROMANCES
1953 - #23, Dec, 1956
Quality Comics Group

#1	2.00	4.00	6.00
2-10	1.00	2.00	3.00
11-23	.60	1.20	1.80

BRIDE'S SECRETS
Mar-Apr, 1954 - #19, Mar, 1958
Ajax/Farrell(Excellent Publ.)/Four-Star Comic

#1	1.50	3.00	4.50
2-19	1.00	2.00	3.00

BRIDE-TO-BE-ROMANCES (See True --)

Brenda Starr #13, © SUPR

Brick Bradford #6, © KING

Brides Romances #8, © QUA

B.U.F., The Big Book #1, © C&L

Broncho Bill #7, © STD

Bruce Gentry #7, © SUPR

BRIGAND, THE (See Fawcett Movie Comics #18)

BRINGING UP FATHER (See Large Feature Comic
#9 and 4-Color Comics #37)

BRINGING UP FATHER
1917 (16½x5½"; cardboard cover; 100pgs.;B&W)
Star Co. (King Features)
	Good	Fine	Mint
(Rare) Daily strip reprints by George McManus-			
(No price on cover)	25.00	62.50	100.00

BRINGING UP FATHER
1919 - 1934   (by George McManus)
(9½x9½"; stiff cardboard covers; B&W; daily
strip reprints; 52 pgs.)
Cupples & Leon Co.

#1	15.00	30.00	45.00
2-10	7.00	14.00	21.00
11-26 (Scarcer)	10.00	20.00	30.00
The Big Book #1(1926)-Thick book(hard cover)			
	20.00	40.00	60.00
The Big Book #2(1929)	15.00	30.00	45.00

NOTE: The Big Books contain 3 regular issues
rebound and probably with dust jackets.

BRINGING UP FATHER, THE TROUBLE OF
1921   (9x15") (Sunday reprints in color)
Embee Publ. Co.

(Rare)	25.00	62.50	100.00

BROADWAY HOLLYWOOD BLACKOUTS
3/54 - #3, 7-8/54
Stanhall (Trojan)

#1-3	1.75	3.50	5.25

BROADWAY ROMANCES
January, 1949 - #9, 1951
Quality Comics Group

#1-Ward cvr/9pg. story; Gustavson story			
	7.00	14.00	21.00
2-Ward 9pg. story	4.00	8.00	12.00
3-9	2.00	4.00	6.00

BROKEN ARROW (See 4-Color #855,947)

BROKEN CROSS, THE (See The Crusaders)

BRONCHO BILL
1939 - 1940; 1949 - 1950
United Features Syndicate/Standard/Visual

Single Series #2('39)	12.00	24.00	36.00
Single Series #19('40)(#2 on cover)			

	Good	Fine	Mint
	8.00	16.00	24.00
#1(1949-Standard)	5.00	10.00	15.00
2	2.50	5.00	7.50
3-10	2.00	4.00	6.00
11-16	1.75	3.35	5.00

NOTE: Schomburg covers-#12,13.

BROTHER POWER, THE GEEK
Sept-Oct, 1968 - #2, Nov-Dec, 1968
National Periodical Publications

#1-Origin; Simon art	.40	.80	1.20
2-Simon art	.20	.40	.60

BROTHERS OF THE SPEAR (Also see Tarzan)
June, 1972 - #17, Feb, 1976
Gold Key

#1	1.00	2.00	3.00
2-10	.40	.80	1.20
11-17	.25	.50	.75

BROWNIES (See 4-Color #192,244,293,337,365,
398,436,482,522,605)

BRUCE GENTRY
1/48 - #2, 11/48; #3, 1/49 - #8, 7/49
Better/Standard/Four Star Publ./Superior #3

#1-Ray Bailey strip reprints begin, end #3;			
Kamen/Feldstein art; E.C. letters in			
style of the E.C. emblem appears as a			
monogram on stationery	9.00	18.00	27.00
2,3-Feldstein art(#2-5pgs.)			
	6.00	12.00	18.00
4-8	4.00	8.00	12.00

NOTE: Kamen stories-#4,6,7; covers-#1-4,6,7.

BRUTE, THE
Feb, 1975 - #3, July, 1975
Seaboard Publ. (Atlas)

#1-Origin & 1st app.	.35	.70	1.05
2	.20	.40	.60
3-Brunner/Starlin/Weiss pencils			
	.25	.50	.75

BUCCANEER
No date (1963)
I.W. Enterprises

I.W. Reprint #1(reprints Quality #20),#8(re-			
prints #23)	1.50	3.00	4.50
Super Reprint #12('64, reprints #21)			
	1.50	3.00	4.50

BUCCANEERS (Formerly Kid Eternity)
#19, 1/50 - #27, 5/51   (#24-27, 52 pgs.)

(Buccaneers cont'd)
Quality Comics Group

	Good	Fine	Mint
#19-Captain Daring, Black Roger, Eric Falcon & Spanish Man begin; Crandall story			
	6.00	12.00	18.00
20,23-Crandall story	6.00	12.00	18.00
21-Crandall cover/story	8.00	16.00	24.00
22,24,26: #24-Adam Peril, U.S.N. begins; last Spanish Man	3.00	6.00	9.00
25-Origin & 1st app. Corsair Queen			
	3.00	6.00	9.00
27-Crandall cover/story	7.00	14.00	21.00

BUCCANEERS, THE (See 4-Color Comics #800)

BUCK DUCK
June, 1953 - #4, Dec, 1953
Atlas Comics (ANC)

#1-4 (Funny Animal)	.40	.80	1.20

BUCK JONES (Also see Big Thrill Booklet)
#2, Apr-June, 1951 - #8, Oct-Dec, 1952
Dell Publishing Co.

4-Color #299(#1)(1950)	4.50	9.00	13.50
#2(4-6/51)	2.50	5.00	7.50
3-8	2.00	4.00	6.00
4-Color #460,500,546,589	2.00	4.00	6.00
4-Color #652,733,850	1.50	3.00	4.50

BUCK ROGERS (In the 25th Century)
1933 (36 pgs. in color) (6x8")
Kelloggs Corn Flakes Giveaway

(Rare) by Phil Nolan & Dick Calkins; 1st Buck Rogers radio premium	50.00	100.00	150.00

BUCK ROGERS (Also see Famous Funnies & Vicks
Winter/40-41 - #6, 9/43   Comics)
Famous Funnies

#1-Sunday strip reprints by Rick Yager; be- gins with strip #190	75.00	150.00	225.00
2	55.00	110.00	165.00
3,4	45.00	90.00	135.00
5-Story continues with Famous Funnies #80; ½ Buck Rogers, ½ Sky Roads			
	35.00	70.00	105.00
6-Reprints of 1939 dailies; contain B.R. story "Crater of Doom"(2pgs.) by Calkins not reprinted from Famous Funnies			
	35.00	70.00	105.00

BUCK ROGERS
#100, Jan, 1951 - #9, May-June, 1951
Toby Press

	Good	Fine	Mint
#100(7),#101(8),#9-All Anderson art			
	6.00	12.00	18.00

BUCK ROGERS
October, 1964
Gold Key

#1(10128-410)	1.35	2.75	4.00

BUCKSKIN (See 4-Color #1011,1107 (Movie))

BUDDIES IN THE U.S. ARMY
Nov, 1952 - #2, 1953
Avon Periodicals

#1,2	4.00	8.00	12.00

BUDDY TUCKER & HIS FRIENDS
1906   (11"x17") (In Color)
Cupples & Leon Co.

1905 Sunday strip reprints by R. F. Outcault			
	15.00	37.50	60.00

BUFFALO BEE (See 4-Color #957,1002,1061)

BUFFALO BILL (See Super Western Comics)

BUFFALO BILL CODY (See Cody of the Pony Exp.)

BUFFALO BILL, JR. (TV)
Jan, 1956 - #13, Aug-Oct, 1959; 1965
Dell Publishing Co./Gold Key

4-Color #673,742,766,798,828,856(11/57)			
	1.00	2.00	3.00
#7(2-4/58)-#13	.80	1.60	2.40
1(6/65-G.K.)	.60	1.20	1.80

BUFFALO BILL'S PICTURE STORIES
1909   (Soft cardboard cover)
Street & Smith Publications

	10.00	20.00	30.00

BUFFALO BILL'S PICTURE STORIES
June-July, 1949 - #2, Aug-Sept, 1949
Street & Smith Publications

#1,2-Wildey art in ea.; Powell in both			
	2.00	4.00	6.00

BUGALOOS (TV)
Sept, 1971 - #4, Feb, 1972
Charlton Comics

#1-4		.15	.30

Buccaneers #27, © QUA

Buck Rogers-1933 Giveaway, © KING

Buck Rogers #100 (Toby), © KING

Bugs Bunny Four Color #298, © L. Schlesinger   B.B's. Christmas Funnies #1, © L. Schlesinger   Bulletman #14, © FAW

(Bugaloos cont'd)
NOTE: #3(1/72) went on sale late in 1972
(after #4) with the 1/73 issues.

BUGHOUSE
March-April, 1954 - #4, Sept-Oct, 1954
Ajax/Farrell (Excellent Publ.)

	Good	Fine	Mint
V1#1	3.00	6.00	9.00
2-4	2.00	4.00	6.00

BUG MOVIES
1931   (52 pgs.) (B&W)
Dell Publishing Co.

Not reprints; Stookie Allen art

	7.00	14.00	21.00

BUGS BUNNY
1942 - Present
Dell Publishing Co./Gold Key #86 on

	Good	Fine	Mint
Large Feature Comic #8(1942)-(Rarely found in Fine-Mint condition)	50.00	125.00	200.00
4-Color #33('43)	35.00	70.00	105.00
4-Color #51	25.00	50.00	75.00
4-Color #88	12.00	24.00	36.00
4-Color #123('46),142,164	7.00	14.00	21.00
4-Color #187,200,217,233	5.00	10.00	15.00
4-Color #250,266,274,281,289,298('50)	3.00	6.00	9.00
4-Color #307,317(#1),327(#2),338,347,355,366, 376,393	2.50	5.00	7.50
4-Color #407,420,432	2.25	4.50	6.75
#28-30(1953)	1.00	2.00	3.00
31-50	.70	1.40	2.10
51-85	.40	.80	1.20
86-88-Bugs Bunny's Showtime-(80pgs.)(25¢)	.80	1.60	2.40
89-120	.30	.60	.90
121-140	.25	.50	.75
141-170	.20	.40	.60
171-206		.20	.40
Christmas Funnies #1('50)	4.00	8.00	12.00
Christmas Funnies #2-5('51-54) (Becomes Christmas Party #6)	2.00	4.00	6.00
Christmas Funnies #7-9(12/56-12/58)	1.75	3.50	5.25
Christmas Party #6('55)(Formerly Christmas Funnies #5)(Giant)	1.75	3.50	5.25
County Fair #1('57)(Giant)	2.00	4.00	6.00
Florida Power & Light Giveaway(1960,'68)	.60	1.20	1.80
Halloween Parade #1('53)(Giant)	3.50	7.00	10.50
Halloween Parade #2('54)(Trick 'N' Treat Halloween Fun #3 on)	1.75	3.50	5.25
Trick 'N' Treat Halloween Fun #3('55), #4 (10/56)(Formerly Halloween Fun)			

	Good	Fine	Mint
	1.75	3.50	5.25
Vacation Funnies #1('51)-112 pgs.	5.00	10.00	15.00
Vacation Funnies #2-9('52-'59)-100 pgs.	2.00	4.00	6.00
Winter Fun #1(12/67)(G.K.)	.60	1.20	1.80

BUGS BUNNY   (See The Best of --; Comic Album #2,6,10,14; Dell Giant #28,32,46; Golden Comics Digest #1,3,5,6,8,10,14,15,17,21,26,30, 35,39,42,47; March of Comics #44,59,75,83,97, 115,132,149,160,179,188,201,220,231,245,259, 273,287,301,315,329,343,363,367,380,392,403; Super Book #14,26; and Whitman Comic Books)

BUGS BUNNY   (Puffed Rice Giveaway)
1949   (32 pgs. each, 3-1/8"x6-7/8")
Quaker Cereals

A1-Traps the Counterfeiters, A2-Aboard Mystery Submarine, A3-Rocket to the Moon, A4-Lion Tamer, A5-Rescues the Beautiful Princess, B1-Buried Treasure, B2-Outwits the Smugglers, B3-Joins the Marines, B4-Meets the Dwarf Ghost, B5-Finds Aladdin's Lamp, C1-Lost in the Frozen North, C2-Secret Agent, C3-Captured by Cannibals, C4-Fights the Man From Mars, C5-And the Haunted Cave

each....	2.00	4.00	6.00

BUGS BUNNY   (3-D)
1953   (Pocket size)   (15 titles)
Cheerios Giveaway

each....	2.50	5.00	7.50

BUGS BUNNY & PORKY PIG
Sept, 1965   (100pgs.)(Paper Cover)(Giant)
Gold Key

#1(30025-509)	1.00	2.00	3.00

BUGS BUNNY'S ALBUM (See 4-Color #498,585,647, 724)

BUGS BUNNY LIFE STORY ALBUM (See 4-Color#838)

BUGS BUNNY MERRY CHRISTMAS (See 4-Color#1064)

BULLETMAN   (See Master Comics & Fawcett Min.)
1941 - #16, Fall, 1946
Fawcett Publications

#1	75.00	150.00	225.00
2	45.00	90.00	135.00
3	30.00	60.00	90.00
4,5	27.50	55.00	82.50

(Bulletman cont'd)

	Good	Fine	Mint
6-10	25.00	50.00	75.00
11-16 (#13 exist?)	20.00	40.00	60.00
-- Well Known Comics (Scarce) (1942)-Paper cover, glued binding (Bestmaid/Samuel Lowe giveaway)	25.00	50.00	75.00

NOTE: *#2,3,5 have* Mac Raboy *covers.*

BULLS-EYE
July-Aug, 1954 - #11, Mar-Apr, 1956
Mainline(Prize)#1-5/Charlton #6-11

	Good	Fine	Mint
#1-S&K cover only	10.00	20.00	30.00
2-S&K cover/story	10.00	20.00	30.00
3-5-S&K cvr/stys(2)	8.00	16.00	24.00
6-S&K story	6.00	12.00	18.00
7-S&K cover, 3 stories	8.00	16.00	24.00
8-11	2.50	5.00	7.50
Great Scott Shoe Store giveaway-Reprints #2 with new cover	5.00	10.00	15.00

BULLS-EYE COMICS
#11, 1944
Harry 'A' Chesler

#11-Origin K-9, Green Knight's sidekick, Lance; The Green Knight, Lady Satan, Yankee Doodle Jones app.	6.00	12.00	18.00

BULLWHIP GRIFFIN (See Movie Comics)

BULLWINKLE (TV)(See March of Comics #233)
3-5/62 - #11, 4/74; #12, 6/76 - #19, 3/78
Dell/Gold Key

4-Color #1270(3-5/62)	.60	1.20	1.80
#01-090-209(Dell, 7-9/62)	.50	1.00	1.50
#1,2(2/63-G.K.)	.50	1.00	1.50
#3(4/72)-#11(4/74-G.K.)	.25	.50	.75
12(6/76)-reprints	.25	.50	.75
13(9/76),#14-new stories	.25	.50	.75
15-19	.25	.50	.75
Mother Moose Nursery Pomes #01-530-207 (5-7/62-Dell)	.70	1.40	2.10

BULLWINKLE (TV)
July, 1970 - #7, July, 1971
Charlton Comics

#1	.25	.50	.75
2-7	.15	.30	.45

BUNNY
1967 - #20, Dec, 1971; #21, 11/76
Harvey Publications

#1	.25	.50	.75
2-21	.15	.30	.45

BURKE'S LAW (TV)
Jan-Mar, 1964 - #3, Mar-May, 1965
Dell Publishing Co.

	Good	Fine	Mint
#1	.30	.60	.90
2,3	.20	.40	.60

BURNING ROMANCES
1950   (132 pgs.)
Fox Feature Publications (Hero Books)

#1-See Fox Giants. Contents can vary and determines price.

BUSINESS WEEK PRESENTS - THE AMAZING ADVENTURES OF THE MEN FROM PACIFIC PLANTRONICS
May, 1971   (Oversized)
Business Week Giveaway

#AR-444-Twenty pgs. Dick Ayers art in color	.60	1.20	1.80

BUSTER BEAR
Dec, 1953 - #10, June, 1955
Quality Comics Group (Arnold Publ.)

#1	.60	1.20	1.80
2-10	.40	.80	1.20
IW Reprint #9,10(Super on inside)	.25	.50	.75

BUSTER BROWN
1903 - 1906 (11x17" strip reprints in color)
Frederick A. Stokes Co.

-- & His Resolutions(1903) by R. F. Outcault	30.00	75.00	120.00
-- Abroad(1904)-Hardback, 8x10½", B&W, by R.F. Outcault (76pgs.)	25.00	62.60	100.00
-- His Dog Tige & Their Troubles(1904)	25.00	62.50	100.00
-- Pranks(1905)	25.00	62.50	100.00
-- Mary Jane & Tige(1906)	25.00	62.50	100.00
-- His Dog Tige & Their Jolly Times(1906)	25.00	62.50	100.00
-- My Resolutions(1906)-68pgs., B&W; hard cover; Sunday panel reprints	25.00	62.50	100.00
Collection of Buster Brown Comics(1908)	25.00	62.50	100.00
Buster Brown Up to Date(1909)	25.00	62.50	100.00

NOTE: *Rarely found in fine or mint condition.*

BUSTER BROWN
1908 - 1917 (11x17" strip reprints in color)
Cupples & Leon Co./N.Y. Herald Co.

Bulls-Eye #7, © PRIZE

Burning Romances #1, © FOX

Buster Brown (1904), © F.A. Stokes

B.B.'s Safety Coloring Book, © F.A. Stokes

Buster Crabbe #5, © LEV

Buzzy #8, © DC

(Buster Brown cont'd)

	Good	Fine	Mint
(By R. F. Outcault)			
-- Amusing Capers(1908)	20.00	50.00	80.00
-- And His Pets(1909)	20.00	50.00	80.00
-- On His Travels(1910)	20.00	50.00	80.00
-- Happy Days(1911)	20.00	50.00	80.00
-- In Foreign Lands(1912)	20.00	50.00	80.00
-- And the Cat(1917)	15.00	37.50	60.00

NOTE: *Rarely found in fine or mint condition.*

BUSTER BROWN COMICS
1945 - 1959   (#5,9-soft covers)
Brown Shoe Co.

	Good	Fine	Mint
#1	4.00	8.00	12.00
2-10	1.75	3.50	5.25
11-20	1.00	2.00	3.00
21-24,26-28	.80	1.60	2.40
25,31,33-37,40,41-Crandall art in all	2.50	5.00	7.50
29,30,32-"Interplanetary Police Vs. the Space Siren" by Crandall	2.50	5.00	7.50
38,39,42,43	.70	1.40	2.10
--Goes to Mars('58, Western Printing)	1.20	2.40	3.60
--In "Buster Makes the Team!"(1959-Custom Comics)	1.00	2.00	3.00
--Of the Safety Patrol('60, Custom Comics)	1.00	2.00	3.00
--Out of This World('59-Custom Comics)	1.00	2.00	3.00
--Safety Coloring Book(1958)-Slick paper, 16pgs.	1.00	2.00	3.00

BUSTER BUNNY
Nov, 1949 - #15, July, 1953
Standard Comics(Animated Cartoons)/Pines

	Good	Fine	Mint
#1,2-Frazetta 1 pg. text illos. in both	2.00	4.00	6.00
3-15	.70	1.40	2.10

BUSTER CRABBE
Nov, 1951 - #12, 1953
Famous Funnies

	Good	Fine	Mint
#1-Frazetta back cover showing drug pusher	8.00	16.00	24.00
2-Williamson/Evans cvr.	10.00	20.00	30.00
3-Williamson/Evans cover & story	15.00	30.00	45.00
4-Cover & 1pg. by Frazetta	17.50	35.00	52.50
5-Frazetta cover & 11 pg. story by William-son/Krenkel/Orlando (per Mr. Williamson) (Rare)	140.00	280.00	420.00
6,8,10-12	2.00	4.00	6.00
7,9-One pg. of Frazetta in each			

	Good	Fine	Mint
	2.50	5.00	7.50

BUSTER CRABBE
Dec, 1953 - #4, June, 1954
Lev Gleason Publications

	Good	Fine	Mint
#1	3.00	6.00	9.00
2,3-Toth art	5.00	10.00	15.00
4	2.00	4.00	6.00

BUTCH CASSIDY
June, 1971 - #3, Oct, 1971 (52 pgs.)
Skywald Comics

	Good	Fine	Mint
#1-Red Mask reprint, retitled Maverick; Bolle art	.25	.50	.75
2-Whip Wilson reprint	.20	.40	.60
3-Dead Canyon Days reprt/Crack Western #63; Sundance Kid app.	.20	.40	.60

BUTCH CASSIDY   (-- & the Wild Bunch)
1951
Avon Periodicals

	Good	Fine	Mint
No#-Kinstler cover/story	5.00	10.00	15.00

BUTCH CASSIDY   (See Fun-In #11)

BUZ SAWYER
1948 - 1949
Standard Comics

	Good	Fine	Mint
#1-Roy Crane	4.00	8.00	12.00
2-5	3.00	6.00	9.00

BUZ SAWYER'S PAL, ROSCOE SWEENEY (See Sweeney)

BUZZY
Winter, 1944-45 - #77, Oct, 1959
National Periodical Publ./Detective Comics

	Good	Fine	Mint
#1	4.00	8.00	12.00
2-5	2.00	4.00	6.00
6-10	1.25	2.50	3.75
11-40: #33-Scribbly by Mayer	.70	1.40	2.10
41-77	.50	1.00	1.50

BUZZY THE CROW   (See Harvey Hits #18)

CADET GRAY OF WEST POINT
1958   (Giant)
Dell Publishing Co.

	Good	Fine	Mint
#1-Williamson story-10pgs.	3.00	6.00	9.00

CAIN'S HUNDRED   (TV)
May-July, 1962 - #2, Sept-Nov, 1962

(Cain's Hundred cont'd)
Dell Publishing Co.

	Good	Fine	Mint
No#(01-094-207),#2	.50	1.00	1.50

CALL FROM CHRIST
1952
Catholic Education Society

	Good	Fine	Mint
	2.00	4.00	6.00

CALLING ALL BOYS (Tex Granger #18 on)
Jan, 1946 - #17, May, 1948
Parents' Magazine Institute

#1	2.00	4.00	6.00
2-17	1.25	2.50	3.75

CALLING ALL GIRLS
Sept, 1941 - #44, Nov, 1945? (Movie reviews)
Parents' Magazine Institute

#1,2	2.00	4.00	6.00
3-10	1.25	2.50	3.75
11-20	.80	1.60	2.40
21-44	.50	1.00	1.50

CALLING ALL KIDS
Dec-Jan, 1945-46 - #26, Aug, 1949
Parents' Magazine/Quality Comics

#1	1.20	2.40	3.60
2	.80	1.60	2.40
3-10	.50	1.00	1.50
11-26	.40	.80	1.20

CALVIN (See Li'l Kids)

CALVIN & THE COLONEL (TV)
1962 - #2, Jul-Sept, 1962
Dell Publishing Co.

4-Color #1354	.50	1.00	1.50
#2	.30	.60	.90

CAMERA COMICS
July, 1944 - #9, 1946
U.S. Camera Publishing Corp.

No#(7/44 & 9/44 issues)	1.50	3.00	4.50
#1(10/44)-The Grey Comet	1.50	3.00	4.50
2-9: All ½ photos	1.00	2.00	3.00

CAMP COMICS
Feb, 1942 - #3, April, 1942
Dell Publishing Co.

#1-"Seaman Sy Wheeler" by Kelly, 7 pgs.;

	Good	Fine	Mint
Bugs Bunny app.	35.00	70.00	105.00
2-Kelly story, 12pgs.; Bugs Bunny app.			
	25.00	50.00	75.00
3-(Scarce)-Kelly story	30.00	60.00	90.00

CAMP RUNAMUCK (TV)
April, 1966
Dell Publishing Co.

#1	.25	.50	.75

CAMPUS LOVES
Dec, 1949 - #5, Aug, 1950
Quality Comics Group (Comic Magazines)

#1-Ward cover, 9pg. story	7.00	14.00	21.00
2-Ward cover/story	5.00	10.00	15.00
3,4	2.50	5.00	7.50
5-Ill. in Seduction of the Innocent (spanking panel); reprint/Frontier Romances #1?			
	4.00	8.00	12.00

NOTE: *Gustavson stories-#1-5. Photo covers-#3-5.*

CAMPUS ROMANCE (-- Romances on cover)
Sept-Oct, 1949 - #3, Feb-Mar, 1950
Avon Periodicals

#1-Walter Johnson art; painted covers(#1-3)			
	4.00	8.00	12.00
2,3: #2-Grandenetti sty.	3.00	6.00	9.00

CANADA DRY PREMIUMS (See Swamp Fox, The)

CANCELLED COMIC CAVALCADE
Summer, 1978 - #2, Fall, 1978 (8½x11")(B&W)
(Xeroxed pages on 1 side only w/blue cover
and taped spine)
DC Comics, Inc.

#1-(412pgs.) Contains xeroxed copies of art for: Black Lightning #12, cover to #13; Claw #13,14; The Deserted #1; Doorway to Nightmare #6; Firestorm #6; The Green Team #2,3.
#2-(532 pgs.) Contains xeroxed copies of art for: Kamandi #60(including Omac),#61; Prez #5, Shade #9(including The Odd Man); Showcase #105(Deadman),#106(The Creeper); The Vixen #1; and covers to Army at War #2, Battle Classics #3, Demand Classics #1&2, Dynamic Classics #3, Mr. Miracle #26, Ragman #6, Weird Mystery #25&26, & Western Classics #1&2. (Rare)
(One set sold in 1978 for $250.00)
NOTE: *In June, 1978, DC cancelled several of their titles. For copyright purposes, the*

Calling All Kids #2, © PMI

Camp Comics #1, © DELL

Campus Loves #2, © QUA

Candy #11, © QUA   Canteen Kate #1, © STJ   Captain Aero Comics #2, © HOKE

(Cancelled Comic Cavalcade cont'd)
unpublished original art for these titles
was xeroxed, bound in the above books, pub-
lished and distributed. Only 35 copies were
made.

CANDID TALES
April, 1950 (Digest size)(144pgs.)
Kirby Publishing Co.   (Full Color)
                    Good   Fine   Mint
(Very Rare) Contains Wally Wood Female
 Pirate story, 15pgs. 25.00 50.00 75.00

CANDY
Fall, 1944 - #3, Spring, 1945
William H. Wise & Co.

#1-Two Scoop Scuttle stories by Basil Wolver-
 ton   8.00 16.00 24.00
 2,3-Scoop Scuttle by Basil Wolverton
  (2-4 pgs.)   6.00 12.00 18.00

CANDY
Fall, 1947 - #64, July, 1956
Quality Comics Group

#1   2.50   5.00   7.50
 2-10   1.20   2.40   3.60
 11-63   .80   1.60   2.40
 64-Ward cover pencils? 1.00 2.00 3.00
 Super Reprint #2,10,16,17('64),18
                      .50   1.00   1.50

CANNONBALL COMICS
Feb, 1945 - #2, Mar, 1945
Rural Home Publishing Co.

#1-The Crash Kid, Thunderbrand, The Captive
 Prince & Crime Crusader begin
                     3.50   7.00 10.50
 2   2.50   5.00   7.50

CANTEEN KATE (Also see All Picture All True
Love Story & Fightin' Marines)
June, 1952 - #3, Nov, 1952
St. John Publishing Co.

#1-Matt Baker cvr/stys. 15.00 30.00 45.00
 2,3-Matt Baker cvr/stys. 9.00 18.00 27.00

CAP'N CRUNCH COMICS (See Quaker Oats)
1963; 1965 (16pgs.; Miniature giveaways;
Quaker Oats Co.   2½x5½")

(4 titles)-"The Picture Pirates," "The Fount-
 ain of Youth," "I'm Dreaming of a Wide
 Isthmus," "Bewitched, Betwitched, & Be-
 tweaked"('65)   .20   .40   .60

CAPTAIN ACTION
Oct-Nov, 1968 - #5, June-July, 1969
National Periodical Publications
                    Good   Fine   Mint
#1-Origin Captain Action; Wood art; Superman
 cameos   .60   1.20   1.80
 2,3,5-Kane/Wood art .40   .80   1.20
 4-Gil Kane art   .30   .60   .90
-- & Action Boy('67)-Ideal Toy Co. giveaway
                     .25   .50   .75

CAPTAIN AERO COMICS (Samson #1-6)
V1#7(#1), Dec, 1941 - V2#4(#10), Jan, 1943;
V3#9(#11), Sept, 1943 - V4#3(#17), Oct, 1944;
#21, Dec, 1944 - #26, Aug, 1946 (No #18-20)
Holyoke Publishing Co.

V1#7(#1)-Flag-Man & Solar, Master of Magic,
 Captain Aero, Cap Stone, Adventurer begin   17.50 35.00 52.50
 8(#2)-Pals of Freedom app.
                    10.00 20.00 30.00
 9(#3)-Alias X begins; Pals of Freedom app.
                    10.00 20.00 30.00
 10(#4)-Origin The Gargoyle; Kubert art
                    11.00 22.00 33.00
 11,12(#5,6)-Kubert art; Miss Victory app.
  in #6   8.00 16.00 24.00
V2#1(#7)   6.00 12.00 18.00
 2(#8)-Origin The Red Cross
                     6.00 12.00 18.00
 3(#9)-Miss Victory app.5.00 10.00 15.00
 4(#10)   3.00   6.00   9.00
V3#9 - V3#13(#11-15) 2.50   5.00   7.50
V4#2, V4#3(#16,17)   2.50   5.00   7.50
#21-23   2.00   4.00   6.00
 24-26-L.B. Cole covers 3.50 7.00 10.50

CAPTAIN AMERICA (See All-Select, All Winners,
Aurora, Book & Record Set, Giant Comics to
Color, & USA Comics)

CAPTAIN AMERICA COMICS
3/41 - #75, 1/50; #76, 5/54 - #78, 9/54
(#74 & 75 titled Capt. America's Weird Tales)
Timely #1-75/Atlas #76-78 (CCC/MJMC/CMPS)

#1-Origin & 1st app. Captain America & Bucky
 by S&K; Hurricane, Tuk the Caveboy begin
 by S&K; Red Skull app.
                    800.00 1600.00 2400.00
 (Prices vary widely on this book)
 2-S&K Hurricane; Tuk by Avison(Kirby splash)
                    350.00 700.00 1050.00
 3-Red Skull app.   225.00 450.00 675.00
 4   160.00 320.00 480.00
 5   130.00 260.00 390.00
 6-Origin Father Time; Tuk the Caveboy ends
                    120.00 240.00 360.00

64

Captain America Comics #12. © MCG

Captain America Comics #32. © MCG

Captain America Comics #75. © MCG

(Captain Atom cont'd)

	Good	Fine	Mint
84-86,88,89	1.20	2.40	3.60
87-Nightshade begins	1.20	2.40	3.60
#83,84(Modern Comics-1977)-reprints		.15	.30

NOTE: *All issues have* Ditko *art & stories.*

CAPTAIN BATTLE (Boy #3 on)(See Silver Streak)
Summer, 1941 - #2, Fall, 1941
Comic House/Fun

	Good	Fine	Mint
#1-Origin Blackout; Captain Battle begins	25.00	50.00	75.00
2	15.00	30.00	45.00

CAPTAIN BATTLE (2nd Series)
1943 - #5, Sum/43 (#3-52pgs,no date)(#5-68pgs.)
Picture Scoop

	Good	Fine	Mint
#3-Origin Silver Streak	10.00	20.00	30.00
4	8.00	16.00	24.00
5-Origin Blackout retold	8.00	16.00	24.00

CAPTAIN BATTLE, JR.
Fall, 1943 - #2, Winter, 1943-44
Comic House

	Good	Fine	Mint
#1-The Claw vs. The Ghost	12.50	25.00	37.50
2-Wolverton's Scoop Scuttle; Don Rico art	15.00	30.00	45.00

CAPTAIN BRITAIN
10/13/76 - #39, 1977 (Weekly)
Marvel Comics International

	Good	Fine	Mint
#1-Origin; with Capt. Britain's face mask inside	1.50	3.75	6.00
2-Origin, conclusion. Britain's Boomerang inside	1.35	2.75	4.00
3-Vs. Bank Robbers	.80	1.60	2.40
4-7-Vs. Hurricane	.80	1.60	2.40
8-Vs. Bank Robbers	.80	1.60	2.40
9-13-Vs. Dr. Synne	.60	1.20	1.80
14,15-Vs. Mastermind	.60	1.20	1.80
16-20-With Capt. America; #17 misprinted & color section reprinted in #18	.60	1.20	1.80
21-23,25,26-With Capt. America	.60	1.20	1.80
24-With C.B.'s Jet Plane inside	1.00	2.00	3.00
27-Origin retold	.60	1.20	1.80
28-32-Vs. Lord Hawk	.50	1.00	1.50
33-35-More on origin	.60	1.20	1.80
36-Star Sceptre	.50	1.00	1.50
37-39-Vs. Highwayman & Munipulator	.50	1.00	1.50

NOTE: *#1,2,&24 are rarer in mint due to in-*
serts. *Distributed in Great Britain only.*
Story from #39 continues in Super Spider-Man
(British weekly) #231-253.

CAPTAIN CANUCK
July, 1975 - Present (Distributed in U.S.)
Comely Comix (Canada)

	Good	Fine	Mint
#1	.50	1.00	1.50
2,3	.30	.60	.90
4(1st printing-2/77)-11x17", B&W. Only 15 copies printed; signed by creator Richard Comely, serially numbered & 2 certificates of authenticity inserted; orange cardboard covers (Very Rare)	20.00	40.00	60.00
4(2nd printing-7/77)-10x14" ($5.00) B&W; 300 copies printed, numbered and signed	7.00	14.00	21.00

CAPTAIN CARVEL AND HIS CARVEL CRUSADERS
(See The Amazing Advs. of --)

CAPTAIN COURAGEOUS (Banner #3-5)
March, 1942
Ace Magazines

	Good	Fine	Mint
#6-Origin & 1st app. The Sword; Lone Warrior, Capt. Courageous app.	18.00	36.00	54.00

CAPT'N CRUNCH COMICS (See Cap'n --)

CAPTAIN DAVY JONES (See 4-Color #598)

CAPTAIN EASY
1939 - 1956
Dell Publ./Standard(Visual Editions)/Argo

	Good	Fine	Mint
Hawley(1939)-Contains reprints from The Funnies & 1938 Sunday strips	20.00	40.00	60.00
4-Color #24('43)	15.00	30.00	45.00
4-Color #111	6.00	12.00	18.00
#10(Standard, 10/47)	4.00	8.00	12.00
11-17: All-30's & 40's strip reprints	3.00	6.00	9.00
Argo #1(4/56)-Reprints	2.50	5.00	7.50

CAPTAIN EASY & WASH TUBBS (See Famous Comics Cartoon Books)

CAPTAIN FEARLESS COMICS (See Holyoke One-Shot #6)

CAPTAIN FEARLESS COMICS
August, 1941 - #2, Sept, 1941
Holyoke Publishing Co.

#1-Origin Mr. Miracle, Alias X, Captain Fear-

Captain Britain #1, © MCG

Captain Courageous #6, © ACE

Captain Easy #13, © NEA Services, Inc.

Captain Flash #1, © Sterling

Captain Flight #3, © Four Star

Captain Marvel #29, © MCG

	Good	Fine	Mint
(Captain Fearless cont'd) less, Citizen Smith, Son of the Unknown Soldier; Miss Victory begins	20.00	40.00	60.00
2	10.00	20.00	30.00

CAPTAIN FLASH
Nov, 1954 - #4, July, 1955
Sterling Comics

#1-Origin by Mike Sekowsky(not Toth); Tomboy begins	5.00	10.00	15.00
2-4	3.00	6.00	9.00

CAPTAIN FLEET
Fall, 1952
Ziff-Davis Publishing Co.

#1	1.50	3.00	4.50

CAPTAIN FLIGHT COMICS
Mar, 1944 - #11, Feb-Mar, 1947
Four Star Publications

#1	4.00	8.00	12.00
2	2.50	5.00	7.50
3-5: #4-Rock Raymond begins, ends #7. #5- Red Rocket begins; the Grenade app.	2.00	4.00	6.00
6-8: #8-Yankee Girl, Black Cobra begin; Intro. Cobra Kid	2.50	5.00	7.50
9-Torpedoman app.; last Yankee Girl; Kinstler story	2.50	5.00	7.50
10-Deep Sea Dawson, Zoom of the Jungle, & Rock Raymond app.; no Red Rocket, Black Cobra	2.00	4.00	6.00
11-Torpedoman, Blue Flame app.; last Black Cobra, Red Rocket	2.00	4.00	6.00

CAPTAIN FORTUNE PRESENTS
1955 - 1959 (16pgs., 3¾x6-7/8")(Giveaway)
Vital Publications

"Davy Crockett in Episodes of the Creek War,"
"Davy Crockett at the Alamo," "In Sherwood
Forest Tells Strange Tales of Robin Hood"
('57), "Meets Bolivar the Liberator"('59),
"Tells How Buffalo Bill Fights the Dog Sol-
iers"('57), "Young Davy Crockett"
.60   1.20   1.80

CAPTAIN GALLANT (--of the Foreign Legion)(TV)
1955 - 1956
Charlton Comics

#1-Buster Crabbe	3.00	6.00	9.00
2-4	1.75	3.50	5.25

Heinz Foods Premium(1955, regular size) U.S.
Pictorial; contains Buster Crabbe photos;

	Good	Fine	Mint
Don Heck art	1.50	3.00	4.50
Non-Heinz version(same as above except pict- ures of show replaces ads)	1.50	3.00	4.50

CAPTAIN HERO (See Jughead As --)

CAPTAIN HOBBY COMICS
Feb, 1948   (Canadian)
Export Publication Ent. Ltd. (Dist. in U.S.
by Kable News Co.)

#1	1.50	3.00	4.50

CAPTAIN HOOK & PETER PAN (See 4-Color #446
and Peter Pan)

CAPTAIN JET
May, 1952 - #5, Jan, 1953
Comic Media/Four Star Publ./Farrell

#1	2.00	4.00	6.00
2-5	1.25	2.50	3.75

CAPTAIN KANGAROO (See 4-Color #721,780,872)

CAPTAIN KIDD (Formerly Dagar)
1949
Fox Features Syndicate

#24,25	2.00	4.00	6.00

CAPTAIN MARVEL (See All Hero, America's
Greatest, Fawcett Min., Gift, Marvel Family,
Master #21, Shazam, Whiz, Wisco, & Xmas)

CAPTAIN MARVEL (--Presents the Terrible 5 #5)
April, 1966 - #4, Nov, 1966   (25¢)
M. F. Enterprises

No#-(#1 on page 5)-Origin	.60	1.20	1.80
#2	.40	.80	1.20
3-(#3 on page 4)-Fights the Bat,			
4	.40	.80	1.20

CAPTAIN MARVEL (See Marvel Super-Heroes #12)
May, 1968 - #19, Dec, 1969; #20, June, 1970-
#21, Aug, 1970; #22, Sept, 1972 - Present
Marvel Comics Group

#1	2.00	4.00	6.00
2-5	1.00	2.00	3.00
6-10	.60	1.20	1.80
11-Smith/Trimpe cover; Death of Una	1.00	2.00	3.00
12-20	.50	1.00	1.50
21-24	.40	.80	1.20
25-Starlin cover/story	1.50	3.00	4.50

(Captain Marvel cont'd)	Good	Fine	Mint
26-34-Starlin cvr/story	1.00	2.00	3.00
35-40	.30	.60	.90
41,43-Wrightson part inks; cover #43(inks)			
	.50	1.00	1.50
42,44-48,50	.25	.50	.75
49-Starlin in part	.40	.80	1.20
51-60: #53-Inhumans app.	.20	.40	.60
Giant-Size #1(12/75)	.70	1.40	2.10

NOTE: *Alcala* story-#35. *Gil Kane* stories-
#17-22; covers-#17-25.

CAPTAIN MARVEL ADVENTURES
1941 - #150, Nov, 1953
Fawcett Publications

No#(#1)-Captain Marvel & Sivana by Jack Kirby. The cover was printed on unstable paper stock and is rarely found in Fine or
Mint condition   500.00 1500.00 2500.00
(Prices vary widely on this book)

	Good	Fine	Mint
#2-Art by George Tuska	175.00	350.00	525.00
3	80.00	160.00	240.00
4- 3 Lt. Marvels app.	60.00	120.00	180.00
5	50.00	100.00	150.00
6-10	37.50	75.00	112.50

11-15: #15-comic cards on back cover begin,
end #26   27.50   55.00   82.50
16,17   22.50   45.00   67.50
18-Origin & 1st app. Mary Marvel & Marvel
Family; painted cvr. 30.00 60.00 90.00
19,20: #19-Mary Marvel x-over
20.00   40.00   60.00
20-With miniature comic still attached to
cover; miniature's cover same as Whiz #22
(other variations possible)(See Fawcett
Miniatures & Mighty Midget)
25.00   50.00   75.00
21   13.50   26.75   40.00
22-Mr.Mind serial begins 20.00 40.00 60.00
23-25   15.00   30.00   45.00
26-30   13.50   26.75   40.00
31-35: #35-Origin Radar 10.00 20.00 30.00
36-40: #37-Mary Marvel x-over
9.00   18.00   27.00
41-46: #43-Captain Marvel 1st meets Uncle
Marvel; Mary Batson cameo. #46-Mr. Mind
serial ends   8.00   16.00   24.00
47-50   6.00   12.00   18.00
51-53,55-60: #52-Origin & 1st app. Sivana Jr.;
Capt.Marvel Jr. x-over 4.00 8.00 12.00
54-Special oversize 68pg. ish.
5.00   10.00   15.00
61-The Cult of the Curse serial begins
6.00   12.00   18.00
62-66-Serial ends; Mary Marvel x-over in #65
4.00   8.00   12.00
67-79: #69-Billy Batson's Xmas; Uncle Marvel,

	Good	Fine	Mint
Mary Marvel, Capt. Marvel Jr. x-over. #71-3 Lt. Marvels app. #78-Origin Mr. Atom.			
#79-Origin Mr. Tawny	4.00	8.00	12.00
80-Origin retold	5.00	10.00	15.00
81-90: #81,90-Mr. Atom app. #85-Freedom Train issue. #86-Mr. Tawny app.			
	4.00	8.00	12.00
91-99: #96-Mr. Tawny app.	3.00	6.00	9.00
100-Origin retold	5.00	10.00	15.00
101-120	3.00	6.00	9.00
121-Origin retold	3.50	7.00	10.50
122-149	2.50	5.00	7.50
150-(Low distribution)	7.00	14.00	21.00

Bond Bread Giveaways(24 pgs.; Pocket size-
7¼x3½"; soft cover): "-- & the Stolen
City," "The Boy Who Never Heard of C.M."-
('50)(reprint) each...15.00 30.00 45.00

CAPTAIN MARVEL ADVENTURES (Also see Whiz)
1945   (6x8") (Full Color, Soft Cover)
Fawcett Publications (Wheaties Giveaway)

"Captain Marvel & the Threads of Life" plus
2 other stories(32pgs.) 5.00 15.00 25.00
NOTE: *All copies were taped at each corner
to a box of Wheaties and are never found in
Fine or Mint condition.*

CAPTAIN MARVEL AND THE GOOD HUMOR MAN
1950
Fawcett Publications

No#   10.00 20.00 30.00

CAPTAIN MARVEL AND THE LTS. OF SAFETY
1950 - 1951   (3 issues - no #'s)
Fawcett Publications

"Danger Flies a Kite," "Danger Smashes the
Lights," "Takes to Climbing"
4.00   8.00 12.00

CAPTAIN MARVEL COMIC STORY PAINT BOOK
(See Comic Story Paint Book)

CAPTAIN MARVEL, JR. (See Fawcett Miniatures)

CAPTAIN MARVEL, JR. (See Marvel Family,
Master Comics, and Shazam)
Nov, 1942 - #119, June, 1953   (No #34)
Fawcett Publications

#1-Origin Capt. Marvel Jr. retold (Whiz #25);
Capt. Nazi app.   85.00 170.00 255.00
2-Vs. Capt. Nazi   45.00 90.00 135.00
3,4   35.00 70.00 105.00
5-Vs. Capt. Nazi   25.00 50.00 75.00

Captain Marvel Adventures #2, © FAW

Captain Marvel Adventures #57, © FAW

Captain Marvel Adventures #96, © FAW

Captain Marvel Jr. #19, © FAW

Captain Midnight #43, © FAW

Captain Science #1, © YM

(Capt. Marvel Jr. cont'd)	Good	Fine	Mint
6-10: #8-Vs. Capt. Nazi	20.00	40.00	60.00
11-20: #16-Captain Marvel & Sivana x-over			
	12.00	24.00	36.00
21-30	6.00	12.00	18.00
31-33,35-40: #35-has #34 on inside			
	4.00	8.00	12.00
41-50	2.50	5.00	7.50
51-70	2.50	5.00	7.50
71-119	2.00	4.00	6.00

NOTE: _Mac Raboy covers-#1-10,12,13,16, among others._

CAPTAIN MARVEL JR. WELL KNOWN COMICS
1944   (12pgs.) (Printed in Blue) (8½x10½")
(Paper cover; glued binding)
Bestmaid/Samuel Lowe (Giveaway)

(Scarce)   30.00 60.00 90.00

CAPTAIN MARVEL PRESENTS THE TERRIBLE FIVE
Aug, 1966; V2#5, Sept, 1967 (No #2-4)(25¢)
M. F. Enterprises

#1	.40	.80	1.20
V2#5-(Formerly Capt.Marvel).30		.60	.90

CAPTAIN MARVEL'S FUN BOOK
1944   (1/2" thick)(Cardboard covers)
Samuel Lowe Co.

Contain puzzles, games, magic, etc.
                          5.00 10.00 15.00

CAPTAIN MARVEL SPECIAL EDITION (See Special Edition)

CAPTAIN MARVEL STORY BOOK
Summer, 1946 - 1948
Fawcett Publications

#1	15.00	30.00	45.00
2-4	10.00	20.00	30.00

CAPTAIN MARVEL THRILL BOOK (Large-Size)
1941   (Black & White) (Color Cover)
Fawcett Publications

#1-Reprints from Whiz #8,10,& Special
   Edition #1 (Rare)   125.00 375.00 625.00
NOTE: _Rarely found in Fine or Mint condition._

CAPTAIN MARVEL WELL KNOWN COMICS
1944   (12 pgs.) Printed in red (8½x10½")
(Paper cover; glued binding)
Bestmaid/Samuel Lowe Co. (Giveaway)

(Scarce)   30.00 60.00 90.00

CAPTAIN MIDNIGHT (Sweethearts #68 on)
Sept, 1942 - #67, Fall, 1948
Fawcett Publications

	Good	Fine	Mint
#1-Origin Captain Midnight; Captain Marvel cameo on cover	40.00	80.00	120.00
2	20.00	40.00	60.00
3-5	14.00	28.00	42.00
6-10	8.00	16.00	24.00
11-20	5.00	10.00	15.00
21-30	3.00	6.00	9.00
31-40	2.50	5.00	7.50
41-67	2.00	4.00	6.00

(See Super Book #3)

CAPTAIN NICE (TV)
Nov, 1967   (One Shot)
Gold Key

#1(10211-711)   .35   .70 1.05

CAPTAIN PUREHEART (See Archie As --)

CAPTAIN ROCKET
1950
Fox Features Publ.

#1-(Reprinted in Canada by P. L. Publ. in
   Nov, 1951)   5.00 10.00 15.00

CAPTAIN SAVAGE (-- & His Leatherneck Raiders)
Jan, 1968 - #19, Mar, 1970 (See Sgt. Fury #10)
Marvel Comics Group

#1-Sgt. Fury & Howlers cameo			
	.50	1.00	1.50
2-Origin Hydra	.25	.50	.75
3-10	.20	.40	.60
11-19(Severin art #8,9,16-19)-#11-Sgt. Fury			
& Howlers x-over	.20	.40	.60

CAPTAIN SCIENCE (Also see Fantastic)
Nov, 1950 - #7, Dec, 1951
Youthful Magazines

#1-Wood story	20.00	40.00	60.00
2,3,6,7	8.00	16.00	24.00
4,5-Wood & Orlando covers & 2 stories each			
	15.00	30.00	45.00

CAPTAIN SILVER'S LOG OF SEA HOUND (See Sea Hound)

CAPTAIN SINDBAD (Movie Adaptation)(See Movie Comics)

CAPTAIN STEVE SAVAGE
1950 - #13, May-June, 1956
Avon Periodicals

(Captain Steve Savage cont'd)

	Good	Fine	Mint
No#(1st series)-Wood art, 22 pgs. (titled-"--Over Korea")	10.00	20.00	30.00
#1(4/51)-Reprints No# ish.(Canadian)	7.00	14.00	21.00
2-Kamen story	3.00	6.00	9.00
3-13: #9-Kinstler art	2.00	4.00	6.00

NOTE: _Kinstler covers-#2-4,7,8,11._

#1(1954-2nd series)	2.50	5.00	7.50
2-5,7('55)	1.50	3.00	4.50
6-Reprints No# ish.	4.00	8.00	12.00
8-13	1.20	2.40	3.60

CAPTAIN STONE (See Holyoke One-Shot #10)

CAPTAIN STORM
May-June, 1964 - #18, Mar-Apr, 1967
National Periodical Publications

#1-Origin	1.00	2.00	3.00
2-18: #12-Kubert cover	.60	1.20	1.80

CAPTAIN 3-D
December, 1953
Harvey Publications

#1-Kirby art	10.00	20.00	30.00

CAPTAIN TOOTSIE & THE SECRET LEGION
1950
Toby Press

#1-Not Beck art	5.00	10.00	15.00
2- " " "	3.00	6.00	9.00

CAPTAIN VENTURE & THE LAND BENEATH THE SEA
Oct, 1968 - #2, Oct, 1969
Gold Key

#1,2	.80	1.60	2.40

CAPTAIN VIDEO (TV)
Feb, 1951 - #6, Dec, 1951
Fawcett Publications

#1-George Evans art	8.00	16.00	24.00
2-6-All Evans art	5.00	10.00	15.00

CAPTAIN WIZARD
1946
Rural Home

#1-Capt. Wizard reprint/Meteor #1	3.00	6.00	9.00

CAREER GIRL ROMANCES

Jan, 1965 - #77, 1972
Charlton Comics

	Good	Fine	Mint
V4#24-77	.15	.30	.45

CAR 54, WHERE ARE YOU? (TV)
3-5/62 - #7, 9-11/63; 1964 - 1965
Dell Publishing Co.

4-Color #1257(3-5/62)	.50	1.00	1.50
#2(7-9/62)-#7	.25	.50	.75
#2,3(10-12/64),#4(1-3/65)-Reprints #2,3,&4 of 1st series	.25	.50	.75

CARNATION MALTED MILK GIVEAWAYS (See Wisco)

CARNIVAL COMICS
1945
Harry 'A' Chesler/Pershing Square Publ. Co.

#1	1.20	2.40	3.60

CARNIVAL OF COMICS
1954   (Giveaway)
Fleet-Air Shoes

No#-Contains a comic bound with new cover; Several combinations possible; Charlton's Eh! known	.60	1.20	1.80

CAROLINE KENNEDY
1961   (One Shot)
Charlton Comics

	2.50	5.00	7.50

CAROUSEL COMICS
V1#8, April, 1948
F. E. Howard, Toronto

V1#8	.60	1.20	1.80

CARTOON KIDS
1957
Atlas Comics (CPS)

#1	1.00	2.00	3.00

CARTOONS (Magazine)(Also see Drag Cartoons)
1961 - Present (52 pgs.) (Automobile humor)
Petersen Publ. Co.

#1	.80	1.60	2.40
2-20	.40	.80	1.20
21-25	.30	.60	.90
26-Toth art	1.50	3.00	4.50
27-101	.25	.50	.75

Captain Steve Savage #2, © AVON

Captain Video #3, © FAW

Caroline Kennedy, © CC

Casey Crime Photographer #4, © MCG   Casper #4, © STJ   The Cat #2, © MCG

CARVEL COMICS (Amaz. Advs. of Capt. Carvel)
1973 (25¢; #3-35¢)
Carvel Corp. (Ice Cream)

	Good	Fine	Mint
#1-3		.15	.30

CASE OF THE SHOPLIFTER'S SHOE (See Feature
Book #50(Perry Mason), & McKay)

CASE OF THE WASTED WATER, THE
1974 (Giveaway)
Rheem Water Heating

	Good	Fine	Mint
Neal Adams art	1.00	2.00	3.00

CASE OF THE WINKING BUDDHA, THE
1950 (132 pgs.)(25¢)(B&W)(5½x7-5/8")
St. John Publ. Co.

	Good	Fine	Mint
Charles Raab, artist; reprinted in Authentic Police Cases #25	2.50	5.00	7.50

CASEY-CRIME PHOTOGRAPHER (Two-Gun Western
Aug, 1949 - #4, Feb, 1950   #5 on?)
Marvel Comics (BFP)

	Good	Fine	Mint
#1	2.00	4.00	6.00
2-4	1.20	2.40	3.60

CASEY JONES (See 4-Color Comics #915)

CASPER AND NIGHTMARE (See Harvey Hits #37,
45,52,56,59,62,65,68)

CASPER AND NIGHTMARE (Nightmare & Casper#1-5)
#6, Nov, 1964 - #42, June, 1973 (25¢)
Harvey Publications

	Good	Fine	Mint
#6	1.00	2.00	3.00
7-10	.40	.80	1.20
11-42	.25	.50	.75

CASPER AND SPOOKY (See Harvey Hits #20)
Oct, 1972 - #7, Oct, 1973
Harvey Publications

	Good	Fine	Mint
#1	.25	.50	.75
2-7	.15	.30	.45

CASPER AND THE GHOSTLY TRIO
Nov, 1972 - #7, Nov, 1973
Harvey Publications

	Good	Fine	Mint
#1	.25	.50	.75
2-7	.15	.30	.45

CASPER AND WENDY
Sept, 1972 - #8, 1973
Harvey Publications

	Good	Fine	Mint
#1	.25	.50	.75
2-8	.15	.30	.45

CASPER CAT
1958; 1963
I.W. Enterprises/Super

	Good	Fine	Mint
#1,7-Reprint, Super #14('63)	.20	.40	.60

CASPER HALLOWEEN TRICK OR TREAT
January, 1976
Harvey Publications

	Good	Fine	Mint
#1	.15	.30	.45

CASPER IN SPACE (Formerly Casper Spaceship)
#6, June, 1973 - #8, Oct, 1973
Harvey Publications

	Good	Fine	Mint
#6-8		.15	.30

CASPER'S GHOSTLAND
April, 1959 - Present (25¢)
Harvey Publications

	Good	Fine	Mint
#1	2.50	5.00	7.50
2-10	1.50	3.00	4.50
11-20	1.00	2.00	3.00
21-40	.50	1.00	1.50
41-60	.25	.50	.75
61-98	.20	.40	.60

CASPER SPACESHIP (Casper in Space #6)
Aug, 1972 - #5, April, 1973
Harvey Publications

	Good	Fine	Mint
#1	.25	.50	.75
2-5	.15	.30	.45

CASPER STRANGE GHOST STORIES
October, 1974 - #15, ?
Harvey Publications

	Good	Fine	Mint
#1	.25	.50	.75
2-15:(#13-40¢)	.15	.30	.45

CASPER, THE FRIENDLY GHOST (See The Friendly
Ghost --, Harvey Hits #61 & Tastee-Freez)

CASPER, THE FRIENDLY GHOST
Sept, 1949 - #3, Aug, 1950; 9/50 - #5, 5/51
St. John Publishing Co.

	Good	Fine	Mint
#1(1949)-Origin & 1st app. Baby Huey	12.00	24.00	36.00
2,3(8/50)	5.00	10.00	15.00
#1(9/50-St. John)	7.00	14.00	21.00

(Casper cont'd)	Good	Fine	Mint
2-5(5/51)	4.00	8.00	12.00

CASPER, THE FRIENDLY GHOST (Paramount Picture
Dec, 1951 - #70, July, 1958   Star --)
Harvey Publications (Family Comics)

	Good	Fine	Mint
#1	7.00	14.00	21.00
2-5	3.00	6.00	9.00
6-20	2.00	4.00	6.00
21-40	1.00	2.00	3.00
41-70	.60	1.20	1.80

CASTILIAN (See Movie Classics)

CAT, T.H.E. (TV) (See T.H.E. Cat)

CAT, THE (See Movie Classics)

CAT, THE
Nov, 1972 - #4, June, 1973
Marvel Comics Group

	Good	Fine	Mint
#1-Origin The Cat; Wally Wood inks	.80	1.60	2.40
2-Mooney/Marie Severin art,			
3-Everett inks	.60	1.20	1.80
4-Starlin/Weiss art	.70	1.40	2.10

CATHOLIC COMICS (See Heroes All Catholic --)
June, 1946 - V3#10, July, 1949
Catholic Publications

	Good	Fine	Mint
#1	2.50	5.00	7.50
2-12	1.35	2.75	4.00
V2#1-10	1.00	2.00	3.00
V3#1-10	.70	1.40	2.10

CATHOLIC PICTORIAL
1947
Catholic Guild

	Good	Fine	Mint
#1-Two Toth stys.(Rare)	8.00	16.00	24.00

CATMAN COMICS (Crash #1-5)
5/41 - #17, 1/43; #18, 7/43 - #22, 12/43;
#23, 3/44 - #26, 11/44; #27, 4/45 - #30,
12/45; #31, 6/46 - #32, 8/46
Holyoke Publishing Co.

	Good	Fine	Mint
#1(V1#6)-Origin The Deacon & Sidekick Mickey; Dr. Diamond & Rag-Man; The Black Widow app.; The Catman by Chas. Quinlan & Blaze Baylor begin	30.00	60.00	90.00
2(V1#7)	15.00	30.00	45.00
3(V1#8)-The Pied Piper begins,			
4(V1#9)	12.00	24.00	36.00
5(V2#10)-Origin Kitten; The Hood begins,			

	Good	Fine	Mint
6,7(V2#11,12)	8.00	16.00	24.00
8(V2#13,3/42)-Origin Little Leaders; Volton by Kubert begins(1st comic book work)	12.00	24.00	36.00
9(V2#14)	7.00	14.00	21.00
10(V2#15)-Origin Blackout; Phantom Falcon begins	7.00	14.00	21.00
11(V3#1)-#15(V3#13)-#19(V2#6),#20(V2#7)	6.00	12.00	18.00
21-23(V3#13,5/44)	5.00	10.00	15.00
24(V2#12,7/44)	5.00	10.00	15.00
25-The Reckoner begins	4.00	8.00	12.00
26-Origin The Golden Archer; Leatherface app.	3.00	6.00	9.00
27-Origin Kitten retold	4.00	8.00	12.00
28-Catman learns Kitten's I.D.; Dr. Macabre, Deacon app.	3.00	6.00	9.00
29-32	3.00	6.00	9.00

NOTE: *Later issues have L. B. Cole covers.*

CAUGHT
Aug, 1956 - #5, April, 1957
Atlas Comics (VPI)

	Good	Fine	Mint
#1	1.20	2.40	3.60
2,4	.80	1.60	2.40
3-Torres story	1.25	2.50	3.75
5-Crandall + Krigstein stories	2.00	4.00	6.00

CAVALIER COMICS
1945; 1952   (Early DC reprints)
A. W. Nugent Publ. Co.

	Good	Fine	Mint
#2(1945)-Speed Saunders, Fang Gow	2.50	5.00	7.50
#2(1952)	1.20	2.40	3.60

CAVE GIRL
1953 - 1954
Magazine Enterprises

	Good	Fine	Mint
#11(A-1#82)-Origin	15.00	30.00	45.00
12(A-1#96),13(A-1#116),14(A-1#125)-Thunda by Powell	10.00	20.00	30.00

NOTE: *Powell covers, stories in all.*

CAVE KIDS
Feb, 1963 - #16, Mar, 1967   (Hanna-Barbera)
Gold Key

	Good	Fine	Mint
#1	.20	.40	.60
2-5	.15	.30	.45
6-16		.15	.30

CENTURION OF ANCIENT ROME, THE
1958 (No month listed) (36 pgs.)(B&W)

Catman Comics #31, © HOKE

Cavalier Comics #2, © A.W. Nugent

Cave Girl #14, © ME

Challengers Of The Unknown #12, © DC   Chamber Of Chills #19, © HARV   Chamber Of Darkness #7, © MCG

(Centurion of Ancient Rome cont'd)
Zondervan Publishing House

	Good	Fine	Mint
(Rare) All by Jay Disbrow			
Estimated value			45.00

CENTURY OF COMICS
1933 (100pgs.)(Probably the 3rd comic book)
Eastern Color Printing Co.

Bought by Wheatena, Milk-O-Malt, John Wanamaker, Kinney Shoe Stores, & others to be
used as premiums and radio giveaways. No
publisher listed.

No#-Mutt & Jeff, Joe Palooka, etc. reprints			
	125.00	250.00	375.00

CHALLENGE OF THE UNKNOWN
#6, Sept, 1950   (Formerly Love Experiences)
Ace Magazines

#6	2.00	4.00	6.00

CHALLENGER, THE
1945 - #4, Oct-Dec, 1946
Interfaith Publications

No#; No date; 32pgs.; Origin the Challenger
    Club; Anti-Fascist with filler Funny

Animal	4.00	8.00	12.00
#2-4-Kubert art	5.00	10.00	15.00

CHALLENGERS OF THE UNKNOWN (See Showcase &
4-5/58 - #77, 12-1/70-71;   Super DC Giant)
#78, 2/73 - #80, 6-7/73; #81, 6-7/77 -
#87, 6-7/78
National Periodical Publications/DC Comics

#1-Two Kirby-Stein stys.	25.00	50.00	75.00
2- " " " "	15.00	30.00	45.00
3- " " " "	10.00	20.00	30.00
4-8-Kirby/Wood stories + cover #8			
	7.00	14.00	21.00
9,10	2.50	5.00	7.50
11-20: #14-Origin Multi-Man. #18-Intro. Cosmo,			
the Challs Spacepet	1.50	3.00	4.50
21-40: #31-Retells origin of the Challengers			
	1.00	2.00	3.00
41-60: #48-Doom Patrol app. #49-Intro. Chall-			
enger Corps. #55-Death of Red Ryan. #51-			
Sea Devils app.	.70	1.40	2.10
61-63,66-73: #69-Intro. Corinna			
	.35	.70	1.05
64,65-Kirby origin reprint, parts 1 & 2			
	.50	1.00	1.50
74-Deadman by Adams; Wrightson art			
	1.50	3.00	4.50

	Good	Fine	Mint
75-80	.25	.50	.75
81('77)-87	.20	.40	.60

NOTE: *Adams covers-#67,68,70,72,74(inks),81.*
*Kirby reprints-#75-80; covers-#75,77,78. Kub-
ert covers-#64,66,69,76,79.*

CHALLENGE TO THE WORLD
1951
Catechetical Guild

No#	3.00	6.00	9.00

CHAMBER OF CHILLS (-- of Clues #27 on)
#21, June, 1951 - #26, Dec, 1954
Harvey Publications/Witches Tales

#21	2.00	4.00	6.00
22,23,5(2/52)	1.75	3.50	5.25
24-Bondage cover	2.00	4.00	6.00
#6-10	1.50	3.00	4.50
11-12	1.25	2.50	3.75
13-23-Nostrand stories in all (#20 cover			
also)	2.50	5.00	7.50
24-26	1.00	2.00	3.00

NOTE: *Powell stories-#21,23,24('51),5-8,11,
13,18,20,21. Bondage covers-#21('51),7.
#25 reprints #5; #26 reprints #9.*

CHAMBER OF CHILLS
Nov, 1972 - #25, Nov, 1976
Marvel Comics Group

#1-Adkins inks	.40	.80	1.20
2,3	.25	.50	.75
4-Brunner art	.50	1.00	1.50
5-7-Last new story	.20	.40	.60
8-10,12-20,22-25	.15	.30	.45
11-Everett story reprt/Menace #3,			
21-8pg. Everett Venus reprt/Venus #18			
	.15	.30	.45

NOTE: *Brunner story-#2-4. Everett inks-#3.
Robert E. Howard horror story adaptation-#3.*

CHAMBER OF CLUES (Formerly Chamber of Chills)
Feb, 1955 - #28, April, 1955
Harvey Publications

#27-Kerry Drake reprint/#19; Heroine story;			
Powell story	4.00	8.00	12.00
28-Kerry Drake	2.50	5.00	7.50

CHAMBER OF DARKNESS (Monsters on the Prowl #9)
Oct, 1969 - #8, Dec, 1970
Marvel Comics Group

#1-Buscema art	.60	1.20	1.80
2-Adams script	.65	1.35	2.00

(Chamber of Darkness cont'd)

	Good	Fine	Mint
3-Smith story	.80	1.60	2.40
4-A Conanesque tryout by Smith; reprinted			
in Conan #16	4.00	8.00	12.00
5,6,8	.40	.80	1.20
7-Wrightson story/cover	1.00	2.00	3.00
#1(1/72-25¢ Special)	.40	.80	1.20

NOTE: *Adkins/Everett story-#8. Craig story-*
#5. Ditko reprints-#6-8. Kirby story-#4,5,7.
Kirby/Everett cover-#5. Wrightson covers-#7,8.

CHAMP COMICS (Champion #1-10)
#11, Oct, 1940 - #29, March, 1944
Champ Publ./Greenwald/Harvey Publications

#11-Human Meteor cont'd.	9.00	18.00	27.00
12-18: #14-Crandall cvr.	8.00	16.00	24.00
19-The Wasp app.; Kirby cover			
	8.00	16.00	24.00
20-The Green Ghost app.	8.00	16.00	24.00
21-29: #22-The White Mask app.			
	7.00	14.00	21.00

CHAMPION (See Gene Autry's --)

CHAMPION COMICS (Champ #11 on)
#2, Dec, 1939 - #10, Aug, 1940 (No #1)
Worth Publ. Co./Harvey Publications

#2-The Champ, The Blazing Scarab, Neptina,			
Liberty Lads, Jungleman, Bill Handy, Swing-			
time Sweetie begin	20.00	40.00	60.00
3-7: #6-The Human Meteor begins			
	10.00	20.00	30.00
8-10-Kirby covers	15.00	30.00	45.00

CHAMPIONS, THE
October, 1975 - #17, Jan, 1978
Marvel Comics Group

#1-The Angel, Black Widow, Ghost Rider,			
Hercules, Ice Man (The Champions) begin;			
Kane/Adkins cover; Venus x-over			
	1.00	2.00	3.00
2-5: #2,3-Venus x-over	.60	1.20	1.80
6-10	.35	.70	1.05
11-17-Byrne stories in all	.20	.40	.60

CHAMPION SPORTS
Oct-Nov, 1973 - #3, Feb-Mar, 1974
National Periodical Publications

#1-3	.15	.30	.45

CHAOS (See The Crusaders)

CHARLIE CHAN (The Adventures of)
6-7/48 - #5, 2-3/49; #6, 6/55 - #9, 3/56

Crestwood(Prize)#1-5; Charlton #6(6/55) on

	Good	Fine	Mint
#1-S&K cover, 2pgs.; Infantino stories			
	5.00	10.00	15.00
2-5-All S&K covers	4.00	8.00	12.00
6(6/55-Charlton)S&K cvr.	3.00	6.00	9.00
7-9	2.00	4.00	6.00

CHARLIE CHAN
Oct-Dec, 1965 - #4, Jul-Sept, 1966
Dell Publishing Co.

#1-Springer art	1.00	2.00	3.00
2-4	.50	1.00	1.50

CHARLIE CHAPLIN
1917 (9x16", Large size, softcover, B&W)
Essanay/M. A. Donohue & Co.

Series 1, #315-Comic Capers. #316-In the			
Movies	25.00	50.00	75.00
Series 1, #317-Up in the Air. #318-In the			
Army	25.00	50.00	75.00
-- Funny Stunts(12½x16-3/8") in color			
	15.00	30.00	45.00

NOTE: *#315-318: partially by Segar - Pre-*
Thimble Theatre.

CHARLIE McCARTHY (See Edgar Bergan Presents--)
1947 - 1954
Dell Publishing Co.

4-Color #171,196, #1	2.00	4.00	6.00
#2-9	1.20	2.40	3.60
4-Color #445,478,527,571	1.20	2.40	3.60

CHARLTON CLASSICS LIBRARY (1776)
V10#1, March, 1973 (One Shot)
Charlton Comics

1776 (Title)-Adaptation of the film musical,			
"1776"	.50	1.00	1.50

CHARLTON PREMIERE (Formerly Marine War Heroes)
V1#19, 7/67; V2#1, 9/67 - #4, 5/68
Charlton Comics

V1#19-Marine War Heroes	.25	.50	.75
V2#1-Trio; intro. Shape, Tyro Team, & Spook-			
man	.25	.50	.75
V2#2-Children of Doom	.25	.50	.75
3-Sinistro Boy Fiend; Blue Beetle Peace-			
maker x-over	.25	.50	.75
4-Unlikely Tales; Ditko art			
	.25	.50	.75

CHARLTON SPORT LIBRARY - PROFESSIONAL FOOTBALL
Winter, 1969-70 (Jan. on cover) (68 pgs.)
Charlton Comics

Champ Comics #12, © HARV

The Champions #1, © MCG

Charlie McCarthy #2, © DELL

(Charlton Sport Library cont'd)

	Good	Fine	Mint
#1	.15	.30	.45

CHASING THE BLUES
1912 (52 pgs.) (7½x10" - B&W) (Hardcover)
Doubleday Page

	Good	Fine	Mint
by Rube Goldberg	10.00	20.00	30.00

CHECKMATE (TV)
Oct, 1962 - #2, Dec, 1962
Gold Key

	Good	Fine	Mint
#1,2	.25	.50	.75

CHEERIOS PREMIUMS (Disney)
1947 (32 pgs.)(Pocket size - 16 titles)
Walt Disney Productions

Set "W"-Donald Duck & the Pirates

	Good	Fine	Mint
	4.00	8.00	12.00
Pluto Joins the F.B.I.			
	2.50	5.00	7.50
Bucky Bug & the Cannibal King			
	2.50	5.00	7.50
Mickey Mouse & the Haunted House			
	3.00	6.00	9.00
Set "X"-Donald Duck, Counter Spy			
	3.00	6.00	9.00
Goofy Lost in the Desert			
	2.50	5.00	7.50
Br'er Rabbit Outwits Br'er Fox			
	2.50	5.00	7.50
Mickey Mouse at the Rodeo			
	3.00	6.00	9.00
Set "Y"-Donald Duck's Atom Bomb by Carl			
Barks	80.00	160.00	240.00
Br'er Rabbit's Secret			
	2.50	5.00	7.50
Dumbo & the Circus Mystery			
	3.00	6.00	9.00
Mickey Mouse Meets the Wizard			
	3.00	6.00	9.00
Set "Z"-Donald Duck Pilots a Jet Plane (Not			
by Barks)	3.00	6.00	9.00
Pluto Turns Sleuth Hound			
	2.50	5.00	7.50
The Seven Dwarfs & the Enchanted Mtn.			
	3.00	6.00	9.00
Mickey Mouse's Secret Room			
	3.00	6.00	9.00

CHEERIOS 3-D GIVEAWAYS (Disney)
1954 (Pocket Size) - 24 titles
Walt Disney Productions
(Glasses were cut-outs on boxes)

	Good	Fine	Mint
Glasses only....	2.00	4.00	6.00

(Set 1)
#1 Donald Duck & Uncle Scrooge, the Fire-
    fighters
 2 Mickey Mouse & Goofy, Pirate Plunder
 3 Donald Duck's Nephews, the Fabulous
    Inventors
 4 Mickey Mouse, Secret of the Ming Vase
 5 Donald Duck with Huey, Dewey & Louie;
    -- the Seafarers (title on 2nd page)
 6 Mickey Mouse, Moaning Mountain
 7 Donald Duck, Apache Gold
 8 Mickey Mouse, Flight to Nowhere

	Good	Fine	Mint
(per book)......	2.50	5.00	7.50

(Set 2)
#1 Donald Duck, Treasure of Timbuktu
 2 Mickey Mouse & Pluto, Operation China

	Good	Fine	Mint
3 Donald Duck in the Magic Cows			
4 Mickey Mouse & Goofy, Kid Kokonut			
5 Donald Duck, Mystery Ship			
6 Mickey Mouse, Phantom Sheriff			
7 Donald Duck, Circus Adventures			
8 Mickey Mouse, Arctic Explorers			
(per book)......	2.50	5.00	7.50

(Set 3)
#1 Donald Duck & Witch Hazel
 2 Mickey Mouse in Darkest Africa
 3 Donald Duck & Uncle Scrooge, Timber
    Trouble
 4 Mickey Mouse, Rajah's Rescue
 5 Donald Duck in Robot Reporter
 6 Mickey Mouse, Slumbering Sleuth
 7 Donald Duck in the Foreign Legion
 8 Mickey Mouse, Airwalking Wonder

	Good	Fine	Mint
(per book)......	2.50	5.00	7.50

CHESTER GUMP (See Lemix-Korlix)

CHESTY AND COPTIE
1946 (4 pgs.) (Giveaway) (Disney)
Los Angeles Community Chest

(Very Rare) by Floyd Gottfredson

	Good	Fine	Mint
	5.00	10.00	15.00

CHEWING GUM BOOKLET
1930's-40's? (2x2½", 8pgs., color cover &
illos inside with text (30 booklets known)
Chewing Gum Giveaway

Titles: each in several issues (6 each?)
    The Soldier of Fortune, Reckless Steele,
    Mirtho, the Clown, Operator #7 of the Sec-
    ret Service, Flash Brown the Super-Scien-

	Good	Fine	Mint
tist. each....	1.50	3.00	4.50

CHEYENNE (TV)
Oct, 1956 - #25, Dec-Jan, 1961-62
Dell Publishing Co.

	Good	Fine	Mint
4-Color #734,772,803	1.00	2.00	3.00
#4(8-10/57) - #12	.75	1.50	2.25
13-25	.50	1.00	1.50

CHEYENNE AUTUMN (See Movie Classics)

CHEYENNE KID (Wild Frontier #1-7)
#8, 1957 - #99, Nov, 1973
Charlton Comics

	Good	Fine	Mint
#8,9,13,15-20	.60	1.20	1.80
10-Three Williamson/Torres stories			
	3.50	7.00	10.50
11,12-Two Williamson/Torres stories each;			
#11-68pgs.	3.00	6.00	9.00
14-Williamson sty., 5pgs.	2.50	5.00	7.50
21,25-Severin cover & 3 stories each			
	1.20	2.40	3.60
22-24,27-29	.40	.80	1.20
26,30-Severin art	.80	1.60	2.40
31-59	.20	.40	.60
60-99: #66-Wander begins, ends #87. Apache			
Red begins #88, origin #89			
	.15	.30	.45

CHICAGO MAIL ORDER (See C-M-O Comics)

CHICAGO SUNDAY TRIBUNE COMIC BOOK MAGAZINE
1940 - 1943 (Similar to Spirit Sections)
(7-3/4"x10-3/4"; Full color; 16-24 pgs. each)
Chicago Tribune

	Good	Fine	Mint
1940 issues	6.00	12.00	18.00

(Chicago Sunday Tribune Comic Book Mag. cont'd)

	Good	Fine	Mint
1941, 1942 issues	5.00	10.00	15.00
1943 issues	4.00	8.00	12.00

NOTE: *Published weekly. Texas Slim, Kit Carson, Spooky, Josie, Nuts & Jolts, Lew Loyal, Brenda Starr, Daniel Boone, Captain Storm, Rocky, Smokey Stover, Tiny Tim, Little Joe, Fu Manchu appear among others. Early issues had photo stories with pictures from the movies; later issues had comic art.*

CHIEF, THE (Indian Chief #3 on)
1950, 1951
Dell Publishing Co.

	Good	Fine	Mint
4-Color #290, #2	1.75	3.50	5.25

CHIEF CRAZY HORSE
1950
Avon Periodicals

	Good	Fine	Mint
No#	5.00	10.00	15.00

CHIEF VICTORIO'S APACHE MASSACRE
1951
Avon Periodicals

	Good	Fine	Mint
No#-Williamson/Frazetta story(7pgs.); Kinstler cover	20.00	40.00	60.00

CHILDREN'S BIG BOOK
1945 (68 pgs.) (Stiff covers) (25¢)
Dorene Publ. Co.

Comics & fairy tales; art by David Icove

	Good	Fine	Mint
	2.50	5.00	7.50

CHILI (Millie's Rival)
April, 1969 - 1973
Marvel Comics Group

		Fine	Mint
#1		.15	.30
2-25		.10	.20
Special #1(12/71)		.15	.30

CHILLING ADVENTURES IN SORCERY (--As Told By Sabrina #1,2)(Red Circle Sorcery #6 on)
Sept, 1972 - #5, Feb, 1974
Archie Publications (Red Circle Prod.)

	Good	Fine	Mint
#1,2-Sabrina cameo in both	.70	1.40	2.10
3-Morrow art/covers, all	.50	1.00	1.50
4,5-Morrow cvr/art, 5,6pgs.	.40	.80	1.20

CHILLING TALES (Formerly Beware)
#13, Dec, 1952 - #17, Oct, 1953
Youthful Magazines

	Good	Fine	Mint
#13(#1)-Matt Fox cvr/sty.	2.50	5.00	7.50
14,16	1.25	2.50	3.75
15,17-Matt Fox covers	1.75	3.50	5.25

CHILLING TALES OF HORROR (Magazine)
V1#1, 6/69 - V1#7, 12/70; V2#2, 2/71 - V2#5, 10/71 (52 pgs.) (Black & White) (50¢)
Stanley Publications

	Good	Fine	Mint
V1#1	.65	1.35	2.00
2-7: #7-Cameron story	.40	.80	1.20
V2#2-Spirit of Frankenstein reprt/Adv. Into Unknown #16; V2#3,5	.35	.70	1.05
V2#4-Reprints 9pg. Feldstein story from Advs. Into Unknown #3	.65	1.35	2.00

CHILLY WILLY (See 4-Color #740,852,967, 1017,1074,1122,1177,1212,1281)

CHINA BOY (See Wisco)

CHIP 'N' DALE (Walt Disney)
11/53 - #30, 6-8/62; 9/67 - Present
Dell Publishing Co./Gold Key

	Good	Fine	Mint
4-Color #517,581,636	1.20	2.40	3.60
#4(12/55-2/56)-#10	.60	1.20	1.80
11-30	.40	.80	1.20
#1(G.K. reprints, '67)	.35	.70	1.05
2-10	.25	.50	.75
11-20	.20	.40	.60
21-57	.20	.20	.40

NOTE: *All Gold Key issues have reprints except #32-35,38-41,45-47. #23-28,30-42,45-47,49 have new covers.*

CHITTY CHITTY BANG BANG (See Movie Comics)

CHOICE COMICS
Dec, 1941 - #3, Feb, 1942
Great Publications

	Good	Fine	Mint
#1-Origin Secret Circle; Atlas the Mighty app.; Zomba, Jungle Fight, Kangaroo Man, & Fire Eater begin	15.00	30.00	45.00
2,3	8.00	16.00	24.00

CHOO CHOO CHARLIE
Dec, 1969
Gold Key

	Good	Fine	Mint
#1-John Stanley art	.70	1.40	2.10

CHOPPERTOONS (Magazine)
Summer, 1971 - #2, Fall, 1971 (52 pgs.)
TRM Publications

	Good	Fine	Mint
#1,2 (Motorcycle humor)	.40	.80	1.20

The Chief #2, © DELL

Chief Crazy Horse No #, © AVON

Chilly Willy Four Color #740, © DELL

Christmas In Disneyland #1, © WDP

Christmas Parade #2(1950), © WDP

Christmas Parade #4, © WDP

CHRISTIAN HEROES OF TODAY
1964   (36 pgs.)
David C. Cook

	Good	Fine	Mint
	.50	1.00	1.50

CHRISTMAS   (See A-1 #28)

CHRISTMAS ADVENTURE, A
1969
Gilberton (Stacey's Dept. Store Giveaway)

Some Alex Blum art - Reprint/Picture Parade #4 with new cvr.(1953)	1.00	2.00	3.00

CHRISTMAS ADVENTURE, THE
1963   (16 pgs.)
S. Rose (H.L. Green Giveaway)

	.40	.80	1.20

CHRISTMAS ALBUM   (See March of Comics #312)

CHRISTMAS & ARCHIE   ($1.00)
Jan, 1975   (68 pgs.)   (10¼x13¼")
Archie Comics

#1	1.00	2.00	3.00

CHRISTMAS AT THE ROTUNDA (Titled Ford Rotunda
Christmas Book 1957 on)   (Regular size)
Given away every Christmas at one location
1954 - 1961
Ford Motor Co.   (Western Printing)

1954-56 issues(no #'s)	1.35	2.75	4.00
1957-61 issues(no #'s)	.65	1.35	2.00

CHRISTMAS BELLS   (See March of Comics #297)

CHRISTMAS CARNIVAL
1952   (100 pgs.) (One Shot)
Ziff-Davis Publ. Co.

No#	3.00	6.00	9.00

CHRISTMAS CAROL, A   (See March of Comics #33)

CHRISTMAS DREAM, A
1950   (16 pgs.) (Kinney Shoe Store Giveaway)
Promotional Publishing Co.

No#	1.20	2.40	3.60

CHRISTMAS EVE, A   (See March of Comics #212)

CHRISTMAS IN DISNEYLAND
Dec, 1957   (25¢) (Disney)
Dell Publishing Co.

	Good	Fine	Mint
#1-Barks art, 18 pgs.	6.00	12.00	18.00

CHRISTMAS JOURNEY THROUGH SPACE
1960
Promotional Publishing Co.

Reprints 1954 issue Jolly Christmas Book with new slick cover	1.00	2.00	3.00

CHRISTMAS PARADE   (Walt Disney's)
Nov, 1949 - #9, Dec, 1957 (25¢) (#9-35¢)
Dell Publishing Co.

#1-Barks art-reprinted in G.K. Christmas Parade #5	30.00	60.00	90.00
2-Barks art-reprinted in G.K. Christmas Parade #6	16.00	32.00	48.00
3-7	3.00	6.00	9.00
8,9-(12/56-12/57)-Barks art	7.00	14.00	21.00

CHRISTMAS PARADE   (See March of Comics #284
and Dell Giant #26)

CHRISTMAS PARADE   (Walt Disney's)
1/63 - #9, 1/72; #1,5(80pgs.)#2-4,6-9(36pgs.)
Gold Key

#1 (30018-301)	3.00	6.00	9.00
2-Reprints 4-Color #367 by Barks	5.00	10.00	15.00
3-Reprints 4-Color #178 by Barks	5.00	10.00	15.00
4-Reprints 4-Color #203 by Barks	5.00	10.00	15.00
5-Reprints Christmas Parade #1(Dell) by Barks	5.00	10.00	15.00
6-Reprints Christmas Parade #2(Dell) by Barks	4.00	8.00	12.00
7,9: #7-Pull-out poster	2.00	4.00	6.00
8-Reprints 4-Color #367 by Barks; pull-out poster	5.00	10.00	15.00

CHRISTMAS PARTY   (See March of Comics #256)

CHRISTMAS ROUNDUP
1960
Promotional Publishing Co.

Marv Levy cvr/art	1.00	2.00	3.00

CHRISTMAS STORY   (See March of Comics #326)

CHRISTMAS STORY BOOK   (See Woolworth's
Christmas Book)

CHRISTMAS TREASURY, A   (See March of Comics
1954   (100 pgs.)   #227)

(A Christmas Treasury cont'd)
Dell Publishing Co.

	Good	Fine	Mint
#1	3.00	6.00	9.00

CHRISTMAS USA   (Through 300 Years)
1956   (Also see Uncle Sam's --)
Promotional Publ. Co.   (Giveaway)

	Good	Fine	Mint
Marv Levy cvr/art	1.00	2.00	3.00

CHRISTMAS WITH ARCHIE
1973   (52 pgs.) (49¢)
Spire Christian Comics (Fleming H. Revell Co.)

No#	.25	.50	.75

CHRISTMAS WITH MOTHER GOOSE (See 4-Color
#90,126,172,201,253)

CHRISTMAS WITH SANTA (See March of Comics #92)

CHUCKLE, THE GIGGLY BOOK OF COMIC ANIMALS
1945   (132 pgs.) (One Shot)
R. B. Leffingwell Co.

#1-Funny animal	2.50	5.00	7.50

CHUCK WAGON (See Sheriff Bob Dixon's --)

CICERO'S CAT
July-Aug, 1959 - #2, Sept-Oct, 1959
Dell Publishing Co.

#1,2	1.35	2.75	4.00

CIMARRON STRIP (TV)
January, 1968
Dell Publishing Co.

#1	.35	.70	1.05

CINDERELLA (See 4-Color #272,786, & Movie
Comics)

CINDERELLA IN "FAIREST OF THE FAIR"
1955   (14 pgs.) (Walt Disney)
American Dairy Assn.   (Premium)

No#	3.00	6.00	9.00

CINDERELLA LOVE
10-11/49 - #11, 4-5/51; #12, 2/54 - #15,
8/54; #25, 12/54 - #29, 10/55
Ziff-Davis/St. John Publ. Co. #12 on

#1(1st Series)	2.00	4.00	6.00
2-8,12(9/51)	.90	1.80	2.70

	Good	Fine	Mint
9-Kinstler story	1.50	3.00	4.50
10-Ogden Whitney painted cover			
	1.25	2.50	3.75
11-Crandall story; Saunders painted cover			
	2.25	4.50	6.75
12(St. John-10/53)-#14	.80	1.60	2.40
15-Matt Baker cover	1.50	3.00	4.50
25(2nd Series)(Formerly Romantic Marriage)			
	1.00	2.00	3.00
26-Baker cover	1.50	3.00	4.50
27,28	.70	1.40	2.10
29-Matt Baker cover (Formerly Crazy Comics?)			
	1.50	3.00	4.50

CINDY (-- Smith #40; Crime Can't Win #41?)
1947 - #40, July, 1950
Timely Comics

#27-Kurtzman art, 3 pgs.	3.00	6.00	9.00
28-31-Kurtzman art	2.00	4.00	6.00
32-40	1.00	2.00	3.00

NOTE: *Kurtzman's "Hey Look"-#27,29-31;
"Giggles 'N' Grins"-#28.*

CIRCUS (-- the Comic Riot)
June, 1938 - #3, Aug, 1938
Globe Syndicate

#1-Spacehawk (2 pgs.), Disk Eyes by Wolverton (2 pgs.), Pewee Throttle by Cole(1st comic book work), Beau Gus, Ken Craig & The Lords of Crillon, Jack Hinton by Eisner, Van Bragger by Kane	60.00	120.00	180.00
2,3-Eisner, Cole, Wolverton, Bob Kane art in each	30.00	60.00	90.00

CIRCUS BOY (See 4-Color #759,785,813)

CIRCUS COMICS
1945 - #2, June, 1945; Winter, 1948-49
Farm Women's Publishing Co./D.S. Publ.

#1	1.20	2.40	3.60
2	.60	1.20	1.80
1(1948)-D.S. Publ.; 2pgs. Frazetta			
	8.00	16.00	24.00

CIRCUS OF FUN COMICS
1945 - 1947 (A book of games & puzzles)
A. W. Nugent Publishing Co.

#1-3	1.00	2.00	3.00

CIRCUS WORLD (See Movie Classics)

CISCO KID
Winter, 1944 - #3, 1945

Cinderella Love #4, © Z-D

Cindy #33, © MCG

Circus Of Fun #3, © A.W. Nugent

The Cisco Kid #33, © DELL   Claire Voyant #4, © STD   Classic Comics #9, © GIL

(Cisco Kid cont'd)
Bernard Bailey/Swappers Quarterly

	Good	Fine	Mint
#1-Giunta art	4.00	8.00	12.00
2,3	2.50	5.00	7.50

CISCO KID COMICS (TV)
July, 1951 - #41, Oct-Dec, 1958
Dell Publishing Co.

4-Color #292(#1)-1950	3.00	6.00	9.00
#2(1/51)-#5	1.75	3.50	5.25
6-20	1.20	2.40	3.60
21-41	.80	1.60	2.40

CITIZEN SMITH (See Holyoke One-Shot #9)

CITY OF THE LIVING DEAD (Movie?)
1952   (See Fantastic Tales #1)
Avon Periodicals

No#-One pg. Kinstler art	8.00	16.00	24.00

CITY SURGEON (Blake Harper --)
August, 1963
Gold Key

#1(10075-308)	.50	1.00	1.50

CIVIL WAR MUSKET, THE
(Kadets of America Handbook)
1960   (36 pgs.) (1/2 Size) (25¢)
Custom Comics, Inc.

No#	1.00	2.00	3.00

CLAIRE VOYANT (Also see Keen Teens)
1946 - 1947   (Sparling strip reprints)
Leader Publ./Standard/Pentagon Publ.

#1	17.50	35.00	52.50
2-Kamen cover	12.00	24.00	36.00
3-Bridal cover by Kamen; contents mentioned in Love and Death, a book by Gershom Legman('49) referenced by Dr. Wertham	25.00	50.00	75.00
4-Classic Kamen bondage cover	14.00	28.00	42.00

CLANCY THE COP
1930 - 1931   (52 pgs.) (B&W) (Not reprints)
Dell Publishing Co.

#1,2-Vep art	4.00	8.00	12.00

UNDERSTANDING THE CLASSICS
By Charles Heffelfinger

The Classic Comics section of the Price Guide, divided as it is into several categories and subcategories, may appear quite formidable to those unfamiliar with the series. For those who hesitate to wade through the listings section by section, here is a brief background and a few definitions which we hope will simplify the detailed listings which follow.

I. SERIES TITLE. The series commonly known as Classic Comics began as "Classic Comics Presents" in 1941. The first five issues were titled "Classic Comics Presents;" Nos. 6 and 7 were "Classic Comics Library," but basically the first 34 issues were known as "Classic Comics." With No. 35, published in March, 1947, the title was changed to "Classics Illustrated," which was thought to more accurately represent the contents. All reprints and new issues from that date on have the "Classics Illustrated" logo.

II. ORIGINALS VS. REPRINTS. Unlike most comic books, most issues of Classics were reprinted regularly, usually every year or two, since the first time they were issued, much like many paperback books. The resulting multiplicity of editions of each title, with a variety of different covers, interior art, logos, dates, and number of pages, is very confusing to the general public and dealers alike. Basically, though, it is important to be able to distinguish between an **original** or **first edition** and reprints. Virtually all first editions have, usually on the inside cover, a promotional ad for the issue to be published next, while on reprints this ad was removed. There are few exceptions to this. Reprints of No. 55 and 57 published at the time of No. 75 have been found in which the "Coming Next" ad was inadvertently left in. Also, the last two issues, Nos. 168 and 169, which were published after the series changed ownership, do not have the "Coming Next" ad, even though first editions. Some collectors believe No. 169 was published before No. 168 in the U. S.

III. DATING AND REORDER LIST. Nearly all Classics contain, usually on the back cover, a list of titles in the series that were available at the time that issue was published. The publishers kept all titles in print up through the first 57 issues; after that, gaps started appearing in the checklist. The order list on a first edition only goes up to that issue's number or the one preceding it following it. The number of the last title on the list, known as the Highest Reorder Number (HRN) is very important, since in the case of reprints, it often provides the only clue to the date of the comic. Reprints with a HRN between 78 and 161, covering the period from December 1950 to March 1961, carried the date of the first printing of that issue regardless of the actual age of the reprint. Thus it is common to see a Classic with a checklist of titles ending in the 150's with a date in the 1940's, though the comic was actually published in 1959! In such cases, the date of the reprint is the same as that of the last title on the list. (You must have a first edition of the latter title to obtain the approximate date.) Obviously, a copy of No. 28 with an order list ending in No. 115 was printed much later than the original No. 28.

During the 1940's, most issues were undated, and starting in September 1963 the actual date of reprinting was used for the first time. Reprints and originals of the first 80 issues can also be distinguished by the price; first editions of Nos. 1-80 were all marked 10 cents on the front cover, while on reprints no price, or simply "15 cents in Canada" was shown.

IV. COVERS. The first 80 issues of Classics had what is known as line drawing covers, which were reproduced, like the interior art, from drawings pencilled and inked by the artist. All issues from No. 81 on, however, had painted covers, which were reproduced from actual paintings in oil, gauche, or acrylic. Gradually all but 10 of the first 80 issues had their covers replaced with new painted covers, too. Except for minor variations, only four issues had more than one line drawing cover, while about 31 issues had a second painted cover. About 30 issues got new interior art as well, thus resulting in a variety of different issues of the same title. Many collectors try to obtain copies of each different cover and interior art for each title.

If, after reading this, you are still confused, don't worry. Even the publisher apparently kept poor records of the earliest issues, and thus often listed supposedly original dates for reprints that were at variance by as much as a year from the actual date of the original printing of that issue!

CLASSIC COMICS (See America in Action, Stories by Famous Authors, Story of the Commandos, & The World Around Us)

CLASSIC COMICS (--'s Illustrated #35 on)
Oct, 1941 - #34, Feb, 1947
Gilberton Publications

(Classic Comics cont'd)

CLASSIC COMICS. Classic Comics first appeared in October 1941 and were issued randomly until July 1945, at which time a monthly schedule was established. Reprints of first editions appeared almost immediately and are described in detail in the reprint listing. The last Classic Comics title was "Mysterious Island," published in February 1947. The first Classics Illustrated was "The Last Days of Pompeii," published in March 1947. The original covers of issues 29, 35, 38, 41, 53, 56, 61, 65, 66, 71, 73, 74, 90 and 93 were never reprinted. The last issue with a line drawing cover was No. 80, "White Fang." Starting in September 1963, the date of reprinting rather than the original printing date was listed inside the front cover. NOTE: All originals (first editions) of Classics have a promotional ad for the next issue, except No. 168 and 169. Reprints rarely have this ad.

	Good	Fine	Mint
#1-The Three Musketeers	80.00	160.00	240.00
2-Ivanhoe	40.00	80.00	120.00
3-The Count of Monte Cristo	30.00	60.00	90.00
4-The Last of the Mohicans	25.00	50.00	75.00
5-Moby Dick	25.00	50.00	75.00
6-A Tale of Two Cities	18.00	36.00	54.00
7-Robin Hood	20.00	40.00	60.00
8-Arabian Nights	40.00	80.00	120.00
9-Les Miserables	20.00	40.00	60.00
10-Robinson Crusoe-Used in <u>Seduction of the Innocent</u>, pg. 142	17.50	35.00	52.50
11-Don Quixote	17.50	35.00	52.50
12-Rip Van Winkle & the Headless Horseman	25.00	50.00	75.00
13-Dr. Jekyll & Mr. Hyde	15.00	30.00	45.00
14-Westward Ho!	60.00	120.00	180.00
15-Uncle Tom's Cabin-Used in <u>Seduction of the Innocent</u>, pg.102,103	20.00	40.00	60.00
16-Gulliver's Travels	15.00	30.00	45.00
17-The Deerslayer	12.00	24.00	36.00
18-The Hunchback of Notre Dame	14.00	28.00	42.00
19-Huckleberry Finn	10.00	20.00	30.00
20-The Corsican Brothers	12.00	24.00	36.00
21-Three Famous Mysteries-"The Sign of the 4," "The Murders in the Rue Morgue," "The Flayed Hand"	20.00	40.00	60.00
22-The Pathfinder	10.00	20.00	30.00
23-Oliver Twist	10.00	20.00	30.00
24-Connecticut Yankee in King Arthur's Court	10.00	20.00	30.00
25-Two Years Before the Mast	12.00	24.00	36.00
26-Frankenstein	20.00	40.00	60.00
27-The Adventures of Marco Polo	10.00	20.00	30.00
28-Michael Strogoff	10.00	20.00	30.00
29-The Prince & the Pauper	15.00	30.00	45.00
30-The Moonstone	10.00	20.00	30.00
31-The Black Arrow	10.00	20.00	30.00
32-Lorna Doone-Matt Baker art	12.00	24.00	36.00
33-Adventures of Sherlock Holmes	30.00	60.00	90.00
34-Mysterious Island	10.00	20.00	30.00

CLASSIC COMICS REPRINTS. The first reprinting of Classic Comics occurred in April 1943, when Numbers 1, 2, 3 and 5 received their second printing. Two months later (June 1943) No. 4 was reprinted and from then on reprintings were scheduled every few months. Besides Elliot Publishing Company (a Gilberton name) and Gilberton, eight other printers published Classic Comics during the period April 1943 to October 1944. Many of these printers were neighborhood weeklies in the greater New York City area. The known printers are:

Conray Products	The Richmond Courier
Island Publishing	The Long Island Independent
The Nassau Bulletin	Queens County Times
Queens Home News	Sunrise Times

One reason suggested for so many printers was the lack of newsprint available because of World War II. Another was the wholesale purchases by the American Red Cross for distribution to servicemen around the world. Issues 18-22 had several printers for original editions. This was the only period when a publisher other than Elliot or Gilberton printed first editions. Reprints from this period have reorder lists to 10-22 when printed by other publishers. The last two reprints occurred in June 1946 (28) and September 1946 (30). Classic Comics 28-34 were never reprinted as "Comics" as the new look of "Illustrated" was planned for March 1947 with the issuance of "The Last Days of Pompeii."

The following three sections have descriptions of the particular editions appropriate to each period. Specific comments applicable to the editions discussed should be reviewed for a complete understanding of this most complicated printing schedule.

SECTION I

Section I lists Classic Comics Reprints with Highest Reorder Number (HRN) of 15 or lower. These editions represent the first or second reprint of early Classic Comics and are very much in demand. In most cases they are identical to originals, except for the price on the cover (10 cents) and the promotion for the next issue, which occupied the entire back cover up through title number 14.

NOTE: Title Number 11 has not been reported with a HRN of 15 or lower. Letters in Parenthesis after edition refer to printers: "E" for Elliot Publishing Company (a Gilberton front!), "L" for Long Island Independent and "C" for Conray Products.

Title#	Eds./Publishers				
1	2	(E - L)	8.00	16.00	24.00
2	2	(E - L)	8.00	16.00	24.00
3	2	(E - L,C)	8.00	16.00	24.00
4	2	(E - L)	8.00	16.00	24.00
5	2	(E - C)	8.00	16.00	24.00
6	1	(E)	12.00	24.00	36.00
7	1	(E)	12.00	24.00	36.00
8	1	(E)	17.00	34.00	51.00
9	1	(E)	12.00	24.00	36.00
10	1	(E)	8.00	16.00	24.00
12	1	(L)	8.00	16.00	24.00
13	1	(L)	8.00	16.00	24.00
14	1	(L)	17.00	34.00	51.00
15	1	(L)	12.00	24.00	36.00

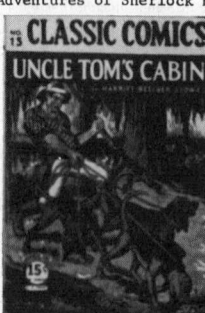

Classic Comics #15, © GIL

Classic Comics #18, © GIL

Classic Comics #20, © GIL

80

Classic Comics #23, © GIL

Classic Comics #27, © GIL

Classic Comics #33, © GIL

(Classic Comics cont'd)

SECTION II

This section lists Classic Comics reprints with Highest Reorder Numbers (HRN's) between 17 and 22. these editions are from the most confusing period in Gilberton's history. Many editions were being printed at the same time by different printers. In some cases, entire printings were purchased by the American Red Cross and sent overseas to servicemen or placed in the now famous boxes, or both, and hence saw very limited distribution on the newsstands. The first Canadian reprint editions also began showing up during this era. The reprint for title number 20 is unique as it represents the only known edition with a white background for the "Classic Comics" banner. It was printed by the Queen's County Times (T). Other codes used for printers are: Island Publishing (I), Nassau Bulletin (N), Queen's Home News (Q), Sunrise Times (S) and Richmond Courier (R). Another feature of this period was the multiple printings of originals or first printings advertising the subsequent title. This was unique in the printing history of first editions and saw the following: First editions of "The Hunchback of Notre Dame" by Gilberton and Island Publishing; "Corsican Brothers" by Gilberton, Richmond Courier and Long Island Independent; "Three Famous Mysteries" by Gilberton, Richmond Courier and Island Publishing; "Pathfinder" by Gilberton, Island Publishing and Queen's County times, and "Huckleberry Finn" by Gilberton and Island Publishing Company.

Title#	Eds./Publishers		Good	Fine	Mint
1	2	(R – S)	6.00	12.00	18.00
2	2	(R – S)	6.00	12.00	18.00
3	2	(R – S)	6.00	12.00	18.00
4	2	(L – Q)	6.00	12.00	18.00
5	2	(S)	6.00	12.00	18.00
6	2	(L – S)	9.00	18.00	27.00
7	2	(L – N)	9.00	18.00	27.00
8	2	(L – N)	12.00	24.00	36.00
9	2	(N – R,T)	9.00	18.00	27.00
10	2	(N – Q)	6.00	12.00	18.00
11	2	(N – Q)	6.00	12.00	18.00
12	1	(T)	6.00	12.00	18.00
13	1	(T)	6.00	12.00	18.00
14	1	(Q)	12.00	24.00	36.00
15	1	(N)	9.00	18.00	27.00
16	2	(Q – T)	6.00	12.00	18.00
17	2	(N – T,Q)	6.00	12.00	18.00
18	2	(Q – T)	6.00	12.00	18.00
19	2	(N – T)	6.00	12.00	18.00
20	1	(T)	7.00	14.00	21.00
21	1	(N)	8.00	16.00	24.00

SECTION III

The final section of Classic Comic Reprints is refreshing for its rationality and integrity of printing sequence. All of these editions were published by Gilberton. There was only one edition of each title number. For title numbers 1-20 the Highest Reorder Number (HRN) was (28), for 21-27 the reorder number was (30). All of these editions had identical logos, the now familiar "Classic Comics" one inch black and yellow banner across the top of the front cover. This banner first appeared with title number 9 and replaced the many false starts, in searching for an enduring logo, such as "Classic Comics Presents" (1-5) and "Classic Comics Library" (6,7). Title numbers 8 and 11, while using the logo "Classic Comics" had individualized presentations until later editions formalized the described banner.

Title#	Good	Fine	Mint
1	4.00	8.00	12.00
2	4.00	8.00	12.00
3	4.00	8.00	12.00
4	4.00	8.00	12.00
5	4.00	8.00	12.00
6	6.00	12.00	18.00
7-Saks 34th Ave. Christmas Giveaway (Diff. cover-same interior art) (Rare)	20.00	40.00	60.00
7-Robin Hood & His Merry Men, The Ill. Story of (Flour giveaway) Circa 1947	20.00	40.00	60.00
7	6.00	12.00	18.00
8	9.00	18.00	27.00
9	6.00	12.00	18.00
10	4.00	8.00	12.00
11	4.00	8.00	12.00
12	4.00	8.00	12.00
13	4.00	8.00	12.00
14	9.00	18.00	27.00
15	6.00	12.00	18.00
16	4.00	8.00	12.00
17	4.00	8.00	12.00
18	4.00	8.00	12.00
19	4.00	8.00	12.00
20	6.00	12.00	18.00
21	7.00	14.00	21.00
22	4.00	8.00	12.00
23	4.00	8.00	12.00
24	4.00	8.00	12.00
25	4.00	8.00	12.00
26	8.00	16.00	24.00
27	4.00	8.00	12.00

CLASSIC COMICS LIBRARY GIFT BOX
(Later boxes titled Classics Illustrated --)

These Gift Boxes first appeared in November 1943. They were (at least according to the advertising) designed with the boys in service in mind. The buyer was told that "the boys relax with Classic Comics." The boxes held five Classics. They began to sell for 50 cents and ceased publication at a price of 79 cents. The earlier series is worth more and are more colorful.

Classic Comics boxes:

	Good	Fine	Mint
Box A,B,C,D	20.00	40.00	60.00
1952 Christmas Box-held #64,76,83 & 98 (reprints)	12.00	24.00	36.00

NOTE: *These boxes were priced at 50¢. Box A held reprints of #1-5; Box B-#6-10; Box C-#11-15; & Box D-#16-20.*

Classics Illustrated boxes:

	Good	Fine	Mint
Boxes with 59¢ price	12.00	24.00	36.00
Boxes with 69¢ price	9.00	18.00	27.00
Boxes with 79¢ price	8.00	16.00	24.00

NOTE: *Condition of box should be graded, also.*

CLASSICS ILLUSTRATED (Formerly Classic Comics)
#35, Mar, 1947 - #169, Winter, 1971
Gilberton Publications

	Good	Fine	Mint
#35-The Last Days of Pompeii	14.00	28.00	42.00
36-Typee	6.00	12.00	18.00
37-The Pioneers	6.00	12.00	18.00
38-The Advs. of Cellini	10.00	20.00	30.00
39-Jane Eyre	10.00	20.00	30.00
40-Mysteries - "The Pit and the Pendulum," "The Advs. of Hans Pfall," "The Fall of the House of Usher"; Used in <u>Seduction of the Innocent</u>	15.00	30.00	45.00
41-Twenty Yrs. After	15.00	30.00	45.00
42-Swiss Family Robinson	7.00	14.00	21.00
43-Great Expectations-Used in <u>Seduction of the Innocent</u>, pg.311	40.00	80.00	120.00
44-Mysteries of Paris-Used in <u>Seduction of the Innocent</u>, pg.323	15.00	30.00	45.00
45-Tom Brown's School Days	8.00	16.00	24.00
46-Kidnapped	5.00	10.00	15.00
47-Twenty Thousand Leagues Under the Sea	5.00	10.00	15.00
48-David Copperfield	5.00	10.00	15.00
49-Alice in Wonderland	8.00	16.00	24.00
50-The Advs. of Tom Sawyer-Used in <u>Seduction of the Innocent</u>, pg.37	7.00	14.00	21.00
51-The Spy	4.00	8.00	12.00
52-The House of 7 Gables	4.00	8.00	12.00
53-A Christmas Carol	6.00	12.00	18.00
54-The Man in the Iron Mask	4.00	8.00	12.00
55-Silas Marner-Used in <u>Seduction of the Innocent</u>, pg.311,312	4.00	8.00	12.00
56-Toilers of the Sea	7.00	14.00	21.00
57-The Song of Hiawatha	3.00	6.00	9.00
58-The Prairie	3.50	7.00	10.50
59-Wuthering Heights	6.00	12.00	18.00
60-Black Beauty	3.50	7.00	10.50
61-The Woman in White	4.00	8.00	12.00
62-Western Stories - "The Luck of Roaring Camp" and "The Outcasts of Poker Flat"	4.00	8.00	12.00
63-The Man Without a Country	3.50	7.00	10.50
64-Treasure Island	3.50	7.00	10.50
65-Biography of Ben Franklin	3.00	6.00	9.00
65-Ben Franklin Store giveaway, 52pgs. (Rare)	20.00	40.00	60.00
66-The Cloister & the Hearth	9.00	18.00	27.00
67-The Scottish Chiefs	3.00	6.00	9.00
68-Julius Caesar	3.00	6.00	9.00
69-Around the World in 80 Days	5.00	10.00	15.00

	Good	Fine	Mint
70-The Pilot	2.50	5.00	7.50
71-The Man Who Laughs	4.00	8.00	12.00
72-The Oregon Trail	2.50	5.00	7.50
73-The Black Tulip	8.00	16.00	24.00
74-Mr. Midshipman Easy	8.00	16.00	24.00
75-The Lady of the Lake	4.00	8.00	12.00
76-The Prisoner of Zenda	3.00	6.00	9.00
77-The Iliad	2.50	5.00	7.50
78-Joan of Arc	2.50	5.00	7.50
79-Cyrano de Bergerac	2.50	5.00	7.50
80-White Fang - last issue with line drawn cover	3.00	6.00	9.00
81-The Odyssey	2.50	5.00	7.50
82-The Master of Ballantrae	2.50	5.00	7.50
83-The Jungle Book	2.50	5.00	7.50
84-The Gold Bug & other stories - "The Gold Bug," "The Tell-Tale Heart," "The Cask of Amontillado"	3.50	7.00	10.50
85-The Sea Wolf	2.50	5.00	7.50
86-Under Two Flags	2.50	5.00	7.50
87-A Midsummer Night's Dream	2.50	5.00	7.50
88-Men of Iron	2.00	4.00	6.00
89-Crime & Punishment	2.25	4.50	6.75
90-Green Mansions	2.50	5.00	7.50
91-The Call of the Wild	2.00	4.00	6.00
92-The Courtship of Miles Standish	2.50	5.00	7.50
93-Pudd'nhead Wilson	2.00	4.00	6.00
94-David Balfour	2.00	4.00	6.00
95-All Quiet on the Western Front	3.50	7.00	10.50
96-Daniel Boone	2.50	5.00	7.50
97-King Solomon's Mines	2.00	4.00	6.00
98-The Red Badge of Courage	1.50	3.00	4.50
99-Hamlet	2.00	4.00	6.00
100-Mutiny on the Bounty	1.50	3.00	4.50
101-William Tell	1.50	3.00	4.50
102-The White Company	2.50	5.00	7.50
103-Men Against the Sea	1.50	3.00	4.50
104-Bring 'em Back Alive	1.50	3.00	4.50
105-From the Earth to the Moon	2.00	4.00	6.00
106-Buffalo Bill	2.00	4.00	6.00
107-The King of the Khyber Rifles	1.50	3.00	4.50
108-Knights of the Round Table	2.00	4.00	6.00
109-Pitcairn's Island	1.50	3.00	4.50
110-A Study in Scarlet	4.00	8.00	12.00
111-The Talisman-Kiefer's last art	4.00	8.00	12.00
112-The Adventures of Kit Carson	3.00	6.00	9.00
113-The 45 Guardsmen	3.00	6.00	9.00

Classics Illustrated #35, © GIL

Classics Illustrated #45, © GIL

Classics Illustrated #55, © GIL

Classics Illustrated #63, © GIL   Classics Illustrated #89, © GIL   Classics Illustrated #163, © GIL

(Classics Ill. cont'd)	Good	Fine	Mint
114-The Red Rover	3.00	6.00	9.00
115-How I Found Livingstone			
	2.50	5.00	7.50
116-The Bottle Imp	2.50	5.00	7.50
117-Captains Courageous	2.50	5.00	7.50
118-Rob Roy	3.00	6.00	9.00
119-Soldiers of Fortune	3.00	6.00	9.00
120-The Hurricane	2.50	5.00	7.50
121-Wild Bill Hickok	3.00	6.00	9.00
122-The Mutineers	2.00	4.00	6.00
123-Fang and Claw	3.00	6.00	9.00
124-The War of the Worlds	1.75	3.50	5.25
125-The Ox-Box Incident	1.75	3.50	5.25
126-The Downfall	1.75	3.50	5.25
127-The King of the Mtns.	1.75	3.50	5.25
128-Macbeth-A. Blum art	2.00	4.00	6.00
129-Davy Crockett	2.50	5.00	7.50
130-Caesar's Conquests	1.75	3.50	5.25
131-The Covered Wagon	2.50	5.00	7.50
132-The Dark Frigate	2.50	5.00	7.50
133-The Time Machine	2.50	5.00	7.50
134-Romeo & Juliet	1.60	3.20	4.80
135-Waterloo	1.75	3.50	5.25
136-Lord Jim	1.75	3.50	5.25
137-The Little Savage	2.50	5.00	7.50
138-A Journey to the Center of the Earth			
	2.50	5.00	7.50
139-In the Reign of Terror			
	1.75	3.50	5.25
140-On Jungle Trails	1.50	3.00	4.50
141-Castle Dangerous	1.50	3.00	4.50
142-Abraham Lincoln	2.50	5.00	7.50
143-Kim - Orlando art	1.50	3.00	4.50
144-The First Men in the Moon - Williamson/			
Evans art	3.00	6.00	9.00
145-The Crisis	1.50	3.00	4.50
146-With Fire & Sword	1.50	3.00	4.50
147-Ben Hur - Orlando art	2.50	5.00	7.50
148-The Buccaneer	1.50	3.00	4.50
149-Off on a Comet	1.50	3.00	4.50
150-The Virginian	2.50	5.00	7.50
151-Won by the Sword	1.50	3.00	4.50
152-Wild Animals I Have Known			
	2.50	5.00	7.50
153-The Invisible Man	2.00	4.00	6.00
154-The Conspiracy of Pontiac			
	1.75	3.50	5.25
155-The Lion of the North	1.50	3.00	4.50
156-The Conquest of Mexico			
	1.75	3.50	5.25
157-Lives of the Hunted	1.50	3.00	4.50
158-The Conspirators	1.50	3.00	4.50
159-The Octopus	1.75	3.50	5.25
160-The Food of the Gods	1.75	3.50	5.25
161-Cleopatra	3.00	6.00	9.00
162-Robur the Conqueror - Gray Morrow art			
	2.00	4.00	6.00

	Good	Fine	Mint
163-Master of the World	2.00	4.00	6.00
164-The Cossack Chief	1.50	3.00	4.50
165-The Queen's Necklace	2.00	4.00	6.00
166-Tigers & Traitors	2.00	4.00	6.00
167-Faust	4.00	8.00	12.00
168-In Freedom's Cause	1.25	2.50	3.75
169-Negro Americans-The Early Years (Scarce)			
	5.00	10.00	15.00

CLASSICS ILLUSTRATED (Line Drawing Reprints). The first Classics Illustrated reprint was issued in April 1947. At that time Gilberton reprinted issues 1—5. In September 1948, Issues 6—10, 28 and 31 were reprinted, then 14, 15 and 33 in November 1948, and 21 in January 1949. After this period the deluge of reprints began with June 1949 through May 1950 seeing reprints of almost all issues. In all cases but four, the covers bearing the new logo are unchanged from the original comics. The issues changed (13, 18, 29 and 41) were objected to by Dr. Wertham because of violent covers. Several others which had been reprinted were terminated because of "violent" covers. Among these were 20, 36, 40, 43 and 44. No reason is known for not reprinting 11, 35, 53, 56, 61, 65 and 66. Issue 38 was said to be suppressed because of religious bias; 71, 73 and 74 may have been destroyed in the Spring flood in 1951 which damaged much of Gilberton's plant in Brooklyn, New York. Generally, the line drawing reprints continued to be published until May 1955, although several continued further and 17 and 37 were reprinted as late as 1966 with line covers. Either because of higher quality control or new color presses, the line drawing reprints from August 1953 (110) to November 1955 (129) are brilliant when compared to earlier reprints and first editions. From a collector's standpoint these reprints, while not as old as others, are more desirable than one with a lower number. Another consideration in valuing line reprints is the contents. In several cases, whole pages of art were clipped; in others panels were omitted and rearranged. Some original 56-page issues were clipped to 48 pages and some 64-page issues to 56, etc. Only a page-by-page comparison with a first edition can show whether or not a reprint has been clipped. The older the reprint the more likely all original art is included. Numbers omitted below have never been reported as line reprints. Editions refers to the number of editions reprinted.

The following listing differentiates LDR's into two sections, April 1947 (36) to October 1949 (64) and April 1950 (70) and later. The first section generally consists of first or extremely early reprintings with the new "Classics Illustrated" logo, clearly more desirable from a collector's standpoint than the later reprintings. To list the LDR's all together does not accurately reflect the everyday activity of market forces and, consequently, they are described here in two sections. The LDR's in Section I generally have all original artwork intact from the first edition. Many are 64 pages in length, as the first edition Classic Comics was, and therefore in demand. The LDR's in Section II generally have pages clipped to get down to a 48-page size and, consequently, are less in demand by collectors.

SECTION I

All issues listed below have HRN ( )'s of 64 or lower. Where issue numbers are not listed, the title does not exist as a Line Drawn Reprint (LDR) in the range specified.

*Indicates cover changed from Classic Comics or first edition.

Title#	Editions			
1	3	1.75	3.50	5.25
2	3	1.75	3.50	5.25
3	3	1.75	3.50	5.25
4	3	1.75	3.50	5.25
5	3	1.75	3.50	5.25

Title#	Editions	Good	Fine	Mint
6	2	1.75	3.50	5.25
7	3	1.75	3.50	5.25
8	2	6.00	12.00	18.00
9	1	3.00	6.00	9.00
10	2	1.75	3.50	5.25
12	2	1.75	3.50	5.25
13*	2	1.75	3.50	5.25
14	1	6.00	12.00	18.00
15	1	3.00	6.00	9.00
16	3	1.75	3.50	5.25
17	2	1.75	3.50	5.25
18*	2	1.75	3.50	5.25
19	2	1.75	3.50	5.25
20	2	4.00	8.00	12.00
21	2	5.00	10.00	15.00
22	1	1.75	3.50	5.25
23	2	1.75	3.50	5.25
24	2	1.75	3.50	5.25
25	2	1.75	3.50	5.25
26	2	3.00	6.00	9.00
28	1	6.00	12.00	18.00
29*	2	1.75	3.50	5.25
30	1	3.00	6.00	9.00
31	1	1.75	3.50	5.25
32	1	1.75	3.50	5.25
33	1	9.00	18.00	27.00
34	2	1.75	3.50	5.25
36	1	3.00	6.00	9.00
37	1	3.00	6.00	9.00
39	2	3.00	6.00	9.00
40	1	6.00	12.00	18.00
41*	1	1.75	3.50	5.25
42	1	1.75	3.50	5.25
43	1	20.00	40.00	60.00
44	1	6.00	12.00	18.00
45	1	4.00	8.00	12.00
46	1	1.75	3.50	5.25
47	1	1.75	3.50	5.25
48	1	1.75	3.50	5.25
49	1	3.00	6.00	9.00
50	1	3.00	6.00	9.00

Title#	Editions	Good	Fine	Mint
23	4	1.25	2.50	3.75
24	3	1.25	2.50	3.75
25	3	1.25	2.50	3.75
26	3	2.50	5.00	7.50
27	3	1.25	2.50	3.75
29*	3	1.25	2.50	3.75
30	1	2.50	5.00	7.50
31	3	1.25	2.50	3.75
32	2	1.25	2.50	3.75
33	2	7.00	14.00	21.00
34	4	1.25	2.50	3.75
37	7	1.25	2.50	3.75
39	3	1.25	2.50	3.75
40	2	6.00	12.00	18.00
41*	1	1.25	2.50	3.75
42	3	1.25	2.50	3.75
44	1	6.00	12.00	18.00
46	3	1.25	2.50	3.75
47	3	1.25	2.50	3.75
48	1	1.25	2.50	3.75
49	1	2.50	5.00	7.50
50	5	1.25	2.50	3.75
51	2	1.25	2.50	3.75
52	2	1.25	2.50	3.75
54	2	1.25	2.50	3.75
55	2	1.25	2.50	3.75
57	3	1.25	2.50	3.75
58	4	1.25	2.50	3.75
59	2	2.50	5.00	7.50
60	2	2.50	5.00	7.50
62	2	1.25	2.50	3.75
63	1	2.50	5.00	7.50
64	2	1.25	2.50	3.75
67	2	1.25	2.50	3.75
68	2	1.25	2.50	3.75
69	2	1.25	2.50	3.75
70	2	1.25	2.50	3.75
72	2	1.25	2.50	3.75
75	2	1.25	2.50	3.75
76	2	1.25	2.50	3.75
77	2	1.25	2.50	3.75
78	2	1.25	2.50	3.75
79	2	1.25	2.50	3.75
80	2	1.25	2.50	3.75

SECTION II

All issues listed below have HRN's ( )'s of 70 or higher. Where issue numbers are not listed the title does not exist as a Line Drawn Reprint (LDR) in the range specified.

I*Indicates cover art changed from Classic Comics or first edition.

NOTE: Because of unusually fine brilliance in cover reproduction, CI's LDR's with Highest Reorder Numbers (HRN's) between 110 and 129, inclusive, generally command a premium (10 to 15 per cent) over other editions in this range. This premium should be added only if the item is in fine or better condition. With this exception, as a general rule the lower the HRN, the more desirable the item.

Title#	Editions	Good	Fine	Mint
1	3	1.25	2.50	3.75
2	4	1.25	2.50	3.75
3	3	1.25	2.50	3.75
4	3	1.25	2.50	3.75
5	3	1.25	2.50	3.75
6	3	1.25	2.50	3.75
7	4	1.25	2.50	3.75
8	1	4.50	9.00	13.50
9	2	2.50	5.00	7.50
10	3	1.25	2.50	3.75
12	3	1.25	2.50	3.75
13*	2	1.25	2.50	3.75
15	2	2.50	5.00	7.50
16	2	1.25	2.50	3.75
17	4	1.25	2.50	3.75
18*	3	1.25	2.50	3.75
19	3	1.25	2.50	3.75
20	2	3.50	7.00	10.50
21	2	4.00	8.00	12.00
22	5	1.25	2.50	3.75

INTRODUCTION OF NEW ART AND NEW COVERS

The following title numbers were changed as to interior art, covers or both, at period indicated. Where integrity of the Highest Reorder Number (HRN) system is maintained (through 163) this number in parenthesis identifies the first introduction of the new art/cover. Where HRN identification is not meaningful, the date of the reprint is shown in parenthesis. The month/season and year is shown in these cases, e. g. 11/63: November 1963; R/68: Reissued 1968, etc. Where (62/63) is shown, the reprint allowed no discernable method of determining date of publication, however, all of these editions appeared between July 1961 and September 1963 and are grouped together as 1962 or 1963, i. e. (62/63). Highest reorder number can be 149, 164, 165 or 167. This was a very unstable period for Gilberton which saw them going into bankruptcy and reorganization. Title numbers omitted below are not reported to have changes in either art or covers.

NOTE: Many Classics were extensively changed in terms of interior art by clipping panels and omitting complete pages. Comparisons of title numbers 11, 13, 15 and many other early editions on a page-by-page comparison with a first edition can show whether or not a reprint has been clipped.

("A2" indicates second art, "C2" second cover, etc.)

Title#	A2	C2	C3
1	(150)	(134)	
2	(142)	(136)	
3	(135)	(135)	
4	(150)	(135)	
5	(131)	(131)	(W/69)
6	(132)	(132)	(F/68)
7	(136)	(129)	
8	(62/63)	(62/63)	
9	(161)	(161)	(R/68)
10	(140)	(130)	
11		(110)	(R/68)

Title#	A2	C2	C3
12	(150)	(132)	(R/68)
13	(112)	(60)	(112)
15		(117)	(W/69)
16		(155)	
17		(R/68)	
18	(158)	(60)	(140)

(#18 had a fourth cover – (158).)

Title#	A2	C2	C3
19	(131)	(131)	
21		(114)	
22		(11/63)	
23	(62/63)	(136)	
24	(140)	(140)	
25		(156)	
26		(146)	
27		(154)	
28		(115)	(SU/69)
29		(60)	(128)
30		(155)	
31		(131)	
32		(138)	(R/68)
34		(140)	
35	(161)	(161)	
36		(155)	
37		(R/68)	
38	(62/63)	(62/63)	
39	(62/63)	(142)	(R/68)
41		(62)	(156)
42	(152)	(131)	
45	(161)	(161)	
46		(131)	
47		(128)	(R/68)
48		(121)	
49		(155)	(F/68)
50	(62/63)	(140)	
51		(139)	
52	(142)	(142)	
54	(142)	(142)	
55		(121)	
56	(62/63)	(62/63)	
57		(134)	
58		(146)	
59		(156)	
60	(158)	(158)	(R/68)
61		(156)	
62		(137)	(R/68)
63	(62/63)	(156)	
64		(131)	
65		(131)	
67		(136)	
68	(62/63)	(156)	
69		(136)	
70		(156)	
71	(62/63)	(62/63)	
72		(131)	
75		(139)	
76		(128)	
77		(139)	
78		(128)	(W/69)
79		(133)	
80		(132)	
81		(SP/69)	
82		(F/68)	
83	(R/68)	(R/68)	
90		(148)	
93		(62/63)	
96		(W/69)	
98		(R/68)	
99		(SP/69)	
103		(131)	
112		(W/69)	
134		(W/69)	
144		(F/68)	
147		(F/68)	
149		(F/68)	

CLASSICS ILLUSTRATED (Painted Cover Reprints). In March 1951, with the publication of "The Odyssey," Gilberton introduced their painted covers designed to make the scenes more real or photographic. Shortly thereafter, the early line covers began converting to the "new" style. Initially, interior art remained the same. Sometime later, many were replaced with new art, previously described, indicating contents redrawn by new artists.

This period also saw the reappearance of some issues discontinued before. Numbers 11, 35, 38 and 56 were reprinted with new art and new covers. Issues released prior to an inside date of "Reissued 1967" have a 15 cents cover price. After this the cover price was 25 cents. Of the millions of Classics Illustrated issued, perhaps 90 per cent are of the painted cover variety. Consequently, they constitute an overwhelming portion of this title available on the market. With the exceptions noted below, most numbers are readily available to collectors willing to accept any edition of a particular title. In a few cases in Section I below, complete, first edition artwork is available (such as No. 1 (143), No. 2 (136), No. 4 (141) and No. 7 (129) in the original 64-page size.) Obviously, these represent real "finds" and are much more desirable from a collector's standpoint than painted covers with new art. The last painted reprints, Numbers 2, 5, 50 and 133 were dated Winter 1971.

The painted cover reprints are shown in two sections below. The first section lists the original painted cover reprint for the title shown. In some unusual cases, the painted cover reprint, because of scarcity due to low press runs, etc., will have a higher value than the first edition painted cover.

Some titles have two different painted covers, none had three. When a date or highest reorder number (HRN) is shown in parenthesis in Section II, any later date or higher reorder number brings the value listed.

All covers in Section II are different from those title numbers listed in Section I. In order to assist differentiation between the second painted cover in Section II, the highest reorder number or edition date, is listed in parenthesis. The edition date is shown at the bottom of the inside front cover.

The following codes are used in Section II: W—Winter, F—Fall, R—Reissued, SP—Spring.

When two painted covers exist, those listed in Section I will all have dates or HRN's prior/lower to the date/HRN listed in Section II.

Some painted cover reprints (e. g. 90 & 93) were never reprinted with the original painted cover. Title numbers not listed in Section I or II do not exist as painted cover reprints in the category described.

Title#	Editions	Good	Fine	Mint
1	11	1.25	2.50	3.75
2	12	1.25	2.50	3.75
2 (Twin Circle edition)		1.50	3.00	4.50
3	10	1.25	2.50	3.75
4	10	1.25	2.50	3.75
4 (Twin Circle edition)		1.50	3.00	4.50
5	8	1.25	2.50	3.75
6	10	1.25	2.50	3.75
7	11	1.25	2.50	3.75
8	1	3.00	6.00	12.00
9	3	1.50	3.00	4.50
10	11	1.25	2.50	3.75
10 (Twin Circle edition)		1.50	3.00	4.50
11	5	1.25	2.50	3.75
12	7	1.25	2.50	3.75
13	9	1.25	2.50	3.75
13 (Twin Circle edition)		1.50	3.00	4.50
15	10	1.25	2.50	3.75
16	6	1.25	2.50	3.75
17	2	1.25	2.50	3.75
18	2	1.25	2.50	3.75
19	12	1.25	2.50	3.75
21	1	4.00	8.00	12.00
22	3	1.50	3.00	4.50
23	8	1.25	2.50	3.75
24	8	1.25	2.50	3.75
25	5	1.25	2.50	3.75
26	11	1.25	2.50	3.75
27	4	1.50	3.00	4.50
28	4	1.25	2.50	3.75
29	9	1.25	2.50	3.75

(Classics Ill. cont'd)

Title#	Editions	Good	Fine	Mint
30	5	1.50	3.00	4.50
31	8	1.25	2.50	3.75
32	5	1.25	2.50	3.75
34	6	1.25	2.50	3.75
35	4	2.00	4.00	6.00
36	4	2.00	4.00	6.00
37	1	2.50	5.00	7.50
38	4	1.50	3.00	4.50
39	5	2.00	4.00	6.00
41	4	1.25	2.50	3.75
42	10	1.25	2.50	3.75
45	3	1.50	3.00	4.50
46	11	1.25	2.50	3.75
47	10	1.25	2.50	3.75
48	11	1.25	2.50	3.75
48 (Twin Circle edition)		1.50	3.00	4.50
49	3	2.00	4.00	6.00
50	9	1.25	2.50	3.75
51	5	1.25	2.50	3.75
52	7	1.25	2.50	3.75
54	6	1.25	2.50	3.75
55	8	1.25	2.50	3.75
56	3	2.00	4.00	6.00
57	7	1.25	2.50	3.75
58	5	1.25	2.50	3.75
59	4	1.25	2.50	3.75
60	3	2.00	4.00	6.00
61	3	2.00	4.00	6.00
62	5	1.25	2.50	3.75
63	4	1.25	2.50	3.75
64	10	1.25	2.50	3.75
65	3	1.25	2.50	3.75
65-Ben Franklin Store Giveaway ('50-'51)		2.50	5.00	7.50
67	4	1.50	3.00	4.50
68	6	1.25	2.50	3.75
68 (Twin Cirlce edition)		1.50	3.00	4.50
69	9	1.50	3.00	4.50
70	3	1.50	3.00	4.50
71	2	4.00	8.00	12.00
72	8	1.25	2.50	3.75
75	6	1.25	2.50	3.75
76	6	1.25	2.50	3.75
77	7	1.25	2.50	3.75
78	8	1.25	2.50	3.75
79	3	1.50	3.00	4.50
80	8	1.25	2.50	3.75
81	2	1.25	2.50	3.75
82	1	1.25	2.50	3.75
83	10	.90	1.80	2.70
84	1	2.50	5.00	7.50
85	7	1.25	2.50	3.75
86	6	.90	1.80	2.70
87	4	1.25	2.50	3.75
88	3	1.25	2.50	3.75
89	4	.90	1.80	2.70
91	10	.90	1.80	2.70
92	3	1.25	2.50	3.75
94	2	.90	1.80	2.70
95	2	1.25	2.50	3.75
96	8	.90	1.80	2.70
97	7	.90	1.80	2.70
98	7	.90	1.80	2.70
99	5	.90	1.80	2.70
100	9	.90	1.80	2.70
101	7	.90	1.80	2.70
102	2	1.50	3.00	4.50
103	1	.90	1.80	2.70
104	7	.90	1.80	2.70
105	11	.90	1.80	2.70
106	7	.90	1.80	2.70
107	6	.90	1.80	2.70
108	6	.90	1.80	2.70
109	3	1.25	2.50	3.75

Title#	Editions	Good	Fine	Mint
110	1	2.50	5.00	7.50
111	3	.90	1.80	2.70
112	7	.90	1.80	2.70
113	1	1.25	2.50	3.75
114	1	1.50	3.00	4.50
115	1	1.50	3.00	4.50
116	1	1.50	3.00	4.50
117	2	1.50	3.00	4.50
118	1	1.50	3.00	4.50
119	2	1.50	3.00	4.50
120	1	1.50	3.00	4.50
121	7	1.25	2.50	3.75
122	6	.90	1.80	2.70
123	5	.90	1.80	2.70
124	10	.90	1.80	2.70
125	7	.90	1.80	2.70
126	2	.90	1.80	2.70
126 (Twin Circle edition)		1.50	3.00	4.50
127	2	.90	1.80	2.70
128	7	.90	1.80	2.70
128 (Twin Circle edition)		1.50	3.00	4.50
129	1	1.50	3.00	4.50
130	6	.90	1.80	2.70
131	7	.90	1.80	2.70
132	3	.90	1.80	2.70
133	8	.90	1.80	2.70
134	3	1.25	2.50	3.75
135	4	.90	1.80	2.70
136	4	.90	1.80	2.70
137	5	.90	1.80	2.70
138	7	.90	1.80	2.70
139	4	.90	1.80	2.70
140	4	.90	1.80	2.70
141	3	1.25	2.50	3.75
142	6	1.50	3.00	4.50
143	3	.90	1.80	2.70
144	4	.90	1.80	2.70
145	4	.90	1.80	2.70
146	3	1.50	3.00	4.50
147	6	.90	1.80	2.70
148	4	.90	1.80	2.70
149	5	.90	1.80	2.70
150	3	2.00	4.00	6.00
151	3	1.25	2.50	3.75
152	4	.90	1.80	2.70
153	6	.90	1.80	2.70
154	3	2.00	4.00	6.00
155	2	.90	1.80	2.70
156	3	1.25	2.50	3.75
157	2	2.00	4.00	6.00
158	2	2.00	4.00	6.00
159	2	.90	1.80	2.70
160	2	1.25	2.50	3.75
161	2	2.50	5.00	7.50
162	2	1.25	2.50	3.75
163	2	.90	1.80	2.70
164	2	.90	1.80	2.70
165	2	.90	1.80	2.70
166	2	1.25	2.50	3.75
167	2	3.00	6.00	9.00
168		1.25	2.50	3.75
169	1	1.25	2.50	3.75

SECTION II

Title#	Editions	Good	Fine	Mint
5(W/69)	2	.50	1.00	1.50
6(F/68)	2	.75	1.50	2.25
9(R/68)	1	.90	1.80	2.70
11(R/68)	1	.60	1.20	1.80
12(R/68)	2	.60	1.20	1.80
15(W/69)	2	.60	1.20	1.80
18(158)	7	.50	1.00	1.50
28(169)	1	.90	1.80	2.70
32(R/68)	1	.50	1.00	1.50

Title#	Editions	Good	Fine	Mint
39(R/68)	1	2.50	5.00	7.50
47(R/68)	2	.60	1.20	1.80
49(F/68)	1	2.50	5.00	7.50
60(R/68)	1	1.50	3.00	4.50
62(R/68)	1	1.50	3.00	4.50
78(W/69)	1	.90	1.80	2.70
81(169)	1	.60	1.20	1.80
82(F/68)	1	.60	1.20	1.80
83(R/68)	1	.60	1.20	1.80
90(Any)	5	.50	1.00	1.50
93(Any)	3	.50	1.00	1.50
96(W/69)	1	.60	1.20	1.80
98(R/68)	1	2.50	5.00	7.50
99(SP/69)	1	.60	1.20	1.80
103(131)	4	.80	1.60	2.40
112(W/69)	1	.90	1.80	2.70
134(W/69)	1	.60	1.20	1.80
144(F/68)	2	.60	1.20	1.80
147(F/68)	1	.60	1.20	1.80
149(F/68)	1	.90	1.80	2.70

CLASSICS ILLUSTRATED LIBRARY GIFT BOX (See Classics Comics --)

CLASSICS ILLUSTRATED EDUCATIONAL SERIES
1951; 1953 (16 pgs.)
Gilberton Corp.

#1-Shelter Through the Ages (Ruberoid Co.) (1951-15¢) Kiefer art 10.00 20.00 30.00
No#-The Westinghouse Story-The Dreams of a Man (Westinghouse Co.-1953) H. C. Kiefer art 10.00 20.00 30.00

CLASSICS ILLUSTRATED GIANTS
February, 1950 (One Shots - "OS")
Gilberton Publications

These Giant Editions were on sale for two years, beginning in 1950. They were 50 cents on the newsstand and 60 cents by mail. They are actually four classics in one volume. All the stories are reprints of the Classics Illustrated Series.

"An Illustrated Library of Great Adventure Stories" - Reprints of #6,7,8,10 15.00 30.00 45.00
"An Illustrated Library of Exciting Mystery Stories" - Reprints of #13,30 & others 17.00 34.00 51.00
"An Illustrated Library of Great Indian Stories" - Reprints of #4,17,22,37 15.00 30.00 45.00

CLASSICS ILLUSTRATED "GOLDEN RECORDS GREAT LITERATURE SERIES" ($2.49 retail for comic & record)
Mar, 1966 (All issues)(Record with comic sets)
Gilberton (Comics)/A.A. Records (Records)

SLP-189--Black Beauty, SLP-190--Mutiny on the Bounty, SLP-191--The Time Machine, SLP-192--The Call of the Wild
Comic & Record...Each..... 7.50
NOTE: Comics are all dated March, 1966 and the last reorder number on the back is 167.

CLASSICS ILLUSTRATED JUNIOR
Oct, 1953 - Spring, 1971
Famous Authors Ltd. (Gilberton Publications)

Original editions have ad for the next issue. Originals (first prints) are worth 50% more than reprints. Prices listed are for originals.

#501-Snow White & the Seven Dwarfs-Alex Blum art & cover 6.00 12.00 18.00

	Good	Fine	Mint
502-The Ugly Duckling	1.50	3.00	4.50
503-Cinderella	.60	1.20	1.80
504-The Pied Piper	.60	1.20	1.80
505-The Sleeping Beauty	.60	1.20	1.80
506-The 3 Little Pigs	.60	1.20	1.80
507-Jack & the Beanstalk	1.00	2.00	3.00
508-Goldilocks & the 3 Bears	.60	1.20	1.80
509-Beauty & the Beast	1.00	2.00	3.00
510-Little Red Riding Hood	1.00	2.00	3.00
511-Puss-N-Boots	.60	1.20	1.80
512-Rumpel Stiltskin	1.00	2.00	3.00
513-Pinocchio	1.50	3.00	4.50
514-The Steadfast Tin Soldier	1.20	2.40	3.60
515-Johnny Appleseed	1.00	2.00	3.00
516-Aladdin & His Lamp	1.50	3.00	4.50
517-The Emperor's New Clothes	1.00	2.00	3.00
518-The Golden Goose	.60	1.20	1.80
519-Paul Bunyan	.60	1.20	1.80
520-Thumbelina	1.00	2.00	3.00
521-King of the Golden River	1.00	2.00	3.00
522-The Nightingale	1.00	2.00	3.00
523-The Gallant Tailor	.60	1.20	1.80
524-The Wild Swans	.60	1.20	1.80
525-The Little Mermaid	.60	1.20	1.80
526-The Frog Prince	.60	1.20	1.80
527-The Golden-Haired Giant	.60	1.20	1.80
528-The Penny Prince	.60	1.20	1.80
529-The Magic Servants	.60	1.20	1.80
530-The Golden Bird	.60	1.20	1.80
531-Rapunzel	1.00	2.00	3.00
532-The Dancing Princesses	.60	1.20	1.80
533-The Magic Fountain	.60	1.20	1.80
534-The Golden Touch	.60	1.20	1.80
535-The Wizard of Oz	1.50	3.00	4.50
535-Twin Circle edition	2.00	4.00	6.00
536-The Chimney Sweep	.60	1.20	1.80
537-The Three Fairies	.60	1.20	1.80
538-Silly Hans	.60	1.20	1.80
539-The Enchanted Fish	.60	1.20	1.80
540-The Tinder-Box	1.50	3.00	4.50
541-Snow White & Rose Red	1.00	2.00	3.00
542-The Donkey's Tale	1.20	2.40	3.60
543-The House in the Woods	.60	1.20	1.80
544-The Golden Fleece	1.50	3.00	4.50
545-The Glass Mountain	1.00	2.00	3.00
546-The Elves & the Shoemaker	1.00	2.00	3.00
547-The Wishing Table	.60	1.20	1.80
548-The Magic Pitcher	.60	1.20	1.80
549-Simple Kate	.60	1.20	1.80
550-The Singing Donkey	.60	1.20	1.80
551-The Queen Bee	.60	1.20	1.80
552-The 3 Little Dwarfs	1.20	2.40	3.60
553-King Thrushbeard	.60	1.20	1.80
554-The Enchanted Deer	.60	1.20	1.80
555-The 3 Golden Apples	1.00	2.00	3.00
556-The Elf Mound	.60	1.20	1.80
557-Silly Willy	.60	1.20	1.80
558-The Magic Dish	.60	1.20	1.80
559-The Japanese Lantern	1.00	2.00	3.00
560-The Doll Princess	.60	1.20	1.80
561-Hans Humdrum	.60	1.20	1.80
562-The Enchanted Pony	1.00	2.00	3.00
563-The Wishing Well	1.00	2.00	3.00
564-The Salt Mountain	.60	1.20	1.80
565-The Silly Princess	.60	1.20	1.80
566-Clumsy Hans	.60	1.20	1.80
567-The Bearskin Soldier	.60	1.20	1.80

(Classics Ill. Junior cont'd)

	Good	Fine	Mint
568-The Happy Hedgehog	1.00	2.00	3.00
569-The Three Giants	1.00	2.00	3.00
570-The Pearl Princess	.60	1.20	1.80
571-How Fire Came to the Indians			
	1.00	2.00	3.00
572-The Drummer Boy	.60	1.20	1.80
573-The Crystal Ball	.60	1.20	1.80
574-Brightboots	.60	1.20	1.80
575-The Fearless Prince	.60	1.20	1.80
576-The Princess Who Saw Everything			
	1.00	2.00	3.00
577-The Runaway Dumpling	1.00	2.00	3.00

NOTE: *Last reprint - Spring, 1971.*

CLASSICS ILLUSTRATED SPECIAL ISSUE
Dec, 1955 - July, 1962 (100 pgs.)(35¢)
Gilberton Co. (Came out semi-annually)

	Good	Fine	Mint
129A-The Story of Jesus(titled --Special Edition)"Three Camels" cover	6.00	12.00	18.00
"Jesus on Mountain"cvr.	3.00	6.00	9.00
132A-The Story of America(6/56)	2.50	5.00	7.50
135A-The Ten Commandments(12/56) Adapted from C. B. DeMille movie	4.00	8.00	12.00
138A-Adventures in Science(6/57)-C.C. Beck art	4.00	8.00	12.00
141A-The Rough Rider (Teddy Roosevelt)	2.50	5.00	7.50
144A-Blazing the Trail West(6/58)-73pgs. of Evans & Severin art	2.50	5.00	7.50
147A-Crossing the Rockies(12/58)-Crandall/ Evans art	3.00	6.00	9.00
150A-Royal Canadian Police(6/59)-Ingels, Sid Check art	3.00	6.00	9.00
153A-Men, Guns & Cattle(12/59)-Evans art, 26pgs.	2.50	5.00	7.50
156A-The Atomic Age(6/60)-Crandall/Evans, Torres art	2.50	5.00	7.50
159A-Rockets, Jets, Missiles(12/60)-Evans, Morrow art	3.00	6.00	9.00
162A-War Between the States(6/61)-Kirby & Crandall/Evans art	2.50	5.00	7.50
165A-To the Stars(12/61)-Torres & Crandall/ Evans art	3.00	6.00	9.00
166A-World War II('62)-Torres art	2.50	5.00	7.50
167A-Prehistoric World(7/62)-Torres & Crandall/Evans art	4.00	8.00	12.00
No# Special Issue-The United Nations (50¢) Williamson art (Rare)	7.00	14.00	21.00

NOTE: *158A appeared as DC's Showcase #43, "Dr. No" and was only published in Great Britain as 158A with different cover.*

CLASSICS LIBRARY (Also see King Classics)
1977(?) - Present   (85¢ each) (30 pgs.)
King Feat. (Printed in Spain for U.S. distr.)

	Good	Fine	Mint
#1-Connecticut Yankee, 2-Last of the Mohicans, 3-Moby Dick, 4-Robin Hood, 5-Swiss Family Robinson, 6-Robinson Crusoe, 7-Treasure Island, 8-20,000 Leagues, 9-Christmas Carol, 10-Huck Finn, 11-Around the World in 80 Days, 12-Davy Crockett, 13-Don Quixote, 14-Gold Bug, 15-Ivanhoe, 16-Three Musketeers, 17-Baron Munchausen, 18-Alice in Wonderland, 19-Black Arrow, 20-Five Weeks in a Balloon, 21-Great Expectations, 22-Gulliver's Travels, 23-Prince & Pauper, 24-Uncle Tom's Cabin, 25-Tale of 2 Cities, 26-Ben-Hur, 27-Heidi, 28-Little Women, 29-Mysterious Island, 30-The Pirate, 31-The Phantom Ship, 32-A Journey to the Center of the Earth each....	.30	.60	.90

CLAW THE UNCONQUERED (See Cancelled Comic Cavalcade)
May-June, 1975 - #9, Sept-Oct, 1976; #10, Apr-May, 1978 - #12, Aug-Sept, 1978
National Periodical Publications/DC Comics

	Good	Fine	Mint
#1	.35	.70	1.05
2,3	.25	.50	.75
4-12: #9-Origin	.20	.40	.60

NOTE: *Kubert covers-#10-12.*

CLAY CODY, GUNSLINGER
Fall, 1957
Pines Comics

#1	.65	1.35	2.00

CLEAN FUN, STARRING "SHOOGAFOOTS JONES"
1944 (24 pgs.)(B&W)(Oversized covers)(10¢)
Specialty Book Co.

Humorous situations involving Negroes in the Deep South

White cover issue....	7.00	14.00	21.00
Dark grey cvr issue..	8.00	16.00	24.00

CLEMENTINA THE FLYING PIG (See Dell Jr. Treasury)

CLEOPATRA (See Ideal, A Classical Comic #1)

CLIFF MERRITT
Giveaway   (2 different)
Brotherhood of Railroad Trainmen

--And the Very Candid Candidate by Al Williamson	.65	1.35	2.00

Claw The Unconquered #8, © DC

Clean Fun #1, © Specialty Book

Climax! #1, © Gilmor

(Cliff Merritt cont'd) Good Fine Mint
--Sets the Record Straight by Al Williamson
   (2 different covers-one by Williamson;
   the other-McWilliams) .65 1.35 2.00

CLIMAX!
July, 1955
Gilmor

#1,2 (Mystery)   1.00 2.00 3.00

CLINT & MAC (See 4-Color Comics #889)

CLOAK AND DAGGER
Fall, 1952
Ziff-Davis Publishing Co.

#1-Painted cover   2.50 5.00 7.50

CLOSE SHAVES OF PAULINE PERIL, THE
1970 - #4, March, 1971
Gold Key

#1-4   .20   .40   .60

CLOWN COMICS
1945; May-June, 1946 - #3, Sept-Oct, 1946
Home Comics/Harvey Publications

No# (1945)   1.75 3.50 5.25
#1-3   1.40 2.80 4.20

CLUBHOUSE PRESENTS
June, 1956
Sussex Publ. Co./Magazine Enterprises

#1   .65 1.35 2.00

CLUBHOUSE RASCALS
June, 1945 - #2, Oct, 1956
Sussex Publ. Co. (Magazine Enterprises)

#1,2-The Brain app. #2 .60 1.20 1.80

CLUB "16"
June, 1948 - #4, Dec, 1948
Famous Funnies

#1-4   1.20 2.40 3.60

CLUE COMICS (Real Clue Crime V2#4 on)
Jan, 1943 - #15(V2#3), May, 1947
Hillman Periodicals

#1-Origin The Boy King, Nightmare, Micro-
   Face, Twilight, & Zippo
                  27.50 55.00 82.50
2   14.00 28.00 42.00

                 Good Fine Mint
3   12.00 24.00 36.00
4   10.00 20.00 30.00
5   7.00 14.00 21.00
6-9   6.00 12.00 18.00
10-Origin The Gun Master 5.00 10.00 15.00
11   4.00 8.00 12.00
12-Origin Rackman 5.00 10.00 15.00
V2#1-Nightro new origin; Iron Lady app.;
   Simon & Kirby art 6.00 12.00 18.00
V2#2-Two S&K stories, Infantino story
                  6.00 12.00 18.00
V2#3-Three S&K stories 7.00 14.00 21.00

CLUTCHING HAND, THE
July-Aug, 1954
American Comics Group

#1   1.75 3.50 5.25

CLYDE BEATTY
October, 1953   (84 pgs.)
Commodore Productions

#1   3.00 6.00 9.00
--African Jungle Book('53)-Richfield Oil Co.
   giveaway   1.50 3.00 4.50

CLYDE CRASHCUP (TV)
Aug-Oct, 1963 - #5, Sept-Nov, 1964
Dell Publishing Co.

#1-5   .25   .50   .75

C-M-O COMICS
1942
Chicago Mail Order Co.

#1-Invisible Terror, Super Ann, & Plymo the
   Rubber Man app. (All costume heroes)
                  5.00 10.00 15.00
 2-Invisible Terror, Super Ann app.
                  4.00 8.00 12.00

COBALT BLUE
1977   (One Shot) (50¢)
Power Comics

#1   .20   .40   .60

COCOMALT BIG BOOK OF COMICS
1938   (Regular size - Full color)
Harry 'A' Chesler

#1-Biro cover; Little Nemo, Dan Hastings;
   Guardineer art 20.00 40.00 60.00

CODE NAME: ASSASSIN (See 1st Issue Special)

Clubhouse Rascals #1, © ME

Clue Comics V2#1, © HILL

Clyde Crashcup #5, © DELL

Cody Of The Pony Express #1, © FOX   Combat Casey #24, © MCG   Combat Kelly #2, © MCG

CODY OF THE PONY EXPRESS (See Colossal
Feature Magazine)
Sept, 1950 - #3, Jan, 1951
Fox Features Syndicate

	Good	Fine	Mint
#1-3	1.75	3.50	5.25

CODY OF THE PONY EXPRESS (Buffalo Bill --)
(Outlaws of the West #11 on)(See Colossal Feat.)
#8, Oct, 1955; #9, Jan, 1956; #10, June, 1956
Charlton Comics

#8-Bullseye on splash page-not Simon & Kirby

	1.00	2.00	3.00
9,10	.75	1.50	2.25

CO-ED ROMANCES
November, 1951
P. L. Publishing Co.

#1	1.00	2.00	3.00

COLLECTORS ITEM CLASSICS (See Marvel C.I.C.)

COLOSSAL FEATURES MAGAZINE (Formerly I Loved)
(See Cody of the Pony --)
#33, 5/50 - #34, 7/50; #3, 9/50
Fox Features Syndicate

#33,34-Cody of the Pony Express begins

(Based on serial)	1.75	3.50	5.25
#3-Authentic criminal cases			
	2.00	4.00	6.00

COLOSSAL SHOW, THE (TV)
October, 1969
Gold Key

#1	.20	.40	.60

COLOSSUS COMICS
March, 1940
Sun Publications

#1-Tulpa of Tsang(hero)	17.50	35.00	52.50

COLT 45 (TV)
1958 - 11-1/60; #4, 2-4/60 - #9, 5-7/61
Dell Publishing Co.

4-Color #924,1004,1058; #4-9

	.80	1.60	2.40

COLUMBIA, THE GEM OF THE COMICS
1943
William H. Wise Co.

#1-Joe Palooka, Charlie Chan, Capt. Yank,

Sparky Watts, Dixie Dugan begin

	Good	Fine	Mint
	6.00	12.00	18.00
2-4	5.00	10.00	15.00

COMANCHE (See 4-Color #1350)

COMANCHEROS, THE (See 4-Color #1300)

COMBAT
June, 1952 - #11, April, 1953
Atlas Comics (ANC)

#1	1.50	3.00	4.50
2,3,5-11	.80	1.50	2.40
4-Krigstein story	1.50	3.00	4.50

NOTE: _Combat Casey_ in #7,8,10,11.

COMBAT
Oct-Nov, 1961 - #40, Oct, 1973 (No #9)
Dell Publishing Co.

#1	.80	1.60	2.40
2-7	.50	1.00	1.50
8(4-6/63),#8(7-9/63)	.35	.70	1.05
10-27	.25	.50	.75
28-40(reprints #1-14)	.15	.30	.45

NOTE: _Glanzman covers/stories-#1-27._

COMBAT CASEY (Formerly War Combat)
#6, Jan, 1953 - #34, July, 1957
Atlas Comics (SAI)

#6-9	1.00	2.00	3.00
10-Battle Brady x-over	.80	1.60	2.40
11-34	.60	1.20	1.80

NOTE: _Everett story-#6. Powell story-#29,30,
34._

COMBAT KELLY
Nov, 1951 - #44, Aug, 1957
Atlas Comics (SPI)

#1-Heath art	2.00	4.00	6.00
2-10	1.00	2.00	3.00
11-44: #17-Combat Casey app.; #18-Battle			
Brady app. #38-Green Berets story(8/56)			
	.80	1.60	2.40

NOTE: _Berg stories-#14,21-23,25,28,31-36.
Whitney story-#5._

COMBAT KELLY (and the Deadly Dozen)
June, 1972 - #9, Oct, 1973
Marvel Comics Group

#1-Intro. Combat Kelly	.20	.40	.60
2,3-Origin C. Kelly #3	.15	.30	.45
4-Sgt. Fury x-over		.15	.30
5-9: #9-Deadly Dozen dies		.10	.20

COMBINED OPERATIONS (See The Story of the Commandos)

COMEDY CARNIVAL (See Carnival)

COMEDY COMICS (1st Series) (Daring Mystery #1-8) (Margie #35 on)
#9, April, 1942 - #34, Fall, 1946
Timely Comics

	Good	Fine	Mint
#9-The Fin by Everett, Capt. Dash, Citizen V, & The Silver Scorpion app.; Wolverton art	40.00	80.00	120.00
10-Origin The Fourth Musketeer, Victory Boys; Monstro, the Mighty app.	25.00	50.00	75.00
11-Vagabond app.	7.00	14.00	21.00
12,13,15-32	2.00	4.00	6.00
14-Origin & 1st app. Super Rabbit	2.50	5.00	7.50
33-Kurtzman art-5pgs.	5.00	10.00	15.00
34-Wolverton art, 5pgs.	5.00	10.00	15.00

COMEDY COMICS (2nd Series)
May, 1948 - #10, 1949
Marvel Comics (ACI)

	Good	Fine	Mint
#1,3,4-Hedy, Tessie, Millie begin; Kurtzman's "Hey Look"	5.00	10.00	15.00
2	1.50	3.00	4.50
5-10	.80	1.60	2.40

COMIC ALBUM
Mar-May, 1958 - #18, June-Aug, 1962
Dell Publishing Co.

#1-Donald Duck	1.75	3.50	5.25
2-Bugs Bunny	.80	1.60	2.40
3-Donald Duck; Barks cvr.	1.20	2.40	3.60
4-Tom & Jerry	.50	1.00	1.50
5-Woody Woodpecker	.50	1.00	1.50
6-Bugs Bunny	.50	1.00	1.50
7-Popeye	.60	1.20	1.80
8-Tom & Jerry	.50	1.00	1.50
9-Woody Woodpecker	.50	1.00	1.50
10-Bugs Bunny	.50	1.00	1.50
11-Popeye(9-11/60)	.60	1.20	1.80
12-Tom & Jerry	.50	1.00	1.50
13-Woody Woodpecker	.50	1.00	1.50
14-Bugs Bunny	.50	1.00	1.50
15-Popeye	.60	1.20	1.80
16-Flintstones	.50	1.00	1.50
17-Space Mouse	.50	1.00	1.50
18-Three Stooges	1.00	2.00	3.00

COMIC BOOK (Also see Comics From Weatherbird)
1954 (Giveaway)
American Juniors Shoe

Contains a comic rebound with new cover. Several combinations possible. Contents determines price.

COMIC CAPERS
1944 - #6, Summer, 1946
Red Circle Mag./Marvel Comics

	Good	Fine	Mint
#1-Super Rabbit	1.50	3.00	4.50
2-6	1.00	2.00	3.00

COMIC CAVALCADE
Winter, 1942-43 - #63, 6-7/54
(#30, Dec-Jan, 1948 on, contents change)
All-American/National Periodical Publ.

#1-The Flash, Green Lantern, Wonder Woman, Wildcat, The Black Pirate by Moldoff(also #2), Ghost Patrol, & Red White & Blue begin; Scribbly app., Minute Movies	80.00	160.00	240.00
2-Mutt & Jeff begin; last Ghost Patrol & Black Pirate; Minute Movies	45.00	90.00	135.00
3-Hop Harrigan & Sargon, the Sorcerer begin; The King app.	30.00	60.00	90.00
4-The Gay Ghost, The King, Scribbly, & Red Tornado app.	25.00	50.00	75.00
5	20.00	40.00	60.00
6-10: #7-Red Tornado & Black Pirate app.; last Scribbly	17.00	34.00	51.00
11,12,14-20: #12-Last Red White & Blue. #15-Johnny Peril begins, ends #29	14.00	28.00	42.00
13-Solomon Grundy app.	25.00	50.00	75.00
21-23	12.00	24.00	36.00
24-Solomon Grundy x-over in Green Lantern	15.00	30.00	45.00
25-29: #25-Black Canary app. #26,27-Johnny Peril app. #28-Last Mutt & Jeff. #29-Last Flash, Wonder Woman, Green Lantern & Johnny Peril	10.00	20.00	30.00
30-The Fox & the Crow begin, 31-63	1.20	2.40	3.60

NOTE: *Toth* art-*#26-28(Green Lantern); covers-#23,27. Atom app.-#22,23.*

COMIC COMICS
1946 - #10, 1947
Fawcett Publications

#1-Capt. Kidd	1.80	3.60	5.40
2-10-Wolverton art, 4pgs. each	3.00	6.00	9.00

COMIC CUTS (Also see The Funnies)
1934 (5¢) (Tabloid size in full color)(Not reprints; published weekly; created for news-

Comedy Comics #1, © MCG

Comic Cavalcade #6, © DC

Comic Cavalcade #28, © DC

Comic Land #1, © Fast & Fiction   Comic Pages V3#4, © CEN   The 1946 Comics Calendar, © True Comics

(Comic Cuts cont'd)
stand sale)
H. L. Baker Co., Inc.

	Good	Fine	Mint
V1#7(6/30/34), V1#8(7/14/34), V1#9(7/28/34)-			
Idle Jack strips	10.00	20.00	30.00

COMIC LAND
March, 1946
Fact and Fiction

#1-Sandusky & the Senator, Sam Stuper, Marvin
  the Great, Sir Passer, Phineas Gruff app.;
  Irv Tirman & Perry Williams art
                              2.50   5.00   7.50

COMIC MONTHLY
Feb, 1921 - #7, Jul, 1922 (24pgs)(8½x9")(10¢)
(1st monthly newsstand comic publication;
B&W dailies)
Embee Dist. Co.

#1-Polly & Her Pals	50.00	100.00	150.00
2-Mike & Ike	10.00	20.00	30.00
3-S'Matter, Pop?	10.00	20.00	30.00
4-Barney Google	20.00	40.00	60.00
5-Tillie the Toiler	15.00	30.00	45.00
6-Indoor Sports	7.00	14.00	21.00
7-Little Jimmy	7.00	14.00	21.00

COMIC PAGES (Formerly Funny Picture Stories)
V3#4, July, 1939 - V3#6, Dec, 1939
Centaur Publications

V3#4-6	6.00	12.00	18.00

COMIC PAINTING AND CRAYONING BOOK
1917   (32pgs.)(10x13½")(No price on cover)
Saalfield Publ. Co.

Tidy Teddy by F. M. Follett, Clarence the
  Cop, Mr. & Mrs. Butt-In. Regular comic-
  drawn stories to read or color
                              7.00   14.00   21.00

COMICS   (See All Good)

COMICS, THE (--Funny Pages #2,3; Funny Pages
April, 1936 - #3, July, 1936   #4 on)
Centaur Publications

#1-Siegel & Shuster, Kelly art			
	25.00	50.00	75.00
2,3	12.00	24.00	36.00

NOTE: See Taylor's Christmas Tabloid for
other early Siegel & Shuster work.

COMICS, THE

3/1937 - #11, 1938 (Newspaper strip reprints)
Dell Publishing Co.

	Good	Fine	Mint
#1-Wash Tubbs, Tom Mix, Tom Beatty, & Ariz-			
ona Kid begin	20.00	40.00	60.00
2	12.00	24.00	36.00
3-11: #3-Alley Oop	10.00	20.00	30.00

COMICS CALENDAR, THE   (The 1946 --)
1946   (116 pgs.) (25¢) (Stapled at top)
True Comics Press

(Rare) Has a "strip" story for every day of
  the year in color   12.00   24.00   36.00

COMICS DIGEST   (Pocket Size)
Winter, 1942-43   (100 pgs.) (Black & White)
Parents' Magazine Institute

#1-Reprints from True Comics (non-fiction
  World War II stories) 3.00   6.00   9.00

COMIC SELECTIONS   (Shoe store giveaway)
1944-46 (Reprints from Calling All Girls,
True Comics, True Aviation, & Real Heroes)
Parents' Magazine Press

#1	1.00	2.00	3.00
2-5	.65	1.35	2.00

COMICS FOR KIDS
1945
London Publishing Co./Timely

#1,2	1.50	3.00	4.50

COMICS FROM WEATHER BIRD (Also see Comic Book,
Free Comics To You, Weather Bird & Edward's
1954 - 1957   (Giveaway)   Shoes)
Weather Bird Shoes

Contains a comic bound with new cover - Many
combinations possible. Contents would determine price. Some issues do not contain complete
comics, but only parts of comics. Value equals
40-60% of contents.

COMICS MAGAZINE, THE
May, 1936 - #5, Sept, 1936
Quality Comics Group

#1	20.00	40.00	60.00
2	12.00	24.00	36.00
3-5	10.00	20.00	30.00

COMICS MAN, THE
1937   (One Shot)

(Comics Man cont'd)	Good	Fine	Mint
#1	12.00	24.00	36.00

COMICS NOVEL (Anarcho, Dictator of Death)
1947
Fawcett Publications

	Good	Fine	Mint
#1-All Radar	9.00	18.00	27.00

COMICS ON PARADE (#30 on, continuation of
4/1938 – #104, 2/1955   Single Series)
United Features Syndicate

	Good	Fine	Mint
#1-Tarzan by Foster; Captain & the Kids, Little Mary Mixup, Abbie & Slats, Ella Cinders, Broncho Bill, Li'l Abner begin			
	60.00	120.00	180.00
2	30.00	60.00	90.00
3	22.00	44.00	66.00
4,5	15.00	30.00	45.00
6-10	12.00	24.00	36.00
11-20	10.00	20.00	30.00
21-29-Last Tarzan ish.	8.00	16.00	24.00
30-Li'l Abner	5.00	10.00	15.00
31-The Captain & the Kids	4.00	8.00	12.00
32-Nancy & Fritzi Ritz	2.50	5.00	7.50
33-Li'l Abner	5.00	10.00	15.00
34-The Captain & the Kids	3.00	6.00	9.00
35-Nancy & Fritzi Ritz	2.50	5.00	7.50
36-Li'l Abner	5.00	10.00	15.00
37-The Captain & the Kids	3.00	6.00	9.00
38-Nancy & Fritzi Ritz	2.50	5.00	7.50
39-Li'l Abner	5.00	10.00	15.00
40-The Captain & the Kids	3.00	6.00	9.00
41-Nancy & Fritzi Ritz	2.00	4.00	6.00
42-Li'l Abner	4.00	8.00	12.00
43-The Captain & the Kids	3.00	6.00	9.00
44-Nancy & Fritzi Ritz	2.00	4.00	6.00
45-Li'l Abner	4.00	8.00	12.00
46-The Captain & the Kids	3.00	6.00	9.00
47-Nancy & Fritzi Ritz	2.00	4.00	6.00
48-Li'l Abner	4.00	8.00	12.00
49-The Captain & the Kids	3.00	6.00	9.00
50-Nancy & Fritzi Ritz	2.00	4.00	6.00
51-Li'l Abner	3.00	6.00	9.00
52-The Captain & the Kids	2.00	4.00	6.00
53-Nancy & Fritzi Ritz	1.50	3.00	4.50
54-Li'l Abner	3.00	6.00	9.00
55-Nancy & Fritzi Ritz	1.50	3.00	4.50
56-The Captain & the Kids	1.75	3.50	5.25
57-Nancy & Fritzi Ritz	1.50	3.00	4.50
58-Li'l Abner	3.00	6.00	9.00
59-The Captain & the Kids	1.50	3.00	4.50
60-70-Nancy & Fritzi Ritz	1.50	3.00	4.50
71-76-Nancy only	1.25	2.50	3.75
77-104-Nancy & Sluggo	1.25	2.50	3.75
Special Issue, 7/46; Summer, 1948- The Capt. & the Kids app.	1.50	3.00	4.50

	Good	Fine	Mint
Bound Volume (Very Rare) includes #1-12; bound by publisher in pictorial comic boards & distributed at the 1939 World's Fair & through mail order from ads in com- ic books (Also see Tip Top)			
	135.00	270.00	405.00

NOTE: *Li'l Abner reprinted from Tip Top.*

COMICS READING LIBRARIES (Educational Series)
1973, 1977 (36pgs. in color)(Giveaways)
King Features (Charlton Publ.)

	Good	Fine	Mint
R-01-Tiger, Quincy app.		.15	.30
R-02-Beetle Bailey, Blondie & Popeye app.			
		.15	.30
R-03-Blondie, Beetle Baily app.			
	.20	.40	.60
R-04-Tim Tyler's Luck, Felix the Cat app.			
	.20	.40	.60
R-05-Quincy, Henry app.		.15	.30
R-06-The Phantom, Mandrake app.			
	.50	1.00	1.50
R-07-Popeye, Little King app.			
	.40	.80	1.20
R-08-Prince Valiant, Flash, Gordon app.			
	6.00	12.00	18.00
R-09-Hagar the Horrible, Boner's Ark app.			
		.15	.30
R-10-Redeye, Tiger app.		.15	.30
R-11-Blondie, Hi & Lois app.	.15	.30	.45
R-12-Popeye-Swee'pea, Brutus app.			
	.20	.40	.60
R-13-Beetle Bailey, Little King app.			
		.15	.30
R-14-Quincy-Hamlet app.		.15	.30
R-15-The Phantom, The Genius app.			
	.50	1.00	1.50
R-16-Flash Gordon, Mandrake app.			
	6.00	12.00	18.00
1977 editions...		.15	.30

NOTE: *Above giveaways available with purchase
of $45.00 in merchandise. Used as a reading
skills aid for small children.*

COMICS REVUE
June, 1947 - #5, Jan, 1948
St. John Publ. Co. (United Features Synd.)

	Good	Fine	Mint
#1-Ella Cinders & Blackie	2.50	5.00	7.50
2-Hap Hopper (7/47)	2.00	4.00	6.00
3-Iron Vic (8/47)	2.00	4.00	6.00
4-Ella Cinders (9/47)	2.00	4.00	6.00
5-Gordo #1 (1/48)	2.00	4.00	6.00

COMIC STORY PAINT BOOK
1943   (68 pgs.) (Large Size)
Samuel Lowe Co.

Comics Novel #1, © FAW

Comics On Parade #66, © UFS

Comics Revue #4, © UFS

(Comic Story Paint Book cont'd)

	Good	Fine	Mint
#1055-Captain Marvel & a Captain Marvel Jr. story to read & color; 3 panels in color per page (reprints)	25.00	50.00	75.00

COMIX BOOK (B&W Magazine - $1.00)
1974 - Present
Marvel Comics Group/Krupp Comics Works #4

	Good	Fine	Mint
#1-Underground comic artists; 2pg. Wolverton story	1.00	2.00	3.00
2	.65	1.35	2.00
3-Low distribution(3/75)	1.00	2.00	3.00
4(2/76), 4(5/76), 5	.65	1.35	2.00

NOTE: Print run #1-3, 200-250M; #4&5, 10M ea.

COMIX INTERNATIONAL
July, 1974 - Present   (Full Color)
Warren Magazines

#1-Low distribution; all Corben reprints from Warren Magazines	5.00	10.00	15.00
2-Wood, Wrightson reprts.	2.00	4.00	6.00
3-5	.75	1.50	2.25

COMMANDER BATTLE AND THE ATOMIC SUB
Jul-Aug, 1954 - #7, Jul-Aug, 1955
American Comics Group (Titan Publ. Co.)

#1 (3-D effect)	3.50	7.00	10.50
2-7	1.50	3.00	4.50

COMMANDMENTS OF GOD
1954, 1958
Catechetical Guild

Same contents in both editions; different covers	2.00	4.00	6.00

COMMANDO ADVENTURES
June, 1957 - #2, Aug, 1957
Atlas Comics (MMC)

#1,2-Severin covers; #2-Drucker story	1.00	2.00	3.00

COMMANDO YANK (See Mighty Midget Comics)

COMPLETE BOOK OF COMICS AND FUNNIES
1944   (196 pgs.)   (One Shot)
Better Publications

#1-Origin Brad Spencer, Wonderman; The Magnet, The Silver Knight by Kinstler, & Zudo the Jungle Boy app.	6.00	12.00	18.00

COMPLETE BOOK OF TRUE CRIME COMICS

No date (Mid 1940's) (132 pgs.) (25¢)
William H. Wise & Co.

	Good	Fine	Mint
No#-Contains Crime Does Not Pay rebound (includes #22)	25.00	50.00	75.00

COMPLETE COMICS (Formerly Amazing #1)
Winter, 1944-45
Marvel Comics

#2-The Destroyer, The Whizzer, The Young Allies & Sergeant Dix	25.00	50.00	75.00

COMPLETE LOVE MAGAZINE (Formerly a pulp with same title)
V26#2, 5-6/51 - V32#4(#191), 9/56
Ace Periodicals (Periodical House)

V26#2-6(2/52), V27#1-6	.60	1.20	1.80
V28#1-6, V29#1-6	.60	1.20	1.80
V30#1(#176,4/54) - V30#6(#181,1/55)	.60	1.20	1.80
V31#1(#182,3/55) - V31#6(#187,1/56)	.50	1.00	1.50
V32#1(#188,3/56) - V32#4(#191,9/56)	.50	1.00	1.50

COMPLETE MYSTERY (True Complete Mystery #5
8/48 - #4, 2/49 (Full length stories)   on)
Marvel Comics (PrPI)

#1-Seven Dead Men	2.50	5.00	7.50
2-Jigsaw of Doom!	2.00	4.00	6.00
3-Fear in the Night-Burgos art	2.00	4.00	6.00
4-A Squealer Dies Fast	2.00	4.00	6.00

COMPLETE ROMANCE
1949
Avon Periodicals

#1	3.00	6.00	9.00

CONAN, THE BARBARIAN
Oct, 1970 - Present
Marvel Comics Group

#1-Origin Conan by Barry Smith; Kull app.	15.00	30.00	45.00
2	7.00	14.00	21.00
3-(low distribution in some areas)	12.00	24.00	36.00
4,5	5.00	10.00	15.00
6-10: #10-52pgs.; Black Knight reprt.; Kull by Severin app.	4.00	8.00	12.00
11-13	3.00	6.00	9.00
14,15-Elric app.	3.00	6.00	9.00

16-20: #16-Conan reprint from Savage Tales

Commando Adventures #1, © MCG

Complete Mystery #3, © MCG

Conan The Barbarian #4, © MCG

94

Conan The Barbarian #13, © MCG   Confessions Of Love #5, © STAR   Confessions Of Romance #11, © STAR

(Conan cont'd)	Good	Fine	Mint
#1	2.00	4.00	6.00
21,22,24: #22-has reprints from #1. #24-Last Smith issue; Red Sonja's 2nd app.			
	2.00	4.00	6.00
23-1st app. Red Sonja	2.00	4.00	6.00
25-Buscema art begins	1.25	2.50	3.75
26-30	.75	1.50	2.25
31-36,38-40	.50	1.00	1.50
37-Adams cover/story	1.20	2.40	3.60
41-43,46,48,50	.40	.80	1.20
44,45-Adams inks; cvr-#45	.50	1.00	1.50
47-Wood reprint	.40	.80	1.20
49-Kane/Adams art	.50	1.00	1.50
51-60: #57-Ploog story	.30	.60	.90
61-70: #64 reprints/Savage Tales #5; Starlin art on Conan	.25	.50	.75
71-80: #78-reprints/Savage Sword of Conan #1	.20	.40	.60
81-93: #87-Reprint/Savage Sword of Conan #3	.15	.30	.45

NOTE: _Buckler_ cover-#40. _Buscema_ stories-#25-36,38,39,41-56,58-63,65-68,70-78,83-91, 93; covers-#26,36,44,52,56,58,59,64,72,78,79, 83-91,93. _Chaykin_ stories-#79-83. _Ditko_ story-#40. _Kane_ stories-Giant Size #1-4; covers-#12,17(w/_Brunner_),17,18,23,25,27-32,34, 35,38,39,41-43,45-48,50,51,53-55,57,60-63, 65-71, Giant Size #1,3,4. _Smith_ art-#1-16, 19-21,23,24; layouts only-#21; covers-#1-11, 13-16,19-22,24. _Sutton_ inks-Giant Size #1-3. Issues #3-5,7-9,11,16,18,21,23,25,27-30,35, 37,38,42,45,52,57,58,65 have original Robert E. Howard stories adapted. Issues #32-34 adapted from Norvell Page's novel _Flame Winds_.

--Book & Record set	.60	1.20	1.80
Giant Size #1(9/74)-Smith reprint from #3; start adaptation of Howard's "Hour of the Dragon"	1.20	2.40	3.60
Giant Size #2(12/74)-Smith reprint from #5; Sutton art; Buscema cvr	.90	1.80	2.70
Giant Size #3(1975-Smith reprint from #6; Sutton art), Giant Size #4(6/75; Smith reprint from #7), Giant Size #5('75; Smith reprint from #14,15; Kirby cover)			
	.60	1.20	1.80
King Size #1(9/73-35¢)-Smith reprints from #2,4; Smith cover	2.00	4.00	6.00
Annual #2(6/76)-50¢ - new stories			
	.70	1.40	2.10
Annual #3(2/78)-reprints	.40	.80	1.20
Annual #4(10/78)	.25	.50	.75

CONAN (See Savage Tales, Savage Sword of --, & Chamber of Darkness #4)

CONFESSIONS ILLUSTRATED (Magazine)
Jan-Feb, 1956 - #2, Spring, 1956
E.C. Comics

	Good	Fine	Mint
#1-Craig, Kamen, Wood, Orlando art			
	5.00	10.00	15.00
2-Craig, Crandall, Kamen, Orlando art			
	7.00	14.00	21.00

CONFESSIONS OF LOVE (Conf. of Romance #7)
#11, July, 1952 - #6, Aug, 1953
Star Publications

#11	1.50	3.00	4.50
12,13-Disbrow stories	2.00	4.00	6.00
14,#6	1.20	2.40	3.60
#4-Disbrow story	2.00	4.00	6.00
5-Wood/? story	3.00	6.00	9.00

NOTE: _L. B. Cole_ covers-#12,5 among others.

CONFESSIONS OF ROMANCE (Formerly Conf. of Love)
#7, Nov, 1953 - #11, Nov, 1954
Star Publications

#7,8	1.50	3.00	4.50
9-Wood story	3.50	7.00	10.50
10,11-Disbrow stories	2.00	4.00	6.00

NOTE: _L. B. Cole_ covers-#11 among others.

CONFESSIONS OF THE LOVELORN (Formerly Love-
#52, Aug, 1954 - #111, Oct, 1959   lorn)
American Comics Group (Regis Publ./Best Synd. Features)

#52-54-(3-D effect)	2.00	4.00	6.00
55-90	.60	1.20	1.80
91-Williamson story	3.00	6.00	9.00
92-111	.40	.80	1.20

NOTE: _Ogden Whitney_ art in most issues.

CONFIDENTIAL DIARY
#14, Sept, 1962 - #17, Mar, 1963
Charlton Comics

#14-17	.15	.30	.45

CONGO BILL
Aug-Sept, 1954 - #7, Aug-Sept, 1955
National Periodical Publications

#1 (Scarce)	5.00	10.00	15.00
2-7	3.00	6.00	9.00

CONNECTICUT YANKEE, A (See King Classics)

CONQUEROR, THE (See 4-Color Comics #690)

CONQUEROR COMICS
Winter, 1945
Albrecht Publishing Co.

No#	2.50	5.00	7.50

CONQUEST
1953   (6¢)
Store Comics

	Good	Fine	Mint
#1-Richard the Lion Hearted, Beowulf, Swamp			
Fox	1.50	3.00	4.50

CONQUEST
1955
Famous Funnies

	Good	Fine	Mint
#1-Crandall art, 1 pg.	2.00	4.00	6.00

CONTACT COMICS
July, 1944 - #12, May, 1946
Aviation Press

#1-Black Venus, Flamingo, Golden Eagle, Tommy Tomahawk begin	6.00	12.00	18.00
2-5: #3-Last Flamingo. #4-Black Venus by L. B. Cole. #5-The Phantom Flyer app.	3.00	6.00	9.00
6,11-Kurtzman's Black Venus; #11-Last Golden Eagle, last Tommy Tomahawk; Feldstein art, 4 pgs.	8.00	16.00	24.00
7-10,12: #12-Sky Rangers, Air Kids, Ace Diamond app.	2.50	5.00	7.50

NOTE: *Infantino* story-#4. *L.B. Cole cover-#11*.

COO COO COMICS (-- the Bird Brain #57 on)
Oct, 1942 - 1952
Nedor Comics/Standard(Animated Cartoons)

#1-Super Mouse origin	2.00	4.00	6.00
2-10	1.00	2.00	3.00
11-33	.70	1.40	2.10
34-40,43,46,48-50-Text illos by Frazetta in all	2.50	5.00	7.50
41-Two Frazetta stories	6.00	12.00	18.00
42,44,45,47-All contain Frazetta stories & text illos.	5.00	10.00	15.00
51-62	.60	1.20	1.80

"COOKIE"
April, 1946 - #54, Apr-May, 1955
Michel Publ./American Comics Group(Regis Publ.)

#1	1.20	2.40	3.60
2-10	.80	1.60	2.40
11-20	.50	1.00	1.50
21-54	.40	.80	1.20

COOL CAT (Formerly Black Magic)
V8#6, 3-4/62 - V9#2, 7-8/62
Prize Publications

V8#6, No#(V9#1), V9#2	.40	.80	1.20

COPPER CANYON (See Fawcett Movie Comics)

CORKY & WHITE SHADOW (See 4-Color #707)

CORLISS ARCHER (See Meet --)

CORPORAL RUSTY DUGAN (See Rusty Dugan)

CORPSES OF DR. SACOTTI, THE (See Ideal A Classical Comic)

CORSAIR, THE (See A-1 Comics #5,7,10)

COSMO CAT
July-Aug, 1946 - 1949; 1959
Fox Publications/Green Publ. Co./Norlen Mag.

	Good	Fine	Mint
#1	2.00	4.00	6.00
2-10	1.20	2.40	3.60
2-4(1957-Green Publ. Co.)	.40	.80	1.20
2-4(1959-Norlen Mag.)	.40	.80	1.20
I.W. Reprint #1	.30	.60	.90

COSMO THE MERRY MARTIAN
Sept, 1958 - #6, Oct, 1959
Archie Publications (Radio Comics)

#1-Bob White art	3.00	6.00	9.00
2-6-Bob White art	2.00	4.00	6.00

COTTON WOODS (See 4-Color Comics #837)

COUGAR, THE
April, 1975 - #2, June, 1975
Seaboard Periodicals (Atlas)

#1	.30	.60	.90
2-Origin	.20	.40	.60

COUNTDOWN (See Movie Classics)

COUNT OF MONTE CRISTO, THE (See 4-Color #794)

COURAGE COMICS
1945
J. Edward Slavin

#1,2,77	1.00	2.00	3.00

COURTSHIP OF EDDIE'S FATHER (TV)
Jan, 1970 - #2, May, 1970
Dell Publishing Co.

#1,2	.25	.50	.75

COVERED WAGONS, HO (See 4-Color #814)

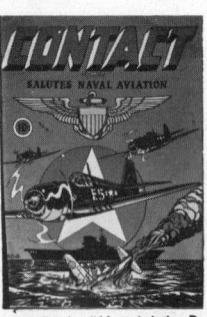

Contact Comics #11, © Aviation Press

Coo Coo Comics #48, © STD

Courage Comics #2, © J. E. Slavin

Cowgirl Romances #28, © FH

Cow Puncher #7, © AVON

Crackajack Funnies #29, © DELL

COWBOY ACTION (Western Thrillers #1-4;
Quick Trigger Western #12 on)
#5, March, 1955 - #11, March, 1956
Atlas Comics (ACI)

	Good	Fine	Mint
#5-10	1.00	2.00	3.00
11-Williamson story, 4pgs.	2.25	4.50	6.75

COWBOY COMICS (-- Stories #14)
1937 - 1938
Centaur Publishing Co.

#13,14	8.00	16.00	24.00

COWBOY IN AFRICA (TV)
March, 1968
Gold Key

#1(10219-803)	.60	1.20	1.80

COWBOY LOVE
July, 1949 - V2#7, 1955
Fawcett Publications/Charlton Comics

V1#1(52pgs.)	2.00	4.00	6.00
V1#2,3	1.50	3.00	4.50
V1#4-27, V1#28,29(4/55)	.80	1.60	2.40
V2#7-Williamson/Evans art	3.00	6.00	9.00

NOTE: _Powell story-#10._

COWBOY ROMANCES (Young Men #4 on?)
Oct, 1949 - #3, Mar, 1950
Marvel Comics (IPC)

#1-Photo cover	2.50	5.00	7.50
2,3	1.75	3.50	5.25

COWBOYS AND INDIANS (Formerly Cowboys 'N'
#6, 1949 - #8, 1952   Injuns)
Magazine Enterprises

#6(A-1#23), 7(A-1#41), 8(A-1#48)			
	1.20	2.40	3.60

COWBOYS 'N' INJUNS COMICS (--& Indians #6 on)
1946 - 1949
Compix/Magazine Enterprises

#1	1.25	2.50	3.75
2-5	.75	1.50	2.25
I.W. Reprint #1,7 (reprinted in Canada by			
Superior, #7)	.50	1.00	1.50

COWBOY WESTERN COMICS (Becomes Wild Bill
1947 - #67, 1/58 (Hickok & Jingles #18 on)
Fawcett/Charlton(Capitol Stories)

#2-10	2.00	4.00	6.00

	Good	Fine	Mint
11-20	1.50	3.00	4.50
21-30	1.25	2.50	3.75
31-50	1.00	2.00	3.00
51-66	.80	1.60	2.40
67-Williamson/Torres story, 5 pgs.			
	3.50	7.00	10.50

NOTE: _This title did not begin with #1;_
earliest issue?

COWGIRL ROMANCES (Formerly Jeanie)
#28, Jan, 1950
Marvel Comics (CCC)

#28(#1)	2.50	5.00	7.50

COWGIRL ROMANCES
1950 - #12, Winter, 1952-53
Fiction House Magazines

#1	3.50	7.00	10.50
2-12	2.25	4.50	6.75

COW PUNCHER (-- Comics)
Jan, 1947 - 1949
Avon Periodicals

#1-Clint Cortland, Texas Rancher, Kit West,			
Pioneer Queen begin; Kubert story; Alabam			
stories begin	10.00	20.00	30.00
2-Kubert story; Kamen bondage cover			
	8.00	16.00	24.00
3-7: #3-Kiefer story	6.00	12.00	18.00

COWPUNCHER
1953 (No #) (Reprints Avon's #2)
Realistic Publications

Kubert story	4.00	8.00	12.00

COWSILLS, THE (See Harvey Pop Comics)

CRACKAJACK FUNNIES (Giveaway)
1937 (32 pgs.)(Full Size, Soft Cover, Full
Color) (Before #1?)
Malto-Meal

Features Dan Dunn, G-Man, Speed Bolton, Freckles, Buck Jones, Clyde Beatty, The Nebbs, Maj-
or Hoople, Wash Tubbs 18.00 36.00 54.00

CRACKAJACK FUNNIES
June, 1938 - #43, Jan, 1942
Dell Publishing Co.

#1-Dan Dunn, Freckles, Myra North, Wash Tubbs,			
Apple Mary, The Nebbs, Don Winslow, Tom			
Mix, Buck Jones begin	33.00	66.50	100.00

(Crackajack Funnies cont'd)	Good	Fine	Mint
2	16.50	33.25	50.00
3	13.50	26.75	40.00
4,5	10.00	20.00	30.00
6-8,10	9.00	18.00	27.00
9-Red Ryder begins	9.00	18.00	27.00
11-14	7.00	14.00	21.00
15-Tarzan text feature begins; not in #26,35			
	8.00	16.00	24.00
16-24	7.00	14.00	21.00
25-The Owl begins; in new costume #26 by Frank Thomas	15.00	30.00	45.00
26-30	10.00	20.00	30.00
31-Owl covers begin	8.00	16.00	24.00
32-Origin Owl Girl	10.00	20.00	30.00
33-39: #36-Last Tarzan ish. #39-Andy Panda begins	8.00	16.00	24.00
40-43-Last Owl cover #42	7.00	14.00	21.00

NOTE: *McWilliams art in most issues.*

CRACK COMICS (-- Western #63 on)
May, 1940 - #62, Sept, 1949
Quality Comics Group

#1-Origin The Black Condor by Lou Fine, Madame Fatal, Red Torpedo & The Space Legion; The Clock, Alias the Spider, Wizard Wells, & Ned Bryant begin; Powell art

	Good	Fine	Mint
	125.00	250.00	375.00
2	60.00	120.00	180.00
3	50.00	100.00	150.00
4	35.00	70.00	105.00
5	32.50	65.00	97.50
6-10: #10-Tor, the Magic Master begins	30.00	60.00	90.00
11-20	27.50	55.00	82.50
21-24-Last Fine Black Condor	25.00	50.00	75.00
25,26	12.00	24.00	36.00
27-Origin Captain Triumph by Alfred Andriola (Kerry Drake artist)	25.00	50.00	75.00
28-30	11.00	22.00	33.00
31-39	7.00	14.00	21.00
40-47	5.00	10.00	15.00
48-57,60-Capt. Triumph by Crandall	5.00	10.00	15.00
58,59,61,62	3.50	7.00	10.50

NOTE: *Black Condor by Fine-#1-24. McWilliams art-#15-27.*

CRACK WESTERN (Formerly Crack; Jonesy #85 on)
#63, Nov, 1949 - #84, May, 1953
Quality Comics Group

	Good	Fine	Mint
#63-Origin & 1st app. Two-Gun Lil(ends #84), Arizona Ames, Frontier Marshal, & Dead Canyon Days	4.00	8.00	12.00
64,65,67,69-Crandall stories; #67-Arizona			

	Good	Fine	Mint
Ames becomes A. Raines. #69-Last Dead Canyon Days	2.50	5.00	7.50
66,68,72-81: #75,78,81-Crandall covers			
	1.75	3.50	5.25
70-Origin & 1st app. The Whip; Crandall story	2.00	4.00	6.00
71,83-Crandall cvr/sty.	2.50	5.00	7.50
82,84-Crandall story	2.00	4.00	6.00

CRACKED (Magazine) (See Biggest Greatest --)
Feb-Mar, 1958 - Present (Satire)
Major Magazines

	Good	Fine	Mint
#1-One pg. Williamson	6.00	12.00	18.00
2-1st Shut-Ups & Bonus Cut-Outs			
	2.50	5.00	7.50
3-6	1.75	3.50	5.25
7-Reprints 1st 6 covers on cover			
	1.00	2.00	3.00
8-12,14-17,19,20: #10-Last ish edited by Sol Brodsky	1.00	2.00	3.00
13-(No#, 3/60)	.65	1.35	2.00
18-(No#, 2/61)	.65	1.35	2.00
21-27(11/62)	.50	1.00	1.50
27(#28, 2/63, misnumbered)	.50	1.00	1.50
29(5/63),30	.50	1.00	1.50
31-60	.35	.70	1.05
61-98,100	.25	.50	.75
99-Alfred E. Neuman featured on cover			
	.25	.50	.75
101-145	.20	.40	.60
Biggest, Greatest Cracked-No#('65)			
	.35	.70	1.05
Biggest, Greatest Cracked #2('66)-#12('76)			
	.25	.50	.75
Extra Special--#1('76),#2('76)			
	.20	.40	.60
Giant -- No#('65)	.50	1.00	1.50
Giant --#2('66)-#12('76), No#(9/77),			
King Sized -- #1('67)	.25	.50	.75
King Sized -- #2('68)-#11('77)			
	.20	.40	.60
Super -- #1('68)	.25	.50	.75
Super -- #2('69)-#10('77)	.20	.40	.60

NOTE: *Burgos stories-#1-10. Davis stories-#5, 11-18,24,80(art); covers-#12-14,16. Elder stories-#5,6,10-13; cover-#10. Everett stories-#1-10,23-25,61; cover-#1. Heath stories-#1-3, 6,13,14,17,110; cover-#6. Jaffee story-#5,6. Morrow story-#8-10. Reinman (Paul) story-#1-4. Severin art & stories in most all issues #1 on. Shores (Syd) stories-#3-7. Stone (Chic) stories-#16,17. Torres story-#7-10. Williamson art-#1 (1 pg.). Wolverton art-#10(2pgs.), Giant No#('65).*

Crackajack Funnies #37, © DELL

Crack Comics #9, © QUA

Crack Comics #16, © QUA

Crack Western #67, © QUA   Crash Comics #1, © Tem Publ.   Creatures On The Loose #10, © MCG

CRACKED COLLECTORS' EDITION(Formerly --Special)
#4, 1973 - Present
Major Magazines

	Good	Fine	Mint
#4	.40	.80	1.20
5-16	.25	.50	.75

CRACKED SHUT-UPS (Cracked Special #3)
Feb, 1972 - #2, 1972
Major Magazines

#1,2	.30	.60	.90

CRACKED SPECIAL (Formerly Cracked Shut-Ups;
-- Collectors' Edition #4 on)
#3, 1973
Major Magazines

#3	.30	.60	.90

CRASH COMICS (Catman #6 on)
May, 1940 - #5, Nov, 1940
Tem Publishing Co.

#1-The Blue Streak, Strongman (origin), The
   Perfect Human begin; Simon & Kirby art

	Good	Fine	Mint
	35.00	70.00	105.00
2-Simon & Kirby art	20.00	40.00	60.00
3- " " " "	15.00	30.00	45.00
4-Origin & 1st app. The Catman; S&K art			
	20.00	40.00	60.00
5-S&K art	15.00	30.00	45.00

NOTE: Solar Legion by Kirby #1-5 (5pgs. ea.)

CRAZY
Dec, 1953 - #7, July, 1954
Atlas Comics (CSI)

#1-Everett art	2.50	5.00	7.50
2-7	1.75	3.50	5.25

NOTE: Berg story-#2. Drucker story-#6. Everett story-#1,4.

CRAZY (People Who Buy This Magazine Is --)
(Formerly This Magazine Is --)
V3#3, 11/57 - V4#8, 2/59 (Magazine) (Satire)
Charlton Publications

V3#3 - V4#7	.60	1.20	1.80
V4#8-Davis art 8 pgs.	1.50	3.00	4.50

CRAZY (Satire)
Feb, 1973 - #3, June, 1973
Marvel Comics Group

#1-3-Not Brand Echh reprints; Kirby reprint-
   #3   .20   .40   .60

CRAZY (Magazine) (Satire)
Oct, 1973 - Present   (40¢) (Black & White)
Marvel Comics Group

	Good	Fine	Mint
#1-1pg. Wolverton, Ploog story, Bode' art; 3pg. photo story of Adams & Giordano			
	.50	1.00	1.50
2-Adams story; Kurtzman's "Hey Look" reprint 2 pgs.; Buscema art	.40	.80	1.20
3,5,6,8: #3-Drucker art	.25	.50	.75
4,7-Ploog art	.25	.50	.75
9-16-Eisner art	.25	.50	.75
17-44	.20	.40	.60
Super Special #1(Sum.'75,100pgs.)-Ploog, Adams reprint	.50	1.00	1.50

NOTE: Cardy covers-#7,8. Freas covers-#1,4,
6; art-#7.

CRAZY, MAN, CRAZY (Magazine) (Satire)
June, 1956
Humor Magazines

V2#2-Three pgs. Wolverton	2.50	5.00	7.50

CREATURE, THE (See Movie Classics)

CREATURES ON THE LOOSE (Tower of Shadows #1-9)
#10, March, 1971 - #37, Sept, 1975
Marvel Comics Group

#10-First King Kull story; Wrightson story			
	4.00	8.00	12.00
11-15: #13-Crandall art	.50	1.00	1.50
16-Origin Warrior of Mars	.50	1.00	1.50
17-20	.40	.80	1.20
21,22: Steranko cover; Thongor begins #22, ends #29	.40	.80	1.20
23-29	.30	.60	.90
30-Manwolf begins	.20	.40	.60
31-37	.20	.40	.60

NOTE: Everett inks-#16. Morrow art-#20,21.

CREEPER, THE (See Beware -- & First Issue
Special)

CREEPY (Magazine)
1964 - Present
Warren Publishing Co.

#1-Frazetta story	2.50	5.00	7.50
2	1.75	3.50	5.25
3-13	1.50	3.00	4.50
14-25	1.00	2.00	3.00
26-40	.80	1.60	2.40
41-60	.70	1.40	2.10
61-80	.60	1.20	1.80
81-102	.50	1.00	1.50
Year Book 1968, '69	1.50	3.00	4.50

(Creepy cont'd)

	Good	Fine	Mint
Year Book 1970-Adams, Ditko art			
	1.35	2.75	4.00
Annual 1971,'72	1.00	2.00	3.00
Annual 1973	.80	1.60	2.40
Annual 1974-All Crandall reprints			
	.80	1.60	2.40

   (NOTE: Annuals are included in regular numbering.)

NOTE: *Above books contain many good artists works: Adams, Brunner, Corben, Craig (Taycee), Crandall, Ditko, Evans, Frazetta, Heath, Jeff Jones, Krenkel, McWilliams, Morrow, Orlando, Ploog, Severin, Torres, Toth, Williamson, Wood & Wrightson; covers by Crandall, Davis, Frazetta, Morrow, SanJulian, Todd/Bode; Otto Binder's "Adam Link" stories in #2,4,6,8,9, 12,13,15 with Orlando art.*

CREEPY THINGS
July, 1975 – #6, June, 1976
Charlton Comics

#1	.15	.30	.45
2-6: #3,4-Sutton covers		.15	.30
3-'77 reprint-Modern Comics		.15	.30

CRIME AND JUSTICE
March, 1951 – 1955
Capitol Stories/Charlton Comics

#1	1.50	3.00	4.50
2-10,12-17,19-26: Shuster cover-#19, story-#21	.80	1.60	2.40
11-Narcotics story	2.00	4.00	6.00
18-Ditko art	1.20	2.40	3.60

CRIME AND PUNISHMENT
April, 1948 – #74, Aug, 1955
Lev Gleason Publications

#1	5.00	10.00	15.00
2-5	2.50	5.00	7.50
6-10	1.60	3.20	4.80
11-20	1.20	2.40	3.60
21-30	1.00	2.00	3.00
31-45	.80	1.60	2.40
46-One pg. Frazetta	1.50	3.00	4.50
47-58,60-65,68,70-74	.60	1.20	1.80
59-Used in Seduction of the Innocent, illo- "What comic-book America stands for"			
	6.00	12.00	18.00
66-Toth cover + all stys.	6.00	12.00	18.00
67,69-Drug stories	3.00	6.00	9.00

NOTE: *Guardineer story-#2,3,10. Kinstler cover-#69. McWilliams stories-#41,48,49.*

CRIME CAN'T WIN   (Formerly Cindy Smith?)

	#41, 1950 – #43, 2/51; #4, 4/51 – #12, 9/53		
Marvel/Atlas Comics (CCC)			

	Good	Fine	Mint
#41-43	.90	1.80	2.70
#4(4/51), 5-12	.70	1.40	2.10

NOTE: *Robinson story-#9,10.*

CRIME CASES   (Formerly Willie Comics)
#24, 8/50 – #27, 3/51; #5, 5/51 – #12, 7/52
Marvel/Atlas Comics(CnPC #24-8/MJMC #9-12)

#24-26	.80	1.60	2.40
27-Everett art	1.00	2.00	3.00
#5-12: #11-Robinson story	.70	1.40	2.10

CRIME CLINIC, THE
1951 – #11, Sept-Oct, 1951
Ziff-Davis Publ. Co.

#1	1.50	3.00	4.50
2-11-Painted covers	1.00	2.00	3.00

CRIME DETECTIVE COMICS
Mar-Apr, 1948 – V3#8, 1952
Hillman Periodicals

V1#1	1.50	3.00	4.50
2-4,6,7,10-12	1.20	2.40	3.60
5-Krigstein story	2.00	4.00	6.00
8-Kirby story	2.00	4.00	6.00
9-Used in Seduction of the Innocent, pg. 16 & "Caricature of the author in a position comic book publishers wish he were in permanently" illo.			
	10.00	20.00	30.00
V2#1,4,7-Krigstein stys.	1.80	3.60	5.40
2,3,5,6,8-10	.70	1.40	2.10
V3#1-8	.60	1.20	1.80

NOTE: *Powell story-#11.*

CRIME DETECTOR
Jan, 1954 – #5, Sept, 1954
Timor Publications

#1	1.20	2.40	3.60
2-4	1.00	2.00	3.00
5-Disbrow story (classic)	2.50	5.00	7.50

CRIME DOES NOT PAY   (Silver Streak #1-21)
#22, 6/42 – #147, 7/55   (1st Crime Comic)
Comic House/Lev Gleason/Golfing

#22-Origin The War Eagle & only app.; Chip Gardner begins; #22 rebound in True Crime, Complete Book of			
(Scarce)	40.00	80.00	120.00
23 (Scarce)	25.00	50.00	75.00
24-Intro. & 1st app. Mr. Crime			

Crime & Justice #5, © CC

The Crime Clinic #11, © Z-D

Crime Detective V2#10, © HILL

Crime Does Not Pay #94, © LEV   Crimefighters #2, © MCG   Crime Must Pay The Penalty ! #5, © ACE

(Crime Does Not Pay cont'd)

	Good	Fine	Mint
(Scarce)	20.00	40.00	60.00
25-30	12.00	24.00	36.00
31-40	6.00	12.00	18.00
41-50	4.00	8.00	12.00
51-70	2.50	5.00	7.50
71-100: #87-Chip Gardner begins, ends #99			
102	1.50	3.00	4.50
101-105,107	1.00	2.00	3.00
106,114-Frazetta, 1 pg.	2.00	4.00	6.00
108-113,115-130	.80	1.60	2.40
131-140,144-147	.80	1.60	2.40
141-143-One Kubert story in each			
	1.75	3.50	5.25
#1(Golfing-'45)	1.00	2.00	3.00

The Best of--(1944)128pgs. Series contains

4 rebound issues	14.00	28.00	42.00
1945 issue	12.00	24.00	36.00
1946-48 issues	9.00	18.00	27.00
1949,'50 issues	7.00	14.00	21.00
1951-53 issues	6.00	12.00	18.00

NOTE: *Kubert cover-#143. McWilliams story-#91,93,95,102. Whodunnit by Guardineer-#40-104; Chip Gardner by Bob Fujitani (Fuje)-#88-103.*

CRIME EXPOSED
June, 1948; Dec, 1950 - #14, June, 1952
Marvel/Atlas Comics(PrPI/PPI)

#1(6/48)	1.75	3.50	5.25
1(12/50)	1.20	2.40	3.60
2-11,14	.80	1.60	2.40
12,13-Krigstein stories	1.75	3.50	5.25

CRIMEFIGHTERS
April, 1948 - #10, Nov, 1949
Marvel Comics (CmPS/CCC #4-10)

#1	1.20	2.40	3.60
2-10	.80	1.60	2.40

CRIME FIGHTERS (-- Always Win)
#11, Sept, 1954 - #13, Jan, 1955
Atlas Comics (CnPC)

#11-13	.80	1.60	2.40

CRIME FIGHTING DETECTIVE (Shock Det. Cases
1950 - #19, June, 1952   #20 on)
Star Publishing Co.

#11-19: #17-Young King Cole & Dr. Doom app.;			
L.B. Cole covers	1.20	2.40	3.60

CRIME FILES
#5, Sept, 1952 - #6, Nov, 1952
Standard Comics

#5,6-Alex Toth art	Good	Fine	Mint
	2.50	5.00	7.50

CRIME ILLUSTRATED (Magazine)
Nov-Dec, 1955 - #2, Spring, 1956
E.C. Comics

#1-Ingels & Crandall art	6.00	12.00	18.00
2- " " "	5.00	10.00	15.00

NOTE: *Craig story-#2. Crandall stories-#1,2; cover-#2. Evans story-#1. Davis story-#2. Ingels stories-#1,2. Krigstein/Crandall story-#1. Orlando stories-#1,2; cover-#1.*

CRIME INCORPORATED (Formerly My Past Confess-
#12, 6/50 - #2, 8/50; #3, 8/51   ions)
Fox Features Syndicate

#12(6/50), 2	2.50	5.00	7.50
3(1951)	1.50	3.00	4.50

CRIME MACHINE (Magazine)
Feb, 1971 - #2, May, 1971
Skywald Publications

#1-Two Kubert stories reprint (Avon)			
	1.00	2.00	3.00
2	.65	1.35	2.00

CRIME MUST LOSE!
#4, Oct, 1950 - #12, April, 1952
Sports Action (Atlas Comics)

#4-12	.80	1.60	2.40

CRIME MUST PAY THE PENALTY (Formerly Four
Favorites; Penalty #47)
#33, 2/48 - #48, 1/57; 1956 - 1957
Ace Magazines (Current Books)

#33(2/48)-Drug story	3.00	6.00	9.00
34-48	.70	1.40	2.10
#1(1955)	.60	1.20	1.80
2-12	.40	.80	1.20

CRIME MUST STOP
October, 1952
Hillman Periodicals

V1#1-Similar to Monster Crime; Krigstein			
story	5.00	10.00	15.00

CRIME MYSTERIES (Secret Mysteries #16 on)
May, 1952 - #15, 1954
Ribage Publishing Corp. (Trojan Magazines)

#1	2.50	5.00	7.50
2-Marijuana story(7/52)	7.00	14.00	21.00

Crime Patrol #13, © WMG

Crime Patrol #16, © WMG

Crime Reporter #3, © STJ

	Good	Fine	Mint
(Crime Mysteries cont'd)			
3,4-One pg. Frazetta	2.00	4.00	6.00
5-15: #13-Woodbridge art	1.50	3.00	4.50

NOTE: *Bondage covers-#1,8,12.*

CRIME ON THE RUN
1949; June, 1954
St. John Publishing Co./Approved Comics

#8(1949)	1.00	2.00	3.00
#8(Reprint-1954)	.50	1.00	1.50

CRIME ON THE WATERFRONT (Formerly Famous
#4, May, 1952 (Painted cover)   Gangsters)
Realistic Publications

#4-Drug mentioned	3.00	6.00	9.00

CRIME PATROL (International #1-5; Inter-
national Crime Patrol #6, becomes Crypt of
Terror #17 on)
#7, Summer, 1948 - #16, Feb-Mar, 1950
E.C. Comics

#7-14: #12-Ingels art	16.00	32.00	48.00
15-Intro. of Crypt Keeper & Crypt of Terror			
	55.00	110.00	165.00
16-2nd Crypt Keeper app.	40.00	80.00	120.00

CRIME PHOTOGRAPHER (See Casey --)

CRIME REPORTER
Aug, 1948 - #3, Dec, 1948 (Shows Oct.)
St. John Publ. Co.

#1	5.00	10.00	15.00

2-Used in Seduction of the Innocent: illo-
"Children told me what the man was going
to do with the red-hot poker"; reprint/
Dynamic #17 with editing; Baker cover;

	Good	Fine	Mint
Tuska story	10.00	20.00	30.00
3-Baker cover; Tuska sty.	5.00	10.00	15.00

CRIMES BY WOMEN
June, 1948 - #15, 1949; 1954
Fox Features Syndicate

#1	8.00	16.00	24.00
2-15	5.00	10.00	15.00
#54(M.S.Publ.,'54)-Reprint (formerly My Love			
Secret)	4.00	8.00	12.00

CRIMES INCORPORATED
1950   (132 pgs.)
Fox Features Syndicate

No#-See Fox Giants. Contents can vary and
    determines price.

CRIME SMASHER
Summer, 1948   (One Shot)
Fawcett Publications

#1 (Spy Smasher)	3.00	6.00	9.00

CRIME SMASHERS (Secret Mysteries #16 on)
Oct, 1950 - #15, Sept, 1954
Ribage Publishing Corp.(Trojan Magazines)

#1-Used in Seduction of the Innocent, pg.19,
    20 & illo-"A girl raped and murdered";
    Sally the Sleuth begins

	9.00	18.00	27.00
2-Kubert cover	4.00	8.00	12.00
3-7	2.50	5.00	7.50
8-Cocaine issue	3.00	6.00	9.00
9-Bondage cover	2.50	5.00	7.50
10-12,14,15	2.00	4.00	6.00
13-One pg. Frazetta	2.50	5.00	7.50

Crimes By Women #6, © FOX

Crimes Inc. #12, © FOX

Crime Smashers #2, © TM

Crime SuspenStories #24, © WMG   Crown Comics #1, © McCombs Publ.   Crusader From Mars #1, © Z-D

CRIME SUSPENSTORIES (Formerly Vault of Horror
#15, 10-11/50 - #27, 2-3/55   #12-14)
E.C. Comics

	Good	Fine	Mint

#15- identical to No. 1 in content; No. 1 printed on outside front cover. No. 15 (formerly "The Vault of Horror") printed and blackened out on inside front cover with Vol. 1, No. 1 printed over it. Evidently, several of No. 15 were printed before a decision was made not to drop the V. O. H. & Haunt of Fear series. The print run was stopped on No. 15 and continued on No. 1. All of No. 15 were changed as described above.

	Good	Fine	Mint
	60.00	120.00	180.00
#1	50.00	100.00	150.00
2	30.00	60.00	90.00
3-5	25.00	50.00	75.00
6-10	15.00	30.00	45.00
11,12,14,15	11.00	22.00	33.00
13,16-Williamson art	17.50	35.00	52.50
17-Williamson/Frazetta story, 6 pgs.			
	22.00	44.00	66.00
18,19	10.00	20.00	30.00
20-Cover used in Seduction of the Innocent, illo-"Cover of a children's comic book"			
	14.00	28.00	42.00
21,23-27	8.00	16.00	24.00
22-Used in Senate investigation on juvenile delinquency	9.00	18.00	27.00

NOTE: *Craig stories-#1-21; covers-#1-18, 20-22. Crandall stories-#18-26. Davis stories-#4,5, 7,9-12,20. Elder stories-#17,18. Evans stories-#15,19,21,23,25,27; covers-#23,24. Feldstein cover-#19. Ingels stories-#1-12,14,15, 27. Kamen stories-#2,4-18,20-27; covers-#25-27. Krigstein stories-#22,24,25,27. Kurtzman stories-#1,3. Orlando stories-#16,22,24,26. Wood stories-#1,3. Issues 11-15 have E.C. "quickie" stories. #25 contains the famous "Are you a Red Dupe?" editorial.*

CRIMINALS ON THE RUN (Formerly Young King
8-9/48 - #10, 11-1/49-50   Cole)
Premium Group (Novelty Press)

V4#1-6: #6-Young King Cole & Dr. Doom app.; McWilliams art	1.00	2.00	3.00
7-Classic "Fish in the Face" cover			
	1.75	3.50	5.25
V5#1,2	1.00	2.00	3.00
#10	1.00	2.00	3.00

NOTE: *Some issues have L. B. Cole covers.*

CROSS AND THE SWITCHBLADE, THE
1972   (35¢) (Religious)
Spire Christian Comics/Fleming H. Revell Co.

#1	.30	.60	.90

CROSSFIRE
1973

Spire Christian Comics(Fleming H. Revell Co.)

	Good	Fine	Mint
	.25	.50	.75

CROSSING THE ROCKIES (See Classics Special)

CROWN COMICS
Winter, 1944 - #19, Winter, 1949
Golfing/McCombs Publ.

#1-"The Oblong Box" story	4.00	8.00	12.00
2,3	2.00	4.00	6.00
4,5,8-Voodah app.	4.00	8.00	12.00
6-Matt Baker cover/sty.	6.00	12.00	18.00
7-Feldstein story	5.00	10.00	15.00
9-12,14-19: Voodah in #10-16			
	2.50	5.00	7.50
13-Leonard Starr/Bolle stories			
	2.50	5.00	7.50

CRUSADER FROM MARS (See Tops in Adventure)
Jan-Mar, 1952 - #2, Fall, 1952
Ziff-Davis Publ. Co.

#1	6.00	12.00	18.00
2-Bondage cover	5.00	10.00	15.00

CRUSADER RABBIT (See 4-Color #735,805)

CRUSADERS, THE
1974 - 1975 (36 pgs.)(39¢)(Religious)
Chick Publications

Vol. 1-Operation Bucharest ('74). Vol.2-The Broken Cross ('74). Vol.3-Scarface ('74). Vol.4-Exorcists ('75). Vol.5-Chaos ('75). each....	.25	.50	.75

CRYIN' LION, THE
Fall, 1944 - #3, Spring, 1945
William H. Wise

#1-3	.65	1.35	2.00

CRYPT OF SHADOWS
Jan, 1973 - #21, Nov, 1975
Marvel Comics Group

#1-Wolverton reprint/Advs. Into Terror #7			
	.40	.80	1.20
2-10	.25	.50	.75
11-21	.15	.30	.45

NOTE: *Briefer story-#2. Everett story-#6,14 (reprt./Mystery Tales #3). Moldoff story-#8. Powell reprint-#12(Uncanny Tales #38),#14(Mystery #4).*

CRYPT OF TERROR (Tales From the Crypt #20
on; formerly Crime Patrol)
#17, Apr-May, 1950 - #19, Aug-Sept, 1950
E.C. Comics

	Good	Fine	Mint
#17	70.00	140.00	210.00
18,19	50.00	100.00	150.00

NOTE: *Craig stories/covers-#17-19. Feldstein
stories-#17-19. Ingels story-#19. Kurtzman
story-#18. Wood story-#18. Canadian reprints
known; see Table of Contents.*

CUPID
Jan, 1950 - #2, Mar, 1950
Marvel Comics (U.S.A.)

#1,2	1.20	2.40	3.60

CURIO
1930's (?) (Tabloid size, 16-20 pgs.)
Harry 'A' Chesler

	7.00	14.00	21.00

CURLY KAYOE COMICS
1946 - 1948; 1948 - 1950
United Features Syndicate/Dell Publ. Co.

#1(1946)	2.00	4.00	6.00
2-8	1.20	2.40	3.60

United Presents--(Fall, 1948)

	1.50	3.00	4.50
4-Color #871(Dell)	1.20	2.40	3.60

CUSTER'S LAST FIGHT
1950
Avon Periodicals

No#-Partial reprint of Cowpuncher #1

	4.00	8.00	12.00

CUTIE PIE
May, 1955 - #5, Aug, 1956
Junior Reader's Guild/Lev Gleason

#1	.70	1.40	2.10
2-5	.40	.80	1.20

CYCLONE COMICS
June, 1940 - #5, Nov, 1940
Bilbara Publishing Co.

#1-Origin Tornado Tom; Volton begins, Mister Q app.	20.00	40.00	60.00
2	10.00	20.00	30.00
3-5	8.00	16.00	24.00

CYNTHIA DOYLE, NURSE IN LOVE
#66, Oct, 1962 - 1963
Charlton Publications

	Good	Fine	Mint
#66-73	.25	.50	.75

DAFFY (-- Duck #18 on)
1953 - Present
Dell Publishing Co./Gold Key #31 on

4-Color #457,536,615('55)	1.00	2.00	3.00
#4-11(1956-'57)	.60	1.20	1.80
12-19(1958-'59)	.50	1.00	1.50
20-40(1960-'64)	.35	.70	1.05
41-60(1964-'68)	.30	.60	.90
61-90(1969-'73)	.20	.40	.60
91-121(1974-'78)	.15	.30	.45
Mini-Comic #1(1976, 3¼x6½").15	.30	.45	

*(See March of Comics #277,288,313,331,347,
357,375,387,397,402,413)*

DAFFYDILS
1911 (52pgs.) (6x8") (B&W) (Hardcover)
Cupples & Leon Co.

by Tad	6.00	12.00	18.00

DAFFY TUNES COMICS
June, 1947 - #2, Aug, 1947
Four Star Publications

No#	1.00	2.00	3.00
#12-Al Fago cover/story	1.00	2.00	3.00

DAGAR, DESERT HAWK (Capt. Kidd #24; formerly
#14, 2/48 - #23, 4/49 (No#17,18) All Great)
Fox Features Syndicate

#14-Tangi & Safari Cary begin; Edmond Good bondage cover/stories	17.50	35.00	52.50
15,16-E. Good stories	12.00	24.00	36.00
19-22	9.00	18.00	27.00
23-Bondage cover	11.00	22.00	33.00

NOTE: *Tangi by Kamen-#14-16,19; cover-#21.*

DAGAR THE INVINCIBLE (Tales of Sword & Sorc-
Oct, 1972 - #18, 12/76   ery --)
Gold Key   (See Dan Curtis)

#1-Origin; intro. Villains Olstellon & Scorpio	.80	1.60	2.40
2-5: #3-Intro. Graylin, Dagar's woman; Jarn x-over	.50	1.00	1.50
6-1st Dark Gods story	.35	.70	1.05
7-10: #9-Intro. Torgus. #10-1st 3 Witches story	.35	.70	1.05
11-18: #13-Durak & Torgus x-over; story continues in Dr. Spector #15. #14-Dagar's			

Crypt Of Terror #19. © WMG

Curly Kayoe Comics #5. © UFS

Dagar Desert Hawk #23. © FOX

Dagwood #8, © KING   Daisy Comics #1, © EAS   Dale Evans Comics #2, © DC

(Dagar cont'd)	Good	Fine	Mint
origin retold. #18-Origin retold			
	.25	.50	.75

NOTE: *Durak app.-#7,12,13. Tragg app.-#5,11.*

DAGWOOD (Chic Young's)
Sept, 1950 - #140, Nov, 1965
Harvey Publications

#1	4.00	8.00	12.00
2-10	2.00	4.00	6.00
11-30: #30-1pg. Popeye	1.20	2.40	3.60
31-70	.70	1.40	2.10
71-100	.40	.80	1.20
101-128,130,135,138	.25	.50	.75
129,131-134,136,137,139,140-All are 68 pg.			
issues	.30	.60	.90

DAGWOOD SPLITS THE ATOM
1949   (Science comic with King Features
characters) (Giveaway)
King Features Syndicate

No#	2.50	5.00	7.50

DAISY AND DONALD (See W. D. Showcase #8)
May, 1973 - Present
Gold Key

#1-Barks reprint from WDC&S #308			
	.40	.80	1.20
2,3,5	.20	.40	.60
4-Barks reprt/WDC&S #224	.25	.50	.75
6-10	.20	.40	.60
11-34	.15	.30	.45

DAISY & HER PUPS (Blondie's Dogs)
#21, 7/51 - #27, 7/52; #8, 9/52 - #25, 7/55
Harvey Publications

#21-27: #26,27 have #6 & 7 on cover but #26			
& 27 on inside	1.00	2.00	3.00
#8-25	.70	1.40	2.10

DAISY COMICS
Dec, 1936   (Small size: 5¼x7½")
Eastern Color Printing Co.

Joe Palooka, Buck Rogers (2pgs. from Famous			
Funnies #18), Napoleon Flying to Fame,			
Butty & Fally	20.00	40.00	60.00

DAISY DUCK & UNCLE SCROOGE PICNIC TIME
(See Dell Giant #33)

DAISY DUCK & UNCLE SCROOGE SHOW BOAT
(See Dell Giant #55)

DAISY DUCK'S DIARY (See 4-Color #600,659,
743,858,948,1055,1150,1247)

DAISY HANDBOOK
1946 - 1948   (132 pgs.)(50¢)(Pocket-size)
Daisy Manufacturing Co.

	Good	Fine	Mint
#1-Buck Rogers, Red Ryder			
	15.00	30.00	45.00
2-Captain Marvel & Ibis the Invincible, Boy			
Commandos, & Robotman; 2 pgs. Wolverton			
art	15.00	30.00	45.00

DAISY'S RED RYDER GUN BOOK
1955   (132 pgs.)(25¢)(Pocket-size)
Daisy Manufacturing Co.

Boy Commandos, Red Ryder, 1 pg. Wolverton			
art	10.00	20.00	30.00

DAISY MAE (See Oxydol-Dreft)

DAKOTA LIL (See Fawcett Movie Comics)

DAKTARI (Ivan Tors) (TV)
July, 1967 - #4, 1969
Dell Publishing Co.

#1	.25	.50	.75
2-4	.20	.40	.60

DALE EVANS (See Queen of the West --)

DALE EVANS COMICS
Sept-Oct, 1948 - #24, July-Aug, 1952
National Periodical Publications

#1-Sierra Smith begins by Alex Toth			
	6.00	12.00	18.00
2-11-Alex Toth art	3.00	6.00	9.00
12-24	1.75	3.50	5.25

DALTON BOYS, THE
1951
Avon Periodicals

No#-Kinstler cover	5.00	10.00	15.00

DAN CURTIS GIVEAWAYS
1974   (24 pgs.) (3x6") (In color)
Dan Curtis Productions

#1-Dark Shadows, #2-Star Trek, #3-The Twilight
Zone, #4-Ripley's Believe It or Not! True
Ghost Stories, #5-Turok, Son of Stone, #6-
Star Trek, #7-The Occult Files of Dr. Spektor,
#8-Dagar the Invincible, #9-Grimm's Ghost

Stories	Set....	2.50	5.00	7.50

DANDEE
1947
Four Star Publications

	Good	Fine	Mint
	.60	1.20	1.80

DAN DUNN (See Super Book (No#), & Detective
Dan)

DAN DUNN & GANGSTER'S FRAME-UP
1937 (68 pgs.)(5½x7½")(B&W)(Hardcover)
Whitman Publishing Co.

Reprints	5.00	10.00	15.00

DANDY COMICS (Also see Happy Jack Howard)
Spring, 1947 - #7, Spring, 1948
E.C. Comics

#1-Vince Fago art	15.00	30.00	45.00
2-7	10.00	20.00	30.00

DANGER
January, 1953 - #12, 1955
Comic Media/Allen Hardy Assoc.

#1-Heck art	1.50	3.00	4.50
2-10	1.20	2.40	3.60
11,12	.90	1.80	2.70

DANGER
#12, June, 1955 - #14, Nov, 1955
Charlton Comics

#12(#1)-Nyoka begins	2.00	4.00	6.00
13,14	1.50	3.00	4.50

DANGER
1964
Super Comics

Super Reprint #10-12:(Black Dwarf; #11-re-
prints from Johnny Danger),#15,16(Yankee
Girl & Johnny Rebel),#17(Capt. Courage &
Enchanted Dagger),#18(no date)(Gun-Master,
Annie Oakley, The Chameleon)

	1.00	2.00	3.00

DANGER AND ADVENTURE (Formerly Danger)
#15, Feb, 1955 - #27, Feb, 1956
Charlton Comics

#15-No Nyoka	.70	1.40	2.10
16-21	.65	1.35	2.00
22-Ibis the Invincible app.			
	1.50	3.00	4.50
23-Lance O'Casey app.	1.00	2.00	3.00
24-27	.60	1.20	1.80

DANGER IS OUR BUSINESS!
Dec, 1953 - #10, June, 1955
Toby Press

	Good	Fine	Mint
#1-Williamson/Frazetta story, 6pgs. (Science Fiction)	15.00	30.00	45.00
2-10	1.40	2.80	4.20
I.W. Reprint #9('64)-Williamson/Frazetta story reprint from #1; Kinstler cover			
	6.00	12.00	18.00

DANGER IS THEIR BUSINESS (See A-1 Comics #50)

DANGER MAN (See 4-Color Comics #1231)

DANGER TRAIL
July-Aug, 1950 - #5, Mar-Apr, 1951
National Periodical Publications

#1-King Farraday begins, ends #4; Toth art			
	7.00	14.00	21.00
2-5-Toth art in all; Johnny Peril app. #5			
	4.50	9.00	13.50

DANIEL BOONE (See The Exploits of --, 4-
Color #1163, The Legends of --, Frontier Scout
--, Fighting --, & March of Comics #306)

DAN'L BOONE
Sept, 1955 - #8, Sept, 1957
Magazine Enterprises/Sussex Publ. Co. #2 on

#1	1.50	3.00	4.50
2-8	1.00	2.00	3.00

DANIEL BOONE (TV)(See March of Comics #306)
Jan, 1965 - #15, Apr, 1969
Gold Key

#1('64)(TV)	.60	1.20	1.80
2-15	.30	.60	.90

DANNY BLAZE
Aug, 1955 - #2, Oct, 1955
Charlton Comics

#1,2	1.50	3.00	4.50

DANNY DINGLE (See Single Series #17)

DANNY KAYE'S BAND FUN BOOK
1959
H & A Selmer (Giveaway)

	1.20	2.40	3.60

DANNY THOMAS SHOW, THE (See 4-Color#1180,1249)

Danger Is Their Business #11, © ME

Danger Trail #2, © DC

Dan'l Boone #2, © Sussex

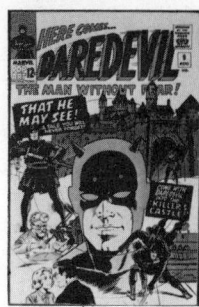

Daredevil #9, © MCG   Daredevil Comics #3, © LEV   Daredevil Comics #69, © LEV

DAN O'NEILL'S COMICS & STORIES
Dec, 1947   (46pgs.)(B&W)(50¢)(Regular size)
Co. & Sons

	Good	Fine	Mint
V1#2	.80	1.60	2.40

DARBY O'GILL & THE LITTLE PEOPLE (See
4-Color #1024 & Movie Comics)

DAREDEVIL (-- & the Black Widow #92-107)
April, 1964 - Present
Marvel Comics Group

	Good	Fine	Mint
#1-Origin Daredevil; Kirby pencils			
	20.00	40.00	60.00
2-Fantastic Four cameo	10.00	20.00	30.00
3-Origin, 1st app. The Owl			
	7.00	14.00	21.00
4,5: #4-dons new costume	4.50	9.00	13.50
6-10: #7-dons new costume	2.50	5.00	7.50
11-20: #12-Facts about Ka-Zar's origin; Kirby art	1.50	3.00	4.50
21-30	.70	1.40	2.10
31-40	.60	1.20	1.80
41-49	.50	1.00	1.50
50-52-Smith art	1.00	2.00	3.00
53-Origin retold	.50	1.00	1.50
54-60	.40	.80	1.20
61-80	.35	.70	1.05
81-90: #81-Black Widow begins. #83-Smith layouts	.30	.60	.90
91-104,106,108-113,115-120	.25	.50	.75
105-Starlin story	.40	.80	1.20
107-Starlin cover	.30	.60	.90
114-1st app. Deathstalker	.30	.60	.90
121-140: #125-1st app. Copperhead			
	.20	.40	.60
141,143-150	.15	.30	.45
142-Nova cameo	.20	.40	.60
151-158	.15	.30	.45
Giant Size #1('75)	.50	1.00	1.50
Special #1(9/67)-new art	1.00	2.00	3.00
Special #2(2/71)(Wood reprint), #3(1/72)-reprints	.50	1.00	1.50
Annual #4(10/76)	.40	.80	1.20

NOTE: _John Buscema stories-#136,137; cover-
#142. Craig inks-#50,52. Everett story & cov-
er-#1, inks-#21,81,83. Kirby covers-#2-4,5(w/
Wood); layouts-#13. Orlando stories-#2-4.
Powell pencils-#11. Wood stories-#5-10; inks-
#11; covers-#5-11._

DAREDEVIL COMICS (See Silver Streak)
7/41 - #134, 9/56 (Charles Biro stories)
Lev Gleason Publications
    (#1 titled "Daredevil Battles Hitler")

#1-The Silver Streak, Lance Hale, Dickey

	Good	Fine	Mint
Dean, Pirate Prince & Cloud Curtis team up with Daredevil and battle Hitler; Daredevil battles the Claw			
	225.00	450.00	675.00
2-London, Pat Patriot, Nightro, Real American #1, Dickie Dean, Pirate Prince, & Times Square begin; intro. & only app. The Pioneer, Champion of America			
	120.00	240.00	360.00
3-Origin of 13	65.00	130.00	195.00
4	55.00	110.00	165.00
5-Intro. Sniffer & Jinx; Ghost vs. Claw begins by Bob Wood	45.00	90.00	135.00
6-10	35.00	70.00	105.00
11	25.00	50.00	75.00
12-Origin of The Claw; Scoop Scuttle by Wolverton begins(2-4pgs.), ends #22, not in #21	35.00	70.00	105.00
13-Intro. of Little Wise Guys			
	35.00	70.00	105.00
14	20.00	40.00	60.00
15-Death of Meatball	25.00	50.00	75.00
16,17	16.00	32.00	48.00
18-New origin of Daredevil-Not same as Silver Streak #6	27.50	55.00	82.50
19,20	14.00	28.00	42.00
21-Reprints cover of Silver Streak #6(on inside) + intro. of The Claw from Silver Streak #1	12.00	24.00	36.00
22-30	7.00	14.00	21.00
31-Death of The Claw	10.00	20.00	30.00
32-37	5.00	10.00	15.00
38-Origin of Daredevil retold from #18			
	7.00	14.00	21.00
39,40	5.00	10.00	15.00
41-50: #42-Intro. Kilroy in Daredevil			
	3.50	7.00	10.50
51-69-Last Daredevil ish.	2.25	4.50	6.75
70-Little Wise Guys take over book; McWilliams art; Hot Rock Flanagan begins, ends #80	1.50	3.00	4.50
71-79,81: #79-Daredevil returns			
	1.50	3.00	4.50
80-Daredevil x-over	1.50	3.00	4.50
82,90-One pg. Frazetta ad in both			
	2.00	4.00	6.00
83-89	1.25	2.50	3.75
91-100	1.20	2.40	3.60
101-134	1.20	2.40	3.60

NOTE: _Wolverton's Scoop Scuttle-#12-20,22.
Bolle art-#125. McWilliams art-#73,75,79._

DARING ADVENTURES
May, 1954 - 1956
St. John Publishing Co.

	Good	Fine	Mint
#6-Two Krigstein stories	2.00	4.00	6.00

(Daring Advs. cont'd)   Good   Fine   Mint
7-10   1.20   2.40   3.60
11-18   1.00   2.00   3.00
3-D #1(11/53)-Reprints lead story/Son of Sinbad #1 by Kubert   8.00   16.00   24.00

DARING ADVENTURES
1963 - 1964
I.W. Enterprises/Super Comics

IW Reprint #9-Three Disbrow stories
                           2.00   4.00   6.00
Super Reprint #10,11('63)-Dynamic Man
                           1.00   2.00   3.00
Super Reprint #12('64)-Phantom Lady from
  Fox(reprints #14,15)   6.00   12.00   18.00
Super Reprint #15('64)-Hooded Menace
                           4.00   8.00   12.00
Super Reprint #16('64)-Mr. E, Dynamic Man
                           1.00   2.00   3.00
Super Reprint #17('64)-Green Lama by Raboy
  from Green Lama #3   2.00   4.00   6.00
Super Reprint #18-Origin Atlas
                           1.00   2.00   3.00

DARING COMICS (Formerly Daring Mystery)
#9, Fall/44 - #12, Fall/45   (Jeanie #13 on)
Timely Comics

#9-Human Torch & Sub-Mariner begin
                          20.00   40.00   60.00
10-The Angel only app.   16.00   32.00   48.00
11,12-The Destroyer app. 16.00   32.00   48.00

DARING CONFESSIONS (Formerly Youthful Hearts)
#4, 1952 - #7, May, 1953
Youthful Magazines

#4-Doug Wildey art   .80   1.60   2.40
 5-7: #6-Wildey art   .80   1.60   2.40

DARING LOVE (Radiant Love #2 on)
Sept-Oct, 1953
Gillmore Magazines

#1   1.75   3.50   5.25

DARING LOVE (Formerly Youthful Romances)
#15, Dec, 1952
Ribage/Pix

#15   1.00   2.00   3.00

DARING MYSTERY COMICS (Comedy #9 on; title
changed to Daring with #9)
Jan, 1940 - #8, Jan, 1942
Timely Comics

#1-Origin The Fiery Mask by Joe Simon; Mon-
  ako, Prince of Magic, John Steele, Soldier of Fortune, Doc Doyle begin; Flash
  Foster & Barney Mullen, Sea Rover only
  app.   350.00 700.00 1050.00
 2-Origin The Phantom Bullet & only app.;
  The Laughing Mask & Mr. E only app.; Tro-
  jak the Tiger Man begins, ends #6; Zephyr
  Jones & K-4 & His Sky Devils app., also
  #4   175.00 350.00 525.00
 3-The Phantom Reporter, Dale of FBI, Breeze
  Barton, Captain Strong & Marvex, the
  Super-Robot only app.; The Purple Mask
  begins   120.00 240.00 360.00
 4-Last Purple Mask; Whirlwind Carter begins;
  Dan Gorman, G-Man app.
                  100.00 200.00 300.00
 5-The Falcon begins; The Fiery Mask, Little
  Hercules app. by Sagendorf in the Segar
  style   85.00 170.00 255.00
 6-Origin of Marvel Boy by S&K & only app.;
  Flying Flame, Dynaman, & Stuporman only
  app.; The Fiery Mask by S&K; S&K cover
                  105.00 210.00 315.00
 7-Origin The Blue Diamond, Captain Daring
  by S&K, The Challenger, The Fin by Everett, The Silver Scorpion & The Thunderer
  by Burgos; Mr. Millions app.
                  120.00 240.00 360.00
 8-Origin Citizen V; Last Fin, Silver Scorpion, Capt. Daring by Borth, Blue Diamond
  & The Thunderer; S&K cover; Rudy the Robot
  only app.   80.00 160.00 240.00
NOTE: *Simon art-#2,3.*

DARK MANSION OF FORBIDDEN LOVE, THE (Becomes
Forbidden Tales of Dark Mansion #5 on)
Sept-Oct, 1971 - #4, Mar-Apr, 1972
National Periodical Publications

#1   .40   .80   1.20
 2-Adams cover   .50   1.00   1.50
 3-Jeff Jones cover   .50   1.00   1.50
 4   .25   .50   .75

DARK MYSTERIES
June-July, 1951 - #30, 1955
"Master"-"Merit" Publications

#1-Wood cover/story,8pgs. 8.00   16.00   24.00
 2-Wood cover/story w/Harrison, 8pgs.
                           7.00   14.00   21.00
 3-10: #7-Harrison story 1.00   2.00   3.00
11-30: #20-Bondage cover   .80   1.60   2.40
NOTE: *Hollingsworth stories-#7-9.*

Daring Mystery #1, © MCG

Daring Mystery #4, © MCG

Dark Mysteries #3, © Master Publ.

Dark Shadows #26, © GK   Darling Love #5, © AP   Date With Danger #5, © STD

DARK SHADOWS
October, 1957 - 1958
Steinway Comic Publications (Ajax)

	Good	Fine	Mint
#1	.80	1.60	2.40
2,3	.50	1.00	1.50

DARK SHADOWS (TV) (See Dan Curtis)
May, 1969 - #35, Feb, 1976
Gold Key

#1(30039-903)-with pull-out poster			
	.60	1.20	1.80
2-5: #3-with pull-out poster; #4-photo			
cover	.40	.80	1.20
6-10	.30	.60	.90
11-20	.25	.50	.75
21-35	.20	.40	.60
Story Digest #1(6/70)	.40	.80	1.20

DARLING LOVE
Oct-Nov, 1949 - #11, 1952 (no month)
Close Up/Archie Publ.(A Darling Magazine)

	Good	Fine	Mint
#1	2.00	4.00	6.00
2-8,10,11	1.25	2.50	3.75
9-Krigstein story	2.00	4.00	6.00

DARLING ROMANCE
Sept-Oct, 1949 - #7, 1951
Close Up (MLJ Publications)

#1	2.00	4.00	6.00
2-7	1.25	2.50	3.75

DASTARDLY & MUTTLEY IN THEIR FLYING MACHINES
(See Fun-In #1-4,6)

DASTARDLY & MUTTLEY KITE FUN BOOK (Giveaway)
1969 (16pgs.;5x7") (Hanna-Barbera's)
Florida Power & Light Co./Sou. Calif. Edison/
Pacific Gas & Electric

	.15	.30	.45

DATE WITH DANGER
#5, Dec, 1952 - #6, Feb, 1953
Standard Comics

#5,6	1.00	2.00	3.00

DATE WITH DEBBI
Jan-Feb, 1969 - #18, Oct-Nov, 1972
National Periodical Publications

#1	.20	.40	.60
2-18	.15	.30	.45

DATE WITH JUDY, A (Radio/TV)
Oct-Nov, 1947 - #79, Oct-Nov, 1960
National Periodical Publications

	Good	Fine	Mint
#1	3.00	6.00	9.00
2	1.50	3.00	4.50
3-10	1.20	2.40	3.60
11-20	.70	1.40	2.10
21-40	.50	1.00	1.50
41-79	.40	.80	1.20

DATE WITH MILLIE, A
Oct, 1959 - #35, 1964
Atlas/Marvel Comics (MPC)

#1	1.50	3.00	4.50
2-10	.70	1.40	2.10
11-20	.40	.80	1.20
21-35	.20	.40	.60

DATE WITH PATSY, A
Sept, 1957
Atlas Comics

#1	1.00	2.00	3.00

DAVID AND GOLIATH (See 4-Color #1205)

DAVID CASSIDY
Feb, 1972 - #13, July, 1973?
Charlton Comics

#1	.50	1.00	1.50
2-13	.25	.50	.75

DAVID LADD'S LIFE STORY (See Movie Classics)

DAVY CROCKETT (See Fighting --, Frontier
Fighters, It's Game Time, & Western Tales)

DAVY CROCKETT
1951
Avon Periodicals

No#	4.00	8.00	12.00

DAVY CROCKETT (TV)
May, 1955 - #2, Nov, 1969 (Walt Disney)
Dell Publishing Co./Gold Key

4-Color #631,639	1.50	3.00	4.50
4-Color #664,671(Marsh art)			
	1.75	3.50	5.25
Annual #1('55-25¢-Marsh art-100pgs.)			
	3.50	7.00	10.50
#1(9/63-Gold Key)	.40	.80	1.20
2	.25	.50	.75

DAVY CROCKETT FRONTIER FIGHTER
Aug, 1955 - #8, 1957
Charlton Comics

	Good	Fine	Mint
#1	1.00	2.00	3.00
2-8	.60	1.20	1.80
Hunting With --('55, 16pgs.)-Ben Franklin Store giveaway(Publ.-S. Rose)	.80	1.60	2.40

DAVY CROCKETT IN THE RAID AT PINEY CREEK
1955 (16pgs.)(5x7½")(Premium)(Walt Disney)
Hudson Div. of American Motors

	2.00	4.00	6.00

DAYS OF THE MOB (See In the Days of the Mob)

DAZEY'S DIARY
June-Aug, 1962
Dell Publishing Co.

#01-174-208	.30	.60	.90

DC COMICS PRESENTS
July-Aug, 1978 - Present
DC Comics

#1-Superman & Flash, #2-Superman & Flash, #3-Superman & Adam Strange, #4-Superman & Metal Men, #5-Superman & Aquaman, #6-Superman & Green Lantern, #7-Superman & Red Tornado, #8-Superman & Swamp Thing

each....	.20	.40	.60

DC 100 PG. SUPER SPECTACULAR (50¢)(No #1-3)
1971 - #13, 6/72; #14, 2/73 - #22, 11/73
National Periodical Publications

#4-Weird Mystery Tales-Johnny Peril & Phantom Stranger; cover & chapter headings by Wrightson; origin Jungle Boy of Jupiter	.80	1.60	2.40
5-Love stories	.50	1.00	1.50
6-"World's Greatest Super-Heroes"-JLA, JSA, Spectre, Johnny Quick, Vigilante, Wildcat & Hawkman; Adams wrap-around cover	1.00	2.00	3.00
7-(See Superman #245)			
8-(See Batman #238)			
9-(See Our Army at War #242)			
10-(See Adventure #416)			
11-(See Flash #214)			
12-(See Superboy #185)			
13-(See Superman #252)			
14-Batman-(reprints Detective #31,32); Dollman, Wonder Woman, The Atom, Wildcat, & Blackhawk reprints	.60	1.20	1.80

	Good	Fine	Mint
15-Superboy, Boy Commandos, Sandman, & Aquaman reprints; S&K art	.50	1.00	1.50
16-Sgt. Rock & Capt. Storm reprints	.50	1.00	1.50
17-JLA-Sandman & All-Star #37 reprint	.50	1.00	1.50
18-Superman, Hourman, Captain Triumph, The G.A. Atom reprint	.50	1.00	1.50
19-Tarzan newspaper reprints by Russ Manning	.50	1.00	1.50
20-Batman origin Two-Face; Dr. Mid-Nite, Starman, Black Canary, Blackhawk, The Spectre reprints	.50	1.00	1.50
21-Superboy reprints	.50	1.00	1.50
22-The Flash reprints	.50	1.00	1.50

NOTE: _Anderson story-#11,22. Crandall art-#14. Drucker reprint-#4. Infantino stories-#17,20,22. Kubert stories-#6,7,16,17; covers-#16,19. Meskin art-#4,22. Toth stories-#17,20._

DC SPECIAL (Also see Super DC --)
10-12/68 - #15, 11-12/71; #16, Spr/75 - #29,
National Periodical Publ.   8-9/77

#1-All Infantino ish; Flash, Batman, Adam Strange reprints	.80	1.60	2.40
2-Teen Favorites	.50	1.00	1.50
3-All Heroine ish. Unpubbed G.A. Black Canary & Wonder Woman sty.	.60	1.20	1.80
4-Mystery Tales	.40	.80	1.20
5-All Kubert ish. Viking Prince, Sgt. Rock reprints	.80	1.60	2.40
6-Wild Frontier	.50	1.00	1.50
7-Strange Sports Stories	.40	.80	1.20
8-Wanted	.50	1.00	1.50
9-Strange Sports Stories	.50	1.00	1.50
10-Stop! In the Name of the Law; reprints/Showcase #1,5	.50	1.00	1.50
11-The Monsters Are Here; Neal Adams/Wrightson cvr; 2 Kirby stys.	.50	1.00	1.50
12-Viking Prince; Kubert cover; reprints from Brave & the Bold #1,5,9,16; new Kubert splashes	.80	1.60	2.40
13-Strange Sports Stories	.50	1.00	1.50
14-Wanted	.50	1.00	1.50
15-G.A. Plastic Man origin reprint(Police#1) & origin Woozy by Cole	1.00	2.00	3.00
16-Super Heroes Battle Super Gorillas	.50	1.00	1.50
17-Green Lantern	.50	1.00	1.50
18-Earth Shaking Stories-Flash, Green Lantern, Captain Marvel	.50	1.00	1.50
19-War Against the Giants	.50	1.00	1.50
20-Green Lantern	.50	1.00	1.50
21-War Against the Monsters	.40	.80	1.20
22-25-The 3 Musketeers(new) & Robin Hood (reprints)	.40	.80	1.20

Davy Crockett No#, © AVON

DC Special #12, © DC

DC Special #17, © DC

DC Super-Stars #4, © DC   D-Day #1, © CC   Dead-Eye Western V2#6, © HILL

	Good	Fine	Mint
(DC Special cont'd)			
26-Enemy Ace reprts/Kubert	.40	.80	1.20
27-Captain Comet	.40	.80	1.20
28-Earth Shattering Disaster Stories			
	.40	.80	1.20
29-Secret Origin of the Justice Society			
	.40	.80	1.20

NOTE: _Adams covers-#3,4,6,11,29. Infantino
stories-#13. Kubert story-#22. Newton story-
#27. Staton story-#29. Toth story-#13._

DC SPECIAL SERIES
Sept, 1977 - Present
National Periodical Publ./DC Comics

	Good	Fine	Mint
#1-Five-Star Super-Hero Spectacular; Adams			
cover; Staton story	.40	.80	1.20
2(#1)-Original Swamp Thing Saga, The(9-10/77)			
reprints Swamp Thing #1&2 by Wrightson;			
Wrightson wrap-around cover			
	.40	.80	1.20
3(#2)-Sgt. Rock Special(10/77); Kubert			
cover	.35	.70	1.05
4(#1)-Unexpected Annual, The(10/77)			
	.35	.70	1.05
5(No#)-Superman Spectacular(11/77, 68pgs.)			
	.35	.70	1.05
6(No#)-Secret Society of Super-Villains			
Special(11/77)	.35	.70	1.05
7(No#)-Ghosts Special(12/77)			
	.35	.70	1.05
8(No#)-Brave & the Bold Special with Batman			
	.35	.70	1.05
9(No#)-Wonder Woman Spectacular(3/78)-Heath,			
Ditko art	.25	.50	.75
10(No#)-Secret Origins of Super-Heroes(4/78)			
	.25	.50	.75
11(No#)-The Flash Spectacular(5/78)-Anderson,			
Wood art	.25	.50	.75
12-Secrets of Haunted House Special(6/78)-			
Starlin cover	.25	.50	.75
13(No#)-Sgt. Rock Spectacular(Summer/78)-			
Kubert cover	.25	.50	.75
14(No#)-Original Swamp Thing Saga(Summer/78)-			
original Wrightson wrap-around cover			
	.25	.50	.75
15(No#)-Batman Spectacular(Summer/78)			
	.25	.50	.75
16-Jonah Hex Spectacular(Fall/78)			
	.25	.50	.75

NOTE: _# in () is cover #; the actual # of
#1-4 is on inside._

DC SUPER-STARS
March, 1976 - #18, Winter, 1978
National Periodical Publications/DC Comics

	Good	Fine	Mint
#1-Teen Titans	.40	.80	1.20

	Good	Fine	Mint
2-Adam Strange, Hawkman	.35	.70	1.05
3-Superman, Legion of Super-Heroes			
	.35	.70	1.05
4-Adam Strange	.35	.70	1.05
5-The Flash	.35	.70	1.05
6-Adam Strange, Capt. Comet, Tommy Tomorrow,			
Space Cabby	.35	.70	1.05
7-Aquaman	.35	.70	1.05
8-Adam Strange, Star Rovers, Space Ranger			
	.35	.70	1.05
9-Superman, Nighthawk	.35	.70	1.05
10-Nine super-heroes & 9 super-villains			
	.35	.70	1.05
11-Magic; Morrow cover	.35	.70	1.05
12-Superboy	.35	.70	1.05
13-Aragones cover/art	.35	.70	1.05
14-Secret Origins of Super-Villains			
	.35	.70	1.05
15-War Heroes-Kubert cover	.35	.70	1.05
16-Star Hunters (1st appearance)-Newton sty/			
cover	.35	.70	1.05
17-Secret Origins of Super-Heroes(1st app. &			
origin of The Huntress)-Staton story/cover,			
18-Deadman & The Phantom Stranger			
	.35	.70	1.05

D-DAY (Also see Special War Series)
Summer, 1963 - #6, Nov, 1968
Charlton Comics

	Good	Fine	Mint
#1(1963)-Montes/Bache cvr.	.40	.80	1.20
2(Fall, '64)-3 Wood stys.	1.00	2.00	3.00
3-6('68)-Montes/Bache art #5			
	.25	.50	.75

DEAD END CRIME STORIES
April, 1949   (52 pgs.)
Kirby Publishing Co.

	Good	Fine	Mint
No#-Powell, Roussos art	1.50	3.00	4.50

DEAD EYE CRIME STORIES
1950
Hillman Periodicals

	Good	Fine	Mint
#1-Roussos art	1.00	2.00	3.00

DEAD-EYE WESTERN COMICS
11-12/48 - V3#1, 1952
Hillman Periodicals

	Good	Fine	Mint
V1#1(1948-52pgs.)-Krigstein story			
	3.00	6.00	9.00
No#(3-4/49, 52pgs.)	1.75	3.50	5.25
V1#2-12	1.00	2.00	3.00
V2#1,2,5-8,10-12	.80	1.60	2.40
3,4-Krigstein art	1.80	3.60	5.40

(Dead-Eye Western cont'd)

	Good	Fine	Mint
9-1pg. Frazetta ad	1.50	3.00	4.50
V3#1	.60	1.20	1.80

NOTE: *Kinstleresque* stories by *McCann*-#12, *V2#1,2,V3#1.*

DEADLIEST HEROES OF KUNG FU
Summer, 1975
Marvel Comics Group

	Good	Fine	Mint
#1	.40	.80	1.20

DEADLY HANDS OF KUNG FU, THE
6/74 - #33, 2/77 (75¢)(Magazine-B&W)
Marvel Comics Group

#1-Origin Sons of the Tiger; Shang-Chi, Master of Kung Fu begins; Bruce Lee photo			
pin-up	1.50	3.00	4.50
2-5	1.00	2.00	3.00
6-15	.70	1.40	2.10
16-33	.60	1.20	1.80
Special Album Edition #1(Summer, '74)			
	.60	1.20	1.80

NOTE: *Adams* covers-#1,2-4,11,12,14,17. *Starlin* stories-#1,2,15(reprint). *Staton* stories-#31,32. *Sons of the Tiger* in #1,3,4, 6-9.

DEAD OF NIGHT
Dec, 1973 - #11, Aug, 1975
Marvel Comics Group

#1-Reprints	.20	.40	.60
2-10: #9-Kirby reprint	.15	.30	.45
11-Intro. & 1st app. The Scarecrow; Kane/Wrightson cover	.25	.50	.75

DEAD WHO WALK, THE
1952
Realistic Comics

No#	7.00	14.00	21.00

DEADWOOD GULCH
1931 (52 pgs.) (B&W)
Dell Publishing Co.

By Gordon Rogers	6.00	12.00	18.00

DEAN MARTIN & JERRY LEWIS (See Advs. of —)

DEAR BEATRICE FAIRFAX
Nov, 1949 - #9, Sept, 1951 (Vern Greene art)
Best/Standard Comics(King Features)

#1	1.50	3.00	4.50
2-9	1.20	2.40	3.60

NOTE: *Schomburg painted covers-#5-7,9.*

DEAR HEART
1956
Ajax

	Good	Fine	Mint
#15	.60	1.20	1.80

DEAR LONELY HEART (-- Illustrated #1-6)
Mar, 1951; #3, 12/51 - #8, 10/52
Artful Publications

#1	4.00	8.00	12.00
2,4-8	2.50	5.00	7.50
3-Matt Baker Jungle Girl story			
	3.50	7.00	10.50

DEAR LONELY HEARTS
#4, Feb, 1954 - #8, Oct, 1954
Harwell Publ./Mystery Publ. Co.

#4-8	1.20	2.40	3.60

DEARLY BELOVED
Fall, 1952
Ziff-Davis Publishing Co.

#1	1.50	3.00	4.50

DEAR NANCY PARKER
June, 1963 - #2, Sept, 1963
Gold Key

#1,2	.25	.50	.75

DEATH VALLEY
Oct, 1953 - #9, 1955
Comic Media/Magazine Enterprises

#1-Old Scout	1.00	2.00	3.00
2-9	.70	1.40	2.10

DEBBIE DEAN, CAREER GIRL
April, 1945 - #2, 1945
Civil Service Publ.

#1,2-Newspaper reprints by Bert Whitman			
	2.00	4.00	6.00

DEBBIE'S DATES
Apr-May, 1969 - #11, Dec-Jan, 1970-71
National Periodical Publications

#1-11: #4-Adams text illo.	.15	.30	.45

DEEP, THE (Movie)
November, 1977
Marvel Comics Group

Dead Of Night #11, © MCG

Dear Beatrice Fairfax #9, © KING

Dear Lonely Hearts #4, © Mystery Publ.

The Defenders #3, © MCG

Dell Giant Comics #25, © ERB

Dell Giant Comics #41, © DELL

	Good	Fine	Mint
(The Deep cont'd)			
#1-Infantino story/cover	.20	.40	.60

DEFENDERS, THE (TV)
Sept-Nov, 1962 - #2, Feb-Apr, 1963
Dell Publishing Co.

	Good	Fine	Mint
#12-176-211(#1), 304(#2)	.40	.80	1.20

DEFENDERS, THE (Also see Marvel Feature)
Aug, 1972 - Present
Marvel Comics Group

	Good	Fine	Mint
#1-The Hulk, Doc Strange, & Sub-Mariner begin	3.50	7.00	10.50
2	1.75	3.50	5.25
3-5: #4-Valkyrie joins	1.25	2.50	3.75
6-10	1.00	2.00	3.00
11-20: #11-X-Men, The Titan app. #13,14-Squadron Sinister app.; Sub-Mariner leaves, Nighthawk joins. #15,16-Magneto app.; #17-19-Wrecking Crew app.	.70	1.40	2.10
21-30: #26-29-Guardians of the Galaxy app.	.50	1.00	1.50
31,32-Origin Nighthawk	.35	.70	1.05
33-40: #36-Intro. Red Guardian	.35	.70	1.05
41-50: #43-Kirby cover. #44-Hellcat joins. #45-Dr. Strange leaves. #47-Wonderman app.	.30	.60	.90
51-60	.20	.40	.60
61,65-67	.15	.30	.45
62-64-Nova & others cameo	.20	.40	.60

NOTE: *J. Buscema* cover-#66. *Kirby covers-#43-45. Silver Surfer in #2,3,6,8-11.*

	Good	Fine	Mint
Annual #1(11/76)	.70	1.40	2.10
Giant Size #1(7/74)-Silver Surfer app.; Starlin art; Everett & Ditko reprint	1.00	2.00	3.00
Giant Size #2(10/74)	.60	1.20	1.80
Giant Size #3(1/75)-Starlin art	.60	1.20	1.80
Giant Size #4(4/75), #5(7/75)-Guardians app.	.50	1.00	1.50

DELECTA OF THE PLANETS (See Fawcett Miniatures & Don Fortune)

DELLA VISION
April, 1955 - #3, Aug, 1955
Atlas Comics

	Good	Fine	Mint
#1-3	1.50	3.00	4.50

DELL GIANT COMICS
#21, 9/59 - #55, 9/61 (Most 80 pgs., 25¢)
Dell Publishing Co.

	Good	Fine	Mint
#21-Tom & Jerry Picnic Time	.90	1.80	2.70
22-Huey, Dewey & Louie Back to School(10/59)	1.20	2.40	3.60
23-Little Lulu & Tubby Halloween Fun	3.50	7.00	10.50
24-Woody Woodpecker Family Fun (11/59)	.80	1.60	2.40
25-Tarzan's Jungle World(11/59)-Marsh art	2.50	5.00	7.50
26-Christmas Parade-Barks art(Disney)	6.00	12.00	18.00
27-Man in Space-Reprints 4-Color #716,866, & 954(100pgs., 35¢)(Disney)	1.75	3.50	5.25
28-Bugs Bunny's Winter Fun (2/60)	1.00	2.00	3.00
29-Little Lulu & Tubby in Hawaii (4/60)	3.00	6.00	9.00
30-Disneyland USA(6/60)-Reprinted in Vacation in Disneyland	1.50	3.00	4.50
31-Huckleberry Hound Summer Fun (7/60)	.70	1.40	2.10
32-Bugs Bunny Beach Party	1.00	2.00	3.00
33-Daisy Duck & Uncle Scrooge Picnic Time (9/60)	2.25	4.50	6.75
34-Nancy & Sluggo Summer Camp (8/60)	1.00	2.00	3.00
35-Huey, Dewey & Louie Back to School (10/60)	1.20	2.40	3.60
36-Little Lulu & Witch Hazel Halloween Fun (10/60)	2.50	5.00	7.50
37-Tarzan, King of the Jungle(11/60)-Marsh art	2.50	5.00	7.50
38-Uncle Donald & His Nephews Family Fun (11/60)	1.20	2.40	3.60
39-Walt Disney's Merry Christmas(12/60)-Not by Barks	1.40	2.80	4.20
40-Woody Woodpecker Christmas Parade(12/60)	.70	1.40	2.10
41-Yogi Bear's Winter Sports(12/60)	.70	1.40	2.10
42-Little Lulu & Tubby in Australia (1961)	2.50	5.00	7.50
43-Mighty Mouse in Outer Space (5/61)	1.50	3.00	4.50
44-Around the World with Huckleberry & His Friends (7/61)	.70	1.40	2.10
45-Nancy & Sluggo Summer Camp (8/61)	1.00	2.00	3.00
46-Bugs Bunny Beach Party	1.75	3.35	5.00
47-Mickey & Donald in Vacationland (8/61)	1.50	3.00	4.50
48-The Flintstones (Bedrock Bedlam) (7/61)	.60	1.20	1.80

(Dell Giant Comics cont'd)	Good	Fine	Mint
49-Huey, Dewey & Louie Back to School (9/61)	1.20	2.40	3.60
50-Little Lulu & Witch Hazel Trick 'N' Treat (10/61)	2.50	5.00	7.50
51-Tarzan, King of the Jungle by Jesse Marsh (11/61)	2.00	4.00	6.00
52-Uncle Donald & His Nephews Dude Ranch (11/61)	1.50	3.00	4.50
53-Donald Duck Merry Christmas-Not by Barks (12/61)	1.50	3.00	4.50
54-Woody Woodpecker Christmas Party(12/61) issued after #55	.70	1.40	2.10
55-Daisy Duck & Uncle Scrooge Showboat(9/61)	1.50	3.00	4.50

DELL JUNIOR TREASURY (15¢)
June, 1955 - #10, Oct, 1957
Dell Publishing Co.

	Good	Fine	Mint
#1-Alice in Wonderland-reprints 4-Color #331 (52 pgs.)	2.50	5.00	7.50
2-Aladdin & the Wonderful Lamp	2.50	5.00	7.50
3-Gulliver's Travels	2.00	4.00	6.00
4-Advs. of Mr. Frog & Miss Mouse	2.00	4.00	6.00
5-The Wizard of Oz	2.50	5.00	7.50
6-Heidi (10/56)	2.00	4.00	6.00
7-Santa & the Angel	2.00	4.00	6.00
8-Raggedy Ann & the Camel with the Wrinkled Knees	2.00	4.00	6.00
9-Clementina the Flying Pig	2.00	4.00	6.00
10-Advs. of Tom Sawyer	2.50	5.00	7.50

DEMON, THE
Aug-Sept, 1972 - #16, Jan, 1974
National Periodical Publications

#1-Origin; Kirby art in all			
	1.00	2.00	3.00
2-5	.60	1.20	1.80
6-10	.50	1.00	1.50
11-16	.40	.80	1.20

DEMON-HUNTER
Sept, 1975
Seaboard Periodicals (Atlas)

#1-Origin	.20	.40	.60

DENNIS THE MENACE (See The Best of --)
Aug, 1953 - Present
Standard Comics/Pines #15-31/Hallden/
Fawcett #32 on

#1	12.00	24.00	36.00

	Good	Fine	Mint
2	5.00	10.00	15.00
3-10	2.50	5.00	7.50
11-20	1.75	3.50	5.25
21-40	1.35	2.75	4.00
41-60	1.00	2.00	3.00
61-90	.60	1.20	1.80
91-160	.30	.60	.90
-- & Dirt('68)-Soil Conservation giveaway	.50	1.00	1.50
-- Away We Go('70)-Caladayl giveaway	.50	1.00	1.50
Food & Drug giveaway('61-16pgs.)("Takes a Poke at Poison")	1.00	2.00	3.00
Fun Book #1('60)(100pgs.)	2.00	4.00	6.00
Takes a Poke at Poison(F.D.A. giveaway)-1961 (revised 1/66, 11/70)	.50	1.00	1.50

DENNIS THE MENACE (Giants)
(#1 titled Giant Vacation Special; becomes Bonus Magazine #76 on)
#1-8,18,23,25,30,38, 100pgs.; rest to #41 are 84pgs.; #42-75, 68pgs.
Summer, 1955 - #75, 1970
Standard/Pines/Hallden(Fawcett)

No#-Giant Vacation Special(Summer, 1955-Standard)	2.50	5.00	7.50

No#-Christmas issue(Winter/55)
#2-Giant Vacation Special (Summer'56, Pines)
 3-Giant Christmas issue(Winter,'56, Pines)
 4-Giant Vacation Special(Summer'57, Pines)
 5-Giant Christmas issue(Winter'57, Pines)
 6-In Hawaii(Giant Vacation Special)(Sum.'58-Pines)-Reprint Summer'60 + 3 more times
 6-Giant Christmas issue(Winter'58)
 7-In Hollywood(Winter'59, Hallden)
 8-In Mexico(Winter'60,100pgs.-Hallden/Fawcett)
 9-Goes to Camp(Summer'61, 84pgs., 2nd printing Summer'62)-1st CCA approved ish.
10-X-Mas issue(Winter '61)

	each....	1.40	2.80	4.20

11-Giant Christmas issue(Winter'62)
12-Triple Feature(Winter'62)
13-Best of Dennis the Menace(Spr'63)-reprints
14-And His Dog Ruff(Summer'63)
15-In Washington, D.C.(Summer'63)
16-Goes to Camp(Summer'63)-reprints #9
17-& His Pal Joey(Winter'63)
18-In Hawaii(reprints #6)
19-Giant Christmas issue(Winter'63)
20-Spring Special(Spring'64)

	each....	1.20	2.40	3.60

21-The Best of--(Spring'64)-reprints
22-T.V. Special(Spring'64)
23-In Hollywood(Summer'64-100pgs.)reprints#7
24-Goes to Camp(Summer'64)-reprints #9
25-In Mexico - reprints #8

Dell Jr. Treasury #5, © DELL

The Demon #1, © DC

Dennis The Menace Giant #14, © FAW

(Dennis the Menace cont'd)

(Dennis the Menace cont'd)

	Good	Fine	Mint
26-In Washington, D.C.(Summer'64)-reprts.#15
27-Giant Christmas issue(Winter'64)
28-Triple Feature(Spring'65)
29-Best of --(Spring'65)-reprints
30-In Hawaii(Summer'65)-reprints #6
31-All Year 'Round(Summer'65)
32-And His Pal Joey!(Summer'65)-reprints #17
33-In California(Summer'65)
34-And His Dog Ruff(Sum.'65)-reprts. all #14
35-Christmas Special(Winter'65)
36-Spring Special(Spring'66)
37-Television Special(Spring'66)
38-In Mexico(Summer'66)-reprints #8
39-Goes to Camp(Summer'66)-reprints #9
40-In Washington, D.C.(Summer'66)-reprts.#15

each.... .80 1.60 2.40

41-From A to Z(Summer'66)
42-In Hollywood(Summer'66)-reprints #7
43-Christmas Special(Winter'66)
44-Around the Clock(Spring'67)
45-And His Pal Joey!(Spring'67)
46-Triple Feature(Summer'67)-reprints #28
47-In California(Summer'67)-reprints most#33
48-Way Out Stories(Summer'67)
49-All Year 'Round(Fall'67)-reprints #31
50-At the Circus(Summer'67)
51-Christmas Special(Winter'67)
52-Sports Special(Spring'68)-last CCA approved ish
53-Spring Special(Spr'68)-reprints most #36
54-And His Dog Ruff(Summ'68)-reprts.most #14
55-Tall Stories(Spring'68)
56-Television Special(Spring'68)-reprints TV show scripts
57-Pet Parade(Summer'68)
58-The Best of --(Summer'68)-reprints
59-Day By Day(Summer'68)
60-In Hollywood(Fall'68)-reprints most #7
61-Christmas Favorites(Winter'68)
62-Fun Book(Winter'68)-reprints most D.T.M. Fun Book #1
63-& His Wish I Was Book(Winter'69)
64-In Mexico(Spr'69)-reprints most #8
65-Around the Clock(Spring'69)-reprints #44
66-Gags 'n' Games(Summer'69)
67-Goes to Camp(Summer'69)reprints most #16
68-In Hawaii(Summer'69)-part reprint #6
69-The Best of --(Aug'69)-reprints
70-Tangled Tales(Aug'69)
71-Highlights(Sept'69)-reprints
72-In Washington, D.C.(Aug'69)-reprts.most#15
73-Way-Out Stories(Sept'69)-reprints #48
74-Mr. Wilson & His Gang at Christmas(Dec.'69)-reprints
75-Merry Christmas to You(Dec'69)

each.... .40 .80 1.20

DENNIS THE MENACE AND HIS DOG RUFF
Summer, 1961
Hallden/Fawcett

#1	2.00	4.00	6.00

DENNIS THE MENACE AND HIS FRIENDS
1969; #5, Jan, 1970 - Present
Fawcett Publications

Dennis T.M. & Joey #1,2(7/69)			
	1.00	2.00	3.00
Dennis T.M. & Ruff #1,2(9/69)			
	1.00	2.00	3.00
Dennis T.M. & Mr. Wilson #1(10/69)			
	1.00	2.00	3.00
Dennis & Margaret #1(Winter, '69)			

	Good	Fine	Mint
	1.00	2.00	3.00

#5-10: #5-Dennis T.M. & Margaret. #6-& Joey. #7-& Ruff. #8-& Mr. Wilson. #9-& Margaret. #10-& Joey .40 .80 1.20
11-20: #11-& Ruff. #12-& Mr. Wilson. #13-& Margaret. #14-& Joey. #15-& Ruff. #16-& Mr. Wilson. #17-& Margaret. #18-& Joey. #19-& Ruff. #20-& Mr. Wilson. .40 .80 1.20
21-35: #21-& Margaret. #22-& Joey. #23-& Ruff. #24-& Mr. Wilson. #25-& Margaret. #26-& Joey. #27-& Ruff. #28-& Mr. Wilson. #29-& Margaret. #30-& Joey. #31-& Ruff. #32-& Mr. Wilson. #33-& Margaret. #34-& His Pal Joey. #35-& Ruff. .35 .70 1.05

DENNIS THE MENACE AND HIS PAL JOEY
Summer, 1961 (10¢)(See D.T.M. Giants #45)
Fawcett Publications

#1	2.00	4.00	6.00

DENNIS THE MENACE BONUS MAGAZINE
#76, 1970 - Present (#76-124, 68pgs.; #125-163, 52pgs.; #164 on, 36pgs.)
Fawcett Publications

#76-In the Carribean(1/70)
77-Sports Special(2/70)-reprints #52
78-Spring Special(3/70)-reprints most #20
79-Tall Stories(4/70)-reprints #55
80-Day By Day(5/70)-reprints #59
81-Summer Funner(6/70)
82-In California(6/70)-reprints most #33
83-Mama Goose(7/70)
84-At the Circus(7/70)-reprint
85-The Fall Ball(8/70)
86-Mr. Wilson & His Gang at Christmas(10/70) reprints
87-Christmas Special(10/70)
88-In London(1/71)
89-Spring Fling(2/71)
90-Highlights(3/71)-reprints

each.... .40 .80 1.20

91-Fun Book(4/71)-reprints most D.T.M. Fun Book #1
92-In Hollywood(5/71)-reprints most #7
93-Visits Paris(6/71)
94-Jackpot(6/71)-reprint
95-That's Our Boy(7/71)-reprints
96-(Some numbered #95)-Summer Games(7/71)
97-Comicapers(8/71)
98-Mr. Wilson & His Gang at Christmas(10/71)
99-Christmas Special(10/71)
100-Up in the Air(1/72)
101-Rise and Shine(2/72)
102-Wish-I-Was Book(3/72)-reprints #63
103-Short Stuff Special(4/72)
104-In Mexico(5/72)-reprints most #8
105-Birthday Special(6/72)-reprints part D.T.M. #1
106-Fast & Funny(6/72)
107-Around the Clock(7/72)-reprints #44
108-Goes to Camp(7/72)-reprints most #9
109-Gags and Games(7/72)-reprints #66 w/new cover
110-Mr. Wilson & His Gang at Christmas(10/72)

each.... .30 .60 .90

111-Christmas Special(10/72)
112-Go-Go Special(1/73)
113-Tangled Tales(2/73)-reprints #70
114-In Hawaii(3/73)-reprints #68 w/new cover
115-Ting-A-Ling Special(4/73)
116-In Washington, D.C.(5/73)-reprts.most #15

(Dennis the Menace Bonus Mag. cont'd)

	Good	Fine	Mint
117-Encore(6/73)-reprints #69 w/new cover			
118-Here's How(6/73)			
119-The Summer Number(7/73)			
120-Strikes Back(7/73)			
121-Way-Out Stories(8/73)-reprints #48			
122-& Mr. Wilson & His Gang at Christmas(10/73)			
123-Christmas Special(10/73)			
124-Happy Holidays!(1/74)			
125-In London(2/74)-reprts. most #88			
126-Sports Special(3/74)-reprints most #52			
127-Visits Paris(4/74)-partially reprints #93			
128-Visits the Queen(Queen Mary)(5/74)			
129-At the Circus(6/74)-part reprint #50			
130-In Hollywood(6/74)-reprints half #7			
131-What in the World?! (7/74)			
132-Follow the Leader(7/74)-reprints			
133-That's the Spirit!(8/74)			
134-Christmas Special(10/74)			
135-& Mr. Wilson & His Gang at Christmas (10/74)-reprints			
136-"Crazy Daze"(1/75)			
137-"Up and at 'Em"(2/75)			
138-Fun Book(3/75)-reprts. ½ D.T.M.Fun Book#1			
139-Jackpot(4/75)-reprints most #94			
140-Big Deal(5/75)			
each....	.25	.50	.75
141-Gags & Games(6/75)-reprints most #109			
142-Just Kidding(6/75)-Intro. Hot Dog(Dennis' cat)			
143-Ireland(7/75)			
144-In Washington, D.C.(7/75)(Bicentennial)- reprints most #116			
145-Yankee Doodle Dennis 1776-1976(8/75)			
146-Christmas Special(10/75)			
147-& Mr. Wilson & His Gang at Christmas(10/75)			
148-In Florida(1/76)			
149-The Cookie Kid!(2/76)-reprints			
150-The Daffy Dozen(3/76)			
151-Yearbook(4/76)			
152-The Best of --(5/76)-reprints			
153-Yankee Doodle Dennis 1776-1976(6/76)- reprints #145			
154-Yours Truly Dennis(6/76)-reprints part #101,106			
155-Making Movies!(Summer Special, 7/76)			
156-Pretty Tricky!(7/76)-reprints			
157-Dare-Devil Dennis(8/76)-reprints			
158-Christmas Special(10/76)			
159-& Mr. Wilson & His Gang at Christmas(10/76)			
160-Yearbook(1/77)			
161-Off and Running!(2/77)-reprints half D.T.M. Fun Book #1			
162-At Marriott's Great America(3/77)			
163-Cherry Blossom Festival(4/77)			
164-"Just Kid-ding"(5/77)-reprints			
165-The Best of Dennis(6/77)-reprints			
166-Vacation Sensation(6/77)-reprints			
167-At the National Air & Space Museum of the Smithsonian Instit. Washington, D.C.(6/77)			
168-Tough and Tricky(7/77)-reprints			
each....	.20	.40	.60
169-178	.15	.30	.45

DENNIS THE MENACE POCKET FULL OF FUN!
Spring, 1969 - Present (196pgs.)(Digest Size)
Fawcett Publications (Hallden)

#1-Reprints in all issues	.40	.80	1.20
2-10	.30	.60	.90
11-34	.20	.40	.60

NOTE: #1-28 are 192 pgs., #29 on, 160 pgs.
#8,11,15,21,25,29 all contain strip reprints.

DENNIS THE MENACE TELEVISION SPECIAL
Summer, 1961 - #2, Spring, 1962 (Giant)
Fawcett Publications (Hallden Div.)

	Good	Fine	Mint
#1	1.50	3.00	4.50
2	1.25	2.50	3.75

DENNIS THE MENACE TRIPLE FEATURE
Winter, 1961 (Giant)
Fawcett Publications

#1	1.50	3.00	4.50

DEPUTY, THE (See 4-Color #1077,1130,1225)

DEPUTY DAWG (TV)
10-12/61 - #1, 8/65
Dell Publishing Co./Gold Key

4-Color #1238,1299	.40	.80	1.20
#1(10164-508)	.20	.40	.60

DEPUTY DAWG PRESENTS DINKY DUCK AND HASHIMOTO SAM
August, 1965
Gold Key

#1(10159-508)		.15	.30

DESIGN FOR SURVIVAL (Gen. Thomas S. Power's--)
1968 (36 pgs. in Color) (25¢)
American Security Council Press

No#-Propaganda against the Threat of Commun- ism	2.00	4.00	6.00

DESPERADO (Black Diamond Western #9 on)
1948 - #8, Jul-Aug, 1949
Lev Gleason Publications

#1-Biro art	2.00	4.00	6.00
2-8	1.20	2.40	3.60

DESTINATION MOON (See Fawcett Movie Comics & Strange Advs. #1

The Destructor #1, © Seaboard

DESTRUCTOR, THE
February, 1975 - #4, Aug, 1975
Atlas/Seaboard

#1-Origin; Ditko/Wood art	.50	1.00	1.50
2-4: #2,3-Wood/Ditko; #4-Ditko art			
	.30	.60	.90

DETECTIVE COMICS
March, 1937 - Present
National Periodical Publ./DC Comics

Detective Comics #3, © DC

Detective Comics #11, © DC

Detective Comics #19, © DC

(Detective Comics cont'd)

	Good	Fine	Mint
#1-(Scarce)-Slam Bradley & Spy by Siegel & Shuster, Speed Saunders by Guardineer, Flat Foot Flannigan by Gustavson, Cosmo, the Phantom of Disguise, Buck Marshall, Bruce Nelson begin; Fu Manchu cover	275.00	550.00	825.00
2 (Rare)	100.00	200.00	300.00
3 (Rare)	90.00	180.00	270.00
4,5	60.00	120.00	180.00
6,7,9,10	50.00	100.00	150.00
8-Fu Manchu cover	60.00	120.00	180.00
11-17,19	35.00	70.00	105.00
18-Fu Manchu cover	50.00	100.00	150.00
20-The Crimson Avenger begins (intro. & 1st app.)	50.00	100.00	150.00
21,23-25	22.50	45.00	67.50
22-Crimson Avenger cvr.	30.00	60.00	90.00
26	25.00	50.00	75.00
27-1st app. The Batman & Commissioner Gordon by Bob Kane; #27 reprinted in Famous 1st Edition	1200.00	2850.00	4500.00
(Prices vary widely on this book)			
28	450.00	900.00	1350.00
29-Batman cover; Doctor Death app.	200.00	400.00	600.00
30,32: #30-Dr.Death app.	125.00	250.00	375.00
31-Batman cover	175.00	350.00	525.00
33-Origin The Batman; Batman cover	300.00	600.00	900.00
34-Steve Malone & Larry Steele begin	85.00	170.00	255.00
35-37: Batman covers. #36-Origin Hugo Strange #37-Cliff Crosby begins	85.00	170.00	255.00
38-Origin & 1st app. Robin the Boy Wonder	225.00	450.00	675.00
39	75.00	150.00	225.00
40-Origin & 1st app. Clay Face	60.00	120.00	180.00

	Good	Fine	Mint
41-Robin's 1st solo	40.00	80.00	120.00
42-45: #44-Crimson Avenger dons new costume	30.00	60.00	90.00
46-50: #48-1st time car called Batmobile. #49-Last Clay Face	25.00	50.00	75.00
51-57,59: #59-Last Steve Malone; 2nd Penguin; Wing becomes Crimson Avenger's aide	22.50	45.00	67.50
58-1st Penguin app.; last Speed Saunders	25.00	50.00	75.00
60-Intro. Air Wave	22.50	45.00	67.50
61-63: #63-Last Cliff Crosby; 1st app. Mr. Baffle	20.00	40.00	60.00
64-Origin & 1st app. Boy Commandos by Simon & Kirby	50.00	100.00	150.00
65-Boy Commandos cover	30.00	60.00	90.00
66-Origin & 1st app. Two-Face	22.50	45.00	67.50
67,69,70	15.00	30.00	45.00
68-Two-Face app.	18.00	36.00	54.00
71-75: #74-1st Tweedledum & Tweedledee; S&K art	12.00	24.00	36.00
76-Newsboy Legion & The Sandman x-over in Boy Commandos; S&K art	15.00	30.00	45.00
77-80: All S&K art; Two-Face in #80	12.00	24.00	36.00
81,82,84-90: #81-1st Cavalier app. #85-Last Spy. #82-Last S&K art? #89-Last Crimson Avenger	10.00	20.00	30.00
83-1st "Skinny" Alfred	12.00	24.00	36.00
91-100	10.00	20.00	30.00
101-120	8.00	16.00	24.00
121-130	7.00	14.00	21.00
131-137,139: #137-Last Airwave	6.00	12.00	18.00
138-Origin Robotman (See Star Spangled #7, 1st app.)	8.00	16.00	24.00
140-1st app. The Riddler	17.00	34.00	51.00
141-150: #142-2nd Riddler app. #150-Last Boy			

Detective Comics #27, © DC

Detective Comics #34, © DC

Detective Comics #72, © DC

Detective Comics #86, © DC

Detective Comics #131, © DC

Detective Eye #1, © CEN

	Good	Fine	Mint
(Detective Comics cont'd) Commandos	5.00	10.00	15.00

151-160: #151-Origin & 1st app. Pow Wow Smith. #152-Last Slam Bradley. #153-1st Roy Raymond app. #156(2/50)-The new classic

	Good	Fine	Mint
Batmobile	4.50	9.00	13.50
161-180	4.00	8.00	12.00

181-210: #187-Two-Face app. #202-Last Robotman & Pow Wow Smith

	Good	Fine	Mint
	3.50	7.00	10.50

211-224: #213-Origin Mirror Man

	Good	Fine	Mint
	3.00	6.00	9.00

225-(Scarce)-Intro. & 1st app. Martian Manhunter-John Jones, later changed to J'onn J'onzz (1st National Silver Age hero)

	Good	Fine	Mint
	40.00	80.00	120.00

226-230: #230-1st app. Mad Hatter

	Good	Fine	Mint
	3.00	6.00	9.00
231,232,234-240	2.50	5.00	7.50
233-Origin & 1st app. Batwoman	3.00	6.00	9.00

241-260: #246-Intro. Diane Meade, J. Jones' girl. #257-Intro. & 1st app. Lohirly Bats

	Good	Fine	Mint
	1.80	3.60	5.40

261-264,266-280: #261-1st app. Dr. Double. #267-Origin & 1st app. Bat-Mite

	Good	Fine	Mint
	1.50	3.00	4.50
265-Batman's origin retold	1.75	3.50	5.25

281-300: #292-Last Roy Raymond. #293-Aquaman begins, ends #300

	Good	Fine	Mint
	1.00	2.00	3.00

301-327,329,330: #311-Intro. Zook in J'onzz; 1st app. Catman. #322-Batgirl's only app. in Det. #326-Last J'onn J'onzz; intro. Idol-Head of Diabolu. #327-Elongated Man begins

	Good	Fine	Mint
	.80	1.60	2.40
328-Death of Alfred	1.00	2.00	3.00

331-368,370: #355-Zatanna x-over in Elongated Man. #356-Alfred brought back in Batman. #359-Intro. new Batgirl

	Good	Fine	Mint
	.70	1.40	2.10
369-Adams story	2.00	4.00	6.00

371-390: #383-Elongated Man series ends. #387-Reprints 1st Batman story from #27

	Good	Fine	Mint
	.50	1.00	1.50

391-394,396,398,399,401,403,405,406,409,411-420: #414-52pgs. begin, end #424. #418-Creeper x-over

	Good	Fine	Mint
	.50	1.00	1.50

395,397,400,402,404,407,408,410-Adams stories. #400-Origin & 1st app. Man-Bat

	Good	Fine	Mint
	1.50	3.00	4.50

421-436: #424-Last Batgirl. #425-1st Jason Bard

	Good	Fine	Mint
	.40	.80	1.20

437-Manhunter begins by Simonson, ends #443

	Good	Fine	Mint
	.50	1.00	1.50

438-441,443-445: All 100pgs. #441-G.A. Plastic Man reprt. #443-Origin The Creeper reprint. #444-Elongated Man begins

	Good	Fine	Mint
	.40	.80	1.20
442-New 12pg. Toth art	.50	1.00	1.50

	Good	Fine	Mint

446-460: #446-Hawkman begins, ends #455. #458-Man-Bat begins. #460-Tim Trench begins

	Good	Fine	Mint
	.25	.50	.75
461-466,469,470	.20	.40	.60
467,468,471-476,478,479-Marshall Rogers art			
	.50	1.00	1.50
477-Adams reprt.;Rogers art	.60	1.20	1.80
480-Newton, Anderson, Rogers art			
	.50	1.00	1.50

481-(Combined with Batman Family, 12/78-1/79) begin $1.00 issues. Starlin/Russell, Rogers art; Newton/Starlin wraparound cover

	Good	Fine	Mint
	.60	1.20	1.80
482-Starlin/Russell, Rogers stories			
	.50	1.00	1.50

483-40th Anniversary ish.; origin retold; Newton Batman begins

	Good	Fine	Mint
	.40	.80	1.20
484	.40	.80	1.20
Special Edition(1944)-Giveaway-(68pgs.) Regular comic format	25.00	50.00	75.00

NOTE: *Adams* covers-#369,370,372,385,389,391, 392,394-422,439. *Anderson* art-#359,360,377, 390,440,442; covers-#359,361-365,369,371, 431,433. *Ditko* story-#443. *Infantino* art-#327-357,361-363,366,367,369,439,442; covers-#327-331,333-347,351-368,371. *Kaluta* covers-#423,424,426-428,431,434,438. *Kubert* art-#438,439; covers-#348-350. *Newton* art-#481. *Robinson* stories-part #72&73, 74-76,79,80; covers-#62,64,66-69,72,74,76,79,86,88. *Roussos* Airwave-#105. *Simon/Kirby* art-#440,442. *Simonson* pencils-#469,470. *Toth* art-#424,440-444. *Wrightson* cover-#425.

DETECTIVE DAN, SECRET OP. 48
1933 (36pgs.)(9½x12"-B&W-Softcover)
Humor Publ. Co.

By Norman Marsh - forerunner of Dan Dunn

	6.00	12.00	18.00

DETECTIVE EYE
Nov, 1940 - #2, Dec, 1940
Centaur Publications

	Good	Fine	Mint
#1-Air Man & The Eye Sees begins; The Masked Marvel app.	25.00	50.00	75.00
2	15.00	30.00	45.00

DETECTIVE PICTURE STORIES
Dec, 1936 - #7, 1937
Quality Comics Group

	Good	Fine	Mint
#1	25.00	50.00	75.00
2	12.00	24.00	36.00
3-The Clock begins	15.00	30.00	45.00
4-Eisner art	15.00	30.00	45.00
5-7: #5-Kane art	12.00	24.00	36.00

DETECTIVES, THE (See 4-Color#1168,1219,1240)

DEVIL DINOSAUR
April, 1978 - #9, Dec, 1978
Marvel Comics Group

	Good	Fine	Mint
#1	.20	.40	.60
2-9	.15	.30	.45

NOTE: *All Kirby covers/stories.*

DEVIL-DOG DUGAN (Tales of the Marines #4 on)
July, 1956 - #3, Nov, 1956
Atlas Comics (OPI)

#1-Severin cover	1.25	2.50	3.75
2-Iron Mike McGraw x-over; Severin cover,			
3	1.00	2.00	3.00

DEVIL DOGS
1942
Street & Smith Publishers

#1-Boy Rangers	5.00	10.00	15.00

DEVILINA
Feb, 1975 - #2, May, 1975 (Magazine)(B&W)
Atlas/Seaboard

#1,2	1.00	2.00	3.00

DEVIL KIDS STARRING HOT STUFF
1962 - Present
Harvey Publications (Illustrated Humor)

#1	2.50	5.00	7.50
2	1.00	2.00	3.00
3-10	.40	.80	1.20
11-30	.20	.40	.60
31-91	.15	.30	.45

DEXTER COMICS
Summer, 1948 - #5, July, 1949
Dearfield Publ.

#1	1.00	2.00	3.00
2-5	.65	1.35	2.00

DEXTER THE DEMON (Formerly Melvin the Monster)
#6, July, 1957 - #7, Sept, 1957
Atlas Comics (HPC)

#6,7	.40	.80	1.20

DIARY CONFESSIONS (Formerly Ideal Romance)
May, 1955 - 1956
Stanmor/Key Publ.

#9-14	.60	1.20	1.80

DIARY LOVES (G.I. Sweethearts #32 on)
Nov, 1949 - #31, April, 1953
Quality Comics Group

	Good	Fine	Mint
#1-Crandall & Colan art	5.00	10.00	15.00
2-Ward cover, 9pgs.	5.00	10.00	15.00
3,5-7,10	1.50	3.00	4.50
4-Crandall art	3.00	6.00	9.00
8,9-Ward art-6,8pgs. + Gustavson-#8			
	3.00	6.00	9.00
11,13,14,17-20	1.00	2.00	3.00
12,15,16-Ward art-9,7,8pgs.			
	2.50	5.00	7.50
21-Ward art, 7pgs.	2.00	4.00	6.00
22-31: #31-Whitney art	.80	1.60	2.40

NOTE: *Most early issues have photo covers.*

DIARY OF HORROR
December, 1952
Avon Periodicals

#1-One pg. Kinstler	5.00	10.00	15.00

DIARY SECRETS (Formerly Teen-Age Diary Secrets)
#10, 6/50 - #30, 9/55
St. John Publishing Co.

#10	2.50	5.00	7.50
11-16,18,19,21-30	2.00	4.00	6.00
17,20-Kubert stories	2.50	5.00	7.50
Annual-No#(25¢)	4.00	8.00	12.00

NOTE: *Baker stories/covers most issues.*

DICK COLE (Sport Thrills #11 on)
Dec-Jan, 1948-49 - #10, Jun-Jul, 1950
Premium Group(Novelty)/Star Publications

#1-Sgt. Spook	2.00	4.00	6.00
2	1.25	2.50	3.75
3-10: #9,10-L.B. Cole covers			
	1.00	2.00	3.00
Accepted Reprint #7(V1#6 on cover)-(1950's reprints #9)	.60	1.20	1.80

DICKIE DARE
1941
Eastern Color Printing Co.

#1-Caniff art, Everett cover			
	10.00	20.00	30.00
2,3	7.00	14.00	21.00
4-Half Scorchy Smith by Noel Sickles who was very influential in Milton Caniff's development	8.00	16.00	24.00

DICK POWELL (See A-1 Comics #22)

Diary Loves #9, © QUA

Diary Secrets #14, © STJ

Dickie Dare #4, © Famous Funnies

Dick Tracy Four Color #1, © N.Y. News Synd.

Dick Tracy Black & White #11
© N.Y. News Synd.

Dick Tracy #9, © N.Y. News Synd.

DICK QUICK, ACE REPORTER
Jan-Feb, 1947   (Formerly Picture News)
Lafayette St. Corp.

	Good	Fine	Mint
#10-Krigstein + Milt Gross story	2.50	5.00	7.50

DICK'S ADVENTURES IN DREAMLAND (See 4-Color
Comics #245)

DICK TRACY (See Big Thrill Booklet, Lemix-
Korlix, Merry Christmas, Tastee-Freez, Limited
Coll. Ed., Harvey Comics Library, & Super Book
#1,7,13,25)

DICK TRACY
1939 - #24, Dec, 1949
Dell Publishing Co.

	Good	Fine	Mint
Black & White #1(1939)	70.00	175.00	280.00
Black & White #4,8,11,13,15	35.00	87.50	140.00
4-Color #1(1939)('35 reprint)	100.00	200.00	300.00
4-Color #6 (Scarce) (1940)('37 reprint)	60.00	120.00	180.00
4-Color #8(1940)('38-'39 reprint)	45.00	90.00	135.00
Large Feature Comics #3(1941)	30.00	75.00	120.00
4-Color #21('41)('38 reprint)	35.00	70.00	105.00
4-Color #34('43)('39-'40 reprint)	25.00	50.00	75.00
4-Color #56('44)('40 rpt)	17.50	35.00	52.50
4-Color #96('46)('40 rpt)	10.00	20.00	30.00
4-Color #133('47)('40-'41 reprint)	10.00	20.00	30.00
4-Color #163('47)('41 rpt)	8.00	16.00	24.00

4-Color #215('48)-titled "Sparkle Plenty,"
Tracy reprints   7.00 14.00 21.00
Buster Brown Shoes giveaway-36pgs. in color
(1938 reprints)   20.00 40.00 60.00
Gillmore Giveaway-(See Super Book)
--Hatful of Fun(no date, 1950-52)-32pgs.,
8½x10"-Dick Tracy hat promotion; D. Tracy
games, magic tricks. Miller Bros. premium
4.00   8.00 12.00
Motorola Giveaway('53)-reprints Harvey Comics
Library #2   4.00   8.00 12.00
Popped Wheat Giveaway('47)-'40 reprint-16pgs.
in color; Sig Feuchtwanger publ.
1.50   3.00   4.50
--Presents the Family Fun Book-Tip Top Bread
Giveaway, no date, # (Mid '40's)16pgs. in
color; Spy Smasher, Ibis, Lance O'Casey
app.   25.00 50.00 75.00
Same as above but without app. of heroes &
Dick Tracy on cover only

	Good	Fine	Mint
	8.00	16.00	24.00
#1(1/48)('34 reprints)	20.00	40.00	60.00
2,3	10.00	20.00	30.00
4-10	8.00	16.00	24.00
11-18	6.00	12.00	18.00
19-24-Not by Gould	3.50	7.00	10.50

DICK TRACY (Cont'd. from Dell series)
#25, Mar, 1950 - #145, April, 1961
Harvey Publications

	Good	Fine	Mint
#25	8.00	16.00	24.00
26-30: #30-1st app. Gravel Gertie	7.00	14.00	21.00
31-40: #36-1st app. B.O. Plenty	6.00	12.00	18.00
41-50	5.00	10.00	15.00
51-56,58-80	4.00	8.00	12.00
57-1st app. Sam Catchem	5.00	10.00	15.00
81-140	3.00	6.00	9.00
141-145 (25¢)	5.00	10.00	15.00

NOTE: #110-120,141-145 are all reprints from
earlier issues.

DICK TRACY
May, 1937 - Jan, 1938
David McKay Publications

Feature Book No#, 100pgs. Part reprinted as
4-Color #1(appeared before Black & Whites,
1st Dick Tracy comic book)
(Very Rare)   300.00 600.00 900.00
Feature Book #4-Reprints No# issue but with
new cover added   90.00 180.00 270.00
Feature Book #6,9   70.00 140.00 210.00

DICK TRACY & DICK TRACY JR. CAUGHT THE
RACKETEERS, HOW
1933   (88 pgs.) (7x8½") (Hardcover)
Cupples & Leon Co.

#2(#'d on pg.84)-Continuation of Stooge
Viller daily strip reprints from
8/3/33 thru 11/8/33
(Rarer than #1)   40.00 80.00 120.00
with dust jacket.... 60.00 120.00 180.00

DICK TRACY & DICK TRACY JR. AND HOW THEY
CAPTURED "STOOGE" VILLER (See Treasure Box
of Famous Comics)
1933 (7x8½") Hard cover; One Shot; 100pgs.
Reprints 1932 & 1933 Dick Tracy daily strips
Cupple & Leon Co.

No#(#1)-1st app. of "Stooge" Viller
30.00 60.00 90.00
with dust jacket.... 40.00 80.00 120.00

DICK TRACY, EXPLOITS OF
1946 (Strip reprints)(Hard Cover)($1.00)
No publisher listed

	Good	Fine	Mint
#1-Reprints the compete case of "The Brow"			
from early 1940's	20.00	40.00	60.00
with dust jacket....	25.00	50.00	75.00

DICK TRACY SHEDS LIGHT ON THE MOLE
1949 (16 pgs.) (Ray-O-Vac Flashlights Give-
Western Printing Co.   away)

Not by Gould	3.00	6.00	9.00

DICK TURPIN (See Legend of Young --)

DICK WINGATE OF THE U.S. NAVY
1951; 1953
Toby Press/Superior Publ.

No#-U.S. Navy giveaway	.65	1.35	2.00
#1(1953)	1.00	2.00	3.00

DIE, MONSTER, DIE (See Movie Classics)

DIG 'EM
1973 (16 pgs.) (2-3/8"x6")
Kellogg's Sugar Smacks Giveaway

4 different	.15	.30	.45

DILLY (The Little Wise Guys)
May, 1953 - #3, Sept, 1953
Lev Gleason Publications

#1-3: #2,3-Biro covers	1.00	2.00	3.00

DIME COMICS
1945 (Gleason reprints); 1951
Newsbook Publ. Corp.

#1-Silver Streak app.; L. B. Cole cover			
	5.00	10.00	15.00
1(1951), #5	1.50	3.00	4.50

DINGBATS (See First Issue Special)

DING DONG
1946
Compix/Magazine Enterprises

#1	1.00	2.00	3.00
2-5	.50	1.00	1.50

DINKY DUCK (Paul Terry's--)(See Blue Ribbon
Comics)
11/51 - #16, 9/55; #16, Fall, 1956; #17, 5/57 -
#19, Summer, 1958

St. John Publishing Co./Pines #16 on

	Good	Fine	Mint
#1	1.20	2.40	3.60
2-10	.60	1.20	1.80
11-16(9/55)	.40	.80	1.20
16(Fall,'56)-#19	.30	.60	.90

DINKY DUCK & HASHIMOTO SAM (See Deputy Dawg
Presents --)

DINO (The Flintstones)
Aug, 1973 - #20, Jan, 1977
Charlton Publications

#1	.15	.30	.45
2-20		.15	.30

DINOSAURUS (See 4-Color Comics #1120)

DIPPY DUCK
October, 1957
Atlas Comics (OPI)

#1-Maneely art	.75	1.50	2.25

DIRTY DOZEN (See Movie Classics)

DISNEYLAND BIRTHDAY PARTY
1958   (25¢)
Dell Publishing Co.

#1-Carl Barks art, 16pgs.	6.00	12.00	18.00

DISNEYLAND, USA (See Dell Giant #30)

DIVER DAN
Feb-Apr, 1962 - #2, June-Aug, 1962
Dell Publishing Co.

4-Color #1254, #2	.80	1.60	2.40

DIXIE DUGAN
1942 - 1949
McNaught Syndicate/Columbia/Publication Ent.

#1-Joe Palooka x-over in Dixie Dugan by			
Ham Fisher	5.00	10.00	15.00
2,3	2.50	5.00	7.50
4,5(1945-46)	1.75	3.50	5.25
6-13(1948-49)	1.20	2.40	3.60

DIXIE DUGAN
Nov, 1951 - 1954
Prize Publications (Headline)

V3#1-4	1.00	2.00	3.00
V4#1-4 (#5-8)	.80	1.60	2.40

Dick Tracy #99, © N.Y. News Synd.

Disneyland Birthday Party #1, © WDP

Dixie Dugan #9, © CCG

Dizzy Duck #32, © STD   Doc Savage Comics #8, © S&S   Doctor Solar #11, © GK

DIZZY DAMES
Sept-Oct, 1952 - #6, Jul-Aug, 1953
American Comics Group (B&M Distr. Co.)
	Good	Fine	Mint
#1	1.00	2.00	3.00
2-6	.60	1.20	1.80

DIZZY DON
1947 - #4, 1947
F. E. Howard Publications (Canada)

#1	1.00	2.00	3.00
2-4	.50	1.00	1.50

DIZZY DUCK
#32, Nov, 1950 - #39, 1952
Standard Comics

#32-39	.40	.80	1.20

DOBERMAN (See Sgt. Bilko's Private --)

DOBIE GILLIS (See The Many Loves of --)

DOC CARTER VD COMICS
1949   (16pgs.)(Paper cover)(In Color)
Health Publications Institute,
Raleigh, N. C.   (Giveaway)

	25.00	50.00	75.00

DOC SAVAGE (-- Comics)
May, 1940 - #20, Oct, 1943
Street & Smith Publications

#1-Doc Savage, Cap Fury, Danny Garrett, Mark
    Mallory, The Whisperer, Captain Death,
    Billy the Kid, Sheriff Pete & Treasure
    Island begin; Norgil, the Magician app.
                60.00 120.00 180.00
  2-Origin & 1st app. Ajax, the Sun Man;
    Danny Garrett, The Whisperer end
                30.00 60.00 90.00
  3   25.00 50.00 75.00
  4-Treasure Island ends 20.00 40.00 60.00
  5-Origin & 1st app. Astron, the Crocodile
    Queen, not in #9 & 11; Norgil the Magici-
    an app.   15.00 30.00 45.00
  6-9: #6-Cap Fury ends; origin & only app.
    Red Falcon in Astron story. #8-Mark Mall-
    ory ends. #9-Supersnipe app.
                12.00 24.00 36.00
 10-Origin The Thunderbolt
                12.00 24.00 36.00
 11,12   9.00 18.00 27.00
V2#1-8(#13-20): #16-The Pulp Hero, The Aveng-
    er app. #18-Sun Man ends; Nick Carter be-
    gins.   9.00 18.00 27.00

DOC SAVAGE
Nov, 1966
Gold Key
	Good	Fine	Mint
#1-Adaptation of the Thousand-Headed Man;			
James Bama cover	1.75	3.50	5.25

DOC SAVAGE
Oct, 1972 - #8, Jan, 1974
Marvel Comics Group

#1	.60	1.20	1.80
2,3-Steranko covers	.40	.80	1.20
4-8	.30	.60	.90
Giant-Size #1(1975)-Reprints #1 & 2			
	.30	.60	.90

DOC SAVAGE (Magazine)
Aug, 1975 - #8, 1976   (Black & White)
Marvel Comics Group

#1-Cover from movie poster	.60	1.20	1.80
2(10/75),3-8	.40	.80	1.20
NOTE: *John Buscema story-#1-3.*

DR. ANTHONY KING, HOLLYWOOD LOVE DOCTOR
Jan, 1952 - #3, May, 1953; #4, May, 1954
Minoan Publishing Corp.

#1	1.50	3.00	4.50
2-4	1.00	2.00	3.00

DR. ANTHONY LOVE CLINIC (See Mr. Anthony's--)

DR. BOBBS (See 4-Color Comics #212)

DR. FATE (See More Fun, First Issue Special,
Showcase, & Justice League)

DR. FU MANCHU (See The Mask of --)
1964
I.W. Enterprises

#1-Reprints Avon's "Mask of Dr. Fu Manchu";			
Wood art	5.00	10.00	15.00

DOCTOR GRAVES (See The Many Ghosts of --)

DR. JEKYLL AND MR. HYDE (See A Star Presentation)

DR. KILDARE (TV)
1962 - #9, Apr-June, 1965
Dell Publishing Co.

4-Color #1337('62)	.50	1.00	1.50
#2-9	.30	.60	.90

DR. MASTERS (See The Adventures of Young --)

DOCTOR SOLAR, MAN OF THE ATOM
Oct, 1962 - #27, April, 1969
Gold Key

	Good	Fine	Mint
#1-Origin Dr. Solar	2.00	4.00	6.00
2-Prof. Harbinger begins	1.20	2.40	3.60
3-5: #5-Intro. Man of the Atom in costume			
	.80	1.60	2.40
6-10	.60	1.20	1.80
11-14,16-27	.50	1.00	1.50
15-Origin retold	.60	1.20	1.80

NOTE: _Frank Bolle_ art-#6-19. _Bob Fugitani_
art in early issues. _Al McWilliams_ art-#20-23.

DOCTOR SPEKTOR (See The Occult Files of --)

DOCTOR STRANGE (Strange Tales #1-168)
#169, June, 1968 - #183, Nov, 1969; June,
1974 - Present (Also see Marvel Premiere)
Marvel Comics Group

	Good	Fine	Mint
#169(#1)	1.00	2.00	3.00
170-183: #177-New costume for Dr. Strange			
	.60	1.20	1.80
#1(6/74)-Brunner cvr/stys.	1.00	2.00	3.00
2-Brunner cvr/stories	.60	1.20	1.80
3-Ditko reprints & Brunner story/cover			
	.50	1.00	1.50
4,5-Brunner cvr/stys end	.50	1.00	1.50
6-Brunner cover	.40	.80	1.20
7-10	.25	.50	.75
11-21	.20	.40	.60
22-Brunner cover	.25	.50	.75
23-26-Starlin stories; covers-#25,26			
	.35	.70	1.05
27-32	.15	.30	.45

NOTE: _Alcala story-#19_
Annual #1(1976)-Russell art | .60 | 1.20 | 1.80
King Size Annual #1(1/77) | .35 | .70 | 1.05

DR. TOM BRENT, YOUNG INTERN
Feb, 1963 - #5, Oct, 1963
Charlton Publications

#1	.25	.50	.75
2-5	.20	.40	.60

DR. VOLTZ (See Mighty Midget Comics)

DR. WHO & THE DALEKS (See Movie Classics)

DO-DO
1951 (5x7¼" Minature) (5¢)
Nation Wide Publishers

#1-7	.50	1.00	1.50

DODO & THE FROG, THE (Formerly Funny Stuff)
Sept-Oct, 1954 - #92, 1957
National Periodical Publ. (Arleigh)

	Good	Fine	Mint
#80-92: Doodles Duck by Sheldon Mayer in			
many issues	.50	1.00	1.50

DOGFACE DOOLEY
1951 - 1953
Magazine Enterprises

#1(A-1#40)	1.25	2.50	3.75
2(A-1#43),3(A-1#49),4(A-1#53),5(A-1#64)			
	1.25	2.50	3.75
IW Reprint #1('64), Super Reprint #17			
	.50	1.00	1.50

DOG OF FLANDERS, A (See 4-Color #1088)

DOGPATCH (See Al Capp's -- & Mammy Yokum)

DOINGS OF THE DOO DADS, THE
1922 (34pgs.)(7-3/4"x7-3/4")(B&W)(50¢)
(Red & White cover)(Square binding)
Detroit News (Universal Feat.& Specialty Co.)

Reprints 1921 newspaper strip "Text & Pictures" given away as prize in the Detroit
News Doo Dads contest; by Arch Dale
6.00 12.00 18.00

DOLLFACE & HER GANG (See 4-Color #309)

DOLL MAN
Fall, 1941 - #47, Oct, 1953
Quality Comics Group

#1-Dollman (by Cassone) & Justice Wright be-			
gin	70.00	140.00	210.00
2-The Dragon begins; 5 Crandall stories			
	40.00	80.00	120.00
3	25.00	50.00	75.00
4	20.00	40.00	60.00
5-Crandall art	17.00	34.00	51.00
6,7,9,10	10.00	20.00	30.00
8-1st app. Torchy by Bill Ward			
	15.00	30.00	45.00
11-20	8.00	16.00	24.00
21-30	7.00	14.00	21.00
31-36,38-40: Jeb Rivers app. #32-34			
	5.00	10.00	15.00
37-Origin Dollgirl	6.00	12.00	18.00
41-47	3.00	6.00	9.00
IW Reprint #1('63)-Crandall art			
	1.50	3.00	4.50
Super Reprint #11('64),15(reprts.#23),17,18:			
Torchy app.-#15,17	2.00	4.00	6.00

NOTE: _Ward Torchy in #8,9,11,12,14-24,27; by_

Doctor Strange #4, © MCG

Doll Man #9, © QUA

Doll Man #43, © QUA

Donald Duck Firestone 1947, © WDP

Donald Duck, 1938 Whitman, © WDP

Donald Duck Four Color #4, © WDP

(Doll Man cont'd)
Fox-#30,35-47. Crandall stories-*#2,5,7,10,13
& Super #11,17,18.*

DOLLY DILL
1945
Marvel Comics/Newsstand Publ.

	Good	Fine	Mint
#1	1.50	3.00	4.50

DOLLY DILL
1951 - #10, 1951

#1	1.00	.200	3.00
2-10	.60	1.20	1.80

DOLLY DIMPLES & BOBBY BOONCE'
1933
Cupples & Leon Co.

	5.00	10.00	15.00

DONALD AND MICKEY IN DISNEYLAND
1958   (25¢)
Dell Publishing Co.

#1 (Giant)	2.00	4.00	6.00

DONALD AND MICKEY MERRY CHRISTMAS
1943 - 1949 (20 pgs.)(Giveaway) Put out each
Christmas; 1943 issue titled "Firestone Presents Comics"   (Disney)
K.K. Publ./Firestone Tire & Rubber Co.

1943-D.Duck reprint from WDC&S #32 by Carl
  Barks   130.00 260.00 390.00
1944-D.Duck reprint from WDC&S #35 by Barks
            110.00 220.00 330.00
1945-"Donald Duck's Best Christmas", 8 pgs.

	Good	Fine	Mint
Carl Barks; intro. & 1st app. Grandma Duck in comic books	160.00	320.00	480.00

1946-D.Duck in "Santa's Stormy Visit", 8pgs.
  Carl Barks   115.00 230.00 345.00
1947-D.Duck in "Three Good Little Ducks,"
  8pgs. Carl Barks 115.00 230.00 345.00
1948-D.Duck in "Toyland," 8 pgs. Carl Barks
            115.00 230.00 345.00
1949-D.Duck in "New Toys," 8 pgs. Carl Barks
            115.00 230.00 345.00

DONALD AND THE WHEEL   (See 4-Color #1190)

DONALD DUCK   (Also see The Wise Little Hen)
1935, 1936 (linen-like text & color pictures;
1st Donald Duck book ever) (9½x13")
Whitman Publishing Co./Grosset & Dunlap/K.K.

#978(1935)-16 pgs.; story book
            120.00 240.00 360.00
No#(1936)-36pgs.-Reprints '35 edition with
  expanded ill. & text 70.00 140.00 210.00
...with dust jacket.... 90.00 180.00 270.00

DONALD DUCK   (Walt Disney's) (10¢)
1938   (B&W)(8½x11½")(Cardboard covers)
Whitman/K.K. Publications
  (Has D.D. smoking pike on front cover)

No#-The first Donald Duck comic book; 1936 &
  1937 Sunday strip reprints(in black and
  white)same format as Black & Whites
            250.00 500.00 750.00
  (Prices vary widely on this book)

DONALD DUCK   (See 4-Color listings for titles)
(Also see Cheerios, Whitman Comic Books)
1940 - Present
Dell Publishing Co./Gold Key #85 on

Donald Duck Black & White #20, © WDP

Donald Duck Four Color #29, © WDP

Donald Duck Four Color #108, © WDP

Donald Duck Four Color #199, © WDP   Donald Duck Four Color #263, © WDP   Donald Duck Four Color #275, © WDP

(Donald Duck cont'd)   Good   Fine   Mint
4-Color #4(1940)Daily('39)strip reprints by
  Al Taliaferro   450.00 900.00 1350.00
Black & White #16(1/41?)-Reprints 1940 Sun-
  day strips in B&W   350.00 875.00 1400.00
Black & White #20('41)400.00 1000.00 1600.00
4-Color #9('42)-"Finds Pirate Gold;" 68pgs.
  by Carl Barks & Jack Hannah
                   500.00 1150.00 1800.00
4-Color #29(9/43)-"Mummy's Ring" by Carl
  Barks-reprinted in Uncle Scrooge & Donald
  Duck #1('65) & W.D. Comics Digest #44('73)
                   400.00 800.00 1200.00
  (Prices vary widely on all above books)
4-Color #62(1/45)-"Frozen Gold;" 52pgs. by
  Carl Barks, reprinted in The Best of W.D.
  Comics   200.00 400.00 600.00
4-Color #108(1946)-"Terror of the River;"
  52pgs. by Carl Barks 120.00 240.00 360.00
4-Color #147(5/47)-in "Volcano Valley" by
  Carl Barks   80.00 160.00 240.00
4-Color #159(8/47)-in "The Ghost of the
  Grotto;" 52pgs. by Carl Barks-reprinted in
  Best of Uncle Scrooge & Donald Duck #1('66)
  & The Best of W.D. Comics; two Barks stories   70.00 140.00 210.00
4-Color #178(12/47)-1st Uncle Scrooge by
  Carl Barks-reprinted in Gold Key Christmas Parade #3 & The Best of W.D. Comics
                   70.00 140.00 210.00
4-Color #189(6/48)-by Carl Barks-reprinted
  in Best of Donald Duck & Uncle Scrooge #1
  ('64)   60.00 120.00 180.00
4-Color #199(10/48)-by Carl Barks
                   60.00 120.00 180.00
4-Color #203(12/48)-by Barks-reprinted as
  Gold Key Christmas Parade #4
                   35.00 70.00 105.00
4-Color #223(4/49)-by Barks-reprinted as
  Best of D. Duck #1('65)
                   40.00 80.00 120.00
4-Color #238(8/49),256(12/49)-by Barks; #256-
  reprinted in Best of Donald Duck & Uncle
  Scrooge #2('67) & W.D. Comics Digest #44
  ('73)   30.00 60.00 90.00
4-Color #263(2/50)-Two Barks stories
                   30.00 60.00 90.00
4-Color #275(5/50),282(7/50),291(9/50)-All
  by Carl Barks; #275,282 reprinted in W.D.
  Comics Digest#44('73) 25.00 50.00 75.00
4-Color #300(11/50),308(1/51),318(3/51)-by
  Barks; #318 reprinted in W.D. Comics
  Digest #34   22.00 44.00 66.00
4-Color #328(5/51)-by Carl Barks (drug issue)   25.00 50.00 75.00
4-Color #339(7-8/51),379-not by Barks
                    4.00 8.00 12.00

                          Good   Fine   Mint
4-Color #348(9-10/51),356,394-Barks covers
  only   5.00 10.00 15.00
4-Color #367(1-2/52)-by Barks: reprinted as
  G.K. Christmas Parade #2 & again as #8
                   18.00 36.00 54.00
4-Color #408(708/52),422(9-10/52)-All by
  Carl Barks. #408-reprinted in Best of
  Duck & Uncle Scrooge #1('64)
                   16.00 32.00 48.00
#26(11-12/53)-In "Trick or Treat"(36pgs. of
  Barks art)-reprinted in Walt Disney Digest
  #16   15.00 30.00 45.00
27-30-Barks covers only 4.00 8.00 12.00
31-40   2.00 4.00 6.00
41-44,47-50   1.20 2.40 3.60
45-Barks art(6pgs.) 5.00 10.00 15.00
46-"Secret of Hondorica" by Barks, 24pgs.-
  reprinted in D.D. #98 & #154
                    8.00 16.00 24.00
51-Half-pg. Barks 1.75 3.50 5.25
52-"Lost Peg-Leg Mine" by Barks, 10pgs.
                    6.00 12.00 18.00
53,55-59   1.20 2.40 3.60
54-"Forbidden Valley" by Barks, 26pgs.
                    8.00 16.00 24.00
60-"D.D. & the Titanic Ants" by Barks, 20pgs.
  + 6 more pgs.   7.00 14.00 21.00
61-67,69,70   .75 1.50 2.25
68-Barks art, 5pgs. 3.50 7.00 10.50
71,79,81-½pg.Barks reprt.1.75 3.50 5.25
72-78,80,82-97,100: #96-D.D. Album
                     .70 1.40 2.10
98-Reprints #46 (Barks) 2.00 4.00 6.00
99-Xmas Album   1.00 2.00 3.00
101-133: #112-1st Moby Duck.30 .60 .90
134-Barks reprint(#52) + a WDC&S reprint
                    1.00 2.00 3.00
135-Barks reprints, 19pgs..80 1.60 2.40
136-153   .25 .50 .75
154-Barks reprint(#46) .70 1.40 2.10
155,156,158   .25 .50 .75
157-Barks reprint(#45) .40 .80 1.20
159-Reprints/WDC&S #192 .25 .50 .75
160,164-Barks reprint(#26) .25 .50 .75
161-163,165-170   .20 .40 .60
171,177-Reprints   .20 .40 .60
172,173,175,176   .15 .30 .45
174-Reprints 4-Color #394 .20 .40 .60
178-187,189-191   .15 .30 .45
188-5pg. Barks reprint .20 .40 .60
192-Barks reprints(40pgs.) from D.D. #60 &
  WDC&S #226,234(52pgs.) .20 .40 .60
193-203   .15 .30 .45
Mini-Comic #1(1976)(3⅓x6½")-Reprints/D.D.#150
                     .15 .30 .45

NOTE: Carl Barks wrote #117,126,138 only.
Issues 4-Color #189,203,223,238,256,263,275,

125

(Donald Duck cont'd)
348,356,367,394,408,422,#26-30,34,35,44,51,57,
65,70,71,73,78-81,83 all have Barks covers.
#96 titled "Comic Album," #99-"Christmas
Album."

DONALD DUCK (Has Paper Cover)
1944 (16pg. Christmas giveaway)(2 different)
K. K. Publications

	Good	Fine	Mint
Kelly cover reprint	70.00	140.00	210.00

DONALD DUCK ALBUM (See Duck Album & Comic
May-July, 1959 - Oct, 1963   Album #1,3)
Dell Publishing Co./Gold Key

4-Color #995,1099,1140,1182,1239(Barks cover),			
#01204-207('62-Dell)	1.20	2.40	3.60
#1(8/63-G.K.)	.70	1.40	2.10
2(10/63)	.30	.60	.90

DONALD DUCK AND THE BOYS (Also see Story Hour
1948 (Hardcover book; 5¼x5½")   Series)
Whitman Publishing Co.

(Scarce) Partial reprint/WDC&S #74 by Barks			
	20.00	40.00	60.00

(Prices vary widely on this book)

DONALD DUCK AND THE RED FEATHER
1948 (4 pgs.) (8½x11") (B&W)
Red Feather Giveaway

	2.50	5.00	7.50

DONALD DUCK BEACH PARTY
1954 - 1959; 1965 (25¢)
Dell Publishing Co./Gold Key('65)

#1	3.00	6.00	9.00
2-6	1.50	3.00	4.50
1(G.K. #10158-509 reprints Barks story from			
WDC&S #45)	2.50	5.00	7.50

DONALD DUCK BOOK (See Story Hour Series)

DONALD DUCK COMIC PAINT BOOK (See Black &
White #20)

DONALD DUCK FUN BOOK (Annual)
1953 - 1954 (100 pgs.) (25¢)
Dell Publishing Co.

#1('53), #2('54)	2.50	5.00	7.50

DONALD DUCK IN DISNEYLAND
1955 (Giant)
Dell Publishing Co.

	Good	Fine	Mint
#1	2.00	4.00	6.00

DONALD DUCK IN "THE LITTERBUG"
1963 (15 pgs.) (Disney giveaway)
Keep America Beautiful

	1.20	2.40	3.60

DONALD DUCK MARCH OF COMICS
1947 - 1951 (Giveaway) (Disney)
K. K. Publications

No#(#4)-"Maharajah Donald;" 32pgs. by Carl			
Barks-(1947)	600.00	1200.00	1800.00
#20-"Darkest Africa" by Carl Barks-1948			
(24 pgs.)	400.00	800.00	1200.00
#41-"Race to South Seas" by Carl Barks-1949			
(24 pgs.)	300.00	600.00	900.00
#56-(1950)-Not Barks	25.00	50.00	75.00
#69-(1951)-Not Barks	20.00	40.00	60.00
#263	3.00	6.00	9.00

DONALD DUCK MERRY XMAS (See Dell Giant #53)

DONALD DUCK PICNIC PARTY (See Picnic Party)

DONALD DUCK "PLOTTING PICNICKERS"
1962 (14 pgs.) (Disney)
Fritos Giveaway

	1.50	3.00	4.50

DONALD DUCK'S SURPRISE PARTY
1948 (16 pgs.)(Giveaway for Icy Frost Twins
Walt Disney Productions   Ice Cream Bars)

Kelly art	40.00	80.00	120.00

DONALD DUCK TELLS ABOUT KITES
1954 (Giveaway) (8 pgs.-no cover) (Disney)
Southern California Edison Co./Pacific Gas
and Electric Co.

S.C.E. issue-Barks pencils-8pgs.; inks-7pgs.			
(Rare)	700.00	1400.00	2100.00
P.G.&E. issue-7th page redrawn changing			
middle 3 panels to show P.G.&E. in story			
line(All Barks; last page Barks pencils			
only) (Rare)	600.00	1200.00	1800.00

(Prices vary widely on above books)
NOTE: *These books appeared one month apart*
in the fall and were distributed on the West
Coast only.

DONALD DUCK, THIS IS YOUR LIFE (See 4-Color
Comics #1109)

Donald Duck 1944, KK, © WDP

Donald Duck Fun Book #1, © WDP

D.D. Tells About Kites, PG&E, © WDP

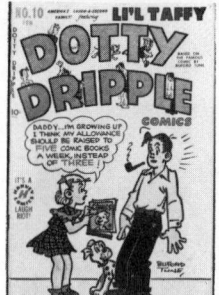

Don Winslow #8, © FAW   Dorothy Lamour #2, © FOX   Dotty Dripple #10, © HARV

DONALD DUCK XMAS ALBUM (See Reg. Series #99)

DONALD IN MATHMAGIC LAND (See 4-Color #1051, #1198)

DONDI (See 4-Color Comics #1176,1276)

DON FORTUNE MAGAZINE
Aug, 1946 - #6, Feb, 1947
Don Fortune Publishing Co.

	Good	Fine	Mint
#1-Delecta of the Planets begins by C.C. Beck			
	2.50	5.00	7.50
2-6	1.75	3.50	5.25

DON NEWCOMBE
1950 (Baseball)
Fawcett Publications

No#	2.00	4.00	6.00

DON'T GIVE UP THE SHIP (See 4-Color #1049)

DON WINSLOW OF THE NAVY (See 4-Color #2,22, & Super Book #5,6)

DON WINSLOW OF THE NAVY (See TV Teens)
Feb, 1943 - #73, Sept, 1955
Fawcett Publications/Charlton #70 on

#1-Capt. Marvel on cover	20.00	40.00	60.00
2	10.00	20.00	30.00
3	6.00	12.00	18.00
4,5	5.00	10.00	15.00
6-10	3.50	7.00	10.50
11-20	3.00	6.00	9.00
21-40	2.00	4.00	6.00
41-64(12/48)	1.50	3.00	4.50
65(1/51)-73: #70,71, & 72 reprints #26,58,			
& 59	1.20	2.40	3.60

DOOM PATROL (My Greatest Adv. #1-85)
3/64 - #121, 9-10/68; 2/73 - #124, 6-7/73
National Periodical Publications

#86	1.00	2.00	3.00
87-99: #88-Origin the Chief. #91-Intro. Mento. #94-Intro. Beast Boy			
	.50	1.00	1.50
100-Origin Beast Boy; Robot-Maniac series begins	.50	1.00	1.50
101-110: #105-Robot-Maniac series ends. #106-Negative Man begins(origin)			
	.40	.80	1.20
111-120	.30	.60	.90
121-Death of Doom Patrol; Orlando cover			
	.30	.60	.90
122-124(reprints)	.20	.40	.60

DOOMSDAY + 1
7/75 - #6, 5/76; #7, 6/78 - Present
Charlton Comics

	Good	Fine	Mint
#1	.35	.70	1.05
2-6,V3#7(reprints)-10	.20	.40	.60
#5(Modern Comics reprint, 1977)	.15	.30	

DOORWAY TO NIGHTMARE (See Cancelled Comic
1-2/78 - #5, 9-10/78   Cavalcade)
DC Comics

#1	.20	.40	.60
2-5: #4-Craig story		.25	.45

NOTE: *Kaluta covers on all.*

DOPEY DUCK COMICS (Wacky Duck #3)
Fall, 1945 - #2, Apr, 1946 (See Super Funnies)
Timely Comics (NPP)

#1,2	1.20	2.40	3.60

DOROTHY LAMOUR-JUNGLE PRINCESS (Formerly Jun-
#2, 6/50 - #3, 8/50   gle Li'l)
Fox Features Syndicate

#2,3-Wood story in each	7.00	14.00	21.00

DOT DOTLAND (Formerly Little Dot --)
#63, Nov, 1974
Harvey Publications

#63	.15	.30	.45

DOTTY (-- & Her Boy Friends)(Glamorous Rom-
#35, 7/48 - #40, 5/49   ances #41 on)
Ace Magazines (A.A. Wyn)

#35-40	1.50	3.00	4.50

DOTTY DRIPPLE (Horace & Dotty Dripple #25 on)
1944 - #24, June, 1952
Magazine Ent.(Life's Romances)/Harvey #3 on

#1(no date)	1.50	3.00	4.50
No#(no date)(10¢)	1.50	3.00	4.50
A-1#1(no date)(M.E.-'44)	1.50	3.00	4.50
#2-24	.60	1.20	1.80

DOTTY DRIPPLE
Aug, 1955 - 1958
Dell Publishing Co.

4-Color #646,691,718,746,801,903,			
#7-11	.60	1.20	1.80

DOUBLE ACTION COMICS
#2, 1/40 (Reg.Size, 68pgs., B&W, color cover)
National Periodical Publications

(Double Action cont'd)

Contains original stories; no costume heroes;
only one known copy. Same cover as Adventure
#37.   Estimated value.... $1,500.00

DOUBLE COMICS
1940 - 1944   (132 pgs.)
Elliot Publications

	Good	Fine	Mint
1940 issues	25.00	50.00	75.00
1941 issues	15.00	30.00	45.00
1942 issues	10.00	20.00	30.00
1943,44 issues	8.00	16.00	24.00

NOTE: Double Comics consisted of an almost endless
combination of pairs of remaindered, unsold issues of comics
representing most publishers and usually mixed publishers in the
same book; e. g., a Captain America with a Silver Streak, or a
Feature with a Detective, etc., could appear inside the same
cover. The actual contents would have to determine its price.
Prices listed are for average contents. Any containing rare origin
or first issues are worth much more. Covers also vary in same
year. Value would be approximately 50% of contents.

DOUBLE DARE ADVENTURES
Dec, 1966 - #2, Mar, 1967   (25¢)
Harvey Publications

#1-Origin Bee-Man, Glowing Gladiator, & Mag-			
ic-Master; Kirby art .90	1.80	2.70	
2-Al Williamson/Crandall art; reprint Alarm-			
ing Adv. #3('63) 1.25	2.50	3.75	

DOUBLE LIFE OF PRIVATE STRONG, THE
June, 1959 - #2, Aug, 1959
Archie Publications/Radio Comics

#1-Origin The Shield by Simon & Kirby			
	12.00	24.00	36.00
2-S&K Shield	6.00	12.00	18.00

DOUBLE UP
1941   (200 pgs.) (Pocket-Size)
Elliott Publications

#1-Contains rebound copies of digest sized			
issues of Pocket Comics, Speed Comics, &			
Spitfire Comics 15.00	30.00	45.00	

DOUBLE TROUBLE
1958
St. John Publishing Co.

#1,2	.50	1.00	1.50

DOUBLE TROUBLE WITH GOOBER
1952 - 1953
Dell Publishing Co.

4-Color #417,471,516,556	.60	1.20	1.80
#1	.50	1.00	1.50

DOVER BOYS   (See Adventures of the --)

DOVER THE BIRD
1955
Famous Funnies Publishing Co.

	Good	Fine	Mint
#1	.40	.80	1.20

DOWN WITH CRIME
Nov, 1952 - #7, 1953
Fawcett Publications

#1	1.50	3.00	4.50
2,4,6,7	1.00	2.00	3.00
3-Heroin drug cvr/story	3.00	6.00	9.00
5-Bondage cover	2.00	4.00	6.00

DO YOU BELIEVE IN NIGHTMARES?
Nov, 1957 - #2, Jan, 1958
St. John Publishing Co.

#1-Ditko art	2.50	5.00	7.50
2-Ayers art	1.00	2.00	3.00

DRACULA   (See Book & Record --, Tomb of --,
& Movie Classics under Universal Presents as
well as Dracula)

DRACULA   (See Movie Classics for #1)
9/66 - #4, 3/67; #6, 7/72 - #8, 7/73 (No#5)
Dell Publishing Co.

#2-Origin Dracula(9/66)	.40	.80	1.20
3,4-Intro. Fleeta #4('67)	.30	.60	.90
6-('72)-reprints #2	.25	.50	.75
7,8: #7-reprts.#3, #8-#4	.20	.40	.60

DRACULA LIVES!   (Magazine)
1973(no month - #14, 9/75   (B&W) (75¢)
Marvel Comics Group

#1-Buckler art	1.00	2.00	3.00
2-Origin; Adams story/cover; Starlin art			
	1.00	2.00	3.00
3-Adams cover; story inks .90	1.80	2.70	
4-Ploog story .80	1.60	2.40	
5(V2#1)-#14: #7-Evans story. #9-Alcala art			
	.60	1.20	1.80

DRAG CARTOONS   (Magazine)
#1, 6-7/63; #2, 12/63 - 1970's
(Later issues-no numbers)
Millar Publ./Professional Serv./Lopez Publ.

#1-Russ Manning + Warren Tufts art			
	1.50	3.00	4.50
2-Russ Manning art .80	1.60	2.40	
3-5,7,9-11,13-24	.35	.70	1.05

Double Comics 1940, © EP

Double Life Of Private Strong #1, © AP

Down With Crime #1, © FAW

Dream Book Of Love #3, © ME   Dumbo Weekly #6, © WDP   Durango Kid #10, © ME

	Good	Fine	Mint
(Drag Cartoons cont'd)			
6,8-Toth art	.60	1.20	1.80
12-Griffin & Toth art	1.50	3.00	4.50
25-49: Wonder Wart-Hog by Gilbert Shelton in all; The Adventures of Bull O' Fuzz & other strips	.70	1.40	2.10
50-60	.25	.50	.75

DRAG 'N' SURF
1969
Charlton Comics

#1	.20	.40	.60

DRAG 'N' WHEELS (Formerly Top Eliminator)
#30, Sept, 1968 - #59, May, 1973
Charlton Comics

#30-59-Scot Jackson feat.	.10	.15

DRAGOON WELLS MASSACRE (See 4-Color #815)

DRAGSTRIP HOTRODDERS (World of Wheels #17 on)
Nov-Dec, 1963 - #16, May-June, 1967
Charlton Comics

#1	.20	.40	.60
2-16	.20	.40	

DRAMA OF AMERICA, THE
1973   (224 pgs.) ($1.95)
Action Text

#1-"Students' Supplement to History"			
	1.00	2.00	3.00

DREAM BOOK OF LOVE (See A-1 Comics #106,114, 123)

DREAM BOOK OF ROMANCE (See A-1 Comics #92, 101,109,110,124)

DREAM OF LOVE
1958   (Reprints)
I.W. Enterprises

#1,2,8,9	.50	1.00	1.50

DRIFT MARLO
May-July, 1962 - #2, Oct-Dec, 1962
Dell Publishing Co.

#01-232-207, #2(12-232-212).50	1.00	1.50

DRISCOLL'S BOOK OF PIRATES
1934   (124 pgs.)(B&W)(Hardcover)(7x9")
David McKay Publ.   (Not reprints)

	Good	Fine	Mint
By Montford Amory	6.00	12.00	18.00

DRUM BEAT (See 4-Color Comics #610)

DUCK ALBUM (See Donald Duck Album)
Oct, 1951 - Sept, 1957
Dell Publishing Co.

4-Color #353,450	1.75	3.50	5.25
4-Color #492,531,560,586	1.25	2.50	3.75
4-Color #611,649,686	1.20	2.40	3.60
4-Color #726,782,840	.90	1.80	2.70

DUDLEY
Nov-Dec, 1949 - #3, Mar-Apr, 1950
Feature/Prize Publications

#1-By Boody Rogers	1.00	2.00	3.00
2,3	.65	1.35	2.00

DUDLEY DO-RIGHT (TV)
Aug, 1970 - #7, Aug, 1971   (Jay Ward)
Charlton Comics

#1-7	.15	.35

DUKE OF THE K-9 PATROL
April, 1963
Gold Key

#1(10052-304)	.50	1.00	1.50

DUMBO (See 4-Color #17,234,668, Movie Comics & Walt Disney Showcase #12)

DUMBO (Walt Disney's --)
1941   (K. K. Publ. Giveaway)
Weatherbird Shoes/Ernest Kern Co.(Detroit)

16pgs., 9x10" (Rare) -	25.00	50.00	75.00
52pgs., 5½x8½", slick cover in color; B&W interior; half text, half reprints/ 4-Color #17	12.00	24.00	36.00

DUMBO COMIC PAINT BOOK (See Black & White#19)

DUMBO WEEKLY
1942 (Premium supplied by Diamond D-X Gas
Walt Disney Productions   Stations)

16 known issues - each...	10.00	20.00	30.00

DUNC AND LOO (#1 titled "Around the Block with Dunc and Loo")
1961 - #8, Oct-Dec, 1963
Dell Publishing Co.

#1	.60	1.20	1.80

(Dunc and Loo cont'd)

	Good	Fine	Mint
2-8	.35	.70	1.05

NOTE: *Written by John Stanley; Bill Williams art.*

DURANGO KID (Also see White Indian)
Oct-Nov, 1949 - #41, 1955
Magazine Enterprises

	Good	Fine	Mint
#1-White Indian by Frazetta begins(origin); Frazetta art continues through #16	30.00	60.00	90.00
2-5	15.00	30.00	45.00
6-16-Last Frazetta ish.	12.00	24.00	36.00
17-Origin Durango Kid	6.00	12.00	18.00
18-30	2.50	5.00	7.50
31-41	1.75	3.50	5.25

NOTE: *#6,8,14,15 contain Frazetta stories not reprinted in White Indian.*

DWIGHT D. EISENHOWER
December, 1969
Dell Publishing Co.

#01-237-912 - Life story	2.00	4.00	6.00

DYNAMIC ADVENTURES
#9, 1964
I.W. Enterprises

#9-Reprints Avon's "Escape From Devil's Island"	1.50	3.00	4.50
No#,no date-Reprts. Risks Unlimited with Rip Carson, Senorita Rio	1.00	2.00	3.00

DYNAMIC CLASSICS (See Cancelled Comic Cavalcade)
Sept-Oct, 1978
DC Comics

#1-Batman	.15	.30	.45

DYNAMIC COMICS (No #4-7)
Oct, 1941 - #25, May, 1948
Harry 'A' Chesler

	Good	Fine	Mint
#1-Origin Major Victory by Charles Sultan(reprinted in Major Victory #1), Dynamic Man & Hale the Magician; The Black Cobra only app.	25.00	50.00	75.00
2-Origin Dynamic Boy & Lady Satan; Intro. the Green Knight & Sidekick Lance Cooper	12.00	24.00	36.00
3	7.00	14.00	21.00
8-Dan Hastings, The Echo, The Master Key, Yankee Boy begin; Yankee Doodle Jones app.	6.00	12.00	18.00
9-Mr. E begins; Mac Raboy cover	8.00	16.00	24.00

	Good	Fine	Mint
10-Drug story	6.00	12.00	18.00
11-14	4.50	9.00	13.50
15-Drug mentioned in one story; The Sky Chief app.	6.00	12.00	18.00
16-Marijuana story	8.00	16.00	24.00
17(1/46)-Illust. in Seduction of the Innocent, "The children told me what the man was going to do with the hot poker", but Wertham saw this in Crime Reporter #2 (this is a drug story)	12.00	24.00	36.00
18-22,24,25	4.00	8.00	12.00
23-Yankee Girl app.	5.00	10.00	15.00
IW Reprint #1-Yankee Girl('64), #8	1.00	2.00	3.00

NOTE: *Tuska art in many issues.*

DYNAMITE (Johnny Dynamite #10 on)
May, 1953 - #9, Dec, 1955?
Comic Media/Allen Hard Publ.

#1-Pete Morisi art	1.25	2.50	3.75
2	.80	1.60	2.40
3-Johnny Dynamite begins by Pete Morisi; F. Robbins art	1.20	2.40	3.60
4-9: #9-Morisi art	.80	1.60	2.40

DYNAMO
Aug, 1966 - #4, June, 1967   (25¢)
Tower Comics

#1-Crandall, Ditko art; Weed series begins; NoMan & Lightning cameos; Wood cover & stories	1.35	2.75	4.00
2-4: Wood covers & stories in all	1.00	2.00	3.00

DYNOMUTT (TV)
Nov, 1977 - #8, Jan, 1979
Marvel Comics Group

#1-8	.15	.30	.45

EAGLE, THE (1st Series)
July, 1941 - #4, Jan, 1942
Fox Features Syndicate

#1-The Eagle begins; Rex Dexter of Mars app.	30.00	60.00	90.00
2-Origin The Spider Queen	17.50	35.00	52.50
3-Origin Joe Spook	12.00	24.00	36.00
4	12.00	24.00	36.00

EAGLE (2nd Series)
Feb-Mar, 1945 - #2, Apr-May, 1945
Rural Home Publ.

Dynamic Comics #16, © H.A. Chesler

Dynamo #1, © TC

The Eagle #1, © FOX

An Earth Man On Venus No#, © AVON

Eerie #8, © AVON

Eerie #60, © WP

	Good	Fine	Mint
(Eagle cont'd)			
#1-Aviation stories	2.50	5.00	7.50
2-Lucky Aces	1.50	3.00	4.50

NOTE: *L. B. Cole* covers.

EARTH MAN ON VENUS (An --)
1951   (Also see Strange Planets)
Avon Periodicals

No#-Wood story, 26pgs. 100.00 200.00 300.00

EASTER BONNET SHOP (See March of Comics #29)

EASTER WITH MOTHER GOOSE (See 4-Color #103,
140,185,220)

EAT RIGHT TO WORK AND WIN
1942   (16 pgs.) (Giveaway)
Swift & Company

Blondie, Henry, Flash Gordon by A. Raymond,
Toots & Casper, Thimble Theatre(Popeye),
Tillie the Toiler, The Phantom, The Little
King, & Bringing Up Father - original strips
just for this book - (in daily strip form
which shows what foods we should eat & why)
                       30.00 60.00 90.00

E.C. CLASSIC REPRINTS
May, 1973 - #12, 1976 (E.C. Comics reprint-
ed in full color minus ads)
East Coast Comix Co.

#1-The Crypt of Terror #1(Tales From the			
Crypt #46)	2.00	4.00	6.00
2-Weird Science #15('52)	1.35	2.65	4.00
3-Shock SuspenStories #12	.60	1.20	1.80
4-Haunt of Fear #12	.60	1.20	1.80
5-Weird Fantasy #13('52)	.60	1.20	1.80
6-Crime SuspenStories #25	.60	1.20	1.80
7-Vault of Horror #26	.60	1.20	1.80
8-Shock SuspenStories #6	.60	1.20	1.80
9-Two-Fisted Tales #34	.60	1.20	1.80
10-Haunt of Fear #23	.60	1.20	1.80
11-Weird Science #12(#1)	.60	1.20	1.80
12-Shock SuspenStories #2	.60	1.20	1.80

E.C. 3-D CLASSICS (See Three Dimensional --)

EDDIE STANKY (Baseball Hero)
1951   (New York Giants)
Fawcett Publications

No#   2.00 4.00 6.00

EDGAR BERGEN PRESENTS CHARLIE McCARTHY
1938 (36 pgs.)(15x10½")(In Color)
Whitman Publishing Co.(Charlie McCarthy Co.)

	Good	Fine	Mint
#764	12.00	24.00	36.00

EDWARD'S SHOES GIVEAWAY
1954   (Has clown on cover)
Edward's Shoe Store

Contains comic with new cover. Many combinations possible. Contents determines price,
50-60% of original. (Similar to Comics From
Weatherbird & Free Comics to You)

ED WHEELAN'S JOKE BOOK STARRING FAT & SLAT
(See Fat & Slat)

EERIE (Strange Worlds #18 on)
#1, 1/47; #1, 5-6/51 - #17, 8-9/54
Avon Periodicals

#1(1947)-1st horror comic; Kubert art			
	10.00	20.00	30.00
1(1951)	7.00	14.00	21.00
2-Wood cover & story	8.00	16.00	24.00
3-Wood cover, Kubert, Wood/Orlando stories			
	8.00	16.00	24.00
4,5-Wood covers + 1 pg. art			
	5.00	10.00	15.00
6,10,11,13,14: #10-Kinstler cover			
	2.00	4.00	6.00
7-Wood/Orlando cover; Kubert story			
	4.00	8.00	12.00
8-Kinstler story; bondage cover			
	2.50	5.00	7.50
9-Kubert sty; Check cvr.	3.00	6.00	9.00
12-25pg. Dracula story from novel			
	2.50	5.00	7.50
15-Reprints most #1('51)	2.00	4.00	6.00
16-Wood story reprt./#2	4.00	8.00	12.00
17-Wood/Orlando & Kubert stories; reprints			
#3 minus inside & outside Wood cover			
	4.00	8.00	12.00

EERIE
1964
I.W. Enterprises

IW Reprint #1(Wood cover reprint)('64)			
	1.00	2.00	3.00
IW Reprint #2,6,8(Dr. Drew by Grandenetti-			
Ghost #9)	.80	1.60	2.40
IW Reprint #9-From Eerie #2(Avon)-Wood cover			
	1.50	3.00	4.50

EERIE (Magazine)
#1, Sept, 1965; #2, Mar, 1966 - Present
Warren Publishing Co.

#1
24 pgs., B&W, small size (5¼x7¼"), low distribution; cover from
inside back cover of Creepy No. 2; stories reprinted from Creepy
No. 7, 8. At least three different versions exist.

Good Fine Mint

First Printing — B&W, 5¼" wide x 7¼" high, evenly trimmed. On page 18, panel 5, in the upper left-hand corner, the large rear view of a bald headed man blends into solid black and is unrecognizable. Overall printing quality is poor.

50.00 100.00 150.00

Second Printing — B&W, 5¼x7¼", with uneven, untrimmed edges (if one of these were trimmed evenly, the size would be less than as indicated). The figure of the bald headed man on page 18, panel 5 is cleared and discernible. The staples have a ¼" blue stripe.

15.00 30.00 45.00

Other unauthorized reproductions for comparison's sake would be practically worthless. One known version was probably shot off a first printing copy with some loss of detail; the finer lines tend to disappear.in this version which can be determined by looking at the lower right-hand corner of page one, first story. The roof of the house is shaded with straight lines. These lines are sharp and distinct on original, but broken on this version.

1.50 3.00 4.50

NOTE: *THE PRICE GUIDE recommends that, before buying, you consult an expert.*

	Good	Fine	Mint
#2-Frazetta cover	2.50	5.00	7.50
3-Frazetta cover, 1pg.	1.75	3.35	5.00
4-10: #4-Frazetta ½ pg.	1.50	3.00	4.50
11-19	1.20	2.40	3.60
20-25	1.00	2.00	3.00
26-42: #39-1st Dax by Maroto. #42-Williamson reprint	.75	1.50	2.25
43-46	.70	1.40	2.10
47-78: #78-The Mummy reprts.	.60	1.20	1.80
79,80-Origin Darklon the Mystic by Starlin	.60	1.20	1.80
81-97	.50	1.00	1.50
Year Book 1970,71 reprts.	1.50	3.00	4.50
Year Book 1972,73 reprts.	1.00	2.00	3.00
Year Book 1974,75 reprts.	.75	1.50	2.25

NOTE: *The above books contain art by many good artists: Adams, Brunner, Corben, Craig (Taycee), Crandall, Ditko, Eisner, Evans, Jeff Jones, Kinstler, Krenkel, McWilliams, Morrow, Orlando, Ploog, Severin, Starlin, Torres, Toth, Williamson, Wood, & Wrightson; covers by Bode', Corben, Davis, Frazetta, Morrow, & Orlando.*

EERIE ADVENTURES
Winter, 1951
Ziff-Davis Publ. Co.

	Good	Fine	Mint
#1-Two Powell stories	2.00	4.00	6.00

EERIE TALES (Magazine)
1959   (Black & White)
Hastings Associates

	Good	Fine	Mint
#1-Williamson + Torres, Powell(2), & Morrow 2 stories	6.00	12.00	18.00

EERIE TALES
1964
Super Comics

Good Fine Mint

	Good	Fine	Mint
Super Reprint #10,11,12,18: Purple Claw in #11,12	.75	1.50	2.25
15-Wolverton story-Spacehawk reprt/Blue Bolt W. Tales #113	2.00	4.00	6.00

EGBERT
Spring, 1946 - #20, 1950
Arnold Publications/Quality Comics Group

	Good	Fine	Mint
#1	2.50	5.00	7.50
2-10	1.25	2.50	3.75
11-20	.80	1.60	2.40

EH! (-- Dig This Crazy Comic)(From Here To Insanity #8 on)
Dec, 1953 - 1954   (Satire)
Charlton Comics

	Good	Fine	Mint
#1	3.00	6.00	9.00
2-7	2.00	4.00	6.00

80 PAGE GIANT (-- Magazine #1-15) (25¢)
8/64 - #15, 10/65; #16, 11/65 - #89, 7/71
National Periodical Publ.   (#57-89, 68pgs.)

	Good	Fine	Mint
#1-Superman	2.75	5.50	8.25
2-Jimmy Olsen	1.75	3.50	5.25
3-Lois Lane	1.50	3.00	4.50
4-Flash-G.A. reprint; Infantino art	1.20	2.40	3.60
5-Batman	1.20	2.40	3.60
6-Superman	1.20	2.40	3.60
7-Sgt. Rock's Prize Battle Tales; Kubert cover + stories	1.00	2.00	3.00
8-More Secret Origins-origins of JLA, Aquaman, Robin, Atom, & Superman; Infantino art	2.50	5.00	7.50
9-Flash(Reprints Flash #123)-Infantino art	1.00	2.00	3.00
10-Superboy	1.00	2.00	3.00
11-Superman	.80	1.60	2.40
12-Batman	.80	1.60	2.40
13-Jimmy Olsen	.80	1.60	2.40
14-Lois Lane	.80	1.60	2.40
15-World's Finest	.80	1.60	2.40

Continued as part of regular series under each title in which that particular book came out, a Giant being published instead of the regular size. Issues No. 16 to No. 89 are listed for your information. See individual titles for prices.

16-JLA #39(11/65)	23-Superman #187
17-Batman #176	24-Batman #182
18-Superman #183	25-Jimmy Olsen #95
19-Our Army at War #164	26-Lois Lane #68
20-Action #334	27-Batman #185
21-Flash #160	28-World's Finest #161
22-Superboy #129	29-JLA #48
	30-Batman #187

Eh! #5, © CC

80 Page Giant #9, © DC

80 Page Giant #16, © DC

Ella Cinders Single Series #28. © **UFS**

Ellery Queen #4. © **SUPR**

Elsie The Cow =2. © **DS**

(80 Page Giant cont'd)

31-Superman #193	60-Superman #217
32-Our Army at	61-Batman #213
War #177	62-Jimmy Olsen #122
33-Action #347	63-Lois Lane #95
34-Flash #169	64-World's Finest #188
35-Superboy #138	65-JLA #76
36-Superman #197	66-Superman #222
37-Batman #193	67-Batman #218
38-Jimmy Olsen #104	68-Our Army at
39-Lois Lane #77	War #216
40-World's Finest #170	69-Adventure #390
41-JLA #58	70-Flash #196
42-Superman #202	71-Superboy #165
43-Batman #198	72-Superman #227
44-Our Army at	73-Batman #223
War #190	74-Jimmy Olsen #131
45-Action #360	75-Lois Lane #104
46-Flash #178	76-World's Finest #197
47-Superboy #147	77-JLA #85
48-Superman #207	78-Superman #232
49-Batman #203	79-Batman #228
50-Jimmy Olsen #113	80-Our Army at
51-Lois Lane #86	War #229
52-World's Finest #179	81-Adventure #403
53-JLA #67	82-Flash #205
54-Superman #212	83-Superboy #174
55-Batman #208	84-Superman #239
56-Our Army at	85-Batman #233
War #203	86-Jimmy Olsen #140
57-Action #373	87-Lois Lane #113
58-Flash #187	88-World's Finest #206
59-Superboy #156	89-JLA #93

87TH PRECINCT (TV)
Apr-June, 1962 - #2, July-Sept, 1962
Dell Publishing Co.

	Good	Fine	Mint
4-Color #1309(Krigstein art)			
	2.50	5.00	7.50
#2	1.00	2.00	3.00

EL BOMBO COMICS
1946
Standard Comics/Frances M. McQueeny

No#(1946)	2.00	4.00	6.00
#1(no date)	2.00	4.00	6.00

EL CID (See 4-Color Comics #1259)

EL DORADO (See Movie Classics)

ELLA CINDERS (See Famous Comics Cartoon Book)

ELLA CINDERS
1938 - 1940
United Features Syndicate

	Good	Fine	Mint
Single Series #3('38)	10.00	20.00	30.00
Single Series #21(#2 on cover, #21 on inside),
#28('40)	8.00	16.00	24.00

ELLA CINDERS (See Comics Revue #1,4)
1948 - #5, 1949
United Features Syndicate

#1	2.25	4.50	6.75
2-5	1.50	3.00	4.50

ELLERY QUEEN
May, 1949 - #4, Nov, 1949
Superior Comics Ltd.

#1	6.00	12.00	18.00
2,3	3.50	7.00	10.50
4-Kamen story	4.00	8.00	12.00

NOTE: *Kamen covers-#1-4.*

ELLERY QUEEN
1-3/52 - #2, Summer/52   (Painted covers)
Ziff-Davis Publishing Co.

#1	4.00	8.00	12.00
2-Bondage, torture cvr.	5.00	10.00	15.00

ELLERY QUEEN (See 4-Color #1165,1243,1289)

ELMER FUDD
May, 1953 - #1293, Mar-May, 1962
Dell Publishing Co.

4-Color #470,558,628,689('56)
	.80	1.60	2.40
4-Color #725,783,841,888,938,977,1032,1081,
1131,1171,1222,1293('61).	60	1.20	1.80
(See Super Book #10,22, & No#)

ELMO
January, 1948
St. John Publishing Co.

#1-Daily newspaper strip reprints
	1.35	2.75	4.00

ELSIE THE COW
Oct-Nov, 1949 - #3, Jul-Aug, 1950
D.S. Publishing Co.

#1-(36pgs.)	10.00	20.00	30.00
2,3	3.00	6.00	9.00
Borden Milk Giveaway(16pgs., No#),(3 issues,
1957)	2.00	4.00	6.00
Elsie's Fun Book(1950, Borden Milk)
	2.50	5.00	7.50
Everyday Birthday Fun With--(1957, 20pgs.-
100th Anniversary)	1.50	3.00	4.50

E-MAN
Oct, 1973 - #10, Sept, 1975
Charlton Comics

	Good	Fine	Mint
#1-Origin E-Man by Joe Staton			
	1.50	3.00	4.50
2-Ditko art	1.00	2.00	3.00
3,4: #3-Howard art. #4-Ditko art			
	1.00	2.00	3.00
5-Miss Liberty Belle app.			
	.75	1.50	2.25
6-10	.75	1.50	2.25
#1-5,9,10(Modern Comics reprts., 1977)			
		.15	.30

EMERGENCY (Magazine)
June, 1976 - #4, Jan, 1977   (B&W)
Charlton Comics

#1-Adams cover/stories	.70	1.40	2.10
2,3-Adams cvrs; sty.#3	.60	1.20	1.80
4	.50	1.00	1.50

EMERGENCY (TV)
June, 1976 - #4, Dec, 1976
Charlton Comics

#1	.25	.50	.75
2-4	.15	.30	.45

EMERGENCY DOCTOR
Summer, 1963   (One Shot)
Charlton Comics

#1	.25	.50	.75

EMIL & THE DETECTIVES (See Movie Comics)

EMMA PEEL & JOHN STEED (See The Avengers)

ENCHANTMENT VISUALETTES (Magazine)
#4, Feb, 1950 - #5, Apr, 1950
World Editions

V1#4,5-Contains two romance comic strips			
each; painted covers	8.00	16.00	24.00

ENCHANTING LOVE
Oct, 1949 - #6, July, 1950
Kirby Publishing Co.

#1	1.50	3.00	4.50
2-4,6: #2-Powell art	1.00	2.00	3.00
5-Ingels art, 9pgs.	3.00	6.00	9.00

ENEMY ACE (See Star-Spangled War Stories)

ENSIGN O'TOOLE (TV)

Aug-Oct, 1963 - #2, 1964
Dell Publishing Co.

	Good	Fine	Mint
#1,2	.35	.70	1.05

ENSIGN PULVER (See Movie Classics)

ERNIE COMICS (All Love Romances #26 on)
Sept, 1948 - #25, Mar, 1949
Current Books/Ace Periodicals

No#(9/48,11/48)	.80	1.60	2.40
#24,25	.60	1.20	1.80

ESCAPADE IN FLORENCE (See Movie Comics)

ESCAPE FROM DEVIL'S ISLAND
1952
Avon Periodicals

#1-Kinstler cover-reprinted as Dynamic Adv.#9			
	7.00	14.00	21.00

ESCAPE TO WITCH MOUNTAIN (See Walt Disney
Showcase #29)

ESPIONAGE (TV)
May-July, 1964 - #2, Aug-Oct, 1964
Dell Publishing Co.

#1,2	.35	.70	1.05

ETERNAL BIBLE, THE
1946   (Large Size)   (16 pgs. in Color)
Authentic Publications

#1	2.00	4.00	6.00

ETERNALS, THE
July, 1976 - #19, Jan. 1978
Marvel Comics Group

#1	.50	1.00	1.50
2-5	.35	.70	1.05
6-19	.30	.60	.90
Annual #1(10/77)	.35	.70	1.05

NOTE: *Kirby covers/stories in all.*

ETTA KETT
#11, Dec, 1948 - #14, Sept, 1949
King Features Syndicate/Standard

#11-14	1.80	3.60	5.40

EVA THE IMP
1957
Red Top Comic/Decker

#1,2	.40	.80	1.20

E-Man #2, © CC

The Eternals #6, © MCG

Etta Kett #13, © KING

Exciting Comics #47. © STD

Exciting Comics #62. © STD

Explorer Joe #1. © Z-D

EVEL KNIEVEL
1974   (16 pgs.)   (Giveaway)
Marvel Comics Group (Ideal Toy Corp.)

	Good	Fine	Mint
No#-Sekowsky art	.35	.70	1.05

EVERYBODY'S COMICS
1944 - 1947
Fox Features Syndicate

	Good	Fine	Mint
#1(1944)-The Green Mask, The Puppeteer; 194 pgs.	5.00	10.00	15.00
#1(1946)-Contents vary-Green Lama, The Puppeteer app.	3.50	7.00	10.50
#1(1946)-Same as the 1945 Ribtickler	1.35	2.75	4.00
1947 (132 pgs.)	2.35	4.75	7.00

EVERYTHING HAPPENS TO HARVEY
Sept-Oct, 1953 - #7, Sept-Oct, 1954
National Periodical Publications

#1	1.50	3.00	4.50
2-7	.70	1.40	2.10

EVERYTHING'S ARCHIE
May, 1969 - Present
Archie Publications

#1(Giant)	1.00	2.00	3.00
2-10(Giants)	.50	1.00	1.50
11-20	.25	.50	.75
21-68	.15	.30	.45

EVERYTHING'S DUCKY   (See 4-Color #1251)

EXCITING COMICS
April, 1940 - #69, Sept, 1949
Nedor/Better Publications/Standard Comics

#1-Origin The Mask, Jim Hatfield, Sgt, Bill King, Dan Williams begin	35.00	70.00	105.00
2-The Sphinx begins; The Masked Rider app.	17.50	35.00	52.50
3	12.00	24.00	36.00
4	10.00	20.00	30.00
5	8.00	16.00	24.00
6-8	7.00	14.00	21.00
9-Origin & 1st app. of The Black Terror & sidekick Tim	40.00	80.00	120.00
10-13	20.00	40.00	60.00
14-Last Sphinx, Dan Williams	12.00	24.00	36.00
15-Origin The Liberator	15.00	30.00	45.00
16-20: #20-The Mask ends	10.00	20.00	30.00
21,23-30: #28-Crime Crusader begins, ends #59	8.00	16.00	24.00

22-Origin The Eaglet; The American Eagle

	Good	Fine	Mint
begins	9.00	18.00	27.00
31-38	6.00	12.00	18.00
39-Origin Kara, Jungle Princess	7.00	14.00	21.00
40-50: #42-The Scarab begins. #49-Last Kara, Jungle Princess	6.00	12.00	18.00
51-Miss Masque begins	8.00	16.00	24.00
52-54	6.00	12.00	18.00
55-Judy of the Jungle (origin); 1pg. Ingels art	8.00	16.00	24.00
56-58: All airbrush cvrs.	6.00	12.00	18.00
59-Frazetta art in Caniff style; signed Frank Frazeta, 9 pgs.	10.00	20.00	30.00
60-66-Rick Howard, the Mystery Rider begins-#60	5.00	10.00	15.00
67-69-Last Black Terror	4.00	8.00	12.00

NOTE: _Schomburg (Xela) covers-#56-66. #66-last airbrush cover. Black Terror by R. Moreira-#65._

EXCITING ROMANCES
1949 - 1953
Fawcett Publications

#1	1.25	2.50	3.75
2-12	.80	1.60	2.40

NOTE: _Powell art-#8-10._

EXCITING ROMANCE STORIES
1949   (132 pgs.)
Fox Features Syndicate

No#-See Fox Giants. Contents can vary and determines price.

EXCITING WAR
#5, Sept, 1952 - #8, May, 1953; #9, 11/53
Standard Comics (Better Publ.)

#5-7,9	1.00	2.00	3.00
8-Toth story	2.00	4.00	6.00

EXORCISTS   (See The Crusaders)

EXOTIC ROMANCES   (Formerly True War Romances)
#22, Oct, 1955 - #31, Nov, 1956
Quality Comics Group (Comic Magazines)

#22-26,29	1.50	3.00	4.50
27,31-Matt Baker cover/story	2.50	5.00	7.50
28,30-Baker story	2.00	4.00	6.00

EXPLOITS OF DANIEL BOONE
Nov, 1955 - #8, Dec, 1956
Quality Comics Group

(Expl. of D. Boone cont'd)	Good	Fine	Mint
#1	2.00	4.00	6.00
2-8	1.35	2.75	4.00

EXPLOITS OF DICK TRACY (See Dick Tracy)

EXPLORER JOE
Winter, 1951 - #2, 10-11/52
(Painted covers by N. Saunders)
Ziff-Davis Publ. Co.

	Good	Fine	Mint
#1	1.50	3.00	4.50
2-Krigstein story	2.50	5.00	7.50

EXPOSED (-- True Crime Cases)
Mar-Apr, 1948 - #9, July-Aug, 1949
D.S. Publishing Co.

#1	1.80	3.60	5.40
2,3,7-9	1.20	2.40	3.60
4-Orlando story	2.00	4.00	6.00
5-Breeze Lawson, Sky Sheriff by E. Good; 2pgs. Wood art	2.00	4.00	6.00
6-Ingels art; used in Seduction of the Innocent, "How to prepare an alibi" illo.	4.50	9.00	13.50

EXTRA (Magazine)
1949
Magazine Enterprises

#1-Funny Man by Siegel & Shuster, Space Ace, Undercover Girl	8.00	16.00	24.00

EXTRA!
Mar-Apr, 1955 - #5, Nov-Dec, 1955
E.C. Comics

#1	5.00	10.00	15.00
2-5	4.00	8.00	12.00

NOTE: _Craig_, _Crandall_, _Severin_ art in all.

FACE, THE (Tony Trent, the Face #3 on)
1941
Columbia Comics Group

#1-The Face	12.00	24.00	36.00
2	7.00	14.00	21.00

FAIRY TALE PARADE (See Famous Fairy Tales)
June-July, 1942 - 1946   (All by Walt Kelly)
Dell Publishing Co.

#1-All by Kelly	120.00	240.00	360.00
2(1943)	70.00	140.00	210.00
3-5	50.00	100.00	150.00
6-9: #7-Kelly cover	35.00	70.00	105.00
4-Color #50('44)	30.00	60.00	90.00

	Good	Fine	Mint
4-Color #69('45)	25.00	50.00	75.00
4-Color #87('45)	22.00	44.00	66.00
4-Color #104,114('46)	17.00	34.00	51.00
4-Color #121('46)-Not Kelly	10.00	20.00	30.00

NOTE: _#2-9, Four-Color #50,69 have Kelly cover/stories; Four Color #87,104,114-Kelly stories only._

FAIRY TALES
#10, 1951 - #11, June-July, 1951
Ziff-Davis Publ. Co. (Approved Comics)

#10,11	2.00	4.00	6.00

FAITHFUL
November, 1949
Marvel Comics/Lovers' Magazine

#1	1.50	3.00	4.50

FALLING IN LOVE
Sept-Oct, 1955 - #143, Oct-Nov, 1973
Arleigh Publ. Co./National Periodical Publ.

#1	2.50	5.00	7.50
2-10	1.00	2.00	3.00
11-20	.60	1.20	1.80
21-40	.40	.80	1.20
41-100	.30	.60	.90
101-143		.20	.45

FALL OF THE ROMAN EMPIRE (See Movie Comics)

FAMILY AFFAIR (TV)
Feb, 1970 - #4, Oct, 1970   (25¢)
Gold Key

#1-Pull-out poster	.50	1.00	1.50
2-4	.25	.50	.75

FAMILY FUNNIES
#9, Aug-Sept, 1946
Parents' Magazine Institute

#9	1.35	2.75	4.00

FAMILY FUNNIES
Sept, 1950 - 1953
Harvey Publications

#1-Mandrake	3.00	6.00	9.00
2-10: #4-Flash Gordon	2.50	5.00	7.50
#1(Black & white)	1.35	2.75	4.00

FAMOUS AUTHORS ILL. (See Stories by --)

Extra! #4, © WMG

Fairy Tale Parade #2, © DELL

Falling In Love #2, © DC

Famous Crimes #10. © FOX

Famous Funnies #1. © EAS

Famous Funnies #27. © EAS

FAMOUS COMICS
No date; Mid 1930's (24 pgs.) (no cover)
Zain-Eppy/United Features Syndicate
Reprinted from 1934 newspaper strips in color; Joe Palooka, Hairbreadth Harry, Napoleon,
The Nebbs, etc.

	Good	Fine	Mint
	17.50	35.00	52.50

FAMOUS COMICS (1st King Features comic book)
1934 (100pgs., daily newspaper reprints)
3½x8½", soft cover (came in a box)
King Features Synd. (Whitman Publ. Co.)

	Good	Fine	Mint
#684(#1)-Little Jimmy, Polly & Her Pals & Katzenjammer Kids, Barney Google	15.00	30.00	45.00
#684(#2)-Polly, Little Jimmy, Katzenjammer Kids	10.00	20.00	30.00
#684(#3)-Little Annie Rooney, Polly, Katzenjammer Kids	10.00	20.00	30.00
...Box price...	3.00	6.00	9.00

FAMOUS COMICS CARTOON BOOKS
1934 (72pgs.)(8x7¾")(Daily strip reprints)
Whitman Publishing Co. (B&W; Hardbacks)

#1200-The Captain & the Kids; Dirks reprints credited to Bernard Dibble	10.00	20.00	30.00
#1202-Captain Easy & Wash Tubbs by Roy Crane	15.00	30.00	45.00
#1203-Ella Cinders	10.00	20.00	30.00
#1204-Freckles & His Friends	8.00	16.00	24.00

NOTE: *Called Famous Funnies Cartoon Books inside.*

FAMOUS CRIMES
June, 1948 - 1953
Fox Features Syndicate

#1-Blue Beetle app. & crime story reprt/Phantom Lady #16	6.00	12.00	18.00
2-6	3.00	6.00	9.00
7-"Tarzan, the Wyoming Killer" used in Seduction of the Innocent, pg. 44	4.50	9.00	13.50
8-11,14-16	2.50	5.00	7.50
12,13-Drug story in ea.	4.00	8.00	12.00
51(no date)-Drug story	3.50	7.00	10.50

FAMOUS FAIRY TALES
1943 (32pgs.); 1944 (16pgs.) (Soft Covers)
K.K. Publ. Co. (Giveaway)

1942-Reprints from Fairy Tale Parade #2 & 3; Kelly inside art	60.00	120.00	180.00
1944-Kelly inside art	30.00	60.00	90.00

FAMOUS FEATURE STORIES
1938
Dell Publishing Co.

	Good	Fine	Mint
#1-Tarzan, Terry & the Pirates, King of the Royal Mtd., Buck Jones, Dick Tracy, Smilin' Jack, Dan Dunn, Don Winslow, G-Man, Tailspin Tommy, Mutt & Jeff, & Little Orphan Annie reprints-All illustrated text	22.00	44.00	66.00

FAMOUS FIRST EDITION (See Limited Collectors Edition) ($1.00) (10x13½"-Giant Size)
(72pgs.; #6-84pgs.; #7,8-68pgs.)
1974 - #8, 8-9/75; #1, 9/78 - Present
National Periodical Publ./DC Comics

C-26-Action #1	1.35	2.75	4.00
C-28-Detective #27	1.00	2.00	3.00
C-30-Sensation #1(1974)	.65	1.35	2.00
F-4-Whiz #2(#1)(10-11/74)	.65	1.35	2.00
F-5-Batman #1(F-6 on inside)	.65	1.35	2.00
F-6-Wonder Woman #1	.65	1.35	2.00
F-7-All-Star Comics #3	.65	1.35	2.00
F-8-Flash #1(8-9/75)	.65	1.35	2.00
C-61-Superman #1(9/78)	.65	1.35	2.00
Hardbound editions w/dust jacket ($5.00) (Lyle Stuart, Inc.) C-26,C-28,C-30,F-4,F-6, known	2.50	5.00	7.50

WARNING: The above books are **exact** reprints of the originals that they represent except for the Giant-Size format. None of the originals are Giant-Size. The first five issues were printed with two covers. Reprint information can be found on the outside cover but not on the inside cover which was reprinted exactly like the original (inside & out).

FAMOUS FUNNIES
1933 - #218, July, 1955
Eastern Color/Dell Publ./Eastern Color

A Carnival of Comics (probably the second comic book), 36 pgs., no date given, no publisher, no number; contains strip reprints of The Bungle Family, Dixie Dugan, Hairbreadth Harry, Joe Palooka, Keeping Up With the Jones, Mutt & Jeff, & Reg'lar Fellers, S'Matter Pop, Strange As It Seems & others. This book was sold by M. C. Gaines to Wheatena, Milk-O-Malt, John Wanamaker, Kinney Shoe Stores & others to be given away as premiums & radio giveaways (1933).

180.00	360.00	540.00

Series I—(No date-early 1934) (68 pgs.) No publisher given; sold in chain stores 10 cents. 35,000 print run (produced by Eastern Color for Dell Publ. Co.) Contains Sunday strip reprints of Mutt & Jeff, Reg'lar Fellers, Hairbreadth Harry, Strange As It Seems, Joe Palooka, Dixie Dugan, the Nebbs, Keeping Up With the Jones, & others. Inside front & back covers & pages 1-16 of Famous Funnies Series I Nos. 49-64 reprinted from Famous Funnies, A Carnival of Comics, & most of pages 17-48 reprinted from Funnies on Parade. This was the first comic book sold.

150.00	300.00	450.00

No. 1 (7/34-on stands 5/34)—Eastern Color Printing Co. First monthly newsstand comic book. Contains Sunday strip reprints of Toonerville Folks, Mutt & Jeff, Hairbreadth Harry, 'S Matter Pop, Nipper, Dixie Dugan, Connie, Ben Webster, Tailspin Tommy, The Nebbs, Joe Palooka & others.

(Famous Funnies cont'd)

	Good	Fine	Mint
	125.00	250.00	375.00
2	40.00	80.00	120.00

3-Buck Rogers Sunday strip rerprints by Rick
Yager begins, ends #218; not in #131,191-
208; the # of the 1st strip reprinted is
Page #190, Series #1 60.00 120.00 180.00

4	30.00	60.00	90.00
5	22.00	44.00	66.00
6-10	18.00	36.00	54.00

11,12,14,18-4pgs. of Buck Rogers in each issue, completes stories in <u>Buck Rogers</u> #1
which lacks these pages; #14 has two Buck
Rogers panels missing; #18-2pgs. of Buck
Rogers reprinted in Daisy Comics #1

	20.00	40.00	60.00
13,15-17,19,20	16.00	32.00	48.00

21,23-30: #27-War on Crime begins

	10.00	20.00	30.00

22-4pgs. of Buck Rogers needed to complete
stories in <u>Buck Rogers</u> #1

	12.00	24.00	36.00
31-34,36,37,39,40	9.00	18.00	27.00

35-2pgs. Buck Rogers omitted in <u>Buck Rogers</u>
#2 12.00 24.00 36.00

38-Full color portrait of Buck Rogers

	10.00	20.00	30.00
41-60	8.00	16.00	24.00
61-64,66,67,69,70	7.00	14.00	21.00

65,68-2pgs. Kirby art-"Lightnin & the Lone
Rider" 7.00 14.00 21.00

71,73,77-80: #80-Buck Rogers story continues from B.R. #5 5.00 10.00 15.00

72,74-76-2pgs. Kirby art in all

	6.00	12.00	18.00

81-Origin Invisible Scarlet O'Neil; strip
begins #82, ends #167 5.00 10.00 15.00

82-Buck Rogers cover 6.00 12.00 18.00

83-87,90: #87 has last B.R. full pg. reprint
5.00 10.00 15.00

88-Buck Rogers in "Moon's End" by Calkins,
2pgs.(not reprints). Beginning with #88,
all Buck Rogers pages have rearranged
panels 6.00 12.00 18.00

89-Origin Fearless Flint, the Flint Man
4.00 8.00 12.00

91-93,95,96,98-110: #105-Series 2 begins
(Strip Page #1) 4.00 8.00 12.00

94-Buck Rogers in "Solar Holocaust" by Calkins, 3pgs.(not reprts.)5.00 10.00 15.00

97-War Bond promotion, B. Rogers by Calkins,
2pgs.(not reprints) 5.00 10.00 15.00

111-130	3.50	7.00	10.50

131-150: #137-Strip page #110½ omitted.

	3.00	6.00	9.00
151-169	2.50	5.00	7.50

170-Two text illos. by Williamson, his 1st
comic book work 5.00 10.00 15.00

171-180: #171-Strip pgs. 227,229,230, Series
2 omitted. #172-Strip pg. 232 omitted

	2.50	5.00	7.50

181-190: Buck Rogers ends with start of strip
pg. 302, Series 2 1.75 3.50 5.25

191-197,199,201,203,204,206-208: No Buck
Rogers 1.50 3.00 4.50

198,200,202,205-One pg. Frazetta ads; no Buck
Rogers 2.00 4.00 6.00

209-Buck Rogers begins with strip pg. #480,
Series 2; Frazetta cover

	30.00	60.00	90.00

210-216: Frazetta covers. #215-Contains Buck
Rogers strip pg. #515-518, Series 2 followed by pgs. #179-181, Series 3

	30.00	60.00	90.00

217,218-Buck Rogers ends with pg. 199, Series
3 1.75 3.50 5.25

NOTE: Rick Yager did the Buck Rogers Sunday strips reprinted
in Famous Funnies. The Sundays were formerly done by Russ
Keaton & Lt. Dick Calkins did the dailies, but would sometimes
assist Yager on a panel or two from time to time. No. 184 is
Yager's first full Buck Rogers page. Yager did the strip until 1958
when Murphy Anderson took over. Tuska at from 4/26/59 —
1965. Virtually every panel was rewritten for Famous Funnies.
Not identical to the original Sunday page. The Buck Rogers reprints run continuously through Famous Funnies issue No. 190
(Strip No. 302) with no break in story line. The story line has no
continuity after No. 190. The Buck Rogers newspaper strips came
out in four series: Series 1, 3/30/30 — 9/21/41 (No. 1 — 600);
Series 2, 9/28/41 — 10/21/51 (No. 1 — 525)(Strip No. 110½
(½ pg.) published in only a few newspapers); Series 3, 10/28/51
— 2/9/58 (No. 100 — 428) (No No. 1 — 99); Series 4, 2/16/58
— 6/13/65 (No numbers, dates only).

FAMOUS FUNNIES
1964
Super Comics

Reprint #15-18	.60	1.20	1.80

FAMOUS GANG
1942 (Giveaway)
Firestone Tire & Rubber Co.

Bugs Bunny	15.00	30.00	45.00

FAMOUS GANGSTERS (Crime on the Waterfront #4)
April, 1951 – #3, Feb, 1952
Avon Periodicals/Realistic

#1-Capone, Dillinger 3.50 7.00 10.50
2-Wood cover + 1 pg.-Reprints Saint story/
Saint #7, retitled "Mike Strong"
4.00 8.00 12.00
3-Lucky Luciano & Murder, Inc. (has drug
story) 5.00 10.00 15.00

FAMOUS INDIAN TRIBES
July-Sept, 1962; July, 1972
Dell Publishing Co.

Famous Funnies #211, © EAS

Famous Funnies #216, © EAS

Famous Gangsters #1, © AVON

Famous Stars #1, © Z-D

Fantastic #10, © AJAX

Fantastic Comics #21, © FOX

(Famous Indian Tribes cont'd)

	Good	Fine	Mint
#12-264-209 (The Sioux)	.40	.80	1.20
#2(7/72)-reprints above	.15	.30	.45

FAMOUS STARS
Nov-Dec, 1950 - #6, Spring, 1952
Ziff-Davis Publ. Co.

	Good	Fine	Mint
#1-Shelley Winters, Susan Peters, Ava Gardner, Shirley Temple	4.00	8.00	12.00
2-Betty Hutton, Bing Crosby, Colleen Townsend, Gloria Swanson; 2 Everett stories	3.00	6.00	9.00
3-Farley Granger, Judy Garland's ordeal, Alan Ladd	3.50	7.00	10.50
4-Al Jolson, Bob Mitchum, Ella Raines, Richard Conte, Vic Damone; 6 pgs. Crandall	3.00	6.00	9.00
5-Liz Taylor, Betty Grable, Esther Williams, George Brent; Krigstein story	3.50	7.00	10.50
6-Gene Kelly, Hedy Lamar, June Allyson, Wm. Boyd, Janet Leigh, Gary Cooper	3.00	6.00	9.00

NOTE: *Whitney story-#1,3.*

FAMOUS STORIES (-- Book #2)
1942
Dell Publishing Co.

#1-Treasure Island	8.00	16.00	24.00
2-Tom Sawyer	8.00	16.00	24.00

FAMOUS TV FUNDAY FUNNIES
1961
Harvey Publications

#1-Casper the Ghost	1.00	2.00	3.00

FAMOUS WESTERN BADMEN
#13, Dec, 1952 - #15, 1953
Youthful Magazines

#13-15	.80	1.60	2.40

FANTASTIC (Beware #10 on)
1951 - #9, April, 1952
Youthful Magazines

#1	1.50	3.00	4.50
2-7,9	1.00	2.00	3.00
8-Capt. Science by Harrison	2.00	4.00	6.00

FANTASTIC (Fantastic Fears #1-9)
#10, Nov-Dec, 1954 - #11, Jan-Feb, 1955
Ajax/Farrell Publ.

	Good	Fine	Mint
#10,11	1.00	2.00	3.00

FANTASTIC ADVENTURES
1963 - 1964   (Reprints)
Super Comics

#9-12,15,16,18: #11-Reprints Disbrow/Blue Bolt #118. #16-Briefer art. #18-Reprints/Superior Stories #1	1.00	2.00	3.00
#17-South Sea Girl by Baker	1.50	3.00	4.50

FANTASTIC COMICS
Dec, 1939 - #23, Nov, 1941
Fox Features Syndicate

#1-Origin Samson; Stardust, The Super Wizard, Space Smith, Sub Saunders, Capt. Kidd begin	50.00	100.00	150.00
2	25.00	50.00	75.00
3-5	20.00	40.00	60.00
6-9: #6,7-Simon cover	15.00	30.00	45.00
10-Intro. David	13.50	26.75	40.00
11-17	10.00	20.00	30.00
18-Intro. Black Fury & sidekick Chuck	12.00	24.00	36.00
19,20	10.00	20.00	30.00
21-Origin The Banshee	12.00	24.00	36.00
22	10.00	20.00	30.00
23-Origin The Gladiator	12.00	24.00	36.00

NOTE: *Lou Fine covers-#1-5.*

FANTASTIC FEARS (Fantastic #10 on)
#7, May, 1953 - #9, Sept-Oct, 1954
Ajax/Farrell Publ.

#7(5/53)	2.00	4.00	6.00
8(7/53)	1.50	3.00	4.50
3,4	1.25	2.50	3.75
5-1st Ditko story written by Bruce Hamilton reprtd. in Weird V2#8	6.00	12.00	18.00
6-Decapitation of girl's head with paper cutter (classic)	2.00	4.00	6.00
7(5-6/54), 9(9-10/54)	1.20	2.40	3.60
8(7-8/54)-Contains story intended for Jo-Jo; name changed to Kaza	1.50	3.00	4.50

FANTASTIC FOUR (See Book & Record --)
Nov, 1961 - Present
Marvel Comics Group

#1-Origin & 1st app. The Fantastic Four (Reed Richards-Mr. Fantastic, Johnny Storm-The Human Torch, Sue Storm-The Invisible Girl, & Ben Grimm-The Thing); origin The Mole Man	250.00	575.00	900.00
1-Reprint from the Golden Record Comic Set	1.50	3.00	4.50

(Fantastic Four cont'd)	Good	Fine	Mint
with record....	2.00	4.00	6.00
2-Vs. The Skrulls	100.00	200.00	300.00

3-Fantastic Four don costumes & establish
Headquarters 60.00 120.00 180.00
4-1st Silver Age Sub-Mariner app.
50.00 100.00 150.00
5-Origin & 1st app. Doctor Doom
35.00 70.00 105.00
6-10: #6-Sub-Mariner, Dr. Doom team up
20.00 40.00 60.00
11-Origin The Impossible Man
15.00 30.00 45.00
12-Fant. Four Vs. The Hulk
15.00 30.00 45.00
13-15: #13-Intro. The Watcher
12.00 24.00 36.00
16-20: #18-Origin The Super Skrull. #19-
Intro. Rama-Tut. #20-Origin The Molecule
Man 8.00 16.00 24.00
21-30: #21-Intro. The Hate Monger. #25,26-
The Thing Vs. The Hulk. #30-Intro. Diablo
5.00 10.00 15.00
31-40: #35-Intro. & 1st app. Dragon Man.
#36-Intro. & 1st app. Madam Medusa & the
Frightful Four(Sandman, Wizard, & Paste
Pot Pete). #39-Wood inks on Daredevil
3.50 7.00 10.50
41-47: #41-43-Frightful Four app. #44-Intro.
Gorgan. #45-Intro. The Inhumans
2.50 5.00 7.50
48-Intro. & 1st app. The Silver Surfer
7.00 14.00 21.00
49,50-Silver Surfer x-over
3.50 7.00 10.50
51-60: #52-Intro. The Black Panther; origin-
#53. Silver Surfer x-over in #55-60,61
(cameo) 2.00 4.00 6.00
61-65,68-70 1.50 3.00 4.50
66,67-1st app. Him (Warlock)
2.00 4.00 6.00
71,73,75,78-80 1.00 2.00 3.00
72,74,76,77: Silver Surfer app.
1.25 2.50 3.75
81-90: #81-Crystal joins & dons costume.
#84-87-Dr. Doom app. .70 1.40 2.10
91-99,101,102: #94-Intro. Agatha Harkness.
#102-Last Kirby issue .60 1.20 1.80
100 1.50 3.00 4.50
103-120: #112-Hulk Vs. Thing. #116-(52pgs.)
.40 .80 1.20
121-140: #121-123-Silver Surfer x-over. #126-
Origin F.F. retold. #128-4pg. glossy insert of F.F. Friends & Fiends. #129-Intro.
Thundra. #130-Sue leaves F.F. #132-Medu-
sa joins. #133-Thundra Vs. Thing
.35 .70 1.05
141-154,158-160: #142-Kirbyish art by Buckler

	Good	Fine	Mint

begins. #150-Crystal & Quicksilver's
wedding. #151-Origin Thundra. #159-Medusa
leaves, Sue rejoins .30 .60 .90
155-157: Silver Surfer in all
.40 .80 1.20
161-180: #164-The Crusader (old Marvel Boy)
revived; origin #165. #166-Hulk Vs. F.F.
#167-Hulk & Thing Vs. F.F. #175-Return of
Impossible Man. #177,178-Frightful Four
app. .20 .40 .60
181-190: #190-F.F. breaks up.20 .40 .60
191-196 .15 .30 .45
197-199-Son of Dr. Doom app..15 .30 .45
200-Giant size .25 .50 .75
201 .15 .30 .45
NOTE: *John Buscema stories-#107,108(w/Kirby
& Romita),109-132,134-141,160,173-175,Annual
#11, Giant-Size #1-4; covers-#107-122,124-129,
133-139, Special #10. Ditko inks-#13. Kirby
stories-#1-102, Special #1-10, Giant-Size #5,
6(reprts); covers-#1-101,164,167,171-177,180,
181,190,200, Annual #11, Giant-Size #5, Special #1-7,9. Steranko covers-#130-132.*

Giant-Size #2(8/74) - #4: Formerly G-S
Super-Stars .75 1.50 2.25
Giant-Size #5(5/75),6(8/75).50 1.00 1.50
Special #1('63)-Origin F.F.; Ditko art
8.00 16.00 24.00
Special #2('64)-Dr. Doom origin & x-over
5.00 10.00 15.00
Special #3('65)-Reed & Sue wed
2.50 5.00 7.50
Special #4(11/66)-G.A. Torch x-over & origin
retold 1.75 3.50 5.25
Special #5(11/67)-Intro. Pscho-Man; no re-
reprints; Silver Surfer app.
1.25 2.50 3.75
Special #6(11/68)-Intro. Annihilus; no re-
prints; Birth of Franklin Richards
1.00 2.00 3.00
Special #7(11/69), #8(12/70), #9(12/71), #10
('73) .60 1.20 1.80
Annual #11(6/76),#12(2/78) .40 .80 1.20
Annual #13(10/78) .30 .60 .90
NOTE: *Buscema stories-#172-175(pencils),
Annual #11. Kirby stories-#1-6; covers-#1-7.*

FANTASTIC GIANTS (Konga #1-23)
Sept, 1966 (25¢)
Charlton Comics

V2#24-Origin Konga & Gorgo reprinted; two
new Ditko stories 2.00 4.00 6.00

FANTASTIC TALES
1958 (No date) (Reprint)

Fantastic Four #1, © MCG

Fantastic Four #10, © MCG

Fantastic Four #121, © MCG

Fantastic Tales #1, © I.W.

Fantasy Masterpieces #5, © MCG

Fat & Slat #1, © WMG

(Fantastic Tales cont'd)
I.W. Enterprises

	Good	Fine	Mint
#1-Reprints Avon's "City of the Living Dead"	1.50	3.00	4.50

FANTASTIC VOYAGE (See Movie Comics)
Aug, 1969 - #2, Dec, 1969
Gold Key

#1,2 (TV)	.40	.80	1.20

FANTASTIC VOYAGES OF SINDBAD, THE
Oct, 1965 - #2, June, 1967
Gold Key

#1,2	1.00	2.00	3.00

FANTASTIC WORLDS
#5, Sept, 1952 - #7, Jan, 1953
Standard Comics

#5-Toth & Anderson art	3.00	6.00	9.00
6-Toth story	3.00	6.00	9.00
7	1.50	3.00	4.50

FANTASY MASTERPIECES (Becomes Marvel Super
2/66 - #11, 10/67   Heroes #12 on)
Marvel Comics Group

#1-Photo of Stan Lee	.80	1.60	2.40
2	.60	1.20	1.80
3-G.A. Captain America reprints begin; 1st			
25¢ ish.	.70	1.40	2.10
4-6-Capt. America reprts.	.60	1.20	1.80
7-Begin G.A. Sub-Mariner, Torch reprint			
	.50	1.00	1.50
8-Torch battles the Sub-Mariner reprint			
(Marvel Mystery #9)	.50	1.00	1.50
9-Origin Human Torch reprint (Marvel Comics			
#1)	.50	1.00	1.50
10-All Winners reprint	.50	1.00	1.50
11-Reprint of origin Toro & Black Knight			
	.50	1.00	1.50

FANTASY QUARTERLY
1978   (50¢)
Power Comics

#1	.20	.40	.60

FANTOMAN (Formerly Amazing Adv. Funnies)
#2, Aug, 1940 - #4, Dec, 1940
Centaur Publications

#2-The Fantom of the Fair; reprints; The			
Arrow app.	15.00	30.00	45.00
3,4	12.00	24.00	36.00

FARGO KID (Formerly Justice Traps the Guilty)
V11#3(#1), 6-7/58 - V11#5, 10-11/58
Prize Publications

	Good	Fine	Mint
V11#3(#1)-Origin Fargo Kid, Severin cover &			
two Williamson stys.	3.50	7.00	10.50
V11#4,5-Severin cvr/stys.	1.50	3.00	4.50

FARMER'S DAUGHTER, THE
2-3/54 - #3, 6-7,54; 8-9/54 - #4, 2-3/55
Stanhall Publ./Trojan Magazines

#1	2.50	5.00	7.50
2,3('54)(Stanhall)	2.00	4.00	6.00
#1(Trojan)	2.00	4.00	6.00
2-4	1.50	3.00	4.50

FASTEST GUN ALIVE, THE (See 4-Color #741)

FAST FICTION (-- Action)(Stories By Famous
Authors Illustrated #6 on)
March, 1950 - #5, July, 1950
Seaboard Publ./Famous Authors Ill.

#1-Scarlet Pimpernel; Jim Lavery art			
	5.00	10.00	15.00
2-Captain Blood; H. C. Kiefer art			
	4.00	8.00	12.00
3-She, by H. Rider Haggard; Vincent Napoli			
art	7.00	14.00	21.00
4-The 39 Steps; Lavery art			
	4.00	8.00	12.00
5-Beau Geste-Kiefer art	4.00	8.00	12.00

FAST WILLIE JACKSON
October, 1976 - Present
Fitzgerald Periodicals, Inc.

#1	.15	.30	.45
2-7		.15	.30

FAT ALBERT (-- & the Cosby Kids) (TV)
March, 1974 - Present
Gold Key

#1	.15	.30	.45
2-29		.15	.30

FAT AND SLAT (Ed Wheelan)(Gunfighter #5 on)
Summer, 1947 - #4, Spring, 1948
E.C. Comics

#1	12.00	24.00	36.00
2-4	9.00	18.00	27.00

FAT AND SLAT JOKE BOOK
Summer, 1944   (One Shot)
All-American Comics (William H. Wise)

(Fat and Slat cont'd)	Good	Fine	Mint
by Ed Wheelan	9.00	18.00	27.00

FATE (See Hand of Fate, & Thrill-O-Rama)

FATMAN, THE HUMAN FLYING SAUCER
April, 1967 - #3, Aug-Sept, 1967
Lightning Comics

#1-Origin Fatman & Tinman by C.C. Beck,			
2-Beck art	2.50	5.00	7.50
3-(Scarce)-Beck art	3.00	6.00	9.00

FAUNTLEROY COMICS (Superduck Presents --)
1953
Close-Up/Archie Publications

#1	2.00	4.00	6.00
2,3	1.00	2.00	3.00

FAWCETT MINIATURES (See Mighty Midget)
1946 (12-24pgs.)(4x5")(Wheaties Giveaways)
Fawcett Publications

Captain Marvel-"And the Horn of Plenty"			
	2.00	4.00	6.00
Captain Marvel-"& the Raiders From Space"			
	2.00	4.00	6.00
Captain Marvel Jr.-"The Case of the Poison			
Press!"	2.00	4.00	6.00
Delecta of the Planets-C.C. Beck art. B&W inside; 12pgs.; 3 different issues			
	10.00	20.00	30.00

FAWCETT MOTION PICTURE COMICS (See M.P.C.)

FAWCETT MOVIE COMICS
1949 - #20, Dec, 1952
Fawcett Publications

No#-"Dakota Lil"-Geo. Montgomery & Rod Cameron('49)			
	5.00	10.00	15.00
No#-"Copper Canyon"-Ray Milland & Hedy Lamarr('50)	6.00	12.00	18.00
No#-"Destination Moon"-(1950)			
	12.00	24.00	36.00
No#-"Montana"-Errol Flynn & Alexis Smith('50)			
	5.00	10.00	15.00
No#-"Pioneer Marshal"-Monte Hale(1950)			
	6.00	12.00	18.00
No#-"Powder River Rustlers"-Rocky Lane(1950)			
	5.00	10.00	15.00
No#-"Singing Guns"-Vaughn Monroe & Ella Raines(1950)	5.00	10.00	15.00
#7-"Gunmen of Abilene"-Rocky Lane; Bob Powell art (1950)	6.00	12.00	18.00
8-"King of the Bullwhip"-Lash LaRue; Bob Powell art (1950)	7.00	14.00	21.00

	Good	Fine	Mint
9-"The Old Frontier"-Monte Hale; Bob Powell art (2/51)	5.00	10.00	15.00
10-"The Missourians"-Monte Hale (4/51)			
	5.00	10.00	15.00
11-"The Thundering Trail"-Lash LaRue (6/51)			
	5.00	10.00	15.00
12-"Rustlers on Horseback"-Rocky Lane (8/51)			
	5.00	10.00	15.00
13-"Warpath"-Edmond O'Brien & Forrest Tucker (10/51)	5.00	10.00	15.00
14-"Last Outpost"-Ronald Reagan(12/51)			
	5.00	10.00	15.00
15-"The Man From Planet X"-Robert Clark; Shaffenberger art (2/52)			
(Scarce)	15.00	30.00	45.00
16-"10 Tall Men"-Burt Lancaster			
	4.00	8.00	12.00
17-"Rose of Cimarron"-Jack Buetel & Mala Powers	4.00	8.00	12.00
18-"The Brigand"-Anthony Dexter; art by Shaffenberger	4.00	8.00	12.00
19-"Carbine Williams"-James Stewart; art by Costanza	4.00	8.00	12.00
20-"Ivanhoe"-Liz Taylor	5.00	10.00	15.00

FAWCETT'S FUNNY ANIMALS (#1-26 titled "Funny Animals")
12/42 - #91, 2/56
Fawcett Publications/Charlton Comics

#1-Capt. Marvel on cover	6.00	12.00	18.00
2-10-Marvel Bunny	2.50	5.00	7.50
11-20-Marvel Bunny	1.75	3.35	5.00
21-40-Marvel Bunny	1.35	2.75	4.00
41-88,90,91	1.00	2.00	3.00
89-Merry Mailman ish	1.35	2.75	4.00

F.B.I., THE
April-June, 1965
Dell Publishing Co.

#1-Sinnott art	.25	.50	.75

F.B.I. STORY, THE (See 4-Color #1069)

FEAR (Adventure Into --)
Nov, 1970 - #31, Dec, 1975
Marvel Comics Group

#1-Reprints Fantasy & Sci-Fi stories			
	.25	.50	.75
2-5	.20	.40	.60
6-9: #9-Everett art	.20	.40	.60
10-Man-Thing begins; Morrow cover & pencils			
	1.80	3.60	5.40
11-Adams cover	1.00	2.00	3.00
12-Starlin art	.80	1.60	2.40
13-18	.50	1.00	1.50

Fawcett Movie Comics, © FAW

Fawcett Movie Comics #10, © FAW

Fawcett's Funny Animals #2, © FAW

Feature Book #34, © KING

Feature Book #52, © KING

Feature Comics #62, © QUA

(Fear cont'd)

	Good	Fine	Mint
19-Intro. Howard the Duck by Val Mayerick	5.00	10.00	15.00
20-Morbius, the Living Vampire begins, ends #31; Gulacy pencils	.40	.80	1.20
21-31: #30-Evans art	.20	.40	.60

NOTE: *Brunner covers-#15-17.*

FEAR IN THE NIGHT (See Complete Mystery #3)

FEARLESS FAGAN (See 4-Color Comics #441)

FEATURE BOOK (Dell) (See Black & White and
Large Feature Book)

FEATURE BOOK (All newspaper reprints)
May, 1937 - #57, 1947
David McKay Publications

	Good	Fine	Mint
No#-Popeye & the Jeep; thought to be reprinted as Feature Book #3			
(Very Rare)	125.00	250.00	375.00
No#-Dick Tracy-Reprinted as Feature Book #4 (100pgs.) & in part as 4-Color #1			
(Very Rare)	300.00	600.00	900.00

NOTE: *Above books were advertised together
with different covers from Feature Books
#3 & 4.*

	Good	Fine	Mint
#1-King of the Royal Mtd.	40.00	80.00	120.00
2-Popeye(6/37) by Segar	60.00	120.00	180.00
3-Popeye(7/37) by Segar	40.00	80.00	120.00
4-Dick Tracy(8/37)-Same as No# issue listed but a new cover added	90.00	180.00	270.00
5-Popeye(9/37) by Segar	35.00	70.00	105.00
6-Dick Tracy(10/37)	70.00	140.00	210.00
7-Little Orphan Annie (Rare)	80.00	160.00	240.00
8-Secret Agent X-9-Not by Raymond	20.00	40.00	60.00
9-Dick Tracy (1/38)	70.00	140.00	210.00
10-Popeye(2/38)	35.00	70.00	105.00
11-Little Annie Rooney	15.00	30.00	45.00
12-Blondie(4/38)(Rare)	40.00	80.00	120.00
13-Inspector Wade	8.00	16.00	24.00
14-Popeye(6/38) by Segar (Scarce)	50.00	100.00	150.00
15-Barney Baxter(7/38)	12.00	24.00	36.00
16-Red Eagle	8.00	16.00	24.00
17-Gangbusters	12.00	24.00	36.00
18,19-Mandrake	20.00	40.00	60.00
20-Phantom	40.00	80.00	120.00
21-Lone Ranger	20.00	40.00	60.00
22-Phantom	40.00	80.00	120.00
23-Mandrake	20.00	40.00	60.00
24-Lone Ranger(1941)	20.00	40.00	60.00
25-Flash Gordon-Reprints not by Alex Raymond	60.00	120.00	180.00

	Good	Fine	Mint
26-Prince Valiant(1941)-Harold Foster art-1st 64 newspaper strips reprinted	130.00	260.00	390.00
27-29,31,34-Blondie	6.00	12.00	18.00
30,32,35,37,41,44-Katzenjammer Kids	5.00	10.00	15.00
33-			
36,38,40,42,43,45,47-Blondie	4.00	8.00	12.00
39-Phantom	17.00	34.00	51.00
46-Mandrake	12.00	24.00	36.00
48-Maltese Falcon('46)	12.00	24.00	36.00
49,50-Perry Mason	5.00	10.00	15.00
51,54-Rip Kirby by Alex Raymond; origin-#51	12.00	24.00	36.00
52,55-Mandrake	10.00	20.00	30.00
53,56,57-Phantom	14.00	28.00	42.00

NOTE: *All Feature Books through #25 are over-
sized 8½"x11-3/8" comics with color covers
and black & white interiors. The covers are
rough, heavy stock. The page counts, including covers, are as follows: No#,#3,4-100pgs.;
#1,2-52pgs.; #5-25 are all 76 pgs.*

FEATURE COMICS (Formerly Feature Funnies)
#21, June, 1939 - #144, May, 1950
Quality Comics Group

	Good	Fine	Mint
#21-26: #23-Charlie Chan begins	10.00	20.00	30.00
27-Origin & 1st app. of Dollman	90.00	180.00	270.00
28-1st Fine Dollman	35.00	70.00	105.00
29,30	25.00	50.00	75.00
31-Last Clock & Charlie Chan issue	20.00	40.00	60.00
32-37: #32-Rusty Ryan & Samar begin. #37-Last Fine Dollman	20.00	40.00	60.00
38-41: #38-Origin the Ace of Space. #39-Origin The Destroying Demon, ends #40. #40-Bruce Blackburn in costume	12.00	24.00	36.00
42-USA, the Spirit of Old Glory begins	8.00	16.00	24.00
43,45-50: #46-Intro. Boyville Brigadiers in Rusty Ryan	8.00	16.00	24.00
44-Dollman by Crandall begins, ends #63	9.00	18.00	27.00
51-55	6.00	12.00	18.00
56-Marijuana story in "Swing Session"	7.00	14.00	21.00
57-Spider Widow begins	6.00	12.00	18.00
58-60	6.00	12.00	18.00
61-68	5.00	10.00	15.00
69,70-Phantom Lady x-over in Spider Widow	8.00	16.00	24.00
71-80	4.00	8.00	12.00

(Feature Comics cont'd)	Good	Fine	Mint
81-100	3.00	6.00	9.00
101-144	2.00	4.00	6.00

NOTE: *Celardo* art-#37-43. *Gustavson* art (*Rusty Ryan*)-#32-47. *Powell* art-#64-73.

FEATURE FILMS MAGAZINE
Mar-Apr, 1950 - #5, Nov-Dec, 1950
National Periodical Publications

	Good	Fine	Mint
#1-"Captain China" with John Payne & Gail Russell	9.00	18.00	27.00
2-"Riding High" with Bing Crosby	7.00	14.00	21.00
3-"The Eagle & the Hawk" with John Payne, R. Fleming & D. O'Keefe	6.00	12.00	18.00
4-"Fancy Pants"-Bob Hope & Lucille Ball,			
5-(Exist?)	7.00	14.00	21.00

FEATURE FUNNIES (Feature Comics #21 on)
Oct, 1937 - #20, May, 1939
Quality Comics Group

	Good	Fine	Mint
#1-Joe Palooka, Mickey Finn, The Bungles, Jane Arden, Dixie Dugan, Big Top, Ned Bryant, Strange As It Seems, & Off the Record strip reprints begin	50.00	100.00	150.00
2-The Clock begins(11/37)-Masked hero	30.00	60.00	90.00
3-Hawks of Seas begins by Eisner, ends #12	15.00	30.00	45.00
4,5	12.00	24.00	36.00
6-12: #11-Archie O'Toole by Bud Thomas begins, ends #22	8.00	16.00	24.00
13-Espionage, Starring Black X begins by Eisner, ends #22	10.00	20.00	30.00
14-20	9.00	18.00	27.00

FEATURE PRESENTATION, A (Feat. Pres. Mag. #6)
#5, April, 1950
Fox Features Syndicate

	Good	Fine	Mint
#5-Black Tarantula	7.00	14.00	21.00

FEATURE PRESENTATIONS MAGAZINE (Formerly A Feature Pres. #5; becomes Feat. Stories Mag. #3 on)
#6, July, 1950
Fox Features Syndicate

	Good	Fine	Mint
#6-Moby Dick; Wood cover	6.00	12.00	18.00

FEATURE STORIES MAGAZINE (Formerly A Feat. Presentation #5, Feat. Pres. Mag. #6)
#3, Aug, 1950 - #4, Oct, 1950
Fox Features Syndicate

#3-Jungle Lil, Zegra stories

	Good	Fine	Mint
	7.00	14.00	21.00
4	4.00	8.00	12.00

FEDERAL MEN COMICS
1945 - #5, 1946   (DC reprints from 1930's)
Gerard Publ. Co.

	Good	Fine	Mint
#1-5: #2-Siegel & Shuster	4.00	8.00	12.00

FELIX THE CAT
1927 - 1931 (24pgs.)(1926,'27 color strip reprints)(8x10¼")
McLoughlin Bros.

	Good	Fine	Mint
#260-(Rare)-by Otto Messmer	35.00	70.00	105.00

FELIX THE CAT (See Inky & Dinky & March of Comics)
1943 - #12, 7-9/65
Dell Publ#1-19/Toby#20-61/Harvey#62-118/Dell

	Good	Fine	Mint
4-Color #15	30.00	60.00	90.00
4-Color #46('44)	17.50	35.00	52.50
4-Color #77('45)	12.00	24.00	36.00
4-Color #119('46)	8.00	16.00	24.00
4-Color #135('46)	7.00	14.00	21.00
4-Color #162('47)	6.00	12.00	18.00
#1(2-3/48)(Dell)	8.00	16.00	24.00
2	4.00	8.00	12.00
3-5	3.00	6.00	9.00
6-19(2-3/51-Dell)	2.00	4.00	6.00
20-30(Toby): #28-2/52 has #29 on cover, #28 on inside	1.50	3.00	4.50
31-61(6/55)(Toby)-Last Messmer ish.	1.25	2.50	3.75
62(8/55)-#100(Harvey)	.60	1.20	1.80
101-118(11/61)	.50	1.00	1.50
#12-269-211(9-11/62)(Dell)	1.00	2.00	3.00
#2-12(7-9/65)(Dell)	.50	1.00	1.50
-- & His Friends #1(12/53-Toby)	1.50	3.00	4.50
-- & His Friends #2-4	1.00	2.00	3.00
3-D Comic Book #1(1953-One Shot)	8.00	16.00	24.00
Summer Annual #2('52)-Early '30's Sunday strip reprints	12.00	24.00	36.00
Summer Annual No#('53,100pgs.,Toby)	8.00	16.00	24.00
Winter Annual #2('54)	5.00	10.00	15.00

(See March of Comics #24,36,51)
NOTE: *4-Color #15,46,77 are all daily or Sunday newspaper reprints from the 1930s drawn by Otto Messmer, who created Felix in 1915 for the Sullivan animation studio. He drew Felix from the beginning under contract to Pat Sullivan. In 1946 he went to work for Dell & wrote & drew most of the stories thru the Toby Press issues. He did not work for*

Feature Films #3, © DC

Feature Presentations Magazine #6, © FOX

Felix The Cat #12, © KING

Fight Against Crime #8, © Story Comics   Fight Comics #13, © FH   Fight Comics #56, © FH

(Felix the Cat cont'd)
*Harvey or the 1960s Dells. #107 reprints #71
interior; #110 reprints #56 interior.*

FERDINAND THE BULL
1938 (10c)(Large size; some color, rest B&W)
Dell Publishing Co.

	Good	Fine	Mint
No#	7.00	14.00	21.00

FIBBER McGEE & MOLLY (See A-1 Comics #25)

FICTION ILLUSTRATED (Digest size)
1/76 - Present (4-3/4"x6-3/4")($1.00)
Pyramid Publ. (Byron Preiss Visual Publ.)

Vol. 1-Schlomo Raven, Detective begins
Vol. 2-Starfawn, Vol.3-Chandler

	.60	1.20	1.80

55 DAYS AT PEKING (See Movie Comics)

FIGHT AGAINST CRIME (Fight Against the Guilty
May, 1951 - #21, Sept, 1954   #22)
Story Comics

	Good	Fine	Mint
#1	1.50	3.00	4.50
2,3	1.20	2.40	3.60
4-Drug story	3.00	6.00	9.00
5-Frazetta, 1 pg.	1.50	3.00	4.50
6-11,13,15	1.00	2.00	3.00
12-Drug story	2.50	5.00	7.50

14,16-Tothish art by Ross Andru; #16-Bondage
cover & E.C. story swipe, also #21

	1.50	3.00	4.50
17-21	.70	1.40	2.10

FIGHT AGAINST THE GUILTY (Formerly Fight
#22, 12/54 - #23, 3/55   Against Crime)
Story Comics

#22-Tothish art by Ross Andru; E.C. story

swipe	1.00	2.00	3.00
23	.70	1.40	2.10

FIGHT COMICS
Jan, 1940 - #86, Summer, 1953
Fiction House Magazines

#1-Origin Spy Fighter, Starring Saber; cover

by Lou Fine & Eisner	40.00	80.00	120.00
2-Eisner cover	20.00	40.00	60.00

3-Rip Regan, the Powerman begins; Eisner

cover	15.00	30.00	45.00
4,5: #4-Fine cover	10.00	20.00	30.00
6-10	8.00	16.00	24.00
11-14: Rip Regan ends	7.00	14.00	21.00
15-1st Super American	12.00	24.00	36.00

	Good	Fine	Mint
16-Captain Fight begins	12.00	24.00	36.00
17,18	10.00	20.00	30.00

19-Captain Fight ends; origin & 1st app.
Senorita Rio; Rip Carson, Chute Trooper

begins	10.00	20.00	30.00
20	7.00	14.00	21.00
21-30	5.00	10.00	15.00
31,33-40	4.00	8.00	12.00
32-Tiger Girl begins	6.00	12.00	18.00

41-47,49,50: #44-1st Capt. Fight

	4.00	8.00	12.00

48-Used in Love and Death by Legman

	6.00	12.00	18.00
51-Origin Tiger Girl	5.00	10.00	15.00
52-60	3.00	6.00	9.00

61-Origin Tiger Girl retold

	4.00	8.00	12.00
62-65-Last Baker issue	3.00	6.00	9.00
66-78	2.50	5.00	7.50
79-The Space Rangers app.	2.50	5.00	7.50
80-85	2.00	4.00	6.00

86-Two Tigerman stories by Evans; Moreira

story	2.50	5.00	7.50

NOTE: *Bondage cover-#40. Tiger Girl by Baker-
#36-60,62-65. Kayo Kirby by Baker-#52-64.*

FIGHT FOR LOVE
1952 (No month)
United Features Syndicate

No#-(Scarce)-Abbie and Slats newspaper

reprints	3.50	7.00	10.50

FIGHTING AIR FORCE
1952 - 1959
Superior Comics Ltd.

#1	1.20	2.40	3.60
2-10	.70	1.40	2.10
11-53	.50	1.00	1.50

FIGHTIN' AIR FORCE
#3, Feb, 1956 - #53, Feb, 1966
Charlton Comics

V1#3-10,11(68pgs., 3/58)	.40	.80	1.20
12-(100pgs.)	.60	1.20	1.80
13-50: #50-American Eagle begins			
	.20	.40	.60
51-53	.15	.30	.45

FIGHTING AMERICAN
Apr-May, 1954 - #7, Apr-May, 1955
Headline Publications/Prize

#1-Origin Fighting American & Speedboy;

S&K cvr.+ 3 stories	30.00	60.00	90.00

```
(Fighting Amer. cont'd)   Good   Fine   Mint                     Good   Fine   Mint
2-Three S&K stories     20.00  40.00  60.00      2-5: #2,3-Powell art   .80   1.60   2.40
3,4-Three S&K stories   17.00  34.00  51.00
5-Two S&K stories, Kirby/? story              FIGHTING INDIAN STORIES  (See Midget Comics)
                        15.00  30.00  45.00
6-4pg. reprint of origin, + 2pgs. by S&K      FIGHTING INDIANS OF THE WILD WEST!
                        12.00  24.00  36.00    Mar, 1952 - #2, Nov, 1952
7-Kirby story            9.00  18.00  27.00    Avon Periodicals
NOTE: Simon & Kirby covers on all.
                                               #1-Kinstler art          2.50   5.00   7.50
                                               2-Kinstler art           1.75   3.50   5.25
FIGHTING AMERICAN                              100pg. Annual(1952,25¢)-Contains three comics
Oct, 1966      (25¢)                              rebound               4.00   8.00  12.00
Harvey Publications
                                               FIGHTING LEATHERNECKS
#1-Origin Fighting American & Speedboy by      Feb, 1952 - #6, Dec, 1952
   S&K-reprint, plus 3 original S&K stories;   Toby Press
   1pg. Adams ad        2.00   4.00   6.00
                                               #1-"Duke's Diary"-full pg. pin-ups by
FIGHTIN' ARMY                                     Sparling              2.00   4.00   6.00
#16, 5/56 - #127, 12/76; #128, 9/77 - Present  2-"Duke's Diary"         1.50   3.00   4.50
Charlton Comics                                3-5-"Gil's Gals"-full-pg. pin-ups
                                                                        1.50   3.00   4.50
#16-30                    .35    .70   1.05     6-(Same as #3-5?)        1.00   2.00   3.00
31-60                    .25    .50    .75
61-80-The Lonely War of Willy Schultz be-      FIGHTING MAN, THE
   gins #75, ends #92    .20    .40    .60      May, 1-52 - #8, July, 1953
81-136: #89,90,92-Ditko art; Devil Brigadein   Ajax/Farrell Publications(Excellent Publ.)
   #79,82,83            .15    .30    .45
#108(Modern Comics reprint-1977) .15    .30     #1                      1.20   2.40   3.60
NOTE: Montes/Bache art-#48,49,51,69,75,76.     2-8                      .70   1.40   2.10
                                               Annual #1(132 pgs.)      2.50   5.00   7.50
FIGHTING DANIEL BOONE
1953                                           FIGHTING MAN MANUAL, THE
Avon Periodicals                               1952
                                               Ajax/Farrell Publications
No#-Kinstler cvr/22pgs.  5.00  10.00  15.00
IW Reprint #1-Kinstler cover/story             #1                       1.75   3.50   5.25
                        1.25   2.50   3.75
                                               FIGHTIN' MARINES  (The Texan #1-15)(2 #15's)
FIGHTING DAVY CROCKETT  (Formerly Kit Carson)  #15, 8/51 - #132, 11/76; #133, 10/77 - Present
#9, Oct-Nov, 1955                              St. John(Approved Comics)/Charlton Comics
Avon Periodicals
                                               #15(#1)-Matt Baker cover & story "Leatherneck
#9-Kinstler cover        2.00   4.00   6.00        Jack"                3.00   6.00   9.00
                                               2-9-Canteen Kate by Matt Baker plus Baker
FIGHTIN' 5, THE  (Formerly Space War)             covers                2.50   5.00   7.50
July, 1964 - #41, Jan, 1967                    10-Baker cover/story     2.00   4.00   6.00
Charlton Comics                                11-Baker cover           1.25   2.50   3.75
                                               12-16,18-20-Not Baker covers
V2#28-Origin F. Five     .40    .80   1.20                              1.00   2.00   3.00
29-39,41                .25    .50    .75      17-Canteen Kate by Baker 2.00   4.00   6.00
40-Peacemaker begins    .50   1.00   1.50      21-24                    .60   1.20   1.80
                                               25-(68pgs.)              1.00   2.00   3.00
FIGHTING FRONTS!                               26-(100pgs.)(8/58)       1.20   2.40   3.60
Aug, 1952 - #5, Jan, 1953                       27-50                    .30    .60    .90
Harvey Publications                            51-100: #78-Shotgun Harker & the Chicken
                                                  series begin          .20    .40    .60
#1                       1.20   2.40   3.60
```

Fighting American #2, © **PRIZE**

The Fighting Man #7, © **AJAX**

Fightin' Marines #5, © **STJ**

Fighting Yank #23. © STD   Film Stars Romances #3. © STAR   Firehair #8(IW). © FH

(Fightin' Marines cont'd)	Good	Fine	Mint
101-121	.15	.30	.45

122-Pilot issue for "War" title (Fightin'

Marines Presents War)		.15	.30
123-141		.15	.30
#120(Modern Comics reprint,'77)		.15	.30

NOTE: *#14 & 16 (CC) reprints St. John issue;
#16 reprints St. John insignia on cover.*
Montes/Bache art-#48,53,55,64,65,72-74,77-83.

FIGHTING MARSHAL OF THE WILD WEST
(See The Hawk)

FIGHTIN' NAVY
#74, May, 1956 - #125, Apr-May, 1966
Charlton Comics

#74-125	.15	.30	.45

NOTE: *Montes/Bache art-#109.*

FIGHTING PRINCE OF DONEGAL, THE (See Movie
Comics)

FIGHTIN' TEXAN
#16, Oct, 1952 - #17, Dec, 1952
St. John Publishing Co.

#16,17	1.00	2.00	3.00

FIGHTING UNDERSEA COMMANDOS
1952 - #5, April, 1953
Avon Periodicals

#1	2.00	4.00	6.00
2-5: #4-Kinstler cover	1.50	3.00	4.50

FIGHTING WAR STORIES
Aug, 1952 - 1953
Men's Publications

#1	1.00	2.00	3.00
2-5	.70	1.40	2.10

FIGHTING YANK(See Startling & America's Best)
Sept, 1942 - #29, Aug, 1949
Nedor/Better Publ./Standard

#1-The Fighting Yank begins; Mystico, the

Wonder Man app.	35.00	70.00	105.00
2	17.50	35.00	52.50
3	14.00	28.00	42.00
4	12.00	24.00	36.00
5,6,8-10	9.00	18.00	27.00
7-The Grim Reaper app.	9.00	18.00	27.00
11-The Oracle app.	6.00	12.00	18.00
12-17	6.00	12.00	18.00
18-The American Eagle app.	4.50	9.00	13.50
19,20	4.50	9.00	13.50

	Good	Fine	Mint
21-25: #21-Kara, Jungle Princess app. #22,24-			

Miss Masque app. #25-The Cavalier app.

	5.00	10.00	15.00
26-29: #27-Robinson/Meskin art. #28-One pg.			

Williamson; Robinson/Meskin story

	5.00	10.00	15.00

NOTE: *Many issues have Schomburg (Xela) cvrs.*

FIGHT THE ENEMY
Aug, 1966 - #3, Mar, 1967   (25¢)
Tower Comics

#1-Lucky 7 & Mike Manly begin; Grandenetti

art	.60	1.20	1.80
2,3: ½-pg. Wood art #3; McWilliams art			
	.40	.80	1.20

FILM FUNNIES
Nov, 1949 - #2, Feb, 1950
Marvel Comics (CPC)

#1	2.00	4.00	6.00
2	1.50	3.00	4.50

FILM STARS ROMANCES
Jan-Feb, 1950 - #3, May-June, 1950
Star Publications

#1-R. Valentino story; L. B. Cole cover

	6.00	12.00	18.00
2-Liz Taylor/Robert Taylor photo cover,			
3-photo cover	5.00	10.00	15.00

FIRE BALL XL5 (See Steve Zodiac)

FIREHAIR COMICS (Pioneer West Romances #3-6)
Winter/48-49 - #2, Spr/49; #7, Spr/51 - #11,
Spr/52
Fiction House Magazines

#1	4.00	8.00	12.00
2,7-11	2.50	5.00	7.50

IW Reprint #8-Kinstler cover; reprints Rangers #57; Dr. Drew story by Grandenetti

(no date)	1.00	2.00	3.00

FIRESTONE (See Donald & Mickey)

FIRESTORM (See Cancelled Comic Cavalcade)
March, 1978 - #5, Oct-Nov, 1978
DC Comics

#1	.20	.40	.60
2-5	.15	.30	.45

FIRST AMERICANS, THE (See 4-Color #843)

FIRST CHRISTMAS, THE (3-D)
1953 (25¢) (Oversized - 8¼"x10¼")
Fiction House Magazines(Real Adv.Publ. Co.)

	Good	Fine	Mint
No#-Kelly Freas cover	7.00	14.00	21.00

FIRST ISSUE SPECIAL
April, 1975 - #13, April, 1976
National Periodical Publications

#1-Intro. Atlas by Kirby	.40	.80	1.20
2-Green Team (See Cancelled Comic Cavalcade)			
	.20	.40	.60
3-Metamorpho	.25	.50	.75
4-Lady Cop	.25	.50	.75
5-Manhunter by Kirby	.30	.60	.90
6-Dingbats by Kirby	.30	.60	.90
7-The Creeper by Fleisher/Ditko			
	.40	.80	1.20
8-The Warlord (origin)	.80	1.60	2.40
9-Dr. Fate; Kubert cover; Simonson art			
	.40	.80	1.20
10-The Outsiders	.25	.50	.75
11-Code Name: Assassin; Redondo art			
	.25	.50	.75
12-New Starman-Kubert cvr.	.25	.50	.75
13-Return of the New Gods	.25	.50	.75

FIRST KISS
Dec, 1957 - #35, Dec, 1963
Charlton Comics

V1#1	.50	1.00	1.50
V1#2-35	.25	.50	.75

FIRST LOVE ILLUSTRATED
Feb, 1949 - #90, Feb, 1963
Harvey Publications(Home Comics)(True Love)

#1-Two Powell stories	2.50	5.00	7.50
2-10	1.50	3.00	4.50
11-30	1.00	2.00	3.00
31-34,36,37,39-90	.80	1.60	2.40
35-Used in Seduction of the Innocent, illo-			
"The title of this comic book is First			
Love"	5.00	10.00	15.00
38-Nostrand art	1.50	3.00	4.50

NOTE: *Powell art-#1,3-5,7,10,11,13-17,19,21-
24,26-29,33,35-41,43,45,46,50,54,57,58,61-63,
71-73,76,82,84,88.*

FIRST MEN IN THE MOON (See Movie Comics)

FIRST ROMANCE MAGAZINE
Aug, 1949 - #51, Sept, 1958
Home Comics(Harvey Publ.)/True Love

#1	2.50	5.00	7.50

	Good	Fine	Mint
2-5	1.50	3.00	4.50
6-10	1.20	2.40	3.60
11-20	1.00	2.00	3.00
21-27,29-51	.80	1.60	2.40
28-Nostrand art	1.50	3.00	4.50

NOTE: *Powell art-#1,3-5,8-10,14,18,20-22,24,
25,28,36,46,48,51.*

FIRST TRIP TO THE MOON (See Space Advs. #20)

5-STAR SUPER-HERO SPEC. (See DC Special
Series #1)

FLAME, THE
Summer, 1940 - #8, Jan, 1942
Fox Features Syndicate

#1-Flame stories from WonderWorld #5-9;			
origin the Flame; Lou Fine art, 50 pgs.			
	70.00	140.00	210.00
2-Two stories by Fine	30.00	60.00	90.00
3-8	14.00	28.00	42.00

FLAME, THE (Formerly Lone Eagle)
#5, Dec-Jan, 1954-55 - #4, Jun-Jul, 1955
Ajax/Farrell Publications(Excellent Publ.)

#5(#1)	4.50	9.00	13.50
2-4	2.50	5.00	7.50

FLAMING LOVE
Dec, 1949 - #6, Oct, 1950 (photo cvrs.#2-6)
Quality Comics Group (Comic Magazines)

#1-Ward cover, 9pgs.	6.00	12.00	18.00
2,5,6	2.00	4.00	6.00
3-Ward art, 9pgs.; Crandall story			
	5.00	10.00	15.00
4-Gustavson story	2.50	5.00	7.50

FLAMING WESTERN ROMANCES
Nov-Dec, 1949 - #3, Mar-Apr, 1950
Star Publications

#1	3.00	6.00	9.00
2	2.50	5.00	7.50
3-Robert Taylor, Arlene Dahl photo cover			
with biographies inside; L.B. Cole cover;			
spanking panel	4.00	8.00	12.00

FLASH (Miniature)
1946 (One Shot) (Wheaties giveaway)
National Periodical Publications

#1-Johnny Thunder, Ghost Patrol, The Flash &			
Kubert Hawkman app.	12.00	36.00	60.00

NOTE: *All known copies were taped to Wheaties
boxes and never found in Fine & Mint condition.*

The Flame #3, © AJAX

Flaming Love #5, © QUA

Flaming Western Romances #3, © STAR

The Flash #106, © DC

Flash Comics #27, © DC

Flash Comics #67, © DC

FLASH, THE (Formerly Flash Comics) (See Showcase, The Brave & the Bold, World's Finest, & Super Team Family)
#105, Feb-Mar, 1959 - Present
National Periodical Publications/DC Comics

	Good	Fine	Mint
#105-Origin Flash(retold), & Mirror Master	60.00	120.00	180.00
106-Origin Grodd & Pied Piper	25.00	50.00	75.00
107-110: #110-Intro. & origin Kid Flash & The Weather Wizard	12.00	24.00	36.00
111,114,115	6.00	12.00	18.00
112-Origin Elongated Man	7.00	14.00	21.00
113-Origin Trickster	6.00	12.00	18.00
116-120: #117-Origin Capt. Boomerang	4.50	9.00	13.50
121	2.50	5.00	7.50
122-Origin & 1st app. The Top	2.50	5.00	7.50
123-Re-intro. Golden Age Flash; origins of both Flashes	5.00	10.00	15.00
124-130: #127-G.A. Flash x-over, J.S.A. cameo. #128-Origin Abra Kadabra	1.75	3.50	5.25
131-140: #131-Green Lantern x-over. #136-1st Dexter Miles. #137-G.A. Flash x-over, J.S.A. cameo. #139-Origin Prof. Doom. #140-Origin Heat Wave	1.25	2.50	3.75
141-150: #143-Green Lantern x-over	1.00	2.00	3.00
151-160: #151-G.A. Flash x-over. #160-25¢ ish G-21: G.A. reprints of Flash & Johnny Quick	.70	1.40	2.10
(84pg. Giant G-21)	1.00	2.00	3.00
161-170: #167-New facts about Flash's origin. #169-25¢ ish G-34. #170-Dr. Mid-Nite, Dr. Fate, G.A. Flash x-over	.50	1.00	1.50
(84pg. Giant G-34)	.60	1.20	1.80
171-180: #171-JLA, Green Lantern, Atom flashbacks. #173-G.A. Flash x-over. #178-25¢ ish G-46	.40	.80	1.20
(84pg. Giant G-46)	.60	1.20	1.80
181-190: #186-Re-intro. Sargon. #187-25¢ ish G-58	.35	.70	1.05
(84pg. Giant G-58)	.50	1.00	1.50
191-200: #191-Green Lantern x-over. #196-25¢ ish G-70	.30	.60	.90
(84pg. Giant G-70)	.50	1.00	1.50
201-210: #205-25¢ ish G-82. #208-52pg. begin, end #213,15,16. #214-Origin Metal Men reprint	.30	.60	.90
(84pg. Giant G-82)	.40	.80	1.20
211-216,220: #211-G.A. Flash origin (#104). #213-All reprints. #214-50¢ ish DC-11, origin Metal Men. #215-G.A. Flash x-over, reprint in #216	.25	.50	.75

	Good	Fine	Mint
(Giant DC-11)	.60	1.20	1.80
217-219: Adams stories in all. #217-Green Lantern/Green Arrow series begins. #219-Last Green Arrow	1.50	3.00	4.50
221-225,227,228,230,231	.25	.50	.75
226-Adams story	1.00	2.00	3.00
229,232-(100pgs. each)	.50	1.00	1.50
233-250: #243-Death of the Top	.20	.40	.60
251-270	.15	.30	.45
Annual #1(10-12/63)-Origin Elongated Man & Kid Flash reprint	2.50	5.00	7.50

NOTE: *Adams* covers-#194,195,202-204,206-208, 211,213,215,246. *Anderson* inks-#110,111,114, 115,117-119,148-150,168,176,194,200-204,206-208,210; covers-#165,176,196,205,210,212,232. *Infantino* art-#105-174,178,187,194,196,201, 203,209,210,213-215,229,Annual #1; covers-#105-164,166-174,176,200,201. *Kubert/Infantino* story-#108. *Kubert* covers-#189-191. *Meskin* reprint-#229. *Staton* covers-#263,264.

FLASH BROWN, THE SUPER-SCIENTIST (See Chewing Gum Booklet)

FLASH COMICS (The Flash #105 on; also see 1/40 - #104, 2/49   All-Flash)
National Periodical Publ./All-American

	Good	Fine	Mint
#1-Origin The Flash by Harry Lampert, Hawkman by Garner Fox, The Whip & Johnny Thunder; Cliff Cornwall by Moldoff, Minute Movies begin; Moldoff (Shelly) cover; 1st app. Shiera Sanders who later becomes Hawkgirl,#24; reprinted in Famous First Edition	275.00	550.00	825.00
2-Rod Rian begins, ends #11	100.00	200.00	300.00
3-The King begins	80.00	160.00	240.00
4-Moldoff (Shelly) Hawkman begins	75.00	150.00	225.00
5	60.00	120.00	180.00
6,7	50.00	100.00	150.00
8-10	40.00	80.00	120.00
11-20: #12-Les Watts begins; "Sparks" #16 on. #17-Last Cliff Cornwall	25.00	50.00	75.00
21-23	20.00	40.00	60.00
24-Shiera becomes Hawkgirl	25.00	50.00	75.00
25-30: #28-Last Les Sparks. #29-Origin Ghost Patrol	17.50	35.00	52.50
31-40: #35-Origin Shade	15.00	30.00	45.00
41-50	12.00	24.00	36.00
51-61: #59-Last Minute Movies. #61-Last Moldoff Hawkman	8.00	16.00	24.00
62-Hawkman by Kubert begins	12.00	24.00	36.00

(Flash Comics cont'd)   Good Fine Mint
63-70: #66-68-Hop Harrigan in all
                   9.00 18.00 27.00
71-80: #80-Atom begins 9.00 18.00 27.00
81-85   8.00 16.00 24.00
86-Intro. The Black Canary in Johnny Thunder
               30.00 60.00 90.00
87-90: #88-Origin Ghost 12.00 24.00 36.00
91,93-103: #98-Atom dons new costume
               14.00 28.00 42.00
92-1st solo Black Canary 20.00 40.00 60.00
104-Origin The Flash retold (Rare)
               50.00 100.00 150.00
NOTE: *Infantino stories-#90,93-95,99-104.*
Kinstler stories-#87,89(Hawkman). Krigstein
story-#94. Kubert stories-#82-76,83,85,86,88-
104; covers-#63,65,67,70,71,73,75,83,85,86,
88,89,91,94,96,98,100,104.

FLASH GORDON (See Eat Right to Work--,
Feature Book #25(McKay, King Classics, King
Comics, March of Comics #118,133,142 &
Street Comix)

FLASH GORDON
#10, 1943 - #512, Nov, 1953
Dell Publishing Co.

4-Color #10-by Alex Raymond(1943)-Reprints/
  "The Ice Kingdom" 100.00 200.00 300.00
4-Color #84-by Alex Raymond(1945)-Reprints/
  "The Fiery Desert" 50.00 100.00 150.00
4-Color #173,190   10.00 20.00 30.00
4-Color #204,247   8.00 16.00 24.00
4-Color #424   6.00 12.00 18.00
#2(5-7/53)(Dell)   4.00   8.00 12.00
4-Color #512   4.00   8.00 12.00
Macy's Giveaway(1943-20pgs.)(Rare)-Not by
  Raymond   80.00 160.00 240.00

FLASH GORDON
Oct, 1950 - April, 1951
Harvey Publications

#1-Alex Raymond art 25.00 50.00 75.00
2-4-Alex Raymond   20.00 40.00 60.00
5-(Extremely Rare)-Small size(5½x8½";B&W;
  32pgs.)Distributed to some mail subscribers only   Estimated value......$700.00
(Also see All-New #15, Boy Explorers #2, and
Stuntman #3)

FLASH GORDON
June, 1965
Gold Key

#1(1947 reprint)   1.25   2.50   3.75

FLASH GORDON (Also see Comics Reading Librs.)
9/66 - #18, 1/70; #19, 10-11/78 - Present
King, #1-11(12/67)/Charlton, #12(2/69)-18/
Gold Key #19 on
                  Good Fine Mint
#1-Army giveaway(1968)("Complimentary" on
  cover)(Same as regular #1 minus Mandrake
  story & back cover) 2.00   4.00   6.00
1-Williamson cover & 2 stories; Mandrake
  app.   2.00   4.00   6.00
2-Bolle, G. Kane art   1.50   3.00   4.50
3-Williamson cover, Estrada art
               1.75   3.50   5.25
4-Secret Agent X-9 begins, Williamson cover
  and art   1.75   3.50   5.25
5-Williamson cover/art 1.75   3.50   5.25
6,8-Crandall art. #6-Crandall cover
               1.50   3.00   4.50
7-Raboy art   1.25   2.50   3.75
9,10-Raymond reprint + Buckler story
               2.00   4.00   6.00
11-Crandall story   1.50   3.00   4.50
12-Crandall cover/story 1.75   3.50   5.25
13-Jeff Jones art   1.20   2.40   3.60
14-17: #17-Brick Bradford app.
             .65   1.35   2.00
18-Kaluta story   1.20   2.40   3.60
19(10-11/78,G.K.),#20 .15   .30   .45

FLASH SPECTACULAR, THE (See DC Special
Series #11)

FLAT TOP
Nov, 1953 - #5, 1954
Mazie Comics/Harvey Publ.(Magazine Publ.)

#1   .80   1.60   2.40
2-5   .50   1.00   1.50

FLINTSTONES, THE (TV)(See Dell Giant #48 for
#2, 11-12/61 - #60, 9/70 (Hanna-Barbera) #1)
Dell Publ. Co./Gold Key #7 on

#2   .30   .60   .90
3-10   .25   .50   .75
11-30: #11-1st app. Pebbles(6/63)
             .20   .40   .60
31-60(9/70): #34-1st app. the Great Gazoo
             .15   .30   .45
At N.Y. World's Fair('64)-J.W. Books(25¢),
  re-issued in 1965(1965 on cover)
             .65   1.35   2.00
Bigger & Boulder #1(30013-211)G.K. Giant(25¢)
  84 pgs.   .65   1.35   2.00
Bigger & Boulder #2-(25¢)(1966)-reprints
  B&B #1   .40   .80   1.20
Pebbles & Bamm Bamm(100pgs.)-#30028-511(paper
  cover-25¢)   .35   .70   1.05

Flash Gordon Four Color #190, © KING

Flash Gordon #1(Harv), © KING

Flash Gordon #2(Dell), © KING

Advs. Of The Fly #4, © AP   Flying A's Range Rider #20, © DELL   Flyin' Jenny #2, © Pentagon Publ.

(Flintstones cont'd)

(See Comic Album #16, Bamm-Bamm & Pebbles
Flintstone, Dell Giant #48, March of Comics
#229,243,271,280,289,299,317,327,341, Pebbles
Flintstone, and Whitman Comic Books.)

FLINTSTONES, THE
Nov, 1970 - #50, Feb, 1977
Charlton Comics

	Good	Fine	Mint
#1	.20	.40	.60
2-7,9-50		.15	.30
8-"Flintstones Summer Vacation", 52pgs.			
(Summer, 1971)	.20	.40	.60

(Also see Barney & Betty Rubble, Dino, The
Great Gazoo, and Pebbles & Bamm-Bamm)

FLINTSTONES, THE (TV)
October, 1977 - #8, Dec, 1978
Marvel Comics Group

#1-8		.15	.30

FLINTSTONES CHRISTMAS PARTY, THE (See The
Funtastic World of Hanna-Barbera #1)

FLIP
1954 - #2, June, 1954   (Satire)
Harvey Publications

#1,2-Nostrand art in ea.	3.00	6.00	9.00

FLIPPER (TV)
April, 1966 - #3, Nov, 1967
Gold Key

#1-3		.25	.50	.75

FLIPPITY & FLOP
Dec-Jan, 1951-52 - #47, Sept-Nov, 1960
National Periodical Publ.(Signal Publ. Co.)

#1	1.50	3.00	4.50
2-20	.75	1.50	2.25
21-47	.40	.80	1.20

FLY, ADVENTURES OF THE (Flyman #31-39)
Aug, 1959 - #30, Oct, 1964; #31, Aug, 1965
Archie Publications

#1-Shield app.; origin The Fly by Simon &			
Kirby	10.00	20.00	30.00
2-Williamson & Simon & Kirby stories			
	7.00	14.00	21.00
3-Origin retold; Davis story			
	5.00	10.00	15.00
4-Adams pencils(1 panel); S&K cover			
	3.50	7.00	10.50

	Good	Fine	Mint
5-10: #7-Black Hood app. #8,9-Shield x-over.			
#10-Black Hood app.	1.50	3.00	4.50
11-13,15-20	.80	1.60	2.40
14-Intro. & origin Fly Girl	.80	1.60	2.40
21-31: #23-Jaguar cameo. #30-Comet x-over in			
Fly Girl	.60	1.20	1.80

FLY BOY
Spring, 1952 - #5, May, 1954
Ziff-Davis Publ. Co. (Approved)

#1-Saunders painted cvrs.	1.20	2.40	3.60
2-5- " " "	.80	1.60	2.40

FLYING ACES
July, 1955 - 1956
Key Publications

#1	1.00	2.00	3.00
2-5	.60	1.20	1.80

FLYING A'S RANGE RIDER (TV)(See 4-Color #404
#2, 6-8/53 - #24, 12-2/59   for #1)
Dell Publishing Co.

#2	1.75	3.50	5.25
3-10	1.00	2.00	3.00
11-16,18-24	.80	1.60	2.40
17-Toth story	2.00	4.00	6.00

FLYING CADET (WW II Plane Photos)
Jan, 1943 - 1947   (½ photos, ½ comics)
Flying Cadet Publishing Co.

V1#1-9	1.20	2.40	3.60
V2#1-8(#10-17)	.80	1.60	2.40

FLYIN' JENNY
1946 - 1947   (1945 strip reprints)
Pentagon Publ. Co.

No#	2.50	5.00	7.50
#2-Baker cover	2.50	5.00	7.50

FLYING MODELS
May, 1954   (16 pgs.) (5c)
H-K Publ. (Harvey Kurtzman)

V61#3 (Rare)	10.00	20.00	30.00

FLYING NUN (TV)
Feb, 1968 - #4, Nov, 1968
Dell Publishing Co.

#1-4		.15	.30	.45

FLYING NURSES (See Sue & Sally Smith --)

FLYING SAUCERS
1950 - 1953
Avon Periodicals/Realistic

	Good	Fine	Mint
#1-(1950)-21pg.Wood sty.	20.00	40.00	60.00
No#(1952)-cover altered + 2pgs. of Wood art			
not in original	15.00	30.00	45.00
No#(1953)-reprints above	10.00	20.00	30.00

FLYING SAUCERS (Comics)
April, 1967 - #5, Oct, 1969
Dell Publishing Co.

#1	.60	1.20	1.80
2-5	.40	.80	1.20

FLYMAN (Formerly The Fly #1-30; Mighty
Comics Presents #40 on)
#31, May, 1965 - #39, Sept, 1966
Mighty Comics Group(Radio Comics)(Archie)

#31-Comet, Shield, Black Hood			
	.80	1.60	2.40
32,33-Comet, Shield, Black Hood x-over; re-intro. Wizard, Hangman-#33			
	.65	1.35	2.00
34-Shield begins	.65	1.35	2.00
35-Origin Black Hood	.65	1.35	2.00
36-Hangman x-over in Shield; re-intro. & origin of Web	.65	1.35	2.00
37-Hangman, Wizard x-over in Flyman; last Shield issue	.65	1.35	2.00
38-Web story	.65	1.35	2.00
39-Steel Sterling story	.65	1.35	2.00

FOLLOW THE SUN (TV)
May-July, 1962 - #2, Sept-Nov, 1962
Dell Publishing Co.

#01-280-207(#1), 208(#2)	.50	1.00	1.50

FOODINI (See The Great --, Pinhead & --, &
Mar, 1950 - #5, 1950   Jingle Dingle)
Continental Publications (Holyoke)

#1	1.00	2.00	3.00
2-5	.65	1.35	2.00

FOOEY (Magazine) (Satire)
Feb, 1961 - #4, May, 1961
Scoff Publishing Co.

#1	.80	1.60	2.40
2-4	.60	1.20	1.80

FOOTBALL THRILLS
Fall-Winter, 1951-52 - #2, 1952
Ziff-Davis Publ. Co.

	Good	Fine	Mint
#1,2-Painted covers by Saunders			
	1.50	3.00	4.50

FOR A NIGHT OF LOVE
1951
Avon Periodicals

No#-Two stories adapted from the works of Emile Zola	5.00	10.00	15.00

FORBIDDEN LOVE
Mar, 1950 - #4, Sept, 1950
Quality Comics Group

#1-Classic photo cover; Crandall story			
	25.00	50.00	75.00
2,3	3.00	6.00	9.00
4-Ward/Cuidera art	5.00	10.00	15.00

FORBIDDEN LOVE (See Dark Mansion of --)

FORBIDDEN TALES OF DARK MANSION (Dark
Mansion of Forbidden Love #1-4)
#5, May-June, 1972 - #15, Feb-Mar, 1974
National Periodical Publications

#5-15	.25	.50	.75

NOTE: *Alcala* stories-#9-11,13. *Chaykin* stories-#7-15. *Kaluta* covers-#7-13. *Kane* story-#13. *Kirby* story-#6. *Redondo* story-#14.

FORBIDDEN WORLDS (--Presents Herbie #114,116)
7-8/51 - #145, 8/67 (#1-5,52pgs.; #6,44pgs.)
American Comics Group

#1-10pg. Williamson/Frazetta story			
	20.00	40.00	60.00
2	5.00	10.00	15.00
3-7pg. Williamson/Wood story			
	10.00	20.00	30.00
4	4.00	8.00	12.00
5-8pg. Williamson/Krenkel story			
	9.00	18.00	27.00
6-Williamson inks/Harrison pencils, 8pgs.			
	8.00	16.00	24.00
7-10	2.00	4.00	6.00
11-20	1.50	3.00	4.50
21-34-Last pre-code ish.	1.25	2.50	3.75
35-62	1.00	2.00	3.00
63,69,76,78-Williamson stories in all			
	2.50	5.00	7.50
64,66-68,70-72,74,75,77,79-90			
	.60	1.20	1.80
65-"There's a New Moon Tonight" listed in #114 as holding 1st record fan mail response	1.00	2.00	3.00

73-Intro., 1st app. Herbie by Whitney

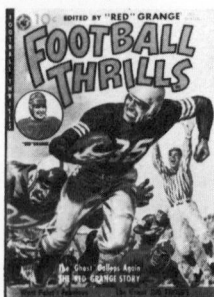
Football Thrills #1, © Z-D

Forbidden Love #1, © QUA

Forbidden Worlds #3, © ACG

Forever People #3. © DC

Four Color #2. © DELL

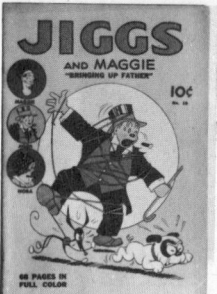

Four Color #18. © DELL

(Forbidden Worlds cont'd)	Good	Fine	Mint
	9.00	18.00	27.00
91-93,95-100	.60	1.20	1.80
94-Herbie app.	2.50	5.00	7.50
101-109,111-113,115,117-120	.35	.70	1.05

110,114,116-Herbie app.; #114 contains list
of editor's top 20 ACG stories

	1.50	3.00	4.50

121-124: #124-Magic Agent app.

	.35	.70	1.05

125-Magic Agent app.; intro. & origin Magicman series, ends #141 .40 .80 1.20

126-130	.35	.70	1.05

131,132,134-141: #136-Nemesis x-over in Magicman. #140-Mark Midnight app. by Ditko

	.30	.60	.90

133-Origin & 1st app. Dragonia in Magicman
(1-2/66); returns #138 .30 .60 .90

142-145	.25	.50	.75

NOTE: *Buscema story-#75,79,81,82. Disbrow
story-#10. Ditko story-#137,138,140. Moldoff
story-#31.*

FORD ROTUNDA CHRISTMAS BOOK (See Christmas
at the Rotunda)

FOREIGN INTRIGUE
1956
Charlton Comics

#1-Johnny Dynamite begins, ends #15

	1.25	2.50	3.75
2-15	.80	1.60	2.40

FOREVER, DARLING (See 4-Color #681)

FOREVER PEOPLE
Feb-Mar, 1971 - #11, Oct-Nov, 1972
National Periodical Publications

#1-Superman x-over; Jack Kirby art begins

	2.00	4.00	6.00
2	1.20	2.40	3.60
3-5: #4-G.A. reprints begin	1.00	2.00	3.00
6-8,11	.80	1.60	2.40
9,10-Deadman x-over	1.00	2.00	3.00

NOTE: *Kirby art & covers-#1-11; #4-9 contain
Sandman reprints from Adventure #85,84,75,80,
77,74 in that order.*

FOR GIRLS ONLY
Nov, 1952 (Digest size, 100 pgs.)
Bernard Bailey Enterprises

#1-Half comic book, half magazine

	1.50	3.00	4.50

FOR LOVERS ONLY
#38, Dec, 1968 - #98, Nov, 1976
Charlton Comics

	Good	Fine	Mint
#38-98		.15	.30

40 BIG PAGES OF MICKEY MOUSE
1936 (44pgs., 10¾x12½", cardboard cover)
Whitman Publishing Co.

#945-Reprints Mickey Mouse Magazine #1, but
with a different cover. Ads were eliminated and some illustrated stories had
expanded text. The book is 3/4" shorter
than M.M.Mag.#1, but the reprints are
the same size. (Rare) 50.00 100.00 150.00

48 FAMOUS AMERICANS
1947 (Giveaway) (Half-size in color)
J. C. Penney Co. (Cpr. Edwin H. Stroh)

Simon & Kirby art	6.00	12.00	18.00

FOUR COLOR
1939 - #1354, 1962
Dell Publishing Co.

NOTE: *Four Color only appears on issues #19-
25, 1-99. Dell Publishing Co. filed these as
Series I, #1-25, and Series II, #1-1354.
Later issues were printed with & without ads
on back cover. Issues without ads are worth
more.*

SERIES I:

#1(no#)-Dick Tracy	100.00	200.00	300.00
2(no#)-Don Winslow(Rare)	40.00	80.00	120.00
3(no#)-Myra North	12.00	24.00	36.00
4-Donald Duck by Al Taliaferro('40)(Disney)			
	450.00	900.00	1350.00

(Prices vary widely on this book)

5-Smilin' Jack	27.00	54.00	81.00
6-Dick Tracy (Scarce)	60.00	120.00	180.00
7-Gangbusters	12.00	24.00	36.00
8-Dick Tracy	45.00	90.00	135.00
9-Terry & the Pirates-Reprints #5 & The Pir-			
ate from Super #9-29	40.00	80.00	120.00
10-Smilin' Jack	27.00	54.00	81.00
11-Smitty	13.50	26.75	40.00
12-Little Orphan Annie	22.00	44.00	66.00

13-Reluctant Dragon('41)-Contains 2pgs. of
photos from film; 2pg. foreword to Fantas-
ia by Leopold Stokowski; Donald Duck(1st
to appear in a comic book), Goofy, Baby
Weems & Mickey Mouse(as the Sorcerer's
Apprentice) app. 55.00 110.00 165.00

14-Moon Mullins	12.00	24.00	36.00

Four Color #2, © Dell

Four Color #4, © N.Y. News Synd.

Four Color #15, © KING

	Good	Fine	Mint
(Four Color cont'd)			
15-Tillie the Toiler	10.00	20.00	30.00
16-Mickey Mouse(Disney)by Gottfredson			
	350.00	875.00	1400.00
(Prices vary widely on this book)			
17-Dumbo(1941)-Mickey Mouse, Donald Duck, &			
Pluto app.(Disney)	70.00	140.00	210.00
18-Jiggs & Maggie(1936-'38 reprints)			
	15.00	30.00	45.00
19-Barney Google-(1st issue with Four Color			
on the cover)	17.50	35.00	52.50
20-Tiny Tim	12.00	24.00	36.00
21-Dick Tracy	35.00	70.00	105.00
22-Don Winslow	10.00	20.00	30.00
23-Gangbusters	10.00	20.00	30.00
24-Captain Easy	15.00	30.00	45.00
25-Popeye	40.00	80.00	120.00

SERIES II:			
#1-Little Joe	17.00	34.00	51.00
2-Harold Teen	12.00	24.00	36.00
3-Alley Oop	25.00	50.00	75.00
4-Smilin' Jack	25.00	50.00	75.00
5-Raggedy Ann & Andy	22.00	44.00	66.00
6-Smitty	10.00	20.00	30.00
7-Smokey Stover	15.00	30.00	45.00
8-Tillie the Toiler	7.00	14.00	21.00
9-Donald Duck "Finds Pirate Gold" by Carl			
Barks & Jack Hannah (Disney) (1942)			
	500.00	1150.00	1800.00
(Prices vary widely on this book)			
10-Flash Gordon by Alex Raymond-Reprints			
from "The Ice Kingdom"			
	100.00	200.00	300.00
11-Wash Tubbs	17.00	34.00	51.00
12-Bambi (Disney)	30.00	60.00	90.00
13-Mr. District Attorney	10.00	20.00	30.00
14-Smilin' Jack	22.00	44.00	66.00
15-Felix the Cat	30.00	60.00	90.00
16-Porky Pig(1942)-"Secret of the Haunted			

	Good	Fine	Mint
House"	40.00	80.00	120.00
17-Popeye	27.00	54.00	81.00
18-Little Orphan Annie's Jr. Commandos			
	17.50	35.00	52.50
19-Thumper Meets the 7 Dwarfs (Disney)-re-			
printed in Silly Symphonies			
	30.00	60.00	90.00
20-Barney Baxter	12.00	24.00	36.00
21-Oswald the Rabbit	20.00	40.00	60.00
22-Tillie the Toiler	6.00	12.00	18.00
23-Raggedy Ann	17.00	34.00	51.00
24-Gangbusters	10.00	20.00	30.00
25-Andy Panda	25.00	50.00	75.00
26-Popeye	22.00	44.00	66.00
27-Mickey Mouse & the 7 Colored Terror			
(Disney)	55.00	110.00	165.00
28-Wash Tubbs	12.00	24.00	36.00
29-Donald Duck-"Mummy's Ring" by Carl Barks			
(Disney)(9/43)	400.00	800.00	1200.00
(Prices vary widely on this book)			
30-Bambi's Children(1943)-Disney			
	27.50	55.00	82.50
31-Moon Mullins	9.00	18.00	27.00
32-Smitty	6.00	12.00	18.00
33-Bugs Bunny-Public Nuisance #1			
	35.00	70.00	105.00
34-Dick Tracy	25.00	50.00	75.00
35-Smokey Stover	8.00	16.00	24.00
36-Smilin' Jack	10.00	20.00	30.00
37-Bringing Up Father	8.00	16.00	24.00
38-Roy Rogers	25.00	50.00	75.00
39-Oswald the Rabbit('44)	16.00	32.00	48.00
40-Barney Google	7.00	14.00	21.00
41-Mother Goose & Nursery Rhyme Comics-			
All by Kelly	16.00	32.00	48.00
42-Tiny Tim('34 reprts)	7.00	14.00	21.00
43-Popeye('38-'42 rprts)	14.00	28.00	42.00
44-Terry & the Pirates	20.00	40.00	60.00
45-Raggedy Ann	12.00	24.00	36.00

Four Color #24, © DELL

Four Color #25, © Walter Lantz

Four Color #27, © WDP

Four Color #48, © L. Schlesinger

Four Color #51, © L. Schlesinger

Four Color #55, © KING

	Good	Fine	Mint
(Four Color cont'd)			
46-Felix the Cat & the Haunted Castle	17.50	35.00	52.50
47-Gene Autry	17.50	35.00	52.50
48-Porky Pig of the Mounties by Carl Barks (7/44)	120.00	240.00	360.00
49-Snow White & the 7 Dwarfs	25.00	50.00	75.00
50-Fairy Tale Parade-Walt Kelly art (1944)	30.00	60.00	90.00
51-Bugs Bunny	25.00	50.00	75.00
52-Little Orphan Annie	10.00	20.00	30.00
53-Wash Tubbs	7.00	14.00	21.00
54-Andy Panda	15.00	30.00	45.00
55-Tillie the Toiler	5.00	10.00	15.00
56-Dick Tracy	17.50	35.00	52.50
57-Gene Autry	14.00	28.00	42.00
58-Smilin' Jack	10.00	20.00	30.00
59-Mother Goose & Nursery Rhyme Comics-Kelly cover only	12.00	24.00	36.00
60-Tiny Folks Funnies	7.00	14.00	21.00
61-Santa Claus Funnies(11/44)-Kelly art	22.00	44.00	66.00
62-Donald Duck-"Frozen Gold" by Carl Barks (Disney)(1/45)	200.00	400.00	600.00
63-Roy Rogers	15.00	30.00	45.00
64-Smokey Stover	5.00	10.00	15.00
65-Smitty	5.00	10.00	15.00
66-Gene Autry	14.00	28.00	42.00
67-Oswald the Rabbit	10.00	20.00	30.00
68-Mother Goose by Walt Kelly	18.00	36.00	54.00
69-Fairy Tale Parade by Walt Kelly	25.00	50.00	75.00
70-Popeye	10.00	20.00	30.00
71-Three Caballeros by Walt Kelly (1945) (Disney)	80.00	160.00	240.00
72-Raggedy Ann & Andy	10.00	20.00	30.00
73-The Gumps	4.00	8.00	12.00
74-Little Lulu	80.00	160.00	240.00

	Good	Fine	Mint
75-Gene Autry	10.00	20.00	30.00
76-Little Orphan Annie	8.00	16.00	24.00
77-Felix the Cat	12.00	24.00	36.00
78-Porky Pig & the Bandit Twins	10.00	20.00	30.00
79-Mickey Mouse in The Riddle of the Red Hat by Carl Barks (Disney)(8/45)	80.00	160.00	240.00
80-Smilin' Jack	8.00	16.00	24.00
81-Moon Mullins	5.00	10.00	15.00
82-Lone Ranger	14.00	28.00	42.00
83-Gene Autry	10.00	20.00	30.00
84-Flash Gordon by Alex Raymond-Reprts. from "The Fiery Desert"	50.00	100.00	150.00
85-Andy Panda & the Mad Dog Mystery	8.00	16.00	24.00
86-Roy Rogers	12.00	24.00	36.00
87-Fairy Tale Parade by Walt Kelly; Dan Noonan cover	22.00	44.00	66.00
88-Bugs Bunny	12.00	24.00	36.00
89-Tillie the Toiler	4.00	8.00	12.00
90-Xmas with Mother Goose by Walt Kelly (11/45)	17.50	35.00	52.50
91-Santa Claus Funnies by Walt Kelly (11/45)	17.00	34.00	51.00
92-Pinocchio(1945); Donald Duck by Kelly, 16pgs. (Disney)	25.00	50.00	75.00
93-Gene Autry	8.00	16.00	24.00
94-Winnie Winkle(1945)	5.00	10.00	15.00
95-Roy Rogers	12.00	24.00	36.00
96-Dick Tracy	10.00	20.00	30.00
97-Little Lulu(1946)	40.00	80.00	120.00
98-Lone Ranger	12.00	24.00	36.00
99-Smitty	4.00	8.00	12.00

(#99-Smitty is last issue to carry "Four Color" logo on cover; all issues beginning with #100 are marked "-- O.S."(One Shot) which can be found in the bottom left-hand panel on the first page; the numbers follow-

Four Color #62, © WDP

Four Color #63, © Roy Rogers

Four Color #71, © WDP

Four Color #101, © News Synd.

Four Color #105, © Walt Kelly

Four Color #120, © WEST

(Four Color cont'd)
ing "O.S." relate to the year/month issued.

	Good	Fine	Mint
100-Gene Autry	8.00	16.00	24.00
101-Terry & the Pirates	13.00	26.00	39.00
102-Oswald the Rabbit-Walt Kelly art, 1 pg.			
	10.00	20.00	30.00
103-Easter with Mother Goose by Walt Kelly			
	17.50	35.00	52.50
104-Fairy Tale Parade by Walt Kelly			
	17.00	34.00	51.00
105-Albert the Alligator & Pogo Possum by			
Kelly(4/46)	60.00	120.00	180.00
106-Tillie the Toiler	3.00	6.00	9.00
107-Little Orphan Annie	7.00	14.00	21.00
108-Donald Duck-"Terror of the River" by			
Carl Barks (Disney)(1946)			
	120.00	240.00	360.00
109-Roy Rogers	8.00	16.00	24.00
110-Little Lulu	24.00	48.00	72.00
111-Captain Easy	6.00	12.00	18.00
112-Porky Pig's Adv. in Gopher Gulch			
	7.00	14.00	21.00
113-Popeye	4.00	8.00	12.00
114-Fairy Tale Parade by Walt Kelly			
	17.00	34.00	51.00
115-Little Lulu	24.00	48.00	72.00
116-Mickey Mouse & "The House of Many Myster-			
ies" (Disney)	12.00	24.00	36.00
117-Roy Rogers	6.00	12.00	18.00
118-The Lone Ranger	12.00	24.00	36.00
119-Felix the Cat	8.00	16.00	24.00
120-Little Lulu	20.00	40.00	60.00
121-Fairy Tale Parade-(not Kelly)			
	10.00	20.00	30.00
122-Henry (10/46)	2.00	4.00	6.00
123-Bugs Bunny's Dangerous Venture			
	7.00	14.00	21.00
124-Roy Rogers	6.00	12.00	18.00
125-The Lone Ranger	8.00	16.00	24.00

	Good	Fine	Mint
126-Christmas with Mother Goose by Walt			
Kelly (1946)	14.00	28.00	42.00
127-Popeye	4.00	8.00	12.00
128-Santa Claus Funnies-"Santa & the Angel"			
by Gollub; "A Mouse in the House" by Kelly			
	14.00	28.00	42.00
129-Uncle Remus & Tales of Brer Rabbit(1946)			
(Disney)	12.00	24.00	36.00
130-Andy Panda	4.00	8.00	12.00
131-Little Lulu	20.00	40.00	60.00
132-Tillie the Toiler('47)	3.00	6.00	9.00
133-Dick Tracy	10.00	20.00	30.00
134-Tarzan & the Devil Ogre			
	25.00	50.00	75.00
135-Felix the Cat	7.00	14.00	21.00
136-The Lone Ranger	8.00	16.00	24.00
137-Roy Rogers	6.00	12.00	18.00
138-Smitty	3.00	6.00	9.00
139-Little Lulu(1947)	18.00	36.00	54.00
140-Easter with Mother Goose by Walt Kelly			
	14.00	28.00	42.00
141-Mickey Mouse & the Submarine Pirates			
(Disney)	12.00	24.00	36.00
142-Bugs Bunny & the Haunted Mtn.			
	7.00	14.00	21.00
143-Oswald the Rabbit	4.00	8.00	12.00
144-Roy Rogers (1947)	6.00	12.00	18.00
145-Popeye	4.00	8.00	12.00
146-Little Lulu	18.00	36.00	54.00
147-Donald Duck in "Volcano Valley" by Carl			
Barks (Disney)(5/47)	80.00	160.00	240.00
148-Albert the Alligator & Pogo Possum by			
Walt Kelly	50.00	100.00	150.00
149-Smilin' Jack	6.00	12.00	18.00
150-Tillie the Toiler (6/47)			
	2.25	4.50	6.75
151-The Lone Ranger	6.00	12.00	18.00
152-Little Orphan Annie	6.00	12.00	18.00
153-Roy Rogers	5.00	10.00	15.00

Four Color #134, © ERB

Four Color #138, © N.Y. News Synd.

Four Color #147, © WDP

Four Color #156, © L. Schlesinger   **Four Color #163,** © N.Y. News Synd.   **Four Color #172,** © DELL

(Four Color cont'd)	Good	Fine	Mint
154-Andy Panda	4.00	8.00	12.00
155-Henry (7/47)	2.00	4.00	6.00
156-Porky Pig & the Phantom			
	5.00	10.00	15.00
157-Mickey Mouse & "The Beanstalk" (Disney)			
	10.00	20.00	30.00
158-Little Lulu	18.00	36.00	54.00
159-Donald Duck in "The Ghost of the Grotto"			
by Carl Barks (Disney)(8/47)			
	70.00	140.00	210.00
160-Roy Rogers	5.00	10.00	15.00
161-Tarzan & the Fires of Tohr			
	20.00	40.00	60.00
162-Felix the Cat (9/47)	6.00	12.00	18.00
163-Dick Tracy	8.00	16.00	24.00
164-Bugs Bunny "Finds the Frozen Kingdom"			
	7.00	14.00	21.00
165-Little Lulu	18.00	36.00	54.00
166-Roy Rogers	5.00	10.00	15.00
167-The Lone Ranger	6.00	12.00	18.00
168-Popeye (10/47)	4.00	8.00	12.00
169-Woody Woodpecker-"Manhunter in the North"			
	3.00	6.00	9.00
170-Mickey Mouse on "Spook's Island" (11/47)			
(Disney)-reprinted in M.M. #103			
	10.00	20.00	30.00
171-Charlie McCarthy	2.00	4.00	6.00
172-Christmas with Mother Goose by Walt			
Kelly (11/47)	14.00	28.00	42.00
173-Flash Gordon	10.00	20.00	30.00
174-Winnie Winkle	3.00	6.00	9.00
175-Santa Claus Funnies by Walt Kelly ('47)			
	14.00	28.00	42.00
176-Tillie the Toiler (12/47)			
	2.25	4.50	6.75
177-Roy Rogers	5.00	10.00	15.00
178-Donald Duck in "Christmas on Bear Mtn."			
by Carl Barks; 1st app. Uncle Scrooge			
(Disney)(12/47)	70.00	140.00	210.00

	Good	Fine	Mint
179-Uncle Wiggily-Walt Kelly cover			
	7.00	14.00	21.00
180-Ozark Ike	4.00	8.00	12.00
181-Mickey Mouse in "Jungle Magic" (Disney)			
	10.00	20.00	30.00
182-Porky Pig (2/48)	5.00	10.00	15.00
183-Oswald the Rabbit	4.00	8.00	12.00
184-Tillie the Toiler	2.25	4.50	6.75
185-Easter with Mother Goose by Walt Kelly			
(1948)	14.00	28.00	42.00
186-Bambi(Disney)-Reprinted as Bambi #3('56)			
	7.00	14.00	21.00
187-Bugs Bunny-"The Dreadful Dragon"			
	5.00	10.00	15.00
188-Woody Woodpecker(5/48)	3.00	6.00	9.00
189-Donald Duck in "The Old Castle's Secret"			
by Carl Barks (Disney)(6/48)			
	60.00	120.00	180.00
190-Flash Gordon ('48)	10.00	20.00	30.00
191-Porky Pig "To the Rescue"			
	5.00	10.00	15.00
192-The Brownies by Walt Kelly (7/48)			
	12.00	24.00	36.00
193-Tom & Jerry (1948)	3.50	7.00	10.50
194-Mickey Mouse in "The World Under the Sea"			
(Disney)-Reprinted in M.M. #101			
	10.00	20.00	30.00
195-Tillie the Toiler	2.00	4.00	6.00
196-Charlie McCarthy	2.00	4.00	6.00
197-Spirit of the Border (Zane Grey)(1948)			
	3.00	6.00	9.00
198-Andy Panda	4.00	8.00	12.00
199-Donald Duck in "Sheriff of Bullet Valley"			
by Carl Barks(Disney)(10/48)			
	60.00	120.00	180.00
200-Bugs Bunny-Super Sleuth (10/48)			
	5.00	10.00	15.00
201-Christmas with Mother Goose by Walt Kelly			
	10.00	20.00	30.00

Four Color #173, © KING   **Four Color #178,** © WDP   **Four Color #196,** © DELL

Four Color #215, © N.Y. News Synd.　　Four Color #216, © Walter Lantz　　Four Color #236, © DELL

(Four Color cont'd)	Good	Fine	Mint
202-Woody Woodpecker	2.25	4.50	6.75
203-Donald Duck in "The Golden Christmas Tree" by Carl Barks (Disney)(12/48)			
	35.00	70.00	105.00
204-Flash Gordon (1948)	8.00	16.00	24.00
205-Santa Claus Funnies by Walt Kelly			
	12.00	24.00	36.00
206-Little Orphan Annie	5.00	10.00	15.00
207-King of the Royal Mtd.	5.00	10.00	15.00
208-Brer Rabbit Does It Again (Disney)(1/49)			
	6.00	12.00	18.00
209-Harold Teen	1.50	3.00	4.50
210-Tippie & Cap Stubbs	1.50	3.00	4.50
211-Little Beaver	3.00	6.00	9.00
212-Dr. Bobbs	1.25	2.50	3.75
213-Tillie the Toiler	2.00	4.00	6.00
214-Mickey Mouse & "His Sky Adventure"(2/49) (Disney)-reprinted in M.M. #105			
	7.00	14.00	21.00
215-Sparkle Plenty (Dick Tracy reprints by Gould)			
	7.00	14.00	21.00
216-Andy Panda	2.50	5.00	7.50
217-Bugs Bunny in "Court Jester"			
	5.00	10.00	15.00
218-The Three Little Pigs (Disney)(3/49)			
	4.00	8.00	12.00
219-Swee'pea	3.50	7.00	10.50
220-Easter with Mother Goose by Walt Kelly			
	11.00	22.00	33.00
221-Uncle Wiggily-Walt Kelly cover in part			
	5.00	10.00	15.00
222-West of the Pecos (Zane Grey)			
	3.00	6.00	9.00
223-Donald Duck "Lost in the Andes" by Carl Barks (Disney-4/49)(Square egg story)			
	40.00	80.00	120.00
224-Little Iodine (4/49)	2.00	4.00	6.00
225-Oswald the Rabbit	2.50	5.00	7.50
226-Porky Pig & Spoofy, the Spook			

	Good	Fine	Mint
	3.50	7.00	10.50
227-Seven Dwarfs(Disney)	5.00	10.00	15.00
228-Mark of Zorro ('49)	5.00	10.00	15.00
229-Smokey Stover	2.00	4.00	6.00
230-Sunset Pass(Zane Grey)	3.00	6.00	9.00
231-Mickey Mouse & "The Rajah's Treasure" (Disney)	7.00	14.00	21.00
232-Woody Woodpecker(6/49)	2.25	4.50	6.75
233-Bugs Bunny-"Sleepwalking Sleuth"			
	5.00	10.00	15.00
234-Dumbo in "Sky Voyage" (Disney)			
	4.00	8.00	12.00
235-Tiny Tim	2.50	5.00	7.50
236-Heritage of the Desert (Zane Grey-'49)			
	3.00	6.00	9.00
237-Tillie the Toiler	2.00	4.00	6.00
238-Donald Duck in "Voodoo Hoodoo" by Carl Barks (Disney)(8/49)	30.00	60.00	90.00
239-Adventure Bound(8/49)	2.00	4.00	6.00
240-Andy Panda	2.50	5.00	7.50
241-Porky Pig	3.50	7.00	10.50
242-Tippie & Cap Stubbs	1.50	3.00	4.50
243-Thumper Follows His Nose (Disney)			
	10.00	20.00	30.00
244-The Brownies by Walt Kelly			
	10.00	20.00	30.00
245-Dick's Adventures in Dreamland (9/49)			
	2.50	5.00	7.50
246-Thunder Mountain (Zane Grey)			
	2.00	4.00	6.00
247-Flash Gordon	8.00	16.00	24.00
248-Mickey Mouse & "The Black Sorcerer" (Disney)	7.00	14.00	21.00
249-Woody Woodpecker-"The Globetrotter" (10/49)	2.25	4.50	6.75
250-Bugs Bunny	3.00	6.00	9.00
251-Hubert at Camp Moonbeam			
	2.00	4.00	6.00
252-Pinocchio(Disney)-not Kelly; origin			

Four Color #239, © DELL　　Four Color #248, © WDP　　Four Color #252, © WDP

Four Color #256, © WDP   Four Color #266, © L. Schlesinger   Four Color #269, © DELL

(Four Color cont'd)	Good	Fine	Mint
	6.00	12.00	18.00
253-Christmas with Mother Goose by Walt Kelly			
	10.00	20.00	30.00
254-Santa Claus Funnies by Walt Kelly; Pogo & Albert story by Kelly (11/49)			
	12.00	24.00	36.00
255-The Ranger (Zane Grey)(1949)			
	2.00	4.00	6.00
256-Donald Duck in "Luck of the North" by Carl Barks (Disney)(12/49)-Shows #257 on inside	30.00	60.00	90.00
257-Little Iodine	2.00	4.00	6.00
258-Andy Panda & "The Balloon Race"			
	2.50	5.00	7.50
259-Santa & the Angel (Gollub art-condensed from #128) & Santa at the Zoo (12/49)- two books in one	3.00	6.00	9.00
260-Porky Pig-"Hero of the Wild West"(12/49)			
	3.50	7.00	10.50
261-Mickey Mouse & "The Missing Key"(Disney)			
	7.00	14.00	21.00
262-Raggedy Ann & Andy	3.00	6.00	9.00
263-Donald Duck in "Land of the Totem Poles" by Carl Barks (Disney)(2/50)-has two Barks stories	30.00	60.00	90.00
264-Woody Woodpecker-in "The Magic Lantern"			
	2.25	4.50	6.75
265-King of the Royal Mtd.	4.00	8.00	12.00
266-Bugs Bunny-"Isle of Hercules"(2/50)-re- printed Best of B.B.#1	3.00	6.00	9.00
267-Little Beaver	2.00	4.00	6.00
268-Mickey Mouse's "Surprise Visitor"-(1950) (Disney)	7.00	14.00	21.00
269-Johnny Mack Brown	3.50	7.00	10.50
270-Drift Fence (Zane Grey)(3/50)			
	2.00	4.00	6.00
271-Porky Pig-"Phantom of the Plains"			
	3.50	7.00	10.50
272-Cinderella (Disney)	3.00	6.00	9.00

	Good	Fine	Mint
273-Oswald the Rabbit	2.50	5.00	7.50
274-Bugs Bunny-"Hair Brained Reporter"			
	3.00	6.00	9.00
275-Donald Duck in "Ancient Persia" by Carl Barks(Disney)(5/50)	25.00	50.00	75.00
276-Uncle Wiggily	3.00	6.00	9.00
277-Porky Pig-"Desert Adventure" (5/50)			
	3.50	7.00	10.50
278-Wild Bill Elliott	3.00	6.00	9.00
279-Mickey Mouse & Pluto Battle the Giant Ants(Disney)-reprinted in M.M. #102			
	6.00	12.00	18.00
280-Andy Panda	2.50	5.00	7.50
281-Bugs Bunny-"In the Great Circus Mystery"			
	3.00	6.00	9.00
282-Donald Duck and "The Pixilated Parrot" by Carl Barks(Disney)	25.00	50.00	75.00
283-King of the Royal Mounted (7/50)			
	4.00	8.00	12.00
284-Porky Pig-"Kingdom of Nowhere"			
	3.50	7.00	10.50
285-Bozo the Clown & His Minikin Circus (TV)			
	1.75	3.50	5.25
286-Mickey Mouse-"& the Uninvited Guest" (Disney)	6.00	12.00	18.00
287-Gene Autry's Champion	2.25	4.50	6.75
288-Woody Woodpecker-"Klondike Gold"			
	2.25	4.50	6.75
289-Bugs Bunny in Indian Trouble			
	3.00	6.00	9.00
290-The Chief	1.75	3.50	5.25
291-Donald Duck in "The Magic Hourglass" by Carl Barks (Disney)(9/50)			
	25.00	50.00	75.00
292-The Cisco Kid	3.00	6.00	9.00
293-The Brownies-Kelly cover/art			
	12.00	24.00	36.00
294-Little Beaver	2.00	4.00	6.00
295-Porky Pig in "President Porky" (9/50)			

Four Color #272, © WDP   Four Color #284, © L. Schlesinger   Four Color # 286, © WDP

159

Four Color #299, © DELL

Four Color #304, © WDP

Four Color #310, © NEA Service

(Four Color cont'd)	Good	Fine	Mint
	3.50	7.00	10.50
296-Mickey Mouse in "Private Eye for Hire"			
(Disney)	6.00	12.00	18.00
297-Andy Panda (10/50)	2.50	5.00	7.50
298-Bugs Bunny "Sheik for a Day"			
	3.00	6.00	9.00
299-Buck Jones	4.50	9.00	13.50
300-Donald Duck in "Big-Top Bedlam" by Carl			
Barks(Disney)(11/50)	22.00	44.00	66.00
301-The Mysterious Rider (Zane Grey)			
	2.00	4.00	6.00
302-Santa Claus Funnies (11/50)			
	2.50	5.00	7.50
303-Porky Pig in "The Land of the Monstrous			
Flies"	2.00	4.00	6.00
304-Mickey Mouse in "Tom-Tom Island"			
(Disney)(12/50)	5.00	10.00	15.00
305-Woody Woodpecker	1.50	3.00	4.50
306-Raggedy Ann	2.50	5.00	7.50
307-Bugs Bunny-"Lumber Jack Rabbit"			
	2.50	5.00	7.50
308-Donald Duck in "Dangerous Disguise" by			
Carl Barks (Disney)(1/51)			
	22.00	44.00	66.00
309-Dollface & Her Gang('51)			
	1.75	3.50	5.25
310-King of the Royal Mounted (1/51)			
	2.50	5.00	7.50
311-Porky Pig in "Midget Horses of Hidden			
Valley"	2.00	4.00	6.00
312-Tonto(#1)	3.00	6.00	9.00
313-Mickey Mouse(#1) in "The Mystery of the			
Double-Cross Ranch" (Disney)			
	5.00	10.00	15.00
314-Ambush (Zane Grey)	2.00	4.00	6.00
315-Oswald the Rabbit	1.75	3.50	5.25
316-Rex Allen(#1)	3.00	6.00	9.00
317-Bugs Bunny in "Hair Today Gone Tomorrow"			
(#1)	2.50	5.00	7.50

	Good	Fine	Mint
318-Donald Duck in "No Such Varmint" by Carl			
Barks(#1)(Disney)	22.00	44.00	66.00
319-Gene Autry's Champion	1.50	3.00	4.50
320-Uncle Wiggily	2.25	4.50	6.75
321-The Little Scouts	1.20	2.40	3.60
322-Porky Pig(#1)	2.00	4.00	6.00
323-Suzie Q. Smith(3/51)	1.25	2.50	3.75
324-I Met a Handsome Cowboy (3/51)			
	3.00	6.00	9.00
325-Mickey Mouse(#2) in "The Haunted Castle"			
(Disney)(4/61)	5.00	10.00	15.00
326-Andy Panda	1.40	2.80	4.20
327-Bugs Bunny	2.50	5.00	7.50
328-Donald Duck in "Old California"(#2) by			
Carl Barks-drug issue (Disney)(5/51)			
	25.00	50.00	75.00
329-Trigger (5/51)	2.00	4.00	6.00
330-Porky Pig (#2)	2.00	4.00	6.00
331-Alice in Wonderland (Disney)(1951)			
	3.00	6.00	9.00
332-Little Beaver	2.00	4.00	6.00
333-Wilderness Trek (Zane Grey)(5/51)			
	2.00	4.00	6.00
334-Mickey Mouse & "Yukon Gold" (Disney)			
(6/51)	5.00	10.00	15.00
335-Francis the Mule	1.20	2.40	3.60
336-Woody Woodpecker	1.50	3.00	4.50
337-The Brownies-not by Walt Kelly			
	2.50	5.00	7.50
338-Bugs Bunny	2.50	5.00	7.50
339-Donald Duck and "The Magic Fountain"-not			
by Carl Barks (Disney)(7-8/51)			
	4.00	8.00	12.00
340-King of the Royal Mounted (7/51)			
	2.50	5.00	7.50
341-Unbirthday Party with Alice in Wonder-			
land (Disney)(7/51)	3.50	7.00	10.50
342-Porky Pig	1.40	2.80	4.20
343-Mickey Mouse in "The Ruby Eye of Homar-			

Four Color #328, © WDP

Four Color #329, © Roy Rogers

Four Color #341, © WDP

Four Color #358, © Walter Lantz

Four Color #366, © L. Schlesinger

Four Color #375, © ERB

	Good	Fine	Mint
(Four Color cont'd)			
Guy-Am" (Disney)-reprinted in M.M. #104			
	4.50	9.00	13.50
344-Sgt. Preston (TV)	2.00	4.00	6.00
345-Andy Panda in Scotland Yard (8-10/51)			
	1.40	2.80	4.20
346-Hideout (Zane Grey)	2.00	4.00	6.00
347-Bugs Bunny-"The Frigid Hare" (8-9/51)			
	2.50	5.00	7.50
348-Donald Duck "The Crocodile Collector"-			
Barks cover only (Disney)(9-10/51)			
	5.00	10.00	15.00
349-Uncle Wiggily	2.25	4.50	6.75
350-Woody Woodpecker	1.50	3.00	4.50
351-Porky Pig-"Grand Canyon Giant" (9-10/51)			
	1.40	2.80	4.20
352-Mickey Mouse-"The Mystery of Painted			
Valley" (Disney)	4.50	9.00	13.50
353-Duck Album-Barks cover (Disney)			
	1.75	3.50	5.25
354-Raggedy Ann & Andy	2.50	5.00	7.50
355-Bugs Bunny Hot-Rod Hare			
	2.50	5.00	7.50
356-Donald Duck in "Rags to Riches"-Barks			
cover only (Disney)	5.00	10.00	15.00
357-Comeback (Zane Grey)	1.75	3.50	5.25
358-Andy Panda (11-1/52)	1.40	2.80	4.20
359-Frosty the Snowman	1.00	2.00	3.00
360-Porky Pig-"In Tree of Fortune" (11-12/51)			
	1.40	2.80	4.20
361-Santa Claus Funnies	2.50	5.00	7.50
362-Mickey Mouse & "The Smuggled Diamonds"			
(Disney)	4.50	9.00	13.50
363-King of the Royal Mtd.	2.00	4.00	6.00
364-Woody Woodpecker	1.25	2.50	3.75
365-The Brownies-not by Kelly			
	2.50	5.00	7.50
366-Bugs Bunny-"Uncle Buckskin Comes to Town"			
(12-1/52)	2.50	5.00	7.50
367-Donald Duck in "A Christmas for Shack-			

	Good	Fine	Mint
town" by Carl Barks (Disney)(1-2/52)			
	18.00	36.00	54.00
368-Beany & Cecil (1/52)	2.00	4.00	6.00
369-The Lone Ranger's Famous Horse-Hi-Yo			
Silver	2.00	4.00	6.00
370-Porky Pig "Trouble in the Big Trees"			
	1.40	2.80	4.20
371-Mickey Mouse-"The Inca Idol Case" ('52)			
(Disney)	4.50	9.00	13.50
372-Riders of the Purple Sage (Zane Grey)			
	1.75	3.50	5.25
373-Sgt. Preston (TV)	2.00	4.00	6.00
374-Woody Woodpecker	1.25	2.50	3.75
375-John Carter of Mars (E. R. Burroughs)-			
Jesse Marsh art; origin			
	6.00	12.00	18.00
376-Bugs Bunny	2.50	5.00	7.50
377-Suzie Q. Smith	1.25	2.50	3.75
378-Tom Corbett, Space Cadet (TV)-McWilliams			
art	3.50	7.00	10.50
379-Donald Duck in "Southern Hospitality"-			
not by Barks (Disney)	4.00	8.00	12.00
380-Raggedy Ann & Andy	2.50	5.00	7.50
381-Tubby (#1)	9.00	18.00	27.00
382-Snow White & 7 Dwarfs(Disney)-origin;			
partial reprint of 4-Color #49 (Movie)			
	4.00	8.00	12.00
383-Andy Panda	1.20	2.40	3.60
384-King of the Royal Mounted (3/52)			
	2.00	4.00	6.00
385-Porky Pig-"The Isle of Missing Ships"			
(3-4/52)	1.40	2.80	4.20
386-Uncle Scrooge #1 by Carl Barks (Disney)			
in "Only a Poor Old Man" (3/52)			
	100.00	200.00	300.00
387-Mickey Mouse in "High Tibet" (Disney)			
(4-5/52)	4.50	9.00	13.50
388-Oswald the Rabbit	1.75	3.50	5.25
389-Andy Hardy	1.20	2.40	3.60

Four Color #378, © DELL

Four Color #385, © L. Schlesinger

Four Color #386, © WDP

Four Color #391, © DELL

Four Color #405, © Walter Lantz

Four Color #421, © DELL

	Good	Fine	Mint
(Four Color cont'd)			
390-Woody Woodpecker	1.25	2.50	3.75
391-Uncle Wiggily	1.75	3.50	5.25
392-Hi-Yo Silver	2.00	4.00	6.00
393-Bugs Bunny	2.50	5.00	7.50
394-Donald Duck in "Malayalaya"-Barks cover			
only (Disney)	5.00	10.00	15.00
395-Forlorn River (Zane Grey)(1952)-First			
Nevada (5/52)	1.75	3.50	5.25
396-Tales of the Texas Rangers (TV)			
	1.75	3.50	5.25
397-Sgt. Preston (TV)	2.00	4.00	6.00
398-The Brownies-not by Kelly			
	2.50	5.00	7.50
399-Porky Pig in "The Lost Gold Mine"			
	1.40	2.80	4.20
400-Tom Corbett-Space Cadet(TV)-McWilliams			
art	3.50	7.00	10.50
401-Mickey Mouse & Goofy's Mechanical Wizard			
(Disney)(6-7/52)	3.50	7.00	10.50
402-Mary Jane & Sniffles	1.50	3.00	4.50
403-Li'l Bad Wolf(Disney)(6/52)			
	1.40	2.80	4.20
404-The Range Rider (TV)	2.00	4.00	6.00
405-Woody Woodpecker	1.25	2.50	3.75
406-Tweety & Sylvester	1.00	2.00	3.00
407-Bugs Bunny "Foreign-Legion Hare"			
	2.25	4.50	6.75
408-Donald Duck and "The Golden Helmet" by			
Carl Barks (Disney)(7-8/52)			
	16.00	32.00	48.00
409-Andy Panda (7-9/52)	1.20	2.40	3.60
410-Porky Pig in "The Water Wizard"			
	1.40	2.80	4.20
411-Mickey Mouse & "The Old Sea Dog" (Disney)			
(8-9/52)	3.50	7.00	10.50
412-Nevada (Zane Grey)	1.75	3.50	5.25
413-Robin Hood (Disney-Movie)(8/52)			
	2.50	5.00	7.50
414-Beany & Cecil(TV)('52)	1.20	2.40	3.60

	Good	Fine	Mint
415-Rootie Kazootie (TV)	1.00	2.00	3.00
416-Woody Woodpecker	1.25	2.50	3.75
417-Double Trouble with Goober			
	.60	1.20	1.80
418-Rusty Riley-A Boy, A Horse, and A Dog-			
Frank Godwin art(strip reprints)(8/52)			
	1.50	3.00	4.50
419-Sgt. Preston (TV)	2.00	4.00	6.00
420-Bugs Bunny-"Mysterious Buckaroo"(8-9/52)			
	2.25	4.50	6.75
421-Tom Corbett-Space Cadet(TV)-McWilliams			
art	3.50	7.00	10.50
422-Donald Duck and "The Gilded Man" by Carl			
Barks (Disney)(9-10/52) (#423 on inside)			
	16.00	32.00	48.00
423-Rhubarb, Owner of the Brooklyn Ball Club			
(The Millionaire Cat)	1.00	2.00	3.00
424-Flash Gordon-Test Flight in Space (9/52)			
	6.00	12.00	18.00
425-Zorro, the Return of	3.50	7.00	10.50
426-Porky Pig in "The Scalawag Leprechaun"			
	1.40	2.80	4.20
427-Mickey Mouse & "The Wonderful Whizzix"			
(Disney)(1952)-reprinted in M.M. #100			
	3.50	7.00	10.50
428-Uncle Wiggily	1.50	3.00	4.50
429-Pluto in "Why Dogs Leave Home" (Disney)			
	2.00	4.00	6.00
430-Tubby	5.00	10.00	15.00
431-Woody Woodpecker	1.25	2.50	3.75
432-Bugs Bunny & "The Rabbit Olympics"			
	2.25	4.50	6.75
433-Wildfire (Zane Grey)	1.75	3.50	5.25
434-Rin Tin Tin-"In Dark Danger" (11/52)			
	1.25	2.50	3.75
435-Frosty the Snowman	1.00	2.00	3.00
436-The Brownies-not by Kelly (11/52)			
	2.00	4.00	6.00
437-John Carter of Mars (E. R. Burroughs)-			

Four Color #422, © WDP

Four Color #423, © DELL

Four Color #429, © WDP

Four Color #443, © DELL

Four Color #444, © WEST

Four Color #460, © DELL

	Good	Fine	Mint
(Four Color cont'd)			
art by Marsh	5.00	10.00	15.00
438-Annie Oakley (TV)	2.00	4.00	6.00
439-Little Hiawatha(Disney)(12/52)			
	1.75	3.50	5.25
440-Black Beauty (12/52)	1.50	3.00	4.50
441-Fearless Fagan	1.25	2.50	3.75
442-Peter Pan (Disney)(Movie)			
	3.00	6.00	9.00
443-Ben Bowie	1.50	3.00	4.50
444-Tubby	5.00	10.00	15.00
445-Charlie McCarthy	1.20	2.40	3.60
446-Captain Hook & Peter Pan (Disney)(Movie)			
(1/53)	3.50	7.00	10.50
447-Andy Hardy	1.00	2.00	3.00
448-Beany & Cecil (TV)	1.20	2.40	3.60
449-Tappan's Burro (Zane Grey)(2-4/53)			
	1.75	3.50	5.25
450-Duck Album-Barks cover (Disney)			
	1.75	3.50	5.25
451-Rusty Riley-Frank Godwin art(strip reprints)(2/53)	1.50	3.00	4.50
452-Raggedy Ann & Andy('53)			
	2.50	5.00	7.50
453-Suzie Q. Smith (2/53)	1.00	2.00	3.00
454-Krazy Kat-not by Herriman (2/53)			
	1.75	3.50	5.25
455-Johnny Mack Brown (3/53)			
	2.00	4.00	6.00
456-Uncle Scrooge in "Back to the Klondike"			
(#2) by Barks (3/53)	50.00	100.00	150.00
457-Daffy Duck	1.00	2.00	3.00
458-Oswald the Rabbit	1.20	2.40	3.60
459-Rootie Kazootie (TV)	1.00	2.00	3.00
460-Buck Jones (4/53)	2.00	4.00	6.00
461-Tubby	5.00	10.00	15.00
462-Little Scouts	.80	1.60	2.40
463-Petunia Pig (4/53)	1.25	2.50	3.75
464-Bozo (4/53)	.80	1.60	2.40
465-Francis the Mule	.75	1.50	2.25

	Good	Fine	Mint
466-Rhubarb, the Millionaire Cat			
	.80	1.60	2.40
467-Desert Gold (Zane Grey)(5-7/53)			
	1.75	3.50	5.25
468-Goofy (Disney)	1.20	2.40	3.60
469-Beetle Bailey (5/53)	1.00	2.00	3.00
470-Elmer Fudd	.80	1.60	2.40
471-Goober, Double Trouble with			
	.60	1.20	1.80
472-Wild Bill Elliott (6/53)			
	1.75	3.50	5.25
473-Li'l Bad Wolf(Disney)	1.25	2.50	3.75
474-Mary Jane & Sniffles	1.25	2.50	3.75
475-The Two Mouseketeers	.70	1.40	2.10
476-Rin Tin Tin	1.25	2.50	3.75
477-Beany & Cecil (TV)	1.20	2.40	3.60
478-Charlie McCarthy	1.20	2.40	3.60
479-Dale Evans	2.00	4.00	6.00
480-Andy Hardy	1.00	2.00	3.00
481-Annie Oakley (TV)	1.75	3.50	5.25
482-Brownies-not by Kelly	1.50	3.00	4.50
483-Little Beaver ('53)	1.75	3.50	5.25
484-River Feud (Zane Grey)(8-10/53)			
	1.75	3.50	5.25
485-The Little People-Walt Scott			
	1.50	3.00	4.50
486-Rusty Riley-Frank Godwin strip reprints			
	1.50	3.00	4.50
487-Mowgli, the Jungle Book (Rudyard Kipling's)	1.50	3.00	4.50
488-John Carter of Mars (Burroughs)-Marsh			
art	5.00	10.00	15.00
489-Tweety & Sylvester	1.00	2.00	3.00
490-Jungle Jim	2.00	4.00	6.00
491-Silvertip (Max Brand)-Kinstler art(8/53)			
	2.00	4.00	6.00
492-Duck Album (Disney)	1.25	2.50	3.75
493-Johnny Mack Brown	2.00	4.00	6.00
494-The Little King	1.25	2.50	3.75

Four Color #467, © DELL

Four Color #479, © Roy Rogers

Four Color #485, © DELL

Four Color #496, © DELL   Four Color #531, © WDP   Four Color #544, © WDP

(Four Color cont'd)	Good	Fine	Mint
495-Uncle Scrooge(#3)(Disney)-by Carl Barks			
(9/53)	28.00	56.00	84.00
496-The Green Hornet(TV)	3.50	7.00	10.50
497-Zorro(Sword of--)	3.50	7.00	10.50
498-Bugs Bunny's Album	1.20	2.40	3.60
499-Spike & Tyke (9/53)	.60	1.20	1.80
500-Buck Jones	2.00	4.00	6.00
501-Francis the Mule	.75	1.50	2.25
502-Rootie Kazootie (TV)	1.00	2.00	3.00
503-Uncle Wiggily (10/53)	1.50	3.00	4.50
504-Krazy Kat-not by Herriman			
	1.75	3.50	5.25
505-The Sword & the Rose(Disney)(10/53)(TV)			
	2.00	4.00	6.00
506-The Little Scouts	.80	1.60	2.40
507-Oswald the Rabbit	1.20	2.40	3.60
508-Bozo (10/53)	.80	1.60	2.40
509-Pluto (Disney)(10/53)	2.00	4.00	6.00
510-Son of Black Beauty	1.25	2.50	3.75
511-Outlaw Trail (Zane Grey)-Kinstler stories			
	2.00	4.00	6.00
512-Flash Gordon (11/53)	4.00	8.00	12.00
513-Ben Bowie's Mountain Men (11/53)			
	1.25	2.50	3.75
514-Frosty the Snowman	.70	1.40	2.10
515-Andy Hardy	1.00	2.00	3.00
516-Goober, Double Trouble with			
	.60	1.20	1.80
517-Chip 'N' Dale (Disney)	1.20	2.40	3.60
518-Rivets (11/53)	1.00	2.00	3.00
519-Steve Canyon-not by Milton Caniff			
	2.50	5.00	7.50
520-Wild Bill Elliott	1.75	3.50	5.25
521-Beetle Bailey (12/53)	1.00	2.00	3.00
522-The Brownies	1.50	3.00	4.50
523-Rin Tin Tin	1.25	2.50	3.75
524-Tweety & Sylvester	1.00	2.00	3.00
525-Santa Claus Funnies	1.20	2.40	3.60
526-Napoleon	1.00	2.00	3.00
527-Charlie McCarthy	1.20	2.40	3.60
528-Dale Evans	1.75	3.50	5.25
529-Little Beaver	1.75	3.50	5.25
530-Beany & Cecil (1/54)	1.20	2.40	3.60
531-Duck Album (Disney)	1.25	2.50	3.75
532-The Rustlers (Zane Grey)(2-4/54)			
	1.50	3.00	4.50
533-Raggedy Ann & Andy	2.50	5.00	7.50
534-Western Marshal(Ernest Haycox's)-			
Kinstler art	2.00	4.00	6.00
535-I Love Lucy (TV)('54)	.60	1.20	1.80
536-Daffy (3/54)	1.00	2.00	3.00
537-Stormy, the Thoroughbred--(Disney-Movie)			
on top 2/3 of each page; Pluto story on			
bottom 1/3 of each page (2/54)			
	2.00	4.00	6.00
538-Zorro(Mask of--)-Kinstler art			
	4.00	8.00	12.00

	Good	Fine	Mint
539-Ben & Me (Disney)	1.25	2.50	3.75
540-Knights of the Round Table (3/54)(Movie)			
	2.00	4.00	6.00
541-Johnny Mack Brown	1.75	3.50	5.25
542-Super Circus Featuring Mary Hartline (TV)			
(3/54)	1.00	2.00	3.00
543-Uncle Wiggily (3/54)	1.50	3.00	4.50
544-Rob Roy (Disney-Movie)-Russ Manning art			
	2.25	4.50	6.75
545-Pinocchio-Partial reprint of 4-Color #92			
(Disney-Movie)	2.25	4.50	6.75
546-Buck Jones	2.00	4.00	6.00
547-Francis the Mule	.75	1.50	2.25
548-Krazy Kat-not by Herriman (4/54)			
	1.50	3.00	4.50
549-Oswald the Rabbit	1.20	2.40	3.60
550-The Little Scouts	.80	1.60	2.40
551-Bozo (4/54)	.80	1.60	2.40
552-Beetle Bailey	1.00	2.00	3.00
553-Suzie Q. Smith	1.00	2.00	3.00
554-Rusty Riley (Frank Godwin strip reprints)			
	1.50	3.00	4.50
555-Range War (Zane Grey)	1.50	3.00	4.50
556-Goober, Double Trouble with (5/54)			
	.60	1.20	1.80
557-Ben Bowie & His Mountain Men			
	1.25	2.50	3.75
558-Elmer Fudd (5/54)	.80	1.60	2.40
559-I Love Lucy (TV)	.60	1.20	1.80
560-Duck Album (Disney)	1.25	2.50	3.75
561-Mr. Magoo (5/54)	1.50	3.00	4.50
562-Goofy (Disney)	1.20	2.40	3.60
563-Rhubarb, the Millionaire Cat (6/54)			
	.75	1.50	2.25
564-Li'l Bad Wolf (Disney)	1.25	2.50	3.75
565-Jungle Jim	2.00	4.00	6.00
566-Son of Black Beauty	1.25	2.50	3.75
567-Prince Valiant-by Bob Fuje (Movie)			
	5.00	10.00	15.00
568-Gypsy Colt (Movie)	1.25	2.50	3.75
569-Priscilla's Pop	.80	1.60	2.40
570-Beany & Cecil (TV)	1.20	2.40	3.60
571-Charlie McCarthy	1.20	2.40	3.60
572-Silvertip (Max Brand)	1.40	2.80	4.20
573-The Little People by Walt Scott			
	1.00	2.00	3.00
574-Zorro (Hand of --)	3.00	6.00	9.00
575-Annie Oakley (TV)	1.75	3.50	5.25
576-Angel (8/54)	.70	1.40	2.10
577-Spike & Tyke	.60	1.20	1.80
578-Steve Canyon (8/54)	2.25	4.50	6.75
579-Francis the Talking Mule			
	.75	1.50	2.25
580-Six Gun Ranch (Luke Short-8/54)			
	1.50	3.00	4.50
581-Chip 'N' Dale (Disney)	1.20	2.40	3.60
582-Mowgli-Jungle Book	1.25	2.50	3.75

(Four Color cont'd)   Good Fine Mint

583-The Lost Wagon Train (Zane Grey)
                    1.50 3.00 4.50
584-Johnny Mack Brown 1.75 3.50 5.25
585-Bugs Bunny's Album 1.20 2.40 3.60
586-Duck Album (Disney) 1.25 2.50 3.75
587-The Little Scouts   .80 1.60 2.40
588-King Richard & the Crusaders(Movie)(10/54)
  Matt Baker art   2.00 4.00 6.00
589-Buck Jones   2.00 4.00 6.00
590-Hansel & Gretel   1.50 3.00 4.50
591-Western Marshal (Ernest Haycox's)-
  Kinstler art   2.00 4.00 6.00
592-Super Circus (TV)   1.00 2.00 3.00
593-Oswald the Rabbit   1.20 2.40 3.60
594-Bozo (10/54)   .80 1.60 2.40
595-Pluto (Disney)   1.25 2.50 3.75
596-Turok, Son of Stone(#1)
               10.00 20.00 30.00
597-The Little King   1.00 2.00 3.00
598-Captain Davy Jones 1.20 2.40 3.60
599-Ben Bowie & His Mountain Men (11/54)
                1.25 2.50 3.75
600-Daisy Duck's Diary (Disney)(11/54)
                1.25 2.50 3.75
601-Frosty the Snowman   .70 1.40 2.10
602-Mr. Magoo & Gerald McBoing-Boing
                1.50 3.00 4.50
603-The Two Mouseketeers .70 1.40 2.10
604-Shadow on the Trail (Zane Grey)
                1.50 3.00 4.50
605-The Brownies-not by Kelly (12/54)
                1.50 3.00 4.50
606-Sir Lancelot (not TV)-J. Buscema art
                2.00 4.00 6.00
607-Santa Claus Funnies 1.20 2.40 3.60
608-Silvertip-Valley of Vanishing Men (Max
  Brand)-Kinstler art 2.00 4.00 6.00
609-The Littlest Outlaw (Disney-Movie)(1/55)
                2.00 4.00 6.00
610-Drum Beat (Movie) 1.35 2.75 4.00
611-Duck Album (Disney) 1.20 2.40 3.60
612-Little Beaver (1/55) 1.20 2.40 3.60
613-Western Marshal (Ernest Haycox's)(2/55)
  Kinstler art   2.00 4.00 6.00
614-20,000 Leagues Under the Sea (Disney)
  (Movie)(2/55)   2.00 4.00 6.00
615-Daffy   1.00 2.00 3.00
616-To the Last Man (Zane Grey)
                1.50 3.00 4.50
617-Zorro (Quest of --) 3.00 6.00 9.00
618-Johnny Mack Brown 1.75 3.50 5.25
619-Krazy Kat-not by Herriman
                1.50 3.00 4.50
620-Mowgli-Jungle Book 1.25 2.50 3.75
621-Francis the Talking Mule (4/55)
                 .60 1.20 1.80
622-Beetle Bailey   1.00 2.00 3.00

                  Good Fine Mint

623-Oswald the Rabbit   .80 1.60 2.40
624-Treasure Island (Disney-Movie)(4/55)
                2.00 4.00 6.00
625-Beaver Valley (Disney-Movie)
                1.25 2.50 3.75
626-Ben Bowie & His Mountain Men
                1.25 2.50 3.75
627-Goofy (Disney)(5/55) 1.20 2.40 3.60
628-Elmer Fudd   .80 1.60 2.40
629-Lady & the Tramp with Jock (Disney)
  (5/55)   2.00 4.00 6.00
630-Priscilla's Pop   .80 1.60 2.40
631-Davy Crockett (Disney)(5/55)(--Indian
  Fighter)(TV)   1.50 3.00 4.50
632-Fighting Caravans (Zane Grey)
                1.50 3.00 4.50
633-The Little People by Walt Scott
                1.00 2.00 3.00
634-Lady & the Tramp Album (Disney)(6/55)
                1.75 3.50 5.25
635-Beany & Cecil (TV)   1.20 2.40 3.60
636-Chip 'N' Dale(Disney) 1.20 2.40 3.60
637-Silvertip (Max Brand)-Kinstler art
                2.00 4.00 6.00
638-Spike and Tyke (8/55) .60 1.20 1.80
639-Davy Crockett (Disney)(7/55)(--At the
  Alamo)(TV)   1.50 3.00 4.50
640-Western Marshal (Ernest Haycox's)
  Kinstler art   2.00 4.00 6.00
641-Steve Canyon ('55)-not by Caniff
                2.25 4.50 6.75
642-The Two Mouseketeers .70 1.40 2.10
643-Wild Bill Elliott   1.75 3.50 5.25
644-Sir Walter Raleigh(5/55)-Based on movie
  "The Virgin Queen" 2.00 4.00 6.00
645-Johnny Mack Brown 1.75 3.50 5.25
646-Dotty Dripple & Taffy .60 1.20 1.80
647-Bugs Bunny Album(9/55) .80 1.60 2.40
648-Texas Rangers(Jace Pearson's)
                1.50 3.00 4.50
649-Duck Album (Disney) 1.20 2.40 3.60
650-Prince Valiant - by Bob Fuje
                3.00 6.00 9.00
651-King Colt(Luke Short)(9/55)-Kinstler art
                1.75 3.50 5.25
652-Buck Jones   1.50 3.00 4.50
653-Smokey the Bear(10/55) .80 1.60 2.40
654-Pluto (Disney)   1.25 2.50 3.75
655-Francis the Talking Mule (10/55)
                 .60 1.20 1.80
656-Turok, Son of Stone (#2)(10/55)
                7.00 14.00 21.00
657-Ben Bowie & His Mountain Men
                1.25 2.50 3.75
658-Goofy (Disney)   1.20 2.40 3.60
659-Daisy Duck's Diary 1.25 2.50 3.75
660-Little Beaver   1.25 2.50 3.75

Four Color #629, © WDP

Four Color #654, © WDP

Four Color #659, © WDP

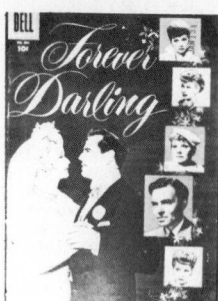

Four Color #681, © DELL   Four Color #684, © DELL   Four Color #725, © L. Schlesinger

	Good	Fine	Mint
(Four Color cont'd)			
661-Frosty the Snowman	.70	1.40	2.10
662-Zoo Parade(TV)-Marlin Perkins (11/55)			
	.80	1.60	2.40
663-Winky Dink (TV)	.75	1.50	2.25
664-Davy Crockett in the Great Keelboat Race			
(TV)(Disney)	1.75	3.50	5.25
665-The African Lion (Disney-Movie)(11/55)			
	1.25	2.50	3.75
666-Santa Claus Funnies	1.20	2.40	3.60
667-Silvertip & the Stolen Stallion (Max			
Brand-12/55)	1.40	2.80	4.20
668-Dumbo (Disney)(12/55)	1.50	3.00	4.50
668-Dumbo (Disney)(1/58) different cover,			
same contents	1.50	3.00	4.50
669-Robin Hood (Disney-Movie)(12/55)-reprint			
of #413	1.50	3.00	4.50
670-Mouse Musketeers(1/56)-Formerly the Two			
Mouseketeers	.60	1.20	1.80
671-Davy Crockett & the River Pirates (TV)			
(Disney)(12/55)-Jesse Marsh art			
	1.75	3.50	5.25
672-Quentin Durward(1/56)(Movie)			
	2.50	5.00	7.50
673-Buffalo Bill, Jr.(TV)	1.00	2.00	3.00
674-The Little Rascals	1.00	2.00	3.00
675-Steve Donovan, Western Marshal (TV)-			
Kinstler art	2.00	4.00	6.00
676-Will-Yum!	.80	1.60	2.40
677-Little King	1.00	2.00	3.00
678-The Last Hunt (Movie)	1.50	3.00	4.50
679-Gunsmoke (TV)	1.25	2.50	3.75
680-Out Our Way with the Worry Wart(2/56)			
	1.00	2.00	3.00
681-Forever, Darling(Movie)with Lucille Ball			
& Desi Arnaz (2/56)	1.50	3.00	4.50
682-When Knighthood Was in Flower(Disney-Mov-			
ie)-reprint of #505	2.00	4.00	6.00
683-Hi & Lois (3/56)	.80	1.60	2.40
684-Helen of Troy (Movie)-Buscema art			
	2.50	5.00	7.50
685-Johnny Mack Brown	1.75	3.50	5.25
686-Duck Album (Disney)	1.20	2.40	3.60
687-The Indian Fighter (Movie)			
	1.50	3.00	4.50
688-Alexander the Great (Movie)(5/56)			
	2.00	4.00	6.00
689-Elmer Fudd (3/56)	.80	1.60	2.40
690-The Conqueror (Movie)	1.00	2.00	3.00
691-Dotty Dripple & Taffy	.60	1.20	1.80
692-The Little People-Walt Scott			
	1.00	2.00	3.00
693-Song of the South (Disney)(1956)-Partial			
reprint of #129	1.75	3.50	5.25
694-Super Circus (TV)	1.00	2.00	3.00
695-Little Beaver	1.25	2.50	3.75
696-Krazy Kat-not by Herriman(4/56)			
	1.50	3.00	4.50

	Good	Fine	Mint
697-Oswald the Rabbit	.80	1.60	2.40
698-Francis the Talking Mule			
	.60	1.20	1.80
699-Prince Valiant-by Bob Fuje			
	3.00	6.00	9.00
700-Water Birds & the Olympic Elk (Disney-			
Movie)	1.50	3.00	4.50
701-Jiminy Crickett (Disney)(5/56)			
	1.25	2.50	3.75
702-The Goofy Success Story (Disney)			
	1.50	3.00	4.50
703-Scamp (Disney)	1.00	2.00	3.00
704-Priscilla's Pop(5/56)	.80	1.60	2.40
705-Brave Eagle	1.40	2.80	4.20
706-Bongo & Lumpjaw(Disney)			
	1.40	2.80	4.20
707-Corky & White Shadow (Disney)(5/56)-Mick-			
ey Mouse Club (TV)	1.20	2.40	3.60
708-Smokey the Bear	.80	1.60	2.40
709-The Searchers (Movie)	1.20	2.40	3.60
710-Francis the Mule	.60	1.20	1.80
711-MGM's Mouse Musketeers	.60	1.20	1.80
712-The Great Locomotive Chase(Disney-Movie)			
(9/56)	2.00	4.00	6.00
713-The Animal World (Movie)(8/56)			
	1.50	3.00	4.50
714-Spin & Marty(TV)(Disney)-Mickey Mouse			
Club (6/56)	1.25	2.50	3.75
715-Timmy (8/56)	.60	1.20	1.80
716-Man in Space (Disney-Movie)			
	1.50	3.00	4.50
717-Moby Dick (Movie)	2.00	4.00	6.00
718-Dotty Dripple & Taffy	.60	1.20	1.80
719-Prince Valiant - by Bob Fuje			
	3.00	6.00	9.00
720-Gunsmoke (TV)	1.00	2.00	3.00
721-Capt. Kangaroo (TV)	1.00	2.00	3.00
722-Johnny Mack Brown	1.75	3.50	5.25
723-Santiago (Movie)-Kinstler art			
	2.25	4.50	6.75
724-Bugs Bunny's Album	.80	1.50	2.40
725-Elmer Fudd (9/56)	.60	1.20	1.80
726-Duck Album	.90	1.80	2.70
727-The Nature of Things(TV)(Disney)-Jesse			
Marsh art	1.75	3.50	5.25
728-Mouse Musketeers	.60	1.20	1.80
729-Bob, Son of Battle	1.00	2.00	3.00
730-Smokey Stover	1.50	3.00	4.50
731-Silvertip-the Fighting Four (Max Brand)			
Kinstler art	2.00	4.00	6.00
732-Zorro, the Challenge of (10/56)			
	3.00	6.00	9.00
733-Buck Jones	1.50	3.00	4.50
734-Cheyenne (TV)(10/56)	1.00	2.00	3.00
735-Crusader Rabbit	1.00	2.00	3.00
736-Pluto (Disney)	1.00	2.00	3.00
737-Steve Canyon	2.25	4.50	6.75

	Good	Fine	Mint
(Four Color cont'd)			
738-Westward Ho, the Wagons (Disney-Movie)			
	1.75	3.50	5.25
739-Bounty Guns(Luke Short)-Drucker art			
	1.50	3.00	4.50
740-Chilly Willy (Walter Lantz)			
	.60	1.20	1.80
741-The Fastest Gun Alive (Movie)(9/56)			
	2.00	4.00	6.00
742-Buffalo Bill, Jr.(TV)	1.00	2.00	3.00
743-Daisy Duck's Diary (Disney)(11/56)			
	1.25	2.50	3.75
744-Little Beaver	1.25	2.50	3.75
745-Francis the Famous Talking Mule			
	.60	1.20	1.80
746-Dotty Dripple & Taffy	.60	1.20	1.80
747-Goofy (Disney)	1.00	2.00	3.00
748-Frosty the Snowman (11/56)			
	.60	1.20	1.80
749-Secrets of Life (Disney-Movie)			
	1.75	3.50	5.25
750-The Great Cat Family (Disney-Movie)			
	1.75	3.50	5.25
751-Our Miss Brooks (TV)	1.00	2.00	3.00
752-Mandrake the Magician	2.50	5.00	7.50
753-Walt Scott's Little People (11/56)			
	1.00	2.00	3.00
754-Smokey the Bear	.80	1.60	2.40
755-The Littlest Snowman (12/56)			
	.70	1.40	2.10
756-Santa Claus Funnies	1.20	2.40	3.60
757-The True Story of Jesse James (Movie)			
	2.00	4.00	6.00
758-Bear Country (Disney-Movie)			
	1.50	3.00	4.50
759-Circus Boy (TV)	1.00	2.00	3.00
760-The Hardy Boys(TV)(Disney)-Mickey Mouse			
Club	1.25	2.50	3.75
761-Howdy Doody(TV)(1/57)	1.20	2.40	3.60
762-The Sharkfighters (Movie)(1/57)(Scarce)			
	2.50	5.00	7.50
763-Grandma Duck's Farm Friends (Disney)			
	1.50	3.00	4.50
764-MGM's Mouse Musketeers	.60	1.20	1.80
765-Will-Yum!	.60	1.20	1.80
766-Buffalo Bill, Jr. (TV)	1.00	2.00	3.00
767-Spin & Marty (TV)(Disney)-Mickey Mouse			
Club (2/57)	1.25	2.50	3.75
768-Steve Donovan, Western Marshal (TV)			
Kinstler stories	2.00	4.00	6.00
769-Gunsmoke (TV)	1.00	2.00	3.00
770-Brave Eagle	1.25	2.50	3.75
771-Brand of Empire(Luke Short)(3/57)-Drucker			
art	1.50	3.00	4.50
772-Cheyenne (TV)	1.00	2.00	3.00
773-The Brave One(Movie)	1.40	2.80	4.20
774-Hi & Lois (3/57)	.80	1.60	2.40
775-Sir Lancelot(TV)-Buscema art			

	Good	Fine	Mint
776-Johnny Mack Brown	2.50	5.00	7.50
	1.75	3.50	5.25
777-Scamp (Disney)	1.00	2.00	3.00
778-The Little Rascals	1.00	2.00	3.00
779-Lee Hunter, Indian Fighter (3/57)			
	1.00	2.00	3.00
780-Capt. Kangaroo (TV)	1.00	2.00	3.00
781-Fury (TV)(3/57)	.90	1.80	2.70
782-Duck Album (Disney)	.90	1.80	2.70
783-Elmer Fudd	.60	1.20	1.80
784-Around the World in 80 Days (Movie)(2/57)			
	2.00	4.00	6.00
785-Circus Boy (TV)(4/57)	1.00	2.00	3.00
786-Cinderella (Disney)(3/57)-Partial reprint			
of #272	1.75	3.50	5.25
787-Little Hiawatha (Disney)(4/57)			
	1.50	3.00	4.50
788-Prince Valiant - by Bob Fuje			
	3.00	6.00	9.00
789-Silvertip-Valley Thieves(Max Brand)(4/57)			
	1.40	2.80	4.20
790-The Wings of Eagles (Movie)-Toth art			
	2.50	5.00	7.50
791-The 77th Bengal Lancers (TV)			
	1.50	3.00	4.50
792-Oswald the Rabbit	.80	1.60	2.40
793-Morty Meekle	1.00	2.00	3.00
794-The Count of Monte Cristo (5/57)(Movie)			
Buscema art	3.00	6.00	9.00
795-Jiminy Cricket(Disney)	1.25	2.50	3.75
796-Ludwig Bemelman's Madeleine & Genevieve			
	1.75	3.50	5.25
797-Gunsmoke (TV)	1.00	2.00	3.00
798-Buffalo Bill, Jr. (TV)	1.00	2.00	3.00
799-Priscilla's Pop	.80	1.60	2.40
800-The Buccaneers (TV)	1.50	3.00	4.50
801-Dotty Dripple & Taffy	.60	1.20	1.80
802-Goofy (Disney)(5/57)	1.00	2.00	3.00
803-Cheyenne (TV)	1.00	2.00	3.00
804-Steve Canyon (1957)	2.25	4.50	6.75
805-Crusader Rabbit	1.00	2.00	3.00
806-Scamp (Disney)(6/57)	1.00	2.00	3.00
807-Savage Range (Luke Short)-Drucker art			
	1.50	3.00	4.50
808-Spin & Marty (TV)(Disney)-Mickey Mouse			
Club	1.25	2.50	3.75
809-The Little People-Walt Scott			
	1.00	2.00	3.00
810-Francis the Mule	.60	1.20	1.80
811-Howdy Doody(TV)(7/57)	1.20	2.40	3.60
812-The Big Land (Movie)	1.75	3.50	5.25
813-Circus Boy (TV)	1.00	2.00	3.00
814-Covered Wagons, Ho! (Disney)-Donald Duck			
(6/57)	1.50	3.00	4.50
815-Dragoon Wells Massacre (Movie)			
	1.50	3.00	4.50
816-Brave Eagle	1.00	2.00	3.00

Four Color #737, © M. Caniff

Four Color #758, © WDP

Four Color #775, © DELL

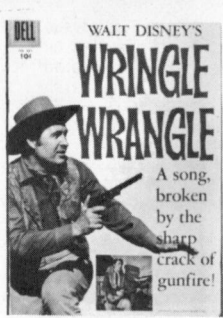

Four Color #821, © WDP

Four Color #845, © DELL

Four Color #866, © WDP

(Four Color cont'd)	Good	Fine	Mint
817-Little Beaver	1.25	2.50	3.75
818-Smokey the Bear (6/57)	.80	1.60	2.40
819-Mickey Mouse in Magicland (Disney)(7/57)			
	1.50	3.00	4.50
820-The Oklahoman (Movie)	1.75	3.50	5.25
821-Wringle Wrangle (Disney)-Based on movie "Westward Ho, the Wagons"-Marsh art			
	2.00	4.00	6.00
822-Paul Revere's Ride with Johnny Tremain (TV)(Disney)-Toth art	2.50	5.00	7.50
823-Timmy	.60	1.20	1.80
824-The Pride & the Passion (Movie)(8/57)			
	1.50	3.00	4.50
825-The Little Rascals	.80	1.60	2.40
826-Spin & Marty & Annette(TV)(Disney)-Mickey Mouse Club	1.25	2.50	3.75
827-Smokey Stover (8/57)	1.50	3.00	4.50
828-Buffalo Bill, Jr.(TV)	1.00	2.00	3.00
829-Tales of the Pony Express (TV)(8/57)			
	1.25	2.50	3.75
830-The Hardy Boys (TV)(Disney)-Mickey Mouse Club (8/57)	1.25	2.50	3.75
831-No Sleep 'Til Dawn (Movie)(9/57)			
	1.50	3.00	4.50
832-Lolly & Pepper	.60	1.20	1.80
833-Scamp (Disney)(9/57)	1.00	2.00	3.00
834-Johnny Mack Brown	1.75	3.50	5.25
835-Silvertip-The Fake Rider (Max Brand)			
	1.40	2.80	4.20
836-Man in Flight (Disney)(9/57)			
	1.25	2.50	3.75
837-All-American Athlete Cotton Woods			
	.95	1.50	2.25
838-Bugs Bunny's Life Story Album (9/57)			
	.80	1.60	2.40
839-The Vigilantes (Movie)	1.50	3.00	4.50
840-Duck Album (Disney)	.90	1.80	2.70
841-Elmer Fudd	.60	1.20	1.80
842-The Nature of Things (Disney-Movie)('57) Jesse Marsh art (TV series)			
	1.75	3.50	5.25
843-The First Americans (Disney)-Jesse Marsh art	1.75	3.50	5.25
844-Gunsmoke (TV)	1.00	2.00	3.00
845-The Land Unknown (Movie)-Alex Toth art			
	3.50	7.00	10.50
846-Gun Glory (Movie) by Alex Toth			
	2.25	4.50	6.75
847-Perri(Squirrels)(Disney-Movie)-Two different cvrs. published	1.50	3.00	4.50
848-Marauder's Moon(Movie)	1.50	3.00	4.50
849-Prince Valiant-by Bob Fuje			
	3.00	6.00	9.00
850-Buck Jones	1.50	3.00	4.50
851-The Story of Mankind (Movie)(1/58)			
	1.50	3.00	4.50
852-Chilly Willy (2/58)	.60	1.20	1.80

	Good	Fine	Mint
853-Pluto (Disney)(10/57)	1.00	2.00	3.00
854-The Hunchback of Notre Dame (Movie)			
	3.50	7.00	10.50
855-Broken Arrow (TV)	1.00	2.00	3.00
856-Buffalo Bill, Jr.(TV)	1.00	2.00	3.00
857-The Goofy Adventure Story (Disney-11/57)			
	1.00	2.00	3.00
858-Daisy Duck's Diary (Disney)(11/57)			
	1.20	2.40	3.60
859-Topper & Neil (11/57)	.80	1.60	2.40
860-Hugh O'Brian Famous Marshal Wyatt Earp (TV)-Manning art	1.60	3.20	4.80
861-Frosty the Snowman	.60	1.20	1.80
862-The Truth About Mother Goose (Movie-Disney)(11/57)	2.00	4.00	6.00
863-Francis the Mule	.60	1.20	1.80
864-The Littlest Snowman	.70	1.40	2.10
865-Andy Burnett(TV)(Disney)(12/57)			
	1.50	3.00	4.50
866-Mars & Beyond (Disney-Movie)			
	1.50	3.00	4.50
867-Santa Claus Funnies	1.20	2.40	3.60
868-Walt Scott's Little People (12/57)			
	1.00	2.00	3.00
869-Old Yeller (Disney-Movie)(1/58)			
	1.50	3.00	4.50
870-Little Beaver (1/58)	1.25	2.50	3.75
871-Curly Kayoe	1.20	2.40	3.60
872-Capt. Kangaroo (TV)	1.00	2.00	3.00
873-Grandma Duck's Farm Friends (Disney)			
	1.20	2.40	3.60
874-Old Ironsides (Disney-Movie with J. Tremain)(1/58)	2.00	4.00	6.00
875-Trumpets West (Luke Short)(2/58)			
	1.50	3.00	4.50
876-Tales of Wells Fargo (TV)(2/58)			
	1.40	2.80	4.20
877-Frontier Doctor with Rex Allen(TV)-Alex Toth art	2.50	5.00	7.50
878-Peanuts-Schulz cover only (2/58)			
	2.00	4.00	6.00
879-Brave Eagle (2/58)	1.00	2.00	3.00
880-Steve Donovan, Western Marshal-Drucker art	1.25	2.50	3.75
881-The Capt. & the Kids	1.25	2.50	3.75
882-Zorro(Disney)-1st Disney issue by Alex Toth(TV)(2/58)	2.50	5.00	7.50
883-The Little Rascals	.80	1.60	2.40
884-Hawkeye & the Last of the Mohicans (TV)			
	1.25	2.50	3.75
885-Fury (TV)(3/58)	.90	1.80	2.70
886-Bongo & Lumpjaw(Disney)			
	1.40	2.80	4.20
887-The Hardy Boys(Disney)(TV)-Mickey Mouse Club (1/58)	1.25	2.50	3.75
888-Elmer Fudd (3/58)	.60	1.20	1.80
889-Clint & Mac (Disney)-Alex Toth art (TV)			

	Good	Fine	Mint
(Four Color cont'd)			
(3/58)	2.50	5.00	7.50
890-Hugh O'Brian Famous Marshal Wyatt Earp (TV)-by Russ Manning	1.60	3.20	4.80
891-Light in the Forest(Disney-Movie)(3/58)			
	1.50	3.00	4.50
892-Maverick (TV)(4/58)	1.25	2.50	3.75
893-Jim Bowie (TV)	1.20	2.40	3.60
894-Oswald the Rabbit	.80	1.60	2.40
895-Wagon Train (TV)(3/58)	1.00	2.00	3.00
896-Tinker Bell (Disney)	2.50	5.00	7.50
897-Jiminy Cricket(Disney)	1.25	2.50	3.75
898-Silvertip's Trap(Max Brand)-Kinstler art (5/58)	2.00	4.00	6.00
899-Goofy (Disney)	1.00	2.00	3.00
900-Prince Valiant-by Bob Fuje	3.00	6.00	9.00
901-Little Hiawatha (Disney)	1.40	2.80	4.20
902-Will-Yum!	.60	1.20	1.80
903-Dotty Dripple & Taffy	.60	1.20	1.80
904-Lee Hunter, Indian Fighter	1.00	2.00	3.00
905-Annette(TV)(Disney)-Mickey Mouse Club	2.00	4.00	6.00
906-Francis the Mule	.60	1.20	1.80
907-Sugarfoot(TV)Toth art	2.00	4.00	6.00
908-The Little People-Walt Scott (5/58)	1.00	2.00	3.00
909-Smitty & Herby	1.00	2.00	3.00
910-The Vikings (Movie)-Buscema art	2.00	4.00	6.00
911-The Gray Ghost of the Confederacy (TV) (Movie)	1.50	3.00	4.50
912-Leave It to Beaver(TV)	.60	1.20	1.80
913-The Left-Handed Gun (Movie)(7/58)	1.75	3.50	5.25
914-No Time For Sergeants (Movie)	1.25	2.50	3.75
915-Casey Jones (TV)	.50	1.00	1.50
916-Red Ryder	1.50	3.00	4.50
917-The Life of Riley(TV)	.80	1.60	2.40
918-Beep Beep, the Roadrunner(7/58)-Two different back cvrs. publ.	1.00	2.00	3.00
919-Boots & Saddles (TV)	.75	1.50	2.25
920-Zorro(Disney)(TV)-Alex Toth art (6/58)	2.50	5.00	7.50
921-Hugh O'Brian Famous Marshal Wyatt Earp (TV)-Manning art	1.60	3.20	4.80
922-Johnny Mack Brown by Russ Manning	2.00	4.00	6.00
923-Timmy	.60	1.20	1.80
924-Colt 45 (TV)(8/58)	.80	1.60	2.40
925-Last of the Fast Guns (Movie)(8/58)	1.50	3.00	4.50
926-Peter Pan (Disney)-reprint of #442	2.50	5.00	4.50
927-Top Gun (Luke Short)	1.50	3.00	4.50

	Good	Fine	Mint
928-Sea Hunt (TV)	1.00	2.00	3.00
929-Brave Eagle	1.00	2.00	3.00
930-Maverick (TV)(7/58)	1.25	2.50	3.75
931-Have Gun, Will Travel (TV)	.75	1.50	2.25
932-Smokey the Bear-origin	.80	1.60	2.40
933-Zorro(Disney)-by Alex Toth (9/58)	2.50	5.00	7.50
934-The Restless Gun (TV)	.90	1.80	2.70
935-King of the Royal Mtd.	1.50	3.00	4.50
936-The Little Rascals	.80	1.60	2.40
937-Ruff and Reddy(TV)(Hanna-Barbera)(9/58)	.50	1.00	1.50
938-Elmer Fudd (9/58)	.60	1.20	1.80
939-Steve Canyon - not by Caniff	2.25	4.50	6.75
940-Lolly & Pepper	.60	1.20	1.80
941-Pluto (Disney)(10/58)	1.00	2.00	3.00
942-Pony Express (TV)	1.25	2.50	3.75
943-White Wilderness (Disney-Movie)(10/58)	1.50	3.00	4.50
944-The 7th Voyage of Sindbad(Movie)(9/58) Buscema art	5.00	10.00	15.00
945-Maverick (TV)	1.25	2.50	3.75
946-The Big Country(Movie)	1.40	2.80	4.20
947-Broken Arrow (TV)	1.00	2.00	3.00
948-Daisy Duck's Diary (Disney)(11/58)	1.20	2.40	3.60
949-Lowell Thomas' High Adventures (TV)	.75	1.50	2.25
950-Frosty the Snowman	.60	1.20	1.80
951-The Lennon Sisters Life Story - 36pgs. Toth art	2.00	4.00	6.00
952-Goofy (Disney)(11/58)	1.00	2.00	3.00
953-Francis the Mule	.60	1.20	1.80
954-Man in Space (Disney-Movie)	1.40	2.80	4.20
955-Hi & Lois (11/58)	.80	1.60	2.40
956-Ricky Nelson (TV)	1.50	3.00	4.50
957-Buffalo Bee	.50	1.00	1.50
958-Santa Claus Funnies	.90	1.80	2.70
959-Walt Scott's Christmas Stories-(Little People)(1951-56 strip reprints)	1.00	2.00	3.00
960-Zorro(Disney)(TV)(12/58)-Toth art	2.50	5.00	7.50
961-Jace Pearson's Tales of the Texas Rangers (TV)-Toth art	2.00	4.00	6.00
962-Maverick (TV)(1/59)	1.25	2.50	3.75
963-Johnny Mack Brown	1.75	3.50	5.25
964-The Hardy Boys(TV)(Disney)-Mickey Mouse Club (1/59)	1.25	2.50	3.75
965-Grandma Duck's Farm Friends (Disney) (1/59)	1.20	2.40	3.60
966-Tonka-Starring Sal Mineo(Disney-Movie)	1.50	3.00	4.50
967-Chilly Willy (2/59)	.60	1.20	1.80

Four Color #943. © WDP

Four Color #959. © DELL

Four Color #961. © DELL

Four Color #973, © DELL   Four Color #994, © DELL   Four Color #1028, © DELL

(Four Color cont'd)	Good	Fine	Mint
967-Johnny Mack Brown	1.75	3.00	5.25
968-Tales of Wells Fargo (TV)			
	1.20	2.40	3.60
969-Peanuts (2/59)	2.00	4.00	6.00
970-Lawman (TV)	.80	1.60	2.40
971-Wagon Train (TV)	1.00	2.00	3.00
972-Tom Thumb (Movie)-George Pal			
	2.00	4.00	6.00
973-Sleeping Beauty & the Prince (Disney)			
(5/59)	1.75	3.50	5.25
974-The Little Rascals (3/59)			
	.75	1.50	2.25
975-Fury (TV)	.90	1.80	2.70
976-Zorro (Disney)(TV)-Toth art			
	2.50	5.00	7.50
977-Elmer Fudd	.60	1.20	1.80
978-Lolly & Pepper	.60	1.20	1.80
979-Oswald the Rabbit	.80	1.60	2.40
980-Maverick(TV)(4-6/59)	1.25	2.50	3.75
981-Ruff & Reddy (TV)(Hanna-Barbera)			
	.50	1.00	1.50
982-Tinker Bell(TV-Disney)	2.50	5.00	7.50
983-Have Gun, Will Travel (TV)(4-6/59)			
	.75	1.50	2.25
984-Sleeping Beauty's Fairy Godmothers			
(Disney)	1.75	3.50	5.25
985-Shaggy Dog(Disney-Movie)(5/59)			
	1.50	3.00	4.50
986-Restless Gun (TV)	.90	1.80	2.70
987-Goofy (Disney)(7/59)	1.00	2.00	3.00
988-Little Hiawatha (Disney)			
	1.40	2.80	4.20
989-Jiminy Cricket (Disney)(5-7/59)			
	1.20	2.40	3.60
990-Huckleberry Hound (TV)(Hanna-Barbera)			
	.50	1.00	1.50
991-Francis the Mule	.60	1.20	1.80
992-Sugarfoot(TV)Toth art	2.00	4.00	6.00
993-Jim Bowie (TV)	1.00	2.00	3.00
994-Sea Hunt (TV)	1.00	2.00	3.00
995-Donald Duck Album (Disney)(5-7/59)			
	1.20	2.40	3.60
996-Nevada (Zane Grey)	1.50	3.00	4.50
997-Walt Disney Presents-Tales of Texas John			
Slaughter(TV)(Disney)	1.25	2.50	3.75
998-Ricky Nelson (TV)	1.50	3.00	4.50
999-Leave It To Beaver (TV)	.60	1.20	1.80
1000-The Gray Ghost of the Confederacy(Movie)			
(6-8/59)	1.25	2.50	3.75
1001-Lowell Thomas' High Adventure (TV)			
(8-10/59)	.75	1.50	2.25
1002-Buffalo Bee (TV)	.50	1.00	1.50
1003-Zorro (TV)(Disney)	1.75	3.50	5.25
1004-Colt 45 (TV)(6-8/59)	.80	1.60	2.40
1005-Maverick (TV)	1.25	2.50	3.75
1006-Hercules (Movie)-Buscema art			
	3.00	6.00	9.00

	Good	Fine	Mint
1007-John Paul Jones (Movie)(7-9/59)			
	1.50	3.00	4.50
1008-Beep Beep, the Road Runner (7-9/59)			
	1.00	2.00	3.00
1009-The Rifleman (TV)	1.40	2.80	4.20
1010-Grandma Duck's Farm Friends (Disney) by			
Carl Barks	4.00	8.00	12.00
1011-Buckskin (TV)	1.00	2.00	3.00
1012-Last Train from Gun Hill(Movie)(7/59)			
	1.50	3.00	4.50
1013-Bat Masterson(TV)(8/59)	.80	1.60	2.40
1014-The Lennon Sisters - Toth art			
	2.00	4.00	6.00
1015-Peanuts-cvr.by Schulz	2.00	4.00	6.00
1016-Smokey the Bear	.60	1.20	1.80
1017-Chilly Willy	.60	1.20	1.80
1018-Rio Bravo(Movie)(6/59)-Toth art			
	2.50	5.00	7.50
1019-Wagon Train (TV)	1.00	2.00	3.00
1020-Jungle Jim	1.25	3.50	5.25
1021-Jace Pearson's Tales of the Texas			
Rangers (TV)	1.20	2.40	3.60
1022-Timmy	.60	1.20	1.80
1023-Tales of Wells Fargo (TV)(8-10/59)			
	1.20	2.40	3.60
1024-Darby O'Gill & the Little People(Disney-			
Movie)-Toth art	2.50	5.00	7.50
1025-Vacation in Disneyland (8-10/59)-Carl			
Barks art	5.00	10.00	15.00
1026-Spin & Marty(TV)(Disney)-Mickey Mouse			
Club (9-11/59)	1.00	2.00	3.00
1027-The Texan (TV)	1.20	2.40	3.60
1028-Rawhide (TV)	.80	1.60	2.40
1029-Boots & Saddles (TV)	.75	1.50	2.25
1030-Spanky & Alfalfa, the Little Rascals			
	.75	1.50	2.25
1031-Fury (TV)	.80	1.60	2.40
1032-Elmer Fudd	.60	1.20	1.80
1033-Steve Canyon - not by Caniff			
	2.25	4.50	6.75
1034-Nancy & Sluggo Summer Camp (9-11/59)			
	.80	1.60	2.40
1035-Lawman (TV)	.80	1.60	2.40
1036-The Big Circus(Movie)	1.20	2.40	3.60
1037-Zorro (Disney)(TV)-Tufts art			
	1.75	3.50	5.25
1038-Ruff & Reddy (TV)(Hanna-Barbera)(1959)			
	.50	1.00	1.50
1039-Pluto(Disney)(11-1/60)	1.00	2.00	3.00
1040-Quick Draw McGraw(TV)(Hanna-Barbera)			
(12-2/60)	.50	1.00	1.50
1041-Sea Hunt(TV)-Toth art	2.00	4.00	6.00
1042-The Three Chipmunks (Alvin, Simon &			
Theodore)(10-12/59)	.50	1.00	1.50
1043-The Three Stooges	1.50	3.00	4.50
1044-Have Gun, Will Travel (TV)(10-12/59)			
	.75	1.50	2.25

(Four Color cont'd)	Good	Fine	Mint
1045-The Restless Gun (TV)	.90	1.80	2.70
1046-Beep Beep, the Road Runner (11-1/60)			
	1.00	2.00	3.00
1047-Gyro Gearloose (Disney)-by Carl Barks			
	4.00	8.00	12.00
1048-The Horse Soldiers (Movie)			
	1.50	3.00	4.50
1049-Don't Give Up the Ship (Movie)(8/59)			
	1.50	3.00	4.50
1050-Huckleberry Hound (TV)(Hanna-Barbera)			
(10-12/59)	.50	1.00	1.50
1051-Donald in Mathmagic Land(Disney-Movie)			
	1.50	3.00	4.50
1052-Ben Hur (Movie)(11/59)-by Russ Manning			
	2.00	4.00	6.00
1053-Goofy(Disney)(11-1/60)	1.00	2.00	3.00
1054-Huckleberry Hound Winter Fun(TV)(Hanna-			
Barbera)(12/59)	.50	1.00	1.50
1055-Daisy Duck's Diary(Disney)-by Carl Barks			
(11-1/60)	4.00	8.00	12.00
1056-Yellowstone Kelly (Movie)(11-1/60)			
	1.50	3.00	4.50
1057-Mickey Mouse Album (Disney)			
	1.00	2.00	3.00
1058-Colt 45 (TV)(11-1/60)	.80	1.60	2.40
1059-Sugarfoot (TV)	1.00	2.00	3.00
1060-Journey to the Center of the Earth(Movie)			
	2.00	4.00	6.00
1061-Buffalo Bee (TV)	.50	1.00	1.50
1062-Walt Scott's Christmas Stories-Little			
People(strip reprints)	1.00	2.00	3.00
1063-Santa Claus Funnies	.90	1.80	2.70
1064-Bugs Bunny's Merry Christmas (12/59)			
	.80	1.60	2.40
1065-Frosty the Snowman	.60	1.20	1.80
1066-77 Sunset Strip(TV)-Toth art (1-3/60)			
	2.00	4.00	6.00
1067-Yogi Bear (TV)(Hanna-Barbera)			
	.50	1.00	1.50
1068-Francis the Talking Mule (11/59-1/60)			
	.60	1.20	1.80
1069-The FBI Story (Movie)-Toth art			
	2.25	4.50	6.75
1070-Solomon & Sheba(Movie)	1.75	3.50	5.25
1071-The Real McCoys (TV)	.50	1.00	1.50
1072-Blythe (Marge's)	1.00	2.00	3.00
1073-Grandma Duck's Farm Friends-by Carl Barks			
(Disney)	4.00	8.00	12.00
1074-Chilly Willy	.60	1.20	1.80
1075-Tales of Wells Fargo (TV)(2-4/60)			
	1.20	2.40	3.60
1076-The Rebel (TV)	1.00	2.00	3.00
1077-The Deputy(TV)-Buscema art			
	1.50	3.00	4.50
1078-The Three Stooges	1.50	3.00	4.50
1079-Spanky & Alfalfa, the Little Rascals			
	.75	1.50	2.25

	Good	Fine	Mint
1080-Fury (TV)	.80	1.60	2.40
1081-Elmer Fudd	.60	1.20	1.80
1082-Spin & Marty (Disney)	1.00	2.00	3.00
1083-Men Into Space (TV)-Anderson art			
	1.50	3.00	4.50
1084-Speedy Gonzales	.80	1.60	2.40
1085-The Time Machine (Movie)(3/60)-Alex			
Toth art	2.50	5.00	7.50
1086-Lolly & Pepper	.60	1.20	1.80
1087-Peter Gunn (TV)	1.00	2.00	3.00
1088-A Dog of Flanders (Movie)(4/60)			
	1.25	2.50	3.75
1089-Restless Gun (TV)	.90	1.80	2.70
1090-Francis the Mule	.60	1.20	1.80
1091-Jacky's Diary(4-6/60)	1.00	2.00	3.00
1092-Toby Tyler (Disney-Movie)(3/60)			
	1.50	3.00	4.50
1093-MacKenzie's Raiders (Movie)(6-8/60)			
	1.40	2.80	4.20
1094-Goofy (Disney)	1.00	2.00	3.00
1095-Gyro Gearloose (Disney)-Carl Barks art			
(4-6/60)	4.00	8.00	12.00
1096-The Texan (TV)	1.20	2.40	3.60
1097-Rawhide(TV)-Manning art	.80	1.60	2.40
1098-Sugarfoot (TV)	1.00	2.00	3.00
1099-Donald Duck Album (Disney)(5-7/60)			
	1.20	2.40	3.60
1100-Annette's Life Story (Disney-Movie)			
	2.00	4.00	6.00
1101-Kidnapped (Disney-Movie)(5/60)			
	1.50	3.00	4.50
1102-Wanted: Dead or Alive (TV)(5-7/60)			
	1.20	2.40	3.60
1103-Leave It To Beaver(TV)	.60	1.20	1.80
1104-Yogi Bear Goes to College (TV)(Hanna-			
Barbera)(6-8/60)	.50	1.00	1.50
1105-Oh, Susanna(TV)-Toth art			
	2.25	4.50	6.75
1106-77 Sunset Strip (TV)-Toth art(6-8/60)			
	2.00	4.00	6.00
1107-Buckskin (Movie)	1.25	2.50	3.75
1108-The Troubleshooters (TV)			
	1.00	2.00	3.00
1109-This Is Your Life, Donald Duck (Disney)			
(8-10/60)-Gyro flashback written by Carl			
Barks	1.50	3.00	4.50
1110-Bonanza (TV)(6-8/60)	1.00	2.00	3.00
1111-Shotgun Slade (TV)	.80	1.60	2.40
1112-Pixie & Dixie & Mr. Jinks (TV)(Hanna-			
Barbera)(7-9/60)	.60	1.20	1.80
1113-Tales of Wells Fargo (TV)			
	1.20	2.40	3.60
1114-Huckleberry Finn (Movie)(7/60)			
	1.50	3.00	4.50
1115-Ricky Nelson (TV)-Manning art			
	1.75	3.50	5.25
1116-Boots & Saddles (TV)	.75	1.50	2.25

Four Color =1052. © DELL

Four Color =1066. © DELL

Four Color #1083. © DELL

Four Color #1136, © WDP

Four Color #1163, © DELL

Four Color #1167, © DELL

(Four Color cont'd)

	Good	Fine	Mint
1117-The Boy & the Pirates (Movie)			
	1.50	3.00	4.50
1118-The Sword & the Dragon (Movie)(6/60)			
	1.50	3.00	4.50
1119-Smokey the Bear	.60	1.20	1.80
1120-Donosaurus (Movie)	1.50	3.00	4.50
1121-Hercules Unchained (Movie)(8/60)			
Crandall/Evans art	2.50	5.00	7.50
1122-Chilly Willy	.60	1.20	1.80
1123-Tombstone Territory (TV)			
	1.00	2.00	3.00
1124-Whirlybirds (TV)	.80	1.60	2.40
1125-Laramie (TV)	.90	1.80	2.70
1126-Hotel DeParee-Sundance (TV)(8-10/60)			
	.65	1.35	2.00
1127-The Three Stooges	1.50	3.00	4.50
1128-Rocky & His Friends (Jay Ward)(8-10/60)			
	.60	1.20	1.80
1129-Pollyanna (Disney-Movie)(8/60)			
	1.75	3.50	5.25
1130-The Deputy (TV)-Buscema art			
	1.50	3.00	4.50
1131-Elmer Fudd (9-11/60)	.60	1.20	1.80
1132-Space Mouse (8-10/60)	.70	1.40	2.10
1133-Fury (TV)	.80	1.60	2.40
1134-Real McCoys (TV)-Toth art			
	2.00	4.00	6.00
1135-Mouse Musketeers	.50	1.00	1.50
1136-Jungle Cat (Disney-Movie)(9-11/60)			
	1.50	3.00	4.50
1137-The Little Rascals	.75	1.50	2.25
1138-The Rebel (TV)	.90	1.80	2.70
1139-Spartacus (Movie)(11/60)-Buscema art			
	2.50	5.00	7.50
1140-Donald Duck Album (Disney)(10-12/60)			
	1.20	2.40	3.60
1141-Huckleberry Hound for President (TV)			
(Hanna-Barbera)(10/60)	.50	1.00	1.50
1142-Johnny Ringo (TV)	.75	1.50	2.25
1143-Pluto (Disney)	1.00	2.00	3.00
1144-The Story of Ruth (Movie)			
	1.50	3.00	4.50
1145-The Lost World (Movie)-Gil Kane art			
	1.75	3.50	5.25
1146-The Restless Gun (TV)	.90	1.80	2.70
1147-Sugarfoot (TV)	1.00	2.00	3.00
1148-I Aim at the Stars-the Wernher Von Braun			
Story(Movie)(11-1/61)	1.50	3.00	4.50
1149-Goofy(Disney)(11-1/61)	1.00	2.00	3.00
1150-Daisy Duck's Diary (Disney)(12-1/61) by			
Carl Barks	4.00	8.00	12.00
1151-Mickey Mouse Album (Disney)(11-1/61)			
	1.00	2.00	3.00
1152-Rocky & His Friends (Jay Ward)(TV)			
(12-2/61)	.60	1.20	1.80
1153-Frosty the Snowman	.50	1.00	1.50
1154-Santa Claus Funnies	.90	1.80	2.70

	Good	Fine	Mint
1155-North to Alaska(Movie)	1.50	3.00	4.50
1156-Swiss Family Robinson (Disney-Movie)			
(12/60)	1.50	3.00	4.50
1157-Master of the World (Movie)(7/61)			
	1.50	3.00	4.50
1158-3 Worlds of Gulliver (2 issues with different covers)(Movie)	1.75	3.50	5.25
1159-77 Sunset Strip(TV)-Toth art			
	2.00	4.00	6.00
1160-Rawhide (TV)	.80	1.60	2.40
1161-Grandma Duck's Farm Friends (Disney) by			
Carl Barks (2-4/61)	4.00	8.00	12.00
1162-Yogi Bear Joins the Marines (TV)(Hanna-Barbera)(5-7/61)	.50	1.00	1.50
1163-Daniel Boone (3-5/61)	1.00	2.00	3.00
1164-Wanted: Dead or Alive (TV)			
	1.20	2.40	3.60
1165-Ellery Queen	1.75	3.50	5.25
1166-Rocky & His Friends (Jay Ward)(TV)			
(3-5/61)	.60	1.20	1.80
1167-Tales of Wells Fargo (TV)			
	1.20	2.40	3.60
1168-The Detectives (TV)	1.00	2.00	3.00
1169-New Adventures of Sherlock Holmes			
	2.00	4.00	6.00
1170-The Three Stooges	1.50	3.00	4.50
1171-Elmer Fudd	.60	1.20	1.80
1172-Fury (TV)	.80	1.60	2.40
1173-The Twilight Zone by Reed Crandall (TV)			
(5/61)	2.50	5.00	7.50
1174-The Little Rascals	.75	1.50	2.25
1175-MGM's Mouse Musketeers (3-5/61)			
	.50	1.00	1.50
1176-Dondi (Movie)-origin	1.25	2.50	3.75
1177-Chilly Willy (4-6/61)	.60	1.20	1.80
1178-Ten Who Dared (Disney-Movie)(12/60)			
	1.50	3.00	4.50
1179-The Swamp Fox (TV)(Disney)(3-5/61)			
	1.50	3.00	4.50
1180-The Danny Thomas Show (TV)-Manning art			
	1.75	3.50	5.25
1181-Texas John Slaughter (TV)(Disney)			
(4-6/61)	1.25	2.50	3.75
1182-Donald Duck Album (Disney)(5-7/61)			
	1.20	2.40	3.60
1183-101 Dalmatians (Disney-Movie)(3/61)			
	1.50	3.00	4.50
1184-Gyro Gearloose by Carl Barks (Disney)			
	4.00	8.00	12.00
1185-Sweetie Pie	.60	1.20	1.80
1186-Yak Yak (#1) by Jack Davis (2 versions - one minus 3pg. Davis art)			
	2.50	5.00	7.50
1187-The 3 Stooges (6/61)	1.50	3.00	4.50
1188-Atlantis the Lost Continent (Movie)(5/61)			
	1.75	3.50	5.25
1189-Greyfriars Bobby (Disney-Movie)(11/61)			

(Four Color cont'd)	Good	Fine	Mint
	1.50	3.00	4.50

1190-Donald & the Wheel (Disney-Movie)(11/61)
    1.75 3.50 5.25
1191-Leave It To Beaver(TV) .60 1.20 1.80
1192-Ricky Nelson (TV)-Manning art
    1.75 3.50 5.25
1193-The Real McCoys (TV) .50 1.00 1.50
1194-Pepe (Movie)(4/61) 1.25 2.50 3.75
1195-National Velvet (TV) .70 1.40 2.10
1196-Pixie & Dixie & Mr. Jinks (TV)(Hanna-
    Barbera)(7-9/61) .60 1.20 1.80
1197-The Aquanauts (TV) 1.00 2.00 3.00
1198-Donald in Mathmagic Land - reprint of
    #1051 (Disney-Movie) 1.25 2.50 3.75
1199-The Absent-Minded Professor(Disney-Movie)
    (4/61) 1.50 3.00 4.50
1200-Hennessey (TV)(8-10/61)-Gil Kane art
    1.00 2.00 3.00
1201-Goofy(Disney)(8-10/61)1.00 2.00 3.00
1202-Rawhide (TV) .80 1.60 2.40
1203-Pinocchio (Disney)(3/62)
    1.50 3.00 4.50
1204-Scamp (Disney) .80 1.60 2.40
1205-David & Goliath (Movie)(7/61)
    1.50 3.00 4.50
1206-Lolly & Pepper(9-11/61).60 1.20 1.80
1207-The Rebel (TV)-Sekowsky art
    1.50 3.00 4.50
1208-Rocky & His Friends (Jay Ward)(TV)
    .60 1.20 1.80
1209-Sugarfoot (TV) 1.00 2.00 3.00
1210-The Parent Trap (Disney-Movie)(8/61)
    1.50 3.00 4.50
1211-77 Sunset Strip (TV)-Manning art
    1.50 3.00 4.50
1212-Chilly Willy (7-9/61) .60 1.20 1.80
1213-Mysterious Island (Movie)
    1.75 3.50 5.25
1214-Smokey the Bear .60 1.20 1.80
1215-Tales of Wells Fargo (TV)(10-12/61)
    1.20 2.40 3.60
1216-Whirlybirds (TV) .80 1.60 2.40
1218-Fury (TV) .80 1.60 2.40
1219-The Detectives (TV) 1.00 2.00 3.00
1220-Gunslinger (TV) 1.00 2.00 3.00
1221-Bonanza (TV)(9-11/61) 1.00 2.00 3.00
1222-Elmer Fudd (9-11/61) .60 1.20 1.80
1223-Laramie (TV)-Gil Kane art
    .90 1.80 2.70
1224-The Little Rascals .75 1.50 2.25
1225-The Deputy (TV) 1.00 2.00 3.00
1226-Nikki, Wild Dog of the North (Disney-
    Movie)(9/61) 1.50 3.00 4.50
1227-Morgan the Pirate (Movie)
    2.00 4.00 6.00
1229-Thief of Baghdad (Movie)-Evans art
    3.00 6.00 9.00

1230-Voyage to the Bottom of the Sea (Movie)
    1.50 3.00 4.50
1231-Danger Man (TV) 1.00 2.00 3.00
1232-On the Double (Movie) 1.50 3.00 4.50
1233-Tammy Tell Me True (Movie)(1961)
    1.50 3.00 4.50
1234-The Phantom Planet (Movie)(1961)
    1.75 3.50 5.25
1235-Mister Magoo (12-2/62)1.00 2.00 3.00
1235-Mister Magoo(3-5/65) 2nd printing -
    reprints of '61 issue .50 1.00 1.50
1236-King of Kings (Movie) 1.50 3.00 4.50
1237-The Untouchables (TV)-not by Toth
    1.00 2.00 3.00
1238-Deputy Dawg (TV) .40 .80 1.20
1239-Donald Duck Album (Disney)(10-12/61)
    Barks cover 1.20 2.40 3.60
1240-The Detectives (TV) 1.00 2.00 3.00
1241-Sweetie Pie .60 1.20 1.80
1242-King Leonardo (TV)(11-1/62)
    .50 1.00 1.50
1243-Ellery Queen 1.75 3.50 5.25
1244-Space Mouse (11-1/62) .70 1.40 2.10
1245-New Adventures of Sherlock Holmes
    2.00 4.00 6.00
1246-Mickey Mouse Album (Disney)(11-1/62)
    1.00 2.00 3.00
1247-Daisy Duck's Diary (Disney)(12-2/62)
    1.20 2.40 3.60
1248-Pluto (Disney) 1.00 2.00 3.00
1249-The Danny Thomas Show (TV)-Manning art
    1.75 3.50 5.25
1250-The Four Horsemen of the Apocalypse
    (Movie) 1.50 3.00 4.50
1251-Everything's Ducky (Movie)(1961)
    1.40 2.80 4.20
1252-Andy Griffith (TV) .80 1.60 2.40
1253-Space Man (1-3/62) .90 1.80 2.70
1254-Diver Dan (TV)(2-4/62) .80 1.60 2.40
1255-The Wonders of Aladdin (Movie)(1961)
    1.50 3.00 4.50
1256-Kona, Monarch of Monster Isle (2-4/62)
    1.75 3.50 5.25
1257-Car 54, Where Are You? (TV)(3-5/62)
    .50 1.00 1.50
1258-The Frogmen-Evans art 2.00 4.00 6.00
1259-El Cid (Movie)(1961) 2.00 4.00 6.00
1260-The Horsemasters (TV, Movie - Disney)
    (12-2/62) 1.50 3.00 4.50
1261-Rawhide (TV) .80 1.60 2.40
1262-The Rebel (TV) 1.00 2.00 3.00
1263-77 Sunset Strip(TV)-Manning art(12-2/62)
    1.50 3.00 4.50
1264-Pixie & Dixie & Mr. Jinks (TV)(Hanna-
    Barbera) .60 1.20 1.80
1265-The Real McCoys (TV) .50 1.00 1.50
1266-Spike & Tyke (12-2/62) .40 .80 1.20
1267-Gyro Gearloose by Carl Barks, 4pgs.

Four Color #1221. © DELL

Four Color #1243. © DELL

Four Color #1260. © WDP

Four Color #1275, © DELL

Four Color #1333, © DELL

Four Favorites #20, © ACE

	Good	Fine	Mint
(Four Color cont'd)			
(Disney)(12-2/62)	3.50	7.00	10.50
1268-Oswald the Rabbit	.80	1.60	2.40
1269-Rawhide (TV)	.80	1.60	2.40
1270-Bullwinkle & Rocky (Jay Ward)(TV)(3-5/62)			
	.60	1.20	1.80
1271-Yogi Bear Birthday Party (TV)(Hanna-Barbera)(11/61)	.35	.70	1.05
1272-Frosty the Snowman	.50	1.00	1.50
1273-Hans Brinker (Disney-Movie)(1962)			
	1.50	3.00	4.50
1274-Santa Claus Funnies	.90	1.80	2.70
1275-Rocky & His Friends (Jay Ward)(TV)(12-2/62)	.60	1.20	1.80
1276-Dondi	1.25	2.50	3.75
1278-King Leonardo (TV)	.50	1.00	1.50
1279-Grandma Duck's Farm Friends (Disney)(2-4/62)	1.20	2.40	3.60
1280-Hennessey (TV)	.75	1.50	2.25
1281-Chilly Willy (4-6/62)	.60	1.20	1.80
1282-Babes in Toyland (Disney-Movie)(1/62)			
	2.00	4.00	6.00
1283-Bonanza (TV)(2-4/62)	1.00	2.00	3.00
1284-Laramie (TV)-Heath art	.90	1.80	2.70
1285-Leave It To Beaver (TV)	.60	1.20	1.80
1286-The Untouchables (TV)	1.00	2.00	3.00
1287-Man From Wells Fargo (TV)			
	1.00	2.00	3.00
1288-The Twilight Zone (TV)(4/62)-Evans/Crandall art	2.50	5.00	7.50
1289-Ellery Queen	1.75	3.50	5.25
1290-Mouse Musketeers	.50	1.00	1.50
1291-77 Sunset Strip (TV)-Manning art			
	1.50	3.00	4.50
1293-Elmer Fudd (3-5/62)	.60	1.20	1.80
1294-Ripcord (TV)	.80	1.60	2.40
1295-Mister Ed (TV)(3-5/62)	.50	1.00	1.50
1296-Fury (TV)(3-5/62)	.80	1.60	2.40
1297-Spanky, Alfalfa & the Little Rascals			
	.75	1.50	2.25
1298-The Hathaways (TV)	.50	1.00	1.50
1299-Deputy Dawg (TV)	.40	.80	1.20
1300-The Comancheros (Movie)(1961)			
	1.50	3.00	4.50
1301-Adventures in Paradise (TV)(2-4/62)			
	1.00	2.00	3.00
1302-Johnny Jason, Teen Reporter (2-4/62)			
	.50	1.00	1.50
1303-Lad: A Dog (Movie)	1.25	2.50	3.75
1304-Nellie the Nurse (3-5/62)-John Stanley art	2.00	4.00	6.00
1305-Mister Magoo (3-5/62)	1.00	2.00	3.00
1306-Target: the Corrupters (TV)(3-5/62)			
	.70	1.40	2.10
1307-Margie (TV)(3-5/62)	.50	1.00	1.50
1308-Tales of the Wizard of Oz (TV)(3-5/62)			
	1.50	3.00	4.50
1309-87th Precinct (TV)(4-6/62)-Krigstein art			

	Good	Fine	Mint
	2.50	5.00	7.50
1310-Huck & Yogi Winter Sports (TV)(Hanna-Barbera)(3/62)	.60	1.20	1.80
1311-Rocky & His Friends (Jay Ward)(TV)			
	.60	1.20	1.80
1312-National Velvet (TV)	.70	1.40	2.10
1313-Moon Pilot (Disney-Movie)(3/62)			
	1.50	3.00	4.50
1324-The Underwater City (Movie)-Evans art			
	2.00	4.00	6.00
1328-The Underwater City (Movie)-Evans art (1961)	2.00	4.00	6.00
1329-Gyro Gearloose-Barks cover			
	2.50	5.00	7.50
1330-Brain Boy-G.Kane art	1.00	2.00	3.00
1332-Bachelor Father (TV)	.70	1.40	2.10
1333-Short Ribs	.80	1.60	2.40
1335-Aggie Mack	1.00	2.00	3.00
1336-On Stage - not by Leonard Starr			
	1.00	2.00	3.00
1337-Dr. Kildare (TV)	.50	1.00	1.50
1341-Andy Griffith (TV)	.80	1.60	2.40
1348-Yak Yak(#2)-by Jack Davis			
	2.50	5.00	7.50
1349-Yogi Bear Visits the U.N. (TV)(Hanna-Barbera)(1/62)	.35	.70	1.05
1350-Comanche(Disney-Movie)(1962)-Reprints 4-Color #966(title change from "Tonka" to "Comanche")(4-6/62)	1.25	2.50	3.75
1354-Calvin & the Colonel (TV)			
	.50	1.00	1.50

NOTE: *Missing numbers probably do not exist.*

FOUR FAVORITES (Crime Must Pay the Penalty
Sept, 1941 - #32, Dec, 1947   #33 on)
Ace Magazines

	Good	Fine	Mint
#1-Vulcan, Lash Lightning, Magno the Magnetic Man & The Raven begin	25.00	50.00	75.00
2-The Black Ace only app.			
	12.00	24.00	36.00
3-Last Vulcan	10.00	20.00	30.00
4,5: #4-The Raven ends; Unknown Soldier begins. #5-Captain Courageous begins			
	8.00	16.00	24.00
6-8	6.00	12.00	18.00
9-11-Kurtzman art	7.00	14.00	21.00
12-20	5.00	10.00	15.00
21	3.00	6.00	9.00
22-Captain Courageous drops costume			
	3.00	6.00	9.00
23-26-Last Magno	3.00	6.00	9.00
27-32	1.50	3.00	4.50

FOUR HORSEMEN OF THE APOCALYPSE, THE
(See 4-Color Comics #1250)

174

FOUR MOST (-- Boys #37-41)
Winter, 1941-42 - V8#5, 9-10/49; 1950
Novelty Publications

	Good	Fine	Mint
V1#1-The Target, The Cadet & Dick Cole, Wonder Boy begin	8.00	16.00	24.00
2	4.00	8.00	12.00
3,4	3.00	6.00	9.00
V2#1-4, V3#1-4	1.50	3.00	4.50
V4#1-4	1.00	2.00	3.00
V5#1-The Target & Targeteers app., 2-4	1.00	2.00	3.00
V6#1-White Rider & Super Horse begins, 2-6	1.00	2.00	3.00
V7#1-6-Last Dick Cole	1.00	2.00	3.00
V8#1-5, #37-41(1950)	1.00	2.00	3.00

FOUR STAR BATTLES TALES
Feb-Mar, 1973 - #5, Nov-Dec, 1973
National Periodical Publications

#1-All reprints	.15	.30	.45
2-4		.15	.30
5-Krigstein reprint	.15	.30	.45

NOTE: *Drucker reprints-#1,3-5. Kubert reprint-#4, cover-#2.*

FOUR STAR SPECTACULAR
Mar-Apr, 1976 - #6, Jan-Feb, 1977   (68 pgs.)
National Periodical Publications

#1	.25	.50	.75
2-6	.20	.40	.60

NOTE: *All contain DC Superhero reprints. #6 has a Blackhawk G.A. reprint.*

FOUR TEENERS
April, 1948   (Teen-age comic)
A. A. Wyn

#34	.80	1.60	2.40

FOX AND THE CROW (Stanley & His Monster
12-1/51-52 - #108, 2-3/68   #105 on)
National Periodical Publications

#1	7.00	14.00	21.00
2-5	3.50	7.00	10.50
6-10	2.50	5.00	7.50
11-20	1.75	3.50	5.25
21-40	1.20	2.40	3.60
41-60	1.00	2.00	3.00
61-108	.50	1.00	1.50

NOTE: *Many covers by Mort Drucker.*

FOX GIANTS

Each of these usually contain four remainder-

ed Fox books minus covers. Since these missing covers often had the first page of the first story, most Giants therefore are incomplete. The value should be approximately 50% of the listed price of each individual title included in the Giant.

FOXHOLE
Sept-Oct, 1954 - 1955
Simon & Kirby Publ.(Prize)/Charlton Comics

	Good	Fine	Mint
#1-Kirby cover	1.75	3.00	5.25
2-Kirby cvr./2 stories	2.00	4.00	6.00
3,5-Kirby cvrs. only	1.25	2.50	3.75
4,7-10	.80	1.60	2.40
6-Kirby cvr./2 stories	2.00	4.00	6.00
11-18	.50	1.00	1.50
Super Reprints #10-12,15-18			
	.50	1.00	1.50

NOTE: *Kirby art-#11,12,18. Powell art-#15,16.*

FOXY FAGAN
1946 - #7, Summer, 1948
Dearfield Publishing Co.

#1-Foxy Fagan & Little Buck begin			
	1.50	3.00	4.50
2-7	1.00	2.00	3.00

FOXY GRANDPA
1901 - 1916   (Hardcover; strip reprints)
N.Y. Herald/Frederick A. Stokes Co./M.A.
Donahue & Co./Bunny Publ.

1901-9x15" in color-N.Y. Herald			
	25.00	62.50	100.00
1902-"Latest Larks of--", 32pgs. in color, 9½x15½"	25.00	62.50	100.00
1903-"Latest Advs.", 9x15", 24pgs. in color, Hammersly Co.	25.00	62.50	100.00
1903-"--'s New Advs.", 10x15", 32 pgs. in color, Stokes	25.00	62.50	100.00
1904-"Up to Date", 10x15", 28pgs. in color, Stokes	25.00	62.50	100.00
1905-"The Latest Advs. of", 9x15", 24pgs., B&W, M.A. Donahue Co.	8.00	20.00	32.00
1905-"Merry Pranks of", 9½x15½", 24pgs. in color, Donahue	15.00	37.50	60.00
1905-"Latest Larks of", 9½x15½", 32pgs. in color, Donahue	15.00	37.50	60.00
1906-"Frolics", 10x15", 30pgs. in color, Stokes	15.00	37.50	60.00
1908?-"Triumphs", 10x15"	8.00	20.00	32.00
1908?-"& Little Brother", 10x15"			
	8.00	20.00	32.00
1908?-"& Flip Flaps", 10x15"			
	8.00	20.00	32.00
1914-9½x15½", 24pgs., 6 color cartoons/page,			

Four Most #58, © NOVP

The Fox & The Crow #78, © DC

Foxhole #1, © PRIZE

Frank Buck #70, © FOX

Frankenstein Comics #13, © **PRIZE**

Frankenstein #18, © MCG

(Foxy Grandpa cont'd)	Good	Fine	Mint
Bunny Publ.	8.00	20.00	32.00

1916-"Merry Book", 10x15", 30pgs. in color,

| Stokes | 8.00 | 20.00 | 32.00 |

FOXY GRANDPA SPARKLETS SERIES
1908   (6½x7-3/4"; 24pgs. in color)
Donahue & Co.

--"Rides the Goat", --"And His Boys",
--"Playing Ball", --"Fun on the Farm",
--"Fancy Shooting", --"Show the Boys Up
Sports", --"Plays Santa Claus"

each....	15.00	37.50	60.00

FRACTURED FAIRY TALES
October, 1952
Gold Key

#1(10022-210)	.50	1.00	1.50

FRANCIS THE FAMOUS TALKING MULE (All based
on movie)(See 4-Color #335,465,501,547,579,
621,655,698,710,745,810,863,906,953,991,1068,
1090)

FRANK BUCK (Formerly My True Love)
#70, May, 1950 - #3, Sept, 1950
Fox Features Syndicate

#70,71,#3-Wood pencils?	5.00	10.00	15.00
72	2.50	5.00	7.50

FRANKENSTEIN (See Movie Classics)
8-10/64; #2, 9/66 - #4, 3/67
Dell Publishing Co.

#1(12-283-410)('64)	.50	1.00	1.50
2-Intro. & origin Super-Hero character(9/66),			
3,4	.25	.50	.75

FRANKENSTEIN COMICS
1945 - V5#5(#33), Oct-Nov, 1954
Prize Publications (Crestwood/Feature)

#1-Frankenstein begins by Dick Briefer			
(origin)	9.00	18.00	27.00
2	5.00	10.00	15.00
3-10: #8-(7-8/47)-Superman satire			
	3.50	7.00	10.50
11-17(1948)-Last humor issue			
	3.00	6.00	9.00
18(3/52)-New origin, horror series begins			
	2.00	4.00	6.00
19	2.00	4.00	6.00
20(V3#4, 8-9/52)	2.00	4.00	6.00
21(V3#5),22(V3#6)	2.00	4.00	6.00
23(V4#1)-#28(V4#6)	1.50	3.00	4.50

	Good	Fine	Mint
29(V5#1-#33(V5#5)	1.50	3.00	4.50

FRANKENSTEIN (The Monster of--)(See Book &
Jan, 1973 - #18, Sept, 1975   Record--)
Marvel Comics Group

#1-Ploog art begins	.60	1.20	1.80
2-6-Last Ploog art	.40	.80	1.20
7-17	.25	.50	.75
18-Wrightson cover	.35	.70	1.05
Power Record giveaway-(12½x12½"; 16pgs.);			
Adams art	.50	1.00	1.50

FRANKENSTEIN, JR. (--& the Impossibles)(TV)
January, 1967   (Hanna-Barbera)
Gold Key

#1	.15	.30	.45

FRANKIE (--& Lana)(Formerly Movie Tunes;
Frankie Fuddle #16 on)
#4, Spring, 1947 - 1948
Marvel Comics (MgPC)

#4-8	.75	1.50	2.25
9-15	.50	1.00	1.50

FRANKIE DOODLE (See Single Series #7 and
Sparkler #2)

FRANKIE FUDDLE (Formerly Frankie & Lana)
1949
Marvel Comics

#16,17	.50	1.00	1.50

FRANK LUTHER'S SILLY PILLY COMICS
1950   (10¢)   (See Jingle Dingle --)
Children's Comics

#1-Characters from radio, records, & TV			
	1.00	2.00	3.00

FRANK MERRIWELL AT YALE
June, 1955 - #4, Dec, 1955
Charlton Comics

#1	1.00	2.00	3.00
2-4	.75	1.50	2.25

FRANTIC (Magazine) (See Zany & Ratfink)
Oct, 1958 - V2#2, April, 1959   (Satire)
Pierce Publishing Co.

V1#1,2	1.00	2.00	3.00
V2#1,2	.60	1.20	1.80

FRECKLES AND HIS FRIENDS (See Famous Comics
Cartoon Book & Honeybee Birdwhistle --)

FRECKLES AND HIS FRIENDS
#5, 11/47 - #12, 8/49; 11/55 - 1956
Standard Comics/Argo

	Good	Fine	Mint
#5-12-Reprints	2.00	4.00	6.00

NOTE: #8 & 9 contain a printing oddity. The
negatives were elongated in the engraving
process, probably to conform to page dimensions on the filler pages. Those pages only
look normal when viewed at a 45 degree angle.

#1(Argo,'55)-Reprints	1.50	3.00	4.50
2,3	1.20	2.40	3.60

FREDDY (See Blue Bird)
March, 1958 - #47, Feb, 1965
Charlton Comics

V2#12-47	.20	.40	.60

FREDDY
May-July, 1963 - #3, Oct-Dec, 1964
Dell Publishing Co.

#1-3	.20	.40	.60

FREE COMICS TO YOU FROM(--name of shoe store)
(Has clown on cover & another with a rabbit)
Circa 1956   (Like comics from Weather Bird
Shoe Store Giveaway   & Edward's Shoes)

Contains a comic bound with new cover - several combinations possible; contents determines price.

FREEDOM AGENT (Also see John Steele)
April, 1963
Gold Key

#1(10054-304)	.60	1.20	1.80

FREEDOM FIGHTERS (See Justice League#107,108)
Mar-Apr, 1976 - #15, Jul-Aug, 1978
National Periodical Publications/DC Comics

#1-Uncle Sam, The Ray, Black Condor, Doll
  Man, Human Bomb, & Phantom Lady begin

	.30	.60	.90
2,3	.20	.40	.60
4-Redondo art, Kubert cvr	.20	.40	.60
5-15	.15	.30	.45

FREEDOM TRAIN
1948   (Giveaway)
Street & Smith Publ.

1.50	3.00	4.50

FRENZY (Magazine) (Satire)
April, 1958 - #6, March, 1959
Picture Magazine

	Good	Fine	Mint
#1	1.20	2.40	3.60
2-6	.80	1.60	2.40

FRIDAY FOSTER
October, 1972
Dell Publishing Co.

#1	.40	.80	1.20

FRIENDLY GHOST, CASPER, THE (See Casper --)
Aug, 1958 - Present
Harvey Publications

#1	6.00	12.00	18.00
2	3.00	6.00	9.00
3-10	2.00	4.00	6.00
11-20	1.25	2.50	3.75
21-50	.60	1.20	1.80
51-100	.35	.70	1.05
101-150	.20	.40	.60
151-201		.20	.40
American Dental Assoc. giveaway-Small size			
(1967, 16pgs.)	.35	.70	1.05

FRIGHT
June, 1975 (August on inside)
Atlas/Seaboard Periodicals

#1-Origin The Son of Dracula; Frank Thorne

cover/art	.25	.50	.75

FRISKY ANIMALS (Formerly Frisky Fables)
#49, 1951 - #55, Sept, 1953
Star Publications

#49-55-Super Cat; L.B. Cole covers

	.35	.70	1.05

FRISKY ANIMALS ON PARADE (Formerly Parade;
#2, 11/57 - #3, 1958   Becomes Superspook)
Ajax-Farrell Publ. (Four Star Comic Corp.)

#2,3	.35	.70	1.05

FRISKY FABLES (Frisky Animals #49 on)
Spring, 1945 - #48, Jan, 1952
Premium Group/Novelty/Star Publ.

V1#1	2.00	4.00	6.00
2,3(1945)	1.50	3.00	4.50
4-7(1946)	1.00	2.00	3.00
V2#1-12(1947)	.80	1.60	2.40
V3#1-12(1948)	.60	1.20	1.80
#32-48(V4#1-12,V5#?;'49-50): #39-48-L.B.			
Cole covers	.50	1.00	1.50

Freckles #5, © NEA Service

Freddy #16, © CC

Freedom Fighters #3, © DC

The Frogmen #5, © DELL

Frontier Romances #1, © AVON

Frontier Western #4, © MCG

FRITZI RITZ (See Single Series #5,1(reprint),
United Comics & Comics on Parade)

FRITZI RITZ
Fall/48-#54,6/57; #55,9-11/57 - #59, 9-11/58
United Features Synd./St. John/Dell #55 on

	Good	Fine	Mint
No#(1948)-Special fall ish.			
	2.50	5.00	7.50
2-5	1.50	3.00	4.50
6-10	1.00	2.00	3.00
11-28,30-33,35-59	.75	1.50	2.25
29-5pg. Abbie & Slats; 1pg. Mamie by Russell			
Patterson	.90	1.80	2.70
34-Li'l Abner dressed as a woman (transvest-			
ism) cameo	1.50	3.00	4.50

NOTE: *Abbie & Slats in #11,18,27,29. Li'l
Abner in #35.*

FROGMAN COMICS
Jan-Feb, 1952 - #11, May, 1953
Hillman Periodicals

#1	1.25	2.50	3.75
2-4,6-11	.80	1.60	2.40
5-Krigstein story	2.00	4.00	6.00

FROGMEN, THE
#1258, Feb-Apr, 1962 - #12, Feb-Mar, 1965
Dell Publishing Co.

4-Color #1258-Evans art	2.00	4.00	6.00
#2,3-Evans art; partial Frazetta inks in			
both	2.50	5.00	7.50
4,6-12	.80	1.60	2.40
5-Toth art	2.00	4.00	6.00

FROM BEYOND THE UNKNOWN
10-11/69 - #25, 11-12/73 (#7-11,64pgs;#12-17,
National Periodical Publ.   52pgs.)

#1	.35	.70	1.05
2-5	.20	.40	.60
6-10: #7-Intro. Col. Glenn Merrit; Anderson			
art #7,8	.20	.40	.60
11-25: Star Rovers reprints begin #18,19.			
Space Museum in #23-25	.15	.30	.45

NOTE: *Adams covers-#3,6,8,9. Anderson covers-
#2,5,10,11,15-17,22; reprints-#3,4,6-8,10,11,
13-16,24,25. Infantino reprints-#1-5,7-19,23-
25. Kaluta cover-#18. Kubert covers-#1,7,12-
14. Toth reprint-#2. Wood inks-#13.*

FROM HERE TO INSANITY (Satire) (Eh #1-7)
(See Frantic & Frenzy)
#8, Feb, 1955 - V3#1, 1956
Charlton Comics

	Good	Fine	Mint
#8,9	2.00	4.00	6.00
10-Ditko cover, 3pgs.	3.00	6.00	9.00
11,12-All Kirby except 4 pgs.			
	5.00	10.00	15.00
V3#1(1956)-5pgs. Wolverton, 3pgs. Ditko;			
magazine format	2.50	5.00	7.50

FRONTIER DAYS
1956   (Giveaway)
Robin Hood Shoe Store (Brown Shoe)

#1	.50	1.00	1.50

FRONTIER DOCTOR (See 4-Color Comics #877)

FRONTIER FIGHTERS
Sept-Oct, 1955 - #8, Nov-Dec, 1956
National Periodical Publications

#1-Davy Crockett, Buffalo Bill by Kubert,			
Kit Carson begin	5.00	10.00	15.00
2-8	2.50	5.00	7.50

NOTE: *Buffalo Bill by Kubert in all.*

FRONTIER ROMANCES
Nov-Dec, 1949 - #2, Jan-Feb, 1950
Avon Periodicals/I.W.

#1-Used in Seduction of the Innocent, pg.180			
& ill."Erotic spanking in a western comic			
book"; reprinted/Campus Loves #5?			
	10.00	20.00	30.00
2 (Scarce)	4.00	8.00	12.00
#1-IW(reprints Avon's #1)	2.50	5.00	7.50
IW Reprint #9	1.00	2.00	3.00

FRONTIER SCOUT, DAN'L BOONE
#10, Jan, 1956 - 1965
Charlton Comics

#10-13	.50	1.00	1.50
V2#14(3/65)	.25	.50	.75

FRONTIER TRAIL (The Rider #1-5)
#6, May, 1958
Ajax/Farrell Publ.

#6	.50	1.00	1.50

FRONTIER WESTERN
Feb, 1956 - #10, Aug, 1957
Atlas Comics (PrPI)

#1	1.75	3.50	5.25
2,3,6-Williamson stories, 4pgs. each			
	2.50	5.00	7.50
4,7,9,10	.90	1.80	2.70

(Frontier Western cont'd) Good   Fine   Mint
5-Crandall, Baker, Wildey, Davis stories
                      2.50   5.00   7.50
  8-Crandall, Morrow, & Wildey stories
                      1.50   3.00   4.50
NOTE: *Drucker story-#4. Ringo Kid in #4.*

FRONTLINE COMBAT
July-Aug, 1951 - #15, Jan, 1954
E.C. Comics

	Good	Fine	Mint
#1-Kurtzman cover	40.00	80.00	120.00
2- " "	30.00	60.00	90.00
3- " "	22.00	44.00	66.00
4,5	14.00	28.00	42.00
6-10	10.00	20.00	30.00
11-15	8.00	16.00	24.00

NOTE: *Davis stories in all; covers-#11,12.*
Evans stories-#10-15. Heath story-#1. Kubert
story-#14. Kurtzman stories-#1-5; covers-
#1-9. Severin stories-#5-7,9,13,15. Severin/
Elder stories-#2-11; cover-#10. Toth stories-
#8,12. Wood stories-#1-4,6-10,12-15; covers-
#13-15. Special issues: #7(Iwo Jima), #9
(Civil War), #12(Air Force). (Canadian re-
prints known; see Table of Contents.)

FRONT PAGE COMIC BOOK
1945
Harvey Publications

#1-Kubert art; Man in Black by Powell
                    6.00 12.00 18.00

FROSTY THE SNOWMAN
1951 - 1961
Dell Publishing Co.

	Good	Fine	Mint
4-Color #359,435	1.00	2.00	3.00
4-Color #514,601,661	.70	1.40	2.10
4-Color #748,861,950,1065	.60	1.20	1.80
4-Color #1153,1272	.50	1.00	1.50

FRUITMAN SPECIAL
Dec, 1969   (68 pgs.)
Harvey Publications

#1-Funny Super Hero   .35   .70   1.05

F-TROOP (TV)
Aug, 1966 - #7, Aug, 1967
Dell Publishing Co.

	Good	Fine	Mint
#1	.25	.50	.75
2-7	.15	.30	.45

FUGITIVES FROM JUSTICE
Feb, 1952 - #5, Oct, 1952

St. John Publishing Co.

	Good	Fine	Mint
#1	2.00	4.00	6.00

  2-Matt Baker story; Vic Flint strip reprints
     begin, end #5   2.50   5.00   7.50
  3-Reprints panel from Authentic Police Cases
     that was used in Seduction of the Innocent,
     with changes   5.00 10.00 15.00

	Good	Fine	Mint
4	2.00	4.00	6.00
5-Bondage cover	3.00	6.00	9.00

FULL COLOR COMICS
1946
Fox Features Syndicate

No#   2.00   4.00   6.00

FULL OF FUN
Aug, 1957 - #2, Nov, 1957; 1964
Red Top(Decker Publ.)(Farrell)/I.W. Ent.

#1(1957)   .40   .80   1.20
2-reprints Bingo, the Monkey Doodle Boy
                  .40   .80   1.20
8-I.W. Reprint('64)   .25   .50   .75

FUN AT CHRISTMAS (See March of Comics #138)

FUN CLUB COMICS (See Interstate Theatres—)

FUN COMICS (Mighty Bear #13 on)
Jan, 1953 - #12, Oct, 1953
Star Publications

	Good	Fine	Mint
#9(Giant)	1.20	2.40	3.60
10-12-L. B. Cole covers	.80	1.60	2.40

FUNDAY FUNNIES (See Famous TV --, and
Harvey Hits #35,40)

FUN-IN (Hanna-Barbera)
Feb, 1970 - #10, 1/72; #11, 4/74 - #15, 12/74
Gold Key

#1-4,6-Dastardly & Muttley in Their Flying
   Machines-Perils of Penelope Pitstop in #1-
   4; It's the Wolf in all; Cattanooga Cats
   in #2-4   .15   .30   .45
  5,7-Motormouse & Autocat-Dastardly & Muttley in both; It's the Wolf in #7
                         .15   .30
  8,10-The Harlem Globetrotters-Dastardly &
   Muttley in #10   .15   .30
  9-Where's Huddles?-Dastardly & Muttley, Mot-
   ormouse & Autocat app.   .15   .30
11-Butch Cassidy   .15   .30
12,15-Speed Buggy; #15-52pgs. .20   .40
13-The Hair Bear Bunch   .15   .30

Frontline Combat #5, © WMG

Fugitives From Justice #2, © STJ

Funland Comics #1, © Croyden

The Funnies #2, © DELL

The Funnies #56, © DELL

Funny Book #5, © PMI

(Fun-In cont'd)	Good	Fine	Mint
14-Inch High Private Eye		.15	.30

NOTE: *52pg. issues had 16pgs. of adv. added.*

FUNKY PHANTOM, THE (TV)
Dec, 1971 - #13, Mar, 1975 (Hanna-Barbera)
Gold Key

#1	.20	.40	.60
2-13	.15	.30	.45

FUNLAND COMICS
1945
Croyden Publishers

#1	1.00	2.00	3.00

FUNNIES, THE (Also see Comic Cuts)
1929 - #36, 10/18/30 (10¢; 5¢ #22 on)(16pgs.)
Full tabloid size in color (not reprints)
Published every Saturday
Dell Publishing Co.

#1-My Big Brudder, Johnathan, Jazzbo & Jim,
Foxy Grandpa, Sniffy, Jimmy Jams & other
strips begin; first four-color comic newsstand publication; also contains magic,

puzzles & stories	40.00	80.00	120.00
2-21(1930, 30¢)	15.00	30.00	45.00
22(no#-7/12/30-5¢)	10.00	20.00	30.00

23(no#-7/19/30-5¢), #24(no#-7/26/30-5¢),
25(no#-8/2/30), #26(no#-8/9/30),
27(no#-8/16/30), #28(no#-8/23/30),
29(no#-8/30/30), #30(no#-9/6/30),
31(no#-9/13/30), #32(no#-9/20/30),
33(no#-9/27/30), #34(no#-10/4/30),
35(no#-10/11/30), #36(no#, no date-10/18/30)

each....	10.00	20.00	30.00

FUNNIES, THE (New Funnies #65 on)
Oct, 1936 - #64, May, 1942
Dell Publishing Co.

#1-Tailspin Tommy, Mutt & Jeff, Alley Oop,
Capt. Easy, Don Dixon begin

	40.00	80.00	120.00
2	20.00	40.00	60.00
3	15.00	30.00	45.00
4	10.00	20.00	30.00
5	9.00	18.00	27.00
6-10	8.00	16.00	24.00
11-29	7.00	14.00	21.00
30-John Carter of Mars begins by Edgar Rice			
Burroughs	15.00	30.00	45.00

31-44: #33-John Coleman Burroughs art begins

on John Carter	10.00	20.00	30.00

45-Origin Phantasmo, the Master of the World
& intro. his sidekick Whizzer McGee

	10.00	20.00	30.00

	Good	Fine	Mint
46-The Black Knight begins,			
47-50	9.00	18.00	27.00
51-56-Last ERB John Carter of Mars			
	9.00	18.00	27.00
57-Intro. & origin Captain Midnight			
	15.00	30.00	45.00
58-60	9.00	18.00	27.00
61-Andy Panda begins by Walter Lantz,			
62-64-Last C. Midnight	10.00	20.00	30.00

NOTE: *McWilliams art in many issues on "Rex
King of the Deep."*

FUNNIES ANNUAL, THE
1959 (B&W)($1.00)(Tabloid-size, approx.
Avon Periodicals   7"x10")

#1-(Rare)-Features the best newspaper comic
strips of the year: Archie, Snuffy Smith,
Beetle Baily, Henry, Blondie, Steve Canyon,
Buz Sawyer, The Little King, Hi & Lois,
Popeye & others. Also has a chronological
history of the comics from 2000 B.C. to

1959.	7.00	14.00	21.00

FUNNIES ON PARADE (Premium)
1933 (Probably the 1st comic book)(36 pgs.)
No date or publisher listed   (Slick cover)
Eastern Color Printing Co.

No#-Contains Sunday page reprints of Mutt &
Jeff, Joe Palooka, Hairbreadth Harry,
Reg'lar Fellers, Skippy, & others (10,000
print run). This book was printed for
Proctor & Gamble to be given away & came
out before Famous Funnies or Century of

Comics.	175.00	350.00	525.00

FUNNY ANIMALS (See Fawcett's Funny Animals)

FUNNYBONE
1944   (132 pgs.)
La Salle Publishing Co.

	1.20	2.40	3.60

FUNNY BOOK (-- Magazine)(Hocus Pocus #9)
Dec, 1942 - #8, June-July, 1946
Parents' Magazine Press

#1-Funny animal	1.50	3.00	4.50
2-8	1.00	2.00	3.00

FUNNY COMIC TUNES (See Funny Tunes)

FUNNY FABLES
Sept, 1957 - #2, Nov, 1957
Decker Publications (Red Top Comics)

(Funny Fables cont'd)	Good	Fine	Mint
V2#1,2	.20	.40	.60

FUNNY FILMS
Sept-Oct, 1949 - #29, May-June, 1954
American Comics Group(Michel Publ/Titan Publ)

	Good	Fine	Mint
#1	1.75	3.50	5.25
2-10	1.25	2.50	3.75
11-29	.80	1.60	2.40

FUNNY FOLKS (Hollywood--, on cvr.only #17-30; becomes Hollywood Funny Folks #31 on)
4-5/46 - #30, 1/51
National Periodical Publications

	Good	Fine	Mint
#1	3.00	6.00	9.00
2-5	1.50	3.00	4.50
6-10	1.20	2.40	3.60
11-30	.80	1.60	2.40

FUNNY FROLICS
Summer, 1945 - #5, Dec, 1946
Timely/Marvel Comics (SPI)

	Good	Fine	Mint
#1-4	1.00	2.00	3.00
5-Kurtzman art	2.50	5.00	7.50

FUNNY FUNNIES
1943   (68 pgs.)
Nedor Publishers

	Good	Fine	Mint
#1	2.00	4.00	6.00

FUNNYMAN
Dec, 1947; #1, Jan, 1948 - #7, Aug, 1948
Magazine Enterprises

No#(12/47)-Prepublication B&W undistributed
    copy by Siegel & Shuster-(5-3/4x8"),16pgs;
    Sold in San Francisco in 1976 for $300.00

#1-By Siegel & Shuster	5.00	10.00	15.00
2-5-By Siegel & Shuster	3.00	6.00	9.00
6,7-(#7 exist?)	2.00	4.00	6.00

FUNNY MOVIES (See 3-D Funny Movies)

FUNNY PAGES (The Comics #1; Comics Funny
#4, Sept, 1936 - #45, 1942   Pages #2,3)
Centaur Publications

#4,5	8.00	16.00	24.00
6-The Clock begins(2pg. strip), ends #11	10.00	20.00	30.00
7-11	8.00	16.00	24.00
12-20(V2#1-9)	7.00	14.00	21.00
21-1st app. of the Arrow by Gustavson (V2#10)	15.00	30.00	45.00

	Good	Fine	Mint
22,23(V2#11,12)	10.00	20.00	30.00
24-33(V3#1-10)	10.00	20.00	30.00
34-The Owl & The Phantom Rider app.; origin Mantoka, Maker of Magic by Jack Cole	12.00	24.00	36.00
35-42-Last Arrow	10.00	20.00	30.00
43-45	8.00	16.00	24.00

FUNNY PICTURE STORIES (Becomes Comic Pages
Nov, 1936 - V3#3, May, 1939   with V3#4)
Centaur Publications

V1#1-The Clock begins	20.00	40.00	60.00
2	10.00	20.00	30.00
3,5-11	7.00	14.00	21.00
4-Eisner art	8.00	16.00	24.00
V2#1-Jack Strand begins	6.00	12.00	18.00
2-11	5.00	10.00	15.00
V3#1-3	5.00	10.00	15.00

FUNNY STUFF (Becomes The Dodo & the Frog #80)
Summer, 1944 - #79, July-Aug, 1954
All-American/National Periodical Publ.

#1-The 3 Mouseketeers & The "Terrific What- zit" begin	5.00	10.00	15.00
2-5	2.50	5.00	7.50
6-15	1.50	3.00	4.50
16-21	1.20	2.40	3.60
22-Superman cameo	2.50	5.00	7.50
23-30	1.00	2.00	3.00
31-79-Dodo & the Frog	.60	1.20	1.80
Wheaties Giveaway(1946, 6½x8¼")	4.00	8.00	12.00

FUNNY 3-D
December, 1953
Harvey Publications

#1	5.00	10.00	15.00

FUNNY TUNES (Animated Funny Comic Tunes #16-
#22; Funny Comic Tunes #23, on covers only;
formerly Human Torch; Oscar #24 on)
#16, Summer, 1944 - #23, Fall, 1946
U.S.A. Comics Magazine Corp. (Timely)

#16-22	1.50	3.00	4.50
23-Kurtzman art	2.50	5.00	7.50

FUNNY TUNES
Aug-Sept, 1953 - #3, Dec-Jan, 1953-54
Avon Periodicals

#1-Space Mouse	1.50	3.00	4.50
2,3-Space Mouse-#3	1.20	2.40	3.60

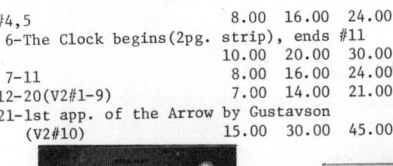

Funny Folks #1. © DC   Funny Picture Stories V3#2, © CEN   Funny Stuff #34, © DC

Funny World #1, © Marbak Press

Future World #2, © G.W. Dougherty

Gabby Hayes #21, © FAW

FUNNY WORLD
1947 - 1948
Marbak Press

	Good	Fine	Mint
#1-3-Newspaper strip reprints			
	1.35	2.75	4.00

FUNTASTIC WORLD OF HANNA-BARBERA, THE
Dec, 1977 - #4, Dec, 1978 ($1.25)(Oversized)
Marvel Comics Group

#1-The Flintstones Christmas Party(12/77);
#2-Yogi Bear's Easter Parade(3/78); #3-Laff-
a-lympics(6/78), #4

each.... .40	.80	1.20

FUN TIME
1953 - #4, Winter, 1953-54
Ace Periodicals

#1,2	.50	1.00	1.50
3,4(100pgs. each)	1.00	2.00	3.00

FUN WITH SANTA CLAUS   (See March of Comics
#11,108,325)

FURY (Straight Arrow's Horse--)(See A-1 #119)

FURY   (TV)
Aug, 1957 - 1962
Dell Publishing Co./Gold Key

4-Color #781,885,975	.90	1.80	2.70
4-Color #1031,1080,1133,1172,1218,1296,			
#01292-208(#1-'62)	.80	1.60	2.40
#10020-211(11/62-G.K.)	.80	1.60	2.40
(See March of Comics #200)			

FUTURE COMICS
June, 1940 - #4, Sept, 1940
David McKay Publications

#1-The Lone Ranger, The Phantom, & Saturn
  Against the Earth begin

	20.00	40.00	60.00
2-4	12.00	24.00	36.00

FUTURE WORLD COMICS
Summer, 1946 - #2, Fall, 1946
George W. Dougherty

#1,2	1.50	3.00	4.50

G-8   (See G-Eight)

GABBY   (Formerly Ken Shannon)
#11, July, 1953; #2, 9/53 - #9, 9/54
Quality Comics Group

	Good	Fine	Mint
#11(#1)(7/53)	1.00	2.00	3.00
2-9	.65	1.35	2.00

GABBY GOB   (See Harvey Hits #85,90,94,97,100,
103,106,109)

GABBY HAYES WESTERN
Nov, 1948 - #50, Jan, 1953; 12/54 - #59, 1/57
Fawcett/Toby Press/Charlton Comics #51 on

#1	7.00	14.00	21.00
2-10	3.00	6.00	9.00
11-20	2.00	4.00	6.00
21-50	1.75	3.50	5.25
51-59(Charlton '54-57)	1.35	2.75	4.00
#1(Toby)(12/53)	3.00	6.00	9.00
Quaker Oats Giveaway #1-5(1951)			
	2.00	4.00	6.00

GAGS
7/37; 7/42 (13-3/4"x10-3/4")
United Features Synd./Triangle Publ. #9

#1(7/37)-52pgs.;20pgs. Grin & Bear It, Fell-			
ow Citizen	4.00	8.00	12.00
V1#9-(36pgs., 15¢)	2.50	5.00	7.50

GAG STRIPS
Aug, 1942 (13-3/4"x10-3/4")(36pgs.)(15¢)
Triangle Publications

V1#1-Comic strips by 24 different cartoonists			
	2.50	5.00	7.50

GALLANT MEN, THE   (TV)
October, 1963
Gold Key

#1(10085-310)-Manning art	.90	1.80	2.70

GALLEGHER, BOY REPORTER   (TV)
May, 1965   (Disney)
Gold Key

#1(10149-505)	.60	1.20	1.80

GANDY GOOSE
3/53 - #5, 11/53; #5, Fall/56 - #6, Sum/58
St. John Publ. Co./Pines #5,6

#1	1.00	2.00	3.00
2-5(1953)(St. John)	.50	1.00	1.50
5,6(Pines,'56-58)	.35	.70	1.05

GANG BUSTERS
1938 - 1943
David McKay/Dell Publishing Co.

(Gang Busters cont'd)	Good	Fine	Mint
Feature Book #17(McKay)('38)			
	12.00	24.00	36.00
Black & White #10('39) (Scarce)			
	20.00	50.00	80.00
Black & White #17('41)	12.00	30.00	48.00
4-Color #7(1940)	12.00	24.00	36.00
4-Color #23,24('42-43)	10.00	20.00	30.00

GANG BUSTERS (Radio/TV)
Dec-Jan, 1947-48 - #67, Dec-Jan, 1958-59
National Periodical Publications

	Good	Fine	Mint
#1	5.00	10.00	15.00
2	2.50	5.00	7.50
3-10	1.75	3.50	5.25
11-13,15,16,18-30	1.25	2.50	3.75
14,17-Frazetta story in both, 8pgs. each			
	10.00	20.00	30.00
31-67	1.00	2.00	3.00

GANGSTERS AND GUN MOLLS
Sept, 1951 - #4, June, 1952
Avon Periodical/Realistic Comics

#1-Wood art, 1pg.	8.00	16.00	24.00
2-Check story, 8pgs. + Kamen story			
	6.00	12.00	18.00
3,4	5.00	10.00	15.00

GANGSTERS CAN'T WIN
1948 - 1951
D. S. Publishing Co.

#1	2.50	5.00	7.50
2,3	1.50	3.00	4.50
4,5,7-10	1.25	2.50	3.75
6-Ingels story	2.00	4.00	6.00
11-24 (exist?)	1.00	2.00	3.00

GANG WORLD
#5, Nov, 1952 - #6, Jan, 1953
Standard Comics

#5-Bondage cover	1.50	3.00	4.50
6	1.00	2.00	3.00

GARRISON'S GORILLAS (TV)
Jan, 1968 - #5, Oct, 1969
Dell Publishing Co.

#1-5: #5-reprints #1	.25	.50	.75

GASOLINE ALLEY (Hardcover)
1929 (B&W daily strip reprints)(7x8-3/4")
Reilly & Lee Publishers

By King (84 pgs.)	8.00	16.00	24.00

GASOLINE ALLEY
Sept, 1950 - #2, 1950   (Newspaper reprints)
Star Publications

	Good	Fine	Mint
#1-Contains 1 pg. intro. history of the strip (The Life of Skeezix); reprints 15 scenes of highlights from 1921-35, + an adventure from 1935 & 36 strips; a 2-page filler is included on the life of the creator Frank King, with photo of the cartoonist			
	5.00	10.00	15.00
2-('36,'37 reprints)	3.00	6.00	9.00

(See Super Book #21)

GASP!
March, 1967 - #4, Aug, 1967
American Comics Group

#1-L.S.D. story	.80	1.60	2.40
2-4	.35	.70	1.05

GAY COMICS (Honeymoon #41)
1944 (no month) - #40, Oct, 1949
Timely Comics/USA Comic Mag. Co. #17-24

#1-Wolverton's Powerhouse Pepper; Tessie the Typist begins	10.00	20.00	30.00
2-10	2.50	5.00	7.50
11-16	1.50	3.00	4.50
17-29-Wolverton art in all; Kurtzman in #24, 29	5.00	10.00	15.00
30,31,33,36,37-Kurtzman's "Hey Look"			
	2.00	4.00	6.00
32,35,38-40	1.20	2.40	3.60
34-Three Kurtzman's "Hey Look"			
	3.00	6.00	9.00

GAY COMICS (Also see Tickle & Smile Comics)
1955   (52 pgs.; 5x7¼")   (7¢)
Modern Store Publ.

#1	.40	.80	1.20

GAY PURR-EE (See Movie Comics)

GEEK, THE (See Brother Power --)

G-8 AND HIS BATTLE ACES
October, 1966
Gold Key

#1(10184-610)	1.50	3.00	4.50

GEM COMICS
April, 1942; 1945
Spotlight Publishers

#1(1942)	3.00	6.00	9.00

Gang Busters #10, © DC

Gangsters & Gun Molls #3, © AVON

Gangsters Can't Win #6, © DS

Gene Autry #4, © FAW   George Pal's Puppetoons #17, © FAW   Georgie #18, © MCG

(Gem Comics cont'd)   Good   Fine   Mint
#1(1945)-Classic bondage cover; Little Mohee,
   Steve Strong   3.00   6.00   9.00

GENE AUTRY (See March of Comics #25,28,39,
54,78,90,104,120,135,150)

GENE AUTRY COMICS (Dell takes over with #11)
1941 - 1944   (68 pgs.)
Fawcett Publications

#1 (Rare)   50.00 100.00 150.00
2   25.00   50.00   75.00
3-5   22.00   44.00   66.00
6-10   15.00   30.00   45.00

GENE AUTRY COMICS (-- & Champion #102 on)
June, 1946 - #121, Jan, 1959
Dell Publishing Co.

#11,12(1943-44)-Continuation of Fawcett
   series   17.50   35.00   52.50
4-Color #47(1944)   17.50   35.00   52.50
4-Color #57('44),66('45)   14.00   28.00   42.00
4-Color #75,83('45)   10.00   20.00   30.00
4-Color #93,100('45)   8.00   16.00   24.00
#1(5-6/46)   12.00   24.00   36.00
2(7-8/46)   7.00   14.00   21.00
3-5   4.50   9.00   13.50
6-10   3.50   7.00   10.50
11-30   2.50   5.00   7.50
31-60   1.50   3.00   4.50
61-80   1.20   2.40   3.60
81-121: #118-Manning art   1.00   2.00   3.00
Pillsbury Premium('47)-36pgs., 6½x7½" -
   Games, Comics, Puzzles 5.00   10.00   15.00
2½"x6-3/4" Quaker Oats Giveaway (5 different-
   1950)   each.... 2.50   5.00   7.50
3-D Giveaway (5 different-1953, pocket-size)
                            2.50   5.00   7.50
NOTE: *Jesse Marsh* art: 4-Color #66,75,93,
100, #1-25,27-37,39,40.

GENE AUTRY TIM (Formerly Superman-Tim)
(Becomes Tim in Space)
1950   (Half-Size)(Black & White Giveaway)
Tim Stores

Several issues (All Scarce)
                            4.00   8.00   12.00

GENE AUTRY'S CHAMPION
1950; #3, Aug-Oct, 1951 - #19, Aug, 1955
Dell Publishing Co.

4-Color #287('50)   2.25   4.50   6.75
4-Color #319('51), #3   1.50   3.00   4.50
#4-19   1.00   2.00   3.00

GENERAL DOUGLAS MACARTHUR
1951
Fox Features Syndicate
                            Good   Fine   Mint
No#   3.00   6.00   9.00

GENTLE BEN (TV)
Feb, 1968 - #5, Oct, 1969
Dell Publishing Co.

#1   .20   .40   .60
2-5: #5-reprints #1   .15   .30   .45

GEORGE OF THE JUNGLE (TV)
Feb, 1969 - #2, Oct, 1969 (Jay Ward)
Gold Key

#1,2   .25   .50   .75

GEORGE PAL'S PUPPETOONS
Dec, 1945 - #18, Dec, 1947; #19, 1950
Fawcett Publications

#1-Capt. Marvel on cover   6.00   12.00   18.00
2-10   2.50   5.00   7.50
11-19   2.00   4.00   6.00

GEORGIE (-- & Judy #24 on)
Spring, 1945 - #39, Oct, 1952
Timely Comics/GPI #1-34

#1-Dave Berg art   2.00   4.00   6.00
2-8   1.50   3.00   4.50
9,10-Kurtzman's "Hey Look"
                            2.00   4.00   6.00
11,12   .90   1.80   2.70
13-Kurtzman's "Hey Look", 3 pgs.
                            2.50   5.00   7.50
14-Wolverton art(1pg.) & Kurtzman's "Hey
   Look"   3.00   6.00   9.00
15,16,18-24,26-39   .80   1.60   2.40
17-Kurtzman's "Hey Look", 1pg.
                            1.75   3.50   5.25
25-Painted cover by classic pin-up artist
   Peter Driben   1.50   3.00   4.50

GERALD McBOING-BOING AND THE NEARSIGHTED MR.
MAGOO (Mr. Magoo #6)
Aug-Oct, 1952 - #5, Aug-Oct, 1953
Dell Publishing Co.

#1   2.00   4.00   6.00
2-5   1.20   2.40   3.60

GERONIMO
1950 - #4, Feb, 1952
Avon Periodicals

#1-Indian Fighter-Maneely art

184

(Geronimo cont'd)	Good	Fine	Mint
	5.00	10.00	15.00
2-On the Warpath; Kit West app.; Kinstler cover/story	4.00	8.00	12.00
3-And His Apache Murderers; Kinstler cover/ two stories	4.00	8.00	12.00
4-Savage Raids of; Kinstler cover	3.00	6.00	9.00

GERONIMO JONES
Sept, 1971 - #9, Jan, 1973
Charlton Comics

	Good	Fine	Mint
#1	.15	.30	.45
2-9		.15	.30

GET LOST
Feb-Mar, 1954 - #3, June-July, 1954 (Satire)
Mikeross Publications

	Good	Fine	Mint
#1	3.00	6.00	9.00
2-Has 4pg. E.C. parady featuring the "Sewer Keeper"	2.50	5.00	7.50
3	2.00	4.00	6.00

GET SMART (TV)
June, 1966 - #8, Sept, 1967
Dell Publishing Co.

	Good	Fine	Mint
#1	.35	.70	1.05
2-Ditko art	.40	.80	1.20
3-8	.25	.50	.75

GHOST
1951 - 1954
Fiction House Magazines

	Good	Fine	Mint
#1	4.00	8.00	12.00
2-8	2.50	5.00	7.50
9-Bondage cover	3.00	6.00	9.00
10,11-Dr. Drew by Grandenetti in each- Reprinted from Rangers; Evans story-#11	3.00	6.00	9.00

GHOST BREAKERS (Also see (CC) Sherlock Holmes & Racket Squad in Action)
Sept, 1948 - #2, Nov, 1948   (52 pgs.)
Street & Smith Publications

	Good	Fine	Mint
#1-Powell art; Dr. Neff (magician) app.	4.00	8.00	12.00
2	3.00	6.00	9.00

GHOST CASTLE (See Tales of --)

GHOSTLY HAUNTS (Formerly Ghost Manor)
#20, 9/71 - #53, 12/76; #54, 9/77 - #55, 10/77; #56, 1/78 - #58, 4/78

Charlton Comics

	Good	Fine	Mint
#20,21		.15	.30
22-41,43-58: #27-Dr. Graves x-over. #39-origin & 1st app. Destiny Fox	.10	.20	
42-Newton cover/story	.15	.30	.45
#40(Modern Comics reprint,1977)		.15	.30

NOTE: _Ditko stories-#22-25,27,28,32-34,36-39, 44; covers-#22-27,30,33-38. Glanzman story- #20. Howard story-#42. Sutton cover-#39._

GHOSTLY TALES (Blue Beetle #50-54)
#55,4-5/66 - #124,12/76; #125,9/77 - Present
Charlton Comics

	Good	Fine	Mint
#55-Intro. Dr. Graves	.20	.40	.60
56-70: Dr. Graves ends	.15	.30	.45
71-113,115-133		.15	.30
114-Newton story	.15	.30	.45

NOTE: _Ditko stories-#55,57,58,60,61,67,69,70, 72,73,75-89,92,95,97,99,100-110,112-114,115, 120; covers-#67,69,77,78,83,84,86-90,92-97, 99,107,122. Howard stories-#95,98,117; covers- #98,107,120,121. Newton cover-#115. Sutton story-#112,113._

GHOSTLY WEIRD STORIES (Formerly Blue Bolt Weird)
#120, 9/53 - #124, Sept, 1954
Star Publications

	Good	Fine	Mint
#120,121-Jo-Jo reprints	3.00	6.00	9.00
122-The Mask, Rulah reprt	3.00	6.00	9.00
123-Jo-Jo, 2 Disbrow stys	3.00	6.00	9.00
124-Torpedo Man	2.50	5.00	7.50

NOTE: _Disbrow art-#120-124. L. B. Cole covers-all issues._

GHOST MANOR (Ghostly Haunts #20 on)
July, 1968 - #19, July, 1971
Charlton Comics

	Good	Fine	Mint
#1	.25	.50	.75
2-10	.20	.40	.60
11-19	.15	.30	.45

NOTE: _Ditko stories-#13-16,18,19; covers-#15, 18,19._

GHOST MANOR (2nd Series)
10/71 - #32, 12/76; #33, 9/77 - Present
Charlton Comics

	Good	Fine	Mint
#1	.20	.40	.60
2-7,9,10		.15	.30
8-Wood story	.15	.30	.45
11-17,19,20		.10	.20
18,22-Newton cover/art	.15	.30	.45
21-E-Man, Blue Beetle, Capt. Atom cameos	.15	.30	.45

Ghost #4. © FH

Ghostly Weird Stories #120. © STAR

Ghost Rider #12. © ME

The Ghost Rider #1,(1967), © MCG   Giant Comics Edition #8, © STJ   Giant Comics Edition #12, © STJ

(Ghost Manor cont'd)

	Good	Fine	Mint
23-41		.10	.20
#19(Modern Comics reprint,1977)		.15	.30

NOTE: *Ditko stories-#1-5,7,8,12,13,15-18,20-22,29; covers-#2-7,28. Howard story-#21.*

GHOST RIDER (See A-1 Comics)
1950 - 1954
Magazine Enterprises

	Good	Fine	Mint
#1(A-1#27)-Origin G.R.	20.00	40.00	60.00
#2(A-1#29),3(A-1#31),4(A-1#34),5(A-1#37)-All Frazetta covers only	18.00	36.00	54.00
#6(A-1#44),7(A-1#51)	6.00	12.00	18.00
#8(A-1#57),9(A-1#69),10(A-1#71)	5.00	10.00	15.00
11(A-1#75),12(A-1#80),13(A-1#84),14(A-1#112)	4.50	9.00	13.50

NOTE: *Dick Ayers art in all.*

GHOST RIDER (See Night Rider)
Feb, 1967 - #7, Nov, 1967
Marvel Comics Group

	Good	Fine	Mint
#1-Origin G.R.; Kid Colt reprint	.60	1.20	1.80
2-7	.40	.80	1.20

GHOST RIDER (See Marvel Spotlight)
Sept, 1973 - Present (Super-Hero)
Marvel Comics Group

	Good	Fine	Mint
#1	.70	1.40	2.10
2-5	.50	1.00	1.50
6-9	.30	.60	.90
10-Ploog art	.40	.80	1.20
11-20	.25	.50	.75
21-33	.20	.40	.60

NOTE: *Kirby covers-#21-23. Mooney art-#6,8. Newton story-#23.*

GHOSTS
Sept-Oct, 1971 - Present (#1-5, 52pgs.)
National Periodical Publications/DC Comics

	Good	Fine	Mint
#1	.40	.80	1.20
2-Wood art	.25	.50	.75
3-10	.20	.40	.60
11-30	.15	.30	.45
31-73: #40-68pgs.		.15	.30

NOTE: *Alcala stories-#9,15,17-19,21,23-25,28, 33,34. Kaluta cover-#7. Redondo story-#13,45.*

GHOSTS SPECIAL (See DC Special Series #7)

GHOST STORIES (See Amazing Ghost Stories)

GHOST STORIES

9-11/62; #2, 4-6/63 - #37, 10/73
Dell Publishing Co.

	Good	Fine	Mint
#12-295-211-Written by John Stanley	1.20	2.40	3.60
#2-10	.35	.70	1.05
11-37	.25	.50	.75

NOTE: *#21-34,36,37 all reprint earlier issues.*

GHOUL TALES (Magazine)
Nov, 1970 - #5, July, 1971 (52pgs.) (B&W)
Stanley Publications

	Good	Fine	Mint
#1-Aragon pre-code reprints; Mr. Mystery as host; bondage cover	.80	1.60	2.40
2-(1/71)Reprint/Climax#1	.40	.80	1.20
3-(3/71)	.40	.80	1.20
4-(5/71)Reprints story "The Way to a Man's Heart" used in Seduction of the Innocent	1.35	2.75	4.00
5-ACG reprints	.40	.80	1.20

NOTE: *#1-4 contain pre-code Aragon reprints.*

GIANT BOY BOOK OF COMICS (See Boy)
1945 (Hardcover) (240 pgs.)
Newsbook Publications (Gleason)

	Good	Fine	Mint
#1-Crimebuster & Young Robin Hood	15.00	30.00	45.00

GIANT COMIC ALBUM
1972 (52 pgs.) (11x14")(B&W)(59¢)
King Features Syndicate

Newspaper reprints: Little Iodine, Katzen-jammer Kids, Henry, Mandrake the Magician ('59 Falk), Popeye, Beetle Bailey, Barney Google, Blondie, Flash Gordon ('68-69 Dan Barry), & Snuffy Smith 1.50 3.00 4.50

GIANT COMICS
Summer, 1957 - #3, Winter, 1957 (100pgs.)(25¢)
Charlton Comics

	Good	Fine	Mint
#1-Atomic Mouse, Hoppy app.	.50	1.00	1.50
2,3-Atomic Mouse, Rabbit, Christmas Book	.50	1.00	1.50

GIANT COMICS (See Wham-O Giant Comics)

GIANT COMICS EDITION (See Terry-Toons)
1947 - 1950 (All 100-164 pgs.) (25¢)
St. John Publishing Co.

	Good	Fine	Mint
#1-Mighty Mouse	4.00	8.00	12.00
2	2.00	4.00	6.00
3-Terry-Toons Album-100pgs.	4.00	8.00	12.00

(Giant Comics Ed. cont'd)　Good　Fine　Mint
4-Crime comics　　　　4.00　8.00　12.00
5-Police Case Book(4/49)-Contents varies;
　contains remaindered St. John books - some
　volumes contain 5 copies rather than 4,
　with 160 pages. Matt Baker cover
　　　　　　　　　　4.00　8.00　12.00
5A-Terry-Toons Album, 132 pgs.
　　　　　　　　　　4.00　8.00　12.00
6-Western Picture Stories; Baker cover, 3
　stories; The Sky Chief, Blue Monk, Ven-
　trilo app.; Tuska art　3.00　6.00　9.00
7-Contains a teen-age romance + 3 Mopsy
　comics　　　　　　　2.50　5.00　7.50
8-The Adventures of Mighty Mouse (10/49)
　　　　　　　　　　4.00　8.00　12.00
9-Romance confession stories; 4 Kubert stor-
　ies + Baker　　　　6.00　12.00　18.00
10-Terry-Toons　　　　3.50　7.00　10.50
11-Western Picture Stories-Baker cover, 4
　stories; The Sky Chief, Desperado, & Blue
　Monk app.　　　　　3.00　6.00　9.00
12-Baker cover; 4 St. John romance comics;
　Many Baker stories　6.00　12.00　18.00
13-Four romance comics; Baker, Kubert art
　　　　　　　　　　6.00　12.00　18.00
14-Mighty Mouse Album　3.50　7.00　10.50
15-Romances(4 love comics)6.00　12.00　18.00
16-Little Audrey, Abbott & Costello, Casper
　　　　　　　　　　3.00　6.00　9.00
NOTE: *The above books contain remaindered
comics and contents could vary with each issue.*

GIANT COMICS EDITIONS
1940's　(132 pgs.)
United Features Syndicate

#1-Abbie & Slats, Abbott & Costello, Jim
　Hardy, Ella Cinders, Iron Vic
　　　　　　　　　　5.00　10.00　15.00
　2-Jim Hardy & Gordo　4.00　8.00　12.00
NOTE: *Above books contain rebound copies;
contents can vary.*

GIANT COMICS TO COLOR
1975 - 1976　(16x11")　(69¢)
Whitman Publishing Co.

1714-Wonder Woman "The Menace of the Mole
　Men"(1975)
1715-Shazam! "Double Trouble(1975)
1716-Superman "Luthor's Lost Land"(1975)
1717-Batman "Comedy of Tears"(1975)
1642-Spider-Man "Weather Forecast: Danger"
　(1976)
1663-Captain America "The Challenge of Super
　Sport"(1976)
1664-Superman "Braniac's Biggest Plot"(1976)

　　　　　　　　　　Good　Fine　Mint
1671-Batman "Four Birds of a Feather"(1976)
　　　　　　　　　　.40　.80　1.20

GIANT GRAB BAG OF COMICS　(See Archie All-
Star Specials)

GIANTS　(See Thrilling True Stories of --)

GIANT-SIZE　(Avengers, Captain America, Capt-
ain Marvel, Conan, Daredevil, Defenders, Fantastic Four, Hulk, Invaders, Iron Man, Kid
Colt, Man-Thing, Master of Kung Fu, Power
Man, Spider-Man, Super-Villain Team-Up, Thor,
Werewolf, and X-Men are listed under their
own titles.)

GIANT-SIZE CHILLERS　(G-S Dracula #2)
June, 1974; Feb, 1975 - #3, Aug, 1975 (35¢)
Marvel Comics Group

#1-(6/74)-Tomb of Dracula(52pgs.)-Origin &
　1st app. Lilith, Dracula's daughter
　　　　　　　　　　.50　1.00　1.50
　1-(2/75)(50¢)(68pgs.)-Alcala story
　　　　　　　　　　.40　.80　1.20
　2-(5/75)　　　　　.35　.70　1.05
　3-(8/75)-Wrightson cover/story; Smith
　reprint　　　　　　.50　1.00　1.50
NOTE: *Everett reprint-#2/Advs. Into Weird
Worlds #10.*

GIANT SIZE CREATURES　(G-S Werewolf #2)
July, 1974　(52 pgs.)　(35¢)
Marvel Comics Group

#1-Werewolf, Tigra app.; Crandall reprint
　　　　　　　　　　.40　.80　1.20

GIANT-SIZE DRACULA　(Formerly G-S Chillers)
#2, Sept, 1974 - #5, June, 1975　(50¢)
Marvel Comics Group

#2　　　　　　　　　.60　1.20　1.80
　3-Wolverton reprt/Uncanny Tales #6
　　　　　　　　　　.50　1.00　1.50
　4,5　　　　　　　.40　.80　1.20

GIANT-SIZE SUPER HEROES
June, 1974　(35¢)
Marvel Comics Group

#1-Spider-Man vs. Man-Wolf .80　1.60　2.40

GIANT-SIZE SUPER-STARS　(G-S Fantastic-4 #2)
May, 1974　(35¢)
Marvel Comics Group

Giant Comics Edition #13. © STJ

Giant-Size Chillers #1. © MCG

Giant-Size Super-Stars #1. © MCG

G.I. Combat #33, © QUA

G.I. In Battle #1, © AJAX

G.I. Jane #1, © TM

(Giant-Size Super-Stars cont'd)

	Good	Fine	Mint
#1-Fantastic-4, Thing, Hulk by Buckler; Kirbyish art	.80	1.60	2.40

GIANT SPECTACULAR COMICS (See Archie All-Star Specials)

GIANT SUMMER FUN BOOK (See Terry-Toons --)

GIANTS (Baseball) (See New York --)

G.I. COMBAT
Oct, 1952 - #43, Dec, 1956
Quality Comics Group

#1-Crandall cover	5.00	10.00	15.00
2,7-9	2.00	4.00	6.00
3-5,10-Crandall cvr/sty.	3.50	7.00	10.50
6-Crandall story	2.50	5.00	7.50
11-20	1.80	3.60	5.40
21-33,35-43	1.50	3.00	4.50
34-Crandall story	2.00	4.00	6.00

G.I. COMBAT
#44, Jan, 1957 - Present
National Periodical Publications/DC Comics

#44	3.00	6.00	9.00
45	2.00	4.00	6.00
46-50	1.50	3.00	4.50
51-60	1.00	2.00	3.00
61-66,68-80	.90	1.80	2.70
67-1st Tank Killer	1.00	2.00	3.00
81,82,84-86,88-100	.60	1.20	1.80
83-1st Big Al, Little Al, & Charlie Cigar			
	1.00	2.00	3.00
87-1st Haunted Tank	1.20	2.40	3.60
101-113,115-120	.40	.80	1.20
114-Origin Haunted Tank	.70	1.40	2.10
121-137,139,140	.25	.50	.75
138-Intro. The Losers (Capt. Storm, Gunner/ Sarge, Johnny Cloud) in H. T.			
	.25	.50	.75
141-150,152,154	.20	.40	.60
151,153-Medal of Honor series by Maurer			
	.20	.40	.60
155-208	.15	.30	.45
209-211 ($1.00 size)	.20	.40	

NOTE: _Adams covers-#168,201,202. Drucker stories-#48,61,63,66,71,72,76,134,140,141,144,147, 148,153. Evans stories-#135,138,158,164,166. Kubert/Heath stories in many issues. Morrow art-#159-161(2pgs.). Redondo story-#189. Wildey story-#153. Johnny Cloud app.-#112, 115,120. Mlle. Marie app.-#123,132,200. Sgt. Rock app.-#111-113,115,120,125,141,146,147, 149,200. USS Stevens by Glanzman-#145,150-53, 157._

G.I. COMICS (Also see Jeep & Overseas Comics)
1945 (distributed to U.S. armed forces)
Giveaways

	Good	Fine	Mint
#33-49-Contains Prince Valiant by Foster, Blondie, Smilin' Jack, Mickey Finn, Terry & the Pirates, Donald Duck, Alley Oop, Moon Mullins, & Capt. Easy strip reprints			
	3.00	6.00	9.00

GIDGET (TV)
April, 1966 - #2, Dec, 1966
Dell Publishing Co.

#1,2	.20	.40	.60

GIFT COMICS (50¢)
1941 - #4, 1949 (#1-3, 324pgs.; #4, 152pgs.)
Fawcett Publications

#1-Captain Marvel, Bulletman, Golden Arrow, Ibis the Invincible, Mr. Scarlet, & Spy Smasher app.	75.00	187.50	300.00
2	60.00	150.00	240.00
3	30.00	75.00	120.00
4-The Marvel Family, Captain Marvel, etc. Each issue can vary in contents			
	18.00	45.00	72.00

GIFTS FROM SANTA (See March of Comics #137)

GIGGLE COMICS (Spencer Spook #99)
Oct, 1943 - #98, Dec, 1954 (Also see Ha Ha)
Creston #1-63/American Comics Group #64 on

#1	2.50	5.00	7.50
2-5	1.20	2.40	3.60
6-20: #9-1st Superkatt	.80	1.60	2.40
21-40	.50	1.00	1.50
41-54,56-59,61-98	.40	.80	1.20
55,60-Milt Gross art	.75	1.50	2.25

G-I IN BATTLE (G-I #1 only)
Aug, 1952 - #9, July, 1953; 1/57 - #6, 5/58
Ajax-Farrell Publ./Four Star

#1	1.20	2.40	3.60
2-9	.80	1.60	2.40
Annual (1953)-100pgs.	2.00	4.00	6.00
#1('57-Ajax)	.70	1.40	2.10
2-6	.40	.80	1.20

G.I. JANE
May, 1953 - #13, Aug-Sept, 1955
Trojan Magazines

#1	1.50	3.00	4.50
2-13	1.20	2.40	3.60

G.I. JOE (Also see Advs. of-- & Showcase#53,
1950 - #51, June, 1957   54)
Ziff-Davis Publ. Co.

	Good	Fine	Mint
#10(#1)	1.20	2.40	3.60
11-14('51-'52)	.75	1.50	2.25
V2#6-17,19,20	.70	1.40	2.10
18-(100pg. Giant-'52)	1.50	3.00	4.50
21-51	.50	1.00	1.50

NOTE: *Norman Saunders painted covers-#6-11,
13,14. Powell stories-#7,11.*

G.I. JOE (America's Moveable Fighting Man)
1967   (32 pgs.)   (5-1/8"x8-3/8")
Custom Comics

	Good	Fine	Mint
Schaffenberger art	.20	.40	.60

G.I. JUNIORS (See Harvey Hits #86,91,95,98,
101,104,107,110,112,114,116,118,120,122)

GIL THORP
May-July, 1963
Dell Publishing Co.

	Good	Fine	Mint
#1	1.00	2.00	3.00

GINGER
1951 - 1954
Archie Publications

	Good	Fine	Mint
#1	2.00	4.00	6.00
2-10	1.00	2.00	3.00

GIRL COMICS (Girl Confessions #13 on)
1949 - #12, Jan, 1952
Marvel/Atlas Comics(CnPC)

	Good	Fine	Mint
#1	3.00	6.00	9.00
2-Kubert story	2.50	5.00	7.50
3-Everett story	2.50	5.00	7.50
4-11	2.00	4.00	6.00
12-Krigstein story	2.50	5.00	7.50

GIRL CONFESSIONS (Formerly Girl Comics)
#13, Mar, 1952 - #35, Aug, 1954
Atlas Comics (CnPC/ZPC)

	Good	Fine	Mint
#13,16-18-Everett stories	1.50	3.00	4.50
14,15,19,20	1.00	2.00	3.00
21-35	.75	1.50	2.25

GIRL FROM U.N.C.L.E., THE (TV)
Oct, 1966 - #5, Oct, 1967
Gold Key

	Good	Fine	Mint
#1-McWilliams art	.80	1.60	2.40
2-5-Leonard Swift-Courier #5			

	Good	Fine	Mint
	.40	.80	1.20

GIRLS' FUN & FASHION MAGAZINE (Formerly Polly
V5#44, 1/50 - V5#47, 7/50   Pigtails)
Parents' Magazine Institute

	Good	Fine	Mint
V5#44-47	.50	1.00	1.50

GIRLS IN LOVE
May, 1950 - #57, Dec, 1956
Fawcett #1/Quality Comics Group

	Good	Fine	Mint
#1	1.20	2.40	3.60
2-10	.75	1.50	2.25
11-56	.60	1.20	1.80
57-Matt Baker cvr/story	1.50	3.00	4.50

GIRLS IN WHITE (See Harvey Comics Hits #58)

GIRLS' LIFE
Jan, 1954 - #6, 1954
Atlas Comics (BFP)

	Good	Fine	Mint
#1-Patsy Walker	1.20	2.40	3.60
2-6	.70	1.40	2.10

GIRLS' LOVE STORIES
Aug-Sept, 1949 - #180, Nov-Dec, 1973
National Per. Publ.(Signal Publ. #28-65/
Arleigh #83-117)

	Good	Fine	Mint
#1-Toth + Kinstler art, 8pgs. each	6.00	12.00	18.00
2	3.00	6.00	9.00
3-10	1.80	3.60	5.40
11-20	1.20	2.40	3.60
21-50	.80	1.60	2.40
51-100	.50	1.00	1.50
101-146: #113-117-April O'Day app.	.30	.60	.90
147-151-"Confessions" serial	.20	.40	.60
152-180		.20	.40

GIRLS' ROMANCES
Feb-Mar, 1950 - #160, Sept, 1971
National Per. Publ. (Signal Publ. #32-79/
Arleigh #84)

	Good	Fine	Mint
#1	5.00	10.00	15.00
2	2.50	5.00	7.50
3-10	1.75	3.50	5.25
11-20	1.20	2.40	3.60
21-50	.80	1.60	2.40
51-100	.35	.70	1.05
101-133,135-160	.15	.30	.45
134-Adams cover	.40	.80	1.20

G.I. Joe #51, © Z-D

Girl Comics #6, © MCG

Girls' Love Stories #4, © DC

G.I. Sweethearts #37, © QUA

G.I. War Brides #5, © SUPR

Going Steady #14, © STJ

G.I. SWEETHEARTS (Formerly Diary Loves)
June, 1952 - #45, May, 1955
Quality Comics Group

	Good	Fine	Mint
#22-45	1.00	2.00	3.00

G.I. TALES (Sgt. Barney Barker #1-3)
#4, Feb, 1957 - #6, July, 1957
Atlas Comics (MCI)

	Good	Fine	Mint
#4-Four Severin stories	1.20	2.40	3.60
5	.70	1.40	2.10
6-Orlando, Powell, & Woodbridge stories			
	1.00	2.00	3.00

G.I. WAR BRIDES
1954 - #8, June, 1955
Superior Publishers Ltd.

	Good	Fine	Mint
#1	1.20	2.40	3.60
2-8	.80	1.60	2.40

G.I. WAR TALES
Mar-Apr, 1973 - #4, Oct-Nov, 1973
National Periodical Publications

#1-Reprints		.15	.30
2-Adams reprint	.15	.30	.45
3-Reprints		.10	.20
4-Krigstein art reprint	.15	.30	.45

NOTE: _Drucker reprints-#3,4. Kubert stories-_
_#2,3._

GJDRKZLXCBWQ COMICS
Oct, 1973 (36pgs.)(50¢)(Small Size)(B&W)
Glenn Bray

Wolverton art	.40	.80	1.20

GLAMOROUS ROMANCES (Formerly Dotty)
#41, Sept, 1949 - #90, Oct, 1956
Ace Magazines (A.A. Wyn)

#41-90	.60	1.20	1.80

GNOME MOBILE, THE (See Movie Comics)

GOD IS
1973
Spire Christian Comics(Fleming H.Revell Co.)

By Al Hartley	.25	.50	.75

GOD'S HEROES IN AMERICA
1956 (No#) (68 pgs.) (25¢)
Catechetical Guild Educational Society

No#	2.00	4.00	6.00

GOD'S SMUGGLER (Religious)
1972 (35¢)
Spire Christian Comics/Fleming H. Revell Co.

	Good	Fine	Mint
#1	.25	.50	.75

GODZILLA
August, 1977 - Present
Marvel Comics Group

#1	.30	.60	.90
2	.20	.40	.60
3-Champions x-over	.20	.40	.60
4,5-Sutton art	.20	.40	.60
6-10	.15	.30	.45
11-20		.20	.40

GO-GO
June, 1966 - #9, Oct, 1967
Charlton Comics

#1-Miss Bikini Luv begins	.35	.70	1.05
2	.20	.40	.60
3-Blooperman begins, ends #6,			
4	.40	.80	1.20
5-Super Hero & TV satire by J. Aparo &			
Grass Green begin	1.00	2.00	3.00
6-9	.35	.70	1.05

GO-GO AND ANIMAL (See Tippy's Friends --)

GOING STEADY (Formerly Teen-Age Temptations)
#10, 1954 - #13, 6/55, #14, 10/55;
V3#4, 9-10/60 - #6, 1-2/61
St. John Publishing Co./Prize(Headline)

#10(1954)-Matt Baker cover/story			
	2.50	5.00	7.50
11(2/55),12(4/55)-Baker covers			
	1.00	2.00	3.00
13(6/55)-Cover/story by Matt Baker			
	2.00	4.00	6.00
14(10/55)-Matt Baker cover, art-25pgs.			
	2.50	5.00	7.50
V3#4-6(1960-61)	.20	.40	.60

GOING STEADY WITH BETTY (Betty & Her Steady
Nov-Dec, 1949   #2)
Avon Periodicals

#1	2.50	5.00	7.50

GOLDEN ARROW (See Fawcett Miniatures)

GOLDEN ARROW (-- Western #6)
1942 - #6, Spring, 1947
Fawcett Publications

	Good	Fine	Mint
#1-Golden Arrow begins	10.00	20.00	30.00
2	7.00	14.00	21.00
3-6: #6-Krigstein story	4.00	8.00	12.00

GOLDEN ARROW WELL KNOWN COMICS
1944 (12 pgs.) (8½x10⅜")
Paper cover; Glued binding
Bestmaid/Samuel Lowe (Giveaway)

	15.00	30.00	45.00

GOLDEN COMICS DIGEST
May, 1969 - #48, Jan, 1976
Gold Key

NOTE: *Whitman editions exist of many titles
and are generally valued less.*

#1-Tom & Jerry, Woody Woodpecker, Bugs Bunny	1.50	3.00	4.50
2-Hanna-Barbera TV Fun Favorites	.35	.70	1.05
3-Tom & Jerry, Woody Woodpecker	.50	1.00	1.50
4-Tarzan-Manning & Marsh art	1.20	2.40	3.60
5,8-Tom & Jerry, Woody Woodpecker, Bugs Bunny	.50	1.00	1.50
6-Bugs Bunny	.50	1.00	1.50
7-Hanna-Barbera TV Fun Favorites	.35	.70	1.05
9-Tarzan	1.20	2.40	3.60
10-Bugs Bunny	.40	.80	1.20
11-Hanna-Barbera TV Fun Favorites,			
12-Tom & Jerry, Bugs, W. Woodpecker Journey to the Sun	.25	.50	.75
13-Tom & Jerry	.25	.50	.75
14-Bugs Bunny Fun Packed Funnies	.25	.50	.75
15-Tom & Jerry, W. Woodpecker, B. Bunny	.25	.50	.75
16-W. Woodpecker Cartoon Special	.25	.50	.75
17-Bugs Bunny	.25	.50	.75
18-Tom & Jerry	.25	.50	.75
19-Little Lulu	1.50	3.00	4.50
20-W. Woodpecker Falltime Funtime	.25	.50	.75
21-Bugs Bunny Showtime	.25	.50	.75
22-Tom & Jerry Winter Wingding	.25	.50	.75
23-Little Lulu & Tubby Fun Fling	1.50	3.00	4.50
24-W. Woodpecker Fun Festival	.25	.50	.75
25,28-Tom & Jerry	.25	.50	.75
26-Bugs Bunny Halloween Hulla-Boo-Loo; Dr.			

Spektor article, also #25			
	.25	.50	.75
27-Little Lulu & Tubby in Hawaii	1.20	2.40	3.60
29-Little Lulu & Tubby	1.20	2.40	3.60
30-Bugs Bunny Vacation Funnies	.25	.50	.75
31-Turok, Son of Stone-reprints 4-Color #596, 656	1.00	2.00	3.00
32-W. Woodpecker Summer Fun	.25	.50	.75
33-Little Lulu & Tubby Halloween Fun; Dr. Spektor app.	1.20	2.40	3.60
34-Tom & Jerry Snowtime Funtime	.25	.50	.75
35-Bugs Bunny Winter Funnies	.25	.50	.75
36-Little Lulu & Her Friends	1.20	2.40	3.60
37-W. Woodpecker County Fair	.25	.50	.75
38-The Pink Panther	.20	.40	.60
39-Bugs Bunny Summer Fun	.20	.40	.60
40-Little Lulu & Tubby Trick or Treat - all by Stanley	1.20	2.40	3.60
41-Tom & Jerry Winter Carnival	.20	.40	.60
42-Bugs Bunny	.20	.40	.60
43-Little Lulu in Paris	1.20	2.40	3.60
44-W. Woodpecker Family Fun Festival	.20	.40	.60
45-The Pink Panther	.30	.60	.90
46-Little Lulu & Tubby	1.20	2.40	3.60
47-Bugs Bunny	.20	.40	.60
48-The Lone Ranger	.30	.60	.90

NOTE: *#1-30, 164 pgs.; #31 on, 132 pgs.*

GOLDEN LAD
July, 1945 - #5, June, 1946
Spark Publications

#1-Origin Golden Lad & Swift Arrow	8.00	16.00	24.00
2-Mort Meskin art	5.00	10.00	15.00
3-Mort Meskin art	4.00	8.00	12.00
4	4.00	8.00	12.00
5-Origin Golden Girl; Shaman & Flame app.	5.00	10.00	15.00

GOLDEN LEGACY
1966 - 1972 (Black History) (25¢)
Fitzgerald Publishing Co.

#1-Toussaint L'Ouverture ('66)
 2-Harriet Tubman ('67)
 3-Crispus Attucks & the Minutemen ('67)
 4-Benjamin Banneker ('68)
 5-Matthew Henson ('69)
 6-Alexander Dumas & Family ('69)

Going Steady With Betty #1. © AVON

Golden Arrow #6. © FAW

Golden Comics Digest #2, © GK

Golden Picture Story Book ST-3, © WDP

Golden West Love #3, © Kirby Publ.

Goofy Comics #11, © STD

	Good	Fine	Mint

(Golden Legacy cont'd)
7-Frederick Douglass, Part 1 ('69)
8-Frederick Douglass, Part 2 ('70)
9-Robert Smalls ('70)
10-J. Cinque & the Amistad Mutiny ('70)
11-The Life of Alexander Pushkin ('71)
12-Black Cowboys ('72)
13-The Life of Martin Luther King, Jr. ('72)
14-Men of Action: White, Marshall J. Wilkins ('72)
15-Ancient African Kingdoms ('72)

	Good	Fine	Mint
each....	.35	.70	1.05
#11,14('76)-reprints	.15	.30	

GOLDEN LOVE STORIES (Formerly Golden West
#4, April, 1950   Love)
Kirby Publishing Co.

#4-Powell art; cover features picture of Glenn Ford & Janet Leigh	2.00	4.00	6.00

GOLDEN PICTURE STORY BOOK
Dec, 1961 (52pgs.; 50¢; Large size)(Disney)
Racine Press (Western)

#ST-1-Huckleberry Hound	1.00	2.00	3.00
ST-2-Yogi Bear	1.00	2.00	3.00
ST-3-Babes in Toyland (Walt Disney's --)	2.50	5.00	7.50
ST-4-(--of Disney Ducks)-Walt Disney's Wonderful World of Ducks(Donald Duck, Uncle Scrooge, Donald's Nephews, Grandma Duck, Ludwig Von Drake, & Gyro Gearloose stories)	4.00	8.00	12.00

GOLDEN WEST LOVE (Golden Love Stories #4)
Sept-Oct, 1949 - #3, Feb, 1950
Kirby Publishing Co.

#1-Powell art	2.00	4.00	6.00
2,3-Powell art	1.50	3.00	4.50

GOLDEN WEST RODEO TREASURY
1957   (25¢-Giant)
Dell Publishing Co.

#1	3.00	6.00	9.00

GOLDILOCKS (See March of Comics #1)

GOLDILOCKS & THE THREE BEARS
1943   (Giveaway)
K. K. Publications

	6.00	12.00	18.00

GOLD KEY CHAMPION
3/78 - #2, 5-6/78   (52 pgs.) (50¢)
Gold Key

	Good	Fine	Mint
#1-Space Family Robinson	.15	.30	.45
2-Mighty Samson	.15	.30	.45

GOLD KEY SPOTLIGHT
May, 1976 - #11, Feb, 1978
Gold Key

#1-Tom, Dick & Harriet		.15	.30
2-Wacky Advs. of Cracky		.15	.30
3-Wacky Witch		.15	.30
4-Tom, Dick & Harriet		.15	.30
5-Wacky Advs. of Cracky		.15	.30
6-Dagar the Invincible-Santos art; origin Demonomicon	.15	.30	.45
7			
8-The Occult Files of Dr. Spector-Santos art,			
9-Tragg	.15	.30	.45
10-O.G. Whiz		.15	.30
11-Tom, Dick & Harriet		.15	.30

GOLD MEDAL COMICS
1945   (132 pgs.)
Cambridge House

#1-Captain Truth	4.00	8.00	12.00
2-5	2.50	5.00	7.50

GOMER PYLE (TV)
July, 1966 - #3, Jan, 1967
Gold Key

#1-3	.25	.50	.75

GOODBYE, MR. CHIPS (See Movie Comics)

GOOFY
May, 1953 - Sept-Nov, 1962
Dell Publishing Co.

4-Color #468,562,627,658	1.20	2.40	3.60
4-Color #747,802,899,952,987,1053,1094,1149, 1201	1.00	2.00	3.00
#12-308-211(Dell,9-11/62)	.50	1.00	1.50

GOOFY ADVENTURE STORY (See 4-Color #857)

GOOFY COMICS
June, 1943 - 1953
Nedor Publ. Co. #1-14/Standard #18-48(Animated Cartoons)

#1	2.50	5.00	7.50
2	1.20	2.40	3.60
3-19	.70	1.40	2.10
20-35-Frazetta text illos in all	2.00	4.00	6.00
36-48	.50	1.00	1.50

GOOFY SUCCESS STORY (See 4-Color #702)

GOOSE (Humor Magazine)
Sept, 1976 - #3, 1976 (52 pgs.) (75¢)
Cousins Publ. (Fawcett)

	Good	Fine	Mint
#1-3	.25	.50	.75

GORDO (See Comics Revue #5)

GORGO (Based on movie) (See Return of --)
May, 1961 - #23, Sept, 1965
Charlton Comics

#1-Ditko art, 22pgs.	5.00	10.00	15.00
2,3-Ditko cvr.& stories	2.50	5.00	7.50
4-10: #4-Ditko cover	1.75	3.50	5.25
11,13-16-Ditko art	1.25	2.50	3.75
12,17-23: #12-Reptisaurus x-over; Montes/ Bache art-#17-23	1.00	2.00	3.00
Gorgo's Revenge('62)-Becomes Return of Gorgo	2.00	4.00	6.00

GOSPEL BLIMP, THE
1973 (36 pgs.) (35¢)
Spire Christian Comics(Fleming H. Revell Co.)

No#	.25	.50	.75

GOTHIC ROMANCES
January, 1975 (B&W Magazine) (75¢)
Atlas/Seaboard Publ.

#1-Adams art	.50	1.00	1.50

GOVERNOR & J.J., THE (TV)
Feb, 1970 - #3, Aug, 1970
Gold Key

#1	.20	.40	.60
2,3	.15	.30	.45

GRANDMA DUCK'S FARM FRIENDS (See 4-Color #763,873,965,1010,1073,1161,1279)

GRAND PRIX (Formerly Hot Rod Racers)
1967 - #44, May, 1972
Charlton Comics

#16-44: Features Rick Roberts	.15	.30

GRAY GHOST, THE (See 4-Color #911,1000)

GREAT ACTION COMICS
1958 (Reprints)
I.W. Enterprises

#1-Captain Truth	1.50	3.00	4.50
8,9-Phantom Lady #15&?	5.00	10.00	15.00

GREAT AMERICAN COMICS PRESENTS - THE SECRET VOICE
1945 (10¢)
Peter George 4-Star Publ./Amer.Features Synd.

	Good	Fine	Mint
#1-All anti-Nazi	5.00	10.00	15.00

GREAT CAT FAMILY, THE (See 4-Color #750)

GREAT COMICS
Nov, 1941 - #3, Jan, 1942
Great Publications

#1-Origin The Great Zarro; Madame Strange begins; Captain Power & The Defender app.	15.00	30.00	45.00
2	10.00	20.00	30.00
3-Futuro Takes Hitler to Hell	12.00	24.00	36.00

GREAT COMICS
1945
Novack Publishing Co.

#1-The Defenders, Capt. Power app.; L. B. Cole cover	4.00	8.00	12.00

GREAT DOGPATCH MYSTERY (See Mammy Yokum & the --)

GREAT EXPLOITS
Oct, 1957
Decker Publ./Red Top

#1-Two Krigstein stories (re-issue on cover) reprts/Daring Advs.#6	1.50	3.00	4.50

GREAT FOODINI, THE (See Foodini)

GREAT GAZOO, THE (The Flintstones)
Aug, 1973 - #20, Jan, 1977 (Hanna-Barbera)
Charlton Comics

#1	.15	.30
2-20	.10	.20

GREAT GRAPE APE, THE
Sept, 1976 - #2, Nov, 1976 (Hanna-Barbera)
Charlton Comics

#1,2	.15	.30

GREAT LOCOMOTIVE CHASE, THE(See 4-Color #712)

GREAT LOVER ROMANCES
March, 1951 - #22, May, 1955
Toby Press

Gorgo #17, © CC

Great Comics #1, © GP

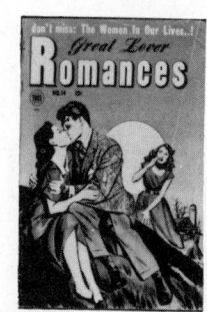

Great Lover Romances #14, © TOBY

Green Giant Comics #1, © Pelican Publ.   Green Hornet Comics #5, © HARV   Green Lama #6, © Spark Publ.

(Great Lover Rom. cont'd)

	Good	Fine	Mint
#1-Jon Juan reprt/JJ #1 by Schomburg; Dr. Anthony King app.	2.50	5.00	7.50
2-5,7,9-22	1.00	2.00	3.00
6-Kurtzman art	2.00	4.00	6.00
8-Five full pgs. of "Pin-Up Pete" by Sparling	2.00	4.00	6.00

GREAT PEOPLE OF GENESIS, THE
No date (64pgs.) (Religious giveaway)
David C. Cook Publ. Co.

Reprint/Sunday Pix Weekly	1.00	2.00	3.00

GREAT RACE, THE (See Movie Classics)

GREAT SCOTT SHOE STORE (See Bulls-Eye)

GREAT SOCIETY, THE (Political Satire)
1966 ($1.00) (Also see Bobman & Teddy)
Parallax

Along Ranger; Captain Marvelous; Colonel
America; Phantasm; Super LBJ; Wonderbird

	1.00	2.00	3.00

GREAT WEST (Magazine)
1969 (52 pgs.) (Black & White)
M. F. Enterprises

V1#1	.25	.50	.75

GREAT WESTERN
Jan-Mar, 1954 - #11, Oct-Dec, 1954
Magazine Enterprises

#8(A-1#93)-origin The Ghost Rider	4.00	8.00	12.00
#9(A-1#105),10(A-1#113),11(A-1#127)-Ghost Rider in #9-11, Durango Kid in all	2.00	4.00	6.00
IW Reprint #1,2,9: Straight Arrow app. in #1,2	.65	1.35	2.00
IW Reprint #8-Origin Ghost Rider(Tim Holt #11); Tim Holt app.; Bolle art	1.50	3.00	4.50

GREEN BERET, THE (See Tales of --)

GREEN GIANT COMICS
1940 (no price on cover)
Pelican Publications (Funnies, Inc.?)

#1-Dr. Nerod, Green Giant & Master Mystic app. (Rare)	200.00	400.00	600.00

NOTE: *Three copies found in estate that produced the Motion Picture Funnies Weekly issues, although other copies exist. (This book*
*had very limited circulation as copies do
turn up, but very rarely.) Contains 5 pgs.
reprinted from Motion Picture Funnies Weekly.*

GREEN HORNET (TV)
Feb, 1967 - #3, Aug, 1967
Gold Key

	Good	Fine	Mint
#1	1.50	3.00	4.50
2,3	1.00	2.00	3.00

GREEN HORNET (See 4-Color Comics #496)

GREEN HORNET COMICS (-- Fights Crime #37)
Dec, 1940 - #47, Sept, 1949
Helnit Publ.(Holyoke)#1/Harvey Publ.

#1-Green Hornet begins	65.00	130.00	195.00
2	35.00	70.00	105.00
3	25.00	50.00	75.00
4	16.00	32.00	48.00
5	14.00	28.00	42.00
6	12.00	24.00	36.00
7-Origin The Zebra; Robin Hood & Spirit of 76 begin	16.00	32.00	48.00
8-10	12.00	24.00	36.00
11,12-Mr. Q in both	10.00	20.00	30.00
13-20: #20-Kubert art	8.00	16.00	24.00
21-30: #30-Kubert art	6.00	12.00	18.00
31-The Man in Black Called Fate begins	7.00	14.00	21.00
32-36	6.00	12.00	18.00
37-Shock Gibson app.; S&K Kid Adonis reprtd. from Stuntman #3	8.00	16.00	24.00
38-Shock Gibson, Kid Adonis app.	6.00	12.00	18.00
39-Stuntman story by S&K	12.00	24.00	36.00
40,41	4.00	8.00	12.00
42-45,47-Kerry Drake in all	4.00	8.00	12.00
46-"Case of the Marijuana Racket"; Kerry Drake app.	6.00	12.00	18.00

NOTE: *Powell art-#7-10,31-34 (Man in Black).
Schomburg cover-#20.*

GREEN JET COMICS, THE
1950 (5½x8½")(16pgs. in color)(Paper cover)
Metropolitan Printing Co. (Giveaway)

#1-Green Lama by Raboy	18.00	36.00	54.00
2-No Green Lama	1.50	3.00	4.50

GREEN LAMA (Also see Green Jet #1)
Dec, 1944 - #8, March, 1946
Spark Publications

#1-Intro. The Green Lama, Lt. Hercules & The
Boy Champions; Mac Raboy art #1-8

(Green Lama cont'd)	Good	Fine	Mint
	20.00	40.00	60.00
2	15.00	30.00	45.00
3,5-8	10.00	20.00	30.00
4-Dick Tracy take-off in Lt. Hercules story;			
Robinson story	12.00	24.00	36.00

GREEN LANTERN (1st Series)(See All-American)
Fall, 1941 - #38, May-June, 1949
National Periodical Publ./All-American

#1-Origin retold	120.00	240.00	360.00
2	75.00	150.00	225.00
3	50.00	100.00	150.00
4	40.00	80.00	120.00
5	35.00	70.00	105.00
6,7	30.00	60.00	90.00
8-Hop Harrigan begins	30.00	60.00	90.00
9	25.00	50.00	75.00
10-Origin Vandal Savage	25.00	50.00	75.00
11-20: #12-Origin Gambler			
	20.00	40.00	60.00
21-30: #27-Origin Sky Pirate			
	15.00	30.00	45.00
31-38: #27-Sargon the Sorcerer app.			
	14.00	28.00	42.00

NOTE: *Book-length stories #2-8. Toth art-#28, 30,31,34-38; covers-#30,34,36-38.*

GREEN LANTERN(2nd Series)(See Showcase,Flash)
7-8/60 - #89, 4-5/72; #90, 8-9/76 - Present
National Periodical Publications/DC Comics

#1-Origin retold; Gil Kane art begins			
	28.00	56.00	84.00
2-1st Pieface, #3	12.00	24.00	36.00
4,5: #5-Origin & 1st app. Hector Hammond;			
1st 5700 A.D. story	7.00	14.00	21.00
6-10: #7-Origin Sinestro. #9-1st Jordan			
Brothers	4.00	8.00	12.00
11-20: #13-Flash x-over. #14-Origin Sonar.			
#16-Origin Star Sapphire. #20-Flash x-over			
	2.50	5.00	7.50
21-30: #21-Origin Dr. Polaris. #23-1st			
Tatooed Man. #24-Origin Shark. #29-JLA			
cameo; 1st Blackhand	1.50	3.00	4.50
31-40: #40-G.A. Green Lantern x-over; origin			
The Guardians	1.00	2.00	3.00
41-50: #42-Zatanna x-over. #43-Flash x-over.			
#45-G.A. Green Lantern x-over			
	.70	1.40	2.10
51-75: #52,61-G.A. Green Lantern x-over. #67-			
G.A. Green Lantern origin retold. #69-			
Wood inks	.50	1.00	1.50
76-Begin Green Lantern/Green Arrow series by			
Neal Adams	8.00	16.00	24.00
77	4.00	8.00	12.00
78-80	3.00	6.00	9.00

	Good	Fine	Mint
81-83	2.50	5.00	7.50
84-Adams/Wrightson story	2.50	5.00	7.50
85,86-DC drug books	3.00	6.00	9.00
87,89: #89-G.A. Green Lantern stories,			
52pgs.	2.00	4.00	6.00
88('72)	.40	.80	1.20
90('76)-99	.20	.40	.60
100(Giant)-113	.35	.70	1.05

NOTE: *Adams stories-#76-87,89; covers-#63, 76-89. Anderson inks-#1,4,9,10,16,21,71,73, 74,87,88; cover inks-#2,9,10,12,14-16,19-44, 52-56,59,61,69. Infantino stories-#53,88; cover-#53. Gil Kane stories-#1-61,68-75,85, 87,88; covers-#1-52,54-61,67-75. Staton cover-#107. Toth reprint-#86.*

GREEN MASK, THE (The Bouncer #11 on?)
Summer, 1940 - V2#6, Oct-Nov, 1946
Fox Features Syndicate

V1#1-Origin The Green Mask & Domino; reprints/			
Mystery Men #1-3,5-7	30.00	60.00	90.00
2	15.00	30.00	45.00
3	10.00	20.00	30.00
4-Navy Jones begins	10.00	20.00	30.00
5	10.00	20.00	30.00
6-The Nightbird begins	8.00	16.00	24.00
7-9	6.00	12.00	18.00
10-Origin One Round Hogan & Rocket Kelly,			
11	6.00	12.00	18.00
V2#1-6	5.00	10.00	15.00
#1(1955-2nd Series)	3.00	6.00	9.00

GREEN PLANET, THE
1962 (One Shot)
Charlton Comics

No#	1.20	2.40	3.60

GREEN TEAM (See First Issue Special)

GREETINGS FROM SANTA (See March of Comics #48)

GREYFRIARS BOBBY (See 4-Color Comics #1189)

GRIM GHOST, THE
Jan, 1975 - #3, July, 1975
Atlas/Seaboard Publ.

#1-Origin	.25	.50	.75
2,3-Heath cover	.15	.30	.45

GRIMM'S GHOST STORIES (See Dan Curtis)
Jan, 1972 - Present
Gold Key

#1	.35	.70	1.05

Green Lantern #16, © DC

Green Lantern #12, © DC

Green Lantern #86, © DC

The Gumps #3, © News Synd.   The Gumps #6 (C&L), © News Synd.   Gunfighter #7, © WMG

(Grimm's Ghost Stories cont'd)

	Good	Fine	Mint
2-4,6,7,9,10	.25	.50	.75
5,8-Williamson story	.50	1.00	1.50
11-16,18-20	.20	.40	.60
17-Crandall story	.30	.60	.90
21-35: #25-Bolle art; #32,34-reprints			
	.20	.40	.60
36-48: #43,44-52pgs.		.20	.40
Mini-Comic #1(3¼x6½",'76)	.15	.30	.45

GRIN (The American Funny Book) (Magazine)
Nov, 1972 - #3, April, 1973 (52pgs.)(Satire)
APAG House Pubs

#1	.35	.70	1.05
2,3	.25	.50	.75

GRIN & BEAR IT (See Large Feat. Comic #28)

GRIT GRADY (See Holyoke One-Shot #1)

GROOVY (Cartoon Comics-not CCA approved)
March, 1968 - #3, July, 1968
Marvel Comics Group

#1-3	.25	.50	.75

GUADALCANAL DIARY
1945   (One Shot)
David McKay Publishing Co.

No#	2.50	5.00	7.50

GUERRILLA WAR (Formerly Jungle War Stories)
#12, Jul-Sept, 1965 - #14, Mar, 1966
Dell Publishing Co.

#12-14	.25	.50	.75

GUILTY (See Justice Traps the --)

GULF FUNNY WEEKLY (In full color)
1933 - #422, 5/23/41 (4pgs; tabloid size to
2/3/39; 2/10/39 on, reg. comic book size);
early issues undated   (Giveaway)
Gulf Oil Company

#1	5.00	10.00	15.00
2-30	2.50	5.00	7.50
31-100	2.00	4.00	6.00
101-196	1.50	3.00	4.50
197-Wings Winfair begins(1/29/37); by Fred Mea-			
gher beginning in '38	15.00	30.00	45.00
198-300(Last tabloid size)	5.00	10.00	15.00
301-350 (Reg. size)	3.00	6.00	9.00
351-422	2.00	4.00	6.00

GULLIVER'S TRAVELS (See Dell Jr. Treasury #3)
Sept-Nov, 1965 - #3, May, 1966
Dell Publishing Co.

	Good	Fine	Mint
#1-3	.65	1.35	2.00

GUMPS, THE
1918 - #8, 1931   (9½x9½") (Black & White)
Cupples & Leon Co./Landfield-Kupfer #4('27)on

1918-(5-3/4"x14")-48pgs. dailies

	15.00	30.00	45.00
No#(1924)by Sidney Smith	10.00	20.00	30.00
#2,3	8.00	16.00	24.00
4-7: #6-(10x10")48pgs.	6.00	12.00	18.00
8-(10x14")32pgs. B&W	6.00	12.00	18.00

GUMPS, THE (-- in Radioland)
1937   (95 pgs.) (Mostly text)
Pebco Tooth Paste Premium

	8.00	16.00	24.00

GUMPS, THE (Also see Merry Christmas --)
Mar-Apr, 1947 - #5, Nov-Dec, 1947
Dell Publ. Co./All-American(National?)

4-Color #73(Dell)	4.00	8.00	12.00
#1(1947)	3.00	6.00	9.00
2-5	2.50	5.00	7.50

GUNFIGHTER (Fat & Slat #1-4)(Becomes Haunt
of Fear #15 on)
#5, Summer, 1948 - #14, Mar-Apr, 1950
E.C. Comics

#5,6-Moon Girl in each	25.00	50.00	75.00
7-14	22.00	44.00	66.00

NOTE: *Craig & H.C. Kiefer art in most issues.*
Feldstein/Craig story-#10. Feldstein stories-
#7-11. Ingels stories-#5-14; covers-#7-12.
Wood stories-#13,14.

GUNFIGHTERS, THE
1963 - 1964
Super Comics   (Reprints)

#10,11(Billy the Kid),12(Swift Arrow),
15(Straight Arrow),16,18-All reprints

	.65	1.35	2.00

GUNFIGHTERS, THE (Formerly Kid Montana)
#51, 10/66 - #52, 10/67
Charlton Comics

#51,52	.20	.40	.60

GUN GLORY (See 4-Color Comics #846)

GUNHAWK, THE (Whip Wilson #10,11)
#12, Nov, 1950 - #18, Dec, 1951
Marvel Comics/Atlas (MCI)

	Good	Fine	Mint
#12-18	1.50	3.00	4.50

GUNHAWKS, THE (The Gunhawk #7)
October, 1972 - #7, October, 1973
Marvel Comics Group

#1-Reno Jones, Kid Cassidy	.20	.40	.60
2-5	.15	.30	.45
6-Kid Cassidy dies. #7-Reno Jones solo			
		.15	.30

GUNMASTER (Judo Master #89 on; formerly
Six-Gun Heroes) (Two #89's)
9/64; 3-4/66 - #89, 10/67
Charlton Comics

V1#1	.60	1.20	1.80
2-4,V5#84-86	.40	.80	1.20
V5#87-89	.30	.60	.90

NOTE: *Vol. 5 was originally cancelled with
#88(3-4/66). #89 on became Judo Master, then
later in 1967, Charlton issued #89 as a Gun-
master one-shot.*

GUNS AGAINST GANGSTERS
Sept-Oct, 1948 - V2#2, 1949
Curtis Publications/Novelty Press

#1-Toni Gayle begins by Schomburg			
	3.00	6.00	9.00
2-5	2.00	4.00	6.00
6-Toni Gayle cover/story by L. B. Cole			
	2.50	5.00	7.50
V2#1-Toni Gayle bondage cover			
	3.00	6.00	9.00
2	2.00	4.00	6.00

NOTE: *L. B. Cole covers-#1,3,5,6.*

GUNSLINGER (See 4-Color Comics #1220)

GUNSLINGER (Formerly Tex Dawson --)
#2, April, 1973 - #3, June, 1973
Marvel Comics Group

#2,3		.15	.30

GUNSMOKE
Apr-May, 1949 - #16, Jan, 1952
P. L. Publishing Co./Western Comics

#1-Gunsmoke, Masked Marvel begin, both by			
Ingels-#1	5.00	10.00	15.00
2-Ingels cover/story	4.00	8.00	12.00
3,4-Ingels story each	2.50	5.00	7.50

	Good	Fine	Mint
5-16	1.20	2.40	3.60

NOTE: *Ingels covers-#1-6; bondage-#1,3.*

GUNSMOKE (TV)
1955 - #27, Jun-Jul, 1961; 2/69 - #6, 2/70
Dell Publishing Co./Gold Key

4-Color #679	1.25	2.50	3.75
4-Color #720,769,797,844	1.00	2.00	3.00
#6(11/57), #7	.60	1.20	1.80
8,9,11,12-Williamson stories in all, 4pgs.			
each	1.80	3.60	5.40
10-Williamson/Crandall story, 4pgs.			
	1.80	3.60	5.40
13-27	.40	.80	1.20
Gunsmoke Film Story (11/62-G.K. Giant)			
#30008-211	1.00	2.00	3.00
#1(G.K.)	.30	.60	.90
2-6('69-70)	.20	.40	.60

GUNSMOKE TRAIL
June, 1957 - #4, 1957
Ajax-Farrell Publ./Four Star Comic Corp.

#1	1.00	2.00	3.00
2-4	.60	1.20	1.80

GUNSMOKE WESTERN (Formerly Western Tales of
Dec, 1955 - #77, 7/63   Black Rider)
Atlas Comics,#32-35(CPS/NPI); Marvel, #36 on

#32	1.50	3.00	4.50
33,36-Williamson stories in both, 5 & 4 pgs.			
+ Drucker #33	2.50	5.00	7.50
34-3pg. Baker story	1.50	3.00	4.50
35,38,39	.80	1.60	2.40
37-Two Davis stories; Williamson text illo			
	1.50	3.00	4.50
40-Williamson/Mayo story, 4pgs.			
	2.50	5.00	7.50
41,42,45-49,51-55,57-59: #49,52-Kid From			
Texas story. #57-1st Two Gun Kid by Sev-			
erin. #60-Sam Hawk app. in Kid Colt			
	.75	1.50	2.25
43,44-Torres story	1.20	2.40	3.60
50,60,61-Crandall story	1.50	3.00	4.50
56-Matt Baker story	1.50	3.00	4.50
62-71,73-77	.60	1.20	1.80
72-Origin Kid Colt Outlaw	.70	1.40	2.10

NOTE: *Colan story-#37. Davis art-#37,50,52,
54,55; cover-#54. Ditko story-#66. Kirby
stories-#47,50,51,59,62,63,65-67,69,71,73,77;
cover-#56(w/Ditko),57,58,61(w/Ayers),63,66,
68,69,71-77. Wildey story-#37,42,57. Kid
Colt in all. Two-Gun Kid in #57,59,60-62,63,
66. Wyatt Earp in #45,48,49,52,54,55,58.*

Gunsmoke #3, © P.L. Publ.   Gunsmoke Trail #1, © AJAX   Gunsmoke Western #68, © MCG

Ha Ha Comics #70, © ACG

Hand Of Fate #13, © ACE

Hangman Comics #2, © MLJ

GUNS OF FACT & FICTION (See A-1 Comics #13)

GUN THAT WON THE WEST, THE
1956   (28 pgs.)(Regular size)(Giveaway)
Winchester-Western Division & Olin Mathieson
Chemical Corp.

	Good	Fine	Mint
No#-Painted cover	1.20	2.40	3.60

GYPSY COLT (See 4-Color Comics #568)

GYRO GEARLOOSE (See Walt Disney Showcase #18)
Nov, 1959 - May-July, 1962   (Disney)
Dell Publishing Co.

4-Color #1047,1095,1184-All by Carl Barks			
	4.00	8.00	12.00
4-Color #1267-Barks cover, 4pgs.			
	3.50	7.00	10.50
4-Color #1329, #01329-207(5-7/62)-Barks cover only			
	2.50	5.00	7.50

HAGAR THE HORRIBLE (See Comics Reading Librs.)

HA HA COMICS (Teepee Tim #100 on)
Oct, 1943 - #99, Jan, 1955 (Also see Giggle)
Scope Mag.(Creston Publ.)#1-90/Amer.Com.Group

#1	2.50	5.00	7.50
2-5	1.20	2.40	3.60
6-20	.80	1.60	2.40
21-40	.50	1.00	1.50
41-99	.40	.80	1.20

HAIR BEAR BUNCH, THE (TV) (See Fun-In #13)
Feb, 1972 - #9, Feb, 1974 (Hanna-Barbera)
Gold Key

#1-9		.15	.30

HALLELUJAH TRAIL, THE (See Movie Classics)

HAND OF FATE (Formerly Mr. Risk)
#8, Dec, 1951 - #26, March, 1955
Ace Magazines

#8	1.50	3.00	4.50
9-24	1.00	2.00	3.00
25(11/54),25(12/54),26-All Nostrand art			
	1.50	3.00	4.50

NOTE: *Cameron art-#20-23,25.*

HANDS OF THE DRAGON
June, 1975
Seaboard Periodicals (Atlas)

#1-Origin; Craig art	.30	.60	.90

HANGMAN COMICS (Special #1; Black Hood #9 on)
#2, Spring, 1942 - #8, Fall, 1943
MLJ Magazines

	Good	Fine	Mint
#2-The Hangman, Boy Buddies begin			
	30.00	60.00	90.00
3-8	20.00	40.00	60.00

HANK
1946
Pentagon Publications

No#-Coulton Waugh's newspaper reprint			
	1.50	3.00	4.50

HANNA-BARBERA(See Golden Comics Dig. #2,7,11)

HANNA-BARBERA BAND WAGON
Oct, 1962 - #3, April, 1963
Gold Key

#1,2-Giants, 84pgs.	.35	.70	1.05
3-Regular size	.25	.50	.75

HANNA-BARBERA HI-ADVENTURE HEROES (See Hi --)

HANNA-BARBERA PARADE
Sept, 1971 - #10, Dec, 1972
Charlton Comics

#1,2,4-10	.35	.70	1.05
3-"Summer Picnic"-52pgs.	.25	.50	.75

NOTE: *#4 (1/72) went on sale late in 1972
with the Jan. 1973 issues.*

HANNA-BARBERA SPOTLIGHT (See Spotlight)

HANNA-BARBERA SUPER TV HEROES
April, 1968 - #7, Oct, 1969 (Hanna-Barbera)
Gold Key

#1-The Birdman, The Herculoids, Moby Dick, Samson & Goliath, & The Mighty Mightor begin	.50	1.00	1.50
2-The Galaxy Trio only app.; Shazzan begins- no Samson & Goliath	.35	.70	1.05
3-7: #3-The Space Ghost app.; also #3,6,7, no Herculoids; no Samson & Goliath in #4-7	.50	1.00	1.50

HANNA-BARBERA (TV STARS) (See TV Stars)

HANS AND FRITZ
1917 (16pgs)10x13½" B&W Sunday strip reprts)
The Saalfield Publishing Co.

By R. Dirks, 16 pgs.	15.00	37.50	60.00

HANS BRINKER (See 4-Color Comics #1273)

HANS CHRISTIAN ANDERSON
1953   (100 pgs.-Special Issue)
Ziff-Davis Publ. Co.

	Good	Fine	Mint
No#-Danny Kaye (movie)	3.00	6.00	9.00

HANSEL & GRETEL   (See 4-Color #590)

HANSI, THE GIRL WHO LOVED THE SWASTIKA
1973   (39¢)
Spire Christian Comics(Fleming H.Revell Co.)

	.20	.40	.60

HAP HAZARD COMICS   (Real Love #25 on)
1944 - #24, Feb, 1949
Ace Magazines (Readers' Research)

#1	1.50	3.00	4.50
2-10	1.20	2.40	3.60
11-13,15-24	1.00	2.00	3.00
14-Feldstein cover(4/47)	3.00	6.00	9.00

HAP HOPPER   (See Comics Revue #2)

HAPPIEST MILLIONAIRE, THE   (See Movie Comics)

HAPPI TIM   (See March of Comics #182)

HAPPY COMICS   (Happy Rabbit #41 on)
1943 - #40, Dec, 1950
Nedor Publ./Standard Comics(Animated Cartoons)

#1	2.50	5.00	7.50
2-10	1.00	2.00	3.00
11-19	.60	1.20	1.80
20-31,34-37-Frazetta text illos in all; 2 in			
#34, 3 in #30	2.00	4.00	6.00
32-Frazetta story, 7pgs. + text illos.			
	5.00	10.00	15.00
33-Two Frazetta stories, 6pgs. each (Scarce)			
	10.00	20.00	30.00
38-40	.40	.80	1.20

HAPPY HOLIDAY   (See March of Comics #181)

HAPPY HOOLIGAN   (See Alphonse --)
1903 (18pgs.)(Sunday strip reprints in color)
Hearst's New York American-Journal

Book 1-by Fred Opper	20.00	50.00	80.00
50pg. Edition(1903)-10x15" in color			
	25.00	62.50	100.00

HAPPY HOOLIGAN   (Handy --)
1908 (32pgs. in color)(10x15",cardboard cvrs)
Frederick A. Stokes Co.

	Good	Fine	Mint
	15.00	37.50	60.00

HAPPY HOOLIGAN   (Story of --)
1932   (16pgs.)(9½x12")(Softcover)
McLoughlin Bros.

#281-Three-color text, pictures on heavy			
paper	7.00	14.00	21.00

HAPPY HOULIHANS   (Saddle Justice #3 on)
Fall, 1947 - #2, Winter, 1947-48
E.C. Comics

#1-Origin Moon Girl	20.00	40.00	60.00
2	9.00	18.00	27.00

HAPPY JACK
August, 1957
Red Top (Decker)

V1#1	1.00	2.00	3.00

HAPPY JACK HOWARD
1957
Red Top(Farrell)/Decker

No#-Reprints Handy Andy story from E.C.			
Dandy Comics #5, renamed "Happy Jack"			
	1.00	2.00	3.00

HAPPY RABBIT   (Formerly Happy Comics)
#41, 1950 - #48, April, 1952
Standard Comics (Animated Cartoons)

#41-48	.35	.70	1.05

HAPPY TIME XMAS BOOK
1952   (Christmas Giveaway)
F. W. Woolworth Co.

	2.00	4.00	6.00

HARDY BOYS, THE   (See 4-Color #760,830,887,
964-Disney)

HARDY BOYS, THE   (TV)
April, 1970 - #4, Jan, 1971
Gold Key

#1	.40	.80	1.20
2-4	.30	.60	.90

HARLEM GLOBETROTTERS   (TV)(See Fun-In #8,10)
April, 1972 - #12, Jan, 1975 (Hanna-Barbera)
Gold Key

#1-12	.10	.20

Hans Christian Anderson No#, © Z-D

Hap Hazard #2, © ACE

Happy Houlihans #1, © WMG

Harold Teen (1929, C&L), © Chicago Tribune   Harvey Comics Hits #52, © HARV   Harvey Comics Library #1, © HARV

(Harlem Globetrotters cont'd)
NOTE: *#4,8 and 12 contain 16 extra pages of advertising.*

HAROLD TEEN (See 4-Color #2,209, & Treasure Box of Famous Comics)

HAROLD TEEN (Adv. of --)
1929-31 (36-52pgs.) (Paper covers)
Cupples & Leon Co.

	Good	Fine	Mint
B&W daily strip reprints by Carl Ed	10.00	20.00	30.00

HARVEY
Oct, 1970; #2, 12/70; #3, 6/72 - #6, 12/72
Marvel Comics Group

#1-6		.10	.20

HARVEY COLLECTORS COMICS (Richie Rich Collectors Comics #10 on)
Sept, 1975 - #9, 1976   (52 pgs.) (35¢)
Harvey Publications

#1	.20	.40	.60
2-9		.20	.40

NOTE: *All reprints: Casper-#2,3, Richie Rich-#1,6,8, Wendy-#4.*

HARVEY COMICS HITS
Oct, 1951 - #61, Oct, 1952
Harvey Publications

#51-The Phantom	8.00	16.00	24.00
52-Steve Canyon	6.00	12.00	18.00
53-Mandrake the Magician	7.00	14.00	21.00
54-Tim Tyler's Tales of Jungle Terror	5.00	10.00	15.00
55-Mary Worth	3.00	6.00	9.00
56-The Phantom	7.00	14.00	21.00
57-Rip Kirby by Alex Raymond-"Kidnap Racket"	12.00	24.00	36.00
58-Girls in White	2.50	5.00	7.50
59-Tales of the Invisible Scarlet O'Neil	6.00	12.00	18.00
60			
61-Casper the Friendly Ghost	3.00	6.00	9.00

HARVEY COMICS LIBRARY
April, 1952 - #2, 1952
Harvey Publications

#1-Teen-Age Dope Slaves as exposed by Rex Morgan, M.D.; used in Seduction of the Innocent, pg. 27	120.00	240.00	360.00

(Prices vary widely on this book)

	Good	Fine	Mint
2-Sparkle Plenty (Dick Tracy in "Blackmail Terror")	8.00	16.00	24.00

HARVEY HITS
Sept, 1957 - #122, Nov, 1967
Harvey Publications

#1-The Phantom	7.00	14.00	21.00
2-Rags Rabbit(10/57)	1.00	2.00	3.00
3-Richie Rich(11/57)-See Little Dot for 1st app.	30.00	60.00	90.00
4-Little Dot's Uncles	1.75	3.50	5.25
5-Stevie Mazie's Boy Friend	1.00	2.00	3.00
6-The Phantom-Kirby cvr.	4.00	8.00	12.00
7-Wendy the Witch	2.00	4.00	6.00
8-Sad Sack	1.00	2.00	3.00
9-Richie Rich's Golden Deeds	5.00	10.00	15.00
10-Little Lotta	1.00	2.00	3.00
11-Little Audrey Summer Fun(7/58)	1.00	2.00	3.00
12-The Phantom-Kirby cvr.	4.00	8.00	12.00
13-Little Dot's Uncles(9/58)	1.50	3.00	4.50
14-Herman & Katnip(10/58)	.75	1.50	2.25
15-The Phantom(1958)	3.00	6.00	9.00
16-Wendy the Witch	1.00	2.00	3.00
17-Sad Sack's Army Life(2/59)	.75	1.50	2.25
18-Buzzy & the Crow	.75	1.50	2.25
19-Little Audrey?	1.00	2.00	3.00
20-Casper & Spooky	1.00	2.00	3.00
21-Wendy the Witch	1.00	2.00	3.00
22-Sad Sack's Army Life	.75	1.50	2.25
22-Baby Huey-the Baby Giant	1.00	2.00	3.00
23-Wendy the Witch	1.00	2.00	3.00
24-Little Dot's Uncles(9/59)	1.00	2.00	3.00
25-Herman & Katnip(10/59)	.75	1.50	2.25
26-The Phantom(11/59)	3.00	6.00	9.00
27-Wendy the Good Little Witch	.75	1.50	2.25
28-Sad Sack's Army Life	.75	1.50	2.25
29-Harvey-Toon('60)-Casper, Buzzy	.75	1.50	2.25
30-Wendy the Witch(3/60)	.75	1.50	2.25
31-Herman & Katnip(4/60)	.75	1.50	2.25
32-Sad Sack's Army Life	.75	1.50	2.25
33-Wendy the Witch(6/60)	.75	1.50	2.25
34-Harvey-Toon(7/60)	.75	1.50	2.25
35-Funday Funnies(8/60)	.75	1.50	2.25
36-The Phantom(1960)	2.50	5.00	7.50
37-Casper & Nightmare	.75	1.50	2.25
38-Harvey-Toon	.75	1.50	2.25
39-Sad Sack's Army Life(12/60)			

Harvey Hits #2, © HARV

Harvey Hits #48, © HARV

Haunted Thrills #14, © AJAX

The Haunt Of Fear #10, © WMG

The Haunt Of Fear #27, © WMG

The Hawk & The Dove #2, © DC

	Good	Fine	Mint
(Haunted cont'd)			
#1	.25	.50	.75
2-16,18-20,22-40	.15	.30	.45
17,21-Newton story	.15	.30	.45

NOTE: _Ditko_ _art-#1-5,7,8,13,15,16,18; covers-#1-7. Howard story-#18. Newton covers-#21,22._

HAUNTED LOVE
April, 1973 - #11, Sept, 1975
Charlton Comics

#1-Tom Sutton love story, 16 pgs.			
	.20	.40	.60
2,3,6-11		.15	.30
4,5-Ditko stories	.15	.30	.45

NOTE: _Howard story-#8. Newton cover-#8,9._

HAUNTED THRILLS
June, 1952 - #21, Nov, 1954
Ajax/Farrell Publications

#1	2.00	4.00	6.00
2-5	1.20	2.40	3.60
6-21	1.00	2.00	3.00

HAUNT OF FEAR (Formerly Gunfighter)
#15, May-June, 1950 - #28, Nov-Dec, 1954
E.C. Comics

#15(1950)	90.00	180.00	270.00
16	50.00	100.00	150.00
17-Origin of Crypt of Terror, Vault of Horror, & Hunt of Fear	40.00	80.00	120.00
#4	30.00	60.00	90.00
5	25.00	50.00	75.00
6-10	20.00	40.00	60.00
11-13,15-18,20	15.00	30.00	45.00
14-Origin Old Witch by Ingels	20.00	40.00	60.00
19-Used in _Seduction of the Innocent_, ill.-"A comic book baseball game"	22.00	44.00	66.00
21-28	11.00	22.00	33.00

(Canadian reprints known; see Table of Contents.)
NOTE: _Craig stories-#15-17,5,7,10,12,13; covers-#15-17,5-7. Crandall stories-#20,21,26,27. Davis stories-#4-26,28. Evans stories-#15-19, 23-25,27. Feldstein stories-#15-17,20; covers-#4,8-10. Ingels stories-#16,17,4-28; covers-#11-28. Kamen stories-#16,4,6,7,9-11,13-19, 21-28. Krigstein story-#28. Kurtzman stories-#15/1,17/3. Orlando stories-#9,12. Wood stories-#15,16,4-6._

HAUNT OF HORROR, THE (Magazine) (75¢)
May, 1974 - #5, Jan, 1975 (B&W)
Cadence Comics Publ. (Marvel)

	Good	Fine	Mint
#1-Alcala art	.65	1.35	2.00
2-Origin & 1st app. Gabriel the Devil Hunter; Satana begins	.50	1.00	1.50
3	.50	1.00	1.50
4-Adams art	.75	1.50	2.25
5-Two Evans stories	.50	1.00	1.50

HAVE GUN, WILL TRAVEL (TV)
1958 - #14, July-Sept, 1962
Dell Publishing Co.

4-Color #931,983,1044	.75	1.50	2.25
#4-14	.50	1.00	1.50

HAWAIIAN EYE (TV)
July, 1963
Gold Key

#1(10073-307)	.50	1.00	1.50

HAWAIIAN ILLUSTRATED LEGENDS SERIES
1975 (B&W)(Cover printed w/blue,yellow,green)
Hogarth Press

#1-Kalelealuaka, the Mysterious Warrior	.35	.70	1.05
2,3	.25	.50	.75

HAWK, THE (Also see Approved Comics)
Winter, 1951 - #12, May, 1955
Ziff-Davis/St. John Publ. Co. #3 on

#1-Anderson art	4.00	8.00	12.00
2-Kubert art	3.00	6.00	9.00
3-8,10-12: #8-reprints #3 with different cover. #10-reprts. 1 story/#2; #11-Buckskin Belle app.	1.50	3.00	4.50
9-Kubert story reprt/#2	2.50	5.00	7.50
3-D#1(11/53)-Baker cover	5.00	10.00	15.00

NOTE: _Baker covers-#8,9,11._

HAWK & THE DOVE, THE (See Showcase)
Aug-Sept, 1968 - #6, June-July, 1969
National Periodical Publications

#1-Ditko cover/art	.65	1.35	2.00
2- " " "	.50	1.00	1.50
3-6: #5-Teen Titans cameo	.40	.80	1.20

NOTE: _Gil Kane art/cover-#3-6._

HAWKEYE & THE LAST OF THE MOHICANS
(See 4-Color Comics #884)

HAWKMAN (See The Brave & the Bold, Mystery in Space, Atom & Hawkman)
April-May, 1964 - #27, Aug-Sept, 1968
National Periodical Publications

THE FANTASTIC FIVE!

A Special Magazine Collector's Series!

Platinum Publications is proud to present these five unique magazines to the memorabilia-minded collector:

FIRST TIME IN PRINT! 12 YEARS IN PRODUCTION!

THE COMPLETE ELVIS

COMPLETE ELVIS LISTS
SONGS
ALBUMS
SINGLES
INTERVIEWS
MOVIES
TELEVISION
CONCERTS
ILLEGAL BOOTLEG RECORDINGS
FOREIGN RELEASES
UNRELEASED SONGS
SONGS OTHERS SING ABOUT THE KING
HUNDREDS OF ALBUM COVERS, RECORD LABELS & PICTURES
MANY NEVER BEFORE PUBLISHED PHOTOS
THE MOST VALUABLE RECORD IN THE WORLD

KISS MEETS THE PHANTOM
Superscoops From The 1st KISS Movie!

EXCLUSIVE, NEVER-BEFORE-PUBLISHED KISS PHOTOS & INTERVIEWS!

PLATINUM PRESENTS

The Love of ELVIS

$2.50 PDC 54120-2

THE ONE AND ONLY MAGAZINE COLLECTION OF ELVIS MEMORABILIA!

ELVIS PHOTOS,
ELVIS DOLLS,
ELVIS JEWELRY,
ELVIS EVERYTHING!
PLUS A GIANT, PULL-OUT POSTER OF THE KING!

SPECTACULAR, COLOR-FULL COLLECTOR'S EDITION!

HE COMPLETE ELVIS: A fact-filled, fully illustrated directory to the King's entire recording career. Albums, singles, television concerts, released songs, foreign releases, bootleg recordings and 100s of photos!

NG ELVIS: A King-sized tribute to the King! 8 gigantic pull-out pinups, plus a colorful portrait portfolio. The only Presley poster book in print.

KISS MEETS THE PHANTOM: The exclusive magazine edition of the first KISS made-for-TV movie. Thrills, chills, blood, monsters and action! Exclusive interviews with the KISS stars and zillions of color photos!

THE FILMS OF ELVIS PRESLEY: A complete, color-full guide to every movie Elvis made. Cast lists, stories, songs, film stills, movie posters and theater lobby cards!

A KING-SIZE PRESLEY PICTORIAL

8 FABULOUS GIANT FOLD-OUT PIN-UPS! Plus A COLORFUL PORTRAIT PORTFOLIO

SPECIAL COLLECTOR'S MEMORIAL ISSUE

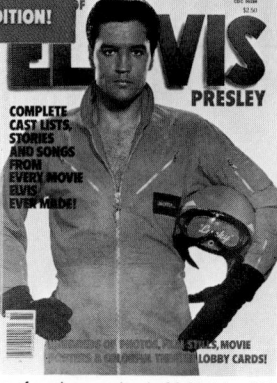

ELVIS PRESLEY

COMPLETE CAST LISTS, STORIES AND SONGS FROM EVERY MOVIE ELVIS EVER MADE!

THE LOVE OF ELVIS: The one-and-only magazine collection of Elvis memorabilia. Elvis jewelry, Elvis lipstick, Elvis notebooks, Elvis everything! Plus many never-before-published photos.

> **SPECIAL OFFER: Save $3.75!**
> Order all five for $12.50
> and we pay the postage!

HOW TO ORDER:

Type or print the name of each magazine you wish to order on a piece of paper and indicate the number of copies of each you

sh to buy. Type or print (legibly please!) your name, address and zip code. The price of each magazine is $2.50 (plus 75¢ ch for postage and handling). Enclose a check or money order for the entire amount and mail to:

PLATINUM PUBLICATIONS, INC. Dept. P
211 East 43rd Street, New York, N.Y. 10017

JOHN CULLEN MURPHY

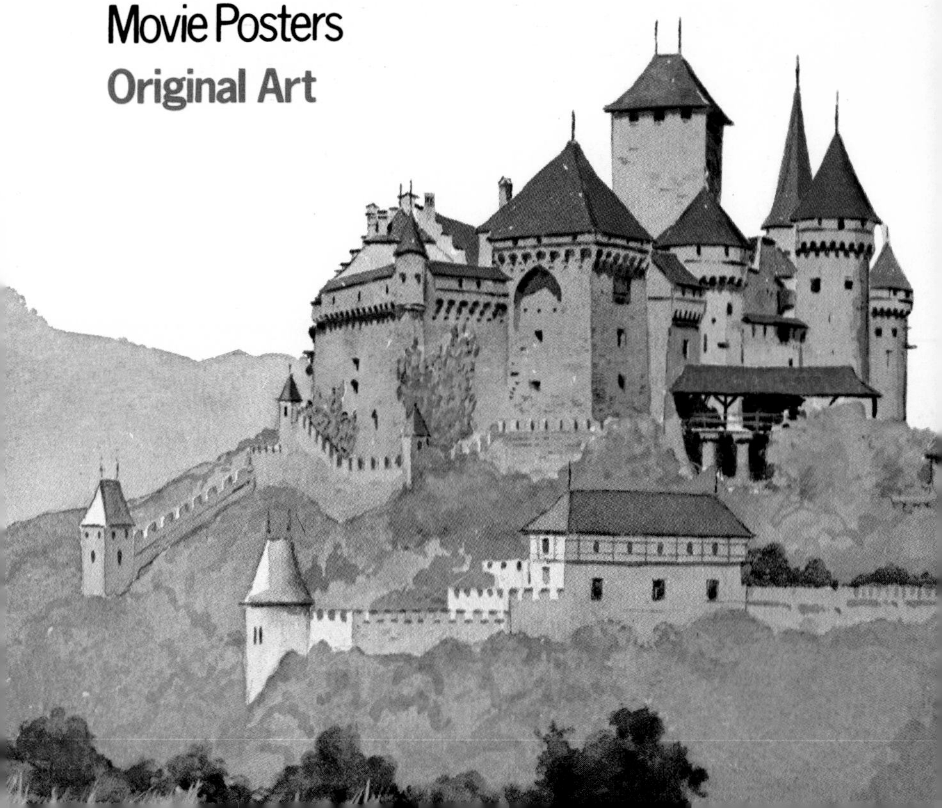

(Hawkman cont'd)	Good	Fine	Mint
#1	4.00	8.00	12.00
2	2.00	4.00	6.00
3-5: #4-Zatanna x-over	1.50	3.00	4.50
6-10: #9-Atom cameo	1.25	2.50	3.75
11-15	.80	1.60	2.40
16-27: Adam Strange x-over #18, cameo #19.
#25-G.A. Hawkman reprint.60		1.20	1.80

NOTE: _Anderson stories-#1-21; covers-#1-21. Kubert cover-#27._

HAWKSHAW THE DETECTIVE (See Okay)
1917   (10½x13½") (Sunday strip reprints)
(Black & White) (24 pgs.)
The Saalfield Publishing Co.

By Gus Mager	6.00	12.00	18.00

HAWTHORN-MELODY FARMS DAIRY COMICS
No Date ('50's)   (Giveaway)
Everybody's Publishing Co.

Cheerie Chick, Tuffy Turtle, Robin Koo Koo,
Donald & Longhorn Legends	1.00	2.00	3.00

HEADLINE COMICS (-- Crime #32-39)
2/43 - #22, 11-12/46; 1947 - #77, 10/56
Prize Publications

#1-Yank & Doodle x-over in Junior Rangers
	5.00	10.00	15.00
2,3	2.50	5.00	7.50
4-10	1.80	3.60	5.40
11,12,17,18	1.25	2.50	3.75
13-15-Blue Streak in all	1.50	3.00	4.50
16-Origin Atomic Man	2.00	4.00	6.00
19-S&K art	5.00	10.00	15.00
20-22: #21-Atomic Man ends
	1.50	3.00	4.50
23,24-(100% S&K)	6.00	12.00	18.00
25-35-S&K covers/stories	3.50	7.00	10.50
36-S&K story	3.00	6.00	9.00
37-1pg. S&K, Severin art	2.00	4.00	6.00
38,40-Meskin art	1.50	3.00	4.50
39,41-43,45-55	.75	1.50	2.25
44-S&K cover, Severin/Elder story, Meskin
story	2.50	5.00	7.50
56,57-S&K art	2.00	4.00	6.00
58-77	.80	1.60	2.40

HEAP, THE
Sept, 1971   (52 pgs.)
Skywald Publications

#1-Kinstler story reprint from Strange
Worlds #8	.50	1.00	1.50

HEART AND SOUL

1954
Mikeross Publications
	Good	Fine	Mint
#1	.50	1.00	1.50
2	.35	.70	1.05

HEART THROBS (Love Stories #147 on)
Aug, 1949 - #146, Oct, 1972
Quality/National #47(4-5/57)on(Arleigh#48-101)

#1-Ward cover, 9pgs. + Gustavson art
	10.00	20.00	30.00
2-Ward cover, 9pgs. + Gustavson art
	5.00	10.00	15.00
3-Gustavson story	3.00	6.00	9.00
4,6,8-Ward art, 8-9pgs.	3.50	7.00	10.50
5,7,9	1.50	3.00	4.50
10,15-Ward art	2.50	5.00	7.50
11-14,16-20	1.00	2.00	3.00
21-Ward cover	1.75	3.50	5.25
22,23-Ward story pencils	1.50	3.00	4.50
24-39	.70	1.40	2.10
40-Ward story; reprints 7pgs./#21
	1.50	3.00	4.50
41-50	.60	1.20	1.80
51-70	.35	.70	1.05
71-119,121-146: #102-123:Serial-Three Girls,
Their Lives, Their Loves.20		.40	.60
120-Adams cover	.40	.80	1.20

NOTE: _Gustavson story-#8._

HEAVY METAL (Magazine) ($1.50)
April, 1977 - Present
HM Communications

#1	1.00	2.00	3.00
2-5	.75	1.50	2.25
6-19	.50	1.00	1.50

HECKLE AND JECKLE (See Blue Ribbon Comics)
10/51 - #24, 10/55; #25, Fall/56 - #34, 6/59
St. John Publ. Co. #1-24/Pines #25 on

#1	2.00	4.00	6.00
2-10	1.00	2.00	3.00
11-20	.60	1.20	1.80
21-34	.40	.80	1.20

HECKLE AND JECKLE (TV) (See New Terrytoons)
Nov, 1962 - #4, Aug, 1963
Gold Key

#1-4	.20	.40	.60

(See March of Comics #379)

HECKLE AND JECKLE (TV)
May, 1966 - #2, Oct, 1966; #3, Aug, 1967
Dell Publishing Co.

Hawkman #5, © DC

Headline Comics #2, © PRIZE

Heart Throbs #2, © QUA

Hedy Devine Comics #23, © MCG

Hello Pal Comics #3, © HARV

He-Man #1, © Z-D

(Heckle and Jeckle cont'd)

	Good	Fine	Mint
#1-3	.15	.30	.45

HECTOR COMICS
1953 - 1954
Key Publications

#1-3	.50	1.00	1.50

HECTOR HEATHCOTE (TV)
March, 1964
Gold Key

#1(10111-403)	.15	.30	.45

HEDY DEVINE COMICS (Formerly USA #17)
(Hedy of Hollywood #36 on)
#22, Aug, 1947 - #50, Sept, 1952
Marvel Comics (RCM)   (#18-21 exist?)

#22	1.50	3.00	4.50
23-Wolverton art(1pg.) + Kurtzman's "Hey			
Look", 2pgs.	4.00	8.00	12.00
24,25,27-30-"Hey Look" by Kurtzman, 1-3pgs.,			
26-"Giggles & Grins" by Kurtzman			
	2.50	5.00	7.50
31-34,36-50	1.25	2.50	3.75
35-Four pgs. "Rusty" by Kurtzman			
	3.50	7.00	10.50

HEDY-MILLIE-TESSIE COMEDY (See Comedy)

HEDY WOLFE
August, 1957
Atlas Publishing Co. (Emgee)

#1	1.00	2.00	3.00

HEE HAW (TV)
July, 1970 - #7, Aug, 1971
Charlton Press

#1-7		.10	.20

HEIDI (See Dell Jr. Treasury #6)

HELEN OF TROY (See 4-Color Comics #684)

HELLO PAL COMICS (Short Story Comics)
Jan, 1943 - #3, May, 1943
Harvey Publications

#1-Rocketman & Rocketgirl begin; Yankee Doo-			
dle Jones app.; Mickey Rooney cover			
	8.00	16.00	24.00
2-Charlie McCarthy cover	6.00	12.00	18.00
3-Bob Hope cover	6.00	12.00	18.00

HELL-RIDER (Magazine)
Aug, 1971 - #2, Oct, 1971   (B&W)
Skywald Publications

	Good	Fine	Mint
#1-Origin & 1st app.; Butterfly & Wildbunch			
begins; drug story (heroin)			
	1.00	2.00	3.00
2	.65	1.35	2.00

NOTE: #3 advertised in Psycho #5 but did not
come out (Morrow cover). Buckler art-#1,2.

HELP! (Magazine)
8/60 - #12, 9/61; V2#1(#13), 2/62 - V2#8(#20),
2/64; #21, 10/64 - #26, 9/65
Edited by Harvey Kurtzman
General Promotions/Warren Publishing Co.

V1#1	5.00	10.00	15.00
2-4	1.50	3.00	4.50
5,9-Little Nemo reprint by Winsor McCay			
(3pgs. & 2pgs.)	2.00	4.00	6.00
6-8,10,12	1.50	3.00	4.50
11-Krazy Kat by George Herriman(2pgs.)			
	1.75	3.50	5.25
V2#1(#13, 2/62)-Spirit reprint by Eisner			
(7pgs.)	3.00	6.00	9.00
2-8(#14-20): #2-The Humor of Charles Dana			
Gibson(6pgs.). #5-Miss Lace by Caniff			
(5pgs.). #6-Skippy by P. Crosby(6pgs.).			
#8-Mutt & Jeff by Ham Fisher(4pgs.)			
	2.00	4.00	6.00
21-(75¢ Annual-10/64)	1.50	3.00	4.50
22(1/65)-Robert Crumb-Fritz the Cat(2pgs.)			
in Public Gallery(Early Underground Comix			
Development)	3.00	6.00	9.00
23,26	1.50	3.00	4.50
24-Fritz the Cat, 2pgs.	3.00	6.00	9.00
25-Sketchbook-Life in Bulgaria			
	2.50	5.00	7.50

NOTE: Robert Crumb art-#22,24,25. Gilbert
Sheldon's Wonder Warthog-V2#4(16), V2#6(18),
V2#8(20),22-26. Covers feature photos of:
#1-Sid Caesar, #2-Ernie Kovacs, #3-Jerry Lew-
is, #4-Mort Sahl, #5-Dave Garroway, #6-Jona-
than Winters, #7-Tom Poston, #8-Hugh Downs,
#9-Phil Ford/Mime Hines, #10-Jackie Gleason.

HE-MAN
Fall, 1952
Ziff-Davis Publ. Co. (Approved Comics)

#1-Kinstler cover	2.00	4.00	6.00

HE-MAN
1954 - #2, July, 1954
Toby Press

#1	3.00	6.00	9.00
2	1.50	3.00	4.50

HENNESSEY (See 4-Color Comics #1200,1280)

HENRY
1935 (52pgs.)(Daily B&W strip reprints)
David McKay Publications

	Good	Fine	Mint
#1-by Carl Anderson	5.00	10.00	15.00

HENRY
1946 - #65, Apr-June, 1961
Dell Publishing Co.

	Good	Fine	Mint
4-Color #122,155	2.00	4.00	6.00
#1	2.00	4.00	6.00
2	.65	1.35	2.00
3-10	.50	1.00	1.50
11-20	.40	.80	1.20
21-65	.30	.60	.90

HENRY (See March of Comics #43,58,84,101,
112,129,147,162,178,189)

HENRY ALDRICH COMICS
Aug-Sept, 1950 - #22, 1954
Dell Publishing Co.

#1-Series written by John Stanley; Bill Williams art	3.00	6.00	9.00
2-5	2.00	4.00	6.00
6-22	1.25	2.50	3.75

HENRY BREWSTER
Feb, 1966 - V2#7, Sept, 1967 (All Giants)
Country Wide (M.F. Ent.)

#1-6(12/66)-Powell art in most	.25	.50	.75
V2#7	.20	.40	.60

HERBIE (See Forbidden Worlds)
April-May, 1964 - #23, Feb, 1967
American Comics Group

#1	7.00	14.00	21.00
2-5	4.00	8.00	12.00
6,7,9,10	2.50	5.00	7.50
8-Origin The Fat Fury	3.50	7.00	10.50
11-22	2.00	4.00	6.00
23-Reprts.1st sty/F.W.#73	2.00	4.00	6.00

NOTE: *All have* Whitney *art/covers.*

HERBIE GOES TO MONTE CARLO, -- RIDES AGAIN
(See Walt Disney Showcase #24,41)

HERCULES
Oct, 1967 - #13, Sept, 1960; Dec, 1968
Charlton Comics

	Good	Fine	Mint
#1-Thane of Bagarth series begins	.60	1.20	1.80
2-13	.50	1.00	1.50
8-(Low distribution)-35¢ magazine format (B&W)(12/68)-reprints	3.00	6.00	9.00

HERCULES (See The Mighty --)

HERCULES UNBOUND
Oct-Nov, 1975 - #12, Aug-Sept, 1977
National Periodical Publications

#1-Wood inks	.30	.60	.90
2-5	.20	.40	.60
6-12	.15	.30	.45

NOTE: Simonson *art-#7,9-12.* Wood *inks-#1-12.*

HERCULES UNCHAINED (See 4-Color #1006,1121)

HERE COMES SANTA (See March of Comics #30,
213,340)

HERE'S HOWIE!
Jan-Feb, 1952 - #20, Mar-Apr, 1955
National Periodical Publications

#1	2.50	5.00	7.50
2-5	1.75	3.50	5.25
6-10	1.00	2.00	3.00
11-20	.60	1.20	1.80

HERMAN & KATNIP (See Harvey Hits#14,25,31,41)

HERO FOR HIRE (Power Man #17 on)
June, 1972 - #16, Dec, 1973
Marvel Comics Group

#1-Origin Luke Cage	1.00	2.00	3.00
2,3	.70	1.40	2.10
4-10	.50	1.00	1.50
11-16	.40	.80	1.20

HEROES ALL CATHOLIC ACTION ILLUSTRATED
V4#9, 11/45 - V4#10, 3/46 (16pgs)(Soft cover)
Heroes All Co.

V4#9,10	.80	1.60	2.40

HEROES, INC. PRESENTS CANNON
1969 - #2, 1976
Wally Wood/CPL/Gang Publ. #2

No#-Wood/Ditko art	3.00	6.00	9.00
2-Wood cover (8½x10½")(B&W)($2.00)-Ditko & Wood stories	1.00	2.00	3.00

NOTE: *First issue not distributed by publisher; it is rumored that 9,000 copies were storied in a warehouse and stolen.*

Herbie #19. © ACG

Here's Howie #6. © DC

Heroes Inc. #2, © Wally Wood

205

Heroic Comics #22, © EAS   Hickory #1, © QUA   High Adventure #1, © Decker

HEROES OF THE WILD FRONTIER (Formerly Baff-
#26, 3/55 - #2, 4/56   ling Mysteries)
Ace Periodicals
                         Good   Fine   Mint
#26(#1),27,28   .80   1.60   2.40
#2   .60   1.20   1.80

HEROIC COMICS (Reg'lar Fellas #1-15; New Her
Aug, 1940 - #97, June, 1955   oic #41 on)
Eastern Color Printing Co./Famous Funnies

#1-Origin Hydroman by Bill Everett & the
   Purple Zombie   35.00   70.00 105.00
 2   20.00   40.00   60.00
 3,4   15.00   30.00   45.00
 5,6   12.00   24.00   36.00
 7-Origin Man O'Metal, 1 pg.
                          12.00   24.00   36.00
 8-10   7.00   14.00   21.00
11,13   6.00   12.00   18.00
12-Origin Music Master   8.00   16.00   24.00
14-Hydroman x-over in Rainbow Boy; also in
   #15. Origin Rainbow Boy
                           8.00   16.00   24.00
15-Intro. Downbeat   7.00   14.00   21.00
16-Hydroman & Man O'War begin
                           5.00   10.00   15.00
17-20: #17-Rainbow Boy x-over in Hydroman.
   #19-Rainbow Boy x-over in Hydroman & vice
   versa   5.00   10.00   15.00
21-30: #23-Rainbow Boy x-over in Hydroman
                           2.50   5.00   7.50
31,34   1.50   3.00   4.50
32,33,35-38-Toth art   2.25   4.50   6.75
39-Ingels art   2.00   4.00   6.00
40-42-Toth, Ingels stys.   2.50   5.00   7.50
43-47,49,50-Toth stories; Everett story-#44
                           2.00   4.00   6.00
48,52-55,57,59   1.00   2.00   3.00
51-Williamson story; Kiefer cover
                           4.00   8.00   12.00
56,58-Toth covers   1.50   3.00   4.50
60,61,64-Everett stories   1.25   2.50   3.75
62,63-Everett covers   2.00   4.00   6.00
65-Williamson/Frazetta story; Evans story,
   2pgs.   5.00   10.00   15.00
66,75,94-Frazetta(2pgs.) in each
                           2.50   5.00   7.50
67,73-Two Frazetta stories, 2pgs. each
                           3.00   6.00   9.00
68,74,76-80,84,85,88-93,95-97
                           .75   1.50   2.25
69,72-Two Frazetta stories (6&8 pgs. total)
                           5.00   10.00   15.00
70,71,86,87-Frazetta, 3-4pgs. each
                           3.00   6.00   9.00
81,82-1pg. Frazetta art   1.50   3.00   4.50
83-½pg. Frazetta art   1.50   3.00   4.50
NOTE: Everett stories (Hydroman)-#1-9,60;
covers-#1-9,62,63.

HEY THERE, IT'S YOGI BEAR (See Movie Comics)

HI-ADVENTURE HEROES (Hanna-Barbera)
May, 1969 - #2, Aug, 1969
Gold Key
                         Good   Fine   Mint
#1-Three Musketeers, Gulliver, Arabian
   Knights stories   .35   .70   1.05
 2-Three Musketeers, Micro-Venture, Arabian
   Knights   .25   .50   .75

HI AND LOIS (See 4-Color #683,774,955)

HI AND LOIS
Nov, 1969 - #11, July, 1971
Charlton Comics

#1   .25   .50   .75
2-11   .20   .40

HICKORY
Oct, 1949 - #6, Aug, 1950
Quality Comics Group

#1-Sahl art/covers   3.50   7.00   10.50
2,4-6   2.50   5.00   7.50
3-Wardish cover by Sahl 3.00   6.00   9.00

HIDDEN CREW, THE (See The United States A.F.)

HIDE-OUT (See 4-Color Comics #346)

HIDING PLACE, THE (Religious)
1973   (35¢)
Spire Christian Comics/Fleming H. Revell Co.

#1   .20   .40   .60

HIGH ADVENTURE
October, 1957
Red Top(Decker)Comics (Farrell)

#1-Krigstein reprint from Explorer Joe
   (re-issue on cover)   1.00   2.00   3.00

HIGH ADVENTURE (See 4-Color #949,1001)

HIGH CHAPPARAL (TV)
August, 1968
Gold Key

#1(10226-808)   .25   .50   .75

HIGH SCHOOL CONFIDENTIAL DIARY
June, 1960 - #11, Mar, 1962
Charlton Comics

#1   .25   .50   .75
2-11   .15   .30   .45

206

HI-HO COMICS
1946
Four Star Publications

	Good	Fine	Mint
#1-Cole cover	1.50	3.00	4.50
2,3	1.00	2.00	3.00

HI-JINX
July-Aug, 1947 - 1949
B&I Publ. Co.(American Comics Group)/Creston/
LaSalle

#1-3	1.25	2.50	3.75
4-7-Milt Gross	1.25	2.50	3.75
132pg. issue, no#, no date (LaSalle)			
	2.00	4.00	6.00

HI-LITE COMICS
Fall, 1945
E. R. Ross Publishing Co.

#1-Miss Shady	4.00	8.00	12.00

HILLBILLY COMICS
Aug, 1955 - #4, July, 1956 (Satire)
Charlton Comics

#1	1.00	2.00	3.00
2-4	.60	1.20	1.80

HIP-IT-TY HOP (See March of Comics #15)

HI-SCHOOL ROMANCE DATE BOOK
Nov, 1962 - #3, Mar, 1963 (25¢ Giant)
Harvey Publications

#1-Powell, Baker art	1.75	3.50	5.25
2,3	1.25	2.50	3.75

HI-SCHOOL ROMANCES (-- Romance #1-15)
Oct, 1949 - #71, Jan, 1958
Harvey Publications/True Love(Home Comics)

#1-Powell art-most issues	1.50	3.00	4.50
2-20	.80	1.60	2.40
21-71	.50	1.00	1.50

NOTE: *Powell art-#1-3,5,8,12-14,16,18,21-23,
25-27,30-34,36,37,39,45-48,50,57,58,60,65,67,
69.*

HIS NAME IS SAVAGE (Magazine format)
#1, June, 1968 (One Shot)
Adventure House Press

#1-Gil Kane art	2.50	5.00	7.50

HI-SPOT COMICS (Red Ryder #1 & 3 on)
#2, Nov, 1940

Hawley Publications

	Good	Fine	Mint
#2-David Innes of Pellucidar; art by J. C. Burroughs; written by Edgar R. Burroughs (Rare)			
	130.00	260.00	390.00

HIT COMICS
July, 1940 - #65, July, 1950
Quality Comics Group

#1-Origin Neon, the Unknown & Hercules; intro. The Red Bee; Blaze Barton, the Strange Twins, X-5 Super Agent, Casey Jones, Jack & Jill(ends #7), & Bob & Swab begin			
	150.00	300.00	450.00
2-The Old Witch begins, ends #14			
	70.00	140.00	210.00
3-Casey Jones ends	60.00	120.00	180.00
4-Super Agent(ends #17), & Betty Bates(ends #65) begin; X-5 ends	45.00	90.00	135.00
5-(classic cover)	60.00	120.00	180.00
6-10: #10-Old Witch by Crandall, 4pgs.			
	35.00	70.00	105.00
11-17: #13-Bob & Swab, Blaze Barton ends. #17-Last Neon; Crandall Hercules in all			
	30.00	60.00	90.00
18-Origin Stormy Foster, the Great Defender; The Ghost of Flanders begins; Crandall cover	35.00	70.00	105.00
19,20	30.00	60.00	90.00
21-24: #21-Last Hercules. #24-Last Red Bee & Strange Twins	25.00	50.00	75.00
25-Origin Kid Eternity by Moldoff			
	27.50	55.00	82.50
26-Blackhawk x-over in Kid Eternity			
	20.00	40.00	60.00
27-29	12.00	24.00	36.00
30,31-"Bill the Magnificent" by Kurtzman, 11pgs. in each	10.00	20.00	30.00
32-40: #34-Last Stormy Foster			
	6.00	12.00	18.00
41-50	4.50	9.00	13.50
51-60-Last Kid Eternity	3.00	6.00	9.00
61,63-Crandall cover/story; Jeb Rivers begins #61	4.00	8.00	12.00
62	2.50	5.00	7.50
64,65-Crandall art	3.50	7.00	10.50

NOTE: *Crandall stories-#11-17(Hercules),#23,
24(Stormy Foster); covers-#18-20,23,24. Fine
covers-#1-17; story #22 only. Ward cover-#33.*

HI-YO SILVER (See Lone Ranger's Famous
Horse --, March of Comics #215, & The Lone
Ranger)

HOCUS POCUS (Formerly Funny Book)
#9, Aug-Sept, 1946
Parents' Magazine Press

Hi-School Romances #35. © HARV

Hit Comics #9. © QUA

Hit Comics #37. © QUA

Hollywood Confessions #1, © STJ   Hollywood Pictorial #3, © STJ   Hollywood Secrets #5, © QUA

(Hocus Pocus cont'd)	Good	Fine	Mint
#9	1.00	2.00	3.00

HOGAN'S HEROES (TV)
June, 1966 - #9, Oct, 1969
Dell Publishing Co.

#1	.25	.50	.75
2,4-9: #9-reprints #1	.15	.30	.45
3-Ditko/Trapani story	.35	.70	1.05

HOLIDAY COMICS
1942 (196 pgs.) (25¢)
Fawcett Publications

#1-Reprints three Fawcett comics; Capt. Marvel, Nyoka(#1) & Whiz	40.00	100.00	160.00

HOLIDAY COMICS
January, 1951 - 1952
Star Publications

#1-8-Funny animal contents (Frisky Fables); L. B. Cole covers	.80	1.60	2.40

HOLI-DAY SURPRISE (Formerly Summer Fun)
1967 (25¢)
Charlton Comics

V2#55-Giant	.15	.30

HOLLYWOOD COMICS
1944
New Age Publications

#1	2.50	5.00	7.50

HOLLYWOOD CONFESSIONS
October, 1949 - #2, Dec, 1949
St. John Publishing Co.

#1-Kubert cover/3 stys.	7.00	14.00	21.00
2-Kubert cvr/sty.(Scarce)	10.00	20.00	30.00

HOLLYWOOD DIARY
Dec, 1949 - #5, July-Aug, 1950
Quality Comics Group

#1-Ward cover	4.00	8.00	12.00
2-5: #2-Photo cover	2.50	5.00	7.50

HOLLYWOOD FILM STORIES
April, 1950 - #4, 1950
Feature Publications/Prize

#1	4.00	8.00	12.00
2-4	3.00	6.00	9.00

HOLLYWOOD FUNNY FOLKS (Formerly Funny Folks; Nutsy Squirrel #61 on)
#31, Feb, 1951 - #60, Jul-Aug, 1954
National Periodical Publications

	Good	Fine	Mint
#31-40	.80	1.60	2.40
41-60	.40	.80	1.20

HOLLYWOOD LOVE DOCTOR (See Doctor Anthony King --)

HOLLYWOOD PICTORIAL (-- Romances on cover)
#3, Jan, 1950
St. John Publishing Co.

#3-Matt Baker story	3.00	6.00	9.00

(Becomes a movie magazine - Hollywood Pictorial Western with #4.)

HOLLYWOOD ROMANCES
V2#46, 11/66; V2#47, 10/67 - #59, June, 1971
Charlton Comics

V2#46-Rolling Stones cover/story	.35	.70	1.05
V2#47-59: #56-"Born to Heart Break" begins		.15	.30

HOLLYWOOD SECRETS
Nov, 1949 - #6, Sept, 1950
Quality Comics Group

#1-Ward cover, 9pgs.	9.00	18.00	27.00
2-Crandall art, Ward cover, 9pgs.	6.00	12.00	18.00
3-6: All photo covers	2.50	5.00	7.50
-- of Romance, I.W. Reprint #9	.40	.80	1.20

HOLYOKE ONE-SHOT
1944 - 1945 (All reprints)
Holyoke Publishing Co. (Tem Publ.)

#1-Grit Grady (on cover only), Miss Victory, Alias X(origin)-All reprints from Captain Fearless	2.00	4.00	6.00
2-Rusty Dugan (Corporal); Capt. Fearless (origin), Mr. Miracle (origin), app.	2.00	4.00	6.00
3-Miss Victory-Crash #4 reprints; Cat Man-(origin), Solar Legion by Kirby app.; Miss Victory on cover only (1945)	5.00	10.00	15.00
4-Mr. Miracle-The Blue Streak app.	2.00	4.00	6.00
5-U.S. Border Patrol Comics(Sgt. Dick Carter of the--), Miss Victory (story matches cover #3), Citizen Smith, & Mr. Miracle			

(Holyoke O-S cont'd)	Good	Fine	Mint
app.	2.00	4.00	6.00

6-Capt. Fearless, Alias X, Capt.Stone(splash used as cover-#10); Diamond Jim & Rusty Dugan(splash from cover-#2)
| | 2.00 | 4.00 | 6.00 |

7-Z-2, Strong Man, Blue Streak(story matches cover-#8)-Reprints from Crash #2
| | 3.00 | 6.00 | 9.00 |

8-Blue Streak, Strong Man(story matches cover-#7)-Crash reprints 2.00 4.00 6.00

9-Citizen Smith-The Blue Streak, Solar Legion by Kirby & Strongman, the Perfect Human app.; reprints from Crash #4 & 5; Citizen Smith on cover only-from story in #5(1944-before #3) 4.00 8.00 12.00

10-Captain Stone(Crash reprints); Solar Legion by S&K 4.00 8.00 12.00

HOMER COBB (See Adventures of --)

HOMER HOOPER
July, 1953 - #3, Sept, 1953
Atlas Comics

#1-3	.50	1.00	1.50

HOMER, THE HAPPY GHOST (See Adventures of--)
3/55 - #22, 11/58; V2#1, 11/69 - V2#5, 7/70
Atlas(ACI/PPI/WPI)/Marvel Comics

V1#1	.65	1.35	2.00
2-22	.35	.70	1.05
V2#1-V2#5(1969-70)		.10	.20

HOME RUN (See A-1 Comics #89)

HONEYBEE BIRDWHISTLE AND HER PET PEPI (Introducing)
1969   (24pgs.)(B&W)(Slick cover)
Newspaper Enterprise Association (Giveaway)

No#-Contains Freckles newspaper strips with a short biography of Henry Fornhals (artist) & Fred Fox (writer) of the strip.
| | 2.00 | 4.00 | 6.00 |

HONEYMOON (Formerly Gay Comics)
#41, January, 1950
A Lover's Magazine(USA) (Marvel)

#41	.60	1.20	1.80

HONEYMOON ROMANCE
April, 1950   (25¢) (Digest Size)
Artful Publications

#1 (Scarce)	3.00	6.00	9.00

HONEY WEST (TV)
Sept, 1966
Gold Key

	Good	Fine	Mint
#1(10186-609)	.70	1.40	2.10

HONG KONG PHOOEY (Hanna-Barbera)
June, 1975 - #9, Nov, 1976
Charlton Comics

#1-9		.10	.20

HOODED HORSEMAN, THE (Formerly Blazing West)
#23, 5-6/52 - #27, 1-2/53; #18, 12-1/54-55 - #27, 6-7/56
American Comics Group (Michel Publ.)

#23(5-6/52)-Hooded Horseman, Injun Jones continues	1.50	3.00	4.50
24-27(1-2/53)	1.20	2.40	3.60
#18(11-12/54)(Formerly Out of the Night), 19	1.20	2.40	3.60
20-Origin Johnny Injun	1.20	2.40	3.60
21-25,27(6-7/56)	.80	1.60	2.40
26-Origin & 1st app. Cowboy Sahib; 11pgs. Starr art	1.20	2.40	3.60

NOTE: *Whitney stories/covers-#20-22.*

HOODED MENACE, THE (Also see Daring Advs.)
1951   (One Shot)
Realistic/Avon Periodicals

No#-Based on a band of hooded outlaws in the Pacific Northwest, 1900-1906; reprinted in Daring Advs. #15   30.00 60.00 90.00

HOOT GIBSON WESTERN
#3, Sept, 1950 - #9, 1951
Fox Features Syndicate

#3(#1)-Wood story	6.00	12.00	18.00
4-9	3.50	7.00	10.50
Western Roundup('50)(25¢-132pgs.)			
	5.00	10.00	15.00

HOPALONG CASSIDY (Also see Master Comics)
1943 - #91, July, 1954
Fawcett Publications

#1	20.00	40.00	60.00
2	10.00	20.00	30.00
3-5	7.00	14.00	21.00
6-14	5.00	10.00	15.00
15-30	3.50	7.00	10.50
31-50	2.25	4.50	6.75
51-91	1.50	3.00	4.50
Grape Nuts Flakes giveaway(1950)			
	2.50	5.00	7.50

Holyoke One-Shot #4. © HOKE

Hoot Gibson's Western Roundup. © FOX

Hopalong Cassidy #9. © FAW

Hoppy The Marvel Bunny #7, © FAW   Horrific #4, © Harwell   Horror From The Tomb #1, © PG

(Hopalong Cassidy cont'd)

	Good	Fine	Mint
--in the Strange Legacy	3.50	7.00	10.50
--Gives a Helping Hand(1951,52pgs.)B&W,Samuel Lowe Co. #517-5	2.50	5.00	7.50
--& the Mad Barber(1951)-Bond Bread giveaway (7"x5")	4.00	8.00	12.00
--Meets the Brend Brothers Bandits	3.50	7.00	10.50

HOPALONG CASSIDY
#92, Aug, 1954 - #135, May-June, 1959
National Periodical Publications

#92-135	1.75	3.50	5.25

NOTE: *Gil Kane art-1956 up.*

HOPE SHIP
June-Aug, 1963
Dell Publishing Co.

#1	.65	1.35	2.00

HOPPY THE MARVEL BUNNY
Dec, 1945 - 1947 (See Fawcett Funny Animal)
Fawcett Publications

#1	3.50	7.00	10.50
2-15	1.75	3.50	5.25

HORACE & DOTTY DRIPPLE (Dotty Dripple #1-24)
#25, Aug, 1952 - #43, Oct, 1955
Harvey Publications

#25-43	.50	1.00	1.50

HORIZONTAL LIEUTENANT, THE(See Movie Classics)

HORRIFIC (Terrific #14 on)
Sept, 1952 - #13, Sept, 1954
Artful/Comic Media/Harwell/Mystery

#1	2.00	4.00	6.00
2-10	1.00	2.00	3.00
11-13	.80	1.60	2.40

HORROR FROM THE TOMB (Mysterious Stories #2)
Sept, 1954
Premier Magazine Co.

#1-Woodbridge/Torres sty.	3.00	6.00	9.00

HORRORS (-- of Mystery)
#13, 6/53 - #15, 1953
Star Publications

#13-Crime stories	1.75	3.50	5.25
14,15-L. B. Cole covers	1.75	3.50	5.25

HORRORS OF THE UNDERWORLD
#14, 1953 - #15, April, 1954
Star Publications

	Good	Fine	Mint
#14,15-L. B. Cole covers	1.75	3.50	5.25

HORRORS OF WAR
#11, Jan, 1953 - #12, Mar, 1953?
Star Publications

#11-Two Disbrow stories	2.50	5.00	7.50
12-L. B. Cole covers	1.75	3.50	5.25

HORROR TALES (Magazine)
V1#7, 6/69 - V6#6, 12/74; V7#2, 5/76 - Present
(V1-V6, 52pgs; V7,v8#2, 112pgs; V8#4 on, 68pgs)
(No V5#3, V7#1, V8#1,3)
Eerie Publications

V1#7-9	.35	.70	1.05
V2#1-6('70),V3#1-6('71)	.25	.50	.75
V4#1-3,5,6('72)	.25	.50	.75
V4#4-LSD story reprint/Weird V3#5	.50	1.00	1.50
V5#1,2,4,5(6/73),5(10/73)	.25	.50	.75
V6#1-6('74),V7#2-4('76)	.25	.50	.75
V8#2,4,5('77)	.25	.50	.75

NOTE: *Bondage covers-V6#1,3.*

HORSE FEATHERS COMICS
Nov, 1945
Lev Gleason Publications

#1-Wolverton's Scoop Scuttle	7.00	14.00	21.00
2-4	2.00	4.00	6.00

HORSEMASTERS, THE (See 4-Color #1260)

HORSE SOLDIERS, THE (See 4-Color #1048)

HORSE WITHOUT A HEAD, THE (See Movie Comics)

HOT DOG
June-July, 1954 - #4, Dec-Jan, 1954-55
Magazine Enterprises

#1(A-1#107),2,3(A-1#115), 4(A-1#136)	.80	1.60	2.40

HOTEL DEPAREE-SUNDANCE (See 4-Color #1126)

HOT ROD AND SPEEDWAY COMICS
Feb-Mar, 1952 - #5, Apr-May, 1953
Hillman Periodicals

#1	1.25	2.50	3.75
2-Krigstein story	1.80	3.60	5.40
3-5	.80	1.60	2.40

HOT ROD CARTOONS (Magazine)
Nov, 1964 - 1974 (35¢)
Petersen Publ. Co.

	Good	Fine	Mint
#1	1.75	3.50	5.25
2-5,8,9	.75	1.50	2.25
6,7,10-12,15-Toth art	1.25	2.50	3.75
13,14,16-20	.40	.80	1.20
21-46,48-59	.35	.70	1.05
47-Toth art, 2pgs.	1.00	2.00	3.00
60-Robert Williams art	1.00	2.00	3.00

HOT ROD COMICS
Nov, 1951 - V2#7, Feb, 1953
Fawcett Publications

V1#1-Powell art in all	1.50	3.00	4.50
2-6, V2#7	1.00	2.00	3.00

"HOT ROD" KING
Fall, 1952
Ziff-Davis Publ. Co.

#1-Giacoia art	1.00	2.00	3.00

HOT ROD RACERS (Grand Prix #16 on)
Dec, 1964 - #15, 1967
Charlton Comics

#1	.20	.40	.60
2-15		.20	.40

HOT RODS AND RACING CARS
Nov, 1951 - #120, June, 1973
Charlton Comics (Motor Mag. #1)

#1	1.25	2.50	3.75
2-10	.60	1.20	1.80
11-20	.25	.50	.75
21-50	.20	.40	.60
51-120		.15	.30

HOT SHOT CHARLIE
1947 (Lee Elias)
Hillman Periodicals

#1	1.25	2.50	3.75

HOT STUFF CREEPY CAVES
Nov, 1974 - Present
Harvey Publications

#1-7		.15	.25

HOT STUFF SIZZLERS
1960 - #59, Mar, 1974
Harvey Publications

	Good	Fine	Mint
#1	1.00	2.00	3.00
2-20	.35	.70	1.05
21-59		.15	.35

HOT STUFF, THE LITTLE DEVIL
Oct, 1957 - Present
Harvey Publications (Illustrated Humor)

#1	3.00	6.00	9.00
2-5	1.20	2.40	3.60
6-20	.40	.80	1.20
21-60	.25	.50	.75
61-146		.15	.35
Shoestore Giveaway('63)	.35	.70	1.05

HOT WHEELS (TV)
Mar-Apr, 1970 - #6, Jan-Feb, 1971
National Periodical Publications

#1	.80	1.60	2.40
2,4,5	.60	1.20	1.80
3-Adams story	1.20	1.40	3.60
6-Adams cover/story	1.50	3.00	4.50

NOTE: *Toth art-#1-5; covers-#1,4,5.*

HOUSE OF MYSTERY (See Limited Collectors'
Edition & Super DC Giant)

HOUSE OF MYSTERY
Dec-Jan, 1951-52 - Present
National Periodical Publications/DC Comics

#1	12.00	24.00	36.00
2,3	6.00	12.00	18.00
4,5	5.00	10.00	15.00
6-15	4.00	8.00	12.00
16-34-Last pre-code ish	2.50	5.00	7.50
35-60	1.25	2.50	3.75
61,66,72-Kirby stories	1.75	3.35	5.00
62-65,67-71,73-75	.70	1.40	2.10
76,82,84,85-Kirby stys.	1.40	2.80	4.20
77-81,83,86-100	.50	1.00	1.50
101-108,110-119	.40	.80	1.20
109,120-Toth art + Kubert #109			
	1.25	2.50	3.75
121-142	.30	.60	.90
143-J'onn J'onzz, Manhunter begins, ends #173			
(6/64)	.70	1.40	2.10
144-148,150	.25	.50	.75
149-Toth story	.70	1.40	2.10
151-155,157,159	.20	.40	.60
156-Origin Robby Reed in Dial H for Hero(begins; ends #173)	.40	.80	1.20
158-Origin & last app. Diabolu Idol-Head in J'onn J'onzz	.25	.50	.75
160-Intro. Marco Xavier (Martian Manhunter) & Vulture Crime Organization in J'onn J'onzz			

Hot Rods & Racing Cars =35. © CC

House Of Mystery =2. © DC

House Of Mystery #185. © DC

House Of Mystery #204, © DC

House Of Secrets #7, © DC

House Of Secrets #66, © DC

(House of Mystery cont'd)	Good	Fine	Mint
(7/66), ends #173; Plastic Man x-over			
	.25	.50	.75
161-168,170	.20	.40	.60
169-Origin & 1st app. Gem Girl in Dial H for Hero			
	.20	.40	.60
171-177: #174-Mystery format begins			
	.20	.40	.60
178-Adams story	1.25	2.50	3.75
179-Adams/Orlando + Wrightson (1st pro work)			
	1.50	3.00	4.50
180,181,183: Wrightson stys.+ Wood in #180,183			
	1.00	2.00	3.00
182-Toth reprint	.25	.50	.75
184-Kane/Wood + Toth story	.80	1.60	2.40
185-Williamson/Kaluta story; 3pgs. Wood art			
	1.20	2.40	3.60
186-Adams + Wrightson	1.40	2.80	4.20
187,190-Toth reprints	.40	.80	1.20
188-Wrightson story	1.20	2.40	3.60
189-Wood story	.60	1.20	1.80
191,195-Wrightson story + Redondo #195			
	1.20	2.40	3.60
192,193,198,200	.20	.40	.60
194,196-Toth reprints	.40	.80	1.20
197-Redondo story	.50	1.00	1.50
199-Wood & Kirby story	.80	1.60	2.40
201,205,206,208-210	.15	.30	.45
202,203,207,211: Redondo art in all			
	.25	.50	.75
204-Wrightson art, 9pgs.	.90	1.80	2.70
212,213,215,216,218,220,222,223,225			
	.15	.30	.45
214,217,219-Redondo stories	.25	.50	.75
221-Wrightson/Kaluta story	.60	1.20	1.80
224-Adams inks + Wrightson stories; begin 100 pg. issues; Phantom Stranger reprint			
	.80	1.60	2.40
226-Wrightson + Redondo stories; Phantom Stranger reprint			
	.50	1.00	1.50
227-Redondo story	.25	.50	.75
228-Adams + Wrightson stys.	.90	1.80	2.70
229-Wrightson(reprint) + Redondo story; Toth story; last 100pg. ish	.50	1.00	1.50
230-234,237-240,242,243: #230-68pgs.			
	.15	.30	.45
235-Redondo story	.25	.50	.75
236-Adams inks, Ditko sty.	.25	.50	.75
241-Redondo story	.20	.40	.60
244-Wrightson Spectre app.	.25	.50	.75
245-250		.15	.35
251-($1.00 size)-Wood art	.50	1.00	1.50
252-265	.40	.80	1.20

NOTE: *Adams covers-#175-192,196,197,199,251-254. Alcala stories-#209,211-215,217,219,220, 222,224-228. Ditko story-#254,258. Drucker story-#37. Howard story-#254. Infantino stories-#110,111. Bob Kane story-#84. Kaluta*
story-#109,195,200,202,250; covers-#200-202, 210,212,233,260,261,263. Kirby story-#63, 194,199; covers-#76,78,79,85. Morrow stories-#192,196,255. Newton story-#259. Orlando art-#175(2pgs.). Reese story-#195,200,205(inks). Starlin art-#207(2pgs.). Wrightson covers-#193-195,204,207,209,211,213,214,217,221,231, 236,255,256.

HOUSE OF SECRETS

11-12/56 - #80, 9-10/66; #81, 8-9/69 - #140, 2-3/76; #141, 8-9/76 - #154, 10-11/78
National Periodical Publications/DC Comics

	Good	Fine	Mint
#1-Drucker story	12.00	24.00	36.00
2-Moreira art	6.00	12.00	18.00
3-Kirby cover/story	6.00	12.00	18.00
4,8-Kirby art	4.00	8.00	12.00
5-7,9,10	3.50	7.00	10.50
11,12-Kirby cover/story	3.50	7.00	10.50
13-20	2.00	4.00	6.00
21,22,24-47,49,50	1.20	2.40	3.60
23-Origin Mark Merlin	1.40	2.80	4.20
48-Toth story	1.40	2.80	4.20
51-60,62: #58-Origin Mark Merlin retold			
	.60	1.20	1.80
61-First Eclipso	.70	1.40	2.10
63-67-Toth stories	1.20	2.40	3.60
68-80: #73-Mark Merlin ends, Prince Ra-Man begins. #80-Eclipso, Prince Ra-Man end			
	.30	.60	.90
81,84,86-89: #81-Mystery format begins			
	.20	.40	.60
82-Adams story(inks)	.80	1.60	2.40
83-Toth story	.60	1.20	1.80
85-Adams story(inks)	.80	1.60	2.40
90-Buckler(1st art in comics)/Adams story			
	.90	1.80	2.70
91-Wood story	.60	1.20	1.80
92-Intro. Swamp Thing; Wrightson story (6-7/71)	8.00	16.00	24.00
93,96-98-Toth reprints + Wood-#96			
	.65	1.35	2.00
94-Wrightson inks + Toth story-#94 (reprint)			
	1.00	2.00	3.00
95,99,102,104-Redondo stys.	.30	.60	.90
100,101,103,105-112,114,115	.20	.40	.60
113,116-Redondo stories	.25	.50	.75
117,119,120-122,124-130	.20	.40	.60
118-Evans story	.25	.50	.75
123-12pgs. Toth art	.30	.60	.90
131-134,136-138	.15	.30	.45
135,139-Wrightson covers; Redondo story-#139			
	.25	.50	.75
140-Origin the Patchworkman; Redondo & Wrightson art	.50	1.00	1.50
141-154: #150-Phantom Stranger, Dr. 13 app.			
	.25	.45	

(House of Secrets cont'd)
NOTE: _Adams covers-#81,82,84-88,90,91. Alcala_
stories-#100,104-107,109,115,117,119,120,122,
125. Anderson story-#91. Colan story-#63.
Ditko story-#139. Finley story-#7. Infantino
story-#53. Kaluta story-#87,98; covers-#98,99,
101,102,151,154. Bob Kane stories-#15,18,21.
Kirby cover-#11. Kubert story-#39(with Mesk-
in?). Morrow stories-#86,89,90; covers-#89,
147,148. Redondo cover-#95. Starlin cover-#150.
Wrightson covers-#92-94,96,99,100,103,106,107,
_135,139._

HOUSE OF TERROR (3-D)
October, 1953
St. John Publishing Co.

	Good	Fine	Mint
#1-Kubert art	6.00	12.00	18.00

HOUSE OF YANG, THE (See Yang)
July, 1975 - #6, June, 1976
Charlton Comics

#1	.25	.50	.75
2-6	.15	.30	.45

HOWARD THE DUCK (See Fear, Man-Thing & Marvel
Jan, 1976 - Present   Treasury Ed.)
Marvel Comics Group

#1-Brunner cover/art; Spider-Man x-over			
(Low distribution)	5.00	10.00	15.00
2-Brunner cover/art + Starlin			
(Low distribution)	2.00	4.00	6.00
3-Buscema art	1.00	2.00	3.00
4,5-Colan art	.75	1.50	2.25
6-9	.40	.80	1.20
10-15: #12-1st app. Kiss	.40	.80	1.20
16-Album ish.	.35	.70	1.05
17-20	.25	.50	.75
21-28: #22-Manthing app.	.15	.30	.45
Annual #1(9/77)	.50	1.00	1.50

NOTE: _Infantino art-#21. Leialoha art-#10-13._
Mayerik art-#23,24.

HOW BOYS AND GIRLS CAN HELP WIN THE WAR
1942   (One Shot)   (10¢)
The Parents' Magazine Institute

#1	3.50	7.00	10.50

HOWDY DOODY (TV)
1949 - #38, July-Sept, 1956
Dell Publishing Co.

#1	3.00	6.00	9.00
2-5	2.00	4.00	6.00
6-Used in Seduction of the Innocent, pg. 309			

	Good	Fine	Mint
	4.00	8.00	12.00
7-10	1.50	3.00	4.50
11-38	1.00	2.00	3.00
4-Color #761,811	1.20	1.40	3.60

HOW IT BEGAN (See Single Series #15)

HOW SANTA GOT HIS RED SUIT (See March of
Comics #2)

HOW STALIN HOPES HE WILL DESTROY AMERICA
1951   (Giveaway)
Joe Lowe Co.

	4.00	8.00	12.00

HOW THE WEST WAS WON (See Movie Comics)

H.R. PUFNSTUF (TV)
Oct, 1970 - #8, July, 1972
Gold Key

#1-8		.10	.20

(See March of Comics #360)

HUBERT (See 4-Color Comics #251)

HUCK & YOGI WINTER SPORTS(See 4-Color #1310)

HUCK FINN (See New Advs. of --)

HUCKLEBERRY FINN (See 4-Color Comics #1114)

HUCKLEBERRY HOUND (See Dell Giant #31,44,
March of Comics #199,214,235, Whitman Comic
Books & Golden Picture Story Book)

HUCKLEBERRY HOUND (TV)
May-July, 1959 - #43, Oct, 1970(Hanna-Barbera)
Dell/Gold Key #15 on

4-Color #990,1050	.50	1.00	1.50
#3(1-2/60)-#17	.20	.40	.60
18-20: All titled Huckleberry Hound Chuckle-			
berry Tales; #18,19-84pgs.			
	.20	.40	.60
21-43	.15	.30	.45
4-Color #1054,1141	.50	1.00	1.50

HUCKLEBERRY HOUND (TV)
Nov, 1970 - #8, Jan, 1972 (Hanna-Barbera)
Charlton Comics

#1-8		.15	.25

HUCKLEBERRY HOUND CHUCKLEBERRY TALES
(See #18-20 in regular series)

Howard The Duck #1, © MCG

Howard The Duck #5, © MCG

Howdy Doody #3, © DELL

Hugh O'Brian--#5, © DELL   The Human Torch #7, © MCG   The Human Torch #34, © MCG

HUEY, DEWEY, & LOUIE BACK TO SCHOOL
1958 (25¢) (See Dell Giant #22,35,49)
Dell Publishing Co.

	Good	Fine	Mint
#1-Giant	1.20	2.40	3.60

HUEY, DEWEY, AND LOUIE JUNIOR WOODCHUCKS
Aug, 1966 - Present (Disney)
Gold Key

	Good	Fine	Mint
#1-Written by Carl Barks	1.75	3.50	5.25
2,3-Written by C. Barks	1.20	2.40	3.60
4,5-Barks reprints	1.00	2.00	3.00
6-17-Written by Barks	.60	1.20	1.80
18-21,24,27-30	.25	.50	.75
22,23,25,26-Barks reprints	.30	.60	.90
31-54: #41-Reprints	.15	.30	.45

HUGH O'BRIAN FAMOUS MARSHAL WYATT EARP
1957 - 1958; #4, 9-11/58 - #20, 1962
Dell Publishing Co.

	Good	Fine	Mint
4-Color #860,890,921-All Manning art	1.60	3.20	4.80
#4-12-Manning art	1.00	2.00	3.00
13-20	.75	1.50	2.25

HULK, THE (See The Incredible --)

HULK, THE (Formerly The Rampaging Hulk)
#11, 10/78 - Present (Magazine)($1.50)(in
Marvel Comics Group   color)

#11-Moon Knight app.	.50	1.00	1.50

HUMAN FLY
1963 - 1964 (Reprints)
I.W. Enterprises/Super

IW Reprint #1-Reprints Blue Beetle #44('46)	1.00	2.00	3.00
Super Reprint #10-Reprints Blue Beetle #46 ('47)	1.00	2.00	3.00

HUMAN FLY, THE
Sept, 1977 - #19, Mar, 1979
Marvel Comics Group

#1-Origin; Spider-Man x-over	.35	.70	1.05
2-Infantino pencils(1st work at Marvel); Ghost Rider x-over	.20	.40	.60
3-10: #9-Daredevil x-over	.20	.40	.60
11-19	.15	.30	.45

HUMAN TORCH, THE (Formerly Red Raven #1)
(See Marvel Mystery)
#2, Fall/40 - #15, Spr/44 (becomes Funny

Tunes); #16, Fall/44 - #35, 3/49 (becomes
Love Tales); #36, 4/54 - #38, 8/54
Timely Comics #1-35(SnPC#16-35)/Atlas #36-38

	Good	Fine	Mint
#2(#1)-Origin Toro; The Falcon, The Fiery Mask, Mantor the Magician, & Microman only app.; Human Torch, Sub-Mariner by Everett begin	400.00	800.00	1200.00
(Prices vary widely on this book)			
3(#2)	175.00	350.00	525.00
4(#3)-The Patriot app.; last Everett Sub-Mariner	125.00	250.00	375.00
5(#4)-The Patriot app. (Summer, 1941)	85.00	170.00	255.00
5-Human Torch battles Sub-Mariner(Fall,'41)	130.00	260.00	390.00
6,7,9	45.00	90.00	135.00
8-Human Torch battles Sub-Mariner; Wolverton art(1pg.)	85.00	170.00	255.00
10-Human Torch battles Sub-Mariner; Wolverton art(1pg.)	65.00	130.00	195.00
11-15	35.00	70.00	105.00
16-20	27.50	55.00	82.50
21-30	20.00	40.00	60.00
31-Namora x-over in Sub-Mariner	15.00	30.00	45.00
32-Sungirl, Namora app.	15.00	30.00	45.00
33-Capt. America x-over in Sub-Mariner	15.00	30.00	45.00
34-Sungirl solo	15.00	30.00	45.00
35-Captain America & Sungirl app. (1949)	15.00	30.00	45.00
36-38(1954)-Sub-Mariner in all issues except #34 & #35	12.00	24.00	36.00

NOTE: *Since there is a ½-year delay between
#15 & 16, it is believed that Funny Tunes
#16 continued after Human Torch #15.*

HUMAN TORCH, THE
Sept, 1974 - #8, Nov, 1975
Marvel Comics Group

#1	.40	1.20	1.80
2-8	.25	.50	.75

HUMBUG (Satire by Harvey Kurtzman)
Aug, 1957 - #11, Oct, 1958
Humbug Publications

#1	6.00	12.00	18.00
2-9	3.00	6.00	9.00
10,11-Magazine format	3.00	6.00	9.00
Bound Volume(#1-6)-Sold by publisher	15.00	30.00	45.00
Bound Volume(#1-9)	20.00	40.00	60.00

NOTE: *Davis art-#1-9,11. Elder art-#2-4,6-9,
11. Heath art-#2,4-8. Jaffee art-#2,4-9.
Kurtzman art-#11. Wood art-#1.*

HUMDINGER
May-June, 1946 - 1947
Novelty Press/Premium Group

	Good	Fine	Mint
#1-Jerkwater Line, Mickey Starlight by Don			
Rico, Dink begin	2.00	4.00	6.00
2-6,V2#1,2	1.00	2.00	3.00

HUMOR (See All Humor Comics)

HUMPHREY COMICS
Oct, 1948 - #40, 1954
Harvey Publications

	Good	Fine	Mint
#1-Joe Palooka's pal (reprints); Powell art			
	2.00	4.00	6.00
2,3	1.25	2.50	3.75
4-Boy Heroes app.	2.50	5.00	7.50
5-10	1.25	2.50	3.75
11-20	.80	1.60	2.40
21-40	.60	1.20	1.80

HUNCHBACK OF NOTRE DAME, THE
(See 4-Color Comics #854)

HUNK
Aug, 1961 - 1963
Charlton Comics

#1-11		.15	.30

HUNTED (Formerly My Love Memoirs)
#13, July, 1950 - #2, Sept, 1950
Fox Features Syndicate

#13(#1), 2	1.75	3.50	5.25

HURRICANE COMICS
1945
Cambridge House

#1-(Humor)	1.50	3.00	4.50

HYPER MYSTERY COMICS
May, 1940 - #2, June, 1940
Hyper Publications

#1-Hyper, the Phenomenal begins			
	16.50	33.25	50.00
2	12.00	24.00	36.00

I AIM AT THE STARS (See 4-Color #1148)

IBIS, THE INVINCIBLE (See Fawcett Min. & Whiz)
1942 - #6, Spring, 1948
Fawcett Publications

#1-Origin Ibis; Raboy cover

	Good	Fine	Mint
	45.00	90.00	135.00
2	25.00	50.00	75.00
3-Wolverton art #3-6(4pgs. each)			
	15.00	30.00	45.00
4-6	12.00	24.00	36.00

IDAHO
June-Aug, 1963 - #8, July-Sept, 1965
Dell Publishing Co.

#1	.65	1.35	2.00
2-8	.40	.80	1.20

IDEAL (-- a Classical Comic) (2nd Series)
July, 1948 - #5, Mar, 1949
Timely Comics

#1-Antony & Cleopatra	5.00	10.00	15.00
2-The Corpses of Dr. Sacotti			
	4.00	8.00	12.00
3-Joan of Arc	4.00	8.00	12.00
4-Richard the Lion-hearted; titled "-- the			
World's Greatest Comics"; The Witness app.			
	5.00	10.00	15.00
5-Ideal Love & Romance	3.50	7.00	10.50
(Feature-length stories in all)			

IDEAL COMICS (1st Series) (Willie #5 on)
Fall, 1944 - #4, Spring, 1946
Timely Comics (MgPC)

#1	1.50	3.00	4.50
2-4-Super Rabbit	1.00	2.00	3.00

IDEAL LOVE & ROMANCE (See Ideal, a Classical Comic)

IDEAL ROMANCE (Diary Confessions #9 on)
April, 1954 - #7, Dec, 1954
Key Publications

#3	1.20	2.40	3.60
4-7	.80	1.60	2.40

IDEAL ROMANCES
1950
Stanmor

#6	.80	1.60	2.40

I DREAM OF JEANNIE (TV)
1966 - #2, Dec, 1966
Dell Publishing Co.

#1,2	.25	.50	.75

IF THE DEVIL WOULD TALK
1950   (32 pgs.)   (Soft cover)

Humdinger #3. © NOVP

Hyper Mystery #2. © Hyper

Ideal #3. © MCG

I Loved #29, © FOX

I Love Lucy #11, © DELL

The Incredible Hulk #3, © MCG

(If the Devil Would Talk cont'd)
Roman Catholic Catechetical Guild

	Good	Fine	Mint
No# (Rare)	250.00	500.00	750.00

ILLUSTRATED GAGS (See Single Series #16)

ILLUSTRATED LIBRARY OF --, AN (See Classics Illustrated Giants)

ILLUSTRATED STORIES OF THE OPERAS
1943 (16pgs.; B&W)(25c) (cover-B&W & Red)
Baily (Bernard) Publ. Co.

	Good	Fine	Mint
No#-Faust (part reprinted in Cisco Kid #1)	6.00	12.00	18.00
No#-Aida	6.00	12.00	18.00

ILLUSTRATED STORY OF ROBIN HOOD & HIS MERRY MEN, THE (See Robin Hood)

ILLUSTRATED TARZAN BOOK, THE (See Tarzan Book)

ILLUSTRATED WEEKENDER COMIC
1945 (Canadian)
Harry 'A' Chesler

	Good	Fine	Mint
#2-Mr. E, Echo, Sky Chief app.	2.50	5.00	7.50

I LOVED (Formerly Rulah; Colossal Feat. Mag.
#28, 7/49 - #32, 3/50   #33 on)
Fox Features Syndicate

	Good	Fine	Mint
#28-32	2.00	4.00	6.00

I LOVE LUCY COMICS (TV)
Summer, 1953; 8-10/54 - #35, 4-6/62
Dell Publishing Co.

	Good	Fine	Mint
3-D(Summer, '53)	6.00	12.00	18.00
4-Color #535,559	.60	1.20	1.80
#3-10	.40	.80	1.20
11-35	.25	.50	.75

I LOVE YOU
June, 1950 - #6, 1951
Fawcett Publications

	Good	Fine	Mint
#1	2.00	4.00	6.00
2-6	1.00	2.00	3.00

I LOVE YOU (Formerly In Love)
#7, Sept, 1955 - #121, Dec, 1976
Charlton Comics

	Good	Fine	Mint
#7-Kirby cvr, Powell sty.	1.75	3.50	5.25

	Good	Fine	Mint
8-20	.65	1.35	2.00
21-50	.30	.60	.90
51-121: #113-Jonnie Love app.	.20		.40

I'M A COP
1954
Magazine Enterprises

	Good	Fine	Mint
#1(A-1#111)	2.00	4.00	6.00
2(A-1#126),3(A-1#128),4	1.50	3.00	4.50

I'M DICKENS-HE'S FENSTER (TV)
May-July, 1963 - #2, Aug-Oct, 1963
Dell Publishing Co.

	Good	Fine	Mint
#1,2	.30	.60	.90

I MET A HANDSOME COWBOY (See 4-Color #324)

IMPACT
Mar-Apr, 1955 - #5, Nov-Dec, 1955
E.C. Comics

	Good	Fine	Mint
#1	7.00	14.00	21.00
2-5: #4-Crandall story	5.00	10.00	15.00

NOTE: Crandall stories-#1-4. Davis stories-#2-4; covers-#1-5. Evans stories-#1,4,5. Ingels stories in all. Kamen story-#3. Krigstein story-#1,5. Orlando story-#2,5.

INCREDIBLE HULK, THE (See Aurora, Book & Record Set, & Rampaging --)
5/62 - #6, 3/63; #102, 4/68 - Present
Marvel Comics Group

	Good	Fine	Mint
#1-Origin	120.00	240.00	360.00
2	40.00	80.00	120.00
3-Origin retold	20.00	40.00	60.00
4-6: #6-Intro. Teen Brigade			
	15.00	30.00	45.00
#102-Origin retold	2.25	4.50	6.75
103-110	1.00	2.00	3.00
111-120	.80	1.60	2.40
121-130	.60	1.20	1.80
131-140	.50	1.00	1.50
141-1st app. Doc Samson	.60	1.20	1.80
142-150: #145-52pgs.	.40	.80	1.20
151-176,179,180	.35	.70	1.05
177,178-Warlock app.	.50	1.00	1.50
181-1st app. Wolverine	.40	.80	1.20
182-200	.25	.50	.75
201-220	.20	.40	.60
221,223-231	.15	.30	.45
222-Starlin story	.25	.50	.75
Giant-Size #1('75)	.60	1.20	1.80
Special #1(10/68)-New material; Steranko cover	2.00	4.00	6.00

(The Incredible Hulk cont'd)

	Good	Fine	Mint
Special #2(10/69)-Origin retold			
	1.00	2.00	3.00
Special #3(1/71),#4(1/72)	.60	1.20	1.80
Annual #5(10/76)	.40	.80	1.20
Annual #6(11/77),#7(8/78)	.30	.60	.90

NOTE: *Buscema* cover-#202. *Ditko* stories-#2,6; covers-#2,6. *Kirby* stories-#1-5; covers-#1-5, Annual #5. *Starlin* cover-#217. *Staton* stories-#207-209. *Wrightson* cover-#197.

INCREDIBLE MR. LIMPET, THE (See Movie Classics)

INCREDIBLE SCIENCE FICTION (Formerly Weird
7-8/55 - #33, 1-2/56   Science-Fantasy)
E.C. Comics

#30,33	17.00	34.00	51.00
31,32-Williamson/Krenkel in both; #31-Two			
Wood stories	24.00	48.00	72.00

NOTE: *Davis* stories-#30,32,33; covers-#30-32. *Krigstein* stories in all. *Orlando* stories-#30,32,33("Judgement Day" reprint). *Wood* stories-#30,31,33; cover-#33.

INDIAN BRAVES (Baffling Mysteries #5 on)
March, 1951 - #4, Sept, 1951
Ace Magazines

#1	1.25	2.50	3.75
2-4	.80	1.60	2.40
I.W. Reprint #1(no date)	.40	.80	1.20

INDIAN CHIEF (White Eagle --)(Formerly The
1951 - #33, Jan-Mar, 1959   Chief)
Dell Publishing Co.

#3-11: #6-White Eagle app.	1.20	2.40	3.60
12-1st White Eagle(10-12/53)-Not same as			
earlier character	1.50	3.00	4.50
13-29	.90	1.80	2.70
30-33-Buscema stories	1.20	2.40	3.60

INDIAN CHIEF (See March of Comics #94,110,
127,140,159,170,187)

INDIAN FIGHTER, THE (See 4-Color #687)

INDIAN FIGHTER
May, 1950 - #11, Jan, 1952
Youthful Magazines

#1	1.40	2.80	4.20
2-11: #3,4-Wildey art	.80	1.60	2.40

INDIAN LEGENDS OF THE NIAGARA (See American
Graphics)

INDIANS
Spring, 1950 - #17, 1953
Fiction House Magazines (Wings Publ. Co.)

	Good	Fine	Mint
#1-Manzar, White Indian,	Long	Bow &	Orphan of
the Storm begin	2.50	5.00	7.50
2-Starlight begins	1.50	3.00	4.50
3-5	1.00	2.00	3.00
6-17	.80	1.60	2.40

INDIANS OF THE WILD WEST
Circa 1958? (No date)
I.W. Enterprises

#9-Reprints	.50	1.00	1.50

INDIANS ON THE WARPATH
No date   (132 pgs.)
St. John Publishing Co.

No#-Matt Baker cover; contains St. John comics			
rebound. Many combinations possible			
	3.00	6.00	9.00

INDIAN TRIBES (See Famous Indian Tribes)

INDIAN WARRIORS (Formerly White Rider --)
#7, June, 1951 - #11, 1952
Star Publications

#7-11: #11-White Rider & Superhorse app.			
L. B. Cole covers	1.00	2.00	3.00
3-D #1 (12/53)	5.00	10.00	15.00
Accepted Reprint(No#)(inside cover shows			
White Rider & Superhorse #11)-Reprints			
cover/#7; origin White Rider & --			
	.50	1.00	1.50

INDOORS-OUTDOORS (See Wisco)

INDOOR SPORTS
No Date (64pgs.)(6x9";B&W reprints;Hardcover)
National Specials Co.

By Tad	3.00	6.00	9.00

INFERIOR 5, THE (See Showcase)
Mar-Apr, 1967 - #10, Sept-Oct, 1968; #11,
Aug-Sept, 1972 - #12, Oct-Nov, 1972
National Periodical Publications

#1	.50	1.00	1.50
2-Plastic Man app.	.40	.80	1.20
3-9	.25	.50	.75
10-Superman x-over	.30	.60	.90
11,12-Orlando cover/art; both reprints Show-			
case #62,63	.20	.40	.60

Incredible Science Fiction #33, © WMG

Indian Chief #4, © DELL

Indian Fighter #4, © YM

The Inhumans #1, © MCG   International Comics #4, © WMG   Intimate Confessions #4, © REAL

INFORMER, THE
April, 1954 - #5, Dec, 1954
Feature Television Productions

	Good	Fine	Mint
#1-Sekowsky art begins	1.25	2.50	3.75
2-5	.80	1.60	2.40

INHUMANS, THE (See Amazing Advs.)
Oct, 1975 - #12, Aug, 1977
Marvel Comics Group

#1	.70	1.40	2.10
2-5	.40	.80	1.20
6-12: #9-reprints	.25	.50	.75

NOTE: *Gil Kane* art-#5-7.

INKY & DINKY (Felix's Nephews)
Sept, 1957 - #7, Oct, 1958
Harvey Publications

#1	2.00	4.00	6.00
2-7	1.00	2.00	3.00

IN LOVE (I Love You #7 on)
Sept, 1954 - #6, July, 1955
Prime Publ./Mainline(Prize)/Charlton #5 on

#1-Simon & Kirby art	5.00	10.00	15.00
2-S&K story	2.00	4.00	6.00
3,4-S&K art	2.50	5.00	7.50
5-S&K cover only	1.60	3.20	4.80
6-No S&K art	.70	1.40	2.10

IN LOVE WITH JESUS
1952   (Giveaway)
Catechetical Educational Society

	2.50	5.00	7.50

IN SEARCH OF THE CASTAWAYS (See Movie Comics)

INSIDE CRIME (Formerly My Intimate Affair)
1950; #3, July, 1950 - #2, Sept, 1950
Fox Features Syndicate (Hero Books)

No#(no publ. listed; I.W. reprint?)

	2.00	4.00	6.00
#3-Wood story, 10pgs.; L. B. Cole cover			
	6.00	12.00	18.00
#2(9/50)	1.50	3.00	4.50

INSPECTOR, THE
July, 1974 - #19, Feb, 1978
Gold Key

#1	.15	.30	.45
2-5		.15	.30
6-19		.10	.20

INSPECTOR WADE (See Feature Book #13, McKay)

INTERNATIONAL COMICS (-- Crime Patrol #6)
Spring, 1947 - #5, Nov-Dec, 1947
E. C. Comics

	Good	Fine	Mint
#1	16.00	32.00	48.00
2-5	12.00	24.00	36.00

INTERNATIONAL CRIME PATROL (Formerly International Comics #1-5; becomes Crime Patrol #7 on)
Spring, 1948
E.C. Comics

#6-Moon Girl app.	22.00	44.00	66.00

INTERSTATE THEATRES' FUN CLUB COMICS
Mid 1940's (10¢ on cover)(B&W cover)(Premium)
Interstate Theatres

Cover features MLJ characters looking at a copy of Top-Notch Comics, but contains an early Detective Comic on inside; many combinations possible   6.00 12.00 18.00

IN THE DAYS OF THE MOB (Magazine)
Fall, 1971   (Black & White)
Hampshire Dist. Ltd. (National)

#1-Jack Kirby art; has John Dillinger wanted poster inside   1.20   2.40   3.60

IN THE PRESENCE OF MINE ENEMIES
1973   (35¢)
Spire Christian Comics/Fleming H. Revell Co.

	.25	.50	.75

INTIMATE
December, 1957
Charlton Comics

#1	.50	1.00	1.50

INTIMATE CONFESSIONS
1950   (132 pgs.)
Fox Features Syndicate

No#-See Fox Giants. Contents could vary and determines price.

INTIMATE CONFESSIONS
July-Aug, 1951 - #8, Mar, 1953
Realistic Comics

#1-Kinstler story; cover reprinted from Avon paperback showing lady of the night with Las Vegas background 60.00 120.00 180.00

(Intimate Confessions cont'd)

	Good	Fine	Mint
(Prices vary widely on this book)			
2	5.00	10.00	15.00
3,8-Kinstler story	6.00	12.00	18.00
4-7: #7-Spanking panel	4.00	8.00	12.00

INTIMATE CONFESSIONS
1964
I.W. Enterprises/Super Comics

I.W. Reprint #9	.90	1.80	2.70
Super Reprint #12,18	.90	1.80	2.70

INTIMATE LOVE
1950 - #28, Aug, 1954
Standard Comics

#5	1.20	2.40	3.60
6-8-Severin/Elder story	2.00	4.00	6.00
9,10	1.00	2.00	3.00
11-18,20,23-25,27,28	.80	1.60	2.40
19,21,22,26-Toth art	2.50	5.00	7.50

NOTE: *Celardo story-#8,10.*

INTIMATE ROMANCES
1950 - 1954
Standard Comics

#1	1.20	2.40	3.60
2-19	.70	1.40	2.10

INTIMATE SECRETS OF ROMANCE
Sept, 1953 - #2, April, 1954
Star Publications

#1-L. B. Cole cover	1.50	3.00	4.50
2	1.00	2.00	3.00

INTRIGUE
January, 1955
Quality Comics Group

#1(Horror)-Jack Cole art	3.50	7.00	10.50

INVADERS, THE (TV)
Oct, 1967 - #4, Oct, 1968
Gold Key

#1	.60	1.20	1.80
2-4	.40	.80	1.20

INVADERS, THE
August, 1975 - Present
Marvel Comics Group

#1-Captain America, Sub-Mariner & Human Torch begin	1.00	2.00	3.00

	Good	Fine	Mint
2	.60	1.20	1.80
3-5	.50	1.00	1.50
6-10: #7-Intro. Union Jack	.40	.80	1.20
11-Origin Spitfire	.40	.80	1.20
12-19: #19-New Union Jack	.30	.60	.90
20-Reprints Sub-Mariner story/Motion Picture Funnies Weekly with brief write-up about MPFW	.80	1.60	2.40
21-35: #24-Burgos & Everett reprint/1940	.25	.50	.75
Annual #1(9/77)-Schomburg, Rico stories; Schomburg cover; Avengers app.	.50	1.00	1.50

NOTE: *Gil Kane covers-#13,17,18,20-27. Kirby covers-#3-9,12,14-16,32,33.*
Giant-Size--#1(6/75)(50¢)-Origin; Captain America, Sub-Mariner, Human Torch reprint from Sub-Mariner #1('41) .60 1.20 1.80

INVISIBLE BOY (Also see Approved Comics)
March, 1954
St. John Publishing Co.

#2-Origin	3.00	6.00	9.00

INVISIBLE MAN, THE (See Superior Stories #1)

INVISIBLE SCARLET O'NEIL
Dec, 1950 - #3, April, 1951
Famous Funnies (Harvey)

#1	8.00	16.00	24.00
2,3	5.00	10.00	15.00

(See Harvey Comics Hits #59)

IRON FIST
November, 1975 - #15, Sept, 1977
Marvel Comics Group

#1-McWilliams art; Iron Man app.	.80	1.60	2.40
2	.50	1.00	1.50
3-5	.40	.80	1.20
6-10	.30	.60	.90
11,13,14	.25	.50	.75
12-Capt. America app.	.25	.50	.75
15-X-Men app.	.25	.50	.75

NOTE: *Byrne stories-#1-15.*

IRON HORSE (TV)
March, 1967 - #2, June, 1967
Dell Publishing Co.

#1,2	.40	.80	1.20

Intrigue #1, © QUA

The Invaders #1, © MCG

Invisible Boy #2, © STJ

Iron Man #2, © MCG   Isis #2, © DC   It Really Happened #6, © STD

IRON JAW (Also see The Barbarians)
January, 1975 - #4, July, 1975
Atlas/Seaboard Publ.

	Good	Fine	Mint
#1-Adams cover	.50	1.00	1.50
2-Adams cover	.40	.80	1.20
3,4-Origin	.25	.50	.75

IRON MAN
May, 1968 - Present
Marvel Comics Group

	Good	Fine	Mint
#1-Origin	5.00	10.00	15.00
2	2.50	5.00	7.50
3-5	1.20	2.40	3.60
6-10	.90	1.80	2.70
11-20	.70	1.40	2.10
21-40: #22-Death of Janice Cord			
	.40	.80	1.20
41-46,48-50: #43-52pgs.	.30	.60	.90
47-Origin retold; Smith art			
	1.20	2.40	3.60
51,52	.30	.60	.90
53-Starlin part pencils	.40	.80	1.20
54-Everett Sub-Mariner in part			
	.30	.60	.90
55,56-Starlin art + cover-#55			
	.80	1.60	2.40
57-68,70	.30	.60	.90
69-Starlin cover	.40	.80	1.20
71,73-80: #76 reprts.#9	.25	.50	.75
72-Brunner draws himself & wife, pg. 14,			
panel 1	.30	.60	.90
81-86,89,90	.20	.40	.60
87-1st app. Blizzard	.20	.40	.60
88-Origin Blizzard	.20	.40	.60
91-99,101-119	.15	.30	.45
100-Starlin cover	.25	.50	.75

NOTE: _Craig pencils-#2-4,15,24,25; inks-#1-19,26-28; covers-#2-4. Infantino pencils-#108,109. Kirby covers-#80,90,92-95._

Giant Size #1('75)	.50	1.00	1.50
Special #1(8/70)	.80	1.60	2.40
Special #2(11/71)	.50	1.00	1.50
Annual #3(6/76)-Manthing app.			
	.40	.80	1.20
Annual #4(8/77)-Newton story; Champions app.			
	.40	.80	1.20

IRON MAN AND SUBMARINER
April, 1968   (One Shot)
Marvel Comics Group

#1-Craig inks-Iron Man	1.50	3.00	4.50

IRON VIC (See Comics Revue #3)
1940; Aug, 1947 - #3, 1947
United Features Syndicate/St. John Publ. Co.

	Good	Fine	Mint
Single Series #22	7.00	14.00	21.00
#2,3(St. John)	1.25	2.50	3.75

ISIS (TV) (Also see Shazam)
Oct-Nov, 1976 - #8, Dec-Jan, 1977-78
National Periodical Publications/DC Comics

#1-Wood inks	.25	.50	.75
2-8: #7-origin	.20	.40	.60

ISLAND AT THE TOP OF THE WORLD (See Walt
Disney Showcase #27)

ISLAND OF DR. MOREAU, THE (Movie)
October, 1977
Marvel Comics Group

#1	.25	.50	.75

I SPY (TV)
Aug, 1966 - #6, Sept, 1968
Gold Key

#1	.50	1.00	1.50
2-6	.30	.60	.90

IS THIS TOMORROW?
1947   (One Shot)   (3 editions)
Catechetical Guild

#1-Theme of communists taking over the USA			
	20.00	40.00	60.00

IT! (See Supernatural Thrillers #1 and
Astonishing Tales #21-24)

IT HAPPENS IN THE BEST FAMILIES
1920   (48 pgs.)   (B&W Sundays)
Powers Photo Engraving Co.

By Briggs	6.00	12.00	18.00

IT REALLY HAPPENED
1944 - #11, Oct, 1947
William H. Wise #1,2/Standard(Visual Editions)

#1	2.00	4.00	6.00
2-7,9-11	1.25	2.50	3.75
8-Story of Roy Rogers	1.50	3.00	4.50

NOTE: _Guardineer story-#7(2); Schomburg cover-#8,9._

IT RHYMES WITH LUST
1951?   (Digest-size) (128 pgs.)
St. John Publishing Co.?

(Scarce)-All by Matt Baker			
	10.00	20.00	30.00

IT'S ABOUT TIME (TV)
January, 1967
Gold Key

	Good	Fine	Mint
#1(10195-701)	.35	.70	1.05

IT'S A DUCK'S LIFE
Feb, 1950 - #11, Feb, 1952
Marvel Comics/Atlas(MMC)

#1-Buck Duck, Super Rabbit begin			
	1.20	2.40	3.60
2-11	.80	1.60	2.40

IT'S FUN TO STAY ALIVE (Giveaway)
1948 (16 pgs.) (Heavy stock paper)
National Automobile Dealers Association

Featuring: Bugs Bunny, The Berrys, Dixie
Dugan, Elmer, Tim Tyler, Bruce Gentry, Abbie
& Slats, Joe Jinks, The Toodles, & Cokey; all
art copyright '46-'48 drawn especially for
this book   6.00 12.00 18.00

IT'S GAME TIME
Sept-Oct, 1955 - #4, Mar-Apr, 1956
National Periodical Publications

#1-(Scarce)-Davy Crockett app. in puzzle			
	5.00	10.00	15.00
2-4 (Scarce)	3.00	6.00	9.00

IT'S LOVE, LOVE, LOVE
November, 1957 (10¢)
St. John Publishing Co.

#1	1.00	2.00	3.00

IVANHOE (See Fawcett Movie Comics #20)

IVANHOE
July-Sept, 1963
Dell Publishing Co.

#1(12-373-309)	.80	1.60	2.40

IWO JIMA (See A Spectacular Feature)

JACE PEARSON (See Texas Rangers)

JACK ARMSTRONG
Nov, 1947 - #13, Sept, 1949
Parents' Magazine Institute

#1	4.00	8.00	12.00
2-5	2.50	5.00	7.50
6-13	2.00	4.00	6.00

JACKIE GLEASON
1948; Sept, 1955 - #5, Dec, 1955
St. John Publishing Co.

	Good	Fine	Mint
#1,2(1948)	3.00	6.00	9.00
1(1955)	2.00	4.00	6.00
2-5	1.00	2.00	3.00

JACKIE GLEASON & THE HONEYMOONERS (TV)
June-July, 1956 - #12, April-May, 1959
National Periodical Publications

#1	2.50	5.00	7.50
2-12	1.25	2.50	3.75

JACKIE JOKERS (Richie Rich & -- #5 on)
March, 1973 - #4, Sept, 1973
Harvey Publications

#1-4		.15	.30

JACKIE ROBINSON (Famous Plays of --)
May, 1950 - #6, 1952 (Baseball hero)
Fawcett Publications

#1	5.00	10.00	15.00
2-6	3.50	7.00	10.50

JACK IN THE BOX (Yellowjacket #1-10)
Feb, 1946; #11, 1946 - #16, 1947
Frank Comunale/Charlton Comics #12 on

#1-Stitches, Marty Mouse & Nutsy McKrow			
	1.35	2.75	4.00
11-Yellowjacket	2.00	4.00	6.00
12,14-16	1.50	3.00	4.50
13-Wolverton art	7.00	14.00	21.00

JACKPOT COMICS (Jolly Jingles #10 on)
Spring, 1941 - #9, Spring, 1943
MLJ Magazines

#1-The Black Hood, Mr. Justice, Steel Sterling			
& Sgt. Boyle begin	60.00	120.00	180.00
2	30.00	60.00	90.00
3,5	20.00	40.00	60.00
4-Archie begins (on sale 12/41)			
	25.00	50.00	75.00
6-9	15.00	30.00	45.00

JACK Q FROST (See Unearthly Spectaculars)

JACK THE GIANT KILLER (See Movie Classics)

JACK THE GIANT KILLER (New Advs. of --)
Aug-Sept, 1953
Bimfort & Co.

V1#1-H.C. Kiefer art	4.00	8.00	12.00

It's Game Time #4, © DC

Jack Armstrong #3, © PMI

Jackpot Comics #6, © MLJ

Jane Arden #1, © UFS

Jeanie Comics #17, © MCG

Jesse James #26, © AVON

JACKY'S DIARY   (See 4-Color Comics #1091)

JAGUAR, THE   (See The Advs. of --)

JAMBOREE
Feb, 1946 - #3, April, 1946
Round Publishing Co.

	Good	Fine	Mint
#1-3	.80	1.60	2.40

JANE ARDEN   (See Pageant of Comics)
March, 1948 - #2, June, 1948
St. John (United Features Syndicate)

#1-Newspaper reprints	5.00	10.00	15.00
2	3.50	7.00	10.50

JANN OF THE JUNGLE   (Jungle Tales #1-7)
#8, Nov, 1955 - #17, June, 1957
Atlas Comics (CSI)

#8(#1)	3.50	7.00	10.50
9,11-15	2.50	5.00	7.50
10-Williamson/Colleta cvr	4.00	8.00	12.00
16,17-Three Williamson/Mayo stories, 5pgs.			
each	6.00	12.00	18.00

JASON & THE ARGONAUTS   (See Movie Classics)

JAWS 2   (See Marvel Super Special, A)

JEANIE COMICS (Cowgirl Romances #28)(Formerly
#13, April, 1947 - #27, 1949   Daring)
Marvel Comics/Atlas(CPC)

#13	2.00	4.00	6.00
14,15	1.20	2.40	3.60
16-Used in Love and Death by Legman; Kurtz-			
man's "Hey Look"	6.00	12.00	18.00
17-19,22-Kurtzman's "Hey Look", 1-3pgs. ea.			
	2.50	5.00	7.50
20,21,23-27	1.00	2.00	3.00

JEEP COMICS   (Also see G.I. & Overseas Com-
Winter/44 - #3, 3-4/48   ics)
R. B. Leffingwell & Co.

#1-3-Capt. Power in #1,2; Criss Cross & Jeep			
& Peep(costumed)in all	2.00	4.00	6.00
#1-29(Giveaway)-Strip reprints in all; Tar-			
zan, Flash Gordon, Blondie, The Nebbs,			
Little Iodine, Red Ryder, Don Winslow,			
The Phantom, Johnny Hazard, Katzenjammer			
Kids; distributed to U.S. Armed Forces in			
mid '40's	4.00	8.00	12.00

NOTE: _L. B. Cole covers-#3._

JEFF JORDAN, U.S. AGENT
Dec, 1947 - Jan, 1948

D. S. Publishing Co.

	Good	Fine	Mint
#1	2.00	4.00	6.00

JERRY DRUMMER
1957
Charlton Comics

V2#10,11, V3#12	.40	.80	1.20

JERRY LEWIS   (See Advs. of --)

JESSE JAMES   (See 4-Color #757 & The Legend
of --)

JESSE JAMES   (Also see Badmen of the West)
Aug, 1950 - #29, Aug-Sept, 1956
Avon Periodicals

#1-"Alabam" reprints begin by Kubert, end #3			
	7.00	14.00	21.00
2-Three Kubert stories	6.00	12.00	18.00
3-Kubert Alabam story reprt/Cowpuncher #2			
	4.00	8.00	12.00
4-No Kubert	2.50	5.00	7.50
5,6-Three Kubert Jesse James stories + 1pg.			
Wood-#5	5.00	10.00	15.00
7-Two Kubert Jesse James stories			
	4.00	8.00	12.00
8-Three Kinstler stories	3.00	6.00	9.00
9,10-No Kubert	2.50	5.00	7.50
11-14	2.00	4.00	6.00
15-Kinstler reprt/#3	2.00	4.00	6.00
16-Kinstler reprt/#3, & Sheriff Bob Dixon's			
Chuck Wagon #1 with name changed to Sher-			
iff Tom Wilson	2.50	5.00	7.50
17-Jesse James reprt/#4; Kinstler cover idea			
from Kubert splash in #6			
	2.00	4.00	6.00
18-Kubert Jesse James reprint/#5			
	2.00	4.00	6.00
19-Kubert Jesse James rpt.	2.00	4.00	6.00
20-Williamson/Frazetta story; reprint-Chief			
Vic. Apache Massacre; Kubert Jesse James			
reprint/#6	8.00	16.00	24.00
21-Two J.James reprts/#4, Kinstler/#4			
	2.00	4.00	6.00
22,23-No Kubert	1.50	3.00	4.50
24-New McCarty strip by Kinstler + Kinstler			
reprt/#9	1.75	3.50	5.25
25-New McCarty Jesse James strip by Kinst-			
ler; Kinstler J. James reprt/#7,#9			
	1.75	3.50	5.25
26,27-New McCarty J. James strip + a Kinst-			
ler/McCann Jesse James reprint			
	1.75	3.50	5.25
28-Reprints most of Red Mountain, Featuring			
Quantrells Raiders	1.75	3.50	5.25

(Jesse James cont'd)	Good	Fine	Mint
29	1.75	3.50	5.25

Annual(No#, 1952-25¢)"--Brings Six-Gun Justice to the West"(100pgs.)-3 earlier issues rebound. Kubert, Kinstler art
7.00 14.00 21.00

NOTE: *Mostly reprints #10 on. Kinstler stories-#3,4,7,8,15(reprt),16(2 stories),21-27; covers-#3,4,9,17,18,20,21,24-27.*

JESSE JAMES
July, 1953
Realistic Publications

No#-Reprints Avon's #1, same cover, colors
different 2.50 5.00 7.50

JEST (Kayo #12) (Formerly Snap)
1944
Harry 'A' Chesler

#10-Johnny Rebel & Yankee Boy app. in text
2.50 5.00 7.50
11-Little Nemo in Adventure Land
2.50 5.00 7.50

JESTER
1945
Harry 'A' Chesler

#10 1.75 3.50 5.25

JET (Jet Powers #2-4) (Space Ace #5)
1950 - 1951
Magazine Enterprises

#1(A-1#30)-Powell art begins
6.00 12.00 18.00
2(A-1#32) 4.00 8.00 12.00
3(A-1#35)-Williamson story
10.00 20.00 30.00
4(A-1#38)-Williamson/Wood story
12.00 24.00 36.00

JET ACES
1952 - 1953
Fiction House Magazines

#1	2.00	4.00	6.00
2-4	1.25	2.50	3.75

JET DREAM (-- & Her Stuntgirl Counterspies)
June, 1968
Gold Key

#1 .50 1.00 1.50

JET FIGHTERS

#5, Nov, 1952 - #7, March, 1953
Standard Magazines

	Good	Fine	Mint
#5,7-Toth art	2.50	5.00	7.50
6	1.20	2.40	3.60

JETMAN
1950's
Superior Publ. Ltd.

#1 1.50 3.00 4.50

JET POWER (-- Powers #1) (See Jet)
1963
I.W. Enterprises

#1,2(Powell art)-reprints Jet #1 & 2
1.20 2.40 3.60

JET POWERS (See Jet)

JET PUP (See 3-D Features)

JETSONS, THE (TV)
Jan, 1963 - #36, Oct, 1970 (Hanna-Barbera)
Gold Key

#1	.25	.50	.75
2-36	.15	.30	.45

(See March of Comics #276,330,348)

JETSONS, THE (TV) (Hanna-Barbera)
Nov, 1970 - #20, Dec, 1973
Charlton Comics

#1-20 .15 .25

JETTA OF THE 21ST CENTURY
#5, 1952 - 1953 (Teen-age Archie type)
Standard Comics

#5-7 1.50 3.00 4.50

JIGGS & MAGGIE (See 4-Color #18)

JIGGS & MAGGIE
#11, 1949 - #26, Dec-Jan, 1953-54
Standard Comics/Harvey Publications

#11	2.50	5.00	7.50
12-20: #16-Wood text illos.			
	2.25	4.50	6.75
21-25	1.50	3.00	4.50
26-4pgs. partially in 3-D			
	3.50	7.00	10.50

NOTE: *Sunday page reprints by McManus loosely blended into story continuity. Advertised on covers as "All New".*

Jet #4, © ME

Jet Fighters #6, © STD

Jiggs & Maggie #12, © STD

Jim Hardy Giant-1944, © UFS

Jimmy Wakely #1, © DC

Jingle Jangle #6, © EAS

JIGSAW (Big Hero Adventures)
Sept, 1966 - #2, Dec, 1966
Harvey Publications (Funday Funnies)

	Good	Fine	Mint
#1-Origin; Crandall art	.80	1.60	2.40
2-Man From S.R.A.M.	.50	1.00	1.50

JIGSAW OF DOOM (See Complete Mystery #2)

JIM BOWIE
1953 - #19, April, 1957
Charlton Comics

#1	1.00	2.00	3.00
2-19	.50	1.00	1.50

JIM BOWIE (See 4-Color #893,993 & Western
Tales)

JIM DANDY
May, 1956 - #3, Sept, 1956 (Charles Biro)
Dandy Magazine (Lev Gleason)

#1	1.20	2.40	3.60
2,3	.60	1.20	1.80

JIM HARDY (Also see Treasury of Comics &
1939 - 1940; 1947; 1/48   Sparkler)
United Feat. Synd./Spotlight Publ./St. John

Single Series #6	10.00	20.00	30.00
Single Series #27('40)	8.00	16.00	24.00
#1('47)-Spotlight Publ.	2.00	4.00	6.00
2	1.50	3.00	4.50
1(1/48)-St. John-(Feat. Windy & Paddles)			
	1.50	3.00	4.50

JIM HARDY
1944; 1948 (132 pgs.) (25¢) (Giant)
(Tip Top, Sparkler reprints)
Spotlight/United Features Syndicate

(1944)-Origin Mirror Man; Triple Terror app.

	7.00	14.00	21.00
(1948)	5.00	10.00	15.00

JIMINY CRICKET (See 4-Color #701,795,897,
989 & Walt Disney Showcase #37)

JIMMY (James Swinnerton)
1905 (10x15") (40 pgs. in color)
N. Y. American & Journal

	15.00	37.50	60.00

JIMMY DURANTE (See A-1 Comics #18,20)

JIMMY OLSEN (See Superman's Pal --)

JIMMY WAKELY
Sept-Oct, 1949 - #18, July-Aug, 1952
National Periodical Publications

	Good	Fine	Mint
#1-Alex Toth art; Kit Colby Girl Sheriff begins			
	9.00	18.00	27.00
2-Toth art	6.00	12.00	18.00
3,4,6,7-Frazetta art in all, 3pgs. each; Kurtzman in #4; Toth in all			
	7.00	14.00	21.00
5,8-15,18-Toth art; #12,14-Kubert art, 3 & 2pgs.			
	5.00	10.00	15.00
16,17	3.00	6.00	9.00

JIM RAY'S AVIATION SKETCH BOOK
Feb, 1946 - #2, May-June, 1946
Vital Publishers

#1,2-Picture stories about planes and pilots			
	2.50	5.00	7.50

JIM SOLAR (See Wisco/Klarer)

JINGLE BELLS (See March of Comics #65)

JINGLE DINGLE CHRISTMAS STOCKING COMICS
V2#1, 1951 (no date listed)(100pgs;Giant-Size)
Stanhall Publications (Pub-annually)(25¢)

V2#1-Foodini & Pinhead, Silly Pilly plus games & puzzles	1.25	2.50	3.75

JINGLE JANGLE COMICS (Also see Puzzle Fun)
Feb, 1942 - #42, Dec, 1949
Eastern Color Printing Co.

#1-Pie-Face Prince of Old Pretzelburg, & Jingle Jangle Tales by George Carlson, Hortense, & Benny Bear begin			
	22.00	44.00	66.00
2,3-No Pie-Face Prince	10.00	20.00	30.00
4-Pie-Face Prince cover	10.00	20.00	30.00
5	8.00	16.00	24.00
6-10	7.00	14.00	21.00
11-15	5.00	10.00	15.00
16-30: #17,18-No Pie-Face Prince			
31-42	3.50	7.00	10.50
	2.50	5.00	7.50

NOTE: *George Carlson art(2 stories) in all
except #2,3,17,18; covers-#1-6.*

JING PALS
1946
Victory Magazine Corporation

#1-3	1.50	3.00	4.50

JINKS, PIXIE, AND DIXIE (See Whitman Comic--)
1965 (Giveaway) (Hanna-Barbera)

224

(Jinks, Pixie, and Dixie cont'd)
Florida Power & Light

	Good	Fine	Mint
	.15	.30	.45

JOAN OF ARC (See A-1 Comics #21 & Ideal A
Classical Comic)

JOE COLLEGE
1949 - #2, Winter, 1950
Hillman Periodicals

#1,2-Powell art; Briefer story-#1			
	1.75	3.50	5.25

JOE JINKS (See Single Series #12)

JOE LOUIS
Sept, 1950 - #2, Nov, 1950
Fawcett Publications

#1	6.00	12.00	18.00
2	4.00	8.00	12.00

JOE PALOOKA
1933 (B&W daily strip reprints)(52pgs.)
Cupples & Leon Co.

#1-(Scarce)-by Fisher	15.00	30.00	45.00

JOE PALOOKA (1st Series)
1942 - 1944
Columbia Comic Corp.

#1	12.00	24.00	36.00
2	7.00	14.00	21.00
3,4	6.00	12.00	18.00

JOE PALOOKA (2nd Series)(Battle Adv. #68-73)
Nov, 1945 - #118, 1961 (--Advs. #74-115)
Harvey Publications

#1	7.00	14.00	21.00
2	4.00	8.00	12.00
3,4,6	3.50	7.00	10.50
5-Boy Explorers by S&K + Powell art(7-8/46)			
	7.00	14.00	21.00
7-1st Powell Flyin' Fool, ends #25,			
8-10	3.00	6.00	9.00
11-14,16-20	2.50	5.00	7.50
15-Origin Humphrey	3.00	6.00	9.00
21-30	2.00	4.00	6.00
31-61: #44-Joe Palooka marries Ann Howe			
	1.50	3.00	4.50
62-S&K Boy Explorers(reprint)			
	2.50	5.00	7.50
63-80	1.25	2.50	3.75
81-115	1.00	2.00	3.00

	Good	Fine	Mint
116-S&K Boy Explorers (reprint)(1960)			
	1.50	3.00	4.50
117,118-Giants	2.00	4.00	6.00

Joe Palooka Fights His Way Back(1945 Giveaway, 24pgs.) Family Comics
	12.00	24.00	36.00
--Visits the Lost City(1945)(One-Shot)(No#)			
(50¢)-164pg. continuous story strip re-			
print. Has biography & photo of Ham Fish-			
er; possibly the single longest comic			
book story published (159pgs.?)			
	22.00	44.00	66.00

NOTE: _Powell art-#26-53 at least._

JOE YANK
March, 1952 - 1954
Standard Comics (Visual Editions)

#5,7	1.00	2.00	3.00
6-Toth + Severin/Elder story			
	2.50	5.00	7.50
8-Toth cover	2.00	4.00	6.00
9-16	.75	1.50	2.25

JOHN CARTER OF MARS(See 4-Color #375,437,488)

JOHN CARTER OF MARS
April, 1964 - #3, Oct, 1964
Gold Key

#1(10104-404)-Reprints 4-Color #375; Jesse			
Marsh art	2.00	4.00	6.00
2(407), 3(410)-Reprints 4-Color #437 & 488;			
Marsh art	1.50	3.00	4.50

JOHN CARTER OF MARS
1970 (72pgs.)(Paper cover; 10½x16½"; B&W)
House of Greystoke

1941-42 Sunday strip reprints; John Coleman			
Burroughs art	4.00	8.00	12.00

JOHN CARTER, WARLORD OF MARS
June, 1977 - Present
Marvel Comics Group

#1-Origin by Gil Kane	.50	1.00	1.50
2-5	.30	.60	.90
6-10	.25	.50	.75
11-Origin Dejah Thorie	.30	.60	.90
12-20	.20	.40	.60
Annual #1(10/77), 2(9/78)	.60	1.20	1.80

NOTE: _Gil Kane pencils-#1-10._

JOHN F. KENNEDY, CHAMPION OF FREEDOM
1964 (no month) (25¢)
Worden & Childs

Joe Palooka #75. © HARV

John Carter Of Mars #3(GK). © ERB

John Carter #1(MCG). © ERB

John Hix Scrap Book #2, © EAS

Johnny Hazard #6, © STD

John Wayne #3, © TOBY

(John F. Kennedy cont'd)	Good	Fine	Mint
No#	2.50	5.00	7.50

JOHN F. KENNEDY LIFE STORY
Aug-Oct, 1964; Nov, 1965; June, 1966 (12¢)
Dell Publishing Co..

#12-378-410	2.50	5.00	7.50
#12-378-511 (reprint)	1.50	3.00	4.50
#12-378-606 (reprint)	1.20	2.40	3.60

JOHN FORCE (See Magic Agent)

JOHN HIX SCRAP BOOK, THE
Late 1930's (no date)(68pgs.-Reg. size)(10¢)
Eastern Color Printing Co.(McNaught Synd.)

#1-Strange As It Seems (resembles Single			
Series books)	8.00	16.00	24.00
2-Strange As It Seems	7.00	14.00	21.00

JOHNNY DANGER
1950
Toby Press

#1-Drug story (opium)	3.00	6.00	9.00

JOHNNY DANGER PRIVATE DETECTIVE
1954 (Reprinted in Danger #11 (Super))
Toby Press

#1	1.50	3.00	4.50

JOHNNY DYNAMITE (Formerly Dynamite #1-9)
1955 - 1956
Charlton Comics

#10-12	1.00	2.00	3.00

JOHNNY HAZARD
#5, Aug, 1948 - #8, May, 1949
Best Books (Standard Comics)

#5,6,8-Strip reprints by Frank Robbins			
	3.00	6.00	9.00
7-New art, not Robbins	2.00	4.00	6.00
#35	2.00	4.00	6.00

JOHNNY JASON (-- Teen Reporter)
Feb-Apr, 1962 - #2, June-Aug, 1962
Dell Publishing Co.

4-Color #1302,#2(01380-208)	.50	1.00	1.50

JOHNNY JINGLE'S LUCKY DAY
1956 (16pgs.) (7¼x5-1/8")(Giveaway)(Disney)
American Dairy Association

	2.00	4.00	6.00

JOHNNY LAW, SKY RANGER
April, 1955 - #3, Aug, 1955; #4, Nov, 1955
Good Comics (Lev Gleason)

	Good	Fine	Mint
#1-Edmond Good art	2.00	4.00	6.00
2-4	1.50	3.00	4.50

JOHNNY MACK BROWN
#2, Oct-Dec, 1950 - #10, Sept-Nov, 1952
Dell Publishing Co.

4-Color #269('50)-Marsh art			
	3.50	7.00	10.50
#2(1950)-Marsh art	2.00	4.00	6.00
3-10: Marsh art #3-9	1.50	3.00	4.50
4-Color #455,493	2.00	4.00	6.00
4-Color #541,584,618,645,685,722,776,834,			
963,967	1.75	3.50	5.25
4-Color #922-Manning art	2.00	4.00	6.00

JOHNNY RINGO (See 4-Color #1142)

JOHNNY STARBOARD (See Wisco)

JOHNNY THUNDER
Feb-Mar, 1973 - #3, July-Aug, 1973
National Periodical Publications

#1-Johnny Thunder & Nighthawk reprints begin			
	.30	.60	.90
2-Trigger Twins app., #3	.25	.50	.75

NOTE: *Drucker* stories-#2,3. *Infantino* story-
#2. *Toth* stories-#1,3. Also see *All-American*
& *All-Star Western*.

JOHN PAUL JONES
Sept, 1959 - 1959
Dell Publishing Co.

4-Color #1007, #1	1.50	3.00	4.50

JOHN STEED & EMMA PEEL (See The Avengers)

JOHN STEELE SECRET AGENT
Dec, 1964 (Freedom Agent)
Gold Key

#1	.60	1.20	1.80

JOHN WAYNE ADVENTURE COMICS (See Oxydol-Dreft)
Winter, 1949 - #31, May, 1955
Toby Press

#1	6.00	12.00	18.00
2-Two Williamson/Frazetta stories(one reprt/			
Billy the Kid #1), 6 & 2 pgs.,			
3,4-Two Williamson/Frazetta stories, 16pgs.			
total each	12.00	24.00	36.00

(John Wayne Adv. cont'd)   Good Fine Mint

5-Kurtzman art-(Alfred "L" Newman in Potshot
   Pete)   3.50 7.00 10.50
6,7-Williamson/Frazetta story in both; Kurtzman art in #6 10.00 20.00 30.00
8-Two Williamson/Frazetta stories, 12 & 9
   pgs.   12.00 24.00 36.00
9-11,13-15   1.50   3.00   4.50
12-Kurtzman art   2.50   5.00   7.50
16-Williamson/Frazetta reprint from Billy
   the Kid #1   4.00   8.00 12.00
17,19-24,26-28,30 1.50   3.00   4.50
18-Williamson/Frazetta stories reprts./John
   Wayne #4 & 8   6.00 12.00 18.00
25-Williamson/Frazetta reprinted from Billy
   the Kid #3   6.00 12.00 18.00
29-Williamson/Frazetta story reprint from #4
             6.00 12.00 18.00
31-Williamson/Frazetta story reprint from #2
             6.00 12.00 18.00
NOTE: *Williamsonish art in later issues by
Gerald McCann.*

JO-JO COMICS (--Congo King #7-29; My Desire
#30 on)(Also see Fantastic Fear & Jungle Jo)
1945 - #29, July, 1949 (2 #7's; no #13)
Fox Features Syndicate

No#(1945)-Funny animal 1.50 3.00 4.50
#2(4-5/47)-6-Funny animal 1.20 2.40 3.60
7(7/47)-Jo-Jo, Congo King begins
            15.00 30.00 45.00
7(#8)-(9/47)   13.00 26.00 39.00
8-10(#9-11): #8-Tanee begins
            12.00 24.00 36.00
11,12(#12,13)   9.00 18.00 27.00
14-16   9.00 18.00 27.00
17-Kamen bondage cover 10.00 20.00 30.00
18-20   8.00 16.00 24.00
21-29   7.00 14.00 21.00
NOTE: *Many bondage covers & art by Baker/
Kamen/Feldstein. #7's have Princesses Gwenna,
Geesa, Yolda & Safra before settling down on
Tanee.*

JO-JOY (Adventures of --)
1945 - 1953 (Christmas gift comic)
W. T. Grant Dept. Stores

1945-53 issues   1.00 2.00 3.00

JOKEBOOK COMICS DIGEST ANNUAL
Oct, 1977 - Present (192pgs.-Digest Size)
Archie Publications

#1(10/77)-Reprints   .40 .80 1.20
2(4/78)   .40 .80 1.20

JOKER, THE (See Batman & Detective)
May, 1975 - #9, Sept-Oct, 1976
National Periodical Publications
              Good Fine Mint
#1-Two-Face app.   .30   .60   .90
2-5: #3-The Creeper app. #4-Green Arrow,
   Black Canary app. .20   .40   .60
6-9: #9-Catwoman app. .20   .40   .60

JOKER COMICS (Adventures Into Terror #43 on)
April, 1942 - #42, March, 1950
Timely/Marvel Comics #36 on

#1-1st app. Powerhouse Pepper by Wolverton;
   Stuporman app. from Daring
           50.00 100.00 150.00
2-Wolverton art cont'd. 25.00 50.00 75.00
3-5-   "   "   "   14.00 28.00 42.00
6-10- "   "   "   10.00 20.00 30.00
11-20- "   "   "   6.00 12.00 18.00
21-27,29,30-Wolverton cont'd. & Kurtzman's
   "Hey Look" in #23-27 5.00 10.00 15.00
28,32,34,37-42   1.00   2.00   3.00
31-Last Powerhouse Pepper; not in #28
             5.00 10.00 15.00
33,35,36-Kurtzman's "Hey Look"
             2.25   4.50   6.75

JOLLY CHRISTMAS, A (See March of Comics #269)

JOLLY CHRISTMAS BOOK (See Christmas Journey
Through Space)
1951; 1954; 1955 (36pgs.; 24pgs.)
Promotional Publ. Co.

1951-Slightly oversized; no slick cover
   (Woolworth giveaway)-Marv Levy cover/art
             1.75   3.35   5.00
1954-Regular size-reprints '51 issue; slick
   cover added (24pgs., no ads)(Hot Shoppes
   giveaway)   1.75   3.35   5.00
1955-Regular size (J.M. McDonald Co. giveaway)   1.35   2.75   4.00

JOLLY COMICS
1947
Four Star Publishing Co.

#1   1.00 2.00 3.00

JOLLY JINGLES (Formerly Jackpot)
1944 - 1945
MLJ Magazines

#10-Super Duck begins 2.00 4.00 6.00
11-25   1.50   3.00   4.50

Jo-Jo Comics #9, © FOX

Jo-Jo Comics #17, © FOX

Joker Comics #17, © MCG

Jon Juan #1, © TOBY

Journey Into Fear #6, © SUPR

Journey Into Mystery #9, © MCG

JONAH HEX
Mar-Apr, 1977 - Present
National Periodical Publications/DC Comics

	Good	Fine	Mint
#1	.40	.80	1.20
2-8,10: #10-Morrow cover	.25	.50	.75
9-Wrightson cover	.35	.70	1.05
11,13-21	.15	.30	.45
12-Starlin cover	.20	.40	.60

JONAH HEX SPECTACULAR (See DC Special Series #16)

JONESY (Formerly Crack Western)
#85, 8/53; #2, 10/53 - #8, 1954
Comic Favorite/Quality Comics Group

	Good	Fine	Mint
#85(#1)	.50	1.00	1.50
#2-8	.35	.70	1.05

JON JUAN (Also see Great Lover Romances)
Spring, 1950
Toby Press

	Good	Fine	Mint
#1-All Schomburg art (signed Al Reid); written by Siegel; used in Seduction of the Innocent, pg. 38	6.00	12.00	18.00

JONNY QUEST (TV)
Dec, 1964   (Hanna-Barbera)
Gold Key

	Good	Fine	Mint
#1(10139-412)	.50	1.00	1.50

JOSEPH & HIS BRETHREN (See The Living Bible)

JOSIE (She's --#1-13)(-- & the Pussycats #45
Feb, 1963 - Present   on)
Archie Publ./Radio Comics

	Good	Fine	Mint
#1	1.50	3.00	4.50
2-10	.80	1.60	2.40
11-20	.60	1.20	1.80
21,23-30	.50	1.00	1.50
22-Mighty Man & Mighty (Josie Girl) app.	.60	1.20	1.80
31-49,51-54	.40	.80	1.20
50-Meet William Hanna & Joseph Barbera, the cartoon producers	.40	.80	1.20
55-74(Giants)(52pgs.)	.25	.50	.75
75-97		.15	.35

JOURNAL OF CRIME
1949   (132 pgs.)
Fox Features Syndicate

No#-See Fox Giants. Contents can vary and determines price.

JOURNEY INTO FEAR
May, 1951 - #21, Sept, 1954
Superior-Dynamic Publications

	Good	Fine	Mint
#1-Two Baker stories	3.50	7.00	10.50
2-4-Kamen stories	2.50	5.00	7.50
5-10	1.50	3.00	4.50
11-21	1.20	2.40	3.60

JOURNEY INTO MYSTERY (1st Series)(Thor #126
6/52 - #48,8/57; #49,11/58 - #125,2/66 on)
Atlas(CPS #1-48/AMI #49-82/Marvel #83 on)

	Good	Fine	Mint
#1	30.00	60.00	90.00
2	15.00	30.00	45.00
3,4	12.00	24.00	36.00
5-10: #5-Briefer story	6.00	12.00	18.00
11-20,22-Last pre-code ish	3.50	7.00	10.50
21-Kubert story	5.00	10.00	15.00
23-32,35-38,40	2.40	4.80	7.20
33-Williamson story	5.00	10.00	15.00
34-Williamson, Krigstein stories	6.00	12.00	18.00
39-Wood story	5.00	10.00	15.00
41-Crandall story	3.00	6.00	9.00
42-Torres story	2.00	4.00	6.00
43,44-Williamson/Mayo story in both	3.50	7.00	10.50
45,47-49,52,53	1.75	3.50	5.25
46-Torres & Krigstein sty.	3.00	6.00	9.00
50-Davis story	2.50	5.00	7.50
51-Kirby/Wood story	2.50	5.00	7.50
54-Williamson story	2.50	5.00	7.50
55-61,63-73: #66-Return of Xemu	1.75	3.50	5.25
62-1st app. Xemu (Titan) called "The Hulk"	2.50	5.00	7.50
74-82-Contents change to Fantasy with #74	1.25	2.50	3.75
83-Reprint from the Golden Record Comic Set	1.00	2.00	3.00
with the record...	2.00	4.00	6.00
83-Origin & 1st app. The Mighty Thor by Kirby (8/62)	90.00	180.00	270.00
84	27.00	54.00	81.00
85-1st app. Loki & Heimdall	18.00	36.00	54.00
86-1st app. Odin	12.00	24.00	36.00
87-90	8.00	16.00	24.00
91-100: #97-Tales of Asgard series begins	5.00	10.00	15.00
101-110: #108-Doctor Strange x-over	2.50	5.00	7.50
111,113-125	1.40	2.80	4.20
112-Thor Vs. Hulk; origin Loki	2.00	4.00	6.00
Annual #1('65)-1st app. Hercules; Kirby			

(Journey Into Mystery cont'd)

	Good	Fine	Mint
cover/story	3.00	6.00	9.00

NOTE: *Ditko stories-#50,53,86,93,95,96; cover-#71. Ditko/Kirby art-#38,50-83. Everett story-#9(reprt.),20,40; covers-#4-6,37,39,40, 41,44,45. Russ Heath cover-#51. Kirby stories-#83-89,93,97,101-125; covers-#50-82(w/Ditko), 83,84,86,87,89,90,92,94,97-125. Morrow story-#41,42. Orlando story-#16,30,45,57.*

JOURNEY INTO MYSTERY (2nd Series)
Oct, 1972 - #19, Oct, 1975
Marvel Comics Group

	Good	Fine	Mint
#1-Robert Howard adaptation; Kane art; Starlin/Ploog story	.40	.80	1.20
2-Robert Bloch adaptation; Starlin/Ploog art; Adams inks	.35	.70	1.05
3,5-Bloch adaptation; #5-Last new story	.25	.50	.75
4-H.P. Lovecraft adapt.	.25	.50	.75
6-19: #16-Orlando reprt.	.15	.30	.45

NOTE: *Ditko reprints-#7,10,12,15,19. Everett reprint-#9. Kirby reprints-#7,13,18,19; cover-#7. Orlando reprint-#16. Wildey reprints-#9,14.*

JOURNEY INTO UNKNOWN WORLDS (Formerly Teen)
#36, Sept, 1950 - #59, Aug, 1957
Atlas Comics (WFP)

	Good	Fine	Mint
#36(#1)-Science fiction	6.00	12.00	18.00
37(#2)-Science fiction; Everett cover/story	6.00	12.00	18.00
38(#3)-Science fiction	4.00	8.00	12.00
#4-6,8-10-All horror	2.50	5.00	7.50
7,14,15-Wolverton art	9.00	18.00	27.00
11,12-Krigstein stories	2.50	5.00	7.50
13,16,17,20	1.25	2.50	3.75
18,19-Matt Fox stories	1.75	3.50	5.25
21-26,28-33,36,37,39-42	1.00	2.00	3.00
27-Sid Check story	1.50	3.00	4.50
34-Kubert & Torres story	2.50	5.00	7.50
35-Torres story	1.75	3.50	5.25
38-Severin story	1.20	2.40	3.60
43-Krigstein story	2.00	4.00	6.00
44-Davis story	2.00	4.00	6.00
45,55,59-Williamson stories in all with Mayo #55,59+Crandall sty#55	3.00	6.00	9.00
46,47,49,52,56-58	1.00	2.00	3.00
48,51-Wood + Crandall #48	3.00	6.00	9.00
50-Davis + Crandall story	2.50	5.00	7.50
53-Crandall story	1.50	3.00	4.50
54-Torres story	1.40	2.80	4.20

NOTE: *Lou Cameron story-#33. Ditko story-#51; cover-#31. Everett story-#11,14,41,47,48,55; covers-#13,17,22,47,50,53-55,59. Morrow*

story-#48. Orlando story-#44,57. Powell stories-#53,54.

JOURNEY OF DISCOVERY WITH MARK STEEL
(See Mark Steel)

JOURNEY TO THE CENTER OF THE EARTH (See 4-Color Comics #1060)

JUDGE COLT
Oct, 1969 - #4, Sept, 1970
Gold Key

	Good	Fine	Mint
#1-4	.30	.60	.90

JUDGE PARKER
1956
Argo

#1	2.00	4.00	6.00
2	1.50	3.00	4.50

JUDO JOE
Aug, 1953 - #3, Dec, 1953
Jay-Jay Corp.

#1-Drug story	2.50	5.00	7.50
2,3	1.20	2.40	3.60

JUDOMASTER (Gun Master #84-90)(See Special #89, 5-6/66 - #98, 12/67 War Series)
Charlton Comics (Two #89's)

#89-98: #91-Sarge Steel begins. #93-Intro. Tiger	.70	1.40	2.10
#93(Modern Comics reprint, 1977)		.15	.30

JUDY CANOVA (Formerly My Experience)
May, 1950 - #3, Sept, 1950
Fox Features Syndicate

#23(#1),24	2.50	5.00	7.50
3-Wood cover/Orlando sty	5.00	10.00	15.00

JUDY GARLAND (See Famous Stars)

JUDY JOINS THE WAVES
1951 (For U.S. Navy)
Toby Press

No#	1.00	2.00	3.00

JUGHEAD (Formerly Archie's Pal --)
#127, Dec, 1965 - Present
Archie Publications

#127-130	.60	1.20	1.80

Journey Into Mystery #85, © MCG

Journey Into Unknown Worlds #36, © MCG

Judy Canova #23(#1), © FOX

Jumbo Comics #3, © FH

Jumbo Comics #113, © FH

Jumbo Comics #145, © FH

	Good	Fine	Mint
(Jughead cont'd)			
131,133,135-160	.40	.80	1.20
132-Shield cover, #134-Sheild cover & app.			
	.50	1.00	1.50
161-200	.25	.50	.75
201-240	.20	.40	.60
241-282		.15	.35

JUGHEAD AS CAPTAIN HERO
Oct, 1966 - #7, Nov, 1967
Archie Publications

#1	1.00	2.00	3.00
2-7	.60	1.20	1.80

JUGHEAD JONES COMICS DIGEST
June, 1977 - Present   (160 pgs.)
Archie Publications

#1-Capt. Hero reprint	.40	.80	1.20
2(9/77)-#5	.30	.60	.90
6-Origin Jaguar reprint	.30	.60	.90

JUGHEAD'S EAT-OUT COMIC BOOK MAGAZINE
(See Archie Giant Series Mag. #170)

JUGHEAD'S FANTASY
Aug, 1960 - #3, Dec, 1960
Archie Publications

#1	2.50	5.00	7.50
2,3	1.20	2.40	3.60

JUGHEAD'S FOLLY
1957
Archie Publications (Close-Up)

#1-Jughead a la Elvis	4.00	8.00	12.00

JUGHEAD'S JOKES
Aug, 1967 - Present
#1-8,38 on-reg.size;#9-23, 68pgs;#24-37,52pgs.
Archie Publications

#1	1.50	3.00	4.50
2-10	.90	1.80	2.70
11-30	.40	.80	1.20
31-58		.20	.40

JUGHEAD WITH ARCHIE (-- Plus Betty & Veronica & Reggie Too #1,2)
March, 1974 - Present (Digest Size-160 pgs.)
Archie Publications

#1	.60	1.20	1.80
2-10	.25	.50	.75
11-29: Capt. Hero reprint in #14-16; Pure-			

heart the Powerful #18,21,22; Capt. Pure-

heart reprts. in #17,19 .20 .40 .60

JUKE BOX COMICS
March, 1948 - #6, 1949
Famous Funnies

#1-Toth art	6.00	12.00	18.00
2-6	3.00	6.00	9.00

JUMBO COMICS (#1-8 oversized-10½x14½"; B&W)
9/38 - #167, 4/53 (#1-3, 68pgs; #4-8, 52pgs.)
Fiction House Magazines(Real Adv. Publ. Co.)

#1-(Rare)-Sheena Queen of the Jungle by Meskin, The Hawk by Eisner, The Hunchback by Dick Briefer(ends #8) begin; 1st comic art by Jack Kirby (Count of Monte Cristo & Wilton of the West); Mickey Mouse appears(1 panel) with brief biography of Walt Disney   140.00 350.00 560.00

2-Diary of Dr. Hayward by Kirby (also #3) plus 2 other stories; contains strip from Universal Film featuring Edgar Bergen & Charlie McCarthy   70.00 175.00 280.00

3-Last Kirby issue   50.00 125.00 200.00

4-Origin The Hawk by Eisner; Wilton of the West by Fine(ends #14); Count of Monte Cristo by Fine(ends #15); The Diary of Dr. Hayward by Fine(cont'd. #8,9)
50.00 125.00 200.00

5   40.00 100.00 160.00

6-8-Last B&W issue. #8 was a N.Y. World's Fair Special Edition 30.00 75.00 120.00

9-Stuart Taylor begins by Fine; Fine cover; 1st color issue-8¼x10¼"
30.00 60.00 90.00

10-14: #10-68pg. issues begin
25.00 50.00 75.00

15-Lightning begins   18.00 36.00 54.00

16-20   15.00 30.00 45.00

21-30: #22-1st Tom, Dick & Harry; origin The Hawk retold   12.00 24.00 36.00

31-40: #35 shows V2#11 (correct # does not appear)   9.00 18.00 27.00

41-50   8.00 16.00 24.00

51-60   6.00 12.00 18.00

61-70: #68-Sky Girl begins, ends #130
5.00 10.00 15.00

71-80   4.00   8.00 12.00

81-93,95-100: #89-2x5 becomes a private eye
4.00   8.00 12.00

94-Used in Love and Death by Legman
6.00 12.00 18.00

101-110   3.00   6.00   9.00

111-140: #131-Long Bow, Indian Boy begins, ends #159   2.50   5.00   7.50

141-158   2.00   4.00   6.00

159-163: Space Scouts serial in all; #163-

(Jumbo Comics cont'd)	Good	Fine	Mint
Suicide Smith app.	2.00	4.00	6.00
164-The Star Pirate begins	2.00	4.00	6.00
165-167: The Space Rangers app. #165,167			
	2.00	4.00	6.00

NOTE: *Hawk by Eisner-#10-15; Eisner covers-*
#6,12,13,15. Sheena by Meskin-#1,4; by Powell-
#2,3,5-28. Sky Girl by Matt Baker-#69-78,80-
124. Bailey art-#3-8. Briefer art-#1-8. Fine
covers-#9-11. Kamen story-#123. Bob Kane art-
#1-8.

JUMPING JACKS PRESENTS THE WHIZ KIDS
1978 (In 3-D) with glasses (4pgs.)
Jumping Jacks Stores giveaway

No#	.25	.50	.75

JUNGLE ACTION
Oct, 1954 - #6, Aug, 1955
Atlas Comics (IPC)

#1-Leopard Girl begins	4.00	8.00	12.00
2-(3-D effect cover)	3.50	7.00	10.50
3-6	3.00	6.00	9.00

JUNGLE ACTION
Oct, 1972 - #24, Nov, 1976
Marvel Comics Group

#1-Lorna, Jann reprints	.35	.70	1.05
2,4	.20	.40	.60
3-Tharn reprints; Starlin/Giacola cover			
	.25	.50	.75
5-Black Panther begins	.50	1.00	1.50
6-10-All new stories	.35	.70	1.05
11-24: All new stories. #18-Kirby cover. #23-			
reprint/#22, Buscema cvr.	.25	.50	.75

JUNGLE ADVENTURES
1963 - 1964   (Reprints)
Super Comics

#10,12(Rulah),15(Kaanga/Jungle #152)			
	1.50	3.00	4.50
17(Jo-Jo)	1.50	3.00	4.50
18-Reprints/White Princess of the Jungle #1;			
No Kinstler art; origin of both White Prin-			
cess & Cap'n Courage	2.00	4.00	6.00

JUNGLE ADVENTURES
March, 1971 - #3, June, 1971
Skywald Comics

#1-Zangar origin; reprints of Jo-Jo, Blue Gor-			
illa(origin)/White Princess #3, Kinstler			
story/White Princess #2	.50	1.00	1.50
2-Zangar, Sheena/Sheena #17 & Jumbo #162,			

		Good	Fine	Mint
Jo-Jo, origin Slave Girl Princess reprints				
		.50	1.00	1.50
3-Zangar, Jo-Jo, White Princess reprints				
		.50	1.00	1.50

JUNGLE BOOK, THE (See Movie Comics)

JUNGLE CAT (See 4-Color Comics #1136)

JUNGLE COMICS
Jan, 1940 - #163, Summer, 1954
Fiction House Magazines

#1-Origin The White Panther, Kaanga, Lord of			
the Jungle, Tabu, Wizard of the Jungle;			
Wambi, the Jungle Boy & Camilla begin			
	70.00	140.00	210.00
2-Fantomah, Mystery Woman of the Jungle			
begins	40.00	80.00	120.00
3,4	30.00	60.00	90.00
5	20.00	40.00	60.00
6-10	16.00	32.00	48.00
11-20	12.00	24.00	36.00
21-30: #25 shows V2#1(correct # does not			
appear). #27-New origin Fantomah, Daught-			
er of the Pharoahs; Camilla dons new cos-			
tume	9.00	18.00	27.00
31-40	7.00	14.00	21.00
41-50	5.00	10.00	15.00
51-60	4.50	9.00	13.50
61-70	3.50	7.00	10.50
71-80: #79-New origin Tabu			
	3.00	6.00	9.00
81-90	2.75	5.50	8.25
91-97,99-110	2.50	5.00	7.50
98-Used in Seduction of the Innocent, pg. 185			
& illo-"In ordinary comic books, there are			
pictures within pictures for children who			
know how to look"	5.00	10.00	15.00
111-150: #135-Desert Panther begins in Terry			
Thunder(origin), not in #137; ends(dies)			
#138	2.25	4.50	6.75
151-157,159-163: #152-Tiger Girl begins			
	2.00	4.00	6.00
158-Sheena app.	2.50	5.00	7.50
IW Reprint #1,9: #9-reprints #151			
	1.35	2.75	4.00

NOTE: *Kaanga by John Celardo-#90-110; by*
Maurice Whitman-#124-163. Tabu by Whitman-
#94-110. Eisner cover-#2,5. Fine cover-#1.
Bondage covers are common.

JUNGLE GIRL (See Lorna, --)

JUNGLE GIRL (Nyoka, -- #2 on)
Fall, 1942
Fawcett Publications

Jungle Action #6. © MCG

Jungle Comics #73. © FH   Jungle Comics #156, © FH

Jungle Jo #1, © FOX

Junie Prom #3, © Dearfield Publ.

Junior Comics #11, © FOX

(Jungle Girl cont'd)	Good	Fine	Mint
#1	25.00	50.00	75.00

JUNGLE JIM
Jan, 1949 - #20, April, 1951
Standard Comics (Best Books)

#11-20	1.50	3.00	4.50

JUNGLE JIM
1953 - #1020, Aug-Oct, 1959
Dell Publishing Co.

4-Color #490,565('53-'54)	2.00	4.00	6.00
#3(10-12/54)-#5	1.50	3.00	4.50
6-20(4-6/59)	1.25	2.50	3.75
4-Color #1020(#21)	1.75	3.50	5.25

JUNGLE JIM
December, 1967
King Features Syndicate

#5-Reprints Dell #5; Wood cover			
	.60	1.20	1.80

JUNGLE JIM (Continued from Dell)
#22, Feb, 1969 - #28, Feb, 1970 (no #21)
Charlton Comics

#22-Dan Flagg begins, ends #23; Wood & Ditko			
art	.75	1.50	2.25
23-28: #23-Wood cvr. #24-Jungle People be-			
gin. #27-Wood, Ditko art. #28-Ditko			
	.50	1.00	1.50

JUNGLE JO
Mar, 1950 - #6, Mar, 1951
Fox Features Syndicate (Hero Books)

No#-Jo-Jo blanked out, leaving Congo King;			
came out after Jo-Jo #29(intended as Jo-Jo			
#30?)	6.00	12.00	18.00
#1-Tangi begins	8.00	16.00	24.00
2-6	5.00	10.00	15.00

JUNGLE LIL (Dorothy Lamour, Jungle Princess
#2 on) (Also see Feature Stories Magazine)
April, 1950
Fox Features Syndicate/Hero Books

#1	8.00	16.00	24.00

JUNGLE TALES (Jann of the Jungle #8 on)
Sept, 1954 - #7, Sept, 1955
Atlas Comics (CSI)

#1-Jann of the Jungle	3.50	7.00	10.50
2-7	2.50	5.00	7.50

JUNGLE TALES OF TARZAN
Dec, 1964 - #5, 1965
Charlton Comics

	Good	Fine	Mint
#1	2.00	4.00	6.00
2-4	1.50	3.00	4.50

5-(Very Rare)-Cardboard covers in color;
Glanzman art-This series was unauthorized
& killed after #5 was printed - all but a
few issues of #5 were destroyed

Estimated value..... $350.00

NOTE: *Glanzman did not get has art back; was
told had to be destroyed with other Tarzan
art.*

JUNGLE TERROR (See Harvey Comics Hits #54)

JUNGLE THRILLS (Terrors of the Jungle #17)
#16, Feb, 1952
Fox Features Syndicate/Star Publications

#16-Phantom Lady & Rulah story-reprint/All			
Top #15	10.00	20.00	30.00
3-D#1(12/53)-Jungle Lil & Jungle Jo appear			
	7.00	14.00	21.00

JUNGLE TWINS, THE (Tono & Kono)
April, 1972 - #17, Nov, 1975
Gold Key

#1	.25	.50	.75
2-5	.20	.40	.60
6-17		.15	.35

JUNGLE WAR STORIES (Guerrilla War #12 on)
July-Sept, 1962 - #11, Apr-June, 1965
Dell Publishing Co.

#01-384-209	.40	.80	1.20
#2-11	.30	.60	.90

JUNIE PROM
Winter, 1947-48 - #7, August, 1949
Dearfield Publishing Co.

#1	1.20	2.40	3.60
2-7	.80	1.60	2.40

JUNIOR COMICS
#9, Sept, 1947 - #16, July, 1948
Fox Features Syndicate

#9-16-Feldstein cvr/stys	18.00	36.00	54.00

JUNIOR FUNNIES (Formerly Tiny Tot Funnies #9)
#10, Aug, 1951 - #13, Feb, 1952
Harvey Publications (King Features Synd.)

(Junior Funnies cont'd)   Good   Fine   Mint
#10-13: Partial reprints-Blondie, Popeye, Felix, Katzenjammer Kids 1.25 2.50 3.75

JUNIOR HOP COMICS (Junior Hopp)
1952 - #3, July, 1952
Atlas Comics/SPM Publ.

	Good	Fine	Mint
#1,2	1.20	2.40	3.60
3-Dave Berg art	1.00	2.00	3.00

JUNIOR MEDICS OF AMERICA, THE
1957   (15¢)
E. R. Squire & Sons

#1359	.65	1.35	2.00

JUNIOR MISS
Winter, 1944 - #39, August, 1950
Timely/Marvel Comics (CnPC)

#1-Frank Sinatra life story	4.00	8.00	12.00
2-10	1.50	3.00	4.50
11-20	1.00	2.00	3.00
21-38	.75	1.50	2.25
39-Kurtzman art	1.75	3.50	5.25

JUNIOR PARTNERS (Formerly Oral Roberts' True
#120, 8/59 - V3#12, 12/61   Stories)
Oral Roberts Evangelistic Assn.

#120(#1)	1.00	2.00	3.00
#2(9/59)	.65	1.35	2.00
3-12(7/60)	.50	1.00	1.50
V2#1(8/60)-5(12/60)	.25	.50	.75
V3#1(1/61)-12	.20	.40	.60

JUNIOR TREASURY (See Dell Junior --)

JUNIOR WOODCHUCKS (See Huey, Dewey & Louie--)

JUSTICE COMICS (Tales of Justice #63 on;
formerly Wacky Duck)
#7, Fall/47 - #9, 6/48; #4, 8/48 - #57, 12/55
Atlas(NPP 7-19/CnPC 20-23/MgMC 24-37/
Male #38-62)

#7-9('47-48)	1.50	3.00	4.50
4-10	.90	1.80	2.70
11-30: #22,25-Robinson art	.60	1.20	1.80
31-57	.50	1.00	1.50

NOTE: *Everett story-#53.*

JUSTICE, INC. (The Avenger)
May-June, 1975 - #4, Nov-Dec, 1975
National Periodical Publications

	Good	Fine	Mint
#1-McWilliams sty.; origin	.30	.60	.90
2-4	.20	.40	.60

NOTE: *Kirby covers-#2,3; stories-#2-4.*
Kubert covers-#1,4.

JUSTICE LEAGUE OF AMERICA (See Brave & Bold)
Oct-Nov, 1960 - Present
National Periodical Publications/DC Comics

	Good	Fine	Mint
#1-Origin Despero	30.00	60.00	90.00
2	15.00	30.00	45.00
3-Origin Kanjarro	12.00	24.00	36.00
4,5: #4-Green Arrow joins JLA. #5-Origin Dr. Destiny	7.00	14.00	21.00
6-8,10: #6-Origin Prof. Amos Fortune. #10-Origin Felix Faust	4.00	8.00	12.00
9-Origin J.L.A.	5.00	10.00	15.00
11-13,15: #12-Origin Dr. Light. #13-Speedy app.	2.50	5.00	7.50
14-Atom joins JLA	2.75	5.50	8.25
16-20: #17-Adam Strange flashback	2.00	4.00	6.00
21,22: #21-Re-intro. of JSA. #22-JSA x-over	2.50	5.00	7.50
23-28: #28-Robin app.	1.50	3.00	4.50
29,30-JSA x-over	1.75	3.50	5.25
31-Hawkman joins JLA, Hawkgirl cameo	1.20	2.40	3.60
32-Origin Brain Storm	1.20	2.40	3.60
33-36,40	1.00	2.00	3.00
37,38-JSA x-over	1.35	2.75	4.00
39-25¢ Giant G-16	1.50	3.00	4.50
41-Origin The Key	1.00	2.00	3.00
42-45: #42-Metamorpho app.	.75	1.50	2.25
46,47-JSA x-over	.90	1.80	2.70
48-25¢ Giant G-29	1.00	2.00	3.00
49,50-Robin app. #50	.70	1.40	2.10
51-54,56,57,59,60	.70	1.40	2.10
55-Intro. Earth 2 Robin	.70	1.40	2.10
58-25¢ Giant G-41	.90	1.80	2.70
61-63,66,68-70: #69-Wonder Woman quits. #70-Creeper x-over	.50	1.00	1.50
64,65-JSA x-over; intro. Red Tornado #65	.60	1.20	1.80
67-25¢ Giant G-53	.70	1.40	2.10
71,72,75,77-80: #71-Manhunter leaves JLA. #78-Re-intro. Vigilante. #79-Vigilante x-over	.40	.80	1.20
73,74-JSA x-over; #73-Black Canary leaves JSA & joins JLA	.50	1.00	1.50
76-25¢ Giant G-65	.50	1.00	1.50
81,84,86-90	.40	.80	1.20
82-JSA x-over	.50	1.00	1.50
83-JSA x-over; death of Spectre(revived later)	.50	1.00	1.50
85-25¢ Giant G-77	.50	1.00	1.50
91-JSA x-over; Hourman. reprint; 52pgs. begin,			

Junior Miss #31. © MCG

Justice Comics #11, © MCG

Justice League #6, © DC

Justice League #16, © DC   Justice Traps The Guilty #3, © PRIZE   Kaanga Comics #3, © FH

	Good	Fine	Mint
(Justice League cont'd)			
end #99	.40	.80	1.20
92-JSA x-over; Flash reprt.	.40	.80	1.20
93-25¢ Giant G-89	.50	1.00	1.50
94-Origin Sandman(Adv.#40)& Starman(Adv.#61); Deadman x-over; Adams art	1.50	3.00	4.50
95-Origin Dr. Fate & Dr. Midnight reprint (More Fun #67, All-American #25)	.60	1.20	1.80
96-Origin Hourman reprint(Adventure #48)	.60	1.20	1.80
97-Origin JLA retold	.50	1.00	1.50
98,99: #98-G.A. Sargon, Starman reprint. #99-G.A. Sandman, Atom reprint	.40	.80	1.20
100-102-JSA, 7 Soldiers & others x-over	.40	.80	1.20
103-106: #103-Phantom Stranger joins. #105-Elongated Man joins. #106-New Red Tornado joins	.30	.60	.90
107,108-JSA & G.A. Uncle Sam, Black Condor, The Ray, Dollman, Phantom Lady, & The Human Bomb x-over	.40	.80	1.20
109-Hawkman resigns	.30	.60	.90
110-116: All 100pg. issues; JSA Tale & Toth reprint. #113-JSA/JLA team up.	.25	.50	.75
117-120: #117-Hawkman rejoins	.25	.50	.75
121-Adam Strange marries Alanna	.25	.50	.75
122,125-130: #128-Wonder Woman rejoins. #129-Death of Red Tornado	.25	.50	.75
123,124-JSA x-over	.25	.50	.75
131,132	.20	.40	.60
133,134-Part 2&3 of Desparo	.20	.40	.60
135,136: JSA & G.A. Bulletman, Bulletgirl, Spy Smasher, Mr. Scarlet, Pinky & Ibis x-over in all	.20	.40	.60
137-Same as above + Superman battles G.A. Capt. Marvel	.30	.60	.90
138,139-Adams covers; #139-begin 52pg. ishs.	.25	.50	.75
140-150: #144-Origin retold; #148,149-JSA & Legion x-over	.20	.40	.60
151-164: #157-Atom marries Jean Loring. #161-Zatanna joins	.15	.30	.45

NOTE: _Adams_ covers-#63,66,67,70,74,79,81,82, 86-89,91,92,94,96-98,138,139. _Anderson_ covers-#1-4,10,12-14,16,17,19,24,75-77,80,83-85, 95,138,139. _Infantino_ story-#110(reprint); covers-#56-58,90. _Kaluta_ cover-#154. _Krigstein_ story-#96(reprint-Sensation #84). _Kubert_ covers-#72,73. _Staton_ cover-#157.

JUSTICE MACHINE
1978   (50¢)
Power Comics

	Good	Fine	Mint
#1	.20	.40	.60

JUSTICE TRAPS THE GUILTY (Fargo Kid V11#3 on)
Oct-Nov, 1947 - V11#2(#92), Apr-May, 1958
Prize/Headline Publications

	Good	Fine	Mint
V2#1-S&K cover/stories	8.00	16.00	24.00
2-5-S&K cover/stories	4.50	9.00	13.50
6-S&K cover/story, + Feldstein story	5.00	10.00	15.00
7,9-S&K cover/story	2.50	5.00	7.50
8,10-S&K cover/story + Krigstein story	3.00	6.00	9.00
11,19-S&K covers	1.80	3.60	5.40
12-17,20-No S&K	1.20	2.40	3.60
18-S&K cvr, Elder story	1.75	3.50	5.25
21-S&K cover/story	1.75	3.50	5.25
22,23,27-S&K covers	1.50	3.00	4.50
24-26,28-50	1.00	2.00	3.00
51-70	.60	1.20	1.80
71-92	.40	.80	1.20

NOTE: _Meskin_ story-#27. _Severin/Belfi_ story-#11.

JUST KIDS
1932   (16pgs.) (9½x12") (Soft cover)
McLoughlin Bros.

	Good	Fine	Mint
#283-Three-color text, pictures on heavy paper	5.00	10.00	15.00

JUST MARRIED
January, 1958 - Present
Charlton Comics

	Good	Fine	Mint
#1	.60	1.20	1.80
2-20	.25	.50	.75
21-50	.15	.30	.45
51-114		.10	.25

KA'A'NGA COMICS (-- Jungle King)
Spring, 1949 - #20, Summer, 1954
Fiction House Magazines(Glen-Kel Publ. Co.)

	Good	Fine	Mint
#1-Ka'a'nga, Lord of the Jungle begins	8.00	16.00	24.00
2-4	5.00	10.00	15.00
5-Camilla app.	3.00	6.00	9.00
6-10: #9-Tabu, Wizard of the Jungle app.	2.50	5.00	7.50
11-15	2.00	4.00	6.00
16-Sheena app.	2.50	5.00	7.50
17-20	1.75	3.50	5.25
IW Reprint #1(reprts.#18)	.80	1.60	2.40
IW Reprint #8(reprts.#10)	.80	1.60	2.40

KAMANDI, THE LAST BOY ON EARTH (See Cancelled Comic Cavalcade)

(Kamandi cont'd)
Oct-Nov, 1972 - #59, Sept-Oct, 1978
National Periodical Publications/DC Comics

	Good	Fine	Mint
#1-Origin	1.20	2.40	3.60
2-5	.70	1.40	2.10
6-10	.60	1.20	1.80
11-20	.50	1.00	1.50
21-31	.35	.70	1.05
32-Giant, origin from #1	.40	.80	1.20
33-40-Last Kirby issue	.25	.50	.75
41-56,58	.15	.30	.45
57,59-Starlin cvr/stories	.25	.50	.75

NOTE: _Alcala_ stories-#47-52. _Kirby_ stories-
#1-40; covers-#1-33. _Kubert_ covers-#34-41.

KARATE KID (See Action, Adventure & Superboy)
Mar-Apr, 1976 - #15, Jul-Aug, 1978
National Periodical Publications/DC Comics

#1-Estrada/Staton art	.25	.50	.75
2-15	.20	.40	.60

NOTE: _Staton_ stories-#6-9.

KASCO COMICS
1949   (Giveaway)(Reg.Size)(Soft Cover)
Kasko Grainfeed

#1-Similar to Katy Keene; Bill Woggan art			
	9.00	18.00	27.00
2	8.00	16.00	24.00

KATHY
September, 1949 - 1953
Standard Comics

#1	1.00	2.00	3.00
2-5	.60	1.20	1.80
6-16	.50	1.00	1.50

KATHY
Oct, 1959 - #27, Feb, 1964
Atlas Comics/Marvel (ZPC)

#1	.50	1.00	1.50
2-27	.20	.40	.60

KAT KARSON
No date (Reprint)
I.W. Enterprises

#1-Funny animals	.40	.80	1.20

KATY KEENE   (Also see Kasco Komics, Laugh,
Pep, Suzie, & Wilbur)
1950 - 1961
Archie Publ./Close-Up/Radio Comics

	Good	Fine	Mint
#1-Bill Woggon art begins			
	15.00	30.00	45.00
2	8.00	16.00	24.00
3-5	6.00	12.00	18.00
6-10	4.00	8.00	12.00
11-20	3.00	6.00	9.00
21-30,32-40	2.50	5.00	7.50
31-(3-D issue)(1953)	6.00	12.00	18.00
41-62	1.75	3.50	5.25
Annual #1('54)	8.00	16.00	24.00
Annual #2-6('55-'59)	4.00	8.00	12.00
3-D#1(1953-Large size)	6.00	12.00	18.00
Charm #1(9/58)	2.50	5.00	7.50
Glamour #1(1957)	3.00	6.00	9.00
Spectacular #1('56)	3.50	7.00	10.50

KATY KEENE FASHION BOOK
1955 - #23, Winter, 1958
Radio Comics/Archie Publications

#1	6.00	12.00	18.00
2-10	3.00	6.00	9.00
11-23	2.00	4.00	6.00

KATY KEENE HOLIDAY FUN   (See Archie Giant
Series Mag. #7,12)

KATY KEENE PINUP PARADE
1955 - #16, Summer, 1961   (25¢)
Radio Comics/Archie Publications

#1	6.00	12.00	18.00
2-16	2.50	5.00	7.50

KATZENJAMMER KIDS, THE
1903   (50 pgs.) (10x15¼") (In Color)
New York American & Journal

1903 (Rare)	25.00	62.50	100.00
1905-Tricks of --(10x15)	20.00	50.00	80.00
1906-Stokes-10x16",32pgs. in color			
	20.00	50.00	80.00
1910-The Komical--(10x15)	20.00	50.00	80.00
1921-Embee Dist. Co., 10x16", 20pgs. in color			
	15.00	37.50	60.00

KATZENJAMMER KIDS, THE
Summer, 1947 - #27, Feb-Mar, 1954
David McKay Publ./Standard #12-21(Spring,
'50-53)/Harvey #22, 4/53 on

Feature Book #30,32,35,37('45),41,44('46)			
	5.00	10.00	15.00
#1(1947)	4.00	8.00	12.00
2-11	2.50	5.00	7.50
12-14(Standard)	2.00	4.00	6.00
15-21(Standard)	1.50	3.00	4.50
22-27(Harvey)	1.50	3.00	4.50

Kathy #8, © STD

Katy Keene #20, © AP

Katy Keene Fashion Book #15, © AP

The Katzenjammer Kids #2, © KING   Keen Detective Funnies V2#7, © CEN   Ken Maynard Western #3, © FAW

KAYO (Formerly Jest?)
March, 1945
Harry 'A' Chesler

	Good	Fine	Mint
#12-Green Knight, Capt. Glory, Little Nemo			
(not by McCay)	2.00	4.00	6.00

KA-ZAR
Aug, 1970 - #3, March, 1971   (Giant-Size)
Marvel Comics Group

	Good	Fine	Mint
#1-Reprints earlier Ka-Zar stories; Avengers x-over in Hercules	.50	1.00	1.50
2,3-Ka-Zar origin #2; Angel in both	.35	.70	1.05

KA-ZAR
Jan, 1974 - #20, Feb, 1977   (Regular Size)
Marvel Comics Group

	Good	Fine	Mint
#1	.50	1.00	1.50
2-10: #4-Brunner cover	.35	.70	1.05
11-20	.25	.50	.75

NOTE: _Alcala inks-#6,8. Kirby cover-#12._

KEEN COMICS
V2#1, May, 1939 - V2#3, Nov, 1939
Centaur Publications

	Good	Fine	Mint
V2#1	10.00	20.00	30.00
V2#2,3: #3-Burgos art	8.00	16.00	24.00

KEEN DETECTIVE FUNNIES
Dec, 1937 - V3#9, Sept, 1940
Centaur Publications

	Good	Fine	Mint
V1#1	25.00	50.00	75.00
2	15.00	30.00	45.00
3-11: The Clock in #8,9	12.00	24.00	36.00
V2#1,2-The Eye Sees begins; ends V3#8	10.00	20.00	30.00
3-TNT Todd begins	10.00	20.00	30.00
4,5-The Clock in #5	10.00	20.00	30.00
6,8-12	10.00	20.00	30.00
7-The Masked Marvel begins	12.00	24.00	36.00
V3#1-6	10.00	20.00	30.00
7-Origin Air Man	12.00	24.00	36.00
8,9	10.00	20.00	30.00

KEEN TEENS
1945
Life's Romances Publ./Leader/Mag. Ent.

	Good	Fine	Mint
No#-14pgs. Claire Voyant(cont'd. in other No# issue), movie photos, Dotty Dripple, Gertie O'Grady & Sissy	5.00	10.00	15.00

	Good	Fine	Mint
No#-16pgs. Claire Voyant & 16pgs. movie photos	5.00	10.00	15.00
#3-5(M.E.)	1.25	2.50	3.75

KEEPING UP WITH THE JONESES
1920 - #2, 1921 (48pgs;9½x9½";B&W daily strip
Cupples & Leon Co.   reprints)

	Good	Fine	Mint
#1,2-By Pop Momand	5.00	10.00	15.00

KELLYS, THE (Formerly Rusty; Spy Cases #26 on
#23, Jan, 1950 - #25, June, 1950
Marvel Comics (HPC)

	Good	Fine	Mint
#23-25	.80	1.60	2.40

KEN MAYNARD WESTERN
Sept, 1950 - #8, Feb, 1952
Fawcett Publications

	Good	Fine	Mint
#1-with photos	7.00	14.00	21.00
2	4.00	8.00	12.00
3-8	2.00	4.00	6.00

KEN SHANNON (Gabby #11)
Oct, 1951 - #15, 1953   (a private eye)
Quality Comics Group

	Good	Fine	Mint
#1-Crandall story	5.00	10.00	15.00
2-Crandall cvr/2 stories	4.00	8.00	12.00
3-5-Crandall stories	3.00	6.00	9.00
6,7	2.00	4.00	6.00
8-10-Crandall covers	2.50	5.00	7.50
11-15	1.35	2.70	4.05

NOTE: _Jack Cole stories-#1-9. #11-15 published after title change to Gabby._

KEN STUART
1948
Publication

	Good	Fine	Mint
#1-Frank Borth art	2.00	4.00	6.00

KENT BLAKE OF THE SECRET SERVICE (War)
May, 1951 - #14, July, 1953
Marvel/Atlas Comics(20CC)

	Good	Fine	Mint
#1	1.50	3.00	4.50
2-14	.80	1.60	2.40

KERRY DRAKE (-- Racket Buster #32,33)
1944; #6, 1/48 - #33, 8/52
Life's Romances/Magazine Ent.#1-5/Harvey#6 on

	Good	Fine	Mint
No#(1944)(A-1 Comics)	6.00	12.00	18.00
#2-5(1944)	5.00	10.00	15.00
6,8(1948)	3.50	7.00	10.50

(Kerry Drake cont'd)	Good	Fine	Mint
7-Kubert story	4.50	9.00	13.50
9,10-Two-part marijuana story			
	5.00	10.00	15.00
11-15: #13-Powell art	3.00	6.00	9.00
16-18,20-33	2.25	4.50	6.75
19-Drug story	5.00	10.00	15.00

--In the Case of the Sleeping City-(1951-Pub-
lishers Synd.)(16pg. Giveaway-for armed
forces) soft cover 2.00 4.00 6.00
NOTE: _Powell_ stories-#11,13,23.

KERRY DRAKE (Also see Green Hornet)
Jan, 1956 - #2, Mar, 1956
Argo

#1,2-Newspaper reprints	2.00	4.00	6.00

KEWPIES
1949
Will Eisner Publications

#1-Eisner & Feiffer art; used in Seduction
of the Innocent in a non-seductive
context 8.00 16.00 24.00

KEY COMICS
Jan, 1944 - #5, Aug, 1946
Consolidated Magazines

#1-The Key, Will-O-The-Wisp begin			
	3.00	6.00	9.00
2-5	2.00	4.00	6.00

KEY COMICS
1951 - 1956 (32 pgs.) (Giveaway)
Key Clothing Co./Peterson Clothing

Contains a comic from different publishers
bound with new cover. Cover changed each year.
Many combinations possible. Distributed in
Nebraska, Iowa, & Kansas. Contents would determine price, 40-60% of original.

KEY RING COMICS
1941 (16 pgs.) (Sold 5 for 10¢)
Dell Publishing Co.

#1-Features Sleepy Samson	2.00	4.00	6.00
#1-Origin Greg Gilday reprint from War Comics			
#2	2.50	5.00	7.50

KID CARROTS
Sept, 1953
St. John Publishing Co.

#1		.65	1.35	2.00

KID COLT OUTLAW (-- Hero of the West #1-?)
(Also see Wisco)
Aug, 1948 - #139, 3/68; #140, 11/69 - Present
#1-102, Marvel/Atlas(LMC); #103 on, Marvel

	Good	Fine	Mint
#1	10.00	20.00	30.00
2	5.00	10.00	15.00
3-5	4.00	8.00	12.00
6-10	2.50	5.00	7.50
11-Origin	3.50	7.00	10.50
12-30	1.80	3.60	5.40
31-47,49,50	1.20	2.40	3.60
48-Kubert art	1.50	3.00	4.50
51-53,55,56	1.00	2.00	3.00
54-Williamson/Maneely cover only			
	2.00	4.00	6.00
57-60,66: 4pg. Williamson stories in all.			
#59-Reprint Rawhide Kid #79			
	2.25	4.50	6.75
61-63,67-78,80-85	.70	1.40	2.10
64,65-Crandall story	1.20	2.40	3.60
79-Origin retold	1.00	2.00	3.00
86-Kirby story reprint	.80	1.60	2.40
87-Davis stories reprint	1.20	2.40	3.60
88,89-Williamson stories in both(4pgs.).#89-			
redrawn Matt Slade #2	2.00	4.00	6.00
90-92,94,95,97-118,120	.50	1.00	1.50
93,96,119-Kirby story	.50	1.00	1.50

121-140: #121-Rawhide Kid x-over. #125-Two-Gun
Kid x-over. #130-132-68pg. issues with one
new story each; #130-Origin. #132-Last
Jack Keller ish. #140-Reprints begin
.25 .50 .75
141-146,148-160: #141-New Two-Gun Kid story.
#156-Giant; reprints .25 .50 .75

147-Williamson story reprt.	.25	.50	.75
161-169,171	.20	.40	.60
170,172-Williamson story reprints; origin re-			
told #170	.20	.40	.60
173-200	.15	.30	.45
201-227		.15	.35

--Album(No date; 1950's)-132pgs.(Atlas Comics)
Random binding, cardboard cover, B&W stories; contents can vary 4.00 8.00 12.00
Giant Size #1(1/75), 2(4/75), 3(7/75)
.30 .60 .90

NOTE: _Crandall_ story reprint-#140,167. _Ever-
ett_ inks-#137. _Kirby_ covers-#87,92-95,97,99-
112,114-117,121-123,197(reprint). _Morrow_
story-#173(reprint). _Whitney_ reprint-#141.
Wildey story-#82. _Woodbridge_ story-#64,81.
Black Rider in #33,35-37,41,44,74,86. _Iron
Mask_ in #110,114,121,127. _Sam Hawk_ in #84,101,
111,121,146,174,181,188.

KID COWBOY
1950 - 1954 (Painted covers)
Ziff-Davis Publ./St. John (Approved Comics)

Kerry Drake #12, © HARV

Kid Colt Outlaw #5, © MCG

Kid Cowboy #3, © Z-D

(Kid Cowboy cont'd)	Good	Fine	Mint
#1-Lucy Belle begins	1.50	3.00	4.50
2-14,#4(4/54-Approved)	1.00	2.00	3.00

KIDDIE KAPERS
Oct, 1957; 1963 - 1964
Decker Publ. (Red Top-Farrell)

#1(no date)	.40	.80	1.20
#1(10/57)(Decker)-Little Bit reprints from			
Kiddie Karnival	.40	.80	1.20
Super Reprint #10('63),#14('63),#15,17('64),			
#18('64)	.20	.40	.60

KIDDIE KARNIVAL
1952   (100pgs.)   (One Shot)
Ziff-Davis Publ. Co. (Approved Comics)

No#-Rebound Little Bit #1,2			
	1.20	2.40	3.60

KID ETERNITY (Becomes Buccaneers) (See Hit)
Spring, 1946 - #18, 1949
Quality Comics Group

#1	10.00	20.00	30.00
2	6.00	12.00	18.00
3-Mac Raboy story	7.00	14.00	21.00
4-10	3.00	6.00	9.00
11-18	2.00	4.00	6.00

KID FROM DODGE CITY, THE
July, 1957 - #2, Sept, 1957
Atlas Comics (MMC)

#1	1.20	2.40	3.60
2-Everett cover	.80	1.60	2.40

KID FROM TEXAS, THE (A Texas Ranger)
June, 1957 - #2, Aug, 1957
Atlas Comics (CSI)

#1-Powell story	1.20	2.40	3.60
2	.80	1.60	2.40

KID KOKO
1958
I.W. Enterprises

Reprint #1,2-(reprints M.E.'s Koko & Kola			
#4, 1947)	.50	1.00	1.50

KID KOMICS (-- Movie Komics #11)
Feb, 1943 - #10, Spring, 1946
Timely Comics

#1-Origin Captain Wonder & sidekick Tim
    Mullrooney; intro. Subbie, the Sea-Going

	Good	Fine	Mint
Lad, Pinto Pete, & Trixy Trouble; Knuck-			
les & Whitewash Jones only app. Wolverton			
art, 7pgs.	70.00	140.00	210.00
2-The Young Allies, Red Hawk, & Tommy Tyme			
begin; last Captain Wonder & Subbie			
	50.00	100.00	150.00
3-The Vision & Daredevils app.			
	30.00	60.00	90.00
4-The Destroyer begins; Sub-Mariner app.;			
Red Hawk & Tommy Tyme end			
	25.00	50.00	75.00
5,6	18.00	36.00	54.00
7-10: The Whizzer app. #7; Destroyer not in			
#7,8; #10-Last Destroyer, Young Allies &			
Whizzer	12.00	24.00	36.00

KID MONTANA (The Gunfighters #51 on)
V2#9, 11/57 - #50, 3/65
Charlton Comics

V2#9,10	.30	.60	.90
#11-20	.25	.50	.75
21-50	.20	.40	.60

NOTE: *Title change to Montana Kid on cover
only on #44; remained Kid Montana on inside.*

KID MOVIE KOMICS (Formerly Kid Komics; Rusty
#11, Summer, 1946   #12 on)
Timely Comics

#11-Silly Seal & Ziggy Pig; 2pgs. Kurtzman			
"Hey Look" + 6pg. sty.	4.00	8.00	12.00

KIDNAPPED (See 4-Color #1101 & Movie Comics)

KIDNAP RACKET (See Harvey Comics Hits #57)

KID SLADE GUNFIGHTER (Formerly Matt Slade--)
#5, Jan, 1957 - #8, July, 1957
Atlas Comics (SPI)

#5	1.20	2.40	3.60
6,8	.75	1.50	2.25
7-Williamson/Mayo story, 4pgs.			
	2.00	4.00	6.00

KID ZOO COMICS
July, 1948
Street & Smith Publications

#1	.80	1.60	2.40

KILLERS, THE
1947 - 1948
Magazine Enterprises

#1-Mr. Zin, the Hatchet Killer; mentioned in

Kid Eternity #12, © QUA

Kid Komics #5, © MCG

Kid Zoo Comics #1, © S&S

The Kilroys #38, © ACG   King Comics #8, © DMP   King Comics #33, © DMP

(The Killers cont'd)   Good   Fine   Mint
   Seduction of the Innocent, pgs. 179,180;
   L. B. Cole cover   12.00   24.00   36.00
2-(Rare)-Hashish story; Whitney, Ingels art
                         10.00   20.00   30.00

KILROYS, THE
June-July, 1947 - #54, June-July, 1955
B&I Publ. Co. #1-19/American Comics Group

#1   2.00   4.00   6.00
 2-5   1.00   2.00   3.00
 6-10   .80   1.60   2.40
11-30   .40   .80   1.20
31-47,50-54   .30   .60   .90
48,49-(3-D effect)   .75   1.50   2.25

KING CLASSICS SERIES (Also see Classics Libr.)
1977   (School reading aids)
King Features Syndicate

No#'s-Robinson Crusoe, 20,000 Leagues Under
   the Sea, Swiss Family Robinson, Robin Hood,
   A Connecticut Yankee, Treasure Island, The
   Last of the Mohicans, Moby Dick, Flash Gor-
   don(Williamson cover reprint)
                           .20   .40   .60

KING COLT (See 4-Color Comics #651)

KING COMICS (Strip Reprints)
April, 1936 - #159, Feb, 1952(Winter on cvr)
David McKay Publications/Standard #159

#1-Flash Gordon by Alex Raymond; Brick Brad-
   ford, Mandrake, the Magician & Popeye
   begin   150.00 300.00 450.00
 2   70.00 140.00 210.00
 3   45.00   90.00 135.00
 4   30.00   60.00   90.00
 5   25.00   50.00   75.00
 6-10   20.00   40.00   60.00
11-20   14.00   28.00   42.00
21-30   12.00   24.00   36.00
31-40: #33-Last Segar Popeye
              10.00   20.00   30.00
41-49   8.00   16.00   24.00
50-The Lone Ranger begins 8.00 16.00 24.00
51-60: #52-Barney Baxter begins?
               7.00   14.00   21.00
61-The Phantom begins 6.00 12.00 18.00
62-90   5.00   10.00   15.00
91-100   5.00   10.00   15.00
101-115-Last Raymond ish. 4.00 8.00 12.00
116-145   3.00   6.00   9.00
146,147-Prince Valiant in both,
148-155-Flash Gordon ends 2.50 5.00 7.50
156-159: #157-Mandrake ends
               2.00   4.00   6.00

KING KONG (See Movie Comics)

KING LEONARDO & HIS SHORT SUBJECTS (TV)
1962 - #4, Sept, 1963
Dell Publishing Co./Gold Key
                        Good   Fine   Mint
4-Color #1242,1278   .50   1.00   1.50
#01390-207(5-7/62)(Dell) .35   .70   1.05
#1-4(10/62-'63)   .35   .70   1.05

KING LOUIE & MOWGLI
May, 1968   (Disney)
Gold Key

#1(10223-805)   .35   .70   1.05

KING OF BAD MEN OF DEADWOOD
1950
Avon Periodicals

No#-Kinstler cover   4.00   8.00   12.00

KING OF DIAMONDS (TV)
July-Sept, 1962
Dell Publishing Co.

#01-391-209   .60   1.20   1.80

KING OF KINGS (See 4-Color Comics #1236)

KING OF THE ROYAL MOUNTED (See Black & White
#9, Feature Book #1(McKay),& Super Book #2,6)

KING OF THE ROYAL MOUNTED
1937   (64pgs.;5½x7½";B&W daily reprints)
Whitman Publ. Co.   (Hardcover)

                         7.00   14.00   21.00

KING OF THE ROYAL MOUNTED (Zane Grey's)
#8, June-Aug, 1952 - #28, Mar-May, 1958
Dell Publishing Co.

4-Color #207('48)   5.00   10.00   15.00
4-Color #265,283   4.00   8.00   12.00
4-Color #310,340   2.50   5.00   7.50
4-Color #363,384   2.00   4.00   6.00
#8-28('58)   1.50   3.00   4.50
4-Color #935('58)   1.50   3.00   4.50
NOTE: 4-Color #207,265,283,310,340,363,384
are all newspaper reprints with Jim Gary art.
#8 on are all Dell originals.

KING RICHARD & THE CRUSADERS (See 4-Color#588)

KING SOLOMON'S MINES
1951   (Movie)
Avon Periodicals

(King Solomon's Mines cont'd)

	Good	Fine	Mint
No#(#1 on 1st page)	10.00	20.00	30.00

KISS (See Marvel Comics Super Special &
Howard the Duck #12)

KIT CARSON (See Frontier Fighters)

KIT CARSON (Formerly All True Detective
Cases #4; Fighting Davy Crockett #9)
6/51 - #3, 12/51; #5, 11-12/54 - #8, 9/55
Avon Periodicals

	Good	Fine	Mint
No#(#1)	2.50	5.00	7.50
#2(8/51), #3(12/51)	2.00	4.00	6.00
5-8(1954)	1.50	3.00	4.50
IW Reprint #10('63)	.65	1.35	2.00

NOTE: *Kinstler covers-#3,5,8.*

KIT CARSON & THE BLACKFEET WARRIORS
1953
Realistic

No#	2.00	4.00	6.00

KIT KARTER
1962
Dell Publishing Co.

#1	.35	.70	1.05

KITTY
Oct, 1948
St. John Publishing Co.

#1-Lily Renee art	1.25	2.50	3.75

KLARER GIVEAWAYS (See Wisco)

KNIGHTS OF THE ROUND TABLE (See 4-Color #540)

KNIGHTS OF THE ROUND TABLE
#10, April, 1957
Pines Comics

#10	.70	1.40	2.10

KNIGHTS OF THE ROUND TABLE
Nov-Jan, 1964
Dell Publishing Co.

#1(12-397-401)	.50	1.00	1.50

KNOCK KNOCK
1936   (32 pgs.) (B&W)
Gerona Publications

	Good	Fine	Mint
#1-Bob Dunn art	7.00	14.00	21.00

KNOCKOUT ADVENTURES
1954
Fiction House Magazines

#1-Reprints/Fight Comics #53	2.00	4.00	6.00

KNOW YOUR MASS
1958   (100 pg. Giant) (35¢)
Catechetical Guild

#303-In color	2.00	4.00	6.00

KOBRA
Feb-Mar, 1976 - #7, Mar-Apr, 1977
National Periodical Publications

#1-Art plotted by Kirby	.30	.60	.90
2-7	.20	.40	.60

KOKEY KOALA
May, 1952
Toby Press

#1	1.00	2.00	3.00

KOKO & KOLA
Fall, 1946 - #5, May, 1947; #6, 1950
Compix/Magazine Enterprises

#1-5,6(A-1#28)	1.20	2.40	3.60

KO KOMICS
October, 1945
Gerona Publications

#1-The Duke of Darkness & The Menace (hero)	4.00	8.00	12.00

KOMIC KARTOONS
Fall, 1945 - #2, Winter, 1945
Timely Comics

#1,2	1.50	3.00	4.50

KOMIK PAGES
April, 1945
Harry 'A' Chesler, Jr. (Our Army, Inc.)

#10(#1 on inside)-Land O' Nod by Rick Yager (2pgs.), Animal Crackers, Foxy GrandPa, Tom, Dick & Mary, Cheerio Minstrels, Red Starr + other 1-2pg. strips; Cole art; all reprints	2.50	5.00	7.50

King Solomon's Mines, © AVON

Kit Carson #6, © AVON

Kobra #1, © DC

Kona #3, © DELL

Konga #3, © CC

Korak #47, © DC

KONA (-- Monarch of Monster Isle)
Feb-Apr, 1962 - #21, Jan-Mar, 1967
Dell Publishing Co.

	Good	Fine	Mint
4-Color #1256	1.75	3.50	5.25
#2-10: #4-Anak begins	.75	1.50	2.25
11-21	.50	1.00	1.50

KONGA (Fantastic Giants #24)(See Return of--)
1961 - #23, Nov, 1965
Charlton Comics

#1-Based on movie	5.00	10.00	15.00
2-5	2.00	4.00	6.00
6-15	1.25	2.50	3.75
16-23	.90	1.80	2.70

NOTE: _Ditko stories-#1,3-15; covers-#4,6-9._
Montes & Bache art-#16-23.

KONGA'S REVENGE (Formerly Return of --)
#2, Summer, 1963 - #3, Fall, 1954; Dec, 1968
Charlton Comics

#2,3: #2-Ditko cover/sty	1.50	3.00	4.50
#1('68)-Reprints Konga's Revenge #3			
	1.00	2.00	3.00

KONG THE UNTAMED
June-July, 1975 - #5, Feb-Mar, 1976
National Periodical Publications

#1	.50	1.00	1.50
2-5	.30	.60	.90

NOTE: _Alcala stories-#1-3. Wrightson covers-#1,2._

KOOKIE
Feb-Apr, 1962 - #2, May-July, 1962
Dell Publishing Co.

#1,2-Written by John Stanley; Bill Williams art	.90	1.80	2.70

KORAK, SON OF TARZAN (Edgar Rice Burroughs)
Jan, 1964 - #45, Jan, 1972
Gold Key

#1-Russ Manning art	3.00	6.00	9.00
2-11-Russ Manning art	1.75	3.50	5.25
12-21: #14-Jon of the Kalahari ends. #15- Mabu, Jungle Boy begins; Manning art #21			
	1.00	2.00	3.00
22-30	.80	1.60	2.40
31-45	.60	1.20	1.80

KORAK, SON OF TARZAN (Tarzan Family #60 on)
#46, 5-6/72 - #56, 2-3/74; #57, 5-6/75 - #59,
9-10/75 (Edgar Rice Burroughs)
National Periodical Publications

	Good	Fine	Mint
#46-(52pgs.)-Carson of Venus begins(origin); Pellucidar feature	.80	1.60	2.40
47,48,50	.50	1.00	1.50
49-Origin Korak retold	.50	1.00	1.50
51-56-Carson of Venus ends.	.40	.80	1.20
57-59	.30	.60	.90

NOTE: _Anderson stories-#52-55. Kaluta stor-
ies-#46-56. All have covers by Joe Kubert.
Manning strip reprints-#57-59._

KORG: 70,000 B.C.
May, 1975 - #9, Nov, 1976 (Hanna-Barbera)
Charlton Comics

#1	.35	.70	1.05
2-9	.25	.50	.75

KORNER KID COMICS
1947
Four Star Publications

#1	.65	1.35	2.00

KOSHER COMICS
1966 ($1.00)
Parallax

"Supermax" & "Tishman of the Apes"

	1.35	2.75	4.00

KRAZY KAT
1946 (Hardcover)
Holt

Reprints daily & Sunday strips by Herriman

	35.00	70.00	105.00
with dust jacket(Rare)..	55.00	110.00	165.00

KRAZY KAT (--& Ignatz the Mouse early issues)
May-June, 1951 - Jan, 1964 (None by Herriman)
Dell Publishing Co./Gold Key

#1(1951)	2.50	5.00	7.50
2-5	2.00	4.00	6.00
4-Color #454,504	1.75	3.50	5.25
4-Color #548,619,696	1.50	3.00	4.50
#1(10098-401)(1/64-G.K.)	1.00	2.00	3.00

KRAZY KAT (See March of Comics #72,87)

KRAZY KOMICS (1st Series) (Cindy #27 on?)
July, 1942 - #26, 1946
Timely Comics(USA #1-21/JPC #22-26)

#1	7.00	14.00	21.00
2-10	3.00	6.00	9.00
11,13,14	1.75	3.50	5.25
12-Timely's entire art staff drew themselves			

(Krazy Komics cont'd)	Good	Fine	Mint
into a Creeper story	2.50	5.00	7.50

15-Has "Super Soldier" by Pfc. Stan Lee

	Good	Fine	Mint
	2.00	4.00	6.00
16-24,26	1.40	2.80	4.20
25-Kurtzman story, 6pgs.	3.50	7.00	10.50

KRAZY KOMICS (2nd Series)(Also see Ziggy Pig)
Aug, 1948 - #26, 1950
Timely/Marvel Comics

#1-Wolverton(10pgs.)& Kurtzman(8pgs.) stories			
	14.00	28.00	42.00
2-Wolverton art	7.00	14.00	21.00
3-10	1.35	2.75	4.00
11-26	1.00	2.00	3.00

KRAZY KROW
Summer, 1945 - #7, 1946
Marvel Comics (ZPC)

#1	1.00	2.00	3.00
2-5	.50	1.00	1.50
6,7	.40	.80	1.20
IW Reprint #1('57), #2('58), #7			
	.25	.50	.75

KRAZYLIFE
1945 (No month)
Fox Features Syndicate

#1-Funny animal	1.00	2.00	3.00

KRIM-KO COMICS
1936 - 1939 (4 pg. Giveaway) (Weekly)
Krim-ko Chocolate Drink

Lola, Secret Agent; 184 issues-all original
stories   each.... 2.00 4.00 6.00

KROFFT SUPERSHOW
April, 1978 - Present
Gold Key

#1-5		.15	.35

KULL & THE BARBARIANS (Magazine)
May, 1975 - #3, Sept, 1975 (B&W) ($1.00)
Marvel Comics Group

#1-Wood reprt./Kull #1, 2pg. Adams
              1.20   2.40   3.60
2-Red Sonja by Chaykin begins; Adams inks;
  Adams art   1.00   2.00   3.00
3-Origin Red Sonja by Chaykin; Adams inks
              1.00   2.00   3.00

KULL THE CONQUEROR (--the Destroyer #11 on)

6/71 - #2, 8/71; #3, 7/72 - #15, 8/74;
#16, 8/76 - #29, 10/78
Marvel Comics Group

	Good	Fine	Mint
#1-Wood/Ross Andru art; origin Kull			
	2.50	5.00	7.50
2,3	1.20	2.40	3.60
4,5	1.00	2.00	3.00
6-9	.80	1.60	2.40
10-15-Ploog stories	.70	1.40	2.10
16-29	.25	.50	.75

NOTE: *#1,2,7-9,11 are based on Robert E.
Howard stories. Alcala inks-#17,18,20. Severin stories-#2-9. Starlin cover-#14.*

KUNG FU (See Deadly Hands of --, & Master of --)

KUNG FU FIGHTER (See Richard Dragon --)

LABOR IS A PARTNER
1949 (32pgs.)(paper cover)
Catechetical Guild Educational Society

Anti-communism	4.00	8.00	12.00

LAD: A DOG
1961 - #2, July-Sept, 1962
Dell Publishing Co.

4-Color #1303 (movie)	1.25	2.50	3.75
#2	.70	1.40	2.10

LADY AND THE TRAMP (See 4-Color #629,634, & Movie Classics & Comics)

LADY AND THE TRAMP IN "BUTTER LATE THAN NEVER"
1955 (14 pgs.) (Walt Disney)
American Dairy Assn. (Premium)

	2.50	5.00	7.50

LADY BOUNTIFUL
1917 (10¼x13½")(24pgs.)(B&W)(Cardboard cvr)
Saalfield Publ. Co./Press Publ. Co.

by Gene Carr; 2 panels per page
              7.00   14.00   21.00

LADY COP (See First Issue Special)

LADY LUCK (Formerly Smash #1-85)
Dec, 1949 - #90, Aug, 1950
Quality Comics Group

#86(#1)	15.00	30.00	45.00
87-90	12.00	24.00	36.00

Krazy Komics #1(1948), © MCG

Kull The Conqueror #4, © MCG

Lady Luck #90, © QUA

Lana #3, © MCG   Lance O'Casey #4, © FAW   Large Feature Comic #12, © DELL

LAFF-A-LYMPICS (Also see The Funtastic World
of Hanna-Barbera #3)
Mar, 1978 - #11, Jan, 1979
Marvel Comics Group

	Good	Fine	Mint
#1	.20	.40	.60
2-11	.15	.30	.45

LAFFY-DAFFY COMICS
Feb, 1945 - #2, March, 1945
Rural Home Publ. Co.

#1,2	.60	1.20	1.80

LANA (Little Lana #8, or True Life Tales
Aug, 1948 - #7, Aug, 1949   #8 on?)
Marvel Comics (MjMC)

#1	1.35	2.75	4.00
2-Kurtzman's "Hey Look"	2.00	4.00	6.00
3-7	.75	1.50	2.25

LANCELOT & GUINEVERE (See Movie Classics)

LANCELOT LINK, SECRET CHIMP (TV)
April, 1971 - #8, Feb, 1973
Gold Key

#1	.15	.30	.45
2-8		.15	.30

LANCE O'CASEY (See Mighty Midget Comics)
Spr, 1946 - #3, Fall, 1946; #4, Summer, 1948
Fawcett Publications

#1	4.00	8.00	12.00
2-4	2.50	5.00	7.50

LANCER (TV)
Feb, 1969 - #3, 1969
Gold Key

#1	.35	.70	1.05
2,3	.25	.50	.75

LAND OF THE GIANTS (TV)
Nov, 1968 - #5, Sept, 1969
Gold Key

#1	.40	.80	1.20
2-5	.30	.60	.90

LAND OF THE LOST COMICS (Radio)
July-Aug, 1946 - #9, Spring, 1948
E.C. Comics

#1	12.00	24.00	36.00
2-9	8.00	16.00	24.00

LAND UNKNOWN, THE (See 4-Color #845)

LARAMIE (TV)
Aug, 1960 - July, 1962
Dell Publishing Co.

	Good	Fine	Mint
4-Color #1125,1223,1284	.90	1.80	2.70
#01-418-207	.80	1.60	2.40

LAREDO (TV)
June, 1966
Gold Key

#1(10179-606)	.35	.70	1.05

LARGE FEATURE COMIC (Continuation of Black
& White) (Black & White interior)
1941 - 1943 (8½x11-3/8" with thin slick
color covers; 52 pgs.)
Dell Publishing Co.

#25-Smilin' Jack	15.00	37.50	60.00
26-Smitty	8.00	20.00	32.00
27-Terry & the Pirates	25.00	62.50	100.00
28-Grin & Bear It	5.00	12.50	20.00
29-Moon Mullins	9.00	22.50	36.00
30-Tillie the Toiler	7.00	17.50	28.00
1-Peter Rabbit by Cady	25.00	62.50	100.00
2-Winnie Winkle	6.00	15.00	24.00
3-Dick Tracy	30.00	75.00	120.00
4-Tiny Tim	12.00	30.00	48.00
5-Toots & Casper	5.00	12.50	20.00
6-Terry & the Pirates	25.00	62.50	100.00
7-Pluto Saves the Ship (Disney) written by			
Carl Barks, Jack Hannah & Nick George			
	60.00	150.00	240.00
8-Bugs Bunny('42)	50.00	125.00	200.00
9-Bringing Up Father	6.00	15.00	24.00
10-Popeye (Thimble Theatre)			
	20.00	50.00	80.00
11-Barney Google & Snuffy Smith			
	10.00	25.00	40.00
12-Private Buck	4.00	12.00	20.00

NOTE: *Above rarely found in fine or mint
condition.*

LARRY DOBY, BASEBALL HERO
1950   (Cleveland Indians)
Fawcett Publications

No#-Bill Ward art	4.00	8.00	12.00

LARS OF MARS
May-June, 1951 - #11, July-Aug, 1951
Ziff-Davis Publ. Co.

#10,11-Anderson stories (3) in each			
	6.00	12.00	18.00

LASH LARUE WESTERN
June, 1949 – #46, Jan, 1954
Fawcett Publications

	Good	Fine	Mint
#1	12.00	24.00	36.00
2-5	6.00	12.00	18.00
6-10	5.00	10.00	15.00
11-20	3.00	6.00	9.00
21-46	2.25	4.50	6.75

LASH LARUE WESTERN
#47, 1954 – #84, June, 1961
Charlton Comics

	Good	Fine	Mint
#47-67,69,70	1.35	2.75	4.00
68-(68pgs.)	1.75	3.35	5.00
71-84	1.00	2.00	3.00

LASSIE (M-G-M's -- #1-36)
1950 - #70, July, 1969
Dell Publ. Co./Gold Key #59(10/62) on

#1	2.50	5.00	7.50
2-10	1.25	2.50	3.75

11-19: #12-Rocky Langford (Lassie's master)
marries Gerry Lawrence. #15-1st app.
Timbu   1.00   2.00   3.00
20-22-Matt Baker stories 1.75 3.50 5.25
23-40: #39-1st app. Timmy as Lassie picks up
her TV family   .50   1.00   1.50
41-70: #63-Last Timmy. #64-Reprints/#19.
#65-Forest Ranger Corey Stuart begins,
ends #69. #70-Forest Rangers Bob Ericson
& Scott Turner app.(Lassie's new masters)
.40   .80   1.20
The Adventures of --(Red Heart Dog Food
Giveaway, 1949)   1.75   3.50   5.25
Florida Power & Light Giveaway(1973)
.25   .50   .75
Kite Fun Book('73)(No#)-Pacific Gas & Elec.
Co. & Sou. Calif. Edison (16pgs.,5x7")
2.50   5.00   7.50
*(See March of Comics #210,217,230,254,266,
278,296,308,324,334,346,358,370,381,394,411)*

LAST HUNT, THE (See 4-Color Comics #678)

LAST OF THE COMANCHES
1953   (Movie)
Avon Periodicals

No#-Kinstler cover/story 6.00 12.00 18.00

LAST OF THE ERIES, THE (See American Graphics)

LAST OF THE FAST GUNS, THE (See 4-Color #925)

LAST OF THE MOHICANS (See King Classics)

LAST TRAIN FROM GUN HILL (See 4-Color #1012)

LATEST ADVENTURES OF FOXY GRANDPA (See Foxy-

LATEST COMICS (Super Duper #3?)
March, 1945
Spotlight Publ./Palace Promotions(Jubilee)

	Good	Fine	Mint
#1-Super Duper	1.00	2.00	3.00
2-Bee-29 (no date)	1.00	2.00	3.00

LAUGH COMICS (Formerly Black Hood #1-19)
#20, Fall, 1946 - Present (Laugh #226 on)
Archie Publications (Close-Up)

#20-Archie begins	10.00	20.00	30.00
21-23,25	6.00	12.00	18.00
24-"Pipsy" by Kirby,6pgs.7.00	14.00	21.00
26-30	4.00	8.00	12.00
31-40	3.00	6.00	9.00

41-70: #67-Debbi by Bill Woggon
2.00   4.00   6.00

71-100	1.20	2.40	3.60
101-126	.70	1.40	2.10

127,129,130,131,133,135,140-142,144-Jaguar
app. + The Fly-#129 .80   1.60   2.40
128,132,134,136,137,139-Fly app.
.80   1.60   2.40

138-Flyman & Flygirl app.	.80	1.60	2.40
143-Flygirl app.	.80	1.60	2.40
145-160	.50	1.00	1.50
161-180	.30	.60	.90
181-220	.20	.40	.60
221-260	.15	.30	.45
261-332		.15	.30

NOTE: *Josie app.-#145,160,164. Katy Keene
app.-#21,59,65,67,82,88,90,99,103,107,110,
111,113,114,116,121,122,124,130.*

LAUGH COMICS DIGEST
8/74; #2, 9/75; #3, 3/76 - Present (160 pgs.)
Archie Publications(Close-Up #1,3 on)

#1	.50	1.00	1.50
2-19	.30	.60	.90

LAUGH COMIX (Formerly Top Notch Laugh;
becomes Suzie #49 on)
#46, Summer, 1944 - #48, Winter, 1944-45
MLJ Magazines

#46-48-Wilbur & Suzie 3.00 6.00 9.00

LAUGH-IN MAGAZINE (Magazine)
Oct, 1968 - #12, Oct, 1969 (50¢) (Satire)
Laufer Publ. Co.

V1#1   .50   1.00   1.50

Lash Larue Western #3, © FAW

Lassie #6, © DELL

Laugh Comics #53, © AP

244

Law Against Crime #2, © Essenkay Publ.   Lawbreakers Suspense Stories #15, © CC   Leading Comics #5, © DC

	Good	Fine	Mint
(Laugh-In Mag. cont'd)			
2-12	.35	.70	1.05

LAUREL & HARDY (See March of Comics #302,314)

LAUREL AND HARDY (-- Comics)
Mar, 1949 - #28, 1951
St. John Publishing Co.

#1	6.00	12.00	18.00
2,3	3.50	7.00	10.50
4-10	2.50	5.00	7.50
11-28	1.50	3.00	4.50

LAUREL AND HARDY (TV)
Oct, 1962 - #4, Sept-Nov, 1963
Dell Publishing Co.

#12-423-210(8-10/62)	1.00	2.00	3.00
#2-4(Dell)	.65	1.35	2.00

LAUREL AND HARDY
Jan, 1967 - #2, Oct, 1967 (Larry Harmon's)
Gold Key

#1,2	.50	1.00	1.50

LAUREL AND HARDY (-- Comics)
July-Aug, 1972 (Larry Harmon's)
National Periodical Publications

#1	.35	.70	1.05

LAW AGAINST CRIME (Law-Crime on cover)
April, 1948 - #3, Aug, 1948
Essenkay Publishing Co.

#1-(#1-3: ½ funny animal, ½ crime) L. B.			
Cole cover/story	4.00	8.00	12.00
2-L. B. Cole cover	2.50	5.00	7.50
3-L. B. Cole cover/story; used in Seduction of the Innocent, pg. 180,181 & illo-"The wish to hurt or kill couples in lovers' lanes"; reprinted in All-Famous Crime #9			
	5.00	10.00	15.00

LAWBREAKERS (-- Suspense Stories #6 on)
Mar, 1951 - #5, Mar, 1952
Law and Order Magazines (Charlton Comics)

#1	1.25	2.50	3.75
2,3,5	1.00	2.00	3.00
4-Drug story	3.00	6.00	9.00

LAWBREAKERS ALWAYS LOSE!
Spring, 1948 - #10, Oct, 1949
Marvel Comics (CBS)

#1-Kurtzman art, 2pgs.	3.00	6.00	9.00

	Good	Fine	Mint
2-5	1.50	3.00	4.50
6,8-10	1.00	2.00	3.00
7-Used in Seduction of the Innocent, illo- "Comic-book philosophy"	4.00	8.00	12.00

LAWBREAKERS SUSPENSE STORIES (Formerly Law-
breakers; Strange Suspense Stories #16 on)
June, 1952 - #15, Nov, 1953
Capitol Stories/Charlton Comics

#6-10,12-15	1.00	2.00	3.00
11-Severed tongues cover/story & nude woman under open negligee	4.00	8.00	12.00

LAW-CRIME (See Law Against Crime)

LAWMAN (TV)
1958 - #11, Apr-June, 1962
Dell Publishing Co.

4-Color #970,1035('58-60)	.80	1.60	2.40
#3-11	.60	1.20	1.80

LAWRENCE (See Movie Classics)

LEADING COMICS (-- Screen Comics #34 on)
Winter, 1941-42 - #33, 10-11/48
National Periodical Publications

#1-Origin The Seven Soldiers of Victory; Crimson Avenger, Green Arrow & Speedy, Shining Knight, The Vigilante, Star Spangled Kid & Stripsey begin			
	70.00	140.00	210.00
2-Meskin art	35.00	70.00	105.00
3	25.00	50.00	75.00
4	22.00	44.00	66.00
5	17.50	35.00	52.50
6-10	15.00	30.00	45.00
11-14(Spring,1945)	12.00	24.00	36.00
15-Content change to funny animal, 16-30: #23-1st app. Peter Porkchops			
	1.20	2.40	3.60
31-33	.65	1.35	2.00

LEADING SCREEN COMICS(Formerly Leading Comics)
#34, 12-1/48-49 - #77, 8-9/55
National Periodical Publications

#34-77	.60	1.20	1.80

LEATHERNECK THE MARINE (See Mighty Midget
Comics)

LEAVE IT TO BEAVER (TV)
1958 - May-July, 1962
Dell Publishing Co.

(Leave It To Beaver cont'd)

	Good	Fine	Mint
4-Color #912,999,1103,1191,1285,			
#01-428-207	.60	1.20	1.80

LEAVE IT TO BINKY (Binky #72 on)(See Super
DC Giant & Showcase)
Feb-Mar, 1948 - #60, Dec-Jan, 1958; #61,
June-July, 1968 - #71, Feb-Mar, 1970
National Periodical Publications

#1	3.00	6.00	9.00
2-10	1.50	3.00	4.50
11-20	1.20	2.40	3.60
21-60	.75	1.50	2.25
61-71	.50	1.00	1.50

LEE HUNTER, INDIAN FIGHTER (See 4-Color
Comics #779,904)

LEFT-HANDED GUN, THE (See 4-Color #913)

LEGEND OF CUSTER, THE (TV)
January, 1968
Dell Publishing Co.

#1	.65	1.35	2.00

LEGEND OF JESSE JAMES, THE (TV)
February, 1966
Gold Key

#10172-602	.65	1.35	2.00

LEGEND OF LOBO, THE (See Movie Comics)

LEGEND OF YOUNG DICK TURPIN, THE (TV)
May, 1966   (Disney TV episode)
Gold Key

#1(10176-605)	.90	1.80	2.70

LEGENDS OF DANIEL BOONE, THE
Oct-Nov, 1955 - #8, Dec-Jan, 1956-57
National Periodical Publications

#1	3.00	6.00	9.00
2-8	2.00	4.00	6.00

LEGION OF MONSTERS (Magazine)
September, 1975   (Black & White)
Marvel Comics Group

#1-Adams cover; Morrow art; origin & only app.
The Manphibian .70 1.40 2.10

LEGION OF SUPER-HEROES (See Action, Adventure,
2/73 - #4, 7-8/73   & Superboy)

National Periodical Publications

	Good	Fine	Mint
#1-Legion & Tommy Tomorrow	.75	1.50	2.25
2-4	.50	1.00	1.50

LEMIX-KORLIX (Kool-Aid)
1935   (48 pgs.) (15x8")
Lemix-Korlix Giveaways

#1,2-Tarzan	30.00	60.00	90.00
3-Terry	22.00	44.00	66.00
4-Dick Tracy	27.50	55.00	82.50
5-Chester Gump	13.50	26.75	40.00

NOTE: *The above are cut-down versions of Big
Little Books with blank back covers for en-
dorsement imprinting and were given away by
Lemix-Korlix Kool-Aid, shoe stores, variety
stores and gas stations. They were liscen-
sed out from Western/Whitman to a company
called Karmetz who farmed them out to different outlets.*

LENNON SISTERS LIFE STORY, THE (See 4-Color
Comics #951,1014)

LEO THE LION
No date   (10¢)
I.W. Enterprises

#1-Reprint	.20	.40	.60

LEROY
Nov, 1949 - 1950
Standard Comics

#1	.70	1.40	2.10
2-Frazetta text illo.	2.00	4.00	6.00
3-6: #3-Lubbers art	.40	.80	1.20

LET'S PRETEND
May-June, 1950 - #3, Sept-Oct, 1950
D.S. Publishing Co.

#1	2.00	4.00	6.00
2,3	1.50	3.00	4.50

LET'S READ THE NEWSPAPER
1974
Charlton Press

Features Quincy by Ted Sheares
.20   .40   .60

LET'S TAKE A TRIP (TV)
Spring, 1958   (CBS TV Presents)
Pines

The Legion Of Monsters #1, © MCG

Legion Of Super-Heroes #4, © DC

Leroy #5, © STD

Liberty Scouts #2, © CEN   Life Stories Of Amer. Presidents #1, © DELL   Life With Archie #50, © AP

(Let's Take a Trip cont'd)

	Good	Fine	Mint
#1-Marv Levy cover/art	.50	1.00	1.50

LETTERS TO SANTA (See March of Comics #228)

LIBERTY COMICS (Miss Liberty #1)
1945 - 1946   (MLJ reprints)
Green Publishing Co.

	Good	Fine	Mint
#4	4.00	8.00	12.00
10-Hangman & Boy Buddies app.; Suzie & Wilbur begin; reprint of Hangman #8	4.00	8.00	12.00
11-Wilbur in Drag!	5.00	10.00	15.00
12-Black Hood app.	4.00	8.00	12.00
14,15-Patty of Airliner & Leonard Star in both	2.00	4.00	6.00
V2#2(1946)	1.50	3.00	4.50

LIBERTY GUARDS
No Date (1946?)
Chicago Mail Order

	Good	Fine	Mint
No#-Reprints Man of War #1 with cover of Liberty Scouts #1	10.00	20.00	30.00

LIBERTY SCOUTS (See Man of War & Liberty
June, 1941 - #3, Fall, 1941   Guards)
Centaur Publications

	Good	Fine	Mint
#2(#1)-Origin The Fire-Man, Man of War; Vapo-Man & Liberty Scouts begin	25.00	50.00	75.00
3(#2)	20.00	40.00	60.00

LIDSVILLE (TV)
Oct, 1972 - #5, Oct, 1973
Gold Key

#1	.15	.30	.45
2-5		.15	.30

LIEUTENANT, THE (TV)
April-June, 1964
Dell Publishing Co.

#1	.25	.50	.75

LT. ROBIN CRUSOE, U.S.N. (See Movie Comics
and Walt Disney Showcase #26)

LIFE OF CHRIST, THE
1958   (100pgs.) (35¢)
Catechetical Guild Educational Society

#301-Book-length story	1.50	3.00	4.50

	Good	Fine	Mint
304-Reprints from Topix(1949)	1.50	3.00	4.50

LIFE OF CHRIST VISUALIZED
1942 - 1943
Standard Publishers

#1-3	2.00	4.00	6.00

LIFE OF PAUL (See The Living Bible)

LIFE OF RILEY, THE (See 4-Color Comics #917)

LIFE OF THE BLESSED VIRGIN
1950
Catechetical Guild

No#	2.50	5.00	7.50

LIFE'S LITTLE JOKES
No Date (1924)   (52 pgs.) (B&W)
MS Publ. Co.

By Rube Goldberg	7.00	14.00	21.00

LIFE STORIES OF AMERICAN PRESIDENTS
Nov, 1957   (25¢)
Dell Publishing Co.

#1-Buscema art	3.00	6.00	9.00

LIFE STORY
April, 1949 - V8#43, Oct, 1952
Fawcett Publications

V1#1	2.50	5.00	7.50
2-6	1.25	2.50	3.75
V2#7-12	1.00	2.00	3.00
V3#13-Wood story	4.00	8.00	12.00
V3#14-18, V4#19-24	.75	1.50	2.25
V5#25-30, V6#31-36	.60	1.20	1.80
V7#37,39-42	.40	.80	1.20
V7#38, V8#43-Evans stys.	1.00	2.00	3.00

NOTE: *Powell* stories-#13,23,26,28,30,32.

LIFE WITH ARCHIE
Sept, 1958 - Present
Archie Publications

#1	7.00	14.00	21.00
2	4.00	8.00	12.00
3-5	2.00	4.00	6.00
6-10	1.50	3.00	4.50
11-25	.80	1.60	2.40
26-41	.50	1.00	1.50
42-45: #42-Pureheart begins	.40	.80	1.20

(Life With Archie cont'd)

	Good	Fine	Mint
46-Origin Pureheart	.50	1.00	1.50
47-50: #50-United 3 begin	.40	.80	1.20
51-59-Pureheart ends	.30	.60	.90
60-100: #60-Archie band begins			
	.25	.50	.75
101-150	.20	.40	.60
151-199		.15	.35

LIFE WITH MILLIE
Nov, 1958 - #20, Dec, 1962
Atlas/Marvel (Male)

#1	1.50	3.00	4.50
2-10	.80	1.60	2.40
11-20	.50	1.00	1.50

LIFE WITH SNARKY PARKER (TV)
August, 1950
Fox Features Syndicate

#1	2.00	4.00	6.00

LIGHT IN THE FOREST (See 4-Color #891)

LIGHTNING COMICS (Sure-Fire #1-4)(No V3#2)
June, 1940 - #14, June, 1942   (2 #3's)
Ace Magazines

V1#1-Origin Flash Lightning; X-The Phantom Fed, Ace McCoy, Buck Steele, Marvo the Magician, The Raven(not in #2) begin			
	30.00	60.00	90.00
2	20.00	40.00	60.00
3(9/40)	15.00	30.00	45.00
3(#4,10/40)No# on cover, #3 on inside			
	12.00	24.00	36.00
5	10.00	20.00	30.00
6-Dr. Nemesis begins	10.00	20.00	30.00
V2#1-6: #2-"Flash Lightning" becomes "Lash --"	9.00	18.00	27.00
V3#1-Intro. Lightning Girl & The Sword	9.00	18.00	27.00

LI'L (See Little)

LILY OF THE ALLEY IN THE FUNNIES
No Date (1920's?)(10½x15½")(In Color)(28pgs.)
Whitman Publishers

No. W936 - by T. Burke	7.00	14.00	21.00

LIMITED COLLECTORS' EDITION (See Famous 1st Edition & Rudolph the Red Nosed Reindeer; becomes All-New Coll. Edition)
(80pgs. 68pgs.#35-41; 60pgs.#42 on) ($1.00)
C-21, Sum,'73 - Present   (10x13½")

National Periodical Publications/DC Comics

	Good	Fine	Mint
No#(C-20)-Rudolph	.50	1.00	1.50
C-21: Shazam + Captain Marvel Jr. reprint by Raboy	.65	1.35	2.00
C-22: Tarzan-complete origin reprinted from #207-210	1.00	2.00	3.00
C-23: House of Mystery-Wrightson, Adams, Wood, Toth, Orlando art	.60	1.20	1.80
C-24: Rudolph	.50	1.00	1.50
C-25: Batman; Adams cvr/art			
	1.00	2.00	3.00
C-27: Shazam	.60	1.20	1.80
C-29: Tarzan-Reprints "Return of Tarzan" from #219-223	1.00	2.00	3.00
C-31: Superman-Origin retold; Adams art			
	1.00	2.00	3.00
C-32: Ghosts (new stories)	.50	1.00	1.50
C-33: Rudolph (new stories)	.50	1.00	1.50
C-34: Xmas with the Super-Heroes; unpublished Angel & Ape story by Oksner & Wood			
	.50	1.00	1.50
C-35: Shazam-cover features TV's Captain Marvel, Jackson Bostwick	.50	1.00	1.50
C-36: The Bible-all new adaptation beginning with Genesis by Kubert, Redondo & Mayer			
	1.00	2.00	3.00
C-37: Batman	.60	1.20	1.80
C-38: Superman; 1pg. Adams	.60	1.20	1.80
C-39: Secret Origins/Super Villains; Adams story reprint	1.00	2.00	3.00
C-40: Dick Tracy by Gould featuring Flattop; newspaper reprints from 12/21/43-5/17/44			
	1.00	2.00	3.00
C-41: Super Friends-Toth art			
	.60	1.20	1.80
C-42: Rudolph	.40	.80	1.20
C-43: Christmas with the Super-Heroes; Wrightson, S&K, Adams art	.70	1.40	2.10
C-44: Batman	.60	1.20	1.80
C-45: Secret Origins/Super Villains			
	.60	1.20	1.80
C-46: Justice League of America			
	.80	1.60	2.40
C-47: Superman Salutes the Bicentennial (Tomahawk interior)	.40	.80	1.20
C-48: The Superman-Flash Race			
	.80	1.60	2.40
C-49: Superboy & the Legion of Super-Heroes			
	.60	1.20	1.80
C-50: Rudolph	.40	.80	1.20
C-51: Batman-Adams cvr/sty	.60	1.20	1.80
C-52: The Best of DC-Adams cover			
	.50	1.00	1.50
C-57: Welcome Back, Kotter(reprints)(5/78)			
	.35	.70	1.05
C-59: Batman's Strangest Cases-Adams, Wrightson reprints; Adams/Wrightson cover			

Lightning Comics #1, © ACE

Linda #1, © AJAX

Linda Carter #5, © MCG

Li'l Abner #67, © UFS

Little Ambrose #1, © AP

Little Angel #13, © STD

	Good	Fine	Mint
(Limited Collector's Edition cont'd)	.35	.70	1.05

NOTE: *All reprints with exception of some special features & covers.*

LINDA (Phantom Lady #5 on)
Apr-May, 1954 - #4, Oct-Nov, 1955
Ajax-Farrell Publ. Co.

	Good	Fine	Mint
#1	2.50	5.00	7.50
2	1.50	3.00	4.50
3,4-Kamen art	2.00	4.00	6.00

LINDA CARTER, STUDENT NURSE
Sept, 1961 - #9, Jan, 1963
Atlas Comics (AMI)

#1	.40	.80	1.20
2-9	.25	.50	.75

LINDA LARK (--Student Nurse #1; --Nurse#7,8)
Oct-Dec, 1961 - #8, Aug-Oct, 1963
Dell Publishing Co.

#1	.30	.60	.90
2-8	.25	.50	.75

LINUS, THE LIONHEARTED (TV)
September, 1965
Gold Key

#1(10155-509)	.25	.50	.75

LION, THE (See Movie Comics)

LION OF SPARTA (See Movie Classics)

LIPPY THE LION AND HARDY HAR HAR (TV)
March, 1963 (Hanna-Barbera)
Gold Key

#1(10049-303)	.20	.40	.60

LI'L ABNER (See Comics on Parade)
1939 - 1948
United Features Syndicate

Single Series #4('39)	17.50	35.00	52.50
Single Series #18('40)(#18 on inside, #2 on cover)	15.00	30.00	45.00

LI'L ABNER (Al Capp's)(See Oxydol-Dreft)
#61, Dec, 1947 - #97, Jan, 1955
Toby Press/Harvey Publ./Toby Press #70 on

#61(#1)-Wolverton art	7.00	14.00	21.00
62-65	5.00	10.00	15.00

	Good	Fine	Mint
66,67,69,70	4.00	8.00	12.00
68-Full length Fearless Fosdick story			
	5.00	10.00	15.00
71-74,76,80	3.50	7.00	10.50
75,77-79,86,91-All with Kurtzman art; #91 reprints #77	5.00	10.00	15.00
81-85,87-90,92-94,96,97: #93-reprints #71			
	2.50	5.00	7.50
95-Full length Fearless Fosdick story			
	3.50	7.00	10.50
-- & the Creatures from Drop-Outer Space (Giveaway)(No#)	3.50	7.00	10.50
-- Joins the Navy(1950)(Toby Press Premium)			
	3.50	7.00	10.50
-- by Al Capp Giveaway(Circa 1955, no date)			
	3.00	6.00	9.00

NOTE: *Powell story-#61.*

LI'L ABNER
1951
Toby Press

#1	2.50	5.00	7.50

LI'L ABNER'S DOGPATCH (See Al Capp's --)

LITTLE AL OF THE F.B.I.
#10, 1950(no month) - #11, Apr-May, 1951
Ziff-Davis Publications

#10(1950)	1.25	2.50	3.75
11(1951)-Drug story; painted covers by Norman Saunders, #10 &11	3.00	6.00	9.00

LITTLE AL OF THE SECRET SERVICE
1950 - #10, 1951
Ziff-Davis Publications

#1	1.25	2.50	3.75
2-10 (Saunders painted covers)	.80	1.60	2.40

LITTLE AMBROSE
Sept, 1958
Archie Publications

#1	2.50	5.00	7.50

LITTLE ANGEL
#5, Sept, 1954; #6, 9/55 - #16, 9/59
Standard(Visual Editions)/Pines

#5-16	.40	.80	1.20

LITTLE ANNIE ROONEY
1935 (48 pgs.) (B&W dailies) (25¢)
David McKay Publications

(Little Annie Rooney cont'd) | Good | Fine | Mint
Book #1-Daily strip reprints by Darrell
McClure | 12.00 | 24.00 | 36.00

LITTLE ANNIE ROONEY
1938; Aug, 1948 - #3, Oct, 1948
David McKay/St. John/Standard

	Good	Fine	Mint
Feature Book #11(McKay, '38)	15.00	30.00	45.00
#1(St. John)	4.00	8.00	12.00
2,3	3.00	6.00	9.00

LITTLE ARCHIE (The Advs. of --)
1956 - Present   (Giants #3-84)
Archie Publications

#1	7.00	14.00	21.00
2	4.00	8.00	12.00
3-5	3.00	6.00	9.00
6-10	2.50	5.00	7.50
11-20	1.50	3.00	4.50
21-40: Little Pureheart begins #40, ends #42,44	1.00	2.00	3.00
41-60: #42-Intro. The Little Archies. #59- Little Sabrina begins	.50	1.00	1.50
61-100	.25	.50	.75
101-136	.15	.30	.45
--In Animal Land #1('57)	2.50	5.00	7.50
--In Animal Land #17(Winter, 1957-58)-#19 (Summer,'58)-Formerly Li'l Jinx	1.50	3.00	4.50

LITTLE ARCHIE COMICS DIGEST ANNUAL
Oct, 1977 - Present (Digest) (192 pgs.)
Archie Publications

#1(10/77)-Reprints	.40	.80	1.20
2(4/78)	.20	.40	.60
3(11/78)-The Fly reprints by S&K	.20	.40	.60

LITTLE ARCHIE MYSTERY
1963 - #2, Oct, 1963
Archie Publications

#1	3.00	6.00	9.00
2	1.50	3.00	4.50

LITTLE ASPIRIN (See Wisco)
July, 1949 - #3, Dec, 1949   (52 pgs.)
Marvel Comics (CnPC)

#1-4pgs. Kurtzman art	2.50	5.00	7.50
2-4pgs. Kurtzman art	2.00	4.00	6.00
3-No Kurtzman	.70	1.40	2.10

LITTLE AUDREY (See Harvey Hits #11,19)
1948 - 1956
St. John Publ./Harvey Publ. #25 on

	Good	Fine	Mint
#1	5.00	10.00	15.00
2-5	2.50	5.00	7.50
6-10	1.75	3.50	5.25
11-20	1.20	2.40	3.60
21-53	.60	1.20	1.80

NOTE: *Richie Rich appears in #25-30?*

LITTLE AUDREY (-- Yearbook)
1950   (260 pgs.) (50¢)
St. John Publishing Co.

Contains 8 complete 1949 comics rebound;
Little Audrey, Abbott & Costello, Pinocchio,
Moon Mullins, Three Stooges(from Jubilee), &
Little Annie Rooney app. (Rare)

	15.00	30.00	45.00

LITTLE AUDREY (See Playful --)

LITTLE AUDREY & MELVIN (Audrey -- #62 on?)
May, 1962 - #61, 8/74?
Harvey Publications

#1	2.50	5.00	7.50
2-5	1.25	2.50	3.75
6-10	1.00	2.00	3.00
11-25	.50	1.00	1.50
26-61	.20	.40	.60

LITTLE AUDREY TV FUNTIME
1962 - #33, Oct, 1971
Harvey Publications

#1	1.20	2.40	3.60
2-5	.60	1.20	1.80
6-10	.40	.80	1.20
11-33	.20	.40	.60

LITTLE BAD WOLF (See 4-Color #403,473,564, & Walt Disney Showcase #21)

LITTLE BEAVER
1948 - #8, Jan, 1953
Dell Publishing Co.

4-Color #211('48)	3.00	6.00	9.00
4-Color #267,294,332	2.00	4.00	6.00
4-Color #483,529	1.75	3.50	5.25
4-Color #612,660,695,744,817,870	1.25	2.50	3.75
#3(10/51)-#8	1.25	2.50	3.75

LITTLE BIT
March, 1949 - #2, 1949

Little Annie Rooney #1, © STJ   Little Audrey #7, © STJ

Little Beaver Four Color #483, © DELL

Little Dot #1, © HARV

Little Eva #1, © STJ

Little Giant #1, © CEN

(Little Bit cont'd)
Jubilee/St. John Publishing Co.

	Good	Fine	Mint
#1,2	1.20	2.40	3.60

LITTLE DOT (See Tastee-Freez Comics)
9/53 - #150, 7/73; #151 - #164, 4/77
Harvey Publications

	Good	Fine	Mint
#1-Intro. & 1st app. Richie Rich & Little Lotta	30.00	60.00	90.00
2	8.00	16.00	24.00
3-5	5.00	10.00	15.00
6-Richie Rich, Little Lotta, & Little Dot all on cover; 1st Richie Rich cover featured	7.00	14.00	21.00
7-10	2.50	5.00	7.50
11-20	1.75	3.50	5.25
21-30	1.00	2.00	3.00
31-50	.70	1.40	2.10
51-100	.35	.70	1.05
101-150	.20	.40	.60
161-164	.15	.30	.45

NOTE: *Richie Rich & Little Lotta in all to at least #75.*

LITTLE DOT DOTLAND (Dot Dotland #63)
July, 1962 - #62, Sept, 1974
Harvey Publications

#1	1.00	2.00	3.00
2-10	.40	.80	1.20
11-20	.20	.40	.60
21-62	.15	.30	.45

LITTLE DOT'S UNCLES & AUNTS (See Harvey Hits
May, 1962 - Present   #4,13,24)
Harvey Publications

#1	1.00	2.00	3.00
2-10	.50	1.00	1.50
11-20	.25	.50	.75
21-50	.15	.30	.45

LITTLE EVA
May, 1952 - #31, Nov, 1956
St. John Publishing Co.

#1	2.00	4.00	6.00
2-10	1.20	2.40	3.60
11-31	.80	1.60	2.40
3-D#1,2(25¢)(10/53-11/53)	3.00	6.00	9.00
IW Reprint #1,2,7,8	.35	.70	1.05
Super Reprint #10,12('63),14,16,18('64)	.35	.70	1.05

LITTLE FIR TREE, THE
1942   (8½x11") (12 pgs. with cover)
W. T. Grant Co.   (Christmas giveaway)

8 pg. Kelly story reprint/Santa Claus Funnies not signed.
        (One copy sold for $300.00 in 1977)

LI'L GENIUS (Summer Fun #54 on)(See Blue Bird)
1954 - #52, Jan, 1965; #53, Oct, 1965
Charlton Comics

	Good	Fine	Mint
#1	.65	1.35	2.00
2-20	.40	.80	1.20
21-53	.20	.40	.60

LI'L GHOST
Feb, 1958 - #3, Mar, 1959
St. John Publishing Co./Fago #2 on

#1	.50	1.00	1.50
2,3	.40	.80	1.20

LITTLE GIANT COMICS
7/38 - #2, 8/38 (132 pgs.) (6-3/4"x4-1/2")
Centaur Publications

#1,2 (B&W)	15.00	30.00	45.00

LITTLE GIANT DETECTIVE FUNNIES
10/38 - #3, 2/39 (132 pgs.) (6-3/4"x4-1/2")
Centaur Publications

#1	15.00	30.00	45.00
2,3	10.00	20.00	30.00
4(1/39)-B&W-no cover, 36pgs. 6½x9½"	10.00	20.00	30.00

LITTLE GIANT MOVIE FUNNIES
8/38 - #2, 10/38 (132 pgs.)(6-3/4"x4-1/2")
Centaur Publications

#1-Reprints of Ed Wheelan's "Minute Movies"	15.00	30.00	45.00
2- " " " "	10.00	20.00	30.00

LITTLE GROUCHO (--Grouchy #2)(See Tippy Terry)
Feb-Mar, 1955 - #2, June-July, 1955
Reston Publ. Co.

#16,1	.60	1.20	1.80
#2(6-7/55)	.35	.70	1.05

LITTLE HIAWATHA(See 4-Color #439,787,901,988)

LITTLE IKE
April, 1953 - #4, Oct, 1953
St. John Publishing Co.

#1	.65	1.35	2.00
2-4	.40	.80	1.20

251

LITTLE IODINE
April, 1949 - #57, July-Sept, 1962
Dell Publishing Co.

	Good	Fine	Mint
4-Color #224,257	2.00	4.00	6.00
#1	2.50	5.00	7.50
2-10	1.35	2.75	4.00
11-20	1.00	2.00	3.00
21-30	.65	1.35	2.00
31-40	.50	1.00	1.50
41-57	.40	.80	1.20

LITTLE JACK FROST
1951
Avon Periodicals

#1	2.50	5.00	7.50

LI'L JINX (Little Archie in Animal Land #17)
1953 - #16, Sept, 1957; Nov, 1956
Archie Publications

#1	2.50	5.00	7.50
2-16	1.40	2.80	4.20
1(11/56)	1.75	3.50	5.25

LI'L JINX (See Archie Giant Series Mag.)

LI'L JINX CHRISTMAS BAG (See Archie Giant
Series Mag. #195,206,219)

LI'L JINX GIANT LAUGH-OUT
#33, Sept, 1971 - #43, Nov, 1973 (52 pgs.)
Archie Publications

#33-43	.20	.40	.60
(See Archie Giant Series Mag. #176,185)			

LITTLE JOE (See 4-Color Comics #1)

LITTLE JOE
1953
St. John Publishing Co.

#1	.70	1.40	2.10

LITTLE JOHNNY & THE TEDDY BEARS
1907 (10x14") (32 pgs. in color)
Reilly & Britton Co.

By J. R. Bray	15.00	37.50	60.00

LI'L KIDS
Aug, 1970 - #12, June, 1973
Marvel Comics Group

#1		.15	.30
2-12: #10,11-Calvin app.		.10	.20

LITTLE KING (See 4-Color #494,597,677)

LITTLE LANA (Formerly Lana)
#8, Nov, 1949 - #9, Mar, 1950
Marvel Comics (MjMC)

	Good	Fine	Mint
#8,9	.75	1.50	2.25

LITTLE LENNY
June, 1949 - #3, Nov, 1949
Marvel Comics (CDS)

#1	.80	1.60	2.40
2,3	.50	1.00	1.50

LITTLE LIZZIE
June, 1949 - #5, April, 1950
Marvel Comics (PrPI)

#1	1.00	2.00	3.00
2-5	.65	1.35	2.00

LITTLE LOTTA (See Harvey Hits #10)
Nov, 1955 - Present
Harvey Publications

#1	4.00	8.00	12.00
2-5	2.00	4.00	6.00
6-10	1.25	2.50	3.75
11-30	.60	1.20	1.80
31-60	.25	.50	.75
61-121(5/76)		.15	.35

LITTLE LOTTA FOODLAND
September, 1963
Harvey Publications

#1	1.25	2.50	3.75

LITTLE LOTTA FOODTOWN
1963 - #9, 1965
Harvey Publications

#1	1.25	2.50	3.75
2-9	.50	1.00	1.50

LITTLE LOTTA IN FOODLAND
1968 - #38, Oct, 1971
Harvey Publications

#1	.40	.80	1.20
2-38	.20	.40	.60

LITTLE LULU (Marge's --)
June, 1945 - Present
Dell Publishing Co./Gold Key, 12/62 on

4-Color #74('45)	80.00	160.00	240.00

Little Iodine #6, © DELL

Little Lenny #3, © MCG   Little Lizzie #2, © MCG

Little Lulu Four Color #146, © WEST   Little Lulu #17, © WEST   Little Miss Muffet #12, © KING

(Little Lulu cont'd)	Good	Fine	Mint
4-Color #97('46)	40.00	80.00	120.00

(Above two books done entirely by John Stanley - cover, pencils, & inks.)

	Good	Fine	Mint
4-Color #110('46),115	24.00	48.00	72.00
4-Color #120,131	20.00	40.00	60.00
4-Color #139('47),146,158,165	18.00	36.00	54.00
#1(1948)	50.00	100.00	150.00
2	25.00	50.00	75.00
3-5	16.00	32.00	48.00
6-10	10.00	20.00	30.00
11-20	8.00	16.00	24.00
21-30: #30-Alvin's Story Telling Time begins (not in #91)	5.00	10.00	15.00
31-38,40	4.50	9.00	13.50
39-Intro. Witch Hazel in "That Awful Witch Hazel"	5.00	10.00	15.00
41-60: #45-2nd Witch Hazel app. #49-Gives Stanley & others credit	3.50	7.00	10.50
61-80: #80-Intro. Little Itch(2/55)	3.00	6.00	9.00
81-100	2.00	4.00	6.00
101-130	1.50	3.00	4.50
131-164,167-170; #165 & 166 listed below as Giant issues	1.00	2.00	3.00
171-205	.50	1.00	1.50
206-Last issue to carry Marge's name,			
207-220	.25	.50	.75
221-249: #241-Stanley reprt.	.15	.30	.45
--& Alvin Story Telling Time #1(3/59)-reprints/#2,5,3,11,30,10,21,17,8,14,16	5.00	10.00	15.00
--& Her Friends #4(3/56) 100pgs.	4.00	8.00	12.00
--& Her Special Friends #3(3/55), 100pgs.	4.00	8.00	12.00
--& Tubby at Summer Camp #5(1957)	4.00	8.00	12.00
--& Tubby at Summer Camp #2(10/58)	4.00	8.00	12.00
--& Tubby Halloween Fun #6(1957)	3.00	6.00	9.00
--& Tubby Halloween Fun #2(1958)	3.00	6.00	9.00
--& Tubby Halloween Fun #23(1959)(Dell Giant)	3.50	7.00	10.50
--& Tubby in Alaska #1(7/59)	4.00	8.00	12.00
--& Tubby in Australia #42(1961)	2.50	5.00	7.50
--& Tubby in Hawaii #29(4/60)	3.00	6.00	9.00
--& Tubby in Japan (12¢)(5-7/62) #01476-207	2.50	5.00	7.50
--& Tubby Witch Hazel Halloween Fun #36(1960)	2.50	5.00	7.50

	Good	Fine	Mint
--& Witch Hazel Trick & Treat #50(1961)	2.50	5.00	7.50
--Christmas Diary #166(1962-63)(Gold Key)	2.50	5.00	7.50
--in Paris #165(1962-G.K.)	2.50	5.00	7.50
--on Vacation #1(1954)-Reprints/4C-110,14, 4C-146,5,4C-97,4,4C-158,3,1	8.00	16.00	24.00
--Summer Camp #1(1967-G.K.)-reprints '57-58	1.50	3.00	4.50
--Trick 'N' Treat #1 (12¢)(12/62-Gold Key)	3.00	6.00	9.00
--Tubby Annual #1(1953)-reprints from 4-Color #165,4C-74,4C-146,4C-97,4C-158, 4C-139,4C-131	15.00	30.00	45.00
--Tubby Annual #2(1954)-Reprints/4C-139,6, 4C-115,4C-74,4C-97,3,4C-146,18	12.00	24.00	36.00

NOTE: *All Giants by Stanley except Christmas Diary #166, In Paris #165.*

LITTLE LULU (See Golden Comics Digest #19, 23,27,29,33,36,40,43,46 & March of Comics #251,267,275,293,307,323,335,349,355,369,385, 406,417)

LITTLE MARY MIXUP (See Single Series #10,26)

LITTLE MAX COMICS (Joe Palooka's Pal)
Oct, 1949 - #73, 1961
Harvey Publications

	Good	Fine	Mint
#1	2.00	4.00	6.00
2-10	1.00	2.00	3.00
11-20	.50	1.00	1.50
21-73	.35	.70	1.05

LI'L MENACE
Dec, 1958 - #2, Feb, 1959
Fago Magazine Co.

	Good	Fine	Mint
#1-Peter Rabbit app.	.60	1.20	1.80
2- " " (Vincent Fago's)	.40	.80	1.20

LITTLE MISS MUFFET
Dec, 1948 - #13, March, 1949
Standard Comics/King Features Synd.

	Good	Fine	Mint
#11-13-Strip reprints; Fanny Cory art	1.75	3.50	5.25

LITTLE MISS SUNBEAM COMICS
June-July, 1950 - #4, Dec-Jan, 1950-51
Magazine Enterprises/Quality Bakers of Amer.

	Good	Fine	Mint
#1	3.50	7.00	10.50

(Little Miss Sunbeam Comics cont'd)

	Good	Fine	Mint
2-4	2.50	5.00	7.50
Bread Giveaway #1-4(Quality Bakers, 1949-50)			
(14pgs. ea.)	2.00	4.00	6.00

LITTLE MONSTERS, THE
Nov, 1964 - #44, Feb, 1978
Gold Key

#1	.35	.70	1.05
2-10	.20	.40	.60
11-20	.15	.30	.45
21-44: #34-36-reprints	.15		.30

LITTLE NEMO (See Cocomalt, Future Comics, Help, Jest, Kayo, Punch, Red Seal, & Superworld; most by Winsor McCay Jr., son of famous artist)

LITTLE NEMO (-- in Slumberland)
1906, 1909 (Sunday strip reprints in color)
(Cardboard covers)
Doffield & Co.(1906)/Cupples & Leon Co.(1909)

1906-11x16½" in color by Winsor McCay(30pgs.)			
(Very Rare)	150.00	375.00	600.00
1909-10x14" in color by Winsor McCay			
(Very Rare)	120.00	300.00	480.00

LITTLE NEMO (-- in Slumberland)
1945 (28pgs.) (11x7¼") (B&W)
McCay Features/Nostalgia Press('69)

Reprints from 1905 & 1911 by Winsor McCay			
	5.00	10.00	15.00
1969-70 exact reprint	2.00	4.00	6.00

LITTLE ORPHAN ANNIE (See Merry Christmas--, & Super Book #11,23)

LITTLE ORPHAN ANNIE (See Treasury Box of--)
1926 - 1934 (Daily strip reprints)(7x8-3/4")
Cupples & Leon Co.   (B&W)

(Hardcover Editions, 100pgs.)

#1(1926)-Little Orphan Annie			
	15.00	30.00	45.00
2('27)-In the Circus	10.00	20.00	30.00
3('28)-The Haunted House			
	10.00	20.00	30.00
4('29)-Bucking the World			
	10.00	20.00	30.00
5('30)-Never Say Die	10.00	20.00	30.00
6('31)-Shipwrecked	10.00	20.00	30.00
7('32)-A Willing Helper	8.00	16.00	24.00
8('33)-In Cosmic City	8.00	16.00	24.00
9('34)-Uncle Dan	10.00	20.00	30.00

NOTE: *Hardcovers with dust jackets are worth 20-50% more; the earlier the book, the higher the percentage. Each book reprints dailies from the previous year.*

LITTLE ORPHAN ANNIE & THE BIG TOWN GUNMAN
1937 (64pgs.;5½x7½";B&W daily reprints)
Whitman Publishing Co.   (Hardcover)

	Good	Fine	Mint
	8.00	16.00	24.00

LITTLE ORPHAN ANNIE
1937 - 1948
David McKay Publ./Dell Publishing Co.

Feature Book(McKay)#7-('37)(Very Rare)			
	80.00	160.00	240.00
4-Color #12(1941)	22.00	44.00	66.00
4-Color #18('43)	17.50	35.00	52.50
4-Color #52('44)	10.00	20.00	30.00
4-Color #76('45)	8.00	16.00	24.00
4-Color #107('46)	7.00	14.00	21.00
4-Color #152('47)	6.00	12.00	18.00
4-Color #206('49)	5.00	10.00	15.00
#1(3-5/48)	12.00	24.00	36.00
2,3	6.00	12.00	18.00
4	5.00	10.00	15.00
Junior Commandos Giveaway(Same cover as 4-Color #18, K.K. Publ.(Big Shoe Store); same back cover as '47 Popped Wheat giveaway; 16pgs.	15.00	30.00	45.00
Popped Wheat Giveaway('47)-16pgs. full color; '38,'40 reprints	1.20	2.40	3.60
Quaker Giveaway(1940)	6.00	12.00	18.00
Quaker Giveaway(1941,'42)"Advs. of," "The Kidnappers," "The Rescue"			
each....	5.00	10.00	15.00
Sparkies Giveaway(Full color-20pgs.)			
(1941-42)(2 different)	4.00	8.00	12.00

LI'L PALS
Sept, 1972 - #5, May, 1973
Marvel Comics Group

#1-5		.10	.20

LITTLE PAN
#6, Dec-Jan, 1947 - #8, Apr-May, 1947
Fox Features Syndicate

#6-8	1.20	2.40	3.60

LITTLE PEOPLE (See 4-Color #485,573,633,692, 753,809,868,908,959,1024,1062)

LITTLE RASCALS (See 4-Color #674,778,825, 883,936,974,1030,1079,1137,1174,1224,1297)

Little Orphan Annie (1927, C&L)
© News Synd.

Little Orphan Annie Sparkies Giveaway
© News Synd.

Little Sammy Sneeze, © N.Y. Herald

The Little Scouts #4, © DELL   Li'l Willie #20, © MCG   Logan's Run #1, © MCG

LI'L RASCAL TWINS
1957 - #17, March, 1959
Charlton Comics

	Good	Fine	Mint
#6-17-Li'l Genius & Tomboy	.20	.40	.60

LITTLE ROQUEFORT
June, 1952 - #9, 10/53; #10, Summer, 1958
St. John Publishing Co./Pines #10

#1	1.20	2.40	3.60
2-10	.70	1.40	2.10

LITTLE SAD SACK (See Harvey Hits #73,76,79,
Oct, 1964 - #19, 1967   81,83)
Harvey Publications

#1-Richie Rich app.	1.00	2.00	3.00
2-19	.25	.50	.75

LITTLE SAMMY SNEEZE
1905   (28 pgs.) (11x16½") (In Color)
New York Herald Co.

By Winsor McCay (Rare) 120.00 340.00 480.00
NOTE: *Rarely found in Fine-Mint condition.*

LITTLE SCOUTS
1951 - #587, Oct, 1954
Dell Publishing Co.

4-Color #321('51)	1.20	2.40	3.60
#2(10-12/51)-#6(10-12/52)	.80	1.60	2.40
4-Color #462,506,550,587	.80	1.60	2.40

LITTLE SPUNKY
No Date (1963?) (10¢)
I.W. Enterprises

#1-Reprint	.25	.50	.75

LITTLE STOOGES, THE (The Three Stooges' Sons)
Sept, 1972 - #7, Mar, 1974
Gold Key

#1-Norman Maurer cover/stories in all	.25	.50	.75
2-7	.20	.40	.60

LITTLEST OUTLAW (See 4-Color Comics #609)

LITTLEST SNOWMAN, THE
1956; 1964
Dell Publishing Co./Gold Key

4-Color #755,864	.70	1.40	2.10
#1(1964)(Gold Key)	.50	1.00	1.50

LI'L TOMBOY
V14#93, Mar, 1957 - #108, May, 1959
Charlton Comics

	Good	Fine	Mint
V14#93-#108	.15	.30	.45

LI'L WILLIE
July, 1949 - #21, Aug-Sept, 1949
Marvel Comics (MgPC)

#20,21	.60	1.20	1.80

LIVE IT UP
1973
Spire Christian Comics(Fleming H. Revell Co.)

	.25	.50	.75

LIVING BIBLE, THE
Fall, 1945 - 1946
Living Bible Corp.

#1-Life of Paul	2.00	4.00	6.00
2-Joseph & His Brethren	1.50	3.00	4.50
3-Chaplains of War	1.50	3.00	4.50
NOTE: *All have L. B. Cole covers.*

LOBO
Dec, 1965 - #2, Oct, 1966
Dell Publishing Co.

#1,2	.30	.60	.90

LOCO (Magazine) (Satire)
Aug, 1958 - V1#3, Jan, 1959
Satire Publications

V1#1-Chic Stone art	1.00	2.00	3.00
V1#2,3-Severin art, 2pgs. Davis-#3	.75	1.50	2.25

LOGAN'S RUN
Jan, 1977 - #7, July, 1977
Marvel Comics Group

#1	.50	1.00	1.50
2-7: #6-Gulacy cover	.25	.50	.75

LOIS LANE (See Superman's Girlfriend --)

LOLLY AND PEPPER
1957 - July, 1962
Dell Publishing Co.

4-Color #832,940,978,1086,1206,			
#01-459,207	.60	1.20	1.80

LOMAX (See Police Action)

LONE EAGLE (The Flame #5 on)
Apr-May, 1954 - #4, Oct-Nov, 1954
Ajax/Farrell Publications

	Good	Fine	Mint
#1	1.50	3.00	4.50
2-4	1.00	2.00	3.00

LONELY HEART
#9, March, 1955 - #14, Feb, 1956
Ajax/Farrell Publ. (Excellent Publ.)

	Good	Fine	Mint
#9-14	.80	1.60	2.40

LONE RANGER, THE
1939 - 1947
Dell Publishing Co.

Black & White #3('39)-Heigh-Yo Silver; text
with ill. by Robert Weisman
24.00 60.00 96.00
Black & White #7('39)-Ill. by Henry Valleley;
Hi-Yo Silver the Lone Ranger to the Rescue
35.00 87.50 135.00
4-Color #82('45)   14.00 28.00 42.00
4-Color #98('45),#118('46)
12.00 24.00 36.00
4-Color #125('46),#136('47)
8.00 16.00 24.00
4-Color #151,167('47)   6.00 12.00 18.00

LONE RANGER COMICS, THE (10c)
1939 (Ice Cream mail order)(68pgs. in color)
Lone Ranger, Inc.   (Regular size)

(Scarce)-not by Valleley 50.00 100.00 150.00

LONE RANGER, THE (#1-37 strip reprints)
Jan-Feb, 1948 - #145, May-July, 1962
Dell Publishing Co.

#1	20.00	40.00	60.00
2	12.00	24.00	36.00
3-7,9,10	8.00	16.00	24.00
8-Origin retold	10.00	20.00	30.00

11-"Young Hawk" Indian boy serial begins,
ends #145   5.00 10.00 15.00
12-17,19,20   5.00 10.00 15.00
18-Origin retold   7.00 14.00 21.00
21,22,24-30   4.00   8.00 12.00
23-Origin retold   6.00 12.00 18.00
31-37-Last newspaper reprint ish; new outfit
2.50   5.00   7.50
38-60   2.00   4.00   6.00
61-80   1.75   3.50   5.25
81-111   1.50   3.00   4.50
112-1st Clayton Moore cvr. 2.50 5.00 7.50
113-117   1.50   3.00   4.50
118-Origin Lone Ranger, Tonto, & Silver re-

	Good	Fine	Mint

told-Special anniversary issue
3.50   7.00 10.50
119-145: #139-Last issue by Fran Striker
1.50   3.00   4.50
Cheerios Giveaways #1-"The Lone Ranger, Hi
Mask & How He Met Tonto." #2-"The Lone
Ranger & the Story of Silver" (1945)
each.... 3.00   6.00   9.00
Doll Giveaway(Gabriel Ind.)(1973, 3¼x5")
.40   .80   1.20
--Golden West #3('55,100pgs.)
2.50   5.00   7.50
How the L.R. Captured Silver Book(1936)-Sil-
vercup Bread giveaway 17.00 34.00 51.00
--In Milk for Big Mike(1955, Dairy Associa-
tion giveaway)   2.00   4.00   6.00
Merita Bread giveaway('54,16pgs.,5x7¾")-
"How to Be a L.R. Health Safety Scout"
2.50   5.00   7.50
--Movie Story('56,100pgs.)-Origin Lone Ranger
in text   5.00 10.00 15.00
Western Treasury #1('53)-Origin of Lone
Ranger   5.00 10.00 15.00
Western Treasury #2('54)(Becomes Golden West
#3)   5.00 10.00 15.00

LONE RANGER, THE (See March of Comics #165,
174,193,208,225,238,310,322,338,350, Feature
Book #21,24(McKay), & Aurora)

LONE RANGER, THE
9/64 - #16, 12/69; #17, 11/72; #18, 9/74 -
#28, 3/77
Gold Key

#1	.70	1.40	2.10

2-17: Small Bear reprints in #6-12
.35   .70   1.05
18-28   .25   .50   .75
Golden West #1(30029-610)-Giant, '66-reprints
most Golden West #3 1.25   2.50   3.75

LONE RANGER'S COMPANION TONTO, THE
#2, Feb-Apr, 1951 - #33, Nov, 1958
Dell Publishing Co.

4-Color #312(1951)	3.00	6.00	9.00
#2,3	1.75	3.50	5.25
4-10	1.50	3.00	4.50
11-20	1.20	2.40	3.60
21-33	.90	1.80	2.70

(See Aurora Comic Booklets)

LONE RANGER'S FAMOUS HORSE HI-YO SILVER, THE
#3, July-Sept, 1952 - #36, Oct, 1960
Dell Publishing Co.

Lonely Heart #10, © AJAX

The Lone Ranger #12, © Lone Ranger

The Lone Ranger Movie Story, © Lone Ranger

Long Bow #3, © FH

Looney Tunes #23, © DELL

Love Adventures #3, © MCG

(Lone Ranger's Famous Horse contd.)

	Good	Fine	Mint
4-Color #369,392	2.00	4.00	6.00
#3-10	1.35	2.75	4.00
11-36	1.00	2.00	3.00

LONE RIDER
April, 1951 - #26, July, 1955
Ajax/Farrell Publications

#1	1.75	3.35	5.00
2-5	1.00	2.00	3.00
6-10	.80	1.60	2.40
11-26	.60	1.20	1.80

LONG BOW, INDIAN BOY
1951 - 1953
Fiction House Magazines(Real Adventures Publ.)

#1	1.50	3.00	4.50
2-9	.80	1.60	2.40

LONGEST DAY (See Movie Classics)

LONG JOHN SILVER & THE PIRATES (Formerly
Terry & the Pirates)
#30, Aug, 1956 - #32, March, 1957
Charlton Comics

#30-32	1.20	2.40	3.60

LOONEY TUNES & MERRIE MELODIES COMICS
("Looney Tunes" #166 (8/55) on)
1941 - #246, July-Sept, 1962
Dell Publishing Co.

#1-Porky Pig, Bugs Bunny, Elmer Fudd begin			
	120.00	240.00	360.00
2	70.00	140.00	210.00
3-Kandi the Cave Kid by Walt Kelly; also in			
#4,5,8,11	50.00	100.00	150.00
4	30.00	60.00	90.00
5	25.00	50.00	75.00
6-10	17.50	35.00	52.50
11-20: #20-Pat, Patsy & Pete by Kelly begin,			
end-#25	14.00	28.00	42.00
21-30	9.00	18.00	27.00
31-40	7.00	14.00	21.00
41-50	5.00	10.00	15.00
51-60	3.50	7.00	10.50
61-80	2.25	4.50	6.75
81-100	1.50	3.00	4.50
101-150	1.00	2.00	3.00
151-200	.75	1.50	2.25
201-246	.50	1.00	1.50

LOONEY TUNES (2nd Series)
April, 1975 - Present
Gold Key

	Good	Fine	Mint
#1	.25	.50	.75
2-24		.15	.35

LOONY SPORTS (Magazine)
Spring, 1975 (68 pgs.)
3-Strikes Publishing

#1-Sports satire	.35	.70	1.05

LOOY DOT DOPE (See Single Series #13)

LORD JIM (See Movie Comics)

LORNA THE JUNGLE GIRL (--Jungle Queen #1-5)
June, 1953 - #26, Aug, 1957
Atlas Comics (OMC #1-11/NPI #12-26)

#1	5.00	10.00	15.00
2-5: #2-Intro. & 1st app. Greg Knight			
	3.50	7.00	10.50
6-15	3.00	6.00	9.00
16,17,19-26: #23,26-Everett cover			
	2.50	5.00	7.50
18-Williamson/Colleta cvr.	3.50	7.00	10.50

LOST IN SPACE (Space Family Robinson--,
on Space Station One)(Formerly Space Family
#37, Oct, 1973 - #54, Nov, 1978   Robinson)
Gold Key

#37-54	.20	.40	.60

LOST WORLD, THE (See 4-Color Comics #1145)

LOST WORLDS
#5, Oct, 1952 - #6, Dec, 1952
Standard Comics

#5-"Alice in Terrorland" by Toth			
	4.00	8.00	12.00
6-Toth story	2.50	5.00	7.50

LOU GEHRIG (See The Pride of the Yankees)

LOVE ADVENTURES (Actual Confessions #13)
Oct, 1949 - #12, 1952
Marvel/Atlas Comics(MPI)

#1	1.50	3.00	4.50
2-Powell	1.20	2.40	3.60
3-8,10-12	.80	1.60	2.40
9-Everett story	1.20	2.40	3.60

LOVE AND MARRIAGE
March, 1952 - #16, Sept, 1954
Superior Comics Ltd.

#1	1.75	2.50	5.25

(Love & Marriage cont'd)	Good	Fine	Mint
2-16	1.00	2.00	3.00
IW Reprint #1,2,8,11,14	.25	.50	.75
Super Reprint #15,17('64)	.25	.50	.75

NOTE: *All issues have Kamenish art.*

LOVE AND ROMANCE
Sept, 1971 - #24, Sept, 1975
Charlton Comics

	Good	Fine	Mint
#1	.15	.30	.45
2-24		.15	.30

LOVE AT FIRST SIGHT
Oct, 1949 - #42, Aug, 1956
Ace Magazines(RAR Publ.Co./Periodical House)

	Good	Fine	Mint
#1	1.50	3.00	4.50
2-10	.80	1.60	2.40
11-42	.50	1.00	1.50
#6(1960)	.15	.30	.45

LOVE BUG, THE (See Movie Comics)

LOVE CLASSICS
Nov, 1949 - #2, Jan, 1950
A Lover's Magazine/Marvel Comics

	Good	Fine	Mint
#1,2	1.50	3.00	4.50

LOVE CONFESSIONS
Oct, 1949 - #53, 1956 (some issues: photo
Quality Comics Group   covers)

#1-Ward cover, 9pgs. + Gustavson story	Good	Fine	Mint
	6.00	12.00	18.00
2-Gustavson story	2.50	5.00	7.50
3	2.00	4.00	6.00
4-Crandall story	2.50	5.00	7.50
5-Ward art, 7pgs.	3.00	6.00	9.00
6,7,9,10	1.25	2.50	3.75
8-Ward story	2.50	5.00	7.50
11-13,15,16,18,20	1.00	2.00	3.00
14,17,19,22-Ward stories	2.00	4.00	6.00
21,23-38,40-44	.75	1.50	2.25
39-Matt Baker story	1.25	2.50	3.75
45-Ward story	1.50	3.00	4.50
46-53	.60	1.20	1.80

LOVE DIARY
July, 1949 - #47, 1954
Our Publishing Co./Toytown/Patches

	Good	Fine	Mint
#1-Krigstein story	3.50	7.00	10.50
2,3-Krigstein & Mort Leav story in each			
	2.50	5.00	7.50
4-8	1.25	2.50	3.75
9,10-Everett story	1.50	3.00	4.50

	Good	Fine	Mint
11-20	1.00	2.00	3.00
21-47	.75	1.50	2.25

LOVE DIARY
Sept, 1949
Quality Comics Group

	Good	Fine	Mint
#1-Ward cover, 9pgs.	8.00	16.00	24.00

LOVE DIARY
July, 1958 - Present
Charlton Comics

	Good	Fine	Mint
#1	.40	.80	1.20
2-20	.20	.40	.60
21-97		.15	.30

LOVE DOCTOR (See Dr. Anthony King --)

LOVE DRAMAS
Oct, 1949 - #2, Jan, 1950
Marvel Comics (IPS)

	Good	Fine	Mint
#1-Jack Kamen art	3.00	6.00	9.00
2	1.50	3.00	4.50

LOVE EXPERIENCES(Challenge of the Unknown #6)
10/49 - #5, 1950; #6, 4/51 - #35, 12/55
Ace Periodicals(A.A.Wyn/Periodical House)

	Good	Fine	Mint
#1	1.20	2.40	3.60
2-5	.75	1.50	2.25
6-10	.50	1.00	1.50
11-35	.40	.80	1.20

LOVE EXPRESSIONS
1949 ?
Ace Magazines

#1	1.20	2.40	3.60

LOVE JOURNAL
#10, Oct, 1951 - #24, May, 1954
Our Publishing Co.

#10	1.00	2.00	3.00
11-24	.75	1.50	2.25

LOVELAND
Nov, 1949 - 1950
Mutual Mag./Eye Publ. (Atlas)

#1,2	1.00	2.00	3.00

LOVE LESSONS
Oct, 1949 - #5, June, 1950
Harvey Comics/Key Publ. #5

Love & Marriage #16, © SUPR

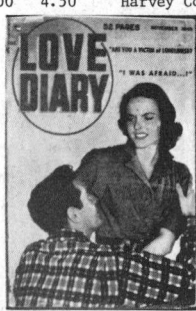

Love Diary #3, © Our Publ.

Love Experiences #30, © ACE

Love Letters #17, © QUA

Love Mystery #1, © FAW

Love Romances #54, © MCG

	Good	Fine	Mint
(Love Lessons cont'd)			
#1-Same cover as Love Letters #1			
	1.40	2.80	4.20
2-5: #2-Powell story	1.00	2.00	3.00

LOVE LETTERS
1949
Harvey Comics

	Good	Fine	Mint
#1-Cover reprinted as Love Lessons #1			
	1.50	3.00	4.50

LOVE LETTERS
Nov, 1949 - #51, Dec, 1956
Quality Comics Group

	Good	Fine	Mint
#1-Ward cover, Gustavson story			
	5.00	10.00	15.00
2-Ward cover, Gustavson story			
	3.00	6.00	9.00
3-Gustavson story	2.50	5.00	7.50
4-Ward story, 9pgs.	3.00	6.00	9.00
5-8,10	1.50	3.00	4.50
9-One pg. Ward-"Be Popular with the Opposite Sex"	2.00	4.00	6.00
11-Ward reprint/Broadway Romances #2 & retitled	2.00	4.00	6.00
12-15,18-20	1.00	2.00	3.00
16,17-Ward stories; #17 has Jane Russell photo cover	2.50	5.00	7.50
21-27,29,32-48	.75	1.50	2.25
28-Ward story pencils	1.75	3.50	5.25
30,31-Ward stories	2.00	4.00	6.00
49,50-Matt Baker stories	1.25	2.50	3.75
51-Matt Baker cover	1.25	2.50	3.75

NOTE: *Photo covers on most #3-28.*

LOVE LIFE
1951
Approved Comics (Ziff-Davis)

	Good	Fine	Mint
#1	1.00	2.00	3.00

LOVELORN (Confessions of the Lovelorn #52 on)
Aug-Sept, 1949 - #51, July, 1954
American Comics Group(Michel Publ./Regis Publ)

	Good	Fine	Mint
#1	1.50	3.00	4.50
2-10	1.00	2.00	3.00
11-48,50: #18-2pgs. Drucker.	.70	1.40	2.10
49,51-Has 3-D effect	2.00	4.00	6.00

LOVE MEMORIES
1949 (no month) - #4, July, 1950
Fawcett Publications

	Good	Fine	Mint
#1	1.75	3.50	5.25
2-4	1.00	2.00	3.00

LOVE MYSTERY
June, 1950 - #3, Oct, 1950
Fawcett Publications

	Good	Fine	Mint
#1,2-Geo. Evans art each	2.50	5.00	7.50
3-Powell art	1.75	3.50	5.25

LOVE PROBLEMS
1949 (132 pgs.)
Fox Features Syndicate

No#-See Fox Giants. Contents can vary and
determines price.

LOVE PROBLEMS AND ADVICE (True Love Problems & Advice Ill. on cover)(Becomes Romance Stories of True Love)
June, 1949 - #44, March, 1957
McCombs/Harvey Publ./Home Comics

	Good	Fine	Mint
V1#1-Powell art	2.00	4.00	6.00
2-10	1.00	2.00	3.00
11-37,39-44	.50	1.00	1.50
38-S&K cover	1.20	2.40	3.60

NOTE: *Powell art-#1,2,7-14,17-25,28,29,33, 40,41.*

LOVE ROMANCES (Formerly True Mysteries?)
#7, July, 1949 - #106, July, 1963
Timely/Marvel/Atlas(TCI #7-71/Male #72-106)

	Good	Fine	Mint
#7	1.20	2.40	3.60
8-Kubert story	2.00	4.00	6.00
9-20	.60	1.20	1.80
21,24-Krigstein stories	2.00	4.00	6.00
22,23,25-35,37,39,40	.50	1.00	1.50
36,38-Krigstein story	1.75	3.50	5.25
41-44,46-48,50-56,58-74	.40	.80	1.20
45,57-Matt Baker stories	1.00	2.00	3.00
49-Toth art, 6pgs.	1.75	3.50	5.25
75,77,82-Matt Baker stys.	.90	1.80	2.70
76,78-81,84,86-95,97,100-104	.35	.70	1.05
83-Kirby cover, Severin story			
	1.00	2.00	3.00
85,96-Kirby cvr/story	1.20	2.40	3.60
98-Four Kirby stories	2.00	4.00	6.00
99,105,106-Kirby stories	1.00	2.00	3.00

NOTE: *Colletta cover-#80. Kirby covers-#80, 85,88.*

LOVERS (Formerly Blonde Phantom)
#23, May, 1949 - #85, June, 1957
Marvel Comics #23,24, Marvel/Atlas #25 on(ANC)

	Good	Fine	Mint
#23,24	.80	1.60	2.40
25,30-Kubert art 7, 10pgs.			
	1.75	3.50	5.25

(Lovers cont'd)	Good	Fine	Mint
26-29,31-36,39,40	.70	1.40	2.10
37,38-Krigstein stories	2.00	4.00	6.00
41-Two Everett stories	1.20	2.40	3.60
42-64	.50	1.00	1.50
65,85-Matt Baker stories	1.00	2.00	3.00
66,68-84	.40	.80	1.20
67-Toth story	1.50	3.00	4.50

NOTE: *Powell story-#27.*

LOVERS' LANE
Oct, 1949 - #40, May, 1954
Lev Gleason Publications

	Good	Fine	Mint
#1	1.20	2.40	3.60
2,3,5-10	.75	1.50	2.25
4-Fuje art, 9pgs.	.75	1.50	2.25
11-19	.60	1.20	1.80
20-Frazetta 1 pg. ad	1.00	2.00	3.00
21-38,40	.40	.80	1.20
39-Story narrated by Frank Sinatra			
	.50	1.00	1.50

NOTE: *Fuje covers-many issues.*

LOVE SCANDALS
2/50 - #5, 10/50 (#4,5-photo covers)
Quality Comics Group

	Good	Fine	Mint
#1-Ward cover, 9pgs. art	6.00	12.00	18.00
2,3	2.00	4.00	6.00
4-Ward art, 18pgs. + Gill Fox story			
	4.00	8.00	12.00
5-C.Cuidera story	2.00	4.00	6.00

LOVE SECRETS
Oct, 1949 - #56, Dec, 1956
Quality Comics Group

	Good	Fine	Mint
#1	2.50	5.00	7.50
2-10	1.25	2.50	3.75
11-33,35-39	.80	1.60	2.40
34,45-Ward stories	1.50	3.00	4.50
40,56-Matt Baker covers	1.25	2.50	3.75
41-44,46-50,53,54	.70	1.40	2.10
51,52-Ward reprints (#52/Love Confessions#17)			
	1.25	2.50	3.75
55-Matt Baker story	1.25	2.50	3.75

LOVE STORIES
#6, 1950 - #18, Aug, 1954
Fox Features Syndicate/Star Publ. #15 on

	Good	Fine	Mint
#6,8-Wood stories	4.00	8.00	12.00
7,9-18	1.75	3.50	5.25

LOVE STORIES (Formerly Heart Throbs)
#147, Nov, 1972 - #152, Oct-Nov, 1973
National Periodical Publications

	Good	Fine	Mint
#147-152		.15	.30

LOVE STORIES OF MARY WORTH (See Harvey Hits
Sept, 1949 - #4, Mar, 1950 #55)
Harvey Publications

	Good	Fine	Mint
#1-1940's newspaper reprints-#1-4			
	2.50	5.00	7.50
2-4	1.75	3.50	5.25

LOVE TALES (Formerly The Human Torch #35)
#36, May, 1949 - #75, Sept, 1957
Marvel/Atlas Comics(ZPC #36-50/MMC #67-75)

	Good	Fine	Mint
#36	1.00	2.00	3.00
37-44,46-50	.60	1.20	1.80
45-Powell story	.80	1.60	2.40
51-Everett story	1.00	2.00	3.00
52-Krigstein story	1.75	3.50	5.25
53-75	.50	1.00	1.50

LOVE, 10 STORIES
July, 1955
Charlton Comics

	Good	Fine	Mint
#6	.25	.50	.75

LOVE TRAILS
Dec, 1949 (52 pgs.)
A Lover's Magazine(CDS)(Marvel)

	Good	Fine	Mint
#1	1.50	3.00	4.50

LOWELL THOMAS' HIGH ADVENTURE (See 4-Color
Comics #949,1001)

LT. (See Lieutenant)

LUCKY COMICS
Jan, 1944; #2, Sum, 1945 - #5, Sum, 1946
Consolidated Magazines

	Good	Fine	Mint
#1-Lucky Starr, Bobbie	2.50	5.00	7.50
2-5	1.50	3.00	4.50

LUCKY DUCK
#5, Jan, 1953 - #8, Sept, 1953
Standard Comics (Literary Ent.)

	Good	Fine	Mint
#5-8-Art by Irving Spector	.80	1.60	2.40

LUCKY FIGHTS IT THROUGH
1949 (16pgs.)(Soft Cover, in color)(Giveaway)
Educational Comics

	Good	Fine	Mint
(Very Rare)-Kurtzman art; V.D. prevention			
	50.00	100.00	150.00

Lovers' Lane #10, © LEV

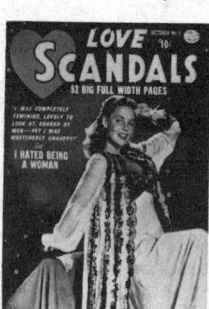

Love Scandals #5, © QUA

Love Tales #47, © MCG

Lucky Star #4, © Nation Wide

Mad #1, © EC

Mad #10, © EC

(Lucky Fights It Through cont'd)
NOTE: *Subtitled "The Story of That Ignorant, Ignorant Cowboy." Prepared for Communications Materials Center, Columbia University.*

LUCKY "7" COMICS
1944
Howard Publishers Ltd.

	Good	Fine	Mint
#1-Congo Raider, Punch Powers			
	2.50	5.00	7.50

LUCKY STAR
1950 - #7, 1951; #8, 1953 - #14, 1955
(5"x7¼") (Full Color)
Nation Wide Publ. Co.

	Good	Fine	Mint
#1-Nostrand art begins	2.50	5.00	7.50
2-7 (52 pgs.)	2.50	5.00	7.50
8-14 (36 pgs.)	2.00	4.00	6.00
Given Away with Lucky Star Western Wear by the Juvenile Mfg. Co.	1.50	3.00	4.50

LUCY SHOW, THE (TV)
June, 1963 - #5, June, 1964
Gold Key

#1	.25	.50	.75
2-5	.20	.40	.60

LUCY, THE REAL GONE GAL(Meet Miss Pepper#5 on)
June, 1953 - #4, Dec, 1953
St. John Publishing Co.

#1-4: #3-Drucker art	1.20	2.40	3.60

LUDWIG BEMELMAN'S MADELEINE & GENEVIEVE
(See 4-Color Comics #796)

LUDWIG VON DRAKE (Walt Disney)
Nov-Dec, 1961 - #4, June-Aug, 1962
Dell Publishing Co.

#1	1.00	2.00	3.00
2-4	.50	1.00	1.50
-- Fish Stampede(15pgs., 1962, Fritos Giveaway)	1.20	2.40	3.60

LUKE CAGE (See Hero For Hire)

LUKE SHORT'S WESTERN STORIES
April, 1954 - 1958
Dell Publishing Co.

#1(4/54)	2.50	5.00	7.50
4-Color #580(8/54), #2(10/54)	1.50	3.00	4.50
4-Color #651-Kinstler art	1.75	3.50	5.25

	Good	Fine	Mint
4-Color #739,771,807,848,875,927			
	1.50	3.00	4.50

LUNATICKLE (Magazine) (Satire)
Feb, 1956 - #2, April, 1956
Whitstone Publ.

#1,2-Kubert art	1.50	3.00	4.50

LYNDON B. JOHNSON
March, 1965
Dell Publishing Co.

#12-445-503	2.00	4.00	6.00

MACHINE MAN (Also see 2001 --)
April, 1978 - #9, Dec, 1978
Marvel Comics Group

#1	.20	.40	.60
2-9	.15	.30	.45

NOTE: *Kirby stories-all; covers-#1-5,7-9.*

MACKENZIE'S RAIDERS (See 4-Color #1093)

MACO TOYS COMIC
1959 (36 pgs.) (Full Color) (Giveaway)
Maco Toys/Charlton Comics

#1-All military stories featuring Maco Toys			
	.80	1.60	2.40

MAD
Oct-Nov, 1952 - Present
(#24 on, magazine format)(Kurtzman editor #1-28, Feldstein #29 on)
E.C. Comics

#1-Wood, Davis, Elder start as regulars			
	70.00	140.00	210.00
2-Davis cover	35.00	70.00	105.00
3	20.00	40.00	60.00
4-Marijuana story "Flob Was a Slob" by Davis	17.50	35.00	52.50
5-(Scarce)-low distribution; Elder cover			
	60.00	120.00	180.00
6-10	12.00	24.00	36.00
11-Wolverton art	10.00	20.00	30.00
12-15	8.00	16.00	24.00
16-23: #22-all by Elder	7.00	14.00	21.00
24-1st magazine issue(25¢); Kurtzman logo & border on cover	12.00	24.00	36.00
25-Jaffee starts as regular writer			
	6.00	12.00	18.00
26-Wood cover	5.00	10.00	15.00
27-Davis cover	5.00	10.00	15.00
28-Elder cvr; Heath back cvr; last issue ed-			

(Mad cont'd)

	Good	Fine	Mint
ited by Kurtzman	5.00	10.00	15.00

29-Wood cvr; Kamen story; Don Martin starts as regular; Feldstein editing begins
5.00 10.00 15.00
30-1st A.E. Neuman cover by Mingo; Crandall inside cover; last Elder story; Bob Clarke starts as regular 5.00 10.00 15.00
31-Freas starts as regular; last Davis art until #99 4.00 8.00 12.00
32-Orlando, Drucker, Woodbridge start as regulars; Wood back cover 4.00 8.00 12.00
33-Orlando back cover 4.00 8.00 12.00
34-Berg starts as regular 3.00 6.00 9.00
35-Mingo wraparound cover; Crandall story
3.00 6.00 9.00
36-40 2.50 5.00 7.50
41-50: #45-Wood art 2.00 4.00 6.00
51-60: #60-Two Clarke cvrs; Prohias starts as regular 1.20 2.40 3.60
61-70: #64-Rickard starts as regular. #68-Martin cover 1.10 2.20 3.30
71-80: #76-Aragones starts as regular
1.00 2.00 3.00
81-90: #86-1st Fold-in. #89-One strip by Walt Kelly. #90-Frazetta back cover; lpg. Wood story .75 1.50 2.25
91-100: #91-Jaffee starts as story artist. #99-Davis art resumes .60 1.20 1.80
101-120: #106-Frazetta back cover
.50 1.00 1.50
121-140: #130-Torres starts as regular. #122-Drucker & Mingo cvr. #128-Last Orlando. #135,139-Davis covers .40 .80 1.20
141-170: #143-2pgs. Wood art. #165-Martin cvr. #169-Drucker cover .35 .70 1.05
171-200: #173,178-Davis cvrs. #176-Drucker cover. #182-Bob Jones starts as regular. #187-Harry North starts as regular
.25 .50 .75
NOTE: *Jules Feiffer story(reprint)-#42. Freas-most covers & back covers-#40-74. Heath stories-#14,27. Kamen story-#29. Krigstein stories-#12,17,24,26. Kurtzman covers-#1,3,4,6-10, 13,14,16,18. John Severin art-#1-6,9,10. Wolverton cover-#11; stories-#11,17,29,31,36, 40,82,137.*

MAD (See --Follies, --Special, More Trash from--, & The Worst from--)

MAD ABOUT MILLIE
April, 1969 - #17, Dec, 1970
Marvel Comics Group

#1	.20	.40	.60
2-17		.15	.30
Annual #1('71),2,3	.25	.50	.75

MAD FOLLIES (Special)
1963 - #7, 1969
E.C. Comics

	Good	Fine	Mint
No#(1963)-Paperback book covers			
	5.00	10.00	15.00
#2(1964)-Calendar	2.50	5.00	7.50
3(1965)-Mischief Stickers			
	2.00	4.00	6.00
4(1966)-Mobile; reprints Frazetta back cvr/ Mad #90	2.00	4.00	6.00
5(1967)-Stencils	2.00	4.00	6.00
6(1968)-Mischief Stickers			
	1.50	3.00	4.50
7(1969)-Nasty Cards	1.50	3.00	4.50

NOTE: *Clarke cover-#4. Mingo covers-#1-3.*

MAD HATTER, THE (Costume Hero)
Jan-Feb, 1946 - #2, Sept-Oct, 1946
O.W. Comics Corp.

#1-Freddy the Firefly begins; Giunta art,
2-Has ad for E.C.'s Animal Fables #1
3.00 6.00 9.00

MADHOUSE
1954; 1957
Ajax/Farrell Publ.(Excellent Publ./4-Star)

#1(1954)	5.00	10.00	15.00
2,3	2.50	5.00	7.50
4-Surrealistic cover	3.00	6.00	9.00
1(1957)	1.50	3.00	4.50
2-4	1.00	2.00	3.00

MADHOUSE (Formerly Madhouse Glads)
#95, 9/74 - #97, 1/75; #98, 8/75 - Present
Red Circle Productions/Archie Publications

#95-97: Horror stories. #97-Intro. Henry Hobson; Morrow art .25 .50 .75
98-113-Satire/humor stys. .20 .40 .60
Annual #8(1970-71)-#12(1974-75)-Formerly Madhouse Ma-ad Annual .25 .50 .75
--Comics Digest #1('75-76)-#3('77-78)
.30 .60 .90
NOTE: *McWilliams art-#97. Morrow covers-#95-97. See Archie Comics Digest #1,13.*

MADHOUSE COMICS DIGEST
1978 - Present
Archie Publications

#1-4 (#4, 8/78) .15 .30 .45

MADHOUSE GLADS (Formerly Madhouse Ma-ad; Madhouse #95 on)
#75, Oct, 1970 - #94, Aug, 1974(#78-92, 52pgs)
Archie Publications

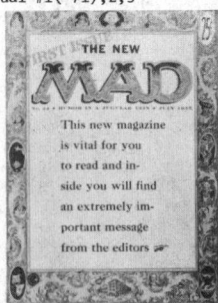

Mad Magazine #24. © EC

Mad Hatter #1, © O.W. Comics

Magic Agent #1, © ACG

Magic Comics #18, © DMP

Magic Comics #106, © DMP

Magnus Robot Fighter #1, © GK

(Madhouse Glads cont'd)	Good	Fine	Mint
#75		.15	.35
76-94		.10	.25

MADHOUSE MA-AD (--Jokes #67-70; --Freak-Out
#71-74)(Formerly Archie's Madhouse)(Becomes
Madhouse Glads #75 on)
#67, Apr, 1969 - #74, Sept, 1970
Archie Publications

	Good	Fine	Mint
#67-74		.15	.35

--Annual #7(1969-70)-Formerly Archie's
Madhouse Annual; becomes Madhouse Annual
.15 .30 .45

MAD MONSTER PARTY (See Movie Classics)

MAD SPECIAL
Fall, 1970 - Present
E.C. Publications, Inc.

Fall '70(#1)-Bonus-Voodoo Doll; contains
17pgs. new material 1.50 3.00 4.50
Spring '71(#2)-Wall Nuts; 17pgs. new material 1.00 2.00 3.00
#3-Protest Stickers 1.00 2.00 3.00
4-8: #4-Mini Posters. #5-Mad Flag. #7-Pres-
idential candidate posters, Wild Shocking
Message posters. #8-TV Guise
.80 1.60 2.40
9(1972)-24pg. color comic insert-Reprints
from Mad comics .80 1.60 2.40
10,11,13: #10-Nonsense Stickers(Don Martin).
#11-33-1/3 RPM record. #13-Sickie Stickers
.60 1.20 1.80
12-32pg. color comic insert; reprints from
Mad comics; Davis art .80 1.60 2.40
14-Vital Message posters & Art Depreciation
paintings .50 1.00 1.50
15-17 .50 1.00 1.50
18-32pg. color comic insert; reprints from
Mad comics .60 1.20 1.80
19-21 .50 1.00 1.50

MAGIC AGENT (See Unknown Worlds)
Jan-Feb, 1961 - #3, May-June, 1961
American Comics Group

#1-Origin & 1st app. John Force
.75 1.50 2.25
2,3 .50 1.00 1.50

MAGIC COMICS
August, 1939 - #123, Nov-Dec, 1949
David McKay Publications

#1-Mandrake the Magician, Henry, Popeye (not
by Segar), Blondie, Barney Baxter, Secret

Agent X-9(not by Raymond), Bunky by Billy
DeBeck & Thornton Burgess text stories
illustrated by Harrison Cady begin

	Good	Fine	Mint
	30.00	60.00	90.00
2	15.00	30.00	45.00
3	12.00	24.00	36.00
4	10.00	20.00	30.00
5	8.00	16.00	24.00
6-10	7.00	14.00	21.00
11-16,18-20	6.00	12.00	18.00
17-The Lone Ranger begins	6.00	12.00	18.00
21-30	5.00	10.00	15.00
31-40	3.50	7.00	10.50
41-50	3.00	6.00	9.00
51-60	2.50	5.00	7.50
61-70	1.80	3.60	5.40
71-100	1.50	3.00	4.50
101-106,109-123	1.20	2.40	3.60
107,108-Flash Gordon in each, not by Raymond			
	4.00	8.00	12.00

MAGICA DE SPELL (See Walt Disney Showcase#30)

MAGIC SWORD, THE (See Movie Classics)

MAGILLA GORILLA (TV) (Hanna-Barbera)
May, 1964 - #10, Dec, 1968
Gold Key/Charlton

#1(Gold Key)	.15	.30	.45
2,4-10		.15	.35
3-Vs. Yogi Bear for President		.15	.35

MAGILLA GORILLA (TV)
Nov, 1970 - #5, July, 1971 (Hanna-Barbera)
Charlton Comics

#1-5		.15	.35

MAGNUS, ROBOT FIGHTER (-- 4000 A.D.)
Feb, 1963 - #46, Jan, 1977
Gold Key

#1-Origin Magnus; Aliens series begins			
	4.00	8.00	12.00
2,3	2.00	4.00	6.00
4-10	1.50	3.00	4.50
11-20	1.00	2.00	3.00
21,22,24-30: #22-Reprint of origin from #1.			
#28-Last new material issue; Aliens series			
ends	.40	.80	1.20
23-Exists with two different prices, 12¢ and			
15¢; the 12¢ blacked out & 15¢ printed			
over it	.40	.80	1.20
31-46: #43,45-reprints	.20	.40	.60

NOTE: *Russ Manning* art-#1-22. *Russ Manning*
reprints-#29-43.

MAID OF THE MIST (See American Graphics)

MAJOR HOOPLE COMICS
1942
Nedor Publications

	Good	Fine	Mint
#1-Mary Worth, Phantom Soldier by Moldoff			
app.	7.00	14.00	21.00

MAJOR INAPAK THE SPACE ACE
1951   (20 pgs.) (Giveaway)
Magazine Enterprises (Inapac Foods)

#1-Bob Powell art	.65	1.35	2.00

NOTE: *Many copies found in warehouse in 1975.*

MAJOR VICTORY COMICS
1944 - #3, Summer, 1945
H.Clay Glover/Service Publ/Harry 'A' Chesler

#1-Origin Major Victory by C. Sultan (reprint from Dynamic #1); Spider Woman 1st app.			
	10.00	20.00	30.00
2-Dynamic Boy app.	5.00	10.00	15.00
3-Rocket Boy app.	4.00	8.00	12.00

MALTESE FALCON (See Feature Book #48(McKay))

MALU IN THE LAND OF ADVENTURE
1964
I.W. Enterprises

#1-Reprints Avon's Slave Girl Princess #1			
	5.00	10.00	15.00

MAMMOTH COMICS
1937   (80 pgs.) (Black & White)
Whitman Publishing Co.

#1-Terry & the Pirates, Dick Tracy, Little Orphan Annie, Wash Tubbs, & other reprints			
	40.00	80.00	120.00

MAMMY YOKUM & THE GREAT DOGPATCH MYSTERY
1951   (Giveaway)
Toby Press

Li'l Abner	4.00	8.00	12.00

MAN-BAT (Also see Detective #400, Brave & the Bold, & Batman Family)
Dec-Jan, 1975-76 - #2, Feb-Mar, 1976
National Periodical Publications

#1-Ditko art	.50	1.00	1.50
2	.30	.60	.90

MAN COMICS

Dec, 1949 - #28, Sept, 1953
Marvel/Atlas Comics(NPI)

	Good	Fine	Mint
#1	1.50	3.00	4.50
2-5	1.00	2.00	3.00
6-15	.70	1.40	2.10
16-21,23-28	.60	1.20	1.80
22-Krigstein story	2.00	4.00	6.00

NOTE: *Everett cover-#25. Kubertish story by Bob Brown-#3.*

MANDRAKE THE MAGICIAN (See Feature Book #18, 19,23,46,52,55)

MANDRAKE THE MAGICIAN (See Harvey C. Hits#53)
1956; Sept, 1966 - #10, Nov, 1967
Dell Publishing Co./King Comics

4-Color #752('56)	2.50	5.00	7.50
#1(King)-Begin S.O.S. Phantom series, ends			
#3	1.00	2.00	3.00
2-5: #4-Girl Phantom app. #5-Brick Bradford			
app., also #6	.65	1.35	2.00
6,7,9: #7-Origin Lothar. #9-Brick Bradford			
app.	.50	1.00	1.50
8-Jeff Jones story	.80	1.60	2.40
10-Rip Kirby app.; 14pgs. art by Raymond			
	1.50	3.00	4.50

MANDRAKE THE MAGICIAN GIANT COMIC ALBUM
1972 (48pgs)(11x14")(B&W)(Cardboard covers)
Modern Promotions

No#-Strip reprints by Lee Falk			
	1.00	2.00	3.00

MAN FROM ATLANTIS, THE
Feb, 1978 - #7, Aug, 1978
Marvel Comics Group

#1-(80-pgs; $1.00)-Buscema cover; origin			
story	.40	.80	1.20
2-7	.20	.40	.60

MAN FROM U.N.C.L.E., THE (TV)
Feb, 1965 - #22, April, 1969
Gold Key

#1	1.00	2.00	3.00
2	.50	1.00	1.50
3-10: #7-Jet Dream begins	.40	.80	1.20
11-22: #21,22-reprints	.25	.50	.75

MAN FROM WELLS FARGO (TV)
July, 1962
Dell Publishing Co.

4-Color #1287, #01-495-207

	1.00	2.00	3.00

Man-Bat #1, © DC

Man Comics #5, © MCG

Mandrake The Magician #8, © KING

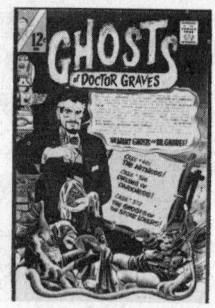

Manhunt #9, © ME   Man-Thing Giant #4, © MCG   Many Ghosts Of Doctor Graves #1, © CC

MANHUNT! (Becomes Red Fox #15 on)
Oct, 1947 - #15, 1953
Magazine Enterprises

	Good	Fine	Mint
#1-Red Fox by L.B. Cole, Undercover Girl by Whitney, Space Ace begin	9.00	18.00	27.00
2-5	6.00	12.00	18.00
6-Bondage cover by Whitney	7.00	14.00	21.00
7-9: Trail Colt begins #7. #8-Space Ace ends	5.00	10.00	15.00
10-G. Ingels story	6.00	12.00	18.00
11-Frazetta art, 7pgs.; Trail Colt app.; The Duke, Scotland Yard begin	12.00	24.00	36.00
12	4.00	8.00	12.00
13(A-1#63)-Frazetta, reprint from Trail Colt #1, 7pgs.; L. B. Cole story	10.00	20.00	30.00
14(A-1#77)-Classic bondage cover	6.00	12.00	18.00
15 (Exist? Was advertised)			

NOTE: *Guardineer art-#1-5; cover-#8. Whitney art-#2-14; covers-#1-6.*

MANHUNTER (See First Issue Special)

MAN IN BLACK (See Thrill-O-Rama)
Sept, 1957 - 1958
Harvey Publications

#1-Bob Powell cover/art	3.50	7.00	10.50
2-5: Powell cover/art	2.50	5.00	7.50

MAN IN FLIGHT (See 4-Color Comics #836)

MAN IN SPACE (See Dell Giant #27 & 4-Color Comics #716,954)

MAN OF PEACE, POPE PIUS XII
1950
Catechetical Guild

	2.00	4.00	6.00

MAN OF WAR (See Liberty Scouts & Liberty
Nov, 1941 - #2, Jan, 1942   Guards)
Centaur Publications

#1-The Fire-Man, Man of War, The Sentinel, & Vapo-Man begin	30.00	60.00	90.00
2-The Ferret app.	20.00	40.00	60.00

MAN O' MARS
1953; 1964
Fiction House Magazines

	Good	Fine	Mint
#1-Space Rangers	6.00	12.00	18.00
IW Reprint #1/Man O'Mars #1; Murphy Anderson art	2.50	5.00	7.50

MAN-THING, THE (See Book & Record and Fear)
Jan, 1974 - #22, Oct, 1975
Marvel Comics Group

#1-Howard the Duck app.	3.00	6.00	9.00
2-4	1.25	2.50	3.75
5-Ploog art	1.00	2.00	3.00
6-11-Ploog art	.70	1.40	2.10
12-20	.40	.80	1.20
21-Origin by Mooney	.25	.50	.75
22-Howard the Duck cameo	.50	1.00	1.50
Giant Size #1(8/74)-Ploog cover/story	.75	1.50	2.25
Giant Size #2,3	.60	1.20	1.80
Giant Size #4-Howard the Duck by Brunner	4.00	8.00	12.00
Giant Size #5-Howard the Duck by Brunner	3.00	6.00	9.00

NOTE: *Alcala story-#14, Giant Size#3. Brunner cover-#1, Giant Size #4. Mooney stories-#18, 20-22. Ploog Man-Thing-#5-11.*

MAN WITH THE X-RAY EYES, THE (See X, --, under Movie Comics)

MANY GHOSTS OF DR. GRAVES, THE
5/67 - #60, 12/76; #61, 9/77 - #62, 10/77;
#63, 2/78 - #65, 4/78
Charlton Comics

#1	.35	.70	1.05
2-10	.20	.40	.60
11-20	.15	.30	.45
21-44		.15	.30
45-1st Newton comic book work	.50	1.00	1.50
46,48,50-65	.15	.30	.45
47,49-Newton stories	.15	.30	.45

NOTE: *Ditko stories-#1,7,9,11-13,15-18,20-22, 24,26,27,29-35,37,38,40-43,47,48,51,52,53,55; covers-#11,12,16-18,22,24,26-35,38,58. Newton covers-#49,52. Sutton cover/art-#42.*

MANY LOVES OF DOBIE GILLIS (TV)
June-July, 1960 - #26, Oct, 1964
National Periodical Publications

#1	1.50	3.00	4.50
2-10	.80	1.60	2.40
11-26	.60	1.20	1.80

MARAUDER'S MOON (See 4-Color Comics #848)

March Of Comics #4, © WDP

March Of Comics #6, © K.K. Publ.

March Of Comics #21, © Loew's Inc.

MARCH OF COMICS (Boys' and Girls' --)
(K.K. Giveaway) (#1-4, No#'s)
1946 - Present (Founded by Sig Feuchtwanger)
K.K. Publications/Western Publ. Co.

Good Fine Mint
Early issues were full size, 32 pages, and were printed with and without an extra cover of slick stock, just for the advertiser. The binding was stapled if the slick cover was added; otherwise the pages were glued together at the spine. 1948-1951 issues were full size, 24 pages, pulp covers. Starting in 1952 they were half-size and 32 pages with slick covers. 1959 and later issues had only 16 pages plus covers. 1952-1959 issues read oblong; 1960 and later issues read upright.

#1(No#)-Goldilocks(1946) 12.00 24.00 36.00
 2(No#)-How Santa Got His Red Suit(1946)-
   Walt Kelly back cover 15.00 30.00 45.00
 3(No#)-Our Gang(Walt Kelly)(1947)
                         40.00 80.00 120.00
 4(No#)-Donald Duck by Carl Barks. "Maharajah
   Donald", 32pgs.; Kelley cover
                     600.00 1200.00 1800.00
 5-Andy Panda   12.00 24.00 36.00
 6-Popular Fairy Tales-Walt Kelly cover; two
   Noonan stories   15.00 30.00 45.00
 7-Oswald the Rabbit; Kelly cover
                      15.00 30.00 45.00
 8-Mickey Mouse, 32pgs. 50.00 100.00 150.00
 9-The Story of the Gloomy Bunny
                       7.00 14.00 21.00
10-Out of Santa's Bag 6.00 12.00 18.00
11-Fun With Santa Claus 5.00 10.00 15.00
12-Santa's Toys   5.00 10.00 15.00
13-Santa's Surprise   5.00 10.00 15.00
14-Santa's Candy Kitchen 5.00 10.00 15.00
15-Hip-It-Ty Top & the Big Bass Viol
                       5.00 10.00 15.00
16-Woody Woodpecker('47) 9.00 18.00 27.00
17-Roy Rogers(1948)   12.00 24.00 36.00
18-Popular Fairy Tales 9.00 18.00 27.00

                      Good   Fine   Mint
19-Uncle Wiggily   8.00 16.00 24.00
20-Donald Duck by Carl Barks. "Darkest
   Africa," 24pgs.; Kelly cover
                     400.00 800.00 1200.00
21-Tom and Jerry   8.00 16.00 24.00
22-Andy Panda   8.00 16.00 24.00
23-Raggedy Ann; Kerr art 10.00 20.00 30.00
24-Felix the Cat,'32 daily strip reprints by
   Otto Messmer   14.00 28.00 42.00
25-Gene Autry   10.00 20.00 30.00
26-Our Gang-Walt Kelly 20.00 40.00 60.00
27-Mickey Mouse   30.00 60.00 90.00
28-Gene Autry   10.00 20.00 30.00
29-Easter Bonnet Shop 3.00 6.00 9.00
30-Here Comes Santa   3.50 7.00 10.50
31-Santa's Busy Corner 3.50 7.00 10.50
32-No book produced
33-A Christmas Carol   3.50 7.00 10.50
34-Woody Woodpecker   6.00 12.00 18.00
35-Roy Rogers(1948)   9.00 18.00 27.00
36-Felix the Cat(1949)-by Messmer; daily
   strip reprints   10.00 20.00 30.00
37-Popeye   8.00 16.00 24.00
38-Oswald the Rabbit   6.00 12.00 18.00
39-Gene Autry   8.00 16.00 24.00
40-Andy and Woody   6.00 12.00 18.00
41-Donald Duck by Carl Barks. "Race to the
   South Seas," 24pgs.; Kelley cover
                     300.00 600.00 900.00
42-Porky Pig   6.00 12.00 18.00
43-Henry   3.50 7.00 10.50
44-Bugs Bunny   6.00 12.00 18.00
45-Mickey Mouse   25.00 50.00 75.00
46-Tom and Jerry   6.00 12.00 18.00
47-Roy Rogers   8.00 16.00 24.00
48-Greetings from Santa 3.00 6.00 9.00
49-Santa Is Here   3.00 6.00 9.00
50-Santa's Workshop('49) 3.00 6.00 9.00
51-Felix the Cat(1950)-by Messmer

March Of Comics #27, © WDP

March Of Comics #37, © KING

March Of Comics #40, © Walter Lantz

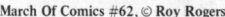

March Of Comics #62, © Roy Rogers   March Of Comics #64, © K.K.Publ.   March Of Comics #118, © KING

(March of Comics cont'd)	Good	Fine	Mint
	9.00	18.00	27.00
52-Popeye	7.00	14.00	21.00
53-Oswald the Rabbit	6.00	12.00	18.00
54-Gene Autry	7.00	14.00	21.00
55-Andy and Woody	5.00	10.00	15.00
56-Donald Duck-not by Barks; Barks art on			
back cover	25.00	50.00	75.00
57-Porky Pig	5.00	10.00	15.00
58-Henry	3.00	6.00	9.00
59-Bugs Bunny	5.00	10.00	15.00
60-Mickey Mouse	20.00	40.00	60.00
61-Tom and Jerry	4.00	8.00	12.00
62-Roy Rogers	6.00	12.00	18.00
63-Welcome Santa	2.50	5.00	7.50
64-Santa's Helpers	2.50	5.00	7.50
65-Jingle Bells(1950)	2.50	5.00	7.50
66-Popeye(1951)	5.00	10.00	15.00
67-Oswald the Rabbit	4.00	8.00	12.00
68-Roy Rogers	5.00	10.00	15.00
69-Donald Duck-not Barks	20.00	40.00	60.00
70-Tom and Jerry	3.50	7.00	10.50
71-Porky Pig	4.00	8.00	12.00
72-Krazy Kat	6.00	12.00	18.00
73-Roy Rogers	5.00	10.00	15.00
74-Mickey Mouse(1951)	12.00	24.00	36.00
75-Bugs Bunny	4.00	8.00	12.00
76-Andy and Woody	3.50	7.00	10.50
77-Roy Rogers	5.00	10.00	15.00
78-Gene Autry(1951)-Last regular size issue			
	5.00	10.00	15.00
79-Andy Panda(1952)-5"x7" size			
	2.50	5.00	7.50
80-Popeye	3.50	7.00	10.50
81-Oswald the Rabbit	2.50	5.00	7.50
82-Tarzan	7.00	14.00	21.00
83-Bugs Bunny	2.50	5.00	7.50
84-Henry	2.00	4.00	6.00
85-Woody Woodpecker	2.00	4.00	6.00
86-Roy Rogers	4.00	8.00	12.00
87-Krazy Kat	4.00	8.00	12.00
88-Tom and Jerry	2.00	4.00	6.00
89-Porky Pig	2.50	5.00	7.50
90-Gene Autry	4.00	8.00	12.00
91-Roy Rogers & Santa	4.00	8.00	12.00
92-Christmas with Santa	2.00	4.00	6.00
93-Woody Woodpecker('53)	2.00	4.00	6.00
94-Indian Chief	2.50	5.00	7.50
95-Oswald the Rabbit	2.00	4.00	6.00
96-Popeye	3.00	6.00	9.00
97-Bugs Bunny	2.50	5.00	7.50
98-Tarzan	6.00	12.00	18.00
99-Porky Pig	2.50	5.00	7.50
100-Roy Rogers	3.50	7.00	10.50
101-Henry	1.50	3.00	4.50
102-Tom Corbett	3.00	6.00	9.00
103-Tom and Jerry	1.75	3.35	5.00
104-Gene Autry	3.50	7.00	10.50

	Good	Fine	Mint
105-Roy Rogers	3.50	7.00	10.50
106-Santa's Helpers	2.00	4.00	6.00
107-Santa's Christmas Book - not published			
108-Fun With Santa('53)	2.00	4.00	6.00
109-Woody Woodpecker('54)	1.50	3.00	4.50
110-Indian Chief	2.00	4.00	6.00
111-Oswald the Rabbit	1.75	3.35	5.00
112-Henry	1.00	2.00	3.00
113-Porky Pig	1.50	3.00	4.50
114-Tarzan(Russ Manning)	6.00	12.00	18.00
115-Bugs Bunny	2.00	4.00	6.00
116-Roy Rogers	3.00	6.00	9.00
117-Popeye	2.50	5.00	7.50
118-Flash Gordon	8.00	16.00	24.00
119-Tom and Jerry	1.50	3.00	4.50
120-Gene Autry	3.00	6.00	9.00
121-Roy Rogers	3.00	6.00	9.00
122-Santa's Surprise('54)	1.50	3.00	4.50
123-Santa's Christmas Book	1.50	3.00	4.50
124-Woody Woodpecker('55)	1.50	3.00	4.50
125-Tarzan	5.00	10.00	15.00
126-Oswald the Rabbit	1.50	3.00	4.50
127-Indian Chief	1.50	3.00	4.50
128-Tom and Jerry	1.50	3.00	4.50
129-Henry	1.25	2.50	3.75
130-Porky Pig	1.50	3.00	4.50
131-Roy Rogers	3.00	6.00	9.00
132-Bugs Bunny	1.50	3.00	4.50
133-Flash Gordon	6.00	12.00	18.00
134-Popeye	2.00	4.00	6.00
135-Gene Autry	2.50	5.00	7.50
136-Roy Rogers	2.50	5.00	7.50
137-Gifts from Santa	1.25	2.50	3.75
138-Fun at Christmas('55)	1.25	2.50	3.75
139-Woody Woodpecker('56)	1.50	3.00	4.50
140-Indian Chief	1.50	3.00	4.50
141-Oswald the Rabbit	1.50	3.00	4.50
142-Flash Gordon	5.00	10.00	15.00
143-Porky Pig	1.50	3.00	4.50
144-Tarzan(Russ Manning)	5.00	10.00	15.00
145-Tom and Jerry	1.25	2.50	3.75
146-Roy Rogers	2.50	5.00	7.50
147-Henry	1.00	2.00	3.00
148-Popeye	2.00	4.00	6.00
149-Bugs Bunny	1.50	3.00	4.50
150-Gene Autry	2.50	5.00	7.50
151-Roy Rogers	2.50	5.00	7.50
152-The Night Before Christmas			
	1.25	2.50	3.75
153-Merry Christmas('56)	1.25	2.50	3.75
154-Tom and Jerry('57)	1.25	2.50	3.75
155-Tarzan	4.00	8.00	12.00
156-Oswald the Rabbit	1.25	2.50	3.75
157-Popeye	1.75	3.50	5.25
158-Woody Woodpecker	1.25	2.50	3.75
159-Indian Chief	1.50	3.00	4.50
160-Bugs Bunny	1.50	3.00	4.50

(March of Comics cont'd)	Good	Fine	Mint
161-Roy Rogers	2.00	4.00	6.00
162-Henry	1.00	2.00	3.00
163-Rin Tin Tin	1.50	3.00	4.50
164-Porky Pig	1.25	2.50	3.75
165-The Lone Ranger	3.50	7.00	10.50
166-Santa and His Reindeer	1.25	2.50	3.75
167-Roy Rogers and Santa	2.00	4.00	6.00
168-Santa's Workshop('57)	1.25	2.50	3.75
169-Popeye('58)	1.50	3.00	4.50
170-Indian Chief	1.50	3.00	4.50
171-Oswald the Rabbit	1.25	2.50	3.75
172-Tarzan	4.00	8.00	12.00
173-Tom and Jerry	1.25	2.50	3.75
174-The Lone Ranger	3.00	6.00	9.00
175-Porky Pig	1.25	2.50	3.75
176-Roy Rogers	2.00	4.00	6.00
177-Woody Woodpecker	1.25	2.50	3.75
178-Henry	1.25	2.50	3.75
179-Bugs Bunny	1.25	2.50	3.75
180-Rin Tin Tin	1.35	2.75	4.00
181-Happy Holiday	.80	1.60	2.40
182-Happi Tim	.80	1.60	2.40
183-Welcome Santa(1958)	.80	1.60	2.40
184-Woody Woodpecker('59)	1.00	2.00	3.00
185-Tarzan	4.00	8.00	12.00
186-Oswald the Rabbit	1.00	2.00	3.00
187-Indian Chief	1.25	2.50	3.75
188-Bugs Bunny	1.00	2.00	3.00
189-Henry	1.00	2.00	3.00
190-Tom and Jerry	1.00	2.00	3.00
191-Roy Rogers	2.00	4.00	6.00
192-Porky Pig	1.00	2.00	3.00
193-The Lone Ranger	2.50	5.00	7.50
194-Popeye	1.25	2.50	3.75
195-Rin Tin Tin	1.35	2.75	4.00
196-Sears Special - not published			
197-Santa Is Coming	.75	1.50	2.25
198-Santa's Helpers(1959)	.75	1.50	2.25
199-Huckleberry Hound('60)	.50	1.00	1.50
200-Fury	.65	1.35	2.00
201-Bugs Bunny	.75	1.50	2.25
202-Space Explorer	1.50	3.00	4.50
203-Woody Woodpecker	.75	1.50	2.25
204-Tarzan	2.50	5.00	7.50
205-Mighty Mouse	1.25	2.50	3.75
206-Roy Rogers	2.00	4.00	6.00
207-Tom and Jerry	.75	1.50	2.25
208-The Lone Ranger	2.50	5.00	7.50
209-Porky Pig	.75	1.50	2.25
210-Lassie	1.25	2.50	3.75
211-Sears Special - not published			
212-Christmas Eve	.75	1.50	2.25
213-Here Comes Santa('60)	.75	1.50	2.25
214-Huckleberry Hound('61)	.50	1.00	1.50
215-Hi Yo Silver	1.50	3.00	4.50
216-Rocky & His Friends	1.00	2.00	3.00
217-Lassie	1.00	2.00	3.00

	Good	Fine	Mint
218-Porky Pig	.75	1.50	2.25
219-Journey to the Sun	1.00	2.00	3.00
220-Bugs Bunny	.75	1.50	2.25
221-Roy and Dale	2.00	4.00	6.00
222-Woody Woodpecker	.75	1.50	2.25
223-Tarzan	3.00	6.00	9.00
224-Tom and Jerry	.75	1.50	2.25
225-The Lone Ranger	2.00	4.00	6.00
226-Sears Special - not published			
227-Christmas Treasury	.75	1.50	2.25
228-Letters to Santa('61)	.75	1.50	2.25
229-The Flintstones('62)	.60	1.20	1.80
230-Lassie	1.00	2.00	3.00
231-Bugs Bunny	.75	1.50	2.25
232-The Three Stooges	1.50	3.00	4.50
233-Bullwinkle	.80	1.60	2.40
234-Smokey the Bear	.50	1.00	1.50
235-Huckleberry Hound	.50	1.00	1.50
236-Roy and Dale	1.50	3.00	4.50
237-Mighty Mouse	1.00	2.00	3.00
238-The Lone Ranger	2.00	4.00	6.00
239-Woody Woodpecker	.75	1.50	2.25
240-Tarzan	2.50	5.00	7.50
241-Santa Claus Around the World			
	.75	1.50	2.25
242-Santa's Toyland('62)	.75	1.50	2.25
243-The Flintstones('63)	.60	1.20	1.80
244-Mister Ed	.60	1.20	1.80
245-Bugs Bunny	.75	1.50	2.25
246-Popeye	1.00	2.00	3.00
247-Mighty Mouse	1.00	2.00	3.00
248-The Three Stooges	1.50	3.00	4.50
249-Woody Woodpecker	.60	1.20	1.80
250-Roy and Dale	1.50	3.00	4.50
251-Little Lulu by Stanley	7.00	14.00	21.00
252-Tarzan	2.50	5.00	7.50
253-Yogi Bear	.50	1.00	1.50
254-Lassie	1.00	2.00	3.00
255-Santa's Christmas List	.65	1.35	2.00
256-Christmas Party('63)	.65	1.35	2.00
257-Mighty Mouse	1.00	2.00	3.00
258-The Sword in the Stone (Disney)			
	2.00	4.00	6.00
259-Bugs Bunny	.75	1.50	2.25
260-Mister Ed	.50	1.00	1.50
261-Woody Woodpecker	.75	1.50	2.25
262-Tarzan	2.50	5.00	7.50
263-Donald Duck-not Barks	3.00	6.00	9.00
264-Popeye	1.00	2.00	3.00
265-Yogi Bear	.50	1.00	1.50
266-Lassie	1.00	2.00	3.00
267-Little Lulu	5.00	10.00	15.00
268-The Three Stooges	1.25	2.50	3.75
269-A Jolly Christmas	.65	1.35	2.00
270-Santa's Little Helpers	.65	1.35	2.00
271-The Flintstones('65)	.50	1.00	1.50
272-Tarzan	2.00	4.00	6.00

March Of Comics #205, © Terrytoons

March Of Comics #221, © Roy Rogers

March Of Comics #267, © WEST

(March of Comics cont'd)	Good	Fine	Mint
273-Bugs Bunny	.75	1.50	2.25
274-Popeye	.75	1.50	2.25
275-Little Lulu	4.00	8.00	12.00
276-The Jetsons	.50	1.00	1.50
277-Daffy Duck	.50	1.00	1.50
278-Lassie	1.00	2.00	3.00
279-Yogi Bear	.50	1.00	1.50
280-The Flintstones('65)	.50	1.00	1.50
281-Tom and Jerry	.50	1.00	1.50
282-Mister Ed	.50	1.00	1.50
283-Santa's Visit	.65	1.35	2.00
284-Christmas Parade('65)	.65	1.35	2.00
285-Astro Boy	1.00	2.00	3.00
286-Tarzan	2.00	4.00	6.00
287-Bugs Bunny	.50	1.00	1.50
288-Daffy Duck	.50	1.00	1.50
289-The Flintstones	.50	1.00	1.50
290-Mister Ed	.50	1.00	1.50
291-Yogi Bear	.50	1.00	1.50
292-The Three Stooges	1.25	2.50	3.75
293-Little Lulu	3.00	6.00	9.00
294-Popeye	.60	1.20	1.80
295-Tom and Jerry	.40	.80	1.20
296-Lassie	.80	1.60	2.40
297-Christmas Bells	.65	1.35	2.00
298-Santa's Sleigh('66)	.65	1.35	2.00
299-The Flintstones('67)	.40	.80	1.20
300-Tarzan	2.00	4.00	6.00
301-Bugs Bunny	.50	1.00	1.50
302-Laurel and Hardy	1.25	2.50	3.75
303-Daffy Duck	.40	.80	1.20
304-The Three Stooges	1.25	2.50	3.75
305-Tom and Jerry	.40	.80	1.20
306-Daniel Boone	1.00	2.00	3.00
307-Little Lulu	2.50	5.00	7.50
308-Lassie	.80	1.60	2.40
309-Yogi Bear	.40	.80	1.20
310-The Lone Ranger	2.00	4.00	6.00
311-Santa's Show	.65	1.35	2.00
312-Christmas Album('67)	.65	1.35	2.00
313-Daffy Duck('68)	.40	.80	1.20
314-Laurel and Hardy	1.25	2.50	3.75
315-Bugs Bunny	.50	1.00	1.50
316-The Three Stooges	1.25	2.50	3.75
317-The Flintstones	.40	.80	1.20
318-Tarzan	2.00	4.00	6.00
319-Yogi Bear	.40	.80	1.20
320-Space Family Robinson	1.50	3.00	4.50
321-Tom and Jerry	.40	.80	1.20
322-The Lone Ranger	2.00	4.00	6.00
323-Little Lulu-not Stanley			
	2.50	5.00	7.50
324-Lassie	.80	1.60	2.40
325-Fun With Santa	.50	1.00	1.50
326-Christmas Story('68)	.50	1.00	1.50
327-The Flintstones('69)	.40	.80	1.20
328-Space Family Robinson	1.25	2.50	3.75
329-Bugs Bunny	.50	1.00	1.50
330-The Jetsons	.40	.80	1.20
331-Daffy Duck	.40	.80	1.20
332-Tarzan	2.00	4.00	6.00
333-Tom and Jerry	.40	.80	1.20
334-Lassie	.60	1.20	1.80
335-Little Lulu	2.50	5.00	7.50
336-The Three Stooges	1.25	2.50	3.75
337-Yogi Bear	.40	.80	1.20
338-The Lone Ranger	1.75	3.50	5.25
339-(Did not come out)			
340-Here Comes Santa('69)	.50	1.00	1.50
341-The Flintstones	.30	.60	.90
342-Tarzan	2.00	4.00	6.00
343-Bugs Bunny	.40	.80	1.20
344-Yogi Bear	.40	.80	1.20
345-Tom and Jerry	.40	.80	1.20
346-Lassie	.60	1.20	1.80

	Good	Fine	Mint
347-Daffy Duck	.40	.80	1.20
348-The Jetsons	.40	.80	1.20
349-Little Lulu-not Stanley			
	1.50	3.00	4.50
350-The Lone Ranger	1.50	3.00	4.50
351-Beep-Beep, the Road Runner			
	.40	.80	1.20
352-Space Family Robinson	1.00	2.00	3.00
353-Beep-Beep, the Road Runner(1971)			
	.40	.80	1.20
354-Tarzan('71)	1.50	3.00	4.50
355-Little Lulu-not Stanley			
	1.50	3.00	4.50
356-Scooby Doo, Where Are You?			
	.40	.80	1.20
357-Daffy Duck & Porky Pig	.40	.80	1.20
358-Lassie	.50	1.00	1.50
359-Baby Snoots	.40	.80	1.20
360-H. R. Pufnstuf (TV)	.40	.80	1.20
361-Tom and Jerry	.35	.70	1.05
362-Smokey the Bear	.35	.70	1.05
363-Bugs Bunny & Yosemite Sam			
	.35	.70	1.05
364-The Banana Splits	.35	.70	1.05
365-Tom and Jerry('72)	.35	.70	1.05
366-Tarzan	1.50	3.00	4.50
367-Bugs Bunny & Porky Pig	.35	.70	1.05
368-Scooby Doo(4/72)	.35	.70	1.05
369-Little Lulu-not Stanley			
	1.25	2.50	3.75
370-Lassie	.50	1.00	1.50
371-Baby Snoots	.30	.60	.90
372-Smokey the Bear	.30	.60	.90
373-The Three Stooges	.40	.80	1.20
374-Wacky Witch	.30	.60	.90
375-Beep-Beep & Daffy Duck	.30	.60	.90
376-The Pink Panther('72)	.30	.60	.90
377-Baby Snoots('73)	.25	.50	.75
378-Turok, Son of Stone	1.00	2.00	3.00
379-Heckle & Jeckle New Terrytoons			
	.25	.50	.75
380-Bugs Bunny & Yosemite Sam			
	.25	.50	.75
381-Lassie	.30	.60	.90
382-Scooby Doo, Where Are You?			
	.35	.70	1.05
383-Smokey the Bear	.25	.50	.75
384-Pink Panther	.25	.50	.75
385-Little Lulu	1.00	2.00	3.00
386-Wacky Witch	.20	.40	.60
387-Beep-Beep & Daffy Duck	.20	.40	.60
388-Tom and Jerry('73)	.20	.40	.60
389-Little Lulu-not Stanley			
	1.00	2.00	3.00
390-Pink Panther	.20	.40	.60
391-Scooby Doo	.20	.40	.60
392-Bugs Bunny & Yosemite Sam			
	.20	.40	.60
393-New Terrytoons (Heckle & Jeckle)			
	.20	.40	.60
394-Lassie	.30	.60	.90
395-Woodsy Owl	.20	.40	.60
396-Baby Snoots	.20	.40	.60
397-Beep-Beep & Daffy Duck	.20	.40	.60
398-Wacky Witch	.20	.40	.60
399-Turok, Son of Stone	.80	1.60	2.40
400-Tom and Jerry	.20	.40	.60
401-Baby Snoots('75)(Reprints #371)			
	.20	.40	.60
402-Daffy Duck(Reprints#313)	.20	.40	.60
403-Bugs Bunny(Reprints#343)	.20	.40	.60
404-Space Family Robinson(Reprints #328)			
	.80	1.60	2.40
405-Cracky	.20	.40	.60
406-Little Lulu (Reprints #355)			

March Of Crime #3, © FOX

Margie Comics #35, © MCG

Marines In Battle #1, © MCG

(March of Comics cont'd)	Good	Fine	Mint
	1.00	2.00	3.00
407-Smokey the Bear (Reprints #362)			
	.20	.40	.60
408-Turok, Son of Stone	.80	1.60	2.40
409-Pink Panther	.20	.40	.60
410-Wacky Witch	.20	.40	.60
411-Lassie (Reprints #324)	.25	.50	.75
412-New Terrytoons('75)	.20	.40	.60
413-Daffy Duck('76)(Reprints #331)			
	.20	.40	.60
414-Space Family Robinson (Reprints #328)			
	.60	1.20	1.80
415-Bugs Bunny(Reprints#329)	.20	.40	.60
416-Road Runner(Reprts.#353)	.20	.40	.60
417-Little Lulu(Reprts.#323)	.50	1.00	1.50
418-Pink Panther(Reprt.#384)	.20	.40	.60
419-Baby Snoots(Reprts.#377)	.20	.40	.60
420-Woody Woodpecker	.20	.40	.60
421-Tweety & Sylvester	.20	.40	.60
422-Wacky Witch(Reprts.#386)	.20	.40	.60
423-Little Monsters	.20	.40	.60
424-Cracky(12/76)	.15	.30	.45
425-Daffy Duck	.15	.30	.45
426-Underdog	.15	.30	.45
427-Little Lulu	.50	1.00	1.50
428-Bugs Bunny	.15	.30	.45
429-The Pink Panther	.15	.30	.45
430-Beep-Beep, the Road Runner			
	.15	.30	.45
431-Baby Snoots	.15	.30	.45
432-Lassie	.15	.30	.45
433-Tweety & Sylvester	.15	.30	.45
434-Wacky Witch	.15	.30	.45
435-New Terrytoons	.15	.30	.45
436-Wacky Advs. of Cracky	.15	.30	.45
437-Daffy Duck	.15	.30	.45
438-Underdog	.15	.30	.45
439-Little Lulu	.20	.40	.60
440-Bugs Bunny	.15	.30	.45
441-The Pink Panther	.15	.30	.45
442-Beep-Beep, the Road Runner			
	.15	.30	.45
443-Baby Snoots	.15	.30	.45
444-Tom and Jerry	.15	.30	.45
445-Tweety and Sylvester	.15	.30	.45
446-Wacky Witch	.15	.30	.45

MARCH OF CRIME (My Love Affair #1-6)
1948 (132pgs); #7, 7/50 - #2, 9/50; #3, 9/51
Fox Features Syndicate

No#(1948,132pgs.)-See Fox Giants. Contents			
can vary and determines price.			
#7(#1)-(7/50)-Wood story	7.00	14.00	21.00
2(9/50)-Wood story	7.00	14.00	21.00
3(9/51)	2.00	4.00	6.00

MARCO POLO
1962 (Movie Classic)
Charlton Comics

	Good	Fine	Mint
No#	2.50	5.00	7.50

MARGARET O'BRIEN, THE ADVENTURES OF
1947 (20pgs. in Color; Slick Cover; Reg.Size)
Bambury Fashions (Clothes)   (Premium)

In "The Big City"-movie adaptation			
	5.00	10.00	15.00

MARGIE (See My Little --)

MARGIE (TV)
Mar-May, 1962 - #2, July-Sept, 1962
Dell Publishing Co.

4-Color #1307, #2	.50	1.00	1.50

MARGIE COMICS (Formerly Comedy)(Reno Browne
#35, Winter/46-47 - #49, 1949   #50 on)
Marvel Comics (ACI)

#35-38,42,45,47-49	1.25	2.50	3.75
39-41,43,44,46-Kurtzman's "Hey Look"			
	2.00	4.00	6.00

MARINES (See Tell It to the --)

MARINES ATTACK
Aug, 1964 - #9, Feb, 1966
Charlton Comics

#1	.25	.50	.75
2-9	.15	.30	.45

MARINES AT WAR (Tales of the Marines #4)
#5, April, 1957 - #7, Aug, 1957
Atlas Comics (OPI)

#5-7: #5-Drucker story. #7-Orlando story			
	.70	1.40	2.10

MARINES IN ACTION
June, 1955 - #14, Sept, 1957
Atlas News Co.

#1-Rock Murdock, Boot Camp Brady begin			
	1.20	2.40	3.60
2-14: #9,11,14-Berg art	.70	1.40	2.10

MARINES IN BATTLE
Aug, 1954 - #25, Sept, 1958
Atlas Comics(ACI #1-12/WPI #13-25)

#1-Heath cover; Iron Mike McGraw by Heath;

(Marines in Battle cont'd) Good Fine Mint
  history of U.S. Marine Corps. begins

	Good	Fine	Mint
	1.25	2.50	3.75
2-6,8-10	.80	1.60	2.40
7-6pg. Kubert/Moskowitz story			
	1.50	3.00	4.50
11-16,18-24: #23-Rock Murdock app.			
	.70	1.40	2.10
17-Williamson story, 3pgs.	2.50	5.00	7.50
25-Torres story	1.20	2.40	3.60

NOTE: *Berg story-#22. Everett story-#4; cover-#21. Orlando story-#14.*

MARINE WAR HEROES (Charlton Premiere #19)
Jan, 1964 - #18, Mar, 1967
Charlton Comics

#1	.25	.50	.75
2-18	.15	.30	.45

NOTE: *Montes/Bache stories-#1,14,18; cover-#1.*

MARK OF ZORRO (See 4-Color Comics #228)

MARK STEEL
1967, 1968, 1972 (24 pgs.) (Color)
American Iron & Steel Institute

1967,1968-"Journey of Discovery with--"
  Neal Adams art   1.50   3.00   4.50
1972-"--Fights Pollution" 1.00   2.00   3.00

MARK TRAIL
Oct, 1955 - #5, Summer, 1959
Standard Magazines (Hall Syndicate)

#1-Sunday strip reprints	2.50	5.00	7.50
2-5	1.80	3.60	5.40

--Adventure Book of Nature #1(Summer, 1958)-
  (Pines, 100pg. Giant-contains 78 Sunday
  strip reprints)   3.00   6.00   9.00

MARMADUKE MONK
No Date; 1963   (10¢)
I.W. Enterprises/Super Comics

#1-I.W. Reprint	.25	.50	.75
#14-(Super Reprint-'63)	.25	.50	.75

MARMADUKE MOUSE
Spring, 1946 - #65, Dec, 1956
Quality Comics Group (Arnold Publ.)

#1	2.00	4.00	6.00
2-30	.80	1.60	2.40
31-65	.50	1.00	1.50
Super Reprint #14('63)	.25	.50	.75

MARS & BEYOND (See 4-Color Comics #866)

M.A.R.S. PATROL TOTAL WAR (Total War #1,2)
#3, Sept, 1966 - #10, Aug, 1969
Gold Key

	Good	Fine	Mint
#3-Wood art	1.20	2.40	3.60
4-10	.40	.80	1.20

MARTHA WAYNE (See The Story of --)

MARTIN KANE (Formerly My Secret Affair)
#4, June, 1950 - #2, Aug, 1950
Fox Features Syndicate (Hero Books)

#4(#1)-Wood cover	3.00	6.00	9.00
2-5pg. Orlando story	3.00	6.00	9.00

MARTY MOUSE
No Date (1958?)   (10¢)
I.W. Enterprises

#1-Reprint	.20	.40	.60

MARVEL ADVENTURE
December, 1975 - #6, Oct, 1976
Marvel Comics Group

#1-Daredevil reprints	.20	.40	.60
2-6	.15	.30	.45

MARVEL BOY (Astonishing #3 on)
Dec, 1950 - #2, Feb, 1951
Marvel Comics (20CC)

#1-Origin Marvel Boy by Russ Heath

	10.00	20.00	30.00
2-Everett art	8.00	16.00	24.00

MARVEL CHILLERS
Oct, 1975 - #7, Oct, 1976
Marvel Comics Group

#1-Intro. Modred the Mystic.	.35	.70	1.05
2,3-Tigra, the Were-Woman begins(origin) #3, ends #7	.25	.50	.75
4-7: #7-Kirby cover	.20	.40	.60

MARVEL CLASSICS COMICS
1976 - #36, Dec, 1978
Marvel Comics Group

#1-Dr. Jekyll and Mr. Hyde; Redondo story	.65	1.35	2.00
2-Time Machine-Nino art	.50	1.00	1.50
3-Hunchback of Notre Dame	.50	1.00	1.50
4-20,000 Leagues Under the Sea			
5-Black Beauty			
6-Gulliver's Travels			
7-Tom Sawyer			

Mark Trail #1, © STD

Martin Kane #2, © FOX

Marvel Classics #2, © MCG

Marvel Coll. Items Classics #2, © MCG

Marvel Comics #1, © MCG

Marvel Family #9, © FAW

(Marvel Classics cont'd)	Good	Fine	Mint
8-Moby Dick-Nino art			
9-Dracula-Redondo story			
10-Red Badge of Courage			
each....	.35	.70	1.05
11-Mysterious Island			
12-The Three Musketeers-Nino art			
13-Last of the Mohicans			
14-War of the Worlds			
15-Treasure Island			
16-Ivanhoe			
17-The Count of Monte Cristo			
18-The Odyssey			
19-Robinson Crusoe			
20-Frankenstein			
each....	.35	.70	1.05
21-Master of the World			
22-Food of the Gods			
23-The Moonstone			
24-She			
25-The Invisible Man			
26-The Illiad-Buscema cover			
27-Kidnapped			
28-The Pit and the Pendulum			
29-Prisoner of Zenda			
30-Arabian Nights			
31-First Man in the Moon			
32-White Fang			
33-The Prince and the Pauper			
34-Robin Hood			
35-Alice in Wonderland			
36-A Christmas Carol			
each....	.25	.50	.75

MARVEL COLLECTORS ITEM CLASSICS
(Marvel's Greatest #23 on)
1965 - #22, Aug, 1969
Marvel Comics Group

#1	2.00	4.00	6.00
2-4	1.20	2.40	3.60
5-10	.80	1.60	2.40
11-22	.50	1.00	1.50

NOTE: *All reprints; Kirby art in all.*

MARVEL COMICS (Marvel Mystery #2 on)
November, 1939
Timely Comics (Funnies, Inc.)

NOTE: The first issue was originally dated October 1939. Most copies have a black circle stamped over the date (on cover & inside) with "November" printed over it. However, some copies do not have the November overprint. Most No. 1's have printing defects, i. e. tilted pages which caused trimming into the panels usually on right side and bottom.

#1-Origin Sub-Mariner by Bill Everett; 1st 8pgs. reprinted from Motion Picture Funnies Weekly #1; Human Torch by Carl Burgos, Kazar the Great, & Jungle Terror (only

app.); Intro. The Angel, The Masked Raider

(ends #12)	Good	Fine	Mint
(ends #12)	3000.00	6500.00	10,000.00

(Prices vary widely on this book)

MARVEL COMICS SUPER SPECIAL (Also see
Howard the Duck #12)(Magazine)($1.50)
September, 1977
Marvel Comics Group

#1-Kiss, 40pgs. comics + photos & features;			
Simonson pencils	1.00	2.00	3.00
2-Conan(3/78)-art by Buscema			
	.80	1.60	2.40
3-Close Encounters of the Third Kind(6/78)			
	.80	1.60	2.40
4-The Ultimate Beatles Book(8/78)			
	.75	1.50	2.25
5-Kiss (12/78)	.75	1.50	2.25
6-Jaws II(12/78)	.60	1.20	1.80
7-Sgt. Pepper	.60	1.20	1.80
8-Battlestar Galactica	.60	1.20	1.80
9-Conan	.60	1.20	1.80

MARVEL DOUBLE FEATURE
Dec, 1973 - #21, Mar, 1977
Marvel Comics Group

#1-Captain America & Iron Man reprints begin			
	.40	.80	1.20
2-5	.35	.70	1.05
6-21: #18-Kirby cover	.20	.40	.60

MARVEL FAMILY (Also see Capt. Marvel #18)
Dec, 1945 - #89, Jan, 1954
Fawcett Publications

#1-Origin Captain Marvel, Captain Marvel Jr.,			
Mary Marvel, & Uncle Marvel retold; Black			
Adam origin & 1st app.	45.00	90.00	135.00
2	22.50	45.00	67.50
3	17.50	35.00	52.50
4,5	10.00	20.00	30.00
6-10: #7-Shazam app.	8.00	16.00	24.00
11-20	6.00	12.00	18.00
21-30	5.00	10.00	15.00
31-40	3.50	7.00	10.50
41-50	3.00	6.00	9.00
51-89	2.50	5.00	7.50

MARVEL FEATURE (See Marvel Two-In-One)
Dec, 1971 - #12, Nov, 1973   (#1,2-25¢)
Marvel Comics Group

#1-Origin The Defenders; Sub-Mariner, The			
Hulk & Dr. Strange; G.A. Sub-Mariner re-			
print, Adams cover	3.00	6.00	9.00
2-G.A. Sub-Mariner reprt.	1.50	3.00	4.50

```
(Marvel Feature cont'd)      Good   Fine   Mint
 3-Defender series ends       1.50   3.00   4.50
 4-Begin Ant-Man series        .40    .80   1.20
 5-7                           .40    .80   1.20
 8-Origin The Wasp; Starlin art; reprint
                               .40    .80   1.20
 9,10-Last Ant-Man             .30    .60    .90
11,12-Thing team-ups; Starlin art
                               .50   1.00   1.50
```

MARVEL FEATURE (Also see Red Sonja)
Nov, 1975 - #7, 1976
Marvel Comics Group

```
#1-Red Sonja begins; Adams reprint/Savage
   Sword of Conan #1          .50   1.00   1.50
2-7                           .35    .70   1.05
```

MARVEL MINI-BOOKS
1966 (50 pgs.)(5/8"x7/8")(6 different)
Marvel Comics Group

```
Captain America, Spider-Man, Sgt. Fury, Hulk,
   Thor                      1.00   2.00   3.00
Millie the Model             .60   1.20   1.80
```

MARVEL MOVIE PREMIERE (Magazine)
Sept, 1975   (One Shot) (Black & White)
Marvel Comics Group

```
#1-Burroughs "The Land That Time Forgot"
   adaptation                .65   1.35   2.00
```

MARVEL MYSTERY COMICS (Formerly Marvel Comics)(Marvel Tales #93 on)
#2, Dec, 1939 - #92, June, 1949
Timely Comics/Marvel Comics

```
#2-American Ace begins, ends #3; Human Torch
   by Burgos, Sub-Mariner by Everett contin-
   ues                    600.00 1200.00 1800.00
3                         400.00  800.00 1200.00
4-Intro. Electro, the Marvel of the Age
   (ends #19), The Ferret, Mystery Detective
   (ends #9)              300.00  600.00  900.00
5-(Rare)                  600.00 1200.00 1800.00
6,7                       200.00  400.00  600.00
8-Human Torch & Sub-Mariner battle
                          250.00  500.00  750.00
9-Human Torch & Sub-Mariner battle
                          300.00  600.00  900.00
10-Human Torch & Sub-Mariner battle, conclu-
   sion; Terry Vance, the Schoolboy Sleuth
   begins, ends #57       175.00 350.00  525.00
11,12: #12-Kirby cover    100.00 200.00  300.00
13-Intro. & 1st app. The Vision by S&K
                          120.00 240.00  360.00
14,15                      75.00 150.00  225.00
```

```
                             Good   Fine   Mint
16-Intro. & 1st app. Toro, Torch's sidekick
                          75.00 150.00 225.00
17-Human Torch/Sub-Mariner x-over
                          75.00 150.00 225.00
18,19                     60.00 120.00 180.00
20-Origin The Angel in text; last S&K Vision
                          50.00 100.00 150.00
21-Intro. & 1st app. The Patriot; not in
   #46-48                 40.00  80.00 120.00
22-25                     35.00  70.00 105.00
26-30: #27-Kazar ends. #28-Jimmy Jupiter in
   the Land of Nowhere begins, ends #48
                          30.00  60.00  90.00
31-40                     27.00  54.00  81.00
41-48-Last Vision         24.00  48.00  72.00
49-Origin Miss America    30.00  60.00  90.00
50-Mary becomes Miss Patriot,
51-60                     20.00  40.00  60.00
61-70                     17.00  34.00  51.00
71-75: #74-Last Patriot. #75-Young Allies
   begin                  15.00  30.00  45.00
76-81: #76-10 Chapter Miss America serial be-
   gins, ends #85. #79-Last Angel
                          15.00  30.00  45.00
82-Origin Namora; Captain America app.
                          25.00  50.00  75.00
83,85: #83-Last Young Allies. #85-Last Miss
   America                15.00  30.00  45.00
84-Blonde Phantom begins; Captain America
   app.                   20.00  40.00  60.00
86,87,89-Captain America app. in all. Sun-
   girl in #89            14.00  28.00  42.00
88-Human Torch & Sungirl x-over; Captain
   America app.           14.00  28.00  42.00
90,91: #90-Capt. America app. #91-Venus app.,
   Blonde Phantom & Sub-Mariner end
                          14.00  28.00  42.00
92-Origin Human Torch retold; Captain America
   app.; no Sub-Mariner   25.00  50.00  75.00
132pg. issue, B&W (25¢)-1944(?)-printed in
   N.Y.; Square binding, blank inside covers
                         120.00 240.00 360.00
```

MARVELOUS WIZARD OF OZ (M.G.M.'s --)
Nov, 1975 (Oversize) ($1.50)
Marvel Comics Group/National Per. Publ.

```
#1-Adaptation of MGM's movie (See Marvel
   Treasury of --)          .80   1.60   2.40
```

MARVEL PREMIERE
April, 1972 - Present
Marvel Comics Group

```
#1-Origin Warlock by Gil Kane/Dan Adkins
                           1.25   2.50   3.75
2-Warlock ends; Kirby Yellow Claw reprint
```

Marvel Feature #2 (1971), © MCG

Marvel Mystery #11, © MCG

Marvel Mystery #83, © MCG

273

Marvel Premiere #13, © MCG

Marvel's Greatest Comics #35, © MCG

Marvel Spotlight #1, © MCG

(Marvel Premiere cont'd)	Good	Fine	Mint
	1.00	2.00	3.00
3-Dr. Strange series begins, Smith pencils			
	1.50	3.00	4.50
4-Smith art	1.00	2.00	3.00
5-7,9	.60	1.20	1.80
8,10,12,13: Starlin stories. #10-Death of			
the Ancient One	.80	1.60	2.40
11,14: #11-Origin reprint by Ditko. #14-Intro.			
God; Last Dr. Strange	.50	1.00	1.50
15-Iron Fist begins(origin), ends #25			
	1.00	2.00	3.00
16-20	.50	1.00	1.50
21-28: #26-Hercules app. #27-Satana app.			
#28-Legion of Monsters	.30	.60	.90
29,30-Liberty Legion	.25	.50	.75
31-Woodgod	.25	.50	.75
32-Monark Starstalker	.30	.60	.90
33,34-Solomon Kane	.20	.40	.60
35-Origin, 1st app. 3-D Man	.30	.60	.90
36,37- 3-D Man	.20	.40	.60
38-Ploog story	.20	.40	.60
39,40-Torpedo, 41-Seeker 3000, 42-Tiara,			
43-Paladin	.20	.40	.60
44-The Jack of Hearts, 45-Man-Wolf			
	.20	.40	.60

NOTE: *Adams stories(inks)-#10,13. Brunner*
stories-#4,6,9-14; covers-#9-14. Chaykin sto-
ries-#32-34. Kirby covers-#29-31,35. Nino
inks-#38. Ploog cover-#7.

MARVEL PRESENTS
October, 1975 - #12, Aug, 1977
Marvel Comics Group

#1-Bloodstone app.	.50	1.00	1.50
2-Bloodstone app.	.25	.50	.75
3-Guardians of the Galaxy	.25	.50	.75
4-7,9,11,12	.20	.40	.60
8-Reprts. Silver Surfer#2	.25	.50	.75
10-Starlin pencils	.25	.50	.75

MARVEL PREVIEW (Magazine)
1975 - Present (B&W) ($1.00)
Marvel Comics Group

#1-Man Gods From Beyond the Stars; Adams			
cover; Nino art	1.25	2.50	3.75
2-Origin The Punisher & 1st app. Dominic			
Fortune; Morrow cover	.80	1.60	2.40
3-Blade the Vampire	.60	1.20	1.80
4-Star-Lord & Sword in the Star (origins &			
1st app.)	.75	1.50	2.25
5,6-Sherlock Holmes	.75	1.50	2.25
7-Satana, Sword in the Star app.			
	.50	1.00	1.50
8-Legion of Monsters	.50	1.00	1.50
9-Man-God	.50	1.00	1.50

	Good	Fine	Mint
10-Thor the Mighty; Starlin art			
	.70	1.40	2.10
11-Starlord; Starlin art	.60	1.20	1.80
12-Haunt of Horror	.40	.80	1.20
13,14-Starlin covers	.50	1.00	1.50
15-Kaluta cover	.40	.80	1.20

NOTE: *Byrne story-#10. Chaykin story-#2.*
Infantino story-#14. Morrow covers-#2-4.
Ploog art-#8.

MARVEL'S GREATEST COMICS
(Marvel Collectors Item Classics #1-22)
#23, Oct, 1969 - Present
Marvel Comics Group

#23,24-Dr. Strange, Fantastic Four, Iron Man,			
Watcher	.50	1.00	1.50
25-28-Capt. America, Dr. Strange, Iron Man,			
Fantastic Four	.50	1.00	1.50
29-34	.40	.80	1.20
35-Silver Surfer & Fantastic-4 reprts.begin,			
36-50	.30	.60	.90
51-60	.25	.50	.75
61-80: #75,80-Kirby covers	.20	.40	.60

NOTE: *Kirby reprints in all.*

MARVELS OF SCIENCE
March, 1946 - #4, June, 1946
Charlton Comics

#1-(1st Charlton comic)	3.00	6.00	9.00
2-4	2.00	4.00	6.00

MARVEL SPECIAL EDITION (Also see Special Coll-
1975 - Present (84pgs.) ectors' Edition)
Marvel Comics Group (Oversized)

#1-Spider-Man reprints	1.00	2.00	3.00
1-Star Wars(1977)-reprints Star Wars #1-3			
	.70	1.40	2.10
2-Star Wars(1978)-reprints Star Wars #4-6			
	.70	1.40	2.10
3-Star Wars(1978)-reprints Star Wars #1-6			
	.70	1.40	2.10

NOTE: *Chaykin covers/stories-#1(1977),#2.*

MARVEL SPECTACULAR
Aug, 1973 - #19, Nov, 1975
Marvel Comics Group

#1-Thor reprints begin by Kirby			
	.50	1.00	1.50
2-5	.30	.60	.90
6-10	.20	.40	.60
11-19	.15	.30	.45

MARVEL SPOTLIGHT
Nov, 1971 - #33, April, 1977
Marvel Comics Group

(Marvel Spotlight cont'd)　　Good　Fine　Mint
#1-Origin Red Wolf; Wood inks, Adams cover
　　　　　　　　　　1.00　2.00　3.00
2-Venus reprint by Everett; origin Werewolf
　by Ploog; Adams cover　1.00　2.00　3.00
3,4-Werewolf ends #4　　.60　1.20　1.80
5-Origin Ghost Rider　　.70　1.40　2.10
6-8-Last Ploog ish.　　.50　1.00　1.50
9-11-Last Ghost Rider　.40　.80　1.20
12-Origin The Son of Satan - begin series,
13-20　　　　　　　　　.30　.60　.90
21-27: #25-Sinbad. #26-Scarecrow. #27-Sub-
　Mariner　　　　　　　.20　.40　.60
28,29-Moon Night app.　.20　.40　.60
30-The Warriors Three　.20　.40　.60
31-Nick Fury app.　　　.20　.40　.60
32-1st app. Spider-Woman.50　1.00　1.50
33-Deathlok　　　　　　.25　.50　.75
NOTE: *Buscema story-#30. Kirby cover-#29.*
Mooney stories-#8,10(inks),14-17,24. Ploog
stories-#2-8; covers-#2-9.

MARVEL SUPER ACTION　(Magazine)
January, 1976　(One Shot)　(Black & White)
Marvel Comics Group

#1-Origin & 2nd app. Dominic Fortune; The
　Punisher & Weird World app.; The Huntress;
　Evans & Ploog art　.75　1.50　2.25

MARVEL SUPER-ACTION
May, 1977 - Present
Marvel Comics Group

#1-Capt. America reprints by Kirby begin;
　Chaykin story　　　.20　.40　.60
2-5: #4-Marvel Boy reprts..15　.30　.45
6-12　　　　　　　　　　.15　.35

MARVEL SUPER HEROES　(Fantasy Masterpieces)
#12, 12/67 - #31, 11/71　　　　　(#1-11)
#32, Sept, 1972 - Present
Marvel Comics Group

#12-Origin & 1st app. Capt. Marvel of the
　Kree; G.A. Torch, Destroyer, Capt. Ameri-
　ca, Black Knight, Sub-Mariner reprints
　　　　　　　　　　1.50　3.00　4.50
13-G.A. Black Knight, Torch, Vision, Capt.
　America, Sub-Mariner reprints; Capt.
　Marvel app.　　　　.75　1.50　2.25
14-G.A. Sub-Mariner, Torch, Mercury, Black
　Knight, Capt. America reprints; Spider-
　Man app.　　　　　.75　1.50　2.25
15-Black Bolt cameo in Medusa; G.A. Black
　Knight, Sub-Mariner, Black Marvel, Capt.
　America reprints　.75　1.50　2.25
16-Origin & 1st app. Phantom Eagle; G.A.

　　　　　　　　　　　Good　Fine　Mint
　Torch, Capt. America, Bl. Knight, Patriot,
　Sub-Mariner reprints　.50　1.00　1.50
17-Origin Black Knight; G.A. Torch, Sub-
　Mariner, All-Winners Squad reprints
　　　　　　　　　　.50　1.00　1.50
18-Origin Guardians of the Galaxy; G.A. Sub-
　Mariner, All-Winners Squad reprints
　　　　　　　　　　.80　1.60　2.40
19-G.A. Torch, Marvel Boy, Black Knight,
　Sub-Mariner reprints; Smith/Trimple cover
　　　　　　　　　　.60　1.20　1.80
20-G.A. Sub-Mariner, Torch, Capt. America
　reprints; Dr. Doom app. .50　1.00　1.50
21-Avengers, Sub-Mariner, Hulk, X-Men re-
　prints　　　　　　　.50　1.00　1.50
22-Daredevil & X-Men reprt.40　.80　1.20
23-X-Men & Daredevil reprint; new Watcher
　story　　　　　　　.40　.80　1.20
24-Daredevil & X-Men reprt.40　.80　1.20
25-27-Hulk, X-Men & Daredevil reprints
　　　　　　　　　　.40　.80　1.20
28-Daredevil & Iron Man reprints; Iron Man
　origin retold　　.40　.80　1.20
29-31-Iron Man & Daredevil reprints
　　　　　　　　　　.40　.80　1.20
32-40-All Sub-Mariner/Hulk reprints
　　　　　　　　　　.20　.40　.60
41-46,48-50　　　　　.20　.40　.60
47-Starlin cover　　.25　.50　.75
51-55　　　　　　　　.20　.40　.60
56-61-Hulk reprints　.20　.40　.60
62-80　　　　　　　　.15　.30　.45
NOTE: *Everett inks-#14,15. New Kirby covers-*
#22,27.

MARVEL SUPER HEROES SPECIAL
October, 1966
Marvel Comics Group

#1-Reprints origin Daredevil; G.A. Sub-Mari-
　ner & Torch app.　1.50　3.00　4.50

MARVEL SUPER SPECIAL　(See Marvel Comics
Super --)

MARVEL TALES　(Marvel Mystery #1-92)
#93, Aug, 1949 - #159, Aug, 1957
Marvel/Atlas Comics (MCI)

#93　　　　　　　7.00　14.00　21.00
94-Classic Everett story 6.00　12.00　18.00
95,99-101,103,105　3.50　7.00　10.50
96-Bondage cover　4.00　8.00　12.00
97-Sun Girl, 2pgs.　6.00　12.00　18.00
98-Krigstein story　5.00　10.00　15.00
102-Wolverton's End of the World story, 6pgs.
　　　　　　　　10.00　20.00　30.00

Marvel Super-Action #1, © MCG

Marvel Super Heroes #1, © MCG

Marvel Tales #96, © MCG

Marvel Tales #102, © MCG

Marvel Tales #2, © MCG

Marvel Team-Up #3, © MCG

	Good	Fine	Mint
(Marvel Tales cont'd)			
104-Wolverton story	9.00	18.00	27.00
106,107-Krigstein stories	3.50	7.00	10.50
108-121,123-131-Last pre-code issue; #120-			
Jack Katz story	1.75	3.50	5.25
122-Krigstein, Kubert sty.	3.50	7.00	10.50
132,133,135-141,143	1.50	3.00	4.50
134-Krigstein, Kubert sty.	3.50	7.00	10.50
142-Krigstein story	3.00	6.00	9.00
144-Williamson/Krenkel story, 3pgs.			
	3.00	6.00	9.00
145,146,148-151,153-155,158			
	1.00	2.00	3.00
147,156-Torres stories	1.75	3.50	5.25
152-Wood, Morrow art	3.00	6.00	9.00
157,159-Krigstein stories	2.00	4.00	6.00

NOTE: *Sid Check story-#147. Ditko story-#145, 147. Drucker stories-#127,135,146,150. Everett stories-#98,104,106,108,131,151,153; covers-#111,117,127,143,148-151,153. Gil Kane art-#117. Morrow stories-#150,152,156. Orlando stories-#149,151,157. Powell story-#136, 137,154. Whitney story-#107. Wildey story-#126,138.*

MARVEL TALES
1964 - Present
Marvel Comics Group

	Good	Fine	Mint
#1-Origin Spider-Man, Hulk, Ant/Giant Man, Iron Man, Thor & Sgt. Fury-All reprints			
	6.00	12.00	18.00
2-Origin X-Men, Dr. Strange, Avengers, re-printed	3.50	7.00	10.50
3	2.00	4.00	6.00
4,5	1.25	2.50	3.75
6-12,14,15	.70	1.40	2.10
13-Reprints origin Marvel Boy from Marvel Boy #1	.75	1.50	2.25
16-23: Last 68pg. ish.	.50	1.00	1.50
24-30	.40	.80	1.20
31-60	.30	.60	.90
61-70: #63-Mooney story	.25	.50	.75
71-74,76-80	.20	.40	.60
75-Origin Spider-Man reprt.	.20	.40	.60
81-97	.15	.30	.45
98-Death of Gwen Stacy reprt/Amazing Spider-Man #121	.20	.40	.60

NOTE: *#1-12 are reprints.*

MARVEL TEAM-UP
March, 1972 - Present
Marvel Comics Group

	Good	Fine	Mint
#1-Spider-Man, H. Torch	2.50	5.00	7.50
2,3-SpM/H-T x-over	1.20	2.40	3.60

4-10: #4-SpM/X-Men. #5-SpM/Vision. #6-SpM/Thing. #7-SpM/Thor. #8-SpM/The Cat. #9-

	Good	Fine	Mint
SpM/Iron-Man. #10-SpM/Torch			
	.90	1.80	2.70

11-20: #11-SpM/Inhumans. #12-SpM/Werewolf. #13-SpM/Capt. America. #14-SpM/S-M. #15-SpM/Ghost Rider(new). #16-SpM/Capt.Marvel. #17-SpM/Mr. Fantastic. #18-H-T/Hulk. #19-SpM/Ka-Zar. #20-SpM/Black Panther
| | .60 | 1.20 | 1.80 |

21-30: #21-SpM/Dr. Strange. #22-SpM/Hawkeye. #23-H-T/Iceman. #24-SpM/Brother Voodoo. #25-SpM/Daredevil. #26-H-T/Thor. #27-SpM/Hulk. #28-SpM/Hercules. #29-H-T/Iron Man. #30-SpM/Falcon.
| | .60 | 1.20 | 1.80 |

31-40: #31-SpM/Iron Fist. #32-H-T/Son of Satan. #33-SpM/Nighthawk. #34-SpM/Valkyrie. #35-H-T/Dr. Strange. #36-SpM/Frankenstein. #37-SpM/Man-Wolf. #38-SpM/Beast. #39-SpM/H-T. #40-SpM/Sons of the Tiger/H-T
| | .30 | .60 | .90 |

41-50: #41-SpM/Scarlet Witch. #42-SpM/The Vision. #43-SpM/Dr. Doom; retells origin. #44-SpM/Moondragon. #45-SpM/Killraven. #46-SpM/Deathlok. #47-SpM/Thing. #48-SpM/Iron Man. #49,50-SpM/Dr. Strange/Iron Man
| | .25 | .50 | .75 |

51-60: #51-SpM/Dr. Strange/Iron Man. #52-SpM/Capt. America. #53-SpM/Woodgod/Hulk. #54-SpM/Woodgod/Hulk. #55-SpM/Warlock. #56-SpM/Daredevil. #57-SpM/Black Widow. #58-SpM/Ghost Rider. #59-SpM/Yellowjacket/The Wasp. #60-SpM/The Wasp
| | .20 | .40 | .60 |

61-70: #61-SpM/H-T. #62-SpM/Ms. Marvel. #63-SpM/Iron Fist. #64-SpM/Daughters of the Dragon. #65-SpM/Capt. Britain(1st U.S. app.) #66-SpM/Capt. Britain. #67-SpM/Tigra. #68-SpM/Man-Thing. #69-SpM/Havock. #70-SpM/Thor
| | .20 | .40 | .60 |

71-76: #71-SpM/Falcon. #72-SpM/Iron Man. #73-SpM/Daredevil. #74-SpM/Not Ready for Prime Time Players. #75-SpM/Power Man. #76-SpM/Dr. Strange/Ms. Marvel; Chaykin art
	.15	.30	.45
Annual #1(1/77)-X-Men app.	.40	.80	1.20
Annual #2-Starlin art; Thing app.			
	.30	.60	.90

NOTE: *Byrne stories-#53-55,59-70; cover-#71. Kane art in #4-6,13,14,16-19,23. Starlin cover-#27. "H-T" means Human Torch; "SpM" means Spider-Man; "S-M" means Sub-Mariner.*

MARVEL TREASURY EDITION ($1.50)
Sept, 1974 - Present   (100 pgs.) (Oversized)
Marvel Comics Group

	Good	Fine	Mint
#1-Spider-Man reprints	1.50	3.00	4.50
2-Fantastic Four	1.25	2.50	3.75
3-The Mighty Thor	1.25	2.50	3.75

(Marvel Treasury Edition cont'd)

	Good	Fine	Mint
4-Conan-Smith reprints, Smith cover			
	1.50	3.00	4.50
5-The Hulk (origin)	1.25	2.50	3.75
6-Doctor Strange-Brunner cover/art; Ditko art; Adams reprt.inks	1.00	2.00	3.00
7-Avengers-Kirby cover	1.00	2.00	3.00
8-Christmas stories-Spider-Man, Hulk, Nick Fury	1.00	2.00	3.00
9-Super Hero team-up	1.00	2.00	3.00
10-Thor reprints-Kirby	1.00	2.00	3.00
11-Fantastic 4 reprts-Kirby	.80	1.60	2.40
12-Howard the Duck-reprts.	1.20	2.40	3.60
13-Giant Superhero Holiday Grab-Bag			
	.60	1.20	1.80
14-Spider-Man	.80	1.60	2.40
15-Conan-Smith, Buscema, Adams reprints			
	1.00	2.00	3.00
16-The Defenders-origin of The Defenders & Valkyrie	.60	1.20	1.80
17-The Hulk	.60	1.20	1.80
18-Marvel Team-up-Spider-Man's 1st team-ups with the X-Men, Werewolf By Night, Ghost Rider, Iron Fist. All reprints			
	.60	1.20	1.80
19-Conan the Barbarian by Buscema			
	.75	1.50	2.25

MARVEL TREASURY OF OZ (See MGM's Marvelous--)
1975   (Over-Sized) ($1.50)
Marvel Comics Group

#1-The Marvelous Land of Oz; Alcala art			
	1.00	2.00	3.00

MARVEL TREASURY SPECIAL
1974; 1976 (84pgs.) ($1.50) (Over-Sized)
Marvel Comics Group

Vol.1-Spider-Man, Torch, Sub-Mariner, Avengers "Giant Superhero Holiday Grab-Bag;" Smith art	1.00	2.00	3.00
Vol.1-Capt. America's Bicentennial Battles (6/76)-Kirby art; Smith inks			
	1.00	2.00	3.00

MARVEL TRIPLE ACTION
2/72 - #24, 3/75; #25, 8/75 - Present
Marvel Comics Group

#1	1.00	2.00	3.00
2-4	.50	1.00	1.50
5,6,8-10	.40	.80	1.20
7-Starlin cover	.50	1.00	1.50
11-15,17-20	.25	.50	.75
16-Wood inks	.30	.60	.90
21-30	.20	.40	.60

	Good	Fine	Mint
31-46	.15	.30	.45
Giant-Size #1(5/75)	.40	.80	1.20
Giant-Size #2(7/75)	.30	.60	.90

NOTE: *Fantastic Four* reprints-#1-4; *Avengers* reprints-#5 on.

MARVEL TWO-IN-ONE
Jan, 1974 - Present
Marvel Comics Group

#1-Thing team-ups begin	1.00	2.00	3.00
2-4: #2-Kane art	.60	1.20	1.80
5-Guardians of the Galaxy	.50	1.00	1.50
6-Starlin cover	.40	.80	1.20
7-10	.25	.50	.75
11-20	.20	.40	.60
21-48	.15	.30	.45

NOTE: *John Buscema* cover & story-#30. *Kirby* covers-#20,25,27.

Annual #1(6/76)-Liberty Legion x-over; Kirby cover	1.00	2.00	3.00
Annual #2(2/77)-Starlin cover/story			
	.60	1.20	1.80
Annual #3(7/78)-Nova app.	.35	.70	1.05

MARVIN MOUSE
Sept, 1957
Atlas Comics (BPC)

#1-Everett/Maneely art	1.50	3.00	4.50

MARY JANE & SNIFFLES   (See 4-Color #402,474)

MARY MARVEL COMICS (Monte Hale #29 on)(Also see Capt. Marvel #18, Marvel Family, & Shazam)
Dec, 1945 - #28, Sept, 1948
Fawcett Publications

#1	35.00	70.00	105.00
2	16.00	32.00	48.00
3	14.00	28.00	42.00
4	12.00	24.00	36.00
5	9.00	18.00	27.00
6,7	8.00	16.00	24.00
8-Bulletgirl x-over in Mary Marvel			
	8.00	16.00	24.00
9,10	6.00	12.00	18.00
11-20	5.00	10.00	15.00
21-28	4.00	8.00	12.00

MARY POPPINS (See Walt Disney Showcase #17 and Movie Comics)

MARY WORTH (See Love Stories of --)
March, 1956
Argo

#1	2.00	4.00	6.00

Marvel Triple Action #2, © MCG

Marvel Two-In-One #1, © MCG

Mary Marvel Comics #11, © FAW

Mask Of Dr. Fu Manchu, © AVON   Master Comics #26, © FAW   Master Comics #30, © FAW

MASK COMICS
2-3/45 - #2, 4-5/45; #2, Fall, 1945
Rural Home Publications

	Good	Fine	Mint
#1-L. B. Cole cvr/story	6.00	12.00	18.00
2-Black Rider, The Boy Magician & The Collector; L.B.Cole cover	5.00	10.00	15.00
2(Fall,'45)-No Publ.-same as regular #2; L.B. Cole cover	3.00	6.00	9.00

MASKED BANDIT, THE
1952
Avon Periodicals

No#-Kinstler art	3.50	7.00	10.50

MASKED MARVEL
Sept, 1940 - #3, Dec, 1940
Centaur Publications

#1-The Masked Marvel begins			
	25.00	50.00	75.00
2,3	15.00	30.00	45.00

MASKED RAIDER, THE (See Blue Bird)
June, 1955 - #30, June, 1961
Charlton Comics

#1	1.20	2.40	3.60
2-10	.50	1.00	1.50
11-14,16-30: #22-Rocky Lane app.			
	.30	.60	.90
15-Williamson story, 7pgs.	2.00	4.00	6.00

MASKED RANGER
April, 1954 - #9, Aug, 1955
Premier Magazines

#1-Woodbridge story; two Sid Check stories			
	3.00	6.00	9.00
2,3-Crimson Avenger app.	1.60	3.20	4.80
4-8-All Woodbridge	2.00	4.00	6.00
9-Torres story	2.50	5.00	7.50

NOTE: *Woodbridge covers/stories-#1,4-8.*

MASK OF DR. FU MANCHU, THE (See Dr. Fu Manchu)
1951
Avon Periodicals

#1-Wood cover + 26 pgs.	120.00	240.00	360.00

MASQUE OF THE RED DEATH (See Movie Classics)

MASTER COMICS (#1-6 over-sized issues)
March, 1940 - #133, April, 1953
Fawcett Publications

#1-Origin Masterman; The Devil's Dagger, El

	Good	Fine	Mint
Carim, Master of Magic, Rick O'Say, Morton Murch, White Rajah, Shipwreck Roberts, Frontier Marshall, Streak Sloan, Mr. Clue begin.(All features end #6)			
	120.00	300.00	480.00
2	50.00	125.00	200.00
3-5	30.00	75.00	120.00
6-Last Masterman	30.00	60.00	90.00
7-(10/40)-Bulletman, Zorro, the Mystery Man (ends #22), Lee Granger, Jungle King, & Buck Jones begin; only app. The War Bird & Mark Swift & the Time Retarder			
	60.00	120.00	180.00
8-The Red Gaucho(ends #13), Captain Venture(ends #22) & The Planet Princess begin			
	30.00	60.00	90.00
9,10: #10-Lee Granger ends			
	25.00	50.00	75.00
11-Origin Minute-Man	55.00	110.00	165.00
12	35.00	70.00	105.00
13-Origin Bulletgirl	50.00	100.00	150.00
14-16: #14-Companions Three begin, ends #31			
	30.00	60.00	90.00
17-20: #17-Raboy art on Bulletman begins			
	35.00	70.00	105.00
21-(Scarce)-Captain Marvel x-over in Bulletmanp Capt. Nazi origin			
	150.00	300.00	450.00
22-Captain Marvel Jr. x-over in Bulletman; Capt. Nazi app.	125.00	250.00	375.00
23-Captain Marvel Jr. begins, vs. Capt. Nazi			
	90.00	180.00	270.00
24,25,29	35.00	70.00	105.00
26-28,30-Captain Marvel Jr. vs. Capt. Nazi			
	35.00	70.00	105.00
31,32: #32-Last El Carim & Buck Jones. Balbo, the Boy Magician intro. in El Carim			
	25.00	50.00	75.00
33-Balbo, the Boy Magician(ends #47), Hopalong Cassidy(ends #49) begins			
	25.00	50.00	75.00
34-Capt. Marvel Jr. vs. Capt. Nazi			
	25.00	50.00	75.00
35	25.00	50.00	75.00
36-40	20.00	40.00	60.00
41-Bulletman, Capt. Marvel Jr. & Bulletgirl x-over in Minute-Man; only app. Crime Crusaders Club(Capt. Marvel Jr., Minute-Man, Bulletman & Bulletgirl)-Only team in Fawcett Comics	16.50	33.25	50.00
42-49: #48-Intro. Bulletboy; Capt. Marvel cameo in Minute-Man. #49-Last Minute-Man			
	12.00	24.00	36.00
50-Radar, Nyoka the Jungle Girl begin. Capt. Marvel x-over in Radar; origin Radar			
	8.00	16.00	24.00
51-58	4.00	8.00	12.00

278

(Master Comics cont'd)	Good	Fine	Mint
59-62: Nyoka serial "Terrible Tiara" in all; #61-Capt. Marvel Jr. 1st meets Uncle Marvel	5.00	10.00	15.00
63-80	4.00	8.00	12.00
81-100: #88-Hopalong Cassidy begins(ends #94). #95-Tom Mix begins(ends #133)	3.00	6.00	9.00
101-106-Last Bulletman	2.50	5.00	7.50
107-133	2.00	4.00	6.00

NOTE: _Mac Raboy_ stories-#17-39,40 in part, 42; covers-#21-49,52,56,58,59.

MASTER DETECTIVE
1964   (Reprint)
Super Comics

#10,17(Young King Cole), #18	.50	1.00	1.50

MASTER OF KUNG FU (Formerly Spec. Marvel Ed.)
#17, April, 1974 - Present
Marvel Comics Group

#17-Starlin art	.70	1.40	2.10
18-20: #19-Man-Thing app.	.60	1.20	1.80
21-23,25-30	.50	1.00	1.50
24-Starlin art	.60	1.20	1.80
31-40	.40	.80	1.20
41-50	.30	.60	.90
51-53,55-60	.25	.50	.75
54-Starlin cover	.30	.60	.90
61-73	.15	.30	.45
Giant Size #1(9/74)	.70	1.40	2.10
Giant Size #2-4(6/75): #4-Reprints 2 Kirby stys/Yellow Claw #2	.50	1.00	1.50
Annual #1(4/76)-Iron Fist	.50	1.00	1.50

NOTE: _Gulacy_ stories-#18-20,25-27,29-31,33-35,39,40,42-50; covers-#51,64,67.

MASTERS OF TERROR (Magazine)
July, 1975 - #2, 1975   (Black & White)
Marvel Comics Group

#1-Brunner, Smith art; Morrow cover; Adams reprint inks; Starlin pencils; Gil Kane art	.60	1.20	1.80
2	.40	.80	1.20

MASTER OF THE WORLD (See 4-Color #1157)

MATT SLADE GUNFIGHTER (Kid Slade #5 on)
May, 1956 - #4, Nov, 1956
Atlas Comics (SPI)

#1-Williamson/Torres art	3.00	6.00	9.00
2-Williamson story	2.50	5.00	7.50
3,4	1.00	2.00	3.00

MAUD
1906   (32pgs. in color) (10x15½")
Frederick A. Stokes Co.   (Cardboard covers)

	Good	Fine	Mint
By Fred Opper	15.00	37.50	60.00

MAVERICK (TV)
1958 - #19, Apr-June, 1962
Dell Publishing Co.

4-Color #892,930,945,962,980,1005	1.25	2.50	3.75
#7-19	.80	1.60	2.40

MAVERICK MARSHAL
Nov, 1958 - #7, May, 1960
Charlton Comics

#1	.40	.80	1.20
2-7	.25	.50	.75

MAX BRAND (See Silvertip)

MAYA (See Movie Classics)
March, 1968
Gold Key

#1(10218-803)(TV)	.30	.60	.90

MAZIE (-- & Her Freinds)(See Tastee-Freez)
1950 - 1958
Mazie Comics(Magazine Publ.)/Harvey Publ.

#1	1.00	2.00	3.00
2-10	.50	1.00	1.50
11-28	.25	.50	.75

MAZIE (5¢)
1950 - 1951   (5x7¼"-Miniature)
Nation Wide Publishers

#1-7	.50	1.00	1.50

McCRORY'S TOYLAND BRINGS YOU SANTA'S PRIVATE EYES
1956   (16 pgs.)
Promotional Publ. Co.   (Giveaway)

Has 9-pg. story + 7pgs. toy ads	.60	1.20	1.80

McHALE'S NAVY (TV) (See Movie Classics)
May-July, 1963 - #3, Nov-Jan, 1963-64
Dell Publishing Co.

#1-3	.25	.50	.75

Master Comics #104, © FAW

Matt Slade Gunfighter #1, © MCG

Maverick Marshal #1, © CC

Meet Corliss Archer #2, © FOX   Mel Allen's Sports Comics #5, © STD   Menace #5, © MCG

McKEEVER & THE COLONEL (TV)
Feb-Apr, 1963 - #3, Aug-Oct, 1963
Dell Publishing Co.

	Good	Fine	Mint
#1-3	.20	.40	.60

McLINTOCK (See Movie Comics)

MD
April-May, 1955 - #5, Dec-Jan, 1955-56
E.C. Comics

| #1-Not approved by code | 4.00 | 8.00 | 12.00 |
| 2-5 | 3.50 | 7.00 | 10.50 |

NOTE: *Crandall, Evans, Ingels, Orlando* stories in all issues; *Craig* covers-#1-5.

MEDAL OF HONOR COMICS
Spring, 1946
A. S. Curtis

| #1 | 2.00 | 4.00 | 6.00 |

MEET ANGEL (Formerly Angel & the Ape)
#7, Nov-Dec, 1969
National Periodical Publications

| #7 | .15 | .30 | .45 |

MEET CORLISS ARCHER (My Life #4 on)
March, 1948 - #3, July, 1948
Fox Features Syndicate

#1-Feldstein cover/art	15.00	30.00	45.00
2-Feldstein cover only	10.00	20.00	30.00
3-Part Feldstein cover only; #1-3 used in Seduction of the Innocent, pg. 39			
	8.00	16.00	24.00

MEET HERCULES (See Three Stooges)

MEET MERTON
1954 - #4, June, 1954
Toby Press

#1-Dave Berg art	.80	1.60	2.40
2-4: Dave Berg art	.40	.80	1.20
IW Reprint #9	.30	.60	.90
Super Reprint #11('63),18	.25	.50	.75

MEET MISS BLISS
May, 1955 - #3, Sept, 1955
Atlas Comics (LMC)

| #1 | 1.25 | 2.50 | 3.75 |
| 2,3 | 1.00 | 2.00 | 3.00 |

MEET MISS PEPPER (Formerly Lucy --)

#5, April, 1954 - #6, June, 1954
St. John Publishing Co.

	Good	Fine	Mint
#5-Kubert/Maurer art	7.00	14.00	21.00
6-Kubert art	6.00	12.00	18.00

MEL ALLEN'S SPORTS COMICS
#5, Nov, 1949 - #6, Jan, 1950?
Standard Comics

| #5-Tuska art | 1.00 | 2.00 | 3.00 |
| 6 | .70 | 1.40 | 2.10 |

MELVIN MONSTER
April-June, 1965 - #10, Oct, 1969
Dell Publishing Co.

| #1-by John Stanley | 1.50 | 3.00 | 4.50 |
| 2-10-All by Stanley | 1.00 | 2.00 | 3.00 |

MELVIN THE MONSTER (Dexter the Demon #6 on)
July, 1956 - #5, June, 1957
Atlas Comics (HPC)

| #1-5 | .50 | 1.00 | 1.50 |

MENACE
March, 1953 - #11, May, 1954
Atlas Comics (HPC)

#1-Everett story	2.50	5.00	7.50
2-4,6-Everett stories	1.50	3.00	4.50
5-Origin & 1st app. The Zombie by Everett (reprinted in Tales of Zombie #1)(7/53)			
	1.50	3.00	4.50
7,8,10,11	1.25	2.50	3.75
9-Everett story reprinted in Vampire Tales			
#1	1.50	3.00	4.50

NOTE: *Everett* covers-#1,2,5. *Heath* stories-#1-8. *Powell* art-#11.

MEN AGAINST CRIME (Also see Mr. Risk)
1950 - #7, Oct, 1951
Ace Magazines

| #1 | 1.25 | 2.50 | 3.75 |
| 2-7: #2,3-Mr. Risk app. | .70 | 1.40 | 2.10 |

MEN FROM PACIFIC PLANTRONICS, THE
(See Business Week --)

MEN, GUNS, & CATTLE (See Classics Special)

MEN IN ACTION (Battle Brady #10 on)
April, 1952 - #9, Dec, 1952
Atlas Comics (IPS)

| #1 | 1.20 | 2.40 | 3.60 |

(Men in Action cont'd)	Good	Fine	Mint
2-6,8,9	.70	1.40	2.10
7-Krigstein story	2.00	4.00	6.00

MEN IN ACTION
1957 - 1958
Ajax/Farrell Publications

#1	.80	1.60	2.40
2-9	.50	1.00	1.50

MEN INTO SPACE (See 4-Color Comics #1083)

MEN OF BATTLE (See New --)

MEN OF WAR
August, 1977 - Present
DC Comics, Inc.

#1-Origin Gravedigger, cont'd. in #2			
	.20	.40	.60
2-13	.15	.30	.45

NOTE: *Chaykin story-#9. Kubert covers-#2-11.*

MEN'S ADVENTURES (Formerly True Adventures)
#4, Aug, 1950 - #28, July, 1954
Marvel/Atlas Comics (CCC)

#4(#1)	2.00	4.00	6.00
5-10	1.25	2.50	3.75
11-20	1.00	2.00	3.00
21,22,24-26	1.25	2.50	3.75
23-Crandall art	2.00	4.00	6.00
27,28-Captain America, Human Torch, & Sub-			
Mariner app. in ea.	12.00	24.00	36.00

NOTE: *Everett story-#10,25; cover-#22. Adventure-#4-10; War-#11-20; Horror-#21-26.*

MEN WHO MOVE THE NATION
(Giveaway - Black & White)

Neal Adams art	1.50	3.00	4.50

MERLIN JONES AS THE MONKEY'S UNCLE (See Movie Comics & The Misadventures of -- under Movie Comics)

MERRILL'S MARAUDERS (See Movie Classics)

MERRY CHRISTMAS, A
1948 (No#) (Giveaway)
K.K. Publications (Child Life Shoes)

	2.00	4.00	6.00

MERRY CHRISTMAS (See Donald Duck --, Dell Giant #39, & March of Comics #153)

MERRY CHRISTMAS FROM MICKEY MOUSE
1939 (16 pgs.)(Color & B&W)
K.K. Publications (Shoe store giveaway)

	Good	Fine	Mint
Donald Duck & Pluto app.; text with art			
(Rare)	125.00	250.00	375.00

MERRY CHRISTMAS FROM SEARS TOYLAND
1939 (16 pgs.) (In Color)
Sears Roebuck Giveaway

Dick Tracy, Little Orphan Annie, The Gumps,			
Terry & the Pirates	15.00	30.00	45.00

MERRY COMICS
December, 1945
Carlton Publishing Co.

No#-Boogeyman app.	1.35	2.75	4.00

MERRY COMICS
1947
Four Star Publications

#1	1.00	2.00	3.00

MERRY-GO-ROUND COMICS
1944(132pgs.)(25¢); 1946; Sept-Oct, 1947
LaSalle Publ. Co./Croyden Publ./Rotary Litho.

#1(1944)(LaSalle)	2.75	5.50	8.00
#21	1.35	2.75	4.00
#1(1946-Croyden)	1.00	2.00	3.00
V1#1(9-10/47-52pgs.)(Rotary Litho. Co. Ltd.,			
Canada)	1.00	2.00	3.00

MERRY MAILMAN
1955
Charlton Comics

#1	.65	1.35	2.00

MERRY MOUSE
June, 1953 - #4, Jan-Feb, 1954
Avon Periodicals

#1-4	1.00	2.00	3.00

METAL MEN (See Showcase & Brave & the Bold)
4-5/63 - #41, 12-1/69-70; #42, 2-3/73 - #44,
7-8/73; #45, 4-5/76 - #56, 2-3/78
National Periodical Publications/DC Comics

#1	2.50	5.00	7.50
2	1.50	3.00	4.50
3-5	1.25	2.50	3.75
6-10	.80	1.60	2.40
11-26	.50	1.00	1.50

Men's Adventures #5, © MCG

Merry Christmas From M.M.('39), © WDP

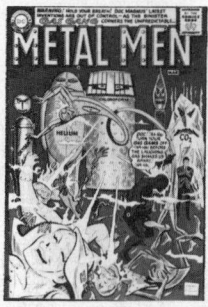

Metal Men #6, © DC

Metamorpho #8, © DC

Mickey Mouse #4('34, McKay), © WDP

Mickey Mouse Four Color #79, © WDP

(Metal Men cont'd)	Good	Fine	Mint
27-Origin Metal Men	.60	1.20	1.80
28-41(1970)	.30	.60	.90
42-44(1973)-Reprints	.20	.40	.60
45('76)-49-Simonson art in all			
	.30	.60	.90
50-56	.20	.40	.60

NOTE: _Kane_ stories/covers-#30,31. _Staton_ stories-#52-56.

METAMORPHO (See Brave & the Bold, Action, First Issue Special, & World's Finest)
July-Aug, 1965 - #17, Mar-Apr, 1968
National Periodical Publications

#1	1.50	3.00	4.50
2-5	.80	1.60	2.40
6-9	.60	1.20	1.80
10-Origin & 1st app. Element Girl(1-2/67)			
	.60	1.20	1.80
11-17	.40	.80	1.20

NOTE: _Orlando_ story pencils-#5-11; covers-#5-9,11.

METEOR COMICS
Nov, 1945
L. L. Baird (Croyden)

#1-Captain Wizard, Impossible Man, Race Wilkins app.; origin Baldy Bean, Capt. Wizard's sidekick   4.00   8.00   12.00

MGM'S MARVELOUS WIZARD OF OZ (See Marvelous--)

MICKEY AND DONALD IN VACATIONLAND (See Dell Giant #47)

MICKEY & THE BEANSTALK (See Story Hour Series)

MICKEY & THE SLEUTH (See Walt Disney Showcase #38,39)

MICKEY FINN
1942 - 1952
McNaught Syndicate #5 on (Columbia)

#1	7.00	14.00	21.00
2	3.50	7.00	10.50
3-Charlie Chan app.	2.50	5.00	7.50
4	2.00	4.00	6.00
5-15(1949)	1.25	2.50	3.75
V3#1,2(1952)	1.25	2.50	3.75

MICKEY MOUSE
1931 - 1934 (48pgs.)(10x9-3/4")(Cardboard cvrs)
David McKay Publications

#1('31)	100.00	200.00	300.00

	Good	Fine	Mint
2('32)	80.00	160.00	240.00
3('33)-All color Sunday reprints; pgs.#5-17, #32-48 reissued in Whitman #948			
	120.00	240.00	360.00
4('34)	70.00	140.00	210.00

NOTE: _Each book reprints strips from previous year - dailies in B&W in #1,2,4; Sundays in color in #3. Later reprints exist; i.e., #2 (1934)._

MICKEY MOUSE
1933 (Copyright date, printing date unknown)
30 pgs.; 10x8-3/4"; Cardboard covers
Whitman Publishing Co.

#948-1932 Sunday strips in color
NOTE: Some copies were bound with a second front cover upside-down instead of the regular back cover; both covers have the same art, but different right & left margins.
   100.00   200.00   300.00
NOTE: _The above book is an exact, but abbreviated reissue of David McKay #3 but with ½" of border trimmed from the top and bottom._

MICKEY MOUSE (See Cheerios giveaways, 40 Big Pages --, Merry Christmas From --, & The Best of Walt Disney Comics)

MICKEY MOUSE (-- Secret Agent #107-109)
1941 - Present
Dell Publishing Co./Gold Key #85 on

4-Color #16(1941)-1st M.M. comic book-"vs. the Phantom Blot" by Gottfredson
   350.00   875.00   1400.00
   (Prices vary widely on this book)
4-Color #27(1943)-"7 Colored Terror"
   55.00   110.00   165.00
4-Color #79(1945)-By Carl Barks(1 story)
   80.00   160.00   240.00

4-Color #116(1946)	12.00	24.00	36.00
4-Color #141(1947)	12.00	24.00	36.00
4-Color #157('47),170,181,194('48)			
	10.00	20.00	30.00
4-Color #214('49),231,248,261			
	7.00	14.00	21.00

4-Color #268-Reprints/WDC&S #22-24 by Gottfredson (Surprise Visitor)
   7.00   14.00   21.00

4-Color #279,286,296	6.00	12.00	18.00
4-Color #304,313(#1),325(#2),334			
	5.00	10.00	15.00
4-Color #343,352,362,371,387			
	4.50	9.00	13.50
4-Color #401,411,427('52)	3.50	7.00	10.50

(Mickey Mouse cont'd)

	Good	Fine	Mint
4-Color #819-M.M. in Magicland	1.50	3.00	4.50
4-Color #1057,1151,1246(1959-61)-Album	1.00	2.00	3.00
#28-32,34	1.25	2.50	3.75
33-(Exists with 2 dates, 10-11/53 & 12-1/54)	1.25	2.50	3.75
35-50	.80	1.60	2.40
51-80	.60	1.20	1.80
81-99: #93,95-titled "Mickey Mouse Club Album"	.50	1.00	1.50
100-105: Reprints 4-Color #427,194,279,170, 343,214 in that order	1.20	2.40	3.60
106-130	.40	.80	1.20
131-146	.30	.60	.90
147-Reprints "The Phantom Fires" from WDC&S #200-202	.70	1.40	2.10
148-Reprints "The Mystery of Lonely Valley" from WDC&S #208-210	.70	1.40	2.10
149-158	.25	.50	.75
159-Reprints "The Sunken City" from WDC&S #205-207	.50	1.00	1.50
160-170: #162-170-reprints	.20	.40	.60
171-194 (#179, 52pgs.)	.15	.30	.45
Album #01-518-210(Dell), #1(10082-309)(9/63- Gold Key)	.60	1.20	1.80
Almanac #1('57)-Barks art	5.00	10.00	15.00
--& Goofy Explore Energy(1976, Walt Disney Educational Media)	.25	.50	.75
--& Goofy "Bicep Bungle"(1952, 14pgs.) Fritos giveaway	2.00	4.00	6.00
--& Goofy Explore Energy(1976-1978) 36pg. Exxon Giveaway in color-reg. size	.15	.30	.45
--& Goofy Explore Energy Conservation(1976- 1978)-Exxon	.15	.30	.45
Birthday Party #1('53)(25th Anniversary) Reprints entire 48 pgs. of Gottfredson's "M.M. in Love Trouble" from WDC&S #36-39. Quality equal to original. Also reprints one story each from 4-Color #27,79 & 181 plus 6 panels of highlights in the career of M.M.	14.00	28.00	42.00
Club #1(1/64-G.K.)(TV)	1.20	2.40	3.60
Club Parade #1(12/55)-Reprints 4-Color #16 with some art redrawn & recolored with night scenes turned into day; quality much poorer than original	7.00	14.00	21.00
In Fantasy Land #1('57)	2.00	4.00	6.00
In Frontier Land #1('56)-M.M. Club ish.	2.00	4.00	6.00
Mini Comic #1(1976)(3¼x6½")Reprints #158	.15	.30	.45
Surprise Party #1(30037-901, G.K.)(1/69) 40th Anniversary	1.00	2.00	3.00

MICKEY MOUSE BOOK
1930   (2 printings)
Bibo & Lang

	Good	Fine	Mint
Very 1st Disney book; origin of Mickey Mouse (1st Printing)	200.00	400.00	600.00

MICKEY MOUSE CLUB MAGAZINE(See Walt Disney--)

MICKEY MOUSE CLUB SPECIAL
Oct, 1977   (224 pgs.)
Gold Key

#1	.60	1.20	1.80

MICKEY MOUSE MAGAZINE
Vol.1#1, Jan, 1933 - Vol.1#9, Sept, 1933
#1-3 published by Kamen-Blair(Kay Kamen, Inc.)
Walt Disney Productions

(Very Rare)-Distributed by leading stores
thru their local theatres. 1st few issues
had 5¢ listed on the cover, later ones had
no price.

V1#1	150.00	300.00	450.00
2-9	70.00	140.00	210.00

MICKEY MOUSE MAGAZINE
V1#1, Nov, 1933 - V2#12, Oct, 1935
Mills giveaways issued by different dairies
Walt Disney Productions

V1#1	30.00	60.00	90.00
2-12	15.00	30.00	45.00
V2#1-12	12.00	24.00	36.00

MICKEY MOUSE MAGAZINE   (No V3#1)
(Becomes Walt Disney's Comics & Stories)
Summer, 1935 - V5#12, Sept, 1940
K.K. Publications

V1#1-John Stanley cover & interior art	80.00	160.00	240.00
2	40.00	80.00	120.00
3	20.00	40.00	60.00
4-6	15.00	30.00	45.00
7-9	12.00	24.00	36.00
10-12	10.00	20.00	30.00
V2#1-9,11-13: Gottfredson Mickey Mouse (B&W) reprints begin #?	9.00	18.00	27.00
10-1st Mickey Mouse in four color	10.00	20.00	30.00
V3#2-12-(Gottfredson Mickey Mouse reprints begin V3#?)	9.00	18.00	27.00
V4#1-12	9.00	18.00	27.00
V5#1-8	15.00	30.00	45.00
9-Regular comic book size begins	25.00	50.00	75.00

Mickey Mouse Four Color #296, © WDP

Mickey Mouse Book 1930, © WDP

Mickey Mouse Mag. V2#13, © WDP

Midnight #2, © AJAX

Midnight Tales #1, © CC

Mighty Comics #40, © AP

(Mickey Mouse Mag. cont'd)	Good	Fine	Mint
10,11	30.00	60.00	90.00

12-(Rare)-The transition issue that changed
the magazine into a comic book; strip
reprints   175.00 437.50 700.00

| V4#1 (Giveaway) | 12.00 | 24.00 | 36.00 |

NOTE: *#1-9 sold 150,000 copies per month;
#10 on sold 500,000 per month.*

MICKEY MOUSE MARCH OF COMICS
1947 - 1951   (Giveaway)
K.K. Publications

#8(1947)-32pgs.	50.00	100.00	150.00
27(1948)	30.00	60.00	90.00
45(1949)	25.00	50.00	75.00
60(1950)	20.00	40.00	60.00
74(1951)	12.00	24.00	36.00

MICKEY MOUSE SUMMER FUN   (Summer Fun #2)
1958
Dell Publishing Co.

| #1 | 2.00 | 4.00 | 6.00 |

MICKEY MOUSE'S SUMMER VACATION   (See Story
Hour Series)

MICROBOTS, THE
Dec, 1971   (One Shot)
Gold Key

| #1(10271-112) | .15 | .30 | .45 |

MICRONAUTS, THE
Feb, 1979 - Present
Marvel Comics Group

| #1 | .15 | .30 | .45 |

MIDGET COMICS   (Fighting Indian Stories)
Feb, 1950 - #2, Apr, 1950   (5-3/8x7-3/8")
St. John Publishing Co.

#1-Matt Baker cover	1.50	3.00	4.50
2-Tex West, Cowboy Marshall			
	1.25	2.50	3.75

MIDNIGHT
1957 - #6, June, 1958
Ajax/Farrell Publ. (Four Star Comic Corp.)

#1-Reprints from Voodoo & Strange Fantasy			
with some changes	1.00	2.00	3.00
2-6	.60	1.20	1.80

MIDNIGHT MYSTERY
Jan-Feb, 1961 - #7, Oct, 1961
American Comics Group

	Good	Fine	Mint
#1	.70	1.40	2.10
2-7	.40	.80	1.20

MIDNIGHT TALES
Dec, 1972 - #18, May, 1976
Charlton Press

V1#1	.20	.40	.60
2-10,15-18		.15	.35
11-14-Newton stories	.15	.30	.45
#17(Modern Comics reprint, 1977)	.15	.30

NOTE: *Howard stories(Wood imitator)-#1-12,14,
15,17,18; covers-#1-18.*

MIGHTY ATOM (-- & the Pixies #6)(Formerly
The Pixies #1-5)
#6, 1949; Nov, 1957 - #6, Aug-Sept, 1958
Magazine Enterprises

#6(1949-M.E.)No month(1st Series)			
	1.00	2.00	3.00
#1-6(2nd Series)-Pixies reprints			
	.75	1.50	2.25
IW Reprint #1(no date)	.40	.80	1.20
Giveaway('59)-Evans art	1.50	3.00	4.50

MIGHTY BEAR (Formerly Fun Comics)
#13, Jan, 1954 - #14, Mar, 1954; 1957
Star Publ.#13,14/Ajax-Farrell(Four Star)

#13,14	.40	.80	1.20
No#(1957)(Ajax)	.30	.60	.90
#2(11/57)Four Star(Ajax)	.30	.60	.90

MIGHTY COMICS (-- Presents)(Formerly Flyman)
#40, Nov, 1966 - #50, Oct, 1967
Radio Comics (Archie)

#40-Web	.50	1.00	1.50
41-Shield, Black Hood	.50	1.00	1.50
42-Black Hood	.50	1.00	1.50
43-Shield & Web	.50	1.00	1.50
44-Black Hood, Steel Sterling & The Shield			
	.50	1.00	1.50
45-Shield & Hangman	.50	1.00	1.50
46-Steel Sterling & Web	.50	1.00	1.50
47-Bl. Hood & Mr. Justice	.50	1.00	1.50
48-Shield & Hangman; Wizard x-over in Shield			
	.50	1.00	1.50
49-Steel Sterling & Fox; Black Hood x-over			
in Steel Sterling	.50	1.00	1.50
50-Black Hood & Web; Inferno x-over in Web			
	.50	1.00	1.50

MIGHTY CRUSADERS, THE
Nov, 1965 - #7, Oct, 1966
Mighty Comics Group(Radio Comics)(Archie)

284

(Mighty Crusaders cont'd)

	Good	Fine	Mint
#1-Origin The Shield	1.50	3.00	4.50
2-Origin Comet	1.00	2.00	3.00
3-Origin Fly-Man	.75	1.50	2.25
4-Fireball, Inferno, Firefly, Web, Fox, Bob Phantom, Blackjack, Hangman, Zambini, Kardak, Steel Sterling, Mr. Justice, Wizard, Capt.Flag, Jaguar x-over	1.00	2.00	3.00
5-Intro. Ultra-Men(Fox, Web, Capt. Flag) & Terrific Three(Jaguar, Mr. Justice Steel Sterling)	.75	1.50	2.25
6,7: #7-Steel Sterling feature; origin Fly-Girl	.75	1.50	2.25

MIGHTY GHOST
#4, 1958
Ajax/Farrell Publ.

#4	.40	.80	1.20

MIGHTY HERCULES, THE (TV)
July, 1963 - #2, Oct, 1963
Gold Key

#1,2(10072-307,311)	.40	.80	1.20

MIGHTY HEROES, THE (TV) (Funny)
Mar, 1967 - #4, July, 1967
Dell Publishing Co.

#1-Reprints 1957 Heckle & Jeckle	.20	.40	.60
2,3	.15	.30	
4-Two 1958 Mighty Mouse reprints	.20	.40	.60

MIGHTY MARVEL WESTERN, THE
10/68 - #46, 9/76 (#1-14,68pgs; #15,16,52pgs)
Marvel Comics Group

#1-Begin Kid Colt, Rawhide Kid, Two-Gun Kid reprints	.25	.50	.75
2-10	.20	.40	.60
11-20	.15	.30	.45
21-30: #24-Kid Colt reprints end. #25-Matt Slade reprints begin	.15	.30	.45
31,33-36,38-46	.15	.30	
32-Origin reprint/Ringo Kid #23; Williamson reprt/Kid Slade #7	.15	.30	.45
37-5pg. Williamson reprint	.15	.30	.45

NOTE: #21-24 Jack Davis reprints. Kirby reprints #1-3,6,9,12,14,16,26,29,32,36,41,43,44; cover-#29. No Matt Slade-#43.

MIGHTY MIDGET COMICS, THE (Miniature)
No Date; Circa 1943 (5"x3-3/4")
Black & White & Red)(Sold 2 for 5¢)

Samuel E. Lowe & Co.

	Good	Fine	Mint
Bulletman #11(1943)	2.50	5.00	7.50
Captain Marvel #11(2 issues; one issue has ad on back for C.M. comics & is believed to be the small comic glued to cover of Capt.Marvel #20)-Golden Arrow, Spysmasher, Ibis, Lance O'Casey x-over	2.50	5.00	7.50
Captain Marvel Jr. #11	2.50	5.00	7.50
Golden Arrow #11	1.50	3.00	4.50
Ibis the Invincible #11	2.00	4.00	6.00
Spy Smasher #11	2.00	4.00	6.00

NOTE: The above books came in a box called "box full of books" and was distributed with other Samuel Lowe puzzles, paper dolls, coloring books, etc. They are not titled Mighty Midget Comics. All have a war bond seal on back cover. These books came in a "Mighty Midget" counter display rack.

Balbo, the Boy Magician #12	2.00	4.00	6.00
Bulletman #12	2.00	4.00	6.00
Commando Yank #12	2.00	4.00	6.00
Dr. Voltz the Human Generator	1.50	3.00	4.50
Lance O'Casey #12	1.75	3.35	5.00
Leatherneck the Marine	1.50	3.00	4.50
Minute Man #12	2.00	4.00	6.00
Mister Q #12	1.50	3.00	4.50
Mr. Scarlet & Pinky #12	2.00	4.00	6.00
Pat Wilton & His Flying Fortress	1.00	2.00	3.00
The Phantom Eagle #12	2.00	4.00	6.00
Tornado Tom-reprints from Cyclone #1-3; origin	2.50	5.00	7.50

MIGHTY MOUSE (See Adventures of --, Dell Giant #43, Giant Comics Edition, March of Comics #205,237,247,257, Oxydol-Dreft, Paul Terry's, & Terry-Toons Comics)

MIGHTY MOUSE (1st Series)
Fall, 1946 - #4, Summer, 1947
Timely/Marvel Comics

#1	8.00	16.00	24.00
2-4	5.00	10.00	15.00

MIGHTY MOUSE (2nd Series)(Paul Terry's--#69-71)
Aug, 1947 - #83, June, 1959
St. John Publishing Co./Pines

#1	6.00	12.00	18.00
2-5	3.00	6.00	9.00
6-10	2.50	5.00	7.50
11-19	1.75	3.50	5.25
20-25(52pgs.)	1.75	3.50	5.25

Mighty Crusaders #4, © AP   Mighty Mouse #5, © Terry Toons

Mighty Mouse #69, © Terry Toons

Mike Barnett #6, © FAW

Military Comics #9, © QUA

Military Comics #34, © QUA

(Mighty Mouse cont'd)	Good	Fine	Mint
26-37	1.25	2.50	3.75
38-45(100pgs.)	2.50	5.00	7.50
46-83	.90	1.80	2.70

Album(No#,date)-Giant Comics Edition, 100pgs. on cover but contains 148 pgs.

		3.50	7.00	10.50
Album #2(11/52-St. John)	3.00	6.00	9.00

Fun Club Magazine #1(Fall,'57-Pines)

		2.00	4.00	6.00

Fun Club Magazine #2-6(Winter '58-Pines)

		1.50	3.00	4.50

3-D #1-1st printing-9/53, stiff covers

(St. John)	6.00	12.00	18.00

3-D #1-2nd printing-10/53-slick, glossy covers, slighty smaller 5.00 10.00 15.00

3-D #2(11/53),#3(12/53)-St. John

		3.50	7.00	10.50

MIGHTY MOUSE ADVENTURES (Advs.of--#2 on, 1st Nov, 1951 Series)
St. John Publishing Co.

#1	4.00	8.00	12.00

MIGHTY MOUSE (TV)(3rd Series)(Formerly Adventures of Mighty Mouse)
#161, Oct, 1964 - #172, Oct, 1968
Gold Key/Dell Publishing Co.

#161(10/64)-#165(9/65)-Gold Key			
	.65	1.35	2.00
#166(3/66)-#172(10/68)Dell	.65	1.35	2.00

MIGHTY SAMSON
7/64 - #20, 11/67; #21, 8/72 - #31, 3/76
Gold Key

#1-Origin	1.00	2.00	3.00
2-5	.50	1.00	1.50
6-10: #7-Tom Morrow begins, ends #20			
	.40	.80	1.20
11-20	.30	.60	.90
21-31: #21,22-Reprints	.20	.40	.60

MIGHTY THOR (See Thor)

MIKE BARRETT, MAN AGAINST CRIME
1952
Fawcett Publications

#1	1.50	3.00	4.50
2-4,6	1.00	2.00	3.00
5-"Market for Morphine"	5.00	10.00	15.00

MIKE SHAYNE PRIVATE EYE
Nov-Jan, 1962 - #3, Sept-Nov, 1962
Dell Publishing Co.

	Good	Fine	Mint
#1	.60	1.20	1.80
2,3	.40	.80	1.20

MILITARY COMICS (Becomes Modern #44 on)
Aug, 1941 - #43, Oct, 1945
Quality Comics Group

#1-Origin Blackhawk by C. Cuidera, Miss America, The Death Patrol by Jack Cole(also #2-4), & The Blue Tracer by Guardineer; X of the Underground, The Yankee Eagle, Q-Boat & Shot & Shell, Archie Atkins, Loops & Banks by Bud Ernest (Bob Powell) begin

	175.00	350.00	525.00
2-Secret War News begins (by McWilliams #7); Cole art	90.00	180.00	270.00
3-Origin Chop Chop	60.00	120.00	180.00
4	50.00	100.00	150.00
5-The Sniper begins; Miss America in costume #4-7	40.00	80.00	120.00
6-10: #8-X of the Underground begins(ends #13). #9-The Phantom Clipper begins (ends #16)	30.00	60.00	90.00
11	25.00	50.00	75.00
12-Blackhawk by Crandall begins, ends #22	35.00	70.00	105.00
13-15: #14-Private Dogtag begins(ends #83)	25.00	50.00	75.00
16-20: #16-Blue Tracer ends	20.00	40.00	60.00
21-31: #22-Last Crandall Blackhawk	15.00	30.00	45.00
32-43	12.00	24.00	36.00

NOTE: *Crandall stories-#6-38; covers-#13-22. Eisner covers-#9,10,12. Ward Blackhawk-#30, 31(15pgs.each); cover-#29,30.*

MILITARY WILLY
1907 (12pgs.) ½ in color(every other page) (regular comic book format)(stapled)
J. I. Austin Co.

By F. R. Morgan	15.00	30.00	45.00

MILLIE, THE LOVABLE MONSTER
Sept-Nov, 1962 - #6, Jan, 1973
Dell Publishing Co.

#12-523-211, #2(8-10/63)	.25	.50	.75
#3(8-10/64), #4(7/72), #5(10/72), #6(1/73)			
	.15	.30	.45

NOTE: *Woggon stories-#3,6; cover-#3.*

MILLIE THE MODEL (See Modeling With --, A Date With --, & Life With --)
1945 - #207, 1974
Marvel/Atlas/Marvel Comics(SPI/Male/VPI)

(Millie Model cont'd)	Good	Fine	Mint
#1	8.00	16.00	24.00
2	4.00	8.00	12.00
3-7	2.50	5.00	7.50
8,10-Kurtzman's "Hey Look"			
	3.00	6.00	9.00
9-Powerhouse Pepper by Wolverton, 4pgs.			
	6.00	12.00	18.00
11-Kurtzman art	2.00	4.00	6.00
12,15,17-30	1.00	2.00	3.00
13,14,16-Kurtzman's "Hey Look"			
	1.50	3.00	4.50
31-60	.50	1.00	1.50
61-100	.30	.60	.90
101-106,108-207: #192-52pgs..15		.30	.45
107-Jack Kirby app. in story.20		.40	.60
Annual #1(1962)	1.00	2.00	3.00
Annual #2-10(11/71)	.50	1.00	1.50
Queen-Size #11('73), #12(9/74)			
	.25	.50	.75

MILT GROSS FUNNIES
Aug, 1947 - #2, Sept, 1947
Rotary Lithograph Co.

#1,2	3.00	6.00	9.00

MILTON THE MONSTER & FEARLESS FLY (TV)
May, 1966
Gold Key

#1(10175-605)	.15	.30	.45

MINUTE MAN (See Mighty Midget Comics)
1941 - #3, Spring, 1942
Fawcett Publications

#1	35.00	70.00	105.00
2,3	20.00	40.00	60.00

MINUTE MAN
No Date (B&W-16pgs.-paper cover Blue & Red)
Sovereign Service Station giveaway

American history	.60	1.20	1.80

MIRACLE COMICS
Feb, 1940 - #4, March, 1941
Hillman Periodicals

#1-Sky Wizard, Master of Space, Dash Dixon,
Man of Might, Dusty Doyle, Pinkie Parker,
The Kid Cop, K-7, Secret Agent, The Scorp-
ion, & Blandu, Jungle Queen begin; Masked
Angel only app.   15.00 30.00 45.00
2-4: #3-Bill Colt, the Ghost Rider begins.
#4-The Veiled Prophet & Bullet Bob app.
                         10.00 20.00 30.00

MIRACLE OF THE WHITE STALLIONS, THE
(See Movie Comics)

MIRTH OF A NATION
#5, 1941   (Small size)
William Wise & Co. (Harry 'A' Chesler)
                          Good Fine Mint
#5-Art by Harry 'A' Chesler, Jr. + a strip
   called Private Chesler 3.50 7.00 10.50

MIRTHO, THE CLOWN (See Chewing Gum Booklet)

MISADVENTURES OF MERLIN JONES, THE
(See Movie Comics & Merlin Jones as the Monkey's Uncle under Movie Comics)

MISS AMERICA COMICS (Miss America Mag. #2 on)
1944   (One Shot)
Marvel Comics (MAP)

#1	35.00	70.00	105.00

MISS AMERICA MAGAZINE (Formerly Miss America)
V1#2, Nov, 1944 - #98, 1957
Miss America Publ. Corp./Marvel/Atlas(MAP)

V1#2: Photo cover of teenage girl in Miss
America costume; Miss America, Patsy Walk-
er(intro.)comic stories + movie reviews &
stories; intro. Buzz Baxter & Hedy Wolfe
                         35.00 70.00 105.00
3-5-Miss America stories + Patsy Walker			
	12.00	24.00	36.00
6-Patsy Walker only	2.00	4.00	6.00
7-10	1.25	2.50	3.75
11-40: #24-Kamen story	.70	1.40	2.10
41-98	.40	.80	1.20

MISS BEVERLY HILLS OF HOLLYWOOD
Mar-Apr, 1949 - #11, Oct-Nov, 1950
National Periodical Publications

#1	5.00	10.00	15.00
2-11	3.00	6.00	9.00

MISS CAIRO JONES
1945
Croyden Publishers

#1-Bob Oksner daily newspaper reprints
   (1st strip story)   5.00 10.00 15.00

MISS FURY COMICS (Newspaper strip reprints)
Winter, 1942-43 - #8, Winter, 1946
Timely Comics

#1-Origin Miss Fury by Tarpe' Mills(68pgs.)
   in costume w/pin-ups 140.00 280.00 420.00

Millie The Model #26, © MCG

Miss America Magazine #50, © MCG

Miss Beverly Hills #3, © DC

Miss Fury #1, © MCG

Mr. District Attorney #8, © DC

Mister Miracle #2, © DC

(Miss Fury cont'd)	Good	Fine	Mint
2-60pgs.; In costume w/pin-ups			
	75.00	150.00	225.00
3-60pgs.; In costume w/pin-ups			
	60.00	120.00	180.00
4-52pgs.; Costume, 2pgs. w/pin-ups			
	50.00	100.00	150.00
5-52pgs.; In costume w/pin-ups			
	45.00	90.00	135.00
6-52pgs.; Not in costume in inside stories,			
w/pin-ups	30.00	60.00	90.00
7,8-36pgs.; In costume lpg. ea., no pin-ups			
	30.00	60.00	90.00

MISSION IMPOSSIBLE (TV)
May, 1967 - #5, Oct, 1969
Dell Publishing Co.

#1	.40	.80	1.20
2-5	.25	.50	.75

MISS LIBERTY (Becomes Liberty)
1944 (MLJ Reprints)
Burten Publishing Co.

#1-The Shield & Dusty, The Wizard, & Roy, the Super Boy app.; reprint/Shield-Wizard			
#13	8.00	16.00	24.00

MISS MELODY LANE OF BROADWAY
Feb-Mar, 1950 - #4, Sept-Oct, 1950
National Periodical Publications

#1	4.00	8.00	12.00
2-4	2.50	5.00	7.50

MISS PEACH
Oct-Dec, 1963; 1969
Dell Publishing Co.

#1-John Stanley art	1.50	3.00	4.50
--Tells You How to Grow('69,25¢)-Mell Lazarus art; also given away (36pgs.)			
	1.20	2.40	3.60

MISS PEPPER (See Meet Miss Pepper)

MISS SUNBEAM (See Little Miss --)

MISS VICTORY (See Holyoke One-Shot #3)
1945
Holyoke Publishing Co. (Tem)

#1	4.00	8.00	12.00
2	3.00	6.00	9.00

MR. & MRS.
1922 (48 pgs.) (B&W)
Whitman Publishing Co.

	Good	Fine	Mint
By Briggs	6.00	12.00	18.00

MR. & MRS. BEANS (See Single Series #11)

MR. & MRS. J. EVIL SCIENTIST
Nov, 1963 - #6, Oct, 1966 (Hanna-Barbera)
Gold Key

#1(11093-311)	.25	.50	.75
2-6	.15	.30	.45

MR. ANTHONY'S LOVE CLINIC
Nov, 1949 - #5, Apr-May, 1950
Hillman Periodicals

#1	1.75	3.50	5.25
2-5	1.00	2.00	3.00

MR. DISTRICT ATTORNEY
Jan-Feb, 1948 - #67, Jan-Feb, 1959
National Periodical Publications

#1	4.00	8.00	12.00
2-10	2.00	4.00	6.00
11-20	1.50	3.00	4.50
21-40	1.20	2.40	3.60
41-67	.80	1.60	2.40

MR. DISTRICT ATTORNEY (See 4-Color #13)

MISTER ED, THE TALKING HORSE (TV)
Mar-May, 1962 - #6, Feb, 1964
Dell Publishing Co./Gold Key

4-Color #1295	.50	1.00	1.50
#1(11/62)-#6 (G.K.)	.30	.60	.90
(See March of Comics #244,260,282,290)			

MR. MAGOO (TV)(The Nearsighted --, --& Gerald McBoing Boing 1954 issues; formerly Gerald--)
#6, 11-1/53-54; 1963 - 1965
Dell Publishing Co.

#6	1.25	2.50	3.75
4-Color #561,602('54)	1.50	3.00	4.50
4-Color #1235,1305('61)	1.00	2.00	3.00
#3-5(9-11/63)	.60	1.20	1.80
4-Color #1235(12-536-505)(3-5/65)-2nd Printing	.50	1.00	1.50

MISTER MIRACLE (See Cancelled Comic Cavalcade)
Mar-Apr, 1971 - #18, Feb-Mar, 1974; #19, Sept, 1977 - #25, Aug-Sept, 1978
National Periodical Publications/DC Comics

#1	2.00	4.00	6.00
2	1.25	2.50	3.75

(Mister Miracle cont'd)	Good	Fine	Mint
3	1.00	2.00	3.00
4-Boy Commando reprints begin,			
5-Young Scott Free begins	.90	1.80	2.70
6-8	.80	1.60	2.40
9-Origin Mr. Miracle	.80	1.60	2.40
10-14,16,17	.50	1.00	1.50
15-Origin Shilo Norman	.60	1.20	1.80
18-Barda & Scott Free wed; New Gods app.			
	.50	1.00	1.50
19-Adams part inks; Rogers pencils			
	.60	1.20	1.80
20-22-Rogers pencils	.40	.80	1.20
23-25	.15	.30	.45

NOTE: _Heath_ story-#24,25; cover-#25. _Kirby art & covers-#1-18. Rogers_ covers-#19-24. #4-8 contain _Simon & Kirby Boy Commando_ reprints from _Detective_ #82,76, Boy Commandos #1,3, Detective #64 in that order.

MR. MIRACLE (See Holyoke One-Shot #4)

MR. MUSCLES (Formerly Blue Beetle #18-21)
#22, Mar, 1956 - #23, May-June, 1956
Charlton Comics

#22,23	1.00	2.00	3.00

MISTER MYSTERY
Sept, 1951 - #19, Oct, 1954
Mr. Publ.(Media Publ.)#1-3/SPM Publ./
Stanmore (Aragon)

#1-Kurtzman horror story swiped			
	4.00	8.00	12.00
2,4,6: Bondage covers + torture-#6			
	2.50	5.00	7.50
3,5,8	2.00	4.00	6.00
7-"The Brain Bats of Venus" by Wolverton; partially re-used in Weird Tales of the Future #7	20.00	40.00	60.00
9,10-Nostrand art	2.25	4.50	6.75
11-Wolverton "Robot Woman" story/Weird Mysteries #2, cut up, rewritten & partially redrawn	12.00	24.00	36.00
12-Classic injury to eye cover			
	12.00	24.00	36.00
13-15,17,19	1.25	2.50	3.75
16-Bondage cover	2.00	4.00	6.00
18-"Robot Woman" by Wolverton reprinted from Weird Mysteries #2	12.00	24.00	36.00

MISTER Q (See Mighty Midget Comics)

MR. RISK (Formerly All Romances; becomes
Hand of Fate #8 on)(See Men Against Crime)
#7, Oct, 1950 - #2, Dec, 1950
Ace Magazines

	Good	Fine	Mint
#7,2	.80	1.60	2.40

MR. SCARLET & PINKY (See Mighty Midget Comics)

MR. UNIVERSE
1951
Mr. Publications Media Publ.(Stanmore,
Aragon)

#1-Drug story	3.50	7.00	10.50
2,3	1.25	2.50	3.75
4,5-"Goes to War"	1.50	3.00	4.50

MITZI COMICS
Spring, 1948 - #4, Winter, 1948
Timely Comics

#1-Kurtzman's "Hey Look" + 3pgs. "Giggles 'n' Grins"	3.00	6.00	9.00
2-4	1.00	2.00	3.00

MITZI'S BOY FRIEND (Becomes Mitzi's Romances)
#2, June, 1948 - #7, April, 1949
Marvel Comics

#2-7	.75	1.50	2.25

MITZI'S ROMANCES (Formerly Mitzi's Boy --)
#8, Oct, 1949 - #10, Dec, 1949
Timely/Marvel Comics

#8-10	.75	1.50	2.25

MOBY DICK (See 4-Color #717, Feature Presentations #6, & King Classics)

MOBY DUCK (See Walt Disney Showcase #2,11)
10/67 - #11, 10/70; #12, 1/74 - #30, 2/78
Gold Key (Disney)

#1	.80	1.60	2.40
2-5	.50	1.00	1.50
6-15	.30	.60	.90
16-30	.20	.40	.60

MODEL FUN (With Bobby Benson)
#4, Spring, 1955 - #5, July, 1955
Harle Publications

#4,5-Bobby Benson	1.00	2.00	3.00

MODELING WITH MILLIE
1961 - #54, June, 1967
Atlas/Marvel Comics Group (Male Publ.)

#1	1.50	3.00	4.50
2-10	.60	1.20	1.80

Mister Mystery #1, © Stanmore Publ.

Mister Mystery #6, © Stanmore Publ.

Mitzi's Boy Friend #7, © MCG

Modern Comics #86, © QUA

Modern Love #7, © WMG

Molly O'Day #1, © AVON

(Modeling w/Millie cont'd)	Good	Fine	Mint
11-30	.30	.60	.90
31-54	.15	.30	.45

MODERN COMICS (Military #1-43)
#44, Nov, 1945 - #102, Oct, 1950
Quality Comics Group

	Good	Fine	Mint
#44	10.00	20.00	30.00
45-52: #49-1st app. Fear, Lady Adventuress			
	8.00	16.00	24.00
53-Torchy by Ward begins(9/46)			
	12.00	24.00	36.00
54-60	8.00	16.00	24.00
61-80	7.00	14.00	21.00
81-101	6.00	12.00	18.00
102-(Scarce)	8.00	16.00	24.00

NOTE: _Crandall Blackhawk-#46-51,54,56-102._
Ward Blackhawk-#52-53,55 (15pgs. each). Tor-
chy in #53-102; by Ward only in #53-89(9/49).

MODERN LOVE
June-July, 1949 - #8, Aug-Sept, 1950
E.C. Comics

#1	35.00	70.00	105.00
2-Craig/Feldstein cover	25.00	50.00	75.00
3	20.00	40.00	60.00
4-6 (Scarce)	30.00	60.00	90.00
7,8	20.00	40.00	60.00

NOTE: _Feldstein art in most issues._ _Ingels_
art in #1,2,4-7. _Wood story-#7. (Canadian re-_
prints known; See Table of Contents.)

MOD LOVE
1967   (36 pgs.) (50¢)
Western Publishing Co.

#1	.25	.50	.75

MODNIKS, THE
Aug, 1967 - #2, Aug, 1970
Gold Key

#10206-708(#1),2		.15	.30

MOD SQUAD (TV)
Jan, 1969 - #8, April, 1971
Dell Publishing Co.

#1	.25	.50	.75
2-8: #8 reprints #2	.15	.30	.45

MOD WHEELS
March, 1971 - #19, Jan, 1976
Gold Key

#1	.15	.30
2-19	.10	.20

MOE & SHMOE COMICS
Spring, 1948 - #2, Summer, 1948
O. S. Publ. Co.

	Good	Fine	Mint
#1	1.20	2.40	3.60
2	1.00	2.00	3.00

MOLLY MANTON'S ROMANCES (My Love #3)
Sept, 1949 - #2, Nov, 1949
Marvel Comics

#1	1.25	2.50	3.75
2	.75	1.50	2.25

MOLLY O'DAY (Super Sleuth)
Feb, 1945   (1st Avon comic?)
Avon Periodicals

#1-Molly O'Day, The Enchanted Dagger by Tuska (reprt/Yankee #1), Capt'n Courage, Corporal Grant app.	20.00	40.00	60.00

MONKEES, THE (TV)
March, 1967 - #17, Oct, 1969
Dell Publishing Co.

#1	1.00	2.00	3.00
2-17: #17 reprints #1	.50	1.00	1.50

MONKEY & THE BEAR, THE
Sept, 1953 - #3, Jan, 1954
Atlas Comics (ZPC)

#1-3	.40	.80	1.20

MONKEYSHINES COMICS
Summer, 1944 - #26, May, 1949
Ace Periodicals/Publishers Specialists/
Current Books

#1	1.35	2.75	4.00
2-10	1.00	2.00	3.00
11-26	.75	1.50	2.25

MONKEY SHINES OF MARSELEEN
1909   (11½x17") (28 pgs. in 2 colors)
Cupples & Leon Co.

By Norman E. Jennett	12.00	24.00	36.00

MONKEY'S UNCLE, THE (See Movie Comics under Merlin Jones as the --)

MONROES, THE (TV)
April, 1967
Dell Publishing Co.

#1	.15	.30	.45

MONSTER
1953
Fiction House Magazines

	Good	Fine	Mint
#1-Dr. Drew by Grandenetti; reprint from Rangers Comics	4.00	8.00	12.00
2	2.50	5.00	7.50

MONSTER CRIME COMICS (Also see Crime Must
October, 1952   Stop)
Hillman Periodicals

	Good	Fine	Mint
#1 (Scarce)	12.00	24.00	36.00

MONSTER HOWLS (Magazine)
Dec, 1966   (Satire) (35¢) (68 pgs.)
Humor-Vision

#1	.40	.80	1.20

MONSTER HUNTERS
8/75 - #9, 1/77; #10, 10/77 - Present
Charlton Comics

#1-Howard art, Newton cvr.	.20	.40	.60
2-18	.15	.30	.45
#1,2(Modern Comics reprints, 1977)		.15	.30

NOTE: _Ditko_ story-#2. _Sutton_ story-#2,4;
cover-#2,4.

MONSTER OF FRANKENSTEIN (See Frankenstein)

MONSTERS ON THE PROWL (Chamber of Darkness
#1-8) (#13,14-52pgs.)
#9, 2/71 - #27, 11/73; #28, 6/74 - #30, 10/74
Marvel Comics Group

#9-Smith inks	1.00	2.00	3.00
10-13,15	.25	.50	.75
14,17-30-All reprints	.15	.30	.45
16-Kull app.	1.20	2.40	3.60

NOTE: _Kirby_ reprints-#10-17,21,23,25,27,28,
30; covers-#9,25. _Kirby/Ditko_ reprints-#17,
18-20,22,24,26,29. _Marie/John Severin_ art-
#16(Kull). #9-13,15-contain _one new story._
Woodish art by Reese-#11.

MONSTERS UNLEASHED (Magazine)
July, 1973 - #11, April, 1975   (B&W)
Marvel Comics Group

#1-Morrow cover	1.00	2.00	3.00
2-The Frankenstein Monster begins; Brunner reprint	.65	1.35	2.00
3-Adams cover; The Man-Thing begins (origin reprint by Morrow); Adams art	.80	1.60	2.40

	Good	Fine	Mint
4-Intro. Satana, the Devil's daughter; Krigstein reprint	.80	1.60	2.40
5	.75	1.50	2.25
6-Ploog story	.75	1.50	2.25
7-Williamson reprint	.75	1.50	2.25
8-Adams reprint	.60	1.20	1.80
9-1st app. Wendigo	.50	1.00	1.50
10,11: #11-Brunner cover	.50	1.00	1.50
Annual #1(Summer,'75)	.50	1.00	1.50

MONTANA KID, THE (See Kid Montana)

MONTE HALE WESTERN (Mary Marvel #1-28)
#29, Oct, 1948 - #88, 1955
Fawcett Publications/Charlton #51 on

#29(#1)	6.00	12.00	18.00
30-40	3.00	6.00	9.00
41-50	2.50	5.00	7.50
51-86,88	2.00	4.00	6.00
87-Wolverton reprint	2.50	5.00	7.50

MONTY HALL OF THE U.S. MARINES (See With the
Aug, 1951 - #11, 1953   Marines--)
Toby Press

#1	2.50	5.00	7.50
2-5	2.00	4.00	6.00
6-11	1.75	3.50	5.25

NOTE: _3-5 full page pin-ups (Pin-Up Pete)
by Jack Sparling in #1-8 at least._

A MOON, A GIRL...ROMANCE (Becomes Weird
Fantasy #13 on; formerly Moon Girl #1-8)
#9, Sept-Oct, 1949 - #12, Mar-Apr, 1950
E.C. Comics

#9-Moon Girl cameo	35.00	70.00	105.00
10,11	25.00	50.00	75.00
12-(Scarce)	35.00	70.00	105.00

NOTE: _Feldstein_, _Ingels_ art in all. _Canadian
reprints known; see Table of Contents._

MOON GIRL AND THE PRINCE (#1)
(Moon Girl #2-6; Moon Girl Fights Crime #7,8;
Becomes A Moon, A Girl, Romance #9 on)
Fall, 1947 - #8, Summer, 1949
E.C. Comics   (Also see Happy Houlihans)

#1-Origin Moon Girl by Moldoff(44 pgs.); intro. assistant Star	40.00	80.00	120.00
2	25.00	50.00	75.00
3,4-Moon Girl vs. a vampire #4	20.00	40.00	60.00
5-E.C.'s 1st horror story, "Zombie Terror"	45.00	90.00	135.00
6-8 (Scarce)	27.00	54.00	81.00

Monte Hale Western #30, © FAW

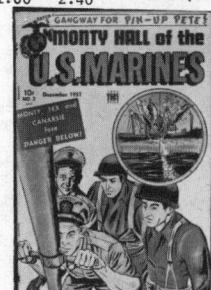
Monty Hall Of The U.S. Marines #3, © TOBY

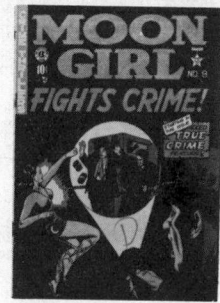
Moon Girl #8, © WMG

Moon Mullins #3(C&L), © N.Y. News Synd.   More Fun Comics #8. © DC

More Fun Comics #39, © DC

(Moon Girl and the Prince cont'd)
(#2 & #3 are 52pgs., #4 on, 36pgs. Canadian reprints known; see Table of Contents.)

MOON MULLINS
1927 - 1933 (52pgs.)(Daily B&W strip reprints)
Cupples & Leon Co.

	Good	Fine	Mint
Series 1('27)-By Willard	15.00	30.00	45.00
Series 2('28), Series 3('29), Series 4('30)			
	10.00	20.00	30.00
Series 5('31), 6('32), 7('33)			
	8.00	16.00	24.00
Big Book #1('30)-B&W	20.00	40.00	60.00

MOON MULLINS (See Superbook #3)
1941 - 1945
Dell Publishing Co.

4-Color #14(1941)	12.00	24.00	36.00
Large Feature Comic #29(1941)			
	9.00	22.50	36.00
4-Color #31(1943)	9.00	18.00	27.00
4-Color #81(1945)	5.00	10.00	15.00

MOON MULLINS
Dec-Jan, 1947-48 - #8, 1949   (52 pgs.)
Michel Publ. (American Comics Group)

#1-Willard reprt., alternating Sunday & daily newspaper reprints	3.50	7.00	10.50
2-8-Willard reprint + Milt Gross-#8			
	2.50	5.00	7.50

MOON PILOT   (See 4-Color Comics #1313)

MOON-SPINNERS, THE   (See Movie Comics)

MOPSY (See TV Teens & Pageant of Comics)
Feb, 1948 - #19, Sept, 1953
St. John Publ. Co.

#1-Partial reprints; also reprints "Some Punkins" by Neher	4.00	8.00	12.00
2-19(1953)	2.25	4.50	6.75

MORE FUN COMICS (Formerly New Fun #1-6)
#7, 1/36 - #127, 4-5/49
National Periodical Publications

#7(1/36),#8(2/36)-Both oversized; 1pg. Kelly in each	50.00	100.00	150.00
9(3-4/36)-11(7/36) Last soft cover & Henri Duval by Siegel & Shuster			
	40.00	80.00	120.00
12(8/36)-1st slick cover,			
V2#1(9/36,#13), V2#2(10/36,#14)-Dr. Occult in costume begins, ends #17			
	35.00	70.00	105.00

	Good	Fine	Mint
V2#3(11/36,#15),16(V2#4),17(V2#5) cover numbering begins #16	27.00	54.00	81.00
18-20(V2#8,5/37)	22.00	44.00	66.00
21(V2#9)-24(V2#12,9/37)	17.00	34.00	51.00
25(V3#1,10/37)-27(V3#3,12/37)			
	17.00	34.00	51.00
28-30: #30-1st non-funny cover			
	17.00	34.00	51.00
31-35: #32-Last Dr. Occult			
	15.00	30.00	45.00
36-40: #36-The Masked Ranger begins, ends #41			
	14.00	28.00	42.00
41-50	12.00	24.00	36.00
51-1st app. The Spectre(in costume) in one panel ad at end of Buccaneer story			
	20.00	40.00	60.00
52-Origin The Spectre(out of costume), Part 1 by Bernard Baily; last Wing Brady			
(Rare)	800.00	1600.00	2400.00
53-Origin The Spectre(out of costume), Part 2; Capt. Desmo begins			
(Rare)	600.00	1200.00	1800.00
(Prices vary widely on above 2 books)			
54-The Spectre in costume; last King Carter			
	200.00	400.00	600.00
55-Intro. & 1st app. Dr. Fate; last Bulldog Martin	140.00	280.00	420.00
56-60: #56-Congo Bill begins			
	90.00	180.00	270.00
61-66: #63-Last St. Bob Neal. #64-Lance Larkin begins	70.00	140.00	210.00
67-Origin Dr. Fate; last Congo Bill & Biff Bronson	85.00	170.00	255.00
68-70: #68-Clip Carson begins. #70-Last Lance Larkin	55.00	110.00	165.00
71-Origin & 1st app. Johnny Quick			
	70.00	140.00	210.00
72-Dr. Fate's new helmet; last Sgt. Carey, Sgt. O'Malley & Capt. Desmo			
	45.00	90.00	135.00
73-(Scarce)-Origin & 1st app. Aquaman; intro. Green Arrow & Speedy	90.00	180.00	270.00
74-80: #76-Last Clip Carson			
	40.00	80.00	120.00
81-88: #85-Johnny Quick by Kubert begins, ends #97. #87-Last Radio Squad			
	30.00	60.00	90.00
89-Origin Green Arrow & Speedy Team-up			
	35.00	70.00	105.00
90-100: #93-Dover & Clover begin. #97-Kubert art. #98-Last Dr.Fate	20.00	40.00	60.00
101-Origin & 1st app. Superboy; last Spectre issue	100.00	200.00	300.00
102	35.00	70.00	105.00
103	30.00	60.00	90.00
104-107: #107-Last Johnny Quick & Superboy	25.00	50.00	75.00

(More Fun Comics cont'd)

	Good	Fine	Mint
108-120: #108-Genius Jones begins			
	3.00	6.00	9.00
121-124,126,127	2.00	4.00	6.00
125-(Scarce)-Superman on cover			
	15.00	30.00	45.00

NOTE: _The Spectre-#52-55,57-60,62-67. Dr. Fate-#55,56,61,68-76. The Green Arrow & Speedy-#77-85,88-97,99,101; w/Dover & Clover- #98,103. Johnny Quick-#86,87,100. Superboy- #101-107; w/Dover & Clover-#102-107. Genius Jones-#108-127._

MORE SEYMOUR (See Seymour My Son)
Oct, 1963
Archie Publications

#1	1.00	2.00	3.00

MORE TRASH FROM MAD (Annual)
1958 - #12, 1969
E.C. Comics

No#(1958)-8pgs. color Mad reprint from #20			
	6.00	12.00	18.00
#2(1959)-Market Product Labels			
	5.00	10.00	15.00
3(1960)-Text book cvrs.	4.00	8.00	12.00
4(1961)-Sing Along with Mad booklet			
	3.00	6.00	9.00
5(1962)-Window Stickers-reprint from Mad			
#39	2.50	5.00	7.50
6(1963)-TV Guise booklet	3.00	6.00	9.00
7(1964)-Alfred E. Neuman commemorative			
stamps	2.00	4.00	6.00
8(1965)-Life size poster-A. E. Neuman			
	2.00	4.00	6.00
9,10('66,'67)-Mischief Sticker			
	2.00	4.00	6.00
11(1968)-Campaign poster & bumper sticker			
	2.00	4.00	6.00
12(1969)-Pocket medals	2.00	4.00	6.00

NOTE: _Kelly Freas_ covers-#1,2,4. _Mingo_ cov- ers-#3,5-9.

MORGAN THE PIRATE (See 4-Color Comics #1227)

MORLOCK 2001 (-- & the Midnight Men #3)
Feb, 1974 - #3, July, 1975
Atlas/Seaboard Publ.

#1-Origin	.30	.60	.90
2	.20	.40	.60
3-Ditko/Wrightson story; origin The Midnight			
Man & The Midnight Men	.40	.80	1.20

MORTIE (Mazie's Friend)
Dec, 1952 - #3, June, 1953

Magazine Publishers/Harvey Publications

	Good	Fine	Mint
#1	1.00	2.00	3.00
2,3	.65	1.35	2.00

MORTY MEEKLE (See 4-Color Comics #793)

MOSES & THE TEN COMMANDMENTS
1957   (100 pgs.) (25¢)
Dell Publishing Co.

#1-Not based on movie; Dell's adaptation			
	2.50	5.00	7.50

MOTHER GOOSE (See Christmas With Mother Goose & 4-Color #41,59,68, & 862)

MOTION PICTURE COMICS (See Faw. Movie Comics)
1950 - #114, Jan, 1953
Fawcett Publications

#101-"The Vanishing Westerner"-Monte Hale			
(1950)	7.00	14.00	21.00
102-"Code of the Silver Sage"-Rocky Lane			
(1/51)	7.00	14.00	21.00
103-"Covered Wagon Raid"-Rocky Lane(3/51)			
	7.00	14.00	21.00
104-"Vigilante Hideout"-Rocky Lane(5/51)			
	7.00	14.00	21.00
105-"Red Badge of Courage"-Audie Murphy;			
Bob Powell art(7/51)	8.00	16.00	24.00
106-"The Texas Rangers"-George Montgomery			
(9/51) Bill Ward art	8.00	16.00	24.00
107-"Frisco Tornado"-Rocky Lane(11/51)			
	6.00	12.00	18.00
108-"Mask of the Avenger"-John Derek			
	7.00	14.00	21.00
109-"Rough Rider of Durango"-Rocky Lane			
	6.00	12.00	18.00
110-"When Worlds Collide"-George Evans art			
(1951)	15.00	30.00	45.00
111-"The Vanishing Outpost"-Lash LaRue			
	7.00	14.00	21.00
112-"Brave Warrior"-Jon Hall & Jay Silver-			
heels	5.00	10.00	15.00
113-"Walk East on Beacon"-George Murphy;			
Shaffenberger art	6.00	12.00	18.00
114-"Cripple Creek"-George Montgomery (1/53)			
	5.00	10.00	15.00

MOTION PICTURE FUNNIES WEEKLY
1939   (36pgs.)(Giveaway)(Black & White)
(No month given; last panel in Sub-Mariner
story dated 4/39) (Also see Green Giant &
Invaders #20)
First Funnies, Inc.

#1-Origin & 1st app. Sub-Mariner by Bill

More Fun Comics #87, © DC

More Fun Comics #102, © DC

Motion Picture Comics #101, © FAW

Motion Picture Funnies Weekly #1, © MCG   The Hallelujah Trail, © DELL   Masque Of The Red Death, © DELL

(Motion Picture Funnies Weekly cont'd)

	Good	Fine	Mint
Everett(8pgs.)-Reprinted in Marvel Mystery #1 with color added over the craft tint which was used to shade the black & white version; Spy Ring, American Ace (reprinted in Marvel Mystery #3) app. (Very Rare)-only five(5) known copies	2500.00	5000.00	7500.00

NOTE: The only five known copies (with a sixth suspected) were discovered in 1974 in the estate of the deceased publisher. Covers only to issues No. 2-4 were also found which evidently were printed in advance along with No. 1. No. 1 was to be distributed only through motion picture movie houses. However it is believed that only advanced copies were sent out and the motion picture houses not going for the idea. Possible distribution at local theatres in Boston suspected. The last panel of Sub-Mariner contains a rectangular box with "Continued Next Week" printed in it. When reprinted in M. Mystery, the box was left in with lettering omitted.

MOUNTAIN MEN (See Ben Bowie)

MOUSE MUSKETEERS(Formerly The Two Mouseketeers)
Jan, 1956 - 1962   (M-G-M)
Dell Publishing Co.

4-Color #670,711,728,764	.60	1.20	1.80
#8-21(4/57-3-5/60)	.40	.80	1.20
4-Color #1135,1175,1290	.50	1.00	1.50

MOUSE ON THE MOON, THE (See Movie Classics)

MOVIE CLASSICS
January, 1953 - Dec, 1969
Dell Publishing Co.

(Before 1962, most movie adaptations were part of the 4-Color Series)

Around the World Under the Sea-#12-030-612
(12/66-Dell)   1.20   2.40   3.60
Bambi-#3(4/56-Dell)-Disney; reprints 4-Color
#186   1.35   2.75   4.00
Battle of the Bulge-#12-056-606(6/66-Dell)
   1.00   2.00   3.00
Beach Blanket Bingo-#12-058-509(Dell)
   1.25   2.50   3.75
Bon Voyage-#01-068-212(12/62-Dell)-Disney
   1.00   2.00   3.00
Castilian, The-#12-110-401(Dell)
   1.00   2.00   3.00
Cat, The-#12-109-612(12/66-Dell)
   .80   1.60   2.40
Cheyenne Autumn-#12-112-506(4-6/65-Dell)
   1.50   3.00   4.50
Circus World, Samuel Bronston's-#12-115-411
(Dell)   1.00   2.00   3.00
Countdown-#12-150-710(10/67-Dell)
   1.00   2.00   3.00
Creature, The-#1(12-142-302)(12-2/62-63 Dell)

	Good	Fine	Mint
	1.00	2.00	3.00
Creature, The-#12-142-410(10/64-Dell)	.65	1.35	2.00
David Ladd's Life Story-#12173-212(10-12/62-Dell)	1.25	2.50	3.75
Die, Monster, Die-#12-175-603(3/66-Dell)	1.00	2.00	3.00
Dirty Dozen-#12-180-710(10/67-Dell)	1.00	2.00	3.00
Dr. Who & the Daleks-#12-190-612(12/66-Dell)	1.00	2.00	3.00
Dracula-#12-231-212(10-12/62-Dell)	1.00	2.00	3.00
El Dorado-#12-240-710(10/67-Dell)	1.25	2.50	3.75
Ensign Pulver-#12-257-410(8-10/64-Dell)	1.00	2.00	3.00
Frankenstein-#12-283-304(3-5/63-Dell)	1.00	2.00	3.00
Great Race, The-#12-299-603(3/66-Dell)	1.00	2.00	3.00
Hallelujah Trail, The-#12-307-602(2/66-Dell) (Says 1/66 inside)	1.00	2.00	3.00
Hatari-#12-340-301(1/63-Dell)	1.00	2.00	3.00
Horizontal Lieutenant, The-#01-348-210(10/62-Dell)	1.00	2.00	3.00
Incredible Mr. Limpet, The-#12-370-408(Dell)	1.00	2.00	3.00
Jack the Giant Killer-#12-374-301(1/63-Dell)	1.50	3.00	4.50
Jason & the Argonauts-#12-376-310(8-10/63-Dell)	2.00	4.00	6.00
Lady and the Tramp-#1(6/55-Dell Giant,100pgs) Disney	1.20	2.40	3.60
Lancelot & Guinevere-#12-416-310(10/63-Dell)	1.00	2.00	3.00
Lawrence-#12-426-308(8/63-Dell)-Story of Lawrence of Arabia-Movie ad on back cover; not exactly like movie	1.00	2.00	3.00
Lion of Sparta-#12-439-301(1/63-Dell)	1.00	2.00	3.00
Longest Day, The-('62-Dell)	1.00	2.00	3.00
Mad Monster Party-#12-460-801(9/67-Dell)	.90	1.80	2.70
Magic Sword, The-#01-496-209(9/62-Dell)	1.50	3.00	4.50
Masque of the Red Death-#12-490-410(8-10/64-Dell)	1.20	2.40	3.60
Maya-#12-495-612(12/66-Dell)	1.00	2.00	3.00
McHale's Navy-#12-500-412(10-12/64-Dell)	1.00	2.00	3.00
Merrill's Marauders-#12-510-301(1/63-Dell)	.80	1.60	2.40

Mouse on the Moon, The-#12-530-312(10/12/63-

(Movie Classics cont'd)	Good	Fine	Mint
Dell)	1.00	2.00	3.00

Mummy, The-#12-537-211(9-11/62-Dell) 2 different back cvr. ishs.   1.00 2.00 3.00

Music Man, The-#12-538-301(1/63-Dell)
    1.20 2.40 3.60

Naked Prey, The-#12-545-612(12/66-Dell)
    1.20 2.40 3.60

Night of the Grizzly, The-#12-558-612(12/66-Dell) .80 1.60 2.40

None But the Brave-#12-565-506(4-6/65-Dell) .90 1.80 2.70

Operation Bikini-#12-597-310(10/63-Dell)
    1.00 2.00 3.00

Operation Crossbow-#12-590-512(10-12/65-Dell) 1.20 2.40

Peter Pan Treasure Chest-#1(1/53-Dell)-
Disney; contains movie adaptation plus
other stories 12.00 24.00 36.00

Prince & the Pauper, The-#01-654-207(5-7/62-Dell)-Disney 1.20 2.40 3.60

Raven, The-#12-680-309(9/63-Dell)
    1.00 2.00 3.00

Ring of Bright Water-#01-701-910(10/69-Dell, inside #12-701-909) .80 1.60 2.40

Runaway, The-#12-707-412(10-12/64-Dell)
    .80 1.60 2.40

Santa Claus Conquers the Martians-#12-725-603 (3/66-Dell) 1.00 2.00 3.00

Six Black Horses-#12-750-301(1/63-Dell)
    .80 1.60 2.40

Ski Party-#12-743-511(9-11/65-Dell)
    1.00 2.00 3.00

Sleeping Beauty-#1(1959-Dell Giant,100 pgs.) Disney 2.00 4.00 6.00

Smoky-#12-746-702(2/67-Dell)
    .80 1.60 2.40

Sons of Katie Elder-#12-748-511(9-11/65-Dell)
    1.00 2.00 3.00

Sword of Lancelot-(1963-Dell)
    1.35 2.75 4.00

Tales of Terror-#12-793-302(2/63-Dell)
    1.00 2.00 3.00

Taras Bulba-(1962-Dell) 2.50 5.00 7.50

Three Stooges Meet Hercules-#01828-208(8/62-Dell) 2.00 4.00 6.00

Tomb of Ligeia-#12-830-506(4-6/65-Dell)
    1.00 2.00 3.00

Treasure Island-#01-845-211(7-9/62-Dell)-Disney; reprts.4-Color#624 .80 1.60 2.40

Twice Told Tales (Nathaniel Hawthorne)-#12-840-401(11-1/63-64-Dell)
    1.00 2.00 3.00

Two on a Guillotine-#12-850-506(4-6/65-Dell)
    .90 1.80 2.70

Universal Presents-Dracula-The Mummy & other stories-#02-530-311(9-11/63-Dell Giant, 84pgs.)-reprints Dracula #12-231-212, The

	Good	Fine	Mint
Mummy #12-537-211, & part of Ghost Stories #1	1.75	3.50	5.25

Valley of Gwangi-#01-880-912(12/69-Dell)
    1.50 3.00 4.50

War Gods of the Deep-#12-900-509(7-9/65-Dell)
    1.20 2.40 3.60

War Wagon, The-#12-533-709(9/67-Dell)
    1.20 2.40 3.60

Who's Minding the Mint?-#12-924-708(8/67-Dell)
    .80 1.60 2.40

Wolfman, The-#12-922-308(6-8/63-Dell)
    1.00 2.00 3.00

Wolfman, The-#1(12-922-410)(8-10/64-Dell)-2nd printing(reprints #12-922-308)
    .50 1.00 1.50

Zulu-#12-950-410(8-10/64-Dell)
    1.00 2.00 3.00

MOVIE COMICS   (See Fawcett Movie Comics)

MOVIE COMICS
April, 1939 - #9, Dec, 1939
National Periodical Publ./Picture Comics

#1-"Gunga Din","Son of Frankenstein","The Great Man Votes","Fisherman's Wharf", & "Scouts to the Rescue" part I; Wheelan "Minute Movies" begin-70.00 140.00 210.00

2-"Stagecoach","The Saint Strikes Back", "King of the Turf","Scouts to the Rescue" part II, "Arizona Legion"
    50.00 100.00 150.00

3-"East Side of Heaven","Mystery in the White Room","Four Feathers","Mexican Rose" with Gene Autry,"Spirit of Culver","Many Secrets","The Mikado" 40.00 80.00 120.00

4-"Captain Fury", Gene Autry in "Blue Montana Skies","Streets of N.Y." with Jackie Cooper, "Oregon Trail" part I with Johnny Mack Brown, "Big Town Czar" with Barton MacLane, & "Star Reporter" with Warren Hull 40.00 80.00 120.00

5-"Man in the Iron Mask","Five Came Back", "Wolf Call","The Girl & the Gambler","The House of Fear","The Family Next Door", "Oregon Trail" part II
    40.00 80.00 120.00

6-"The Phantom Creeps","Chumps at Oxford", & "The Oregon Trail" part III
    45.00 90.00 135.00

7-9   45.00 90.00 135.00

NOTE: *Above books contain many original movie stills with dialogue from movie scripts.*

MOVIE COMICS
Dec, 1946 - 1947
Fiction House Magazines

Mouse On The Moon, © DELL

Movie Comics #1, © DC

Movie Comics #2, © FH

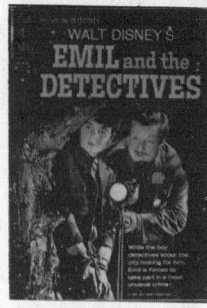

Blackbeard's Ghost, © GK   Emil & The Detectives, © GK   King Kong, © GK

(Movie Comics cont'd)

	Good	Fine	Mint
#1-Big Town & Johnny Danger begin-Celardo art	8.00	16.00	24.00
2-"White Tie & Tails" with William Bendix; Mitzi of the Movies begins by Matt Baker, ends #4	6.00	12.00	18.00
3-Andy Hardy	6.00	12.00	18.00
4-Slave Girl by M.Baker	8.00	16.00	24.00

MOVIE COMICS
Oct, 1962 - March, 1972
Gold Key/Whitman

	Good	Fine	Mint
Alice in Wonderland-#10144-503(3/65-G.Key) Disney; partial reprint of 4-Color #331	.80	1.60	2.40
Aristocats, The-#1(30045-103)(3/71-G.Key) Disney; with pull-out poster(25¢)	.75	1.50	2.25
Bambi #1(10087-309)(9/63-G.Key)-Disney; reprints 4-Color #186	.60	1.20	1.80
Bambi #2(10087-607)-7/66-G.Key)-Disney; reprints 4-Color #186)	.50	1.00	1.50
Beneath the Planet of the Apes-#30044-012 (12/70-G.Key)-with pull-out poster	1.50	3.00	4.50
Big Red-#10026-211(11/62-G.Key)	.80	1.60	2.40
Big Red-#10026-503(3/65-G.Key)-Disney; reprints #10026-211	.65	1.35	2.00
Blackbeard's Ghost-#10222-806(6/68-G.Key) Disney	1.00	2.00	3.00
Bullwhip Griffin-#10181-706(3/67-G.Key)- Disney	.80	1.60	2.40
Captain Sindbad-#10077-309(9/63-G.Key)- Manning art	1.50	3.00	4.50
Chitty Chitty Bang Bang-#1(30038-902)(2/69- G.Key)-with pull-out poster	1.75	3.50	5.25
Cinderella-#10152-508(8/65-G.Key)-Disney; reprints 4-Color #786	1.00	2.00	3.00
Darby O'Gill & the Little People-#1(10251-001) (1/70-G.Key)-Disney; reprints 4-Color #1024 (Toth)	1.50	3.00	4.50
Dumbo #1(10090-310)(10/63-G.Key)-Disney; reprints 4-Color #668	.70	1.40	2.10
Emil & the Detectives-#10120-502(2/65-G.Key) Disney	.80	1.60	2.40
Escapade in Florence-#1(10043-301)(1/63-G. Key)-Disney; starring Annette	1.75	3.50	5.25
Fall of the Roman Empire-#10118-407(7/64- G.Key)	1.20	2.40	3.60
Fantastic Voyage-#10178-702(2/67-G.Key)-Wood/ Adkins art	1.75	3.50	5.25
55 Days at Peking-#10081-309(9/63-G.Key)	1.00	2.00	3.00

	Good	Fine	Mint
Fighting Prince of Donegal, The-#10193-701 (1/67-G.Key)-Disney	1.00	2.00	3.00
First Men in the Moon-#10132-503(3/65-G.Key)	1.00	2.00	3.00
Gay Purr-ee-#1(30017-301)(1/63-G.Key Giant, 84pgs.)	1.00	2.00	3.00
Gnome Mobile, The-#10207-710(10/67-G.Key) Disney	.80	1.60	2.40
Goodbye, Mr. Chips-#10246-006(6/70-G.Key)	1.00	2.00	3.00
Happiest Millionaire, The-#10221-804(4/68- G.Key)-Disney	.80	1.60	2.40
Hey There, It's Yogi Bear-#10122-409(9/64- G.Key)-Hanna-Barbera	.50	1.00	1.50
Horse Without a Head, The-#10109-401(1/64- G.Key)-Disney	.80	1.60	2.40
How the West Was Won-#1(10074-307)(7/63- G.Key)	1.00	2.00	3.00
In Search of the Castaways-#10048-303(3/63- G.Key)-Disney	1.00	2.00	3.00
Jungle Book, The-#1(6022-801)(1/68-Whitman) Disney; large size(10x13½") (59¢)	1.50	3.00	4.50
Jungle Book, The-#1(30033-803)(3/68-G.Key)- Disney; same contents as Whitman #1	.80	1.60	2.40
Kidnapped-#10080-306(6/63-G.Key)-Disney; reprints 4-Color #1101	.80	1.60	2.40
King Kong-#1(30036-809)(9/68-G.Key Giant, 68pgs.)-painted cover	2.50	5.00	7.50
Lady and the Tramp-#10042-301(1/63-G.Key)- Disney; reprints 4-Color #629	.90	1.80	2.70
Lady and the Tramp-#1(1967-G.Key Giant 25¢)- Disney; reprints part of Dell #1	.60	1.20	1.80
Lady and the Tramp-#2(10042-203)(3/72-G.Key) Disney; reprints 4-Color #629	.80	1.60	2.40
Legend of Lobo, The-#1(10059-303)(3/63-G.Key) Disney	.75	1.35	2.00
Lt. Robin Crusoe, U.S.N.-#10191-610(10/66- G.Key)-Disney	.80	1.60	2.40
Lion, The-#10035-301(1/63-G.Key)	.65	1.35	2.00
Lord Jim-#10156-509(9/65-G.Key)	.80	1.60	2.40
Love Bug, The-#10237-906(6/69-G.Key)-Disney	.80	1.60	2.40
Mary Poppins-#10136-501(1/65-G.Key)-Disney	1.25	2.50	3.75
Mary Poppins-#30023-501(1/65-G.Key Giant, 68pgs.)-Disney	2.00	4.00	6.00
McLintock!-#10110-403(3/64-G.Key)	1.00	2.00	3.00
Merlin Jones as the Monkey's Uncle-#10115-510			

(Movie Comics cont'd)   Good   Fine   Mint
  (10/65-G.Key)-Disney   .90   1.80   2.70
Miracle of the White Stallions, The-#10065-
  306(6/63-G.Key)-Disney   .80   1.60   2.40
Misadventures of Merlin Jones, The-#10115-405
  (5/64-G.Key)-Disney   .80   1.60   2.40
Moon-Spinners, The-#10124-410(10/64-G.Key)
  Disney   1.25   2.50   3.75
Mutiny on the Bounty-#1(10040-302)(2/63-
  G.Key)   1.00   2.00   3.00
Nikki, Wild Dog of the North-#10141-412
  (12/64-G.Key)-Disney; reprints 4-Color
  #1226   .65   1.35   2.00
Old Yeller-#10168-601(1/66-G.Key)-Disney;
  reprints 4-Color #869   .65   1.35   2.00
Old Yeller-(1968-G.Key)-Disney; reprint
      .50   1.00   1.50
One Hundred & One Dalmations-#1(10247-002)
  (2/70-G.Key)-Disney; reprints 4-Color
  #1183   .65   1.35   2.00
Peter Pan-#1(10086-309)(9/63-G.Key)-Disney;
  reprints 4-Color #442   .90   1.80   2.70
Peter Pan-#2(10086-909)(9/69-G.Key)-Disney;
  reprints 4-Color #442   .60   1.20   1.80
P.T. 109-#10123-409(9/64-G.Key)-John F.
  Kennedy   1.50   3.00   4.50
Rio Conchos-#10143-503(3/65-G.Key)
      1.00   2.00   3.00
Robin Hood-#10163-506(6/65-G.Key)-Disney;
  reprints 4-Color #413   .60   1.20   1.80
Shaggy Dog & the Absent-Minded Professor-
  #30032-708(8/67-G.Key Giant, 68pgs.)-
  Disney; reprints 4-Color #985,1199
      1.50   3.00   4.50
Sleeping Beauty-#1(30042-009)(9/70-G.Key)-
  Disney; reprints 4-Color #973; with pull-
  out poster   .60   1.20   1.80
Snow White & the Seven Dwarfs-#1(10091-310)
  (10/63-G.Key)-Disney; reprints 4-Color
  #382   1.00   2.00   3.00
Snow White & the Seven Dwarfs-#10091-709
  (9/67-G.Key)-Disney; reprints 4-Color
  #382   .60   1.20   1.80
Son of Flubber-#1(10057-304)(4/63-G.Key)-
  Disney; sequel to "The Absent-Minded Pro-
  fessor"   1.00   2.00   3.00
Summer Magic-#10076-309(9/63-G.Key)-Disney;
  Manning art   2.00   4.00   6.00
Swiss Family Robinson-#10236-904(4/69-G.Key)
  Disney; reprints 4-Color #1156
      .65   1.35   2.00
Sword in the Stone, The-#30019-402(2/64-G.Key
  Giant, 84pgs.)-Disney 1.50   3.00   4.50
That Darn Cat-#10171-602(2/66-G.Key)-Disney
      1.00   2.00   3.00
Those Magnificent Men in Their Flying Mach-
  ines-#10162-510(10/65-G.Key)
      1.00   2.00   3.00

     Good   Fine   Mint
Three Stooges in Orbit-#30016-211(11/62-G.
  Key Giant, 32pgs.)-all photos from movie
      2.50   5.00   7.50
Tiger Walks, A-#10117-406(6/64-G.Key)-Disney;
  Torres art   1.50   3.00   4.50
Toby Tyler-#10142-502(2/65-G.Key)-Disney;
  reprints 4-Color #1092   .75   1.50   2.25
Treasure Island-#1(10200-703)(3/67-G.Key)-
  Disney; reprts.4C-#624   .75   1.50   2.25
20,000 Leagues Under the Sea-#1(10096-312)
  (12/63-G.Key)-Disney; reprints 4-Color
  #614   .75   1.50   2.25
Wonderful Adventures of Pinocchio, The-#1
  (10089-310)(10/63-G.Key)-Disney; reprints
  4-Color #545   .60   1.20   1.80
Wonderful Adventures of Pinocchio, The-#10089-
  109(9/71-G.Key)-Disney; reprints 4-Color
  #545   .75   1.50   1.50
Wonderful World of the Brothers Grimm-#1
  (10008-210)(10/62-G.Key)
      1.00   2.00   3.00
X, the Man with the X-Ray Eyes-#10083-309
  (9/63-G.Key)   1.00   2.00   3.00
Yellow Submarine-#35000-902(2/69-G.Key Giant
  68pgs.)with pull-out poster; The Beatles
  cartoon movie   9.00   18.00   27.00

MOVIE LOVE (See Personal Love)
Feb, 1950 - #22, Aug, 1953
Famous Funnies

#1   2.50   5.00   7.50
2-7,9   1.50   3.00   4.50
8-Williamson/Frazetta story, 6pgs.
      30.00   60.00   90.00
10-Frazetta story, 6pgs. (Rare)
      35.00   70.00   105.00
11-16   1.20   2.40   3.60
17-1pg. Frazetta ad   2.00   4.00   6.00
18-22   1.20   2.40   3.60
NOTE: *Each issue has a full-length movie
adaptation with photo covers.*

MOVIE THRILLERS
1949
Magazine Enterprises

#1-"Rope of Sand" with Burt Lancaster
   7.00   14.00   21.00

MOVIE TOWN ANIMAL ANTICS (Formerly Animal An-
tics; Raccoon Kids #52 on)
#20, May-June, 1949 - #51, July-Aug, 1954
National Periodical Publications

#20-51-Raccoon Kids continue
      .65   1.35   2.00

PT 109, © GK

X, The Man With The X-Ray Eyes, © GK

Movie Love #8, © FF

Murder Inc. #5, © FOX   Murderous Gangsters #3, © AVON   Mutiny #3, © Aragon Mag.

MOVIE TUNES (Frankie #4 on)(Also see Animated--)
Spring, 1946 - #3, Fall, 1946
Marvel Comics (MgPC)

	Good	Fine	Mint
#1-Super Rabbit	1.50	3.00	4.50
2,3-Super Rabbit	1.00	2.00	3.00

MOWGLI JUNGLE BOOK (See 4-Color #487,582,620)

MR. (See Mister)

MS. MARVEL
January, 1977 - Present
Marvel Comics Group

#1-Buscema art	.75	1.50	2.25
2-Origin	.50	1.00	1.50
3-5: #5-Vision app.	.35	.70	1.05
6-10	.25	.50	.75
11-22: #20-New costume	.15	.30	.45

NOTE: *Buscema stories-#1-3; covers-#2,4,7,8,
15. Starlin cover-#12.*

MUGGSY MOUSE
1951 - 1953; 1963
Magazine Enterprises

| #1(A-1#33),2(A-1#36),3(A-1#39),
4(A-1#95),5(A-1#99)	.60	1.20	1.80
Super Reprint #14('63)	.25	.50	.75
I.W. Reprint #1,2(no date)	.25	.50	.75

MUGGY-DOO, BOY CAT
July, 1953 - #4, Jan, 1954
Standard Publications

#1-Art by Irving Spector	1.00	2.00	3.00
2-4	.65	1.35	2.00
Super Reprint #12('63),#16('64)	.20	.40	.60

MUMMY, THE (See Movie Classics)

MUNSTERS, THE (TV)
Jan, 1965 - #16, Jan, 1968
Gold Key

#1(10134-501)	.60	1.20	1.80
2-5	.40	.80	1.20
6-16	.30	.60	.90

MURDER, INC. (My Private Life #16 on)
1/48 - #15, 12/49;(No #10, 2 #9's); 6/50 -
#3, 8/51
Fox Features Syndicate

#1(1st Series)	6.00	12.00	18.00
2-7,9(3/49),9(4/49),11-15: #3-Rico art			

	Good	Fine	Mint
	3.00	6.00	9.00

8-Used in Seduction of the Innocent, pg.

160	7.00	14.00	21.00

5(6/50)(2nd Series)-Formerly My Desire

	2.50	5.00	7.50
3(8/51)	1.75	3.50	5.25

MURDEROUS GANGSTERS
July, 1951 - #4, June, 1952
Avon Periodicals/Realistic #3 on

| #1-Pretty Boy Floyd, Leggs Diamond; 1 pg.
Wood	6.00	12.00	18.00
2-Baby Face Nelson; 1pg. Wood,
3,4	3.00	6.00	9.00

MURDER TALES (Magazine)
V1#10, 11/70 - V1#11, 1/71   (52 pgs.)
World Famous Publications

V1#10-1pg. Frazetta ad	1.20	2.40	3.60
11-Guardineer reprint	.60	1.20	1.80

MUSHMOUSE AND PUNKIN PUSS (TV)
Sept, 1965   (Hanna-Barbera)
Gold Key

#1(10153-509)		.15	.30

MUSIC MAN, THE (See Movie Classics)

MUTINY (Stormy Tales of Seven Seas)
Oct, 1954 - #3, Feb, 1955
Aragon Magazines

#1	1.20	2.40	3.60
2-Capt. Mutiny, #3	.80	1.60	2.40

MUTINY ON THE BOUNTY (See Movie Comics)

MUTT & JEFF (-- Cartoon, The)
1911 - 1914 (5-3/4"x15-1/2")(Hardcover-B&W)
Ball Publications

| #1(1910)-Mutt reading The Oregon Journal on
cover; by Bud Fisher	25.00	50.00	75.00
1(1911)-Mutt reading The American on cover	25.00	50.00	75.00
2(1911),3-5(1914)	18.00	36.00	54.00

NOTE: *Above books were reprinted for several
years after issued.*

MUTT & JEFF
1916 - 1933 (B&W dailies)(9½x9½" large stiff-
cover comic; 52 pgs.)
Cupples & Leon Co.

(Mutt & Jeff cont'd)

	Good	Fine	Mint
#6-10-By Bud Fisher	12.00	24.00	36.00
11-22	9.00	18.00	27.00
No#(1920)(16x11",20pgs., reprts. 1919 Sunday strips)(Advs.of--)	20.00	50.00	80.00
Big Book #1-(1928)-Thick book(hardcovers) w/dust jacket	25.00	50.00	75.00
Big Book #2-(1929)-Thick book (hardcovers) w/dust jacket	25.00	50.00	75.00

NOTE: *The Big Books contain three previous issues rebound.*

MUTT & JEFF
1921 (9x15")
Embee Publ. Co.

Sunday strips in color (Rare)

              25.00 62.50 100.00

MUTT AND JEFF
1939 (no date) - #148, Nov, 1965
All American/National #1-103(6/58)/Dell #104-115(10-12/59)/Harvey #116(2/60)-148

	Good	Fine	Mint
#1(No#)-Lost Wheels	30.00	60.00	90.00
2(No#)-Charging Bull(Summer,'40, no date)	15.00	30.00	45.00
3(No#)-Bucking Broncos(Summer,'41, no date)	12.00	24.00	36.00
4(Wint.'41),5(Sum.'42)	10.00	20.00	30.00
6-10	6.00	12.00	18.00
11-20	3.50	7.00	10.50
21-30	2.00	4.00	6.00
31-74-Last Fisher ish.	1.25	2.50	3.75
75-100	.80	1.60	2.40
101-148: #117,121-Richie Rich	.60	1.20	1.80
--Jokes #1-3(1960-61, Harvey, 84 pgs.)	1.00	2.00	3.00
--New Jokes #1-4(10/63-'65, Harvey, 68pgs.)- Richie Rich in all; Stumbo in #1	.60	1.20	1.80

NOTE: *Issues #1-74 by Bud Fisher. #86 on by Al Smith. Issues from 1963 on have Fisher reprints. Clarification: early issues signed by Fisher are mostly drawn by Smith.*

MUTTSY, THE TALKING DOG (See Harvey Hits Magazine #84,92)

MY BROTHERS' KEEPER
1973 (36 pgs.) (35c)
Spire Christian Comics(Fleming H. Revell Co.)

No#	.25	.50	.75

MY CONFESSIONS (My Confession #7; formerly Western True Crime; A Spec. Feat. Mag. #11 on)

#7, Aug, 1949 - #10, Jan-Feb, 1950
Fox Features Syndicate

	Good	Fine	Mint
#7-Wood story, 10pgs.	6.00	12.00	18.00
8-Wood story	5.00	10.00	15.00
9,10	1.75	3.50	5.25

MY DATE COMICS
July, 1947 - V1#4, Jan, 1948
Hillman Periodicals

#1	5.00	10.00	15.00
2-4-S&K + Dan Barry art	4.00	8.00	12.00

MY DESIRE (Formerly Jo-Jo)(Murder, Inc. #5 on)
#30, Aug, 1949 - #4, April, 1950
Fox Features Syndicate

#30,31(#1,2)	2.50	5.00	7.50
32(12/49)-Wood story	5.00	10.00	15.00
3,4	1.75	3.50	5.25
31 (Canadian edition)	1.00	2.00	3.00

MY DIARY
December, 1949 - #2, March, 1950
Marvel Comics (A Lovers Mag.)

#1,2	1.50	3.00	4.50

MY DOG TIGE (Buster Brown's Dog)
1957 (Giveaway)
Buster Brown Shoes

	1.20	2.40	3.60

MY EXPERIENCE (Formerly All Top; Judy Canova #19, Sept, 1949 - #22, Mar, 1950   #23 on)
Fox Features Syndicate

#19-Wood story	5.00	10.00	15.00
20	1.75	3.50	5.25
21-Two Wood stories	7.00	14.00	21.00
22-Wood story, 9pgs.	5.00	10.00	15.00

MY FAVORITE MARTIAN (TV)
Jan, 1964 - #15, Feb-Apr, 1968
Gold Key

#1-Russ Manning art	1.00	2.00	3.00
2-15 (#11-15 exist?)	.35	.70	1.05

MY FRIEND IRMA (Radio/TV) (Formerly Western Life Romances?)
#3, June, 1950 - #47, Sept, 1954; #48, 2/55
Marvel/Atlas Comics(BFP)

#3	1.50	3.00	4.50
4-Kurtzman story, 10pgs.	6.00	12.00	18.00

Mutt & Jeff #4, © DC

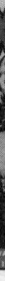

My Experience #20, © FOX

My Friend Irma #10, © MCG

My Great Love #3, © FOX

My Life #9, © FOX

My Love #1('49), © MCG

	Good	Fine	Mint
(My Friend Irma cont'd)			
5-"Egghead Doodle" by Kurtzman, 4pgs.			
	4.00	8.00	12.00
6,8-10	1.00	2.00	3.00
7-1pg. Kurtzman	1.50	3.00	4.50
11-20	.50	1.00	1.50
21,22,24-31,33-48	.40	.80	1.20
23,32-1pg. Frazetta	1.20	2.40	3.60

MY GIRL PEARL
April, 1955 - #6, 9/57; #7, 8/60 - #16, 1961
Atlas Comics

	Good	Fine	Mint
#1	.60	1.20	1.80
2-16	.30	.60	.90

MY GREATEST ADVENTURE (Doom Patrol #86 on)
Jan-Feb, 1955 - #85, Feb, 1964
National Periodical Publications

	Good	Fine	Mint
#1-Before CCA	10.00	20.00	30.00
2-5	5.00	10.00	15.00
6-10	2.50	5.00	7.50
11-16,19,22-27,29,30	1.75	3.50	5.25
17,18-Kirby story/cvr-#18	2.50	5.00	7.50
20,21,28-Kirby art	2.00	4.00	6.00
31-57,59	.80	1.60	2.40
58,60,61,77-Toth art	1.25	2.50	3.75
62-76,78,79	.40	.80	1.20
80-Intro. Doom Patrol	1.20	2.40	3.60
81,85-Toth art	.80	1.60	2.40
82-84	.60	1.20	1.80
NOTE: *Anderson story-#42.*			

MY GREATEST THRILLS IN BASEBALL
(16 pg. Giveaway)
Mission of California

	Good	Fine	Mint
By Mickey Mantle	1.50	3.00	4.50

MY GREAT LOVE
Oct, 1949 - #4, Apr, 1950
Fox Features Syndicate

	Good	Fine	Mint
#1	3.00	6.00	9.00
2-4	2.00	4.00	6.00

MY INTIMATE AFFAIR (Inside Crime #3)
1950
Fox Features Syndicate

	Good	Fine	Mint
#1	3.00	6.00	9.00
2	2.00	4.00	6.00

MY LIFE (Meet Corliss Archer #1-3)
#3, Sept, 1948 - #15, July, 1950
Fox Features Syndicate

	Good	Fine	Mint
#4-Used in *Seduction of the Innocent*, pg. 39;			
Kamen/Feldstein art	10.00	20.00	30.00
5-Kamen art	4.00	8.00	12.00
6-Kamen/Feldstein art	4.00	8.00	12.00
7-Wash cover	3.00	6.00	9.00
8-15	2.00	4.00	6.00

MY LITTLE MARGIE (TV)
1954 - #54, Nov, 1964
Charlton Comics

	Good	Fine	Mint
#1	1.00	2.00	3.00
2-20	.40	.80	1.20
21-53	.25	.50	.75
54-Beatles on cover; lead story spoofs the Beatle haircut craze of the '60's			
	1.75	3.35	5.00

MY LITTLE MARGIE'S BOY FRIENDS
1955 - 1961
Charlton Comics

	Good	Fine	Mint
#1	.80	1.60	2.40
2-20	.40	.80	1.20
21-38	.25	.50	.75

MY LITTLE MARGIE'S FASHIONS
Feb, 1959 - #5, 1959
Charlton Comics

	Good	Fine	Mint
#1	1.50	3.00	4.50
2-5	.75	1.50	2.25

MY LOVE (Formerly Molly Manton's Romances
July, 1949 - #3, Jan, 1950 #1 & 2)
Marvel Comics (CDS)

	Good	Fine	Mint
#1(7/49)(becomes Blaze the Wonder Collie #2?)			
	1.50	3.00	4.50
3(1/50)	.80	1.60	2.40

MY LOVE
Sept, 1969 - #39, Mar, 1976
Marvel Comics Group

		Good	Fine	Mint
#1-9			.15	.30
10-Williamson reprint (My Own Romance #71);				
Kirby story	.35	.70	1.05	
11-20: #14-Morrow art			.15	.30
21,22,24-39: #38,39-Reprints			.15	.30
23-Steranko reprint/Our Love Story #5				
	.15	.30	.45	
Special (12/71)			.15	.35

MY LOVE AFFAIR (March of Crime #7)
July, 1949 - #6, May, 1950
Fox Features Syndicate

(My Love Affair cont'd)	Good	Fine	Mint
#1	3.00	6.00	9.00
2,4	2.00	4.00	6.00
3,5,6-Wood stories	5.00	10.00	15.00

MY LOVE LIFE (Formerly Zegra)
#6, June, 1949 - #12, June, 1950
Fox Features Syndicate

#6-Kamen/Feldstein art	4.00	8.00	12.00
7-12	2.00	4.00	6.00

MY LOVE MEMOIRS (Formerly Women Outlaws; Hunt-
#9, 11/49 - #12, 5/50   ed #13 on)
Fox Features Syndicate

#9,11,12-Wood stories	5.00	10.00	15.00
10	2.00	4.00	6.00

MY LOVE SECRET (Formerly Phantom Lady)(Animal
#24, 6/49 - #30, 6/50; 1954   Crackers #31)
Fox Features Syndicate/M.S. Distr.

#24-Kamen/Feldstein art	3.00	6.00	9.00
25-Possible caricature of Wood on the cover?			
	2.50	5.00	7.50
26,28-Wood stories	5.00	10.00	15.00
27,29,30: #30-photo cvr.	2.00	4.00	6.00
#53-(Reprint, M.S.Distr.)1954? no date given;			
formerly Western Thrillers #52 (Crimes By			
Women #54)	1.50	3.00	4.50

MY LOVE STORY
Sept, 1949 - #4, Mar, 1950
Fox Feaures Syndicate

#1	3.00	6.00	9.00
2	2.00	4.00	6.00
3,4-Wood stories	5.00	10.00	15.00

MY LOVE STORY
April, 1956 - #9, Aug, 1957
Atlas Comics (GPS)

#1-Two Colletta stories	.75	1.50	2.25
2,4-9	.40	.80	1.20
3-Matt Baker story	.80	1.60	2.40
NOTE: *Colletta art in most.*			

MY ONLY LOVE
July, 1975 - #9, Nov, 1976
Charlton Comics

#1,2,4-9		.10	.25
3-Toth art	.25	.50	.75

MY OWN ROMANCE (Formerly My Romance)
#3, May, 1949 - #76, July, 1960

Marvel/Atlas(MjPC/RCM #3-59/ZPC #60-76)
	Good	Fine	Mint
#3-5	.80	1.60	2.40
6-20	.50	1.00	1.50
21-70,72-76	.30	.60	.90
71-Williamson story	3.00	6.00	9.00

MY PAST (-- Confessions) (Formerly Western Thrillers)
#8, Oct, 1949 - #11, April, 1950
Fox Features Syndicate (Crimes Inc. #12)

#8-10	2.00	4.00	6.00
11-Wood story	4.00	8.00	12.00

MY PERSONAL PROBLEM
Nov, 1955 - #3, Sept, 1956; Oct, 1957 - 1958
Ajax/Farrell/Steinway Comic

#1-3	1.00	2.00	3.00
#1(10/57),2('58)-Steinway	.40	.80	1.20

MY PRIVATE LIFE (Formerly Murder, Inc.)
#16, Feb, 1950
Fox Features Syndicate

#16	2.00	4.00	6.00

MY REAL LOVE
#5, June, 1952
Standard Comics

#5-Toth art, 3pgs.; photo cover			
	2.50	5.00	7.50

MYRA NORTH (See 4-Color Comics #3)

MY ROMANCE (My Own Romance #3 on)
Sept, 1948 - #3, Jan, 1949
Marvel Comics (RCM)

#1	1.50	3.00	4.50
2,3	1.25	2.50	3.75

MY ROMANTIC ADVENTURES (Formerly Romantic Ad-
#70, 10/56 - #137, 2/64   ventures)
American Comics Group

#70-85	.40	.80	1.20
86-3pg. Williamson story(2/58)			
	3.00	6.00	9.00
87-137	.25	.50	.75
NOTE: *Whitney art in most.*			

MY SECRET
Aug, 1949 - #3, Oct, 1949
Superior Comics, Ltd.

My Love Memoirs #9, © FOX

My Love Story #4, © FOX

My Secret #3, © SUPR

My Secret Marriage #5, © SUPR   Mysteries #3, © SUPR   Mysterious Adventures #6, © Story Comics

(My Secret cont'd)	Good	Fine	Mint
#1	2.00	4.00	6.00
2,3	1.25	2.50	3.75

MY SECRET AFFAIR (Martin Kane #4)
Dec, 1949 - #3, April, 1950
Hero Book (Fox Features Syndicate)

#1-Harrison/Wood story, 10pgs.			
	7.00	14.00	21.00
2-Wood story (poor)	4.00	8.00	12.00
3-Wood story	5.00	10.00	15.00

MY SECRET CONFESSION
September, 1955
Sterling Comics

#1-Sekowsky art	1.00	2.00	3.00

MY SECRET LIFE (Formerly Western Outlaws;
Romeo Tubbs #28 on)
#22, July, 1949 - #27, May, 1950
Fox Features Syndicate

#22	2.00	4.00	6.00
23,26-Wood story, 6pgs.	5.00	10.00	15.00
24,25,27	1.75	3.50	5.25

MY SECRET LIFE
#20, Nov, 1957 - #47, 1962
Charlton Comics

#20-47	.20	.40	.60

MY SECRET MARRIAGE
May, 1953 - #24, July, 1956
Superior Comics, Ltd.

#1	1.50	3.00	4.50
2-24	.90	1.80	2.70
IW Reprint #9	.25	.50	.75

MY SECRET ROMANCE (A Star Presentation #3)
Jan, 1950 - #2, March, 1950
Hero Book (Fox Features Syndicate)

#1-Wood art	6.00	12.00	18.00
2-Wood art	5.00	10.00	15.00

MY SECRET STORY (Sabu #30 on)
#26, Oct, 1949 - #29, April, 1950
Fox Features Syndicate

#26-29	1.75	3.50	5.25

MYSTERIES (-- Weird & Strange)
May, 1953 - #11, Jan, 1955
Superior/Dynamic Publ.(Randall Publ. Ltd.)

	Good	Fine	Mint
#1	1.75	3.50	5.25
2	1.00	2.00	3.00
3-9,11	.90	1.80	2.70
10-Kamen cover/stories reprinted/Strange Mysteries #2; cover from a panel in S.M.#2			
	2.00	4.00	6.00

MYSTERIES OF SCOTLAND YARD (See A-1 #121)

MYSTERIES OF UNEXPLORED WORLDS (See Blue Bird)
(Son of Vulcan V2#49 on)
April, 1956 - #48, Sept, 1965
Charlton Comics

#1	2.00	4.00	6.00
2-10-Ditko stys. in all	1.25	2.50	3.75
11-18,20	.80	1.60	2.40
19,21-24,26-Ditko stories	1.00	2.00	3.00
25,27-30	.50	1.00	1.50
31-45	.40	.80	1.20
46-Son of Vulcan origin & series begins			
	.70	1.40	2.10
47,48	.50	1.00	1.50

NOTE: *Ditko covers-#2-6,10,19,21-24.*

MYSTERIOUS ADVENTURES
March, 1951 - #25, Aug, 1955
Story Comics

#1	2.00	4.00	6.00
2	1.00	2.00	3.00
3,4,6-10	.80	1.60	2.40
5-Bondage cover	1.50	3.00	4.50
11-22,24,25	.80	1.60	2.40
23-Disbrow story	1.00	2.00	3.00

NOTE: *Cameron story-#6. Hollingsworth stories-#5,6.*

MYSTERIOUS ISLAND (See 4-Color #1213)

MYSTERIOUS ISLE
Nov-Jan, 1964   (Jules Verne)
Dell Publishing Co.

#1	1.00	2.00	3.00

MYSTERIOUS STORIES (Horror From the Tomb #1)
Dec, 1954 - #7, Dec, 1955
Premier Magazines

#2-Woodbridge cover	1.75	3.50	5.25
3-Woodbridge cvr/story	1.75	3.50	5.25
4-7: #6-Woodbridge cover	1.25	2.50	3.75

MYSTERIOUS SUSPENSE
October, 1968
Charlton Comics

Mysterious Suspense cont'd) Good Fine Mint
#1-The Question app. by Ditko
                              2.00   4.00   6.00

<u>MYSTERIOUS TRAVELER</u> (See Tales of the --)

<u>MYSTERIOUS TRAVELER COMICS</u> (Radio)
Nov, 1948 - #4, 1949
Trans-World Publications

#1   3.00   6.00   9.00
2-4   2.00   4.00   6.00

<u>MYSTERY COMICS</u>
1944 - #4, 1944
Better Publications

#1-The Magnet, The Silver Knight, Brad Spen-
   cer, Wonderman, Dick Devins, King of Fut-
   uria, & Zudo the Jungle Boy begin
                             12.00 24.00 36.00
2   7.00 14.00 21.00
3-Lance Lewis, Space Detective begins,
4   6.00 12.00 18.00

<u>MYSTERY COMICS DIGEST</u>
March, 1972 - #26, Oct, 1975
Gold Key

#1-Ripley's-reprint of Ripley's #1; origin
   Ra-Ka-Tep the Mummy; Wood art
                             1.25   2.50   3.75
 2-Boris Karloff-Wood art; 1st app. Werewolf
   Count Wulfstein   .80   1.60   2.40
 3-Twilight Zone-Crandall, Toth & George
   Evans art; 1st app. Tragg & Simbar the
   Lion Lord   .80   1.60   2.40
 4-Ripley's Believe I.O.N.-1st app. Baron
   Tibor, the Vampire   .40   .80   1.20
 5-Boris Karloff Tales of Mystery-1st app.
   Dr. Spektor   .40   .80   1.20
 6-Twilight Zone-1st app. U.S. Marshal Reid
   & Sir Duane   .40   .80   1.20
 7-Ripley's Believe I.O.N.-origin The Lurker
   in the Swamp; 1st app. Duroc
                        .40   .80   1.20
 8-Boris Karloff T.O.M. .40   .80   1.20
 9-Twilight Zone-Williamson, Crandall, McWilliams art; 2nd Tragg app..90   1.80   2.70
10,13-Ripley's--   .35   .70   1.05
11,14-Boris Karloff--   .35   .70   1.05
12,15-Twilight Zone   .35   .70   1.05
16,19,22,25-Ripley's-- .30   .60   .90
17-Boris Karloff T.O.M.-Williamson reprint
                        .60   1.20   1.80
18,21,24-Twilight Zone .30   .60   .90
20,23,26-Boris Karloff-- .30   .60   .90
NOTE: <u>Dr. Spektor</u> app.-#5,10-12,21. <u>Durak</u>

app.-#15. <u>Duroc</u> app.-#14(later called Durak).
<u>King George</u> 1st app.-#8.

<u>MYSTERY IN SPACE</u> (#1-4, 52pgs.)
Apr-May, 1951 - #110, Sept, 1966
National Periodical Publications
                              Good   Fine   Mint
#1-Frazetta art, 8pgs.; Knights of the Galaxy
   begins, ends #8   50.00 100.00 150.00
 2   18.00 36.00 54.00
 3   14.00 28.00 42.00
 4,5   10.00 20.00 30.00
 6-10: #7-Toth art   7.00 14.00 21.00
11-15: #13-Toth art   6.00 12.00 18.00
16-18,20-25: Interplanetary Insurance feature by Infantino in all. #24-Last precode
   issue   5.00 10.00 15.00
19-Virgil Finley story   7.00 14.00 21.00
26-Space Cabbie begins   3.00   6.00   9.00
27-34,36-40   3.00   6.00   9.00
35-Kubert art   4.00   8.00 12.00
41-52: #47-Space Cabbie feature ends
                         2.00   4.00   6.00
53-1st Adam Strange app. 15.00 30.00 45.00
54   8.00 16.00 24.00
55   6.00 12.00 18.00
56-60   4.00   8.00 12.00
61-70: #63-Origin Vandor. #66-1st Star Rov-
   ers. #68-Origin Dust Devil
                         2.50   5.00   7.50
71-74,76-80   1.75   3.50   5.25
75-JLA x-over in Adam Strange
                         1.75   3.50   5.25
81-86   1.25   2.50   3.75
87-90-Hawkman in all   1.00   2.00   3.00
91-102: #91-End Infantino art on Adam Strange.
   #92-Space Ranger begins. #94,98-Adam Stran-
   ge/Space Ranger team-up. #102-Adam Strange
   ends   .40   .80   1.20
103-Origin Ultra, the Multi-Alien; Space
    Ranger ends   .40   .80   1.20
104-110   .30   .60   .90
NOTE: <u>Anderson</u> stories-#2,4,8-10,12-17,19,
45-48,51,57,61-64,70,76,87-98; covers-#9,10,
15-25,87,89,105-108,110. <u>Drucker</u> stories-#13,
14. <u>Infantino</u> stories-#1-8,11,14-25,27-46,48,
49,51,53-91,103; covers-#60-86,88,90,91,105,
107. <u>Gil Kane</u> stories-#100-102; cover-#101.
<u>Simon & Kirby</u> art-#4(2pgs.).

<u>MYSTERY MEN COMICS</u>
Aug, 1939 - #31, Feb, 1942
Fox Features Syndicate

#1-Intro. & 1st app. The Blue Beetle, The
   Green Mask, Rex Dexter of Mars, Zanzibar,
   Lt. Drake, D-13, Secret Agent, Chen Chang,
   Wing Turner, & Captain Denny Scott

Mysterious Stories #5, © PG

Mystery In Space #15, © DC

Mystery Men Comics #10, © FOX

Mystery Tales #37, ©MCG   Mystic #25, © MCG   Mystic Comics #6, © MCG

(Mystery Men cont'd)	Good	Fine	Mint
	70.00	140.00	210.00
2	35.00	70.00	105.00
3	30.00	60.00	90.00
4-Capt. Savage begins	27.00	54.00	81.00
5	22.00	44.00	66.00
6-8	17.00	34.00	51.00
9-The Moth begins	15.00	30.00	45.00
10-Wing Turner by Kirby	15.00	30.00	45.00
11-Intro. Domino	12.00	24.00	36.00
12,13,15-18	10.00	20.00	30.00
14-Intro. Lynx & sidekick Blackie			
	12.00	24.00	36.00
19-Intro. & 1st app. Miss X (ends #21)			
	12.00	24.00	36.00
20-25	10.00	20.00	30.00
26-The Wraith begins	10.00	20.00	30.00
27-31	10.00	20.00	30.00

NOTE: *Lou Fine covers-#1-5,8,9. Simon cover-#10.*

MYSTERY TALES
March, 1952 - #54, Aug, 1957
Atlas Comics (20CC)

#1	3.00	6.00	9.00
2-Krigstein story	2.50	5.00	7.50
3-10: #10-Gil Kane art	1.50	3.00	4.50
11-19,21: Last precode issue			
	1.00	2.00	3.00
20-Torres art	1.75	3.50	5.25
22-35,37,38,40-43,49	.80	1.60	2.40
36,39-Krigstein stories	1.75	3.50	5.25
44,48,51-Williamson stories; with Mayo			
#44,51	2.50	5.00	7.50
45-Ditko story	1.25	2.50	3.75
46-Williamson/Krenkel sty.	2.50	5.00	7.50
47-Crandall + Powell art	1.50	3.00	4.50
50-Torres + Morrow story	1.50	3.00	4.50
52,53	.80	1.60	2.40
54-Crandall story	1.25	2.50	3.75

NOTE: *Everett stories-#2,28,29,33,35,43; covers-#9,11,14,38,46,48-51,53. Kinstler story-#15. Orlando story-#51. Powell story-#21,29,37,38,48. Robinson story-#7(with Lee),42. Wildey story-#37. #26-No code on cover.*

MYSTERY TALES
1964
Super Comics

Super Reprint #16,17('64)	.50	1.00	1.50
Super Reprint #18-Kubert art/Strange Terrors			
#4	.70	1.40	2.10

MYSTIC (3rd Series)
March, 1951 - #61, Aug, 1957
Marvel/Atlas Comics(CSI)

	Good	Fine	Mint
#1	3.00	6.00	9.00
2,3,5,7-10	1.75	3.50	5.25
4,6-Wolverton art	10.00	20.00	30.00
11-20	1.25	2.50	3.75
21-32,34-36-Last precode issue			
	1.00	2.00	3.00
33-Sid Check story	1.25	2.50	3.75
37-51,53-55,57,61	.80	1.60	2.40
52-Wood & Crandall stys.	3.00	6.00	9.00
56-Severin cover, Powell story			
	1.00	2.00	3.00
58,59-Krigstein stories	1.75	3.50	5.25
60-Williamson/Mayo story, 4pgs.			
	2.50	5.00	7.50

NOTE: *Drucker story-#52,56. Everett stories-#8,9,17,40,44,53,57; covers-#18,42,53-55,61. Infantino story-#12. Kane art-#1,8. Morrow story-#51. Orlando stories-#57,61. Robinson story-#5. Whitney story-#33.*

MYSTICAL TALES
June, 1956 - #8, Aug, 1957
Atlas Comics (EPI)

#1-Everett cover/story	2.25	4.50	6.75
2-4-Crandall art	2.00	4.00	6.00
5-Williamson story,4pgs.	2.50	5.00	7.50
6-Torres, Krigstein art	2.25	4.50	6.75
7-Torres, Orlando story	2.25	4.50	6.75
8-Krigstein, Check story	2.00	4.00	6.00

NOTE: *Drucker story-#46. Everett covers-#4,6,7. Krigstein story-#6,8. Orlando stories-#1,2. Powell story-#1,4.*

MYSTIC COMICS (1st Series)
March, 1940 - #10, Aug, 1942
Timely Comics

#1-Origin The Blue Blaze, The Dynamic Man, & Flexo the Rubber Man; Zephyr Jones, 3X's & Deep Sea Demon app.; The Magician begins   275.00 550.00 825.00

2-The Invisible Man & Master Mind Excello begin; Space Rangers, Zara of the Jungle, Taxi Taylor app.   150.00 300.00 450.00

3-Origin Hercules, who last appears in #4   120.00 240.00 360.00

4-Origin The Thin Man & The Black Widow; Merzak the Mystic app.; last Flexo Dynamic Man, Invisible Man & Blue Blaze.(Some issues have date sticker on cover)   140.00 280.00 420.00

5-Origin The Black Marvel, The Blazing Skull, The Sub-Earth Man, Super Slave & The Terror; The Moon Man & Black Widow app.   125.00 250.00 375.00

6-Origin The Challenger & The Destroyer   100.00 200.00 300.00

(Mystic Comics cont'd)   Good   Fine   Mint
7-The Witness begins(origin); origin Davey
   & the Demon; last Black Widow; Simon &
   Kirby cover   75.00 150.00 225.00
8   70.00 140.00 210.00
9-Gary Gaunt app.; last Black Marvel, Mystic
   & Blazing Skull   70.00 140.00 210.00
10-Father Time, World of Wonder, & Red Skeleton app.; last Challenger & Terror
               70.00 140.00 210.00

MYSTIC COMICS (2nd Series)
Oct, 1944 - #4, Winter, 1944-45
Timely Comics

#1-The Angel, The Destroyer, The Human Torch,
   Terry Vance, the Schoolboy Sleuth, & Tommy
   Tyme begin   25.00 50.00 75.00
2,3: #2-Last Human Torch & Terry Vance; #3-
   last Angel(2 stories) & Tommy Tyme
              17.00 34.00 51.00
4-The Young Allies app. 15.00 30.00 45.00

MY STORY (--True Romances in Pictures #5&6)
#5, May, 1949 - #12, Aug, 1940(Formerly Zago)
Hero Books (Fox Features Syndicate)

#5-Kamen/Feldstein art 3.00 6.00 9.00
6-8,11,12   1.50 3.00 4.50
9,10-Wood stories   5.00 10.00 15.00

MY TRUE LOVE (Frank Buck #70 on)
#65, July, 1949 - #69, March, 1950
Fox Features Syndicate

#65-69   1.50 3.00 4.50

NAKED PREY, THE (See Movie Classics)

NAMORA
Fall, 1948 - #3, Dec, 1948
Marvel Comics

#1-Sub-Mariner x-over in Namora; Everett art
              30.00 60.00 90.00
2-The Blonde Phantom app. in Sub-Mariner
   story; Everett art 25.00 50.00 75.00
3-Sub-Mariner app.; Everett art
              17.00 34.00 51.00

NANCY AND SLUGGO
1949 - #23, 1954
United Features Syndicate

#16(#1)   1.35 2.75 4.00
17-23   1.00 2.00 3.00

NANCY & SLUGGO (Nancy #157-173; formerly
Sparkler Comics)
#121, 4/55 - #192, 10/63
St. John/Dell #146-187/Gold Key #188 on
          Good   Fine   Mint
#121(4/55)-#145(7/57)-St. John
          .80 1.60 2.40
146(9/57)-Peanuts begins, ends #192(Dell)
         1.00 2.00 3.00
147-161(Dell)   .80 1.60 2.40
162-180-John Stanley art 1.20 2.40 3.60
181-187(3-4/62)(Dell) .70 1.40 2.10
188(10/62)-192(G.Key) .60 1.20 1.80
4-Color #1034-Summer Camp .80 1.60 2.40
--Travel Time #1('58-Dell)(25¢)
         1.25 2.50 3.75
    (See Dell Giant #34,45)

NANNY AND THE PROFESSOR (TV)
Aug, 1970 - #2, Oct, 1970
Dell Publishing Co.

#1(01-546-008), #2   .15 .30

NAPOLEON & SAMANTHA (See Walt Disney Showcase #10)

NAPOLEON & UNCLE ELBY
1942 (68 pgs.) (One Shot)
Eastern Color Printing Co.

#1   10.00 20.00 30.00
1945-American Book-Strafford Press(128pgs.)
   (8x10½"-B&W reprints-Hardcover)
         7.00 14.00 21.00

NAPOLEON & UNCLE ELBY
1954
Dell Publishing Co.

4-Color #526, #1   1.00 2.00 3.00

NATIONAL COMICS
July, 1940 - #75, 1949
Quality Comics Group

#1-Origin Uncle Sam, Merlin, the Magician
   (ends #26), & Wonder Boy's sidekick Buddy;
   Cyclone, Wonder Boy(ends #26), Kid Patrol,
   Sally O'Neal Policewoman, Pen Miller(ends
   #22, Kid Dixon, Prop Powers(ends #26), &
   Paul Bunyan(ends #22) begin
         135.00 270.00 405.00
2   70.00 140.00 210.00
3   60.00 120.00 180.00
4-Last Cyclone   35.00 70.00 105.00
5-Quick Silver by Jack Cole begins; origin
   Uncle Sam   40.00 80.00 120.00

My Story #10. © FOX

Nancy #166. © UFS

National Comics #16. © QUA

National Comics #36, © QUA   Nature Boy #4, © CC   Navy Tales #2, © MCG

(National Comics cont'd)	Good	Fine	Mint
6-11: #8-Jack & Jill begins(ends #22)			
	30.00	60.00	90.00
12-20-Lou Fine art	25.00	50.00	75.00
21,22	20.00	40.00	60.00
23-The Unknown & Destroyer begin			
	17.50	35.00	52.50
24-26,28,30	15.00	30.00	45.00
27-G-2, the Unknown begins(ends #46)			
	15.00	30.00	45.00
29-Origin The Unknown	15.00	30.00	45.00
31-33: #33-Chic Carter begins(ends #47)			
	9.00	18.00	27.00
34-40: #35-Last Kid Patrol			
	7.00	14.00	21.00
41-47,49,50: #42-The Barker begins			
	5.00	10.00	15.00
48-Origin The Whistler	5.00	10.00	15.00
51-Sally O'Neil by Ward, 8pgs. (12/45)			
	6.00	12.00	18.00
52-60	4.00	8.00	12.00
61-67: #67-Format change; Quicksilver app.			
	3.00	6.00	9.00
68-75: #74-The Barker ends			
	2.25	4.50	6.75

NOTE: *Cole* Quicksilver-#13. *Crandall* Uncle
Sam-#11,13(w/Fine),25,26; covers-#24-26,30-
33. Crandall Paul Benjamin-#11-13. Fine
Uncle Sam-#12,13(w/Crandall)-20; covers-#1-
22. Guardineer Quicksilver-#27. Gustavson
Quicksilver-#14-26. McWilliams art-#23-28,
55,57. Zolnerwich Uncle Sam-#1-3.

NATIONAL CRUMB, THE (Magazine-Size)
August, 1975   (52 pgs.)   (Satire)
Mayfair Publications

#1	.40	.80	1.20

NATIONAL VELVET (TV)
May-July, 1961 - March, 1963
Dell Publishing Co./Gold Key

4-Color #1195,1312	.70	1.40	2.10
#01556-207,210	.70	1.40	2.10
#1(12/62),#2(3/63)-G.Key	.40	.80	1.20

NATURE BOY
#3, March, 1956 - #5, Feb, 1957
Charlton Comics

#3-Origin; Blue Beetle story; Buscema story			
	4.00	8.00	12.00
4,5-Buscema stories each	3.00	6.00	9.00

NATURE OF THINGS (See 4-Color #727,842)

NAVY ACTION (Sailor Sweeney #12-14)

Aug, 1954 - #11, 4/56; #15, 1/57 - #18, 8/57
Atlas Comics (CDS)

	Good	Fine	Mint
#1-Powell story	1.50	3.00	4.50
2-11	.75	1.50	2.25
15-18	.70	1.40	2.10

NOTE: *Berg* story-#9. *Drucker* story-#7,17.

NAVY COMBAT
June, 1955 - #20, Oct, 1958
Atlas Comics (MPI)

#1-Torpedo Taylor begins by D. Heck			
	1.50	3.00	4.50
2-10	.75	1.50	2.25
11-13,15,16,18-20	.60	1.20	1.80
14-Torres story	1.25	2.50	3.75
17-Williamson story,4pgs.	2.50	5.00	7.50

NOTE: *Berg* story-#11. *Everett* stories-#3,20;
covers-#10,15.

NAVY HEROES
1945
Almanac Publishing Co.

#1-Heavy in propaganda	2.50	5.00	7.50

NAVY: HISTORY & TRADITION
1958 - 1961   (No#)   (Giveaway)
Stokes Walesby Co./Dept. of Navy

1772-1778, 1778-1817, 1817-1865, 1865-1936,			
1940-1945	1.35	2.75	4.00

1961-Navy Actions of the Civil War (6 known
issues in all)
each....	1.35	2.75	4.00

NAVY PATROL
May, 1955 - #4, Nov, 1955
Key Publications

#1	1.00	2.00	3.00
2-4	.60	1.20	1.80

NAVY TALES
Jan, 1957 - #4, July, 1957
Atlas Comics (CDS)

#1-Everett cover	1.50	3.00	4.50
2-Williamson/Mayo story, 5pgs. + Crandall			
story	3.00	6.00	9.00
3,4: #3-Krigstein story. #4-Crandall story			
	1.50	3.00	4.50

NAVY TASK FORCE
Feb, 1954 - #8, April, 1956
Stanmor Publications/Aragon Mag. #4-8

(Navy Task Force cont'd)	Good	Fine	Mint
#1	1.00	2.00	3.00
2-8	.60	1.20	1.80

NAVY WAR HEROES
Jan, 1964 - #7, Mar-Apr, 1965
Charlton Comics

#1	.20	.40	.60
2-7		.15	.45

NAZA (Stone Age Warrior)
Nov-Jan, 1964 - #9, March, 1966
Dell Publishing Co.

#1(12-555-401)	1.00	2.00	3.00
2-9	.60	1.20	1.80

NEBBS, THE
1928   (Daily B&W strip reprints, 52pgs.)
Cupples & Leon Co.

By Sol Hess; Carlson art	6.00	12.00	18.00

NEBBS, THE
1941 - 1945
Dell Publishing Co./Croyden Publishers

Black & White #23('41)	6.00	15.00	24.00
#1(1945) reprints	2.50	5.00	7.50

NEGRO (See All-Negro)

NEGRO HEROES (Reprints from True, Real
Heroes, & Calling All Girls)
Spring, 1947 - #2, Summer, 1948
Parents' Magazine Institute

#1 (Scarce)	30.00	60.00	90.00
2 (Scarce)	15.00	30.00	45.00

NEGRO ROMANCE (Negro Romances #4)
June, 1950 - #3, Oct, 1950
Fawcett Publications

#1-Evans art (Scarce)	70.00	140.00	210.00
2,3 (Scarce)	40.00	80.00	120.00

NEGRO ROMANCES (Formerly Negro Romance)
#4, May, 1955
Charlton Comics

#4 (Scarce)-Reprints Fawcett #2			
	30.00	60.00	90.00

NELLIE THE NURSE
1945 - #36, Oct, 1952; 1957
Marvel/Atlas Comics(SPI/LMC)

	Good	Fine	Mint
#1	4.00	8.00	12.00
2-4	2.50	5.00	7.50
5-Kurtzman's "Hey Look"	3.00	6.00	9.00
6-8,10	1.50	3.00	4.50
9-Wolverton art, 1pg.	2.50	5.00	7.50
11,14-16,18-Kurtzman's "Hey Look"			
	2.50	5.00	7.50
12-"Giggles 'n' Grins" by Kurtzman			
	2.00	4.00	6.00
13,17,19-27,29-36	1.00	2.00	3.00
28-Kurtzman's Rusty reprt.	2.00	4.00	6.00
#1('57)-Leading Mag.(Atlas)	.40	.80	1.20

NELLIE THE NURSE (See 4-Color Comics #1304)

NEUTRO
Jan, 1967
Dell Publishing Co.

#1	.70	1.40	2.10

NEVADA (See Zane Grey's Stories of the West#1)

NEVER AGAIN (War stories)
Aug, 1955 - #8, July, 1956
Charlton Comics

#1	2.00	4.00	6.00
2-8	1.50	3.00	4.50

NEW ADVENTURE COMICS (Formerly New Comics;
becomes Adventure Comics #31 on)
V1#12, Jan, 1937 - #30, Sept, 1938
National Periodical Publications

V1#12	30.00	60.00	90.00
V2#1(2/37,#13)	24.00	48.00	72.00
14(V2#2)-#20(V2#8): #15-1st Adventure logo.			
#17-Nadir, Master of Magic begins, ends			
#30	24.00	48.00	72.00
21(V2#9),#22(V2#10,2/37)			
	17.00	34.00	51.00
23-30: #29-Federal Men by Siegel & Shuster			
begins; last New Adventure			
	17.00	34.00	51.00

NEW ADVENTURE OF SNOW WHITE AND THE SEVEN
DWARFS, A (See Snow White Bendix Giveaway)

NEW ADVENTURES OF CHARLIE CHAN, THE
May-June, 1958 - #6, Mar-Apr, 1959
National Periodical Publications

#1	2.50	5.00	7.50
2-6-Sid Greene art	1.50	3.00	4.50

Naza #3, © DELL

Negro Romance #2, © FAW

Nellie The Nurse #16, © MCG

New Advs. Of Peter Pan 1953, © WDP

New Comics #5, © DC

New Gods #2, © DC

NEW ADVENTURES OF HUCK FINN, THE (TV)
September, 1968 (Hanna-Barbera)
Gold Key

	Good	Fine	Mint
#1-"The Curse of Thut"	.25	.50	.75

NEW ADVENTURES OF PETER PAN (Disney)
1953 (36pgs.) (Admiral giveaway) (5x7¼")
Western Publishing Co.

	3.00	6.00	9.00

NEW ADVENTURES OF PINOCCHIO
Oct-Dec, 1962 - #3, 1963
Dell Publishing Co.

#12-562-212	.70	1.40	2.10
#2,3	.50	1.00	1.50

NEW ADVENTURES OF ROBIN HOOD (See Robin Hood)

NEW ADVENTURES OF SHERLOCK HOLMES (See
4-Color Comics #1169,1245)

NEW BOOK OF COMICS
1936; Spring/1938 (100pgs.) (Reprints)
National Periodical Publications

#1	60.00	120.00	180.00
2-Dr. Occult by Siegel & Shuster; #1&2 re-
prints New Comics & More Fun			
	35.00	70.00	105.00

NEW COMICS (New Adventure #12 on)
Dec, 1935 - #11, Dec, 1936 (#1-6, soft cover)
National Periodical Publications

V1#1-Billy the Kid, Sagebrush 'n' Cactus,
Jibby Jones, Needles, The Vikings, Sir
Loin of Beef, Now-When I Was a Boy, &
other 1-2pg. strips. 2pgs. Kelly art
(Gulliver's Travels). (Also see More-
Fun #6)	180.00	360.00	540.00
2	90.00	180.00	270.00
3-5	50.00	100.00	150.00

NOTE: #1-5 rarely occur in mint condition.

6-11	30.00	60.00	90.00

NEW FUN COMICS (More Fun #7 on)
Feb, 1935 - #6, Oct, 1935 (Large Size)
National Periodical Publications

V1#1 (1st DC comic)	200.00	400.00	600.00
2(3/35) (Very Rare)	120.00	240.00	360.00
3-5(8/35)	70.00	140.00	210.00
6(10/35)-1st Dr. Occult by Siegel & Shust-
er; 1st comic book art by Walt Kelly,
1pg.; last "New Fun" title. "New Comics"
#1 begins in Dec. which is reason for
title change to More Fun; Henri Duval
(ends #9), Leger Reuths by Siegel & Shus-
ter begins	100.00	200.00	300.00

	Good	Fine	Mint

NEW FUNNIES (The Funnies, #1-64; #259,260,
272,273 titled New TV--; #261-271-TV Funnies)
#65, July, 1942 - #288, Mar-Apr, 1962
Dell Publishing Co.

#65(#1)-Andy Panda, Felix the Cat by Messmer,
Raggedy Ann, Oswald the Rabbit, & Li'l
Eight Ball begin	60.00	120.00	180.00
66-70: #67-Billy & Bonnie Bee by Frank
Thomas begins	25.00	50.00	75.00
71-75: #72-Kelly illos	12.00	24.00	36.00
76-Andy Panda-(Carl Barks & Pabian art)	100.00	200.00	300.00
77-79-Andy Panda in a World of Real People
ends, becomes all funny animal	12.00	24.00	36.00
80,81	12.00	24.00	36.00
82-Brownies by Kelly?	15.00	30.00	45.00
83-85-Kelly text illos	10.00	20.00	30.00
86-90	4.00	8.00	12.00
91-100	3.00	6.00	9.00
101-120	2.00	4.00	6.00
121-150	1.00	2.00	3.00
151-200: #182-Origin & 1st app. Nuthead &
Splinter	.75	1.50	2.25
201-288	.40	.80	1.20

NOTE: Early issues written by John Stanley.

NEW GODS, THE (Orion of--#2,3)(See 1st Issue
Feb-Mar, 1971 - #11, Oct-Nov, 1972; Spec.)
#12, July, 1977 - #19, Jul-Aug, 1978
National Periodical Publications/DC Comics

#1	2.00	4.00	6.00
2	1.35	2.75	4.00
3,4-Origin Manhunter reprinted in #4	1.20	2.40	3.60
5-8: #5-Young Gods feature. #7-Origin Orion.
#7,8-Young Gods app.	1.00	2.00	3.00
9-11	.80	1.60	2.40
12-14,16-19-Newton/Atkins art	.30	.60	.90
15	.25	.50	.75

NOTE: #4-9 contain Manhunter reprints by
Simon & Kirby from Adventure #73,74,75,76,77,
& 78 in that order. Kirby art/covers in #1-11.
Starlin cover-#17. Staton cover-#19.

NEW HEROIC (See Heroic)

NEWLYWEDS & THEIR BABY'S COMIC PICTURES, THE
1917 (22pgs.)(14x10",oblong,cardboard covers)
Saalfield Publ. Co.

(Newlyweds & -- cont'd)   Good   Fine   Mint
By George McManus. Reprints "Newlyweds"
(Baby Snookums strips) mainly from 1916. Blue
cover; says for painting and crayoning, but
some pages in color. (Scarce)
                              20.00 50.00 80.00

NEW MEN OF BATTLE, THE
No# 1949   (Cardboard covers)
Catechetical Guild

No#(V8#1-V8#6)-192pgs., contains 6 issues
  of Topix rebound   1.50   3.00   4.50
No#(V8#7-V8#11)-160pgs., contains 5 issues
  of Topix   1.50   3.00   4.50

NEW PEOPLE, THE (TV)
Jan, 1970 - #2, May, 1970
Dell Publishing Co.

#1,2   .20   .40   .60

NEW ROMANCES
#5, May, 1951 - #20, Feb, 1954
Standard Comics

#5-9   1.00   2.00   3.00
10,11,16,17-Toth stories   2.00   4.00   6.00
12-15,18-20   .75   1.50   2.25
NOTE: *Tuska art-#7,20.*

NEW TERRYTOONS (TV)
6-8/60 - #8, 3-5/62; 10/62 - Present
Dell Publishing Co./Gold Key

#1('60-Dell)   .50   1.00   1.50
  2-8 ('62)   .25   .50   .75
  1(30010-210)(3/62,G.Key, 84pgs.)
                            .20   .40   .60
  2(30010-301)-84pgs.   .20   .40   .60
  3-16   .15   .30   .45
  17-55   .15   .30
NOTE: *Reprints: #4-12,38,40,47. (See March
of Comics #393,412)*

NEW TV FUNNIES (See New Funnies)

NEW YORK GIANTS (See Thrilling True Story of
the Baseball Giants)

NEW YORK STATE JOINT LEGISLATIVE COMMITTEE TO
STUDY THE PUBLICATION OF COMICS, THE
1951
N. Y. State Legislative Document

This document was referenced by Wertham for
Seduction of the Innocent. Contains numerous
repros from comics showing violence, sadism,

torture, and sex.

NEW YORK WORLD'S FAIR
1939, 1940 (100 pgs.) (Cardboard covers)
National Periodical Publications

                             Good   Fine   Mint
1939-Superman, Sandman, Zatara, Slam Bradley,
  Pep Morgan begin; Ginger Snap by Bob Kane
  app.   175.00 437.50 700.00
1940-Slam Bradley, Batman, Hourman, Johnny
  Thunder app.   100.00 250.00 400.00

NOTE: The 1939 edition was published at 25 cents. Since all
other comics were 10 cents, it didn't sell. Remaining copies were
repriced with 15 cents stickers placed over the 25 cents price.
Four variations on the 15 cents stickers known. It was advertised
in other DC comics at 25 cents. Everyone who sent a quarter
through the mail for it received a free Superman No. 1 or No. 2
to make up the dime difference. The 1940 edition was priced at
15 cents.

NICKEL COMICS
1938 (Pocket size - 7½x5½") (132 pgs.)
Dell Publishing Co.

#1-"Bobby & Chip" by Otto Messmer, Felix the
  Cat artist. Contains some English reprints
                            20.00 40.00 60.00

NICKEL COMICS
5/40 - #8, 8/40 (36 pgs.) (Bi-Weekly) (5c)
Fawcett Publications

#1-Origin Bulletman   80.00 160.00 240.00
2   45.00 90.00 135.00
3   35.00 70.00 105.00
4-The Red Gaucho begins   30.00 60.00 90.00
5-8   25.00 50.00 75.00
NOTE: *Covers on some issues by C. C. Beck.
Jack Binder cover-#1.*

NICK FURY, AGENT OF SHIELD (See Shield)
June, 1968 - #18, March, 1971
Marvel Comics Group

#1   1.75   3.50   5.25
2,3   1.50   3.00   4.50
4-Origin retold   1.25   2.50   3.75
5-Steranko story   1.25   2.50   3.75
6-11: #9-Hate Monger begins(ends #11). #11-
  Smith cover   .60   1.20   1.80
12-Smith cover/art   1.00   2.00   3.00
13-15   .50   1.00   1.50
16-18-All reprints (52pgs) .30   .60   .90
NOTE: *Craig inks-#10. Kirby reprints-#18.
Steranko stories-#1-3,5; covers-#1-7.*

NICK HALIDAY
May, 1956
Argo

New Romances #13, © STD

Nickel Comics #6, © FAW

Nick Fury Agent Of Shield #4, © MCG

Nick Haliday #1, © Argo   Nightmare #2, © STJ   Noman #1, © TC

	Good	Fine	Mint
(Nick Haliday cont'd)			
#1-Daily & Sunday strip reprints by Petree			
	2.00	4.00	6.00

NIGHT BEFORE CHRISTMAS, THE (See March of
Comics #152)

NIGHTMARE
Summer, 1952 - #2, Fall, 1952; #3,4, 1953
Ziff-Davis(Approved Comics)/St. John #3,4

#1-Kinstler art	2.50	5.00	7.50
2-Kinstler story-Poe's "Pit & the Pendulum"			
	1.75	3.50	5.25
3-Kinstler story	1.75	3.50	5.25
4	1.20	2.40	3.60

NIGHTMARE (Formerly Weird Horrors #1-9)
(Amazing Ghost Stories #14 on)
#10, Dec, 1953 - #13, Aug, 1954
St. John Publishing Co.

#10-Reprints Z-D Weird Thrillers #2 with new			
Kubert cover + 2pgs. Kinstler, Toth &			
Anderson stories	2.50	5.00	7.50
11-Krigstein story	2.00	4.00	6.00
12-Kubert bondage cover	1.75	3.50	5.25
13-Reprints Z-D Weird Thrillers #3 with new			
cover + Powell story	1.75	3.50	5.25

NIGHTMARE (Magazine)
Dec, 1970 - #23, Feb, 1975 (B&W) (68pgs.)
Skywald Publishing Corp.

#1-Everett art	1.00	2.00	3.00
2-5	.65	1.35	2.00
6-Kaluta art	1.00	2.00	3.00
7,9,10: #9,10-Wolverton back covers			
	.65	1.35	2.00
8-Features E.C. movie "Tales From the Crypt";			
reprints some E.C. comics panels			
	1.50	3.00	4.50
11-20	.25	.50	.75
21-(1974 Summer Special)-Kaluta art			
	.60	1.20	1.80
22-Tomb of Horror ish.	.35	.70	1.05
23-(1975 Winter Special)	.35	.70	1.05
Annual #1(1972)	.50	1.00	1.50
Winter Special #1(1973)	.50	1.00	1.50
Yearbook-No#(1974)	.35	.70	1.05

NOTE: _Adkins_ story-#5. _Boris_ cover-#5. _Everett_ story-#5. _Jones_ art-#6,21. _Wildey_ art-
#6,'74 Year Book. _Wrightson_ story-#9.

NIGHTMARE & CASPER (See Harvey Hits #71)
(Casper & Nightmare #6 on)
May, 1963 - #5, Aug, 1964 (25¢)
Harvey Publications

	Good	Fine	Mint
#1	.50	1.00	1.50
2-5	.30	.60	.90

NIGHTMARES (See Do You Believe in --)

NIGHT NURSE
Nov, 1972 - #4, May, 1973
Marvel Comics Group

#1-4		.15	.30

NIGHT OF MYSTERY
1953 (No Month) (One Shot)
Avon Periodicals

No#-Kinstler art. 1pg.	4.00	8.00	12.00

NIGHT OF THE GRIZZLY, THE (See Movie Classics)

NIGHT RIDER
Oct, 1974 - #6, Aug, 1975
Marvel Comics Group

#1	.25	.50	.75
2-6	.15	.30	.45

NOTE: _#1-6 reprints Ghost Rider #1-6._

NIKKI, WILD DOG OF THE NORTH (See 4-Color
#1226 & Movie Comics)

1984 (Magazine)
May, 1978 - Present
Warren Publishing Co.

#1	.40	.80	1.20
2-4	.25	.50	.75

NIPPY'S POP
1917 (Sunday strip reprints-B&W)(10½x13½")
The Saalfield Publishing Co.

32pgs.	5.00	10.00	15.00

NOAH'S ARK
1973
Spire Christian Comics/Fleming H. Revell Co.

By Al Hartley	.25	.50	.75

NOMAN
Nov, 1966 - #2, March, 1967
Tower Comics

#1-Wood/Williamson cover; Lightning begins;			
Dynamo cameo; Kane pencils			
	1.20	2.40	3.60
2-Wood cover only; Dynamo x-over; Whitney			
stories-#1,2	1.00	2.00	3.00

NONE BUT THE BRAVE (See Movie Classics)

NOODNIK COMICS (See Pinky the Egghead)
1953; #2, Feb, 1954 - #5, Aug, 1954
Comic Media/Mystery/Biltmore

	Good	Fine	Mint
3-D(1953)(Comic Media)(#1)	6.00	12.00	18.00
#2-5	.70	1.40	2.10

NORTH TO ALASKA (See 4-Color Comics #1155)

NORTHWEST MOUNTIES (Also see Approved Comics)
Oct, 1948 - #4, July, 1949; #12, Aug, 1954
Jubilee Publications/St. John

#1-Rose of the Yukon by Matt Baker; Walter			
Johnson art	4.00	8.00	12.00
2-Baker story; Ventrilo app.			
	3.00	6.00	9.00
3-Bondage cover, Baker story; Sky Chief,			
K-9 app.	4.00	8.00	12.00
4-Baker cover, 2pgs.; Blue Monk app.			
	3.00	6.00	9.00
12(8/54)-Reprints #4 with new Baker cover			
	1.75	3.50	5.25

NO SLEEP 'TIL DAWN (See 4-Color #831)

NOT BRAND ECHH
Aug, 1967 - #13, May, 1969 (#9-13, 68pgs.)
Marvel Comics Group

#1	.75	1.50	2.25
2-4	.50	1.00	1.50
5-Origin & intro. Forbush Man			
	.50	1.00	1.50
6-13-Avengers satire #12	.35	.70	1.05

NOTE: _Kirby art-#1,3,5-7; cover-#1. Archie_
satire-#9.

NO TIME FOR SERGEANTS (TV)
July, 1958 - #3, Aug-Oct, 1965
Dell Publishing Co.

4-Color #914 (Movie)	1.25	2.50	3.75
#1(2-4/65)-#3 (TV)	.35	.70	1.05

NOVA
Sept, 1976 - Present
Marvel Comics Group

#1-Origin; low distribution in some areas			
	1.50	3.00	4.50
2,3	.50	1.00	1.50
4-Thor app.	.50	1.00	1.50
5-Marvel Gang app.	.40	.80	1.20
6-10	.35	.70	1.05
11,13,14,19	.25	.50	.75

	Good	Fine	Mint
12-Spider-Man x-over	.25	.50	.75
15-18-Nick Fury & Shield app.			
	.25	.50	.75
20-Reveals I.D. to family	.25	.50	.75
21,22	.20	.40	.60

NOTE: _John Buscema stories-#1,2,21; cover-#2._
Infantino stories-#10-21. Kirby covers-#5,7.

NUKLA
Oct-Dec, 1965 - #4, Sept, 1966
Dell Publishing Co.

#1-Origin Nukla	.70	1.40	2.10
2,3	.40	.80	1.20
4-Ditko art	.80	1.60	2.40

NURSE BETSY CRANE
Aug, 1961 - #27, Mar, 1964
Charlton Comics

V2#12-27		.15	.35

NURSE HELEN GRANT (The Romances of)
August, 1957
Atlas Comics (VPI)

#1	.30	.60	.90

NURSE LINDA LARK (See Linda Lark)

NURSERY RHYMES
1951
Ziff-Davis Publ. Co.

#2-10-Howie Post art #10	1.20	2.40	3.60

NURSES, THE (TV)
April, 1963 - #3, Oct, 1963
Gold Key

#1	.25	.50	.75
2,3	.20	.40	.60

NUTS! (Satire)
March, 1954 - #5, Nov, 1954
Premiere Comics Group

#1	3.00	6.00	9.00
2-5: #5-Capt. Marvel parody			
	2.00	4.00	6.00

NUTS (Magazine) (Satire)
Feb, 1958 - #2, April, 1958
Health Knowledge

#1	1.50	3.00	4.50
2	1.20	2.40	3.60

Northwest Mounties #2, © STJ

Nova #1, © MCG   Nuts! #1, © PG

Nyoka The Jungle Girl #22, © FAW   Official True Crime Cases #25, © MCG   O.G. Whiz #1, © GK

NUTS & JOLTS (See Black & White #22)

NUTSY SQUIRREL (Formerly Hollywood Funny
#61, 9-10/54 - #72, 11/57   Folks)
National Periodical Publications

	Good	Fine	Mint
#61-72	1.00	2.00	3.00

NUTTY COMICS
Winter, 1946
Fawcett Publications

#1-Capt. Kidd story; Wolverton art

	4.00	8.00	12.00

NUTTY COMICS
1945 - #8, June-July, 1947
Harvey Publications (Home Comics)

No#-Helpful Hank, Bozo Bear & others

	1.00	2.00	3.00
#2-4	.50	1.00	1.50
5-8: #5-Rags Rabbit begins	.50	1.00	1.50

NUTTY LIFE
#2, Summer, 1946
Fox Features Syndicate

#2	1.50	3.00	4.50

NYOKA, THE JUNGLE GIRL (Formerly Jungle Girl)
#2, Winter, 1945 - #77, June, 1953
Fawcett Publications

#2	20.00	40.00	60.00
3	12.00	24.00	36.00
4,5	9.00	18.00	27.00
6-10	8.00	16.00	24.00
11-20	6.00	12.00	18.00
21-30	4.50	9.00	13.50
31-40	3.00	6.00	9.00
41-50	2.50	5.00	7.50
51-60	2.00	4.00	6.00
61-77	1.75	3.50	5.25

NOTE: _Krigstein stories-#11,13,14,17,18._

NYOKA, THE JUNGLE GIRL (Zoo Funnies #1-12)
1955 - #22, Nov, 1957
Charlton Comics

#13-22	2.00	4.00	6.00

OAKEY DOAKES
1942   (One Shot)
Eastern Color Printing Co.

#1	12.00	24.00	36.00

OAKLAND PRESS FUNNYBOOK, THE
9/17/78 - Present (16pgs.)(Weekly)
(Full color in comic book form)
The Oakland Press

	Good	Fine	Mint
Contains Tarzan by Manning, Marmaduke, Bugs Bunny, etc. (Low distribution)	.50	1.00	1.50

OBIE
1953   (6¢)
Store Comics

#1	.40	.80	1.20

OCCULT FILES OF DOCTOR SPEKTOR, THE
May, 1973 - #24, Feb, 1977
Gold Key (Also see Mystery Comics Digest #5)

#1-1st app. Lakota; Baron Tibor begins	.50	1.00	1.50
2-5: #3-Ra-Ka-Tep, the Mummy begins. #4-Intro. Elliott Kane; Duroc(later called Durak) app. #5-Hyde begins; 1st app. Count Dracula	.25	.50	.75
6-10: #6-Origin Simbar, the Lion Lord; 1st app. Frankenstein Monster. #7-Flashbacks to Tragg #8 & Dagar #1; establishes blood-link between Tragg, Dagar, & Spektor. #8-1st app. Cindy Bask(Kane's girlfriend). #9-Dr. Solar app.	.20	.40	.60
11-13: #11-1st app. Spektor as Werewolf. #12-1st app. Dr. Tong & Lu-Sai	.15	.30	.45
14-Dr. Solar app.	.15	.30	.45
15-17: #15-Xorkon app.; Durak flashback(Digest #14). #16-Durak app. #17-1st app. Anne Sara, Spektor's cousin	.15	.30	.45
18-Rutland, Vermont story. The Owl, Dr. Solar, Lurker, Hyde, Frankenstein Monster, Dracula, Count Wulfstein, Ra-Ka-Tep, Simbar, The Purple Zombie app.	.15	.30	.45
19-22: #19-Tragg cameo. #21-Lurker guest-stars. #22-Owl app.	.15	.30	.45
23-Dr. Solar cameo	.15	.30	.45
24-Dr. Tong app.	.15	.30	.45

ODELL'S ADVENTURES IN 3-D (See Adventures
in --)

OFFICIAL SOUPY SALES COMIC (See Soupy Sales)

OFFICIAL TRUE CRIME CASES (Formerly All-
Winner #21; All-True Crime Cases #26 on)
#22, Spring, 1947 - #25, Winter, 1947-48
Timely/Marvel(OCI)

#22-25: #24-Burgos art	1.20	2.40	3.60

O.G. WHIZ
2/71 - #6, 5/72; #7, 5/78 - #10, 11/78
Gold Key

	Good	Fine	Mint
#1,2-John Stanley script, pencils, inks, & lettering	1.00	2.00	3.00
3-6(1972)	.35	.70	1.05
7-10(1978)	.20	.40	.60

OH, BROTHER! (Teen Comedy)
Jan, 1953 - #5, Oct, 1953
Stanhall Publ./Trojan/Standard #5

#1	1.00	2.00	3.00
2-5	.60	1.20	1.80

OH SUSANNA (See 4-Color Comics #1105)

OKAY COMICS
1940
United Features Syndicate

#1-Captain & the Kids & Hawkshaw the Detective reprints	12.00	24.00	36.00

OK COMICS
July, 1940 - #2, 1940
United Features Syndicate

#1-Little Giant, Phantom Knight, Sunset Smith, & The Teller Twins begin	15.00	30.00	45.00
2 (Rare)	15.00	30.00	45.00

OKLAHOMA KID
June, 1957 - #4, 1958
Ajax/Farrell Publ.

#1	1.35	2.75	4.00
2-4	.80	1.60	2.40

OKLAHOMAN, THE (See 4-Color Comics #820)

OLD GLORY COMICS
1944   (Giveaway)
Chesapeake & Ohio Railway

Capt. Fearless reprint	2.00	4.00	6.00

OLD IRONSIDES (See 4-Color Comics #874)

OLD YELLER (See 4-Color #869, Movie Comics, and Walt Disney Showcase #25)

OMAC (One Man Army, -- Corps #4 on)
Sept-Oct, 1974 - #8, Nov-Dec, 1975
National Periodical Publications

	Good	Fine	Mint
#1-Origin	.50	1.00	1.50
2-8	.25	.50	.75

NOTE: *Kirby* art-#1-8; covers-#1-7. *Kubert* covers-#1-8.

O'MALLEY AND THE ALLEY CATS
April, 1971 - #9, Jan, 1974   (Disney)
Gold Key

#1	.25	.50	.75
2-9	.15	.30	.45

OMEGA THE UNKNOWN
March, 1976 - #10, Sept, 1977
Marvel Comics Group

#1	.50	1.00	1.50
2-10: #2-Hulk app.	.25	.50	.75

ONE HUNDRED AND ONE DALMATIANS (See 4-Color #1183, Movie Comics, & W. Disney Showcase #9)

100 PAGES OF COMICS
1937   (Stiff covers)
Dell Publishing Co.

#101(Found on back cover)-Alley Oop, Wash Tubbs, Capt. Easy, Og Son of Fire, Apple Mary, Tom Mix, Dan Dunn, Tailspin Tommy, Doctor Doom	35.00	70.00	105.00

100-PAGE SUPER SPECTACULAR (See DC --)

$1,000,000 DUCK (See W. Disney Showcase #5)

ONE MILLION YEARS AGO (See Tor)

ONE SHOT (See 4-Color --)

1001 HOURS OF FUN
1942   (52pgs.)(11¼x8-3/8")(Like Large Feature Comics)
Dell Publishing Co.

Puzzles & games; by A.W. Nugent	4.00	8.00	12.00

ON STAGE (See 4-Color Comics #1336)

ON THE AIR
1947   (Giveaway)
NBC Network Comic

(Scarce)	2.00	4.00	6.00

ON THE DOUBLE (See 4-Color Comics #1232)

O.K. Comics #1, © UFS

Omac #6, © DC

Omega The Unknown #1, © MCG

Operation Peril #5, © ACG

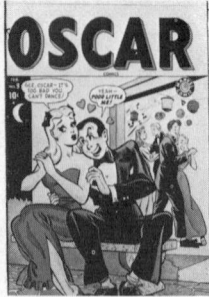

Oscar #9, © MCG

Our Army At War #1, © DC

ON THE LINKS
Dec, 1926   (48 pgs.) (9x10")
Associated Feature Service

	Good	Fine	Mint
Daily strip reprints	7.00	14.00	21.00

ON THE SPOT (Pretty Boy Floyd --)
Fall, 1948
Fawcett Publications

No#-Bondage cover	5.00	10.00	15.00

OPERATION BIKINI (See Movie Classics)

OPERATION BUCHAREST (See The Crusaders)

OPERATION CROSSBOW (See Movie Classics)

OPERATION PERIL
Oct-Nov, 1950 - 1953
American Comics Group (Michel Publ.)

#1-Time Travelers, Danny Danger (by Leonard Starr) & Typhoon Tyler (by Ogden Whitney)			
begin	2.50	5.00	7.50
2-5: #3-Horror story	1.50	3.00	4.50
6-12-Last Time Travelers; change to war format; #7-All horror	1.20	2.40	3.60
13-16	.80	1.60	2.40

NOTE: _Whitney stories-#1,2,8-10; covers-#1, 8,9._

OPERATOR #7 OF THE SECRET SERVICE
(See Chewing Gum Booklet)

ORAL ROBERTS' TRUE STORIES (15¢)(Junior Partners #120 on) (No#, #102-25¢)
1956(no month) - #119, 7/59
TelePix Publ.(Oral Roberts' Evangelistic Assn/Healing Waters)

V1#1(1956)-(Not code approved)-"The Miracle Touch"	2.50	5.00	7.50
#102-(only issue approved by code) (10/56)	2.00	4.00	6.00
103-119: #115-(#114 on inside)	1.75	3.50	5.25

ORIGINAL SWAMP THING SAGA, THE (See DC Special Series #2,14)

OSCAR (Formerly Animated Funny Comic Tunes; Awful -- #12 on)
#24, Spring, 1947 - #11, June, 1949
Marvel Comics

#24(1947)	1.20	2.40	3.60
25(1947)-Wolverton art + Kurtzman's "Hey			

	Good	Fine	Mint
Look"	4.00	8.00	12.00
#3-9,11	1.00	2.00	3.00
10-Kurtzman's "Hey Look"	2.50	5.00	7.50

OSWALD THE RABBIT
1943 - 1962   (Walter Lantz)
Dell Publishing Co.

4-Color #21('43)	20.00	40.00	60.00
4-Color #39('43)	16.00	32.00	48.00
4-Color #67('44)	10.00	20.00	30.00
4-Color #102('46)-Kelly art, 1pg.			
	10.00	20.00	30.00
4-Color #143,183	4.00	8.00	12.00
4-Color #225,273	2.50	5.00	7.50
4-Color #315,388	1.75	3.50	5.25
4-Color #458,507,549,593	1.20	2.40	3.60
4-Color #623,697,792,894,979,1268			
	.80	1.60	2.40

OSWALD THE RABBIT (See March of Comics #7, 38,53,67,81,95,111,126,141,156,171,186, & Super Book #8,20)

OUR ARMY AT WAR (Sgt. Rock #302 on)
Aug, 1952 - #301, Feb, 1977
National Periodical Publications

#1	10.00	20.00	30.00
2,3,5	5.00	10.00	15.00
4-Krigstein story	6.00	12.00	18.00
6,7	4.00	8.00	12.00
8-10-Krigstein stories	5.00	10.00	15.00
11,14-Krigstein stories	4.00	8.00	12.00
12,15-20	2.50	5.00	7.50
13-Krigstein cover/story	6.00	12.00	18.00
21-30	2.00	4.00	6.00
31-40	1.75	3.50	5.25
41-60	1.25	2.50	3.75
61-70	1.00	2.00	3.00
71-80	.90	1.80	2.70
81-1st Sgt. Rock app. by Andru & Esposito in Easy Co. story	5.00	10.00	15.00
82-Sgt. Rock cameo in Easy Co. story(6 panels)			
	3.00	6.00	9.00
83-1st Kubert Sgt. Rock	5.00	10.00	15.00
84-90	1.50	3.00	4.50
91-All Sgt. Rock issue	2.00	4.00	6.00
92-100	.80	1.60	2.40
101-120	.70	1.40	2.10
121-150	.50	1.00	1.50
151-Intro. Enemy Ace by Kubert			
	1.35	2.75	4.00
152-163,165-170: #153,155-Enemy Ace stories.			
#157-2pg. pin-up. #162,163-Viking Prince x-over in Sgt. Rock	1.00	2.00	3.00
164-Giant G-19	1.25	2.50	3.75

(Our Army at War cont'd)	Good	Fine	Mint
171-176,178-181	.40	.80	1.20
177-80pg. Giant G-32	.50	1.00	1.50
182,183,186-Neal Adams art	1.25	2.50	3.75
184,185,187-189,191-199: #189-Intro. The Teen-age Underground Fighters of Unit 3	.30	.60	.90
190-80pg. Giant G-44	.50	1.00	1.50
200-12pg. Rock story told in verse; Krigstein reprint; Evans story	.30	.60	.90
201-Krigstein reprint/#14	.30	.60	.90
202,206-215	.25	.50	.75
203-80pg. Giant G-56-All reprints, no Sgt. Rock	.35	.70	1.05
204,205-All reprints, no Sgt. Rock	.25	.50	.75
216-80pg. Giant G-68	.35	.70	1.05
217-228	.25	.50	.75
229-80pg. Giant G-80	.35	.70	1.05
230-234,236-239	.20	.40	.60
235,241-Toth art	.30	.60	.90
240-Adams art	.50	1.00	1.50
242-50¢ ish. DC-9-Kubert cvr.	.50	1.00	1.50
243-248,250-253	.20	.40	.60
249-Wood art	.40	.80	1.20
254-Toth art	.25	.50	.75
255-301	.20	.40	.60

NOTE: *Alcala* story-#251. *Drucker* stories-#27, 67,68,79,82,83,164,177,203,212,244,269,275, 280. *Evans* stories-#165-175,200,266,269,270, 274,276,278,280. *Kubert* stories-#38,59,67,68 & most issues from #83 on. *Maurer* stories-#233,237,239. *Medal of Honor* by *Maurer*-#233, 237,239,240,280,284,288,290,291,295. *U.S.S. Stevens* by *Glanzman*-#218,220,222,223,225,227, 230-32,238,240,241,244,247,248,256-59,261, 265-67,271,282,283,298.

OUR FIGHTING FORCES
Oct-Nov, 1954 - #181, Sept-Oct, 1978
National Periodical Publications/DC Comics

#1	7.50	15.00	22.50
2	4.50	9.00	13.50
3-Kubert cover/story	5.00	10.00	15.00
4,5	3.50	7.00	10.50
6-9	2.50	5.00	7.50
10-Wood story	4.00	8.00	12.00
11-20	1.75	3.50	5.25
21-30	1.50	3.00	4.50
31-40	1.25	2.50	3.75
41-44	.60	1.20	1.80
45-Gunner & Sarge begin(ends #94)	1.00	2.00	3.00
46-50	.60	1.20	1.80
51-90	.50	1.00	1.50
91-100: #95-Devil-Dog begins, ends #98. #99-Capt. Hunter begins, ends #106			

	Good	Fine	Mint
	.40	.80	1.20
101-122: #106-Hunters Hellcats begin. #116-Mlle. Marie app. #121-Intro. Heller	.30	.60	.90
123-Losers(Capt. Storm, Gunner/Sarge, Johnny Cloud) begin	.25	.50	.75
124-133,135-145	.20	.40	.60
134,146-Toth art	.20	.40	.60
147-181	.20	.40	.60

NOTE: *Adams* cover-#147. *Drucker* stories-#39, 42,43. *Evans* story-#149,165-173(Losers),177-181. *Infantino* story-#135. *Kirby* story-#151-162; covers-#152-159. *Kubert* art in many issues. *Maurer* story-#135. *Redondo* story-#166. *Medal of Honor* by *Maurer*-#135. *U.S.S. Stevens* by *Glanzman*-#125-28,134,138-41,143, 144.

OUR FIGHTING MEN IN ACTION
1957 - 1958
Ajax/Farrell Publ. (Four Star Comic Corp.)

#1	.90	1.80	2.70
2-6	.50	1.00	1.50

OUR FLAG COMICS
Aug, 1941 - #5, April, 1942
Ace Magazines

#1-Captain Victory & the Unknown Soldier begin	50.00	100.00	150.00
2-Origin The Flag	30.00	60.00	90.00
3-5	25.00	50.00	75.00

OUR GANG COMICS (With Tom & Jerry #39-59; becomes Tom & Jerry #60 on)
Sept-Oct, 1942 - #59, June, 1949
Dell Publishing Co.

#1-Our Gang & Barney Bear by Kelly, Tom & Jerry, Pete Smith, Flip & Dip, The Milky Way begin	100.00	200.00	300.00
2	50.00	100.00	150.00
3-5	35.00	70.00	105.00
6-Bumbazine & Albert only app. by Kelly	60.00	120.00	180.00
7-No Kelly story	20.00	40.00	60.00
8-Benny Burro begins by Barks	50.00	100.00	150.00
9-Two Barks stories-B.Burro & Happy Hound; No Kelly story	40.00	80.00	120.00
10-B.Burro by Barks	35.00	70.00	105.00
11-1st Barney Bear & Benny Burro by Barks; Happy Hound by Barks	30.00	60.00	90.00
12-20	20.00	40.00	60.00
21-30	14.00	28.00	42.00

Our Fighting Forces #19, © DC   Our Gang Comics #10, © Loew's Inc.   Our Gang Comics #27, © Loew's Inc.

The Outer Limits #6, © DELL

Outlaw Fighters #1, © MCG

Outlaws #4, © DS

(Our Gang Comics cont'd)	Good	Fine	Mint
31-36-Last Barks ish.	8.00	16.00	24.00
37-40	2.50	5.00	7.50
41-50	2.00	4.00	6.00
51-57	1.75	3.50	5.25
58,59-No Kelly art or Our Gang story			
	1.20	2.40	3.60

NOTE: #31-36 contain *Barks* art in part only. Barks did not write Barney Bear stories #30-34. (See March of Comics #3,26)

OUR LADY FATIMA
1955   (15¢)
Catechetical Guild Educational Society

No#	2.00	4.00	6.00

OUR LOVE
1949 - #2, Jan, 1950
Marvel Comics (SPC)

#1	1.50	3.00	4.50
2	1.20	2.40	3.60

OUR LOVE STORY
Oct, 1969 - #38, Feb, 1976
Marvel Comics Group

#1	.25	.50	.75
2-4,6-13		.15	.35
5-Steranko art	3.00	6.00	9.00
14-New story by Gary Fredrich & Tarpe' Mills (Miss Fury artist)	.65	1.35	2.00
15-38		.15	.35

OUR MISS BROOKS (See 4-Color Comics #751)

OUR SECRET
1950 - #8, Aug, 1950
Superior Comics Ltd.

#5-8	1.25	2.50	3.75

OUTBURSTS OF EVERETT TRUE
1921   (32 pgs.) (B&W)
Saalfield Publ. Co.

1907 (2-panel strips reprint)

	5.00	10.00	15.00

OUTER LIMITS, THE (TV)
Jan-Mar, 1964 - #18, Oct, 1969
Dell Publishing Co.

#1	.70	1.40	2.10
2	.40	.80	1.20
3-10	.30	.60	.90
11-18: #17 reprints #1; #18-#2			

	Good	Fine	Mint
	.25	.50	.75

OUTER SPACE
May, 1958 - #25, Dec, 1959
Charlton Comics

#17-Williamson/Wood art swiped; not by the above artists (Sid Check?)

	1.00	2.00	3.00
18-20: Ditko art	1.25	2.50	3.75
21-25: #21-Ditko cover	.60	1.20	1.80
V2#1(11/68)-Ditko art	.50	1.00	1.50
V3#2-Ditko cover	.30	.60	.90

OUTLAW (See Return of the --)

OUTLAW FIGHTERS
Aug, 1954 - #5, April, 1955
Atlas Comics (IPC)

#1	1.00	2.00	3.00
2-5: #5-7pg. Heath	.70	1.40	2.10

OUTLAW KID, THE (1st Series)
Sept, 1954 - #19, Sept, 1957
Atlas Comics(CCC #1-11/EPI #12-19)

#1-Black Rider app.	2.00	4.00	6.00
2-7,9: #2-Bl. Rider app.	1.00	2.00	3.00
8-Williamson/Woodbridge story, 4pgs.			
	2.50	5.00	7.50
10-Williamson story	2.00	4.00	6.00
11-17,19	.80	1.60	2.40
18-Williamson story	2.00	4.00	6.00

NOTE: *Berg* story-#13. *Wildey* stories-#1,4,5, 7,8,10,11,13-18.

OUTLAW KID, THE (2nd Series)
Aug, 1970 - #30, Oct, 1975
Marvel Comics Group

#1,2-Reprints; Wildey art	.20	.40	.60
3-Williamson story reprt.	.15	.30	.45
4-8		.15	.30
9-Williamson story reprt.	.15	.30	.45
10-Origin Outlaw Kid-new material begins			
		.15	.30
11,12-Bounty Hawk cameo #11, x-over in #12,			
13-26,29,30		.15	.30
27-Origin reprint/#10		.15	.30
28-Williamson reprint		.15	.30

NOTE: *Berg* story-#7. *Wildey* stories-#3,6,7, 19,21,22,26.

OUTLAWS
Feb-Mar, 1948 - #9, June-July, 1949
D.S. Publishing Co.

(Outlaws cont'd)	Good	Fine	Mint
#1	2.50	5.00	7.50
2-Ingels story	3.50	7.00	10.50
3-6: #3-Not Frazetta	1.50	3.00	4.50
7,8-Ingels story in ea.	2.50	5.00	7.50
9-Frazetta story, 7pgs.	12.00	24.00	36.00

NOTE: *#3 was printed in Canada with Frazetta story "Prairie Jinx," 7 pgs.*

OUTLAWS
#10, 5/52 - #13, 9/53; #14, 4/54
Star Publishing Co.

	Good	Fine	Mint
#10-14-L.B. Cole covers	.80	1.60	2.40

OUTLAWS OF THE WEST (Formerly Cody of the Pony Express #10)
#11, July, 1957 - #81, May, 1970
Charlton Comics

	Good	Fine	Mint
#11-13,15-17,19,20	.60	1.20	1.80
14-68pgs. (15¢)	.80	1.60	2.40
18-Ditko art	1.00	2.00	3.00
21-50	.30	.60	.90
51-70: #54-Kid Montana app. #65-Captain Doom begins. #68-Kid Montana begins	.20	.40	.60
71-81: #73-Origin & 1st app. The Sharp Shooter. last app.-#74. #75-Last Capt. Doom. #80,81-Ditko art	.15	.30	.45
64(Modern Comics reprint, 1977)	.15	.30	

OUTLAWS OF THE WILD WEST
1952   (132 pgs.) (25¢)
Avon Periodicals

	Good	Fine	Mint
#1-Wood back cover; Kubert art(3 Jesse James reprints)	6.00	12.00	18.00

OUT OF SANTA'S BAG (See March of Comics #10)

OUT OF THE NIGHT (The Hooded Horseman #18 on)
Feb-Mar, 1952 - #17, Oct-Nov, 1954
American Comics Group (Creston/Scope)

	Good	Fine	Mint
#1-Williamson story, 9pgs. + Torres story	8.00	16.00	24.00
2-Williamson story,5pgs.	5.00	10.00	15.00
3,5-10	1.00	2.00	3.00
4-Williamson story,7pgs.	5.00	10.00	15.00
11-17	.80	1.60	2.40

OUT OF THE SHADOWS
#5, July, 1952 - #14, Aug, 1954
Standard Comics/Visual Editions

	Good	Fine	Mint
#5,14-Toth stories + Moreira-#5	2.00	4.00	6.00

	Good	Fine	Mint
6-8,13	1.00	2.00	3.00
9-Two Crandall stories	2.25	4.50	6.75
10,11-Toth art, 3,2pgs.	1.50	3.00	4.50
12-Two Toth stories	2.50	5.00	7.50

OUT OF THIS WORLD
June, 1950   (One Shot)
Avon Periodicals

	Good	Fine	Mint
#1-Two Kubert stories(one reprt/Eerie #1-'47) + Crom the Barbarian by Giunta (origin)	20.00	40.00	60.00

OUT OF THIS WORLD ADVENTURES (Pulp)
July, 1950 - #2, Dec, 1950; #2, April, 1951
Avon Periodicals

	Good	Fine	Mint
#1-Has Avon's Out of This World #1 comic insert	8.00	16.00	24.00
2-Has Avon's Strange Worlds #1; used in Seduction of the Innocent, pg. 120	6.00	12.00	18.00
2(4/51)-Has Avon's Flying Saucers #1	8.00	16.00	24.00

NOTE: *Comic book inserts can vary.*

OUT OF THIS WORLD
1957 - #16, Dec-Jan, 1960
Charlton Comics

	Good	Fine	Mint
#1	1.50	3.00	4.50
2	.80	1.60	2.40
3-6: #3,4-Ditko stories each	2.00	4.00	6.00
7,8-68pgs.(15¢-Ditko art)	2.50	5.00	7.50
9-12-Ditko stories	1.50	3.00	4.50
13-15	.60	1.20	1.80
16-Ditko cover/story	1.50	3.00	4.50

NOTE: *Ditko covers-#3-5,11,16.*

OUT OUR WAY WITH WORRY WART (See 4-Color#680)

OUTSIDERS, THE (See First Issue Special)

OVERSEAS COMICS (Also see G.I. & Jeep Comics)
1945   (Distributed to U.S. armed forces)
Giveaway

	Good	Fine	Mint
#65-Bringing Up Father, Popeye, Joe Palooka, Dick Tracy, Superman, Gasoline Alley, Buz Sawyer, Li'l Abner	3.00	6.00	9.00

OWL, THE
April, 1967; #2, April, 1968
Gold Key

	Good	Fine	Mint
#1,2	.40	.80	1.20

Out Of The Night #2, © ACG

Out Of The Shadows #5, © STD

Out Of This World #2(Pulp), © AVON

317

Ozark Ike #B11, © STD

Panic #4, © WMG

Parole Breakers #2, © AVON

OXYDOL-DREFT
1950 (Set of 6 pocket-size giveaways-Distributed through the mail as a set) (Scarce)
Oxydol-Dreft

	Good	Fine	Mint
#1-Li'l Abner, #2-Daisy Mae, #3-Shmoo			
	3.50	7.00	10.50
#4-John Wayne-Williamson/Frazetta cover from			
John Wayne #3	5.00	10.00	15.00
#5-Archie	4.00	8.00	12.00
#6-Terrytoons Mighty Mouse	2.50	5.00	7.50

NOTE: *Set is worth more with original envelope.*

OZ (See MGM's Marvelous-- & Marvel Treasury--)

OZARK IKE
2/48; 11/48 - #24, 12/51; #25, 9/52
Dell Publishing Co./Standard Comics

	Good	Fine	Mint
4-Color #180(1948-Dell)	4.00	8.00	12.00
#B11, B12	3.50	7.00	10.50
#13-15	3.00	6.00	9.00
16-25	2.50	5.00	7.50

OZZIE & BABS
1947 - #13, Fall, 1949
Fawcett Publications

	Good	Fine	Mint
#1	1.20	2.40	3.60
2-13	.75	1.50	2.25

OZZIE & HARRIET (See The Adventures of --)

PAGEANT OF COMICS (See Jane Arden & Mopsy)
Sept, 1947 - #2, Oct, 1947
Archer St. John

#1-Mopsy strip reprints	4.00	8.00	12.00
2-Jane Arden strip reprints			
	4.00	8.00	12.00

PANCHO VILLA
1950
Avon Periodicals

No#-Kinstler cover	6.00	12.00	18.00

PANHANDLE PETE AND JENNIFER (TV)
July, 1951 - #3, Nov, 1951
J. Charles Laue Publishing Co.

#1-3	1.25	2.50	3.75

PANIC (Companion to Mad)
Feb-Mar, 1954 - #12, Dec-Jan, 1955-56
E.C. Comics

#1	7.00	14.00	21.00

	Good	Fine	Mint
2	6.00	12.00	18.00
3,4: #3-Kelly parody	5.00	10.00	15.00
5-12	3.50	7.00	10.50

NOTE: *Davis stories-#1-12; cover-#12. Elder stories-#1-12. Feldstein covers-#1-3,5. Kamen story-#1. Orlando stories-#1-9. Wolverton cover-#4. Wood stories-#2-9,11,12.*

PANIC (Magazine) (Satire)
7/58 - #6, 7/59; V2#10, 12/65 - V2#12, 1966
Panic Publications

#1	2.00	4.00	6.00
2-6	1.50	3.00	4.50
V2#10-12: Reprints earlier issues			
	.70	1.40	2.10

NOTE: *Davis art-#3(2pgs.),4,5,10; cover-#10. Elder art-#5. Powell art-V2#10. Torres art-#1-5.*

PARADE (See Hanna-Barbera --)

PARADE COMICS (Frisky Animals on Parade #2 on)
Sept, 1957
Ajax/Farrell Publ. (World Famous Publ.)

#1	.30	.60	.90

NOTE: *Cover title: Frisky Animals on Parade.*

PARAMOUNT ANIMATED COMICS
Feb, 1953 - #22, July, 1956
Harvey Publications

	Good	Fine	Mint
#1-Baby Huey, Herman & Katnip, Buzzy the			
Crow begin	5.00	10.00	15.00
2-6	2.00	4.00	6.00
7-Baby Huey becomes permanent cover feature;			
cover title becomes Baby Huey with #9.			
	2.50	5.00	7.50
8-10	1.75	3.50	5.25
11-22	1.50	3.00	4.50

PARENT TRAP, THE (See 4-Color Comics #1210)

PAROLE BREAKERS
Dec, 1951 - #3, July, 1952
Avon Periodicals/Realistic

#1 (#2 on inside)	6.00	12.00	18.00
2-Kubert story	5.00	10.00	15.00
3-Kinstler cover	3.50	7.00	10.50

PARTRIDGE FAMILY, THE (TV)
March, 1971 - #20, Nov, 1973
Charlton Comics

#1	.30	.60	.90

(Partridge Family cont'd)	Good	Fine	Mint
2-4,6-20	.20	.40	.60
5-Partidge Family Summer Special (52pgs.)			
	.25	.50	.75

PASSION, THE
1955
Catechetical Guild

	2.00	4.00	6.00

PAT BOONE
Sept-Oct, 1959 - #5, May-June, 1960
National Periodical Publications

#1	3.00	6.00	9.00
2-5	1.75	3.50	5.25

PATCHES
Mar-Apr, 1945 - #11, Nov, 1947
Rural Home/Patches Publ. (Orbit)

#1-L.B. Cole cover	1.50	3.00	4.50
2-11	1.25	2.50	3.75

PATORUZU (See Adventures of --)

PATSY & HEDY
1952 - #110, Feb, 1967
Atlas Comics/Marvel(GPI/Male)

#1	2.00	4.00	6.00
2-10	1.20	2.40	3.60
11-20	.75	1.50	2.25
21-50	.40	.80	1.20
51-110	.20	.40	.60
Annual #1('63)	1.20	2.40	3.60

PATSY & HER PALS
1953 - #29, Aug, 1957
Atlas Comics (PPI)

#1	2.00	4.00	6.00
2-10	1.00	2.00	3.00
11-29	.50	1.00	1.50

PATSY WALKER (Also see Girls' Life & Miss America Magazine)
Oct, 1945 - #124, Dec, 1965
Marvel/Atlas Comics(BPC)

#1	8.00	16.00	24.00
2	4.00	8.00	12.00
3-10	2.50	5.00	7.50
11,12,15,16,18,23,24,26-29			
	1.60	3.20	4.80
13,14,17,19-22-Kurtzman's "Hey Look"			
	2.50	5.00	7.50

	Good	Fine	Mint
25-Rusty by Kurtzman	3.00	6.00	9.00
30-60	.80	1.60	2.40
61-100	.40	.80	1.20
101-124	.20	.40	.60
Fashion Parade #1('66, 68pgs.)			
	1.00	2.00	3.00

PAT THE BRAT
June, 1953; Summer, 1955 - #35, Nov, 1959
Archie Publications (Radio)

No#(6/53)	2.50	5.00	7.50
#1(Summer,'55)	2.00	4.00	6.00
2-10	.80	1.60	2.40
11-35	.50	1.00	1.50

PATTY POWERS
1956
Atlas Comics

#5-7	.50	1.00	1.50

PAT WILTON (See Mighty Midget Comics)

PAULINE PERIL (See The Close Shaves of --)

PAUL REVERE'S RIDE (See 4-Color #822)

PAUL TERRY'S ADVENTURES OF MIGHTY MOUSE
(See Adventures of --)

PAUL TERRY'S COMICS (Formerly Terry-Toons Comics; becomes Adv. of Mighty Mouse #126 on)
#85, Mar, 1951 - #125, May, 1955
St. John Publishing Co.

#85-100	1.25	2.50	3.75
101-125-Mighty Mouse	1.00	2.00	3.00

PAUL TERRY'S MIGHTY MOUSE (See Mighty Mouse)

PAUL TERRY'S MIGHTY MOUSE ADVENTURE STORIES
1953 (384pgs.) (50c) (Cardboard covers)
St. John Publishing Co.

No#	8.00	16.00	24.00

PAWNEE BILL
February, 1951 - #3, July, 1951
Story Comics

#1	1.50	3.00	4.50
2,3: #3-Origin Golden Warrior; Cameron art			
	1.20	2.40	3.60

PAY-OFF (This Is the --, --Crime, --Detective Stories)

Pat Boone #1, © DC

Patches #10, © RH

Patsy Walker #22, © MCG

Peanuts #6, © DELL

Pep Comics #2, © MLJ

Pep Comics #33, © MLJ

(Pay-Off cont'd)
July-Aug, 1948 - #5, Mar-Apr, 1949 (52 pgs.)
D. S. Publishing Co.

	Good	Fine	Mint
#1	1.50	3.00	4.50
2-5	1.00	2.00	3.00

PEACEMAKER, THE
Mar, 1967 - #5, Nov, 1967
Charlton Comics

#1-Fightin' Five begins	.60	1.20	1.80
2,3,5	.35	.70	1.05
4-Origin The Peacemaker	.50	1.00	1.50

PEANUTS (Charlie Brown)
2/58 - #13, 1962; 5/63 - #4, 2/64
Dell Publishing Co./Gold Key

4-Color #878,969,1015('59)	2.00	4.00	6.00
#4(2-4/60)	1.75	3.50	5.25
5-13	1.25	2.50	3.75
1(G.K.)	1.00	2.00	3.00
2-4	.70	1.40	2.10
#1('53-'54)-Reprints United Features' Strange As It Seems, Willie, Fernand			
	5.00	10.00	15.00

PEBBLES & BAMM BAMM (TV)
Jan, 1972 - #36, Dec, 1976 (Hanna-Barbera)
Charlton Comics

#1	.15	.30	.45
2-36		.15	.30

PEBBLES FLINTSTONE (TV)
Sept, 1963 (Hanna-Barbera)
Gold Key

#1(10088-309)	.20	.40	.60

PECKS BAD BOY & COUSIN CYNTHIA
1907 - 1908 (Strip reprints)(11¼x15-3/4")
Thompson of Chicago (by Walt McDougal)

--& Cousin Cynthia('07)-In color			
	15.00	37.50	60.00
--& His Chums('08)-Hardcover-in full color 16pgs.	15.00	37.50	60.00
Advs. of--in Pictures('08)-In color-Stanton & Van V. Liet Co.	15.00	37.50	60.00

PEDRO
#18, June, 1950 - #2, Aug, 1950?
Fox Features Syndicate

#18(#1)-Wood cover/stories (in part?)			
	6.00	12.00	18.00

	Good	Fine	Mint
#2	1.20	2.40	3.60

PEE-WEE PIXIES (See The Pixies)

PENALTY (See Crime Must Pay the --)

PENNY
1947 - 1949
Avon Periodicals

#1-Photo & biography of creator; newspaper reprints	2.50	5.00	7.50
2-6	1.50	3.00	4.50

PEP COMICS
Jan, 1940 - Present
MLJ Magazines/Archie Publ. #57 on

#1-Intro. The Shield by Irving Novick(1st patriotic hero); origin The Comet by Jack Cole, The Queen of Diamond & Kayo Ward; The Rocket, The Press Guardian(The Falcon #1 only), Sergeant Boyle, Fu Chang, & Bentley of Scotland Yard			
	120.00	240.00	360.00
2-Origin The Rocket	60.00	120.00	180.00
3	40.00	80.00	120.00
4-Wizard cameo	38.00	76.00	114.00
5-Wizard cameo in Shield story			
	35.00	70.00	105.00
6-10: #8-Last Cole Comet			
	27.00	54.00	81.00
11-Dusty, Shield's sidekick begins; last Press Guardian, Fu Chang			
	25.00	50.00	75.00
12-Origin Fireball; last Rocket & Queen of Diamonds	30.00	60.00	90.00
13-15	25.00	50.00	75.00
16-Origin Madam Satan	30.00	60.00	90.00
17-Origin The Hangman; death of The Comet			
	85.00	170.00	255.00
18-20-Last Fireball	20.00	40.00	60.00
21-Last Madam Satan	18.00	36.00	54.00
22-Intro. & 1st app. Archie, Betty, & Jughead(12/41)	60.00	120.00	180.00
23-29	16.00	32.00	48.00
30-Capt. Commando begins	16.00	32.00	48.00
31-35,37-40	13.00	26.00	39.00
36-1st Archie cover	15.00	30.00	45.00
41-47: #47-Last Hangman issue. #41 on are all Archie covers	10.00	20.00	30.00
48-Black Hood begins(5/44); ends #51,59,60			
	7.00	14.00	21.00
49-60: #52-Suzie begins. #54-Capt. Commando app. #56-Last Capt. Commando. #59-Suzie ends. #60-Katy Keene begins			
	6.00	12.00	18.00

(Pep Comics cont'd)	Good	Fine	Mint
61,63-65-Last Shield	4.00	8.00	12.00
62-1st app. Li'l Jinx	5.00	10.00	15.00
66-70: #66-G-Man Club becomes Archie Club			
(2/48)	3.00	6.00	9.00
71-80	2.50	5.00	7.50
81-100	2.00	4.00	6.00
101-120	1.50	3.00	4.50
121-149: #139,140-Katy Keene app.			
	1.25	2.50	3.75
150,152,157,159-Jaguar stories in all			
	.80	1.60	2.40
151,154,160-The Fly stories in all			
	.80	1.60	2.40
153,155,156,158-Flygirl stories in all			
	.80	1.60	2.40
161,162,164-Katy Keene by Bill Woggan			
	1.00	2.00	3.00
163,165-167,169-200	.60	1.20	1.80
168-Jaguar app.	.80	1.60	2.40
201-240	.25	.50	.75
241-300	.20	.40	.60
301-343		.15	.35

NOTE: _Schomburg cover-#38._

PEPE (See 4-Color Comics #1194)

PERCY & FERDIE
1921 (48pgs.) (B&W dailies)
Cupples & Leon Co.

By H. A. McGill	6.00	12.00	18.00

PERFECT CRIME, THE
Oct, 1949 - 1953
Cross Publications

#1-Powell story	2.00	4.00	6.00
2-7,9,10: #7-Steve Duncan begins, ends #30			
	1.25	2.50	3.75
8-Heroin story	3.00	6.00	9.00
11-Used in Seduction of the Innocent, pg.159			
	2.50	5.00	7.50
12-14,16-25,27-33	.80	1.60	2.40
15-"The Most Terrible Menace"-a two page anti-			
drug editorial	2.50	5.00	7.50
26-Drug cover	4.00	8.00	12.00

NOTE: _Powell stories-#1,2,4. Wildey stories-#5._

PERFECT LOVE
#2, Oct-Nov, 1951 - #10, 1952
Ziff-Davis/Approved Comics

#2	1.20	2.40	3.60
3,4,6,7,9,10	.90	1.80	2.70
5-Woodbridge story?	1.00	2.00	3.00
8-Kinstler story	1.50	3.00	4.50

PERRI (See 4-Color Comics #847)

PERRY MASON (See Feature Book #49,40,McKay)

PERRY MASON MYSTERY MAGAZINE (TV)
June-Aug, 1964 - #2, Oct-Dec, 1964
Dell Publishing Co.

	Good	Fine	Mint
#1,2	.60	1.20	1.80

PERSONAL LOVE (Also see Movie Love)
Jan, 1950 - #33, June, 1955
Famous Funnies

#1	2.50	5.00	7.50
2-7,9,10	1.50	3.00	4.50
8-7pg. Kinstler story	2.00	4.00	6.00
11-Toth story	3.00	6.00	9.00
12-15,18-23	1.20	2.40	3.60
16,17-1pg. Frazetta	2.00	4.00	6.00
24,25,27,28-Frazetta stories in all-8,7,8 & 6pgs. ea.; Everett story-#24			
	30.00	60.00	90.00
26,29-31,33	1.00	2.00	3.00
32-Classic Frazetta story, 8pgs.			
	50.00	100.00	150.00

PERSONAL LOVE
V1#1, Sept, 1957 - V3#1, Sept-Oct, 1959
Prize Publ. (Headline)

V1#1	.60	1.20	1.80
2-6(7-8/58)	.40	.80	1.20
V2#1(9-10/58)-V2#6(7-8/59)	.40	.80	1.20
V3#1	.30	.60	.90

PETER COTTONTAIL
Jan, 1954; Feb, 1954 - #2, Mar, 1954
Key Publications

#1(1/54)-not 3-D	1.50	3.00	4.50
1(3-D)(2/54)-Written by Bruce Hamilton			
	5.00	10.00	15.00
2-Reprints 3-D #1 but not in 3-D			
	1.20	2.40	3.60

PETER GUNN (See 4-Color Comics #1087)

PETER PAN (See New Adventures of--, 4-Color #442,446,926 & Movie Classics & Comics)

PETER PAN TREASURE CHEST (See Movie Classics)

PETER PANDA
Aug-Sept, 1953 - #31, Aug-Sept, 1958
National Periodical Publications

#1	2.50	5.00	7.50

The Perfect Crime #3, © Cross Publ.

Perfect Love #5, © Z-D

Personal Love #30, © FF

Peter Rabbit #1, © AVON   Peter Wheat No#, © Bakers Assoc.   Peter Wheat Fun Book. © Bakers Assoc.

(Peter Panda cont'd)	Good	Fine	Mint
2-10	1.25	2.50	3.75
11-31	.70	1.40	2.10

PETER PARKER (See The Spectacular Spider-Man)

PETER PAT (See Single Series #8)

PETER PAUL'S 4 IN 1 JUMBO COMIC BOOK
No Date (1953)
Capitol Stories

#1-Contains 4 comics bound; Space Adventures,
  Space Western, Crime & Justice, Racket
  Squad in Action   5.00   10.00   15.00

PETER PIG
#5, May, 1953 - #6, Aug, 1953
Standard Comics

#5,6	.40	.80	1.20

PETER PORKCHOPS
Nov-Dec, 1949 - #62, Oct-Dec, 1960
National Periodical Publications

#1	3.50	7.00	10.50
2-10	1.50	3.00	4.50
11-30	1.00	2.00	3.00
31-62	.65	1.35	2.00

PETER POTAMUS (TV)
Jan, 1965   (Hanna-Barbera)
Gold Key

#1	.20	.40	.60

PETER RABBIT (See Large Feature Comic #1)

PETER RABBIT
1922 - 1923   (9¼x6¼")   (Soft Cover)
John H. Eggers Co. The House of Little Books
Publishers

#B1-B4-(Rare)-(Set of 4 books which came in
  a cardboard box) Each book reprints ⅓ of
  a Sunday page per page & contains 8 B&W
  & 2 color pages; by Harrison Cady
          each.... 20.00   40.00   60.00

PETER RABBIT (Adventures of --)
1947 - #34, Aug-Sept, 1956
Avon Periodicals

#1(1947)-Reprints 1943-44 Sunday strips; con-
  tains a biography & drawing of Cady
          15.00   30.00   45.00
2-6(1949)-Last Cady ish.10.00   20.00   30.00

	Good	Fine	Mint
7-10(1950-51)	2.00	4.00	6.00
11(11/51)-#34('56)-Avon's character			
	1.50	3.00	4.50
--Easter Parade(Giant)	4.00	8.00	12.00
--Jumbo Book(1954-Giant size,25c)-6pgs.-Jesse			
James by Kinstler	3.50	7.00	10.50

PETER RABBIT
1958
Fago Magazine Co.

#1	1.50	3.00	4.50

PETER, THE LITTLE PEST (#4 titled Petey)
Nov, 1969 - #4, May, 1970
Marvel Comics Group

#1		.15	.30	.45
2-4('69)-Reprints Dexter the Demon & Melvin				
the Monster			.15	.30

PETER WHEAT (The Adventures of --)
1948 - 1952 (16pgs. in color; paper covers)
Bakers Associates Giveaway

No#(#1)-States on last page, end of 1st Adv-			
enture of--; Kelly art			
	20.00	40.00	60.00
No#(5 issues)-Kelly art	15.00	30.00	45.00
#7-10-All Kelly art	12.00	24.00	36.00
11-20- " " "	10.00	20.00	30.00
21-30- " " "	9.00	18.00	27.00
31-40	7.00	14.00	21.00
41-66	6.00	12.00	18.00

NOTE: *Al Hubbard art #34? on; written by
Del Connell.*

PETER WHEAT FUN BOOK
1952 (32pgs.;paper cover;B&W w/some color)
Bakers Associates   (8¼x10-3/4")

Contains cut-outs, puzzles, games, magic, &			
pages to color	8.00	16.00	24.00

PETER WHEAT NEWS
1948 - #20, 1949   (4 pgs. in color)
Bakers Associates

Vol.1-All have 2pgs. Peter Wheat by Kelly			
	15.00	30.00	45.00
2-10	10.00	20.00	30.00
11-20	6.00	12.00	18.00

NOTE: *Early issues have no date.*

PETEY (See Peter, the Little Pest)

PETTICOAT JUNCTION (TV)
Oct-Dec, 1964 - #5, Oct-Dec, 1965

322

(Petticoat Junction cont'd)
Dell Publishing Co.

	Good	Fine	Mint
#1	.25	.50	.75
2-5	.15	.30	.45

PETUNIA (See 4-Color Comics #463)

PHANTASMO (See Black & White #18)

PHANTOM, THE
1939 - 1949
David McKay Publishing Co.

Feature Book #20,22	40.00	80.00	120.00
Feature Book #39	17.00	34.00	51.00
Feature Book #53,56,57	14.00	28.00	42.00

PHANTOM, THE (See Eat Right to Work --,
Harvey Comics Hits #51,56 & Harvey Hits #1,
6,12,15,26,36,44,48)

PHANTOM, THE (No #29)(Also see Comics Read-
ing Library)
Nov, 1962 - #17, July, 1966; #18, Sept, 1966-
#28, Dec, 1967; #30, Feb, 1969 - #74, 1/77
Gold Key(#1-17)/King(#18-28)/Charlton(#30 on)

#1	1.75	3.50	5.25
2-King, Queen & Jack begins; ends #11			
	1.25	2.50	3.75
3-5	1.00	2.00	3.00
6-10	.80	1.60	2.40
11-17-Track Hunter begins #12			
	.70	1.40	2.10
18-Flash Gordon begins; Wood art			
	1.25	2.50	3.75
19,20-Flash Gordon ends	1.00	2.00	3.00
21-24,26,27: #21-Mandrake begins. #26-Brick			
Bradford app.	.60	1.20	1.80
25-Jeff Jones art, 1pg. Williamson ad			
	.60	1.20	1.80
28(No#)-Brick Bradford app.			
	1.00	2.00	3.00
30-40: #36,39-Ditko art	.40	.80	1.20
41-66: #62-Bolle cover	.25	.50	.75
67-Newton cvr/stys. begin	.30	.60	.90
68-74	.25	.50	.75

PHANTOM BLOT, THE (Disney)
Oct, 1964 - #7, Nov, 1966
Gold Key

#1	1.25	2.50	3.75
2-1st Super-Goof	1.00	2.00	3.00
3-7	.75	1.50	2.25

PHANTOM EAGLE (See Mighty Midget Comics)

PHANTOM LADY (1st Series) (My Love Secret
#24 on; also see All Top, Daring Adventures,
Jungle Thrills & Wonder Boy)
Aug, 1947 - #23, April, 1949
Fox Features Syndicate

	Good	Fine	Mint
#13(#1)-Phantom Lady by Matt Baker begins;			
The Blue Beetle app.	120.00	240.00	360.00
14(#2)	75.00	150.00	225.00
15,16	60.00	120.00	180.00

17-Classic bondage cover; used in Seduction
of the Innocent, illo-"Sexual stimulation
by combining 'headlights' with the sadist's
dream of tying up a woman"

	200.00	400.00	600.00
18-23	40.00	80.00	120.00

NOTE: *Matt Baker covers/stories in all.*

PHANTOM LADY (2nd Series)(See Terrific Comics)
12-1/55 - #4, 6/55   (Formerly Linda)
Ajax/Farrell Publ.

V1#5(#1)-by Matt Baker	20.00	40.00	60.00
V1#2-4-Red Rocket in#3,4	14.00	28.00	42.00

PHANTOM PLANET, THE (See 4-Color #1234)

PHANTOM STRANGER, THE (1st Series)
Aug-Sept, 1952 - 1953
National Periodical Publications

#1	20.00	40.00	60.00
2-6	10.00	20.00	30.00

PHANTOM STRANGER, THE (2nd Series)(See Show-
5-6/69 - #41, 2-3/76   case)
National Periodical Publications

#1	1.25	2.50	3.75
2,3,5-10	.75	1.50	2.25
4-Neal Adams art	1.50	3.00	4.50
11-19: Last 25¢ ish. #15-Toth art(reprint)			
	.50	1.00	1.50
20-22	.40	.80	1.20
23-Spawn of Frankenstein begins by Kaluta,			
ends #25	.70	1.40	2.10
24,25	.60	1.20	1.80
26-30	.30	.60	.90
31-The Black Orchid begins (Dezuniga art)			
	.30	.60	.90
32,35,36-Black Orchid by Redondo			
	.30	.60	.90
33-Deadman app.	.25	.50	.75
34,37,38: #34-New Dr. 13 story			
	.25	.50	.75
39-41-Deadman in all	.25	.50	.75

NOTE: *Adams covers-#3-19. Dezuniga art-#34.
Kaluta cover-#26. Meskin reprints-#15,16,18.*

The Phantom #74, © CC

Phantom Lady #20, © FOX

Phantom Stranger #23, © DC

Pictorial Love Stories #1, © STJ

Pictorial Romances #6, © STJ

Picture Parade #3, © GIL

(The Phantom Stranger cont'd)
*Black Orchid by Carrilo-#38-41. Dr. 13 solo
in #13,18,20. Frankenstein by Kaluta-#23-25;
by Baily-#27-30. No Black Orchid-#33,34.*

PHANTOM WITCH DOCTOR
1952
Avon Periodicals

	Good	Fine	Mint
#1-Kinstler cover, 7pgs.	9.00	18.00	27.00

PHIL RIZZUTO (Baseball Hero)
1951 (New York Yankees)
Fawcett Publications

	Good	Fine	Mint
No#	4.00	8.00	12.00

PHOENIX
Jan, 1975 - #4, Oct, 1975
Atlas/Seaboard Publ.

#1-Origin	.30	.60	.90
2,3: #3-Origin & only app. The Dark Avenger	.25	.50	.75
4-New origin/costume The Protector (formerly Phoenix)	.25	.50	.75

PICNIC PARTY (Walt Disney's)(Vacation Parade
1955 - 1957   #1-5)
Dell Publishing Co.

#6,7-Uncle Scrooge	2.00	4.00	6.00
8-Carl Barks art	5.00	10.00	15.00

PICTORIAL CONFESSIONS (Pictorial Romances
Sept, 1949 - #3, Dec, 1949   #4 on)
St. John Publishing Co.

#1-Baker art	4.00	8.00	12.00
2-Baker stys; photo cvr.	2.50	5.00	7.50
3-Kubert, Baker art	5.00	10.00	15.00

PICTORIAL LOVE STORIES (Formerly Tim McCoy)
#22, Oct, 1949 - #26, July, 1950
Charlton Comics

#22-26-"Me-Dan Cupid" in all			
	2.50	5.00	7.50

PICTORIAL LOVE STORIES
October, 1952
St. John Publ. Co.

#1-Baker cover/story	6.00	12.00	18.00

PICTORIAL ROMANCES (Formerly Pictorial Con-
#4, 1/50 - #24, 3/54   fessions)
St. John Publishing Co.

	Good	Fine	Mint
#4,5,10-All Matt Baker issues			
	3.00	6.00	9.00
6-9,12,13,15,16-Baker covers, 2-3 stories			
	2.50	5.00	7.50
11-Baker cover/3 stories; Kubert story			
	3.50	7.00	10.50
14,17,18,21-24-Baker cover/story each			
	2.00	4.00	6.00
19,20(7/53)-100pgs. ea.; Baker cover/stories			
	2.50	5.00	7.50

NOTE: *Matt Baker art in most issues.*

PICTURE NEWS (Dick Quick #10 on)
Jan, 1946 - #9, Sept, 1946
Lafayette Street Corp.

#1-Milt Gross begins, ends #6; 4pg. Kirby story	2.50	5.00	7.50
2-5	1.25	2.50	3.75
6-9	1.00	2.00	3.00

PICTURE PARADE (Picture Progress #5 on)
Sept, 1953 - V1#4, Dec, 1953   (28 pgs.)
Gilberton Corp.

V1#1-Andy's Atomic Adventures	1.50	3.00	4.50
2-			
3-Adventures of the Lost One (11/53)			
4-A Christmas Adventure			
	1.25	2.50	3.75

PICTURE PROGRESS (Formerly Picture Parade)
V1#5, 1/54 - V3#2, 10/55   (28-36 pgs.)
Gilberton Corp.

V1#5-News in Review 1953			
6-The Birth of America			
7-The Four Seasons			
8-Paul Revere's Ride			
9-The Hawaiian Islands(5/54)			
V2#1-The Story of Flight(9/54)			
2-The Meaning of Elections			
3-Louis Pasteur			
4-The Star Spangled Banner			
5-News in Review 1954			
6-Alaska: The Great Land			
7-Life in the Circus			
V2#8-The Time of the Cave Man			
9-Summer Fun(5/55)			
each....	.80	1.60	2.40
V3#1-The Man Who Discovered America			
2-The Lewis & Clark Expedition			
each....	.80	1.60	2.40
No#-The American Indian	.80	1.60	2.40

PICTURE SCOPE JUNGLE ADVENTURES
1954   (36pgs.)(Says 3-D on cover, but not

(Picture Scope Jungle Advs. cont'd)
Star Publishing Co.   3-D)
                         Good Fine Mint
No#-Disbrow art/script   4.00 8.00 12.00

PICTURE STORIES FROM AMERICAN HISTORY
1945 - 1947   (68 - 52 pgs.)
National/All-American/E.C. Comics

#1   4.00 8.00 12.00
 2-4   3.50 7.00 10.50

PICTURE STORIES FROM SCIENCE
Spring, 1947 - #2, Fall, 1947
E.C. Comics

#1,2   5.00 10.00 15.00

PICTURE STORIES FROM THE BIBLE
Fall, 1942-43 & 1944-46
National/All-American/E.C. Comics

#1-4(Fall'43)-Old Testament (DC)
                         5.00 10.00 15.00
Complete Old Testament Edition, 232 pgs.(DC)
  1943-contains #1-4   8.00 16.00 24.00
Complete Old Testament Edition, 232 pgs.,
  Hardbound, in color with dust jacket;
  published by Bible Pictures Ltd.(1945)
                        10.00 20.00 30.00
NOTE: *Both Old & New Testaments published in*
England by Bible Pictures Ltd. in hardback,
1943, in color, 376 pages.
#1,2(Old Test. reprints in comic book form)
  (52pgs. ea.-E.C.)   4.00 8.00 12.00
 1-3(New Test.)(52pgs. ea.)(1944-46)(DC)
                         4.00 8.00 12.00
The Complete Life of Christ Edition-(1945)-
  Contains #1 & 2 of the New Testament Edition   10.00 20.00 30.00
Complete New Testament Edition, 144pgs.(E.C.)
  (1946)(Contains #1-3) 6.00 12.00 18.00
 1(New Test. reprint in comic book form)
  (52pgs., E.C.)   4.00 8.00 12.00

PICTURE STORIES FROM WORLD HISTORY
Spring, 1947 - #2, Fall, 1947 (52-48pgs.)
E.C. Comics

#1,2   5.00 10.00 15.00

PINHEAD & FOODINI (Also see The Great Foodini)
July, 1951 - #4, Jan, 1952   (TV)
Fawcett Publications

#1   1.75 3.50 5.25
 2-4   1.40 2.80 4.20

PINK PANTHER & THE INSPECTOR, THE   (TV)
April, 1971 - Present
Gold Key
                         Good Fine Mint
#1   .30   .60   .90
 2-10   .20   .40   .60
11-30: Warren Tufts art #16 on
                         .15   .30   .45
31-62   .15   .35
Kite Fun Book-(16pgs., 1972)-Sou. Calif.
  Edison Co. giveaway   1.00 2.00 3.00
Mini-Comic #1(3¾x6½", 1976).15 .30   .45
NOTE: *Pink Panther began as a movie cartoon.*
(See Golden Comics Digest #38,45 & March of
Comics #376,384,390,409)

PINKY LEE   (See The Adventures of --)

PINKY THE EGGHEAD
1963   (Reprints from Noodnik)
I.W./Super Comics

I.W. Reprint #1,2(no date) .20 .40 .60
Super Reprint #14   .20   .40   .60

PINOCCHIO (See 4-Color #92,252,545,1203,
Movie Comics under Wonderful Advs. of -- &
World's Greatest Stories #2, New Advs. of--)

PINOCCHIO
1940   (10 pgs.) (Linen-like paper)
Montgomery Ward   (Giveaway)

                        10.00 20.00 30.00

PINOCCHIO LEARNS ABOUT KITES
(Also see Donald Duck & Brer Rabbit)
1954   (8 pgs.)   (Walt Disney)(Premium)
Pacific Gas & Electric Co.

(Rare)   12.00 24.00 36.00

PIN-UP PETE   (Also see Monty Hall -- & Great
1952   Lover Romances)
Toby Press

#1-Jack Sparling pin-ups 6.00 12.00 18.00

PIONEER MARSHAL   (See Fawcett Movie Comics)

PIONEER PICTURE STORIES
Dec, 1941 - #9, Dec, 1943
Street & Smith Publications

#1   2.50 5.00 7.50
 2-9   1.50 3.00 4.50

Picture Stories F.T. Bible, N.T. #3, © WMG

Pinhead & Foodini #1, © FAW

Pin-Up Pete #1, © TOBY

Pioneer West Romances #6. © FH Planet Comics #24. © FH Planet Comics =39. © FH

PIONEER WEST ROMANCES (Firehair #1,2,7-11)
#3, Summer, 1949 - #6, Winter, 1949-50
Fiction House Magazines

	Good	Fine	Mint
#3-6-Firehair continues	2.50	5.00	7.50

PIPSQUEAK (The Adventures of --)
1953 - #39, July, 1960
Archie Publications (Radio Comics)

#1	2.00	4.00	6.00
2-10	1.00	2.00	3.00
11-39	.60	1.20	1.80

PIRACY
Oct-Nov, 1954 - #7, Oct-Nov, 1955
E.C. Comics

#1-Williamson/Torres art	12.00	24.00	36.00
2-Williamson/Torres art	10.00	20.00	30.00
3-7	9.00	18.00	27.00

NOTE: *Crandall stories in all; covers-#2-4.
Davis stories-#1,2,6. Evans stories-#3-7;
cover-#7. Ingels stories-#3-7. Krigstein
stories-#3-5,7; covers-#5,6. Wood stories-
#1,2; cover-#1.*

PIRANA (See Thrill-O-Rama #2,3)

PIRATE OF THE GULF, THE (See Superior Stories #2)

PIRATES COMICS
Feb-Mar, 1950 - #4, Aug-Sept, 1950
Hillman Periodicals

#1	1.50	3.00	4.50
2-4: #3,4-Berg art	1.20	2.40	3.60

PIXIE & DIXIE & MR. JINKS (TV)
July-Sept, 1960 - Feb, 1963 (Hanna-Barbera)
Dell Publishing Co./Gold Key

4-Color #1112,1196,1264	.60	1.20	1.80
#01-631-207(Dell)	.40	.80	1.20
#1(2/63-G.K.)	.30	.60	.90

PIXIE PUZZLE ROCKET TO ADVENTURELAND
Nov, 1952
Avon Periodials

#1	2.00	4.00	6.00

PIXIES, THE (Advs. of --)(Mighty Atom #6 on)
Winter, 1946 - #4, 1947; #5, 1948
Magazine Enterprises

#1-Mighty Atom	2.00	4.00	6.00

	Good	Fine	Mint
2-5-Mighty Atom	1.20	2.40	3.60

IW Reprint #1('58),#8-(Pee-Wee Pixies),#10-
IW on cover, Super on inside

	.60	1.20	1.80

PLANET COMICS
Jan, 1940 - #73, 1954
Fiction House Magazines

#1-Origin Auro, Lord of Jupiter; Flint Baker & The Red Comet begin; Eisner/Fine cover	120.00	240.00	360.00
2-(Scarce)	80.00	160.00	240.00
3	70.00	140.00	210.00
4-Gale Allen and the Girl Squadron begins	60.00	120.00	180.00
5,6-(Scarce)	50.00	100.00	150.00
7-11	40.00	80.00	120.00
12-The Star Pirate begins	35.00	70.00	105.00
13-15: #13-Reff Ryan begins. #15-Mars, God of War begins	35.00	70.00	105.00
16-20	25.00	50.00	75.00
21-The Lost World & Hunt Bowman begin	30.00	60.00	90.00
22-25	25.00	50.00	75.00
26-The Space Rangers begin	25.00	50.00	75.00
27-30	20.00	40.00	60.00
31-35: #33-Origin Star Pirates Wonder Boots, reprinted in #52. #35-Mysta of the Moon begins	20.00	40.00	60.00
36-45: #41-New origin of "Auro, Lord of Jupiter." #42-Last Gale Allen. #43-Futura begins	17.00	34.00	51.00
46-52,54-60	12.00	24.00	36.00
53-Used in Seduction of the Innocent, pg.32	15.00	30.00	45.00
61-64	8.00	16.00	24.00
65-70-All partial reprints of earlier issues	7.00	14.00	21.00
71-73-No series stories	6.00	12.00	18.00
IW Reprint #1(no date)-reprints #70, which reprints part of #41	2.50	5.00	7.50
IW Reprint #8(reprts.#72),#9-Reprts.#73	2.50	5.00	7.50

NOTE: *#33-38,40-51-Star Pirate by Anderson.
Eisner covers-#2,5,6. Evans art-#50-64(Lost
World). Ingels art-#24-31,56-61/Auro, Lord
of Jupiter). Mysta of the Moon by Maurice
Whitman-#51,52; by Matt Baker-#53-59. Star
Pirate by M. Whitman-#54-56.*

PLANET OF THE APES (Magazine)(See Book&Record)
8/74 - #29, 2/77 (B&W; based on movies)
Marvel Comics Group

#1-Ploog art	1.20	2.40	3.60

(Planet of the Apes cont'd)

	Good	Fine	Mint
2-Ploog art	.80	1.60	2.40
3-10	.60	1.20	1.80
11-20	.50	1.00	1.50
21-29	.40	.80	1.20

NOTE: *Alcala art-#7-11,17-22,24. Ploog art-#1-8,11,13,14,19. Sutton art-#12,15,17,19, 20,23,24.*

PLANET OF VAMPIRES
Feb, 1975 - #3, June, 1975
Seaboard Publications (Atlas)

#1-Adams cover	.30	.60	.90
2-Adams cvr, #3-Heath art	.25	.50	.75

PLASTIC MAN (Also see Police)
1943 - #64, Nov, 1956
Vital Publ. #1,2/Quality Comics #3 on

No#(#1)-"The Game of Death"; Jack Cole art			
begins	80.00	160.00	240.00
No#(#2)-"The Gay Nineties Nightmare"			
	50.00	100.00	150.00
#3	35.00	70.00	105.00
4	30.00	60.00	90.00
5	25.00	50.00	75.00
6-10	17.00	34.00	51.00
11-20	12.00	24.00	36.00
21-30	9.00	18.00	27.00
31-40	7.00	14.00	21.00
41-64	5.00	10.00	15.00
Super Reprint #11('63),#16(reprints #21, Cole art),#18('64-Spirit app. by Eisner)			
	2.00	4.00	6.00

PLASTIC MAN (See DC Special #15 & Brave & the Bold)
11-12/66 - #10, 5-6/68;
#11, 2-3/76 - #20, 10-11/77
National Periodical Publications/DC Comics

#1-Gil Kane cover	1.20	2.40	3.60
2-5('68)	.70	1.40	2.10
6-10('68)	.50	1.00	1.50
11('76)-20	.25	.50	.75

PLAYFUL LITTLE AUDREY
May, 1957 - Present
Harvey Publications

#1	4.00	8.00	12.00
2-5	1.75	3.50	5.25
6-10	1.00	2.00	3.00
11-30	.60	1.20	1.80
31-50	.30	.60	.90
51-121(5/76)	.15	.30	.45
Clubhouse #1('63)	1.00	2.00	3.00

PLOP!
Sept-Oct, 1973 - #24, Nov-Dec, 1976
National Periodical Publications

	Good	Fine	Mint
#1-Wrightson story	.75	1.50	2.25
2-4	.50	1.00	1.50
5-Wrightson story	.50	1.00	1.50
6-10	.30	.60	.90
11-20	.25	.50	.75
21-24-Giant Size, 52pgs.	.20	.40	.60

NOTE: *Alcala stories-#1-3. Ditko story-#16. Orlando art-#21,22. Toth story-#11. Wolverton art-#4(1pg.),22; covers-#1-12,14,17. Wood art-#14,16,18-24; covers-#13,15,16,18,19.*

PLUTO
1942 - 1961 (Walt Disney)
Dell Publishing Co.

Large Feature Comic #7(1942)			
	60.00	150.00	240.00
4-Color #429,509	2.00	4.00	6.00
4-Color #595,654	1.25	2.50	3.75
4-Color #736,853,941,1039,1143,1248			
	1.00	2.00	3.00

(See Cheerios Premiums & Walt Disney Showcase #4,7,13,20,23)

POCAHONTAS
1941 - #2, 1942
Pocahontas Fuel Company

No#(#1), #2	5.00	10.00	15.00

POCKET COMICS (Pocket size - 100 pgs.)
Aug, 1941 - #4, Jan, 1942
Harvey Publications

#1-Origin The Black Cat, Cadet Blakey the Spirit of 76, The Phantom Sphinx, The Red Blazer, & The Zebra; Phantom Ranger, British Agent #99, Spin Hawkins, Satan, Lord of Evil begin	30.00	60.00	90.00
2	20.00	40.00	60.00
3,4	15.00	30.00	45.00

POGO PARADE (Annual)
1953 (100 pgs.)
Dell Publishing Co.

#1-Kelly art(Reprints Pogo from Animal Comics in this order: #11,13,21,14,27,16,23,9,18, 15,17)	22.00	44.00	66.00

POGO POSSUM (Also see Animal Comics)
1949 - 1954
Dell Publishing Co.

Plastic Man =20, © QUA

Plop! =12, © DC

Pogo Possum #14, © Walt Kelly

Police Comics #6, © QUA

Police Comics #19, © QUA

Police Line-Up #3. © AVON

	Good	Fine	Mint
(Pogo Possum cont'd)			
4-Color #105(1946-Kelly)	60.00	120.00	180.00
4-Color #148-Kelly	50.00	100.00	150.00
#1-Kelly art in all	40.00	80.00	120.00
2	20.00	40.00	60.00
3-5	15.00	30.00	45.00
6-10	12.00	24.00	36.00
11-16	8.00	16.00	24.00

NOTE: *#1-4,9-13 (52pgs.); #5-8,14-16 (36pgs.)*

POLICE ACTION
Jan, 1954 - #7, Nov, 1954
Atlas News Co.

#1	1.25	2.50	3.75
2-7: #7-Powell story	.80	1.60	2.40

POLICE ACTION
Feb, 1975 - #3, June, 1975
Atlas/Seaboard Publ.

#1-Lomax, N.Y.P.D., Luke Malone begin;			
McWilliams art	.25	.50	.75
2,3: #2-Origin Luke Malone, Manhunter			
	.20	.40	.60

NOTE: *Ploog art in all.*

POLICE AGAINST CRIME
April, 1954 - #9, Aug, 1955
Premiere Magazines/Ace Periodicals

#1	1.00	2.00	3.00
2-9	.60	1.20	1.80

POLICE BADGE #479 (Spy Thrillers #1-4)
#5, Sept, 1955
Atlas Comics (CPI)

#5	1.00	2.00	3.00

POLICE CASE BOOK (See Giant Comics Editions)

POLICE CASES (See Authentic -- & Record Book of --)

POLICE COMICS
Aug, 1941 - #127, Oct, 1953
Quality Comics Group (Comic Magazines)

#1-Origin Plastic Man by Jack Cole, The Human Bomb by Gustavson, & #711; Intro. Chic Carter by W. Eisner, The Firebrand by R. Crandall, The Mouthpiece, Phantom Lady, & The Sword	200.00	400.00	600.00
2	100.00	200.00	300.00
3	80.00	160.00	240.00
4	70.00	140.00	210.00
5-Plastic Man forced to smoke marijuana			

	Good	Fine	Mint
	70.00	140.00	210.00
6,7	60.00	120.00	180.00
8-Origin Manhunter	65.00	130.00	195.00
9,10	50.00	100.00	150.00
11-Origin The Spirit by Will Eisner-strip reprint('40)	100.00	200.00	300.00
12-Intro. Ebony	50.00	100.00	150.00
13-Intro. Woozy Winks; last Firebrand	50.00	100.00	150.00
14-19: #15-Last #711; Destiny begins	30.00	60.00	90.00
20-The Raven x-over in Phantom Lady; features Jack Cole himself	30.00	60.00	90.00
21,22-Raven & Spider Widow x-over in Phantom Lady #21, cameo in Phantom Lady #22	25.00	50.00	75.00
23-30: #23-Last Phantom Lady. #24-Chic Carter becomes The Sword, only ish. #24-26-Flatfoot Burns by Kurtzman in all	20.00	40.00	60.00
31-41-Last Spirit reprint by Eisner	15.00	30.00	45.00
42-50-(#50 on cvr, #49 on inside, 1/46)	8.00	16.00	24.00
51-60: #58-Last Human Bomb	6.00	12.00	18.00
61,62,64-90	6.00	12.00	18.00
63-(Some issues have #65 printed on cover, but #63 on inside)	6.00	12.00	18.00
91-102: #101-Last Manhunter. #102-Last Plastic Man. #1-102 all by Jack Cole	7.00	14.00	21.00
103-Content change to crime - Ken Shannon	4.00	8.00	12.00
104-112,114-127-Crandall art most issues	2.50	5.00	7.50
113-Crandall cover, 2 stories, 9pgs. each	3.00	6.00	9.00

NOTE: *Most Spirit stories signed by Eisner are not by him; all are reprints. Cole covers-#20,24-26,28,29,31,36-38. Crandall Firebrand-#1-13. Grandenetti Spirit-#94-102. No Spirit in #89,91,93.*

POLICE LINE-UP
Aug, 1951 - #4, July, 1952
Realistic Comics/Avon Periodicals

#1-Wood art, 1pg. + part cover			
	4.00	8.00	12.00
2,4	2.50	5.00	7.50
3-Kubert reprints(1 story + part/cover)			
	3.50	7.00	10.50

POLICE THRILLS
1954
Ajax/Farrell Publ.

(Police Thrills cont'd)	Good	Fine	Mint
#1	1.25	2.50	3.75

POLICE TRAP
Aug-Sept, 1954 - #6, Sept, 1955
Mainline #1-4(Prize)/Charlton #5

	Good	Fine	Mint
#1-S&K cover	2.50	5.00	7.50
2,3-S&K covers	1.75	3.50	5.25
4	1.00	2.00	3.00
5,6-S&K cover/story	3.00	6.00	9.00

POLICE TRAP
#11, 1963; #16-18, 1964
Super Comics

	Good	Fine	Mint
Reprint #11,16-18	.60	1.20	1.80

POLL PARROT
Poll Parrot Shoe Store/International Shoe
1950 - 1951; 1959 - 1962
K.K. Publications (Giveaway)

#1-4-Howdy Doody('50)	1.50	3.00	4.50
#2('59)-#16('61): #8-Mixed Up Mission('60).			
#16---& the Rajah's Ruby('62)			
	.75	1.50	2.25

POLLY & HER PALS (See Comic Monthly #1)

POLLYANNA (See 4-Color Comics #1129)

POLLY PIGTAILS (Girls' Fun & Fashion Mag.
Jan, 1946 - V4#43, 10-11/49   #44 on)
Parents' Magazine Institute/Polly Pigtails

#1	2.50	5.00	7.50
2-5	1.50	3.00	4.50
6-10	1.25	2.50	3.75
11-30	.80	1.60	2.40
31-43	.60	1.20	1.80

PONYTAIL
7-9/62 - #12, 10-12/65; #13, 11/69 - #20, 1/71
Dell Publishing Co./Charlton #13 on

No#(#1)	.30	.60	.90
#2-12	.25	.50	.75
13-20	.20	.40	.60

POPEYE (See Eat Right to Work--, Comic Album
#7,11,15, & March of Comics #37,52,66,80,96,
117,134,148,157,169,194,246,264,274,294)

POPEYE (See Thimble Theatre)
1935 (25¢) (52pgs.) (By Segar) (B&W)
David McKay Publications

	Good	Fine	Mint
#1-Daily strip serial reprints-"The Gold			
Mine Thieves"	50.00	100.00	150.00
2-Daily strip reprints	40.00	80.00	120.00

NOTE: *Popeye first entered Thimble Theatre
in 1929.*

POPEYE
1937 (All color drawings + text taken from
Segar; probably not him)(Cardboard covers)
Whitman Publishing Co.   (8-3/8x9-3/8")

-- Borrows a Baby Nurse(72pgs.)
-- & His Jungle Pet(72pgs.)
each....	20.00	40.00	60.00

-- Goes Duck Hunting(28pgs.)
Wimpy Tricks Popeye & Rough-House(28pgs.)
-- Plays Nursemaid to Sweet Pea(28pgs.)
-- Calls on Olive Oyl(28pgs.)
each....	15.00	30.00	45.00

POPEYE
1937 - 1939   (All by Segar)
David McKay Publications

Feature Book-No#(100pgs.)(Very Rare)			
	125.00	250.00	375.00
Feature Book #2 (52pgs.)	60.00	120.00	180.00
Feature Book #3 (100pgs.)-Thought to be a reprint of the No# issue with a new cover			
	40.00	80.00	120.00
Feature Book #5,10(76pgs)	35.00	70.00	105.00
Feature Book #14 (76pgs.) (Scarce)			
	50.00	100.00	150.00

POPEYE (Also see Comics Reading Libraries)
(Strip reprints through 4-Color #70)
1941 - 1947; #1, 2-4/48 - #65, 7-9/62; #66,
10/62 - #80, 5/66; #81, 8/66 - #92, 12/67;
#94, 2/69 - #138, 1/77 (No #93); #139, 5/78 -
Present
Dell #1-65/Gold Key #66-80/King #81-92/
Charlton #94-138/Gold Key #139 on

Black & White #24('41)-Half by Segar			
	25.00	62.50	100.00
4-Color #25('41)-by Segar			
	40.00	80.00	120.00
Large Feature Comic #10('43)			
	20.00	50.00	80.00
4-Color #17('43)by Segar	27.00	54.00	81.00
4-Color #26('43)by Segar	22.00	44.00	66.00
4-Color #43('44)	14.00	28.00	42.00
4-Color #70('45)	10.00	20.00	30.00
4-Color #113('46-original strips begin),127, 145('47),168	4.00	8.00	12.00
#1(2-4/48)(Dell)	8.00	16.00	24.00
2	5.00	10.00	15.00

Police Trap #4, © PRIZE

Popeye Four Color #17, © KING

Popeye #4, © KING

Popeye #10, © KING

Popular Comics #8, © DELL

Popular Comics #22, © DELL

(Popeye cont'd)	Good	Fine	Mint
3-10	3.00	6.00	9.00
11-20	2.00	4.00	6.00
21-40	1.50	3.00	4.50
41-50	1.00	2.00	3.00
51-60	.75	1.50	2.25
61-65,68-80	.50	1.00	1.50
66,67-both 84pgs.	.60	1.20	1.80
81-92,94-100	.20	.40	.60
101-142	.15	.30	.45
Bold Detergent giveaway(Same as reg. issue #94)	.40	.80	1.20
--& Business & Office Careers('73)(32pg.Giveaway, reg.size)#E-10	.50	1.00	1.50
--& Health Careers, & Environmental Careers ('72, 32pg. Giveaway, reg. size, in color) George Wildman art	.50	1.00	1.50
--Kite Fun Book(PG&E, 1977)	.20	.40	.60
--& Manufacturing Careers(1973 giveaway)	.50	1.00	1.50

POPEYE
1972 - 1974 (36pgs. in color)
Charlton (King Features) (Giveaway)

E-1 Popeye & Health Careers (1972)
E-2 Popeye & Environmental Careers (1973)
E-3 Popeye & Communications & Media Careers (1972)
E-4 Popeye & Transportation Careers (1972)
E-5 Popeye & Construction Careers (1972)
E-6 Popeye & Consumer & Homemaking Careers (1972)
E-7 Popeye & Manufacturing Careers (1972)
E-8 Popeye & Hospitality & Recreation Careers (1972)
E-9 Popeye & Marketing & Distribution Careers (1972)
E-10 Popeye & Business & Office Careers (1972)
E-11 Popeye & Public Service Careers (1972)
E-12 Popeye & Personal Service Careers(1972)
E-13 Popeye & Marine Science Careers (1972)
E-14 Popeye & Fine Arts & Humanities Careers (1972)
E-15 Popeye & Agri-Business & Natural Resources Careers (1972)

No#-Popeye Gettin' Better Grades-4pgs. used as intro. to above giveaways (in color)	.15	.30	.45

POPEYE CARTOON BOOK
1934 (36pgs. plus cover)(8½x13")(Cardboard
The Saalfield Publ. Co.   covers)

#2095-(Rare)-1933 strip reprints in color by
Segar; each pg. contains a vertical half
of a Sunday strip, so the continuity reads
row by row completely across each double

	Good	Fine	Mint

page spread. If each page is read by itself, the continuity makes no sense. Each
double page spread reprints one complete
Sunday page(from 1933).

	100.00	200.00	300.00

POPPO OF THE POPCORN THEATRE
10/29/55 - 1956 (Published weekly)
Fuller Publishing Co. (Publishers Weekly)

#1	1.75	3.50	5.25
2-13	1.00	2.00	3.00

NOTE: *By Charles Biro. 10¢ cover price, given
away by supermarkets such as IGA.*

POP-POP COMICS
No date (Circa 1945)
R. B. Leffingwell Co.

#1	1.35	2.75	4.00

POPSICLE PETE FUN BOOK
1947, 1948
Joe Lowe Corp.

No#-36pgs. in color; Sammy 'n' Claras, The King Who Couldn't Sleep & Popsicle Pete stories, games, cut-outs	3.00	6.00	9.00
Adventure Book('48)	2.50	5.00	7.50

POPULAR COMICS
Feb, 1936 - #145, July-Sept, 1948
Dell Publishing Co.

#1-Terry & the Pirates, Gasoline Alley, Dick Tracy, Moon Mullins, The Gumps begin (All strip reprints)	50.00	100.00	150.00
2	25.00	50.00	75.00
3	20.00	40.00	60.00
4	15.00	30.00	45.00
5	12.00	24.00	36.00
6-10	10.00	20.00	30.00
11-20	9.00	18.00	27.00
21-27-Last Terry & the Pirates	9.00	18.00	27.00
28-37	7.00	14.00	21.00
38-43-Tarzan in all	10.00	20.00	30.00
44-Masked Pilot begins	5.00	10.00	15.00
45	5.00	10.00	15.00
46-Origin Martan, the Marvel Man	6.00	12.00	18.00
47-50	5.00	10.00	15.00
51-Origin The Voice(The Invisible Detective) strip begins	6.00	12.00	18.00
52-59	5.00	10.00	15.00
60-Origin Professor Supermind and Son	6.00	12.00	18.00

(Popular Comics cont'd)	Good	Fine	Mint
61,62,64-71	5.00	10.00	15.00
63-Smilin' Jack begins	5.00	10.00	15.00
72-The Owl & Terry & the Pirates begin; Smok-ey Stover reprts.begin	5.00	10.00	15.00
73-75	5.00	10.00	15.00
76-78-Capt. Midnight in all	5.00	10.00	15.00
79-86-Last Owl	5.00	10.00	15.00
87-100: #98-Felix the Cat, Smokey Stover re-prints begin	3.00	6.00	9.00
101-130	2.50	5.00	7.50
131-145	2.00	4.00	6.00

POPULAR FAIRY TALES (See March of Comics #6,18)

POPULAR ROMANCE
#5, Dec, 1949 - #29, 1954
Better-Standard Publications

#5	1.00	2.00	3.00
6-9,11-21,24,28,29	.80	1.60	2.40
10-Wood art, 2pgs.	2.00	4.00	6.00
22,23,25-27-Toth stories	2.00	4.00	6.00

NOTE: *All have photo cover.* _Tuska_ *art in most issues.*

POPULAR TEEN-AGERS (Secrets of Love)(Former-ly School Day Romances)
July-Aug, 1950? - #23, Nov, 1954
Star Publications

#5-8-Toni Gay, Honey Bunn, etc.; all have L. B. Cole covers	3.00	6.00	9.00
9-(--Romances; change to romance format)	1.75	3.50	5.25
10-(--Secrets of Love)	1.50	3.00	4.50
11,16,18,19,22,23	1.25	2.50	3.75
12,13,17,20,21-Disbrow stories	1.50	3.00	4.50
14-Harrison/Wood story; two spanking scenes	4.00	8.00	12.00
15-Wood/? story + Disbrow art	4.00	8.00	12.00

NOTE: *All have L. B. Cole covers.*

PORE LI'L MOSE
1902 (30pgs.-10½x15"-in full color)
New York Herald Publ. by Grand Union Tea
Cupples & Leon Co.

By R. F. Outcault; 1pg. strips about early Negroes	40.00	80.00	120.00

PORKY PIG
1942 - Present
Dell Publishing Co./Gold Key

	Good	Fine	Mint
4-Color #16(1942)	40.00	80.00	120.00
4-Color #48-Carl Barks art (1944)	120.00	240.00	360.00
4-Color #78('45)	10.00	20.00	30.00
4-Color #112('46)	7.00	14.00	21.00
4-Color #156,182,191('49)	5.00	10.00	15.00
4-Color #226,241('49),260,271,277,284,295 ('50)	3.50	7.00	10.50
4-Color #303,311,322,330	2.00	4.00	6.00
4-Color #342,351,360,370,385,399('52),410, 426	1.40	2.80	4.20
#25-30	.60	1.20	1.80
31-50	.40	.80	1.20
51-81(3-4/62)	.35	.70	1.05
#1(1/65-G.K.)(2nd Series)	.50	1.00	1.50
2,4,5-Reprints 4-Color #226,284 & 271 in that order	.50	1.00	1.50
3,6-10	.25	.50	.75
11-30	.20	.40	.60
31-50	.15	.30	.45
51-88		.15	.35

PORKY PIG (See March of Comics #42,57,71,89, 99,113,130,143,164,175,192,209,218,367, and Super Book #6,18,30)

PORKY'S BOOK OF TRICKS
1942 (48 pgs.) (8½x5½")
K.K. Publications (Giveaway)

7pg. comic story, text stories, + games & puzzles	20.00	40.00	60.00

POWDER RIVER RUSTLERS (See Faw. Movie Comics)

POWER COMICS
1944 - 1945
Holyoke Publ. Co./Narrative Publ.

#1-L. B. Cole cover	3.50	7.00	10.50
2-4: #2-Dr. Mephisto begins. #3,4-L. B. Cole cvr.; Miss Espionage app. each	2.50	5.00	7.50

POWER COMICS
1976 (50¢)
Power Comics

#1-Nightwitch, 2-Cobolt Blue, 3-Nightwitch, 4-Northern Light, 5-Bluebird (Ploog Man-thing reprint-#5) each....	.20	.40	.60

POWERHOUSE PEPPER COMICS (See Gay Comics)
#1, 1943; #2, May, 1948 - #5, Nov, 1948
Marvel Comics (20CC)

Popular Romance #25, © STD   Popular Teen-Agers Of Love #16, © STAR   Porky Pig Four Color #182, © L. Schlesinger

Powerhouse Pepper #1, © MCG   Prison Break! #3, © AVON   Private Secretary #1. © DELL

(Powerhouse Pepper cont'd)

	Good	Fine	Mint
#1-Wolverton art begins	40.00	80.00	120.00
2-4-All by Wolverton	25.00	50.00	75.00
5-Wolverton art(Scarce)	30.00	60.00	90.00

POWER MAN (Formerly Hero for Hire)
#17, Feb, 1974 - Present
Marvel Comics Group

#17-Iron Man app.	.30	.60	.90
18-30	.25	.50	.75
31-Part Adams inks	.35	.70	1.05
32-44: #36-Reprint	.20	.40	.60
45-Starlin cover	.25	.50	.75
46,47	.20	.40	.60
48-53-Iron Fist joins Cage.	15	.30	.45
54	.15	.30	.45
Giant-Size #1('75)	.40	.80	1.20
Annual #1(11/76)	.30	.60	.90

NOTE: *Byrne stories-#48-50. Nino stories-*
#42(inks),43.

POW MAGAZINE (Bob Sproul's)(Satire Magazine)
Aug, 1966 - #3, Feb, 1967   (30¢)
Humor-Vision

#1	.75	1.50	2.25
2-Jones art	.80	1.60	2.40
3-Wrightson art	1.20	2.40	3.60

PREHISTORIC WORLD (See Classics Special)

PREMIERE (See Charlton Premiere)

PRETTY BOY FLOYD (See On the Spot)

PREZ (See Cancelled Comic Cavalcade)
Aug-Sept, 1973 - #4, Feb-Mar, 1974
National Periodical Publications

#1-Origin	.20	.40	.60
2-4		.15	.35

PRIDE AND THE PASSION, THE (See 4-Color #824)

PRIDE OF THE YANKEES, THE
1949   (The Life of Lou Gehrig)
Magazine Enterprises

No#-Ogden Whitney art	5.00	10.00	15.00

PRIMUS (TV)
Feb, 1972 - #7, Oct, 1972
Charlton Comics

#1-5,7-Staton art in all	.25	.50	.75
6-Drug book	.35	.70	1.05

PRINCE & THE PAUPER, THE (See Movie Classics)

PRINCE VALIANT   (See Comics Reading Libraries,
Feature Book #26, McKay)

PRINCE VALIANT (See 4-Color #567,650,699,719,
788,849,900)

PRISCILLA'S POP (See 4-Color #569,630,704,799)

PRISON BARS (See Behind --)

PRISON BREAK!
Sept, 1951 - #5, Sept, 1952
Avon Periodicals/Realistic #4 on

	Good	Fine	Mint
#1-Wood cover + 1pg.; has reprt/Saint #7 re-titled Michael Strong Private Eye	7.00	14.00	21.00
2-Wood cover/Kubert story + 2pgs. Wood art	6.00	12.00	18.00
3-Orlando, Check stories	4.00	8.00	12.00
4,5: Kinstler covers. #5-Infantino art	3.50	7.00	10.50

PRISON RIOT
1952
Avon Periodicals

#1-Kinstler cover	3.50	7.00	10.50

PRISON TO PRAISE
1974
Logos International

True story of Merlin R. Corothers
	.20	.40	.60

PRIVATE BUCK (See Large Feature Comic #12 &
Black & White #21)

PRIVATE EYE
Jan, 1951 - #8, March, 1952
Atlas Comics (MCI)

#1	1.50	3.00	4.50
2-V. Henkel cvr/stories	1.20	2.40	3.60
3-8: #8-Rocky Jorden--	1.00	2.00	3.00

PRIVATE EYE (See Mike Shayne --)

PRIVATE SECRETARY
Dec-Feb, 1962-63 - #2, Mar-May, 1963
Dell Publishing Co.

#1,2	.50	1.00	1.50

PRIVATE STRONG (See The Double Life of --)

<u>PRIZE COMICS</u> (-- Western #69 on)
March, 1940 - #68, Feb-Mar, 1948
Prize Publications

	Good	Fine	Mint
#1-Origin Power Nelson, The Futureman & Jupiter, Master Magician; Ted O'Neal, Secret Agent M-11, Jaxon of the Jungle, Bucky Brady & Storm Curtis begin	35.00	70.00	105.00
2-The Black Owl begins	18.00	36.00	54.00
3	14.00	28.00	42.00
4	12.00	24.00	36.00
5,6: Dr. Dekkar, Master of Monsters app. in each	10.00	20.00	30.00
7-Black Owl by S&K; Dr. Frost, Frankenstein, The Green Lama, Captain Gallant, & Twist Turner begin; Kirby cover	15.00	30.00	45.00
8,9-Black Owl & Ted O'Neil by S&K	15.00	30.00	45.00
10,12,14-20	9.00	18.00	27.00
11-Origin Bulldog Denny	9.00	18.00	27.00
13-Origin Yank & Doodle	12.00	24.00	36.00
21-24	6.00	12.00	18.00
25-30	5.00	10.00	15.00
31-33	3.00	6.00	9.00
34-Origin Airmale, Yank & Doodle, & The Black Owl	4.00	8.00	12.00
35-Flying Fist & Bingo begin,			
36-40: #37-Intro. Stampy, Airmale's sidekick	3.00	6.00	9.00
41-50: #48-Prince Ra begins	2.50	5.00	7.50
51-62,64-68: #55-No Frankenstein. #64-Black Owl retires	2.00	4.00	6.00
63-Simon & Kirby cvr/sty.	4.00	8.00	12.00

<u>PRIZE COMICS WESTERN</u> (Prize #1-68)
#69, 1949 - #119, Nov-Dec, 1956
Prize Publications (Feature)

#69	4.00	8.00	12.00
70-73,75-78,80,81,83,84	2.50	5.00	7.50
74,79-Kurtzman stories	4.00	8.00	12.00
82-1st app. The Preacher by Mart Bailey	3.00	6.00	9.00
85-American Eagle by John Severin begins (1-2/50)	5.00	10.00	15.00
86-98,101-105	3.50	7.00	10.50
99-Three Severin & Elder stories	4.00	8.00	12.00
100	4.00	8.00	12.00
106-108,110-112	3.00	6.00	9.00
109-Severin/Williamson story	5.00	10.00	15.00
113-Two Williamson/Severin stories	6.00	12.00	18.00
114-119: Drifter series in all; by Mort			

	Good	Fine	Mint
Meskin #114-118	2.00	4.00	6.00

NOTE: *Kirby covers-#63,75,83. Severin & Elder stories-#79,81,82,87-92,98(2 ea.); cover-#98. Severin stories-#72,75,83-86,96,97,100-105; covers-most #85-109.*

<u>PRIZE MYSTERY</u>
May, 1955 - #3, 1955
Key Publications

#1	1.00	2.00	3.00
2,3	.75	1.50	2.25

<u>PROFESSIONAL FOOTBALL</u> (See Charlton Sport Library)

<u>PSYCHO</u> (Magazine)
Jan, 1971 - #24, Mar, 1975 (68pgs.)(B&W)
Skywald Publishing Corp.

#1-All reprints	.75	1.50	2.25
2-Origin & 1st app. The Heap, & Frankenstein series by Adkins	.60	1.20	1.80
3-10	.50	1.00	1.50
11-23	.35	.70	1.05
24-1975 Winter Special	.40	.80	1.20
Annual #1('72)	.50	1.00	1.50
Fall Special('74)	.40	.80	1.20
Yearbook(1974-No#)	.40	.80	1.20

NOTE: *Boris cover-#3,5. Buckler story-#4,5. Everett story-#3,4,6. Jones stories-#4,6; cover-#12. Kaluta story-#13. Morrow story-#1. Reese story-#5. Wildey story-#5.*

<u>PSYCHOANALYSIS</u>
Mar-Apr, 1955 - #4, Sept-Oct, 1955
E.C. Comics

#1-All Kamen; not approved by code	5.00	10.00	15.00
2-4-Kamen art in all	4.00	8.00	12.00

<u>P.T. 109</u> (See Movie Comics)

<u>PUBLIC DEFENDER IN ACTION</u>
#7, Mar, 1956 - #12, 1957
Charlton Comics

#7-12	.40	.80	1.20

<u>PUBLIC ENEMIES</u>
1948 - 1949
D.S. Publishing Co.

#1	2.00	4.00	6.00
2-Used in Seduction of the Innocent	5.00	10.00	15.00

Prize Comics #15, © PRIZE

Prize Comics Western #80, © PRIZE

Public Enemies #9, © DS

Punch Comics #15, © CHES   The Purple Claw #2, © TOBY   Queen Of The West Dale Evans #21, © DELL

(Public Enemies cont'd)	Good	Fine	Mint
3-9	1.50	3.00	4.50

PUDGY PIG
Aug-Sept, 1958 - #2, Nov, 1958
Charlton Comics

#1,2	.20	.40	.60

PUNCH & JUDY COMICS
1944 - V3#9, Dec, 1951
Hillman Periodicals

V1#1(60pgs.)	2.50	5.00	7.50
2-12(7/46)	1.35	2.75	4.00
V2#1,3-10	1.25	2.50	3.75
V2#2,11,12,V3#1-Two Kirby stories each			
	6.00	12.00	18.00
V3#2-Kirby story	5.00	10.00	15.00
3-9	1.00	2.00	3.00

PUNCH COMICS
Dec, 1941 - #26, Dec, 1947
Harry 'A' Chesler

#1-Mr. E, The Sky Chief, Hale, the Magician, Kitty Kelly begin	20.00	40.00	60.00
2-Captain Glory app.	12.00	24.00	36.00
3	10.00	20.00	30.00
4	7.00	14.00	21.00
5	6.00	12.00	18.00
6-8	5.00	10.00	15.00
9-Rocketman & Rocket Girl & The Master Key begin	5.00	10.00	15.00
10-Sky Chief app.	4.00	8.00	12.00
11,12: #11-Sky Chief app. #12-Rocket Boy & Capt. Glory app.	3.50	7.00	10.50
13-17,19	3.00	6.00	9.00
18-Bondage cover	3.50	7.00	10.50
20-Used in Seduction of the Innocent? Unique cover with bare-breasted women			
	6.00	12.00	18.00
21-26: #22,23-Little Nemo-not by McCay			
	2.50	5.00	7.50

PUPPET COMICS
Spring, 1946
George W. Dougherty Co.

#1,2	2.00	4.00	6.00

PUPPETOONS (See George Pal's --)

PURPLE CLAW, THE (Also see Tales of Horror)
Jan, 1953 - #3, 1953
Minoan Publishing Co./Toby Press

#1	3.00	6.00	9.00

	Good	Fine	Mint
2,3	2.00	4.00	6.00
IW Reprint #8(reprts.#1)	1.25	2.50	3.75

PUSSYCAT (Magazine)
1968 (B&W reprints from men's magazines)
Marvel Comics Group

#1-(Scarce)-Ward, Everett, Wood art; Everett cover	6.00	12.00	18.00

PUZZLE FUN COMICS (Also see Jingle Jangle)
Spring, 1946 - #2, Summer, 1946; 1957
George W. Dougherty Co./National Per. Publ.

#1(1946)	6.00	12.00	18.00
2	4.00	8.00	12.00
1(National,'57)Exist?	1.00	2.00	3.00

NOTE: #1,2('46) each contain a George Carlson cover + a 6pg. story "Alec in Fumbleland;" also many puzzles in each.

QUAKER OATS (Also see Cap'n Crunch)
1965 (Giveaway) (2½x5½") (16 pgs.)
Quaker Oats Co.

"Plenty of Glutton","Lava Come-Back","Kite Tale","A Witch in Time"	.25	.50	.75

QUEEN OF THE WEST, DALE EVANS
July, 1953 - #22, Jan, 1959
Dell Publishing Co.

4-Color #479('53)	2.00	4.00	6.00
4-Color #528('54)	1.75	3.50	5.25
#3-10-Manning art	2.00	4.00	6.00
11,19,21-No Manning	1.00	2.00	3.00
12-18,20,22-Manning art	1.50	3.00	4.50

QUENTIN DURWARD (See 4-Color Comics #672)

QUESTION, THE (See Mysterious Suspense)

QUICK-DRAW McGRAW (TV) (Hanna-Barbera)
12-2/60 - #15, 6/69
Dell Publ. Co./Gold Key #12 on

4-Color #1040	.50	1.00	1.50
#2(4-6/60)-#6	.30	.60	.90
7-11	.25	.50	.75
12-15-All titled "Q-D McG. Fun-Type Roundup"; #12,13-84pgs.	.40	.80	1.20
(See Whitman Comic Books)			

QUICK-DRAW McGRAW (TV)
Nov, 1970 - #8, Jan, 1972 (Hanna-Barbera)
Charlton Comics

#1-8		.15	.25

QUICK-TRIGGER WESTERN (Formerly Cowboy Action)
#12, May, 1956 - #19, Sept, 1957
Atlas Comics(ACI #12/WPI #13-19)

	Good	Fine	Mint
#12-Baker art	1.75	3.50	5.25
13-Williamson sty.,5pgs.	2.50	5.00	7.50
14-Everett, Crandall, Torres, Heath stories			
	2.50	5.00	7.50
15-Torres, Crandall	1.75	3.50	5.25
16-Orlando + Kirby story	1.50	3.00	4.50
17-Crandall story	1.50	3.00	4.50
18-Baker story	1.25	2.50	3.75
19	1.00	2.00	3.00

NOTE: _Morrow_ story-#18. _Severin_ cover-#13,17.

QUINCY (See Comics Reading Libraries)

RACCOON KIDS, THE (Formerly Movietown Animal
#52, 9-10/54 - #64, 11/57   Antics)
National Periodical Publ. (Arleigh #63,64)

#52-64	.60	1.20	1.80

RACE FOR THE MOON
March, 1958 - #3, Nov, 1958
Harvey Publications

#1-Powell art; ½-pg. S&K art; cover from Gal-			
axy Science Fiction(5/53)pulp			
	3.00	6.00	9.00
2-Three Kirby/Williamson stories			
	6.00	12.00	18.00
3-Four Kirby/Williamson stories			
	8.00	16.00	24.00

RACKET SQUAD IN ACTION
May-June, 1952 - #29, March, 1958
Capitol Stories/Charlton Comics

#1	1.50	3.00	4.50
2	.80	1.60	2.40
3-6-Dr. Neff, Ghost Breaker app.			
	.80	1.60	2.40
7-10	.75	1.50	2.25
11,13-28	.60	1.20	1.80
12-Ditko explosion cover (classic)			
	1.50	3.00	4.50
29-(68pgs.)(15¢)	.75	1.50	2.25

RADIANT LOVE (Formerly Daring Love #1)
#2, Dec, 1953 - #6, Aug, 1954
Gilmor Magazines

#2-6	1.20	2.40	3.60

RAGGEDY ANN AND ANDY (See March of Comics#23)
1942 - #39, 8/49; 1955 - #4, 3/66
Dell Publishing Co.

	Good	Fine	Mint
4-Color #5(1942)	22.00	44.00	66.00
4-Color #23(1943)	17.00	34.00	51.00
4-Color #45(1943)	12.00	24.00	36.00
4-Color #72(1945)	10.00	20.00	30.00
#1(6/46)-Billy & Bonnie Bee by Frank Thomas			
	12.00	24.00	36.00
2,3: #3-Egbert Elephant by Dan Noonan begins			
	8.00	16.00	24.00
4-10	6.00	12.00	18.00
11-20	4.50	9.00	13.50
21-39,4-Color #262	3.00	6.00	9.00
4-Color #306,354,380,452,533			
	2.50	5.00	7.50
Giant #1('55)Tales From-	5.00	10.00	15.00
#1(10-12/64, Dell)	.80	1.60	2.40
2,3(10-12/65),#4(3/66)	.50	1.00	1.50

NOTE: _Kelly_ art("Animal Mother Goose")-#1-34,
36,37; cover-#28. Peterkin Pottle by _John
Stanley_ in #32-38.

RAGGEDY ANN AND ANDY
Dec, 1971 - #6, Sept, 1973
Gold Key

#1	.30	.60	.90
2-6	.25	.50	.75

RAGGEDY ANN & THE CAMEL WITH THE WRINKLED
KNEES (See Dell Jr. Treasury #8)

RAGMAN (See Cancelled Comic Cavalcade)
Aug-Sept, 1976 - #5, June-July, 1977
National Periodical Publications

#1-Origin	.60	1.20	1.80
2-Origin; Kubert cvr/sty.	.35	.70	1.05
3-5	.25	.50	.75

NOTE: _Kubert_ covers-#1-5; stories-#4,5.
Redondo stories-#1,2,4,5.

RAGS RABBIT (See Harvey Hits#2 & Tastee Freez)
1951 - #18, March, 1954
Harvey Publications

#11-18	.60	1.20	1.80

RALPH KINER, HOME RUN KING
1950   (Pittsburgh Pirates)
Fawcett Publications

No#	4.00	8.00	12.00

RAMAR OF THE JUNGLE
1954 - 1956
Toby Press #1,2/Charlton #3-5

#1	3.00	6.00	9.00

Racket Squad In Action =5. © CC

Raggedy Ann And Andy #18. © J. Gruelle

Ragman #1. © DC

Range Romances #5, © QUA

Rangers Comics #3, © FH

Rangers Comics #39, © FH

(Ramar cont'd)	Good	Fine	Mint
2-5	2.00	4.00	6.00

RAMPAGING HULK, THE (Magazine)(The Hulk #11
1/77 - #10, 9/78 on)
Marvel Comics Group

	Good	Fine	Mint
#1-Bloodstone featured	1.00	2.00	3.00
2-10	.60	1.20	1.80

NOTE: *Alcala* inks-#1-4. *Buscema* story-#1.
Nino inks-#4. *Simonson* pencils-#1-3. *Starlin*
story-#4,7; covers-#4,5,7.

RANGE BUSTERS
Sept, 1950 - #8, 1951
Fox Features Syndicate

#1	2.50	5.00	7.50
2-8	1.50	3.00	4.50

RANGE BUSTERS
#8, May, 1955 - #10, Sept, 1955
Charlton Comics

#8-10	.60	1.20	1.80

RANGELAND LOVE
Dec, 1949 - #2, Mar, 1950
Atlas Comics (CDS)

#1,2	1.75	3.50	5.25

RANGER, THE (See 4-Color Comics #255)

RANGE RIDER (See Flying A's --)

RANGE RIDER, THE (See 4-Color Comics #404)

RANGE ROMANCES
Dec, 1949 - #5, Aug, 1950
Comic Magazines (Quality Comics)

#1-Gustavson cover/story	6.00	12.00	18.00
2-Crandall story/cover; "spanking" scene			
	7.00	14.00	21.00
3-Crandall, Gustavson story			
	4.50	9.00	13.50
4-Crandall story	4.00	8.00	12.00
5-Gustavson art; Crandall pencils			
	4.00	8.00	12.00

RANGERS COMICS (-- of Freedom #1-7)
Oct, 1941 - #69, Winter, 1952-53
Fiction House Magazines (Flying stories)

| #1-Intro. Ranger Girl & The Rangers of Free-
dom; ends #4, cover app. only-#5			
	40.00	80.00	120.00

	Good	Fine	Mint
2	25.00	50.00	75.00
3	20.00	40.00	60.00
4,5	12.00	24.00	36.00
6,7-Sky Rangers begin-#6?			
	10.00	20.00	30.00
8-12-Commando Rangers begin-#11			
	9.00	18.00	27.00
13-Commando Ranger begins-not same as Comm.			
Rangers	9.00	18.00	27.00
14-21: #21-Firehair begins			
	8.00	16.00	24.00
22-30: #23-Kazanda begins, ends #28. #28-
Origin Tiger Man. #30-Crusoe Island be-
gins, ends #40	6.00	12.00	18.00
31-40	5.00	10.00	15.00
41-46	3.50	7.00	10.50
47-56-"Eisnerish" Dr. Drew by Grandenetti			
	4.00	8.00	12.00
57-60-Straight Dr. Drew by Grandenetti			
	3.00	6.00	9.00
61-66: #64-Suicide Smith begins			
	2.50	5.00	7.50
67-The Space Rangers begin, end #69,			
68,69	2.50	5.00	7.50

NOTE: *A very large percentage of above have
bondage, discipline, etc. covers. Firehair
art by Lee Elias-#21-28; by Bob Lubbers-#30-
37. Glory Forbes by Matt Baker-#36-38. "I
Confess" by Evans-#47-52. Tiger Man art by
John Celardo-#36-39; by Evans-#40-45,48,52.
Werewolf Hunter by Evans-#39.*

RANGO (TV)
August, 1967
Dell Publishing Co.

#1	.35	.70	1.05

RATFINK (See Frantic & Zany)
October, 1964
Canrom, Inc.

#1-Woodbridge art	1.00	2.00	3.00

RAT PATROL, THE (TV)
March, 1967 - #6, Oct, 1969
Dell Publishing Co.

#1	.35	.70	1.05
2-6	.20	.40	.60

RAVEN, THE (See Movie Classics)

RAWHIDE (TV)
9-11/59 - 6-8/62; 7/63 - #2, 1/64
Dell Publishing Co./Gold Key

4-Color #1028,1097,1160,1202,1261,1269

(Rawhide cont'd)	Good	Fine	Mint
	.80	1.60	2.40
#01-684-208(8/62-Dell)	.60	1.20	1.80
#1(10071-307,G.K.),#2	.40	.80	1.20

RAWHIDE KID
3/55 - #16, 9/57; #17, 8/60 - Present
Atlas/Marvel Comics(CnPC #1-16/AMI #17-30)

	Good	Fine	Mint
#1	8.00	16.00	24.00
2	4.00	8.00	12.00
3-5	3.00	6.00	9.00
6,8-10	2.00	4.00	6.00
7-Williamson story,4pgs.	3.50	7.00	10.50
11-15	1.75	3.50	5.25
16-Torres art	1.75	3.50	5.25
17-Origin by J. Kirby	3.00	6.00	9.00
18-30	.80	1.60	2.40
31,32,36-44: #40-Two-Gun Kid x-over. #42-1st Larry Lieber issue	.75	1.50	2.25
33-35-Davis stories	1.20	2.40	3.60
45-Origin retold	1.50	3.00	4.50
46-Toth story	1.75	3.50	5.25
47-70: #50-Kid Colt x-over. #64-Kid Colt story. #66-Two-Gun Kid story. #67-Kid Colt story	.30	.60	.90
71-78	.25	.50	.75
79-Williamson story reprint/Kid Colt #59, 4pgs.	.25	.50	.75
80-85	.20	.40	.60
86-Origin reprint; Williamson story reprint/ Ringo Kid #13, 4pgs.	.25	.50	.75
87-94: #89,90-Kid Colt x-over. #93-52pgs.	.15	.30	.50
95-Williamson reprint	.20	.40	.60
96-110: #105-Western Kid reprint	.15	.30	.45
111-Williamson reprint	.20	.40	.60
112-115-Last new story	.15	.30	.45
116-148: #125-Davis reprint		.15	.35
Special #1(9/71)-Reprints	.25	.50	.75

NOTE: *Davis reprint-#125. Everett story-#65, 66,88. Kirby story-#17-32,34,42,43,84,86,109, #1(Special); covers-#17-35,40,41,43-47. McWilliams story-#41. Torres reprint-#99. Whitney story-#66.*

REAL ADVENTURE COMICS
April, 1955
Gillmore Magazines

#1	.65	1.35	2.00

REAL CLUE CRIME STORIES (Formerly Clue)
1947 - V8#3, May, 1953
Hillman Periodicals

V2#4(#1)-S&K cover/3 stories; Dan Barry art

	Good	Fine	Mint
	5.00	10.00	15.00
5-7-S&K covers/3-4 stories; #7-Iron Lady app.	4.00	8.00	12.00
8-12	1.20	2.40	3.60
V3#1-12,V4#1-8,10-12	1.00	2.00	3.00
V4#9-Krigstein art	1.75	3.50	5.25
V5#1-5,7,8,10,12	.80	1.60	2.40
V5#6.9,11-Krigstein art	1.50	3.00	4.50
V6#1-5,8,9,11	.80	1.60	2.40
V6#6,7,10,12-Krigstein art	1.50	3.00	4.50
V7#1-3,5,7-11,V8#1-3	.75	1.50	2.25
V7#4,12-Krigstein art	1.50	3.00	4.50
V7#6-McWilliams art; 1pg. Frazetta ad	1.25	2.50	3.75

REAL EXPERIENCES (Formerly Tiny Tessie)
#25, January, 1950
Atlas Comics (20CC)

#25	.60	1.20	1.80

REAL FACT COMICS
Mar-Apr, 1946 - #21, July-Aug, 1949
National Periodical Publications

#1-S&K art	5.00	10.00	15.00
2-S&K art	3.00	6.00	9.00
3	2.00	4.00	6.00
4-"Just Imagine" begins by Virgil Finley, ends #12(2pgs. ea.)	2.50	5.00	7.50
5-Batman app.	7.00	14.00	21.00
6-Origin & 1st app. Tommy Tomorrow	4.00	8.00	12.00
7-(#6 on inside)	2.00	4.00	6.00
8-2nd app. T.Tomorrow	2.50	5.00	7.50
9-S&K art	3.00	6.00	9.00
10-Vigilante by Meskin	3.50	7.00	10.50
11,12: #11-Kinstler art	2.00	4.00	6.00
13-T.Tomorrow cover/story	2.00	4.00	6.00
14,15,17-19	1.60	3.20	4.80
16-Tommy Tomorrow app.	1.75	3.50	5.25
20-Kubert story	2.50	5.00	7.50
21-Kubert art(2pgs.)	2.00	4.00	6.00

REAL FUN OF DRIVING!!, THE
1965, 1967 (Regular Size)
Chrysler Corp.

12pg. Shaffenberger story	.25	.50	.75

REAL FUNNIES
1943
Nedor Publishing Co.

#1	2.50	5.00	7.50
2,3	1.50	3.00	4.50

Real Clue Crime Stories =8. © HILL

Real Fact Comics =17. © DC

Real Funnies #3. © Nedor Publ.

Real Heroes #4, © PMI   Realistic Romances #2, © AVON   Real Screen Comics #34, © DC

REAL HEROES COMICS
Sept, 1941 - #16, Oct, 1946
Parents' Magazine Institute

	Good	Fine	Mint
#1	3.00	6.00	9.00
2-10	2.00	4.00	6.00
11-16	1.00	2.00	3.00

REAL HIT
1944   (Savings Bond premium)
Fox Features Publications

#1-Blue Beetle reprint	5.00	10.00	15.00

REALISTIC ROMANCES
July-Aug, 1951 - #17, Aug-Sept, 1954
Realistic Comics/Avon Periodicals

	Good	Fine	Mint
#1-Kinstler story	5.00	10.00	15.00
2-4	2.50	5.00	7.50
5,6,8-Kinstler stories	3.00	6.00	9.00
7-Evans story?	3.00	6.00	9.00
9,10	2.50	5.00	7.50
11-15,17	2.00	4.00	6.00
16-Kinstler marijuana sty.	5.00	10.00	15.00
IW Reprint #8,9	.50	1.00	1.50

NOTE: *Astarita stories-#2-4,7,8.*

REAL LIFE COMICS
Sept, 1941 - #59, Sept, 1952
Nedor/Better/Standard Publications

#1	5.00	10.00	15.00
2	2.50	5.00	7.50
3-10	1.50	3.00	4.50
11-20	1.25	2.50	3.75
21-49	1.00	2.00	3.00
50,52-Frazetta story in each(5&4pgs.) + Severin/Elder story-#52	8.00	16.00	24.00
51,53-57: Severin/Elder story in each	2.00	4.00	6.00
58-Two Severin/Elder stys.	2.50	5.00	7.50
59-1pg. Frazetta	1.50	3.00	4.50

NOTE: *Some issues had two titles.*

REAL LIFE SECRETS
1949 - #5, May, 1950
Ace Periodicals

#1	1.25	2.50	3.75
2-5	.80	1.60	2.40

REAL LIFE STORY OF FESS PARKER (Magazine)
1955
Dell Publishing Co.

#1	1.50	3.00	4.50

REAL LIFE TALES OF SUSPENSE (See Suspense)

REAL LOVE (Formerly Hap Hazard)
#25, April, 1949 - #75, 1956
Ace Periodicals (A.A. Wyn)

	Good	Fine	Mint
#25,26	1.00	2.00	3.00
27-L. B. Cole story	1.50	3.00	4.50
28-35	.80	1.60	2.40
36-75	.60	1.20	1.80

REAL McCOYS, THE (TV)
1960 - 1962
Dell Publishing Co.

4-Color #1071,1193,1265	.50	1.00	1.50
4-Color #1134-Toth art	2.00	4.00	6.00
#01689-207(5-7/62)	.30	.60	.90

REAL SCREEN COMICS (#1 titled Real Screen Funnies; TV Screen Cartoons #129-138)
Spring, 1945 - #128, May-June, 1959
National Periodical Publications

#1-The Fox & the Crow begin	12.00	24.00	36.00
2	6.00	12.00	18.00
3-5	5.00	10.00	15.00
6-15	3.00	6.00	9.00
16-30	2.00	4.00	6.00
31-50	1.50	3.00	4.50
51-100	1.00	2.00	3.00
101-128	.60	1.20	1.80

REAL SECRETS
1949 - #4, Mar, 1950
Ace Periodicals

#1	1.50	3.00	4.50
2-4	1.00	2.00	3.00

REAL SPORTS COMICS
Oct-Nov, 1948
Hillman Periodicals

#1-12pg. Powell story	1.25	2.50	3.75

REAL WESTERN HERO (Formerly Wow #1-69; becomes Western Hero #76 on)
#70, Sept, 1948 - #75, March, 1949
Fawcett Publications

#70(#1)-Featuring Tom Mix, Gabby Hayes, Monte Hale & Hopalong Cassidy	7.00	14.00	21.00
71-75	4.00	8.00	12.00

REAL WEST ROMANCES
Apr-May, 1949 - V2#1, Apr-May, 1950
Crestwood Publishing Co./Prize Publ.

(Real West Rom. cont'd)   Good Fine Mint
V1#1-S&K pencils   3.50 7.00 10.50
  2,3-Kirby pencils only 2.00 4.00 6.00
  4-7-S&K art   2.50 5.00 7.50
V2#1-Kirby pencils only 2.00 4.00 6.00
NOTE: *Meskin story-V1#5. Severin & Elder*
stories-V1#3-6,V2#1. Leonard Starr story-#1-3.

REBEL, THE (See 4-Color #1076,1138,1207,1262)

RECKLESS STEELE (See Chewing Gum Booklet)

RECORD BOOK OF FAMOUS POLICE CASES
1949   (132 pgs.) (25¢)
St. John Publishing Co.

No#-Three Kubert stories reprt/Son of Sinbad;
  Matt Baker cover   6.00 12.00 18.00

RED ARROW
1951 - #3, Oct, 1951
P.L. Publishing Co.

#1   1.20 2.40 3.60
 2,3   .75 1.50 2.25

RED BALL COMIC BOOK
1947   (Red Ball Shoes giveaway)
Parents' Magazine Institute

Reprints from True Comics 1.50 3.00 4.50

RED BAND COMICS
Feb, 1945 - #4, May, 1945
Enwil Associates

#1   4.00 8.00 12.00
 2-Origin Boogeyman & Santanas
             3.00 6.00 9.00
 3,4-Captain Wizard app. in both; identical
  contents in each   3.00 6.00 9.00

RED CIRCLE COMICS
Jan, 1945 - #4, April, 1945
Rural Home Publications (Enwil)

#1-The Prankster & Red Riot begin
             3.50 7.00 10.50
 2-4-Starr art   2.50 5.00 7.50

RED CIRCLE SORCERY (Chilling Advs. in Sorcery
#6, Apr/74 - #11, Feb/75   #1-5)
Red Circle Productions (Archie)

#6-11   .25   .50   .75
NOTE: *McWilliams story-#10. Morrow stories-*
#5-8,10,11; covers-#6-11. Toth stories-#8,9.
Wood story-#10.

RED DRAGON (1st Series)(Trail Blazers #1-4)
#5, Jan, 1943 - #9, Jan, 1944
Street & Smith Publications
             Good Fine Mint
#5-Origin Red Rover, the Crimson Crimebuster;
  Rex King, Man of Adventure, Captain Jack
  Commando, & The Minute Man begin
           12.00 24.00 36.00
 6-Origin The Black Crusader & Red Dragon
  (3/43)   10.00 20.00 30.00
 7   7.00 14.00 21.00
 8-The Red Knight app. 7.00 14.00 21.00
 9-Origin Chuck Magnon, Immortal Man
           7.00 14.00 21.00

RED DRAGON (2nd Series)
Nov, 1947 - #6, Jan, 1949; #7, July, 1949
Street & Smith Publications

#1-Red Dragon begins; Elliman, Nigel app.;
  Ed Cartier, Powell art
           10.00 20.00 30.00
 2   7.00 14.00 21.00
 3,4-Elliman, Nigel app.-#3
           6.00 12.00 18.00
 5,7-Maneely art   6.00 12.00 18.00
 6   5.00 10.00 15.00
NOTE: *Powell art-#1-5,7.*

REDDY GOOSE
1959 - #15, Jan, 1962 (Giveaway)
International Shoe Co. (Western Printing)

#3-15   .25   .50   .75

REDDY KILOWATT (5¢)(Also see Story of Edison)
1946 - #2, 1947 (no month)(16pgs;soft cover)
Educational Comics (E.C.)

#1-Reddy Made Magic (Rare)
           20.00 40.00 60.00
 2-Edison, the Man Who Changed the World
  (3/4" smaller than #1) (Rare)
           20.00 40.00 60.00

REDEYE (See Comics Reading Libraries)

RED EAGLE (See Feature Book #16, McKay)

RED FOX (Manhunt #1-14)
1954
Magazine Enterprises

#15(A-1#108)-Undercover Girl app.; Red Fox
  by L.B. Cole (cover also); reprints from
  Manhunt   3.50 7.00 10.50

RED GOOSE COMIC SELECTIONS (See Comic Sel.)

Real West Romances V2#1, ©PRIZE

Red Dragon #6('49), ©S&S

Reddy Kilowatt #2, ©WMG

Red Raven =1. ©MCG   Red Ryder =56. ©DELL   Red Seal =20. ©CHES

RED HAWK (See A-1 Comics #90)

RED ICEBERG, THE
1960   (10¢)
Impact Publ.

	Good	Fine	Mint
Cummunist propaganda	2.50	5.00	7.50

RED MASK (Formerly Tim Holt)
#42, June-July, 1954 - #54, 1957
Magazine Enterprises

#42-Ghost Rider continues, ends #50; Black
Phantom continues, ends #50,54

	3.00	6.00	9.00
43-50	2.25	4.50	6.75
51-1st app. The Presto Kid			
	2.25	4.50	6.75
52-Origin The Presto Kid	2.25	4.50	6.75
53,54	2.00	4.00	6.00

IW Reprint #1(reprts./#52),#2(reprts.#51),#8
(no date; Kinstler cvr)1.00 2.00 3.00
NOTE: *Bolle stories in all.*

RED MOUNTAIN FEATURING QUANTRELL'S RAIDERS
1952   (Movie)(Also see Jesse James #28)
Avon Periodicals

(Scarce)-Alan Ladd; Kinstler cover/art
5.00 10.00 15.00

RED RABBIT
Jan, 1947 - #22, Aug-Sept, 1951
Dearfield Comic/J. Charles Laue Publ. Co.

#1	1.20	2.40	3.60
2-10	.65	1.35	2.00
11-22	.40	.80	1.60

RED RAVEN COMICS (Human Torch #2 on)
August, 1940
Timely Comics

#1-Origin Red Raven; Comet Pierce & Mercury
by Kirby, The Human Top & The Eternal
Brain; intro. Magar, the Mystic & only app.;
Kirby cover   600.00 1200.00 1800.00
(Prices vary widely on this book)

RED RYDER COMICS (Hi Spot #2)
#1, Sept, 1940; #3, 8/41 - #151, 4/57
Hawley Publ.#1-4/Dell Publishing Co. #5 on

#1-Red Ryder strip reprints by Harmon; 1st
meeting of Red & Little Beaver
60.00 120.00 180.00
3-(Scarce)-Alley Oop, Freckles & His Friends,
Dan Dunn, Capt. Easy, King of Royal Mtd.,

	Good	Fine	Mint
Red Ryder strip reprints begin			
	30.00	60.00	90.00
4,5	20.00	40.00	60.00
6-10	15.00	30.00	45.00
11-20	8.00	16.00	24.00
21-32-Last Alley Oop, Dan Dunn, Capt. Easy,			
Freckles	6.00	12.00	18.00
33-40	4.50	9.00	13.50
41-49-Last Red Ryder strip reprint			
	3.00	6.00	9.00
50-60-New stories on Red Ryder begin			
	2.25	4.50	6.75
61-80: #73-Last King of the Royal Mtd. strip			
reprints by Jim Gary	2.00	4.00	6.00
81-100	1.75	3.50	5.25
101-120	1.50	3.00	4.50
121-144	1.40	2.80	4.20
145-Title changed to Red Ryder Ranch Magazine			
with photos	1.20	2.40	3.60
146-148	1.20	2.40	3.60
149-151-Title changed to Red Ryder Ranch			
Comics	1.20	2.40	3.60
4-Color #916	1.50	3.00	4.50

Red Ryder Victory Patrol-Superbook #2('43)
Giveaway(reprts.#43,44)6.00 12.00 18.00
Wells Lamont Corp. giveaway('50)-16pgs. in
color; reg. size; paper cover; 1941 reprts.
20.00 40.00 60.00
NOTE: *Fred Harmon covers-#1-98,107,118.
Photo covers-#99,101,108-117. #119-painted
covers begin(not by Harmon).*

RED RYDER PAINT BOOK
1941   (148 pgs.)   (8½x11½")
Whitman Publishing Co.

Reprints 1940 daily strips
12.00 24.00 36.00

RED SEAL
Oct, 1945 - #22, Dec, 1947
Harry 'A' Chesler/Superior Publ. #22

#14-The Black Dwarf begins; Little Nemo app.
5.00 10.00 15.00
15,17: #17-Lady Satan, Yankee Girl & Sky
Chief app.   5.00 10.00 15.00
16-Used in Seduction of the Innocent, illo-
"We'll drain this dame dry"; Veiled Avenger & Barry Kuda app. 8.00 16.00 24.00
18,20-Lady Satan & Sky Chief app.
5.00 10.00 15.00
19-No Black Dwarf-on cover only; Zor, El
Tigre app.   4.50 9.00 13.50
21-Lady Satan & Black Dwarf app.,
5.00 10.00 15.00
22-Zor, Rocketman app. 4.50 9.00 13.50

REDSKIN
Sept, 1950 - #12, Oct, 1952
Youthful Magazines

	Good	Fine	Mint
#1	1.20	2.40	3.60
2-12	.80	1.60	2.40

RED SONJA (Also see Conan #23 & Marvel Feature)
Jan, 1977 - Present
Marvel Comics Group

	Good	Fine	Mint
#1	.50	1.00	1.50
2,3	.40	.80	1.20
4-11	.20	.40	.60
12-J. Buscema story; Brunner cover			
	.15	.30	.45

RED WARRIOR
Jan, 1951 - #6, Dec, 1951
Marvel/Atlas Comics (TCI)

#1	1.50	3.00	4.50
2-6	1.00	2.00	3.00

RED WOLF
May, 1972 - #9, Sept, 1973
Marvel Comics Group

#1	.25	.50	.75
2-9: #9-Origin sidekick, Lobo (wolf)			
	.20	.40	.60

REFORM SCHOOL GIRL!
1951
Realistic Comics

No#-Used in Seduction of the Innocent, pg.
358, & cover ill. with caption "Comic
books are supposed to be like fairy
tales" (Rare)   350.00 700.00 1050.00
      (Prices vary widely on this book)
NOTE: *The cover originated from an Avon paperback book (1951) which also commands high
prices.*

REGGIE (Formerly Archie's Rival--; Reggie &
#15, 9/63 - #18, 11/65   Me #19 on)
Archie Publications

#15(9/63),16(10/64)	1.50	3.00	4.50
17(8/65),18(11/65)	1.50	3.00	4.50

NOTE: *Cover title #15,16 is Archie's Rival--.*

REGGIE AND ME (Formerly Reggie)
#19, 1967 - Present   (#50-68, 52pgs.)
Archie Publications

#19-23-Evilheart app.	.60	1.20	1.80

	Good	Fine	Mint
24-50	.30	.60	.90
51-107		.15	.35

REGGIE'S JOKES (See Reggie's Wise Guy Jokes)

REGGIE'S WISE GUY JOKES
Aug, 1968 - Present   (#5 on are Giants)
Archie Publications

#1	.60	1.20	1.80
2-4	.25	.50	.75
5-28 (All Giants)	.20	.40	.60
29-46		.15	.35

REGISTERED NURSE
Summer, 1963
Charlton Comics

#1-Reprints Nurse Betsy Crane & Cynthia Doyle
                .25   .50   .75

REG'LAR FELLERS (See Treasure Box of --)
1921 - 1929
Cupples & Leon Co./MS Publishing Co.

#1(1921)-52pgs. B&W dailies (Cupples & Leon)
              9.00 18.00 27.00
1925, 48pgs. B&W dailies (MS Publ.)
              9.00 18.00 27.00
Hardcover(1929)-B&W reprints, 96 pgs.
             12.00 24.00 36.00

REG'LAR FELLERS
#5, Nov, 1947 - #6, Mar, 1948
Visual Editions (Standard)

#5,6	2.50	5.00	7.50

REG'LAR FELLERS HEROIC (See Heroic)

RELUCTANT DRAGON, THE (See 4-Color #13)

REMEMBER PEARL HARBOR
1942

No#	3.50	7.00	10.50

RENO BROWNE, HOLLYWOOD'S GREATEST COWGIRL
(Formerly Margie; Apache Kid #53 on)
#50, April, 1950 - #52, Sept, 1950
Marvel Comics (MPC)

#50-52	3.00	6.00	9.00

REPTILICUS (Reptisaurus #3 on)
Aug, 1961 - #2, Oct, 1961

Red Sonja #1, © MCG

Reform School Girl No#, © REAL

Reg'lar Fellers 1929, © C&L

Rex Allen Comics =3. © DELL   Ribtickler =3. © FOX   Richard Dragon =1. © DC

(Reptilicus cont'd)
Charlton Comics

	Good	Fine	Mint
#1(Movie), #2	1.00	2.00	3.00

REPTISAURUS THE TERRIBLE (Reptilicus #1,2)
Jan, 1962 - #8, Dec, 1962; Summer, 1963
Charlton Comics

V2#3-8	.75	1.50	2.25
Special Edition #1('63)	.75	1.50	2.25

RESCUERS, THE (See Walt Disney Showcase #40)

RESTLESS GUN, THE (See 4-Color #934,986,1045,
1089,1146)

RETURN OF GORGO, THE (Formerly Gorgo's Revenge)
#2, Summer, 1963 - #3, Fall, 1964
Charlton Comics

#2,3-Both Ditko art	1.25	2.50	3.75

RETURN OF KONGA, THE (Konga's Revenge #2 on)
1962
Charlton Comics

No#	1.00	2.00	3.00

RETURN OF THE OUTLAW
Feb, 1953 - #11, 1955
Toby Press (Minoan)

#1-Billy the Kid	1.00	2.00	3.00
2-11	.60	1.20	1.80

REVEALING LOVE STORIES
1950   (132 pgs.)
Fox Features Syndicate

No#-See Fox Giants. Contents can vary and
determines price.

REVEALING ROMANCES
Sept, 1949 - #6, Aug, 1950
Ace Magazines

#1	1.20	2.40	3.60
2-6	.60	1.20	1.80

REX ALLEN COMICS (Also see 4-Color #877)
#2, Sept, 1951 - #31, Dec-Jan, 1958-59
Dell Publishing Co.

4-Color #316(#1)('51)	3.00	6.00	9.00
#2-10	1.60	3.20	4.80
11-20	1.20	2.40	3.60
21-23,25-31	1.00	2.00	3.00

	Good	Fine	Mint
24-Toth art	2.50	5.00	7.50

NOTE: *Manning art-#20,27-30.*

REX DEXTER OF MARS
Fall, 1940
Fox Features Syndicate

#1-Rex Dexter, Patty O'Day, & Zanzibar app.; Briefer art	40.00	80.00	120.00

REX HART (Formerly Blaze Carson; Whip Wilson
#6, 8/49 - #8, 2/50   #9 on)
Timely/Marvel Comics (USA)

#6-Black Rider app.	2.00	4.00	6.00
7,8: #8-Blaze the Wonder Collie app. in text	1.75	3.50	5.25

REX MORGAN, M.D. (Also see Harvey Comics
Dec, 1955 - #3, 1956   Library)
Argo Publ.

#1-Reprints R.M. daily newspaper strips & daily panel reprints of "These Women" by D'Alessio & "Timeout" by Jeff Keate	2.50	5.00	7.50
2,3	1.35	2.75	4.00

REX THE WONDER DOG (See The Adventures of--)

RHUBARB, THE MILLIONAIRE CAT (See 4-Color
#423,466,563)

RIBTICKLER (Also see Everybody's Comics)
1945 - #9, Aug, 1947; 1957 - 1959
Fox Feat. Synd./Green Publ.('57)/Norlen('59)

No#(1945)-Chicago Nite Life News-Marvel Mutt app. (194pgs.-50c)	1.50	3.00	4.50
#1	1.50	3.00	4.50
2-9: #7-Cosmo Cat app.	1.20	2.40	3.60
3,8(Green Publ.-'57)	.50	1.00	1.50
3,7,8(Norlen Mag.-'59)	.40	.80	1.20

RICHARD DRAGON, KUNG-FU FIGHTER
Apr-May, 1975 - #18, Nov-Dec, 1977
National Periodical Publications/DC Comics

#1	.50	1.00	1.50
2-Starlin art	.50	1.00	1.50
3-Kirby story	.50	1.00	1.50
4-8,11-Wood inks	.30	.60	.90
9,12-18	.25	.50	.75

RICHARD THE LION-HEARTED(See Ideal a Classic--

RICHIE RICH (See Harvey Hits, Mutt & Jeff,
Little Dot, Super Richie, & 3-D Dolly)

342

RICHIE RICH (-- The Poor Little Rich Boy)
Nov, 1960 - Present   (See Harvey Hits #3,9)
Harvey Publications

	Good	Fine	Mint
#1-(See Little Dot for 1st app.)			
	40.00	80.00	120.00
2	15.00	30.00	45.00
3-5	6.00	12.00	18.00
6-10	3.00	6.00	9.00
11-20	1.75	3.50	5.25
21-40	1.20	2.40	3.60
41-60	1.00	2.00	3.00
61-80	.60	1.20	1.80
81-100	.35	.70	1.05
101-173	.15	.30	.45

RICHIE RICH AND BILLY BELLHOPS
October, 1977
Harvey Publications

#1	.15	.30	.45

RICHIE RICH AND CADBURY
October, 1977 - Present
Harvey Publications

#1	.20	.40	.60
2-4	.15	.30	.45

RICHIE RICH AND CASPER
Aug, 1974 - Present
Harvey Publications

#1	.50	1.00	1.50
2-5	.25	.50	.75
6-26		.20	.40

RICHIE RICH AND DOLLAR THE DOG
Sept, 1977 - Present
Harvey Publications

#1	.20	.40	.60
2-5	.15	.30	.45

RICHIE RICH AND DOT
October, 1974
Harvey Publications

#1	.40	.80	1.20

RICHIE RICH AND GLORIA
Sept, 1977 - Present
Harvey Publications

#1	.20	.40	.60
2-5	.15	.30	.45

RICHIE RICH & JACKIE JOKERS (Formerly Jack-
ie Jokers)
Nov, 1973 - Present
Harvey Publications

#5	.25	.50	.75
6-24		.20	.40

RICHIE RICH AND TIMMY TIME
Sept, 1977   (50¢)
Harvey Publications

#1	.20	.40	.60

RICHIE RICH BANK BOOKS
Oct, 1972 - Present
Harvey Publications

#1	.50	1.00	1.50

	Good	Fine	Mint
2-5	.25	.50	.75
6-37		.20	.40

RICHIE RICH BEST OF THE YEARS
October, 1977 - Present (Digest) (128 pgs.)
Harvey Publications

#1(10/77)-Reprints, #2(10/78)-reprints

	.25	.50	.75

RICHIE RICH BILLIONS
Oct, 1974 - Present   (35¢ - 40¢)
Harvey Publications

#1	.50	1.00	1.50
2-5	.25	.50	.75
6-27		.20	.40

RICHIE RICH CASH
Sept, 1974 - Present
Harvey Publications

#1 ·	.50	1.00	1.50
2-5	.25	.50	.75
6-26		.20	.40

RICHIE RICH, CASPER & WENDY NATIONAL LEAGUE
June, 1976   (52 pgs.)
Harvey Publications

#1	.25	.50	.75

RICHIE RICH COLLECTORS COMICS(Formerly Harvey
#10, Feb, 1977 - Present   Coll. Comics)
Harvey Publications

#10-14	.15	.30	.45

RICHIE RICH DIGEST STORIES
Oct, 1977   (Digest) (132 pgs.)
Harvey Publications

#1-Reprints	.25	.50	.75

RICHIE RICH DIAMONDS
Aug, 1972 - Present
Harvey Publications

#1	.75	1.50	2.25
2-5	.35	.70	1.05
6-39	.15	.30	.45

RICHIE RICH DOLLARS & CENTS
Aug, 1963 - Present   (25¢-40¢)
Harvey Publications

#1	4.00	8.00	12.00
2	2.00	4.00	6.00
3-10	1.25	2.50	3.75
11-20	.80	1.60	2.40
21-30	.50	1.00	1.50
31-50	.25	.50	.75
51-88(#76-40¢)		.20	.40

RICHIE RICH FORTUNES
Sept, 1971 - Present
Harvey Publications

#1	.60	1.20	1.80
2-5	.35	.70	1.05
6-10	.20	.40	.60
11-43		.20	.40

RICHIE RICH GEMS
Sept, 1974 - Present
Harvey Publications

(Richie Rich Gems cont'd)	Good	Fine	Mint
#1	.50	1.00	1.50
2-5	.25	.50	.75
6-24		.20	.40

RICHIE RICH GOLD AND SILVER
Sept, 1975 - Present
Harvey Publications

	Good	Fine	Mint
#1	.35	.70	1.05
2-5	.20	.40	.60
6-21		.20	.40

RICHIE RICH INVENTIONS
Oct, 1977 - Present
Harvey Publications

#1	.20	.40	.60
2-5	.15	.30	.45

RICHIE RICH JACKPOTS
Oct, 1972 - Present
Harvey Publications

#1	.60	1.20	1.80
2-5	.30	.60	.90
6-38		.20	.40

RICHIE RICH MILLIONS
Sept, 1961 - Present
Harvey Publications

#1	5.00	10.00	15.00
2	2.50	5.00	7.50
3-10	1.50	3.00	4.50
11-20	1.00	2.00	3.00
21-30	.60	1.20	1.80
31-50	.25	.50	.75
51-92	.15	.30	.45

RICHIE RICH MONEY WORLD
Sept, 1972 - Present
Harvey Publications

#1	.60	1.20	1.80
2-5	.30	.60	.90
6-37		.20	.40

RICHIE RICH PROFITS
Oct, 1974 - Present
Harvey Publications

#1	.50	1.00	1.50
2-5	.25	.50	.75
6-25		.20	.40

RICHIE RICH RICHES
July, 1972 - Present
Harvey Publications

#1	.60	1.20	1.80
2-5	.30	.60	.90
6-39		.20	.40

RICHIE RICH SUCCESS STORIES
1964 - Present
Harvey Publications

#1	3.50	7.00	10.50
2-5	1.50	3.00	4.50
6-10	.80	1.60	2.40
11-30	.50	1.00	1.50
31-50	.25	.50	.75
51-84		.20	.40

RICHIE RICH VACATIONS DIGEST
Nov, 1977   (Digest)   (132 pgs.)

Harvey Publications

	Good	Fine	Mint
#1-Reprints	.25	.50	.75

RICHIE RICH VAULTS OF MYSTERY
Nov, 1974 - Present
Harvey Publications

#1	.50	1.00	1.50
2-10	.25	.50	.75
11-25		.20	.40

RICHIE RICH ZILLIONZ
Oct, 1976 - Present   (68 pgs.)
Harvey Publications

#1	.25	.50	.75
2-12		.20	.40

RICKY
Sept, 1953
Standard Comics (Visual Editions)

#5	.30	.60	.90

RICKY NELSON   (TV)
1959 - 1961
Dell Publishing Co.

4-Color #956,998	1.50	3.00	4.50
4-Color #1115,1192-Manning art			
	1.75	3.50	5.25
#1-5	.60	1.20	1.80

RIDER, THE   (Frontier Trail #6)
March, 1957 - #5, 1958
Ajax/Farrell Publ.(Four Star Comic Corp.)

#1	1.00	2.00	3.00
2-5	.50	1.00	1.50

RIFLEMAN, THE   (TV)
July-Sept, 1959 - #20, Sept, 1964
Dell Publ. Co./Gold Key

4-Color #1009, #2	1.40	2.80	4.20
#3-Toth art-4pgs.	1.75	3.50	5.25
4-10	.75	1.50	2.25
11-20	.60	1.20	1.80

The Rifleman #2, © DELL

RIMA, THE JUNGLE GIRL
Apr-May, 1974 - #7, Apr-May, 1975
National Periodical Publications

#1-Origin, part 1	.60	1.20	1.80
2,3-Origin, part 2,3	.50	1.00	1.50
4-Origin-conclusion	.50	1.00	1.50
5-7: #7-Origin & only app. Space Marshal			
	.50	1.00	1.50

Rima The Jungle Girl #6. © DC   Riot #4. © MCG   Rip Hunter #1. © DC

(Rima the Jungle Girl cont'd)
NOTE: *Kubert covers-#1-7. Nino art-#1-5.*
Redondo art-#1-6.

RING OF BRIGHT WATER (See Movie Classics)

RINGO KID, THE (2nd Series)
Jan, 1970 - #30, Nov, 1976
Marvel Comics Group

	Good	Fine	Mint
#1(1970)-Williamson story reprint from #10,			
1956	.25	.50	.75
2-19,21-30		.15	.35
20-Williamson reprt./#1	.15	.30	.45

NOTE: *Wildey reprint-#13.*

RINGO KID WESTERN, THE (1st Series)
August, 1954 - #21, Sept, 1957
Atlas Comics(HPC)/Marvel Comics

#1-Maneely, Sinnott art	2.50	5.00	7.50
2-5: #2-Black Rider app.	1.50	3.00	4.50
6-8-Severin covers, 3 stories each			
	1.75	3.50	5.25
9,11,14-21	1.00	2.00	3.00
10,13-Williamson sty,4pgs.	2.50	5.00	7.50
12-Orlando sty,.4pgs.	1.50	3.00	4.50

NOTE: *Wildey stories-#16,17.*

RIN TIN TIN (See March of Comics#163,180,195)

RIN TIN TIN (TV) (-- & Rusty #21 on)
Nov, 1952 - #38, May-July, 1961; 1963
Dell Publishing Co./Gold Key

4-Color #434,476,523	1.25	2.50	3.75
#4(6-8/54) - #10	.60	1.20	1.80
11-38	.40	.80	1.20
#1(11/63-G.K.)--& Rusty	.50	1.00	1.50

RIO BRAVO (See 4-Color Comics #1018)

RIO CONCHOS (See Movie Comics)

RIOT (Satire)
April, 1954 - #3, 8/54; #4, 2/56 - #6, 6/56
Atlas Comics(ACI #1-5/WPI #6)

#1-Russ Heath art	2.50	5.00	7.50
2,3,5,6	2.00	4.00	6.00
4-Infinity cover	2.00	4.00	6.00

NOTE: *Everett stories-#4,6. Severin stories-*
#4-6.

RIPCORD (See 4-Color Comics #1294)

RIP HUNTER TIME MASTER (See Showcase)
Mar-Apr, 1961 - #29, Nov-Dec, 1965
National Periodical Publications

	Good	Fine	Mint
#1	3.00	6.00	9.00
2	1.50	3.00	4.50
3-5	1.00	2.00	3.00
6,7-Toth art in ea.	1.00	2.00	3.00
8-15	.60	1.20	1.80
16-29: #29-G.Kane cover	.50	1.00	1.50

RIP KIRBY (See Feature Book #51,54 & Harvey
Comics Hits #57 & Street Comix)

RIPLEY'S BELIEVE IT OR NOT!
Sept, 1953 - #4, March, 1954
Harvey Publications

#1	3.00	6.00	9.00
2-4	2.00	4.00	6.00
J.C. Penney giveaway('48)	2.50	5.00	7.50

RIPLEY'S BELIEVE IT OR NOT! (Formerly True
War Stories #1(#3))
#4, 4/67 - Present
Gold Key

#4-McWilliams art	.80	1.60	2.40
5-10: #5-Subtitled "True War Stories." #8-			
Orlando art	.70	1.40	2.10
11-20	.50	1.00	1.50
21-40	.25	.50	.75
41-60	.20	.40	.60
61-86: #74-83, 52pgs.		.20	.40
Story Digest Mag. #1(6/70, 4-3/4"x6-1/2")			
	.25	.50	.75

RIPLEY'S BELIEVE IT OR NOT! (See Mystery
Comics Digest #1,4,7,10,13,16,19,22,25)

RIPLEY'S BELIEVE IT OR NOT TRUE GHOST
STORIES (Becomes --True War Stories)
June, 1965 - #2, Oct, 1966 (See Dan Curtis)
Gold Key

#1-Williamson, Wood & Evans stories			
	2.00	4.00	6.00
2-Orlando story	1.00	2.00	3.00
Mini-Comic #1('76-3½x6½")	.15	.30	.45

RIPLEY'S BELIEVE IT OR NOT TRUE WAR STORIES
(Formerly --True Ghost Stories; becomes Rip-
ley's Believe It Or Not #4)
November, 1966
Gold Key

#1(#3)-Williamson story	1.00	2.00	3.00

RIPLEY'S BELIEVE IT OR NOT! TRUE WEIRD
June, 1966 - #2, Aug, 1966 (B&W Magazine)
Ripley Enterprises

345

(Ripley's Believe It or Not! cont'd)

	Good	Fine	Mint
#1,2-Comic stories & text	.70	1.40	2.10

RIP RAIDER
1944

No#	1.75	3.50	5.25

RIVETS (See 4-Color Comics #518)

RIVETS (A dog)
Jan, 1956 - #3, May, 1956
Argo Publ.

#1-Reprints Sunday & daily newspaper strips

	1.20	2.40	3.60
2,3	.80	1.60	2.40

ROAD RUNNER, THE (See Beep Beep --)

ROAD RUNNER KITE FUN BOOK
1971   (8 pgs.) (Giveaway)
Pacific Gas & Electric Co.(Western Printing)

No#	2.50	5.00	7.50

ROBIN (See Aurora)

ROBIN HOOD (See 4-Color #413,669, King
Classics, Movie Comics, The Advs. of --, &
New Advs. of --)

ROBIN HOOD (-- & His Merry Men, The Illustrated Story of --) (See Classic Comics #7)

ROBIN HOOD (New Adventures of --)
1952 (36pgs.) "New Adventures of Robin Hood,"
"Ghosts of Waylea Castle" & "The Miller's
Ransom" (Flour Giveaways) (5x7¼")
Walt Disney Productions

each......	2.00	4.00	6.00

ROBIN HOOD (Adventures of -- #8)
#52, Nov, 1955 - #7, Sept, 1957
Magazine Enterprises (Sussex Publ. Co.)

#52-Origin Robin Hood & Sir Gallant of the

Round Table	1.50	3.00	4.50
53, #3-7	1.25	2.50	3.75

NOTE: *Bolle art in all. Powell art-#6,7.*
IW Reprint #1,2(reprts#4), 9(reprts#52)('63)

	.70	1.40	2.10

Super Reprint #10(reprts#53 or 3),11,15(re-
prts#5),17('64)

	.70	1.40	2.10

ROBIN HOOD
No date (Circa 1955)
Shoe Store Giveaway (Robin Hood Stores)

	Good	Fine	Mint
#1-7-Reed Crandall art	3.00	6.00	9.00

ROBIN HOOD (Not Disney)
May-July, 1963 - #7, Nov-Jan, 1964-65
Dell Publishing Co.

#1	.40	.80	1.20
2-7	.25	.50	.75

ROBIN HOOD ($1.50)
1973 (Disney)(8½x11)(Cardboard covers)
Western Publishing Co.   (52pgs.)

#96151-"Robin Hood", based on movie, #96152-
"The Mystery of Sherwood Forest," #96153-
"In King Richard's Service," #96154-"The
Wizard's King" each.. 1.00 2.00 3.00

ROBIN HOOD AND HIS MERRY MEN
#28, April, 1956 - #38, Aug, 1958
Charlton Comics

#28-37	.80	1.60	2.40
38-Ditko art, 5pgs.	1.20	2.40	3.60

ROBIN HOOD TALES (National Periodical #7 on)
Feb, 1956 - #6, Nov-Dec, 1956
Quality Comics Group (Comic Magazines)

#1	2.25	4.50	6.75
2-5-Matt Baker stories	1.75	3.50	5.25
6	1.40	2.80	4.20

Frontier Days giveaway('56)

	1.25	2.50	3.75

ROBIN HOOD TALES (Cont'd. from Quality)
#7, Jan-Feb, 1957 - #14, Mar-Apr, 1958
National Periodical Publications

#7-14	2.00	4.00	6.00

ROBINSON CRUSOE (Also see King Classics)
Nov-Jan, 1964
Dell Publishing Co.

#1	.40	.80	1.20

ROBOTMEN OF THE LOST PLANET
1952   (Also see Space Thrillers)
Avon Periodicals

#1	20.00	40.00	60.00

ROB ROY (See 4-Color Comics #544)

Robin Hood 1952 Flour Giveaway, © WDP   Robin Hood #29, © CC   Robotmen Of The Lost Planet #1, © AVON

Rocket Ship X =1. © FOX   Rocky Lane Western =13. © FAW   Roger Dodger =5. © STD

ROCK AND ROLLO
V2#14, Oct, 1957 - #19, 1958
Charlton Comics

	Good	Fine	Mint
#14-19	.20	.40	.60

ROCKET COMICS
Feb, 1940 - #3, May, 1940
Hillman Periodicals

	Good	Fine	Mint
#1-Rocket Riley & Red Roberts, Phantom Ranger, The Steel Shark, Electro Man, The Defender, Man With a Thousand Faces begin	20.00	40.00	60.00
2,3	12.00	24.00	36.00

ROCKET KELLY
1944; Fall, 1945 - #5, 1947
Fox Features Syndicate

No#(1944)	2.50	5.00	7.50
#1	2.50	5.00	7.50
2-The Puppeteer app.(a costumed hero),			
3-5	2.00	4.00	6.00

ROCKETMAN
June, 1952
Ajax/Farrell Publications

#1-Rocketman & Cosmo	4.00	8.00	12.00

ROCKETS AND RANGE RIDERS
1957   (16 pgs.) (Giveaway)
Richfield Oil Corp.

Toth art	3.50	7.00	10.50

ROCKET SHIP X
Sept, 1951
Fox Features Syndicate

#1	10.00	20.00	30.00

ROCKET TO ADVENTURE LAND (See Pixie Puzzle--)

ROCKET TO THE MOON
1951
Avon Periodicals

No#-Orlando cover/story; adapts Otis Aldebert Kline's "Maza of the Moon"; used in Seduction of the Innocent	40.00	80.00	120.00

ROCK HAPPENING
1969
Harvey Publications

#1,2	.20	.40	.60

ROCKY AND BULLWINKLE KITE FUN BOOK
1963; 1970 (8pgs; 16pgs)(Soft Cover)(Giveaway)
Pacific Gas & Electric Co./Sou. Calif. Edison

	Good	Fine	Mint
No#-8pgs.(PG&E)(1963)	3.00	6.00	9.00
No#-16pgs.(SCEC)(1970)	2.25	4.50	6.75

ROCKY AND HIS FIENDISH FRIENDS (TV)
Oct, 1962 - #5, Sept, 1963 (Jay Ward)
Gold Key

#1-3(84pgs.)	.50	1.00	1.50
4,5(Reg. size)	.25	.50	.75

ROCKY AND HIS FRIENDS (See 4-Color #1128,1152, 1166,1208,1275,1311 & March of Comics #216)

ROCKY JONES SPACE RANGER (See Space Adventures #15-18)

ROCKY LANE WESTERN (See Black Jack)
May, 1949 - #87, Nov, 1959
Fawcett Publications/Charlton #55 on

#1	7.00	14.00	21.00
2	5.00	10.00	15.00
3-10	3.50	7.00	10.50
11-20	3.00	6.00	9.00
21-30	2.50	5.00	7.50
31-50	2.00	4.00	6.00
51-78,80-87	1.75	3.50	5.25
79-Giant edition, 68pgs.	2.50	5.00	7.50

ROD CAMERON WESTERN
Feb, 1950 - #20, April, 1953
Fawcett Publications

#1	7.00	14.00	21.00
2	4.50	9.00	13.50
3-10	3.00	6.00	9.00
11-20	2.50	5.00	7.50

RODEO RYAN (See A-1 Comics #8)

ROGER BEAN, R.G. (Regular Guy)
1915 - 1917 (34pgs.; B&W; 4-3/4"x16"; Cardboard covers)(#1&4 bound on side, #3 bound at top)
The Indiana News Co.

#1-By Chic Jackson	7.00	14.00	21.00
2-4	5.00	10.00	15.00

ROGER DODGER (Also in Exciting #57 on)
#5, Aug, 1952
Standard Comics

#5	.80	1.60	2.40

ROLY POLY COMIC BOOK
1945 - 1946   (MLJ Reprints)
Green Publishing Co.

	Good	Fine	Mint
#1-Red Rube & Steel Sterling begin	4.00	8.00	12.00
6-The Blue Circle & The Steel Fist app.	2.50	5.00	7.50
10-Origin Red Rube retold; Steel Sterling story(Zip #41)	3.00	6.00	9.00
11,12,14-The Black Hood in all	3.00	6.00	9.00
15-The Blue Circle & The Steel Fist app.			

ROMANCE (See True Stories of --)

ROMANCE AND CONFESSION STORIES (See Giant
Comics Edition)

ROMANCE DIARY
Dec, 1949
Marvel Comics (CDS)

#1	1.50	3.00	4.50

ROMANCE OF FLYING, THE
1941-42   (World War II photos)
David McKay Publications

No#-Illustration with text. 8pgs. of photos
  of The Doolittle Tokyo Raiders
	2.00	4.00	6.00

ROMANCES OF MOLLY MANTON (See Molly Manton)

ROMANCES OF NURSE HELEN GRANT(See Helen Grant)

ROMANCES OF THE WEST
Nov, 1949 - #2, March, 1950
Marvel Comics (SPC)

#1-Movie photo of Calamity Jane & Sam Bass	2.50	5.00	7.50
2	1.50	3.00	4.50

ROMANCE STORIES OF TRUE LOVE (Formerly Love
Problems & Advice)
#45, May, 1957 - #50, Mar, 1958
Harvey Publications

#45-51	.50	1.00	1.50
52-Matt Baker story	.70	1.40	2.10
NOTE: *Powell stories-#45,46,48-50.*

ROMANCE TALES (Formerly Western Winners?)
#8, Jan, 1950 - #9, March, 1950
Marvel Comics (CDS)

	Good	Fine	Mint
#8,9	.80	1.60	2.40

ROMANCE TRAIL
July-Aug, 1949 - #7, July-Aug, 1950
National Periodical Publications

#1-Kinstler story	4.00	8.00	12.00
2-Kinstler story	2.50	5.00	7.50
3-7	2.00	4.00	6.00

ROMAN HOLIDAYS, THE (TV)
Feb, 1973 - #4, Nov, 1973   (Hanna-Barbera)
Gold Key

#1-4	.20	.40	.60

ROMANTIC ADVENTURES (My-- #49-69, covers only)
3-4/49 - #69, 9/56   (My -- #70 on)
American Comics Group (B&I Publ. Co.)

#1	2.00	4.00	6.00
2	1.00	2.00	3.00
3-10	.60	1.20	1.80
11-20	.50	1.00	1.50
21-69	.40	.80	1.20
NOTE: *Whitney art in many issues.*

ROMANTIC CONFESSIONS
Oct, 1949 - V2#9, Aug-Sept, 1952
Hillman Periodicals

V1#1-McWilliams art	1.75	3.50	5.25
V1#2-12	.80	1.60	2.40
V2#1,2,4-8	.70	1.40	2.10
V2#3-Krigstein story	2.00	4.00	6.00
V2#9-1pg. Frazetta ad	1.60	3.20	4.80

ROMANTIC HEARTS
Mar, 1951 - #9, 8/52; 7/53 - #12, 7/55
Story Comics/Master/Merit Pubs.

#1(3/51)(1st Series)-Walter Johnson cover/ story	2.00	4.00	6.00
2-9	1.00	2.00	3.00
#1(3/53)(2nd Series)	1.35	2.75	4.00
2-12	.80	1.60	2.40

ROMANTIC LOVE
#4, June, 1950
Quality Comics Group

#4(6/50)	1.50	3.00	4.50
IW Reprint #2,3,8	.25	.50	.75

ROMANTIC LOVE
Sept-Oct, 1949 - #23, Sept-Oct, 1954
Avon Periodicals/Realistic

Romance Of Flying No#. © DMP

Romantic Adventures =7. © ACG

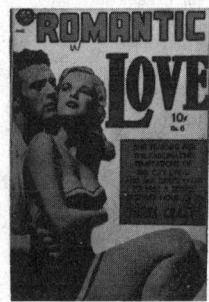

Romantic Love =6. © AVON

Romantic Marriage #2, © Z-D

Romantic Secrets #22, © CC

Roundup #5, © DS

(Romantic Love cont'd)	Good	Fine	Mint
#1-W. Johnson story	4.00	8.00	12.00
2-5,8,10	2.50	5.00	7.50
6,9,11-Kinstler stories	3.00	6.00	9.00
7-Evans? story	3.00	6.00	9.00
12-19,21,22	2.00	4.00	6.00
20-Kinstler cover/story	2.50	5.00	7.50
23-Kinstler cover	2.00	4.00	6.00
No#(1-3/53)(Realistic reprint)			
	1.50	3.00	4.50

NOTE: *Astarita* stories-#7,10,11.

ROMANTIC MARRIAGE (Cinderella Love #25 on)
Nov-Dec, 1950 - #24, Sept, 1954
Ziff-Davis/St. John #13 on

#1	1.75	3.50	5.25
2-10	1.00	2.00	3.00
11-22,24	.70	1.40	2.10
23-Baker cover	1.00	2.00	3.00

ROMANTIC PICTURE NOVELETTES
1946
Magazine Enterprises

#1-Mary Worth reprints	5.00	10.00	15.00

ROMANTIC SECRETS (Becomes Time For Love)
Sept, 1949 - #38, 1/53; #5, 10/55 - #51, 9/64
Fawcett/Charlton Comics #5(10/55) on

#1	2.00	4.00	6.00
2,3	1.00	2.00	3.00
4,9-Evans stories	1.20	2.40	3.60
5-8,10	.75	1.50	2.25
11-23	.50	1.20	1.80
24-Evans story	1.00	2.00	3.00
25-31,33-38	.50	1.00	1.50
32-Drug mentioned in story			
	2.00	4.00	6.00
#5(10/55)-#51('64)-Charlton	.20	.40	.60

NOTE: *Powell* art-#5,7,10,12,16,17,20,26,29, 33,34,36,37.

ROMANTIC STORY
Nov, 1949 - #130, Nov, 1973
Fawcett/Charlton Comics

#1	2.00	4.00	6.00
2-5	1.20	2.40	3.60
6-14,16-20	.90	1.80	2.70
15-Evans story	1.20	2.40	3.60
21-39,41-50	.60	1.20	1.80
40-(100pgs.)	2.00	4.00	6.00
51-80	.25	.50	.75
81-130		.15	.35

NOTE: *Powell* art-#7,8,16,20.

ROMANTIC THRILLS
1950   (Giant) (132 pgs.)
Fox Features Syndicate

No#-See Fox Giants. Contents may vary and determines price.

ROMANTIC WESTERN
Winter, 1949 - #3, June, 1950
Fawcett Publications

	Good	Fine	Mint
#1	2.50	5.00	7.50
2-Williamson story + McWilliams story			
	4.00	8.00	12.00
3	1.75	3.50	5.25

ROMEO TUBBS (Formerly My Secret Life)
#28, July, 1950; #1, 1950
Fox Features Syndicate

#28,1	1.20	2.40	3.60

RONALD McDONALD
Sept, 1970 - #4, March, 1971
Charlton Press (King Features Synd.)

#1	.15	.30	.45
2-4		.15	.25

ROOKIE COP
Nov, 1955 - #33, Aug, 1957
Charlton Comics

#27-33	.60	1.20	1.80

ROOM 222 (TV)
Jan, 1970 - #4, Jan, 1971
Dell Publishing Co.

#1,2,4: #4 reprts. #1	.20	.40	.60
3-Marijuana story	.70	1.40	2.10

ROOTIE KAZOOTIE (See 3-D-e11)
1952 - 1954
Dell Publishing Co.

4-Color #415,459,502	1.00	2.00	3.00
#4(4-6/54)-#6(10/12/54)	.75	1.50	2.25

ROUNDUP (Western Crime)
July-Aug, 1948 - #5, Mar-Apr, 1949
D.S. Publishing Co.

#1	2.00	4.00	6.00
2-5	1.50	3.00	4.50

ROY CAMPANELLA, BASEBALL HERO
1950
Fawcett Publications

(Roy Campanella cont'd)

	Good	Fine	Mint
No#	4.00	8.00	12.00

ROY ROGERS (See March of Comics #17,35,47,62,
68,73,77,86,91,100,105,116,121,131,136,146,
151,161,167,176,191,206,221,236,250)

ROY ROGERS AND TRIGGER
April, 1967
Gold Key

	Good	Fine	Mint
#1-Reprints	.30	.60	.90

ROY ROGERS COMICS
1944 - 1948
Dell Publishing Co.

	Good	Fine	Mint
4-Color #38('44)	25.00	50.00	75.00
4-Color #63('45)	15.00	30.00	45.00
4-Color #86,95('45)	12.00	24.00	36.00
4-Color #109('46)	8.00	16.00	24.00
4-Color #117,124,137,144	6.00	12.00	18.00
4-Color #153,160,166,177	5.00	10.00	15.00

ROY ROGERS COMICS (See Trigger)
Jan, 1948 - #145, Sept-Oct, 1961
Dell Publishing Co.

	Good	Fine	Mint
#1	14.00	28.00	42.00
2	8.00	16.00	24.00
3-5	5.00	10.00	15.00
6-10	4.00	8.00	12.00
11-20	3.00	6.00	9.00
21-30	2.25	4.50	6.75
31-40	2.00	4.00	6.00
41-55: #49-Trigger feature ends; Charley's Tales begins. #55-Last ish. w/back cover picture	1.50	3.00	4.50
56-70	1.40	2.80	4.20
71-91	1.25	2.50	3.75
92-Title changed to Roy Rogers and Trigger (8/55)	1.20	2.40	3.60
93-110,112-118	1.20	2.40	3.60
111,119-124-Toth art	2.00	4.00	6.00
125-145	1.00	2.00	3.00
-- & the Man From Dodge City(Dodge giveaway, 16pgs.,'54)Frontier, Inc. (5x7¼")	3.00	6.00	9.00
-- Riders Club Comics(16pgs.,'52)	3.50	7.00	10.50

NOTE: *Buscema stories*,2ea.-#74-108. *Manning art-#123,124,132-144.* *Marsh art-#110.*

ROY ROGERS' TRIGGER
#2, Sept-Nov, 1951 - #17, June-Aug, 1955
Dell Publishing Co.

	Good	Fine	Mint
4-Color #329(5/51)	2.00	4.00	6.00

	Good	Fine	Mint
#2-5	1.50	3.00	4.50
6-17	1.00	2.00	3.00

RUDOLPH, THE RED NOSED REINDEER (See Limited Collectors Edition #33,50)

RUDOLPH, THE RED NOSED REINDEER
1939   (2,400,000 copies printed)
Montgomery Ward   (Giveaway)

	Good	Fine	Mint
Possible 1st app. in print; written by Robert May	12.00	24.00	36.00

RUDOLPH, THE RED NOSED REINDEER
1950 - #13, Winter, 1963-64; 1972-73
(Issues are not numbered) (15 known issues)
National Periodical Publications

	Good	Fine	Mint
1950 issues	2.50	5.00	7.50
1951-54 issues	2.00	4.00	6.00
1955-63 issues	1.50	3.00	4.50
1972, C-24(1973)80pgs.; oversized 10x13½"	.50	1.00	1.50

RUFF & REDDY (TV) (Hanna-Barbera)
Sept, 1958 - #12, Jan-Mar, 1962
Dell Publishing Co./Gold Key

	Good	Fine	Mint
4-Color #937,981,1038	.50	1.00	1.50
#4(1-3/60)-#12	.30	.60	.90

NOTE: *Existence of #1('66-Gold Key) suspected.*

RUGGED ACTION (Str. Stor. of Suspense #5 on)
Dec, 1954 - #4, June, 1955
Atlas Comics (CSI)

	Good	Fine	Mint
#1	1.40	2.80	4.20
2-4	.90	1.80	2.70

RULAH JUNGLE GODDESS (Formerly Zoot; I Loved #28 on) (Also see Terrors of the Jungle)
#17, Aug, 1948 - #27, June, 1949
Fox Features Syndicate

	Good	Fine	Mint
#17	17.00	34.00	51.00
18-20	14.00	28.00	42.00
21-Used in Seduction of the Innocent, pg. 388,389	16.00	32.00	48.00
22-27	12.00	24.00	36.00

NOTE: *Kamen covers-#17-19,21,22.*

RUNAWAY, THE (See Movie Classics)

RUN BABY RUN
1974   (39¢)
Logos International

Roy Rogers #19, © Roy Rogers

Rugged Action #4, © MCG

Rulah Jungle Goddess #19, © FOX

Saari The Jungle Goddess =1. © P.L. Publ.   Sabu =2. © FOX   Saddle Justice =7. © WMG

(Run Baby Run cont'd)	Good	Fine	Mint
By Tony Tallarico from Nicky Cruz's book			
	.20	.40	.60

RUN, BUDDY, RUN (TV)
June, 1967
Gold Key

#1(10204-706)	.25	.50	.75

RUSTY (Formerly Kid Movie Comics; The Kelleys
#12, 4/47 - #22, 9/49   #23 on)
Marvel Comics (HPC)

#12,13,18,19	1.00	2.00	3.00
14-Wolverton's Powerhouse Pepper(4pgs.) +			
Kurtzman's "Hey Look"	6.00	12.00	18.00
15-17-Kurtzman's "Hey Look",			
20-Kurtzman, 5pgs.	4.00	8.00	12.00
21,22-Kurtzman, 17&22pgs.	7.00	14.00	21.00

RUSTY, BOY DETECTIVE
Mar, 1955 - #5, Nov, 1955
Good Comics/Lev Gleason

#1-Bob Wood, Carl Hubbell art begins			
	1.50	3.00	4.50
2-5	1.20	2.40	3.60

RUSTY DUGAN (See Holyoke One-Shot #2)

RUSTY RILEY (See 4-Color #418,451,486,554)

SAARI, THE JUNGLE GODDESS
Nov, 1951
P.L. Publishing Co.

#1	8.00	16.00	24.00

SABRINA'S CHRISTMAS MAGIC (See Archie Giant
Series Mag. #196,207,220,231,243,455,467)

SABRINA, THE TEEN-AGE WITCH (TV)
(See Archie's TV Laugh-Out)(Giants #1-17)
April, 1971 - Present
Archie Publications

#1	.25	.50	.75
2-5	.15	.30	.45
6-47: #3,4-Archie's Group x-over	.15		.35

SABU, "ELEPHANT BOY"(Formerly My Secret Story)
#30, June, 1950 - #2, Aug, 1950
Fox Features Syndicate

#30(#1)-Wood story	6.00	12.00	18.00
2-Photo cover; Kamen art	5.00	10.00	15.00

SACRAMENTS, THE
October, 1955   (25c)
Catechetical Guild Educational Society

	Good	Fine	Mint
#304	.50	1.00	1.50

SAD CASE OF WAITING ROOM WILLIE, THE
1950?(no date)(14pgs. in color)(paper covers)
(Regular size)
American Visuals Corp.(For Balti.Medical Soc.)

By Will Eisner	5.00	10.00	15.00

SADDLE JUSTICE (Happy Houlihans #1,2;
becomes Saddle Romances #9 on)
#3, Spring, 1948 - #8, Sept-Oct, 1949
E.C. Comics

#3-The first E.C. by Bill Gaines to break
away from M. C. Gaines' old Educational
Comics format. Craig, Feldstein, H. C.
Kiefer, & Stan Asch art

	25.00	50.00	75.00
4-1st Graham Ingels E.C. story			
	25.00	50.00	75.00
5-8-Ingels art in all	22.00	44.00	66.00

NOTE: *Craig & Feldstein art in most issues.
Canadian reprts. known; see Table of Contents.*

SADDLE ROMANCES (Saddle Justice #3-8;
continued as Weird Science #12 on)
#9, Nov-Dec, 1949 - #11, Mar-Apr, 1950
E.C. Comics

#9-Ingels art	22.00	44.00	66.00
10-Wood's 1st work at E.C.; Ingels story			
	25.00	50.00	75.00
11-Ingels art	25.00	50.00	75.00

NOTE: *Canadian reprints known; see Table of
Contents.*

SADIE SACK (See Harvey Hits #93)

SAD SACK AND THE SARGE
Sept, 1957 - Present
Harvey Publications

#1	3.00	6.00	9.00
2-10	1.20	2.40	3.60
11-20	.60	1.20	1.80
21-50	.25	.50	.75
51-134		.20	.40

SAD SACK COMICS (See Tastee Freez & Harvey
Sept, 1949 - Present   Hits #8)
Harvey Publications

#1	9.00	18.00	27.00

(Sad Sack cont'd)	Good	Fine	Mint
2,3	5.00	10.00	15.00
4-10	3.00	6.00	9.00
11-30	1.50	3.00	4.50
31-50	.90	1.80	2.70
51-100	.50	1.00	1.50
101-150	.25	.50	.75
151-265		.20	35.
3-D#1(1/54-titled "Harvey 3-D Hits")			
	5.00	10.00	15.00
Armed Forces Complimentary copies, HD#2-15,			
23-25('56-59),31-38('61).35		.70	1.05

SAD SACK GOES HOME
1951   (16 pgs. in color)
Harvey Publications

No#-by George Baker	2.50	5.00	7.50

SAD SACK FUN AROUND THE WORLD
1974 (no month)
Harvey Publications

#1-About Great Britain	.15	.30	.45

SAD SACK LAUGH SPECIAL
Winter, 1958-59 - #93, Feb, 1977
Harvey Publications

#1	2.50	5.00	7.50
2-10	1.00	2.00	3.00
11-30	.50	1.00	1.50
31-50	.20	.40	.60
51-93		.20	.40

SAD SACK NAVY, GOBS 'N' GALS
Aug, 1972 - #8, Oct, 1973
Harvey Publications

#1	.25	.50	.75
2-8		.20	.40

SAD SACK'S ARMY LIFE   (See Harvey Hits #17, 22,28,32,39,43,47,51,55,58,61,64,67,70)

SAD SACK'S ARMY LIFE (--Parade #1-57,--Today
1963 - Present   #58 on)
Harvey Publications

#1	1.75	3.50	5.25
2-10	.70	1.40	2.10
11-30	.25	.50	.75
31-62		.20	.40

SAD SACK'S FUNNY FRIENDS (See Harvey Hits #75)
1955 - #75, Oct, 1969
Harvey Publications

	Good	Fine	Mint
#1	3.00	6.00	9.00
2-10	1.25	2.50	3.75
11-20	.80	1.60	2.40
21-30	.40	.80	1.20
31-50	.25	.50	.75
51-75		.20	.40

SAD SACK'S MUTTSY (See Harvey Hits #74,77,80, 82,87,89,96,99,102,105,108,111,113,115,117, 119,121)

SAD SACK USA (-- Vacation #8)
Nov, 1972 - #7, Nov, 1973; #8, Oct, 1974
Harvey Publications

#1	.25	.50	.75
2-8		.20	.40

SAD SACK WITH SARGE & SADIE
Sept, 1972 - #8, 1973
Harvey Publications

#1	.25	.50	.75
2-8		.20	.40

SAD SAD SACK WORLD
1964 - #46, Dec, 1973
Harvey Publications

#1	.80	1.60	2.40
2-10	.40	.80	1.20
11-46	.20	.40	.60

SAGA OF BIG RED, THE
Sept, 1976   ($1.25) (In Color)
Omaha World-Herald

No#-by Win Mumma; story of the Nebraska			
Cornhuskers(sports)	.50	1.00	1.50

SAILOR SWEENEY (Navy Action #1-11, 15 on)
#12, July, 1956 - #14, Nov, 1956
Atlas Comics (CDS)

#12-14: #12-Shores art. #13-Severin cover			
	1.00	2.00	3.00

SAINT, THE
Aug, 1947 - #12, Mar, 1952
Avon Periodicals

#1-Kamen bondage cover/stories			
	15.00	30.00	45.00
2-4	9.00	18.00	27.00
5-Everett story; spanking panel			
	12.00	24.00	36.00
6-Miss Fury app.,14pgs; Wood story?			

Sad Sack #19. © HARV

The Saint =5. © AVON

The Saint =8. © AVON

Samson ≠3. © FOX   Sands Of The South Pacific ≠1. © TOBY   Santa Claus Funnies Four Color ≠175. © DELL

(The Saint cont'd)	Good	Fine	Mint
	17.00	34.00	51.00
7-9(12/50): Saint strip reprints in #8-12;			
#9-Kinstler cover	7.00	14.00	21.00
10-Wood art, 1pg.	6.00	12.00	18.00
11,12	5.00	10.00	15.00

NOTE: *Lucky Dale, Girl Detective in #1,4,6.*

SAM HILL PRIVATE EYE
1950 - #7, 1951
Close-Up

#1	1.50	3.00	4.50
2-7	1.00	2.00	3.00

SAMSON (1st Series) (Capt. Aero #7 on)
Fall, 1940 - #6, Sept, 1941
Fox Features Syndicate

#1-Will Eisner art	30.00	60.00	90.00
2	20.00	40.00	60.00
3-Navy Jones app.	14.00	28.00	42.00
4-Yarko the Great, Master Magician begins;			
Fine cover?	12.00	24.00	36.00
5	12.00	24.00	36.00
6-Origin The Topper	12.00	24.00	36.00

SAMSON (2nd Series) (See Spec. Feat. Mag.)
#12, April, 1955 - #14, Aug, 1955
Ajax/Farrell Publications (Four Star)

#12-14-Wonder Boy in #12,13; Rocket Man in			
#13	2.00	4.00	6.00

SAMSON (See Mighty Samson)

SAMSON & DELILAH (See A Spectacular Feat.Mag.)

SAMUEL BRONSTON'S CIRCUS WORLD (See Movie
Comics under Circus World)

SANDMAN, THE
Winter, 1974; #2, 4-5/75 - #6, 12-1/75-76
National Periodical Publications

#1-Simon & Kirby story	.50	1.00	1.50
2,3-Chua art in each	.35	.70	1.05
4,5	.25	.50	.75
6-Kirby/Wood cvr/story	.30	.60	.90

NOTE: *Kirby stories-#4-6; covers-#1-5.*

SANDS OF THE SOUTH PACIFIC
January, 1953
Toby Press

#1	1.50	3.00	4.50

SANTA AND HIS REINDEER (See March of Comics
#166)

SANTA AND POLLYANNA PLAY THE GLAD GAME
1960   (15 pgs.) (Disney giveaway)
Sales Promotion

	Good	Fine	Mint
	1.00	2.00	3.00

SANTA AND THE ANGEL (See 4-Color #259 &
Dell Jr. Treasury #7)

SANTA & THE BUCCANEERS
1959
Promotional Publ. Co. (Giveaway)

Reprints 1952 Santa & the Pirates			
	.50	1.00	1.50

SANTA & THE PIRATES
1952
Promotional Publ. Co. (Giveaway)

Marv Levy cover/art	1.00	2.00	3.00

SANTA AT THE ZOO (See 4-Color Comics #259)

SANTA CLAUS AROUND THE WORLD (See March of
Comics #241)

SANTA CLAUS CONQUERS THE MARTIANS (See Mov-
ie Classics)

SANTA CLAUS FUNNIES
1942 - 1962
Dell Publishing Co.

No#(#1)(1942)-Kelly art	35.00	70.00	105.00
#2(1943)-Kelly art	28.00	56.00	84.00
4-Color #61('44)-Kelly	22.00	44.00	66.00
4-Color #91('45)-Kelly	17.00	34.00	51.00
4-Color #128('46),175('47)-Kelly art			
	14.00	28.00	42.00
4-Color #205,254-Kelly	12.00	24.00	36.00
4-Color #302,361	2.50	5.00	7.50
4-Color #525,607,666,756,867			
	1.20	2.40	3.60
4-Color #958,1063,1154,1274			
	.90	1.80	2.70
#1(1952-Dell Giant)(Dan Noonan-A Christmas			
Carol adaptation)	3.50	7.00	10.50

NOTE: *Most issues contain only one Kelly
story.*

SANTA CLAUS PARADE
1951; 1952; 1955   (25¢)
Ziff-Davis(Approved Comics)/St. John Publ.

No#(1951)-116pgs.(Ziff-Davis)(XMas Special)			
	2.50	5.00	7.50
#2(12/52-Z-D)100pgs.; Dave Berg art			
	2.50	5.00	7.50

(Santa Claus Parade cont'd)

	Good	Fine	Mint
V1#3(1/66-St. John)100pgs.	2.00	4.00	6.00

SANTA IS COMING (See March of Comics #197)

SANTA IS HERE (See March of Comics #49)

SANTA ON THE JOLLY ROGER
1965
Promotional Publ. Co. (Giveaway)

Marv Levy cover/art	.25	.50	.75

SANTA'S BUSY CORNER (See March of Comics #31)

SANTA'S CANDY KITCHEN(See March of Comics #14)

SANTA'S CHRISTMAS BOOK (See March of Comics #123)

SANTA'S CHRISTMAS COMICS
Dec, 1952   (100 pgs.)
Standard Comics (Best Books)

No#	2.00	4.00	6.00

SANTA'S CHRISTMAS LIST (See March of Comics #255)

SANTA'S CIRCUS
1964   (½-Size)
Promotional Publ. Co. (Giveaway)

Marv Levy cover/art	.25	.50	.75

SANTA'S HELPERS (See March of Comics #64, 106,198)

SANTA'S LITTLE HELPERS (See March of Comics #270)

SANTA'S RODEO
1964   (½-Size)
Promotional Publ. Co. (Giveaway)

Marv Levy story only	.25	.50	.75

SANTA'S SHOW (See March of Comics #311)

SANTA'S SLEIGH (See March of Comics #298)

SANTA'S STORIES
1953 (Regular size, soft cover)
K.K. Publications (Klines Dept. Store)

Kelly art	8.00	16.00	24.00

SANTA'S SURPRISE (See March of Comics #13,22)

SANTA'S TINKER TOTS
1958
Charlton Comics

	Good	Fine	Mint
#1-Based on "The Tinker Tots Keep Christmas"	.35	.70	1.05

SANTA'S TOYLAND (See March of Comics #242)

SANTA'S TOYTOWN FUN BOOK
1952
Promotional Publ. Co. (Giveaway)

Marv Levy cover only	.80	1.60	2.40

SANTA'S TOYS (See March of Comics #12)

SANTA'S VISIT (See March of Comics #283)

SANTA'S WORKSHOP (See March of Comics #50,168)

SANTIAGO (See 4-Color Comics #723)

SARGE SNORKEL (Beetle Bailey)
Oct, 1973 - #17, Dec, 1976
Charlton Comics

#1-17		.10	.20

SARGE STEEL (Becomes Secret Agent #9 on)
Dec, 1964 - #8, Mar-Apr, 1966
Charlton Comics

#1-Origin	.50	1.00	1.50
2-8	.30	.60	.90

SAVAGE COMBAT TALES
Feb, 1975 - #3, July, 1975
Atlas/Seaboard Publ.

#1-Sgt. Stryker's Death Squad begins(origin); McWilliams cvr/art	.20	.40	.60
2,3: #2-Toth, McWilliams art; intro., only app. Warhawk	.20	.40	.60

SAVAGE RAIDS OF GERONIMO (See Geronimo #4)

SAVAGE RANGE (See 4-Color Comics #807)

SAVAGE SWORD OF CONAN, THE (Magazine)
Aug, 1974 - Present   (Black & White)
Marvel Comics Group

#1-Smith reprint + Buscema/Adams/Krenkel art; origin Blackmark by G. Kane(part 1) & Red Sonja(3rd app.)	2.50	5.00	7.50
2-Adams cover	1.50	3.00	4.50
3-Smith art; Adams story	1.50	3.00	4.50

Sarge Steel #1. © CC

Savage Sword Of Conan #1. © MCG

Savage Tales #2. © MCG

Savage Tales #3, © MCG

Scamp #11, © WDP

Science Comics #5, © FOX

(Savage Sword of Conan cont'd)

	Good	Fine	Mint
4-Adams/Kane story reprt.	1.25	2.50	3.75
5-10	1.00	2.00	3.00
11-13,15	.90	1.80	2.70
14-Adams pencils	1.20	2.40	3.60
16-Smith pencils	1.20	2.40	3.60
17-25,27,28	.60	1.20	1.80
26-Starlin cover	.70	1.40	2.10
29-Adams inks	.70	1.40	2.10
30-37	.50	1.00	1.50
Annual #1('75)-B&W, Smith reprints(Conan #10, 13)	.80	1.60	2.40

NOTE: _Alcala_ stories-#2,4,7,12,15-20,23,24, 28. _Boris_ covers-#1,4,5,7,9,10,12,15. _Brunner_ story-#30; covers-#8,30. _Buscema_ stories-#1-5, 7,10-12,15-24,26-28,31,32. _Chaykin_ story-#18, 22; cover-#31. _Corbin_ story-#4,16,29. _Finley_ story-#16. _Infantino_ story-#34. _Kaluta_ story-#11,18; cover-#4. _Krenkel_ story-#9,11,14,16, 24. _Morrow_ story-#7. _Newton_ story-#6. _Nino_ cover/art-#6. #8 & #10 contain a Robert E. Howard Conan adaptation.

SAVAGE TALES (Magazine) (B&W)
5/71; #2, 10/73; #3, 2/74 - #12, Summer/75
Marvel Comics Group

	Good	Fine	Mint
#1-Origin & 1st app. The Man-Thing by Morrow; Conan the Barbarian by Barry Smith, Femizons by Romita begin; Ka-Zar app.	16.00	32.00	48.00
2-Smith, Brunner, Morrow, Williamson, Wrightson art (reprt.-Creatures on the Loose(#10); King Kull app.	5.00	10.00	15.00
3-Smith, Brunner, Steranko, Williamson art	3.50	7.00	10.50
4,5-Adams covers; last Conan (Smith reprt./ #4)+ Kane/Adams story. #5-Brak the Barbarian begins, ends #8	1.75	3.50	5.25
6-Ka-Zar begins; Williamson reprint; Adams cover	1.00	2.00	3.00
7-Buscema/Adams story	1.00	2.00	3.00
8-Shanna, the She-Devil begins, ends #10; Adams cover/story	1.00	2.00	3.00
9,11	.80	1.60	2.40
10-Adams story inks	1.00	2.00	3.00
Annual #1(Sum.'75)(#12 on inside)-B&W; Smith reprt./Astonishing Tales.	.80	1.60	2.40

NOTE: _Kaluta_ cover-#9. _Starlin_ story-#5.

SCAMP (Walt Disney)
5/56 - #1204, 8-10/61; 11/67 - Present
Dell Publishing Co./Gold Key

	Good	Fine	Mint
4-Color #703,777,806('57),833	1.00	2.00	3.00
#5(3-5/58)-#10(6-8/59)	.50	1.00	1.50

	Good	Fine	Mint
11-16(12-2/61)	.35	.70	1.05
4-Color #1204('61)	.80	1.50	2.40
#1(12/67,G.K.)-reprts.begin	.25	.50	.75
2(3/69)-#10	.20	.40	.60
11-44		.20	.40

NOTE: _New stories-#20(in part),22-25,27,30, 31,34,37,38,44. New covers-#11,12,14,15,17-25, 27,29-31,34,36-38._

SCAR FACE (See The Crusaders)

SCARECROW, THE (-- of Romney Marsh #1)
April, 1964 - #3, Oct, 1965 (Disney TV Show)
Gold Key

	Good	Fine	Mint
#10112-404 (#1)	1.00	2.00	3.00
#2,3	.60	1.20	1.80

SCARLET O'NEIL (See Harvey Comics Hits #59)

SCARY TALES
8/75 - #9, 1/77; #10, 9/77 - Present
Charlton Comics

	Good	Fine	Mint
#1-Origin & 1st app. Countess Von Bludd, not in #2	.15	.30	.45
2-18: #3-Ditko story. #4-Sutton cover		.15	.30
#1(Modern Comics reprint, 1977)	.15	.30	

SCHOOL DAY ROMANCES (-- of Teen-Agers #4)
(Popular Teen-Agers #5 on)
Nov-Dec, 1949 - #4, May-June, 1950
Star Publications

	Good	Fine	Mint
#1-Tony Gayle(later Gay), Gingersnapp begin	4.00	8.00	12.00
2-4	2.50	5.00	7.50

NOTE: _All have L. B. Cole covers._

SCHWINN BICYCLE BOOK (--Bike Thrills, 1959)
1949; 1952; 1959 (10¢)
Schwinn Bicycle Co.

	Good	Fine	Mint
1949	2.50	5.00	7.50
1952-Believe It or Not type facts; comic format (32pgs.)	1.50	3.00	4.50
1959	1.00	2.00	3.00

SCIENCE COMICS (1st Series)
Feb, 1940 - #8, Sept, 1940
Fox Features Syndicate

	Good	Fine	Mint
#1-Origin Dynamo-(called Electro in #1), The Eagle, & Navy Jones; Marga, the Panther Woman, Cosmic Carson & Perisphere Payne, Dr. Doom begin	60.00	120.00	180.00

(Science Comics cont'd)	Good	Fine	Mint
2	35.00	70.00	105.00
3	25.00	50.00	75.00
4-Kirby art	30.00	60.00	90.00
5-8	18.00	36.00	54.00

NOTE: *Cosmic Carson by Kirby-#4 only. Lou Fine covers-#1-3 only.*

SCIENCE COMICS (2nd Series)
January, 1946 - #5, 1946
Humor Publications

#1	2.00	4.00	6.00
2,4,5	1.50	3.00	4.50
3-Feldstein art, 6pgs.	3.00	6.00	9.00

SCIENCE COMICS
March, 1951
Export Publication Ent., Toronto, Canada
Distr. in U.S. by Kable News Co.

#1-Science adventure stories + some true science features	1.25	2.50	3.75

SCIENCE FICTION SPACE ADVENTURES
(See Space Adventures)

SCOOBY DOO (-- Where Are You? #1-16,26; -- Mystery Comics #17-25, 27 on) (TV)
March, 1970 - #30, Feb, 1975
Gold Key

#1	.20	.40	.60
2-30		.20	.35

(See March of Comics #356,382,391)

SCOOBY-DOO
Oct, 1977 - #8, Dec, 1978
Marvel Comics Group

#1	.20	.40	.60
2-8		.20	.35

SCOOBY DOO, WHERE ARE YOU? (TV)
April, 1975 - #11, Dec, 1976 (Hanna-Barbera)
Charlton Comics

#1		.20	.40
2-11		.15	.30

SCOOP
Nov, 1941 - 1946
Harry 'A' Chesler (Holyoke)

#1-Intro. Rocketman & Rocketgirl; origin The
Master Key; Dan Hastings begins; cover/
stories by Charles Sultan

	20.00	40.00	60.00

	Good	Fine	Mint
2-Rocket Boy app.	10.00	20.00	30.00
3-8	6.00	12.00	18.00

SCOOTER (See Swing With --)

SCOOTER
April, 1946
Rucker Publ. Ltd. (Canadian)

#1	1.25	2.50	3.75

SCORPION, THE
Feb, 1975 - #3, July, 1975
Atlas/Seaboard Publ.

#1-Intro.	.40	.80	1.20
2,3	.25	.50	.75

NOTE: *Chaykin stories-#1,2. Craig story-#3.*

SCOTLAND YARD (Inspector Farnsworth of --)
1955 - #4, March, 1956
Charlton Comics

#1	1.75	3.50	5.25
2-4	1.00	2.00	3.00

SCREAM (-- Comics)
Fall, 1944 - #19, April, 1948
Humor Publications/Current Books

#1	2.00	4.00	6.00
2-15	1.35	2.75	4.00
16-Intro. Lily-Belle	1.75	3.50	5.25
17-19	1.25	2.50	3.75

SCREAM (Magazine)
Aug, 1973 - #11, Feb, 1975 (68 pgs.) (B&W)
Skywald Publishing Corp.

#1	.40	.80	1.20
2-5: #3(12/73)-#3 found on pg. 22	.35	.70	1.05
6-11	.30	.60	.90

SCRIBBLY
Aug-Sept, 1948 - #15, Dec-Jan, 1950-51
National Periodical Publications

#1	10.00	20.00	30.00
2-5	6.00	12.00	18.00
6-10	3.50	7.00	10.50
11-15	2.50	5.00	7.50

NOTE: *Sheldon Mayer art in all.*

SEA DEVILS (See Showcase)
Sept-Oct, 1961 - #35, May-June, 1967
National Periodical Publications

Scotland Yard #1, © CC

Scribbly #4, © DC

Sea Devils #16, © DC

Sea Hound #1. © AVON

Sea Hunt #11. © DELL

Secret Love #3. © AJAX

(Sea Devils cont'd)	Good	Fine	Mint
#1	3.00	6.00	9.00
2	1.50	3.00	4.50
3-5	1.20	2.40	3.60
6-10	.80	1.60	2.40
11,12,14-20	.60	1.20	1.80
13-Kubert + Colan art	1.00	2.00	3.00
21,23-35	.50	1.00	1.50
22-Intro. International Sea Devils; origin & 1st app. Capt. X & Man Fish			
	.50	1.00	1.50

NOTE: _Heath_ covers-#1-11,14-16; story-#11.

SEA HOUND, THE (Capt. Silver's Log of --)
1945 (no month) - #4, Jan-Feb, 1946
Avon Periodicals

#1	3.00	6.00	9.00
2-4	2.00	4.00	6.00

SEA HOUND, THE
#3, July, 1949 - #4, Sept, 1949
Capt. Silver Syndicate

#3,4	1.25	2.50	3.75

SEA HUNT (TV)
1958 - 10-12/59; #4, 1-3/60 - #13, 4-6/62
Dell Publishing Co.

4-Color #928,994,#4-13: Manning art #4-6, 8-11,13	1.00	2.00	3.00
4-Color #1041-Toth art	2.00	4.00	6.00

SEARCH FOR LOVE
Feb-Mar, 1950 - #2, Apr-May, 1950
American Comics Group

#1	1.50	3.00	4.50
2	1.00	2.00	3.00

SEARCHERS (See 4-Color Comics #709)

SEARS (See Merry Christmas From --)

SEASON'S GREETINGS
1935 (6½x5¼") (14 pgs. in color)
Hallmark (King Features)

Cover feat. Mickey Mouse, Popeye, Jiggs & Skippy. "The Night Before Christmas" told one panel per page, each panel by a famous artist featuring their character. Art by Alex Raymond, Gottfredson, Swinnerton, Segar, Chic Young, Milt Gross, Sullivan(Messmer), Herriman, McManus, Percy Crosby & others (22 artists in all)   30.00 60.00 90.00

SECRET AGENT (Formerly Sarge Steel)
Oct, 1966 - V2#10, Oct, 1967
Charlton Comics

	Good	Fine	Mint
V2#9-Sarge Steel begins	.35	.70	1.05
10-Tiffany Sinn, CIA app.-from Career Girl Romances #39	.25	.50	.75

SECRET AGENT (TV)
Nov, 1966 - #2, Jan, 1968
Gold Key

#1,2	.50	1.00	1.50

SECRET AGENT X-9
1934; Book 1(80pgs.), Book 2(120pgs.)(8x7½")
David McKay Publications

Book 1, Book 2-Alex Raymond dailies			
	40.00	80.00	120.00

SECRET AGENT X-9 (See Feature Book #8,McKay)

SECRET AGENT Z-2 (See Z-2)

SECRET DIARY OF EERIE ADVENTURES
1953 (One Shot) (Giant-100pgs.)
Avon Periodicals

Kubert art	8.00	16.00	24.00

SECRET HEARTS
Sept-Oct, 1949 - #154, Sept, 1971
National Per. Publ.(Beverly)(Arleigh #50-113)

#1	3.00	6.00	9.00
2-10	1.50	3.00	4.50
11-30	.90	1.80	2.70
31-50	.50	1.00	1.50
51-109	.25	.50	.75
110-"Reach for Happiness" serial begins; ends #138	.25	.50	.75
111-119,121-133,135-138	.20	.40	.60
120,134-Adams covers	.50	1.00	1.50
139,140		.20	.35
141,142-"20 Miles to Heartbreak", Chapter 2&3 (See Young Love for Chapter 1&4); Toth + Colletta art	.25	.50	.75
143-148,150-154: #144-Morrow art			
		.20	.35
149-Toth art	.20	.40	.60

SECRET LOVE
1949 (Giant Size, 132 pgs.)
Fox Features Syndicate

No#-Contents can vary & determines price. See Fox Giants.

SECRET LOVE
12/55 - #3, 8/56; 4/57 - #5, 2/58; #6, 6/58
Ajax-Farrell/Four Star Comic Corp. #2 on

	Good	Fine	Mint
#1(12/55-Ajax)	1.00	2.00	3.00
2,3	.60	1.20	1.80
1(4/57-Ajax)	.60	1.20	1.80
2-6	.40	.80	1.20

SECRET LOVE (See Sinister House of --)

SECRET LOVES
Nov, 1949 - #6, Sept, 1950
Comic Magazines/Quality Comics Group

#1-Ward cover	5.00	10.00	15.00
2-Ward cover	4.00	8.00	12.00
3-6	1.75	3.50	5.25

SECRET MISSIONS
Feb, 1950
St. John Publishing Co.

#1-Kubert cover	4.00	8.00	12.00

SECRET MYSTERIES (Formerly Crime Mysteries & Crime Smashers)
#17, Mar, 1954; #16, 11/54 - #19, 7/55
Ribage/Merit Publishing Corp.

#17(3/54)	1.25	2.50	3.75
16(Crime stories)	1.25	2.50	3.75
17-19(Horror stories)	1.25	2.50	3.75

SECRET ORIGINS
Feb-Mar, 1973 - #6, 1-2/74; #7, 10-11/74
National Periodical Publications

#1-Origin Superman, Batman, The Ghost, The
   Flash(Showcase #4); Infantino & Kubert

art	.70	1.40	2.10

2-Origin new Green Lantern, the new Atom, &
   Supergirl; Kane art   .50   1.00   1.50
3-Origin Wonder Woman, Wildcat
   .50   1.00   1.50
4-Origin Vigilante by Meskin, Kid Eternity
   .30   .60   .90
5-Origin The Spectre   .50   1.00   1.50
6-Origin Blackhawk & Legion of Super Heroes
   .30   .60   .90
7-Origin Robin, Aquaman   .30   .60   .90

SECRET ORIGINS ANNUAL (See 80 Pg. Giant #8)
Aug-Oct, 1961
National Periodical Publications

#1('61)-Origin Adam Strange(Showcase #17),Gr.
   Lantern(G.L.#1), Challs(partial/Showcase

	Good	Fine	Mint

#6, 6pgs. Kirby art), J'onn J'onzz(Det.
#225), New Flash(Showcase #4), Green Arrow
(1pg. text), Superman-Batman team, & Wonder Woman   8.00 16.00 24.00

SECRET ORIGINS OF SUPER-HEROES (See DC Special Series #10)

SECRET ROMANCE
Oct, 1968 - #41, Nov, 1976
Charlton Comics

#1	.15	.30	.45
2-41: #9-Reese art		.15	.30

NOTE: *Beyond the Stars app. #9,11,12,14.*

SECRET ROMANCES
April, 1951 - #27, July, 1955
Superior Publications Ltd.

#1	2.00	4.00	6.00
2-10	1.40	2.80	4.20
11-27	1.00	2.00	3.00

SECRET SERVICE (See Kent Blake of the --)

SECRET SIX
Apr-May, 1968 - #7, Apr-May, 1969
National Periodical Publications

#1-Origin	.50	1.00	1.50
2-7	.30	.60	.90

SECRET SOCIETY OF SUPER-VILLAINS
May-June, 1976 - #15, June-July, 1978
National Periodical Publications/DC Comics

#1-Origin	.30	.60	.90
2-5: #2-Re-intro. Capt. Comet			
	.25	.50	.75
6-15	.20	.40	.60

SECRET SOCIETY OF SUPER-VILLAINS SPECIAL
(See DC Special Series #6)

SECRETS OF HAUNTED HOUSE
Apr-May, 1975 - #5, Dec-Jan, 1975-76;
#6, June-July, 1977 - #14, Oct-Nov, 1978
National Periodical Publications/DC Comics

#1	.25	.50	.75
2-14: #4-Redondo art. #5-Wrightson cover.			
#9-Ditko story. #11-Kaluta cover. #13-			
Orlando cover	.20	.40	.60
Special (3/78)	.20	.40	.60

SECRETS OF HAUNTED HOUSE SPECIAL (See DC Special Series #12)

Secret Loves #1, © QUA

Secret Mysteries #18, © Ribage Publ.

Secret Romances #23, © SUPR

Secret Story #15, © MCG

Select Detective #2, © DS

Sensation Comics #10, © DC

SECRETS OF LIFE (See 4-Color Comics #749)

SECRETS OF LOVE (See Popular Teen-Agers --)

SECRETS OF LOVE & MARRIAGE
1956 - V2#25, June, 1961
Charlton Comics

	Good	Fine	Mint
V2#1-6	.30	.60	.90
V2#7-9-(All 68pgs.)	.25	.50	.75
10-25	.15	.30	.45

SECRETS OF MAGIC (See Wisco)

SECRETS OF SINISTER HOUSE (Sinister House of Secret Love #1-4)
#5, June-July, 1972 - #18, June-July, 1974
National Periodical Publications

#5	.20	.40	.60
6,8,9	.15	.30	.45
7-Redondo story	.25	.50	.75
10-Adams story(inks)	.80	1.60	2.40
11-16,18		.20	.40
17-Toth reprint	.15	.30	.45

NOTE: *Alcala stories-#13,14. Ambrose Bierce adaptation-#14.*

SECRETS OF TRUE LOVE
Feb, 1958
St. John Publishing Co.

#1	.80	1.60	2.40

SECRETS OF YOUNG BRIDES
#5, 9/57 - #44, 9/64; 7/75 - #9, 11/76
Charlton Comics

#5	.25	.50	.75
6-44	.15	.30	.45
#1-9		.15	.35

SECRET SQUIRREL (TV)
Oct, 1966   (Hanna-Barbera)
Gold Key

#1	.20	.40	.60
Florida Power & Light Giveaway('66)			
	.20	.40	.60

SECRET STORY ROMANCES (Becomes True Tales of Love?)
Nov, 1953 - #21, Mar, 1956
Atlas Comics (TCI)

#1	1.00	2.00	3.00
2-21	.50	1.00	1.50

NOTE: *Colletta stories-#17,21; cover-#17.*

SECRET VOICE, THE (See Great American Comics)

SEDUCTION OF THE INNOCENT (Also see N. Y. State Joint Legis. Comm. to Study --)
1953, 1954 (399 pgs.) (Hardback)
Rinehart & Co., Inc., N. Y. (Also printed in Canada by Clarke, Irwin & Co. Ltd., Toronto)

Written by Dr. Fredric Wertham

	VG	VF
(1st Version)-with bibliographical note intact (only a few copies got out before the comic publishers forced the removal of this page)	25.00	40.00
with dust jacket....	30.00	50.00
(2nd Version)-	VG	VF
	12.00	20.00
with dust jacket....	20.00	30.00

NOTE: *Material from this book appeared in the Ladies' Home Journal under the title "What Parents Don't Know About Comic Books." With the release of this book, Dr. Wertham reveals seven years of research attempting to link juvenile delinquency to comic books. Many illustrations showing excessive violence, sex, sadism, & torture are shown. This book led to the Kefauver Senate hearings and eventually the Comics Code Authority. Because of the influence this book had on the comic industry and the collector's interest in it, we feel this listing is justified.*

SELECT DETECTIVE
Aug-Sept, 1948 - #3, Dec-Jan, 1948-49
D.S. Publishing Co.

	Good	Fine	Mint
#1-Matt Baker art	2.50	5.00	7.50
2-Baker + McWilliams art	2.00	4.00	6.00
3-2pg. Wood art	1.50	3.00	4.50

SENSATIONAL POLICE CASES
1952; 1954
Avon Periodicals

No#-100pg. issue(1952,25¢)-Kubert & Kinstler art	5.00	10.00	15.00
#1(1954)	2.50	5.00	7.50
2,3,5	2.00	4.00	6.00
4-Reprint/Saint #5	2.50	5.00	7.50

SENSATIONAL POLICE CASES
No Date (1963?)
I.W. Enterprises

Reprint #5-Reprints Prison Break #5('52)Avon; Infantino art	.80	1.60	2.40

359

SENSATION COMICS (-- Mystery #110 on)
Jan, 1942 - #109, May-June, 1952
National Periodical Publ./All-American

	Good	Fine	Mint
#1-Origin Mr. Terrific, Wildcat, The Gay Ghost, & Little Boy Blue; Wonder Woman, The Black Pirate begin; intro. Justice & Fair Play Club; #1 reprinted in Famous 1st Editions	150.00	300.00	450.00
2	70.00	140.00	210.00
3	50.00	100.00	150.00
4	40.00	80.00	120.00
5-Intro. Justin, Black Pirate's son	30.00	60.00	90.00
6-10	25.00	50.00	75.00
11-20	20.00	40.00	60.00
21-30	14.00	28.00	42.00
31-33	10.00	20.00	30.00
34-Sargon, the Sorcerer begins, ends #36; begins again #52	9.00	18.00	27.00
35-40	8.00	16.00	24.00
41-50: #43-The Whip app.	7.00	14.00	21.00
51-60: #56,57-Sargon by Kubert	6.00	12.00	18.00
61-70: #63-Last Mr. Terrific. #65,66-Wildcat by Kubert. #68-Origin Huntress	5.00	10.00	15.00
71-80	5.00	10.00	15.00
81-Used in Seduction of the Innocent; Krigstein art	8.00	16.00	24.00
82-90: #83-Last Sargon. #86-The Atom app. #90-Last Wildcat	4.00	8.00	12.00
91-Streak begins by Alex Toth	5.00	10.00	15.00
92(Toth art,2pgs.),93	4.00	8.00	12.00
94-1st all girl issue	6.00	12.00	18.00
95-106: Wonder Woman ends. #99-1st app. Astra, Girl of the Future, ends #106	6.00	12.00	18.00
107-(Scarce)-1st mystery issue; Toth art	5.00	10.00	15.00
108,109-(Scarce)-J. Peril by Toth	5.00	10.00	15.00

NOTE: *Krigstein stories(Wildcat)-#81,84.*
Moldoff Black Pirate-#1-25. Wonder Woman by
H. C. Peter, all issues except #17,19,21.

SENSATION MYSTERY (Sensation #1-109)
#110, Jul-Aug, 1952 - #117, Sept-Oct, 1953
National Periodical Publications

	Good	Fine	Mint
#110-113-Johnny Peril continues, ends #117	2.50	5.00	7.50
114-117-Toth J. Peril in all	3.00	6.00	9.00

NOTE: *Anderson stories-#111,113,116. Giunta*
story-#112. G.Kane covers-#112,113. Infantino
stories-#111,112,114,116; cover-#116.

SERGEANT BARNEY BARKER (G.I. Tales #4 on)
Aug, 1956 - #3, Dec, 1956
Atlas Comics (MCI)

	Good	Fine	Mint
#1-Four Severin stories	1.75	3.50	5.25
2,3-" " "	1.20	2.40	3.60

SGT. BILKO (Phil Silvers) (TV)
May-June, 1957 - #18, Mar-Apr, 1960
National Periodical Publications

#1	2.00	4.00	6.00
2-5	1.20	2.40	3.60
6-18	.90	1.80	2.70

SGT. BILKO'S PRIVATE DOBERMAN (TV)
June-July, 1958 - #11, Feb-Mar, 1960
National Periodical Publications

#1	2.00	4.00	6.00
2-5	1.00	2.00	3.00
6-11	.60	1.20	1.80

SGT. DICK CARTER (See U.S. Border Patrol)

SGT. FURY (& His Howling Commandos)
May, 1963 - Present
Marvel Comics Group

#1-1st app. Sgt. Fury; Kirby art	15.00	30.00	45.00
2-Kirby art	8.00	16.00	24.00
3-5: #3-Reed Richards x-over. #4-Death of Junior Juniper. #5-1st Baron Strucker app; Kirby art	3.00	6.00	9.00
6,7-Kirby art	2.25	4.50	6.75
8-10: #8-Baron Zemo, 1st Percival Pinkerton app. #10-1st app. Capt. Savage (the Skipper)	1.75	3.50	5.25
11,12,14-20: #14-1st Blitz Squad. #18-Death of Pamela Hawley	1.00	2.00	3.00
13-Captain America app.; Kirby art	1.75	3.50	5.25
21-30: #25-Red Skull app. #27-1st Eric Koenig app.	.60	1.20	1.80
31-40: #34-Origin Howling Commandos	.45	.90	1.35
41-60: #44-Flashback of Howlers 1st mission	.30	.60	.90
61-100: #64-Capt. Savage & Raiders x-over. #76-Fury's Father app. in WWI story. #98-Deadly Dozen x-over. #89-Origin Fury's eye patch. #100-Captain America, Fantastic Four cameos	.25	.50	.75
101-Origin retold	.25	.50	.75
102-120: #113-Reprints	.20	.40	.60
121-149-Reprints	.20	.40	
Annual #1('65)-Reprints origin Shield			

Sensation Comics #24. © DC

Sensation Mystery #116. © DC

Sgt. Bilko #15. © DC

Seven Seas Comics =5. © Universal Phoenix

The Shadow #3. © DC

Shadow Comics =4. © S&S

(Sgt. Fury cont'd)	Good	Fine	Mint
	1.20	2.40	3.60
Special #2-7('66-11/71)	.50	1.00	1.50

NOTE: *Ditko inks-#15. Kirby stories-Special #5. Severin story-#44,48, inks-#49-79. Reprints in #80,82,85,87,89,91,93,95,99,101, 103,105,107,109,111.*

SGT. PRESTON OF THE YUKON (TV)
1951 - #29, Nov-Jan, 1958-59
Dell Publishing Co.

4-Color #344,373,397('52),419			
	2.00	4.00	6.00
#5-10	1.50	3.00	4.50
11-29: #13-Origin	1.35	2.75	4.00

SERGEANT PRESTON OF THE YUKON
1956   (4 comic booklets)(7x2½" & 5x2½")
Giveaways with Quaker Cereals

each......	2.50	5.00	7.50

SGT. ROCK (Formerly Our Army at War)
#302, March, 1977 - Present
National Periodical Publications/DC Comics

#302-323: #318-reprints	.20	.40	.60

NOTE: *Most have Kubert covers.*

SGT. ROCK SPECIAL (See DC Special Series #3)

SGT. ROCK SPECTACULAR (See DC Spec.Series#13)

SGT. ROCK'S PRIZE BATTLE TALES
March, 1964   (One Shot) (Giant - 52pgs.)
National Periodical Publications

#1	1.50	3.00	4.50

SEVEN DEAD MEN (See Complete Mystery #1)

SEVEN DWARFS (See 4-Color #227,382)

SEVEN SEAS COMICS
Apr, 1946 - #6, 1947 (no month)
Universal Phoenix Features/Leader #6

#1-South Sea Girl by Matt Baker, Capt. Cutlass begin	15.00	30.00	45.00
2,4-6	10.00	20.00	30.00
3-6pg. Feldstein story	12.00	24.00	36.00

NOTE: *Baker stories-#1-6; covers-#3-6.*

1776 (See Charlton Classic Library)

7TH VOYAGE OF SINBAD, THE (See 4-Color #944)

77 SUNSET STRIP (TV)
Jan-Mar, 1960 - #2, Feb, 1963
Dell Publ. Co./Gold Key

	Good	Fine	Mint
4-Color #1066,1106,1159-Toth art			
	2.00	4.00	6.00
4-Color #1211,1263,1291-Manning art;			
#01742-209(9/62)-Manning	1.50	3.00	4.50
#1(11/62-G.K.), #2-Manning art in each			
	1.00	2.00	3.00

77TH BENGAL LANCERS, THE (See 4-Color #791)

SEYMOUR, MY SON (See More Seymour)
Sept, 1963
Archie Publications (Radio Comics)

#1	1.00	2.00	3.00

SHADE, THE CHANGING MAN (See Cancelled Comic
6-7/77 - #8, 8-9/78   Cavalcade)
National Periodical Publ./DC Comics

#1	.25	.50	.75
2-5-Ditko cover/art	.20	.40	.60
6-8	.15	.30	.45

SHADOW, THE
Aug, 1964 - #8, Sept, 1965
Archie Comics (Radio Comics)

#1	1.20	2.40	3.60
2-8	.50	1.00	1.50

SHADOW, THE
Oct-Nov, 1973 - #12, Aug-Sept, 1975
National Periodical Publications

#1-Kaluta art begins	1.00	2.00	3.00
2	.60	1.20	1.80
3-Kaluta/Wrightson story	.80	1.60	2.40
4,6-Kaluta art ends	.50	1.00	1.50
5,7-12	.30	.60	.90

NOTE: *Craig art-#10. Cruz art-#11,12. Kaluta stories-#1-4,6; covers-#1-4,6,10,11. Kubert cover-#9. Robbins art-#5,7-9.*

SHADOW COMICS
March, 1940 - #107, Nov, 1950
Street & Smith Publications

NOTE: *The Shadow began on radio in 1929 and was featured in pulps beginning in 1931.*

V1#1-Shadow, Doc Savage, Bill Barnes, Nick Carter, Frank Merriwell, Iron Munro, the Astonishing Man begin	75.00	150.00	225.00

(Shadow Comics cont'd)   Good   Fine   Mint
  2-The Avenger begins, ends #6; Capt. Fury
    only app.   40.00 80.00 120.00
  3(No#,5/40)-Norgil the Magician app.(also
    #9);Doc Savage ends 30.00 60.00 90.00
  4,5: #4-The Three Musketeers begins, ends
    #8   25.00 50.00 75.00
  6-9: #7-Origin & 1st app. Hooded Wasp &
    Wasplet; series ends V3#8
             17.00 34.00 51.00
  10-Origin The Iron Ghost, ends #11; The
    Dead End Kids begins, ends #13
             17.00 34.00 51.00
  11-Origin The Hooded Wasp & Wasplet retold
             15.00 30.00 45.00
  12   12.00 24.00 36.00
  V2#1,2(11/41)   10.00 20.00 30.00
  3-Origin & 1st app. Supersnipe
             12.00 24.00 36.00
  4,5: #4-Little Nemo story
             10.00 20.00 30.00
  6-Blackstone, the Magician app.,
  7-9   9.00 18.00 27.00
  10-Supersnipe app.   9.00 18.00 27.00
  11,12   9.00 18.00 27.00
  V3#1-12: #10-Doc Savage begins, not in V5#5,
    V6#10-12,V8#4   8.00 16.00 24.00
  V4#1-12   6.00 12.00 18.00
  V5#1-12   5.50 11.00 16.50
  V6#1-8   5.00 10.00 15.00
    9-Intro. Shadow, Jr. 5.00 10.00 15.00
  10-12   5.00 10.00 15.00
  V7#1-12: #2,5-Shadow, Jr. app.; Powell art
             5.00 10.00 15.00
  V8#1-12-Powell art   5.00 10.00 15.00
  V9#1-5(#107)   4.00   8.00 12.00
NOTE: *Powell art in most issues beginning*
V6#11.

SHADOWS FROM BEYOND   (Formerly Unusual Tales)
October, 1966
Charlton Comics

V2#50   .15   .30

SHAGGY DOG & THE ABSENT-MINDED PROFESSOR
(See 4-Color #985 & Movie Comics)

SHANNA, THE SHE-DEVIL
Dec, 1972 - #5, Aug, 1973
Marvel Comics Group

#1-Steranko cover   .40   .80 1.20
2-5: #2-Steranko cover .25   .50   .75

SHARK FIGHTERS, THE   (See 4-Color #762)

SHARP COMICS   (Slightly large size)

Winter, 1945-46 - V1#2, Spring, 1946 (52pgs.)
H. C. Blackerby
             Good   Fine   Mint
V1#1-Origin Dick Royce Planetarian
             7.00 14.00 21.00
  2-Origin The Pioneer, Michael Morgan, Dick
    Royce, Sir Gallagher, Planetarian, Steve
    Hagen, Weeny and Pop app.
             6.00 12.00 18.00

SHARPY FOX
1958; 1963
I.W. Enterprises/Super

#1,2-IW Reprint('58)   .20   .40   .60
#14-Super Reprint('63)   .20   .40   .60

SHAZAM (See Giant Comics to Color & Limited
Collector's Edition)

SHAZAM!
Feb, 1973 - #35, May-June, 1978
National Periodical Publications/DC Comics

#1-1st revival of the original Captain Marvel,
  by C.C. Beck; Capt. Marvel Jr. & Mary
  Marvel x-over   .50 1.00 1.50
2-5   .35   .70 1.05
6,7,9,10-Last Beck ish. .30   .60   .90
8-100pgs.; reprints Capt. Marvel Jr. by
  Raboy; origin/C.M.#80; origin Mary Marvel/
  C.M.#18   .40   .80 1.20
11-Shaffenberger art begins.25 .50   .75
12-17-All 100pgs.   .25   .50   .75
18-24-(reg. size)   .20   .40   .60
25-1st app. Isis   .20   .40   .60
26-30   .15   .30   .45
31-35: #34-New look for Capt. Marvel & Capt.
  Marvel Jr. #35-Newton story
            .15   .30   .45

SHEENA, QUEEN OF THE JUNGLE (See 3-D --)
Spring, 1942 - #18, Winter, 1952-53
Fiction House Magazines

#1-Sheena begins   50.00 100.00 150.00
2   25.00 50.00 75.00
3(1942)   18.00 36.00 54.00
4(Fall,1948)   8.00 16.00 24.00
5(Sum.'49)-#10(Fall,'50) 7.00 14.00 21.00
11-18   5.00 10.00 15.00
IW Reprint #9-reprts.#17 1.75 3.35   5.00

SHERIFF BOB DIXON'S CHUCK WAGON
Nov, 1950
Avon Periodicals

#1-Kinstler art   3.00   6.00   9.00

Shadow Comics #8. © S&S   Shazam! =1. © DC   Sheena Queen Of The Jungle =5. © FH

Sherlock Holmes #1, © CC

Shield Wizard Comics #9, © MLJ

Shocking Mystery Cases #51, © STAR

SHERIFF OF COCHISE, THE
1957   (20 pgs.)   (TV Show)
Mobil Giveaway

	Good	Fine	Mint
Kurt Shaffenberger art	1.50	3.00	4.50

SHERIFF OF TOMBSTONE
Nov, 1958 - #17, Sept, 1961
Charlton Comics

	Good	Fine	Mint
V1#1-Williamson/Severin cover	1.75	3.50	5.25
2-17	.40	.80	1.20

SHERLOCK HOLMES (See 4-Color #1169,1245 &
Spectacular Stories)

SHERLOCK HOLMES (All New Baffling Advs. of)
1955 - 1956
Charlton Comics

	Good	Fine	Mint
#1-Dr. Neff, Ghost Breaker app.			
(#1 only-26pgs.)	3.00	6.00	9.00
2	2.00	4.00	6.00

SHERLOCK HOLMES
Sept-Oct, 1975
National Periodical Publications

	Good	Fine	Mint
#1-Cruz art; Simonson cvr.	.50	1.00	1.50

SHERRY THE SHOWGIRL
July, 1956 - #7, Aug, 1957
Atlas Comics

	Good	Fine	Mint
#1	.80	1.60	2.40
2-7	.40	.80	1.20

SHIELD (Nick Fury & His Agents of --)
Feb, 1973 - #5, Oct, 1973   (See Nick Fury)
Marvel Comics Group

#1-Steranko cover	.35	.70	1.05
2- "	.25	.50	.75
3-5: #1-5 all contain reprints from Strange			
Tales #146-155; #3-5-cover reprints			
	.20	.40	.60

SHIELD WIZARD COMICS
Summer, 1940 - #13, Spring, 1944
MLJ Magazines

#1-Origin The Shield & The Wizard by Irving			
Novick	70.00	140.00	210.00
2-Origin The Shield retold; intro. Wizard's			
sidekick, Roy	40.00	80.00	120.00
3,4	25.00	50.00	75.00
5-Dusty, the Boy Detective begins			

	Good	Fine	Mint
	22.00	44.00	66.00
6-8: #6-Roy the Super Boy begins			
	17.00	34.00	51.00
9,10	15.00	30.00	45.00
11-13	12.00	24.00	36.00

SHIP AHOY
Nov, 1944
Spotlight Publishers

#1-Feldstein story	2.50	5.00	7.50

SHMOO (See Al Capp's-- & Washable Jones &--)

SHOCK (Magazine)
(Reprints from horror comics)(Black & White)
May, 1969 - V3#4, Sept, 1971
Stanley Publications

V1#1-Cover reprint/Weird Tales of the Future			
#7 by Bernard Baily	.50	1.00	1.50
2-Wolverton reprint; cover reprt/Weird			
Chills #1	.50	1.00	1.50
3,5,6	.25	.50	.75
4-Harrison/Williamson reprint/Forbidden			
Worlds #6	.40	.80	1.20
V2#2, V1#8, V2#4-6, V3#1-4	.25	.50	.75

SHOCK DETECTIVE CASES (Formerly Crime Fight-
#20, 9/52 - #23, 3/53   ing Det.)
Star Publications

#20-23-L. B. Cole covers	1.40	2.80	4.20

SHOCK ILLUSTRATED (Magazine format)
Sept-Oct, 1955 - #3, Spring, 1956
E.C. Comics

#1-All by Kamen	4.00	8.00	12.00
2-Williamson story redrawn from Crime Sus-			
penStories #13 + Ingels, Crandall, &			
Evans	5.00	10.00	15.00
3-(Scarce)-Only 100-200 known copies			
bound & distributed	300.00	600.00	900.00
(Prices vary widely on this book)			

SHOCKING MYSTERY CASES (Formerly Thrilling
#50, 9/52 - #60, 10/54   Crime Cases)
Star Publications

#50-Disbrow "Frankenstein" story			
	2.50	5.00	7.50
51-Disbrow story; L.B. Cole cover			
	2.00	4.00	6.00
52-60	1.40	2.80	4.20
NOTE: *L. B. Cole covers.*			

SHOCK SUSPENSTORIES
Feb-Mar, 1952 - #18, Dec-Jan, 1954-55
E. C. Comics

	Good	Fine	Mint
#1-Feldstein cover	50.00	100.00	150.00
2	25.00	50.00	75.00
3,4	17.00	34.00	51.00
5-7	15.00	30.00	45.00
8-Williamson story	20.00	40.00	60.00
9-12	12.00	24.00	36.00
13-Frazetta's only solo story for E.C., 7pgs.			
	27.00	54.00	81.00
14-18	10.00	20.00	30.00

NOTE: *Craig* story-#11; cover-#11. *Crandall* stories-#9-13,15-18. *Davis* stories-#1-5. *Evans* stories-#7,8,14-18; covers-#16-18. *Feldstein* covers-#1,7-9,12. *Ingels* stories-#1,2,6. *Kamen* stories in all. *Krigstein* stories-#14,18. *Orlando* stories-#1,3-7,9,10,12, 16,17. *Wood* stories-#2-15; covers-#2-6,14. #16 contains the famous "Red Dupe" editorial.

SHOGUN WARRIORS
Mar, 1979 - Present
Marvel Comics Group

#1	.15	.30	.45

SHOOK UP (Magazine) (Satire)
November, 1958
Dodsworth Publ. Co.

V1#1	.75	1.50	2.25

SHORT RIBS (See 4-Color Comics #1333)

SHORT STORY COMICS (See Hello Pal, --)

SHORTY SHINER
June, 1956 - #3, Oct, 1956
Dandy Magazine (Charles Biro)

#1	1.00	2.00	3.00
2,3	.60	1.20	1.80

SHOTGUN SLADE (See 4-Color Comics #1111)

SHOWCASE (See Cancelled Comic Cavalcade)
3-4/56 - #93, 9/70; #94, 9/77 - #104, 9/78
National Periodical Publications/DC Comics

#1-Fire Fighters	50.00	100.00	150.00
2-King of the Wild; Kubert art			
	25.00	50.00	75.00
3-The Frogmen	20.00	40.00	60.00
4-Origin The Flash(Silver Age) & The Turtle; Kubert art	200.00	500.00	800.00
5-Manhunters	15.00	30.00	45.00

6-Origin Challengers by Kirby-partly reprinted in Secret Origins #1 & Challs./Unknown #64,65	35.00	70.00	105.00
7-Challengers by Kirby/reprint Challs./Unknown #75	25.00	50.00	75.00
8-The Flash; origin Capt. Cold	60.00	120.00	180.00
9,10-Lois Lane	20.00	40.00	60.00
11,12-Challengers by Kirby	20.00	40.00	60.00
13-The Flash; origin Mr. Element	45.00	90.00	135.00
14-The Flash; origin Dr. Alchemy, former Mr. Element	45.00	90.00	135.00
15,16-Space Ranger	10.00	20.00	30.00
17-Adam Strange	30.00	60.00	90.00
18,19-Adam Strange	20.00	40.00	60.00
20,21-Rip Hunter. #21-Sekowsky cover/art	6.00	12.00	18.00
22-Origin & 1st app. Silver Age Green Lantern by Gil Kane	25.00	50.00	75.00
23,24-Green Lantern	14.00	28.00	42.00
25-Rip Hunter by Kubert	4.00	8.00	12.00
26-Rip Hunter by Kubert	4.00	8.00	12.00
27-29-Sea Devils by Heath, cover/art	2.50	5.00	7.50
30-Origin Aquaman	2.50	5.00	7.50
31-33-Aquaman	2.00	4.00	6.00
34-Origin & 1st app. Silver Age Atom by Kane	4.00	8.00	12.00
35,36-The Atom by G.Kane	2.50	5.00	7.50
37-40-Metal Men	1.50	3.00	4.50
41,42-Tommy Tomorrow	1.00	2.00	3.00
43-Dr. No(James Bond); Nodel art; originally done for Classics Ill. Series (appeared as British Cl. Ill. #158A)	3.00	6.00	9.00
44-Tommy Tomorrow	.80	1.60	2.40
45-Sgt. Rock; Heath cover	1.00	2.00	3.00
46,47-Tommy Tomorrow	.80	1.60	2.40
48,49-Cave Carson	.80	1.60	2.40
50,51-I Spy(Danger Trail reprints by Infantino), Anderson cover inks; King Farady story(not reprint-#50)	.70	1.40	2.10
52-Cave Carson	.70	1.40	2.10
53,54-G.I.Joe-Heath art	.80	1.60	2.10
55,56-Dr. Fate & Hourman	1.00	2.00	3.00
57,58-Enemy Ace by Kubert	1.00	2.00	3.00
59-Teen Titans	.90	1.80	2.70
60-The Spectre by Anderson	1.25	2.50	3.75
61,64-The Spectre " "	1.00	2.00	3.00
62,63,65-Inferior Five	.40	.80	1.20
66,67-B'wana Beast	.40	.80	1.20
68,69-Maniaks	.25	.50	.75
70-Binky	.25	.50	.75
71-Maniaks	.25	.50	.75
72-Top Gun(Johnny Thunder reprints)-Toth art			

Shock SuspenStories #6, © WMG

Showcase #4, © DC

Showcase #15, © DC

Showcase #38, © DC

Showcase #83, © DC

Silver Streak Comics #2, © LEV

(Showcase cont'd)	Good	Fine	Mint
	.40	.80	1.20
73-Creeper by Ditko	1.20	2.40	3.60
74-Anthro	.50	1.00	1.50
75-Hawk & the Dove by Ditko	.80	1.60	2.40
76-Bat Lash	.80	1.60	2.40
77-Angel & Ape	.30	.60	.90
78-Johnny Double	.40	.80	1.20
79-Dolphin	.60	1.20	1.80
80-Phantom Stranger-Neal Adams cover			
	1.00	2.00	3.00
81-Windy & Willy	.25	.50	.75
82-Nightmaster by Grandenetti; Kubert cover			
	.60	1.20	1.80
83,84-Nightmaster by Wrightson in ea.;			
Kubert covers	2.50	5.00	7.50
85-87-Firehair-Kubert art	.90	1.80	2.70
88-90-Jason's Quest	.30	.60	.90
91-93-Manhunter 2070	.30	.60	.90
94-96-The Doom Patrol	.20	.40	.60
97-99-Power Girl	.20	.40	.60
100-(52pgs.)-Feat. most Showcase characters			
	.25	.50	.75
101-103-Hawkman	.25	.50	.75
104-O.S.S Spies at War	.20	.40	.60

NOTE: *Anderson stories-#50,55,56,60,61,64.
Grandenetti story-#80. Infantino art/covers-
#4,8,13,14. Kane art-#22-24,34-36; covers-
#17-19,22-24,31,34-36,101-103. Kirby covers-
#6,7,11,12. Kubert art-#2,25,26,45,53,54,72;
inks-#4; covers-#25,26,53,54,57,58,82-87,
101-104. Orlando art/covers-#62,63,97(inks).
Staton stories-#94-100; covers-#97-100.*

SHOWGIRLS
June, 1957 - #4, Dec, 1957
Atlas Comics

#1-Millie, Sherry, Chili, Pearl & Hazel be-			
gin	1.50	3.00	4.50
2-4	1.20	2.40	3.60

SICK (Magazine) (Satire)
Aug, 1960 - Present
Feature Publ./Headline Publ./Crestwood Publ.
Co./Hewfred Publ./Pyramid Comm./Charlton Publ.

V1#1-Torres art	3.00	6.00	9.00
2-5-Torres art in all	2.00	4.00	6.00
6	1.50	3.00	4.50
V2#1-8(#7-14)	1.00	2.00	3.00
V3#1-8(#15-22)	.70	1.40	2.10
V4#1-5(#23-27)	.60	1.20	1.80
#28-40	.40	.80	1.20
41-105	.25	.50	.75
Annual 1971	.40	.80	1.20
Annual #2	.35	.70	1.05

NOTE: *Davis covers/stories in most issues of*

#16-27,30-32,34,35. *Simon art-#1-3. Torres
art-V2#7, V4#2. Civil War Blackouts-#23,24.*

SILK HAT HARRY'S DIVORCE SUIT
1912   (5-3/4"x15-1/2")   (B&W)
M. A. Donoghue & Co.

	Good	Fine	Mint
Newspaper reprints by Tad (Thomas Dorgan)			
	10.00	20.00	30.00

SILLY PILLY (See Frank Luther's --)

SILLY SYMPHONIES (Walt Disney)
Sept, 1952 - 1959   (All Giants)
Dell Publishing Co.

#1-Reprints 3 Little Pigs & M. Mouse in "The			
Brave Little Tailor"	7.00	14.00	21.00
2-Mickey Mouse "The Sorcerer's Apprentice"			
	6.00	12.00	18.00
3-(4-Color #71)(not Duck portion),(4-Color			
#157)	6.00	12.00	18.00
4-(4-Color #234)	4.00	8.00	12.00
5-(4-Color Cinderella)	4.00	8.00	12.00
6-Pinocchio (WDC&S #63)& 7 Dwarfs (WDC&S			
#45)	5.00	10.00	15.00
7-(4-Color #13)	6.00	12.00	18.00
8-(4-Color #19)	5.00	10.00	15.00
9	4.00	8.00	12.00

NOTE: *All reprints with some possibly redrawn.*

SILLY TUNES
Fall, 1945 - #7, April, 1947
Timely Comics

#1	2.00	4.00	6.00
2-7	1.50	3.00	4.50

SILVER (See Lone Ranger's Horse --)

SILVER KID WESTERN
Oct, 1954 - 1955
Key/Stanmor Publications

#1	1.00	2.00	3.00
2-5	.60	1.20	1.80
IW Reprint #1,2	.35	.70	1.05

SILVER STREAK COMICS
Dec, 1939 - May, 1942; 1946
Comic House Publ./Newsbook Publ.

#1-Intro. The Claw(reprt. Daredevil #21),Red			
Reeves, Boy Magician, & Captain Fearless;			
The Wasp, Mister Midnight begin; Spirit			
Man app.	150.00	300.00	450.00
2-Simon cover	75.00	150.00	225.00
3-1st app. & origin Silver Streak; Dickie			

```
(Silver Streak cont'd)     Good   Fine   Mint
    Dean, the Boy Inventor, Lance Hale, Ace
    Powers, Bill Wayne, & The Planet Patrol
    begin              90.00 180.00 270.00
4-Sky Wolf begins; Silver Streak by Jack
    Cole; Intro. Jackie, Lance Hale's sidekick
                       45.00  90.00 135.00
5-Jack Cole cvr/story  55.00 110.00 165.00
6-(Scarce)-Origin & 1st app. Daredevil by
    Jack Binder; Cole cover
                      325.00 650.00 975.00
    (Prices vary widely on this book)
7-Claw vs. Daredevil by Jack Cole & 3 other
    Cole stys.(38pgs.) 130.00 260.00 390.00
8-Claw vs. Daredevil by Cole; last Cole
    Silver Streak      75.00 150.00 225.00
9-Claw vs. Daredevil by Cole
                       55.00 110.00 165.00
10-Origin Captain Battle; Claw vs. Daredevil
    by Cole            40.00  80.00 120.00
11-Intro. Mercury, Silver Streak's sidekick;
    conclusion Claw vs. Daredevil by Rico
                       35.00  70.00 105.00
12-14: #12-Intro. Hale. #13-Origin Thun-Dohr
                       30.00  60.00  90.00
15-17-Last Daredevil ish.25.00  50.00  75.00
18-The Saint begins    20.00  40.00  60.00
19-21(1942): #20,21 have Wolverton's Scoop
    Scuttle            15.00  30.00  45.00
22-24(1946)-reprints    9.00  18.00  27.00

No#(11/46)(Newsbook Publ.)-Reprints SS story
    from #4-7 + 2 Captain Fearless stories-
    all in color       20.00  40.00  60.00
NOTE: Jack Cole art: (Daredevil)-#6-10,
(Dickie Dean)-#3-10, (Pirate Prince)-#7,
(Silver Streak)-#4-8, (Silver Streak cover)-
#5. Mac Raboy Lance Hale-#6. Don Rico Dare-
devil-#11-17. Simon Silver Streak-#3. Bob
Wood Silver Streak-#9. Claw covers-#1,2,6-8;
by Cole-#6-8.

SILVER SURFER  (See Fantastic Four)
Aug, 1968 - #18, Sept, 1970 (#1-7, 68pgs.)
Marvel Comics Group

#1-Origin Silver Surfer by John Buscema; Wat-
    cher begins, ends #7 14.00  28.00  42.00
2                       7.00  14.00  21.00
3-1st app. Mephisto     5.00  10.00  15.00
4-Low distribution; Thor app.
                        8.00  16.00  24.00
5-7-Last giant size. #5-The Stranger app.
    #6-Brunner inks. #7-Brunner cover
                        4.00   8.00  12.00
8-10                    3.00   6.00   9.00
11-18: #14-Spider-Man x-over. #18-Kirby
    art/cover           2.00   4.00   6.00
```

SILVERTIP (Max Brand)
1953 - 1958
Dell Publishing Co.

```
                           Good   Fine   Mint
4-Color #491,608,637,731,898-Kinstler art
                           2.00   4.00   6.00
4-Color #572,667,789,835   1.40   2.80   4.20
```

SINBAD, JR. (TV Cartoon)
Sept-Nov, 1965 - #3, May, 1966
Dell Publishing Co.

```
#1                          .50   1.00   1.50
2,3                         .35    .70   1.05
```

SINBAD (See Movie Comics: Capt. Sindbad;
& Fantastic Voyages of Sindbad)

SINGING GUNS (See Fawcett Movie Comics)

SINGLE SERIES (Comics on Parade #30 on)
1938 - 1940 (Also see John Hix --)
United Features Syndicate

```
#1-Captain & the Kids   17.50  35.00  52.50
 2-Broncho Bill(1939)   12.00  24.00  36.00
 3-Ella Cinders         10.00  20.00  30.00
 4-Li'l Abner(1939)     17.50  35.00  52.50
 5-Fritzi Ritz           7.00  14.00  21.00
 6-Jim Hardy by Dick Moores
                        10.00  20.00  30.00
 7-Frankie Doodle        7.00  14.00  21.00
 8-Peter Pat             7.00  14.00  21.00
 9-Strange As It Seems   6.00  12.00  18.00
10-Little Mary Mixup     7.00  14.00  21.00
11-Mr. & Mrs. Beans      5.00  10.00  15.00
12-Joe Jinks             7.00  14.00  21.00
13-Looy Dot Dope         6.00  12.00  18.00
14-Billy Make Believe    6.00  12.00  18.00
15-How It Began('39)     7.00  14.00  21.00
16-Illustrated Gags('40) 3.50   7.00  10.50
17-Danny Dingle          5.00  10.00  15.00
18-Li'l Abner           15.00  30.00  45.00
19-Broncho Bill(#2 on cvr)8.00  16.00  24.00
20-Tarzan by Hal Foster 120.00 240.00 360.00
21-Ella Cinders(#2 on cvr)8.00  16.00  24.00
22-Iron Vic              7.00  14.00  21.00
23-Tailspin Tommy by Hal Forrest
                        10.00  20.00  30.00
24-Alice in Wonderland  12.00  24.00  36.00
25-Abbie & Slats         9.00  18.00  27.00
26-Little Mary Mixup     7.00  14.00  21.00
27-Jim Hardy by Dick Moores
                         8.00  16.00  24.00
28-Ella Cinders & Abbie & Slats
                         9.00  18.00  27.00
 1-Captain & the Kids (1939 reprint)
                        12.00  24.00  36.00
```

Silver Streak Comics #14, © LEV

Silver Surfer #4, © MCG

Single Series #24, © UFS

Six-Gun Heroes #1, © FAW   Skeleton Hand #2, © ACG   Skippy's O.B. Of Comics #1, © Percy Crosby

(Single Series cont'd)   Good   Fine   Mint
1-Fritzi Ritz(1939 reprint) 2nd edition
                 6.00   12.00   18.00
NOTE: *Some issues given away at the 1939-40
New York World's Fair(#6).*

SINISTER HOUSE OF SECRET LOVE, THE
(Secrets of Sinister House #5 on)
Oct-Nov, 1971 - #4, Apr-May, 1972
National Periodical Publications

	Good	Fine	Mint
#1	.40	.80	1.20
2,4	.25	.50	.75
3-Toth story, 36pgs.	.50	1.00	1.50

SIR LANCELOT (See 4-Color Comics #606,775)

SIR WALTER RALEIGH (See 4-Color #644)

6 BLACK HORSES (See Movie Classics)

SIX-GUN HEROES
March, 1950 - #23, Nov, 1953
Fawcett Publications

#1-Rocky Lane, Hopalong Cassidy, Smiley
    Burnette begin   7.00   14.00   21.00
2   5.00   10.00   15.00
3-10: #6-Lash Larue begins
                 3.50   7.00   10.50
11-23   2.25   4.50   6.75

SIX-GUN HEROES (Cont'd. from Fawcett)
(Becomes Gunmasters #84 on)
Jan, 1954 - #83, Mar-Apr, 1965
Charlton Comics

V4#24-46: Tom Mix, Lash Larue
                 1.50   3.00   4.50
   47-Williamson story, 2pgs. + Torres
                 2.50   5.00   7.50
   48,50-75,82   .50   1.00   1.50
   49-Williamson sty,5pgs.2.25   4.50   6.75
   76-81,83-Gunmaster in all
                 .40   .80   1.20

SIXGUN RANCH (See 4-Color Comics #580)

SIX-GUN WESTERN
Jan, 1957 - 1958
Atlas Comics (CDS)

#1-Crandall art   2.50   5.00   7.50
2,3,7-Williamson stories in all; Powell
    story in #3   2.50   5.00   7.50
4-Woodbridge story   1.20   2.40   3.60
5,6,8-10   1.00   2.00   3.00
11-Williamson story   2.50   5.00   7.50

SIX MILLION DOLLAR MAN (Magazine)
June, 1976 - Present   (B&W)
Charlton Comics

	Good	Fine	Mint
#1-Adams cover/art	.60	1.20	1.80
2-Adams cover	.50	1.00	1.50
3-8	.40	.80	1.20

SIX MILLION DOLLAR MAN
June, 1976 - #4, Jan, 1977; #5, Oct, 1977;
#6, Feb, 1978 - #9, June, 1978
Charlton Comics

#1-Staton cover/stories	.35	.70	1.05
2-Adams cover	.30	.60	.90
3-9	.20	.40	.60

SKATING SKILLS
1957   (36 pgs.) (5x7") (10¢)
Custom Comics, Inc.
Chicago Roller Skates

Resembles old ACG cover + interior art
                 .60   1.20   1.80

SKEEZIX
1925 - 1928 (Strip reprints) (Soft covers)
Reilly & Lee Co.   (Pictures & text)

-- and Pal(1925)   7.00   14.00   21.00
-- at the Circus(1926)   7.00   14.00   21.00
-- & Uncle Walt(1927)   7.00   14.00   21.00
-- Out West(1928)   7.00   14.00   21.00
Hardback Editions...   10.00   20.00   30.00

SKELETON HAND(--In Secrets of the Supernatural)
Sept-Oct, 1952 - #6, July-Aug, 1953
American Comics Group (B&M Dist. Co.)

#1	1.50	3.00	4.50
2-6	1.00	2.00	3.00

SKI PARTY (See Movie Classics)

SKIPPY
1925 (68pgs.) (Hardcover-in color) (8½x11")
Greenberg Publ.

Panel & strips   10.00   20.00   30.00

SKIPPY'S OWN BOOK OF COMICS
1934   (52 pgs.) (Giveaway)
No publisher listed

No#-(Rare)-Strip reprints by Percy Crosby
          100.00 200.00 300.00
Published by Max C. Gaines for Phillip's Dental Magnesia to be
advertised on the Skippy Radio Show and given away with the
purchase of a tube of Phillip's Tooth Paste. 500,000 copies
printed. This is the first four-color comic book of reprints about
one character.

SKULL THE SLAYER
August, 1975 - #8, Nov, 1976
Marvel Comics Group

	Good	Fine	Mint
#1-Origin	.25	.50	.75
2-5	.20	.40	.60
6-8	.15	.30	.45

SKY BLAZERS (Radio)
Sept, 1940 - #2, Nov, 1940
Hawley Publications

	Good	Fine	Mint
#1-Sky Pirates, Ace Archer, Flying Aces			
begin	10.00	20.00	30.00
2	6.00	12.00	18.00

SKY KING "RUNAWAY TRAIN"
1964   (16 pgs.) (Regular Size)
National Biscuit Co.

	.80	1.60	2.40

SKYMAN (See Big Shot)
1941 - #4, 1948
Columbia Comics Group

	Good	Fine	Mint
#1-Origin Skyman, The Face app.; Whitney art			
	20.00	40.00	60.00
2-Yankee Doodle	10.00	20.00	30.00
3,4	8.00	16.00	24.00

SKY PILOT
1950 (Painted covers by Norman Saunders)
Ziff-Davis Publ. Co.

#10,11-Frank Borth art	2.00	4.00	6.00

SKY RANGER (See Johnny Law —)

SKYROCKET
1944
Harry 'A' Chesler

#1-Atlas the Dragon, Dr. Vampire, Skyrocket			
app.	5.00	10.00	15.00

SKY SHERIFF (See Breeze Lawson —)

SLAM BANG COMICS (Western Desperado #8)
March, 1940 - #7, Sept, 1940
Fawcett Publications

#1-Diamond Jack, Mark Swift & The Time Retarder, Lee Granger, Jungle King begin			
	30.00	60.00	90.00
2	15.00	30.00	45.00
3	12.00	24.00	36.00
4-7	10.00	20.00	30.00

SLAM BANG COMICS
No date
Post Cereal Giveaway

	Good	Fine	Mint
#9-Dynamic Man, Echo, Mr. E, Yankee Boy app.			
	2.00	4.00	6.00

SLAPSTICK COMICS
No date (1946?) (36 pgs.)
Comic Magazine Publishers

#1-Firetop feature	2.00	4.00	6.00

SLAVE GIRL COMICS (See Malu —)
Feb, 1949 - #2, Apr, 1949
Avon Periodicals

#1	30.00	60.00	90.00
2	25.00	50.00	75.00

SLEEPING BEAUTY (See 4-Color #973,984, Movie Classics & Comics)

SLICK CHICK COMICS
1947
Leader Enterprises

#1	2.50	5.00	7.50
2,3	2.00	4.00	6.00

SLIM MORGAN (See Wisco)

SLUGGER (of the Little Wise Guys)
April, 1956
Lev Gleason Publications

#1	1.20	2.40	3.60

SMASH COMICS (Lady Luck #86 on)
Aug, 1939 - #85, Oct, 1949
Quality Comics Group

#1-Origin Hugh Hazard & His Iron Man, Bozo the Robot, Espionage, Starring Black X by Eisner & Invisible Justice; Chic Carter & Wings Wendell begin	45.00	90.00	135.00
2-The Lone Star Rider app.			
	20.00	40.00	60.00
3	15.00	30.00	45.00
4,5	12.00	24.00	36.00
6-12	10.00	20.00	30.00
13-Magno begins; last Eisner issue			
	10.00	20.00	30.00
14-Intro. The Ray by Lou Fine & others			
	90.00	180.00	270.00
15-17	40.00	80.00	120.00
18-Origin Midnight by Jack Cole			
	60.00	120.00	180.00

Skyrocket #1, © CHES

Slave Girl #2, © AVON

Smash Comics #14, © QUA

Smash Comics #19. © QUA

Smiley Burnette Western #1. © FAW

Smilin' Jack #5. © N.Y. News Synd.

	Good	Fine	Mint
(Smash Comics cont'd)			
19-22: Last Fine Ray; The Jester begins-#22			
	30.00	60.00	90.00
23,24: #24-The Sword app.; last Chic Carter;			
Wings Wendell dons costume #24,25			
	25.00	50.00	75.00
25-Origin Wildfire	27.00	54.00	81.00
26-29,31	25.00	50.00	75.00
30-Classic Lou Fine Ray	30.00	60.00	90.00
32,34: Ray by Rudy Palais; also #33			
	17.00	34.00	51.00
33-Origin The Marksman	18.00	36.00	54.00
35-37	15.00	30.00	45.00
38-The Yankee Eagle begins; last Midnight by			
Jack Cole	15.00	30.00	45.00
39,40-Last Ray issue	12.00	24.00	36.00
41,43-50	6.00	12.00	18.00
42-Lady Luck begins	7.00	14.00	21.00
51-60	5.00	10.00	15.00
61-70	4.00	8.00	12.00
71-85	3.50	7.00	10.50

NOTE: *Cole* stories-(*Midnight*)#18-38,68-85;
covers-#38,60,61. *Crandall* stories-(*Ray*)#23-
29,35-38; covers-#36,39,40,43,44,46. *Fine*
stories-(*Ray*)#14-22,30,31. *Fuji* story-#30.
Guardineer stories-(The Marksman)#39-? Gustavson stories-(The Jester)#22-46; (*Magno*)#13-
21; (*Midnight*)#39(Cole inks). *Kotzky* stories-
(*Espionage*)#33-38; covers-#45,47. *Powell* stor-
ies-(*Abdul the Arab*)#13-24.

SMASH HIT SPORTS COMICS
1949
Essankay Publishing Co.

V2#1	.75	1.50	2.25

S'MATTER POP?
1917 (44pgs.)(B&W)(10x14")(Cardboard covers)
Saalfield Publ. Co.

By Charlie Payne; ½ in full color; pages			
printed on one side	8.00	16.00	24.00

SMILE COMICS (Also see Tickle & Gay Comics)
1955 (52 pgs.) (5x7¼") (7¢)
Modern Store Publ.

#1	.60	1.20	1.80

SMILEY BURNETTE WESTERN
March, 1950 - #4, Oct, 1950
Fawcett Publications

#1	5.00	10.00	15.00
2-4	3.00	6.00	9.00

SMILIN' JACK (See Super Book #1,2,7,19)

1941 - #8, Oct-Dec, 1949
Dell Publishing Co.

	Good	Fine	Mint
4-Color #5,10('40)	27.00	54.00	81.00
Black & White#12,14('41)	15.00	37.50	60.00
Large Feature Comic #25('41)			
	15.00	37.50	60.00
4-Color #4('42)	25.00	50.00	75.00
4-Color #14('43)	22.00	44.00	66.00
4-Color #36,58('43-'44)	10.00	20.00	30.00
4-Color #80('45)	8.00	16.00	24.00
4-Color #149('47)	6.00	12.00	18.00
#1(1-3/48)	6.00	12.00	18.00
2-8(10-12/49)	3.50	7.00	10.50
Popped Wheat Giveaway-(1936,38,40 reprints)			
16pgs. in full color(1947)			
	1.25	2.50	3.75
Shoe Store Giveaway-('36 reprints)-16pgs.			
	4.00	8.00	12.00
Sparked Wheat Giveaway(1942)-16 pgs. in full			
color	3.50	7.00	10.50

SMILING SPOOK SPUNKY (See Spunky)

SMITTY (See Treasure Box of Famous Comics)
1929 - 1932 (B&W newspaper strip reprints)
(Cardboard covers; 9½x9½", 52pgs; 7x8¼", 36pgs)
Cupples & Leon Co.

1929-At the Ball Game, 1930-The Flying Office			
Boy, 1931-The Jockey, 1932-In the North Woods			
each....	8.00	16.00	24.00
Mid 1930's issue(reprint of 1928 Treasure			
Box issue, 36pgs., 7x8-3/4")			
	6.00	12.00	18.00
Hardback Editions(100pgs., 7x8¼") with dust			
jacket each....	12.00	24.00	36.00

SMITTY (See Super Book #2 & #4)
1940 - 1949
Dell Publishing Co.

4-Color #11(1940)	13.50	26.75	40.00
Large Feature Comic #26('41)			
	8.00	20.00	32.00
4-Color #6('42)	10.00	20.00	30.00
4-Color #32('43)	6.00	12.00	18.00
4-Color #65('45)	5.00	10.00	15.00
4-Color #99('46)	4.00	8.00	12.00
4-Color #138('47)	3.00	6.00	9.00
#1(1948)	3.00	6.00	9.00
2-4(1949)	1.75	3.35	5.00
5-7(1949)	1.50	3.00	4.50
4-Color #909	1.00	2.00	3.00

SMOKEY BEAR (TV)
Feb, 1970 - #13, Mar, 1973
Gold Key

369

(Smokey Bear cont'd)

	Good	Fine	Mint
#1		.15	.35
2-13		.10	.20

(See March of Comics #362,372,383,407)

SMOKEY STOVER (See Super Book #5,17,29)

SMOKEY STOVER FIREFIGHTER OF FOO
1937 (64pgs.-5½x7½"-B&W reprints)(Hardcover)
Whitman Publ. Co.

	Good	Fine	Mint
	6.00	12.00	18.00

SMOKEY STOVER
1942 - 1943
Dell Publishing Co.

	Good	Fine	Mint
4-Color #7('42-reprints)	15.00	30.00	45.00
4-Color #35('43)	8.00	16.00	24.00
4-Color #64('44)	5.00	10.00	15.00
4-Color #229	2.00	4.00	6.00
4-Color #730,827	1.50	3.00	4.50
General Motors giveaway('53)			
	2.50	5.00	7.50
National Fire Protection giveaway('53)-16pgs.			
	2.50	5.00	7.50

SMOKEY THE BEAR
Oct, 1955 - 1961
Dell Publishing Co.

	Good	Fine	Mint
4-Color #653,708,754,818,932			
	.80	1.60	2.40
4-Color #1016,1119,1214	.60	1.20	1.80
True Story of --, The('59)-U.S. Forest Serv- ice giveaway-Publ. by Western Printing Co. (reprinted in '64 & '69) Reprints 1st 16pgs. 4-Color #932	.50	1.00	1.50

(See March of Comics #234)

SMOKY (See Movie Classics)

SNAFU
Nov, 1955 - #3, March, 1956
Atlas Comics (RCM)

	Good	Fine	Mint
#1-Heath/Severin art	3.00	6.00	9.00
2,3-Severin art	2.00	4.00	6.00

SNAGGLEPUSS (TV)
Oct, 1962 - #4, Sept, 1963 (Hanna-Barbera)
Gold Key

	Good	Fine	Mint
#1	.15	.30	.45
2-4		.15	.30

SNAP (Jest #10?)
1944

Harry 'A' Chesler

	Good	Fine	Mint
#9-Manhunter, The Voice	2.50	5.00	7.50

SNAPPY COMICS
1945
Cima Publ. Co. (Prize Publ.)

	Good	Fine	Mint
#1-Airmale app.	1.75	3.50	5.25

SNARKY PARKER (See Life with --)

SNIFFY THE PUP
#5, Nov, 1949 - #18, Sept, 1953
Standard Publications (Animated Cartoons)

	Good	Fine	Mint
#5-Two Frazetta text illustrations			
	1.75	3.50	5.25
6-10	.65	1.35	2.00
11-18	.50	1.00	1.50

SNOOPER AND BLABBER DETECTIVES (TV)
Nov, 1962 - #3, May, 1963 (Hanna-Barbera)
Gold Key

	Good	Fine	Mint
#1-3	.15	.30	.45

(See Whitman Comic Books)

SNOW FOR CHRISTMAS
1957 (16 pgs.) (Giveaway)
W. T. Grant Co.

	Good	Fine	Mint
	1.00	2.00	3.00

SNOW WHITE (See 4-Color #49,227,382 & Movie Comics)

SNOW WHITE AND THE SEVEN DWARFS
1952 (32 pgs.) (5x7¼") (Disney)
Bendix Washing Machines

	Good	Fine	Mint
	5.00	10.00	15.00

SNOW WHITE AND THE 7 DWARFS IN "MILKY WAY"
1955 (16pgs.) (Disney Premium)
American Dairy Association

	Good	Fine	Mint
	4.00	8.00	12.00

SNOW WHITE AND THE SEVEN DWARFS
1957 (Small Size)
Promotional Publ. Co.

	Good	Fine	Mint
	2.50	5.00	7.50

SNOW WHITE AND THE SEVEN DWARFS
1958 (16 pgs.) (Disney Premium)
Western Printing Co.

Smitty #7, © N.Y. News Synd.

Snagglepuss #1, © GK

Snappy #1, © PRIZE

Soldier Comics #7. © FAW   Soldiers Of Fortune #2. © ACG   Space Adventures V3#57. © CC

(Snow White & the Seven Dwarfs cont'd)

	Good	Fine	Mint
"Mystery of the Missing Magic"			
	3.00	6.00	9.00

SOJOURN ($1.50)
9/77 - #2, 1978 (Full tabloid size)(Color &
White Cliffs Publ. Co.   B&W)

#1-Tor by Kubert, Eagle by Severin, E.V. Race,
   Private Investigator by Doug Wildey, T. C.
   Mars by S. Aragones begin plus other strips,

2	.50	1.00	1.50

SOLDIER & MARINE COMICS
#11, Dec, 1954 - V2#9, Dec, 1956
Charlton Comics (Toby Press of Conn. V1#11)

V1#11(12/54)-#13(4/55)	.80	1.60	2.40
V1#14(6/55), #15,V2#9	.80	1.60	2.40

NOTE: _Bob Powell_ story-#11.

SOLDIER COMICS
Jan, 1952 - #11, Sept, 1953
Fawcett Publications

#1	1.50	3.00	4.50
2-5	.90	1.80	2.70
6-11	.70	1.40	2.10

SOLDIER OF FORTUNE (See Chewing Gum Booklet)

SOLDIERS OF FORTUNE
Feb-Mar, 1951 - #13, Feb-Mar, 1953
American Comics Group(Creston Publ. Corp.)

#1-Capt. Crossbones by Shelly, Ace Carter,			
Lance Larsen begin	2.00	4.00	6.00
2-10	1.25	2.50	3.75
11-13(War format)	1.00	2.00	3.00
Giant(1951)	1.75	3.50	5.25

NOTE: _Shelly_ art-#1-3,5. _Whitney_ art-#6,8-13;
covers-#1-3,6.

SOLOMON AND SHEBA (See 4-Color #1070)

SONG OF THE SOUTH (See 4-Color #693 & Brer
Rabbit)

SON OF BLACK BEAUTY (See 4-Color #510,566)

SON OF FLUBBER (See Movie Comics)

SON OF SATAN
Dec, 1975 - #8, Feb, 1977
Marvel Comics Group

#1-Starlin pencils, 1pg.	.50	1.00	1.50

	Good	Fine	Mint
2-Origin The Professor	.25	.50	.75
3-8: #8-Heath art	.20	.40	.60

SON OF SINBAD
February, 1950
St. John Publishing Co.

#1-Kubert cover/art	15.00	30.00	45.00

SON OF TOMAHAWK (See Tomahawk)

SON OF VULCAN (Mysteries of Unexplored
Worlds #1-48; Thunderbolt, V3#51 on)
Nov, 1965 - V2#50, Jan, 1966
Charlton Comics

#49,50	.50	1.00	1.50

SONS OF KATIE ELDER (See Movie Classics)

SORCERY (See Chilling Adventures in-- & Red
Circle --)

SORORITY SECRETS
July, 1954
Toby Press

#1	1.50	3.00	4.50

SOUPY SALES COMIC BOOK (The Official --)
1965
Archie Publications

#1	2.00	4.00	6.00

SPACE ACE (Jet #1; Jet Powers #2-4)
1952
Magazine Enterprises

#5(A-1#61)-Guardineer art	5.00	10.00	15.00

SPACE ACTION
June, 1952 - #3, Oct, 1952
Ace Magazines (Junior Books)

#1	2.00	4.00	6.00
2,3	1.25	2.50	3.75

SPACE ADVENTURES
7/52 - #59, 11/64; V3#60, 10/67; V1#1,
5/68 - V1#8, 7/69; #9, 5/78 - Present
Capitol Stories/Charlton Comics

#1	3.50	7.00	10.50
2-5	2.00	4.00	6.00
6-12	1.50	3.00	4.50
13,14-Blue Beetle (Fox reprints, 10-11/54 -			
#14, 12-1/54-55)	3.50	7.00	10.50

(Space Adventures cont'd) Good Fine Mint
15,17-19: #15-18-Rocky Jones
                           1.25 2.50 3.75
16-Krigstein story; Rocky Jones app.
                           2.00 4.00 6.00
20-Reprints Fawcett's "Destination Moon"
                           3.00 6.00 9.00
21-32: #23-Reprints Fawcett's "Space Trip to
    the Moon"   1.00 2.00 3.00
33-Origin & 1st app. Captain Atom by Steve
    Ditko   3.00 6.00 9.00
34-40,42-All Capt. Atom   2.00 4.00 6.00
41,43,46-59   .35   .70 1.05
44,45-Mercury Man in ea.   .50 1.00 1.50
V2#60(10/67)-Origin Paul Mann & The Saucers
    from the Future   .25   .50   .75
#1('68)   .25   .50   .75
 2-8('69)   .20   .40   .60
 9-12('78)-Capt. Atom reprints by Ditko
                           .20   .40   .60
NOTE: *Ditko stories-#10,11,16,24,25-27,29,31,
32,34,35,38,40,#2('68); covers-#10,12. Shuster story-#11.*

SPACE BUSTERS
Spring, 1952 - #3, Fall, 1952 (Painted covers
Ziff-Davis Publ. Co.   by Norman Saunders)

#1-Krigstein art   6.00 12.00 18.00
 2,3   4.00 8.00 12.00
NOTE: *Anderson stories-#2.*

SPACE CADET (See Tom Corbett, --)

SPACE COMICS
#4, Mar-Apr, 1954 - #5, May-June, 1954
Avon Periodicals

#4,5-Space Mouse, Peter Rabbit, Super Pup, &
    Merry Mouse app.   1.00 2.00 3.00
IW Reprint #8-No date-Space Mouse reprints
                           .40   .80 1.20

SPACE DETECTIVE
July, 1951 - #4, July, 1952
Avon Periodicals

#1-Red Hathway, Space Det. begins, ends #4;
    Wood cover/3 stories, 23pgs.; Drug story
                          35.00 70.00 105.00
 2-Tales from the Shadow Squad begins; Wood/
    Orlando cover   17.00 34.00 51.00
 3,4: #3-Kinstler cover   5.00 10.00 15.00
IW Reprint #1(reprts.#2),8(reprts.cover #1 &
    part Famous Funnies #191)
                          1.20 2.40 3.60
IW Reprint #9   1.20 2.40 3.60

SPACE EXPLORER (See March of Comics #202)

SPACE FAMILY ROBINSON (--Lost in Space #15
on) (Lost in Space #37 on)
Dec, 1962 - #36, Oct, 1969
Gold Key

                          Good Fine Mint
#1   5.00 10.00 15.00
 2(3/63)   1.75 3.50 5.25
 3-10   1.00 2.00 3.00
11-20   .60 1.20 1.80
21-36   .50 1.00 1.50
NOTE: *Idea created by Carl Barks.*

SPACE FAMILY ROBINSON (See March of Comics
#320,328,352,404)

SPACE GHOST (TV)
March, 1967   (Hanna-Barbera)
Gold Key

#1(10199-703)   .50 1.00 1.50

SPACE KAT-ETS (In 3-D)
Dec, 1953   (25¢)
Power Publishing Co.

#1   5.00 10.00 15.00

SPACEMAN
Sept, 1953 - #8, Nov, 1954
Atlas Comics (CnPC)

#1   2.50 5.00 7.50
 2-8   1.50 3.00 4.50
NOTE: *Everett covers-#1,3.*

SPACE MAN
1962 - #8, 3-5/64; #9, 7/72 - #10, 10/72
Dell Publishing Co./Gold Key

4-Color #1253(1-3/62)   .90 1.80 2.70
#2,3   .40   .80 1.20
 4-8   .30   .60   .90
 9-Reprints #1253   .20   .40   .60
10-Reprints #2   .20   .40   .60

SPACE MOUSE (Also see Space Comics)
April, 1953 - #5, Apr-May, 1954
Avon Periodicals

#1   2.00 4.00 6.00
 2-5   1.00 2.00 3.00

SPACE MOUSE (See Comic Album #17)
Aug-Oct, 1960 - #5, Nov, 1963 (Walter Lantz)
Dell Publ. Co./Gold Key

Space Busters #2, © Z-D

Space Detective #1. © AVON

Space Family Robinson #8. © GK

Space Patrol #1, © Z-D   Space Thrillers 1954, © AVON   Space War #17, © CC

(Space Mouse cont'd)	Good	Fine	Mint
4-Color #1132,1244	.70	1.40	2.10
#1(11/62)-#5(G.K.)	.35	.70	1.05

SPACE MYSTERIES
1964
I.W. Enterprises

Reprint #1,8,9	.80	1.60	2.40

SPACE: 1999
Nov, 1975 - #7, Nov, 1976
Charlton Comics

#1-Staton art; origin Moonbase Alpha

	.40	.80	1.20
2-Staton art	.30	.60	.90
3-7: #5,6-Morrow art	.25	.50	.75

SPACE: 1999 (Magazine)
November, 1975 - #8, Nov, 1976
Charlton Comics

#1-Origin Moonbase Alpha; Morrow cover/art

	.70	1.40	2.10
2,3-Morrow cover/art	.50	1.00	1.50
4-8(#7 shows #6 on inside)	.50	1.00	1.50

SPACE PATROL
Summer, 1952 - #2, Fall, 1952 (Painted covers
Ziff-Davis Publ. Co.   by Norman Saunders)

#1-Krigstein stories	8.00	16.00	24.00
2-Krigstein stories	6.00	12.00	18.00

SPACE SQUADRON (Space Worlds #6)
June, 1951 - #5, Feb, 1952
Marvel/Atlas Comics (ACI)

#1	2.50	5.00	7.50
2-5	1.50	3.00	4.50

SPACE THRILLERS
1954 (Giant) (25¢)
Avon Periodicals

No#-Robotmen of the Lost Planet; contains 3
rebound comics of The Saint & Strange
Worlds. Contents could vary.

	10.00	20.00	30.00

SPACE TRIP TO THE MOON (See Space Advs. #23)

SPACE WAR (Fightin' Five #28 on)
10/59 - #27, 3/64; #28, 3/78 - Present
Charlton Comics

V1#1	1.25	2.50	3.75

	Good	Fine	Mint
2,3	.80	1.60	2.40
4,5-Ditko cover/story	1.20	2.40	3.60
6,8,10-Ditko stories	1.00	2.00	3.00
7,9,11-27	.70	1.40	2.10
28-33	.50	1.00	1.50

SPACE WESTERN
#40, Oct, 1952 - #45, Aug, 1953
Charlton Comics (Capitol Stories)

#40	6.00	12.00	18.00
41-45	4.00	8.00	12.00

SPACE WORLDS (Space Squadron #1-5)
#6, April, 1952
Atlas Comics (Male)

#6	1.00	2.00	3.00

SPANKY & ALFALFA THE LITTLE RASCALS (See
The Little Rascals)

SPARKIE, RADIO PIXIE (Big John & Sparkie #4)
Winter, 1951 - #3, 1952
Ziff-Davis Publ. Co.

#1-3	1.50	3.00	4.50

SPARKLE COMICS
Oct-Nov, 1948 - #33, Dec-Jan, 1953-54
United Features Syndicate/Ziff-Davis Publ.

#1-Li'l Abner, Nancy, Captain & the Kids

	1.75	3.50	5.25
2-10	1.20	2.40	3.60
11-33	.80	1.60	2.40

SPARKLE PLENTY (See 4-Color #215 & Harvey
Comics Library #2)

SPARKLER COMICS (1st Series)
1940
United Feature Comic Group

#1-Jim Hardy	10.00	20.00	30.00
2-Frankie Doodle	5.00	10.00	15.00

SPARKLER COMICS (2nd Series)(Nancy & Sluggo
July, 1940 - #120, Jan, 1955   #121 on)
United Features Syndicate

#1-Origin Sparkman; Tarzan(by Hogarth in all
issues), Captain & the Kids, Ella Cinders,
Danny Dingle, Dynamite Dunn, Nancy, Abbie
& Slats, Frankie Doodle, Broncho Bill be-

gin	35.00	70.00	105.00
2	18.00	36.00	54.00

(Sparkler Comics cont'd)	Good	Fine	Mint
3	14.00	28.00	42.00
4	12.00	24.00	36.00
5-10	10.00	20.00	30.00

11-13,15-20: #12-Sparkman new costume
| | 8.00 | 16.00 | 24.00 |
| 14-Hogarth Tarzan cover | 12.00 | 24.00 | 36.00 |

21-27,29,30: #22-Race Riley & the Commandos
strips begin, end #44 7.00 14.00 21.00

28,31,34,37,39-Tarzan covers by Hogarth
	10.00	20.00	30.00
32,33,35,36,38,40	6.00	12.00	18.00
41,43,45,46,48,49	3.50	7.00	10.50
42,44,47,50-Tarzan covers	8.00	16.00	24.00

51,52,54-70: #57-Li'l Abner begins
	3.00	6.00	9.00
53-Tarzan cover	7.00	14.00	21.00
71-80	2.50	5.00	7.50
81,82,84-90	2.00	4.00	6.00

83-Tarzan cover; last Li'l Abner
| | 4.00 | 8.00 | 12.00 |
| 91-96,98-100 | 1.75 | 3.50 | 5.25 |

97-Origin Casey Ruggles by Warrne Tufts
	2.00	4.00	6.00
101-107,109-112,114-120	1.40	2.80	4.20
108,113-Toth art	2.50	5.00	7.50

SPARKLING LOVE
June, 1950; 1953
Avon Periodicals/Realistic(1953)

#1(Avon)-Kubert art	8.00	16.00	24.00

No#(1953-reprint)-Kubert story
| | 2.50 | 5.00 | 7.50 |

SPARKLING LOVE STORIES (Pulp Magazine)
July, 1950
Avon Periodicals

Contains Avon comic Sparkling Love #1
| | 7.00 | 14.00 | 21.00 |

SPARKLING STARS
June, 1944 - #33, March, 1948
Holyoke Publishing Co.

#1-Hell's Angels	4.00	8.00	12.00
2-10	1.75	3.50	5.25
11-19,21-33	1.25	2.50	3.75
20-Fangs the Wolf Boy app.	1.50	3.00	4.50

SPARKMAN
1945 (One Shot)
United Features Syndicate

#1-Origin Sparkman	8.00	16.00	24.00

SPARKY WATTS

1942 - 1949
Columbia Comic Group

	Good	Fine	Mint
#1-Skyman & The Face app. (1942)			
	7.00	14.00	21.00
2(1943), 3(1944)	5.00	10.00	15.00
4(1944)-Origin	4.00	8.00	12.00
5('47)-Skyman app.	3.00	6.00	9.00
6('47),7,8('48),9,10('49)	2.50	5.00	7.50

SPARTACUS (See 4-Color Comics #1139)

SPECIAL AGENT (See Steve Saunders --)

SPECIAL COLLECTORS' EDITION
Dec, 1975 (10½x13½")
Marvel Comics Group

#1-Kung Fu, Iron Fist & Sons of the Tiger
| | .75 | 1.50 | 2.25 |

SPECIAL COMICS (Hangman #2 on)
Winter, 1941-42
MLJ Magazines

#1-Origin The Boy Buddies(Shield & Wizard x-
over); death of The Comet; origin The
Hangman retold 80.00 160.00 240.00

SPECIAL EDITION (See Gorgo, Reptisaurus)

SPECIAL EDITION COMICS
1940 (One Shot)
Fawcett Publications

#1-Captain Marvel (came out before Captain
Marvel #1) 300.00 600.00 900.00
(Prices vary widely on this book)

SPECIAL MARVEL EDITION (Master of Kung Fu #17
Jan, 1971 - #16, Feb, 1974 on)
Marvel Comics Group

#1-Thor begins(reprint)	.40	.80	1.20
2-4-Last Thor(reprints)	.35	.70	1.05
5-14: Sgt. Fury reprints; #11 reprints/Sgt. Fury #13(Capt.America)	.20	.40	.60

15-Master of Kung Fu begins; Starlin art
| | 1.00 | 2.00 | 3.00 |
| 16-Starlin art | .70 | 1.40 | 2.10 |

SPECIAL WAR SERIES
Aug, 1965 - #4, Nov, 1965
Charlton Comics

V4#1-D-Day	.30	.60	.90
2-Attack!	.20	.40	.60
3-War & Attack	.20	.40	.60
4-Judomaster	.65	1.35	2.00

Sparkler #28, © UFS

Sparkler #58, © UFS

Sparky Watts #2, © CCG

Spectacular Stories Mag. #4, © FOX

The Spectre #3, © DC

Speed Comics #28, © HARV

SPECTACULAR ADVENTURES
12/49 - #2, 2/50 (just "Adventures" on inside)
St. John Publishing Co.

	Good	Fine	Mint
#1 (Exist?)	8.00	16.00	24.00
2-Slave Girl; L. Starr art; China Bombshell app.; Bolle art	8.00	16.00	24.00

SPECTACULAR FEATURES MAGAZINE, A (Formerly My Confessions)(Spect. Features Mag. #3)
#11, April, 1950 - #12, June, 1950
Fox Features Syndicate

#11-Samson & Delilah	5.00	10.00	15.00
12-Iwo Jima	3.00	6.00	9.00

SPECTACULAR FEATURES MAGAZINE
(Formerly A Spectacular Features Magazine)
#3, Aug, 1950
Fox Features Syndicate

#3	3.00	6.00	9.00

SPECTACULAR SPIDER-MAN, THE (See Marvel Treasury Edition & Marvel Special Edition)

SPECTACULAR SPIDER-MAN, THE (Magazine)
July, 1968 - #2, Nov, 1968 (35¢)
Marvel Comics Group

#1-(Black & White)	2.50	5.00	7.50
2-(Color)	1.75	3.50	5.25

SPECTACULAR SPIDER-MAN, THE (Peter Parker)
Dec, 1976 - Present
Marvel Comics Group

#1	.75	1.50	2.25
2-5	.35	.70	1.05
6-10: #8-Gulacy cover	.20	.40	.60
11-26	.15	.30	.45

SPECTACULAR STORIES MAGAZINE (Formerly A Star Presentation Magazine)
#4, July, 1950
Fox Features Syndicate (Hero Books)

#4-Sherlock Holmes	5.00	10.00	15.00

SPECTRE, THE (See Adventure, Showcase, More
11-12/67 - #10, 5-6/69 Fun)
National Periodical Publications

#1-Anderson cover/art	1.50	3.00	4.50
2-5-Neal Adams cover/art #3; Wildcat x-over	1.75	3.50	5.25
6-8,10: #7-Hourman app.	1.00	2.00	3.00
9-Wrightson story	1.75	3.50	5.25

NOTE: _Anderson inks-#6-8._

SPEED BUGGY (Also see Fun-In #12,15)
July, 1975 - #9, Nov, 1976 (Hanna-Barbera)
Charlton Comics

	Good	Fine	Mint
#1-9		.15	.30

SPEED CARTER SPACEMAN (See Spaceman)

SPEED COMICS (New Speed; #14-16 pocket size,
Oct, 1939 - #44, Jan-Feb, 1947 100 pgs.)
Brookwood Publ./Speed Publ./Harvey Publ.

#1-Origin Shock Gibson; Ted Parrish, the Man with 1000 Faces begins; Bob Powell art	50.00	100.00	150.00
2-Powell art	25.00	50.00	75.00
3	15.00	30.00	45.00
4-Powell art	12.00	24.00	36.00
5	10.00	20.00	30.00
6-12: #7-Mars Mason begins, ends #11. #12-The Wasp begins; Major Colt app. (Capt. Colt #12)	10.00	20.00	30.00
13-Intro. Captain Freedom & Young Defenders; Girl Commandos, Pat Parker, War Nurse begins; Major Colt app.	18.00	36.00	54.00
14-16: #15-Pat Parker dons costume, last in costume #23; no Girl Commandos	10.00	20.00	30.00
17-Black Cat begins(origin)Reprint/Pocket #1-not in #40,41	20.00	40.00	60.00
18-20	10.00	20.00	30.00
21,22,25-30	8.00	16.00	24.00
23-Origin Girl Commandos	12.00	24.00	36.00
24-Pat Parker Team-up with Girl Commandos	8.00	16.00	24.00
31-44	7.00	14.00	21.00

NOTE: _Kubert stories-#7-11(Mars Mason),37,38, 42-44. Powell Shock Gibson-#44._

SPEED DEMONS
1957 - 1958
Charlton Comics

#5-10	.25	.50	.75

SPEED SMITH THE HOT ROD KING
Spring, 1952
Ziff-Davis Publ. Co.

#1-Saunders painted cover	1.40	2.80	4.20

SPEEDY GONZALES (See 4-Color Comics #1084)

SPEEDY RABBIT
No date (1958?); 1963
I.W. Enterprises/Super Comics

IW Reprint #1	.35	.70	1.05
Super Reprint #14('63)	.35	.70	1.05

SPELLBOUND (Tales to Hold You--#1, Stories--)
3/52 - #23, 6/54; #24, 10/55 - #34, 6/57
Atlas Comics(ACI #1-14/Male #15-23/BPC #24-34)

	Good	Fine	Mint
#1	2.50	5.00	7.50
2-5	1.50	3.00	4.50
6-Krigstein story	2.00	4.00	6.00
7-10	1.35	2.75	4.00
11-16,18-20	1.00	2.00	3.00
17-Krigstein story	1.75	3.50	5.25
21-24,26-31	.80	1.60	2.40
25-Orlando story	1.25	2.50	3.75
32,33-Torres stories	1.50	3.00	4.50
34-Williamson/Mayo story, 4pgs.			
	3.00	6.00	9.00

NOTE: _Ditko_ story-#29, _Everett_ stories-#2,5,
31; _covers_-#2,7,14,30. _Heath_ story-#9. _Infan-
tino_ story-#15. _Krigstein_ stories-#6,17.
Orlando story-#25. _Powell_ stories-#20,32.

SPENCER SPOOK (Formerly Giggle)
Jan-Feb, 1955 - #100, Mar-Apr, 1955
American Comics Group

#99,100	.35	.70	1.05

SPIDER-MAN (See Amazing --)

SPIDER-WOMAN
April, 1978 - Present
Marvel Comics Group

#1	.20	.40	.60
2-11	.15	.30	.45

SPIDEY SUPER STORIES (Spider-Man)
Oct, 1974 - Present (35¢) (No ads)
Marvel/Children's TV Workshop

#1-(Stories simplified)	.30	.60	.90
2-5	.20	.40	.60
6-10	.15	.30	.45
11-38		.15	.35

SPIKE & TYKE (M.G.M.)
Sept, 1953 - #1266, Dec-Feb, 1961-62
Dell Publishing Co.

4-Color #499,577,638	.60	1.20	1.80
#4-10	.35	.70	1.05
11-24(12-2/60-61)	.25	.50	.75
4-Color #1266	.40	.80	1.20

SPIN & MARTY (TV) (Walt Disney's)
June, 1956 - #1082, Mar-May, 1960
Dell Publishing Co.

4-Color #714,767,808,826	1.25	2.50	3.75

	Good	Fine	Mint
#5(3-5/58)-#10(6-8/59)	.80	1.60	2.40
4-Color #1026,1082	1.00	2.00	3.00

SPINE-TINGLING TALES
May, 1975 - #4, Jan, 1976
Gold Key

#1-Reprints 1st Tragg/Mystery Comics Digest#3			
	.20	.40	.60
2-Origin Ra-Ka-Tep reprt./Mystery C.Digest			
#1; Dr. Spektor/#12		.15	.35
3-All Durak ish. reprts.		.15	.35
4-Baron Tibor's 1st app. reprt./Mystery Com.			
Digest #4		.15	.35

SPIRIT, THE (Weekly Comic Book) (in color)
Distributed thru various newspapers
6/2/40 - 8/10/52 (16pgs.; 8pgs.)(no cover)
Will Eisner

6/2/40(#1)-Origin by Will Eisner, reprinted			
in Police #11; Lady Luck(Brenda Banks) by			
Ford Davis & Mr. Mystic by S. R. Powell			
begin	60.00	120.00	180.00
6/9/40(#2)-Eisner art	20.00	40.00	60.00
6/16/40(#3)-Eisner art; Black Queen app. in			
Spirit	15.00	30.00	45.00
6/23/40(#4)-Eisner art; Mr. Mystic receives			
magical necklace	12.00	24.00	36.00
6/30/40(#5)-Eisner art	12.00	24.00	36.00
7/7/40(#6)-Eisner art; Black Queen app. in			
Spirit	12.00	24.00	36.00
7/14/40(#7)-8/4/40(#10)-Eisner art			
	10.00	20.00	30.00
8/11/40-9/22/40-Eisner art			
	10.00	20.00	30.00
9/29/40-Eisner art; Ellen drops engagement			
with Homer Creep	9.00	18.00	27.00
10/6/40-11/3/40-Eisner art			
	9.00	18.00	27.00
11/10/40-Eisner art; The Black Queen app.			
	9.00	18.00	27.00
11/17/40,11/24/40-Eisner art			
	9.00	18.00	27.00
12/1/40-Ellen spanking by Spirit on cover &			
inside; Eisner art	10.00	20.00	30.00
12/8/40-3/9/41-Eisner art	8.00	16.00	24.00
3/16/41-Intro. & 1st app. Silk Satin by			
Eisner	12.00	24.00	36.00
3/23/41-6/1/41-Eisner art	7.00	14.00	21.00
6/8/41-2nd app. Satin by Eisner; Spirit			
learns Satin is also a British agent			
	9.00	18.00	27.00
6/15/41-1st app. Twilight by Eisner			
	7.00	14.00	21.00
6/22/41-Hitler app. in Spirit by Eisner			
	6.00	12.00	18.00

Spellbound #18, © MCG

The Spirit 8/25/40, © Will Eisner

The Spirit 12/1/40, © Will Eisner

The Spirit 8/23/42, © Will Eisner

The Spirit 4/21/46, © Will Eisner

The Spirit 9/1/46, © Will Eisner

(The Spirit cont'd)	Good	Fine	Mint
6/29/41-12/14/41,12/28/41-Eisner			
	6.00	12.00	18.00
12/21/41-Not Eisner	4.00	8.00	12.00
1/4/42-1/18/42-Spirit by Lou Fine			
	6.00	12.00	18.00
1/25/42,2/8/42-Not Eisner 4.00	8.00	12.00	
2/1/42-1st app. Duchess by Eisner			
	6.00	12.00	18.00
2/15/42-3/1/42-Eisner art; Lady Luck by			
Klaus Nordling begins 5.00	10.00	15.00	
3/8/42,3/22/42-8/16/42-Most by Lou Fine			
	5.00	10.00	15.00
3/15/42-Not Fine/Eisner	3.00	6.00	9.00
8/23/42-Satin cover splash; Spirit by Lou			
Fine (signed) 6.00	12.00	18.00	
8/30/42-10/3/43-Not Fine or Eisner			
	3.00	6.00	9.00
10/10/43-10/24/43-Mr. Mystic by Guardineer;			
not Eisner art 2.50	5.00	7.50	
10/31/43-12/16/45-Not Eisner: 5/14/44-Last			
Mr. Mystic 2.00	4.00	6.00	
12/23/45-1/13/46-Eisner art			
	5.00	10.00	15.00
1/20/46-1st postwar Satin app. by Eisner			
	6.00	12.00	18.00
1/27/46-3/10/46-Eisner art: 3/3/46-Last Lady			
Luck 4.00	8.00	12.00	
3/17/46-Intro. & 1st app. Nylon by Eisner			
	5.00	10.00	15.00
3/24/46,3/31/46,4/14/46-Eisner			
	4.00	8.00	12.00
4/7/46-2nd app. Nylon by Eisner			
	4.50	9.00	13.50
4/21/46-Intro. & 1st app. Mr. Carrion & His			
Buzzard Pet Julia by Eisner			
	6.00	12.00	18.00
4/28/46-5/12/46,5/26/46-6/30/46-Eisner art			
	4.00	8.00	12.00
5/19/46-2nd app. Mr. Carrion by Eisner			

	Good	Fine	Mint
	5.00	10.00	15.00
7/7/46-Intro. & 1st app. Dulcet Tone & Skinny			
by Eisner 6.00	12.00	18.00	
7/14/46-9/29/46-Eisner art			
	4.00	8.00	12.00
10/6/46-Intro. & 1st app. P'Gell by Eisner			
	6.00	12.00	18.00
10/13/46-11/24/46-Eisner art			
	4.00	8.00	12.00
12/1/46-2nd app. P'Gell by Eisner			
	5.00	10.00	15.00
12/8/46-7/6/47-Eisner art 4.00	8.00	12.00	
7/13/47-"Hansel & Gretel" fairy tales by			
Eisner 5.00	10.00	15.00	
7/20/47-Li'l Abner, Daddy Warbucks, Dick			
Tracy, Fearless Fosdick parady by Eisner			
	5.00	10.00	15.00
7/27/47-9/14/47-Eisner art			
	4.00	8.00	12.00
9/21/47-Pearl Harbor flashback by Eisner			
	4.00	8.00	12.00
9/28/47,10/12/47-11/30/47-Eisner art			
	4.00	8.00	12.00
10/5/47-"Cinderella" fairy tales by Eisner			
	5.00	10.00	15.00
12/7/47-Intro. & 1st app. Powder Puff by			
Eisner 6.00	12.00	18.00	
12/14/47-12/28/47-Eisner art			
	4.00	8.00	12.00
1/4/48-2nd app. Powder Puff by Eisner			
	5.00	10.00	15.00
1/11/48-1st app. Sparrow Fallon by Eisner;			
Powder Puff app. 5.00	10.00	15.00	
1/18/48-He-Man ad cover; satire issue by			
Eisner 5.00	10.00	15.00	
1/25/48-Intro. & 1st app. Castonet by			
Eisner 5.00	10.00	15.00	
2/1/48-2nd app. Castonet by Eisner			
	4.00	8.00	12.00

The Spirit 10/6/46, © Will Eisner

The Spirit 7/27/47, © Will Eisner

The Spirit 10/26/47, © Will Eisner

The Spirit 1/23/49, © Will Eisner

The Spirit 2/13/49, © Will Eisner

The Spirit 9/18/49, © Will Eisner

	Good	Fine	Mint
(The Spirit cont'd)			
2/8/48-3/7/48-Eisner art	4.00	8.00	12.00
3/14/48-Only app. Kretchma by Eisner			
	4.00	8.00	12.00
3/21/48,3/28/48,4/11/48-4/25/48-Eisner art			
	4.00	8.00	12.00
4/4/48-Only app. Wild Rice by Eisner			
	4.00	8.00	12.00
5/2/48-2nd app. Sparrow by Eisner			
	4.00	8.00	12.00
5/9/48-7/18/48-Eisner art	4.00	8.00	12.00
7/25/48-Ambrose Bierce's "The Thing" adapta-			
tion classic by Eisner	6.00	12.00	18.00
8/1/48-8/15/48,8/29/48-9/12/48-Eisner art			
	4.00	8.00	12.00
8/22/48-Poe's "Fall of the House of Usher"			
classic by Eisner	6.00	12.00	18.00
9/19/48-Only app. Lorelei by Eisner			
	4.00	8.00	12.00
9/26/48-10/31/48-Eisner art			
	4.00	8.00	12.00
11/7/48-Only app. Plaster of Paris by Eisner			
	4.50	9.00	13.50
11/14/48-12/19/48-Eisner art			
	4.00	8.00	12.00
12/26/48-Reprints some covers of 1948 with			
flashbacks	4.00	8.00	12.00
1/2/49-1/16/49-Eisner art	4.00	8.00	12.00
1/23/49,1/30/49-1st & 2nd app. Thorne by			
Eisner	4.50	9.00	13.50
2/6/49-8/14/49-Eisner art	4.00	8.00	12.00
8/21/49,8/28/49-1st & 2nd app. Monica Veto			
by Eisner	4.50	9.00	13.50
9/4/49,9/11/49-Eisner art	4.00	8.00	12.00
9/18/49-Love comic cover; has gag love comic			
ads on inside	6.00	12.00	18.00
9/25/49-Only app. Ice by Eisner			
	4.50	9.00	13.50
10/2/49,10/9/40-Autumn News appears & dies			
in 10/9 ish. by Eisner	4.00	8.00	12.00

	Good	Fine	Mint
10/16/49-11/27/49,12/18/49,12/25/49-Eisner			
art	4.00	8.00	12.00
12/4/49,12/11/49-1st & 2nd app. Flaxen by			
Eisner	4.00	8.00	12.00
1/1/50-Flashbacks to all of the Spirit girls-			
Thorne, Ellen, Satin & Monica by Eisner			
	4.50	9.00	13.50
1/8/50-Intro. & 1st app. Sand Sareff by			
Eisner	6.00	12.00	18.00
1/15/50-2nd app. Sareff by Eisner			
	5.00	10.00	15.00
1/22/50-2/5/50-Eisner art	4.00	8.00	12.00
2/12/50-Roller Derby ish. by Eisner			
	5.00	10.00	15.00
2/19/50-Half Dead Mr. Lox-classic horror by			
Eisner	5.00	10.00	15.00
2/26/50-9/3/50-Eisner art	4.00	8.00	12.00
9/8/50-P'Gell returns by Eisner			
	4.50	9.00	13.50
9/17/50-1/7/51-Eisner art	4.00	8.00	12.00
1/14/51-Life Magazine cover; brief biog. of			
Comm. Dolan, Sand Sareff, Silk Satin,			
P'Gell, Sammy & Willum, Darling O'Shea &			
Mr. Carrion & His Pet Buzzard Julia, with			
pin-ups by Eisner			
1/21/51,2/4/51-7/29/51,8/12/51-Last Eisner			
issue	3.50	7.00	10.50
1/28/51-The Meanest Man in the World classic			
by Eisner	4.00	8.00	12.00
8/5/51,8/19/51-7/20/52-Not Eisner			
	2.00	4.00	6.00
7/27/52-8/10/52-(Rare)-Denny Colt in Outer			
Space by Wally Wood in ea.; 7pg. S/F stor-			
ies of EC vintage	30.00	60.00	90.00
Large Tabloid pages from 1946 on (Eisner)			
each....	7.00	14.00	21.00

NOTE: *Spirit sections came out in both large
and small format. Some newspapers went to
the 8-pg. format months before others. Some*

The Spirit 3/12/50, © Will Eisner

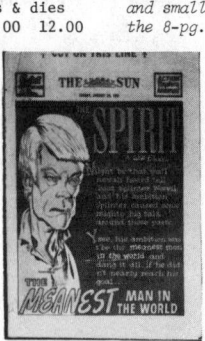

The Spirit 1/28/51, © Will Eisner

The Spirit 8/10/52, © Will Eisner

The Spirit #1(Magazine), © Will Eisner   Spitfire #132, © EP   Spook #27, © STAR

(The Spirit cont'd)
printed the pages so they cannot be folded
into a small comic book section; these are
worth less. (Also see Three Comics Mag.*)*

SPIRIT, THE   (1st Series)
1944 - #22, Aug, 1950
Quality Comics Group (Vital)

	Good	Fine	Mint
No#(#1)-"Wanted Dead or Alive"			
	30.00	60.00	90.00
No#(#2)-"Crime Doesn't Pay"			
	17.00	34.00	51.00
No#(#3)-"Murder Runs Wild"			
	15.00	30.00	45.00
#4,5	12.00	24.00	36.00
6-10	10.00	20.00	30.00
11,17	7.00	14.00	21.00
12-16-Eisner covers	10.00	20.00	30.00
18-21: Strip reprints by Eisner; Eisner			
covers	20.00	40.00	60.00
22-Classic Eisner cover	30.00	60.00	90.00
Super Reprint #11,12-Not Eisner; Sunday strip			
reprints	2.00	4.00	6.00

NOTE: *Crandall cover-#11; Super #11 reprints*
Quality Spirit #19.

SPIRIT, THE   (2nd Series)
Spring, 1952 - 1954
Fiction House Magazines

#1-Not Eisner	12.00	24.00	36.00
2-Two Eisner stories	15.00	30.00	45.00
3	10.00	20.00	30.00
4-One Eisner story/cvr	12.00	24.00	36.00
5-Four Eisner stories	17.00	32.00	48.00

SPIRIT, THE
Oct, 1966 - #2, March, 1967
Harvey Publications

#1-Eisner reprints + 2 new pgs.			
	5.00	10.00	15.00
2-Eisner reprints + 2 new pgs.			
	4.00	8.00	12.00

NOTE: *Existence of a #3 suspected; sent to*
mail subscribers only.

SPIRIT, THE   (Underground)
Jan, 1973 - #2, Sept, 1973   (Black & White)
Kitchen Sink Enterprises (Krupp Comics)

#1-New Eisner cover, 4pgs. new Eisner art +			
reprints (titled Crime Convention)			
	2.00	4.00	6.00
2-New Eisner cover, 4pgs. new Eisner art +			
reprints (titled Meets P'Gell)			
	2.00	4.00	6.00

SPIRIT, THE   (Magazine)
4/74 - #16, 1977; #17, Winter, 1977 - Present
Warren Publ. Co./Krupp Comic Works #17 on

	Good	Fine	Mint
#1-Eisner reprts. begin	1.50	3.00	4.50
2-5	1.25	2.50	3.75
6-9,11-16	.80	1.60	2.40
10-Origin	.90	1.80	2.70
17,18(8/78)	.25	.50	.75
Special #1('75)-All Eisner art			
	.60	1.20	1.80

NOTE: *Covers pencilled by* Eisner *only; one*
color story reprinted in #1-10.

SPIRIT WORLD   (Magazine)
Fall, 1971   (Black & White)
National Periodical Publications

#1-Kirby art/Adams cover	1.35	2.75	4.00

SPITFIRE
1944 - 1945   (Female undercover agent)
Malverne Herald (Elliot)(J. R. Mahon)

#132,133	3.50	7.00	10.50

SPITFIRE COMICS   (Also see Double Up)
Aug, 1942 - #2   (Pocket size - 100pgs.)
Harvey Publications

#1-Origin The Clown, The Fly-Man, The Spit-			
fire & The Magician from Bagdad			
	18.00	36.00	54.00
2	10.00	20.00	30.00

SPOOF!
Oct, 1970; #2, Nov, 1972 - #5, May, 1973
Marvel Comics Group

#1	.20	.40	.60
2-5		.15	.35

SPOOK   (-- Detective Cases #22)
#22, Jan, 1953 - #30, Oct, 1954
Novelty-Star Publications

#22(1/53)	1.50	3.00	4.50
23-27,30-Sgt. Spook	1.25	2.50	3.75
28,29-Rulah app.; Jo-Jo in #29			
	2.50	5.00	7.50

NOTE: *L. B. Cole covers-all issues.* Disbrow
art-#26,28-30; #30 reprint/Blue Bolt Weird
Tales #114.

SPOOK COMICS
1946
Baily Publications/Star

#1-Mr. Lucifer app.	1.25	2.50	3.75

SPOOKY (The Tuff Little Ghost)
Nov, 1956 - Present
Harvey Publications

	Good	Fine	Mint
#1	4.00	8.00	12.00
2-10(1956-57)	1.00	2.00	3.00
11-20(1957-58)	.50	1.00	1.50
21-40(1958-59)	.30	.60	.90
41-100	.20	.40	.60
101-159		.10	.25

SPOOKY HAUNTED HOUSE
Oct, 1972 - #15, Feb, 1975
Harvey Publications

#1	.20	.40	.60
2-15		.10	.25

SPOOKY MYSTERIES
No date (1946)   (10¢)
Your Guide Publ. Co.

No#-Mr. Spooky, Super Snooper, Pinky, Girl Detective app.	1.75	3.50	5.25

SPOOKY SPOOKTOWN
June, 1962 - #66, Sept, 1976
Harvey Publications

#1-Casper, Spooky	2.00	4.00	6.00
2-10	.80	1.60	2.40
11-20	.40	.80	1.20
21-40	.25	.50	.75
41-66		.20	.40

SPORT COMICS (True Sport Picture Stor.#4 on?)
Oct, 1940 - #3, 1940?
Street & Smith Publications

#1-Life story of Lou Gehrig	3.50	7.00	10.50
2,3	2.25	4.50	6.75

SPORT LIBRARY (See Charlton Sport --)

SPORTS ACTION (Formerly Sport Stars)
#2, Feb, 1950 - #14, Sept, 1952
Marvel/Atlas Comics (ACI #2,3/SAI #4-14)

#2	1.00	2.00	3.00
3-12,14	.60	1.20	1.80
13-Krigstein art	1.75	3.50	5.25

SPORT STARS
2-3/46 - #4, 8-9/46 (½ comic, ½ photo mag.)
Parents' Magazine Institute (Sport Stars)

#1-"How Tarzan Got That Way" story of Johnny

	Good	Fine	Mint
Weissmuller	3.00	6.00	9.00
2-Baseball greats	1.20	2.40	3.60
3,4	1.20	2.40	3.60

SPORT STARS (Sports Action #2)
Nov, 1949
Marvel Comics (ACI)

#1-Knute Rockne	2.00	4.00	6.00

SPORT THRILLS (Formerly Dick Cole)
#11, Nov, 1949 - #15, Nov, 1951
Star Publications

#11-Last app. Dick Cole	1.50	3.00	4.50
12-15-All L. B. Cole covers	1.00	2.00	3.00

SPOTLIGHT
Sept, 1978 - #3, Jan, 1979   (Hanna-Barbera)
Marvel Comics Group

#1-3		.15	.30	.45

SPOTLIGHT COMICS
Nov, 1944 - #3, 1945
Harry 'A' Chesler (Our Army, Inc.)

#1-The Black Dwarf, The Veiled Avenger, & Barry Kuda begin	8.00	16.00	24.00
2,3	6.00	12.00	18.00

SPOTTY THE PUP
#3, Dec-Jan, 1953-54
Avon Periodicals

#3	.50	1.00	1.50

SPUNKY (-- Junior Cowboy) (-- Comics #2 on)
April, 1949 - #7, Nov, 1951
Standard Comics

#1,2-Text illos by Frazetta	2.50	5.00	7.50
3-7	.50	1.00	1.50

SPUNKY THE SMILING SPOOK
Aug, 1957 - #4, May, 1958
Ajax/Farrell (World Famous Comics/Four Star Comic Corp.)

#1-Reprints from Frisky Fables	.40	.80	1.20
2-4	.25	.50	.75

SPY AND COUNTERSPY (Spy Hunters #3 on)
Aug-Sept, 1949 - #2, Oct-Nov, 1949
American Comics Group

Spooky Mysteries No#. © Your Guide

Sport Thrills #11. © STAR

Spotlight Comics #1. © CHES

Spy Cases #14. © MCG   Spy Smasher #9. © FAW   Stamps Comics =6. © YM

	Good	Fine	Mint
(Spy & Counterspy cont'd)			
#1-Origin, 1st app. Jonathan Kent, Counterspy			
	1.50	3.00	4.50
2	1.00	2.00	3.00

SPY CASES (Formerly The Kellys)
#26, Sept, 1950 - #19, Oct, 1953
Marvel/Atlas Comics (Hercules Publ.)

#26-29(1950)	1.50	3.00	4.50
4-10	1.00	2.00	3.00
11-19	.75	1.50	2.25

SPY FIGHTERS
March, 1951 - #15, July, 1953
Marvel/Atlas Comics (CSI)

#1	1.50	3.00	4.50
2-15	.90	1.80	2.70

SPY-HUNTERS (Formerly Spy & Counterspy)
#3, 12-1/49-50 - #24, 6-7/53
American Comics Group

#3-Jonathan Kent begins, ends #10			
	1.50	3.00	4.50
4-10: #8-Starr story	1.00	2.00	3.00
11-15,17-24	.80	1.60	2.40
16-9pg. Williamson story	3.00	6.00	9.00

NOTE: _Whitney cvrs.-#8,16; stories-many issues._

SPYMAN (Top Secret Adventures on cover)
Sept, 1966 - #3, Feb, 1967
Harvey Publications

#1	.70	1.40	2.10
2,3	.40	.80	1.20

SPY SMASHER (See Fawcett Miniatures)
1941 - #11, Feb, 1943
Fawcett Publications

#1-Spy Smasher begins	75.00	150.00	225.00
2	35.00	70.00	105.00
3	30.00	60.00	90.00
4,5	25.00	50.00	75.00
6-11	20.00	40.00	60.00

SPY SMASHER WELL KNOWN COMICS
1944 (12pgs.)(Printed in green)(8½x10½")
(Paper cover; glued binding)
Bestmaid/Samuel Lowe (Giveaway)

(Scarce)	25.00	50.00	75.00

SPY THRILLERS (Police Badge #479 #5)
Nov, 1954 - #4, May, 1955
Atlas Comics (PrPI)

	Good	Fine	Mint
#1	1.25	2.50	3.75
2-4	.75	1.50	2.25

SQUEEKS
Oct, 1953 - 1954
Lev Gleason Publications

#1-Biro cover	1.20	2.40	3.60
2-5: #2,3-Biro covers	.80	1.60	2.40

STALKER
June-July, 1975 - #4, Dec-Jan, 1975-76
National Periodical Publications

#1-Ditko/Wood cover-stories begin			
	.50	1.00	1.50
2-4	.35	.70	1.05

STAMP COMICS
Oct, 1951 - #7, Oct, 1952 (#1 - 15¢)
Youthful Magazines/Stamp Comics, Inc.

#1	1.50	3.00	4.50
2-6: #3,4-Kiefer, Wildey stories	1.20	2.40	3.60
7-Roy Krenkel, 4pgs.	1.75	3.50	5.25

NOTE: _Promotes stamp collecting; gives stories behind various commemorative stamps._

STANLEY & HIS MONSTER (Formerly The Fox & the
#109, 4-5/68 - #114, 2-3/69   Crow)
National Periodical Publications

#109-114	.20	.40	.60

STAR COMICS
2/37 - #23(V2#7), 8/39 (#1-6, Large size)
Harry 'A' Chesler/Centaur Publications

V1#1-Dan Hastings begins	15.00	30.00	45.00
2-5: #5-Little Nemo	10.00	20.00	30.00
6-10	8.00	16.00	24.00
11-15	7.00	14.00	21.00
16-The Phantom Rider begins			
	7.00	14.00	21.00
17-23(V2#1-7)	6.00	12.00	18.00

STAR FEATURE COMICS
1963
I.W. Enterprises

Reprint #9-Stunt-Man Stetson app.			
	.65	1.35	2.00

STARFIRE
Aug-Sept, 1976 - #8, Oct-Nov, 1977
National Periodical Publ./DC Comics

(Starfire cont'd)   Good   Fine   Mint
#1-Origin (CCA stamp fell off cover art; so
   it was approved by code).35   .70   1.05
2-8   .25   .50   .75

STAR HUNTERS
10-11/77 - #7, 10-11/78
National Periodical Publications/DC Comics

#1-Newton cover/art   .25   .50   .75
2-7   .20   .40   .60

STARK TERROR (Magazine)
Dec, 1970 - #5, Aug, 1971 (52pgs.) (B&W)
Stanley Publications

#1   .70   1.40   2.10
2-4(Gillmor/Aragon reprts).50   1.00   1.50
5-(ACG reprints)   .40   .80   1.20

STARLET O'HARA IN HOLLYWOOD
1949 - #4, Sept, 1949
Standard Comics

#1   3.50   7.00 10.50
2-4-by Bob Oksner   2.50   5.00   7.50

STARMAN (See Adventure, First Issue Special,
Showcase, & Justice League)

STAR PRESENTATION MAGAZINE, A (Formerly My
Secret Romance #1,2; Spectacular Stories #4)
#3, May, 1950 (Also see This Is Suspense)
Fox Features Syndicate (Hero Books)

#3-Dr. Jekyll & Mr. Hyde by Wood & Harrison
   (reprinted in Startling Terror Tales #10);
   Wood cover   30.00 60.00 90.00

STAR RANGER
Feb, 1937 - #12, 1938 (Large size-#1-6)
Centaur Publications

#1-Ace & Deuce, Air Plunder
                           16.50 33.25 50.00
2-8,V2#9-12(small size) 7.00 14.00 21.00

STAR RANGER FUNNIES
V1#15, Oct, 1958; V2#2, April, 1939
Centaur Publications

V1#15-6pg. Eisner western story
                           12.00 24.00 36.00
V2#2   6.00 12.00 18.00

STARR FLAGG, UNDERCOVER GIRL(See Undercover--)

STARS AND STRIPES COMICS

Feb, 1941 - #6, Dec, 1941
Centaur Publications
                                 Good   Fine   Mint
#2(#1)-The Shark, The Iron Skull, A Man, The
   Amazing Man, Mighty Man, Minimidget begin;
   The Voice & Dash Darwell, the Human Meteor
   app.   35.00 70.00 105.00
3-Origin Dr. Synthe; The Black Panther app.
                          25.00 50.00 75.00
4-The Stars and Stripes origin
                          20.00 40.00 60.00
5(#5 on cover & inside) 17.00 34.00 51.00
5(#6)-(#5 on cover, #6 on inside)
                          17.00 34.00 51.00

STAR SPANGLED COMICS (--War Stories #131 on)
Oct, 1941 - #130, July, 1952
National Periodical Publications

#1-Origin Tarantula; Captain X of the R.A.F.,
   Star Spangled Kid & Armstrong of the Army
   begin   70.00 140.00 210.00
2   35.00 70.00 105.00
3-5   20.00 40.00 60.00
6-Last Armstrong/Army   15.00 30.00 45.00
7-Origin The Guardian by S&K, & Robotman by
   Jimmy Thompson; The Newsboy Legion & TNT
   begin; last Capt. X   95.00 190.00 285.00
8-Origin TNT & Dan the Dyna-Mite
                          55.00 110.00 165.00
9,10   40.00 80.00 120.00
11-17   30.00 60.00 90.00
18-Origin Star Spangled Kid
                          35.00 70.00 105.00
19-Last Tarantula   30.00 60.00 90.00
20-Liberty Belle begins 30.00 60.00 90.00
21-29-Last S&K issue; #23-Last TNT
                          20.00 40.00 60.00
30-40   8.00 16.00 24.00
41-50   7.00 14.00 21.00
51-64: Last Newsboy Legion & The Guardian;
   #53 by S&K   6.00 12.00 18.00
65-Robin begins   7.00 14.00 21.00
66-68,70-80   4.50   9.00 13.50
69-Origin Tomahawk   7.00 14.00 21.00
81-Origin Merry, Girl of 1000 Gimmicks
                          4.00   8.00 12.00
82-Last Star Spangled Kid 3.00   6.00   9.00
83-Capt. Compass begins
                          3.00   6.00   9.00
84-100: #91-Federal Men begin, end #93. #94-
   Manhunters Around the World begin, end
   #121   2.50   5.00   7.50
101-112,114-121   2.25   4.50   6.75
113-Frazetta story,10pgs. 12.00 24.00 36.00
122-Ghost Breaker begins(origin), ends #130
                          2.00   4.00   6.00
123-130   1.75   3.50   5.25

Starfire #1, © DC

Star Ranger =9, © CEN

Star Spangled Comics =20, © DC

Star Spangled War #52, © DC

Startling Comics #14, © BP

Startling Comics #49, © BP

(Star Spangled Comics cont'd)

NOTE: *Most all issues after #29 signed Simon & Kirby are not by them.*

STAR SPANGLED WAR STORIES (Star Spangled
Comics #1-130; The Unknown Soldier #205 on)
#131, 8/52 - #133, 10/52; #3, 11/52 - #204,
2-3/77   (See Showcase)
National Periodical Publications

	Good	Fine	Mint
#131(#1)	8.00	16.00	24.00
132,133	4.50	9.00	13.50
#3-5: #4-Devil Dog Dugan app.			
	4.00	8.00	12.00
6-10	3.00	6.00	9.00
11-20	2.50	5.00	7.50
21-30	2.00	4.00	6.00
31-50	1.60	3.20	4.80
51-83	1.00	2.00	3.00
84-Origin Mlle. Marie	1.25	2.50	3.75
85-89-Mlle. Marie in all	1.00	2.00	3.00
90-1st Dinosaur issue	1.75	3.50	5.25
91-100	.80	1.60	2.40
101-120	.60	1.20	1.80
121-133,135-137-Last dinosaur story; Heath			
Birdman-#129,131	.50	1.00	1.50
134,144-Adams story + Kubert #144			
	1.25	2.50	3.75
138-Enemy Ace begins by Joe Kubert, ends #161			
	1.00	2.00	3.00
139-143,145-148,152,153,155	.60	1.20	1.80
149,150-Viking Prince by Kubert			
	.80	1.60	2.40
151-1st Unknown Soldier	.40	.80	1.20
154-Origin Unknown Soldier	.40	.80	1.20
156-1st Battle Album	.25	.50	.75
157-161-Last Enemy Ace	.25	.50	.75
162-180,184-204: #164-Toth story. #166-The			
Young Commandos app.	.20	.40	.60
181-183-Enemy Ace vs. Balloon Buster serial			
app.	.20	.40	.60

NOTE: *Anderson cover-#120. Drucker stories-
#66,73-84. John Giunta story-#72. Infantino
stories-#21,37,163(reprint); covers-#118,121.
Kaluta cover-#167. Krigstein story-#34.
Kubert stories-#6-138(most issues),800.
Maurer story-#160. Sutton story-#168. Wildey
story-#161. Suicide Squad in #110,116-18,120,
121,127. U.S.S. Stevens by Glanzman-#171,172,
174.*

STARSTREAM (Adventures in Science Fiction)
1976   (68 pgs.) (Cardboard covers) (79¢)
Whitman/Western Publishing Co.

#1-Bolle art	.50	1.00	1.50
2-4-McWilliams & Bolle art.	.40	.80	1.20

STAR STUDDED
1945 (25¢; 132pgs.); 1945 (196pgs.)
Cambridge House/Superior Publishers

	Good	Fine	Mint
#1-Captain Combat, Ghost Woman, Commandette,			
& Red Rogue app.	6.00	12.00	18.00
No#-The Cadet, Edison Bell, Hoot Gibson, Jun-			
gle Lil(196pgs.); copies vary-Blue Beetle			
in some	5.00	10.00	15.00

STARTLING COMICS
June, 1940 - #53, May, 1948
Better Publications (Nedor)

#1-Origin Captain Future, Mystico, the Wonder			
Man; The Masked Rider begins			
	45.00	90.00	135.00
2	24.00	48.00	72.00
3	15.00	30.00	45.00
4	12.00	24.00	36.00
5-9	10.00	20.00	30.00
10-Origin & 1st app. The Fighting Yank			
	30.00	60.00	90.00
11-15	12.00	24.00	36.00
16-Origin The Four Comrades; not in #32,35			
	15.00	30.00	45.00
17-Last Masked Rider & Mystico			
	10.00	20.00	30.00
18-Origin Pyroman	20.00	40.00	60.00
19	10.00	20.00	30.00
20-The Oracle begins; not in #26,28,33,34			
	10.00	20.00	30.00
21-Origin The Ape, Oracle's enemy,			
22-30	7.00	14.00	21.00
31-33	5.00	10.00	15.00
34-Origin The Scarab & only app.			
	5.00	10.00	15.00
35-40: #36-Last Four Comrades. #40-Last Capt.			
Future & Oracle	5.00	10.00	15.00
41-Front Page Peggy begins	5.00	10.00	15.00
42,43-Last Pyroman	5.00	10.00	15.00
44-Lance Lewis, Space Detective begins;			
Ingels cover	7.00	14.00	21.00
45-Tygra begins(origin)	6.00	12.00	18.00
46-Ingels cover/story	6.00	12.00	18.00
47-53: #49-Last Fighting Yank. #50,51-Sea-			
Eagle app.	3.00	6.00	9.00

NOTE: *Ingels covers-#44-46(airbrush). Schomburg (Xela) covers-#47-53(airbrush). Bondage
covers-#46,48,49.*

STARTLING TERROR TALES
5/52 - #14, 2/53; #4, 4/53 - #11, 1954
Star Publications

#10-(1st Series)-Wood/Harrison art(reprints			
A Star Presentation #3)	7.00	14.00	21.00
11-Reprints Fox's "The Black Tarantula"			

383

(Startling Terror Tales cont'd)

	Good	Fine	Mint
	3.00	6.00	9.00
12,14	1.50	3.00	4.50
13-Jo-Jo reprint; Disbrow art			
	2.50	5.00	7.50
#4-11('53-'54)-(2nd Series).80	1.60	2.40

NOTE: *L. B. Cole covers-all issues.*

STAR TREK (TV) (See Dan Curtis)
July, 1967 - Present
Gold Key

#1	5.00	10.00	15.00
2-5	2.50	5.00	7.50
6-10	1.50	3.00	4.50
11-20	.90	1.80	2.70
21-30	.50	1.00	1.50
31-40	.25	.50	.75
41-60	.20	.40	.60

NOTE: *McWilliams art-#38,40-57,60. #29 reprints #1; #35 reprts. #4; #37 reprts. #5; #45 reprts. #7.*

-- the Enterprise Logs #1(8/76)-Whitman, 224pgs.($1.95)-Reprints #1-8 + 7pgs. by

McWilliams	1.50	3.00	4.50
-- the Enterprise Logs #2('76)-Reprts.#9-17
| | 1.00 | 2.00 | 3.00 |
-- the Enterprise Logs #3('77)-Reprts.#18-28
| | .80 | 1.60 | 2.40 |
-- the Enterprise Logs #4(Wint.'77)-Reprts.
| #29-37 | .80 | 1.60 | 2.40 |

STAR WARS (Movie)
July, 1977 - Present
Marvel Comics Group

#1-(35¢ cover price; limited distribution)
	3.00	6.00	9.00
#1-(regular 30¢ price)	2.00	4.00	6.00
2,3	1.00	2.00	3.00
4-Low distribution in some areas
	1.75	3.50	5.25
5-10	.50	1.00	1.50
11-15	.35	.70	1.05
16-20	.15	.30	.45
#1-4(reprints)	.15	.30	.45

NOTE: *Chaykin stories-#1-10; cover-#1. Infantino pencils-#11 on. Leialoha inks-#2-5.*

STAR VENTURE
1964
I.W. Enterprises

Reprint #9	.75	1.50	2.25

STEEL, THE INDESTRUCTIBLE MAN
March, 1978 - #5, Oct-Nov, 1978

DC Comics, Inc.

	Good	Fine	Mint
#1	.20	.40	.60
2-5	.15	.30	.45

STEVE CANYON
Feb, 1948 - #6, Dec, 1948 (Reprints)
Harvey Publications

#1-Origin Steve Canyon	14.00	28.00	42.00
2-6(Caniff art #1-6)	8.00	16.00	24.00

Strictly For the Smart Birds-16pgs., 1951-Information Comics Div.(Harvey) Premium
| | 8.00 | 16.00 | 24.00 |

STEVE CANYON
1959 (96pgs.; no text; 6-3/4"x9"; hardcover)
black & white inside)
Grosset & Dunlap

#100100-Reprints 2 stories from strip(1953, 1957)
	2.50	5.00	7.50
#100100(Softcover edition)2.00	4.00	6.00

STEVE CANYON (See 4-Color #519,578,641,737, 804,939,1033, & Harvey Comics Hits #52)

STEVE DONOVAN, WESTERN MARSHAL (TV)
1956
Dell Publishing Co.

4-Color #675,768-Kinstler art
	2.00	4.00	6.00
4-Color #880, #1	1.25	2.50	3.75

STEVE ROPER
April, 1948 - #5, Dec, 1948
Famous Funnies

#1-Contains 1944 daily newspaper reprints
	3.00	6.00	9.00
2-5	2.00	4.00	6.00

STEVE SAUNDERS SPECIAL AGENT
Dec, 1947 - #8, Sept, 1949
Parents' Magazine Institute

#1	1.50	3.00	4.50
2-8	1.20	2.40	3.60

STEVE SAVAGE (See Captain --)

STEVE ZODIAC & THE FIRE BALL XL-5 (TV)
January, 1964
Gold Key

#1(10108-401)	.40	.80	1.20

Startling Terror Tales #10. © STAR

Star Trek #5. © GK

Steve Saunders #1, © PMI

Stories By Famous Authors #5, © Fam. Authors Stories By Famous Authors #8, © Fam. Authors Stories Of Romance #9, © MCG

STEVIE
1952 - #6, April, 1954
Harvey Magazine Publ./Mazie(Magazine Publ.)

	Good	Fine	Mint
#1	.75	1.50	2.25
2-6	.40	.80	1.20

STEVIE MAZIE'S BOY FRIEND (See Harvey Hits #5)

STONEY BURKE (TV)
June-Aug, 1963 - #2, Sept-Nov, 1963
Dell Publishing Co.

#1,2	.40	.80	1.20

STONY CRAIG
1946 (No#)
Pentagon Publishing Co.

Reprints Bell Syndicate's "Sgt. Stony Craig"
newspaper strips   3.00   6.00   9.00

STORIES BY FAMOUS AUTHORS ILLUSTRATED
Fall, 1950 - #13, May, 1951 (Fast Fiction#1-5)
Seaboard Publ./Famous Authors Ill.

#1-Scarlet Pimpernel-Baroness Orczy
                          4.00   8.00 12.00
2-Capt. Blood-Rafael Sabatini
                          4.00   8.00 12.00
3-She, by Haggard   6.00 12.00 18.00
4-The 39 Steps-John Buchan
                          4.00   8.00 12.00
5-Beau Geste-P.C. Wren   4.00   8.00 12.00
NOTE: The above five issues are exact reprints of Fast Fiction
Nos. 1-5 except for the title change and new Kiefer covers on
Nos. 1 and 2. The above five issues were released before Famous
Authors No. 6.

6-Macbeth, by Shakespeare; Kiefer art(8/50);
  used in Seduction of the Innocent, pg. 22
                          4.00   8.00 12.00
7-The Window; Kiefer art 4.00   8.00 12.00
8-Hamlet, by Shakespeare; Kiefer art; used
  in Seduction of the Innocent
                          6.00 12.00 18.00
9-Nicholas Nickleby, by Dickens;
  G. Schrotter art   4.00   8.00 12.00
10-Romeo & Juliet, by Shakespeare; Kiefer
  art   4.00   8.00 12.00
11-Ben-Hur; Schrotter art 5.00 10.00 15.00
12-LaSvengali; "   "   4.00   8.00 12.00
13-Scaramouche; Kiefer " 4.00   8.00 12.00

STORIES OF CHRISTMAS
1942   (32 pgs.)(Paper cover)(Giveaway)
K.K. Publications

Adaptation of "A Christmas Carol"
                          5.00 10.00 15.00

STORIES OF ROMANCE
#5, 1956 - #13, Aug, 1957
Atlas Comics (LMC)

	Good	Fine	Mint
#5-13	.40	.80	1.20

STORMY (See 4-Color Comics #537)

STORY HOUR SERIES (Disney)
1948(32pgs.); 1952-53(36pgs.) (4-3/4"x6½")
Given away with subscription to Walt Disney's
Comics & Stories
Whitman Publishing Co.

#800-Donald Duck in "Bringing Up the Boys;"
  1948 Soft Cover   6.00 12.00 18.00
  1953   3.00   6.00   9.00
#801-Mickey Mouse's Summer Vacation
  1948 Soft Cover   4.00   8.00 12.00
  1951,1952 edition   2.00   4.00   6.00
#803-Bongo
  1948 Soft Cover   3.00   6.00   9.00
#804-Mickey and the Beanstalk
  1948 Soft Cover   4.00   8.00 12.00
1948 Hard Cover Edition of each...$2-$3 more

STORY OF CHECKS, THE
1972   (5th edition)
Federal Reserve Bank of New York

Severin art   .40   .80   1.20

STORY OF EDISON, THE
1956   (Reddy Killowatt) (16 pgs.)
Educational Comics

Reprint of Reddy Killowatt '47 edition?
                         7.00 14.00 21.00

STORY OF JESUS (See Classics Special)

STORY OF MANKIND, THE (See 4-Color #851)

STORY OF MARTHA WAYNE, THE
April, 1956
Argo Publ.

#1-Newspaper reprints   1.50   3.00   4.50

STORY OF RUTH, THE (See 4-Color #1144)

STORY OF THE COMMANDOS, THE (Combined Opera-
1943   (68 pgs.) (B&W) (15c)   tions)
Long Island Independent (Distr. by Gilberton)

No#-All text (no comics); photos & illustra-
    tions; ads for Classics Comics on back
    cover (Rare)   12.00 24.00 36.00

385

STORY OF THE GLOOMY BUNNY, THE (See March
of Comics #9)

STRAIGHT ARROW
Feb-Mar, 1950 - #55, Mar, 1956
Magazine Enterprises

	Good	Fine	Mint
#1-Whitney art	8.00	16.00	24.00
2-Red Hawk begins by Powell, ends #55			
	5.00	10.00	15.00
3-Frazetta cover	12.00	24.00	36.00
4-10	2.50	5.00	7.50
11-20	1.75	3.50	5.25
21,23-40	1.50	3.00	4.50
22-Frazetta cover	10.00	20.00	30.00
41-55	1.50	3.00	4.50

NOTE: *Powell art in all.*

STRAIGHT ARROW'S FURY (See A-1 Comics #119)

STRANGE
March, 1957 - #6, May, 1958
Ajax-Farrell Publ. (Four Star Comic Corp.)

	Good	Fine	Mint
#1	1.00	2.00	3.00
2-6	.60	1.20	1.80

STRANGE ADVENTURES
8-9/50 - #244, 10-11/73 (#1-12, 52pgs.)
National Periodical Publications

	Good	Fine	Mint
#1-Adaptation of "Destination Moon;" Kris KL-99 & Darwin Jones begin			
	25.00	50.00	75.00
2	14.00	28.00	42.00
3,4: Kirby art ea.	10.00	20.00	30.00
5-8: #7-Origin Kris KL-99			
	8.00	16.00	24.00
9-Intro. & origin Captain Comet (6/51)			
	20.00	40.00	60.00
10-12,14,15	6.00	12.00	18.00
13,17-Toth stories	7.00	14.00	21.00
16,18-20	5.00	10.00	15.00
21-30	4.00	8.00	12.00
31,34-38	3.50	7.00	10.50
32,33-Krigstein stories	4.00	8.00	12.00
39-Used in Seduction of the Innocent			
	6.00	12.00	18.00
40-49-Last Capt. Comet	3.00	6.00	9.00
50-53-Last pre-code ish.	2.00	4.00	6.00
54-70	1.60	3.20	4.80
71-100	1.35	2.75	4.00
101-110: #104-Space Museum begins by Sekowsky			
	1.00	2.00	3.00
111-116,118-120: #114-Star Hawkins begins, ends #185	.80	1.60	2.40
117-Origin Atomic Knights	4.00	8.00	12.00
121-140: #124-Origin Faceless Creature			

	Good	Fine	Mint
	.75	1.50	2.25
141-160: #159-Star Rovers app. #160-Last Atomic Knights	.50	1.00	1.50
161-179: #161-Last Space Museum. #163-Star Rovers app. #177-Origin Immortal Man			
	.40	.80	1.20
180-Origin Animal Man	.50	1.00	1.50
181-186,188-204	.30	.60	.90
187-Origin The Enchantress	.30	.60	.90
205-Origin Deadman by Infantino; by Neal Adams #206 on	4.50	9.00	13.50
206	3.50	7.00	10.50
207-210	3.00	6.00	9.00
211-216-Last Deadman	2.00	4.00	6.00
217-Adam Strange & Atomic Knights reprints begin	.30	.60	.90
218-225: #222-New Adam Strange story			
	.25	.50	.75
226-231(all 68pgs.): #231-Last Atomic Knights reprint	.25	.50	.75
232-236(all 52pgs.): #236-Star Rovers app.			
	.20	.40	.60
237-244-Last Adam Strange reprint			
	.15	.30	.45

NOTE: *Adams stories-#206-216; covers-#207-218,228,235. Anderson stories-#8-52,94,96,97,99,115,117,119-163; covers or reprints-#217-233,235-239,241-243. Ditko story-#188,189. Drucker stories-#42,43,45. Finlay stories-#2,3,6,7(#210,229 reprints). Infantino stories-#10-101,106-151,154,157-163,180; covers or reprints-#197,199-211,218-221,223-244. Kaluta cover-#240. Gil Kane stories-#8-116,124,125,130,138,146-157,173-186; reprints-#204,222,227-231. Kubert stories-#55(2pgs.),226; covers-#219,225-227,232,234. Morrow cover-#230. Powell story-#4. Mike Sekowsky stories-#97-162; cover-#206; reprints-#217-219. Simon & Kirby-#2(2pg. reprint). Toth stories-#8,12,18,19. Wood-#154(inks).*

STRANGE AS IT SEEMS
1932 (64pgs.; B&W; square binding)
Blue-Star Publishing Co.

	Good	Fine	Mint
#1-Newspaper reprints	15.00	30.00	45.00

NOTE: *Published with and without No. 1 and price on cover.*

STRANGE AS IT SEEMS
1939
United Features Syndicate

	Good	Fine	Mint
Single Series #9, #1,2	4.00	8.00	12.00

STRANGE CONFESSIONS
Jan-Mar, 1952 - #4, Fall, 1952
Ziff-Davis Publ. Co. (Approved)

Straight Arrow #4, © ME   Strange Adventures #13, © DC

Strange Adventures #207, © DC

Strange Fantasy #5. © AJAX   Strange Mysteries #12. © SUPR   Strange Stories F.A. World #3. © FAW

	Good	Fine	Mint
(Str. Confessions cont'd)			
#1-Photo cover	5.00	10.00	15.00
2-4	2.50	5.00	7.50

STRANGE FANTASY
Aug, 1952 - #14, Oct-Nov, 1954
Harvey Publ./Ajax-Farrell #2 on

#1-The Black Cat app.	3.00	6.00	9.00
2(8/52)-Jungle Princess story; no Black Cat			
	1.50	3.00	4.50
2(10/52)-No Black Cat or Rulah			
	1.50	3.00	4.50
3-Rulah story	2.00	4.00	6.00
4-Rocket Man app.	1.75	3.50	5.25
5-8,10,12,14	1.20	2.40	3.60
9(w/Black Cat), #9(w/Boy's Ranch; S&K art)			
	2.50	5.00	7.50
9-regular ish.	1.20	2.40	3.60
11-Jungle story	1.50	3.00	4.50
13-Bondage cover; Rulah (Kolah) story			
	2.50	5.00	7.50

STRANGE GALAXY (Magazine)
V1#8, Feb, 1971 - #11, Aug, 1971   (B&W)
Eerie Publications

V1#8-Cover reprinted from Fantastic V19#3			
(2/70)(a pulp)	.40	.80	1.20
9-11	.40	.80	1.20

STRANGE JOURNEY
Sept, 1957 - #4, June, 1958 (Farrell reprints)
America's Best (Steinway Publ.)(Ajax/Farrell)

#1	1.20	2.40	3.60
2-4	.75	1.50	2.25

STRANGE LOVE
1950   (132 pgs.)
Hero Books/Fox Features Syndicate

No#-Photo cover. See Fox Giants. Contents
can vary and determines price.

STRANGE MYSTERIES
Sept, 1951 - #21, Dec, 1954
Superior/Dynamic Publications

#1	2.50	5.00	7.50
2-All Kamen art	2.50	5.00	7.50
3-5	1.40	2.80	4.20
6-8,10	1.00	2.00	3.00
9-Bondage cover	1.25	2.50	3.75
11,13-18,21	.80	1.60	2.40
12-Kamen/Feldstein? story	2.00	4.00	6.00
19-Baker cover/stories; Kamen story			
	2.50	5.00	7.50

	Good	Fine	Mint
20-Kamen stories	2.00	4.00	6.00

STRANGE MYSTERIES
1963 - 1964
I.W. Enterprises/Super Comics

IW Reprint #9	.40	.80	1.20
Super Reprint #10-12,15-17('63-'64): #12-reprints Tales of Horror #5(3/53) less cover. #15,16-reprints The Dead Who Walk			
	.40	.80	1.20
Super Reprint #18-Reprint of Witchcraft #1; Kubert story			
	.70	1.40	2.10

STRANGE PLANETS
1958; 1963-64
I.W. Enterprises/Super Comics

IW Reprint #1(no date)-E.C. Incredible S/F #30 + cover/Strange Worlds #3			
	6.00	12.00	18.00
IW Reprint #8	1.25	2.50	3.75
IW Reprint #9-Orlando/Wood story(Strange Worlds #4); cover from Flying Saucers #1			
	3.00	6.00	9.00
Super Reprint #10-23pg. Wood story from Space Detective #1 minus cvr.	3.00	6.00	9.00
Super Reprint #11-25pg. Wood story from An Earthman on Venus	6.00	12.00	18.00
Super Reprint #12-Orlando story from Rocket to the Moon	5.00	10.00	15.00
Super Reprint #15-Reprints Atlas stories; Heath art	1.20	2.40	3.60
Super Reprint #16-Avon's Strange Worlds #6; Kinstler, Check art	1.50	3.00	4.50
Super Reprint #17	1.20	2.40	3.60
Super Reprint #18-Reprints Daring Adventures; Space Busters, Explorer Joe, The Son of Robin Hood; Krigstein art			
	1.50	3.00	4.50

STRANGE SPORTS STORIES (See Br.& Bold,DC Spec.)
Sept-Oct, 1973 - #6, July-Aug, 1974
National Periodical Publications

#1	.20	.40	.60
2-6		.15	.30

STRANGE STORIES FROM ANOTHER WORLD
(Unknown World #1)
#2, Aug, 1952 - #5, Feb, 1953
Fawcett Publications

#2-5-Saunders painted covers			
	1.75	3.50	5.25

STRANGE STORIES OF SUSPENSE(Rugged Action#1-4)
#5, Oct, 1955 - #16, Aug, 1957
Atlas Comics (CSI)

	Good	Fine	Mint
#5(#1)	1.75	3.35	5.00
6,7,9	1.20	2.40	3.60
8-Williamson/Mayo story, #10-Williamson/			
Crandall + Torres sty.	3.00	6.00	9.00
11,13,16	1.00	2.00	3.00
12-Torres story	1.50	3.00	4.50
14-Williamson story	3.00	6.00	9.00
15-Krigstein story	2.00	4.00	6.00

NOTE: *Everett story-#6,7; covers-#9,11-13.*
Morrow story-#13.

STRANGE STORY
June-July, 1946   (52 pgs.)
Harvey Publications

	Good	Fine	Mint
#1-The Man in Black Called Fate by Powell			
	4.00	8.00	12.00

STRANGE SUSPENSE STORIES (Lawbreakers Suspense Stories #6-15; Captain Atom V1#78 on)
6/52 - #5, 2/53; #16, 1/54 - #77, 10/65;
V3#1, 10/67 - V1#9, 9/69
Fawcett Publications/Charlton Comics

	Good	Fine	Mint
#1-(Fawcett)-Powell art	3.00	6.00	9.00
2-5: #2-4-George Evans horror stories			
	2.00	4.00	6.00
16(1/54)-#23-Last pre-code issue			
	1.25	2.50	3.75
24-35,37-67-Contents change to science fict-			
ion	.50	1.00	1.50
36-68pgs., Ditko stories	1.50	3.00	4.50
68-74	.30	.60	.90
75-Origin Captain Atom by Ditko			
	1.75	3.50	5.25
76,77-Captain Atom	1.20	2.40	3.60
V3#1(10/67)-4	.25	.50	.75
V1#2-9	.20	.40	.60

NOTE: *Ditko stories-#18,20,22,31-35,37,39,41,*
45,47,50-52,57,76,77,2('68); covers-#18-20.

STRANGE TALES (Dr. Strange #169 on)
6/51 - #168, 5/68; #169, 9/73 - #188, 11/76
Atlas(CCPC #1-67/ZPC #68-79/VPI #80-107)/
Marvel #108 on

	Good	Fine	Mint
#1	40.00	80.00	120.00
2	20.00	40.00	60.00
3-5	12.00	24.00	36.00
6-9	8.00	16.00	24.00
10-Krigstein story	9.00	18.00	27.00
11-14,16-20	5.00	10.00	15.00
15-Krigstein story	6.00	12.00	18.00
21,23-32,34	3.00	6.00	9.00

	Good	Fine	Mint
22-Krigstein story	4.00	8.00	12.00
33-Davis story	4.00	8.00	12.00
35-41,43,44,46-52,54,55,57,59,60			
	2.00	4.00	6.00
42,45,59,61-Krigstein stories			
	2.50	5.00	7.50
53-Torres, Crandall stys.	3.00	6.00	9.00
56-Crandall story	2.50	5.00	7.50
58,64-Williamson story in each, with Mayo-			
#58	4.00	8.00	12.00
62-Torres story	2.00	4.00	6.00
63,65,66	1.50	3.00	4.50
67-80-Ditko/Kirby in all	1.50	3.00	4.50
81-90- " " " "	1.25	2.50	3.75
91-96,98-100-Kirby art	1.20	2.40	3.60
97-Aunt May app.; Kirby art			
	2.50	5.00	7.50
101-Human Torch begins by Jack Kirby(10/62)			
	18.00	36.00	54.00
102	9.00	18.00	27.00
103-105	7.00	14.00	21.00
106-109	4.00	8.00	12.00
110-1st app. Dr. Strange by Ditko			
	8.00	16.00	24.00
111-113	2.00	4.00	6.00
114-Acrobat disguised as Captain America-1st			
app. since the G.A.; intro. & 1st app.			
Victoria Bentley	2.50	5.00	7.50
115-Origin Dr. Strange	5.00	10.00	15.00
116-120	1.40	2.80	4.20
121-125	1.00	2.00	3.00
126-129,131-134: Thing/Torch team-up in all;			
last Human Torch-#134	.80	1.60	2.40
130-The Beatles app.	2.00	4.00	6.00
135-Origin Nick Fury, Agent of Shield by			
Kirby	1.40	2.80	4.20
136-150: #146-Last Ditko Dr. Strange who is			
in consecutive stories since #113			
	.70	1.40	2.10
151-John Buscema 1st work at Marvel			
	.75	1.50	2.25
152-168-Steranko art (inks #151-161)			
	.80	1.60	2.40
169,170-Brother Voodoo origin in ea.; series			
ends #173	.20	.40	.60
171-177: #177-Brunner cover	.20	.40	.60
178-181-Warlock by Starlin	.60	1.20	1.80
182-188	.20	.40	.60
Annual #1(1962)-Reprints from Str. Tales #73,			
76,78, Tales of Suspense #7,9, Tales to			
Astonish #1,6,7, & Journey Into Mystery			
#53,55,59	9.00	18.00	27.00
Annual #2(1963)-Reprints from Str. Tales #67,			
Str. Worlds(Atlas) #1-3, World of Fantasy			
#16; Human Torch vs. Spider-Man by Ditko/			
Kirby; Kirby cover	8.00	16.00	24.00

NOTE: *Briefer story-#17. Colan stories-#11,20.*

Strange Stories Of Suspense #10, © MCG

Strange Suspense Stories #4, © FAW

Strange Tales #178, © MCG

388

Strange Tales Of The Unusual #6. © MCG   Strange World Of Your Dreams #4. © PRIZE   Strange Worlds #3. © AVON

(Strange Tales cont'd)
Davis cover-#71. Ditko stories-#50,94,95,102,
103,106-111,114-146. Everett stories-#40-42,
45,73,147-152,164(inks); covers-#11,13,24,50,
51. Jack Katz app.-#26. Kirby Human Torch-
#101-104,108,109,114,120; Nick Fury(pencils)-
#135,141-143; (layouts)-#136-140,144-153;
other Kirby stories-#73,153; layouts-#135-
140,144-153; covers-#68-70,72-92,94,101-140.
Orlando stories-#41,44,46,49,52. Powell stor-
ies-#44,49, Starlin stories/covers-#178-181.
Woodbridge story-#59. Fantastic Four cameo-
#101-134.

STRANGE TALES OF THE UNUSUAL
Dec, 1955 - #11, Sept, 1957
Atlas Comics (ACI #1-4/WPI #5-12)

	Good	Fine	Mint
#1-Powell story	2.00	4.00	6.00
2,4,6,8,11	1.00	2.00	3.00
3-Williamson story,4pgs.	3.00	6.00	9.00
5-Crandall, Ditko stys.	1.75	3.50	5.25
7-Kirby + Orlando	1.20	2.40	3.60
9-Krigstein story	1.75	3.50	5.25
10-Torres + Morrow story	1.25	2.50	3.75

NOTE: *Everett story-#2; cover-#11. Orlando*
story-#7.

STRANGE TERRORS
June, 1952 - #7, June, 1953
St. John Publishing Co.

#1-Bondage cover	2.50	5.00	7.50
2	1.40	2.80	4.20
3-Kubert story	2.50	5.00	7.50
4-Kubert story(reprinted in Mystery Tales			
#18); Ekgren cover; has caricature of			
Jerry Iger	3.00	6.00	9.00
5-Kubert story	2.50	5.00	7.50
6-Giant, 100pgs.; Cameron story(3/53)			
	2.50	5.00	7.50
7-Giant, 100pgs.; Kubert story/cover			
	4.00	8.00	12.00

STRANGE WORLD OF YOUR DREAMS
Aug, 1952 - #4, Jan-Feb, 1953
Prize Publications

#1-Simon & Kirby art	8.00	16.00	24.00
2,3-Simon & Kirby art	7.00	14.00	21.00
4-S&K cover, Meskin sty.	5.00	10.00	15.00

STRANGE WORLDS (#18 continued from Avon's
11/50 - #22, 9-10/55   Eerie #1-17)
Avon Periodicals

#1-Kenton of the Star Patrol by Kubert; Crom
the Barbarian by John Giunta; used in

	Good	Fine	Mint
Seduction of the Innocent, pg. 120			
	20.00	40.00	60.00
2-Wood story; Crom the Barbarian by Giunta; Dara of the Vikings app.; used in Seduction of the Innocent, pg. 112			
	17.00	34.00	51.00
3-Wood/Orlando story(Kenton), Wood/William-son/Frazetta/Krenkel/Orlando story(7pgs.); Malu Slave Girl Princess app.; Kinstler cover	50.00	100.00	150.00
4-Wood cover/story(Kenton) + Orlando story; origin The Enchanted Daggar; Sultan story art	20.00	40.00	60.00
5-Orlando/Wood story(Kenton); Wood cover	17.50	35.00	52.50
6-Two Kinstler stories; Orlando/Wood cover, Check story	6.00	12.00	18.00
7,9,10: #9-Kinstler sty.	4.00	8.00	12.00
8-Kubert + Kinstler sty.	5.00	10.00	15.00
18-Reprints "Attack on Planet Mars" by Kubert	5.00	10.00	15.00
19-Reprints Avon's Robotmen of the Lost Plan-et	5.00	10.00	15.00
20-War stories-Reprints Wood cover/U.S. Para-troops #1	2.00	4.00	6.00
21,22-War stories	2.00	4.00	6.00
IW Reprint #5-Kinstler story reprint/Avon's #9	1.25	2.50	3.75

STRANGE WORLDS
Dec, 1958 - #5, July-Aug, 1959
Marvel Comics(MPI #1,2/Male #3,5)

#1-Kirby & Ditko art	3.00	6.00	9.00
2-Ditko cover/story	2.00	4.00	6.00
3-Two Kirby stories	2.00	4.00	6.00
4-Williamson story	4.00	8.00	12.00
5-Ditko story	1.75	3.50	5.25

NOTE: *Buscema story-#3, Ditko stories-#1-5;*
cover-#2. Kirby story-#1,3; covers-#1,3-5.

STREET COMIX (50¢)
1973 (36 pgs.) (B&W) (20,000 print run)
Street Enterprises/King Features

#1-Rip Kirby	.25	.50	.75
2-Flash Gordon	.25	.50	.75

STRICTLY PRIVATE
1942
Eastern Color Printing Co.

#1,2	10.00	20.00	30.00

STRONG MAN
Mar-Apr, 1955 - #4, Sept-Oct, 1955
Magazine Enterprises

(Strong Man cont'd)

	Good	Fine	Mint
#1(A-1#130)-Powell art	6.00	12.00	18.00
2(A-1#132), 3(A-1#134), 4(A-1#139)-Powell art	4.00	8.00	12.00

STUMBO THE GIANT (See Harvey Hits #49,54, 57,60,63,66,69,72,78,88)

STUMBO TINYTOWN
Oct, 1963 - 1965
Harvey Publications

#1	1.50	3.00	4.50
2-5	.80	1.60	2.40
6-13	.60	1.20	1.80

STUNTMAN COMICS
4-5/46 - #2, 6-7/46; #3, 10-11/46
Harvey Publications

#1-Origin Stuntman by S&K reprinted in Black
   Cat #9   50.00 100.00 150.00
2-S&K art   30.00 60.00 90.00
3-(Extremely Rare)-Small size(5½x8½"; B&W;
   32pgs.)Distributed to mail subscribers only; S&K art; Kid Adonis by S&K reprinted
   in Green Hornet #37. (Sold in San Francisco, 1976 for $700.00)
*(Also see All-New #15, Boy Explorers #2, and
Flash Gordon #5)*

SUBMARINE ATTACK
#11, May, 1958 - #60, Feb, 1967
Charlton Comics

#11-20	.25	.50	.75
21-60	.15	.30	.45

NOTE: *Montes/Bache art-#38,40,41.*

SUB-MARINER (See All-Winners, Blonde Phantom, Daring, Human Torch, Marvel Mystery, Motion Picture Funnies Weekly, & Namora)

SUB-MARINER, THE (2nd Series)
May, 1968 - #72, Sept, 1974 (#43-52pgs.)
Marvel Comics Group

#1-Origin Sub-Mariner   2.25 4.50 6.75
 2-Triton app.   1.20 2.40 3.60
 3-5: #5-1st Tiger Shark .90 1.80 2.70
 6-10: #8-The Thing app. .70 1.40 2.10
11-13,15-18,20   .50 1.00 1.50
14-Sub-Mariner vs. H.Torch .70 1.40 2.10
19-1st app. Sting Ray   .50 1.00 1.50
21-30: #30-Capt. Marvel app.30 .60 .90
31-33,35,37,39,40: #35-Avengers app. #37-
   Death of Lady Dorma   .30 .60   .90
34-Silver Surfer, Hulk app..50 1.00 1.50

	Good	Fine	Mint
36-Wrightson inks	.50	1.00	1.50
38-Origin	.50	1.00	1.50
41-49: #43-52pgs.	.30	.60	.90
50-55,57,58,60-Everett art	.50	1.00	1.50
56	.30	.60	.90
59-Starlin/Everett story	.60	1.20	1.80

61-Last artwork by Everett; 1st 4pgs. completed by Mortimer & Mooney
                          .50 1.00 1.50
62-1st Tales of Atlantis, ends #66; Chaykin
   art   .25 .50   .75
63-72   .20 .40   .60
NOTE: *Chaykin stories-#62-64. Craig inks-
#19-21.*
Special #1(1971)   .80 1.60 2.40
Annual #2(1/72)-Everett art.50 1.00 1.50

SUB-MARINER (1st Series) (--Comics #3 on)
(Best Love #33 on)(Amazing Mysteries #32 on?)
Spring, 1941 - #32, June, 1949; #33, April,
1954 - #42, Oct, 1955
Timely, #1-32(MPC)/Atlas, #33-42(CCC)

#1-The Sub-Mariner by Everett & The Angel
   begin   275.00 550.00 825.00
2-Everett art   140.00 280.00 420.00
3   90.00 180.00 270.00
4-Everett art, 40pgs.; 1pg. Wolverton art
                    85.00 170.00 255.00
5   60.00 120.00 180.00
6-10: #9-Wolverton art, 3pgs.
                    45.00 90.00 135.00
11-15   30.00 60.00 90.00
16-20   27.50 55.00 82.50
21-Last Angel; Everett art
                    20.00 40.00 60.00
22-Young Allies app.; Everett art
                    20.00 40.00 60.00
23-The Human Torch, Namora x-over
                    20.00 40.00 60.00
24-Namora x-over   20.00 40.00 60.00
25-The Blonde Phantom begins, ends #29,31;
   Kurtzman art; Namora x-over
                    25.00 50.00 75.00
26,27   20.00 40.00 60.00
28-Namora cover + story by Everett
                    20.00 40.00 60.00
29-31: #29-The Human Torch app. #31-Capt.
   America app.   20.00 40.00 60.00
32-Origin Sub-Mariner 22.00 44.00 66.00
33-Origin Sub-Mariner; The Human Torch app.
   Namora x-over in Sub-Mariner, #33-42
                    20.00 40.00 60.00
34,35-Human Torch in ea. 12.00 24.00 36.00
36-42: #39-Namora app. 12.00 24.00 36.00
NOTE: *Angel by Gustavson-#1,2. Everett art
in all #33-42.*

The Sub-Mariner #4, © MCG

Sub-Mariner Comics #5, © MCG

Sub-Mariner Comics #39, © MCG

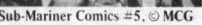

Sugar Bowl #4, © FF

Sun Girl #2, © MCG

Sunny #14, © FOX

SUE & SALLY SMITH (Flying Nurses)
1963
Charlton Comics

	Good	Fine	Mint
V2#48-54		.15	.30

SUGAR & SPIKE
Apr-May, 1956 - #98, Oct-Nov, 1971
National Periodical Publications

#1 (Scarce)	17.00	34.00	52.00
2	8.00	16.00	24.00
3-5	5.00	10.00	15.00
6-10	4.00	8.00	12.00
11-20	2.50	5.00	7.50
21-40	1.20	2.40	3.60

41-98: #85-68pgs., reprints #72. #72-Origin
& 1st app. Bernie the Brain. #96-68pgs.

#97,98-52pgs.	.70	1.40	2.10

NOTE: *All written and drawn by* <u>Sheldon Mayer</u>.

SUGAR BEAR
No date   (16 pgs.)   (2½x4½")
Post Cereal Giveaway

"The Almost Take Over of the Post Office"			
	.15	.30	.45
"The Race Across the Atlantic"			
	.15	.30	.45

SUGAR BOWL COMICS
May, 1948 - 1949
Famous Funnies

#1-Toth cover	2.50	5.00	7.50
2,4,5	1.75	3.50	5.25
3-Toth story	2.50	5.00	7.50

SUGARFOOT (See 4-Color #907,992,1059,1098, 1147,1209)

SUMMER FUN (Walt Disney's--)(Formerly Mickey
#2, 1959   Mouse--)
Dell Publishing Co.

#2-Two Barks stories	5.00	10.00	15.00

SUMMER FUN (Formerly Li'l Genius; Holiday
#54, Oct, 1966   (Giant)   Surprise #55)
Charlton Comics

#54		.15	.35

SUMMER LOVE (Formerly Brides in Love)
V2#46, 10/65 - V2#48, Nov, 1968
Charlton Comics

V2#46-Beatle cover/story	1.50	3.00	4.50

	Good	Fine	Mint
47-Beatle story	1.35	2.75	4.00
48		.15	.30

SUMMER MAGIC (See Movie Comics)

SUNDANCE (See 4-Color Comics #1126)

SUNDANCE KID
June, 1971 - #3, Sept, 1971   (52 pgs.)
Skywald Publications

#1-Durango Kid; 2 Kirby Bullseye reprints			
	.40	.80	1.20
2-Swift Arrow, Durango Kid, Bullseye by S&K;			
Meskin + 1pg. origin	.25	.50	.75
3-Durango Kid, Billy the Kid, Red Hawk re-			
prints	.20	.40	.60

SUNDAY FUNNIES
1950
Harvey Publications

#1	1.50	3.00	4.50

SUN FUN KOMIKS
1939   (Black, white & red)
Sun Publications

#1	6.00	12.00	18.00

SUN GIRL
Aug, 1948 - #3, Dec, 1948
Marvel Comics

#1-Sun Girl begins; Miss America app.			
	25.00	50.00	75.00
2-The Blonde Phantom begins,			
3	18.00	36.00	54.00

SUNNY, AMERICA'S SWEETHEART
#11, Dec, 1947 - #14, June, 1948
Fox Features Syndicate

#11-14-Feldstein cover/stories			
	15.00	30.00	45.00
IW Reprint #8-Feldstein art; reprints Fox			
issue	3.00	6.00	9.00

SUNSET CARSON
Feb, 1951 - #4, 1951
Charlton Comics

#1	3.00	6.00	9.00
2-4	2.00	4.00	6.00

SUPER ANIMALS PRESENTS PIDGY & THE MAGIC GLASSES

(Super Animals Presents Pidgy & -- cont'd)
Dec, 1953
Star Publications

	Good	Fine	Mint
3-D #1	4.00	8.00	12.00

SUPER BOOK OF COMICS
(32pgs.; later issues-16pgs.)(Omar Bread & Pan-Am Motor Oil Co. giveaways)
1943 - 1946   (Some numbers repeated)
Dell Publishing Co.

	Good	Fine	Mint
#1-Smilin' Jack(Omar)	5.00	10.00	15.00
1-Dick Tracy	10.00	20.00	30.00
2-Red Ryder Victory Patrol	7.00	14.00	21.00
2-King of the Royal Mtd.	5.00	10.00	15.00
2-Smitty	3.50	7.00	10.50
2-Smilin' Jack(Omar)	5.00	10.00	15.00
3-Captain Midnight	8.00	16.00	24.00
3-Terry & the Pirates	8.00	16.00	24.00
3-Moon Mullins	3.00	6.00	9.00
4-Smitty	3.00	6.00	9.00
4-Andy Panda	4.00	8.00	12.00
5-Don Winslow	4.00	8.00	12.00
5-Smokey Stover(Omar)	3.00	6.00	9.00
5-Terry & the Pirates	8.00	16.00	24.00
6-Don Winslow-McWilliams art	4.00	8.00	12.00
6-King of the Royal Mtd.	5.00	10.00	15.00
6-Porky Pig	4.00	8.00	12.00
7-Dick Tracy	10.00	20.00	30.00
7-Smilin' Jack(Omar)	4.00	8.00	12.00
8-Oswald the Rabbit	3.00	6.00	9.00
9-Alley Oop	4.00	8.00	12.00
9-Terry & the Pirates	7.00	14.00	21.00
10-Elmer Fudd(Omar)	2.50	5.00	7.50
11-Little Orphan Annie	5.00	10.00	15.00
12-Woody Woodpecker	3.00	6.00	9.00
13-Dick Tracy(16pgs.)(Omar)	10.00	20.00	30.00
14-Bugs Bunny(Omar)	4.00	8.00	12.00
15-Andy Panda	2.50	5.00	7.50
16-Terry & the Pirates	7.00	14.00	21.00
17-Smokey Stover	3.00	6.00	9.00
18-Porky Pig(Omar)	3.00	6.00	9.00
19-Smilin' Jack(Omar)	4.00	8.00	12.00
20-Oswald the Rabbit(Omar)	3.00	6.00	9.00
21-Gasoline Alley(Omar)	4.00	8.00	12.00
22-Elmer Fudd	2.50	5.00	7.50
23-Little Orphan Annie(Omar)	4.00	8.00	12.00
24-Woody Woodpecker(Omar)	2.00	4.00	6.00
25-Dick Tracy	8.00	16.00	24.00
26-Bugs Bunny(Omar)	2.00	4.00	6.00
27-Andy Panda	2.00	4.00	6.00
28-Terry & the Pirates(1946)(Omar)	7.00	14.00	21.00
29-Smokey Stover	2.50	5.00	7.50
30-Porky Pig(Omar)	2.00	4.00	6.00
No#-Bugs Bunny('48)	2.00	4.00	6.00
No#-Dan Dunn('39 reprint)	2.50	5.00	7.50
No#-Dick Tracy	8.00	16.00	24.00
No#-Elmer Fudd('46)	2.00	4.00	6.00
No#-Woody Woodpecker	2.00	4.00	6.00

SUPERBOY
(-- & the Legion of Super Heroes with #197) (See More Fun & Aurora)
Mar-Apr, 1949 - Present
National Periodical Publications/DC Comics

	Good	Fine	Mint
#1 (Scarce)	115.00	230.00	345.00
2	60.00	120.00	180.00
3	40.00	80.00	120.00
4,5: #5-Supergirl app.	30.00	60.00	90.00
6-10	22.00	44.00	66.00
11-15	15.00	30.00	45.00
16-20	12.00	24.00	36.00
21-30	8.00	16.00	24.00
31-40	6.00	12.00	18.00
41-50	4.00	8.00	12.00
51-60	3.00	6.00	9.00
61-67,69,70	2.25	4.50	6.75
68-Origin & 1st app. original Bizarro (10-11/58)	3.00	6.00	9.00
71-77,79,80: #76-1st Supermonkey	1.50	3.00	4.50
78-Origin Mr. Mxyzptlk & Superboy's costume	2.50	5.00	7.50
81,83-97,99,100: #86-Intro. Pete Ross. #89-Intro. Mon-el. #90-Pete Ross learns Superboy's I.D.	1.25	2.50	3.75
82-1st Bizarro Krypto	1.25	2.50	3.75
98-Intro. & origin Ultra Boy	1.50	3.00	4.50
101-103,105-120	.80	1.60	2.40
104-Origin Phantom Zone	.80	1.60	2.40
121-140: #125-1st app. Kid Psycho. #126-Origin Krypto the Super Dog. #129-Giant G-22. #138-Giant G-35	.50	1.00	1.50
(80-pg. Giant G-22,35)	.70	1.40	2.10
141-176: #145-Superboy's parents regain their youth. #147,156,165,174-All Giants G-47, G-59,G-71,G-83. #147-Origin The Legion of Super Heroes.	.40	.80	1.20
(Giants G-47,59,71,83)	.60	1.20	1.80
177-184,186,187(All 52pgs): #184-Origin Dial H for Hero	.35	.70	1.05
185-100pg. Super Spec. #12	.60	1.20	1.80
188-190	.35	.70	1.05
191-196,198,199	.30	.60	.90
197-Legion begins	.50	1.00	1.50
200-Bouncing Boy & Duo Damsel marry	.40	.80	1.20

Super Animals--3-D #1, © STAR

Super Book #21, © News Synd.

Superboy #19, © DC

Supercar #1, © GK

Super Comics #9, © DELL

Super Comics #100, © DELL

(Superboy cont'd)	Good	Fine	Mint
201,204,206,207,209	.30	.60	.90
202,205-100pgs.	.50	1.00	1.50
203-Invisible Kid dies	.50	1.00	1.50
208-68pgs.	.40	.80	1.20
210-Origin Karate Kid	.50	1.00	1.50
211-215,217-220	.25	.50	.75
216-1st app. Tyrol	.25	.50	.75
221-229	.20	.40	.60
230-$1.00 ish.	.35	.70	1.05
231-237,240-246	.20	.40	.60
238-Starlin cover	.20	.40	.60
239-Starlin story	.20	.40	.60
Annual #1(6/64)	1.75	3.50	5.25

NOTE: *Adams covers-#143,145,146,148-155,157-161,163,164,166-168,172,173,175,176,178. Chaykin pencils-#240. Infantino cover-#171. Simonson pencils-#237. Staton story-#227,243-246. Wood inks-#152-155,157-161. Legion app.-#172,173,176,183,184,188,190,191,193,195. See 80-Page Giant #10.*

SUPER BRAT
January, 1954 - #4, July, 1954
Toby Press

#1(1954)	.80	1.60	2.40
2-4: #4-Li'l Teevy by Mel Lazarus			
	.60	1.20	1.80
IW Reprint #1,2,3,7,8('58)	.25	.50	.75
IW(Super) Reprint #10('63)	.25	.50	.75

SUPERCAR (TV)
Nov, 1962 - #4, Aug, 1963
Gold Key

#1-Crandall cover	1.20	2.40	3.60
2-4-Crandall covers	.80	1.60	2.40

SUPER CAT
1953 - 1954; Sept, 1957 - #4, May, 1958
Ajax/Farrell Publ. (Four Star Comic Corp.)

#56-58(1st Series)-L. B. Cole covers			
	.50	1.00	1.50
#1('57-Ajax)(2nd Series)	.40	.80	1.20
2-4	.30	.60	.90

SUPER CIRCUS
January, 1951 - #5, 1951
Cross Publishing Co.

#1	1.00	2.00	3.00
2-5	.50	1.00	1.50

SUPER CIRCUS (TV)
March, 1954 - April, 1956
Dell Publishing Co.

	Good	Fine	Mint
4-Color #542,592,694('54-'56)			
	1.00	2.00	3.00

SUPER COMICS
May, 1938 - #121, Feb-Mar, 1949
Dell Publishing Co.

	Good	Fine	Mint
#1-Terry & the Pirates, The Gumps, Dick Tracy, Little Orphan Annie, Gasoline Alley, Little Joe, Smilin' Jack begin			
	60.00	120.00	180.00
2	30.00	60.00	90.00
3	20.00	40.00	60.00
4	17.00	34.00	51.00
5-10	14.00	28.00	42.00
11-20	12.00	24.00	36.00
21-Origin Magic Morro	10.00	20.00	30.00
22-30	10.00	20.00	30.00
31-40	8.00	16.00	24.00
41-50: #43-Terry & the Pirates ends			
	7.00	14.00	21.00
51-60	6.00	12.00	18.00
61-70	5.00	10.00	15.00
71-80	4.00	8.00	12.00
81-100	3.50	7.00	10.50
101-115-Last Dick Tracy	3.00	6.00	9.00
116-121: #119-121-Terry & the Pirates app.			
	2.00	4.00	6.00

SUPER COPS, THE
July, 1974 (One Shot)
Red Circle Productions (Archie)

#1-Morrow cover/story	.20	.40	.60

SUPER CRACKED (See Cracked)

SUPER DC GIANT (25¢) (No #1-12)
#13, 9-10/70 - #26, 7-8/71; #27, Fall, 1976
National Periodical Publications

S-13-Binky	.25	.50	.75
S-14-Top Guns of the West; Kubert cover; Trigger Twins, Johnny Thunder, Wyoming Kid reprints	.30	.60	.90
S-15-Western comics; Kubert cover; Pow Wow Smith, Vigilante, Buffalo Bill reprints	.30	.60	.90
S-16-Best of the Brave & the Bold; Kubert art	.50	1.00	1.50
S-17-Love 1970	.30	.60	.90
S-18-Three Mouseketeers; Dizzy Dog, Doodles Duck, Bo Bunny reprts.	.25	.50	.75
S-19-Jerry Lewis; 3 stories inked by Adams	.70	1.40	2.10
S-20-House of Mystery-Neal Adams cover; 3 Kirby stories reprinted	.40	.80	1.20

(Super DC Giant cont'd)	Good	Fine	Mint
S-21-Love 1971	.30	.60	.90
S-22-Top Guns of the West	.30	.60	.90
S-23-Unexpected, The	.30	.60	.90
S-24-Supergirl	.50	1.00	1.50
S-25-Challengers of the Unknown-All Kirby/ Wood reprints			
S-26-Aquaman('71)	.50	1.00	1.50
#27-Strange Flying Saucer Adventures(Fall, '76)	.30	.60	.90

SUPER DOOPER
1946   (Soft cover)(10¢)(32pgs.)
Able Publ. Co.

#1-4,6,7	.80	1.60	2.40
5-Capt. Freedom & Shock Gibson	2.00	4.00	6.00

SUPER DUCK COMICS   (The Cockeyed Wonder)
Fall, 1944 - #94, Dec, 1960
MLJ Mag. #1-4/Close-Up #5 on (Archie)

#1-Origin	7.00	14.00	21.00
2-5	3.00	6.00	9.00
6-10	2.00	4.00	6.00
11-20	1.50	3.00	4.50
21-40	1.00	2.00	3.00
41-94	.80	1.60	2.40

SUPER DUPER
1941
Harvey Publications

#5-Captain Freedom & Shock Gibson app.	8.00	16.00	24.00
8,11	4.00	8.00	12.00

SUPER DUPER COMICS   (Formerly Latest Comics?)
May-June, 1947
F. E. Howard Publ.

#3-Mr. Monster app.	1.00	2.00	3.00

SUPER FRIENDS   (TV)
Nov, 1976 - Present
National Periodical Publications/DC Comics

#1-Superman, Batman, Wonder Woman, Aquaman, Robin, Wendy, Marvin & Wonder Dog begin			
	.25	.50	.75
2-10	.15	.30	.45
11-16		.15	.35

SUPER FUN
January, 1956
Gillmor Magazines

	Good	Fine	Mint
#1-Comics, puzzles, cut-outs by A. W. Nugent	1.35	2.75	4.00

SUPER FUNNIES   (-- Western Funnies #3,4)
Dec, 1953 - #4, 1954   (Satire)
Superior Comics Publishers Ltd. (Canada)

#1(3-D)-Dopey Duck	5.00	10.00	15.00
2	.60	1.20	1.80
3,4-(Western-Phantom Ranger)	.60	1.20	1.80

SUPERGEAR COMICS
1976   (4 pgs.) (in color) (slick paper)
Jacobs Corp. (Giveaway)

(Rare)-Superman, Lois Lane; Steve Lombard app.	.25	.50	.75

NOTE: *500 copies printed, over half destroyed.*

SUPERGIRL   (See Super DC Giant, Adventure, Action, & Superman Family)
11/72 - #9, 12-1/73-74; #10, 9-10/74
National Periodical Publications

#1	.50	1.00	1.50
2-5: #5-Zatanna origin reprint	.30	.60	.90
6-10	.25	.50	.75

NOTE: *Anderson art-#5. Zatanna in #1-3,5,7; Wonder Woman-#9; Prez-#10.*

SUPER GOOF   (Walt Disney)
Oct, 1965 - Present
Gold Key

#1	.60	1.20	1.80
2-10	.40	.80	1.20
11-20	.25	.50	.75
21-52	.15	.30	.45

NOTE: *Reprints in #16,24,28,29,37,38,43.*

SUPER GREEN BERET   (Tod Holton --)
April, 1967 - #2, June, 1967   (68 pgs.)
Lightning Comics (Milson Publ. Co.)

#1,2	.75	1.50	2.25

SUPER HEROES   (See Marvel --)

SUPER HEROES
Jan, 1967 - #4, June, 1967
Dell Publishing Co.

#1	.60	1.20	1.80
2-4	.35	.70	1.05

Super Duper #3, © F.E. Howard

Super Funnies #2, © SUPR

Supergirl #1, © DC

Super Magic #1, © S&S

Superman #1, © DC

Superman #10, © DC

SUPER HEROES BATTLE SUPER-GORILLAS
Winter, 1976-77   (One Shot)
National Periodical Publications

	Good	Fine	Mint
#1-Superman, Batman, Flash stories	.25	.50	.75

SUPERHEROES VS. SUPERVILLAINS
July, 1966 (no month given)
Archie Publications

#1-Reprints from Archie Superhero comics	1.00	2.00	3.00

SUPERIOR STORIES
May-June, 1955 - #4, Nov-Dec, 1955
Nesbit Publishing Co.

#1-The Invisible Man app.	2.00	4.00	6.00
2-The Pirate of the Gulf by J. H. Ingrahams	1.25	2.50	3.75
3-Wreck of the Grosvenor	1.25	2.50	3.75
4-O'Henry's "The Texas Rangers"	1.50	3.00	4.50

SUPER MAGIC (Super Magician #2 on)
May, 1941
Street & Smith Publications

V1#1-Blackstone, the Magician app.; origin &
  1st app. Rex King(Black Fury); not Eisner
  cover   20.00 40.00 60.00

SUPER MAGICIAN COMICS (Super Magic #1)
#2, Sept, 1941 - V5#8, Feb-Mar, 1947
Street and Smith Publications

V1#2-Rex King, Man of Adventure app.
                     8.00 16.00 24.00
  3-Tao-Anwar, Boy Magician begins
                     7.00 14.00 21.00
  4-Origin Transo   6.00 12.00 18.00
  5-12: #11-Supersnipe app.
                     5.00 10.00 15.00
V2#1-The Shadow app. 2.50   5.00   7.50
  2-12: #5-Origin Tigerman. #8-Red Dragon
  begins   2.00   4.00   6.00
V3#1-12: #5-Origin Mr. Twilight
                     1.60   3.20   4.80
V4#1-12: #12-Elliman Nigel begins
                     1.50   3.00   4.50
V5#1-6   1.50   3.00   4.50
  7,8-Red Dragon by Cartier
                     3.50   7.00 10.50

SUPERMAN (See Action Comics, All-Star Comics, Book & Record Set, Giant Comics to Color Taylor's Christmas Tabloid, & World's Finest Comics)

SUPERMAN
Summer, 1939 - Present
National Periodical Publications/DC Comics

	Good	Fine	Mint
#1(No#)-1st four Action stories reprinted; origin Superman by Siegel & Shuster; has a new 2pg. origin plus 4pgs. omitted in Action story	1400.00	2800.00	4200.00

(Prices vary widely on this book)

2-All daily strip reprints	350.00	700.00	1050.00
3-2nd story reprint from Action #6	275.00	550.00	825.00
4	175.00	350.00	525.00
5	140.00	280.00	420.00
6,7	100.00	200.00	300.00
8-10	80.00	160.00	240.00
11-15: #13-Jimmy Olsen app.	50.00	100.00	150.00
16-20	35.00	70.00	105.00
21-25	28.00	56.00	84.00
26-29: #28-Lois Lane Girl Reporter series begins #40,42	20.00	40.00	60.00

30-Origin & 1st app. Mr. Mxyztplk (pronounced
  "Mix-it-plk"); name later became Mxyzptlk
  ("Mix-yez-pit-1-ick")-The character was inspired by a combination of the name of Al
  Capp's Joe Blyfstyk(the little man with
  the black cloud over his head) & the devilish antics of Bugs Bunny.
                    40.00 80.00 120.00

31-40	14.00	28.00	42.00
41-50	12.00	24.00	36.00
51,52	10.00	20.00	30.00
53-Origin Superman retold	20.00	40.00	60.00
54-Used in Seduction of the Innocent, pg.33	12.00	24.00	36.00
55-60	9.00	18.00	27.00

61-Origin Superman retold; origin Green Cryp-
  tonite(1st Kryptonite story)
                    12.00 24.00 36.00

62-70	8.00	16.00	24.00
71-75: #73-1st Superbaby story. #75-Some have #74 on cover	7.00	14.00	21.00

76-(Scarce)-Batman x-over; Superman & Batman
  learn each other's I.D.
                    12.00 24.00 36.00

77-80	6.00	12.00	18.00
81-90	5.00	10.00	15.00
91-99	4.50	9.00	13.50
100	7.00	14.00	21.00
101-110	4.00	8.00	12.00
111-120	3.00	6.00	9.00
121,122,124-130: #128-1st use of Red Kryptonite. #129-Origin & 1st app. Lori Lemaris, the Mermaid	2.50	5.00	7.50
123-1st app. Supergirl	6.00	12.00	18.00

	Good	Fine	Mint

(Superman cont'd)   Good Fine Mint

131-140   2.00 4.00 6.00

141-150: #146-Superman's life story. #147-1st
app. Legion of Super-Villains
                1.75 3.50 5.25

151-165: #158-1st app. Flamebird & Nightwing.
#165-Origin Sally Selwyn
                1.50 3.00 4.50

166,168-180   1.25 2.50 3.75

167-New origin Braniac 1.50 3.00 4.50

181,182,184-186,188-192,194-196,198-200: #181-
1st 2965 story/series   .75 1.50 2.25

183(G-18),187(G-23),193(G-31),197(G-36) - All
Giants   .90 1.80 2.70

201,203-206,208-211,213-216,218-221,223-226,
228-231,234-238   .60 1.20 1.80

202(G-42),207(G-48),212(G-54),217(G-60),222
(G-66),227(G-72),232(G-78),239(G-84) -
All Gaints   .75 1.50 2.25

233-1st app. Morgan Edge, Clark Kent switch
from newspaper reporter to TV newscaster,

240-Kaluta story   .50 1.00 1.50

241-244 (52pgs.)   .75 1.50 2.25

245-DC 100pg. Super Spec. #7; Air Wave, Kid
Eternity reprints   .90 1.80 2.70

246-248,250,251,253 (All 52pgs.): #253-2pg.
Finley art   .30   .60   .90

249,254-Adams stories. #249(52pgs.)-origin &
1st app. Terra-Man by Adams (inks)
                1.25 2.50 3.75

252-DC 100pg. Super Spec. #13; Ray, Black Condor, Starman, Hawkman, Dr. Fate, Spectre
app.; Adams cover 1.25 2.50 3.75

255-263   .30   .60   .90

264-1st app. Steve Lombard .30   .60   .90

265-271,273-277,279-283,285-299
                 .25   .50   .75

272,278,284-All 100pgs. .50 1.00 1.50

300-Retells origin   .25   .50   .75

301-330   .20   .40   .60

331   .15   .30   .45

Annual #1(10/60)   8.00 16.00 24.00

Annual #2(1960)   4.00 8.00 12.00

Annual #3(1961)   3.00 6.00 9.00

Annual #4(1961)-Legionairres origins, #5
                2.00 4.00 6.00

Annual #6('62)-Reprints Legion/Adventure#247,

Annual #7('63), #8('64) 1.75 3.50 5.25

The Amazing World of Superman "Official Metropolis Edition"(14x10½"; $2.00)-Reprints
origin   1.50 3.00 4.50

Pizza Hut Giveaway(12/77)-Exact reprints of
#97,113   .30   .60   .90

--Special Edition #5(U.S. Navy giveaway,'45)
52pgs., regular comic book format
             30.00 60.00 90.00

(See Aurora giveaway)

NOTE: *Adams stories-#249(inks),254; covers-*
*#204-208,210,212-215,219,231,233-237,240-243,
249-252,254,263,306-308,313,314,317.* Anderson
stories-#233-270. Wayne Boring *art-late 1940's
to early 1960's.* Infantino *stories-#242,245;
covers-#199,216,238.* Kubert *cover-#216.*
Morrow *story-#238.*

SUPERMAN & THE GREAT CLEVELAND FIRE(Giveaway)
1948 (4pgs., no cover) (Hospital Fund)
National Periodical Publications

               Good Fine Mint

(Rare)-in full color 60.00 120.00 180.00

SUPERMAN COSTUME COMIC
1954   (One Shot)
National Periodical Publications

#1-(Rare)   15.00 30.00 45.00

SUPERMAN FAMILY, THE (Formerly Superman's Pal
#164, 4-5/74 - Present   Jimmy Olsen)
National Periodical Publications/DC Comics

#164   .50 1.00 1.50

165-176-(100-68pgs.) .35   .70 1.05

177-181-(52pgs.)   .25   .50   .75

182($1.00 ish.begin)-#194 .50 1.00 1.50

NOTE: *Adams covers-#182-185.* Anderson *story-
#187.* Staton *stories-#191,192.*

SUPERMAN (Miniature)
1953; 1955 - 1956 (3 issues)(No#'s)(32pgs.)
The pages are numbered in the 1st ish: 1-32;
2nd: 1A-32A, & 3rd: 1B-32B
National Periodical Publications

No date-Py-Co-Pay Tooth Powder giveaway
(8pgs.; Circa late '40's-early '50's)
            10.00 20.00 30.00

#1-The Superman Time Capsule (Kellogg's Sug-
ar Smacks)   8.00 16.00 24.00

1A-Duel in Space   6.00 12.00 18.00

1B-The Super Show of Metropolis (also #1-32,
no B)   6.00 12.00 18.00

NOTE: *Numbering variations exist. Each title
could have any combination-#1,1A, or 1B.*

SUPERMAN RECORD COMIC
1966   (Golden records)
National Periodical Publications

#1 (with record)   1.50 3.00 4.50

8 (with record)-Record reads origin of Superman from comic; came with iron-on patch,
decoder, membership card & button
             2.00 4.00 6.00

Superman #56, © DC   Superman Annual #7, © DC

Superman & The Great Clev. Fire, © DC

Superman's G.F. Lois Lane #10, © DC

Superman's Pal Jimmy Olsen #17, © DC

Superman Tim(1949-Illo), © DC

SUPERMAN'S CHRISTMAS ADVENTURE
1940, 1944 (16pgs.) (Giveaway)
Distr. by Nehi drinks, Bailey Store, Ivey-
Keith Co., Kennedy's Boys Shop, Macy's Store
National Periodical Publications

	Good	Fine	Mint
#1(1940)-by Burnley	100.00	200.00	300.00
No#(1944)	70.00	140.00	210.00

SUPERMAN SCRAPBOOK
1940 (10"x17")
Saalfield

Contains Sundays #135,163-172,198,199 + origin from Action #1   25.00 50.00 75.00

SUPERMAN'S GIRLFRIEND LOIS LANE (See 80 Pg.
Giants #3,14, Showcase & Superman Family)

SUPERMAN'S GIRLFRIEND LOIS LANE
3-4/58 - #136, 1-2/74; #137, 9-10/74
National Periodical Publications

	Good	Fine	Mint
#1	30.00	60.00	90.00
2	15.00	30.00	45.00
3	12.00	24.00	36.00
4,5	8.00	16.00	24.00
6-10	5.00	10.00	15.00
11-20: #14-Supergirl x-over	3.50	7.00	10.50
21-30: #29-Aquaman, Batman, Green Arrow			
cameo	1.75	3.50	5.25
31-50	1.00	2.00	3.00
51-67,69,70	.60	1.20	1.80
68-(Giant G-26)	.75	1.50	2.25
71-76,78	.35	.70	1.05
77-(Giant G-39)	.60	1.20	1.80
79-Adams covers begin, end #95,108			
	.60	1.20	1.80
80-85,87-94: #89-Batman x-over; all Adams			
covers	.50	1.00	1.50
86-(Giant G-51)-Adams cvr.	.60	1.20	1.80
95-(Giant G-63)-Wonder Woman x-over; Adams			
cover	.60	1.20	1.80
96-103,106,107,109-111	.25	.50	.75
104-(Giant G-75)	.50	1.00	1.50
105-Origin & 1st app. The Rose & the Thorn,			
108-Adams cover	.30	.60	.90
112,114-123(52pgs.): #111-Morrow story. #123-			
G.A. Batman reprint	.25	.50	.75
113-(Giant G-87)	.40	.80	1.20
124-137: #136-Wonder Woman x-over			
	.20	.40	.60
Annual #1(8-10/62)	1.50	3.00	4.50
Annual #2(8-10/63)	.80	1.60	2.40

SUPERMAN'S PAL JIMMY OLSEN (Superman Family
#164 on) (See 80 Pg. Giants)

Sept-Oct, 1954 - #163, Feb-Mar, 1974
National Periodical Publications

	Good	Fine	Mint
#1	50.00	100.00	150.00
2	25.00	50.00	75.00
3	17.00	34.00	51.00
4,5	10.00	20.00	30.00
6-10	6.00	12.00	18.00
11-20	4.00	8.00	12.00
21-30	2.00	4.00	6.00
31-40: #31-Origin Elastic Lad. #33-1pg. bio-			
graphy of Jack Larson(T.V. Jimmy Olsen)			
	1.50	3.00	4.50
41-50	1.00	2.00	3.00
51-70	.65	1.35	2.00
71-78,80-90	.50	1.00	1.50
79(9/64)-Titled The Red-headed Beetle of			
1000 B.C.	1.00	2.00	3.00
91-94,96-103,105-110	.40	.80	1.20
95(G-25),104(G-38)-Giants	.50	1.00	1.50
111,112,114-121,123-130,132	.30	.60	.90
113(G-50),122(G-62),131(G-74)-Giants			
	.50	1.00	1.50
133-Newsboy Legion by Kirby begins			
	1.00	2.00	3.00
134-139	.60	1.20	1.80
140-(Giant G-86)	.50	1.00	1.50
141-Newsboy Legion reprints by S&K begin			
(52pg. issues begin)	.50	1.00	1.50
142-148-N.L. reprints	.50	1.00	1.50
149,150-G.A. Plastic Man reprint in both			
(last 52pg. ish.)	.30	.60	.90
151-163	.20	.40	.60

NOTE: *Issues #141-148 contain Simon & Kirby
Newsboy Legion reprints from Star Spangled
#7,8,9,10,11,12,13,14 in that order. Adams
covers-#109-112,115,117,118,120,121,132,134-
136,146-148. Kirby stories-#133-139,141-148;
covers-#133,139. Kirby/Adams covers-#137,
138,141-146.*

SUPERMAN SPECTACULAR (See DC Spec.Series #5)

SUPERMAN 3-D (See 3-D --)

SUPERMAN-TIM (Becomes Gene Autry-Tim)
1945 - 1950 (½-Size) (B&W Giveaway)
Superman-Tim Stores/National Per. Publ.

	Good	Fine	Mint
Issues with a Superman story			
	15.00	30.00	45.00
Issues with Superman text illos			
	10.00	20.00	30.00
Issues without Superman	8.00	16.00	24.00

SUPERMAN VS. SPIDER-MAN
April, 1976 (100pgs.)($2.00)(Over-sized)
National Per. Publ./Marvel Comics Group

	1.50	3.00	4.50

SUPERMAN WORKBOOK
1945   (One Shot) (68pgs.) (B&W)
National Per. Publ./Juvenile Group Foundation

	Good	Fine	Mint
	15.00	30.00	45.00

SUPERMOUSE (-- The Big Cheese)
Dec, 1948 - #45, Fall, 1958
Standard Comics/Pines #12 on(Literary Ent.)

#1	3.50	7.00	10.50
2,3,5,6-Text illos by Frazetta in all			
	2.50	5.00	7.50
4-7pg. text story with Frazetta illos			
	4.00	8.00	12.00
7-10	1.50	3.00	4.50
11-20	.90	1.80	2.70
21-45	.60	1.20	1.80
#1-Summer Holiday issue-Summer'57(Pines)			
(100pgs.)	1.50	3.00	4.50
2-Giant Summer issue-Summer'58(Pines)			
(100pgs.)	1.00	2.00	3.00

SUPER-MYSTERY COMICS
July, 1940 - V8#6, July, 1949
Ace Magazines

V1#1-Magno, the Magnetic Man & Vulcan begin			
	40.00	80.00	120.00
2	20.00	40.00	60.00
3-The Black Spider begins			
	18.00	36.00	54.00
4-Origin Davy	16.50	33.25	50.00
5-Intro. The Clown	15.00	30.00	45.00
6	12.00	24.00	36.00
V2#1-Origin Buckskin	12.00	24.00	36.00
2-6	10.00	20.00	30.00
V3#1,2	8.00	16.00	24.00
3-Intro. The Lancer; Dr. Nemesis & The			
Sword begin; cover & 2 stories by Kurtz-			
man(Mr. Risk & Paul Revere Jr.)			
	12.00	24.00	36.00
4-Kurtzman story	10.00	20.00	30.00
5-Two Kurtzman stys.	11.00	22.00	33.00
6-Mr. Risk app.; Kurtzman's Paul Revere			
Jr.	11.00	22.00	33.00
V4#1-6	4.00	8.00	12.00
V5#1-6	3.00	6.00	9.00
V6#1-5: #4-Last Magno; Mr. Risk app. in #2,			
4-6	2.00	4.00	6.00
V7#1-6, V8#1-6	2.00	4.00	6.00

SUPERNATURAL THRILLERS
12/72 - #6, 11/73; #7, 7/74 - #15, 10/75
Marvel Comics Group

#1-It!	.50	1.00	1.50
2-The Invisible Man	.50	1.00	1.50

	Good	Fine	Mint
3-The Valley of the Worm	.70	1.40	2.10
4-Dr. Jekyll & Mr. Hyde	.30	.60	.90
5-The Living Mummy	.20	.40	.60
6-The Headless Horseman	.20	.40	.60
7-The Living Mummy begins	.20	.40	.60
8-15	.20	.40	.60

NOTE: *Brunner cover-#11. Robert E. Howard*
story-#3. Steranko covers-#1,2.

SUPER PUP
#4, Mar-Apr, 1954 - #5, 1954
Avon Periodicals

#4,5	1.00	2.00	3.00

SUPER RABBIT (See Wisco)
Fall, 1943 - #14, 1949
Timely Comics (CmPI)

#1	3.00	6.00	9.00
2,3	2.00	4.00	6.00
4,5,7-10,12-14	1.25	2.50	3.75
6-Origin	1.50	3.00	4.50
11-Kurtzman's "Hey Look"	2.00	4.00	6.00
IW Reprint #1,2('58),7,10('63)			
	.40	.80	1.20

SUPER RICHIE
Sept, 1975 - Present
Harvey Publications

#1	.25	.50	.75
2-17		.20	.40

SUPERSNIPE COMICS (Army & Navy #1-5)
(Also see Shadow Comics)
Oct, 1942 - V5#1, Aug-Sept, 1949
Street & Smith Publications

V1#6-Rex King Man of Adventure by Jack Binder			
begins; Supersnipe continues from Army			
Navy #5; Bill Ward art			
	8.00	16.00	24.00
7-12: #9-Doc Savage x-over in Supersnipe			
#11-Little Nemo app.	7.00	14.00	21.00
V2#1-12	5.00	10.00	15.00
V3#1-12	4.00	8.00	12.00
V4#1-12, V5#1	3.00	6.00	9.00

NOTE: *Doc Savage in some issues.*

SUPERSPOOK (Formerly Frisky Animals on Parade)
1958
Ajax/Farrell Publications

#4	.40	.80	1.20

Super-Mystery Comics V6#2, © ACE

Supersnipe Comics #7, © S&S

Supersnipe Comics V2#4, © S&S

Surprise Adventures #3, © Sterling Comics   Suspense Comics #5, © MCG   Suspense Detective #4, © FAW

SUPER SPY (See Wham)
Oct, 1940 - #2, Nov, 1940
Centaur Publications

	Good	Fine	Mint
#1-Origin The Sparkler	15.00	30.00	45.00
2	10.00	20.00	30.00

SUPER-TEAM FAMILY
10-11/75 - #15, 3-4/78 (#1-3, 68pgs.)
National Periodical Publications/DC Comics

#1-Reprints; Adams, Wood, Infantino art			
	.50	1.00	1.50
2,3: #2-The Creeper app.; Adams reprt. #3-			
Brunner cover, Wood art; Adams reprint			
	.40	.80	1.20
4-7-Reprints	.25	.50	.75
8-Challs. of Unknown begin.	.25	.50	.75
9,10,12-15	.20	.40	.60
11-Weiss art	.20	.40	.60

SUPER TV HEROES (See Hanna-Barbera --)

SUPER-VILLAIN TEAM-UP
August, 1975 - #14, Oct, 1977
Marvel Comics Group

#1-Sub-Mariner app.	.60	1.20	1.80
2-5: #4-Mooney art	.35	.70	1.05
6-Starlin cover	.30	.60	.90
7-16	.20	.40	.60

NOTE: *Everett pencils-#1,3.*
Giant-Size #1(10/74, 68pgs.)-Craig inks
| | .60 | 1.20 | 1.80 |
Giant-Size #2(7/75, 68pgs.)-Dr. Doom, Sub-
Mariner app. | .50 | 1.00 | 1.50 |

SUPER WESTERN COMICS
Aug, 1950 - #9, Dec, 1951
Youthful Magazines

#1-Buffalo Bill begins; Powell art			
	1.00	2.00	3.00
2-9	.70	1.40	2.10

SUPER WESTERN FUNNIES (See Super Funnies)

SUPERWORLD COMICS
April, 1940 - #3, Aug, 1940
Hugo Gernsback (Komos Publ.)

#1-Origin Hip Knox, Super Hypnotist; Mitey			
Powers & Buzz Allen, the Invisible Aveng-			
er, Little Nemo begin	25.00	50.00	75.00
2-Marvo 1,2 Go+, the Super Boy of the Year			
2680	20.00	40.00	60.00
3	15.00	30.00	45.00

SURE FIRE (See Lightning & Veri Best --)

SURF 'N' WHEELS
Nov, 1969 - #20, 1972
Charlton Comics

	Good	Fine	Mint
#1-20?		.15	.25

SURF'TOONS (Magazine)
1965   (50¢)
Petersen Publishing Co.

#1('65)(no month)	.50	1.00	1.50
Many issues, no #'s	.40	.80	1.20

SURPRISE ADVENTURES
1955 - #5, July, 1955
Sterling Comic Group

#3-5: #5-Sekowsky art	.80	1.60	2.40

SUSPENSE COMICS
Dec, 1943 - #12, Sept, 1946
Holyoke Publications

#1-The Grey Mask begins	7.00	14.00	21.00
2-Intro. The Mask	5.00	10.00	15.00
3-12: #3,5-Schomburg cvr.	4.00	8.00	12.00

NOTE: *L. B. Cole covers-#7-12.*

SUSPENSE COMICS (Radio)(Real Life Tales of --
#1,2)(Amazing Detective Cases #3 on?--change
to horror)
12/49 - #29, 4/53 (#1-7,17,18-52pgs.)
Marvel/Atlas Comics(CnPC #1-10/BFP #11-29)

#1-Powell art	4.00	8.00	12.00
2-Crime stories	2.00	4.00	6.00
3-Change to horror	2.00	4.00	6.00
4,6-17,19-21,23-29	1.50	3.00	4.50
5,18,22-Krigstein story	2.00	4.00	6.00

NOTE: *Briefer story-#27. Everett stories-#5,
6,19,28; covers-#21,22. Robinson story-#29.
Whitney stories-#15,16,22.*

SUSPENSE DETECTIVE
June, 1952 - #5, Feb, 1953
Fawcett Publications

#1	1.75	3.50	5.25
2,3,5	1.20	2.40	3.60
4-Bondage cover	1.50	3.00	4.50

SUSPENSE STORIES (See Strange Suspense Stor.)

SUZIE COMICS (Formerly Laugh Comics)
1945 - 1954
MLJ Mag./Close-Up #51 on (Archie)

(Suzie Comics cont'd)	Good	Fine	Mint
#49-Katie Keene begins, ends #100			
	6.00	12.00	18.00
50-55	3.00	6.00	9.00
56-65	2.50	5.00	7.50
66-80	2.00	4.00	6.00
81-100	1.50	3.00	4.50

SUZIE Q. SMITH (See 4-Color #323,377,453,553)

SWAMP FOX, THE (See 4-Color Comics #1179)

SWAMP FOX, THE
1960 (14 pgs.) (Canada Dry Premiums)
Walt Disney Productions

Titles: A. Tory Masquerade, B. Rindau Rampage, C. Turnabout Tactics	1.20	2.40	3.60

SWAMP THING (See House of Secrets #92)
10-11/72 - #24, 8-9/76; #25, 1978
National Periodical Publications/DC Comics

#1-Cover/stories by Wrightson begin			
	3.00	6.00	9.00
2	1.50	3.00	4.50
3-Intro. Patchworkman	1.50	3.00	4.50
4,5	1.25	2.50	3.75
6-10: #7-Batman app. #10-Last Wrightson issue	1.00	2.00	3.00
11-15-Redondo art	.60	1.20	1.80
16-23-Redondo art; S.T. reverts back to Dr. Holland-#23	.50	1.00	1.50
24,25	.25	.50	.75

(Also see DC Special Series #2)
NOTE: Carrillo & Chua art-#25.

SWAT MALONE
Sept, 1955
Swat Malone Enterprises

V1#1-Hy Fleishman art	1.20	2.40	3.60

SWEENEY (Buz Sawyer's Pal, Roscoe --)
1949
Standard Comics

#4,5-Crane art #5	2.00	4.00	6.00

SWEE'PEA (See 4-Color Comics #219)

SWEETHEART DIARY
1949 - 1969
Fawcett Publications/Charlton Comics

#1	2.50	5.00	7.50
2,5-10	1.00	2.00	3.00
3,4-Wood stories	4.00	8.00	12.00

	Good	Fine	Mint
11-20	.80	1.60	2.40
21-40	.50	1.00	1.50
41-60	.25	.50	.75
61-107		.20	.40

SWEETHEART LOVE STORIES
Oct, 1955
Charlton Comics

#32		.30	.60	.90

SWEETHEARTS (Formerly Captain Midnight)
#68, Oct, 1948 - #125, Sept, 1954
Fawcett/Charlton

#68	1.25	2.50	3.75
69-80	.80	1.60	2.40
81-84,86-93,95-102,104-109,111-116,118-125	.60	1.20	1.80
85,94,103,110,117-All have George Evans stories	1.00	2.00	3.00

SWEETHEARTS
V2#24, 1956 - #134, June, 1973
Charlton Comics

V2#24('56) - 50	.20	.40	.60
51-134		.15	.35

SWEETHEART SCANDALS
1950 (Giant) (132 pgs.)
Fox Features Syndicate

No#-Contents may vary and determines price.
See Fox Giants.

SWEETIE PIE (See 4-Color #1185,1241)

SWEETIE PIE
Dec, 1955 - #15, Fall, 1957
Ajax/Pines (Literary Ent.)

#1-by Napine Seltzer	.60	1.20	1.80
2-15	.30	.60	.90

SWEET LOVE
Sept, 1949 - #5, May, 1950
Home Comics (Harvey)

#1	1.35	2.75	4.00
2-5: #3,5-Powell art	.80	1.60	2.40

SWEET ROMANCE
October, 1968
Charlton Comics

#1		.15	.35

Suzie #59. © AP

Swamp Thing #4. © DC

Sweetheart Diary #36, © FAW

Swift Arrow #1, © AJAX   Taffy #3, © RH   Tales From The Crypt #27, © WMG

SWEET SIXTEEN
Aug-Sept, 1946 - #13, Jan, 1948
Parents' Magazine Institute

	Good	Fine	Mint
#1-Van Johnson's life story; Dorothy Dare, Queen of Hollywood Stunt Artists begins (in all issues)	2.50	5.00	7.50
2-13	1.50	3.00	4.50

SWIFT ARROW
Feb-Mar, 1954 - #5, Oct-Nov, 1954; 1957
Ajax/Farrell Publications

#1(1954)(1st Series)	1.25	2.50	3.75
2-5	.75	1.50	2.25
1(2nd Series)(Swift Arrow's Gunfighters #4)	1.00	2.00	3.00
2,3(9/57)-Lone Rider begins #2	.60	1.20	1.80

SWIFT ARROW'S GUNFIGHTERS (Formerly Swift
#4, Nov, 1957   Arrow)
Ajax/Farrell Publ. (Four Star Comic Corp.)

#4	.60	1.20	1.80

SWING WITH SCOOTER
June-July, 1966 - #36, Oct-Nov, 1972
National Periodical Publications

#1	.50	1.00	1.50
2-10	.30	.60	.90
11-32,35,36	.20	.40	.60
33-Interview with David Cassidy	.20	.40	.60
34-Interview with Ron Ely(Doc Savage)	.20	.40	.60

NOTE: _Orlando covers-#1,2,10,11,13; stories-#1-3,6,11. #20,33,34-68pgs.; #35-52pgs._

SWISS FAMILY ROBINSON (See 4-Color #1156, King Classics, & Movie Comics)

SWORD & THE DRAGON, THE (See 4-Color #1118)

SWORD & THE ROSE, THE (See 4-Color #505,682)

SWORD IN THE STONE, THE (See March of Comics #258 & Movie Comics)

SWORD OF LANCELOT (See Movie Classics)

SWORD OF SORCERY (See Wonder Woman #201)
Feb-Mar, 1973 - #5, Nov-Dec, 1973
National Periodical Publications

#1-Leiber Fafhrd & The Gray Mouser; Adams/
Bunkers inks; also #2; Kaluta cover

	Good	Fine	Mint
	.80	1.60	2.40
2-Wrightson cover inks	.70	1.40	2.10
3-Wrightson story	.70	1.40	2.10
4,5-Starlin art #5	.60	1.20	1.80

NOTE: _Chaykin art-#1-4. Simonson pencils-#4,5._

TAFFY
Mar-Apr, 1945 - #12, 1948
Rural Home/Orbit Publ.

#1-Origin of Wonderworm + 7 chapter WWII Funny Animal Adv.	2.00	4.00	6.00
2-12	1.20	2.40	3.60

TAILSPIN
November, 1944
Spotlight Publishers

No#-Firebird app.	2.00	4.00	6.00

TAILSPIN TOMMY STORY & PICTURE BOOK
1931? (No date)(Color strip reprints)(10½x10")
McLoughlin Bros.

#266-by Forrest	12.00	24.00	36.00

TAILSPIN TOMMY
1932   (100 pgs.)   (Hardcover)
Cupples & Leon Co.

(Rare)-B&W strip reprints from 1930 by Hal Forrest & Glenn Claffin	20.00	40.00	60.00

TAILSPIN TOMMY
1937 - 1940
United Features Synd./Service Publ. Co.

Single Series #23('40)	8.00	16.00	24.00
Best Seller #1('46)-Service Publ. Co.	6.00	12.00	18.00

TALES CALCULATED TO DRIVE YOU BATS
Nov, 1961 - #7, Nov, 1962; 1966
Archie Publications

#1	3.00	6.00	9.00
2	2.00	4.00	6.00
3-6	1.50	3.00	4.50
7-Story line change	1.00	2.00	3.00
1-('66-25¢)(reprts.#1,2)	1.20	2.40	3.60

TALES FROM THE CRYPT (Formerly The Crypt of Terror #17-19)
#20, Oct-Nov, 1950 - #46, Feb-Mar, 1955
E.C. Comics

#20	50.00	100.00	150.00

(Tales From the Crypt cont'd)

	Good	Fine	Mint
21-Kurtzman reprt/Haunt of Fear #15/1			
	30.00	60.00	90.00
22-Moon Girl costume at costume party, one			
panel	22.00	44.00	66.00
23-25	20.00	40.00	60.00
26-30	17.50	35.00	52.50
31-Williamson story	20.00	40.00	60.00
32,34-40	12.00	24.00	36.00
33-Origin The Crypt Keeper			
	17.00	34.00	51.00
41-46	11.00	22.00	33.00

NOTE: *Craig* stories-#20,22-24; *cover*-#20.
Crandall stories-#38,44. *Davis* stories-#23,
24-46; *covers*-#29-46. *Elder* stories-#37,38.
Evans stories-#32-34,36,40,41,43,46. *Feldstein* stories-#20-23; *covers*-#21-25,28.
Ingels stories in all. *Kamen* stories-#20,22,
25,27-31,33-36,39,41-45. *Krigstein* stories-#40,42,45. *Kurtzman* story-#21. *Orlando* stories-#27-30,35,37,39,46. *Wood* stories-#21,24,
25; *covers*-#26,27. *Canadian reprints known;
see Table of Contents.*

TALES FROM THE CRYPT (Magazine)
#10, July, 1968 (35¢) (B&W)
Eerie Publications

#10-Contains Farrell reprints from 1950's
	.40	.80	1.20

TALES FROM THE GREAT BOOK
Feb, 1955 - #4, Jan, 1956
Famous Funnies

#1	1.50	3.00	4.50
2-4-Lehti art in all	1.00	2.00	3.00

TALES FROM THE TOMB
Oct, 1962 - #2, Dec, 1962
Dell Publishing Co.

#1(02-810-210)(Giant)-All stories written by			
John Stanley	2.00	4.00	6.00
2	2.00	4.00	6.00

TALES FROM THE TOMB (Magazine) (52 pgs.)
V1#6, July, 1969 - V6#6, Dec, 1974
Eerie Publications

V1#6-8	.50	1.00	1.50
V2#1-3,5,6	.40	.80	1.20
4-LSD story reprt./Weird V3#5			
	.50	1.00	1.50
V3#1-Rulah reprint	.50	1.00	1.50
2-6('70),V4#1-6('72),V5#1-6('73),			
V6#1-6('74)	.25	.50	.75

TALES OF ASGARD
Oct, 1968 (One Shot) (68 pgs.)
Marvel Comics Group

	Good	Fine	Mint
#1-Thor reprints from Journey into Mystery			
#97-106; new Kirby cvr.	1.00	2.00	3.00

TALES OF DEMON DICK & BUNKER BILL
1934 (78pgs.) (5x10½") (B&W) (Hardcover)
Whitman Publishing Co.

#793-by Dick Spencer	5.00	10.00	15.00

TALES OF EVIL
Feb, 1975 - #3, June, 1975
Atlas/Seaboard Publ.

#1	.20	.40	.60
2-Intro. The Bog Beast	.15	.30	.45
3-Origin The Man-Monster	.15	.30	.45

TALES OF GHOST CASTLE
May-June, 1975 - #3, Sept-Oct, 1975
National Periodical Publications

#1-2pg. Redondo art	.25	.50	.75
2,3	.15	.30	.45

TALES OF HORROR
June, 1952 - #13, Oct, 1954
Toby Press/Minoan Publ. Corp.

#1	2.00	4.00	6.00
2-8	1.40	2.80	4.20
9-Origin Purple Claw	2.50	5.00	7.50
10-13-Purple Claw	1.75	3.50	5.25

TALES OF JUSTICE (Formerly Justice)
#58, Feb, 1956 - #67, Aug, 1957
Atlas Comics (MjMC #63-66/Male #67)

#58,59-Krigstein stories	2.00	4.00	6.00
60-63,65	.70	1.40	2.10
64-Crandall story	1.50	3.00	4.50
66-Torres + Orlando sty.	1.25	2.50	3.75
67-Crandall story	1.50	3.00	4.50

NOTE: *Everett* story-#60. *Orlando* stories-#65,66.

TALES OF SUSPENSE (Capt. America #100 on)
Jan, 1959 - #99, March, 1968
Atlas(WPI #1,2/Male #3-12/VPI #13-40)/Marvel #41 on

#1-Williamson sty.,5pgs.	25.00	50.00	75.00
2,3	12.00	24.00	36.00
4-Williamson story,4pgs.	10.00	20.00	30.00
5-10	5.00	10.00	15.00

Tales From The Crypt #44, © WMG

Tales Of Horror #4, © TOBY

Tales Of Suspense #13, © MCG

Tales Of Suspense #51, © MCG

Tales Of Terror #1, © TOBY

Tales Of The Green Beret #1, © DELL

(Tales of Suspense cont'd)	Good	Fine	Mint
11,13-22	3.00	6.00	9.00
12-Crandall story	3.50	7.00	10.50
23-38	1.75	3.50	5.25
39-Origin & 1st app. Iron Man; 1st Iron Man			
story-Kirby layouts	45.00	90.00	135.00
40-Iron Man in new armor	15.00	30.00	45.00
41-Dr. Strange app.	10.00	20.00	30.00
42-45: #45-Intro. & 1st app. Happy & Pepper			
	5.00	10.00	15.00
46,47	3.00	6.00	9.00
48-New Iron Man armor	3.00	6.00	9.00
49-51: #50-1st app. Mandarin			
	2.00	4.00	6.00
52-1st app. The Black Widow			
	2.25	4.50	6.75
53-Origin The Watcher(5/64); Black Widow			
app.	2.00	4.00	6.00
54-56	1.75	3.50	5.25
57-Origin Hawkeye(9/64)	2.00	4.00	6.00
58-Captain America begins(10/64)			
	2.00	4.00	6.00
59-Iron Man + Captain America features begin			
	1.50	3.00	4.50
60,61,64	1.00	2.00	3.00
62-Origin Mandarin(2/65)	1.00	2.00	3.00
63-Origin Captain America(3/65)			
	1.50	3.00	4.50
65-1st Red Skull(6/65)	1.20	2.40	3.60
66-Origin Red Skull	1.20	2.40	3.60
67-99: #69-1st app. Titanium Man			
	.80	1.60	2.40

NOTE: *Craig inks(Iron Man)-#99. Crandall
story-#12. Davis story-#38. Ditko Iron Man-
#47-49. Ditko/Kirby art in most all issues
#1-35,37,38,41-44,46. Gil Kane stories-#89-
91. Kirby Captain America-#59-75,77-86,92-99;
layouts-#69-75,77; covers-#58-72,74,76,78,80,
82,84,86,92,94,96. Kirby pencils(Iron Man)-
#40,41,43; covers-#39-44,46-56. Wood inks
(Iron Man)-#71.*

TALES OF SWORD & SORCERY (See Dagar)

TALES OF TERROR
1952 (no month) - #6, Aug, 1953
Toby Press Publications

#1	1.50	3.00	4.50
2-6 (exist?)	1.00	2.00	3.00

TALES OF TERROR (See Movie Classics)

TALES OF TERROR (Magazine)
Summer, 1964
Eerie Publications

#1	1.00	2.00	3.00

TALES OF TERROR ANNUAL
1951 - 1953   (25¢)
E.C. Comics

	Good	Fine	Mint
No#(1951) (Rare)	300.00	600.00	900.00
#2(1952) (Scarce)	150.00	300.00	450.00
3(1953)	100.00	200.00	300.00

No. 1 contains three horror and one science fiction comic which
came out in 1950. No. 2 contains a horror, crime, and science
fiction book which generally had cover dates in 1951, and No. 3
had horror, crime, and shock books that generally appeared in
1952. All E. C. annuals contain four complete books that didn't
sell on the stands which were rebound in the annual format,
minus the covers, and sold from the E. C. office and on the stands
in key cities. The contents of each annual may vary in the same
year.

TALES OF TERROR ILLUSTRATED (See Terror Ill.)

TALES OF TEXAS JOHN SLAUGHTER(See 4-Color#997)

TALES OF THE GREEN BERET
Jan, 1967 - #5, Oct, 1969
Dell Publishing Co.

#1	.35	.70	1.05
2-5: #5 reprints #1	.25	.50	.75

NOTE: *Glanzman art-#1-4.*

TALES OF THE INVISIBLE (See Harvey Comics
Hits #59)

TALES OF THE KILLERS (Magazine)
V1#10, 12/70 - V1#11, 2/71 (52pgs.) (B&W)
World Famous Periodicals

V1#10-1pg. Frazetta	1.25	2.50	3.75
11	.90	1.80	2.70

TALES OF THE MARINES (Devil-Dog Dugan #3)
Feb, 1957 (Marines at War #5 on)
Atlas Comics (OPI)

#4-Powell art	1.00	2.00	3.00

TALES OF THE MYSTERIOUS TRAVELER
Aug, 1956 - #13, June, 1959
Charlton Comics

#1-Ditko art	4.00	8.00	12.00
2-10-Ditko art	2.50	5.00	7.50
11,12-Ditko covers only	1.75	3.50	5.25
13-No Ditko	1.25	2.50	3.75

TALES OF THE PONY EXPRESS(See 4-Color#829,942)

TALES OF THE TEXAS RANGERS (Jace Pearson's)
1952 - 1959
Dell Publishing Co./Nesbit Publ.

403

(Tales of the Texas Rangers cont'd)

	Good	Fine	Mint
4-Color #396	1.75	3.50	5.25
#2(5-7/53)	1.50	3.00	4.50
3-10	1.25	2.50	3.75
4-Color #648(9/55)	1.50	3.00	4.50
#11-22	1.20	2.40	3.60
4-Color #961-Toth art	2.00	4.00	6.00
4-Color #1021	1.20	2.40	3.60

TALES OF THE UNEXPECTED(The Unexpected#105 on)
2-3/56 - #104, 12-1/68 (See Super DC Giant)
National Periodical Publications

#1	10.00	20.00	30.00
2	5.00	10.00	15.00
3-5	4.00	8.00	12.00
6-10	3.00	6.00	9.00
11,12,14,15	1.75	3.50	5.25

13,16-18,22,23: Kirby or S&K art. #16-Character named "Thor" with a magic hammer-not like later Thor 2.25 4.50 6.75
19-21,24-39: #24-Cameron story
.80 1.60 2.40
40-Space Ranger begins, ends #82
3.00 6.00 9.00

41-50	1.00	2.00	3.00
51-70	.70	1.40	2.10

71-100: #91-1st Automan(also in #94,97)
.40 .80 1.20
101-104 .25 .50 .75
NOTE: *Adams cover-#104. Anderson story-#50. Bob Kane story-#48. Kirby cover-#22.*

TALES OF THE WEST (See 3-D --)

TALES OF THE WIZARD OF OZ (See 4-Color #1308)

TALES OF THE ZOMBIE (Magazine)
8/73 - #10, 3/75 (75¢) (B&W)
Marvel Comics Group

V1#1-Reprint/Menace #5; origin
.75 1.50 2.25

2,3	.50	1.00	1.50
V2#1(#4),5-7,9,10	.40	.80	1.20
8-Kaluta story	.50	1.00	1.50
Annual #1(Sum,'75)(B&W)	.50	1.00	1.50

NOTE: *Alcala stories-#6-9. Boris covers-#2-4.*

TALES OF VOODOO (Magazine)
V1#11, Nov, 1968 - V7#6, Nov, 1974
Eerie Publications

V1#11	.75	1.50	2.25
V2#1(3/69)-V2#4(9/69)	.40	.80	1.20
V3#1-6('70)	.30	.60	.90

V4#1-6('71), V5#1-6('72), V6#1-6('73),

	Good	Fine	Mint
V7#1-6('74)	.30	.60	.90
Annual #1	1.00	2.00	3.00

TALES OF WELLS FARGO (See 4-Color #876,968, 1023,1075,1113,1167,1215)

TALES TO ASTONISH (The Hulk #102 on)
Jan, 1959 - #101, March, 1968
Atlas(MAP#1/ZPC#2-14/VPI#15-42)/Marvel#43 on

#1-Jack Davis story	25.00	50.00	75.00
2	12.00	24.00	36.00
3	8.00	16.00	24.00
4	6.00	12.00	18.00
5-Williamson story,4pgs.	7.00	14.00	21.00
6-10	4.00	8.00	12.00
11-20	2.50	5.00	7.50
21-26,28-34	1.75	3.50	5.25
27-1st Antman app.(1/62)	60.00	120.00	180.00

35-2nd Antman-begin series
22.00 44.00 66.00

36	10.00	20.00	30.00
37-40	6.00	12.00	18.00
41-43	3.00	6.00	9.00
44-Origin The Wasp	3.50	7.00	10.50
45-48,50	2.50	5.00	7.50

49-Antman becomes Giant Man; origin The Human Top 3.00 6.00 9.00
51-60: #52-Origin & 1st app. Black Knight. #59-Giant Man vs. Hulk feat. story. #60-Giant Man & Hulk double feature begins
1.50 3.00 4.50
61-70: #65-New Giant Man costume. #69-Last Giant Man. #70-Sub-Mariner begins
1.00 2.00 3.00

71-80	.75	1.50	2.25
81-92	.60	1.20	1.80
93-Silver Surfer app.	1.50	3.00	4.50

94-101: #100-Hulk battles Sub-Mariner
.50 1.00 1.50
NOTE: *Ditko art in most issues-#1-42,45-48. Ditko Hulk-#60-67, Giant Man-#61. Everett Hulk-#78-84, Sub-Mariner-#87-91,94-96; inks-#79,85-91,94. Kirby stories-#1-27(most),35-40,44,49-70; layouts-#71-84(Hulk); pencils (Sub-Mariner)-#82,83; covers-#50-70,73,75, 77(w/Romita),78(w/Colan),79,81,85(all w/Everett),90. Powell Hulk-#73,74, Giant-Man-#64.*

TALES TO HOLD YOU SPELLBOUND (See Spellbound)

TALKING KOMICS
1957 (20 pgs.) (Slick Covers)
Belda Record & Publ. Co.

Each comic contained a record that followed the story - much like the Golden Record sets.

Tales Of The Unexpected #78. © DC

Tales To Astonish #36. © MCG

Tales To Astonish #49. © MCG

Target Comics #5, © NOVP   Target Western Romances #107, © STAR   Tarzan #6, © ERB

(Talking Komics cont'd)   Good   Fine   Mint
Known titles: Chirpy Cricket, Lonesome Octo-
pus, Sleepy Santa, Grumpy Shark, Flying Turtle, Happy Grasshopper
    with records......   1.00   2.00   3.00

TALLY-HO COMICS
December, 1944
Swappers Quarterly (Baily Publ. Co.

No#-Frazetta's 1st work as Giunta's assist-
    ant   20.00 40.00 60.00

TAMMY, TELL ME TRUE   (See 4-Color #1233)

TARANTULA   (See Weird Suspense)

TARAS BULBA   (See Movie Classics)

TARGET COMICS   (--Western Romances #106 on)
Feb, 1940 - V10#3, Aug-Sept, 1949
Novelty Publications

V1#1-Origin & 1st app. Manowar, The White
    Streak by Burgos; Bulls-Eye Bill by
    Everett   50.00 100.00 150.00
  2   25.00 50.00 75.00
  3   20.00 40.00 60.00
  4-Jack Cole art   18.00 36.00 54.00
  5-Origin The White Streak in text; Space
    Hawk by Wolverton begins
                          60.00 120.00 180.00
  6-The Chameleon begins; White Streak ori-
    gin cont'd. in text 40.00 80.00 120.00
  7-Wolverton cover   75.00 150.00 225.00
  8,9,12   30.00 60.00 90.00
  10-Intro. & 1st app. The Target; Kirby
    cover   45.00 90.00 135.00
  11-Origin The Target & The Targeteers
                          40.00 80.00 120.00
V2#1,2   20.00 40.00 60.00
  3,5   15.00 30.00 45.00
  4-The Cadet begins   15.00 30.00 45.00
  6-10-Red Seal with White Streak in all
                          15.00 30.00 45.00
  11,12   12.00 24.00 36.00
V3#1-10-Last Wolverton issue
                          12.00 24.00 36.00
  11,12   3.00   6.00   9.00
V4#1-5,7-12   2.00   4.00   6.00
  6-Targetoons by Wolverton, 1pg.
                           2.50   5.00   7.50
V5#1-12   1.50   3.00   4.50
V6#1-12   1.40   2.80   4.20
V7#1-12, V8#1-5,7-12   1.20   2.40   3.60
  6-Krigstein art   1.75   3.50   5.25
V9#1-12, V10#1-3   1.20   2.40   3.60
NOTE: *Jack Cole* art-#1-8.

TARGET: THE CORRUPTORS   (TV)
#1306, Mar-May, 1962 - #3, 1962
Dell Publishing Co.
                          Good   Fine   Mint
4-Color #1306, #2,3   .70   1.40   2.10

TARGET WESTERN ROMANCES   (Formerly Target)
#106, 10-11/49 - #107, 12-1/49-50
Star Publications

#106,107-L. B. Cole cvrs. 2.00   4.00   6.00

TARGITT
March, 1975 - #3, July, 1975
Atlas/Seaboard Publ.

#1-Origin; Nostrand art in all
                           .25   .50   .75
  2,3: #2-1st in costume   .15   .30   .45

TARZAN   (See Aurora, Comics on Parade, DC
100-Pg. Super Spec., Golden Comics Digest #4,
9, Jungle Tales of --, Lemix-Korlix, Limited
Coll. Ed., Sparkler, & Tip Top)

TARZAN
1939 - 1947
Dell Publishing Co./United Features Synd.

Black & White #5('39)-(Scarce)-by Hal Foster;
    reprints 1st dailies from 1929
                          100.00 250.00 400.00
Single Series #20('40)-by Hal Foster
                          120.00 240.00 360.00
4-Color #134('46)   25.00 50.00 75.00
4-Color #161('47)   20.00 40.00 60.00

TARZAN   (-- of the Apes #138 on)
Jan-Feb, 1948 - #206, Feb, 1972
Dell Publishing Co./Gold Key #132 on

#1-Jesse Marsh art begins; Two Against the
    Jungle begins, ends #24
                          40.00 80.00 120.00
  2   20.00 40.00 60.00
  3-5   12.00 24.00 36.00
  6-10   10.00 20.00 30.00
  11-15   7.00 14.00 21.00
  16-20   6.00 12.00 18.00
  21-24,26-30   4.00   8.00 12.00
  25-1st "Brothers of the Spear" episode; ser-
    ies ends #156,160,161,196-206
                           5.00 10.00 15.00
  31-40   3.00   6.00   9.00
  41-50   2.50   5.00   7.50
  51-60   2.00   4.00   6.00
  61,62,64-70   1.75   3.50   5.25
  63-Two Tarzan stories, 1 by Manning

405

(Tarzan cont'd)	Good	Fine	Mint
	2.00	4.00	6.00
71-100	1.50	3.00	4.50
101-109,111-120	1.25	2.50	3.75
110 (Scarce)	1.50	3.00	4.50
121-140	1.00	2.00	3.00
141-154	.80	1.60	2.40
155-Origin Tarzan	1.20	2.40	3.60

156-177: #157-Bantu, Dog of the Arande begins,
  ends #159,195. #162-No Manning
  | | .60 | 1.20 | 1.80 |

178-Tarzan origin reprt./#155; Leopard Girl
  app., also in #179,190,191
  | | .50 | 1.00 | 1.50 |

179-199,201-206	.40	.80	1.20
200-(Scarce)	.60	1.20	1.80
Story Digest #1(G.K.)(6/70).80	1.60	2.40

NOTE: *#162,165,168,171 are TV issues. #1-153-
all have* Marsh *art on Tarzan. #154-161,163,
164,166,167,172-177 all have* Manning *art on
Tarzan. #178,202 have* Manning *Tarzan reprints.
No "Brothers of the Spear" in #1-24,157-159,
162-195. #39-126,128-156 all have* Russ Manning *art on "Brothers of the Spear;" #196-201,
204,205 all have* Manning *B.O.T.S. reprints;
#25-38,127 all have* Jesse Marsh *art on B.O.T.
S. #206 has a* Marsh *B.O.T.S. reprint.* Doug
Wildey *art-#179-187.*

TARZAN (Continuation of Gold Key series)
#207, April, 1972 - #258, Feb, 1977
National Periodical Publications

#207-Origin Tarzan by Joe Kubert, part 1.
  John Carter begins(origin); 52pg. ish.
  through #209 | .90 | 1.80 | 2.70 |
208-210: Origin Tarzan, parts 2-4. #209-
  Last John Carter. #210-Kubert art
  | | .60 | 1.20 | 1.80 |
211-Kubert art | .50 | 1.00 | 1.50 |
212-214: Adaptations from "Jungle Tales of
  Tarzan." #213-Beyond the Farthest Star be-
  gins, ends #218 | .40 | .80 | 1.20 |
215-218,224,225-All by Kubert
  | | .40 | .80 | 1.20 |
219-223: Adapts "The Return of Tarzan" by
  Kubert | .35 | .70 | 1.05 |
226-Manning art | .35 | .70 | 1.05 |
227-229 | .35 | .70 | 1.05 |
230-100pgs.; Kubert, Kaluta art; Korak begins, ends #234; Carson of Venus app.
  | | .50 | 1.00 | 1.50 |
231-234: Adapts "Tarzan and the Lion Man;"
  all 100pgs.; Rex, the Wonder Dog reprts.-
  #232,233 | .40 | .80 | 1.20 |
235-Last Kubert issue; 100pgs.
  | | .40 | .80 | 1.20 |
236,237,239 | .25 | .50 | .75 |

	Good	Fine	Mint
238-68pgs.	.30	.60	.90

240-243: Adapts "Tarzan & the Castaways,"
| 244-249 | .25 | .50 | .75 |
250-256: Adapts "Tarzan the Untamed;" #252,
| 253-reprints #213 | .20 | .40 | .60 |
| 257,258 | .20 | .40 | .60 |

Comic Digest #1(50¢)-160pgs., Digest Size
  (DC), Fall, 1972 - Kubert cover, Manning
  art | 1.00 | 2.00 | 3.00 |
NOTE: *Foster strip reprints-#208,209,211,221.*
Anderson *stories-#207,209,217,218.* Chaykin
story-#216. Finley *reprint-#212.* Infantino
stories-#230 on. Kubert *covers-#207-249,253.*
Manning *strip reprints-#230-235,238.* Morrow
story-#208.

TARZAN BOOK (The Illustrated --)
1929   (80 pgs.)   (7x9")
Grosset & Dunlap

#1-(Rare)-Contains 1st B&W Tarzan newspaper
  comics from 1929. Cloth reinforced spine
  & dust jacket (50¢)
  with dust jacket.... | 80.00 | 160.00 | 240.00 |
  without dust jacket.. | 40.00 | 80.00 | 120.00 |
2nd Printing(1934)-76pgs.(25¢); 4 Foster
  pages dropped; paper spine, circle in lower right cover with 25¢ price. The 25¢ is
  barely visible on some copies.
  | | 25.00 | 50.00 | 75.00 |
1967-House of Greystoke reprint-7x10"; using
  the complete 300 illustrations/text from
  the 1929 edition minus the original indicia, foreword, etc. Initial version bound
  in gold paper & sold for $5.00. Officially
  titled *Burroughs Bibliophile* #2. A very few
  additional copies were bound in heavier
  blue paper.
  Gold binding.... | 4.00 | 8.00 | 12.00 |
  Blue binding.... | 5.00 | 10.00 | 15.00 |

TARZAN FAMILY (Formerly Korak)
#60, Nov-Dec, 1975 - #66, Nov-Dec, 1976
#60-62, 68pgs.; #63 on, 52pgs.
National Periodical Publications

#60-Korak begins; Kaluta reprint
	.30	.60	.90
61-65-All Kaluta reprints	.25	.50	.75
66	.25	.50	.75
NOTE: *Carson of Venus reprints-#60-65. New
John Carter-#62-64(65,66-reprints). New Korak-
#62-66. Pellucidar feature-#66.* Foster *Sunday
reprints-#60('32),63.* Kaluta *Carson of Venus-
#62-65.* Kubert *covers-#60-64.* Manning *strip
reprints-#60-64.* Morrow *reprint-#66.*

Tarzan #14, © ERB

Tarzan #225, © ERB

Tarzan Book #1(1929), © ERB

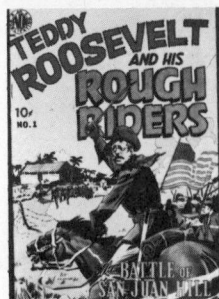

Teddy Roosevelt #1, © AVON   Teena #21, © STD   Teen-Age Confidential Confessions #1, © CC

TARZAN KING OF THE JUNGLE (See Dell Giant
#37,51)

TARZAN, LORD OF THE JUNGLE
1965   (Giant) (Soft paper cover) (25¢)
Gold Key

	Good	Fine	Mint
#1-Marsh reprints	1.60	3.20	4.80

TARZAN, LORD OF THE JUNGLE
June, 1977 - Present
Marvel Comics Group

#1	.25	.50	.75
2-Origin by J. Buscema	.20	.40	.60
3-10	.20	.40	.60
11-21	.15	.30	.45
Annual #1(10/77), 2(11/78)	.30	.60	.90

NOTE: *John Buscema stories-#1-18; covers-#1-19. Annual #1(10/77)-J. Buscema cover/art.*

TARZAN MARCH OF COMICS (See March of Comics
#82,98,114,125,144,155,172,185,204,223,240,
252,262,272,286,300,318,332,342,354,366)

TARZAN OF THE APES TO COLOR
1933 (24pgs.)(10-3/4"x15¼")
Saalfield

#988-(Very Rare)-Contains 1929 daily reprints
   by Hal Foster. Two panels blown up large
   on each page; 25% in color; believed to be
   the only time these panels ever appeared
   in color.   100.00 200.00 300.00

TARZAN'S JUNGLE ANNUAL
Aug, 1952 - 1957 (25¢) (Two #5's)
Dell Publishing Co.

#1	4.50	9.00	13.50
2	3.00	6.00	9.00
3-7: Manning art-#3,5-7	2.00	4.00	6.00

NOTE: *All have Marsh art.*

TARZAN'S JUNGLE WORLD (See Dell Giant #25)

TASMANIAN DEVIL & HIS TASTY FRIENDS
Nov, 1962
Gold Key

#1-Bugs Bunny & Elmer Fudd x-over	.50	1.00	1.50

TASTEE-FREEZ COMICS
1957   (36 pgs.) (10¢) (6 different)
Harvey Comics

#1-Little Dot, #2-Rags Rabbit, #3-Casper,

	Good	Fine	Mint
#4-Sad Sack, #5-Mazie	1.60	3.20	4.80
#6-Dick Tracy	3.50	7.00	10.50

TAYLOR'S CHRISTMAS TABLOID
Mid 1930's, Cleveland, Ohio
Dept. Store Giveaway (Tabloid size, in color)

No#(Very Rare)-Among the earliest pro work
   of Siegel & Shuster; one full color page
   called "The Battle in the Stratosphere,"
   with a pre-Superman look; Shuster art
   throughout
              Estimated value.... $300.00

TEDDY ROOSEVELT & HIS ROUGH RIDERS
1950
Avon Periodicals

#1-Kinstler cover	4.00	8.00	12.00

TEDDY ROOSEVELT ROUGH RIDER (See Classics
Special)

TEE AND VEE CROSLEY IN TELEVISION LAND COMICS
1951 (52pgs.)(8x11")(Soft cover)(in color)
Crosley Divison, Avco Mfg. Corp.

Many stories, puzzles, cut-outs, games, etc.
                    1.00   2.00   3.00

TEENA
1948 - 1949
Magazine Enterprises/Standard Comics

A-1#11,12,15	1.25	2.50	3.75
20-22(Standard)	1.00	2.00	3.00

TEEN-AGE BOOBY TRAP
1970 (36pgs.in color)(Paper cvr)(6-3/4x5")
Malcolm Ater.   (Giveaway)

No#-Contains ill. stories against the use of
   drugs   .40   .80   1.20

TEEN-AGE BRIDES (True Bride's Experiences #8)
Aug, 1953 - #7, Aug, 1954
Harvey/Home Comics

#1	1.50	3.00	4.50
2-7: #1-3,6-Powell art	.75	1.50	2.25

TEEN-AGE CONFESSIONS (See Teen Confessions)

TEEN-AGE CONFIDENTIAL CONFESSIONS
July, 1960 - #22, 1964
Charlton Comics

#1	.50	1.00	1.50
2-22	.15	.30	.45

TEEN-AGE DIARY SECRETS (Formerly Blue Ribbon Comics) (Becomes Diary Secrets #10 on)
Sept, 1949 - #9, April, 1950
St. John Publishing Co.

	Good	Fine	Mint
No#-oversized issue(9/49)	2.50	5.00	7.50
#6-9-Photo covers; Baker stories(2-3) in each	2.50	5.00	7.50

TEEN-AGE DOPE SLAVES (See Harvey Comics Library #1)

TEENAGE HOTRODDERS (Top Eliminator #25 on)
April, 1963 - #24, July, 1967
Charlton Comics

#1	.20	.40	.60
2-24		.15	.35

TEEN-AGE LOVE
1950   (132 pgs.)
Fox Publications (Hero)

No#-See Fox Giants. Contents can vary and determines price.

TEEN-AGE LOVE
V2#4, 7/58 - #96, Dec, 1973
Charlton Comics

V2#4-9	.30	.60	.90
10(9/59)-30	.15	.30	.45
31-96: #61&62-Origin Jonnie Love & begin series		.15	.25

TEEN-AGE ROMANCES
Jan, 1949 - #86, Mar, 1962
St. John Publ. Co.(Approved Comics)/Marvel (ZPC) #65 on

#1-Baker cover/stories	5.00	10.00	15.00
2,3-Baker cover/stories	4.00	8.00	12.00
4-8-Photo covers; 2-3 Baker stories each	3.50	7.00	10.50
9-Baker cover/story; Kubert story	4.00	8.00	12.00
10-12,20-Baker covers + 2-3 stories each	3.00	6.00	9.00
13-19,21-Complete issues by Baker	4.00	8.00	12.00
22-25-Baker covers, 2-3 stories each	2.50	5.00	7.50
26-40-Baker art	1.50	3.00	4.50
41-60-Baker art	1.00	2.00	3.00
61-86	.60	1.20	1.80

TEEN-AGE TALK
1964

I.W. Enterprises

	Good	Fine	Mint
Reprint #5,8,9	.25	.50	.75

TEEN-AGE TEMPTATIONS (Going Steady #10 on)
10/52 - #9, 8/54 (See True Love Pict.)
St. John Publishing Co.

#1-Baker cover/story; has story "Reform School Girl" by Estrada	8.00	16.00	24.00
2-Baker cover only	2.50	5.00	7.50
3-9-Baker cover/stories	3.00	6.00	9.00

TEEN BEAM (Teen Beat #1)
#2, Jan-Feb, 1968
National Periodical Publications

#2	.25	.50	.75

TEEN BEAT (Teen Beam #2)
Nov-Dec, 1967
National Periodical Publications

#1-Photos & text only	.40	.80	1.20

TEEN COMICS (Formerly All Teen; Journey Into Unknown Worlds #36 on)
#21, 1947 - #35, May, 1950
Marvel Comics (WFP)

#21,24,26,28,30-Kurtzman's "Hey Look"	1.75	3.50	5.25
22,23,25,27,29,31-35	.80	1.60	2.40

TEEN CONFESSIONS
August, 1959 - #97, Nov, 1976
Charlton Comics

#1	1.00	2.00	3.00
2-10	.50	1.00	1.50
11-30	.35	.70	1.05
31-88,91-97	.15	.30	.45
89,90-Newton covers	.20	.40	.60

TEENIE WEENIES, THE
1950 - 1951   (Newspaper reprints)
Ziff-Davis Publ. Co.

#10,11	2.25	4.50	6.75

TEEN-IN (Tippy Teen)
Summer, 1968 - #4, Fall, 1969
Tower Comics

No#(Summer,'68), No#(Spring,'69), #3,4	.15	.30	.45

Teen-Age Romances =5. © STJ

Teen-Age Romances #14. © STJ

Teen-Age Temptations #5. © STJ

Teen Titans #4, © DC

Television Comics #5, © STD

Tell It To The Marines #14, © TOBY

TEEN LIFE (Formerly Young Life)
#3, Winter, 1945 - #5, Fall, 1945
New Age/Quality Comics Group

	Good	Fine	Mint
#3-5	.75	1.50	2.25

TEEN ROMANCES
1964
Super Comics

| #15,16-Reprints | .20 | .40 | .60 |

TEEN SECRET DIARY
1959 - #9, Feb, 1961; 1972
Charlton Comics

#1	.40	.80	1.20
2-9(2/61)	.20	.40	.60
#1(1972)	.15	.30	.45

TEEN TALK (See Teen)

TEEN TITANS (See Brave & the Bold & Showcase)
1-2/66 - #43, 1-2/73; #44, 11/76 - #53, 2/78
National Periodical Publications/DC Comics

#1	2.50	5.00	7.50
2	1.25	2.50	3.75
3-5: #4-Speedy app.	1.00	2.00	3.00
6-10	.60	1.20	1.80
11-18: #11-Speedy app.	.50	1.00	1.50
19-Wood art; Speedy begins as regular			
	.50	1.00	1.50
20-22: Adams art in all; #21-Hawk & Dove app.			
#22-Origin Wonder Girl	1.25	2.50	3.75
23-Wonder Girl dons new costume,			
24	.40	.80	1.20
25-Flash, Aquaman, Batman, Green Arrow, Green Lantern, Superman, & Hawk & Dove guests			
	.40	.80	1.20
26-30: #29-Ocean Master app. #29-Hawk & Dove & Ocean Master app. #30-Aquagirl app.			
	.40	.80	1.20
31-43: #31-Hawk & Dove app. #36-Superboy story. #38-Green Arrow/Speedy reprint; Aquaman/Aqualad story. #39-Hawk & Dove story (#36-39, 52pgs.)	.30	.60	.90
44-52: #44-Mal becomes the Guardian. #50-Intro. Teen Titans West	.20	.40	.60
53-Origin	.15	.30	.45

TEEPEE TIM (Formerly Ha Ha Comics)
#100, Feb-Mar, 1955 - #102, June-July, 1955
American Comics Group

| #100-102 | .25 | .50 | .75 |

TEGRA JUNGLE PRINCESS (Zegra #2 on)
August, 1948

Fox Features Syndicate

	Good	Fine	Mint
#1-Blue Beetle, Rocket Kelly app.; used in Seduction of the Innocent			
	14.00	28.00	42.00

TELEVISION (See TV)

TELEVISION COMICS
#5, Feb, 1950 - #8, Nov, 1950
Standard Comics(Animated Cartoons)

| #5-1st app. Willy Nilly | .80 | 1.60 | 2.40 |
| 6-8 | .50 | 1.00 | 1.50 |

TELEVISION PUPPET SHOW
1950 - #2, Nov, 1950
Avon Periodicals

| #1,2 | 2.50 | 5.00 | 7.50 |

TELEVISION TEENS MOPSY (See T.V. Teens)

TELL IT TO THE MARINES
Mar, 1952 - #15, July, 1955
Toby Press Publications

#1-Lover Leary and His Liberty Belles (with pin-ups), ends #5	2.00	4.00	6.00
2-5	1.50	3.00	4.50
6-15	.80	1.60	2.40
IW Reprint #1,9	.30	.60	.90
Super Reprint #16('64)	.30	.60	.90

TEN COMMANDMENTS (See Moses & the-- & Classics Special)

TENDER LOVE STORIES
Feb, 1971 - #4, July, 1971 (All 52pgs.)(25¢)
Skywald Publ. Corp.

| #1-4 | | .15 | .30 |

TENDER ROMANCE
December, 1953 - #2, 1954
Key Publications (Gilmour Magazines)

| #1 | 1.50 | 3.00 | 4.50 |
| 2 | 1.25 | 2.50 | 3.75 |

TENNIS (For Speed, Stamina, Strength, Skill)
1956 (16 pgs.) (Soft cover) (10¢)
Tennis Educational Foundation
Derus Productions

| Book #1-Endorsed by Gene Tunney, Ralph Kiner, etc. showing how tennis has helped them. | | | |
| | 1.00 | 2.00 | 3.00 |

TENSE SUSPENSE
Dec, 1958 - #2, Feb, 1959
Fago Publications

	Good	Fine	Mint
#1,2	.75	1.50	2.25

TEN STORY LOVE (Formerly a pulp magazine
with same title)
V29#6, 1/52 - V36#5(#210), 9/56
Ace Periodicals

	Good	Fine	Mint
V29#6	.60	1.20	1.80
V30#6, V31, V32#1,2	.50	1.00	1.50
V32#3(6/53)-V32#6(12/53)	.50	1.00	1.50
V33, V34#1-4	.50	1.00	1.50
V34#5(#197, 8/54), V34#6(#198), V35#1(#199)-V35#6(#204, 9/55), V36#1(#205, 11/55)-V36#5 (#210, 9/56)	.50	1.00	1.50

TEN WHO DARED (See 4-Color Comics #1178)

TERRIFIC COMICS
Jan, 1944 - #6, Nov, 1944
Holyoke Publishing Co.

	Good	Fine	Mint
#1-Kid Terrific	5.00	10.00	15.00
2-The Boomerang begins	3.50	7.00	10.50
3-Diana becomes Boomerang's costumed aide,			
4,6	3.00	6.00	9.00
5-The Reckoner begins; Boomerang & Diana by L.B. Cole & Ed Wheelan's "Comics" McCormick, called the world's #1 comic book fan; Bondage cover	6.00	12.00	18.00

TERRIFIC COMICS (Horrific #1-13)
#14, May, 1955 - #18, July, 1955
Mystery Publ. (Ajax/Farrell)

	Good	Fine	Mint
#14-16-No Phantom Lady	1.50	3.00	4.50
17,18-Phantom Lady & Wonder Boy in both	7.00	14.00	21.00

TERRIFYING TALES (Terrors of the Jungle#4-10)
#11, Jan, 1953 - #15, Apr, 1954
Novelty-Star Publications

	Good	Fine	Mint
#11,12-All Jo-Jo reprints	5.00	10.00	15.00
13,14-All Rulah reprints	5.00	10.00	15.00
15-Rulah, Zago reprints	5.00	10.00	15.00

NOTE: *All issues have L. B. Cole covers;
bondage covers-#12-14.*

TERROR ILLUSTRATED (Adult Tales of --)
Nov-Dec, 1955 - #2, Spring, 1956 (Magazine)
E.C. Comics

	Good	Fine	Mint
#1	6.00	12.00	18.00
2	5.00	10.00	15.00

NOTE: *Craig story-#1. Crandall stories-#1,2;
covers-#1,2. Evans stories-#1,2. Ingels stories-#1,2.*

TERRORS OF THE JUNGLE (Terrifying Tales
#11 on; formerly Jungle Thrills)
#17, May, 1952 - #10, 1954
Novelty-Star Publications

	Good	Fine	Mint
#17-Reprints Rulah #21; bondage cover	6.00	12.00	18.00
18-Jo-Jo reprint	5.00	10.00	15.00
19,20(1953)-Jo-Jo reprints; Disbrow art	5.00	10.00	15.00
21-Jungle Jo, Tangi reprints	4.50	9.00	13.50
#4,6-10	4.00	8.00	12.00
5-Jo-Jo reprint	5.00	10.00	15.00

NOTE: *Disbrow art-#19,20,4-10. L. B. Cole
covers-all; bondage covers-#17,19,21,5,7.*

TERRORS OF THE UNIVERSE
1953
Novelty-Star Publications

	Good	Fine	Mint
#8,9	2.50	5.00	7.50

TERROR TALES (See Beware Terror Tales)

TERROR TALES (Magazine)
V1#7, 1969 - V6#6, Dec, 1974; V7#1, 4/76 -
Present   (V1-V6, 52pgs.; V7 on, 68pgs.)
Eerie Publications

	Good	Fine	Mint
V1#7	.50	1.00	1.50
V1#8-11('69)	.40	.80	1.20
V2#1-6('70), V3#1-6('71), V4#1-6('72), V5#1-6('73), V6#1-6('74)	.30	.60	.90
V7#1,4(no V7#2),V8#1-3('77)	.30	.60	.90
V7#3-LSD story reprt./Weird V3#5	.30	.60	.90

TERRY AND THE PIRATES (See Lemix-Korlix &
Super Comics)

TERRY AND THE PIRATES
1939 - 1953   (By Milton Caniff)
Dell Publishing Co.

	Good	Fine	Mint
Black & White #2('39)	40.00	100.00	160.00
Black & White #6('39)-1936 dailies	30.00	75.00	120.00
4-Color #9(1940)	40.00	80.00	120.00
Large Feature Comic #27('41), #6('42)	25.00	62.50	100.00
4-Color #44('43)	20.00	40.00	60.00
4-Color #101('45)	13.00	26.00	39.00
Buster Brown Shoes giveaway(1938, 32pgs.)			

Ten Story Love V29#5. © ACE

Terrific Comics #14. © AJAX

Terrors Of The Jungle #5. © STAR

Terry & The Pirates #12, © News Synd.　　Tessie The Typist #9, © MCG　　The Texan #13, © STJ

(Terry & Pirates cont'd)	Good	Fine	Mint
in color	25.00	50.00	75.00
Canada Dry Premiums-Books #1-3; 2"x5", 36pgs.			
(Harvey, 1953)	4.00	8.00	12.00
Family Album(1942)	7.00	14.00	21.00
Gillmore Giveaway('38-24pgs.)			
	6.00	12.00	18.00
Popped Wheat Giveaway('38)-reprints in full			
color	1.50	3.00	4.50
Sparked Wheat Giveaway('42)-16pgs. in full			
color	5.00	10.00	15.00

TERRY AND THE PIRATES (See Superbook #3,5,
9,16,28, & Merry Christmas --)

TERRY AND THE PIRATES (Long John Silvers
#30 on) (Reprints of daily strips)
#3, 4/47 - #26, 4/51; #26, 1955 - #28, 1955
Harvey Publ./Charlton #27-29 (Two #26's)

#3(#1)-Boy Explorers by S&K; Terry & Pirates			
begin by Caniff	18.00	36.00	54.00
4-S&K Boy Explorers	12.00	24.00	36.00
5-10: #7-9-Powell art	6.00	12.00	18.00
11-20	5.00	10.00	15.00
21-26(4/51)-Last Caniff ish.			
	4.00	8.00	12.00
26-28('55)-Not by Caniff	3.00	6.00	9.00

TERRY BEARS COMICS (TerryToons, The-- #4)
June, 1952 - #3, Oct, 1952
St. John/Pines #4

#1-3	1.00	2.00	3.00

TERRY-TOONS COMICS (1st Series) (Becomes
Paul Terry's Comics #87 on; later issues
titled "Paul Terry's--")(See Giant Comics Ed.)
Oct, 1942 - #84, Feb, 1951
Timely/Marvel #1-59(7/47)(Becomes Best West-
ern #58 on?, Marvel)/St. John #60(8/47) on

#1	15.00	30.00	45.00
2	8.00	16.00	24.00
3-5	5.00	10.00	15.00
6-10	3.50	7.00	10.50
11-20	2.50	5.00	7.50
21-37	1.50	3.00	4.50
38-1st Mighty Mouse	8.00	16.00	24.00
39-59(8/47): #50-1st app. Heckle & Jeckle			
	1.50	3.00	4.50
60(8/47)-#84	1.20	2.40	3.60

TERRY-TOONS COMICS (2nd Series)
June, 1952 - #9, Nov, 1953
St. John Publishing Co./Pines

#1	2.00	4.00	6.00

	Good	Fine	Mint
2-9	1.50	3.00	4.50
Giant Summer Fun Book #101,102(Summer,'57-			
Summer,'58)	1.25	2.50	3.75

TERRYTOONS, THE TERRY BEARS (Formerly Terry
#4, Summer, 1958　　　　　　　　　　　　Bears)
Pines Comics

#4	.50	1.00	1.50

TESSIE THE TYPIST (Tiny Tessie #24)
Summer, 1944 - #23, 1948
Timely/Marvel Comics (20CC)

#1-Doc Rockblock & others by Wolverton			
	12.00	24.00	36.00
2-Wolverton's Powerhouse Pepper			
	7.00	14.00	21.00
3-No Wolverton	1.50	3.00	4.50
4-8-Wolverton art; Kurtzman's "Hey Look"-#6			
	6.00	12.00	18.00
9,12,14-Wolverton's Powerhouse Pepper + Kurt-			
zman's "Hey Look"	5.00	10.00	15.00
10,11,13-Powerhouse Pepper	4.00	8.00	12.00
15-18-Kurtzman's "Hey Look" + Giggles 'n'			
Grins #15	2.50	5.00	7.50
19-8pg. Annie Oakley	1.20	2.40	3.60
20-23	1.00	2.00	3.00

TEXAN, THE (Fightin' Marines #15 on)
Aug, 1948 - #15, Oct, 1951 (Two #15's)
St. John Publishing Co.

#1-Buckskin Belle	2.50	5.00	7.50
2-10	1.50	3.00	4.50
11,13-15-Baker cover/2-3 stories each			
	2.50	5.00	7.50
12-All Matt Baker	3.00	6.00	9.00
NOTE: Matt Baker covers-#6-15. Tuska art-#1.			

TEXAN, THE (See 4-Color Comics #1027,1096)

TEXAS JOHN SLAUGHTER (See 4-Color #997,1181)

TEXAS KID
Jan, 1951 - #10, July, 1952
Marvel/Atlas Comics (LMC)

#1-Tuska art	2.00	4.00	6.00
2-10	1.50	3.00	4.50

TEXAS RANGERS, THE (See Superior Stories #4
and Tales of --)

TEXAS RANGERS IN ACTION (See Blue Bird Comics)
#5, July, 1956 - #79, Aug, 1970
Charlton Comics

(Texas Rangers cont'd)

	Good	Fine	Mint
#5-10	.70	1.40	2.10
11-Three Williamson stories, 5,5,& 8 pgs.			
	4.00	8.00	12.00
12,14-20	.40	.80	1.20
13-Williamson story, 5pgs.	2.00	4.00	6.00
21-59	.30	.60	.90
60-Rileys Rangers begin	.25	.50	.75
61-70: #66-1st app. The Man Called Loco,			
origin-#67	.20	.40	.60
71-79		.15	.35
76(Modern Comics reprint, 1977)	.15	.30

TEXAS SLIM (See A-1 Comics #2-8,10)

TEX DAWSON, GUN-SLINGER (Gunslinger #2 on)
January, 1973
Marvel Comics Group

#1-Steranko cover; Williamson reprint; Tex			
Dawson reprts. begin	.20	.40	.60

TEX FARNUM (See Wisco)

TEX FARRELL
Mar-Apr, 1948
D. S. Publishing Co.

#1-Shelly cover	1.75	3.50	5.25

TEX GRANGER (Formerly Calling All Boys)
#18, June, 1948 - #24, Sept, 1949
Parents' Magazine Institute/Commended

#18-24	1.00	2.00	3.00

TEX MORGAN
Aug, 1948 - #9, Feb, 1950
Marvel Comics (CCC)

#1	3.00	6.00	9.00
2-9	2.00	4.00	6.00

TEX RITTER WESTERN
Oct, 1950 - #46, May, 1959
Fawcett, #1-20(1/54)/Charlton #21 on

#1	7.00	14.00	21.00
2	5.00	10.00	15.00
3-5	3.50	7.00	10.50
6-10	3.00	6.00	9.00
11-20	2.25	4.50	6.75
21-38,40-46	1.50	3.00	4.50
39-Williamson art(1/58)	2.50	5.00	7.50

TEX TAYLOR (See Wisco)
Sept, 1948 - #9, March, 1950
Marvel Comics (HPC)

	Good	Fine	Mint
#1	2.50	5.00	7.50
2-9	2.00	4.00	6.00

THAT'S MY POP! GOES NUTS FOR FAIR
1939   (76 pgs.) (B&W)
Bystander Press

No#-by Milt Gross	8.00	16.00	24.00

THAT DARN CAT (See Movie Comics & Walt Disney Showcase #19)

THAT THE WORLD MAY BELIEVE
No date   (Graymoor Friars distr.)
Catechetical Guild

	1.25	2.50	3.75

THAT WILKIN BOY (Meet Bingo --)
Jan, 1969 - Present
Archie Publications

#1	.40	.80	1.20
2-10	.25	.50	.75
11-26(last giant issue)	.20	.40	.60
27-43		.15	.35

T.H.E. CAT (TV)
Oct, 1966 - #4, Oct, 1967
Dell Publishing Co.

#1	.40	.80	1.20
2-4	.25	.50	.75

THERE'S A NEW WORLD COMING
1973
Spire Christian Comics/Fleming H. Revell Co.

	.25	.50	.75

THEY RING THE BELL
1946
Fox Features Syndicate

#1	2.00	4.00	6.00

THIEF OF BAGHDAD (See 4-Color Comics #1229)

THIMBLE THEATRE STARRING POPEYE
1931, 1932   (52pgs.) (25¢) (B&W) (Rare)
Sonnet Publishing Co.

#1-Daily strip serial reprints in both by			
Segar	60.00	120.00	180.00
2	50.00	100.00	150.00

NOTE: *Probably the first Popeye reprint book.
Popeye first entered Thimble Theatre in 1929.*

Texas Slim #4, © ME

Tex Granger #21, © PMI

Thimble Theatre 1931, © Sonnet

The Thing #12, © CC   This Magazine Is Haunted #5, © FAW   Thor #135, © MCG

THIMK (Magazine) (Satire)
May, 1958 - #6, May, 1959
Counterpart

	Good	Fine	Mint
#1	1.50	3.00	4.50
2-6	.80	1.60	2.40

THING!, THE (Blue Beetle #18 on)
Feb, 1952 - #17, Nov, 1954
Song Hits #1/Capitol Stories/Charlton

#1	3.00	6.00	9.00
2-6,8-10	1.75	3.50	5.25
7-Injury to eye cover	5.00	10.00	15.00
12-16-Ditko cover/3-4 stories each			
	5.00	10.00	15.00
17-Ditko cover; classic story-"Through the Looking Glass;" Powell story reprint			
	3.00	6.00	9.00

THIRTEEN (-- Going on 18)
Nov-Jan, 1961-62 - #29, Jan, 1971
Dell Publishing Co.

#1	1.50	3.00	4.50
2-10	1.00	2.00	3.00
11-29	.60	1.20	1.80

NOTE: *John Stanley art/script-#3-29.*

THIRTY SECONDS OVER TOKYO
1943 (Movie)
David McKay Co.

No#	3.00	6.00	9.00

THIS IS SUSPENSE!
1952 - 1955
Charlton Comics

#1 (exist?)	1.00	2.00	3.00
2-22,25,26 (all exist?)	1.00	2.00	3.00
23-Wood story reprt./A Star Presentation #3-"Dr. Jekyll & Mr. Hyde"	5.00	10.00	15.00
24-Evans story	1.50	3.00	4.50

THIS IS THE PAYOFF (See Pay-Off)

THIS IS WAR
#5, July, 1952 - #9, May, 1953
Standard Comics

#5,6,9-Toth art	2.00	4.00	6.00
7,8	1.00	2.00	3.00

THIS IS YOUR LIFE, DONALD DUCK (See 4-Color Comics #1109)

THIS MAGAZINE IS CRAZY (Crazy V3#3 on)

V3#2, 7/57 (68 pgs.) (25¢) (Satire)
Charlton Publ. (Humor Magazines)

	Good	Fine	Mint
V3#2	.75	1.50	2.25

THIS MAGAZINE IS HAUNTED
Oct, 1951 - V3#21, Nov, 1954
Fawcett Publications/Charlton #14 on

#1-Evans art	3.00	6.00	9.00
2,5-Evans art	2.00	4.00	6.00
3,4	1.50	3.00	4.50
6-13	1.25	2.50	3.75
14,19,20	1.00	2.00	3.00
15-18,21-Ditko stories	1.50	3.00	4.50

NOTE: *Ditko cover-V3#16. Powell stories-#5, 11,17.*

THIS MAGAZINE IS HAUNTED (2nd Series) (Formerly Zaza the Mystic)
V2#12, July, 1957 - V2#16, April, 1958
Charlton Comics

V2#12-16-Ditko cover/stories in all			
	1.50	3.00	4.50

THIS MAGAZINE IS WILD (See Wild)

THIS WAS YOUR LIFE (Religious)
1964 (3½x5½") (40pgs.) (Bl.,white & red)
Jack T. Chick Publ.

.15	.30	.45

THOR (Formerly Journey Into Mystery)
March, 1966 - Present
Marvel Comics Group

#126	1.20	2.40	3.60
127-140	1.00	2.00	3.00
141-147,150: #146-Inhumans begin, end #151			
	.60	1.20	1.80
148,149-Origin Black Bolt in ea.			
	.80	1.60	2.40
151-157,159,160	.60	1.20	1.80
158-Reprints origin(#83)	.70	1.40	2.10
161-164,167-179-Last Kirby ish.			
	.60	1.20	1.80
165,166-Warlock app.	.80	1.60	2.40
180,181-Adams art	1.25	2.50	3.75
182-192,194-200	.50	1.00	1.50
193-(52pgs.)-Silver Surfer x-over			
	.80	1.60	2.40
201-212,214-226: #225-Intro. Firelord			
	.40	.80	1.20
213-Starlin cover	.50	1.00	1.50
227-230-Buckler art	.40	.80	1.20
231-250	.25	.50	.75

(Thor cont'd)	Good	Fine	Mint
251-280	.20	.40	.60
Giant-Size #1('75)	.40	.80	1.20
Special #2(9/66)	1.00	2.00	3.00
Special #3,4('67-12/71)(See Journey Into			
Mystery for #1)	.80	1.60	2.40
Annual #5(11/76)	.50	1.00	1.50
Annual #6(10/77),7(9/78)	.30	.60	.90

NOTE: *Adams covers-#179-181. Buscema stories-
#178,182-226,231-253,254(reprint),256-259,
272-278,Annual #5; covers-#175,182-202,254,
256,259,261,262,272-278,Annual #6. Everett
inks-#143,170-175; cover-#241(w/Romita).
Kirby stories-#126-177,179,254(reprint);
covers-#126-169,172-174,176-178,249-253,255,
257,258,Annual #5,Special #1-4. Simonson
pencils-#260-271.*

THOSE MAGNIFICENT MEN IN THEIR FLYING MACHINES (See Movie Comics)

THREE BEARS, THE (See Surprise Books)

THREE CABALLEROS (See 4-Color Comics #71)

THREE CHIPMUNKS, THE (See 4-Color #1042)

THREE COMICS MAGAZINE
1944
Quality Comics Group

#1-Lady Luck, Mr. Mystic, The Spirit app.			
(3 Spirit sections bound together)	10.00	20.00	30.00

3-D (NOTE: *The prices of all the 3-D comics
listed include glasses. Deduct 40-50% if
glasses are missing, and reduce slightly if
glasses are loose.*)

3-D ACTION
Jan, 1954   (Oversized)   (15¢)
Atlas Comics (ACI)

	Good	Fine	Mint
#1-Battle Brady	5.00	10.00	15.00

3-D ANIMAL FUN (See Animal Fun)

3-D BATMAN
1953, Reprinted in 1966
National Periodical Publications

	Good	Fine	Mint
1953-Reprints Batman #48	12.00	24.00	36.00
1966-Tommy Tomorrow app.	3.00	6.00	9.00

3-D CIRCUS
1953   (25¢)
Fiction House Magazines

	Good	Fine	Mint
#1	5.00	10.00	15.00

3-D COMICS (See Tor, 3-D, & Mighty Mouse)

3-D DOLLY
Dec, 1953
Harvey Publications

#1-Richie Rich story redrawn from his 1st app.			
in Little Dot #1	10.00	20.00	30.00

3-D-ELL
1953   (3-D comics)   (25¢)
Dell Publishing Co.

	Good	Fine	Mint
#1,2-Rootie Kazootie	6.00	12.00	18.00
3-Flukey Luke	5.00	10.00	15.00

3-D FEATURES PRESENT JET PUP
Oct-Dec, 1953
Dimensions Public

	Good	Fine	Mint
#1-Two stories by Irving Spector			
	5.00	10.00	15.00

3-D FUNNY MOVIES
1953   (25¢)
Comic Media

	Good	Fine	Mint
#1	5.00	10.00	15.00

3-D LOVE
December, 1953   (25¢)
Steriographic Publ. (Mikeross Publ.)

	Good	Fine	Mint
#1	5.00	10.00	15.00

3-D NOODNICK (See Noodnick)

3-D ROMANCE
January, 1954   (25¢)
Steriographic Publ. (Mikeross Publ.)

	Good	Fine	Mint
#1	5.00	10.00	15.00

3-D SHEENA, JUNGLE QUEEN
1953
Fiction House Magazines

	Good	Fine	Mint
#1	10.00	20.00	30.00

3-D SUPERMAN
1953   (Large size)
National Periodical Publications

	Good	Fine	Mint
Origin Superman	15.00	30.00	45.00

3-D TALES OF TERROR (See E.C. 3-D Classics)

3-D Action #1, © MCG

3-D Dolly #1, © HARV

3-D Sheena #1, © FH

3-D TALES OF THE WEST
Jan, 1954   (Oversized)   (15¢)
Atlas Comics (CPS)

	Good	Fine	Mint
#1 (3-D)	6.00	12.00	18.00

3-D THREE STOOGES (See Three Stooges)

3-D WHACK (See Whack)

THREE DIMENSION COMICS (See Mighty Mouse)

THREE DIMENSIONAL E.C. CLASSICS (Three Dimensional Tales From the Crypt #2)
Spring, 1954   (Prices include glasses)
E.C. Comics

#1-Reprints: Wood(Mad#3), Krigstein(W.S.#7), Evans(F.C.#13), & Ingels(CSS #5); Kurtzman cover

	Good	Fine	Mint
	11.00	22.00	33.00

NOTE: *Stories redrawn to 3-D format. Original stories not necessarily by artists listed. CSS: Crime SuspenStories; F.C.: Frontline Combat; W.S.: Weird Science.*

THREE DIMENSIONAL TALES FROM THE CRYPT
(Formerly Three Dimensional E.C. Classics)
Spring, 1954   (Prices include glasses)
E.C. Comics

#2-Davis(TFTC#25), Elder(VOH#14), Craig (TFTC#24), & Orlando(TFTC#22) stories; Feldstein cover

	Good	Fine	Mint
	8.00	16.00	24.00

NOTE: *Stories redrawn to 3-D format. Original stories not necessarily by artists listed. TFTC: Tales From the Crypt; VOH: Vault of Horror.*

3 FUNMAKERS, THE
1908   (64 pgs.)   (10"x15")
Stokes and Company

Maude, Katzenjammer Kids, Happy Hooligan (1904-06 Sunday strip reprints in color)

	Good	Fine	Mint
	20.00	50.00	80.00

THREE LITTLE PIGS (See 4-Color Comics #218)

3 LITTLE PIGS, THE (See W.C. Showcase #15,21)
May, 1964 - #2, Sept, 1968   (Walt Disney)
Gold Key

		Good	Fine	Mint
#1-Reprints 4-Color #218		.40	.80	1.20
2		.30	.60	.90

THREE MOUSEKETEERS, THE (1st Series)
Mar-Apr, 1956 - #26, Oct-Dec, 1960

National Periodical Publications

	Good	Fine	Mint
#1	1.50	3.00	4.50
2-10	1.00	2.00	3.00
11-26	.60	1.20	1.80

THREE MOUSEKETEERS, THE (2nd Series)
May-June, 1970 - #7, May-June, 1971
National Periodical Publications

	Good	Fine	Mint
#1-4		.15	.30
5-7(68pgs.)	.15	.30	.45

(See Super DC Giant)

THREE NURSES
V3#18, May, 1963 - V3#23, Mar, 1964
Charlton Comics

	Good	Fine	Mint
V3#18-23	.15	.30	.45

THREE RASCALS
1958; 1963
I.W. Enterprises

IW Reprint #1(Says Super Comics on inside) (M.E.'s Clubhouse Rascals), #2('58)

	Good	Fine	Mint
#10('63)-reprints #1	.35	.70	1.05

THREE RING COMICS
March, 1945
Spotlight Publishers

	Good	Fine	Mint
#1	1.50	3.00	4.50

THREE ROCKETEERS (See Blast-Off)

THREE STOOGES (See Comic Album #18, The Little Stooges, March of Comics #232,248, 268,292,304,316,336,373, & Movie Classics & Comics)

THREE STOOGES
2/49 - #2, 5/49; 9/53 - #7, 10/54
Jubilee #1,2/St. John #1(9/53) on

#1-(Scarce)-(1949)Kubert art

	Good	Fine	Mint
	10.00	20.00	30.00
2-(Scarce)-Kubert, Maurer art			
	7.00	14.00	21.00
1(9/53)-Hollywood Stunt Girl by Kubert,7pgs.			
	8.00	16.00	24.00
2,3(3-D)(10-11/53)	5.00	10.00	15.00
4(3/54)-#7(10/54)	2.50	5.00	7.50

NOTE: *All issues have Kubert-Maurer art.*

THREE STOOGES
Oct-Nov, 1959 - #55, June, 1972
Dell Publ. Co./Gold Key #10(10/62) on

(Three Stooges cont'd)

	Good	Fine	Mint
4-Color #1043,1078,1127,1170,1187, #6('61)-			
#9(01-827-208)	1.50	3.00	4.50
#10-14,16-20	1.00	2.00	3.00
15-Go Around the World in a Daze-Movie issue			
	2.00	4.00	6.00
21-55	.60	1.20	1.80

3 WORLDS OF GULLIVER (See 4-Color #1158)

THRILLING ADVENTURES IN STAMPS COMICS
1/53 (25¢)(100pgs.)(Formerly Stamp Comics)
Stamp Comics, Inc.

V1#8-Harrison, Wildey art	2.00	4.00	6.00

THRILLING ADVENTURE STORIES
Feb, 1975 - #2, July-Aug, 1975 (B&W, 68pgs.)
Atlas/Seaboard Publ.

	Good	Fine	Mint
#1-Tigerman, Kromag the Killer begin; Heath			
story	.80	1.60	2.40
2-Toth + Severin story, Adams cover			
	.80	1.60	2.40

THRILLING COMICS
Feb, 1940 - #80, April, 1951
Nedor/Better/Standard Comics

	Good	Fine	Mint
#1-Origin Doc Strange; Nickie Norton begins			
	35.00	70.00	105.00
2-The Rio Kid & The Woman in Red begin			
	17.00	34.00	51.00
3-The Ghost & Lone Eagle begin			
	15.00	30.00	45.00
4-10	10.00	20.00	30.00
11-18,20	8.00	16.00	24.00
19-Origin The American Crusader, ends #39,41			
	15.00	30.00	45.00
21-30: #24-Intro. Mike, Doc Strange's side-			
kick. #29-Last Rio Kid	7.00	14.00	21.00
31-40: #36-Commando Cubs begin			
	4.00	8.00	12.00
41-52-The Ghost ends	3.00	6.00	9.00
53-The Phantom Detective begins; The Cavalier			
app.; no Commando Cubs	3.00	6.00	9.00
54-The Cavalier app.; no Commando Cubs			
	3.00	6.00	9.00
55-Lone Eagle ends	3.00	6.00	9.00
56-Princess Pantha begins	6.00	12.00	18.00
57-60	5.00	10.00	15.00
61-65: #61-The Lone Eagle app. #62-Last Phan-			
tom Detective. #65-Last Commando Cubs;			
Captain Eagle app.	5.00	10.00	15.00
66-Frazetta text illo	6.00	12.00	18.00
67,70-73: Frazetta story in each, 5-7pgs.;			
#72-Sea Eagle app. #73-Last Princess Pan-			
tha; Tara app.	8.00	16.00	24.00

	Good	Fine	Mint
68,69-Two Frazetta stories, 8&6pgs.; 9&7pgs.			
	12.00	24.00	36.00
74-76,78	2.00	4.00	6.00
77-Western format begins	2.00	4.00	6.00
79-Krigstein story	2.50	5.00	7.50
80-Severin & Elder, Celardo & Moreira stories			
	2.50	5.00	7.50

NOTE: *Schomburg (Xela)* covers-#57-69(#62-69, airbrush). *Woman in Red* not in #19,23,31-33, 39-45. #72 exists as a Canadian reprint with no Frazetta story.

THRILLING CRIME CASES (Shocking Myst. Cases
#41, 6-7/50 - #49, 1952   #50 on)
Star Publications

	Good	Fine	Mint
#41,42,44-49	2.00	4.00	6.00
43-Drug story	3.00	6.00	9.00

NOTE: *All have* L. B. Cole *covers*.

THRILLING ROMANCES
1950 - #26, June, 1954
Standard Comics

	Good	Fine	Mint
#7-7pgs.Severin/Elder art	3.00	6.00	9.00
8,9	1.20	2.40	3.60
10-4pgs.Severin/Elder art	2.00	4.00	6.00
11,14-21,23,26	1.00	2.00	3.00
12-Wood art, 2pgs.	2.00	4.00	6.00
13-Severin art	2.00	4.00	6.00
22,24,25-Toth art	2.50	5.00	7.50

NOTE: *All photo covers.* Celardo *story-#16.*

THRILLING TRUE STORY OF THE BASEBALL GIANTS
1952 (2nd issue titled --Baseball Yankees)
Fawcett Publications

	Good	Fine	Mint
Each......	4.00	8.00	12.00

THRILL-O-RAMA
Oct, 1965 - #3, Dec, 1966
Harvey Publications (Fun Films)

	Good	Fine	Mint
#1-Fate(Man in Black) by Powell app.; Doug			
Wildey story	.90	1.80	2.70
2-Pirana begins; Williamson 2pgs.; Fate(Man			
in Black) by Powell app.	.70	1.40	2.10
3-Man in Black(Fate) app.	.50	1.00	1.50

THRILLS OF TOMORROW (Formerly Tomb of Terror)
#17, Oct, 1954 - #20, 1955
Harvey Publications

	Good	Fine	Mint
#17,18-Powell art(horror); #17-reprts. Witch-			
es Tales #7. #18-reprints Tomb of Terror			
#1	1.20	2.40	3.60
19,20-Stuntman by S&K (reprints from Stunt-			
man); #19 has origin	10.00	20.00	30.00

Thrilling Comics #2, © STD

Thrilling Comics #59, © STD

Thrilling Romances #21, © STD

Thrills Of Tomorrow #18, © HARV   Thun'da #1, © ME   Thunder Agents #7, © TC

THROBBING LOVE
1950   (Giant) (132 pgs.)
Fox Features Syndicate

No#-See Fox Giants. Contents may vary and
determines price.

THROUGH GATES OF SPLENDOR
1973   (36 pgs.) (39¢)
Spire Christian Comics(Fleming H. Revell Co.)

	Good	Fine	Mint
No#	.25	.50	.75

THUMPER (See 4-Color Comics #19 & #243)

THUN'DA
1952 - 1953
Magazine Enterprises

	Good	Fine	Mint
#1(A-1#47)-Cave Girl; Frank Frazetta cover/ art	150.00	300.00	450.00
2(A-1#56)	10.00	20.00	30.00
3(A-1#73), #4(A-1#78)	9.00	18.00	27.00
5(A-1#83), #6(A-1#86)	8.00	16.00	24.00

NOTE: *Powell cover/stories-#2-5.*

THUNDER AGENTS
11/65 - #17, 12/67; #18, 9/68, #19, 11/68,
#20, 11/69 (#1-16, 68pgs.; #17 on, 52pgs.)
Tower Comics

	Good	Fine	Mint
#1-Origin & 1st app. Dynamo, Noman, Menthor, & The Thunder Squad; 1st app. The Iron Maiden	3.00	6.00	9.00
2-Death of Egghead	1.75	3.50	5.25
3-5: #4-Guy Gilbert becomes Lightning who joins Thunder Squad; Iron Maiden app.	1.50	3.00	4.50
6-10: #7-Death of Menthor. #8-Origin & 1st app. The Raven	1.25	2.50	3.75
11-15: #13-Undersea Agent app.; no Raven story	.80	1.60	2.40
16-19	.60	1.20	1.80
20-All reprints	.40	.80	1.20

NOTE: *Crandall story-#1,4,5(pencil),18; cover-#18. Ditko story-#6,7(inks),12(pencils), 16,18. Kane story-#1,5(pencils),6(pencils), 14,16; covers-#14,15. Whitney stories-#10, 13,15,17,18; cover-#17. Wood story-#1-11, (w/Ditko-#12,18),(inks-#9,16,17),5-17,19,20 (reprint); cover-#1-8,10-13(#10 w/Williamson).*

THUNDERBOLT (See The Atomic --)

THUNDERBOLT (Peter Cannon --)(Formerly Son of Vulcan #50)
Jan, 1966; #51, 3-4/66 - #60, 11/67
Charlton Comics

	Good	Fine	Mint
#1-Origin	.80	1.60	2.40
51	.50	1.00	1.50
52-58: #56-Sentinels begin. #58-Last Thunderbolt	.40	.80	1.20
59,60: #60-Prankster app.	.30	.60	.90

THUNDER MOUNTAIN (See 4-Color Comics #246)

TICK TOCK TALES
Jan, 1946 - #34, 1951
Magazine Enterprises

	Good	Fine	Mint
#1-The Pixies	1.50	3.00	4.50
2-10	.80	1.60	2.40
11-34	.50	1.00	1.50

TICKLE COMICS (Also see Gay & Smile Comics)
1955   (52 pgs.) (5x7¼") (7¢)
Modern Store Publ.

	Good	Fine	Mint
#1	.65	1.35	2.00

TIGER (Also see Comics Reading Libraries)
March, 1970 - #6, Jan, 1971 (15¢)
Charlton Press (King Features)

	Good	Fine	Mint
#1	.15	.30	.45
2-6		.15	.30

TIGER BOY (See Unearthly Spectaculars)

TIGER GIRL
Sept, 1968
Gold Key

	Good	Fine	Mint
#1(10227-809)	1.25	2.50	3.75

TIGER-MAN
April, 1975 - #3, Sept, 1975
Seaboard Periodicals (Atlas)

	Good	Fine	Mint
#1	.30	.60	.90
2,3-Ditko story in each	.20	.40	.60

TIGER WALKS, A (See Movie Comics)

TILLIE AND TED-TINKERTOTLAND
1945
W. T. Grant Co.

Good	Fine	Mint
1.50	3.00	4.50

TILLIE THE TOILER
1926 - 1933 (B&W daily strip reprints)(52pgs)
Cupples & Leon Co.

	Good	Fine	Mint
#1	7.00	14.00	21.00

417

(Tillie the Toiler cont'd)

	Good	Fine	Mint
2-8	6.00	12.00	18.00

NOTE: *First strip app. was January, 1921.*

TILLIE THE TOILER (See Comic Monthly)
1941 - 1950
Dell Publishing Co.

	Good	Fine	Mint
4-Color #15(1941)	10.00	20.00	30.00
Large Feature Comic #30(1941)	7.00	17.50	28.00
4-Color #8(1942)	7.00	14.00	21.00
4-Color #22(1943)	6.00	12.00	18.00
4-Color #55(1944)	5.00	10.00	15.00
4-Color #89(1945)	4.00	8.00	12.00
4-Color #106('45),132('46)	3.00	6.00	9.00
4-Color #150,176,184	2.25	4.50	6.75
4-Color #195,213,237	2.00	4.00	6.00

TIME FOR LOVE (Formerly Romantic Secrets)
V2#53, Oct, 1966 - #47, May, 1976
Charlton Comics

V2#53(10/66),#2(12/67)	.15	.30	.45
#3-47		.15	.30

TIMELESS TOPIX (See Topix)

TIME MACHINE, THE (See 4-Color Comics #1085)

TIME TO RUN
1973
Spire Christian Comics(Fleming H. Revell Co.)

By Al Hartley (from Billy Graham movie)

	.20	.40	.60

TIME TUNNEL, THE (TV)
Feb, 1967 - #2, July, 1967
Gold Key

#1,2	.65	1.35	2.00

TIM HOLT (Becomes Red Mask #42 on)
1948 - #41, May, 1954
Magazine Enterprises

	Good	Fine	Mint
#1(A-1#14)	15.00	30.00	45.00
2(A-1#17)	8.00	16.00	24.00
3(A-1#19)	7.00	14.00	21.00
4-10: #6-1st app. Calico Kid	5.00	10.00	15.00
11-Origin & 1st app. Ghost Rider; series be- gins in Tim Holt	17.00	34.00	51.00
12-16	3.00	6.00	9.00
17-Frazetta cover	14.00	28.00	42.00
18,19	3.00	6.00	9.00
20-Origin Red Mask	4.00	8.00	12.00

	Good	Fine	Mint
21,23-Frazetta covers	11.00	22.00	33.00
22,24,26-30	2.50	5.00	7.50
25-1st app. Black Phantom	3.00	6.00	9.00
31-38,40,41: #38-Black Phantom begins	2.00	4.00	6.00
39-(3-D effect)	2.50	5.00	7.50

NOTE: *Bolle* art in most issues.

TIM IN SPACE (Formerly Gene Autry Tim)
1950   (1/2 size giveaway) (B&W)
Tim Stores

	1.00	2.00	3.00

TIM McCOY (Pictorial Love Stories #22)
#16, Oct, 1948 - #21, Aug-Sept, 1949
Charlton Comics

#16-21	5.00	10.00	15.00

TIM McCOY, POLICE CAR 17
1934   (32 pgs.) (11x14") (B&W)
Whitman Publishing Co.

1933 movie in pictures	7.00	14.00	21.00

TIMMY (See 4-Color #715,823,923,1022)

TIMMY THE TIMID GHOST (See Blue Bird)
1957 - #45, 9/66; Oct, 1967 - #23, July, 1971
Charlton Comics

#1(1957) (1st Series)	1.00	2.00	3.00
2-5	.50	1.00	1.50
6-10	.40	.80	1.20
11(4/58)(Giant)	.40	.80	1.20
12-45('66)	.20	.40	.60
#1(11/67)-Bluebird	.15	.30	.45
2-23		.15	.30
Shoe Store Giveaway	.25	.50	.75

TIM TYLER (See Harvey Comics Hits #54)

TIM TYLER (Also see Comics Reading Libraries)
1942; 1973
Better Publications/CC

#1	5.00	10.00	15.00

TIM TYLER COWBOY
#11, Nov, 1948 - #18, 1950
Standard Comics

#11-18	2.00	4.00	6.00

TINKER BELL (See 4-Color #896,982 & Walt Disney Showcase #37)

Tillie The Toiler #3(C&L), © KING

The Time Tunnel #1, © GK

Tim Holt #10, © ME

Tiny Tot Comics #8, © WMG   Tip Top Comics #2, © UFS   Tip Top Comics #27, © UFS

TINY FOLKS FUNNIES (See 4-Color Comics #60)

TINY TESSIE (Tessie #1-23; Real Experiences
#24, Oct, 1949   #25)
Marvel Comics (20CC)

	Good	Fine	Mint
#24	.60	1.20	1.80

TINY TIM
1941 - 1949
Dell Publishing Co.

Large Feature Comic #4('41)

	Good	Fine	Mint
	12.00	30.00	48.00
4-Color #20(1941)	12.00	24.00	36.00
4-Color #42(1943)	7.00	14.00	21.00
4-Color #235	2.50	5.00	7.50

TINY TOT COMICS
1946 - #10, Nov-Dec, 1947
E.C. Comics

#1	9.00	18.00	27.00
2-10	7.00	14.00	21.00

TINY TOT FUNNIES (Becomes Junior Funnies)
June, 1951
Harvey Publ. (King Features Synd.)

#9-Flash Gordon, Mandrake	3.00	6.00	9.00

TINY TOTS COMICS
1943   (Not reprints)
Dell Publishing Co.

#1-Two Kelly stories	25.00	50.00	75.00

TIPPY & CAP STUBBS (See 4-Color #210,242)

TIPPY'S FRIENDS GO-GO & ANIMAL
July, 1966 - #15, Oct, 1969   (25¢)
Tower Comics

#1	.20	.40	.60
2-15: #12-15 titled "Tippy's Friend Go-Go"		.15	.30

TIPPY TEEN
Nov, 1965 - #27, Feb, 1970   (25¢)
Tower Comics

#1	.20	.40	.60
2-27		.15	.30
Special Collectors' Editions(1969-No#)(25¢)			
	.15	.30	.45

TIPPY TERRY
1963
Super/I.W. Enterprises

	Good	Fine	Mint
Super Reprint #14('63)-Little Grouchy reprts.			
	.40	.80	1.20
I.W. Reprint #1(no date)	.40	.80	1.20

TIP TOP COMICS
April, 1936 - #225, May-July, 1961
United Features/St. John/Dell Publ. Co.

#1-Tarzan by Hal Foster, Li'l Abner begin; strip reprints	80.00	160.00	240.00
2	40.00	80.00	120.00
3	25.00	50.00	75.00
4	20.00	40.00	60.00
5-10: #7-Photo & biography of Edgar Rice Burroughs	15.00	30.00	45.00
11-20	12.00	24.00	36.00
21-40: #36-Kurtzman panel	10.00	20.00	30.00
41-50: #41-Has 1st Tarzan Sunday. #43-Mort Walker panel	8.00	16.00	24.00
51-53	7.00	14.00	21.00
54-Origin Mirror Man & Triple Terror, also featured on cover	9.00	18.00	27.00
55,56,58,60	6.00	12.00	18.00
57,59,62-Tarzan by Hogarth	10.00	20.00	30.00
61-Last Tarzan by Foster	6.00	12.00	18.00
63-80: #65,67,68,70,73-No Tarzan	5.00	10.00	15.00
81-90	3.50	7.00	10.50
91-100	2.50	5.00	7.50
101-140: #111-Li'l Abner app. #118-No Tarzan. #132-No Tarzan	2.00	4.00	6.00
141-170: #157-Last Li'l Abner	1.50	3.00	4.50
171-188-Tarzan reprints by B. Lubbers in all. #176-Peanuts by Shulz begins	1.75	3.50	5.25
189-225	1.00	2.00	3.00
Bound Volumes (Very Rare) sold at 1939 World's Fair; bound by publ. in pictorial comic boards. (Also see Comics on Parade)			
Bound issues #1-12	160.00	320.00	480.00
Bound issues #13-24	120.00	240.00	360.00
Bound issues #25-36	80.00	160.00	240.00

NOTE: *Tarzan covers-#3,9,13,16,18,21,24,27,30,
32-34,36,37,39,41,43,45,47,50 (all worth 10-
20% more). Tarzan by Foster-#1-40,44-50; by
Rex Maxon-#41-43; by Burne Hogarth-#57,59,62.*

TIP TOPPER COMICS
1949 - 1954
United Features Syndicate

#1-Li'l Abner, Abbie & Slats	1.50	3.00	4.50
2-5	1.00	2.00	3.00

(Tip Topper cont'd)	Good	Fine	Mint
6-25	.80	1.60	2.40
26-28-Twin Earths	2.50	5.00	7.50

T-MAN
Sept, 1951 - #38, Dec, 1956
Quality Comics Group

	Good	Fine	Mint
#1-Jack Cole art	3.00	6.00	9.00
2,6-Crandall covers	2.00	4.00	6.00
3,7,8-Drug stories, Crandall covers			
	5.00	10.00	15.00
4,5-Crandall cover/story each			
	3.00	6.00	9.00
9,10	1.75	3.50	5.25
11-38	1.20	2.40	3.60

TNT COMICS
Feb, 1946
Charles Publishing Co.

#1-Yellowjacket app.	2.50	5.00	7.50

TOBY TYLER (See Movie Comics & 4-Color #1092)

TODAY'S BRIDE
Nov, 1955 - #4, Nov, 1956
Ajax/Farrell Publishing Co.

#1	1.20	2.40	3.60
2-4	.75	1.50	2.25

TODAY'S ROMANCE
#5, March, 1952 - #8, Sept, 1952
Standard Comics

#5	.80	1.60	2.40
6-Toth art	2.00	4.00	6.00

TOKA (Jungle King)
Aug-Oct, 1964 - #10, Jan, 1967
Dell Publishing Co.

#1	.65	1.35	2.00
2	.40	.80	1.20
3-10	.30	.60	.90

TOMAHAWK (Son of -- #131-140 on cover)
Sept-Oct, 1950 - #140, May-June, 1972
National Periodical Publications

#1	12.00	24.00	36.00
2-Frazetta/Williamson story, 4pgs.			
	10.00	20.00	30.00
3-5	5.00	10.00	15.00
6-10	4.00	8.00	12.00
11-20	2.25	4.50	6.75
21-27,30	1.50	3.00	4.50

	Good	Fine	Mint
28-1st app. Lord Shilling(arch-foe)			
	1.75	3.50	5.25
29-Frazetta reprint/Jimmy Wakely #3, 3pgs.			
	8.00	16.00	24.00
31-50	1.00	2.00	3.00
51-56,58-70	.75	1.50	2.25
57-Frazetta reprint/Jimmy Wakely #6, 3pgs.			
	6.00	12.00	18.00
71-80	.40	.80	1.20
81-1st app. Miss Liberty	.50	1.00	1.50
82,84,85,87-95	.35	.70	1.05
83-Origin Tomahawk's Rangers			
	.40	.80	1.20
86-Last Lord Shilling; origin King Colosso (Giant Ape)	.35	.70	1.05
96-Origin & 1st app. The Hood, Alias Lady Shilling	.35	.70	1.05
97-106,108,109	.30	.60	.90
107-Origin & 1st app. Thunder-Man			
	.30	.60	.90
110-The Hood & Miss Liberty app.			
	.30	.60	.90
111-The Hood & Thunder-Man team-up			
	.25	.50	.75
112-130	.25	.50	.75
131-Frazetta reprint/Jimmy Wakely #7, 3pgs.; origin Firehair retold	.50	1.00	1.50
132,134,136-6pg. Kubert	.25	.50	.75
133,135,137,138,140	.20	.40	.60
139-Frazetta reprint/Star Spangled #113			
	.35	.70	1.05

NOTE: _Adams covers-#116-119,121,123-130. Firehair by Kubert-#131-134,136. Maurer story-#138._

TOM AND JERRY (See Comic Album #4,8,12, Dell Giant #21, Golden Comics Digest #1,5,8, 13,15,18,22,25,28,34, & March of Comics #21, 46,61,70,88,103,119,128,145,154,173,190,207, 224,281,295,305,321,333,345,361,365,388,400)

TOM AND JERRY COMICS (M.G.M)(Our Gang #1-59)
#193, 6/48 - #291, 2/75; #292, 3/77 - Present
Dell Publ. Co./Gold Key #213 on

4-Color #193	3.50	7.00	10.50
#60-80	1.50	3.00	4.50
81-100	1.00	2.00	3.00
101-130	.60	1.20	1.80
131-160	.50	1.00	1.50
161-200	.35	.70	1.05
201-212(7-9/62)	.25	.50	.75
213-215-All titled "--Funhouse." #213,214- 84pgs.	.50	1.00	1.50
216-230	.25	.50	.75
231-270	.20	.40	.60
271-316: #286-"Tom & Jerry"	.15		.35

Tip Topper #8, © UFS

T-Man #18, © QUA

Tomahawk #6, © DC

Tom & Jerry Comics #86, © Loew's Inc.   Tomb Of Terror #9, © HARV   Tom Mix Comics #3(Ralston), © Tom Mix

	Good	Fine	Mint
(Tom and Jerry cont'd)			
Back to School #1(9/56)	1.50	3.00	4.50
Mouse From T.R.A.P.#1(7/66)-Giant, Gold Key			
	.50	1.00	1.50
Picnic Time #1(7/58)	1.25	2.50	3.75
Summer Fun #1(7/54)-Droopy written by Carl			
Barks	3.50	7.00	10.50
Summer Fun #2-4(7/57)	1.25	2.50	3.75
Summer Fun #1(G.K.-reprints,'67)-Reprints			
Barks' Droopy/Winter Carnival #2			
	.70	1.40	2.10
--Tells About Kites(1959,PG&E giveaway)			
	1.00	2.00	3.00
Toy Fair #1(100pgs.-'58)	1.50	3.00	4.50
Winter Carnival #1('52)-Droopy written by			
Barks	4.00	8.00	12.00
Winter Carnival #2('53)-Droopy written by			
Barks (Giant)	3.00	6.00	9.00
Winter Fun #3-7('54-'58)	1.00	2.00	3.00

NOTE: *#60-87,98-121,268,277,289,302 are 52pgs.*

TOM OF DARKNESS (Formerly Beware)
#9, July, 1974 - #23, Nov, 1976
Marvel Comics Group

#9-19: #17-Woodbridge reprt./Astonishing #62			
	.15	.30	.45
20-Everett Venus reprint/Venus #19			
	.15	.30	.45
21-23: #23-Everett reprt.	.15	.30	

TOM OF DRACULA (See Giant-Size Dracula)
April, 1972 - Present
Marvel Comics Group

#1	1.75	3.50	5.25
2-5: #3-Intro. Dr. Rachel Van Helsing			
	.80	1.60	2.40
6-9: #6-Intro. Inspector Chelm			
	.60	1.20	1.80
10-1st app. Blade the Vampire Slayer			
	.70	1.40	2.10
11,12,14-20: #12-Brunner cover pencils			
	.40	.80	1.20
13-Origin Blade the Vampire Slayer			
	.50	1.00	1.50
21-Origin Dr. Sun	.40	.80	1.20
22-24,26-28,30	.30	.60	.90
25-Origin & 1st app. Hannibal King			
	.30	.60	.90
29-Origin Taj	.30	.60	.90
31-40: #33-Origin Quincy Harker			
	.25	.50	.75
41,42,44-49	.20	.40	.60
43-Wrightson cover	.25	.50	.75
50-Silver Surfer app.	.25	.50	.75
51-53,55-60	.20	.40	.60

	Good	Fine	Mint
54-Birth Dracula's Son	.20	.40	.60
61-67	.20	.40	.60
Annual #1('75)-Adams reprt.	.50	1.00	1.50

TOMB OF LIGEIA (See Movie Classics)

TOMB OF TERROR (Thrills of Tomorrow #17 on)
June, 1952 - #16, July, 1954
Harvey Publications

#1	2.50	5.00	7.50
2	1.75	3.50	5.25
3-Bondage cover	2.50	5.00	7.50
4-Sid Check story	3.00	6.00	9.00
5-12	2.00	4.00	6.00
13,14,16-Special S/F ish.	2.00	4.00	6.00
15-S/F ish.; cover shows head exploding			
	2.50	5.00	7.50

NOTE: *Nostrand art-#8,9(2pgs.),10-12,15(reprt),
16. Powell art-#1,3,4(1pg.),5,9-16.*

TOMBSTONE TERRITORY (See 4-Color #1123)

TOM CAT
July, 1956 - #7, May, 1957
Charlton Comics

#1-7(CDC)	.25	.50	.75

TOM CORBETT SPACE CADET (TV)
1952 - #11, Sept-Nov, 1954
Dell Publishing Co.

4-Color #378,400,421-All by McWilliams			
	3.50	7.00	10.50
#4-11	2.50	5.00	7.50

TOM CORBETT SPACE CADET (See March of
Comics #102)

TOM CORBETT SPACE CADET
May-June, 1955 - V3#1, Nov-Dec, 1955
Prize Publications

V2#1-3	1.75	3.50	5.25
V3#1	1.50	3.00	4.50

TOM LANDRY & THE DALLAS COWBOYS
1973   (35¢)
Spire Christian Comics/Fleming H. Revell Co.

#1	.25	.50	.75

TOM MIX (-- Commando Comics #10-12)
Sept, 1940 - #12, Nov, 1942   (36 pgs.)
Given away for 2 Ralston box tops
Ralston-Purina Co.

(Tom Mix cont'd)

	Good	Fine	Mint
#1-Origin(life)Tom Mix; Fred Meagher art			
	40.00	80.00	120.00
2	30.00	60.00	90.00
3-9	20.00	40.00	60.00
10-Origin Tom Mix Commando Unit; Speed O'Dare			
begins	15.00	30.00	45.00
11,12	15.00	30.00	45.00

TOM MIX NATIONAL CHICLE GUM CO.
(See Big Thrill Booklet) (46 titles known)
1934   (8pgs.) (2 inside ill. with text)
National Chicle Gum Co.   (2-3/8"x2-3/4")

each......	4.00	8.00	12.00

NOTE: *Like Big Thrill Gum Booklets; color on cover only.*

TOM MIX WESTERN   (Also see Master Comics)
Jan, 1948 - #61, May, 1953
Fawcett Publications

#1	16.00	32.00	48.00
2	9.00	18.00	27.00
3-5	7.00	14.00	21.00
6-9: #8-Tempera cover by Kinstler			
	6.00	12.00	18.00
10-Used in Seduction of the Innocent, pg.			
323-325	8.00	16.00	24.00
11-20: #11-Oil cover by Kinstler			
	4.00	8.00	12.00
21-30	3.50	7.00	10.50
31-40	3.00	6.00	9.00
41-61	2.00	4.00	6.00

TOMMY OF THE BIG TOP
1948 - 1949
King Features Synd./Standard Comics

#10-12	1.20	2.40	3.60

TOM SAWYER   (See Famous Stories & Advs.of--)

TOM SAWYER & HUCK FINN
1925   (48 pgs. in color)
Stoll & Edwards Co.

By Dwiggins	8.00	16.00	24.00

TOM SAWYER COMICS
1951?   (Soft Cover)
Giveaway

Contains a coverless Hopalong Cassidy from
1951; other combinations possible.

	1.00	2.00	3.00

TOM SKINNER-UP FROM HARLEM

1975   (36 pgs.) (39¢)
Spire Christian Comics(Fleming H. Revell Co.)

	Good	Fine	Mint
No#	.25	.50	.75

TOM TERRIFIC!   (TV)
Summer, 1957 - #6, Fall, 1958
Pines Comics

#1	1.20	2.40	3.60
2-6	.80	1.60	2.40

TOM THUMB   (See 4-Color Comics #972)

TOM-TOM, THE JUNGLE BOY
1947; Nov, 1957 - #3, Mar, 1958
Magazine Enterprises

#1	1.40	2.80	4.20
2,3(1947)	1.00	2.00	3.00
1(1957)(& Itchi the Monk),2,3('58)			
	.40	.80	1.20
IW Reprint #1,2,8,10	.25	.50	.75

TONKA   (See 4-Color Comics #966)

TONTO   (See The Lone Ranger's Companion --)

TONY TRENT   (The Face #1,2)
1948 - 1949
Big Shot/Columbia Comics Group

#3,4: #3-The Face app.	2.50	5.00	7.50

TOODLES, THE
1-2/51 - #10, 7-8/51; 1956 (Newspaper reprts.)
Ziff-Davis(Approved Comics)/Argo

#1	1.50	3.00	4.50
2-9	.90	1.80	2.70
10-Painted cover, some newspaper reprints			
	.90	1.80	2.70
#1(Argo, 3/56)	1.20	2.40	3.60

TOONERVILLE TROLLEY
1921   (Daily strip reprints)(B&W)(52pgs.)
Cupples & Leon Co.

#1-By Fontaine Fox	15.00	30.00	45.00

TOOTS & CASPER   (See Large Feature Comic #5)

TOP   (See Tops in Humor?)
1945
Consolidated Book (Lev Gleason)

#2001	3.50	7.00	10.50

Tom Mix Western #2, © Tom Mix

Tony Trent #3, © CCG

Toonerville Trolley 1921, © C&L

| Top Cat #1, © DELL | Topix V5#8, © CG | Top Love Stories #15, © STAR |

TOP ADVENTURE COMICS
1964   (Reprints)
I.W. Enterprises

	Good	Fine	Mint
#1-Reprints/Explorer Joe #2; Krigstein art			
	1.20	2.40	3.60
2-Black Dwarf	1.50	3.00	4.50

TOP CAT (TV) (Hanna-Barbera)
Dec-Feb, 1961-62 - #31, Sept, 1970
Dell Publ. Co./Gold Key #4 on

#1	.50	1.00	1.50
2-5	.25	.50	.75
6-10	.20	.40	.60
11-31	.15	.30	.45

TOP CAT (TV) (Hanna-Barbera)
Nov, 1970 - #20, Nov, 1973
Charlton Comics

#1	.15	.30	.45
2-20		.15	.30

NOTE: #8(1/72) went on sale late in 1972 between #14 & #15 with the Jan., 1973 issues.

TOP COMICS
July, 1967   (All rebound issues)
K.K. Publications/Gold Key

#1-Beagle Boys(#7), Bugs Bunny, Chip 'n' Dale,
  Daffy Duck(#50), Flintstones, Flipper,
  Huckleberry Hound, Huey, Dewey & Louie,
  Junior Woodchucks, The Jetsons, Lassie,
  The Little Monsters(#71), Moby Duck, Porky
  Pig(has Gold Key label - says Top Comics
  on inside), Scamp, Super Goof, Tarzan of
  the Apes(#169), Three Stooges(#35), Tom &
  Jerry, Top Cat(#21), Tweety & Sylvester(#7),
  Walt Disney Comics & Stories(#322), Woody
  Woodpecker, Yogi Bear, Zorro known; each
  character given own book.

	.50	1.00	1.50
#1-Uncle Scrooge(#70)	1.75	3.50	5.25
#1-Donald Duck(not Barks), Mickey Mouse, Tar-			
zan	1.25	2.50	3.75

#2-Bugs Bunny, Daffy Duck, Donald Duck(not
  Barks), Mickey Mouse(#114), Porky Pig, Super Goof, Three Stooges, Tom & Jerry, Tweety
  & Sylvester, Walt Disney's C&S(reprints
  #325), Woody Woodpecker, Zorro

	.40	.80	1.20
#2-Snow White & 7 Dwarfs(6/67-'44 reprint),			
Uncle Scrooge(Barks art)(#71)			
	1.20	2.40	3.60
#3-Donald Duck	.75	1.50	2.25
#3-Uncle Scrooge(#72)	1.20	2.40	3.60
#3-The Flintstones, Mickey Mouse(reprts.#115),			

	Good	Fine	Mint
Tom & Jerry, Woody Woodpecker, Yogi Bear			
	.30	.60	.90
#4-The Flintstones, Mickey Mouse, Woody Wood-			
pecker	.30	.60	.90

NOTE: Each book in this series is identical
to its counterpart except for cover, and
came out at same time. The number in parenthesis is the original issue it contains.

TOP DETECTIVE COMICS
1964   (Reprints)
I.W. Enterprises

#9-Young King Cole & Dr. Drew(not Granden-			
etti)	.40	.80	1.20

TOP ELIMINATOR (Formerly Teenage Hotrodders;
Drag 'n' Wheels #30 on)
#25, Sept, 1967 - #29, July, 1968
Charlton Comics

#26-29	.15	.30	.45

TOP FLIGHT COMICS
1947; July, 1949
Four Star Publications/St. John Publ.

#1	1.00	2.00	3.00
1(7/49)-Hector the Inspector			
	.75	1.50	2.25

TOP GUN (See 4-Color Comics #927)

TOP GUNS (See Super DC Giant & Showcase #72)

TOPIX (--Comics)(Timeless Topix-early issues)
1943 - V10#15, 1/28/52   (Weekly-later issues)
Catechetical Guild Eductional Society

V1-V4	1.25	2.50	3.75
V5#1-15(V5#2-11/46, #4-12/47)			
	.70	1.40	2.10
V6#1-14, V7#1-17 (5/1/49)	.50	1.00	1.50
V8#1-10	.50	1.00	1.50
V8#11(12/5/49)-Soft cover, publ. weekly			
	.40	.80	1.20
V8#12-Ingels art	1.50	3.00	4.50
V8#13-18(2/13/50), #19-30(5/15/50)			
	.40	.80	1.20
V9#1-15, V10#1-15	.40	.80	1.20

TOP JUNGLE COMICS
1964   (R.print)
I.W. Enterprises

#1(no date)-Reprints White Princess of the			
Jungle #3, minus cvr.	1.25	2.50	3.75

423

TOP LOVE STORIES
#3, May, 1951 - #19, Mar, 1954
Star Publications

	Good	Fine	Mint
#3	2.00	4.00	6.00
4,5,7-9,16	1.50	3.00	4.50
6-Wood story	4.00	8.00	12.00
10-15,18,19-Disbrow stys.	2.00	4.00	6.00
17-Wood art(Fox reprint)	2.50	5.00	7.50

NOTE: _L. B. Cole covers-#7,15._

TOP-NOTCH COMICS(--Laugh#28-45; Laugh#46 on)
Dec, 1939 - #45, June, 1944
MLJ Magazines

	Good	Fine	Mint
#1-Origin The Wizard; Kardak, the Mystic Magician begins; J. Cole art	60.00	120.00	180.00
2-Jack Cole art	30.00	60.00	90.00
3-Bob Phantom begins	25.00	50.00	75.00
4	20.00	40.00	60.00
5	15.00	30.00	45.00
6	12.00	24.00	36.00
7-Kalthar, the Giant Man x-over in Kardak; The Shield x-over in Wizard; The Wizard dons new costume	30.00	60.00	90.00
8-Origin The Firefly & Roy, the Super Boy	30.00	60.00	90.00
9-Origin & 1st app. The Black Hood	55.00	110.00	165.00
10	30.00	60.00	90.00
11-20	15.00	30.00	45.00
21-30: #23,24-No Wizard, Roy app. in each. #25-Last Bob Phantom, Roy app. #26-Roy app. #27-Last Firefly. #28-Suzie begins. #29-Last Kardak	12.00	24.00	36.00
31-41,43: Black Hood series ends, not in #35-37	8.00	16.00	24.00
42,44,45	2.50	5.00	7.50

TOPPER & NEIL (See 4-Color Comics #859)

TOPPS COMICS
1947
Four Star Publications

	Good	Fine	Mint
#1	1.00	2.00	3.00

TOPS
1949   (Large Size) (10"x13")
Consolidated Book Co. (Lev Gleason)

	Good	Fine	Mint
#1,2-(Rare)-Crandall/Lubbers, Biro art	25.00	50.00	75.00

TOPS COMICS
1944   (132 pgs.) (10¢)
Consolidated Book Publishers

	Good	Fine	Mint
No#(Color cover, inside in red shade & some in full color)-Ace Kelly by Rick Yager, Black Orchid, Don on the Farm, Dinky Dinkerton (Rare)	8.00	16.00	24.00

NOTE: This book is printed in such a way that when the staple is removed, the strips on the left side of the book correspond with the same strips on the right side. Therefore, if strips are removed from the book, each strip can be folded into a complete comic section of its own.

TOP SECRET
January, 1952
Hillman Publ.

	Good	Fine	Mint
#1	1.20	2.40	3.60

TOP SECRET ADVENTURES (See Spyman)

TOP SECRETS (-- of the F.B.I.)
1947 - #10, July-Aug, 1949
Street & Smith Publications

	Good	Fine	Mint
#1-Powell cover/stories	2.50	5.00	7.50
2-6,8-10-Powell covers/stories	1.75	3.50	5.25
7-"How to Hurt People" ill. in Seduction of the Innocent; Powell cover/story	4.00	8.00	12.00

TOPS IN ADVENTURE
Fall, 1952   (132 pgs.)
Ziff-Davis Publ. Co.

	Good	Fine	Mint
#1-Crusader from Mars & The Hawk; Powell art	4.00	8.00	12.00

TOPS IN HUMOR (See Top?)
1944   (Small size) (7¼x5")
Consolidated Book Publ.(Lev Gleason)

	Good	Fine	Mint
#2001(#1)-Origin The Jack O' Spades, Ace Kelly by Rick Yager, Black Orchid(female crime fighter) app.	6.00	12.00	18.00
#2	4.00	8.00	12.00

TOP SPOT COMICS
1945
Top Spot Publ. Co.

	Good	Fine	Mint
#1-The Menace, Duke of Darkness app.	3.00	6.00	9.00

TOPSY-TURVY
April, 1945
R. B. Leffingwell Publ.

	Good	Fine	Mint
#1	1.25	2.50	3.75

Top-Notch Comics #1, © MLJ

Top-Notch Comics #15, © MLJ

Top Secrets #7, © S&S

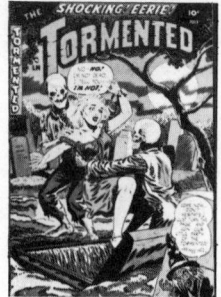

Tor 3-D #2(Nov.), © STJ   Torchy #1, © QUA   The Tormented #1, © Sterling

TOR (#1 titled "One Million Years Ago")(No#2)
#1, Sept, 1953; #3, May, 1954 - #5, Oct, 1954
St. John Publishing Co.

	Good	Fine	Mint
#1-Origin; Kubert art	25.00	50.00	75.00
2-5-Kubert art; Danny Dreams by Toth-#3			
	16.50	33.25	50.00
3-D #2(10/53)-Kubert	8.00	16.00	24.00
3-D #2(10/53)-Oversized, otherwise same			
contents	8.00	16.00	24.00
3-D #2(11/53)-Kubert	8.00	16.00	24.00

NOTE: All 3-D's have Powell art and same
contents.

TOR
May-June, 1975 - #6, Mar-Apr, 1976
National Periodical Publications

#1-New origin by Kubert	.25	.50	.75
2-Origin reprt./St.John#1	.20	.40	.60
3-6	.20	.40	.60

NOTE: All Kubert cover/stories; reprints-
#2-6.

TORCHY (--Blond Bombshell)(See Dollman, Mil-
11/49 - #6, 9/50   itary & Modern)
Quality Comics Group

#1-Bill Ward cover(per Bill Ward), Gil Fox			
stories	150.00	300.00	450.00
2,3-Fox cover/stories	45.00	90.00	135.00
4-Fox cover, 3 stories + 1 Ward story,9pgs.			
	50.00	100.00	150.00
5,6-Ward covers, 9pgs. + 3 Fox stories in			
each	80.00	160.00	240.00
Super Reprint #16('64)-Reprints #4 with new			
cover	8.00	16.00	24.00

TORMENTED, THE
July, 1954 - #2, Sept, 1954
Sterling Comics

#1,2	1.20	2.40	3.60

TORNADO TOM (See Mighty Midget Comics)

TOTAL WAR (M.A.R.S. Patrol #3 on)
July, 1965 - #2, Oct, 1965
Gold Key

#1,2-Wood art	1.75	3.50	5.25

TOUGH KID SQUAD COMICS
March, 1942
Marvel Comics

#1-Origin The Human Top & The Tough Kid Squad;			
The Flying Flame app.	90.00	180.00	270.00

TOWER OF SHADOWS (Creatures on the Loose
Sept, 1969 - #9, Jan, 1971   #10 on)
Marvel Comics Group

	Good	Fine	Mint
#1-Steranko, Craig story	1.20	2.40	3.60
2-Neal Adams story	.75	1.50	2.25
3-Smith story	.75	1.50	2.25
4-Kirby/Everett cover	.60	1.20	1.80
5-Smith, Wood story(Wood draws himself-1st			
pg., 1st panel)	1.00	2.00	3.00
6-8: Wood stories; #8-Wrightson cover			
	.80	1.60	2.40
9-Wrightson cover	.60	1.20	1.80
Special #1(12/71)-Adams sty.	.50	1.00	1.50

NOTE: Issues #1-9 contain new stories with
some pre-Marvel age reprints in #6-9. H.P.
Lovecraft adaptation-#9.

TOWN & COUNTRY
May, 1940

Origin The Falcon	12.00	24.00	36.00

TOWN THAT FORGOT SANTA, THE
1961   (24 pgs.) (Giveaway)
W. T. Grant Co.

No#	1.00	2.00	3.00

TOYLAND COMICS
Jan, 1947 - 1947
Fiction House Magazines

#1	2.50	5.00	7.50
2-4: #3-Tuska story	2.00	4.00	6.00
148pg. Issue	2.50	5.00	7.50

NOTE: All above contain strips by Al Walker.

TOY TOWN COMICS
1945 - 1946
Toytown/Orbit Publ./B. Antin/Swapper Quart.

#1-Mertie Mouse	1.50	3.00	4.50
2-7	.80	1.60	2.40

TRAGG & THE SKY GODS (See Mystery Comics
Digest #3 & Spine Tingling Tales)
June, 1975 - #8, Feb, 1977
Gold Key

#1-Origin	.30	.60	.90
2-8: #4-Sabre-Fang app. #8-Ostellon app.			
	.20	.40	.60

NOTE: Santos art-#1,2; covers-#3-7.

TRAIL BLAZERS (Red Dragon #5 on)
1941 - 1942
Street & Smith Publications

425

(Trail Blazers cont'd)	Good	Fine	Mint
#1	5.00	10.00	15.00
2-4	3.00	6.00	9.00

TRAIL COLT
1949
Magazine Enterprises

#1(A-1#24)-7pg. Frazetta story reprinted in
Manhunt #13; Ingels cover
   (Scarce)   12.00 24.00 36.00
  2(A-1#26)-Undercover Girl; Ingels cover
                9.00 18.00 27.00

TRAPPED
1951   (Giveaway) (16pgs.) (Soft cover)
Harvey Publications (Columbia Univ. Press)

Drug education comic(30,000 printed?) distributed to schools. Mentioned in Seduction
of the Innocent, pgs. 256,350.
                15.00 37.50 60.00

TRAPPED!
Oct, 1954 - #4, 1955
Periodical House Magazines (Ace)

#1	1.00	2.00	3.00
2,3	.75	1.50	2.25
4-Krigstein story	1.75	3.50	5.25

TRAVELS OF JAIMIE McPHEETERS, THE (TV)
December, 1963
Gold Key

#1		.40	.80	1.20

TREASURE BOX OF FAMOUS COMICS
Mid 1930's (36 pgs.) (6-7/8"x8-1/2")
Cupples & Leon Co.   (Soft covers)

Box + 5 titles: Reg'lar Fellers(1928), Little
Orphan Annie(1926), Smitty(1928), Harold
Teen(1931), Dick Tracy & Dick Tracy Jr.
(1933) (These are abbreviated version of
hardcover editions)
       (Set)... 100.00 200.00 300.00
NOTE: *Dates shown are copyright dates; all
books actually came out in 1934 or later.*

TREASURE CHEST (Catholic Guild)
3/12/46 - V27#8, 7/72 (Educational comics)
George A. Pflaum (not publ. during summer)

V1#1	1.50	3.00	4.50
2-12; #5-Dr. Styx app. by Baily			
	.75	1.50	2.25
V2, V3	.50	1.00	1.50

	Good	Fine	Mint
V4#1-20(9/9/48 - 5/31/49)	.50	1.00	1.50
V5#1-20(9/6/49 - 5/31/50)	.30	.60	.90
V6#1-20(9/14/50-5/31/51)	.30	.60	.90
V7#1-20(9/13/51-6/5/52)	.30	.60	.90
V8#1-20(9/11/52-6/4/53)	.30	.60	.90
V9#1-20('53-'54)	.30	.60	.90
V10#1-20('54-'55)	.25	.50	.75
V11('55-'56), V12('56-'57)	.25	.50	.75
V13-V20('57-'65)	.20	.40	.60
V13#2,6,8,11-Ingels story	1.20	2.40	3.60
V21-V25('65-'70)-(2 V24#5's 11/7/68 & 11/21/			
68)(No V24#6)	.20	.40	.60
V21#10-Ingels story	1.20	2.40	3.60
V26,V27#1-8(V26,27-68pgs.)	.20	.40	.60
Summer Edition V1#1-6('66), V2#1-6('67)			
		.15	.35

NOTE: *Anderson story-V18#13. Borth stories-*
V13#2,6,11. Crandall stories (R=Reprints)-
V7#20,V16#7,9,12,14,17,20; V17#1,2,4,5,14,16,
20; V18#1,7,9,9,10,17,19; V19#4,11,13,16,19;
V20#1,2,6,9,10,12,14-16,20; V21#1-3,5,8,9,11,
13,16,17; V22#3,7,9-11,14,16,20; V23#3,6,9,
13,16; V24#8,10; V25#16; V27#1,3-5(R),6(R),
8(2pg); covers-V16#7, V19#4, V21#5,9, V22#7,
11, V23#9,16.

TREASURE CHEST OF THE WORLD'S BEST COMICS
1945   (500pgs.) (Hardcover)
Superior, Toronto, Canada

Contains Blue Beetle, Capt. Combat, John
Wayne, Dynamic Man, Nemo, Li'l Abner; Contents can vary - represents random binding of
extra books   8.00 16.00 24.00

TREASURE COMICS
June-July, 1945 - #12, Fall, 1947
Prize Publications (American Boys' Comics)

#1-Paul Bunyan, Marco Polo, Highwayman &			
Carrot Topp begin	3.00	6.00	9.00
2-4,12	1.50	3.00	4.50
5,6,11-Krigstein art	3.00	6.00	9.00
7,8-Frazetta, 5pgs. ea.	10.00	20.00	30.00
9,10-Jr. Rangers by Kirby in ea.; #10-Kirby			
cover	4.00	8.00	12.00

TREASURE ISLAND (See 4-Color #624, King
Classics, & Movie Classics & Comics)

TREASURY OF COMICS
1947; #2, July, 1947 - #4, Sept, 1947
St. John Publishing Co.

No#(#1)-Abbie 'n' Slats (No# on cover, #1 on			
inside)	3.50	7.00	10.50
#2-Jim Hardy	2.50	5.00	7.50

Trapped! (Giveaway). © HARV

Trapped! #1, © ACE

Treasury Of Comics #4, © STJ

True Aviation Picture Stories #5. © PMI

True Bride's Experiences #8. © HARV

True Comics #71. © PMI

(Treasury of Comics cont'd)	Good	Fine	Mint
3-Bill Bumlin	2.00	4.00	6.00
4-Abbie 'n' Slats	2.50	5.00	7.50

TREASURY OF COMICS
Mar, 1948 - #5, 1948; 1949 (500 pgs.)
St. John Publishing Co.

#1	5.00	10.00	15.00
2(#2 on cvr,#1 on inside)	3.50	7.00	10.50
3-5	3.00	6.00	9.00
#1-(500pgs.)-Abbie & Slats, Abbott & Costello, Little Annie Rooney, Little Audrey, Jim Hardy, Ella Cinders (16 books bound together - $1.00)	12.00	24.00	36.00

TREASURY OF DOGS, A
Oct, 1956 (Giant)
Dell Publishing Co.

#1	2.50	5.00	7.50

TREASURY OF HORSES, A
1955 (Giant)
Dell Publishing Co.

#1	2.50	5.00	7.50

TRIALS OF LULU AND LEANDER, THE
1906 (32 pgs. in color) (10x16")
William A. Stokes Co.

By F. M. Howarth	15.00	30.00	45.00

TRIGGER (See Roy Rogers --)

TRIGGER TWINS
Mar-Apr, 1973 (One Shot)
National Periodical Publications

#1-Trigger Twins & Pow Wow Smith reprints; Infantino art	.15	.30	.45

TRIPLE GIANT COMICS (See Archie All-Star Spec.)

TRIPLE THREAT
Winter, 1945
Special Action/Holyoke/Gerona Publ.

#1-Duke of Darkness, King O'Leary	3.00	6.00	9.00

TROUBLE SHOOTERS, THE (See 4-Color #1108)

TRUE ADVENTURES (Formerly True Western)
#3, May, 1950 (Men's Adventures #4 on)
Marvel Comics (CCC)

#3	1.50	3.00	4.50

TRUE ANIMAL PICTURE STORIES
Winter, 1947 - #2, Spr-Summer, 1947
True Comics Press

	Good	Fine	Mint
#1,2	1.00	2.00	3.00

TRUE AVIATION PICTURE STORIES (Aviation Adventures & Model Building #16)
1942 - #15, Sept-Oct, 1946
Parents' Magazine Institute

#1-(titled --Aviation Comics Digest)(Not digest size)	2.00	4.00	6.00
2-14	1.20	2.40	3.60
15-(titled "True Aviation Advs. & Model Building")	1.20	2.40	3.60

TRUE BRIDE'S EXPERIENCES (Formerly Teen-Age
#8, 10/54 - #16, 2/56 Brides)
True Love (Harvey)

#8-15	.80	1.60	2.40
16-Spanking issue	2.00	4.00	6.00

NOTE: _Powell art-#8-10,12,13._

TRUE BRIDE-TO-BE ROMANCES
Aug, 1953 - #29, Sept, 1958
Home Comics/True Love(Harvey)

#1	1.50	3.00	4.50
2-5	1.00	2.00	3.00
6-15	.75	1.50	2.25
16,18-22,24-28	.60	1.20	1.80
17-S&K cover, Powell sty.	1.25	2.50	3.75
23-Powell story	.50	1.00	1.50
29-Powell, 1pg. Baker art	.80	1.60	2.40

TRUE COMICS
April, 1941 - #84, Aug, 1950
True Comics/Parents' Magazine Press

#1	5.00	10.00	15.00
2-5	3.00	6.00	9.00
6-10	2.00	4.00	6.00
11-30	1.50	3.00	4.50
31-50	1.25	2.50	3.75
51-81,83,84	1.00	2.00	3.00
82-Distr. to subscribers through the mail only (Rare)	5.00	10.00	15.00

NOTE: _#80-84 have soft covers & combined with Tex Granger, Jack Armstrong, & Calling All Kids. #68-78 featured true FBI adventures._

TRUE COMICS AND ADVENTURE STORIES
1965 (Giant) (25c)
Parents' Magazine Institute

#1	.80	1.60	2.40

TRUE COMPLETE MYSTERY (Formerly Complete Mys-
#5, April, 1949 - #7, Aug, 1949   tery)
Marvel Comics

	Good	Fine	Mint
#5-7	1.75	3.50	5.25

TRUE CONFESSIONS
1949
Fawcett Publications

	Good	Fine	Mint
#1	2.00	4.00	6.00

TRUE CONFIDENCES
Fall, 1949 - #4, June, 1950
Fawcett Publications

	Good	Fine	Mint
#1	2.00	4.00	6.00
2-4-Bob Powell art #4	1.20	2.40	3.60

TRUE CRIME CASES
1944; V1#6, 6-7/49 - V2#1, 8-10/49
St. John Publishing Co.

	Good	Fine	Mint
1944-(100pgs.)	7.00	14.00	21.00
V1#6, V2#1	1.50	3.00	4.50

TRUE CRIME COMICS (See Complete Book of --)
1942
Comic House Publications/William H. Wise

	Good	Fine	Mint
#1-The War Eagle	6.00	12.00	18.00

TRUE CRIME COMICS
#2, May, 1947; #3, 7-8/48 - #6, 6-7/49;
V2#1 - 8-9/49
Magazine Village

#2-Jack Cole cover & stories; used in Seduct-
ion of the Innocent, pg. 81,82 + illo.-
"A sample of the injury-to-eye motif" &
illo.-"Dragging living people to death";

	Good	Fine	Mint
drug story	35.00	70.00	105.00
3-Classic Cole cover/story; heroin drug story	25.00	50.00	75.00
4-Jack Cole cover	3.50	7.00	10.50
5-J. Cole cover; drug story	7.00	14.00	21.00
6	3.00	6.00	9.00

V2#1-Used in Seduction of the Innocent, pgs.
81,82 & illo-"Dragging living people to
death"; Toth, Wood(3pgs.), Roussos story;
Cole reprint from #2 + Cole cover

	Good	Fine	Mint
	12.00	24.00	36.00

TRUE GHOST STORIES (See Ripley's --)

TRUE LIFE ROMANCES
Dec, 1955   (Romances on inside)

Ajax/Farrell Publications

	Good	Fine	Mint
#1	1.20	2.40	3.60

TRUE LIFE SECRETS
#2, 5-6/51 - #28, Sept, 1955
Romantic Love Stories/Charlton

	Good	Fine	Mint
#2-9	1.50	3.00	4.50
10-13,15-19	1.75	3.50	5.25
14-Drug story	3.50	7.00	10.50
20-28	1.20	2.40	3.60

TRUE LIFE TALES (Formerly Lana?)
#8, Oct, 1949 - #2, Jan, 1950
Marvel Comics (CCC)

	Good	Fine	Mint
#8(10/49)	1.00	2.00	3.00
2(1/50)-Photo cover	1.00	2.00	3.00

TRUE LOVE CONFESSIONS
May, 1954 - #11, Jan, 1956
Premier Magazines

	Good	Fine	Mint
#1	1.20	2.40	3.60
2-11	.80	1.60	2.40

TRUE LOVE PICTORIAL
1952 - #11, Aug, 1954
St. John Publishing Co.

	Good	Fine	Mint
#1	1.75	3.50	5.25
2	1.50	3.00	4.50
3-5(All 100pgs.): #5-Formerly TeenAge Temp- tations (4/53); Kubert stories-#3,5; Baker stories-#3-5	5.00	10.00	15.00
6,7-Baker cover/stories	3.00	6.00	9.00
8-11-Baker cover/story	2.50	5.00	7.50

TRUE LOVE PROBLEMS & ADVICE ILLUSTRATED
(See Love Problems & Advice)

TRUE MOVIE AND TELEVISION
#1, 8/50 - #3, 11/50 (52pgs.) (10c)
Toby Press

	Good	Fine	Mint
#1-Liz Taylor cover	6.00	12.00	18.00
2	4.00	8.00	12.00
3-June Allyson cover	4.00	8.00	12.00

NOTE: 16 pages in color, rest movie material
in black & white.

TRUE MYSTERIES (Love Romances #7 on?)
June, 1949
Marvel Comics

	Good	Fine	Mint
#6	1.25	2.50	3.75

True Crime Comics V2#1, © Mag. Village

True Life Secrets #23, © CC

True Love Pictorial #11, © STJ

428

True Sport Picture Stories V2#8. © S&S True Stories Of Romance #1. © FAW True To Life Romances #6. © STAR

TRUE SECRETS
#3, 3/50; #4, 2/51 - #40, 9/56
Marvel(IPS)/Atlas Comics(MPI)

	Good	Fine	Mint
#3	1.00	2.00	3.00
4-21,23-40: #34-Colletta art	.50	1.00	1.50
22-Everett story	1.00	2.00	3.00

TRUE SPORT PICTURE STORIES (Formerly Sport
1941 - V5#2, July-Aug, 1949   Comics)
Street & Smith Publications

V1#4-12(1941-42)	2.00	4.00	6.00
V2#1-12(1943-44)	1.25	2.50	3.75
V3#1-12(1945-46)	.80	1.60	2.40
V4#1-12(1947-48), V5#1,2	.70	1.40	2.10

NOTE: *Powell art-V3#10, V4#1,2,4,6,12, V5#2.*

TRUE STORIES OF ROMANCE
Jan, 1950 - #3, May, 1950
Fawcett Publications

#1	1.25	2.50	3.75
2,3	.80	1.60	2.40

TRUE STORY OF JESSE JAMES, THE
(See 4-Color Comics #757)

TRUE SWEETHEART SECRETS
May, 1950 - #10, Nov, 1952
Fawcett Publications

#1	1.50	3.00	4.50
2-Wood art, 11pgs.	3.00	6.00	9.00
3-10: #4,5-Powell art	1.00	2.00	3.00

TRUE TALES OF LOVE (Formerly Secret Story
#22, 4/56 - #31, 9/57   Romances)
Atlas Comics (TCI)

#22	.50	1.00	1.50
23-31: Colleta art in most.	.35	.70	1.05

TRUE 3-D
Dec, 1953 - #2, Feb, 1954
Harvey Publications

#1-Nostrand, Powell art	6.00	12.00	18.00
2	6.00	12.00	18.00

TRUE-TO-LIFE ROMANCES
#3, April, 1950 - #23, Oct, 1954
Star Publications

#3-10	2.00	4.00	6.00
11,22,23	1.50	3.00	4.50
12-14,17-21-Disbrow art	2.50	5.00	7.50

	Good	Fine	Mint
15,16-Wood & Disbrow art in each	4.00	8.00	12.00

NOTE: *Kamen art-#13, Kamen/Feldstein art-#14.
All have L. B. Cole covers.*

TRUE WAR EXPERIENCES
Aug, 1952 - #4, Dec, 1952
Harvey Publications

#1	1.20	2.40	3.60
2-4	.80	1.60	2.40

TRUE WAR ROMANCES
Sept, 1952 - #21, June, 1955
Quality Comics Group

#1-Photo cover	2.50	5.00	7.50
2-10	1.50	3.00	4.50
11-21	1.25	2.50	3.75

TRUE WAR STORIES   (See Ripley's --)

TRUE WESTERN (True Adventures #3)
Dec, 1949 - #2, March, 1950
Marvel Comics (MMC)

#1	2.50	5.00	7.50
2	2.00	4.00	6.00

TRUE WEST ROMANCE
1952
Quality Comics Group

#21	1.50	3.00	4.50

TRUMP (Magazine format)
Jan, 1957 - #2, Mar, 1957
HMH Publishing Co.

#1-Harvey Kurtzman satire	12.00	24.00	36.00
2- " " "	8.00	16.00	24.00

NOTE: *Davis, Elder, Heath, Jaffee art-#1,2;
Wood-#1. #2-article by Mel Brooks.*

TRUMPETS WEST   (See 4-Color Comics #875)

TRUTH ABOUT CRIME
1949   (132 pgs.)
Fox Features Syndicate

No#-See Fox Giants. Contents can vary and
determines price.

TRUTH ABOUT MOTHER GOOSE (See 4-Color #862)

TRUTH BEHIND THE TRIAL OF CARDINAL
MINDSZENTY, THE

(Truth Behind the Trial of -- cont'd)
1949   (24 pgs.)
Catechetical Guild Educational Society

	Good	Fine	Mint
	4.00	8.00	12.00

TRUTHFUL LOVE (Formerly Youthful Love)
#2, July, 1950
Youthful Magazines

		Good	Fine	Mint
#2		.75	1.50	2.25

TUBBY (Marge's --) (Little Lulu)
1952 - #49, Dec-Feb, 1961-62
Dell Publishing Co./Gold Key

	Good	Fine	Mint
4-Color #381-Stanley art	9.00	18.00	27.00
4-Color #430,444,461-All by Stanley			
	5.00	10.00	15.00
#5-Stanley art	5.00	10.00	15.00
6-10	4.00	8.00	12.00
11-20: #18-Stanley art	3.00	6.00	9.00
21-30	2.50	5.00	7.50
31-49	1.50	3.00	4.50

And His Clubhouse Pals #1(1956)-4pgs. art by
  Stanley; wrote Gran'pa Feeb stories
	4.00	8.00	12.00

& the Little Men From Mars #30020-410(10/64-
  G.Key, 25¢)-68pgs. 3.00 6.00 9.00

TUFF GHOSTS (Starring Spooky)
July, 1962 - #43, Oct, 1972
Harvey Publications

	Good	Fine	Mint
#1	1.00	2.00	3.00
2-5	.50	1.00	1.50
6-20	.15	.30	.45
21-43		.15	.30

TUFFY
1949 - 1950
Standard Comics

	Good	Fine	Mint
#1-By Sid Hoff	1.50	3.00	4.50
2-10	.80	1.60	2.40

TUFFY TURTLE
No date
I.W. Enterprises

		Good	Fine	Mint
#1-Reprint		.35	.70	1.05

TUROK, SON OF STONE (See Golden Comics
Digest #33, March of Comics #378,399,408, &
Dec, 1954 - Present   Dan Curtis)
Dell Publ. Co. #1-29/Gold Key #30 on

	Good	Fine	Mint
4-Color #596(12/54)	10.00	20.00	30.00

	Good	Fine	Mint
4-Color #656(10/55)	7.00	14.00	21.00
#3-5	4.00	8.00	12.00
6-10	3.00	6.00	9.00
11-20	2.00	4.00	6.00
21-30	1.50	3.00	4.50
31-40	.80	1.60	2.40
41-50	.60	1.20	1.80
51-60	.40	.80	1.20
61-70	.30	.60	.90
71-83	.25	.50	.75
84-Origin & 1st app. Hutel	.25	.50	.75
85-118: #114-52pgs.	.15	.30	.45
Giant #1(30031-611)(11/61)	1.50	3.00	4.50

TV CASPER & COMPANY
Aug, 1963 - #44, 1973   (25¢)
Harvey Publications

	Good	Fine	Mint
#1	.75	1.50	2.25
2-5	.35	.70	1.05
6-44	.15	.30	.45

TV FUNDAY FUNNIES (See Famous TV --)

TV FUNNIES (See New Funnies)

TV FUNTIME (See Little Audrey)

TV LAUGHOUT (See Archie's --)

TV SCREEN CARTOONS (Formerly Real Screen)
#129, 7-8/59 - #138, 1-2/61
National Periodical Publications

	Good	Fine	Mint
#129-138	.50	1.00	1.50

TV STARS (Hanna-Barbera)
Aug, 1978 - #3, Dec, 1978
Marvel Comics Group

	Good	Fine	Mint
#1-3	.15	.30	.45

TV TEENS
Feb, 1954 - V2#13, July, 1956
Charlton Comics

	Good	Fine	Mint
V1#14,15: #14-Ozzie & Babs	.75	1.50	2.25
V2#3-7-Don Winslow	1.00	2.00	3.00
V2#8(7/55)-#13-Mopsy	1.00	2.00	3.00

TWEETY AND SYLVESTER (1st Series)
June, 1952 - #37, June-Aug, 1962
Dell Publishing Co.

	Good	Fine	Mint
4-Color #406,489,524	1.00	2.00	3.00
#4-20	.50	1.00	1.50
21-37	.30	.60	.90

Tubby Annual #1, © WEST

Tuffy #8, © STD

Turok Son Of Stone #8, © DELL

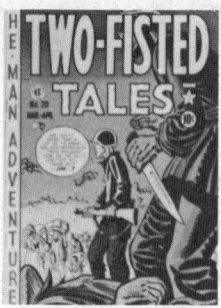

Twilight Zone #4, © DELL   Two-Fisted Tales #20, © WMG   Two-Fisted Tales #32, © WMG

TWEETY AND SYLVESTER (2nd Series)
Nov, 1963; #2, Nov, 1965 - Present
Gold Key

	Good	Fine	Mint
#1	.40	.80	1.20
2-10	.20	.40	.60
11-30	.15	.30	.45
31-89		.15	.30
Mini Comic #1(3¼x6½",1976)	.15	.30	.45

12 O'CLOCK HIGH (TV)
Jan-Mar, 1965 - #2, Apr-June, 1965
Dell Publishing Co.

#1,2	.40	.80	1.20

20,000 LEAGUES UNDER THE SEA (See 4-Color Comics #614, King Classics, & Movie Comics)

TWICE TOLD TALES (See Movie Classics)

TWILIGHT ZONE, THE (TV) (See Dan Curtis)
1961 - #91, April, 1979
Dell Publishing Co./Gold Key

4-Color #1173,1288-Crandall art			
	2.50	5.00	7.50
#01-860-207,#12-860-210(Dell 5-7/63,8-10/62)			
	1.25	2.50	3.75
#1(Gold Key-11/62)-Williamson/Evans story,			
10pgs. + Crandall sty.	2.00	4.00	6.00
2,4,5	1.00	2.00	3.00
3-Toth art	1.50	3.00	4.50
6-11,16-20	.60	1.20	1.80
12-Williamson story	1.25	2.50	3.75
13,15-Crandall story	.90	1.80	2.70
14-Williamson + Orlando + Crandall			
	1.25	2.50	3.75
21-Crandall reprint	.40	.80	1.20
22-24	.30	.60	.90
25-Evans/Crandall reprint	.40	.80	1.20
26-Crandall, Evans reprts.	.40	.80	1.20
27-Two Evans stys.reprts.	.40	.80	1.20
28-31	.25	.50	.75
32-Evans reprint	.25	.50	.75
33-50,52-70	.20	.40	.60
51-Williamson story	.25	.50	.75
71(reprint)-#91: #83,84-52pgs.	.20	.40	
Mini Comic #1(3¼x6½",1976)	.15	.30	.45

NOTE: *Bolle story-#50. McWilliams story-#59. Orlando stories-#19, 20, 22, 23. Sekowsky story-#3. (See Mystery Comics Digest #3,6,9,12,15, 18,21,24)*

TWINKLE COMICS
May, 1945
Spotlight Publishers

	Good	Fine	Mint
#1	1.50	3.00	4.50

TWIST, THE
Sept, 1962
Dell Publishing Co.

#01864-209	.60	1.20	1.80

TWO BIT THE WACKY WOODPECKER (See Wacky --)
1953 - #3, May, 1953
Toby Press

#1-3	.50	1.00	1.50

TWO-FISTED TALES(Formerly Haunt of Fear#15-17)
#18, Nov-Dec, 1950 - #41, Feb-Mar, 1955
E.C. Comics

#18(#1)-Kurtzman cover	70.00	140.00	210.00
19-Kurtzman cover	35.00	70.00	150.00
20-Kurtzman cover	30.00	60.00	90.00
21,22- " "	20.00	40.00	60.00
23-25- " "	15.00	30.00	45.00
26-35	12.00	24.00	36.00
36-41	11.00	22.00	33.00
Two-Fisted Annual, 1952	80.00	160.00	240.00
Two-Fisted Annual, 1953	60.00	120.00	180.00

NOTE: *Berg story-#29. Craig stories-#18,19, 32. Crandall stories-#35,36. Davis stories-#20-36,40; covers-#30,34,35,41,Annual #2. Evans stories-#34,40,41; cover-#40. Feldstein story-#18. Krigstein story-#41. Kubert stories-#18-25; covers-#36-39. Kurtzman stories-#18-25; covers-#18-29,31,Annual #1. Severin stories-#26,28, 29,31,34-41(#37-39 are all-Severin issues); covers-#36-39. Severin/Elder stories-#19-29, 31,33,36. Wood stories-#18-28,30-35,41; covers-#32,33. Special Issues: #26(ChanJin Reservoir), #31(Civil War), #35(Civil War). Canadian reprints known; see Table of Contents.*

TWO-GUN KID
3/48 - #10, 11/49; 12/53 - #59, 4/61; #60, 11/62 - #92, 3/68; #93, 7/70 - #136, 4/77
Marvel/Atlas Comics(MCI #1-10/HPC #11-59/Marvel #60 on)

#1	10.00	20.00	30.00
2	5.00	10.00	15.00
3-5	4.00	8.00	12.00
6-10	3.00	6.00	9.00
11-24,26-29	1.50	3.00	4.50
25,30-Williamson story in both, 5 & 4 pgs.			
	3.00	6.00	9.00
31-33,35,37-40	1.25	2.50	3.75
34-Crandall story	1.50	3.00	4.50
36,41,42,48-origin in all	1.20	2.40	3.60

(Two-Gun Kid cont'd)	Good	Fine	Mint
43,44,47	.80	1.60	2.40
45,46-Davis stories	1.60	3.20	4.80
49,50,52,55,57-Three Severin stories in each			
	1.20	2.40	3.60
51-5pg. Williamson story	2.50	5.00	7.50
53,54,56,59	.60	1.20	1.80
58,60-New origin	.70	1.40	2.10
61-80: #64-Intro.Boom-Boom	.30	.60	.90
81-100: #85-Rawhide Kid x-over. #89-Kid Colt,			
Rawhide Kid x-over. #92,98-Last new story.			
#99-Three Severin reprts.25		.50	.75
101-Origin retold(#58)	.20	.40	.60
102-109,111-136	.15	.30	.45
110-Williamson reprint	.15	.30	.45

NOTE: *Davis* covers-#45-47. *Everett* stories-
#82,91. *Kirby* stories-#54,55,57-62,75-77,90,
95,101,119,120,129; covers-#10,52,54-65,67-72,
74-76,116. *Powell* story-#38,102,104. *Whitney*
stories-#87,89-91,98-113,124,129; covers-#87,
89,91,113. *Black Rider* in #11,12. *Kid Colt* in
#13,14,16-18,21.

TWO-GUN WESTERN (1st Series) (Formerly Casey
Crime Photographer?)
#5, Nov, 1950 - #14, June, 1952
Marvel/Atlas Comics (MPC)

#5-Intro. & origin Apache Kid by Buscema			
	2.50	5.00	7.50
6-14	1.75	3.50	5.25

NOTE: *Crandall* story-#8. *Powell* story-#7.
Wildey story-#8.

2-GUN WESTERN (2nd Series) (Formerly Billy
Buckskin; Two-Gun Western #5 on)
#4, May, 1956
Atlas Comics (MgPC)

#4-Apache Kid; Ditko art	1.50	3.00	4.50

TWO-GUN WESTERN (Formerly 2-Gun Western)
#5, July, 1956 - #12, Sept, 1957
Atlas Comics (MgPC)

#5-8,12	.90	1.80	2.70
9,11-Williamson story in both, 5pgs. each			
	2.50	5.00	7.50
10-Crandall story	1.50	3.00	4.50

NOTE: *Morrow* story-#9. *Powell* story-#11.

TWO MOUSEKETEERS, THE (See 4-Color #475,603,
642) (Becomes Mouse Musketeers)

TWO ON A GUILLOTINE (See Movie Classics)

2001: A SPACE ODYSSEY (Marvel Treasury Special)
Oct, 1976 (One Shot) (Over-Sized)

Marvel Comics Group

	Good	Fine	Mint
#1-Kirby & Giacoia art	1.00	2.00	3.00

2001: A SPACE ODYSSEY
Dec, 1976 - #10, Sept, 1977 (Regular size)
Marvel Comics Group

#1-Kirby cover/story	.35	.70	1.05
2-Kirby cover/story	.25	.50	.75
3-7	.25	.50	.75
8-10-Origin & 1st app. Machine Man			
	.25	.50	.75

UFO & ALIEN COMIX
1978 (One-Shot)
Warren Publ. Co.

Toth, Severin art reprints	.40	.80	1.20

UFO AND OUTER SPACE (Formerly UFO Flying Sau-
#14, 6/78 - Present   cers)
Gold Key

#14-Reprints UFO Flying Saucers #3			
	.25	.50	.75
15,16-reprints	.15	.30	.45
17,18-New material	.20	.40	.60

UFO ENCOUNTERS
May, 1978 (228 pgs.) ($1.95)
Western Publishing Co.

Reprts/UFO Flying Saucers	.75	1.50	2.25

UFO FLYING SAUCERS (UFO & Outer Space #14 on)
Oct, 1968 - #13, Jan, 1977 (#2 on, 36pgs.)
Gold Key

#1(30035-810)(68pgs.)	1.00	2.00	3.00
2(11/70),3(11/72),4(11/74).50		1.00	1.50
5(2/75)-#13: Bolle stories #4 on			
	.40	.80	1.20

UNBIRTHDAY PARTY WITH ALICE IN WONDERLAND
(See 4-Color Comics #341)

UNCANNY TALES
June, 1952 - #57, Sept, 1957
Atlas Comics (PrPI)

#1	4.00	8.00	12.00
2-5,7,9,10	2.00	4.00	6.00
6-Wolvertonish art by Matt Fox			
	2.00	4.00	6.00
8-Toth art	2.50	5.00	7.50
11-20	1.50	3.00	4.50
21-27	1.25	2.50	3.75

Two-Gun Western #5, © MCG

2001: A Space Odyssey #1, © MCG

Uncanny Tales #2, © MCG

Uncle Sam #3, © QUA

Uncle Scrooge #18, © WDP

Uncle Scrooge #52, © WDP

	Good	Fine	Mint
(Uncanny Tales cont'd)			
28-Last pre-code issue; Kubert art			
	2.50	5.00	7.50
29-41,43-49,52	1.00	2.00	3.00
42,54,56-Krigstein stys.	2.00	4.00	6.00
50,53,55-Torres story	1.60	3.20	4.80
51,57-Williamson story	3.00	6.00	9.00

NOTE: _Briefer_ story-#20. _Colan_ story-#16. _Ditko_ reprint-#4. _Drucker_ story-#37,42,45. _Everett_ stories-#12,36,47,48; covers-#7,50, 52,53. _Krenkel_ story-#19. _Krigstein_ stories-#42,54,56. _Moldoff_ art-#23. _Morrow_ story-#46, 51. _Orlando_ stories-#49,50,53. _Powell_ stories-#12,18,38,50,53,56. _Robinson_ stories-#3,13. _Wildey_ story-#48.

UNCANNY TALES
Dec, 1973 - #12, Oct, 1975
Marvel Comics Group

#1		.15	.30	.45
2-12			.15	.30

NOTE: _Ditko_ reprints-#7,11. _Everett_ covers-#7,11.

UNCLE CHARLIE'S FABLES
1951 - #5, Sept, 1952
Lev Gleason Publications

#1-Norman Maurer art; has Biro's picture			
	2.25	4.50	6.75
2-5	1.50	3.00	4.50

UNCLE DONALD & HIS NEPHEWS DUDE RANCH
(See Dell Giant #52)

UNCLE DONALD & HIS NEPHEWS FAMILY FUN
(See Dell Giant #38)

UNCLE JOE'S FUNNIES
1938
Centaur Publications

#1-Games/puzzles, some interior art; Bill			
Everett cover	10.00	20.00	30.00

UNCLE MILTY
Dec, 1950 - #4, June, 1950
Victoria Publications/True Cross

#1-Milton Berle	3.00	6.00	9.00
2-4	2.00	4.00	6.00

UNCLE REMUS & HIS TALES OF BRER RABBIT
(See 4-Color Comics #129,208,693)

UNCLE SAM (Blackhawk #9 on)
Fall, 1941 - #8, Fall, 1943

Quality Comics Group

	Good	Fine	Mint
#1-Origin Uncle Sam; cover, chapter headings, & 2pgs. by Eisner (2 versions: dark cover, no price; light cover with price)			
	60.00	120.00	180.00
2-Cameos by The Ray, Black Condor, Quicksilver, The Red Bee, Alias The Spider, Hercules & Neon the Unknown. Eisner, Fine cover/story	30.00	60.00	90.00
3-Crandall story	20.00	40.00	60.00
4	15.00	30.00	45.00
5-8	10.00	20.00	30.00

NOTE: _Kotzky_ or _Tuska_ stories-#4-8.

UNCLE SAM'S CHRISTMAS STORY
1958
Promotional Publ. Co. (Giveaway)

Reprints 1956 Christmas USA

	.40	.80	1.20

UNCLE SCROOGE (Walt Disney)
March, 1952 - Present
Dell Publishing Co./Gold Key #40 on

4-Color #386(#1)-in "Only a Poor Old Man" by Carl Barks-reprinted in Uncle Scrooge & D. Duck #1('65) & The Best of W.D. Comics ('74)			
	100.00	200.00	300.00
4-Color #456(#2)-in "Back to the Klondike" by Carl Barks-reprinted in Best of U.S. & D.D. #1('66)	50.00	100.00	150.00
4-Color #495(#3)-reprinted in Uncle Scrooge #105	28.00	56.00	84.00
#4	20.00	40.00	60.00
5-Reprinted in W.D. Digest #1	16.00	32.00	48.00
6-Reprinted in U.S. #106 & Best of U.S. & D.D. #1('66)	12.00	24.00	36.00
7-Reprinted in Best of D.D. & U.S. #2('67)	10.00	20.00	30.00
8-10: #9-Reprinted in U.S. #104. #10-Reprinted in U.S. #67	9.00	18.00	27.00
11-20	7.00	14.00	21.00
21-30	5.00	10.00	15.00
31-40	4.50	9.00	13.50
41-50	4.00	8.00	12.00
51-60	3.50	7.00	10.50
61-66,68-70: #70-Last Barks issue with original story	3.00	6.00	9.00
67,72,73-Barks reprints	1.50	3.00	4.50
71-Written by Barks only	1.50	3.00	4.50
74-1pg. Barks reprints	1.00	2.00	3.00
75-81,83-Not by Barks	1.00	2.00	3.00
82,84-Barks reprts. begin	1.00	2.00	3.00
85-100	.80	1.60	2.40
101-110	.60	1.20	1.80

(Uncle Scrooge cont'd)	Good	Fine	Mint
111-120	.50	1.00	1.50
121-141,143-162	.20	.40	.60
142-Reprints 4-Color #456 with cover			
	.35	.70	1.05
Uncle Scrooge & Money(G.K.)-Barks reprint			
from WDC&S #130(3/67)	3.00	6.00	9.00
Uncle Scrooge Goes to Disneyland #1(1957-25¢)			
20pgs. Barks	6.00	12.00	18.00
Mini Comic #1(3½x6½",1976)-Reprint/U.S.#115,			
Barks cover	.30	.60	.90

(See Dell Giants #33 & 55)

UNCLE SCROOGE & DONALD DUCK
June, 1965   (25¢) (paper cover)
Gold Key

#1-Reprint of 4-Color #386(#1) & lead story			
from 4-Color #29	16.00	32.00	48.00

UNCLE WIGGILY (See 4-Color #179,221,276,320, 349,391,428,503,543, & March of Comics #19)

UNDERCOVER CRIME (Underground Crime #5)
1952
Fawcett Publications

#6	1.20	2.40	3.60

UNDERCOVER GIRL (Starr Flagg)
1952 - 1953
Magazine Enterprises

#5(#1)(A-1#62)	12.00	24.00	36.00
#6(A-1#98),#7(A-1#118)-All have Starr Flagg			
	9.00	18.00	27.00

NOTE: *All have Powell cover, Whitney stories.*

UNDERDOG (TV)
July, 1970 - #10, Jan, 1972; 3/75 - Present
Charlton Comics/Gold Key

#1	.25	.50	.75
2-10	.15	.30	.45
#1-24(G.K.): #13-1st app. Shack of Solitude			
		.15	.35
Kite Fun Book('74, 5x7")-16pgs. Sou. Calif.			
Edison	.20	.40	.60

UNDERGROUND CRIME (Undercover Crime #6)
1952
Fawcett Publications

#5	1.20	2.40	3.60

UNDERSEA AGENT
Jan, 1966 - #6, Mar, 1967   (68 pgs.)
Tower Comics

	Good	Fine	Mint
#1-Davy Jones, Undersea Agent begins			
	1.00	2.00	3.00
2-6: #2-Jones gains magnetic powers. #5-Origin & 1st app. of Merman. #6-Wood cover			
	.60	1.20	1.80

NOTE: *Gil Kane story-#3-6; covers-#4,5.*

UNDERSEA FIGHTING COMMANDOS
May, 1952 - #3, Sept, 1952; 1964
Avon Periodicals

#1	2.00	4.00	6.00
2,3	1.50	3.00	4.50
IW Reprint #1,2('64)	.40	.80	1.20

UNDERWATER CITY, THE (See 4-Color #1324,1328)

UNDERWORLD (True Crime Stories)
Feb-Mar, 1948 - #9, June, 1949
D. S. Publishing Co.

#1-Sheldon Moldoff cover; Walter Johnson			
story	3.00	6.00	9.00
2-Moldoff cover; Ma Barker story used in			
Seduction of the Innocent			
	2.50	5.00	7.50
3-McWilliams cvr/story	1.75	3.50	5.25
4-9	1.50	3.00	4.50

UNDERWORLD CRIME
June, 1952 - #9, Oct, 1953
Fawcett Publications

#1	2.25	4.50	6.75
2-6,8,9	1.25	2.50	3.75
7-Bondage/torture cover	2.00	4.00	6.00

UNDERWORLD STORY, THE
1950   (Movie)
Avon Periodicals

No#-(Scarce)	8.00	16.00	24.00

UNEARTHLY SPECTACULARS
Oct, 1965 - #3, Mar, 1967
Harvey Publications

#1-Tiger Boy	.70	1.40	2.10
2-Jack Q. Frost app.; Wood, Williamson,			
Adams, Kane art; reprints Thrill-O-Rama#2			
	1.75	3.50	5.25
3-Jack Q. Frost app.; Williamson/Crandall			
art; reprint from Alarming Adventures #1,			
1962; 2pgs. Kirby art	1.50	3.00	4.50

UNEXPECTED, THE (Formerly Tales of the --)
#105, Feb-Mar, 1968 - Present

Undercover Girl #6, © ME

Underworld #1, © DS

Unearthly Spectaculars #2, © HARV

Unknown Worlds #19, © ACG   Unknown Worlds Of S.F. #1, © MCG   The Unseen #7, © STD

(The Unexpected cont'd)
National Periodical Publications/DC Comics

	Good	Fine	Mint
#105-115,117,118,120,122-127			
	.20	.40	.60
116,119,121,128-Wrightson stories			
	.80	1.60	2.40
129-132,134-136,139-156: #132-136, 52pgs.			
	.25	.50	.75
133,137,138-Wood stories	.25	.50	.75
157-162-(All 100pgs.)	.25	.50	.75
163-188	.20	.40	.60
189,190 ($1.00 size)	.40	.80	1.20

NOTE: _Adams covers-#110,112-118,121,124._
Alcala stories-#140,144,150-153,156,157,168,
169. Anderson story-#122. Kirby stories-#127,
162. Wood inks-#122,137. Wrightson reprint-
#161(2pgs.). Johnny Peril in #106-114,117.

UNEXPECTED ANNUAL, THE (See DC Spec.Series #4)

UNITED COMICS
Aug, 1940 - #26, Jan-Feb, 1953
United Features Syndicate

#1-Fritzi Ritz & Phil Fumble			
	3.50	7.00	10.50
2-9-Fritzi Ritz, Abbie & Slats			
	1.50	3.00	4.50
10-26	.90	1.80	2.70

NOTE: _Abbie & Slats reprinted from Tip Top._

UNITED NATIONS, THE (See Classics Illustrated Special Ed.)

UNIVERSAL PRESENTS DRACULA(See Movie Classics)

UNITED STATES AIR FORCE PRESENTS: THE
HIDDEN CREW
1964   (36 pgs.) (Full Color)
U.S. Air Force

Shaffenberger art	.80	1.60	2.40

UNKEPT PROMISE
1949   (24 pgs.)
Legion of Truth   (Giveaway)

Anti-alcohol	1.50	3.00	4.50

UNKNOWN MAN, THE
1951   (Movie)
Avon Periodicals

No#-Kinstler cover	6.00	12.00	18.00

UNKNOWN SOLDIER (Formerly Star-Spangled War
#205, Apr-May, 1977 - Present   Stories)

National Periodical Publications/DC Comics

	Good	Fine	Mint
#205-222		.20	.35

NOTE: _Most covers by Kubert._

UNKNOWN WORLD (Strange Stories From Another
June, 1952   World #2 on)
Fawcett Publications

#1-Painted cover by Norman Saunders? (Same			
artist did S.S.F.A.W. #2-5)			
	2.50	5.00	7.50

UNKNOWN WORLDS (See Journey Into --)

UNKNOWN WORLDS
Aug, 1960 - #57, Aug, 1967
American Comics Group/Best Synd. Features

#1	1.75	3.50	5.25
2-5	.80	1.60	2.40
6-19	.60	1.20	1.80
20-Herbie cameo	1.20	2.40	3.60
21-35	.40	.80	1.20
36-"The People vs. Hendricks by Craig; most			
popular ACG story ever	.75	1.50	2.25
37-46	.35	.70	1.05
47-Williamson story reprinted from Adventures			
Into the Unknown #96, 3pgs. + Craig story			
	.75	1.50	2.25
48-57: #49,54-Ditko art	.30	.60	.90

NOTE: _John Force, Magic Agent app.-#35,36,48,_
_50,52,54,56._

UNKNOWN WORLDS OF SCIENCE FICTION
12/74 - #6, 11/75; 12/76 (B&W Magazine)($1.00)
Marvel Comics Group

#1-Williamson/Wood reprint/Witzend #1, Neal			
Adams reprint/Phase 1; Brunner & Kaluta			
reprints	1.00	2.00	3.00
2-Brunner & Kaluta story	.80	1.60	2.40
3-6: #4,6-Brunner covers	.70	1.40	2.10
Special #1(12/76)-100pgs.-Newton cover			
	.60	1.20	1.80

NOTE: _Corben story-#4, Kaluta cover-#2._
Morrow story-#3,5. Nino story-#3,6.

UNSANE
June, 1954
Star Publications

#15-Two Disbrow stories; L.B. Cole cover			
	4.00	8.00	12.00

UNSEEN, THE
1952 - #15, July, 1954
Visual Editions/Standard Comics

	Good	Fine	Mint
#5-Toth art	2.00	4.00	6.00

6-8,10,11,13,14: #6-1pg. Toth

	Good	Fine	Mint
	1.00	2.00	3.00
9-Jack Katz story	1.50	3.00	4.50
12,15-Toth art?	1.50	3.00	4.50

UNTAMED LOVE
January, 1950 - #5, Sept, 1950
Quality Comics Group (Comic Magazines)

#1-Ward cover, Gustavson art			
	6.00	12.00	18.00
2,4	2.50	5.00	7.50
3,5-Gustavson stories	3.50	7.00	10.50

UNTOUCHABLES, THE (TV)
1961 - #4, Oct, 1962
Dell Publishing Co.

4-Color #1237,1286	1.00	2.00	3.00
#01879-207,#12-879-210(#01879-210 on inside)			
	.60	1.20	1.80

Topps Bubblegum giveaway-2½x4½", 8pgs.(2 diff.)
"The Organization," "Jamaica Ginger"

	1.25	2.50	3.75

UNUSUAL TALES (Blue Beetle & Shadow From Beyond #50 on)
Nov, 1955 - #49, Mar-Apr, 1965
Charlton Comics

#1	2.00	4.00	6.00
2-7,10	1.00	2.00	3.00
8-Ditko story	1.50	3.00	4.50
9-20pgs. Ditko	1.75	3.50	5.25
11-68pgs.; 4 Ditko stys.	2.00	4.00	6.00
12,13,16-20	.60	1.20	1.80
14,15-Ditko stories	1.00	2.00	3.00
21,24,28-49	.40	.80	1.20
22,23,25-27-Ditko stories	.60	1.20	1.80

NOTE: _Ditko covers-#6,8,14,15,22._

UP FROM HARLEM
1973
Spire Christian Comics(Fleming H. Revell Co.)

	.25	.50	.75

UP-TO-DATE COMICS
No date (1939?) (36 pgs.) (B&W cover) (10c)
King Features Syndicate

No#-Popeye & Henry cover; The Phantom, Jungle
  Jim by Raymond, The Katzenjammer Kids,
  Curley Harper   25.00 50.00 75.00

UP YOUR NOSE AND OUT YOUR EAR (Magazine)

April, 1972 - #2, June, 1972 (52pgs.)(Satire)
Klevart Enterprises

	Good	Fine	Mint
V1#1,2	.40	.80	1.20

USA COMICS (Hedy Devine #18 on)
Aug, 1941 - #17, Fall, 1945
Timely Comics (USA)

#1-Origin Major Liberty, Rockman by Wolverton,
  & The Whizzer by Avison; The Defender with
  sidekick Rusty & Jack Frost begin; The
  Young Avenger only app.; S&K cover + one
  page   300.00 600.00 900.00
2-Origin Captain Terror & The Vagabond; last
  Wolverton Rockman 150.00 300.00 450.00
3-No Whizzer   120.00 240.00 360.00
4-Last Rockman, Major Liberty, Defender,
  Jack Frost & Capt. Terror; Corporal Dix
  app.   80.00 160.00 240.00
5-Origin American Avenger & Roko the Amazing; The Black Widow, The Blue Blade &
  Victory Boys, Gypo, the Gypsy Giant &
  Hills of Horror only app.; Sergeant Dix
  begins; no Whizzer 65.00 130.00 195.00
6-Captain America, The Destroyer, Jap Buster Johnson, Jeep Jones begin; Terror
  Squad only app.   65.00 130.00 195.00
7-Captain Daring, Disk-Eyes, the Detective
  by Wolverton app.; origin & only app.
  Marvel Boy; Secret Stamp begins; no Whizzer, Sergeant Dix 55.00 110.00 165.00
8-10: #9-Last Secret Stamp. #10-The Thunder-
  bird only app.   35.00 70.00 105.00
11-17: #11-No Jeep Jones. #13-No Whizzer;
  Jeep Jones ends. #15-No Destroyer; Jap
  Buster Johnson ends 22.00 44.00 66.00

U.S. AGENT (See Jeff Jordan --)

U.S. AIR FORCE COMICS (Army Attack #38 on)
Oct, 1958 - #37, Mar-Apr, 1965
Charlton Comics

#1	1.00	2.00	3.00
2-10	.50	1.00	1.50
11-20	.30	.60	.90
21-37	.15	.30	.45

NOTE: _Montes/Bache art-#33._

USA IS READY
1941 (68 pgs.) (One Shot)
Dell Publishing Co.

#1-War propaganda	5.00	10.00	15.00

U.S. BORDER PATROL COMICS (Sgt. Dick Carter of the --) (See Holyoke One Shot)

Unusual Tales #8. © CC

USA Comics #1. © MCG

USA Comics #4. © MCG

U.S. Fighting Air Force #27, © SUPR   U.S. Marines #3, © TOBY   Valor #2, © WMG

U.S. FIGHTING AIR FORCE
Sept, 1952 - #29, Oct, 1956
Superior Comics Ltd.

	Good	Fine	Mint
#1	1.50	3.00	4.50
2	1.00	2.00	3.00
3-10	.80	1.60	2.40
11-29	.60	1.20	1.80
IW Reprint #1,9(no date)	.30	.60	.90

U.S. FIGHTING MEN
1963 - 1964   (Reprints)
Super Comics

#10-Avon's-With the U.S. Paratroops			
	.50	1.00	1.50
11,12,15-18	.40	.80	1.20

U.S. JONES
Nov, 1941 - #2, Jan, 1942
Fox Features Syndicate

#1-U.S. Jones & The Topper begin			
	35.00	70.00	105.00
2	17.00	34.00	51.00

U.S. MARINES
1943 - #4, 1944; #5, 1952 - 1953
Magazine Enterprises/Toby Press

#1-Mart Bailey art	4.00	8.00	12.00
2-4	2.50	5.00	7.50
5(A-1#55)-Powell art, #6(A-1#60), #7(A-1#68),			
#8(A-1#72)	1.75	3.50	5.25
7-11(Toby)	.80	1.60	2.40

U.S. MARINES IN ACTION!, THE
1952
Avon Periodicals/Charlton Comics

#1	2.25	4.50	6.75
2,3: #3-Kinstler cover	1.75	3.50	5.25
1(Fall/1964-Charlton)		.20	.40

U.S. PARATROOPS (See With the --)

U.S. PARATROOPS BEHIND ENEMY LINES
1964?
I.W. Enterprises

#1-Wood cover reprt/With the U.S.--#1,			
#8-Kinstler cover	.50	1.00	1.50

U.S. TANK COMMANDOS
July, 1952 - #4, March, 1953
Avon Periodicals

#1	2.50	5.00	7.50

	Good	Fine	Mint
2-4	1.50	3.00	4.50
IW Reprint #1,8	.50	1.00	1.50

NOTE: *Kinstler stories-#3,4,IW#1; covers-#1, 4,IW#1,8.*

VACATION COMICS (See A-1 Comics #16)

VACATION IN DISNEYLAND
Aug, 1958 - Mar, 1965   (Walt Disney)
Dell Publ. Co./Gold Key(1965)

#1(1958-25¢)	2.00	4.00	6.00
4-Color #1025-Barks art	5.00	10.00	15.00
#1(30024-508)(G.K.)-Reprints Dell Giant #30			
& cover to #1('58)	.75	1.50	2.25

VACATION PARADE (Picnic Party #6 on)
1950 - 1954   (116 pgs.) (25¢) (Walt Disney)
Dell Publishing Co.

#1-Donald Duck & Mickey Mouse; Carl Barks			
art, 55 pgs.	70.00	140.00	210.00
2	8.00	16.00	24.00
3-5	4.00	8.00	12.00

VALLEY OF THE DINOSAURS (TV)(Hanna-Barbera)
April, 1975 - #11, Dec, 1976
Charlton Comics

#1-Howard inks	.25	.50	.75
2-11: #2-Howard inks	.20	.40	.60

VALLEY OF GWANGI (See Movie Classics)

VALOR
Mar-Apr, 1955 - #5, Nov-Dec, 1955
E.C. Comics

#1-Williamson/Torres story; Wood cover &			
story	15.00	30.00	45.00
2-Williamson cover & story; Wood story			
	10.00	20.00	30.00
3-Williamson & a Crandall story			
	9.00	18.00	27.00
4-Wood cover	9.00	18.00	27.00
5-Wood cover & story; Williamson/Evans			
story	8.00	16.00	24.00

NOTE: *Crandall stories-#3,4. Ingels stories-#1,2,4,5. Krigstein stories-#1-5. Orlando stories-#3,4; cover-#3. Wood stories-#1,2,5; covers-#1,4,5.*

VAMPIRELLA (Magazine)
Sept, 1969 - Present
Warren Publishing Co.

#1-Intro. Vampirella	8.00	16.00	24.00

(Vampirella cont'd)	Good	Fine	Mint
2	4.00	8.00	12.00
3 (Scarce)	10.00	20.00	30.00
4-7	3.00	6.00	9.00
8-Vampi begins by Tom Sutton as serious strip (early issues-gag line)			
	3.50	7.00	10.50
9-Smith art	4.00	8.00	12.00
10-No Vampi story	3.00	6.00	9.00
11-15: #11-Origin, 1st app. Pendragon. #12-Vampi by Gonzales begins, ends #34			
	2.50	5.00	7.50
16-25	1.75	3.50	5.25
26-40: #28-Intro. Pantha. #31-Origin Luana, the Beast Girl. #32-Pantha ends			
	1.50	3.00	4.50
41-45	1.00	2.00	3.00
46-Origin	1.25	2.50	3.75
47-50: #50-Spirit cameo	.80	1.60	2.40
51-74	.70	1.40	2.10
Annual #1('72)-New origin Vampirella by Gonzales; reprints by Adams(#1), Wood(#9)			
	7.00	14.00	21.00

NOTE: _Adams stories-#1,10,17,19,51. Bode'/ Todd cover-#3. Bode'/Jones cover-#4. Brunner story-#10. Corben stories-#30,31,33,54. Crandall stories-#1,19. Frazetta covers-#1,5,7, 11,31. Jones stories-#5,9,12,27,32,33(w/ Wrightson),34,50,53,56. Ploog story-#14. Barry Smith story-#9. Sutton story-#11. Wood stories-#8-10,12,19,27,74(reprt.); cover-#9. Wrightson story-#33,63._

VAMPIRES & WEREWOLVES (Magazine)
1962   (One Shot)
Charlton Comics

#1	2.50	5.00	7.50

VAMPIRE TALES (Magazine)
Aug, 1973 - #11, June, 1975 (B&W) (75¢)
Marvel Comics Group

#1-Morbius, the Living Vampire begins by Pablo Marcos	.75	1.50	2.25
2-Intro. Satana; Steranko reprint			
	.60	1.20	1.80
3-Satana app.	.50	1.00	1.50
4-6,8-11	.50	1.00	1.50
7-Kaluta art	.60	1.20	1.80
Annual #1(10/75)	.60	1.20	1.80

NOTE: _Alcala stories-#6,8,9. Everett story-#1. Heath story-#9. Infantino reprint-#3._

VARIETY COMICS
1944 - 1945; 1946
Rural Home Publications/Croyden Publ. Co.

	Good	Fine	Mint
#1-Origin Captain Valiant	3.50	7.00	10.50
2-Capt. Valiant	2.50	5.00	7.50
3(Croyden-1946)-Captain Valiant			
	2.00	4.00	6.00
4,5	1.75	3.50	5.25

VARIETY COMICS
1946; 1950   (132 pgs.)
Fox Features Syndicate (Hero Books)

#1(1946)-Blue Beetle & Jungle Jo			
	5.00	10.00	15.00

No#(1950)-See Fox Giants. Contents can vary and determines price.

VARSITY
1945
Parents' Magazine Institute

#1	1.00	2.00	3.00

VAUDEVILLE AND OTHER THINGS
1900   (10½x13") (In Color) (18+ pgs.)
Isaac H. Blandiard Co.

By Bunny	20.00	50.00	80.00

VAULT OF EVIL
Feb, 1973 - #23, Nov, 1975
Marvel Comics Group

#1(Reprints begin)	.15	.30	.45
2-10: #3,4-Brunner cover		.15	.30
11-23		.15	.30

NOTE: _Ditko reprints-#20-22. Drucker reprints-#10(Mystic #52),13(Uncanny Tales)#42). Everett reprints-#11(Menace #2),13(Menace#4); cover-#10. Krigstein reprint-#20(Uncanny Tales #54)._

VAULT OF HORROR (War Against Crime #1-11)
Apr-May, 1950 - #40, Dec-Jan, 1954-55
E.C. Comics

#12	90.00	180.00	270.00
13	45.00	90.00	135.00
14	40.00	80.00	120.00
15	30.00	60.00	90.00
16-19	20.00	40.00	60.00
20-25	17.00	34.00	51.00
26-36,38-40	12.00	24.00	36.00
37-Williamson story	14.00	28.00	42.00

NOTE: _Craig stories in all but #13 & 33; covers-#12-40. Crandall stories-#33,34,39. Davis stories-#17-38. Evans stories-#27,28,30,32,33. Feldstein stories-#12-16. Ingels stories-#13-20,22-40. Kamen stories-#15-22,25,29,35._

Vampirella #46, © WP   Variety Comics No#, © FOX   Vault Of Horror #34, © WMG

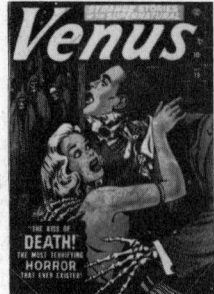

Venus #8, © MCG   Venus #19, © MCG   Vicky 1948, © ACE

(Vault of Horror cont'd)
Krigstein stories-#36,38-40. *Kurtzman* stories-
#12,13. *Orlando* stories-#24,31,40. *Wood* stor-
ies-#12-14.

V...-COMICS(Morse code for "V", 3 dots, 1 dash)
Jan, 1942 - #2, Mar-Apr, 1942
Fox Features Syndicate

	Good	Fine	Mint
#1-Origin V-Man & the Boys; The Banshee & The			
Black Fury, The Queen of Evil, & V-Agents			
begin	30.00	60.00	90.00
2	20.00	40.00	60.00

VENGEANCE SQUAD
July, 1975 - #6, May, 1976
Charlton Comics

#1	.25	.50	.75
2-6	.15	.30	.45
5,6(Modern Comics reprint, 1977)	.15		.30

VENUS
August, 1948 - #19, April, 1952
Marvel/Atlas Comics (LMC)

#1-Venus begins; Kurtzman's "Hey Look"			
	18.00	36.00	54.00
2,3,5	10.00	20.00	30.00
4-Kurtzman's "Hey Look"	12.00	24.00	36.00
6-9: #6-Loki app.	9.00	18.00	27.00
10-S/F end of the world	10.00	20.00	30.00
11,12	8.00	16.00	24.00
13-19-Venus by Everett, 2-3 stories each;			
cover-#13,15-19	12.00	24.00	36.00

VERI BEST SURE FIRE COMICS
No date (Circa 1945) (Reprints Holyoke One-
Holyoke Publ. Co.   Shots)

#1-Captain Aero, Alias X, Miss Victory,			
Commandos of the Devil Dogs, Red Cross,			
Hammerhead Hawley, Capt. Aero's Sky Scouts,			
Flagman app.	9.00	18.00	27.00

VERI BEST SURE SHOT COMICS
No date (Circa 1945)(Reprts.Holyoke One-Shots)
Holyoke Publ. Co.

#1-Capt. Aero, Miss Victory by Quinlan, Alias			
X, The Red Cross, Flagman, Commandos of the			
Devil Dogs, Hammerhead Hawley, Capt. Aero's			
Sky Scouts	12.00	24.00	36.00

VIC FLINT   (Crime Buster --)
Aug, 1948   (Newspaper reprints)
St. John Publishing Co.

#1	3.00	6.00	9.00
2-5	2.00	4.00	6.00

VIC FLINT
Feb, 1956 - #2, May, 1956 (Newspaper reprints)
Argo Publ.

#1,2	1.50	3.00	4.50

VIC JORDAN
April, 1945
Civil Service Publ.

#1-1944 daily newspaper reprints			
	2.00	4.00	6.00

VICKI (Humor)
Feb, 1975 - #4, July, 1975   (#1,2-68pgs.)
Atlas/Seaboard Publ.

#1-Reprints Tippy Teen	.15	.30	.45
2-4		.15	.30

VICKS COMICS
No date (Circa 1937-38) (68pgs. in color)
Eastern Color Printing Co.(Vicks Chemical Co.)

No#-Reprints from Famous Funnies (before #40).			
Contains 5pgs. Buck Rogers, 4pgs. from F.F.			
#15 & 1pg. from #16	75.00	150.00	225.00

VICKY
Oct, 1948 - #5, June, 1949
Ace Magazine

No#(10/48), #4(12/48)	1.25	2.50	3.75
No#(2/49), No#(4/49), #5(6/49)			
	1.25	2.50	3.75

VICTORY COMICS
Aug, 1941 - #4, Dec, 1941
Hillman Periodicals

#1-The Conqueror by Bill Everett, The Crusad-			
er, & Bomber Burns begin; Conqueror's ori-			
gin in text; Everett cover			
	45.00	90.00	135.00
2-Everett story	22.00	44.00	66.00
3,4	12.00	24.00	36.00

VIC TORRY & HIS FLYING SAUCER
1950   (One Shot)
Fawcett Publications

Powell art	7.00	14.00	21.00

VIC VERITY MAGAZINE
1945 - 1946   (A comic book)
Vic Verity Publications

	Good	Fine	Mint
#1-C.C. Beck art	2.50	5.00	7.50
2-7	1.50	3.00	4.50

VIGILANTES, THE (See 4-Color Comics #839)

VIKINGS, THE (See 4-Color Comics #910)

VIRGINIAN, THE (TV)
June, 1963
Gold Key

#10060-306	.25	.50	.75

VOODA (Formerly Voodoo)
#20, Apr, 1955 - #22, Aug, 1955
Ajax-Farrell (Four Star Publ.)

#20-22-Baker story + Kamen/Baker story, Kimbo; Boy of Jungle, & Baker cover (pencils) in all	4.00	8.00	12.00

NOTE: #20-Baker reprint/Seven Seas #4.

VOODOO (Vooda #20 on)
May, 1952 - #19, Feb, 1955
Ajax-Farrell(Four Star Publ.)

#1-South Sea Girl reprt. by Baker	5.00	10.00	15.00
2-Rulah story reprt. + South Sea Girl from Seven Seas #2 by Baker (name changed from Alani to El'nee)	4.00	8.00	12.00
3,4-Baker reprint	3.00	6.00	9.00
5-10	2.00	4.00	6.00
11-19	1.75	3.50	5.25
Annual #1(1952)(25¢)	3.00	6.00	9.00

VOODOO (See Tales of --)

VOYAGE TO THE BOTTOM OF THE SEA (TV)
1961 - #16, April, 1970
Dell Publ. Co./Gold Key

4-Color #1230(Movie-'61)	1.50	3.00	4.50
#10133-412(G.K.-12/64)	.60	1.20	1.80
#2-5	.35	.70	1.05
6-14	.30	.60	.90
15,16-Reprints	.20	.40	.60

VOYAGE TO THE DEEP
Sept-Nov, 1962 - #4, Nov-Jan, 1964
Dell Publishing Co.

#1	.75	1.50	2.25
2-4	.50	1.00	1.50

WACKY ADVENTURES OF CRACKY (Also see Gold
Dec, 1972 - #12, Sept, 1975   Key Spotlight)
Gold Key

	Good	Fine	Mint
#1		.15	.35
2-12		.10	.25

(See March of Comics #405)

WACKY DUCK (Formerly Dopey Duck?; Justice
#3, Fall, 1946 - #6, Summer, 1947; #7 on)
Aug, 1948 - #2, Oct, 1948
Marvel Comics (NPP)

#3,5,6('46-47)	1.25	2.50	3.75
4-Infinity cover	1.50	3.00	4.50
1,2(1948)	1.20	2.40	3.60
IW Reprint #1,2,7('58)	.20	.40	.60
Super Reprint #10(IW on cover, Super on inside)	.20	.40	.60

WACKY QUACKY (See Wisco)

WACKY RACES (TV)
Feb, 1969 - #7, April, 1972 (Hanna-Barbera)
Gold Key

#1-7		.10	.20

WACKY WITCH (See March of Comics #374,398,410)
March, 1971 - #21, Jan, 1976
Gold Key

#1		.15	.35
2-21		.10	.20

WACKY WOODPECKER (See Two Bit --)
1958; 1963
I.W. Enterprises/Super Comics

IW Reprint #1,2,7(no date-reprints Two Bit--)			
	.25	.50	.75
Super Reprint #10('63)	.25	.50	.75

WAGON TRAIN (1st Series) (TV)
1958 - #13, Apr-June, 1962
Dell Publishing Co.

4-Color #895,971,1019	1.00	2.00	3.00
#4(1-3/60)-#13	.80	1.60	2.40

WAGON TRAIN (2nd Series)
Jan, 1964 - #4, Oct, 1964
Gold Key

#1	.30	.60	.90
2-4	.20	.40	.60

Vic Verity Magazine #1, © Vic Verity

Voodoo #8, © AJAX

Voodoo #14, © AJAX

Walt Disney's Comics & Stories #9, © WDP   Walt Disney's Comics & Stories #17, © WDP   Walt Disney's Comics & Stories #21, © WDP

<u>WALLY</u>
Dec, 1962 - #4, Sept, 1963
Gold Key

	Good	Fine	Mint
#1	.20	.40	.60
2-4	.15	.30	.45

<u>WALT DISNEY COMICS DIGEST</u>
June, 1968 - #57, Feb, 1976 (50¢ Digest Size)
Gold Key

#1-Reprints Uncle Scrooge #5			
	5.00	10.00	15.00
2-4-Barks reprints	3.00	6.00	9.00
5-Daisy Duck by Barks(21pgs.)-last published story by Barks(art only)			
	3.50	7.00	10.50
6-13-All Barks reprints	2.00	4.00	6.00
14,15	1.25	2.50	3.75
16-Reprints Donald Duck #26 by Barks			
	2.50	5.00	7.50
17-20-Barks reprints	1.50	3.00	4.50
21-31,33,35-37-Barks reprints; #24-Toth Zorro			
	1.25	2.50	3.75
32	1.00	2.00	3.00
34-Reprints 4-Color #318	2.50	5.00	7.50
38-Reprints Christmas in Disneyland #1			
	1.75	3.50	5.25
39-Two Barks reprts./WDC&S #272, 4-Color#1073 + Toth Zorro reprt.	1.50	3.00	4.50
40-Mickey Mouse reprints	1.00	2.00	3.00
41,45,47-49	.60	1.20	1.80
42,43-Barks reprints	1.00	2.00	3.00
44-(Has Gold Key emblem, 50¢)-Reprints 1st story of 4-Color #29,256,275, & 282			
	4.00	8.00	12.00
44-Republished in 1976 by Whitman; not identical to original; slightly smaller, blank back cover, 69¢ cover price			
	1.50	3.00	4.50
46,50-Barks reprint	1.00	2.00	3.00
51-Reprints 4-Color #71	1.50	3.00	4.50
52-Barks reprt/WDC&S #161,132			
	1.00	2.00	3.00
53-Reprt./Dell Giant #30	.50	1.00	1.50
54-Reprt. Donald Duck Beach Party #2			
	.50	1.00	1.50
55-Reprt/Dell Giant #49	.50	1.00	1.50
56-Reprt/Uncle Scrooge #32(Barks) + another Barks story	1.00	2.00	3.00
57-Reprt/M.Mouse Almanac('57) & two Barks stories	1.00	2.00	3.00

NOTE: #1-10, 196pgs.; #11-41, 164pgs.; #42 on, 132pgs. Old issues were being reprinted & distributed by Whitman in 1976.

<u>WALT DISNEY CHRISTMAS PARADE</u>
Winter, 1977   (228 pgs.) (Cardboard covers)
Whitman Publishing Co. (Golden Press)

	Good	Fine	Mint
#11191-Barks stories reprint/Christmas in Disneyland #1 & Dell Christmas Parade #9			
	.50	1.00	1.50

<u>WALT DISNEY PRESENTS</u>
June-Aug, 1959 - #6, Dec-Feb, 1960-61
Dell Publishing Co.

4-Color #997	1.25	2.50	3.75
#2(12-2/60)-The Swamp Fox, El Fego Baca, Texas John Slaughter (Disney TV Show),			
3-6	.90	1.80	2.70

<u>WALT DISNEY'S COMICS & STORIES</u> (Continuation of Mickey Mouse Magazine) (#1-30 contain Donald Duck newspaper reprints)
Oct, 1940 - Present
Dell Publ. Co./Gold Key #264 on

#1(V2#1)-Donald Duck strip reprints by Al Taliaferro & Gottfredson's Mickey Mouse begin	500.00	1500.00	2500.00
	(Prices vary widely on this book)		
2	250.00	625.00	1000.00
3	150.00	300.00	450.00
4	110.00	220.00	330.00
4-Special promotional, complimentary issue; cover same except one corner was blanked out & boxed in to identify the giveaway (not a pasteover). This special pressing was probably sent out to former subscribers to Mickey Mouse Mag. whose subscriptions had expired. (Very Rare - one known copy)	250.00	500.00	750.00
5	90.00	180.00	270.00
6-10	75.00	150.00	225.00
11-14	65.00	130.00	195.00
15-17	50.00	100.00	150.00
18-21: #15-The 3 Little Kittens(17pgs.).#16-The 3 Little Pigs(29pgs.). #17-The Ugly Duckling(4pgs.)	40.00	80.00	120.00
22-30	30.00	60.00	90.00
31-1st Donald Duck by Carl Barks			
	200.00	400.00	600.00
32-Barks art	120.00	240.00	360.00
33-Barks art(infinity cover)			
	85.00	170.00	255.00
34-Gremlins by Walt Kelly begin, end #41; Barks art	70.00	140.00	210.00
35,36-Barks art	60.00	120.00	180.00
37-D.D. by Jack Hannah	28.00	56.00	84.00
38-40-Barks art	40.00	80.00	120.00
41-50-Barks art	30.00	60.00	90.00
51-60-Barks art; #52-Li'l Bad Wolf begins, ends #203(not in #55)	24.00	48.00	72.00
61-70: Barks art. #61-Dumbo story. #63,64-Pinocchio stories. #65-Pluto story. #66-			

441

(Walt Disney's C&S cont'd)   Good   Fine   Mint
Infinity cvr. #67,68-M.Mouse art(Sunday
  reprts)by Bill Wright 18.00   36.00   54.00
71-80: Barks art. #75-77-Brer Rabbit stories,
  no Mickey Mouse   14.00   28.00   42.00
81-87,89,90: #82-84-Bongo stories. #86-90-
  Goofy & Agnes app. #89-Chip 'n' Dale story
          11.00   22.00   33.00
88-1st app. Gladstone Gander by Barks
          12.00   24.00   36.00
91-97,99,100: Barks art. #96-No Mickey Mouse;
  Little Toot begins, ends #97
          10.00   20.00   30.00
98-1st Uncle Scrooge app. in WDC&S
          14.00   28.00   42.00
101-110-Barks art   8.00   16.00   24.00
111,114,117-All Barks   6.00   12.00   18.00
112-Drug(ether) issue (Donald Duck)
          7.00   14.00   21.00
113,115,116,118,119,121-123: Not by Barks.
  #116-Dumbo x-over. #121-Grandma Duck begins, ends #168; not in #135,142,146,155
          3.00   6.00   9.00
120-Barks pencils   4.00   8.00   12.00
124,126-130-All Barks   5.00   10.00   15.00
125-Intro. & 1st app. Junior Woodchucks;
  Barks art   6.00   12.00   18.00
131,133,135-139-All Barks 4.00   8.00   12.00
132-Two Barks stories (D.Duck & Grandma Duck)
          6.00   12.00   18.00
134-Intro. & 1st app. The Beagle Boys
          6.00   12.00   18.00
140-1st app. Gyro Gearloose by Barks
          5.00   10.00   15.00
141-150-All Barks. #143-Little Hiawatha begins,
  ends #151,159   3.50   7.00   10.50
151-170-All Barks. #164-Has blank inside
  covers   2.50   5.00   7.50
171-200-All Barks   2.00   4.00   6.00
201-240: All Barks. #204-Chip 'n' Dale & Scamp
  begin   1.50   3.00   4.50
241-283: #241-Dumbo x-over. #249-Gyro Gearloose begins, ends #274. #256-Ludwig Von
  Drake begins, ends #274
          1.40   2.80   4.20
284,285,287,290,295,296,309-311-Not by Barks
          .80   1.60   2.40
286,288,289,291-294,297,298,308-All Barks
  stories; #293(Grandma Duck's Farm Friends),
  298(Daisy Duck's Diary-reprint)
          1.25   2.50   3.75
299-307-All contain early Barks reprints
  (#43-117)   1.40   2.80   4.20
312-Last Barks issue with original story
          1.25   2.50   3.75
313-315,317-327,329-334,336-341
          .60   1.20   1.80
316-Last issue published during life of Walt

                    Good   Fine   Mint
  Disney   .60   1.20   1.80
328,335,342-350-Barks reprints
          1.00   2.00   3.00
351-360-w/posters inside; Barks reprints(2
  versions of each with & without posters)
          .80   1.60   2.40
361-400-Barks reprints   .80   1.60   2.40
401-429-Barks reprints   .50   1.00   1.50
430,433,437,438,441,444,445-No Barks
          .20   .40   .60
431,432,434-436,439,440,442,443-Barks reprts.,
446,447(12/77-52pgs.)-Barks .25   .50   .75
448-460-All Barks   .20   .40   .60
(#1-38, 68pgs.; #39-42, 60pgs.; #43-57,61-
134,143-168,446,447, 52pgs.; #58-60,135-142,
169-Present, 36pgs.)

NOTE: **Barks** art in all issues No. 31 on, except where noted.
Kelly covers—(most) Nos. 34-94, 97-103, 105, 106, 110-123. The
whole number can always be found at bottom of title page in the
lower left-hand panel. Walt Disney's Comics & Stories featured
Mickey Mouse Serials which were in practically every issue from
No. 1 through No. 392. The titles of the serials, along with the
issues they are in, are listed in previous editions. **Floyd Gottfred-
son** Mickey Mouse Serials in issues No. 1-60, 63-66, 69-92 plus
"Mickey Mouse in a Warplant" (3 pgs.), and "Pluto Catches a Nazi
Spy" (4 pgs.) in No. 62; "Mythery Next Door," No. 93; "Sunken
Treasure," No. 94; "Aunt Marissa," No. 95; "Gangland," No. 98;
"Thanksgiving Dinner," No. 99; and "The Talking Dog," No. 100.
Mickey Mouse by Paul Murry No. 152 on. **Al Taliaferro** Silly Sym-
phonies in No. 5—"Three Little Pigs;" No. 13—"Birds of a Feather;" No. 14—"The Boarding School Mystery;" No. 15—"Cookie-
land" and "Three Little Kittens;" No. 16—"Three Little Pigs;"
No. 17—"The Ugly Duckling," and "The Robber Kitten;" No.
19—"Penguin Isle;" and "Bucky Bug" in Nos. 20-23, 25, 26, 28
(one continuous story from 1932-34; first 2 pgs. not Taliaferro).

WALT DISNEY'S COMICS & STORIES
1943   (36pgs.) (Dept. Store Xmas giveaway)
Walt Disney Productions

No#   80.00 160.00 240.00

WALT DISNEY'S COMICS & STORIES
Mid 1940's ('45-48) (4pgs. in color)
Dell Publishing Co.   (Slick paper)

Special Xmas offer-subscription form for
WDC&S-(Reprints two different WDC&S covers
with subscription forms printed on inside
covers)   9.00 18.00 27.00

WALT DISNEY SHOWCASE
Oct, 1970 - Present
Gold Key

#1-Boatniks (Movie)   .40   .80   1.20
2-Moby Duck   .25   .50   .75
3-Bongo & Lumpjaw-reprts. .25   .50   .75
4-Pluto-reprints   .25   .50   .75
5-$1,000,000 Duck (Movie) .40   .80   1.20
6-Bedknobs & Broomsticks (Movie)
          .40   .80   1.20
7-Pluto-reprints   .20   .40   .60

Walt Disney's Comics & Stories #34. © WDP   Walt Disney's Comics & Stories #58. © WDP   Walt Disney's Comics & Stories #63, © WDP

WDC&S Subscription Form, Mid 1940's, © WDP

Wambi #8, © FH

(W. Disney Showcase cont'd)	Good	Fine	Mint
8-Daisy & Donald	.20	.40	.60
9-101 Dalmatians (Cartoon feature)-reprints 4-Color #1183	.30	.60	.90
10-Napoleon & Samantha (Movie)	.30	.60	.90
11-Moby Duck-reprints	.20	.40	.60
12-Dumbo-reprints 4-Color #668	.25	.50	.75
13-Pluto-reprints	.20	.40	.60
14-World's Greatest Athlete (Movie)	.35	.70	1.05
15-3 Little Pigs-reprints	.20	.40	.60
16-Aristocats (Cartoon feature)-reprints Aristocats #1	.20	.40	.60
17-Mary Poppins-reprints M.P. #10136-501	.25	.50	.75
18-Gyro Gearloose (Barks reprints-4-Color #1047,1184)	.70	1.40	2.10
19-That Darn Cat-reprints T.D.C.#10171-602	.30	.60	.90
20-Pluto-reprints	.20	.40	.60
21-Li'l Bad Wolf & the Three Little Pigs	.20	.40	.60
22-Unbirthday Party with Alice in Wonderland -reprints 4-Color #341	.35	.70	1.05
23-Pluto-reprints	.20	.40	.60
24-Herbie Rides Again (Movie)-sequel to "The Love Bug"	.30	.60	.90
25-Old Yeller (Movie)-reprints 4-Color #869	.25	.50	.75
26-Lt. Robin Crusoe USN (Movie)-reprints Lt. Robin Crusoe USN #10191-601	.25	.50	.75
27-Island at the Top of the World (Movie)	.35	.70	1.05
28-Brer Rabbit, Bucky Bug reprints	.25	.50	.75
29-Escape to Witch Mountain (Movie)	.35	.70	1.05
30-Magica De Spell-Barks reprints-Uncle Scrooge #36 & WDC&S #258	.50	1.00	1.50
31-Bambi (Cartoon feature)-reprints 4-Color #186	.30	.60	.90
32-Spin & Marty-reprint; Mickey Mouse Club	.20	.40	.60
33-Pluto	.20	.40	.60
34-Paul Revere's Ride with Johnny Tremain-4-Color #822 reprint	.20	.40	.60
35-Goofy	.20	.40	.60
36-Peter Pan-4-Color reprt.	.20	.40	.60
37-Tinker Bell & Jiminy Crickett-reprints 4-Color #982,989	.20	.40	.60
38-Mickey & the Sleuth, Part 1	.20	.40	.60
39-Mickey & the Sleuth, Part 2	.20	.40	.60
40-The Rescuers (Cartoon feature)	.25	.50	.75

	Good	Fine	Mint
41-Herbie Goes to Monte Carlo (Movie)-Sequel to "Herbie Rides Again"	.20	.40	.60
42-Mickey & the Sleuth	.20	.40	.60
43-Pete's Dragon (Movie)	.25	.50	.75
44-Return to Witch Mountain(new) & In Search of the Castaways(reprint) (Movies)(68pgs.)	.25	.50	.75
45-The Jungle Book (Movie)-reprints#30033-803	.25	.50	.75
46-The Cat From Outer Space (Movie)-new, & The Shaggy Dog (Movie)-reprint	.25	.50	.75
47-Mickey Mouse Surprise Party-reprint (68pgs.)	.25	.50	.75
48-The Wonderful Advs. of Pinocchio-reprints; (68pgs.)	.25	.50	.75

WALT DISNEY'S MAGAZINE (Formerly W.D. Mickey Mouse Club Magazine) (50¢) (Bi-Mo.)
V2#4, June, 1957 - V4#6, Oct, 1959
Western Publishing Co.

	Good	Fine	Mint
V2#4-Stories & articles on the Mouseketeers, Zorro, & Goofy & other Disney characters & people	1.75	3.50	5.25
V2#5,V2#6(10/57)	1.75	3.50	5.25
V3#1(12/57)-V3#6(10/58)	1.25	2.50	3.75
V4#1(12/58)-V4#6(10/59)	1.25	2.50	3.75

NOTE: V2#4-V3#6 were 11½x8½", 48pgs.; V4#1 on were 10x8", 52pgs. (Peak circulation of 400,000)

WALT DISNEY'S MERRY CHRISTMAS (See Dell Giant #39)

WALT DISNEY'S MICKEY MOUSE CLUB MAGAZINE
(Becomes Walt Disney Mag.) (Quarterly)
Winter, 1956 - V2#3, 4/57 (11½x8½")(48pgs.)
Western Publishing Co.

	Good	Fine	Mint
V1#1	4.00	8.00	12.00
2-4	2.50	5.00	7.50
V2#1-3	2.00	4.00	6.00
Annual (1956)-Two diff.($1.50) Whitman, 120 pgs., cardboard covers, 11-3/4"x8-3/4"; reprints	6.00	12.00	18.00
Annual (1957)-Same as above	4.00	8.00	12.00

WALT DISNEY'S WHEATIES PREMIUMS
(See Wheaties)

WALT SCOTT'S XMAS STORIES (See 4-Color #959, 1062)

WAMBI, JUNGLE BOY
Spring, 1942 - #3, Spring, 1943; #4, Fall, 1948 - #18, Winter, 1952-53

443

(Wambi, Jungle Boy cont'd)
Fiction House Magazines

	Good	Fine	Mint
#1-Wambi, the Jungle Boy begins	12.00	24.00	36.00
2,3(1943)	7.00	14.00	21.00
4-Origin in text ('48)	2.50	5.00	7.50
5-10	2.00	4.00	6.00
11-18	1.75	3.50	5.25
IW Reprint #8('64)-reprints F.H. #12 with			
new cover	.80	1.60	2.40

WANTED COMICS
#9, Sept-Oct, 1947 - #53, April, 1953
Toytown Publications/Patches/Orbit Publ.

#9-11	1.50	3.00	4.50
12-Used in Seduction of the Innocent, pg. 277	4.00	8.00	12.00
13-Heroin racket story	2.50	5.00	7.50
14-17	1.20	2.40	3.60
18-Marijuana story	8.00	16.00	24.00
19-2pgs. on wanted dopepusher	2.00	4.00	6.00
20,22,23,25-48,53	.90	1.80	2.70
21,24-Krigstein story	2.00	4.00	6.00
49,52-Buscema story	1.20	2.40	3.60
50-Surrealist cover by Buscema	2.00	4.00	6.00
51-Drug story	3.00	6.00	9.00

WANTED: DEAD OR ALIVE (See 4-Color #1102,1164)

WANTED, THE WORLD'S MOST DANGEROUS VILLAINS
(See DC Special)
7-8/72 - #9, 8-9/73   (All reprints)
National Periodical Publications

#1-Reprints Batman, Green Lantern, & Green Arrow	.40	.80	1.20
2-Reprints Batman & The Flash	.30	.60	.90
3-Reprints Dr. Fate, Hawkman, & Vigilante	.30	.60	.90
4-Reprints origin Solomon Grundy from All-American #61	.30	.60	.90
5-Dollman/Green Lantern	.25	.50	.75
6-Starman/Wildcat/Sargon	.25	.50	.75
7-Johnny Quick/Hawkman/Hourman; Baily, Meskin reprints	.25	.50	.75
8-Dr. Fate/Flash	.25	.50	.75
9-S&K Sandman/Superman	.25	.50	.75

NOTE: Infantino stories-#2,8. Kubert stories-#3(inks),6,7.

WAR
7/75 - #9, 11/76; #10, 9/78 - Present
Charlton Comics

	Good	Fine	Mint
#1		.15	.35
2-12		.15	.25
7,9(Modern Comics reprt,'77)		.15	.25

WAR ACTION
April, 1952 - #14, June, 1953
Atlas Comics (CPS)

#1	1.50	3.00	4.50
2-10,14	1.00	2.00	3.00
11-13-Krigstein stories	2.00	4.00	6.00

WAR ADVENTURES
Jan, 1952 - #13, Mar, 1953
Atlas Comics (HPC)

#1	1.50	3.00	4.50
2-13: #3-Robinson story	1.00	2.00	3.00

WAR ADVENTURES ON THE BATTLEFIELD
(See Battlefield)

WAR AGAINST CRIME! (Vault of Horror #12 on)
Spring, 1948 - #11, Feb-Mar, 1950
E.C. Comics

#1	25.00	50.00	75.00
2,3	18.00	36.00	54.00
4-9	15.00	30.00	45.00
10-1st Vault Keeper app.	55.00	110.00	165.00
11-2nd Vault Keeper app.	40.00	80.00	120.00

NOTE: All have Craig covers.

WAR AND ATTACK (Also see Special War Series#1)
Fall, 1964 - V2#63, Dec, 1967
Charlton Comics

#1-Wood art	.60	1.20	1.80
V2#54(6/66)-#63	.15	.30	.45

NOTE: Montes/Bache art-#55,56,60,63.

WAR AT SEA
#22, Nov, 1957 - #42, June, 1961
Charlton Comics

#22-42	.15	.30	.45

WAR BATTLES
Feb, 1952 - #9, Dec, 1959
Harvey Publications

#1	1.75	3.50	5.25
2-5,7-9	1.20	2.40	3.60
6-Nostrand story	1.50	3.00	4.50

NOTE: Powell art-#1-3,7.

WAR BIRDS
1952

Wanted #31, © Toytown

War #13, © MCG

War Against Crime #9, © WMG

War Comics #1, © DELL

War Fury #3, © Harwell

War Heroes #9, © DELL

(War Birds cont'd)
Fiction House Magazines

	Good	Fine	Mint
#1	2.50	5.00	7.50
2-7	1.50	3.00	4.50

WAR COMBAT (Combat Casey #6 on)
March, 1952 - #5, Nov, 1952
Atlas Comics (SAI)

#1	1.25	2.50	3.75
2-5: #2-Berg story	.80	1.60	2.40

WAR COMICS (See Key Ring Comics)
May, 1940 - #8, 1941
Dell Publishing Co.

#1-Sikandur the Robot Master, Sky Hawk, Scoop Mason, War Correspondent begin	8.00	16.00	24.00
2-Origin Greg Gilday	5.00	10.00	15.00
3-Joan becomes Greg Gilday's aide	5.00	10.00	15.00
4-Origin Night Devils	6.00	12.00	18.00
5-8	4.50	9.00	13.50

WAR COMICS
Dec, 1950 - #49, Sept, 1957
Marvel/Atlas (USA #1-41/JPI #42-49)

#1	2.50	5.00	7.50
2-7,9,10	1.40	2.80	4.20
8-Krigstein story	2.00	4.00	6.00
11-20	1.00	2.00	3.00
21,23-37,39-42,44,45,47,48	.80	1.60	2.40
22-Krigstein story	2.00	4.00	6.00
38-Kubert/Moskowitz story	1.75	3.50	5.25
43,49-Torres stories	1.50	3.00	4.50
46-Crandall story	1.50	3.00	4.50

NOTE: _Drucker_ stories-#37,43,48. _Everett_ story-#17. _G. Kane_ story-#19. _Orlando_ story-#42,48. _Robinson_ story-#15.

WAR DOGS OF THE U.S. ARMY
1952
Avon Periodicals

#1-Kinstler cover/story	4.00	8.00	12.00

WARFRONT
9/51 - #35, 1958; #36, 10/65; #37, 9/66 - #39, 2/67
Harvey Publications

#1	2.25	4.50	6.75
2-10	1.25	2.50	3.75
11,12,14,16-20	1.00	2.00	3.00
13,15,22-Nostrand stories	1.50	3.00	4.50

	Good	Fine	Mint
21,23-27,29,31-33,35	.80	1.60	2.40
28,30,34-Kirby covers	1.00	2.00	3.00
36-Dynamite Joe begins, ends #39	.35	.70	1.05
37-39-Wood art, 2-3pgs.; Lone Tiger app.	.80	1.60	2.40

NOTE: _Kirby_ cover-#28,34. _Powell_ art (some w/Nostrand): #2-6,9-12,14,20,23,25,27,28,30, 31,34.

WAR FURY
Sept, 1952 - #4, March, 1953
Comic Media/Harwell

#1	1.20	2.40	3.60
2-4	.75	1.50	2.25

WAR GODS OF THE DEEP (See Movie Classics)

WAR HEROES (See Marine War Heroes)

WAR HEROES
7-9/42 (no month); #2, 10-12/42 - #10, 10-12/44; #11, 3/45
Dell Publishing Co.

#1	5.00	10.00	15.00
2,3,5	2.50	5.00	7.50
4-Disney's Gremlins app.	5.00	10.00	15.00
6-11	2.00	4.00	6.00

NOTE: #1 was to be released in July, but was delayed.

WAR HEROES
1952 - #8, April, 1953
Ace Magazines

#1	1.20	2.40	3.60
2-8	.75	1.50	2.25

WAR HEROES
Feb, 1963 - #27, Nov, 1967
Charlton Comics

#1	.25	.50	.75
2-27: #27-1st Devils Brigade by Glanzman	.15	.30	.45

NOTE: _Montes/Bache_ art-#3-7,21,25,27; covers-#3-7.

WAR IS HELL
Jan, 1973 - #15, Oct, 1975
Marvel Comics Group

#1-Williamson reprint	.25	.50	.75
2-5	.20	.40	.60
6-15		.15	.30

(War Is Hell cont'd)
NOTE: *Bolle reprint-#3. Powell, Woodbridge story-#1. Sgt. Fury reprints-#7,8.*

WARLOCK (The Power of --)
8/72 - #8, 10/73; #9, 10/75 - #15, 10/76
Marvel Comics Group

	Good	Fine	Mint
#1-Origin by Kane	1.50	3.00	4.50
2,3	.80	1.60	2.40
4-8: #4-Death of Eddie Roberts	.60	1.20	1.80
9-15-Starlin art in all	.75	1.50	2.25

WARLORD, THE (See First Issue Special)
1-2/76, #2, 3-4/76; #3, 10-11/76 - Present
National Periodical Publications/DC Comics

#1-Story cont'd. from 1st Issue Special #8; Grell art begins	.70	1.40	2.10
2-16: #11-reprint	.40	.80	1.20

WARPATH
Nov, 1954 - #3, April, 1955
Key Publications/Stanmor

#1	1.00	2.00	3.00
2,3	.60	1.20	1.80

WAR REPORT
Sept, 1952 - #5, May, 1953
Ajax/Farrell Publications (Excellent Publ.)

#1	1.25	2.50	3.75
2-5	.75	1.50	2.25

WARRIOR COMICS
1945   (1930's DC reprints)
H. C. Blackerby

#1-Wing Brady, The Iron Man, Mark Markon	2.00	4.00	6.00

WAR ROMANCES (See True --)

WAR STORIES
1942 - #8, Feb-Apr, 1943
Dell Publishing Co.

#1	6.00	12.00	18.00
2-4	3.50	7.00	10.50
5-Origin The Whistler	4.00	8.00	12.00
6-8-Night Devils	3.50	7.00	10.50

WAR STORIES (Korea)
Sept, 1952 - #5, May, 1953
Ajax/Farrell Publications (Excellent Publ.)

#1	1.25	2.50	3.75

	Good	Fine	Mint
2-5	.80	1.60	2.40

WAR STORIES (See Star Spangled --)

WART AND THE WIZARD
Feb, 1964   (Walt Disney)
Gold Key

#1(10102-402)	.60	1.20	1.80

WARTIME ROMANCES
July, 1951 - #18, Nov, 1953
St. John Publishing Co.

#1-All Baker art	6.00	12.00	18.00
2-4-All Baker art	3.00	6.00	9.00
5-8-Baker cover/2-3 stories each	2.50	5.00	7.50
9-12,16,18-Baker cover/story each	2.20	4.40	6.60
13-15,17-Baker cvrs. only	1.75	3.50	5.25

WAR VICTORY ADVENTURES (#1-War Victory Comics)
Summer, 1942 - #3, Winter, 1943-44 (5¢)
U.S. Treasury Dept./War Victory/Harvey Publ.

#1-(Promotion of Savings Bonds)-Featuring America's greatest comic art by top syndicated cartoonists; Blondie, Joe Palooka, Green Hornet, Dick Tracy, Superman, Gumps, etc.; (36pgs.)	18.00	36.00	54.00
2	7.00	14.00	21.00
3-Capt. Red Cross(cover & text only); Powell art	6.00	12.00	18.00

WAR WAGON, THE (See Movie Classics)

WAR WINGS
October, 1968
Charlton Comics

#1		.15	.35

WASHABLE JONES & SHMOO
1953
Harvey Publications

#1	3.00	6.00	9.00

WASH TUBBS (See 4-Color Comics #11,28,53)

WATCH OUT FOR BIG TALK
1949
Giveaway

Dan Barry art (about crooked politicians)			
	1.50	3.00	4.50

Warlock #9. © MCG

The Warlord #1. © DC

Wartime Romances #2. © STJ

446

Web Of Evil #6, © QUA   Web Of Mystery #6, © ACE   Weekly Comic Magazine, 5/12/40, © FOX

WATER BIRDS AND THE OLYMPIC ELK (See 4-Color
Comics #700)

WEATHER-BIRD (See Comics From --, & Free
Comics to You --) (Giveaway)
1958 - #15, 1962
International Shoe Co./Western Printing Co.

	Good	Fine	Mint
#1	.40	.80	1.20
2-15	.25	.50	.75

NOTE: *The numbers are located at the bottom
of the bottom panel, pg. 1. All feature a
character called Weather-Bird.*

WEATHER BIRD COMICS (See Comics From Weath-
1957 (Giveaway) er Bird)
Weather Bird Shoes

No#-Contains a comic bound with new cover.
Several combinations possible; contents
determines price (30-50% of contents).

WEB OF EVIL
Nov, 1952 - #21, Dec, 1954
Comic Magzines/Quality Comics Group

#1-Jack Cole art	4.00	8.00	12.00
2-11-Jack Cole art	2.50	5.00	7.50
12,13,15-21	1.40	2.80	4.20
14-Crandall cover	2.00	4.00	6.00

WEB OF HORROR (Magazine)
Dec, 1969 - #3, Apr, 1970
Major Magazines

#1-Jones cover; Wrightson story			
	6.00	12.00	18.00
2-Jones cover; 2 Wrightson stories; Kaluta			
story	4.00	8.00	12.00
3-Wrightson cover; Brunner, Kaluta, Bruce			
Jones, Wrightson stys.	4.00	8.00	12.00

WEB OF MYSTERY
Feb, 1951 - #29, Sept. 1955
Ace Magazines (A.A. Wyn)

#1-Lou Cameron art	2.00	4.00	6.00
2-Matt Baker story(pencils)			
	2.00	4.00	6.00
3-10	1.25	2.50	3.75
11-26,28,29: #20-reprints/The Beyond #1			
	1.00	2.00	3.00
27-Matt Baker story(reprint/The Beyond #2)			
	1.20	2.40	3.60

NOTE: *This series was to appear as "Creepy
Stories," but title was changed before publ.
Cameron stories-#17,18-20, 22, 24,27; cover-#17.*

WEDDING BELLS
Feb, 1954 - #19, 1956
Quality Comics Group

	Good	Fine	Mint
#1	2.50	5.00	7.50
2	1.50	3.00	4.50
3-9	1.00	2.00	3.00
10-Ward art, 9pgs.	2.50	5.00	7.50
11-14,17	.80	1.60	2.40
15-Baker cover	1.25	2.50	3.75
16-Baker cover/story	1.75	3.50	5.25
18,19-Baker story each	1.50	3.00	4.50

WEEKENDER, THE
1946 (52 pgs.)
Rucker Publ. Co.

V2#1-36pgs. comics, 16 in newspaper format
with photos; partial Dynamic Comics reprints; 4pgs. of cels from the Disney
film Pinocchio; Little Nemo story by
Winsor McCay, Jr.; Jack Cole story
       4.00   8.00   12.00

WEEKLY COMIC MAGAZINE
5/12/40 (16 pgs.) (Full Color)
Fox Publications

(1st Version)-8pg. Blue Beetle story, 7pg.
Patty O'Day story; 2 copies known to
exist. Estimated value..... $300.00
(2nd Version)-7 two-pg. adventures of Blue
Beetle, Patty O'Day, Yarko, Dr. Fung,
Green Mask, Spark Stevens & Rex Dexter;
1 copy known ot exist.
       Estimated value..... $250.00

Discovered with business papers, letters and exploitation material
promoting **Weekly Comic Magazine** for use by newspapers in the
same manner of **The Spirit** weeklies. Interesting note: these are
dated three weeks before the first Spirit comic. Letters indicate
that samples may have been sent to a few newspapers. These sections were actually 15½x22" pages which will fold down to an
approximate 8x10" comic booklet. Other various comic sections
were found with the above, but were more like the Sunday comic
sections in format.

WEIRD (Magazine)
1/66 - V8#6, 12/74; V9#2, 6/76 - Present
(V1-V8, 52pgs.; V9 on, 68pgs.) (No V9#1)
Eerie Publications

V1#10(#1)-Intro. Morris the Caretaker of			
Weird(ends V2#10); Burgos art			
	.80	1.60	2.40
11,12	.40	.80	1.20
V2#1-4(10/67), V3#1(1/68), V2#6(4/68)-V2#7,			
9,10(12/68), V3#1(2/69)-V3#4			
	.25	.50	.75
V2#8-Reprints Ditko's 1st story/Fantastic			
Fears #5	.50	1.00	1.50

Weird Chills #3, © Key Publ.

Weird Fantasy #16, © WMG

Weird Horrors #8, © STJ

(Weird cont'd)	Good	Fine	Mint

5(12/69)-Rulah reprint-"Rulah" changed to
"Pulah"; LSD story-reprinted in Horror
Tales V4#4, Tales From the Tomb V2#4, &
Terror Tales V7#3   .30   .60   .90
V4#1-6('70), V5#1-6('71), V6#1-7('72), V7#1-6
('73), V8#1-6('74), V9#2-4('76)(no V9#1),
V10#1-3('77)   .25   .50   .75

WEIRD ADVENTURES
May-June, 1951 - #3, Sept-Oct, 1951
P. L. Publishing Co. (Canada)

#1-"The She-Wolf Killer" by Matt Baker			
	4.00	8.00	12.00
2	1.50	3.00	4.50
3-Male bondage-torture cover			
	1.50	3.00	4.50

WEIRD ADVENTURES
#10, July-Aug, 1951
Ziff-Davis Publishing Co.

#10	1.00	2.00	3.00

WEIRD CHILLS
July, 1954 - #3, Nov, 1954
Key Publications

#1-Wolverton story reprt./Weird Mysteries #4			
	10.00	20.00	30.00
2-Injury to eye cover	5.00	10.00	15.00
3-Bondage cover	2.00	4.00	6.00

WEIRD COMICS
April, 1940 - #20, Jan, 1942
Fox Features Syndicate

#1-The Birdman, Thor, God of Thunder(ends#5), The Sorceress of Zoom, Blast Bennett, Typhon, Voodoo Man, & Dr. Mortal begin; Fine cover	45.00	90.00	135.00
2	25.00	50.00	75.00
3,4	20.00	40.00	60.00
5-Intro. Dart & sidekick Ace(ends #20)			
	22.00	44.00	66.00
6,7-Dynamite Thor app. in each			
	17.00	34.00	51.00
8-Dynamo, The Eagle & sidekick Buddy & Marga, the Panther Woman begin			
	17.00	34.00	51.00
9	15.00	30.00	45.00
10-Navy Jones app.	15.00	30.00	45.00
11-16	12.00	24.00	36.00
17-Origin The Black Rider,			
18-20	12.00	24.00	36.00

WEIRD FANTASY
(Formerly A Moon, A Girl, Romance; becomes Weird Science-Fantasy #23 on)
#13, May-June, 1950 - #22, Nov-Dec, 1953
E.C. Comics

	Good	Fine	Mint
#13(#1)(1950)	90.00	180.00	270.00
14	50.00	100.00	150.00
15,16	40.00	80.00	120.00
17(1951)	30.00	60.00	90.00
6-10	25.00	50.00	75.00
11-13(1952)	18.00	36.00	54.00
14-Frazetta/Williamson/Krenkel story, 7pgs.			
	40.00	80.00	120.00
15-Three Williamson/Evans stories 4,3,& 7pgs.			
	25.00	50.00	75.00
16-19-Williamson/Krenkel stories in all. #18-Williamson/Krenkel cover			
	20.00	40.00	60.00
20-Frazetta/Williamson story, 7pgs.			
	28.00	56.00	84.00
21-Frazetta/Williamson cover & Williamson/Krenkel story	45.00	90.00	135.00
22	17.00	34.00	51.00

NOTE: *Crandall story-#22. Elder story-#17. Feldstein stories-#13(#1)-8; covers-#13(#1)-18(#18 w/Krenkel),20. Kamen stories-#13(#1)-16,18-22. Krigstein story-#22. Kurtzman stories-#13(#1)-17(#5),6. Orlando stories-#9-22 (2 stories in #16); covers-#19,22. Severin/Elder stories-#18-21. Wood stories-#13(#1)-14,17(2 stories ea. in #10-13). Canadian reprints exist; see Table of Contents.*

WEIRD HORRORS
(Nightmare #10 on)
Aug, 1952 - #9, Oct, 1953
St. John Publishing Co.

#1	2.50	5.00	7.50
2,5	1.50	3.00	4.50
3,4-Fineish art by Tuska	1.50	3.00	4.50
6-Ekgren cover	3.50	7.00	10.50
7-Ekgren cover; Kubert, Cameron stories			
	5.00	10.00	15.00
8,9-Kubert cvr/stories	4.00	8.00	12.00

WEIRD MYSTERIES
Oct, 1952 - #14, Jan, 1955
Gillmore Publications

#1-Partial Wolverton cover swiped from splash page "Flight to the Future" in Weird Tales of the Future #2			
	7.00	14.00	21.00
2-"Robot Woman" by Wolverton; Bernard Bailey cover-reprinted in Mister Mystery #18			
	20.00	40.00	60.00
3,6,8-14: #8-Nostrand art			
	2.25	4.50	6.75

(Weird Mysteries cont'd)   Good Fine Mint
4-Swiped with editing from "The Man Who Never Smiled" by Wolverton; B. Bailey cover
               10.00 20.00 30.00
5-Wolverton story   10.00 20.00 30.00
7-Used in Seduction of the Innocent, illo-
  "Indeed" & illo-"Sex and blood"
               10.00 20.00 30.00

WEIRD MYSTERIES (Magazine)
Mar-Apr, 1959   (68 pgs.) (35¢) (B&W)
Pastime Publications

#1-Torres art; E.C. swipe from TFTC #46
  by Tuska-"The Ragman" 3.00 6.00 9.00

WEIRD MYSTERY TALES (See DC 100pg.Super Spec.)

WEIRD MYSTERY TALES (See Cancelled Comic Cav-
7-8/72 - #24, 11/75   alcade)
National Periodical Publications

#1-Kirby story   .40   .80 1.20
2,3-Kirby story; #2-2pgs. Starlin
                .25   .50   .75
 4-8,10   .20   .40   .60
 9-Redondo story   .25   .50   .75
11-20,22   .15   .30   .45
21-Wrightson cover .20   .40   .60
23-Wood story   .20   .40   .60
24-Kaluta story   .20   .40   .60
NOTE: Alcala stories-#5,10,13,14. Bolle story-
#8, Kaluta cover-#1. Nino story-#6.

WEIRD SCIENCE (Formerly Saddle Romances)
(Becomes Weird Science-Fantasy #23 on)
#12, May-June, 1950 - #22, Nov-Dec, 1953
E.C. Comics

#12(#1)(1950)   100.00 200.00 300.00
13   55.00 110.00 165.00
14,15(1950)   42.00 84.00 126.00
5-10   25.00 50.00 75.00
11-14(1952)   20.00 40.00 60.00
15-18-Williamson/Krenkel story in each; #15-
  1st Williamson E.C. story
               20.00 40.00 60.00
19,20-Williamson/Frazetta story, 7pgs. ea.
  #19-Used in Seduction of the Innocent,
  illo-"A young girl on her wedding night
  stabs her sleeping husband to death with
  a hatpin..."   25.00 50.00 75.00
21-Williamson/Frazetta story, 6pgs.
               25.00 50.00 75.00
22-Williamson/Frazetta/Krenkel story, 8pgs.
  Wood draws himself in his story-last pg.&
  panel   25.00 50.00 75.00
NOTE: Elder stories-#14,19. Evans story-#22.

Feldstein stories-#12(#1)-8; covers-#12(#1)-
8,11. Ingels story-#15. Kamen stories-#12(#1)-
13,15-18,20,21. Kurtzman stories-#12(#1)-7.
Orlando stories-#10-22. Wood stories-#12(#1),
13(#2),5-22. (#9,10,12,13 all have 2 Wood
stories); covers-#9,10,12-22. Canadian reprints exist; see Table of Contents.

WEIRD SCIENCE-FANTASY(Formerly Weird Science
& Weird Fantasy; becomes Incredible S.F. #30)
#23, Mar, 1954 - #29, May-June, 1955
E.C. Comics

                  Good Fine Mint
#23,24-Williamson & Wood stories in both
               20.00 40.00 60.00
25-Williamson cover; Williamson/Torres/Kren-
  kel story + Wood sty. 22.00 44.00 66.00
26-Flying Saucer Report; Wood, Crandall,
  Orlando art   16.00 32.00 48.00
27   18.00 36.00 54.00
28-Williamson/Krenkel/Torres story; Wood
  story   22.00 44.00 66.00
29-Frazetta cover; Williamson/Krenkel &
  Wood story   50.00 100.00 150.00
NOTE: Crandall stories-#26,27,29. Evans story-
#26. Feldstein covers-#24,26,28. Kamen stories-
#27,28. Krigstein stories-#23-25. Orlando stor-
ies in all. Wood stories in all; covers-#23,27.

WEIRD SCIENCE-FANTASY ANNUAL
1952, 1953 (Sold thru the E.C. office & on
the stands in some major cities)
E.C. Comics

1952   135.00 270.00 405.00
1953   90.00 180.00 270.00
NOTE: The 1952 annual contains books cover-
dated in 1951 & 1952, and the 1953 annual
from 1952 & 1953. Contents of each annual
may vary in same year.

WEIRD SUSPENSE STORIES (Canadian reprint of
Crime SuspenStories #1-3; see Table of Contents)

WEIRD SUSPENSE TALES
Feb, 1975 - #3, July, 1975
Atlas/Seaboard Publ.

#1-Tarantula begins .25   .50   .75
2,3   .15   .30   .45

WEIRD TALES OF THE FUTURE
March, 1952 - #8, July, 1953
S.P.M. Publ. #1,2/Aragon Publ./Stanmor Publ.

#1   8.00 16.00 24.00
2,3-Three Wolverton stories/covers in each.
  #3 has LSD-like story 30.00 60.00 90.00

Weird Mysteries #8, © Gillmore Publ.

Weird Science #5, © WMG

Weird Science #17, © WMG

Weird Tales Of The Future #2. © Aragon   Weird Tales Of The Macabre #2. © Seaboard   Weird Terror #5. © Comic Media

(Weird Tales of the Future cont'd)

	Good	Fine	Mint
4-"Jumpin Jupiter" satire by Wolverton; partial Wolverton cover	12.00	24.00	36.00
5-Two Wolverton stories/cover	40.00	80.00	120.00
6-Bernard Bailey cover	3.00	6.00	9.00
7-"The Mind Movers" from the art to Wolverton's "Brain Bats of Venus" from Mr. Mystery #7 which was cut apart, pasted up, partially redrawn, and rewritten by Harry Kantor, the editor; Bernard Bailey cover	10.00	20.00	30.00
8-Reprints Weird Mysteries #1(10/52) minus cover	2.00	4.00	6.00

WEIRD TALES OF THE MACABRE (Magazine)
Jan, 1975 - #2, Mar, 1975 (B&W) (75¢)
Atlas/Seaboard Publ.

	Good	Fine	Mint
#1-Jones cover	.60	1.20	1.80
2-Boris Valejo cover	.50	1.00	1.50

WEIRD TERROR (Also see Horrific)
Sept, 1952 - #13, Sept, 1954
Allen Hardy Associates (Comic Media)

	Good	Fine	Mint
#1	1.50	3.00	4.50
2-10	1.00	2.00	3.00
11-13	.80	1.60	2.40

WEIRD THRILLERS
Sept-Oct, 1951 - #5, Oct-Nov, 1952
Ziff-Davis Publ. Co. (Approved Comics)

	Good	Fine	Mint
#1-Photo cover	3.00	6.00	9.00
2-Toth, Anderson stories	2.50	5.00	7.50
3-Kinstler + 2 Powell stories	2.00	4.00	6.00
4-Kubert story	2.50	5.00	7.50
5-Powell art	1.75	3.50	5.25

NOTE: *Anderson stories-#1,2,3. Roussos story-#4. #2 & #3 reprinted in Nightmare #10 & 13; #4,5 reprinted in Amazing Ghost Stories #? & #15.*

WEIRD WAR TALES
Sept-Oct, 1971 - Present
National Periodical Publications/DC Comics

	Good	Fine	Mint
#1-Kubert art	.75	1.50	2.25
2-Kubert(2pgs.) + Crandall reprint	.75	1.50	2.25
3,4-Kubert art	.50	1.00	1.50
5,6,10-Toth art	.50	1.00	1.50
7-Kubert art	.50	1.00	1.50
8-Adams cvr/sty.(inks)	1.25	2.50	3.75

	Good	Fine	Mint
9,11,12,14-16,18-20	.25	.50	.75
13-Redondo story	.30	.60	.90
17,22-Evans story	.25	.50	.75
21,23-34,37-40	.20	.40	.60
35-Evans story	.25	.50	.75
36-Crandall, Kubert reprt/#2	.25	.50	.75
41-45,47-50	.20	.40	.60
46-Evans story	.20	.40	.60
51-73	.15	.30	.45

NOTE: *Alcala stories-#9,11,14-16,20,23,25-29, 35,42-44,50,64. Baily story-#21. Chaykin story-#40,61,62,67,69. Ditko story-#46,49. Drucker stories-#2,3. Heath story-#59. Infantino reprint-#5. Kaluta cover-#12. Kubert story-#68,69; covers-#60,62-67. Maurer story-#5. Meskin reprint-#4. Morrow cover-#54. Nino story-#61.*

WEIRD WESTERN TALES (Formerly All-Star Western)
#12, 6-7/72 - Present (#12-52pgs.)
National Periodical Publications/DC Comics

	Good	Fine	Mint
#12-Bat Lash, Pow Wow Smith reprints; El Diablo by Adams/Wrightson	1.40	2.80	4.20
13,15-Adams art + cover #15	1.20	2.40	3.60
14-Toth art	.30	.60	.90
16-20: #19-Last El Diablo	.20	.40	.60
21-28,30-38	.15	.30	.45
29-Origin Jonah Hex	.25	.50	.75
39-Origin, 1st app. Scalphunter; Evans inks	.15	.30	.45
40,42-Evans inks	.15	.30	.45
41,43-50	.20		.35

NOTE: *Alcala stories-#16,17,19. Chaykin story #49. Evans inks-#42-48. Kubert cover-#12. Starlin cover-#44,45. Wildey story-#26.*

WEIRD WONDER TALES
Dec, 1973 - #22, May, 1977
Marvel Comics Group

	Good	Fine	Mint
#1-Wolverton story reprint from Mystic #6	.40	.80	1.20
2-5	.20	.40	.60
6-15	.15	.30	.45
16-18: Venus reprints by Everett/Venus #19, 18 & 17	.20	.40	.60
19-Dr. Druid(Droom)reprts.	.15	.30	.45
20-22	.20		.35

NOTE: *Ditko reprints-#4,5,11-13,19,20,21. Drucker reprint-#12. Everett reprints-#3 (Spellbound #16),#6(Astonishing #10),#9(Adv. Into Mystery #5). Kirby reprints #6,11,13,18-22; cover-#19,20. Krigstein reprint-#19. Kubert reprint-#22. Torres reprint-#7. Wildey reprint-#2.*

WEIRD WORLDS (See Adventures Into --)

WEIRD WORLDS (Magazine)
V1#10(12/70),V2#1(2/71)-#3(6/71) (52pgs.)
Eerie Publications

	Good	Fine	Mint
V1#10	.40	.80	1.20
V2#1-3	.30	.60	.90

WEIRD WORLDS
8-9/72 - #9, 1-2/74; #10, 10-11/74
National Periodical Publications

#1-Edgar Rice Burrough's John Carter of Mars
& David Innes begin; Kubert cover
.75 1.50 2.25
2,3-Adams/Bunkers stories. #2-Wrightson inks
.60 1.20 1.80
4-Kaluta story .60 1.20 1.80
5-7-Last John Carter .60 1.20 1.80
8-Iron Wolf begins by Chaykin
.50 1.00 1.50
9,10-Chaykin art .50 1.00 1.50
NOTE: *John Carter by Anderson-#1-3. Kaluta
covers-#5,6,10. Orlando story-#4.*

WELCOME BACK, KOTTER (TV)
Nov, 1976 - #10, Mar-Apr, 1978
National Periodical Publications/DC Comics

#1	.20	.40	.60
2-10	.15	.30	.45

WELCOME SANTA (See March of Comics #63,183)

WELLS FARGO (See Tales of --)

WENDY PARKER COMICS
July, 1953 - #8, July, 1954
Atlas Comics (OMC)

#1	1.40	2.80	4.20
2-8	.80	1.60	2.40

WENDY, THE GOOD LITTLE WITCH
Aug, 1960 - #93, Jan, 1976
Harvey Publications

#1	3.00	6.00	9.00
2-10	1.40	2.80	4.20
11-20	.70	1.40	2.10
21-30	.50	1.00	1.50
31-60	.20	.40	.60
61-93	.15	.30	.45

(See Harvey Hits #7,16,21,23,27,30,33)

WENDY WITCH WORLD
1962 - #53?, 9/74

Weird Worlds #3. © DC

Harvey Publications

	Good	Fine	Mint
#1	1.50	3.00	4.50
2-10	.75	1.50	2.25
11-20	.30	.60	.90
21-53	15	.30	.45

WEREWOLF (Super Hero)
Dec, 1966 - #3, April, 1967
Dell Publishing Co.

#1	.40	.80	1.20
2,3	.25	.50	.75

WEREWOLF BY NIGHT (See Marvel Spotlight)
Sept, 1972 - #43, Mar, 1977
Marvel Comics Group

#1-Ploog art-cont'd./Marvel Spotlight #4
.90 1.80 2.70
2-7-Ploog art in all .50 1.00 1.50
8-10 .30 .60 .90
11,12,17-20 .25 .50 .75
13-16-Ploog art; #15-New origin Werewolf
.40 .80 1.20
21-30 .25 .50 .75
31 .20 .40 .60
32-Origin & 1st app. Moon Knight
.20 .40 .60
33-Moon Knight concludes .20 .40 .60
34,36-43 .15 .30 .45
35-Starlin/Wrightson cvr. .40 .80 1.20
Giant Size #2(10/74,68pgs.)(Formerly G-S Creatures)-Frankenstein app..40 .80 1.20
Giant-Size #3-5(7/75,68pgs.):#4-Morbius the
Living Vampire app. .30 .60 .90
NOTE: *Ploog covers-#5-8,13-16. Ploog/Bolle
story-#6. Sutton art-#9,11,16.*

WESTERN ACTION
1964
I.W. Enterprises

#7-Reprint .40 .80 1.20

WESTERN ACTION
Feb, 1975
Atlas/Seaboard Publ.

#1-Kid Cody by Wildey & The Comanche Kid app.;
intro. The Renegade .20 .40 .60

WESTERN ACTION THRILLERS
1937 (100 pgs.)

#1-Buffalo Bill & The Texas Kid
12.00 24.00 36.00

Werewolf By Night #13. © MCG   Western Adventure Comics 1948. © ACE

451

Western Bandit Trails #2, © STJ

Western Comics #14, © DC

Western Crime Busters #9, © TM

WESTERN ADVENTURES COMICS
Oct, 1948 - #6, Aug, 1949
Ace Magazines

	Good	Fine	Mint
No#(#1)-Sheriff Sal begins			
	3.00	6.00	9.00
No#(#2)(12/48)	2.00	4.00	6.00
No#(#3,2/49)-#6	1.75	3.50	5.25

WESTERN BANDITS
1952
Avon Periodicals

#1-Butch Cassidy, The Daltons; Kinstler story
4.00 8.00 12.00

WESTERN BANDIT TRAILS
Jan, 1949 - #3, July, 1949; #9, July, 1954
St. John Publishing Co.

#1-Tuska art; Baker cover; Blue Monk, Vent-rilo app.	2.50	5.00	7.50
2-Baker cover	2.00	4.00	6.00
3-Baker cover/story, Tuska story	2.50	5.00	7.50
9(7/54)-Reprints #3 with new Baker cover	1.50	3.00	4.50

WESTERN COMICS (See Super DC Giant)
Jan-Feb, 1948 - #85, Jan-Feb, 1961
National Periodical Publications

#1-The Vigilante, Wyoming Kid begin	7.00	14.00	21.00
2-4-Last Vigilante	4.00	8.00	12.00
5-Nighthawk begins	3.00	6.00	9.00
6,7,9,10	2.50	5.00	7.50
8-Origin Wyoming Kid	2.50	5.00	7.50
11-20	2.00	4.00	6.00
21-40	1.50	3.00	4.50
41-60: #43-Pow Wow Smith begins, ends #85	1.25	2.50	3.75
61-85-Last Wyoming Kid; #77-Origin Matt Savage Trail Boss. #82-1st app. Fleetfoot, Pow Wow's girlfriend	1.00	2.00	3.00

NOTE: *Gil Kane, Infantino art in most.*

WESTERN CRIME BUSTERS
1950 - #10, Mar-Apr, 1952
Trojan Magazines

#1	5.00	10.00	15.00
2-4	3.50	7.00	10.50
5,6-Wood stories	6.00	12.00	18.00
7-Six-Gun Smith by Wood	6.00	12.00	18.00
8	3.00	6.00	9.00
9-Two Wood stories	8.00	16.00	24.00
10-Wood story	6.00	12.00	18.00

WESTERN CRIME CASES
#9, Dec, 1951
Novelty-Star Publications

	Good	Fine	Mint
#9-White Rider & Super Horse; L. B. Cole cover	1.25	2.50	3.75

WESTERN DESPERADO COMICS (Formerly Slam Bang)
1940 (Oct?)
Fawcett Publications

#8   7.00 14.00 21.00

WESTERNER, THE   (Wild Bill Pecos)
#14, June, 1948 - #41, Dec, 1951
"Wanted" Comic Group/Toytown/Patches

#14	2.00	4.00	6.00
15-17,20	1.25	2.50	3.75
18,22-24,27-Krigstein stories	2.00	4.00	6.00
19-Meskin art	1.25	2.50	3.75
26(4/50)-Origin & 1st app. Calamity Kate, series ends #32; Quest app. #33. Krigstein art	2.50	5.00	7.50
28-41: #37-Lobo, the Wolf Boy begins	1.20	2.40	3.60

WESTERNER, THE
1964
Super Comics

Super Reprint #15,16(Crack West. #65), 17
.40   .80   1.20

WESTERN FIGHTERS
Apr-May, 1948 - V4#7, Mar-Apr, 1953
Hillman Periodicals/Star Publ.

V1#1-Simon & Kirby cover	6.00	12.00	18.00
2,3	2.00	4.00	6.00
4,7-Krigstein stories	2.50	5.00	7.50
5,6,8-10,12	1.25	2.50	3.75
11-Williamson/Frazetta story	9.00	18.00	27.00
V2#1-Krigstein story	2.00	4.00	6.00
2-12	1.00	2.00	3.00
V3#1-11	.80	1.60	2.40
12-Krigstein story	2.00	4.00	6.00
V4#1,4-6	.70	1.40	2.10
2,3-Krigstein story	1.75	3.50	5.25
7-Williamson/Frazetta story?	7.00	14.00	21.00
3-D#1(12/53)(Star Publ.)	6.00	12.00	18.00

NOTE: *Kinstlerish stories-V2#6,8,9,12: V3#2, 5-7,11,12.*

WESTERN FRONTIER
1951
P. L. Publishers

	Good	Fine	Mint
#1	1.20	2.40	3.60
2-7	.75	1.50	2.25

WESTERN GUNFIGHTERS (1st Series)(Apache Kid
#20, 6/56 - #27, 8/57   #1-19)
Atlas Comics (CPS)

#20	.90	1.80	2.70
21,25-27	.90	1.80	2.70
22-Wood & Powell art	3.50	7.00	10.50
23-Williamson story	3.00	6.00	9.00
24-Toth story	2.00	4.00	6.00

WESTERN GUNFIGHTERS (2nd Series)
8/70 - #33, 11/75 (#1-6, 68pgs.; #7, 52pgs.)
Marvel Comics Group

#1-Ghost Rider, Fort Rango, Renegades & Gun-			
hawk app.	.40	.80	1.20
2-Williamson, Kubert reprt., 5pgs.; Ghost			
Rider app.; Apache Kid reprints begin;			
origin Nightwind(Apache Kid's horse)			
	.25	.50	.75
3-Black Rider(Black Mask), Western Kid re-			
prints begin, end #6	.20	.40	.60
4-Smith art	.20	.40	.60
5-9: #6-Gunhawk, Wyatt Earp app.; Ghost Rid-			
er dies. #7-Last Gunhawk, Ghost Rider(ori-			
gin retold); death of Jamie Jacobs. #8-			
Outlaw Kid reprint	.20	.40	.60
10-Origin Black Rider by Kirby; sequel to			
Matt Slade's origin	.20	.40	.60
11-17: #12-Matt Slade reprints begin(origin),			
end #15. #16-Kid Colt reprints begin			
	.15	.30	.45
18-Williamson reprint	.15	.30	.45
19-33		.15	.35

NOTE: *Everett inks-#6. Kirby stories-#1,11.
Steranko cover-#14. Torres story-#26('57).
Wildey reprints-#8,9. Woodbridge story-#27
('57). Renegades in #4,5; Ghost Rider-#1-7.*

WESTERN HEARTS
Dec, 1949 - #10, Mar, 1952
Standard Comics

#1-Severin art, photo cvr.	3.50	7.00	10.50
2-Williamson/Frazetta story, 2pgs.			
	12.00	24.00	36.00
3	1.50	3.00	4.50
4-10-Severin & Elder, Al Carreno art			
	2.00	4.00	6.00

WESTERN HERO (Wow #1-69; Real Western Hero

May, 1949 - #112, Mar, 1952   #70-75)
Fawcett Publications

	Good	Fine	Mint
#76-79-Tom Mix, Hopalong Cassidy, & Gabby			
Hayes begin	4.00	8.00	12.00
80-112	2.50	5.00	7.50

WESTERN KID (1st Series)
Dec, 1954 - #17, Aug, 1957
Atlas Comics (CPC)

#1-Origin Western Kid	2.50	5.00	7.50
2-8	1.25	2.50	3.75
9,10-Williamson story in both, 4pgs. each			
	3.00	6.00	9.00
11-17	.90	1.80	2.70

WESTERN KID, THE (2nd Series)
Dec, 1971 - #5, Aug, 1972
Marvel Comics Group

#1-Reprints	.15	.30	.45
2,4,5: #4-Everett reprint		.15	.30
3-Williamson reprint	.15	.30	.45

WESTERN KILLERS
1948 - #64, May, 1949; #6, July, 1949
Fox Features Syndicate

No#,no date-Range Busters	2.00	4.00	6.00
#60-64, 6	2.00	4.00	6.00

WESTERN LIFE ROMANCES (My Friend Irma #3?)
Dec, 1949 - #2, Mar, 1950
Marvel Comics (IPP)

#1	2.00	4.00	6.00
2	1.50	3.00	4.50

WESTERN LOVE
July-Aug, 1949 - #5, Mar-Apr, 1950
Prize Publications

#1-S&K art	4.00	8.00	12.00
2,5-S&K art	3.00	6.00	9.00
3,4	2.00	4.00	6.00

NOTE: *Meskin & Severin & Elder stories-#2-5.*

WESTERN LOVE TRAILS
#9, March, 1950
Ace Magazines

#9	1.50	3.00	4.50

WESTERN MARSHAL (See Steve Donovan-- & Ernest
Haycox's 4-Color #534,591,613,640(Based on
Haycox's "Trailtown"))

Western Fighters #7, © HILL

Western Hearts #2, © STD

Western Love #5, © PRIZE

Western Rough Riders #3, © Stanmore Publ.   Western Roundup #1, © DELL   Western Trails #1, © MCG

WESTERN OUTLAWS (My Secret Life #22 on)
#17, Sept, 1948 - #21, May, 1949
Fox Features Syndicate

	Good	Fine	Mint
#17-Kamen art; Baker/Feldstein story			
	2.50	5.00	7.50
18,20,21	2.00	4.00	6.00
19-Kamen/Feldstein story	2.50	5.00	7.50

WESTERN OUTLAWS
Feb, 1954 - #21, Aug, 1957
Atlas Comics (ACI #1-14/WPI #15-21)

#1-Heath art	2.00	4.00	6.00
2-10: #10-Everett story	1.20	2.40	3.60
11,14-Williamson story in both, 6pgs. each			
	3.00	6.00	9.00
12,13,16,18,20,21	1.00	2.00	3.00
15-Torres story	1.50	3.00	4.50
17-Crandall story, Williamson text illo			
	1.75	3.50	5.25
19-Crandall story	1.50	3.00	4.50

NOTE: *Bolle* story-#21. *Colan* story-#17. *Powell* story-#3. *Romita* story-#7.

WESTERN OUTLAWS & SHERIFFS(Formerly Best West.)
Dec, 1949 - #73, June, 1952
Marvel/Atlas Comics (IPC)

#60-65	1.50	3.00	4.50
66-73: #68-Robinson sty.	1.25	2.50	3.75

WESTERN PICTURE STORIES
Feb, 1937 - #4, 1937
Quality Comics Group

#1-Will Eisner art	20.00	40.00	60.00
2-Will Eisner art	12.00	24.00	36.00
3,4	9.00	18.00	27.00

WESTERN PICTURE STORIES (See Giant Comics Editions #6,11)

WESTERN ROMANCES (See Target --)

WESTERN ROUGH RIDERS
Nov, 1954 - #4, May, 1955
Gillmor Magazines #1/Stanmor Publications

#1	1.00	2.00	3.00
2-4	.60	1.20	1.80

WESTERN ROUNDUP
June, 1952 - #25, Jan-Mar, 1959 (100 pgs.)
Dell Publishing Co.

#1-Gene Autry, Roy Rogers, Elliott, Brown, & Rex Allen begin	6.00	12.00	18.00

	Good	Fine	Mint
2	4.00	8.00	12.00
3-5	3.50	7.00	10.50
6-10	2.50	5.00	7.50
11-13,16,17,19-24-Manning art			
	2.00	4.00	6.00
14,15,25	1.75	3.50	5.25
18-Toth art	2.50	5.00	7.50

WESTERN TALES (Formerly Witches --)
#31, Oct, 1955 - #33, July-Sept, 1956
Harvey Publications

#31,32-All S&K art; Davy Crockett app. in ea.			
	6.00	12.00	18.00
33-S&K art; Jim Bowie app.			
	6.00	12.00	18.00

WESTERN TALES OF BLACK RIDER (Formerly Black Rider; Gunsmoke Western #32 on)
#28, May, 1955 - #31, Nov, 1955
Atlas Comics (CPS)

#28-31	1.50	3.00	4.50

WESTERN TEAM-UP
November, 1973
Marvel Comics Group

#1-The Rawhide Kid & The Dakota Kid reprints; Gunsmoke Kid reprint by Jack Davis			
	.15	.30	.45

WESTERN THRILLERS (My Past Confessions #8 on)
Aug, 1948 - #7, Aug, 1949
Fox Features Syndicate

#1-"Velvet Rose" by Kamen/Feldstein; "Two-Gun Sal," "Striker Sisters"(all women outlaws issue)	5.00	10.00	15.00
2,3,6,7	1.75	3.50	5.25
4,5-Baker/Feldstein story; Butch Cassidy app. #5	2.50	5.00	7.50
#52-(Reprint, M.S.Dist.)1954? No date given (Becomes My Love Secret #53)			
	.75	1.50	2.25

WESTERN THRILLERS (Cowboy Action #5 on)
Nov, 1954 - #4, Feb, 1955
Atlas Comics (ACI)

#1	1.75	3.50	5.25
2-4	1.20	2.40	3.60

WESTERN TRAILS
May, 1957 - #2, July, 1957
Atlas Comics (SAI)

#1	1.25	2.50	3.75

(Western Trails cont'd)   Good   Fine   Mint
2-Severin cover   .80   1.60   2.40

WESTERN TRUE CRIME (Becomes My Confessions)
#15, Aug, 1948 - #6, June, 1949
Fox Features Syndicate

#15-Kamen/Feldstein story 2.50 5.00 7.50
16   2.00 4.00 6.00
3,5,6   1.75 3.50 5.25
4-Johnny Craig story 2.50 5.00 7.50

WESTERN WINNERS (Formerly All-Western Winners; Black Rider #8, or Romance Tales #8 on?)
#5, Sept, 1949 - #7, Dec, 1949
Marvel Comics (CDS)

#5-7-Two-Gun Kid, Kid Colt, Black Rider; #6-
Heath Kid Colt story 3.00 6.00 9.00

WEST OF THE PECOS (See 4-Color Comics #222)

WESTWARD HO, THE WAGONS (See 4-Color #738)

WHACK (Satire)
Oct, 1953 - #3, May, 1954
St. John Publishing Co.

#1-(3-D)-Kubert art   6.00 12.00 18.00
2,3-Kubert art in ea. 3.00 6.00 9.00

WHACKY (See Wacky)

WHAM (See Super Spy)
Nov, 1940 - #2, Dec, 1940
Centaur Publications

#1-The Sparkler, The Phantom Rider, Craig
Carter and the Magic Ring, Detector,
Copper Slug, & Speed Centaur begin
               20.00 40.00 60.00
2-Origin Blue Fire & Solarman; The Buzzard
app.   15.00 30.00 45.00

WHAM-O GIANT COMICS (98¢)
1967 (Newspaper size)(One Shot)(Full Color)
Wham-O Mfg. Co.

#1-Radian & Goody Bumpkin by Wally Wood;
1pg. Stanley art   2.00 4.00 6.00

WHAT IF --?
Feb, 1977 - Present   (#1-52pgs.)
Marvel Comics Group

#1   .75 1.50 2.25
2-5   .50 1.00 1.50
6-13   35   .70 1.05

NOTE: *J. Buscema cover-#10. Craig story-#1,6.*
Gil Kane story-#3. Kirby story-#11; covers-
#9,11.

WHEATIES (Premiums) (32 titles)
1950 & 1951   (32 pgs.) (Pocket size)
Walt Disney Productions

                        Good   Fine   Mint
    (Set A-1 to A-8, 1950)
A-1 Mickey Mouse & the Disappearing Island
A-2 Grandma Duck, Homespun Detective
A-3 Donald Duck & the Haunted Jewels
A-4 Donald Duck & the Giant Ape
A-5 Mickey Mouse, Roving Reporter
A-6 Li'l Bad Wolf, Forest Ranger
A-7 Goofy, Tightrope Acrobat
A-8 Pluto & the Bogus Money
        each.... 2.00 4.00 6.00
    (Set B-1 to B-8, 1950)
B-1 Mickey Mouse & the Pharoah's Curse
B-2 Pluto, Canine Cowpoke
B-3 Donald Duck & the Buccaneers
B-4 Mickey Mouse & the Mystery Sea Monster
B-5 Li'l Bad Wolf in the Hollow Tree Hideout
B-6 Donald Duck, Trail Blazer
B-7 Goofy & the Gangsters
B-8 Donald Duck, Klondike Kid
        each.... 1.75 3.50 5.25
    (Set C-1 to C-8, 1951)
C-1 Donald Duck & the Inca Idol
C-2 Mickey Mouse & the Magic Mountain
C-3 Li'l Bad Wolf, Fire Fighter
C-4 Gus & Jaq Save the Ship
C-5 Donald Duck in the Lost Lakes
C-6 Mickey Mouse & the Stagecoach Bandits
C-7 Goofy, Big Game Hunter
C-8 Donald Duck Deep-Sea Diver
        each.... 1.75 3.50 5.25
    (Set D-1 to D-8, 1951)
D-1 Donald Duck in Indian Country
D-2 Mickey Mouse and the Abandoned Mine
D-3 Pluto & the Mysterious Package
D-4 Bre'r Rabbit's Sunken Treasure
D-5 Donald Duck, Mighty Mystic
D-6 Mickey Mouse & the Medicine Man
D-7 Li'l Bad Wolf and the Secret of the Woods
D-8 Minnie Mouse, Girl Explorer
        each.... 1.75 3.50 5.25
NOTE: *Some copies lack the Wheaties ad.*

WHEELIE AND THE CHOPPER BUNCH
July, 1975 - #7, July, 1976 (Hanna-Barbera)
Charlton Comics

#1-7   .10   .20

WHEN KNIGHTHOOD WAS IN FLOWER (See 4-Color
Comics #505,682)

Western True Crime #4, © FOX

Whack #3, © STJ

What If #1, © MCG

455

Whip Wilson #10, © MCG

White Indian #11, © ME

White Princess Of The Jungle #2, © AVON

WHEN SCHOOL IS OUT (See Wisco)

WHERE CREATURES ROAM
July, 1970 - #8, Sept, 1971
Marvel Comics Group

	Good	Fine	Mint
#1-Kirby/Ditko reprints	.25	.50	.75
2-8-Kirby/Ditko reprints	.15	.30	.45

WHERE MONSTERS DWELL
Jan, 1970 - #38, Oct, 1975
Marvel Comics Group

	Good	Fine	Mint
#1-Kirby/Ditko reprints	.30	.60	.90
2-10: #4-Crandall reprt.	.20	.40	.60
11-37	.15	.30	.45
38-Williamson reprt./World of Suspense #3	.20	.40	.60

WHERE'S HUDDLES? (TV) (See Fun-In #9)
Jan, 1971 - #3, Dec, 1971 (Hanna-Barbera)
Gold Key

#1-3: #3 reprts. most #1		.10	.20

WHIP WILSON(Formerly Rex Hart; Gunhawk #12 on)
#9, April, 1950 - #11, Sept, 1950
Marvel Comics

#9-11	3.00	6.00	9.00
IW Reprint #1('64)-Kinstler cover; reprints			
Marvel #11	1.00	2.00	3.00

WHIRLWIND COMICS
June, 1940 - #3, Sept, 1940
Nita Publication

#1-Cyclone begins(origin)	18.00	36.00	54.00
2,3	10.00	20.00	30.00

WHIRLYBIRDS (See 4-Color #1124,1216)

WHITE CHIEF-PAWNEE INDIANS
1951
Avon Periodicals

No#-Kit West app.	3.50	7.00	10.50
#1,2	3.50	7.00	10.50

WHITE EAGLE INDIAN CHIEF (See Indian Chief)

WHITE INDIAN
1953 - 1954
Magazine Enterprises

#11(A-1#94), 12(A-1#102?), 13(A-1#104)-Frazetta reprints in all from Durango Kid
25.00 50.00 75.00

	Good	Fine	Mint
14(A-1#117), 15(A-1#135)-Not Frazetta;			
Torres art-#15	6.00	12.00	18.00

NOTE: *#11 reprints from Durango Kid #1-4;
#12 from #5,9,10,11; #13 from #7,12,13,16.*

WHITE PRINCESS OF THE JUNGLE (Also see Top
Jungle & Jungle Adventures)
July, 1951 - #5, Nov, 1952
Avon Periodicals

#1-Origin of White Princess & Capt'n Courage (reprt);Kinstler cvr.	10.00	20.00	30.00
2-Reprints origin of Malu, Slave Girl Princess from Avon's Slave Girl Princess #1 w/ Malu changed to Zora; Kinstler cover/story	8.00	16.00	24.00
3-Origin Blue Gorilla by Kinstler	7.00	14.00	21.00
4-Jack Barnum, White Hunter app.; reprint/ Sheena #9	5.00	10.00	15.00
5-Blue Gorilla by Kinstler	5.00	10.00	15.00

WHITE RIDER AND SUPER HORSE (Indian Warriors
1950 - 1951 #7 on)
Novelty-Star Publications/Accepted Publ.

#1-3	1.50	3.00	4.50
4-6-Adapt. "The Last of the Mohicans"	1.50	3.00	4.50
6-(Accepted reprint)	1.00	2.00	3.00

NOTE: *All have L. B. Cole covers.*

WHITE WILDERNESS (See 4-Color Comics #943)

WHITMAN COMIC BOOKS
1962 (136 pgs.) (B&W Reprints)
7-3/4"x5-3/4"; Hardcover)
Whitman Publishing Co.

#1-Yogi Bear
 2-Huckleberry Hound
 3-Mr. Jinks and Pixie and Dixie
 4-The Flintstones
 5-Augie Doggie & Loopy de Loop
 6-Snooper & Blabber Fearless Detectives/
   Quick Draw McGraw of the Wild West
 7-Bugs Bunny-reprints from #47,51,53,54 & 55
   each.... .80 1.60 2.40
 8-Donald Duck-reprints most of WDC&S #209-213.
   Includes 5 Barks stories, 1 complete Mickey
   Mouse serial & 1 Mickey Mouse serial missing the 1st episode 10.00 20.00 30.00
NOTE: *Hanna-Barbera #1-6, original stories.
Dell reprints-#7 & 8.*

WHIZ COMICS
#2, Feb, 1940 - #155, June, 1953
Fawcett Publications

NOTE: *The 1st issue was titled Thrill Comics with "Captain Thunder." Possibly 10 copies were made up and circulated within the office. However, no copies have yet emerged.*

	Good	Fine	Mint
#1-(No# on cover, #2 inside)-Origin & 1st app. Captain Marvel by C. C. Beck, Spy Smasher, Golden Arrow, Ibis the Invincible, Dan Dare, Scoop Smith & Lance O'Casey begin; #1 reprinted in Famous 1st Editions	1250.00	3125.00	5000.00

(Prices vary widely on this book)

	Good	Fine	Mint
2-(No# on cover, #3 inside)	500.00	1000.00	1500.00
3-(#3 on cover, #4 inside)-Spy Smasher reveals I.D. to Eve	300.00	600.00	900.00
4-(#4 on cover, #5 inside)	250.00	500.00	750.00
5-Captain Marvel wears button-down flap on splash page only	175.00	350.00	525.00
6-10: #7-Dr. Voodoo begins	120.00	240.00	360.00
11-14: #14-Dr. Voodoo by Raboy begins, ends #22	70.00	140.00	210.00
15-18-Spy Smasher battles Captain Marvel in all; #15-origin Sivana; Dr. Voodoo by Raboy	90.00	180.00	270.00
19,20	45.00	90.00	135.00
21-Origin & 1st app. Lt. Marvels	50.00	100.00	150.00
22-24: #23-Dr. Voodoo by Tuska begins	35.00	70.00	105.00
25-Origin & 1st app. Captain Marvel Jr., x-over in Capt. Marvel; Capt. Nazi app.	80.00	160.00	240.00
26-30	25.00	50.00	75.00
31,32: #32-1st app. The Trolls	20.00	40.00	60.00
33-Spy Smasher, Captain Marvel x-over	25.00	50.00	75.00
34-40-The Trolls in #37	16.50	33.25	50.00
41-50: #47-1pg. origin recap. #43-Spy Smasher, Ibis, Golden Arrow x-over in Capt. Marvel	10.00	20.00	30.00
51-60: #52-Capt. Marvel x-over in Ibis. #57-Spy Smasher, Golden Arrow, Ibis cameo	7.00	14.00	21.00
61-70	6.00	12.00	18.00
71,74,77-80	5.00	10.00	15.00
72,73,75,76-Two Captain Marvel stories in each; #76-Spy Smasher becomes Crime Smasher	5.00	10.00	15.00
81-100: #86-Captain Marvel battles Sivana Family	4.00	8.00	12.00

	Good	Fine	Mint
101,103-105	3.50	7.00	10.50
102-Commando Yank app.	3.50	7.00	10.50
106-Bulletman app.	3.50	7.00	10.50
107-152	3.00	6.00	9.00
153-155-(Scarce)	7.00	14.00	21.00
Wheaties Giveaway (1946) (Miniature)-6x8", 32pgs.; all copies were taped at each corner to a box of Wheaties and are never found in fine or mint condition.	5.00	15.00	25.00

NOTE: *Krigstein Golden Arrow-#75,78,91,95,96, 98,100. Wolverton ½ pg. "Culture Corner"-#65-68,70-75,77-85,87-96,98-100,102-104,106,108, 109,115,125,126,128,129,133,134,136,143,146.*

WHODUNIT
Aug-Sept, 1948 - #3, Dec-Jan, 1948-49
D.S. Publishing Co.

	Good	Fine	Mint
#1-7pg. Baker story	2.50	5.00	7.50
2,3	1.50	3.00	4.50

WHO IS NEXT?
January, 1953
Standard Comics

	Good	Fine	Mint
#5-Toth story	5.00	10.00	15.00

WHO'S MINDING THE MINT? (See Movie Classics)

WILBUR COMICS
Summer, 1944 - #90, 10/65 (#1-46, 52pgs.)
MLJ Magazines/Archie Publ. #8 on

	Good	Fine	Mint
#1	10.00	20.00	30.00
2-4	5.00	10.00	15.00
5-1st app. Katy Keene	8.00	16.00	24.00
6-10	3.00	6.00	9.00
11-20	2.50	5.00	7.50
21-30(1949)	1.75	3.50	5.25
31-50	1.00	2.00	3.00
51-90	.70	1.40	2.10

NOTE: *Katy Keene in #5-55,58-61,63(1pg.),64-71.*

WILD
Feb, 1954 - #5, Aug, 1954
Atlas Comics (IPC)

	Good	Fine	Mint
#1	3.00	6.00	9.00
2-5	2.00	4.00	6.00

WILD (This Magazine Is --) (Magazine)
Jan, 1968 - #3, 1968 (52pgs.) (Satire)
Dell Publishing Co.

	Good	Fine	Mint
#1-3	.50	1.00	1.50

Whiz Comics #64. © FAW

Who Is Next #5. © STD

Wilbur Comics #38. © AP

Wild #1, © MCG

Wild Bill Hickok #9, © AVON

Wild Boy #10, © Z-D

WILD BILL ELLIOTT
1950 - #17, Apr-June, 1955
Dell Publishing Co.

	Good	Fine	Mint
4-Color #278	3.00	6.00	9.00
#2-17	1.75	3.50	5.25
4-Color #472,520,643	1.75	3.50	5.25

WILD BILL HICKOK
Oct-Nov, 1949 - #28, May-June, 1956
Avon Periodicals

	Good	Fine	Mint
#1-Ingels cover	7.00	14.00	21.00
2-Painted cover	3.50	7.00	10.50
3,5-Painted covers	2.00	4.00	6.00
4-Painted cover by Howard Winfield, not			
Frazetta	2.00	4.00	6.00
6-10,12: #8-10-Painted covers			
	2.00	4.00	6.00
11,14-Kinstler cvr/story	3.00	6.00	9.00
13,15-18,20-24: #13,17,21,22-Kinstler cover.			
#17-Larsen, + Reinman art			
	1.75	3.50	5.25
19-Meskin story	1.75	3.50	5.25
25-27-Kinstler cover/story reprints			
	2.00	4.00	6.00
28-Kinstler cvr/story(new) + reprints/Last			
of the Comanches	2.00	4.00	6.00
IW Reprint #1-Kinstler cvr	.60	1.20	1.80
Super Reprint #10-12	.50	1.00	1.50

NOTE: #25 contains numerous editing deletions in both art & script due to code. *Kinstler* covers-#6, 11-14,18, 20-22,24-28.

WILD BILL HICKOK & JINGLES (Formerly
Cowboy Western) (See Blue Bird)
March, 1958 - 1960
Charlton Comics

	Good	Fine	Mint
#68,69-Williamson art	2.50	5.00	7.50
70-2pgs. Williamson art	1.50	3.00	4.50
71-76	.60	1.20	1.80

WILD BILL PECOS (See The Westerner)

WILD BOY OF THE CONGO(Also see Approved Comics)
#8, Oct-Nov, 1950 - #15, June, 1955
Ziff-Davis #8-12,4-9/St. John #11 on

#8,9	1.75	3.50	5.25
10(2-3/51)-Origin; bondage cover by Saunders			
	2.50	5.00	7.50
11(4-5/51),12(8-9/51)-Norman Saunders covers			
	2.00	4.00	6.00
4(10-11/51)-Saunders bondage cover			
	2.00	4.00	6.00
5(Winter,'51),6,8,9(10/53)			

	Good	Fine	Mint
	1.50	3.00	4.50
7(8-9/52)-Baker cover	1.75	3.50	5.25
11-13,15(10/54-6/55)-St. John			
	1.20	2.40	3.60
14(4/55)-Baker cover; reprints #12('51)			
	1.50	3.00	4.50

WILD FRONTIER (Cheyenne Kid #8 on)
Oct, 1955 - #7, April, 1957
Charlton Comics

#1-Davy Crockett	1.20	2.40	3.60
2-6-Davy Crockett in all	.60	1.20	1.80
7-Origin Cheyenne Kid	.60	1.20	1.80

WILD KINGDOM (TV)
1965 (Giveaway) (Regular size) (16pgs.)
Western Printing Co.

Mutual of Omaha's --	.50	1.00	1.50

WILD WEST (Wild Western #3 on)
Spring, 1948 - #2, July, 1948
Marvel Comics (WFP)

#1-Two-Gun Kid, Arizona Annie, Tex Taylor			
	5.00	10.00	15.00
2	3.00	6.00	9.00

WILD WEST (Black Fury #1-57)
#58, November, 1966
Charlton Comics

V2#58	.15	.30	.45

WILD WESTERN (Wild West #1,2)
#3, Sept, 1948 - #57, Sept, 1957
Marvel/Atlas Comics (WFP)

#3-Two-Gun Kid, Kid Colt, Blaze Carson			
	3.00	6.00	9.00
4-10	1.75	3.50	5.25
11-20: #15-Origin Red Larabee, Gunhawk			
	1.25	2.50	3.75
21-30	1.00	2.00	3.00
31-40	.80	1.60	2.40
41-47,49-51,53,57	.75	1.50	2.25
48-Williamson/Torres story, 4pgs. + Mort			
Drucker story	3.00	6.00	9.00
52-Crandall art	1.50	3.00	4.50
54,55-Williamson story in both, 5 & 4 pgs.,			
#54 with Mayo + two text illos.			
	2.50	5.00	7.50
56-Baker story	2.00	4.00	6.00

NOTE: *Annie Oakley* in #46,47. *Arrowhead* in #35,36. *Black Rider* in #5,12,14,30,33,35,41. *Kid Colt* in #27,30,33,35,36,41,46,47,52,54-

(Wild Western cont'd)
56. Ringo Kid in #29,39,41,46,47,52-56. Two-Gun Kid in #30,33,35,36,41. Wyatt Earp in #47. Severin story-#46.

WILD WESTERN ACTION (Also see The Bravados)
March, 1971 - #3, June, 1971   (52 pgs.)
Skywald Publishing Corp.   (Reprints)

	Good	Fine	Mint
#1-Durango Kid, Straight Arrow; with all references to "Straight" in the story relettered to "Swift"; Bravados begin	.35	.70	1.05
2-Billy Nevada, Durango Kid	.15	.30	.45
3-Red Mask, Durango Kid	.15	.30	.45

WILD WESTERN ROUNDUP
Oct, 1957; 1964
Red Top/Decker Publications/I.W. Enterprises

#1(1957)-Kid Cowboy reprt.	.75	1.50	2.25
IW Reprint #1('60-61)	.40	.80	1.20

WILD WEST RODEO
1953   (15¢)
Star Publications

#1-A comic book coloring book with regular full color cover & B&W inside			
	1.50	3.00	4.50

WILD WILD WEST, THE (TV)
June, 1966 - #7, Oct, 1969
Gold Key

#1,2-McWilliams art	.50	1.00	1.50
3-7	.25	.50	.75

WILKIN BOY (See That --)

WILLIE COMICS (Formerly Ideal #1-4; Crime
#5, Fall, 1946 - #23, 3/50   Cases #24 on)
Marvel Comics (MgPC)

#5(#1)	.80	1.60	2.40
6,8,9,12,14-18,20-23	.70	1.40	2.10
7,10,11,13,19-Kurtzman's "Hey Look"			
	2.00	4.00	6.00

WILLIE MAYS (See The Amazing --)

WILLIE THE PENGUIN (See Wisco)
April, 1951 - #6, April, 1952
Standard Comics

#1	.40	.80	1.20
2-6	.20	.40	.60

WILLIE THE WISE-GUY
Sept, 1957
Atlas Comics (NPP)

	Good	Fine	Mint
#1	.50	1.00	1.50

WILLIE WESTINGHOUSE EDISON SMITH THE BOY INVENTOR
1906   (36 pgs.) (10x16") (in color)
William A. Stokes Co.

By Frank Crane	15.00	37.50	60.00

WILL ROGERS WESTERN (Also see Blazing Comics)
#2, Aug, 1950 - #5, 1951
Fox Features Syndicate

#2-5	2.00	4.00	6.00

WILL-YUM (See 4-Color Comics #676,765,902)

WIN A PRIZE COMICS
Feb, 1955 - #2, 1955
Charlton/Simon & Kirby

V1#1-S&K art	6.00	12.00	18.00
2-S&K art	5.00	10.00	15.00

WINDY & WILLY
May-June, 1969 - #4, Nov-Dec, 1969
National Periodical Publications

#1-4-Reprints of Dobie Gillis with some art changes	.15	.30	.45

WINGS COMICS
Sept, 1940 - #124, 1954
Fiction House Magazines

#1-Skull Squad, Clipper Kirk, Suicide Smith, Jane Martin, War Nurse, Phantom Falcons, Greasemonkey Griffin, Parachute Patrol, & Powder Burns begin	40.00	80.00	120.00
2	20.00	40.00	60.00
3-5	15.00	30.00	45.00
6-10	12.00	24.00	36.00
11-15	8.00	16.00	24.00
16-Origin Captain Wings	12.00	24.00	36.00
17-20	8.00	16.00	24.00
21-30	7.00	14.00	21.00
31-40	6.00	12.00	18.00
41-50	5.00	10.00	15.00
51-60: #60-Last Skull Squad			
	4.00	8.00	12.00
61-67: #66-Ghost Patrol begins (becomes Ghost Squadron #71)	4.00	8.00	12.00
68,69: #68-Clipper Kirk becomes The Phantom Falcon-origin, Part 1; Part 2-#69			

Wild Western Roundup #1. © Decker

Wings Comics #25, © FH

Wings Comics #91, © FH

Wings Comics #112, © FH

(Wings Comics cont'd)	Good	Fine	Mint
	4.00	8.00	12.00

70-72: #70-1st app. The Phantom Eagle in
costume, origin-Part 3; Capt. Wings battles
Col. Kamikaze in all   3.00   6.00   9.00

| 73-80 | 3.00 | 6.00 | 9.00 |
| 81-100 | 3.00 | 6.00 | 9.00 |

101-124: #111-Last Jane Martin

2.00   4.00   6.00

NOTE: *Bondage covers are common. Captain
Wings battles Sky Hag #75,76; --Mr. Atlantis
#85-92; --Mr. Pupin(Red Agent) #98-103. Bob
Lubbers art on Capt. Wings-#70-103. Evans
art-#85-103,108(Jane Martin). Jane Martin by
Fran Hopper-#68-84; Suicide Smith by John
Celardo-#76-103; Ghost Patrol by Maurice
Whitman-#83-103; Skull Squad by M. Baker-
#52-60; Clipper Kirk by Baker-#60,61.*

WINGS OF THE EAGLES, THE   (See 4-Color #790)

WINKY DINK (Adventures of --)
#75, March, 1957   (One Shot)
Pines Comics

| #75-Marv Levy cover/art | .40 | .80 | 1.20 |

WINKY DINK (See 4-Color Comics #663)

WINNIE THE POOH
January, 1977 - Present   (Walt Disney)
Gold Key

| #1 | .20 | .40 | .60 |
| 2-11 | .15 | .30 | .45 |

WINNIE WINKLE
1930 - 1933   (52pgs)(B&W daily strip reprints)
Cupples & Leon Co.

| #1 | 8.00 | 16.00 | 24.00 |
| 2-4 | 7.00 | 14.00 | 21.00 |

WINNIE WINKLE
1941 - 1949
Dell Publishing Co.

Large Feature Comic #2('41)

	6.00	15.00	24.00
4-Color #94('45)	5.00	10.00	15.00
4-Color #174	3.00	6.00	9.00

#1(3-5/48)-Contains daily & Sunday newspaper
reprints from 1939-41   3.50   7.00 10.50

| 2-7 | 2.00 | 4.00 | 6.00 |

WISCO/KLARER COMIC BOOK   (Miniature)
1948 - 1953   (24pgs.)(3-1/2"x6-3/4")
Givean away by Wisco "99" Service Stations,

Carnation Malted Milk, Klarer Health Wieners,
Fleers Dubble Bubble Gum, & Rodeo All-Meat
Wieners
Vital Publications/Fawcett Publications

	Good	Fine	Mint
Blackstone "Solves the Sealed Vault Mystery"			
	2.00	4.00	6.00

Blaze Carson in "The Sheriff Shoots It Out"
(1950)   2.00   4.00   6.00
Captain Marvel & Billy's Big Game
22.00 44.00 66.00
(*Prices vary widely on this book*)
China Boy in "A Trip to the Zoo" #10
1.00   2.00   3.00
Indoors-Outdoors Game Book
1.00   2.00   3.00
Jim Solar Space Sheriff in "Battle for Mars,"
"Between Two Worlds","Conquers Outer Space"
"The Creatures on the Comet","Defeats the
Moon Missile Men","Encounter Creatures on
Comet","Meet the Jupiter Jumpers","Meets
the Man From Mars","On Traffic Duty","Out-
laws of the Spaceways","Pirates of the
Planet X","Protects Space Lanes","Raiders
From the Sun","Ring Around Saturn","Robots
of Rhea","The Sky Ruby","Spacetts of the
Sky","Spidermen of Venus","Trouble on Mer-
cury"   1.50   3.00   4.50
Johnny Starboard & the Underseas Pirates('48)
1.00   2.00   3.00
Kid Colt in "He Lived by His Guns"(1950)
2.50   5.00   7.50
Little Aspirin as "Crook Catcher" #2(1950)
.75   1.50   2.25
Little Aspirin in "Naughty But Nice" #6(1950)
.75   1.50   2.25
Return of the Black Phantom
1.50   3.00   4.50
Secrets of Magic   1.50   3.00   4.50
Slim Morgan "Brings Justice to Mesa City" #3
1.25   2.50   3.75
Super Rabbit(1950)-Cuts Red Tape, Stops
Crime Wave!   1.00   2.00   3.00
Tex Farnum, Frontiersman(1948)
1.00   2.00   3.00
Tex Taylor in "Draw or Die, Cowpoke!"(1950)
1.75   3.50   5.25
Tex Taylor in "An Exciting Adventure at the
Gold Mine"('50)   1.75   3.50   5.25
Wacky Quacky in "All-Aboard"
.75   1.50   2.25
When School Is Out   .75   1.50   2.25
Willie in a "Comic-Comic Book Fall" #1
.75   1.50   2.25
Wonder Duck "An Adventure at the Rodeo of the
Fearless Quack-er!"('50)
1.00   2.00   3.00
Rare uncut version of three; includes Capt.
Marvel, Tex Farnum, Black Phantom
Estimated value...... $75.00

WISE LITTLE HEN, THE
1934 (48pgs.); 1935; 1937   (Story book)
David McKay Publ.

1st book app. Donald Duck; Donald app. on cover with W.L.Hen & Practical Pig; painted
cover; same artist as the B&W's from Silly
Symphony Cartoon, The Wise Little Hen(1934)
30.00 60.00 90.00
1935 Edition with dust jacket; 40pgs. with
color, 8-3/4"x9-3/4"   25.00 50.00 75.00
#888(1937)-9½x13", 12pgs. (Whitman) Donald
Duck app.   20.00 40.00 60.00

WITCHCRAFT
Mar-Apr, 1952 - #6, Mar, 1953
Avon Periodicals

	Good	Fine	Mint
#1-Kubert art	7.00	14.00	21.00
2-Kubert & Check stories	6.00	12.00	18.00
3,4,6	3.00	6.00	9.00
5-Kelly Freas cover	4.00	8.00	12.00

NOTE: *Hollingsworth stories-#5,6.*

WITCHES TALES (Witches Western Tales #29,30)
Jan, 1951 - #27, Oct, 1954; #28, April, 1955
Witches Tales/Harvey Publications

	Good	Fine	Mint
#1-Bondage cover	3.00	6.00	9.00
2-4,7-10	1.75	3.50	5.25
5,6-Bondage covers	2.00	4.00	6.00
11-13,15,16	1.50	3.00	4.50
14,17-Powell/Nostrand art	2.00	4.00	6.00
18-Nostrand art, 2 stys.	2.25	4.50	6.75
19-26-Nostrand art in all	2.00	4.00	6.00
27,28: #27-Reprints #6 with diff. cover. #28-			
Reprints #8 with diff. cover			
	1.75	3.50	5.25

NOTE: *Nostrand stories-#17-26; #14,17(w/Powell). Powell stories-#3-7,10,11,19-25,27. #28 shows date as December on cover.*

WITCHES TALES (Magazine)
V1#7, 7/69 - V7#1, 2/75 (52 pgs.) (B&W)
Eerie Publications

	Good	Fine	Mint
V1#7(7/69)-#9(11/69)	.40	.80	1.20
V2#1-6('70),V3#1-6('71)	.30	.60	.90
V4#1-6('72),V5#1-6('73),V6#1-6('74),V7#1			
	.25	.50	.75

NOTE: *Ajax/Farrell reprints in early issues.*

WITCHES' WESTERN TALES (Formerly Witches Tales) (Western Tales #31 on)
#29, Feb, 1955 - #30, Apr, 1955
Harvey Publications

	Good	Fine	Mint
#29,30-S&K reprints from Boys' Ranch includ-			
ing cover	7.00	14.00	21.00

WITCHING HOUR, THE
Feb-Mar, 1969 - #85, Oct, 1978
National Periodical Publications/DC Comics

	Good	Fine	Mint
#1-Toth + Adams, 3pgs.	1.25	2.50	3.75
2,6,9,10	.30	.60	.90
3,5-Wrightson, Toth stys.	1.00	2.00	3.00
4-Toth sty.; Cardy cvr.	.80	1.60	2.40
7-Kaluta, Toth stories	.80	1.60	2.40
8-Adams story	1.20	2.40	3.60
11,16-20	.25	.50	.75
12-Kane/Wood, Toth stys.	.80	1.60	2.40

	Good	Fine	Mint
13-Adams cover/story	1.00	2.00	3.00
14-Williamson/Garzon, Jones stories; Adams			
cover	1.00	2.00	3.00
15-Wood story	.40	.80	1.20
21,22,24-33,35-37	.20	.40	.60
23,34-Redondo story	.25	.50	.75
38-(100pgs.); Toth reprint	.20	.40	.60
39-64	.20	.40	.60
65-Two Redondo stories	.15	.30	.45
66-85		.20	.35

NOTE: *Adams covers-#7-11,13,14. Alcala stories-#24,27,33,41,43. Anderson story-#38. Morrow stories-#10,13,15,16.*

WITH THE MARINES ON THE BATTLEFRONTS OF THE WORLD
1953 (no month) - #2, March, 1954
Toby Press

	Good	Fine	Mint
#1-John Wayne story	2.50	5.00	7.50
2-Monty Hall in #1,2	1.50	3.00	4.50

WITH THE U.S. PARATROOPS BEHIND ENEMY LINES
1951 - #6, 12/52 (Also see U.S. Paratroops)
Avon Periodicals

	Good	Fine	Mint
#1-Wood cvr & inside cvr.	4.50	9.00	13.50
2-6: #2-Kinstler art. #5-Kinstler cover/sty.			
#6-Kinstler art	2.00	4.00	6.00

WITNESS, THE
Sept, 1948
Marvel Comics (MMC)

	Good	Fine	Mint
#1-Everett cover (Rare)	12.00	24.00	36.00

WITTY COMICS
1945
Irwin H. Rubin Publ./Chicago Nite Life News#2

	Good	Fine	Mint
#1,2-The Pioneer, Junior Patrol			
	2.00	4.00	6.00
3-7-Skyhawk	1.50	3.00	4.50

WIZARD OF OZ (See 4-Color #1308, Dell Jr. Treasury #5, Marvelous --, & Marvel Treasury of Oz)

WOLF GAL (See Al Capp's --).

WOLFMAN, THE (See Book & Record Set, Movie Classics)

WOMAN IN LOVE (A Feature Presentation #5)
Aug, 1949 - #4, Feb, 1950
Fox Features Synd./Hero Books

	Good	Fine	Mint
#1	4.00	8.00	12.00

Witchcraft #2. © AVON

Witches Tales #6. © HARV

The Witness #1. © MCG

Women Outlaws #4, © FOX   Wonder Comics #11, © BP   Wonder Woman #2, © DC

	Good	Fine	Mint
(Woman in Love cont'd)			
2-Kamen/Feldstein cover	3.00	6.00	9.00
3	2.00	4.00	6.00
4-Wood story	5.00	10.00	15.00

WOMAN OF THE PROMISE, THE
1950   (General Distr.)
Catechetical Guild

	Good	Fine	Mint
	3.00	6.00	9.00

WOMEN OUTLAWS (My Love Memories #9 on)
July, 1948 - #8, Sept, 1949
Fox Features Syndicate

#1-Used in Seduction of the Innocent, "Giving children an image of American womanhood"			
illo.	10.00	20.00	30.00
2,4-8	5.00	10.00	15.00
3-Kamen story	6.00	12.00	18.00
No#,no date-Contains Cody of the Pony Express			
	4.00	8.00	12.00

WOMEN TO LOVE
No date (1953)
Realistic

	Good	Fine	Mint
No# (Rare)	9.00	18.00	27.00

WONDER BOY
#16, 1955 - #18, July, 1955
Ajax/Farrell Publ.

#16,17	3.00	6.00	9.00
18-Phantom Lady app.	6.00	12.00	18.00

WONDER COMICS (Wonderworld #3 on)
May, 1939 - #2, June, 1939
Fox Features Syndicate

#1-Wonder Man only app. by Will Eisner; Bob Kane art; Eisner cvr.	90.00	180.00	270.00
2-Yarko the Great, Master Magician by Eisner begins; Bob Kane art; Lou Fine cover			
	50.00	100.00	150.00

WONDER COMICS
May, 1944 - #20, Oct, 1948
Great/Nedor/Better Publications

#1-The Grim Reaper & Spectro, the Mind Reader begin	15.00	30.00	45.00
2-Origin The Grim Reaper; Super Sleuths begin, end #8,17	8.00	16.00	24.00
3-5	7.00	14.00	21.00
6-10: #8-Last Spectro. #9-Wonderman begins			
	6.00	12.00	18.00
11-14-Dick Devens, King of Futuria begins #11,			

	Good	Fine	Mint
ends #14	7.00	14.00	21.00
15-Tara begins(origin), ends #20			
	7.00	14.00	21.00
16,18: #16-Spectro app.	6.00	12.00	18.00
17,19,20: A few Frazetta panels each. #17-Last Grim Reaper. #19-The Silver Knight begins	8.00	16.00	24.00

NOTE: *Ingels* covers-#8,11,12,14,15,18-20.
Schomburg (Xela) covers (line)-#1-10; (painted)-#13-20.

WONDER DUCK (See Wisco)
1949 - #3, Mar, 1950
Marvel Comics (CDS)

#1-3	1.00	2.00	3.00

WONDERFUL ADVENTURES OF PINOCCHIO, THE
(See Movie Comics)

WONDERFUL WORLD OF DUCKS(See Golden Picture
1975   Story Book)
Colgate Palmolive Co.

#1-Mostly reprints	.20	.40	.60

WONDERFUL WORLD OF THE BROTHERS GRIMM
(See Movie Comics)

WONDERLAND COMICS
Summer, 1945 - #9, Feb-Mar, 1947
Feature Publications/Prize

#1	1.50	3.00	4.50
2-9	1.00	2.00	3.00

WONDERS OF ALADDIN, THE (See 4-Color #1255)

WONDER WARTHOG MAGAZINE
Winter, 1967 - #2, Spring, 1967
Millar Publications

#1,2-Kurtzman + Gilbert Shelton art			
	6.00	12.00	18.00

WONDER WOMAN (See All-Star Comics, Giant
Comics to Color, & Sensation Comics)

WONDER WOMAN
Summer, 1942 - Present
National Per. Publ./All-American Publ.

#1-Origin Wonder Woman retold (see All-Star #8); reprinted in Famous 1st Editions; H.G. Peter art begins	135.00	270.00	405.00
2	60.00	120.00	180.00
3	50.00	100.00	150.00

(Wonder Woman cont'd)	Good	Fine	Mint
4,5	30.00	60.00	90.00
6-10	25.00	50.00	75.00
11-20	16.00	32.00	48.00
21-30	12.00	24.00	36.00
31-40	10.00	20.00	30.00
41-44,46-50	6.00	12.00	18.00
45-Origin retold	9.00	18.00	27.00
51-70	5.00	10.00	15.00
71-90	3.50	7.00	10.50
91-100: #94-Robin Hood x-over. #98-Last H.G.			
Peter art	3.00	6.00	9.00
101-104,106-110: #107-1st app. Wonder Girl			
	2.50	5.00	7.50
105-Wonder Woman's secret origin			
	3.00	6.00	9.00
111-120	2.00	4.00	6.00
121-130	1.25	2.50	3.75
131-150	1.00	2.00	3.00
151-170	.70	1.40	2.10
171-194	.50	1.00	1.50
195-Wood inks	.70	1.40	2.10
196-198(52pgs.)	.70	1.40	2.10
199,200-Jones cvrs; 52pgs.	1.40	2.80	4.20
201,204-210: #204-Return to old costume			
	.25	.50	.75
202-Fafhrd & The Grey Mouser debut			
	.60	1.20	1.80
203-Women's Lib issue	.40	.80	1.20
211,214-(100pgs.)	.30	.60	.90
212,213,215,216	.20	.40	.60
217-(68pgs.)	.25	.50	.75
218-230: #224-Steve Trevor returns. #220-Adams			
assist	.20	.40	.60
231-240: #233-Morrow cover	.15	.30	.45
241-Staton story	.20	.40	.60
242-251	.15	.30	.45
Pizza Hut Giveaway(12/77)-Exact reprints of			
#60,62	.25	.50	.75
--Spectacular (12/77,$1.00)-Ditko, Heath art			
	.50	1.00	1.50

NOTE: *Staton covers-#241,245,246.*

WONDER WOMAN SPECTACULAR (See DC Special
Series #9)

WONDERWORLD (Formerly Wonder Comics)
#3, July, 1939 - #33, Jan, 1942
Fox Features Syndicate

#3-The Flame begins; Wonder Man & Yarko the			
Great, Master Magician continues by			
Eisner	30.00	60.00	90.00
4	22.00	44.00	66.00
5-10	20.00	40.00	60.00
11-Origin The Flame	25.00	50.00	75.00
12-21	12.00	24.00	36.00
22-Origin The Black Lion & Cub			

	Good	Fine	Mint
	12.50	25.00	37.50
23-27	10.00	20.00	30.00
28-Lu-Nar, the Moon Man begins; origin U.S.			
Jones	12.00	24.00	36.00
29,31-33	8.00	16.00	24.00
30-Origin Flame Girl	12.00	24.00	36.00

NOTE: *Yarko by Eisner-#3-10 (at least).*
Lou Fine covers/art-#3-11; #12-cover only.

WOODSY OWL (See March of Comics #395)
Nov, 1973 - #10, Feb, 1976
Gold Key

#1		.15	.30
2-10		.10	.20

WOODY WOODPECKER (See Comic Album)
1947 - Present
Dell Publishing Co./Gold Key #73 on

4-Color #169,188	3.00	6.00	9.00
4-Color #202,232,249,264,288			
	2.25	4.50	6.75
4-Color #305,336,350	1.50	3.00	4.50
4-Color #364,374,390,405,416,431(1952)			
	1.25	2.50	3.75
#16-30('53-'55)	.60	1.20	1.80
31-72,76-80('55-'63)	.30	.60	.90
73-75(Giants, 84pgs.)	.50	1.00	1.50
81-100	.25	.50	.75
101-120		.20	.35
121-176		.15	.35
Back to School #1(1952)	2.00	4.00	6.00
Back to School #2-4,6('53-'57)(No#5)(County			
Fair #5)	1.00	2.00	3.00
Christmas Parade #1(11/68-Giant)(G.K.)			
	.40	.80	1.20
Clover Stamp-Newspaper Boy Contest('56)-9pg.			
story-Giveaway	.50	1.00	1.50
County Fair #5('56)-Formerly Back to School			
#2('58)	1.00	2.00	3.00
In Chevrolet Wonderland(1954-giveaway)-20pgs.,			
full story line(Western Publ.)-Chilly			
Willy app.	2.50	5.00	7.50
Meets Scotty McTape(1953-Scotch Tape give-			
away, 16pgs., full size)			
	2.00	4.00	6.00
Summer Fun #1(G.K.-'66,25¢)	.30	.60	.90

NOTE: *15¢ editions exist.*

WOODY WOODPECKER (See Comic Album #5,9,13,
Dell Giant #24,40,54, Golden Comics Digest
#1,3,5,8,15,16,20,24,32,37,44, March of Com-
ics #16,34,85,93,109,124,139,158,177,184,203,
222,239,249,261, & Super Book #12,24)

Wonder Woman #32, © DC

Wonderworld #4, © FOX

Woody Woodpecker Four Color #169, © W. Lantz

The World Around Us #21, © GIL   World Famous Heroes #3, © CEN   World Of Fantasy #3, © MCG

WOOLWORTH'S CHRISTMAS STORY BOOK (See Jolly
Christmas Book & Happy Time Xmas Book)
1952 - 1954
Promotional Publ. Co.

	Good	Fine	Mint
No#	1.25	2.50	3.75

NOTE: *1952 issue-Marv Levy cover/art.*

WORLD AROUND US, THE (Ill. Story of --)
Sept, 1958 - #36, Oct, 1961 (25¢)
Gilberton Publishers (Classics Illustrated)

	Good	Fine	Mint
#1-Dogs	2.50	5.00	7.50
2-Indians	1.50	3.00	4.50
3-Horses	1.50	3.00	4.50
4-Railroads	1.25	2.50	3.75
5-Space-Ingels art	2.50	5.00	7.50
6-F.B.I., The-Evans, Ingels art	2.50	5.00	7.50
7-Pirates-Ingels art	1.75	3.50	5.25
8-Flight-Evans, Ingels, Crandall art	2.50	5.00	7.50
9-Army-Ingels, Orlando art	2.50	5.00	7.50
10-Navy-Kinstler art	1.50	3.00	4.50
11-Marine Corps.	1.50	3.00	4.50
12-Coast Guard	1.50	3.00	4.50
13-Air Force	1.50	3.00	4.50
14-French Revolution-Crandall, Evans art	3.00	6.00	9.00
15-Prehistoric Animals-Al Williamson art, 6pgs. + Morrow art	4.00	8.00	12.00
16-Crusades	1.50	3.00	4.50
17-Festivals	1.50	3.00	4.50
18-Great Scientists-Crandall, Evans, Torres, Williamson, Morrow art	2.50	5.00	7.50
19-Jungle-Crandall, Williamson, Morrow art	4.00	8.00	12.00
20-Communications-Crandall, Evans art	2.50	5.00	7.50
21-Presidents	2.00	4.00	6.00
22-Boating-Morrow art	1.25	2.50	3.75
23-Great Explorers-Crandall, Evans art	2.00	4.00	6.00
24-Ghosts-Morrow, Evans	1.50	3.00	4.50
25-Magic-Evans,Morrow art	3.00	6.00	9.00
26-The Civil War	1.50	3.00	4.50
27-Mountains (High Advs.)-Evans, Morrow, Torres art	1.50	3.00	4.50
28-Whaling-Crandall, Evans, Morrow art	1.50	3.00	4.50
29-Vikings-Crandall, Evans, Torres, Morrow art	1.75	3.50	5.25
30-Undersea Adventure-Evans art	1.25	2.50	3.75
31-Hunting-Kirby art	1.25	2.50	3.75
32-For Gold & Glory-Morrow, Kirby, Crandall, Evans art	1.50	3.00	4.50

	Good	Fine	Mint
33-Famous Teens-Torres, Crandall, Evans art	1.50	3.00	4.50
34-Fishing-Evans art	1.25	2.50	3.75
35-Spies-Kirby, Evans, Morrow art	1.40	2.80	4.20
36-Fight for Life (Medicine)-Kirby art	1.40	2.80	4.20

(See Classics Ill. Special Edition)

WORLD FAMOUS HEROES MAGAZINE
Oct, 1941 - #4, Apr, 1942 (A comic book)
Comic Corp. of America (Centaur)

	Good	Fine	Mint
#1	8.00	16.00	24.00
2-4	5.00	10.00	15.00

WORLD FAMOUS STORIES
1945
Croyden Publishers

	Good	Fine	Mint
#1-Ali Baba, Hansel and Gretel, Rip Van Winkle, Mid-Summer Night's Dream	2.50	5.00	7.50

WORLD IS HIS PARISH, THE
1953   (15¢)
George A. Pflaum

	Good	Fine	Mint
The story of Pope Pius XII	1.50	3.00	4.50

WORLD OF ADVENTURE (Walt Disney's --)
April, 1963 - Oct, 1963
Gold Key

	Good	Fine	Mint
#1-3-Disney TV characters; Savage Sam, Johnny Shiloh, Capt. Nemo, The Mooncussers	.40	.80	1.20

WORLD OF ARCHIE, THE (See Archie Giant Series Mag. #148,151,156,160,165,171,177,182,
188,193,200,208,213,225,232,237,244,249,456,
461,468)

WORLD OF FANTASY
May, 1956 - #19, Aug, 1959
Atlas Comics (CPC #1-15/ZPC #16-19)

	Good	Fine	Mint
#1	3.00	6.00	9.00
2-Williamson, 4pgs.	3.50	7.00	10.50
3-Sid Check story	1.75	3.50	5.25
4-7	1.50	3.00	4.50
8-Matt Fox story	2.00	4.00	6.00
9-Krigstein story	2.00	4.00	6.00
10,13-15	1.20	2.40	3.60
11-Torres story	1.50	3.00	4.50
12-Everett cover	1.35	2.75	4.00

(World of Fantasy cont'd)

	Good	Fine	Mint
16-Williamson, 4pgs.; Ditko, Kirby art			
	3.00	6.00	9.00
17-19-Ditko, Kirby art	2.00	4.00	6.00

NOTE: *Berg story-#5,6,8. Check art-#3. Ditko story-#17,19. Everett covers-#4,5-7,9,13. Kirby covers-#15,17-19. Krigstein story-#9. Morrow stories-#7,8,14. Orlando stories-#8, 13,14. Powell story-#6.*

WORLD OF GIANT COMICS, THE (See Archie All-Star Specials)

WORLD OF JUGHEAD, THE (See Archie Giant Series Mag. #9,14,19,24,30,136,143,149,152,157, 161,166,172,178,183,189,194,202,209,215,227, 233,239,245,251,457,463,469)

WORLD OF MYSTERY
June, 1956 - #7, June, 1957
Atlas Comics (GPI)

#1-Torres, Orlando stys.	2.50	5.00	7.50
2	1.40	2.80	4.20
3-Torres, Davis, Ditko stories,			
4-Davis story	2.50	5.00	7.50
5,7: #5-Orlando story	1.25	2.50	3.75
6-Williamson/Mayo story, 4pgs.; Ditko story			
	3.50	7.00	10.50

WORLD OF SUSPENSE
April, 1956 - #8, July, 1957
Atlas News Co.

#1-Orlando art	2.50	5.00	7.50
2,4-6,8	1.25	2.50	3.75
3,7-Williamson story in both, 4pgs. each;			
#7-with Mayo	3.00	6.00	9.00

NOTE: *Ditko story-#2. Everett story-#5; cover-#2,6. Orlando story-#5. Powell story-#6.*

WORLD OF WHEELS (Formerly Dragstrip Hotrodders)
Oct, 1967 - #32, June, 1970
Charlton Comics

#17-32-Features Ken King	.15	.30

WORLD'S BEST (-- Finest #2 on)
Spring, 1941
National Periodical Publications

#1-The Batman, Superman, Crimson Avenger, Johnny Thunder, The King, Young Dr. Davis, Zatara, Lando, Man of Magic, & Red, White & Blue begin (inside covers blank)			
	150.00	375.00	600.00

WORLDS BEYOND (Worlds of Fear #2 on)
Nov, 1951
Fawcett Publications

	Good	Fine	Mint
#1-Powell art	2.00	4.00	6.00

WORLD'S FAIR COMICS (See N. Y. --)

WORLD'S FINEST COMICS (World's Best #1)
#2, Summer/1941 - Present (early issues-100pgs)
Nat. Per. Publ./DC (#1-17 cardboard covers)

#2	80.00	200.00	320.00
3-The Sandman begins; last Johnny Thunder; origin & 1st app. The Scarecrow			
	70.00	175.00	280.00
4-Hop Harrigan app.; last Young Dr. Davis			
	40.00	100.00	160.00
5-Intro. & only app. TNT & Dan the Dyna-Mite; last King & Crimson Avenger			
	40.00	100.00	160.00
6-Star Spangled Kid begins; Aquaman app.; S&K Sandman with Sandy in new costume begins, ends #7	30.00	75.00	120.00
7-Green Arrow begins; last Lando, King & Red, White & Blue; S&K art			
	30.00	75.00	120.00
8-Boy Commandos begin; last Red, White & Blue	25.00	62.50	100.00
9-Batman cameo in Star Spangled Kid;S&K art,			
10-S&K art	24.00	60.00	96.00
11-17-Last cardboard cover issue			
	20.00	50.00	80.00
18-20: #18-Paper covers begin; last Star Spangled Kid	20.00	40.00	60.00
21-30: #30-Johnny Peril app.			
	15.00	30.00	45.00
31-40: #33-35-Tomahawk app.			
	10.00	20.00	30.00
41-50: #41-Boy Commandos end. #42-Wyoming Kid begins, ends #63. #43-Full Steam Foley begins, ends #48. #49-Tom Sparks, Boy Inventor begins	8.00	16.00	24.00
51-60: #51-Zatara ends. #59-Manhunters Around the World begins, ends #62			
	7.00	14.00	21.00
61-70: #62(?)-Last ish. with square binding. #63-Capt. Compas app. #65-Tomahawk begins, ends #101	5.00	10.00	15.00
71-(Scarce)-Batman & Superman begin as a team			
	10.00	20.00	30.00
72-80	4.00	8.00	12.00
81-90: #88-1st Joker/Luthor team-up. #90-Batwoman's 1st app. in World's Finest			
	3.00	6.00	9.00
91-100: #94-Origin Superman/Batman team. #96-99-Kirby Green Arrow	2.50	5.00	7.50
101-120: #102-Tommy Tomorrow begins, ends#124.			

World Of Mystery #6, © MCG

World Of Suspense #6, © MCG

World's Finest Comics #4, © DC

465

World's Finest Comics #94, © DC   Worlds Of Fear #9, © FAW   World War III #1, © ACE

(World's Finest cont'd)   Good   Fine   Mint
#105-2pgs. Kubert. #113-Intro. Miss Arrow-
ette in Green Arrow; 1st Batmite/Mxyzptlk
team-up   1.75   3.50   5.25
121-150: #125-Aquaman begins, ends #139. #140-
last Green Arrow. #143-1st Mailbag. #148-
Congorilla reprint   1.20   2.40   3.60
151-174: #154-1st Supersons story. #161-25¢
Giant G-28. #170-25¢ Giant G-40
                                  .80   1.60   2.40
(80pg. Giant G-28,G-40)1.20   2.40   3.60
175,176-Adams stories   1.25   2.50   3.75
177-200: #179-25¢ Giant G-52. #182-Silent
Knight reprint/Brave & the Bold #6. #186-
Johnny Quick reprint. #188-25¢ Giant G-64.
#190-193-Robin reprints. #197-25¢ Giant
G-76; Green Arrow app.   .40   .80   1.20
(80pg. Giant G-52-G-76) .60   1.20   1.80
201-Dr. Fate, Green Arrow app.
                            .30   .60   .90
202-204,206,207: #206-25¢ Giant G-88. #204,
204,207-212, 52pgs.   .30   .60   .90
(80pg. Giant G-88)   .50   1.00   1.50
205-6pgs. Shining Knight by Frazetta/Adv.#153
& Tarantula reprints   .60   1.20   1.80
208-Dr. Fate app.; Robotman & Ghost Patrol
reprints   .30   .60   .90
209-Batman, Hawkman reprts. .30   .60   .90
210-214: #210-Green Arrow app.; Black Pirate
reprint. #211-Atom app.; G.A. Green Lantern reprt. #212-Jonn' Jonzz' app.; G.A.
Air Wave & Grim Ghost reprint. #213-Robin
app. #214-Vigilante app.; Two Face begins
                            .30   .60   .90
215-Intro. Batman Jr. & Superman Jr.
                            .30   .60   .90
216-222: #217-Metamorpho begins; Batman/Super-
man team-up begins   .25   .50   .75
223,226-Adams stories reprints; 100pgs.; #226-
S&K & Toth reprints   .60   1.20   1.80
224,225,227-(100pgs.)   .35   .70   1.05
228-Toth story; 100pgs. .35   .70   1.05
229,231-243   .15   .30   .45
230-Adams story reprint .20   .40   .60
244-248: #244-$1.00 size begins
                            .50   1.00   1.50
249-The Creeper begins by Ditko
                            .50   1.00   1.50
250-The Creeper origin retold by Ditko
                            .50   1.00   1.50
251-254   .50   1.00   1.50
NOTE: Adams covers-#174-176,178-180,182,183,
185,186,198-205,208-211,223,226(reprints),
244-246. Anderson stories-#121,122,204,245-
247. Aparo covers-#253,254. Burnley cover-#7.
Infantino story-#225. Kubert Zatara-#40-44.
Morrow stories-#245-248. Newton stories-#253,

254. Orlando story-#224. Robinson Batman-
#14,15; covers-# 3,6. (See 80 Pg. Giant #15)

WORLD'S GREATEST ATHLETE (See Walt Disney
Showcase #14)

WORLD'S GREATEST SONGS
Sept, 1954
Atlas Comics (Male)
                            Good   Fine   Mint
#1-Heath & Harry Anderson art
                            2.50   5.00   7.50

WORLD'S GREATEST STORIES
Jan, 1949 - #2, May, 1949
Jubilee Publications

#1-Alice in Wonderland   4.00   8.00   12.00
2-Pinocchio   3.00   6.00   9.00

WORLDS OF FEAR (World Beyond #1)
V1#2, 1952 - V2#10, June, 1953
Fawcett Publications

V1#2-6(9/52): #3-Evans art. #2,4,5-Powell
art   1.50   3.00   4.50
V2#7-10: #10-Painted cvr. 1.00   2.00   3.00

WORLDS UNKNOWN
May, 1973 - #8, Aug, 1974
Marvel Comics Group

#1-Reprint from Astonishing #54; Torres art
                            .15   .30   .45
2-8   .15   .30
NOTE: Adkins/Mooney art-#5. Kane art-#1,2;
covers-#5,6,8. Sutton art-#2.

WORLD WAR STORIES
Apr-June, 1965 - #3, Dec, 1965
Dell Publishing Co.

#1   .40   .80   1.20
2,3: #1-3-Glanzman art   .30   .60   .90

WORLD WAR II (See Classics Special Ed.)

WORLD WAR III
Mar, 1952 - #2, 1952
Ace Periodicals

#1,2   5.00   10.00   15.00

WORST FROM MAD, THE (Annual)
1958 - #12, 1969 (Each annual cover is reprinted from the cover of the Mad issues
being reprinted)
E.C. Comics

466

(Worst From Mad cont'd)

	Good	Fine	Mint
No#(1958)-Bonus-Record labels & travel stickers; 1st Mad annual; reprints from Mad #29-34	6.00	12.00	18.00
#2(1959)-Bonus is small 33-1/3 rpm record entitled "Meet the Staff of Mad"; reprts./ Mad #35-40	6.00	12.00	18.00
3(1960)-20"x30" campaign poster "Alfred E. Neuman for President;" reprint/Mad #41-46	4.00	8.00	12.00
4(1961)-Sunday comics section; reprints/ Mad #47-54	5.00	10.00	15.00
5(1962)-Small 33-1/3 rpm record; reprints/ Mad #55-62	5.00	10.00	15.00
6(1963)-Small 33-1/3 rpm record; reprints/ Mad #63-70	5.00	10.00	15.00
7(1964)-Mad protest signs; reprints/Mad #71-76	2.50	5.00	7.50
8(1965)-Build a Mad Zeppelin	3.00	6.00	9.00
9(1966)-33-1/3 rpm record	3.50	7.00	10.50
10(1967)-Mad bumper sticker	2.50	5.00	7.50
11(1968)-Mad cover window stickers	2.50	5.00	7.50
12(1969)-Mad picture postcards	2.00	4.00	6.00

NOTE: *Covers: Bob Clarke-#8. Mingo-#7,9-12.*

WOTALIFE COMICS
#3, 8-9/46 - #12, July, 1947; 1959
Fox Features Syndicate/Norlen Mag.

#3-12-Cosmo Cat	.80	1.60	2.40
#1(1959-Norlen)-Atomic Rabbit, Atomic Mouse	.50	1.00	1.50

WOTALIFE COMICS
1957 - #5, 1957
Green Publications

#1-5	.30	.60	.90

WOW COMICS
May, 1936 - #4, Nov. 1936
David McKay Publications/Henle Publ.

#1-Fu Manchu, Eisner story	50.00	100.00	150.00
2-Ken Maynard, Fu Manchu, Popeye; Eisner art	35.00	70.00	105.00
3-Eisner cover; Popeye, Fu Manchu	35.00	70.00	105.00
4-Flash Gordon, Mandrake, Popeye; Eisner art	50.00	100.00	150.00

WOW COMICS (Real Western Hero #70 on)
Spring, 1941 - #69, Fall, 1948
Fawcett Publications

	Good	Fine	Mint
No#(#1)-Origin Mr. Scarlet by S&K; Atom Blake, Boy Wizard begins; Diamond Jack, The White Rajah, Shipwreck Roberts, Jim Dolan, & Rick O'Shay only app.; the cover of this comic was printed on unstable paper stock and is rarely found in fine or mint condition. (Rare)	800.00	1900.00	3000.00

(Prices vary widely on this book)

2-The Hunchback begins	60.00	120.00	180.00
3	30.00	60.00	90.00
4-Origin Pinky	40.00	80.00	120.00
5	30.00	60.00	90.00
6-Origin The Phantom Eagle; Commando Yank begins	20.00	40.00	60.00
7,8	20.00	40.00	60.00
9-Capt. Marvel, Capt. Marvel Jr., Shazam app.; Scarlet & Pinky x-over	25.00	50.00	75.00
10-Mary Marvel begins	17.50	35.00	52.50
11-17,19,20	10.00	20.00	30.00
18-1st app. Uncle Marvel(10/43)	10.00	20.00	30.00
21-30: #28-Pinky x-over in Mary Marvel	6.00	12.00	18.00
31-40	4.00	8.00	12.00
41-50	3.00	6.00	9.00
51-60	2.50	5.00	7.50
61-69	2.00	4.00	6.00

WRECK OF GROSVENOR (See Superior Stories #3)

WRINGLE WRANGLE (See 4-Color Comics #821)

WULF, THE BARBARIAN
Feb, 1975 - #4, Sept, 1975
Atlas/Seaboard Publ.

#1-Origin	.40	.80	1.20
2-Intro. Berithe the Swordswoman; Adams, Wood, Reese art	.30	.60	.90
3,4	.25	.50	.75

WYATT EARP (See Hugh O'Brian Famous Marshal--)

WYATT EARP
11/55 - #29, 6/60; #30, 10/72 - #34, 6/73
Atlas Comics/Marvel #23 on(IPC)

#1	2.00	4.00	6.00
2-Williamson story, 4pgs.	3.00	6.00	9.00
3-6,8-11	1.00	2.00	3.00
7,12-Williamson stories, 4pgs. ea.; #12 with Mayo	3.00	6.00	9.00
13-20	.80	1.60	2.40

Wow Comics #3, © DMP

Wow Comics #3, © FAW

Wow Comics #18, © FAW

X-Men #3, © MCG

X-Men #16, © MCG

X-Venture #2, © Victory Mag.

	Good	Fine	Mint
(Wyatt Earp cont'd)			
21-Davis cover	1.00	2.00	3.00
22-24,26-29: #22-Ringo Kid app. #23-Kid From			
Texas app.	.80	1.60	2.40
25-Davis story	1.50	3.00	4.50
30-Williamson reprt.('72)	.20	.40	.60
31,33,34-Reprints		.15	.35
32-Torres story reprint		.20	.40

NOTE: *Kirby* cover-#25. *Maurer* story-#4.
Wildey stories-#24,28.

WYATT EARP FRONTIER MARSHAL (See Blue Bird)
#12, Jan, 1956 - #72, Dec, 1967
Charlton Comics

	Good	Fine	Mint
#12-19	.40	.80	1.20
20-Four Williamson stories-8,5,5, & 7 pgs.;			
68pg. issue	4.50	9.00	13.50
21-30	.25	.50	.75
31-72	.15	.30	.45

X-MAS COMICS
1941 - #2, 1942 (324 pgs.) (50¢)
#3, 1943 - #7, 1947 (132 pgs.)
Fawcett Publications

	Good	Fine	Mint
#1-Reprints Whiz #21, Capt. Marvel #3, Bullet-man #2, Wow #3, & Master #18; Raboy back			
cover	100.00	250.00	400.00
2-Captain Marvel, Bulletman, Spy Smasher			
reprints	50.00	125.00	200.00
3-7-Funny animals	5.00	10.00	15.00

X-MAS COMICS
1949 - 1952 (196 pgs.)
Fawcett Publications

	Good	Fine	Mint
#4-7-Reprints from Whiz, Master, Tom Mix, &			
Captain Marvel	12.00	24.00	36.00

X-MEN, THE
Sept, 1963 - Present
Marvel Comics Group

	Good	Fine	Mint
#1-Origin X-Men; 1st app. Magneto			
	25.00	50.00	75.00
2-1st app. The Vanisher	12.00	24.00	36.00
3-1st app. The Blob	8.00	16.00	24.00
4,5: #4-1st Quick Silver & Scarlet Witch &			
Brotherhood of the Evil Mutants			
	5.00	10.00	15.00
6-9: #8-1st Unus the Untouchable. #9-Aveng-ers app.	3.00	6.00	9.00
10-1st Silver-Age app. Ka-Zar			
	3.00	6.00	9.00
11,13-20: #11-1st app. The Stranger. #19-1st app. The Mimic	1.50	3.00	4.50
12-Origin Prof. X	1.50	3.00	4.50

	Good	Fine	Mint
21-30: #28-1st app. The Banshee			
	1.00	2.00	3.00
31-37	.75	1.50	2.25
38-Origin The X-Men feature begins, ends #57			
	.75	1.50	2.25
39,40: #39-New costumes	.75	1.50	2.25
41-48: #42-Death of Prof. X (Changeling dis-guised as). #44-Red Raven app.(G.A.)			
	.60	1.20	1.80
49-Steranko cover	.60	1.20	1.80
50,51-Steranko cover/stys.	1.00	2.00	3.00
52	.50	1.00	1.50
53-Smith cover/story; 1st Smith comic book			
work	2.00	4.00	6.00
54,55-Smith cover	1.00	2.00	3.00
56-63,65-Adams art. #65-Return of Prof. X			
	1.40	2.80	4.20
64-1st Sunfire app.	.40	.80	1.20
66	.40	.80	1.20
67-93: #67-All reprints. #72-52pgs.			
	.30	.60	.90
94-New X-Men begin	1.25	2.50	3.75
94-100: #95-Death Thunderbird			
	.50	1.00	1.50
101-Intro. Phoenix	.35	.70	1.05
102-105	.20	.40	.60
106-Intro. Star Jammer	.20	.40	.60
107-118	.15	.30	.45
Giant-Size #1(Sum.'75,60¢)-1st app. new X-Men			
	1.50	3.00	4.50
Giant-Size #2(11/75)-51pgs. Adams art reprint			
	.60	1.20	1.80
Special #1(12/70)-Kirby cover/art; origin			
The Stranger	.75	1.50	2.25
Special #2(11/71)	.60	1.20	1.80

NOTE: *Adams* covers-#56-63,65. *Byrne* stories-
#108,109,111-date. *Everett* cover-#73(w/Kane).
Kirby stories-#1-17(#12-17-layouts); covers-
#1-22,25,26,30,31,35. *Toth* story-#12. *Wood*
inks-#14.

X, THE MAN WITH THE X-RAY EYES
(See Movie Comics)

X-VENTURE
July, 1947 - #2, Nov, 1947 (Super heroes)
Victory Magazines Corp.

	Good	Fine	Mint
#1,2-Atom Wizard, Mystery Shadow, Lester			
Trumble	4.00	8.00	12.00

YAK YAK (See 4-Color Comics #1186,1348)

YAKKY DOODLE & CHOPPER
Dec, 1962 (Hanna-Barbera)
Gold Key

	Good	Fine	Mint
#1		.15	.35

YANG (See House of Yang)
Nov, 1973 - #13, May, 1976
Charlton Comics

	Good	Fine	Mint
#1-Origin	.25	.50	.75
2-5	.20	.40	.60
6-13		.15	.35
3,10,11(Modern Comics reprint, 1977)		.15	.30

YANKEE COMICS (#5,6-Small size)
Sept, 1941 - #6, June, 1942; #7, no date
Harry 'A' Chesler/William H. Wise #7

#1-Origin The Echo, The Enchanted Dagger, Yankee Doodle Jones, The Firebrand, & The Scarlet Sentry; Black Satan app.	20.00	40.00	60.00
2-Origin Johnny Rebel; Major Victory app.; Barry Kuda begins	15.00	30.00	45.00
3	12.00	24.00	36.00
4	10.00	20.00	30.00
5,6(Small size)	4.00	8.00	12.00
7(Wm. H. Wise),Small size)no date; distr. thru Army PX's only	4.00	8.00	12.00

YANKS IN BATTLE
Sept, 1956 - #4, Dec, 1956
Quality Comics Group

#1	1.50	3.00	4.50
2-4	1.00	2.00	3.00

YANKS IN BATTLE
1963
I.W. Enterprises

Reprint #3	.40	.80	1.20

YARDBIRDS, THE (G.I. Joe's Sidekicks)
Summer, 1952
Ziff-Davis Publ. Co.

#1-By Bob Oskner	1.50	3.00	4.50

YARNS OF YELLOWSTONE
1972 (36 pgs.) (50¢)
World Color Press

Ill. by Bill Chapman	.30	.60	.90

YELLOW CLAW
Oct, 1956 - #4, April, 1957
Atlas Comics (MjMC)

#1-Origin by Joe Maneely	10.00	20.00	30.00
2-4-Kirby art in all; #2,4-Severin covers. #3-Everett cover. #4-Kirby/Severin art	10.00	20.00	30.00

YELLOWJACKET (Jack in the Box #11 on)
Sept, 1944 - #10, June, 1946
E. Levy/Frank Comunale

	Good	Fine	Mint
#1-Origin Yellowjacket; Diana, the Huntress begins	8.00	16.00	24.00
2-5	6.00	12.00	18.00
6-10	4.00	8.00	12.00

YELLOWSTONE KELLY (See 4-Color Comics #1056)

YELLOW SUBMARINE (See Movie Comics)

YOGI BEAR (TV) (Hanna-Barbera)
Dec-Feb, 1959-60 - #42, Oct, 1970
Dell Publ. Co./Gold Key #10 on

4-Color #1067,1104,1162	.50	1.00	1.50
#4(8-9/61)-#9(7-9/62)-Dell	.20	.40	.60
#10(10/62-G.K.),#11-titled "Y.B. Jellystone Jollies"-80pgs.	.25	.50	.75
12	.20	.40	.60
13(Surprise Party, 68pgs.)(7/63)	.25	.25	.75
14-42	.20	.40	.60
4-Color #1271,1349	.35	.70	1.05
--Kite Fun Book('62,8pgs.)Soft cover; Pacific Gas & Electric giveaway; No#	2.00	4.00	6.00

YOGI BEAR (See Dell Giant #41, March of Comics #253,265,279,291,309,319,337,344, Whitman Comic Books & Movie Comics under "Hey There It's --")

YOGI BEAR
Nov, 1970 - #35, Jan, 1976 (Hanna-Barbera)
Charlton Comics

#1	.25	.50	.75
2-6,8-35		.15	.35
7-Summer Fun(Giant)52pgs.	.15	.30	.45

YOGI BEAR (TV)
Nov, 1977 - #8, Jan, 1979
Marvel Comics Group

#1		.20	.35
2-8		.10	.20

YOGI BEAR'S EASTER PARADE (See The Funtastic World of Hanna-Barbera #2)

YOGI BERRA (Baseball hero)
1951 (Yankee catcher)
Fawcett Publications

No#	5.00	10.00	15.00

Yankee Comics #1. © CHES

Yellow Claw #1. © MCG

Yellowjacket #4. © F. Communale

Young Allies #4, © MCG

Young Brides #3, © PRIZE

Young Love #2, © PRIZE

YOSEMITE SAM (-- and Bugs Bunny)
Dec, 1970 - Present
Gold Key

	Good	Fine	Mint
#1	.15	.30	.45
2-10		.20	.35
11-58		.15	.25

(See March of Comics #363,380,392)

YOUNG ALLIES COMICS (All-Winners #21)
Summer, 1941 - #20, Oct, 1946
Timely Comics (Young Allies, Inc.)

#1-Origin The Young Allies; 1st meeting of
Captain America & Human Torch; Red Skull
app.; S&K cover & splash page
           150.00 300.00 450.00
2-Captain America & Human Torch app.; Simon
& Kirby cover   70.00 140.00 210.00
3-Fathertime, Captain America & Human Torch
app.   50.00 100.00 150.00
4-The Vagabond & Red Skull, Capt. America,
Human Torch app.   40.00 80.00 120.00
5-Capt. America & Human Torch app.
           35.00 70.00 105.00
6-10: #7-Origin Tommy Tyme & Clock of Ages;
ends #19   20.00 40.00 60.00
11-20   15.00 30.00 45.00

YOUNG BRIDES
Sept-Oct, 1952 - #32?, 1956
Feature/Prize Publications

V1#1-Simon & Kirby art	3.50	7.00	10.50
2-4-S&K art	2.50	5.00	7.50
V2#1,3-6-S&K art	2.00	4.00	6.00
2,7-9-No S&K	.70	1.40	2.10
15-25,27,29-32	.60	1.20	1.80
26-All S&K ish.	2.00	4.00	6.00
28-S&K story	1.00	2.00	3.00

YOUNG DR. MASTERS (See Advs. of Young Dr.
Masters)

YOUNG DOCTORS, THE
January, 1963 - #6, 1963
Charlton Comics

V1#1-6	.15	.30	.45

YOUNG EAGLE
Dec, 1950 - #10, June, 1952; 1957
Fawcett Publications/Charlton

#1	3.00	6.00	9.00
2-9	1.75	3.50	5.25
10-Origin Thunder, Young Eagle's horse			
	1.75	3.50	5.25
4(1/57), 5(4/57)(CC)	.80	1.60	2.40

YOUNG HEARTS
Nov, 1949 - #2, Feb, 1950
Marvel Comics (SPC)

	Good	Fine	Mint
#1	1.25	2.50	3.75
2	1.00	2.00	3.00

YOUNG HEARTS IN LOVE
1964
Super Comics

#17-Reprints Young Love V5#6, 4-5/62
          .15 .30 .45

YOUNG HEROES
#35, Feb-Mar, 1955 - #37, June-July, 1955
American Comics Group (Titan)

#35-37-Frontier Scout 1.25 2.50 3.75

YOUNG KING COLE (Becomes Criminals on the Run)
Fall, 1945 - V3#6, July, 1948
Premium Group/Novelty Press

V1#1-Toni Gayle begins	2.50	5.00	7.50
2-6	1.50	3.00	4.50
V2#1-6	1.25	2.50	3.75
V3#1-6	1.00	2.00	3.00

NOTE: *Toni Gayle covers-V2#1,3,5, V3#1,6.*

YOUNG LAWYERS, THE (TV)
Jan, 1971 - #2, April, 1971
Dell Publishing Co.

#1,2   .20 .40 .60

YOUNG LIFE (Teen Life #3 on)
Summer, 1945 - #2, Fall, 1945
New Age Publ./Quality Comics Group

#1,2   1.25 2.50 3.75

YOUNG LOVE
Feb-Mar, 1949 - #72, Oct-Nov, 1956; V4#1,
Jun-Jul, 1960 - V6#6, Apr-May, 1963
Prize(Feature) Publ. (Crestwood)

V1#1-S&K cvr., 2 stories	5.00	10.00	15.00
2-Photo covers begin; S&K story			
	3.00	6.00	9.00
3-S&K story	2.50	5.00	7.50
4-6-Minor S&K art	2.00	4.00	6.00
V2#1(#7)-Two S&K stories	2.50	5.00	7.50
2-5-Minor S&K art; Severin/Elder story-#3			
	1.50	3.00	4.50
6,8-S&K covers only	1.75	3.50	5.25
7(#14)-S&K cvr./2 stys.	2.00	4.00	6.00
#16-22-S&K covers/stories	1.75	3.50	5.25

470

(Young Love cont'd)

	Good	Fine	Mint
23-25-Photo covers resume; S&K art in all	1.50	3.00	4.50
26-No S&K	.80	1.60	2.40
27-29,32-35-Minor S&K art	1.00	2.00	3.00
30,31,36-S&K stories in all	1.25	2.50	3.75
37-72(V7#1, 10-11/56)-Most have S&K art	1.00	2.00	3.00
V4#1(6-7/60)-6(4-5/61)	.50	1.00	1.50
V5#1(6-7/61)-6(4-5/62)	.50	1.00	1.50
V6#1(6-7/62)-6(4-5/63)	.50	1.00	1.50

NOTE: _S&K art not in #53,57,58,61,63-65._
V1-3(1957-60) exist?

YOUNG LOVE
#39, 9-10/63 - #120, Winter, 1975-76;
#121, Oct, 1976 - Present
National Per. Publ.(Arleigh Publ. Corp.#49-60)/DC Comics

	Good	Fine	Mint
#39-41,43-63,65-67	.35	.70	1.05
42-Diary of Mary Robin begins, ends #52	.35	.70	1.05
64-Simon & Kirby art	.30	.60	.90
68-Life & Loves of Lisa St. Claire serial begins, ends #78; not in #69	.15	.30	.45
69-(68pgs.)	.15	.30	.45
70-72,74-77,81	.15	.30	.45
73-Toth story	.30	.60	.90
78,79-"20 Miles to Heartbreak" by Toth & Coletta(Chapter 1 & 4, see Secret Hearts #141,142 for Chapter 2 & 3)	.30	.60	.90
80,82-Morrow art	.15	.30	.45
83-120: #107-114-(100pgs.)	.15	.30	.45
121,123-126		.15	.35
122-Toth art	.20	.40	.60

YOUNG LOVER ROMANCES
#4, June, 1952 - #5, Aug, 1952
Toby Press

	Good	Fine	Mint
#4,5	.70	1.40	2.10

YOUNG LOVERS
#16, 1956 - #18, May, 1957
Charlton Comics

	Good	Fine	Mint
#16,17('56)	.60	1.20	1.80
18-Elvis Presley photo cover, text story (biography)	15.00	30.00	45.00

YOUNG MARRIAGE
June, 1950
Fawcett Publications

	Good	Fine	Mint
#1-Powell art	1.50	3.00	4.50

YOUNG MEN (Formerly Cowboy Romances?)
(-- on the Battlefield #12-20(4/53))
#4, 6/50 - #11, 10/51; #12, 12/51 - #28, 6/54
Marvel/Atlas Comics (IPC)

	Good	Fine	Mint
#4	1.40	2.80	4.20
5-11	1.20	2.40	3.60
12-23: #19-Everett story	1.00	2.00	3.00
24-Origin Captain America, Human Torch, & Sub-Mariner which are revived thru #28	15.00	30.00	45.00
25-28	10.00	20.00	30.00

NOTE: _#24,26-Sub-Mariner by Everett._

YOUNG REBELS, THE (TV)
January, 1971
Dell Publishing Co.

	Good	Fine	Mint
#1	.15	.30	.45

YOUNG ROMANCE COMICS (The 1st romance comic)
Sept-Oct, 1947 - V16#4, June-July, 1963
Prize/Headline(Feature Publ.)

	Good	Fine	Mint
V1#1-First romance comic; S&K cover, 2 stories	7.00	14.00	21.00
2-5-S&K covers, 2-3 stories each	3.50	7.00	10.50
6-S&K cover, 2 stories; Robinson/Meskin story	3.50	7.00	10.50
V2#1-6(#7-12)-S&K cover, 2-3 stories each	3.00	6.00	9.00
V3, V4(#13-25)-S&K art in all; all have photo covers	1.75	3.50	5.25
V5, V6(#26,27,33,34)-S&K cover/story each	2.00	4.00	6.00
V5(#28-32)-S&K sty. each	1.75	3.50	5.25
#35-48-S&K art in each	1.50	3.00	4.50
49-51-No S&K art	1.00	2.00	3.00
52-71-S&K art in most	1.25	2.50	3.75
72-77-No S&K	.70	1.40	2.10
78,79-S&K story	1.20	2.40	3.60
80,81,83,84,86-91-Some S&K art each	1.00	2.00	3.00
82,85-All S&K art	1.75	3.50	5.25
V11#2,5, V12#1,3-S&K cover/story each	1.50	3.00	4.50
V11#1,3,4, V12#2,4,5-No S&K art	.60	1.20	1.80
V12#6-S&K story	1.00	2.00	3.00
V13#1-S&K cover/2 stories; Powell art	1.50	3.00	4.50
V13#2 - V16#4	.30	.60	.90

Young Men #5, © MCG

Young Men #26, © MCG

Young Romance Comics #6, © PRIZE

Youthful Romances #2, © Ribage

Zago Jungle Prince #2, © FOX

Zegra Jungle Empress #4, © FOX

YOUNG ROMANCE COMICS
#125, Aug-Sept, 1963 - #208, Nov-Dec, 1975
National Per. Publ.(Arleigh Publ. Corp.#127)

	Good	Fine	Mint
#125-153,155-162(Nat.Per.)	.20	.40	.60
154-Adams cover	.35	.70	1.05
163,164-Toth art	.25	.50	.75
165-196: #170-Michell from Young Love ends, Lily Martin, the Swinger begins			
	.15	.30	.45
197(100pgs.)-#208	.15		.35

YOUR DREAMS (See Strange World of --)

YOUR UNITED STATES
1946
Lloyd Jacquet Studios

Used in Seduction of the Innocent, pg. 309, 310   6.00 12.00 18.00

YOUTHFUL HEARTS (Daring Confessions #4 on)
1952 - #3, 1952
Youthful Magazines

#1-"Monkey on Her Back" swipes E.C. drug story from Shock SuspenStories #12
	5.00	10.00	15.00
2,3	2.00	4.00	6.00

NOTE: *Doug Wildey art in all.*

YOUTHFUL LOVE (Truthful Love #2)
May, 1950
Youthful Magazines

#1   1.25 2.50 3.75

YOUTHFUL ROMANCES (Daring Love #15)
Aug-Sept, 1949 - #18, July, 1953
Pix-Parade/Ribage

#1-(titled Youthful Love-Romances) Walter Johnson cover/story	3.50	7.00	10.50
2-5-W. Johnson covers, 1-2 stories each			
	2.50	5.00	7.50
6,7-Johnson story	1.75	3.50	5.25
8-Wood cover	2.50	5.00	7.50
9-18	1.00	2.00	3.00

ZAGO, JUNGLE PRINCE (My Story #5 on)
Sept, 1948 - #4, March, 1949
Fox Features Syndicate

#1-Blue Beetle app.-partial reprint/Atomic #4 (Toni Luck)	10.00	20.00	30.00
2,3-Kamen stories	7.00	14.00	21.00
4-Baker cover	7.00	14.00	21.00

ZANE GREY'S STORIES OF THE WEST
#27, Sept, 1955 - #39, Sept, 1958
Dell Publishing Co./Gold Key 11/64

	Good	Fine	Mint
4-Color #197('48),222,230,236('49)			
	3.00	6.00	9.00
4-Color #246,255,270,301,314,333,346			
	2.00	4.00	6.00
4-Color #357,372,395,412,433,449,467,484			
	1.75	3.50	5.25
4-Color #511-Kinstler art	2.00	4.00	6.00
4-Color #532,555,583,604,616,632,996('59)			
	1.50	3.00	4.50
#27-39	1.20	2.40	3.60
#1(10131-411)-(11/64-G.K.)-Nevada; reprints 4-Color #996	.75	1.50	2.25

ZANY (Magazine)(Satire)(See Ratfink & Frantic)
Sept, 1958 - #4, May, 1959
Candor Publ. Co.

#1-Bill Everett covers	1.50	3.00	4.50
2-4	.80	1.60	2.40

ZAZA, THE MYSTIC (This Magazine Is Haunted
April, 1956 - #11, Sept, 1956   V2#12 on)
Charlton Comics

#10,11   1.25 2.50 3.75

ZEGRA JUNGLE EMPRESS (My Love Life #6 on)
#2, 10/48 - #5, 4/49   (Formerly Tegra)
Fox Features Syndicate

#2	10.00	20.00	30.00
3-5	9.00	18.00	27.00

ZIGGY PIG AND SILLY SEAL
Fall, 1944 - #6, Fall, 1946
Timely Comics (CmPL)

#1-Vs. the Japs	2.50	5.00	7.50
2-6	1.50	3.00	4.50
IW Reprint #1('58)-Reprints/Krazy Komics			
	.40	.80	1.20
IW Reprint #2,7,8	.40	.80	1.20

ZIP COMICS
Feb, 1940 - #47, Summer, 1944
MLJ Magazines

#1-Origin Kalthar the Giant Man, The Scarlet Avenger & Steel Sterling; Mr. Satan, Nevada Jones & Zambini, the Miracle Man, War Eagle, Captain Valor begins
	80.00	160.00	240.00
2	40.00	80.00	120.00
3	30.00	60.00	90.00

Ziggy Pig #5, © MCG   Zip Comics #1, © MLJ   Zip Comics #12, © MLJ

	Good	Fine	Mint
(Zip Comics cont'd)			
4,5	25.00	50.00	75.00
6-9: #9-Last Kalthar & Mr. Satan			
	20.00	40.00	60.00
10-Inferno, the Flame Breather begins, ends			
#13	20.00	40.00	60.00
11,12: #11-Inferno without costume			
	17.00	34.00	51.00
13-19: #17-Last Scarlet Avenger. #18-Wilbur			
begins	17.00	34.00	51.00
20-Origin Black Jack	22.00	44.00	66.00
21-26: #25-Last Nevada Jones. #26-Black Witch			
begins, last Capt. Valor			
	12.00	24.00	36.00
27-Intro. Web	14.00	28.00	42.00
28-Origin Web	14.00	28.00	42.00
29,30	10.00	20.00	30.00
31-38: #34-1st Applejack app. #35-Last Zamb-			
ini, Black Jack. #38-Last Web issue			
	7.00	14.00	21.00
39-Origin Red Rube	7.00	14.00	21.00
40-47: #45-Wilbur ends	4.00	8.00	12.00

ZIP-JET (Hero)
Feb, 1953 - #2, Apr-May, 1953
St. John Publ. Co.

	Good	Fine	Mint
#1,2-Rocketman reprints/Punch Comics			
	5.00	10.00	15.00

ZIPPY THE CHIMP (CBS TV Presents --)
#50, March, 1957 - #51, Aug, 1957
Pines (Literary Ent.)

	Good	Fine	Mint
#50,51	.50	1.00	1.50

ZODY, THE MOD ROB
July, 1970
Gold Key

	Good	Fine	Mint
#1	.25	.50	.75

ZOO ANIMALS
#8, 1954   (36 pgs.) (15¢)
Star Publications

	Good	Fine	Mint
#8-(B&W for coloring)	.70	1.40	2.10

ZOO FUNNIES
1945 - #15, 1947
Charlton Comics/Children Comics Publ.

	Good	Fine	Mint
#101(#1)-1945	1.25	2.50	3.75
#2(9/45)-#5	.80	1.60	2.40
6-15: #8-Diana the Huntress app.			
	.80	1.60	2.40

ZOO FUNNIES (Nyoka #13 on)
July, 1953 - #12, July, 1955
Capitol Stories/Charlton Comics

	Good	Fine	Mint
#1	1.00	2.00	3.00
2-7	.60	1.20	1.80
8-12-Nyoka app.	2.00	4.00	6.00

ZOO PARADE (See 4-Color Comics #662)

ZOOM COMICS
Dec, 1945   (One Shot)
Carlton Publishing Co.

	Good	Fine	Mint
#1-Dr. Mercy, Satanas, from Red Band Comics;			
Capt. Milksop origin retold			
	2.50	5.00	7.50

ZOOT (Rulah #17 on)
1946 - #16, July, 1948   (Two #13's & #14's)
Fox Features Syndicate

Zip Comics #47, © MLJ   Zip-Jet #1, © STJ   Zoot #9, © FOX

Zoot #10, © FOX

Zoot #16, © FOX

Zorro #9, © DELL

(Zoot cont'd)	Good	Fine	Mint
No#-Funny animal only	2.50	5.00	7.50
#2-The Jaguar app.; funny animal bondage			
cover	6.00	12.00	18.00
3(Fall,'46)-#6-Funny animals & teen-age			
	2.00	4.00	6.00
7-Rulah, Jungle Goddess begins(6/47)-			
origin	18.00	36.00	54.00
8-10	11.00	22.00	33.00
11-Kamen bondage cover	15.00	30.00	45.00
12	10.00	20.00	30.00
13(2/48), 14(3/48)	10.00	20.00	30.00
13(4/48), 14(5/48)	10.00	20.00	30.00
15,16	10.00	20.00	30.00

NOTE: *Kamen covers-#10-12; art-many issues.*

ZORRO (Walt Disney with #882)
May, 1949 - #15, Sept-Nov, 1961
Dell Publishing Co.

	Good	Fine	Mint
4-Color #228	5.00	10.00	15.00
4-Color #425,497	3.50	7.00	10.50
4-Color #538-Kinstler art	4.00	8.00	12.00

	Good	Fine	Mint
4-Color #574,617,732	3.00	6.00	9.00
4-Color #882,920,933,960,976-Toth art in all			
	2.50	5.00	7.50
4-Color #1003,1037('59)	1.75	3.50	5.25
#8(12-2/60)	1.20	2.40	3.60
9,12-Toth story	1.50	3.00	4.50
10,11,13-15	1.00	2.00	3.00

ZORRO (Walt Disney)
Oct, 1965 - #9, March, 1968
Gold Key

	Good	Fine	Mint
#1-Toth art	1.20	2.40	3.60
2,5,7,8-Toth art	.80	1.60	2.40
3,4,6,9	.60	1.20	1.80

NOTE: *#1-9: reprints from Zorro 4-Color comics*

Z-2 COMICS (Secret Agent --) (See Holyoke
One-Shot #7)

ZULU (See Movie Classics)

Baseball Comics No. 1, 1949 © Will Eisner
Complete book by Will Eisner

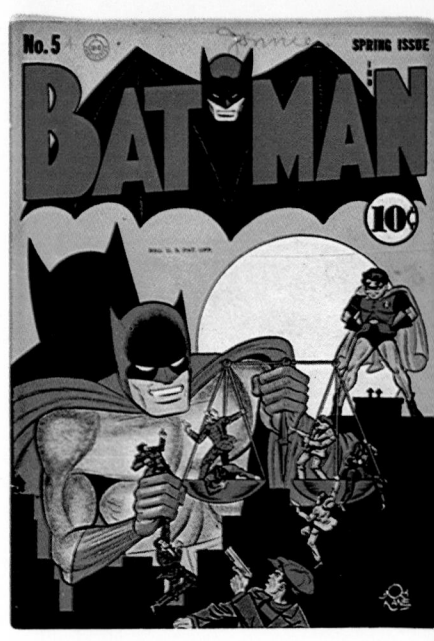

Batman No. 5, 1941 © DC
Bob Kane cover art

Black Cat Mystery No. 36, 1952 © Harv
Used in Seduction Of The Innocent

Blue Bolt Weird Tales No. 119, 1953 © Star
L.B. Cole cover art

Buccaneers No. 21, 1950 © Qua
Crandall cover art

Captain America No. 7, 1941 © MCG
Simon & Kirby cover art

hief Victorio's Apache Massacre, 1951 © Avon
Williamson/Frazetta story

Christmas Parade No. 1, 1949 © WDP
Walt Kelly cover art

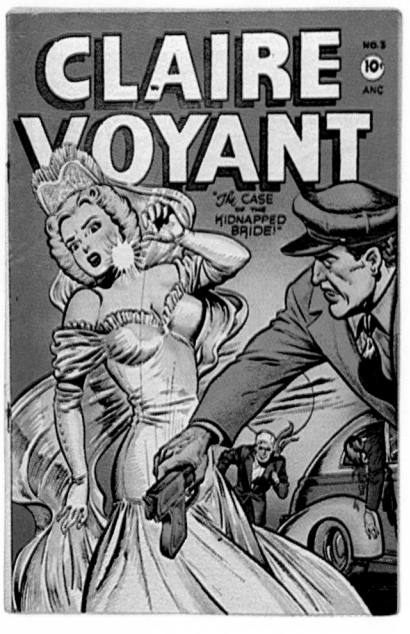

Claire Voyant No. 3, 1947 © Leader Ent.
Jack Kamen cover art

Classics Illustrated No. 40, 1947 © Gil
(Original)

Detective Comics No. 140, 1948 © DC
First appearance The Riddler

Eerie No. 3, 1951 © Avon
Wallace Wood cover art

Famous Funnies A Carnival Of Comics , 1933
© Eas. The second comic book

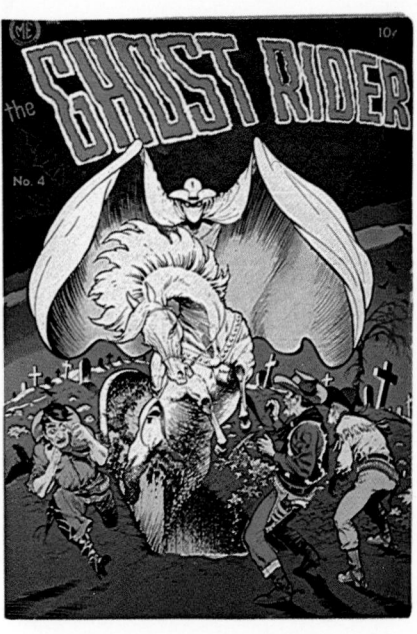

The Ghost Rider No. 4, 1951 © ME
Frank Frazetta cover art

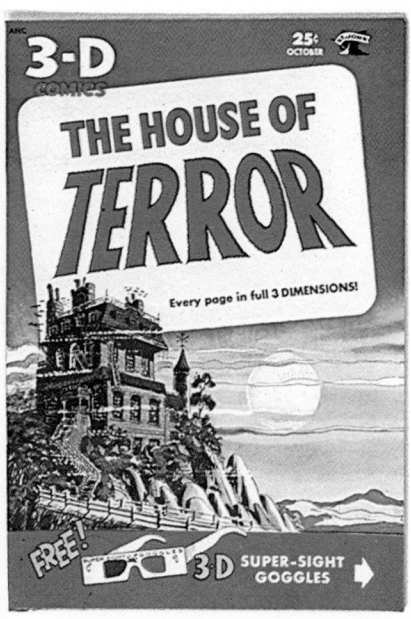

The House Of Terror, 1953 © STJ

If The Devil Would Talk, 1950 © CG

Intimate Confessions No. 3, 1951 © Real
Contains a Kinstler story

Jo-Jo No. 8, 1947 © Fox

Kid Komics No. 1, 1943 © MCG

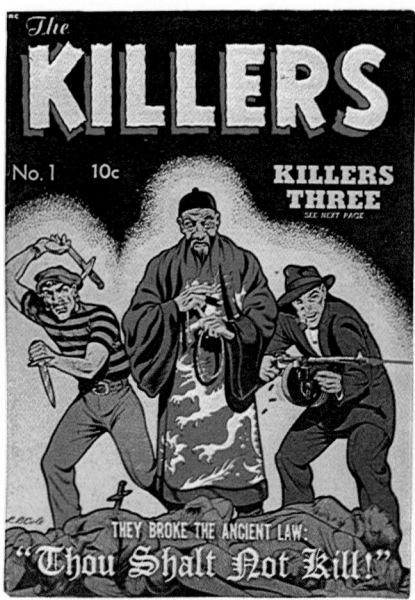

The Killers No. 1, 1947 © ME
Used in Seduction Of The Innocent

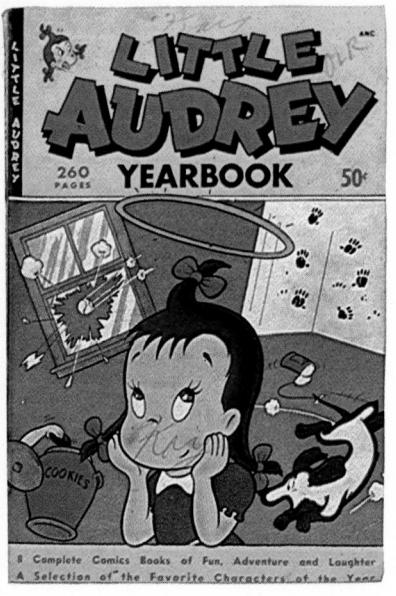

Little Audrey Yearbook, 1950 © STJ

Marvel Mystery Comics No. 4, 1940 © MCG

Motion Picture Comics No. 110, 1952 © Faw

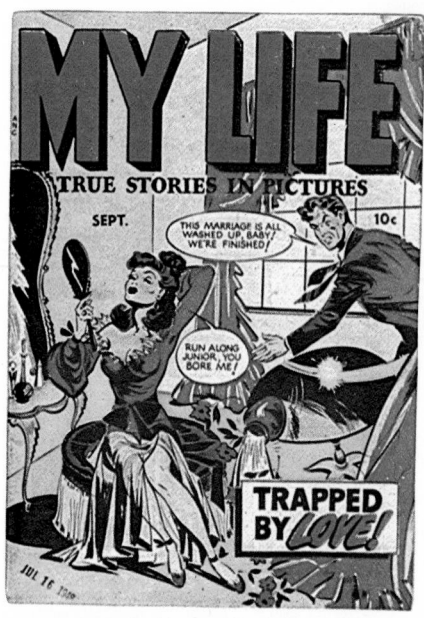

My Life No. 4, 1948 © Fox
Used in Seduction Of The Innocent

Mystery In Space No. 2, 1951 © DC

Negro Romance No. 1, 1950 © Faw

Out Of This World No. 1, 1950 © Avon
Contains a Kubert story

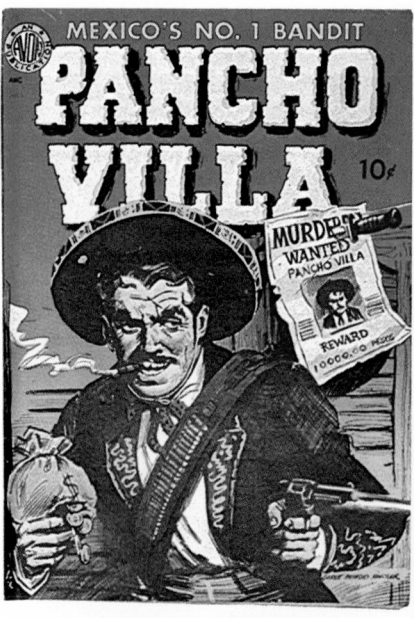

Pancho Villa, 1950 © Avon
Kinstler cover art

Pep Comics No. 17, 1941 © MLJ
Origin The Hangman, Death of
The Comet

Planet Comics No. 54, 1948 © FH
Contains a Matt Baker story

Police Comics No. 11, 1942 © Qua
Contains the origin of The Spirit by
Will Eisner and Jack Cole's Plastic
Man

Popular Teen-Agers No. 11, 1952 © Star
L.B. Cole cover art

Racket Squad In Action No. 12, 1954 © CC
Steve Ditko Explosion cover

Real Screen Funnies No. 1, 1945 © DC

Robotmen Of The Lost Planet No. 1, 1952
© Avon

Seven Seas Comics No. 4, 1947 © Leader Ent.
Matt Baker cover art

Showcase No. 4, 1956 © DC

Spirit Section dated August 3, 1952 © Will Eisner
Seven pages by Wallace Wood

Strange Fantasy No. 9, 1953 © Ajax

The Strange World Of Your Dreams No. 3, 1952
Simon & Kirby cover/stories © Prize

Strange Worlds No. 4, 1951 © Avon
Wood/Orlando cover; Wood story

Superman No. 53, 1948 © DC
Origin retold

Terrors Of The Jungle No. 18, 1952 © Star
L.B. Cole cover art

Uncle Milty No. 1, 1950 © Victoria Publ.

The Underworld Story, 1950   © Avon

Wacky Duck No. 4, 1946   © MCG
Infinity cover

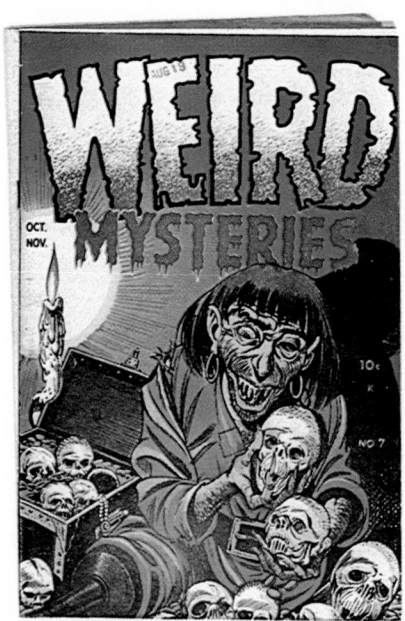

Weird Mysteries No. 7, 1953   © Gilmor Mag.
Used in Seduction Of The Innocent

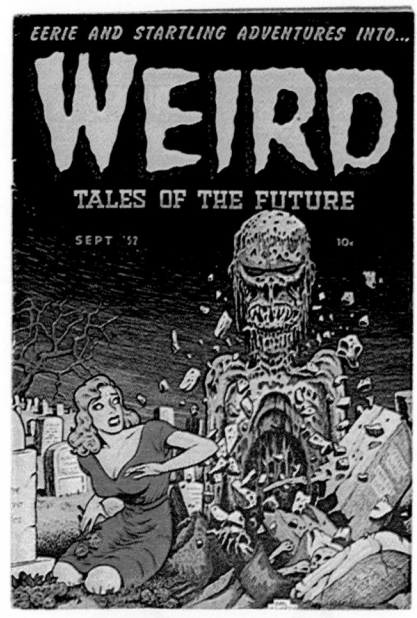

Weird Tales Of The Future No. 3, 1952
© SPM Publ. Wolverton cover/stories

A Book Sail Comic

THE GRAPHIC STORY OF KIDS RUNNING WILD IN THE VIOLENCE-RIDDEN COMIC STORES OF TODAY!

10¢

REFORM SCHOOL COMICS!

WARD

THEY SUCCUMBED TO TEMPTATION!

This is the story of youth gone wrong . . . and of the penalty hundreds of comic collectors have to pay when they allow themselves to fall victim to unscrupulous dealers, their own wayward emotions, and the other hidden pitfalls of a comic-crazed fandom!

The Book Sail, 1186 N. Tustin St., Orange, Ca. 92667. (714) 997-9511
Specialist in 1950's Comics, Good Girl Art, Esoteric, Disney, E.C.'s, B.L.B., Quality Pulp Magazines, D.C. and Marvel.

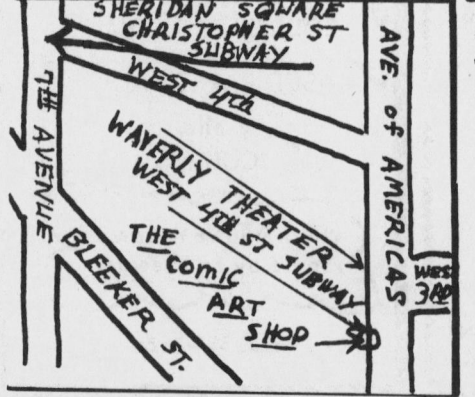

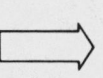

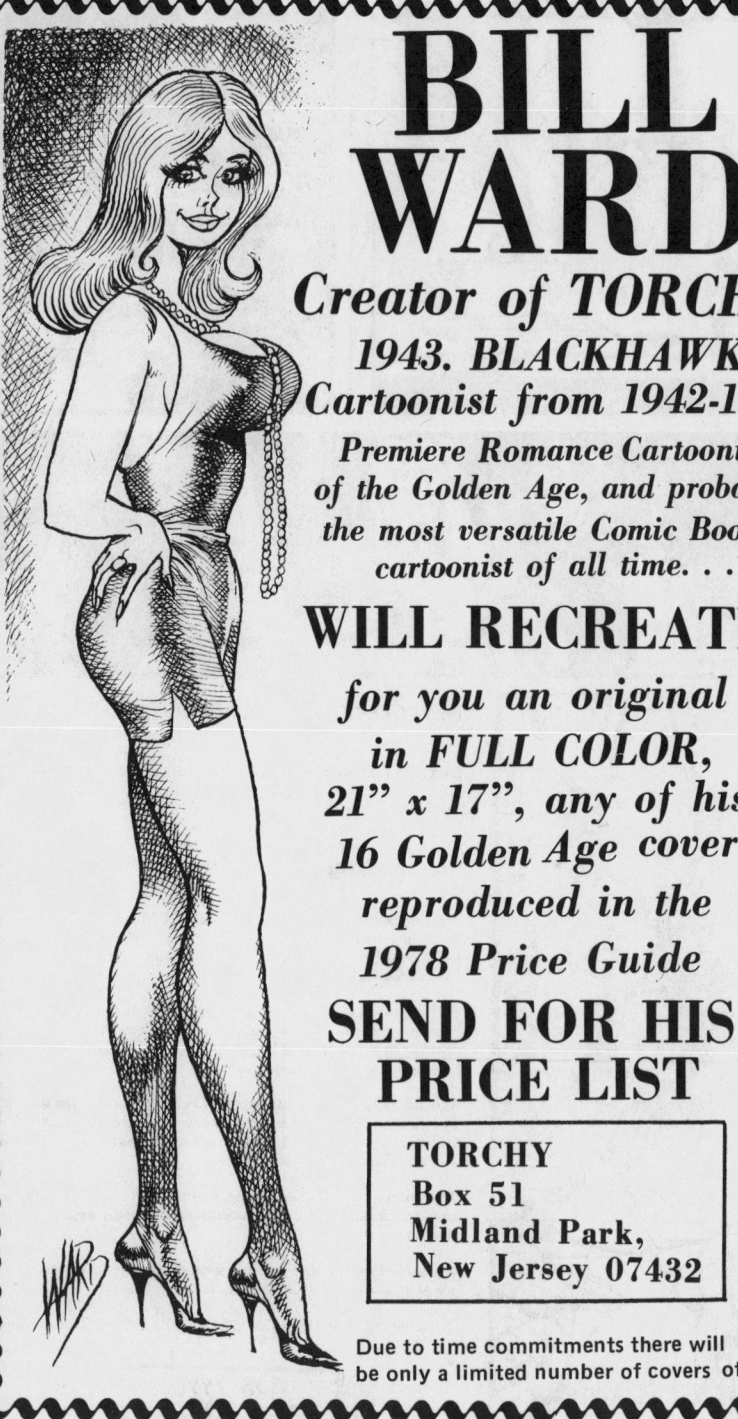

THE Fantasy Mail Co. INC.

NEW COMIC BOOK AND MAGAZINE SERVICE

Dear Comic Book Reader, Collector, Investor, and Dealer,

Do you love—*the thrill of the unknown?*
challenging hopeless odds?
stories that tickle your fancy?
never missing an issue of your favorite
comic book character?

Then join our band of intrepid adventurers at the Fantasy Mail Company, month after month, as they bring all your heart's desires from MARVEL, DC, WARREN, and GOLD KEY, right to your front door, issue after consecutive issue.

Each month you'll receive our latest ordering list with all the new comic book and magazine releases, as well as many high quality fanzines, selective paperbacks, hard bound books, art portfolios, calenders (in season), gum cards, and posters.

As usual, all items are sold at discount (10 to 30%, depending on volume). Orders are sent via UPS or the Post Office, in specially designed, heavy-duty corrugated boxes. Order as many or as few of each title as you like. There is no minimum order.

Why not try us today! Send a long (business) self-addressed, stamped envelope for our current list. Canadian and Overseas inquiries are most welcome.

We look forward to your joining our band and sharing adventures non-stop, issue after issue, after issue!

Please mention THE 1979 COMIC BOOK PRICE GUIDE when writing!

BOX 7476
ROCHESTER, N.Y.
14615

FEATURES

YOJIMBO -- Akira Kurosawa directs and Toshiro Mifune stars in this tongue-in-cheek Japanese answer to the American Western. Mifune portrays a wandering samurai pitted against two merchant families who are battling for control of a country town. 110 minutes................$210

SHAME -- Directed by Ingmar Bergman, with Liv Ullmann and Max von Sydow. SHAME describes personal disintegration in direct relationship to society. Perhaps Bergman's most unrelenting work. 102 minutes...$235

PERSONA -- Hailed by many as Bergman's most intense and complete film, PERSONA stars Liv Ullmann as an actress who suffers a nervous breakdown and is sent to a nurse to recuperate. 81 minutes..$235

IKIRU -- Takashi Shimura plays a lower-echelon bureaucrat who finds that he is about to die in this brilliant film by the renowned Japanese director, Akira Kurosawa. Shimura's quest toward making his last days more meaningful is sensitively and painfully shown. 140 minutes................$260

THE T.A.M.I. SHOW -- This mid-sixties rock and roll spectacular pounds home the sound of contemporary music in the days of the second British invasion. Featuring Billy J. Kramer, Gerry and the Pacemakers, Mick Jagger and the Rolling Stones, Jan and Dean, Chuck Berry, The Supremes, James Brown and more top flight acts. 110 minutes of rocking, bopping excitement...................$179

CUL-DE-SAC -- Donald Pleasance and Jackie Bisset star in this macabre comedy directed by Roman Polanski with demonic elegance. The tale concerns two wounded gangsters who terrorize a middle aged milque-toast and his beautiful young wife. Polanski at his finest! 110 minutes..............$189

BATTLE OF SAN PIETRO -- Directed by John Huston (1944). The meaning of war, not only to the men engaged in combat, but to the civilian population of the ground being fought over is examined. The impact of combat photography is reinforced by unemotional but highly expressive commentary spoken by Huston himself. 30 minutes..$65

THE THIRD MAN -- Orson Welles is Harry Lime, a shadowy and mysterious figure pursued by Joseph Cotten, in the undisputed screen classic. A strong cast and first rate musical score. 104 minutes...$179

PRELUDE TO WAR -- The rise of Fascism in Germany and Italy is powerfully shown in this entry in Frank Capra's "Why We Fight" series produced during World War II. 53 minutes......................$99

THE NAZIS STRIKE -- Another of the highly acclaimed "Why We Fight" series, produced and directed by Frank Capra. Here, Capra shows the rape of Austria and the fall of Poland. 42 minutes.......$95

STAGECOACH TO DENVER -- Allan "Rocky" Lane as Red Ryder. Featuring Bobby Blake. 56 minutes.......$95

EYES OF TEXAS -- A solid Roy Rogers entry from Republic. 75 minutes...........................$125

REPULSION -- Polanski is at his best in this horrifying story about a beautiful woman (Catherine Deneuve) torn apart by her sexual feelings toward men. Her macabre descent into insanity makes for one of the most realistic terror tales ever put on the screen. A must see! 105 minutes..............$235

PUBLIC COWBOY #1 -- Gene Autry and Smiley Burnette tangle with modern day rustlers. 54 minutes.....$95

HOUR OF THE WOLF -- This celebrated Bergman film deals explicitly with madness and demonism, as Alma (Liv Ullmann) reconstructs her life with her husband, an artist who has been driven mad by nightmarish visions. 88 minutes...$235

BELLS OF SAN ANGELO -- Roy Rogers and Andy Devine swing into action. 75 minutes (uncut version)....$125

MY PAL TRIGGER -- The story of how Roy Rogers and his famous equine got together. 75 minutes......$125

NIGHT OF THE LIVING DEAD -- This picture started a new trend of explicitness in horror movies, and has since become a classic of the grotesque. It is an excursion into a nightmarish world of semi-human zombies that is definitely not for faint hearts or weak stomachs. 90 minutes...........$189

WAR COMES TO AMERICA -- This entry in Capra's "Why We Fight" series tells of the events leading up to Pearl Harbor, and includes actual footage of Pearl Harbor itself. 67 minutes..................$125

THE STRANGER -- Orson Welles directed and starred in this excellent film, which details the life of an escaped Nazi official who manages to establish himself as a respected citizen in The US. 95 mn$179

SANTA FE TRAIL -- This action fulled 1940 Warners features Errol Flynn, Olivia de Havilland, Raymond Massey, and Ronald Reagan in the sweeping historical drama of John Brown's fight to free the slaves in pre-Civil War America. Michael Curtiz directs. 110 minutes........................$179

LITTLE SHOP OF HORRORS -- Jonathan Haze, Jackie Joseph, and Mel Welles star in this very funny Roger Corman horror film from 1960. It seems that Haze grows plants, and one of them starts talking one day, demanding human blood. Jack Nicholson does a bit as a masochistic dental patient. 65 mn$135

REEFER MADNESS -- Dope crazed teens get silly, then salacious. High art from 1936. 65 minutes....$135

THE TRIAL -- Orson Welles wrote, produced and directed this extravagantly expressionistic adaptation of Franz Kafka's nightmarish novel about a man obsessed by an undefined guilt. Anthony Perkins stars as the neurotic Everyman figure and Welles himself plays The Advocate in this highly impressive and atmospheric mood piece. 118 minutes.......................................$200

CRY THE BELOVED COUNTRY -- Alan Paton's novel of humanity and faith in the midst of an oppressive system of South African apartheid is brought to the screen most effectively by producer, director Zoltan Korda. Especially noteworthy is Sidney Poitier in an early role. 105 minutes........$189

BELLS OF ROSARITA -- Roy Rogers stars in an action packed Western tale. 54 minutes................$125

GAY RANCHERO -- Ray Rogers as a US Marshall on the trail of dope smugglers. Good action. 54 min..$125

THE BIG SHOW -- Gene Autry unlimbers his voice at the 1936 Texas Exposition. 54 minutes..........$125

NO C.O.D. ORDERS. MINIMUM ORDER $25.00. No charge for postage and handling. Satisfaction is guaranteed on all orders.

BRUCE WEBSTER
426 N.W. 20
OKC, OKLAHOMA 73103
All films 16mm sound Ph. (405) 524-6251 9 A.M. til Midnight

PSYCHO TRAILER -- Alfred Hitchcock takes us on a tour of the PSYCHO sets. An extra long (6 minutes) theatrical trailer, with a shock ending that will rock you out of your seat.........................$18
PIE PIE BLACKBIRD -- Eubie Blake and his band are baked in a giant pie and get burned alive without missing a beat, until they are skeletons who keep right on playing. One-reel surrealism...........$25
CALLING ALL GIRLS -- In typical Hollywood style, this 1935 Warners short tells how those beautiful girls are chosen for Busby Berkeley musicals. The excerpts from GOLD DIGGERS, FOOTLIGHT PARADE, and WONDER BAR are magnificent, and the story is Old Hollywood deluxe. 20 minutes...................$40
HARRYHAUSEN TRAILER REEL -- Our popular group of Harryhausen trailers includes: BEAST FROM 20 THOUSAND FATHOMS, 3 WORLDS OF GULLIVER, 7th VOYAGE OF SINBAD, 20 MILLION MILES TO EARTH, and EARTH VS. THE FLYING SAUCERS. 16 full minutes of animation magic....................................$25
SON OF HARRYHAUSEN -- 5 b&w trailers from his color movies plus surprise trailer......................$30

BLACK AND WHITE CARTOONS (minimum order $22.50)

HAUNTING WE WILL GO -- Bimbo and Koko go on a fur hunting expedition and come back with plenty of furs. The animals are understandably miffed, not to mention cold, and call for Betty Boop.........$17
THE HENPECKED DUCK -- This very good Warners effort features Daffy Duck as a magician who makes an egg containing his future son disappear. Trouble starts when he can't bring it back...............$17
EARLY WARNERS CARTOONS -- The following Cartoons are representative of the period when "All Talking! All Singing! All Dancing" meant just that to moviegoers the world over. Produced by the legendary team of Harmon & Ising, these tuneful cartoons will have you snapping your fingers and tapping your feet. Films include: CROSBY, COLOMBO & VALLE (1932), FREDDY THE FRESHMAN (1931), SMILE, DARN YA, SMILE (1931), ONE MORE TIME (1931), PAGAN MOON (1931), and I LOVE A PARADE..EACH TITLE.....$17
UNCLE TOM AND LITTLE EVA -- An incredible musical cartoon adaption of "Uncle Tom's Cabin," this is the most blatantly racist cartoon we've ever seen, with black characters tap dancing on the auction block, "Liza Jane" running across the ice floes pursued by dancing bloodhounds, all in an animation style that heavily resembles Disney. Must be seen to be believed.........................$17
RHYTHM OF THE RESERVATION -- Betty Boop makes a trip to the Indian reservation, and ends up teaching the braves and squaws a few new moves...$17
MAKING STARS -- Betty Boop introduces and provides color commentary for a group of "Stars of Tomorrow"...$17
BURIED TREASURE -- Here's the rare, early porno cartoon, reportedly animated by Max Fleischer in the days before the talkies. This one stars Everready Horton, who does his best to live up to his name when confronted with various females, human and otherwise. Silent, 6 minutes........$17
ALL THIS AND RABBIT STEW -- Considered by many to be one of the funniest Warner Brothers cartoons ever made, this Bugs Bunny opus has achieved a kind of fame for its stereotyped Negro antagonist, who is out to "get me a rab--bit..." Tex Avery directed...$17
IS MY PALM READ? -- Our most popular Boop. BB goes to have her fortune told by Bimbo, who looks after her with lust in his heart. They end up on an island, pursued by drooling monsters. This cartoon contains footage of Boop in the buff. Move over Hedy Lamarr.................................$17
AFRAID TO COME HOME IN THE DARK -- A drunk, coming home, meets up with all manner of foul creatures in a Max Fleischer Screen Song. Great animation and singalong music...........................$17
I WISHED ON THE MOON -- Abe Lyman and his Californians handle the song, and Fleischer animates an outrageous story, in this Screen Song from the 1930's..$17
SLEEPYTIME DOWN SOUTH -- The unforgettable Boswell Sisters warble the title song in a live-action sequence, and Fleischer takes care of the rest...$17
TAKE A TRIP IN MY AIRSHIP -- A nice Screen Song with excellent Fleischer effects..................$17
WALT DISNEY'S ALICE CARTOONS -- These rare and entertaining cartoons showcase the talents of Walt Disney studios in the late 1920's. Music and sound effects have been added. Titles are: ALICE'S ORPHAN, ALICE SOLVES A PUZZLE, and ALICE RATTLED BY RATS. All 3 cartoons...........................$40
SON OF ALICE CARTOONS -- Another Alice package of the same vintage and quality. Titles are: ALICE'S TIN PONY, ALICE'S BALLOON RACE, and ALICE'S EGGPLANT. Price for all 3.............................$40
THE FLYING HOUSE -- Excellent fantasy effects highlight this early Winsor McCay cartoon, one of the famed "Dreams of a Rarebit Fiend" series. Silent, musical track, 11 minutes.....................$25
THE PET -- The rarebit fiend goes to bed on a full stomach, which causes him to dream about a giant dog-like creature that attacks the city. Silent, 11 minutes.................................$25
GERTIE THE DINOSAUR -- McCay's friends at the club scoff when he says he can make a drawing come to life. He proves it with Gertie, an animation classic. One of the very first of the animated cartoons, with both live action and animation sequences. Silent, 11 minutes......................$25
POPEYE CARTOONS -- We have the following adventures of the world renowned spinach eater. Toot: CUSTOMERS WANTED (1939), WITH POOPDECK PAPPY (1940), I SKI LOVE SKI YOU SKI (1936), I'M IN THE ARMY NOW (1936), and POPEYE PRESENTS EUGENE THE JEEP (1940). Each..................................$17
BETTY BOOP IN POOR CINDERELLA -- Boop meets Prince Charming in the immortal love story. Lots of music and singing highlight this extra long extravaganza..$25
BETTY BOOP IN BLUNDERLAND -- Betty surrealistically parodies Alice's wonderland..................$17
BETTY BOOP'S RISE TO FAME -- Betty struts her stuff in excerpts from three of her greatest screen triumphs. "Uncle Max" Fleischer makes a live action appearance.................................$17
BETTY BOOP'S CRAZY INVENTIONS -- The title tells it all...$17

NO C.O.D's   MINIMUM ORDER $25.00   NO CHARGE FOR POSTAGE AND HANDLING, SATISFACTION GUARANTEED.

Robert D. Crestohl
4732 Circle Road
Montreal, Quebec, Canada
H3W 1Z1

#WE ALSO SELL. SEND FOR FREE LIST.

Comics We are Buying

We are always interested in buying any of the following Marvels in any quantity, although large collections are definitely preferred. Prices listed below are what we are paying for copies in Very good or better condition. Books in VG condition must be in collectable shape with only a minimum of wear. Books dated before 1970 are also accepted in Good condition at one-half (1/2) the listed prices, as long as they are complete with no obvious defects other than wear. Do not send books in poor condition, books with the Marvel stamps cut out (All books are checked carefully) or any books that are not listed, as these will be returned at the sender's expense.

Comics may be sent in for immediate payment (U.S. or Canadian funds). Book rate or Parcel Post are recommended for most shipments, although Air Freight is best for large shipments over 1000 comics. It is not necessary to write before shipping books as we always need to buy. Just pack securely and send an invoice on ahead informing me what you have sent. We will be glad to furnish any additional shipping instructions on request.

We are expecially interested in buying Mint copies of early Marvels (pre-1965) and we will pay substantially higher prices for these books.

MARVEL

Avengers
1	$ 35.00
2	12.00
3,4	10.00
5	5.00
6,7,11	4.00
8,9,10	3.00
12	2.00
13-17	1.00
18-23	.75
24-49	.40
50-56,58-92	.60
57,94-96	2.00
93,100	4.00
97-99	1.00
101-118	.50
119-138	.30
139-152	.20

Capt. America
100	$ 1.50
101,102,109	.60
103-108,112	.50
110,111,113	1.50
114-120	40
121.160	.30
161-200	.20

Capt. Marvel
1	$ 2.00
2-24	.40
25-33	.60

Conan
1,3	$ 15.00
2	6.00
4,5	5.00

Conan
6,7	$ 4.00
8,9,10	3.00
11-14	2.00
15-22	1.50
23-28,37	1.00
29-36	.60
38-40	.40
41-52	.30

Daredevil
1	$ 15.00
2	6.00
3	4.00
4,5	2.00
6,7,8	1.50
9,10	1.00
11-17, 100	.60
18-22	.40
23-49, 53-99	.30
50,51,52	.75
101-127	.20

Defenders
1	$ 4.00
2	1.50
3,4,5	1.00
6-10	.75
11,12,13	.50
14-18	.30
19-28	.20

Fantastic Four
1	$ 150.00
2	60.00
3	40.00

Fantastic Four
4	$ 30.00
5	20.00
6	15.00
7,8,12	12.00
9,10,11	10.00
13,14,15	8.00
16-20	6.00
21-27	4.00
28,29,30	3.00
31-38	2.00
39-47	1.00
48,49,50,100	1.50
51-60,116	.75
61-99,112	.50
101-111,113-115	.40
117-136	.40
137 157	.30
158-162	.20

Hulk
1	$ 50.00
2	25.00
3	15.00
4,5	10.00
6	8.00
102	2.00
103-105	.75
106-130	.50
131-181	.40
182-195	.30
196-216	.20

Iron Man
1	$ 4.00
2	1.50
3	1.00
4,47	.75
5-12	.40
13-46,48-57	.30
58-87,98-102	.20

J.I.M. & Thor
83	$ 40.00
84	20.00
85	10.00
86	8.00
87,88	6.00
89,90	5.00
91,92	4.00
93-95	3.00
96-100	2.00
101-112	1.50
113-115	1.00
116-120, 193	.50
121-192	.30
194-217	.30
218-227	.20

Marvel Team-Up
1	$ 3.00
2,3	1.00

Marvel Team-Up
4,5	.75
6,7,8	.50
9,10,11	.40
12-29	.30
30-39	.20

Marvel Two-in-One
1	$ 1.50
2-10	.30
11-17	.20

Silver Surfer
1	$ 6.00
2,3	3.00
4	4.00
5,6,7	2.00
8-12	1.50
13-18	1.00

Spiderman
AAF No. 15	$ 110.00
1	110.00
2	40.00
3	30.00
4	20.00
5	15.00
6	10.00
7,8,9,10	8.00
11,12	6.00
13,14	5.00
15,16	4.00
17-22	3.00
23-28	2.00
29-35	1.50
36-50	1.00
51-60	.75
61-95,99	.60
96,97,98,100	1.25
101,102,119,120	.75
103-118	.50
121,122	4.00
123-125	.40
126-145	.30
146-152,171	.20

Tales of Suspense
39	$ 35.00

Tales to Astonish
27	$ 40.00
35	20.00
36	5.00
37-40	3.00
41,42	2.00
43-50,59	1.00
51-58,60,93	.60
61-70	.40
71-92,94-101	.30

X-Men
1	$ 20.00
2	8.00
3	5.00
4	4.00
5	3.00
6,7	2.00
8,9,10	1.00
11-20	.50
21-48,52,54,55	.30
49,50,51	.60
53,56	1.50
57-66	1.00
67-75,95	.30
76-93,96-107	.20
94	75

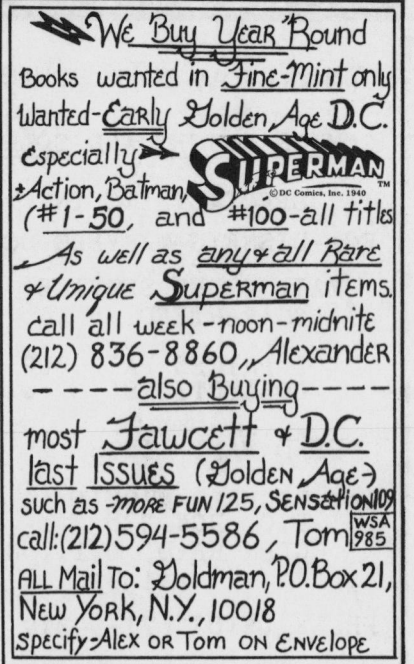

BUYING COMICS
Top Prices Paid!

J&S Comics wants to buy your comics and we'll pay more than *anyone* to get them. But don't take our word for it, check the list of prices we are paying below. The prices listed are for books in STRICT MINT condition. We'll also buy them in lesser condition at lower prices. This list represents just a small sample of books we're interested in. We specialize in buying large golden and silver age collections. For valuable collections we will travel to you and pay cash. We buy Timely, Marvel, DC, EC, Avon, Fox, Disney, Dell and many others. So if you have any books or a whole collection for sale, write or call Jim Walsh at 150 Bridge Ave., Red Bank, N.J. 07701. Phone 201-747-7548. No collect calls please.

PAYING IN STRICT MINT
SEND FOR IMMEDIATE PAYMENT

Amazing Fantasy 15 ....($360)	Justice League I ....($80)
Avengers I ....($120)	Lois Lane I ....($80)
Daredevil I ....($50)	Showcase 4 ....($750)
Fantastic Four I...........($750)	Showcase 8 ....($175)
Hulk I ....($275)	Showcase 22 ....($80)
Journey into Mystery 83.....($250)	All Negro I ....($225)
Spiderman I ....($325)	Attack on Planet Mars ....($50)
Strange Tales 101 ....($40)	Earthman on Venus ....($125)
Tales of Suspense 39 ....($120)	Intimate Confessions........($60)
Tales to Astonish 27 ....($150)	Mask of Fu Manchu ....($200)
X-Men I ....($65)	Phantom Lady 13 ....($300)
Action 252 ....($90)	Phantom Lady 17 ....($350)
Adventure 247 ....($120)	Reform School Girl ....($1,000)
Brave and Bold 28 ....($45)	Teen Age Dope Slaves ......($325)
Challengers I ....($65)	Torchy I ....($350)
Detective 225 ....($125)	Torchy 2-4 ....($100 ea.)
Flash 105 ....($175)	Torchy 5, 6............($200 ea.)
Green Lantern I ....($70)	Weird Science 12 (I) ....($225)
Jimmy Olsen I ....($135)	

* COMPLETE SET OF ABOVE TITLES FROM 1961 THRU 1966 ($5,000)

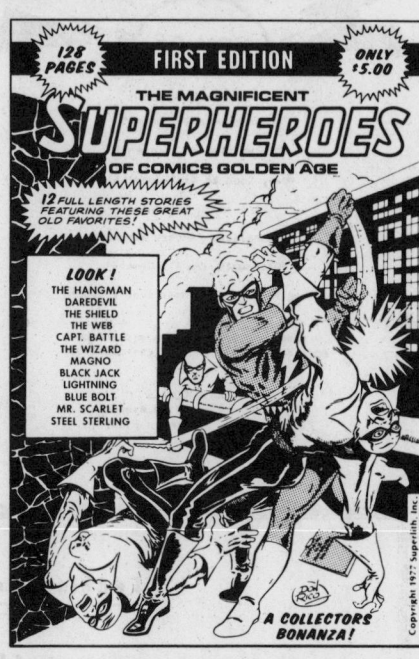

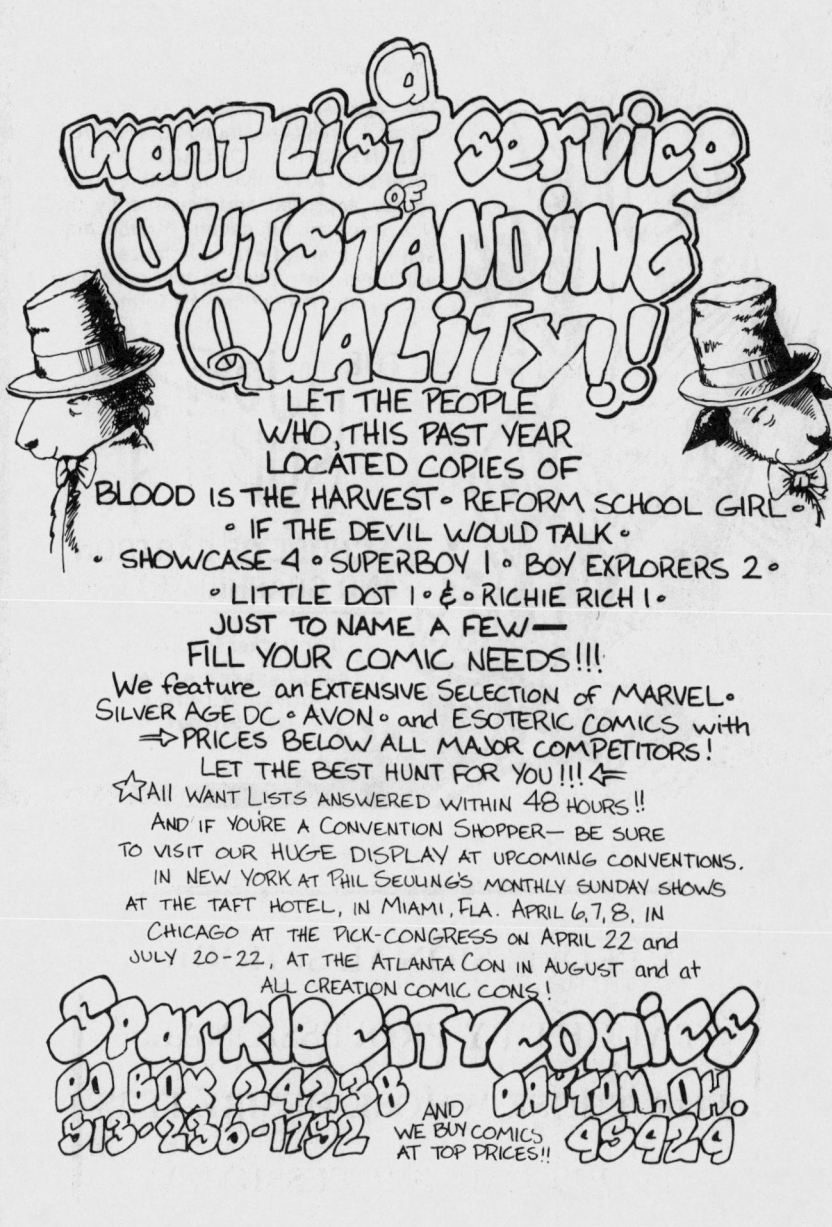

THE COMIC WORLD is a publication for the serious comics enthusiast. If you want to learn more about the history and development of comics both past and present, then this is the publication for you. We are devoted to the principle that any subject worth writing about is worth covering in depth, and detail. You'll find no two and three page shortie articles in COMIC WORLD. What you will find is good substantial writing, well researched, well illustrated, and well laid out. Our material is presented in a clear, informal style that can be appreciated by both the long time collector, or the newcomer to the hobby. Give us a try. COMIC WORLD will help develop your knowledge and enjoyment of the comics field.

THE COMIC WORLD appears on a bi-monthly schedule. A sample copy is just $1.50. A six issue subscription is only $6.00.

Robert Jennings, RFD 2, Whiting Rd., Dudley, Mass. 01570

Our cover illustrations, from the top: Blackhawk © DC Comics; The Blue Tracer © Quality Comics; Phantom Lady © Ajax Pub.; Daredevil © Lev Gleason Pub.; The Ghost Rider © Magazine Enterprises; The Sniper © Quality Comics; The Black Terror © Standard Pub.; The Lost World © Fiction House; Sheena © Fiction House/S.M. Iger; Fighting American © Harvey Pub.; The Blue Beetle © Charlton Pub.; The Green Arrow © DC Comics; The Vigilante © DC Comics.

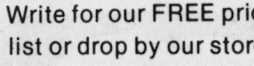

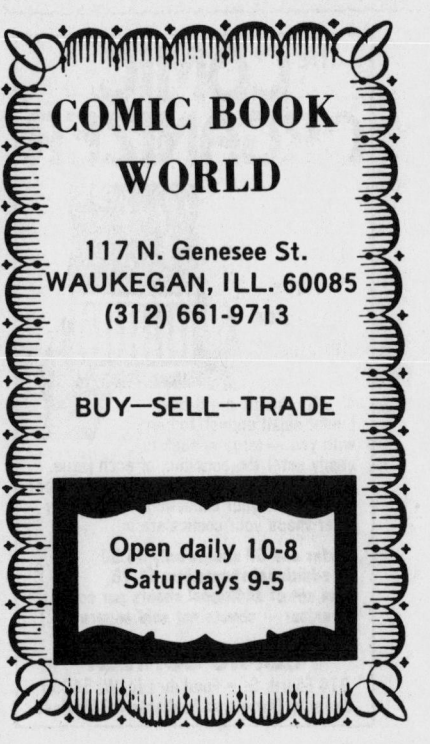

* CLASSIFIED ADVERTISING CONT'D *

WALT KELLY/POGO
Comics, pins, brochures, autographs, orig. art, posters, paperbacks, hardcovers, records, and many other items in stock. Please send a SASE for our next listing. Extensive Search, Squaw Rock, Danielson, CT. 06239. 203-774-1203.

Into Comics? Then get into the COLLECTORS' CLUB To join, send $2.00 to the COLLECTORS' CLUB c/o David Kelley, 4617 Riverview, Fort Worth, Tx 76118 Steve Miller v.p.

30M COMICS, MAGS, MISC. COLLECTIBLES ON SALE. B. J.'S COMIC CORNER, 260 N. ARDMORE, VILLA PARK, ILL. 60181. WE BUY. 312-834-0383.

GUM CARDS: SASE FOR FREE LIST—B. W. YUEN, P. O. BOX 26432 S. F., CA 94126. BUY & TRADE YOUR COMICS WSA 1331-IFICC

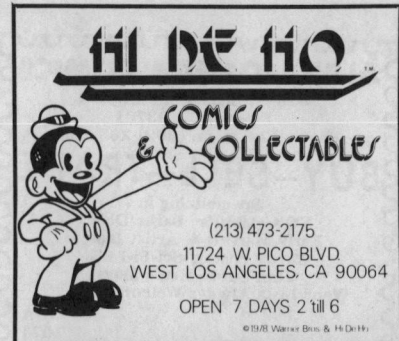

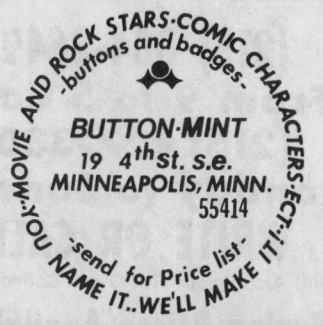

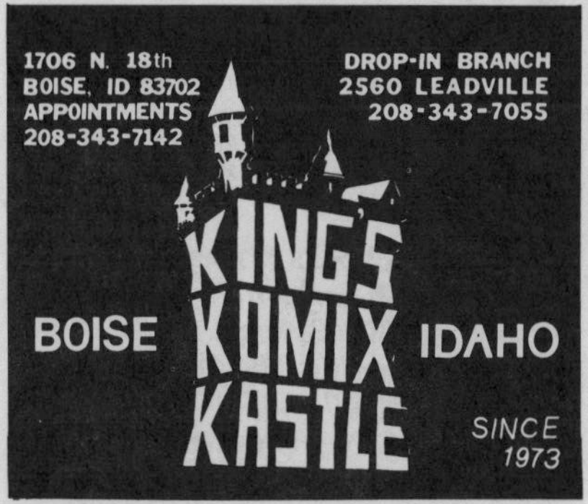

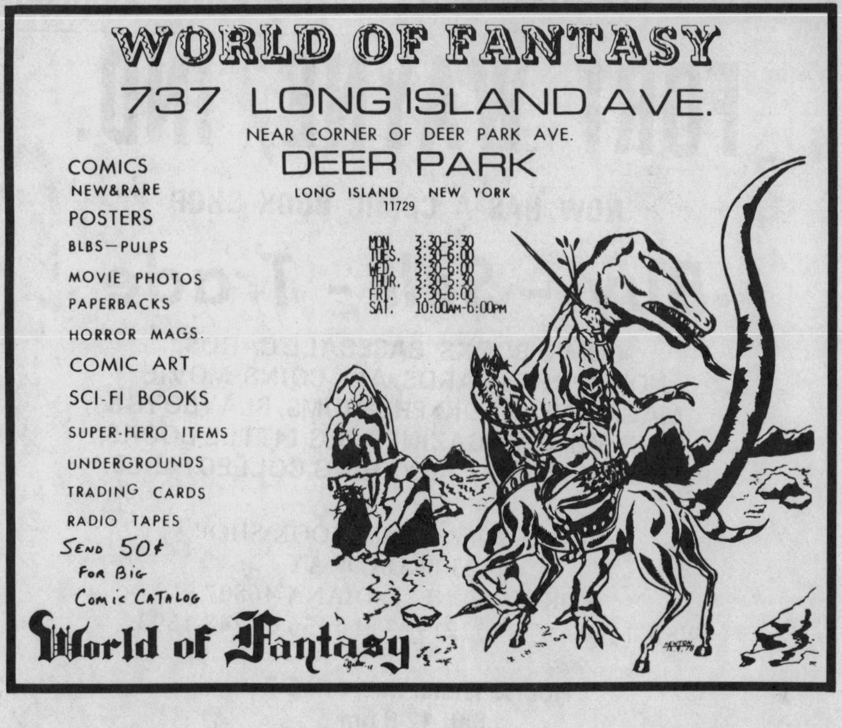